NEW!

for *Scientific American: Child and Adolescent Development*

Engaging Every Student. **Supporting Every Instructor.** **Setting the New Standard for Teaching and Learning.**

Achieve for *Scientific American: Child and Adolescent Development* sets a whole new standard for engaging and appraising your students' progress with ease, by way of **assessments**, **activities**, and **analytics**. It also brings together all of the features that instructors and students loved about our previous platform, LaunchPad—interactive e-book, LearningCurve adaptive quizzing and other assessments, interactive learning activities, extensive instructor resources—in a powerful new platform that offers:

- A cleaner, more intuitive, **mobile-friendly** interface.
- Powerful analytics.
- Self-regulated learning with goal-setting surveys.
- A fully integrated iClicker classroom response system, with questions available for each unit or the option to integrate your own.
- An **expansive Video Collection for *Scientific American: Child and Adolescent Development***

Our resources were **co-designed with instructors and students**, on a foundation of *years* of **learning research**, and rigorous testing over multiple semesters. The result is superior content, organization, and functionality. Achieve's pre-built assignments engage students both *inside and outside of class*. And Achieve is effective for students at *all levels* of motivation and preparedness, whether they are high achievers or need extra support.

Macmillan Learning offers **deep platform integration** of Achieve with all LMS providers, including Blackboard, Brightspace, Canvas, and Moodle. With integration, students can access course content and their grades through one sign-in. And you can pair Achieve with course tools from your LMS, such as discussion boards, chat, and Gradebook functionality. LMS integration is also available with Inclusive Access. For more information, visit MacmillanLearning.com/College/US/Solutions /LMS-Integration or talk to your local sales representative.

Achieve was built with **accessibility** in mind. Macmillan Learning strives to create products that are usable by all learners and meet universally applied accessibility standards. In addition to addressing product compatibility with assistive technologies such as screen reader software, alternative keyboard devices, and voice recognition products, we are working to ensure that the content and platforms we provide are fully accessible. For more information, visit MacmillanLearning.com/College/US /Our-Story/Accessibility.

LearningCurve Adaptive Quizzing

Based on extensive learning and memory research, and proven effective for hundreds of thousands of students, LearningCurve focuses on the core concepts in every chapter, providing individualized question sets and feedback for correct and incorrect responses. The system adapts to each student's level of understanding, with follow-up quizzes targeting areas where the student needs improvement. Each question is tied to a learning objective and linked to the appropriate section of the e-book to encourage students to discover the right answer for themselves. LearningCurve has consistently been rated the #1 resource by instructors and students alike.

- LearningCurve's game-like quizzing promotes retrieval practice through its unique delivery of questions and its point system.

- Students with a firm grasp on the material get plenty of practice but proceed through the activity relatively quickly.

- Unprepared students are given more questions, therefore, requiring that they do what they should be doing anyway if they're unprepared — practice some more.

- Instructors can monitor results for each student and the class as a whole, to identify areas that may need more coverage in lectures and assignments.

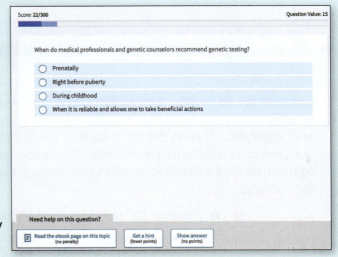

E-book

Macmillan Learning's e-book is an interactive version of the textbook that offers highlighting, bookmarking, and note-taking. Built-in, low-stakes self-assessments allow students to test their level of understanding along the way, and learn even more in the process thanks to the testing effect. Students can download the e-book to read offline or to have it read aloud to them. Achieve allows instructors to assign chapter sections as homework.

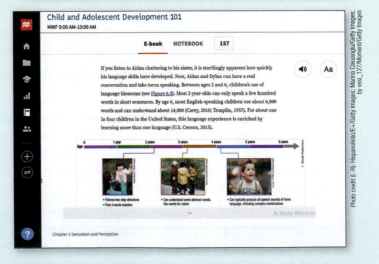

Test Bank

The Test Bank for *Scientific American: Child and Adolescent Development* offers thousands of questions, all meticulously reviewed. Instructors can assign out-of-the-box exams or create their own by:

- Choosing from thousands of questions in our database.

- Filtering questions by type, topic, difficulty, and Bloom's level.

- Customizing multiple-choice questions.

- Integrating their own questions into the exam.

Exam/Quiz results report to a Gradebook that lets instructors monitor student progress individually and classwide.

Practice Quizzes

Practice Quizzes mirror the experience of a quiz or test, with questions that are similar to but distinct from those in the test bank. Instructors can use the quizzes as is or create their own, selecting questions by question type, topic, difficulty, and Bloom's level.

Achieve for *Scientific American: Child and Adolescent Development*:   **Engaging Every Student**

Achieve is designed to support and encourage active learning by connecting familiar activities and practices out of class with some of the most effective and approachable in-class activities, curated from a variety of active learning sources.

Scientific American Profile

Meet Telele

Scientific American Profiles

These short video clips, central to this project, take readers into the homes of the children and families they meet in every chapter. In addition to providing context for the major concepts, these videos foster an emotional connection to the material that will stick with students.

Video Collection for Developmental Psychology

Development comes to life when you see babies taking their first steps or preschoolers participating in Piaget's conservation-of-mass task. This expansive collection is a broad curation of news clips, documentary footage, interviews with leading researchers, and more.

Our faculty and student consultants were instrumental in helping us create this diverse and engaging set of clips. All videos are closed-captioned and found only in **Achieve**.

Spotlight on Science

These interactive activities focus on high-interest studies, such as the connection between age and ADHD diagnoses and the effects of the media on body image in adolescence. They reinforce students' understanding of the steps of the scientific method, walking students through each study, honing critical thinking and scientific literacy skills by posing questions. Students view and interact with data, study stimuli, and are scaffolded through a discussion of the research approach, limitations, and conclusions.

Chapter 4: Physical and Cognitive Development in Infancy and Toddlerhood

Spotlight on Science

Using the Experimental Method to Fight Allergies

Learning Goals

- You will follow the steps of the experimental research design, from hypothesis through random assignment, treatment and control conditions.

Begin Activity

Concept Practice Tutorials

Achieve includes dozens of these dynamic, interactive mini-tutorials that teach and reinforce the course's foundational ideas. Each of these brief activities (only 5 minutes to complete) addresses one or two key concepts, in a consistent format — review, practice, quiz, and conclusion.

Instructor Activity Guides

Instructor Activity Guides provide instructors with a structured plan for using Achieve's active learning opportunities in both face-to-face and remote learning courses. Each guide offers step-by-step instructions — from pre-class reflection to in-class engagement to post-class follow-up. The guides include suggestions for discussion questions, group work, presentations, and simulations, with estimated class time, implementation effort, and Bloom's taxonomy level for each activity.

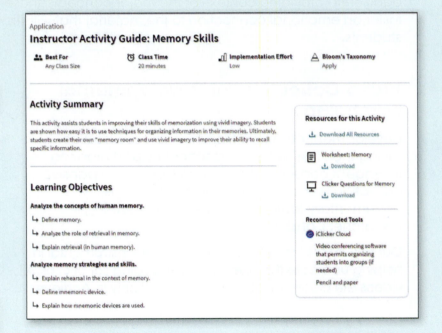

Developing Lives

Developing Lives provides a robust interactive experience in which users "raise" their own child from conception to adolescence. As the child grows, the student responds to events both planned and unforeseen, making important decisions (nutrition choices, doctor visits, and child care) and facing uncertain moments (bullying, substance use, and a new school), with each choice affecting how the child grows. Each stage of development is accompanied by a quiz to help students apply the main concepts of the course to their experience as a virtual caregiver.

iClicker Classroom Response System

Achieve seamlessly integrates iClicker, Macmillan Learning's highly acclaimed classroom response system. iClicker can help make any classroom — in-person or virtual — more lively, engaging, and productive. Access to iClicker is included with Achieve at no additional cost.

- iClicker's attendance feature helps make sure students are actually attending in-person classes.

- Instructors can choose from flexible polling and quizzing options to engage students, check their understanding, and get their feedback in real time.

- iClicker allows students to participate using laptops, mobile devices, or in-class remotes.

- iClicker easily integrates instructors' existing slides and polling questions — there is no need to re-enter them.

- Instructors can take advantage of the questions in our Instructor Activity Guides and our book-specific questions within Achieve to improve the opportunities for all students to be active in class.

© Macmillan Learning

Achieve for *Scientific American: Child and Adolescent Development*:   Supporting Every Instructor

Learning Objectives, Reports, and Insights

Content in Achieve is tagged to specific Learning Objectives, aligning the coursework with the textbook and with the APA Learning Goals and Outcomes. Reporting within Achieve helps students see how they are performing against objectives, and it helps instructors determine if any student, group of students, or the class as a whole needs extra help in specific areas. This enables more efficient and effective instructor interventions.

Achieve provides reports on student activities, assignments, and assessments at the course level, unit level, subunit level, and individual student level, so instructors can identify trouble spots and adjust their efforts accordingly. Within Reports, the Insights section offers snapshots with high-level data on student performance and behavior, to answer such questions as:

- What are the top Learning Objectives to review in this unit?

- What are the top assignments to review?

- What's the range of performance on a particular assignment?

- How many students aren't logging in?

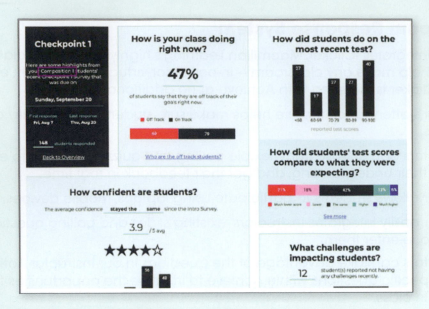

Achieve's **Goal-setting & Reflection Surveys** help students self-direct, and develop confidence in, their own learning:

- The **Intro Survey** asks students to consider their goals for the class and how they plan to manage their time and learning strategies.

- **Checkpoint surveys** ask students to reflect on what's been working and where they need to make changes.

- **Each completed survey generates a report** that reveals how each student is doing, beyond the course grade.

These tools help instructors engage their students in a discussion on soft skills, such as metacognition, effective learning and time management strategies, and other noncognitive skills that impact student success.

Additional Instructor Resources in Achieve: All Within One Place

Image Slides and Tables

Presentation slides feature chapter illustrations and tables and can be used as is or customized to fit an instructor's needs. Alt text for images is available upon request via WebAccessibility@Macmillan.com

Lecture Slides

Accessible, downloadable presentation slides provide support for key concepts and themes from the text, and can be used as is or customized to fit an instructor's needs.

Customer Support

Our Achieve Client Success Team—dedicated platform experts—provides collaboration, software expertise, and consulting to tailor each course to fit your instructional goals and student needs. Start with a demo at a time that works for you to learn more about how to set up your customized course. Talk to your sales representative or visit www.MacmillanLearning.com/College/US/Contact-Us /Training-and-Demos for more information.

Pricing and bundling options are available at the Macmillan Student Store: Store.MacmillanLearning.com

Scientific American:
CHILD AND ADOLESCENT DEVELOPMENT

Allison Sidle Fuligni

California State University, Los Angeles

Andrew J. Fuligni

University of California, Los Angeles

Jessica Bayne

worth publishers
Macmillan Learning
New York

Executive Vice President and General Manager: Charles Linsmeier
Vice President, Social Sciences & High School: Shani Fisher
Program Director: Suzanne Jeans
Executive Program Manager: Daniel DeBonis
Senior Development Editor: Andrea Musick Page
Associate Development Editor: Nick Rizzuti
Editorial Assistant: Emily Kelly
Executive Marketing Manager: Katherine Nurre
Marketing Assistant: Claudia Cruz
Senior Market Development Manager: Stephanie Ellis
Associate Director, Digital Content: Anna Gar
Senior Media Editor: Karissa Venne
Media Editor: Clarah Grossman
Senior Director, Content Management Enhancement: Tracey Kuehn
Executive Managing Editor: Michael Granger
Senior Manager of Publishing Services: Gregory Erb
Lead Content Project Manager: Peter Jacoby
Lead Media Project Manager: Joseph Tomasso
Senior Workflow Supervisor: Jennifer Wetzel
Senior Photo Editor: Sheena Goldstein
Photo Researcher: Cheryl Dubois
Director of Design, Content Management: Diana Blume
Senior Design Services Manager: Natasha A. S. Wolfe
Senior Cover Designer: John Callahan
Interior Design: Tammy Newnam and Lumina Datamatics, Inc.
Art Manager: Matthew McAdams
Illustrations: Lumina Datamatics, Inc., Eli Ensor, Matthew McAdams
Composition: Lumina Datamatics, Inc.
Printing and Binding: Lakeside Book Company
Icon Credits: aslann/Shutterstock, johavel/Shutterstock, Ermin13/Shutterstock, Pro Symbols/Shutterstock,
    Kirill Mlayshev/Shutterstock, fonikum/DigitalVision Vectors/Getty Images
Brief Contents and Contents Photos: © Macmillan, Photo by Sidford House and Point Studio, Inc.

Library of Congress Control Number: 2022948780
ISBN-13: 978-1-319-05326-0
ISBN-10: 1-319-05326-2

Printed in the United States of America
1   2   3   4   5   6   28   27   26   25   24   23

Worth Publishers
120 Broadway
New York, NY 10271
www.macmillanlearning.com

ABOUT THE AUTHORS

Scientific American: Child and Adolescent Development has united experienced classroom teachers and highly respected researchers Allison Sidle Fuligni and Andrew J. Fuligni with writer and producer Jessica Bayne. As developmental scientists with a deep love for the nitty-gritty of research and theory, Andrew and Allison share a deep desire to make sure that this science makes it out into the world to improve lives.

Allison is a professor in the Department of Child and Family Studies at California State University, Los Angeles, and teaches development every semester. She has spent much of her research career focused on understanding and improving the environments where young children develop, at the Columbia University National Center for Children and Families, at the UCLA Center for Improving Child Care Quality, and at California State University, Los Angeles. She was involved with several longitudinal studies of children's development, including the Los Angeles Exploring Children's Early Learning Settings and the National Early Head Start Research and Evaluation Project. Allison received her Ph.D. from the University of Michigan.

Andrew is a professor in the Departments of Psychiatry and Biobehavioral Sciences and Psychology at University of California, Los Angeles, where he teaches courses on child and adolescent development. He also directs the Adolescent Development Lab at UCLA and is co-executive director of the UCLA Center for the Developing Adolescent, which is dedicated to improving the health and well-being of young people through the translation and dissemination of developmental science. He has published extensively on the sociocultural experience and biobehavioral development during adolescence and young adulthood, with a focus on young people from Latin American, Asian, European, and immigrant backgrounds. Andrew has received numerous awards for his teaching and research and is a former associate editor of the journal *Child Development*. Like Allison, he received his Ph.D. at the University of Michigan.

Jessica is a writer, editor, and producer who has been creating videos and media content for college courses for more than 20 years. She has collaborated with leading researchers and educators and led the development of a wide array of products for higher education. Jessica's approach is grounded in her own experiences working in nursing homes, coaching theater, and raising children.

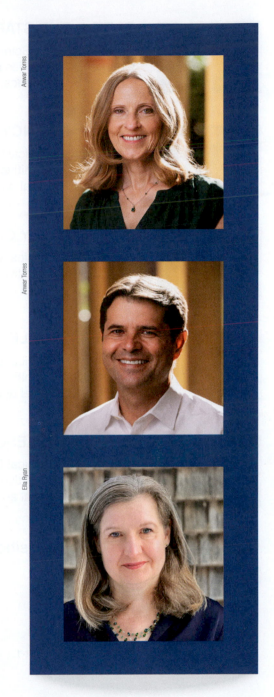

Anwar Torres

Anwar Torres

Ella Ryan

BRIEF CONTENTS

CONTENTS

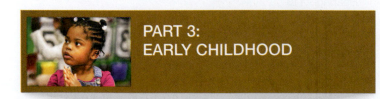

**PART 3:
EARLY CHILDHOOD**

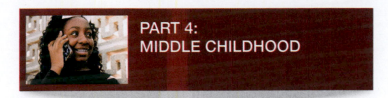

**PART 4:
MIDDLE CHILDHOOD**

**PART 5:
ADOLESCENCE**

Epilogue: The Transition to Adulthood

PREFACE

Welcome! This project is inspired by the idea that developmental science can change lives for the better. Sometimes information can provide inspiration: changing how we work, investigate phenomena on our own, or advocate for others in our community. At other times, science provides us with reassurance: Maybe it is relieving to know that, yes, most 4-year-olds are full of energy and enjoy jumping on the couch. Or, that most toddlers really are sick more than 30 days every year (Vissing et al., 2018). Or, that most of the risks adolescents take are healthy ones—like learning something new or meeting a friend.

At its heart, developmental science combines a long tradition of rigorous scientific research with advocacy designed to support well-being. We know from our own teaching experience (and our own learning experiences when we were in college) that this class can change lives, and empirical research supports this: The classes we take can indeed make us kinder and more prosocial adults (Harrell-Levy & Kerpelman, 2015). This course also enables us to explain how science itself works. Understanding science better can help us think critically about research, evaluate empirical evidence for claims, and understand how what we know changes over time.

Developmental science is a subject we love to teach and share with others, whether in the classroom or through conversations around our own dinner table. One of the reasons we love teaching this course is that developmental science is relevant to everyone. In this project, we take full advantage of this inherent relatability by sharing the science that addresses our curiosity about the world. Why is learning to move so hard, yet so important, for infants? What are the skills that can help adolescents transition to adulthood? Did the COVID-19 pandemic really harm children for a lifetime? Is your personality set at birth? Psychologists find that making the material relevant not only keeps the conversation going after class is over: It helps everyone think more deeply and retain the material.

This is an exciting time in developmental science, with new innovations that strengthen communities and bolster our resilience. Scientists are now able to connect understanding of the brain and the biology of development with our social and cultural

Interventions That Work Throughout this book, you will see examples of ways that developmental science helps build on people's strengths. For example, these parents benefited from a group prenatal health program, Centering Pregnancy, that helps leverage the power of social bonds to improve pregnancy outcomes. They enjoyed the program so much they returned to introduce their babies after they were born.

Meet Some of the Family You will meet Olivia (*left*), learning yoga as she learns yoga in pre-K in Chapter 6. Jesús (*right*) will share how having a sense of purpose and helping others has boosted his resilience in Chapter 15.

context in new ways. Applications of developmental knowledge in child care, schools, and health care, among other arenas, demonstrate that science can make an impact. Developmental science can transform how we work, care for each other, and grow, which is what inspired us to write a textbook that brings all of this into the classroom.

Developmental science is not just about facts and scholarly research: It is also about people. To tell its story, our team has traveled around the United States to find the 16 children, adolescents, and their families who have shared their lives with us. We tracked down professionals in fields from acting to art, library science to literacy promotion, who describe how developmental science has changed how they work. As a result, each chapter includes a profile of a family both in text and on video and a professional in the field in our *Science in Practice* features.

Over the years, our work has given us the honor of getting to know a variety of families. We have been privileged to share the birth of Alizah and Spencer's first child, Courage, and to cheer for Telele as she learns to say her first words in Inupiaq and in English. We have rooted for Jesús as he finishes yet another mural as well as the eleventh grade. We have shared the joy of Mervlyn as she describes her more than 50 years of being a part of a landmark research study. The stories that appear in every chapter, along with the photographs and videos, come from communities across the United States, from Alaska to Florida, and are one way that we have tried to make developmental science memorable.

Key Approaches

In this project, we employ five major strategies for sharing content: (1) stories of real people; (2) inclusive coverage of children and their families; (3) accessible treatment of current science; (4) a strengths-based perspective; and (5) a focus on skills that will help students in their future careers and personal lives.

Storytelling You Will Remember

Scientific American: Child and Adolescent Development presents students with vivid stories of individuals and families. Within our own classes, we talk about real people each day. We talk about our families in class (and even feature them in clicker questions). We bring in guest speakers, from neuroscientists to clinicians who work hands-on with families. When we run into former students or read their course evaluations, we find that those personal stories stick with them.

Contemporary learning science supports our anecdotal experiences: When students have a personal, emotional connection to what they learn, they remember it better and have an easier time applying it (Landrum et al., 2019). Stories even help us relate better to the scientists and theorists who have shaped the field. Drawing on the science of teaching and learning, we know that people relate more to stories of famous people when we emphasize their personal stories, how their successes were not inevitable, and how they surmounted obstacles of their own on their way to being prominent names in a textbook (Lin-Siegler et al., 2016). Therefore, you will learn not just that John Watson is credited with popularizing the science of behaviorism, but also that he was in trouble with the law in high school and needed quarts of Coca-Cola to get through his exams (Moore, 2017).

As we have described, each chapter of this book tells the story of a child or adult and their family in the text and in the accompanying online videos. These include 10-year-old Amara from Los Angeles, who has already helped to write a number of songs and a book, and 3-year-old Olivia, who is adjusting to preschool and learning to share and enjoy circle time in New Jersey. These stories and video profiles help students see the challenges and opportunities of each life stage: We think we remember what it was like to be 10, but the video of Amara reminds us what it is *really* like, for someone whose life experience is different from our own.

In addition, in our *Science in Practice* sections, you will be introduced to 16 professionals who share their personal experiences of how developmental science has made a difference in their lives. You will learn about Nicolle Gonzales, C.N.M., a midwife, who incorporates Indigenous traditions into pregnancy and postpartum care for women near the Diné reservation in New Mexico and Rodrigo Encisco, who provides leadership, insight, and problem solving as a school psychologist for children in schools in San Diego, California.

Inclusive Coverage to Represent the Broad Contexts That Impact Development

Like many instructors, we have often struggled to explain to our students why their textbooks do not reflect their lives or families and describe a world that they often cannot relate to. Textbooks do not always reflect the broad variety of experiences that make up human development. We have always seen this course as a way of connecting people to the experiences of other human beings: Whether we are investigating the impact of urbanization on families in China or the stress of remote schooling for children in Chicago, understanding the impact of context to development is important. Throughout this book, you will find research from Ghana to Geneva and stories from families from Lhasa to Los Angeles.

Building from our experiences, this book casts a broad net over what *diversity* means. We set out to write a book that would better represent the diverse legacy of the science itself, the children and families we interview, and the current issues we discuss. We cover complex family structures, intersectional identities, and challenges faced by those who are affluent and those who are less well-off.

This book includes the stories of people from diverse cultures, family configurations, health and abilities, and access to resources. In this way, we connect to students' own diverse experiences and enable them to stand in someone else's shoes. Students will be able to see themselves reflected in these pages and also learn about populations that they may interact with one day, whether in the supermarket or on the job. Much of this coverage is not just abstract, but also practical: We try to model how to talk about differences and diversity throughout the book. For instance, there is in-depth

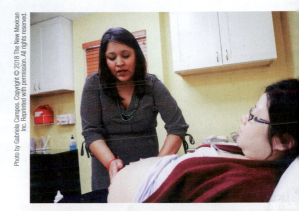

Science at Work Developmental science is not knowledge that stays in the classroom. It is information that enriches careers and lives outside of class. Portraits of professionals like Nicolle Gonzales (*top*), a midwife in New Mexico, and Heather Kosakowski, a researcher in neuroscience in Boston (*bottom*), appear in each chapter.

Developmental Science Changes Lives Whether it is an intervention to understand the strengths of Yazidi refugees (*left*) or to help anxious children recover from trauma such as displacement in Gaza, Palestine (*right*), developmental science can help identify effective practices to make things better.

Joy of Science Developmental scientists studied the effects of early education on children's lives in Brazil: helping build evidence that children benefit from early opportunities.

discussion about what it means to talk about culture, race, and identity labels in Chapter 1. In Chapter 10, we talk about the impact of labels on body size and weight-related stigma.

We know from learning science that this is not just the right thing to do, but also an effective way of building student motivation (Byrd, 2016). However, we also know that we need to apply the principles of cultural humility to our own efforts (Abbott et al., 2019). Working closely with our colleagues at Macmillan Learning, we engaged with many expert reviewers and instructors to ensure that all students would feel represented in this text. Sensitivity reviewers read the manuscript to ensure we were up to date on the most current ways to communicate inclusively. As a result of these efforts, we have written for a broad audience but acknowledge that we may not always get it quite right. Our aim is to make sure that people of all backgrounds and identities feel that this is a course where they belong.

Engaging and Current Science

We teach this course and chose to author this book because we find scientific research exciting and interesting. Every day arrives with new insights into children's development in today's world. Much of the news can seem bleak, as with recent reports of increasing diagnoses of mental health difficulties in children (Lebrun-Harris et al., 2022). But other reports are more positive: This year, more adolescents felt hopeful about the future than they had in decades (Harvard Kennedy School, 2021).

One of the biggest challenges we faced while writing each chapter was in deciding which concepts and topics to omit, many of which we thought students would love to know: Could we have more on glia? Could we squeeze in another example of adolescent activism? What about more theoretical coverage of cultural variations in the acceptance of diversity? What about mental health? We have tried to limit ourselves to what students can realistically get through in a semester, while continuing to channel our enthusiasm.

One of our goals is to make developmental science engaging and accessible, as well as to share the value of science as a discipline. In the spirit of *Scientific American* magazine, this brings the excitement of important breakthroughs in science using language that most anyone can understand. You will find the latest science on prenatal brain maturation in Chapter 4 and the benefits of young people's community involvement in Chapter 15. You will see our excitement about science in the visual program, as well: in the infographics about brain development (see Brain Development in Early Childhood on page 174) and about the impact of context on development (see Contexts of Middle Childhood on page 308). Brief descriptions of current research that inspires us appears in marginal *Share It!* features, designed to encourage students to look beyond the text and delve into the research themselves. Online *Spotlight on Science* activities walk students through current and classic scientific work, from Harlow's research on attachment to empirical tests of intervention research in adolescence. Throughout, we share our curiosity about developmental research. From epigenetics to executive function, you will find cutting-edge science on every page.

A Strengths-Based Perspective

We teach and do research in developmental science because we believe that science is a tool to support well-being in development and break barriers that may limit our growth. Although the world is full of challenges, we want students to view developmental science as a source of solutions that help and empower people throughout all stages of life. While there are many institutional and structural barriers that can keep children from thriving, we highlight throughout the book how to boost resilience and promote positive developmental practices.

A focus on the unique strengths and resilience found in all communities enhances our discussions of challenges and disparities. We incorporate the most current research so that students have the tools they need to make the world a better place for themselves and for others. You will find many major sections that include examples of empirical interventions, from home visiting to tutoring for college students, that have been shown to improve lives. We focus on applications as well as abstraction. For instance, you can read about an intervention that supports early language development on page 134 or that identifies risk factors for suicide on page 385 or that highlights jobs of the future on page 403.

Building Skills

In addition to making developmental science accessible and relevant, as educators we aim to build lasting skills people can use in the real world. Among the most important are critical thinking and scientific literacy to help everyone navigate a world full of information. Many development textbooks introduce the scientific method in the introductory chapters and then never address it again.

We revisit the design and conduct of research in the text, in figures that highlight specific results and in special features. In Chapters 4 and 11, for instance, we examine issues of experimental versus correlational studies. In Chapter 7, we acknowledge where research is still incomplete in our understanding of how to prevent allergies and build a healthier microbiome.

We also demonstrate how to interpret multiple claims and news stories that we encounter every day. Scientific literacy involves learning how to read and interpret graphs, tables, and figures—skills that are addressed throughout the book. Scientific literacy also means being able to communicate about science, which means being able to use appropriate terms to talk about everything from social categories to age stages.

Part of thinking like a scientist means confronting ideas that may run counter to our own upbringing or experience, whether that is research about how to feed a baby or what types of support help children learning to read. One of the joys of developmental science is that it covers topics that are personal and often connected to our lived experiences, so prepare to disagree! Scientific thinking also demands that we master a great deal of vocabulary in order to communicate effectively. Some of these terms may be new and unfamiliar, and, although we have tried to make it accessible, some

Paul J. Richards/AFP via Getty Images

Persevering for the Win The girls' robotics team from Afghanistan impressed the world in 2018 with their strong showing in international competition. Years later, they have been trying to solve new problems: Some have developed cost-effective ventilators and sanitizing devices to help during the COVID-19 pandemic. Others have left Afghanistan and are adjusting to a new life in Mexico and Qatar.

specialized terminology may be difficult. For people who are new to these concepts, please stick with it. We hear from most of our students that after the first few weeks of the course, things get easier, more concrete, and more relevant to everyday life and your future career. Thinking about your goals and knowing how typical it is for course material to seem rigorous, can help you persist (Binning et al., 2020).

Integrated Features

We have integrated a set of highlighted sections into this project to spotlight key aspects of developmental science and build critical-thinking skills.

- *Can You Believe It?* features embedded in every chapter present a controversial topic or common myth in the field and ask readers to unpack the evidence. Each section examines study designs, identifies author biases, and searches for outsized claims in the context of high-interest topics, such as whether mobile apps have changed dating (page 407), or whether screen time can really change the brain (page 273).
- *Making a Difference* features present the important work and interventions from developmental science that promote well-being in the lives of children, adolescents, and adults. For example, we cover how science is changing attitudes about spanking (page 233), how research on the long-term effects of concussions is making sports safer (page 342), and how to incorporate more play into preschool (page 233).
- *Science in Practice* features profile people from a variety of professions who use developmental science at work, such as pre-K teacher Johnathon Hines from Atlanta, Georgia (page 40), who applies the charisma that once helped him on the basketball court to teach phonics. Or robotics engineer Randi Williams from Cambridge, Massachusetts (page 193), who applies lessons from Piaget to designing interactive machines for children. These profiles introduce a variety of potential careers and help explain how research informs the world of work in diverse professions including teaching, nursing, medicine, criminal justice, case work, child care, and neuroscience.

Developmental Science in the Real World Johnathan Hines (*left*) is an award-winning pre-K teacher in Georgia: and a role model. Randi Williams (*right*) studies how children interact with technology to help design robots.

Photo by Vaneeda Thompson, courtesy DeKalb County School

Courtesy Randi Williams, photo by Huili Chen

- *Learn It Together* are interactive group activities that appear in every chapter. One of many lessons from the pandemic is that it can be beneficial to learn in a group; sometimes there is no better way to learn than with others. From asking students to role-play parent–adolescent conflict or parenting styles, to assignments that analyze what makes us feel grown up, these engaging activities will help students take their learning to the next level.

- *Share It!* callouts in the margins address practical and high-interest topics to hook students into the more abstract material, but also to provide information useful for their own lives and careers. They answer some of the practical questions students have on topics such as health and wellness. For example, what does science tell us about how to soothe an inconsolable baby? What are ways developmental scientists have helped adolescents make a positive difference in their communities?

- **Innovative figures and photographs that teach** We employ the latest approaches to visualizing data that *Scientific American* uses to make science clear and accessible to a popular audience. Every chapter also integrates infographics that are designed to visually reinforce the material in the text itself. Graphics review the chronology of major events in development (see Figure 7.1 on page 178) and integrate various theories of development (see Infographic 2.1 on page 44). We know that brain and biological development is often challenging to visualize, so infographics bring together what we know about brain development in every age stage through early adulthood. Context is also important to development, so each age stage includes a diagram showing the factors that promote resilience and risk, including special coverage of the impact technology and the environment have on development around the world.

The World Is Changing Whether it is war in Ukraine or a global pandemic, lives are constantly in flux. Highlighting strength-based interventions helps identify ways we can all develop more resilience to adjust to the constancy of change.

Interactive Features

We take full advantage of online learning tools to enhance the learning process and give students real-time feedback. We have worked closely with a group of video producers, visionary content providers, and the capable team at Macmillan Learning to pull together materials for you to use in your course that we have used in our own teaching.

- *Scientific American Profiles* are the short video clips that are so central to this project. These videos reflect the families that we talk about in every chapter: They take readers into the homes of the children and families. In addition to providing context for the major concepts, these videos foster an emotional connection to the material that will stick with students.

- *Spotlight on Science* activities focus on studies we found particularly interesting and wanted to take more time with. We wrote these activities to walk students through scientific studies, focusing on the nitty-gritty of research and highlighting its methodology. Students will examine and interpret data, reinforce scientific concepts, and make meaningful connections to chapter content, whether the topic relates to an analysis of the experimental method as used to understand childhood allergies for Chapter 4 or the impact of peers on cognition in Chapter 14.

- For the first time, the popular *Concept Practice* tutorials by Thomas Ludwig (Hope College) are available for development. These short activities enable students to practice their understanding of more than 30 important concepts in less than 5 minutes each.

- The ***Video Collection for Developmental Psychology*** is an extensive archive of over 150 video clips that covers the full range of the course and includes classic experiments, research footage, interviews, news clips, and more. This collection is newly updated with recent videos on cyberbullying, food insecurity, online dating, talking about race, body image, gender neutral parenting, and the effects of the COVID-19 pandemic on mental health and learning. All Macmillan Learning videos are closed captioned and accompanied by a transcript to accommodate all learners.
- ***Scientific American Library***. We have chosen several classic and contemporary *Scientific American* articles to supplement the book. Students can read Jean Piaget, Stella Thomas, and Alexander Chess in their own words, bringing science to life in a different way. Each article is accompanied by scaffolding and a brief assessment.
- ***Developing Lives*** provides a robust interactive experience in which users "raise" their own child from conception to adolescence. As the child grows, the student responds to events both planned and unforeseen, making important decisions (nutrition choices, doctor visits, and child care) and facing uncertain moments (bullying, substance use, and a new school), with each choice affecting how the child grows. The entire product has been revised and features new scenarios, including celebrating baby's first birthday, discovering cultural practices around losing baby teeth, and exploring rites of passage.

ACHIEVE for *Scientific American: Child and Adolescent Development*

Achieve for *Scientific American: Child and Adolescent Development* is a comprehensive online learning platform that makes it easy to integrate assessments, activities, and analytics into your teaching. Built from the ground up for today's learners, it includes an interactive e-book, LearningCurve adaptive quizzing, and all of the interactive features of *Scientific American: Child and Adolescent Development*. Achieve can be integrated with all major LMS providers and meets a high level of web accessibility standards. See the very front of the text for more information about these engaging digital resources.

Additional Instructor Resources in Achieve: All in One Place

- The test bank was written specifically to match the content and learning outcomes of *Scientific American: Child and Adolescent Development*. Authors Lora Garrison (Rogers State University), Carmon Weaver Hicks (Ivy Tech Community College), and Christine Park (California State University, Los Angeles) worked in consultation with the authors to craft an assessment package as carefully constructed as the book and media. In total, it comprises over 3,000 multiple-choice and essay items written at several levels of Bloom's taxonomy and tagged to the chapter section.
- The Lecture Slides, authored by Kristine Camacho (Worcester State University), reimagine the content of the text for in-class presentation with abundant images, a concise presentation of the major points, and questions for discussion. Each presentation is also annotated with tips for teaching and other instructor resources to help build effective and engaging classroom experiences.

Also Available: Achieve Read & Practice

Achieve Read & Practice marries Macmillan Learning's mobile-accessible e-book with the acclaimed LearningCurve adaptive quizzing. Instructors can assign reading and quizzing easily, students can complete assignments on any device, and the cost is significantly less than that of a printed book. Find out more at http://macmillanlearning.com/readandpractice.

Thanks

Creating this project has taken many years and help from many, many instructors and students who shared with us what worked for them in the classroom. We are very appreciative for the candid feedback we have received from so many people who care about this course and getting accessible developmental science out into the world. These include:

Andrea Cureton, Spartanburg Community College

Ahni Fritton, Lesley University

AJ Marsden, Beacon College

Alma E. Cortes, Los Angeles Pierce College

Amanda Joyce, Murray State University

Amy Resch, Citrus College

Amy Strimling, Sacramento City College

Angela Bright, Indiana State University

Angie McDonald, Palm Beach Atlantic College

Anika Hunter, Prince George's Community College

Anna Otto, Sacramento City College

April Peterson, California State University–Fullerton

Barbara Gamble, University of the Cumberlands

Barbara Shebloski, University of CA–Davis

Barry Davis, South Florida Bible College and Theological Seminary and Tri-State Bible College

Bernadette Towns, Bakersfield College

Beth Sanders, Atlantic Cape Community College

Brian Belland, PA State University–Main Campus

Candace Lapan, Wingate University

Carolanne Carty, Moravian University

Caroline Millen, Keystone College

Carolyn Hsiao, Immaculata University

Carrie Perock, Waukesha County Technical College

Caryn Huss, Manhattanville College

Cassendra Bergstrom, University of Northern Colorado

Catherine Phillips, Northwest Vista College

Cecilia Cheung, University of California–Riverside

Charisse Nixon, Pa State at Erie Behrend C

Christie Bartholomew, Kent State University–Trumbull

Christie Thiessen Pickel, Ohio University–Main Campus

Christina McIntyre, Midwestern State University

Christina Sinisi, Charleston Southern University

Claire Ford, Bridgewater State University

Cory Brown, Ohio State University–Newark

Cristina Diaconu, University of Texas Rio Grande Valley–Edinburg Campus

Dave Baskind, Delta College

David Devonis, Graceland University–Lamoni

Dean Vesperman, University of Wisconsin–River Falls

Debi Rutledge, Rochester College

Deborah Harris O'Brien, Trinity Washington University

Deirdre Thompson, Prince George's Community College

Diana Kim, University of Hawaii at Manoa

Elaine Barry, Pa State University–Fayette Campus

Elizabeth Barton, Wayne State University

Emily Bollinger, Eastern Kentucky University

Emily Dulle, Washington University–St. Louis

Emily Yearling, University of Connecticut–Storrs

Erica Gelven, Quinnipiac University

Erin Harmeyer, Louisiana State University & A&M College

Grant Canipe, University of North Carolina–Chapel Hill

Guadalupe Espinoza, California State University–Fullerton

Hawai Kwok, City College of New York–Convent Avenue

Heidi Broad Smith, Northern Maine Community College

Helen Runyan, Regent University

Hilary Kalagher, Drew University

James Eckhoff, South Louisiana CC–Lafayette Campus

Jeffrey Gelfer, University of Nevada–Las Vegas

Jennifer Christie, Jefferson Community College

Jerry Green, Tarrant County Community College–Northwest

Jessica Pieuss, Morningside College

Joanna Barr, Salem State University

Jodi Levinthal, Peirce College

Jodi Swanson, Arizona State University–Tempe

John MacDonald, Quincy College

Joy Bolden, Texas Woman's University

Judith Newman, Pennsylvania State University–Ogontz Campus

Karinna Hurley, University of California–Davis

Karleah Harris, Miami University–Oxford

Kasey Magnuson, Grand Valley State University–Allendale

Kathleen Holloway, University of Texas–Austin

Kathy McGuire, Western Illinois University–Macomb

Katie Fleener, Fresno Pacific University

Kelly Champion, Rockford University

Kristi Moore, Angelo State University

Kristin Homan, Grove City College

Kristin Peviani, Virginia Tech–Blacksburg

Kristina Brookshire-Gay, Eastern Michigan University

Kyle Matsuba, Kwantlen Polytechnic University

Larry Kollman, North Iowa Area Community College

Laura Lopez, Laredo Community College

Laura Ochoa, Bergen Community College

Lauren Holleb, Husson University Bangor Campus

LeAnne Syring, Southwest Minnesota State University

Leslie Holley, Nova Southeastern University

Lesly Pogrew-Terrance, Colorado Community College

Lindsay Bonebrake, Midwestern Baptist Theological Seminary

Lindsay Oram, North Central Missouri College

Lindsay Taraban, University of Pittsburgh–Main

Lonny Meinecke, King University

Loreen Huffman, Missouri Southern State College

Lucien Winegar, Ursinus College

Madison Smart-McCarthy, Tidewater CC–Norfolk

Mamta Saxena, SUNY Oswego State University

Margaret Maghan, Ocean County College

Marisa Castronova, Caldwell College

Martha Page, Elizabeth Community College

Mary Hughes Stone, San Francisco State University

Mary Schindler, Sonoma State University

Mary Shuttlesworth, La Roche College

Matthew Wiediger, Richland Community College

Meeta Banerjee, University of South Carolina

Megan Lorenz, Augustana College

Mel Moore, University of Northern Colorado

Melissa Heagy, Eastern University

Michael Coughlin, Bristol Community College

Michael Figuccio, Farmingdale State College

Michelle Chesnut, Trinity University

Michelle Kwok, Texas A&M–Main Campus

Nanci Monaco, SUNY University at Buffalo

Nancy Alwood, University of Arkansas–Main

Nicole Hansen, Fairleigh Dickinson University, College at Florham

Oh Ryeong Ha, University of Missouri–Kansas City

Patrick K. Smith, Virginia Peninsula CC–Hampton

Paula Donohue, Dominican University New York

Paula Mullineaux, Hamline University–St. Paul

Rebecca Castile, Spartanburg Community College

Rebecca Langley, Henderson State University

Robert Hoople, SUNY–Morrisville

Robert McDermid, Missouri Southern State College

Robert Rex Johnson, Delaware County Community College

Rodrigo Rodriguez, CA State University–Fresno

Rosanne Dlugosz, Scottsdale Community College

Shanna Davis, Eastern Washington University

Sharla Snider, Texas Woman's University–Denton

Shawnice Johnson, Virginia Tech

Shubam Sharma, University of Florida–Gainesville

Starlette Sinclair, Florida Gulf Coast University

Stephen Pulos, Roberts Wesleyan College

Steven McCloud, CUNY–Borough of Manhattan Community College

Susan Martinez, Tarrant County Community College–Northeast

Tara Kaser, Ivy Tech Community College–Indianapolis

Tara Stoppa, Eastern College

Terry Stone, University of Nebraska–Omaha

Theresa Kearns-Cooper, Jackson State University

Tianlin Wang, SUNY–Albany

Tingting Xu, Stephen F. Austin State University

Victoria Taylor, Prince George's Community College

Violeta Rodriguez, University of Georgia–Athens

Virtue Sankoh, CUNY–Herbert H Lehman College

Young Suk Hwang, CA State University-San Bernardino

This project is much more than a text. The words created by the dedicated team of Test Bank, Lecture Slide, and LearningCurve authors will be some of the ones our students will pay the most attention to. We are grateful to Lora Garrison, Carmon Weaver Hicks, Kristine Camacho, and Christine Park for accompanying us on this journey. Writing assessment questions is not for the faint of heart: It takes tremendous creativity, empathy, and dogged persistence. We are so fortunate to have this team of instructors to share their energies to help students get the most out of the course.

We are particularly grateful to the team at Macmillan Learning who have worked with us over the years. We have been so fortunate to work on this project with the expert guidance of Dan DeBonis and Andrea Musick Page, who cared about us, the instructors they work with, and the science as much as we did, dreaming and thinking about this project on what was supposed to be their off time. Thank you to the management team at Macmillan Learning, including Charles Linsmeier, Shani Fisher, and Christine Brune, for giving us the support we needed. Over the years, we have also been fortunate to work with other thoughtful editors and publishers, including Rachel Losh, Kevin Feyen, Dan McDonough, Matthew Wright, and Mimi Melek. A first-edition project like this takes a village of people who are inspired, ambitious, and a little obsessive.

We have been lucky to work with a team of people who are also caring and fun. Editorial assistant Emily Kelly kept track of the many, many details and shared her insights with good humor. Associate development editor Nick Rizzuti has worked with us for nearly five years and, throughout her work on the manuscript and on the media activities, has always been a smart, reliable, and creative support. Associate director of digital content Anna Garr and senior media editor Karissa Venne have shared their enthusiasm and expert vision for making this project a truly interactive student experience. Art manager Matthew McAdams helped us make our words into pictures and connected us with the amazingly talented illustrator and designer Eli Ensor, who knows brain anatomy, design, and how to make things beautiful. We are grateful for Eli's time and creativity in helping us make the infographics and figures on these pages. John Callahan created a cover that helps to share the stories and the people that are at the heart of the book.

Cheryl Dubois spent many months helping us find the beautiful photographs that appear in this project, with expert assistance from Sheena Goldstein and Jennifer MacMillan. Our production and copyediting team of Peter Jacoby, Deborah Heimann, Daniel Nighting, and the team at Lumina Datamatics were flexible, careful, and insightful in making sure the details were right. We appreciate the team from Writing Diversely, including Renee Harleston, Isabelle Felix, and Sossity Chiricuzio, who shared their expertise and lived experience in helping us write to a broad group of readers with empathy. Our marketing team, including Stephanie Ellis and Kate Nurre, have helped us get in touch with the many people who teach this course and better understand their needs.

Jessica would like to send a note of thanks for the patience of her family and their help, love, and faith in this project. She would also particularly like to thank Allison and Andrew for continuing on this journey, sharing their enthusiasm about science, and being optimistic even in the grueling bits of this adventure.

Allison and Andrew would also like to thank their families for their love and support throughout this project, for always asking "how's the textbook going?" and never asking "why is it taking so long?" They are grateful to Ben and Gabe, for putting up with endless discussions about textbook details that continued at the dinner table, and to Jessica, for her incredible creativity, vision, and determination—they could not have had a better partner on this adventure. They thank each other for mutual support through yet another collaboration beyond marriage, home, and parenting.

Enormous appreciation to Caroline Losneck and to Kate Super and her team, including Joe Gamez and Jim Arounness, at Point Studio, for coordinating with the profiled families and creating beautiful, moving footage.

Most of all, thank you to the families, the professionals, and the children who shared their stories and homes with us: trusting us to share your stories, your children's first steps, and your own challenges, hopes, and dreams. Thank you for making the story of development come to life.

Allison S. Fuligni   Andrew J. Fuligni   Jessica Bayne

1 The Science of Human Development

© Macmillan, Photo by Sidford House

Development Is a Science
1.1 Define scientific thinking.
1.2 Define developmental science.

The History of Developmental Science
1.3 Describe the historical origins of developmental science.

Themes of Developmental Science
1.4 Analyze four key themes addressed by developmental science.
1.5 Explain the contexts of family, community, country, and historical moments in shaping development.
1.6 Describe the complexity of understanding culture and development.
1.7 Explain the ways in which developmentalists describe human growth and change.

Four-year-old Lucia's biggest dream was to have a Little Mermaid–themed birthday party, with a green cake and all her preschool classmates in attendance. As is true for many young children, birthday parties were part of the cycle of Lucia's life: paper plates and decorated cakes, themed napkins and paper bags filled with treats. Unfortunately, her birthday party had to be scaled back, as were many social events during the first waves of the COVID-19 pandemic.

Lucia lives in Miami, Florida, with her younger sister, Nina, and her parents, Michelle and Patricio. When she is not in school, she spends a lot of time with her grandparents, Hugo and Marta, who watch her in the afternoons (and let her ride her tricycle indoors!). Lucia, like many children her age, thrives on routines, which were forced to change by a global pandemic.

Pandemic restrictions meant that Lucia had "Zoom school" in her grandparents' living room instead of "real school." She spent long days with Nina and had more time to play soccer and learn to balance on a bike with her father, Patricio. She also got better at recognizing when her mother, Michelle, was on a work call, based on the kind of laughter she heard from the other room. And of course, Lucia did not have the Little Mermaid party with her preschool friends that she had wanted so desperately.

Missing a birthday party turned out to be a small sacrifice during a global pandemic. Compared to many other children around the world who were confined to their homes for months, lost family members to the virus, or contracted COVID-19 themselves, Lucia fared easily during the pandemic. The Florida sunshine and her spacious backyard enabled her to spend lots of time outdoors.

Nevertheless, Lucia's life was changed in many ways, and it was not the first time the little girl had been challenged to be flexible.

Just before the pandemic, when Lucia was only 2 and Nina was a newborn, their father, Patricio, was diagnosed with an aggressive form of cancer that had metastasized throughout his body. Fifteen years ago, it would have been considered incurable, but Patricio benefited from recent scientific advances in cancer treatment that employ the body's immune cells to fight off the disease.

For Lucia, this experience meant her parents were worried, her father had to be careful when he picked her up, and he spent a lot of time resting. There were unexpected rides in the car and days when her grandparents put her to bed instead of her parents. Patricio experienced some setbacks during his treatment, but by the time the pandemic began, his scans had started to come back clear. Michelle and Patricio credit science for saving his life.

Lucia's story is exceptional, but it illustrates some universal questions about human development that fascinate scientists, and the rest of us, such as:

- What makes us able to adapt to our environment, as Lucia did when she learned to adjust to Zoom classes and to her father's illness?
- How can we, as Lucia did, develop **resilience**, or the ability to bounce back and recover despite difficult circumstances?
- What is the impact, on Lucia and on other children around the world, of a global pandemic? How do we learn to interpret scientific data about the effect of this unexpected, dramatic event? Will its disruptions and resulting stress lead to long-term emotional or academic repercussions for children, as some have suggested (Deoni, 2021; McCoy et al., 2021; Samji et al., 2022)?

As you will learn, human development is complex — dependent on different factors and elements mixed together over time. Its study is focused on learning how, when, and why development happens — for Lucia and her family and for humanity as a whole (Lerner, 2021; Raeff, 2016). Lucia and her family exemplify the amazing potential of human beings to grow and adapt despite challenges. They also remind us of the power of science. Science helped Patricio survive cancer and will enable researchers to understand the impact of the pandemic on Lucia and other children.

Scientific American Profile

Meet Lucia

Development Is a Science

Learning Objectives

1.1 Define scientific thinking.

1.2 Define developmental science.

resilience The ability to bounce back and recover despite difficult life circumstances.

science A process of gathering and organizing knowledge about the world in a way that is testable and reliable.

Science is the process of gathering and organizing knowledge about the world in a way that is testable and reliable. Science is based on the idea that there are universal, objective truths that can be studied *empirically*, which is to say they can be verified by systematic study. Science is not a set of facts, but a way of learning that is based on rigorously questioning what you know, testing that information, and relying on other people to cross check what you discover.

Scientific breakthroughs helped Patricio attend his daughters' birthdays, even if they were small gatherings with a cake in the backyard. Such breakthroughs have also made people around the globe healthier and enabled more of us, despite the pandemic, to live longer, happier lives than ever before in human history (Aburto et al., 2021; Catillon et al., 2018).

Nearly everyone has ideas about how human beings develop. You probably have your own hunches about the right ways to raise a child, how best to get through elementary school, and how people should act when they reach adolescence. Science is different from opinion, or even your own individual experiences, because it can be supported (or disproven) by evidence.

Science can be surprising: Did you know that getting enough sleep is one of the best ways teenagers can improve their mental health (Urrila et al., 2017)? Or that newborns can recognize their parents on the day they are born (Lee & Kisilevsky, 2014)? Or that being bilingual helps boost children's cognitive function (Cat et al., 2018)?

What Is Development?

Development refers to the changes that happen as we grow and develop, even before birth. It is also the study of what in the environment and in our genes make each of us unique. Worldwide, there are major differences between adults' and children's ability to think, manage their feelings, and survive independently. No one believes that children are simply "short adults": Everyone recognizes that *something* changes between birth and adulthood beyond just getting taller (Garbarino & Bruyere, 2013, p. 259). Developmental science is the study of what exactly that something is.

All living beings, from amoebas to elephants, change as they grow, but only humans have such a long period between birth and adulthood (Hrdy & Burkart, 2020; Stearns, 2017). The two decades that it takes for humans to reach maturity enable children and adolescents to learn how to thrive in a social world, including how to communicate with language and manage their feelings in groups (Gopnik et al., 2020). This has allowed human beings to develop the complex relationships and skills that lead to the cultural and technological innovations of the modern world (Caspari & Lee, 2004). Like some other animals and our early humanoid ancestors, human beings are social animals: We live in groups, nurture our children over many years, and support members of the community who need help (Bribiescas, 2020; Kessler, 2020).

Across time, cultures and communities have distinguished childhood from adulthood. Some of this categorization is informed by biology, as with the milestones of birth and puberty. But culture helps determine what biological milestones are important and even when we meet them. Community practices influence the timing and the pace of these milestones: What you eat and how you live, for instance, affect how quickly you grow or when you reach puberty (Brix et al., 2020). Cultures also have different ways of distinguishing stages of growth throughout childhood and adolescence, like whether you start school at 6 A.M. or 9 A.M. or whether you are expected to finish school, begin working full time, and start a family at age 16 or age 30. Most developmental scientists divide childhood into five major sections, as you see in **Figure 1.1**.

This categorization of development is neither precise nor universal. Diversity is an essential part of development. For instance, a baby does not stop being a toddler on the day they turn 2½, and a child does not transform into an adolescent on their twelfth birthday. Many children develop quickly—learning to walk before they turn 1 or reaching puberty before they are 10. Others take extra time. But regardless of the variations, describing children and adolescents who are about the same age—and how the pace of change sometimes differs between them—is one of the major projects of developmental science.

What Is Developmental Science?

Developmental science is the systematic study of how humans grow and the underlying processes that create change over time. The goal of developmental science is to both explain and improve the lives of people of all ages. Developmental researchers are diverse, but they share a common vocabulary, agree on some basic facts about development, and use common methods for studying how people change. They also share values, such as a commitment to accurate science, an appreciation for all kinds of human beings, and empathy for the people they study.

Development is complex and takes place in multiple interconnected circumstances. Lucia's growth, for instance, will be affected by her genes, family, culture,

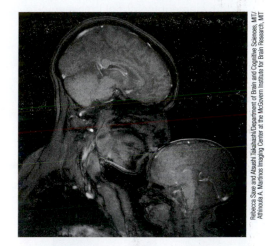

The Brain Is in Everything . . . Even in a parent's love for her child. How did a neuroscientist show her attachment to her baby? She lay down with him in an MRI scanner. There is no single area in the brain of neuroscientist Rebecca Saxe or her 4-month-old son that represents love in this scan. However, you can see signs of attachment in the way she kisses his head and in the fact that she wanted to make this image as a reminder of their bond.

development The pattern of changes and stability in individuals that happens as we grow. It is also the study of what in the environment and in our genes make each of us unique.

developmental science The systematic study of how humans grow and the underlying processes that create change and stability over time.

FIGURE 1.1 Major Periods of Childhood and Adolescence Many distinctions between periods in development are based on cultural expectations. We may think of the stages in childhood and adolescence in terms of where children go to school: preschool (between ages 3 and 5); elementary school (between 6 to 10); middle school (between 11 and 13); and high school ages (14 to 18).

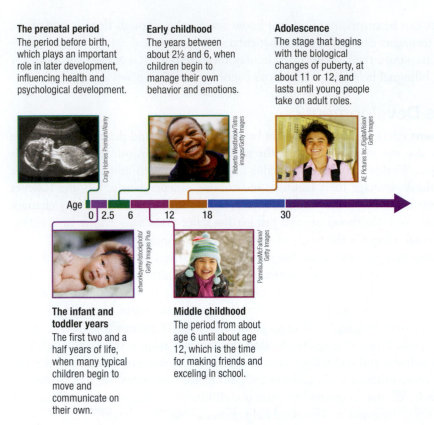

The prenatal period
The period before birth, which plays an important role in later development, influencing health and psychological development.

Early childhood
The years between about 2½ and 6, when children begin to manage their own behavior and emotions.

Adolescence
The stage that begins with the biological changes of puberty, at about 11 or 12, and lasts until young people take on adult roles.

Age   0 2.5 6   12   18   30

The infant and toddler years
The first two and a half years of life, when many typical children begin to move and communicate on their own.

Middle childhood
The period from about age 6 until about age 12, which is the time for making friends and exceling in school.

How Do You Become a Developmental Scientist? For Dr. Deborah Rivas-Drake, it started with majoring in psychology and going on to receive her master's and Ph.D. degrees. She is now a professor at the University of Michigan, where she teaches and directs the Contexts of Academic + Socioemotional Adjustment (CASA) Lab. Dr. Rivas-Drake collaborates with a team of undergraduate, graduate, and postdoctoral students to understand how schools, families, peers, and communities can promote the development of youth of color. She publishes research papers, gives lectures across the country, consults with nonprofit groups (including the makers of Sesame Street), and cowrote an award-winning book. What does Dr. Rivas-Drake seek in her work? "To amplify the ways youth and their families feel empowered by their identities, their narratives, and their roots, so that they may realize a world that is free, in ways beyond what we can imagine ourselves."

and community. Developmental scientists often divide development into *domains*, or broad areas of study, including physical, cognitive, social, and emotional development, areas that often overlap (see **Figure 1.2**). For instance, although brain development, part of the physical domain, is separate from other areas, your brain and its maturation play a crucial role in everything from how you learn language to how you make decisions about fairness in late life. Similarly, it is impossible to consider any of these domains separately from the cultural context. Culture affects how children grow, express their emotions, and even think (Marks & García Coll, 2018; Rogoff et al., 2017).

Developmental science is both interdisciplinary and international. Many researchers come from psychology, but others come from anthropology, neuroscience, pediatrics, sociology, economics, nursing, biology, education, and even engineering. Like other scientists, developmentalists around the world hold each other accountable, review each other's work, and collaborate to create breakthroughs in how we understand both people themselves and how they grow. These researchers are in all seven continents: Understanding what about human development is unique to one community and what is universal is an essential part of developmental science.

Most developmental scientists have advanced degrees, which typically require more than 10 years of studying development after high school. They often have years or even decades of hands-on experience working with people and conducting research, which involves testing new ideas. This education helps them learn the specialized vocabulary, standards, and techniques for contributing to developmental knowledge.

Developmental scientists use a variety of *methods*, or ways of studying development, which will be described in more depth in Chapter 2. Many scientists invite children or adolescents to participate in laboratory experiments. Others study participants' brains with high-tech devices, and still others may work with people in more naturalistic settings, observing children in schools or interviewing families in their homes. Developmental researchers also have differing areas of *focus*. For instance,

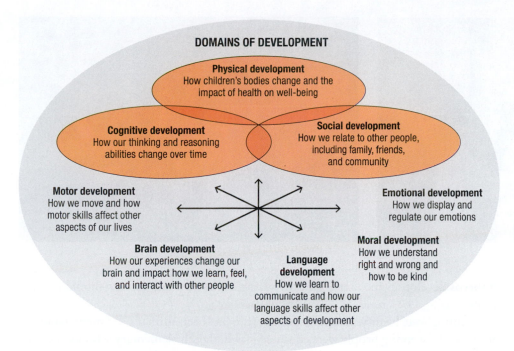

DOMAINS OF DEVELOPMENT

Physical development
How children's bodies change and the impact of health on well-being

Cognitive development
How our thinking and reasoning abilities change over time

Social development
How we relate to other people, including family, friends, and community

Motor development
How we move and how motor skills affect other aspects of our lives

Emotional development
How we display and regulate our emotions

Brain development
How our experiences change our brain and impact how we learn, feel, and interact with other people

Language development
How we learn to communicate and how our language skills affect other aspects of development

Moral development
How we understand right and wrong and how to be kind

FIGURE 1.2 Domains of Development
When developmental scientists analyze how we grow, they often separate our behaviors into broad areas of study, called domains, that overlap and intersect.

some researchers may focus on close relationships, others on the development of thinking, and others on creating policy or advocating for social justice. However, as trained developmental scientists, they all agree on some broad outlines of human development.

Developmental science provides a framework for professionals working with children and adolescents, such as nurses, teachers, social workers, lawyers, probation officers, doctors, coaches, clergy, and many others. These professionals are often able to adapt developmental scientific breakthroughs into interventions that help people thrive. For instance, more than one in four children around the world has survived serious trauma, violence, or war—experiences that do not always wear off (Ellis et al., 2022; Hillis et al., 2016). One research team worked with a group of children in Iraq who lost many of their family members in war, and were forced to flee their homes, in order to understand how their early experiences influenced their ability to focus in school. The researchers' goal was to find out what strengths helped these children succeed in school and overcome the trauma in their early lives (Pellizzoni et al., 2019).

APPLY IT! 1.1 How will Lucia's community affect how she grows up? Do you think your community changed how you developed? Do you think that you might have developed differently if you had lived in a different neighborhood, a different country, or a different family?

1.2 Lucia is in the stage of early childhood. What do you think marked your transition from childhood into adolescence, or from adolescence into adulthood? Do you think these transitions are universal?

Building Strengths with Friends Around the world, more than 20 million children have been forced from their homes as a result of war or natural disaster. Developmental scientists work with children and their families to help them become resilient. These children are playing table football in Sinjar, Iraq. This game is far from the mountainous villages where their families lived until the Islamic State forced them, along with other members of the Yazidi community, from their land.

The History of Developmental Science

People have tried to understand how to nurture development since the beginnings of human life. Some of the oldest archeological discoveries are miniature tools that were designed to teach children (Crawford et al., 2018; Sánchez Romero, 2018). In the earliest written records, dating back more than 2,000 years, thinkers from the Middle East, China, and Europe sought to better understand development by learning how

Learning Objective

1.3 Describe the historical origins of developmental science.

How Do We Support Each Other?
Communities often share a commitment to take care of each other, but that does not mean that everyone lives with advantages. In the past and in the present, some people have been neglected. The photograph on the left shows boys, between 10 and 12, working in a fish cannery in Eastport, Maine, in 1911. The photograph on the right shows children and adolescents who were separated from their parents after seeking refuge in the United States. They are shown here waiting in caged rooms in McLaren, Texas, in 2018.

embryos develop in the uterus and theorizing about how adolescents should become adults (Kinney, 1995; Stearns, 2017; Troyansky, 2015).

Throughout history, as in the present, life has been difficult for many children. Some wealthy young people were educated—whether in elementary schools in China or by private tutors in ancient Egypt—but most lives were short and filled with hard work (Kinney, 1995; Stearns, 2016). Until about 1900, about one in three children in the United States would die before their fifth birthday because of illness, starvation, or complications of birth itself (Coontz, 2016; Mintz, 2004). Despite widespread inequality and the recent global pandemic, improvements in health and human rights make today the best time to be alive for many. For instance, babies born today are twice as likely to live into adulthood as they were 30 years ago (UNICEF, 2020). Even in the wake of the COVID-19 pandemic, nearly 9 in 10 children worldwide attend school (UNICEF, 2022a). Most children in need are cared for by family members or in foster families—and fewer than 6 million worldwide are now housed in institutions like orphanages (Desmond et al., 2020).

The Origins of Modern Developmental Science

While human beings have always had ideas about how people mature, developmental science is a recent invention. It combines scientific methodology with a commitment to the human rights and well-being of all people.

European philosophers from the 1600s and 1700s helped to develop a vocabulary for thinking about development. These philosophers had big ideas about how people developed, but they did not base them in empirical study or observation. However, their thoughts about the core nature of human beings continue to be a reference point today. For instance, the English doctor John Locke (1632–1704) believed that children were born "blank slates" to be written upon by life experiences (Locke, 1690/1847). The Swiss philosopher Jean Jacques Rousseau (1712–1778) argued that children were born good until they were corrupted by the world around them (Rousseau, 2010).

Modern science, with an emphasis on empirical observation and testable ideas, began with the advent of the *scientific method* in the late 1500s. Researchers owe a debt of gratitude to Iraqi neuroscientist Ibn al-Haytham, who lived in the 1100s (Di Ventra, 2018). His idea that building knowledge required rigorous experimental study was adapted by European scientists into the scientific method in the late 1500s, as you will learn in Chapter 2. The scientific method became a shared set of rules and assumptions that helped scientists around the world, who spoke dozens of languages and were often trained quite differently, build on each other's work and create a common body of knowledge.

By the mid-1800s, science began to look much as it does today. Researchers worked in laboratories, published their writing, and challenged each other in scholarly articles (Dear, 2008). Over the next 75 years, the foundations for modern disciplines like psychology, economics, and biology took hold (Poskett, 2019). Important breakthroughs established how we learn, challenged prevailing beliefs, and established that early experiences can shape our adult personalities.

Early Concerns for Social Welfare

From ancient times, governments and religious organizations often intervened in peoples' lives—passing laws to regulate child labor, set ages for marriage, or provide care for the sick (Popple, 2018; Wagner, 2005). But as communities became larger and more complex, institutions took a more active role. By the 1900s, many cities around the world had established rudimentary social services, like schools, hospitals, and orphanages (Oakley, 2018).

Many of these institutions were not equally open to all. They were often harsh and imposed rigid ideas about what kind of behavior was "right." For instance, Indigenous children in the United States, Canada, and Australia were often taken from their families and put into boarding schools where they were forced to become "proper" English-speaking citizens (Lomawaima et al., 2018). Other children were rejected from school if they were immigrants or unfairly deemed to be "unfit" (Stoskopf, 1999). But many early social workers and public health workers were deeply committed to human well-being.

In a time when most of U.S. and European culture was dominated by White men, advocating for the welfare of children was an area of public service that was more open to women, immigrants, and people of color, as you can see in **Infographic 1.1** (Oakley, 2018).

Early Developmental Science

By the early 1900s, university scientists were writing popular books about the "science" of parenting and child development. Much of this work was inspired by efforts to make social progress and reform the world. By 1940, many major organizations were founded, such as the Society for Research in Child Development and the American Association of Pediatrics, which still exist today to promote scientific work that advocates for children and adolescents.

Early advocates and scientists often had disturbing ideas about children, gender, and race. Many, including those who wrote for *Scientific American*, and those who worked for leading organizations in developmental science, embraced inhumane, racist, and sexist beliefs (Hopkins, 1921; Nutall, 1911). For instance, G. Stanley Hall (1846–1924), the first U.S. man to receive a Ph.D. in psychology, a university president, and author of a popular book about parenting, suggested in one of his top-selling books that women were "weaker in body and mind" than men and that people of color were "naturally impulsive and undeveloped" (Arnett, 2006; Fasteland, 2019; Hall, 1904). Unfortunately, these offensive ideas were common. However, even then, many developmental scientists rejected those beliefs, and today's scholars are at the forefront of advancing social justice and equality across the lifespan (Cooper et al., 2022).

Early developmental scientists were eager to use their scientific knowledge to help people thrive—and to change popular misconceptions about development. They demonstrated that learning, and not just inevitable maturation, helped children grow (McGraw, 1943). They worked to end routine separations between children and their caregivers and improved medical care for people of all ages (Bowlby, 2008; Spitz, 1945; Warren, 1948). Developmental scientists even helped change laws in the United States and contributed to ending legal segregation in schools (Clark & Clark, 1940; Kluger, 2011).

In Love and Changing the World
Mamie Phipps Clark and Kenneth Clark were pioneering psychologists and advocates for civil rights (and a married couple for 46 years). In the 1940s, the Clarks studied preschoolers and showed that even 3-year-olds understood racial labels, and that racism was affecting their self-esteem and ability to succeed. Their work was crucial to the landmark 1954 U.S. Supreme Court case, *Brown v. Board of Education*, which established racial integration in public schools.

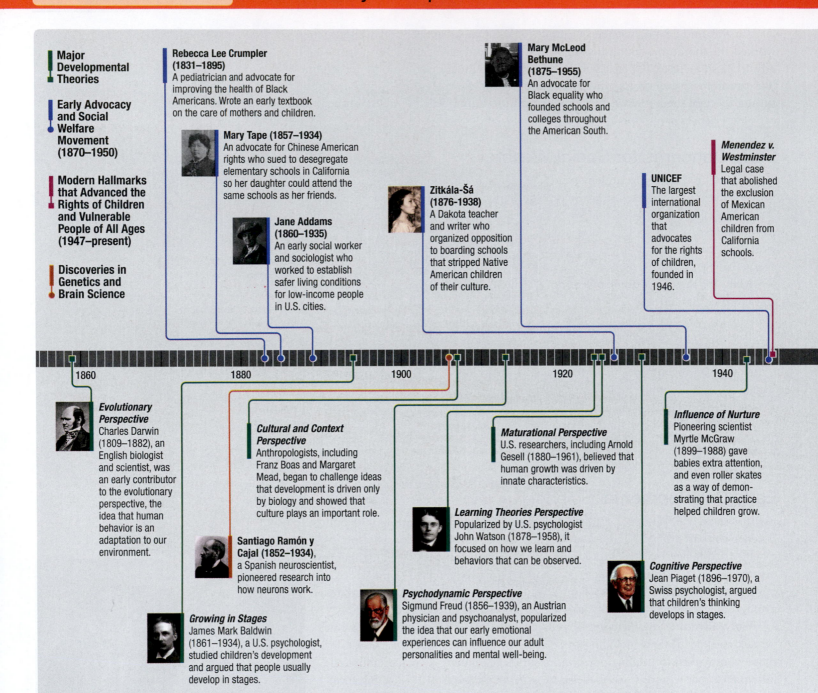

Legend:
- Major Developmental Theories
- Early Advocacy and Social Welfare Movement (1870–1950)
- Modern Hallmarks that Advanced the Rights of Children and Vulnerable People of All Ages (1947–present)
- Discoveries in Genetics and Brain Science

Rebecca Lee Crumpler (1831–1895) A pediatrician and advocate for improving the health of Black Americans. Wrote an early textbook on the care of mothers and children.

Mary Tape (1857–1934) An advocate for Chinese American rights who sued to desegregate elementary schools in California so her daughter could attend the same schools as her friends.

Jane Addams (1860–1935) An early social worker and sociologist who worked to establish safer living conditions for low-income people in U.S. cities.

Mary McLeod Bethune (1875–1955) An advocate for Black equality who founded schools and colleges throughout the American South.

Zitkála-Šá (1876–1938) A Dakota teacher and writer who organized opposition to boarding schools that stripped Native American children of their culture.

UNICEF The largest international organization that advocates for the rights of children, founded in 1946.

Menendez v. Westminster Legal case that abolished the exclusion of Mexican American children from California schools.

Timeline years: 1860, 1880, 1900, 1920, 1940

Evolutionary Perspective Charles Darwin (1809–1882), an English biologist and scientist, was an early contributor to the evolutionary perspective, the idea that human behavior is an adaptation to our environment.

Cultural and Context Perspective Anthropologists, including Franz Boas and Margaret Mead, began to challenge ideas that development is driven only by biology and showed that culture plays an important role.

Santiago Ramón y Cajal (1852–1934), a Spanish neuroscientist, pioneered research into how neurons work.

Growing in Stages James Mark Baldwin (1861–1934), a U.S. psychologist, studied children's development and argued that people usually develop in stages.

Maturational Perspective U.S. researchers, including Arnold Gesell (1880–1961), believed that human growth was driven by innate characteristics.

Learning Theories Perspective Popularized by U.S. psychologist John Watson (1878–1958), it focused on how we learn and behaviors that can be observed.

Psychodynamic Perspective Sigmund Freud (1856–1939), an Austrian physician and psychoanalyst, popularized the idea that our early emotional experiences can influence our adult personalities and mental well-being.

Influence of Nurture Pioneering scientist Myrtle McGraw (1899–1988) gave babies extra attention, and even roller skates as a way of demonstrating that practice helped children grow.

Cognitive Perspective Jean Piaget (1896–1970), a Swiss psychologist, argued that children's thinking develops in stages.

Developmental Science: A Legacy of Theory, Research, and Advocacy People have always had ideas about how we grow and how best to protect children and other vulnerable people. Developmental science is a recent invention that combines modern scientific methodology, classic theories, and a commitment to human rights and the protection of children and adolescents.

Modern Developmental Science

The racist genocide of more than 11 million Jewish, Roma, gay and lesbian, and other marginalized people during World War II had a profound effect on the world and on developmental science. As a result of this atrocity, more scientists and scientific organizations began to reject racism and the idea that personality or behavior is genetic. Scholars turned their attention to focus on the basics about how people grow—and on testing their ideas more rigorously in the laboratory (Hagen et al., 2020). As you will

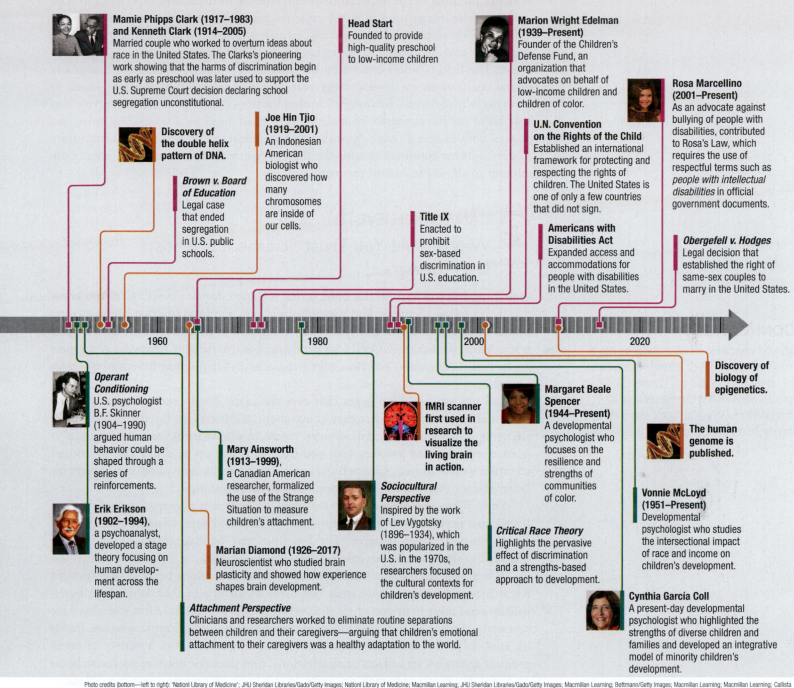

Mamie Phipps Clark (1917–1983) and Kenneth Clark (1914–2005)
Married couple who worked to overturn ideas about race in the United States. The Clarks's pioneering work showing that the harms of discrimination begin as early as preschool was later used to support the U.S. Supreme Court decision declaring school segregation unconstitutional.

Discovery of the double helix pattern of DNA.

Brown v. Board of Education
Legal case that ended segregation in U.S. public schools.

Joe Hin Tjio (1919–2001)
An Indonesian American biologist who discovered how many chromosomes are inside of our cells.

Head Start
Founded to provide high-quality preschool to low-income children

Title IX
Enacted to prohibit sex-based discrimination in U.S. education.

Marion Wright Edelman (1939–Present)
Founder of the Children's Defense Fund, an organization that advocates on behalf of low-income children and children of color.

U.N. Convention on the Rights of the Child
Established an international framework for protecting and respecting the rights of children. The United States is one of only a few countries that did not sign.

Americans with Disabilities Act
Expanded access and accommodations for people with disabilities in the United States.

Rosa Marcellino (2001–Present)
As an advocate against bullying of people with disabilities, contributed to Rosa's Law, which requires the use of respectful terms such as *people with intellectual disabilities* in official government documents.

Obergefell v. Hodges
Legal decision that established the right of same-sex couples to marry in the United States.

1960   1980   2000   2020

Operant Conditioning
U.S. psychologist B.F. Skinner (1904–1990) argued human behavior could be shaped through a series of reinforcements.

Erik Erikson (1902–1994), a psychoanalyst, developed a stage theory focusing on human development across the lifespan.

Mary Ainsworth (1913–1999), a Canadian American researcher, formalized the use of the Strange Situation to measure children's attachment.

Marian Diamond (1926–2017)
Neuroscientist who studied brain plasticity and showed how experience shapes brain development.

Attachment Perspective
Clinicians and researchers worked to eliminate routine separations between children and their caregivers—arguing that children's emotional attachment to their caregivers was a healthy adaptation to the world.

fMRI scanner first used in research to visualize the living brain in action.

Sociocultural Perspective
Inspired by the work of Lev Vygotsky (1896–1934), which was popularized in the U.S. in the 1970s, researchers focused on the cultural contexts for children's development.

Margaret Beale Spencer (1944–Present)
A developmental psychologist who focuses on the resilience and strengths of communities of color.

Critical Race Theory
Highlights the pervasive effect of discrimination and a strengths-based approach to development.

Discovery of biology of epigenetics.

The human genome is published.

Vonnie McLoyd (1951–Present)
Developmental psychologist who studies the intersectional impact of race and income on children's development.

Cynthia García Coll
A present-day developmental psychologist who highlighted the strengths of diverse children and families and developed an integrative model of minority children's development.

Photo credits (bottom—left to right): 'Nationl Library of Medicine'; JHU Sheridan Libraries/Gado/Getty Images; Nationl Library of Medicine; Macmillan Learning; JHU Sheridan Libraries/Gado/Getty Images; Macmillan Learning; Bettmann/Getty Images; Macmillan Learning; Macmillan Learning; Callista Images/ImageSource/AGE Fotostock; Courtesy Margaret Beale Spencer, photo by Ven Sherrod, Chicago, IL; Courtesy Cynthia Garcia-Coll; Pasieka/Science Source

learn in Chapter 2, the theories of child development that are influential today were established after World War II, in the last half of the 1900s. Prominent developmental thinkers explored how learning takes place, the role of relationships in development, and how maturation and cultural contexts influence development.

Technological breakthroughs in the late 1900s also changed how scientists thought about the biology of development (Boddice, 2019; Kandel, 2012). Scientists were able to use computers and scanning devices to look at the living brain. Genetics research made it possible to analyze human genes—and look for patterns associated with how they are activated over time (Hesson & Pritchard, 2019). An international group of researchers, including Zing-Yang Kuo (1898–1970) in Hong Kong and Gilbert Gottlieb (1929–2006) in the United States, discovered experimental and theoretical evidence pointing to the importance of **epigenetics**, or the role of experience in activating genetic information in human maturation (Gottlieb, 2007; Qian et al., 2020).

Today, developmental science is still an international, multidisciplinary enterprise spurred by scientists trying to understand how children grow and how to help them thrive. The field balances basic scientific discoveries—such as measuring how many neural connections we develop every year—with more practical research—such as studying why children have trouble learning fractions or how to develop interventions that build on the strengths of adolescents (National Academies of Sciences, Engineering, and Medicine, 2019; Siegler et al., 2020). Appreciating the importance of culture and community to development continues to spur the field to ensure that the benefits of science are relevant to all people around the world.

CAN YOU BELIEVE IT?
Why Should You Trust Science If Scientists Do Not Agree?

One thing you will learn in this book is that scientists do not always agree. You know this if you follow the news. You may have read reports proposing that breast-feeding boosts intelligence, that video games cause aggression, that moodiness in teenagers is inevitable, or that the COVID-19 pandemic has irretrievably harmed a generation (Gavin, 2020; Gill & Saavedra, 2022; Oster, 2019; Rothman, 2018). Or you may have read the exact opposite.

You just read in these pages that over the years, developmental scientists have made radical changes in what they think about children's development. With these changing and sometimes contradictory pieces of information, you may wonder if science really has any answers. Can you trust what you are reading? Developmental scientists would say yes: Science builds over time, and diversity of opinion makes for better science that you can trust *more*. Remember two things:

First: When you see a claim in the news, know that it may not be the full story. If you read beyond the brief descriptions, you may find that scientists actually agree much more than they disagree. The headlines may be exaggerated or made more dramatic so that you click to read further (Jellison et al., 2020).

When you read about science in the media, it is often because one team of researchers is excited to share what they have discovered in their laboratory. But it usually takes more than one single discovery to build agreement. After scientists have repeatedly discovered the same thing, uncertainty fades and *scientific consensus* builds (Fischhoff, 2013). Scientific consensus means that researchers from a variety of backgrounds agree on a set of facts or observations. This does not mean every researcher is on board, but that a wide majority agree. In this book we present research conclusions that are accepted by most scientists, and we point out where research is still ongoing.

Second: Diversity of ideas and points of view makes science better. When you read about disagreements between experts, it is a sign that science is healthy. Disagreements and contradictions are a crucial part of the research process, because they motivate investigators to test and evaluate their work. Scientific evaluation relies on **critical thinking**, which is the ability to thoughtfully question what you believe or what other people believe (Halonen, 2008). In science, critical thinking means that you evaluate everything carefully against what is accepted and check to make sure that proper procedures have been followed. Scientific disagreements help build new consensus.

In developmental science, strong disagreements have helped to build new consensus. Consensus now exists on a wide variety of subjects. For instance, researchers agree that spanking is unhealthy for children and that separating babies from their families is harmful (Bouza et al., 2018; Butler & Katona, 2019; Sege et al., 2018). Exciting investigations

CONNECTIONS

Are you wondering which of these claims is true? You will find your answers in the Can You Believe It? sections in Chapters 4, 12, and 15. You will find Can You Believe It? sections throughout this book, designed to help build scientific and critical-thinking skills.

epigenetics The role of experience in activating genetic information in human growth.

critical thinking The ability to thoughtfully question what you believe or what other people believe.

continue in other areas. For instance, how can we help children learn to focus more easily, encourage teenagers to stay in school, or support families who are helping their children catch up after the COVID-19 pandemic? Learning about the science of development will arm you with some new ways of understanding what is behind the headlines. You will become skilled in the vocabulary of developmental science. And you will learn about what theories, methods, and cultural biases impact scientific discovery so you can think critically about them yourself.

APPLY IT! **1.3** Early developmental advocates wanted to help improve lives and address inequities they saw in the world around them. Do you see things in your world you would like to change?
1.4 Developmental scientists are looking for answers to help guide our understanding of why we grow and change. Lucia's mother, Michelle, asked us what a developmental scientist would say about the impact of her husband's illness on her young children. What questions do you have about how we develop?

Themes of Developmental Science

Some fields of study are fairly narrow. For instance, doctors may focus on health and educators on learning. But developmental science is a broad field, focusing on health and learning and everything in between and finding patterns in the many factors that influence development.

Four major themes pervade developmental science:

1. Each person's development is a complex interaction between them and the world.
2. The process of development is universal but also unique to each person.
3. Culture and community context are critical.
4. Change is constant, but some elements of ourselves remain the same.

Although these concepts may seem abstract, the goal of developmental science is very concrete: to improve lives (Lerner & Murray, 2016).

Learning Objectives

1.4 Analyze four key themes addressed by developmental science.

1.5 Explain the contexts of family, community, country, and historical moments in shaping development.

1.6 Describe the complexity of understanding culture and development.

1.7 Explain the ways in which developmentalists describe human growth and change.

Beyond Nature Versus Nurture

How did Lucia maintain her sunny, exuberant personality despite the stresses in her life? How does she still have the energy to run her tricycle through the house, sing at the top of her lungs, make up yet another party game with her little sister, and confidently learn how to sound out new words? Many of us might suggest a simple answer: Perhaps Lucia was just born outgoing and optimistic. Or, maybe her mother's positive thinking made her easygoing.

Developmental scientists might call this a trick question. Growth arises from a mind-boggling combination of factors that interact to create who we are. So, a scientist might not give you a simple answer about what makes Lucia so adaptable. Instead, they may draw you a chart of the intersecting and overlapping factors that all contribute to her ability to respond to life's experiences.

This complexity of development offers hope: It allows for change to happen at any point and for a great diversity of possible outcomes. The many factors that impact development are interconnected in a complex, interrelated system (Lerner, 2021; Overton, 2015; Witherington & Boom, 2019). This means, for instance, that it is very unusual that one risk factor in development always leads universally and predictably to another—multiple factors are always in play as people grow (Sameroff, 2020). Small things can add up: Repeated experiences of discrimination or multiple lucky breaks can change a life for better or worse (Hicken et al., 2018; Jackson et al., 2011).

nature The influence of genetics on development.

nurture The influence of experience on development.

Scientific American Profile

Family and Resilience

Outside of developmental science, people often simplify human development as resulting from someone's genetics or from what they've experienced. Researchers often refer to the influence of genetics on development as **nature** and to the influence of experience on development as **nurture**, calling this the question of nature versus nurture. For instance, if you said that Lucia's resilience was something she was born with or inherited from her parents, like a gene for trying new things, you would be attributing her talents to her *nature*. On the other hand, if you said that Lucia's resilience was something she learned from her family, you would be attributing it to her *nurture*.

Developmental scientists have learned that it isn't accurate to label development as either nature *or* nurture (Lerner, 2021). In fact, as you will learn in Chapter 3, even your genetic code is influenced by your environment. Your genes also change your environment. For instance, researchers have found that newborns who have genetically driven characteristics like being very fussy are more likely to evoke irritable responses from their careworn families than those who are more mellow, leading to a cascade of changes for those babies and their families (Quist et al., 2019). Researchers have found that your genes and the environment around you interact and mutually influence each other in a complex and ever-changing dance that occurs over your entire lifespan (Overton, 2013).

It is also common for people to wonder whether the brain drives behavior. Does something in Lucia's brain explain her personality? Developmental scientists believe that complex traits, like personality characteristics, will never be identified as coming from one place inside your skull. Even if they could prove that Lucia's brain is a little different from someone else's, researchers caution that any differences may be caused by the activities associated with what makes Lucia unique—rather than her unique traits being driven by her brain. Just as your genes interact with the environment (and vice versa), your brain interacts with the world.

Development Is Both Universal and Unique

There are about 8 billion people on the Earth right now, each one of them unique (Wilmouth et al., 2022). Even identical twins are, as described in Chapter 3, actually different—right from the beginning (Jonsson et al., 2021). These 8 billion people live in more than 195 countries and 24 time zones, and they speak more than 7,000 different languages (Eberhard et al., 2022). You may wonder how, with so much diversity and variation, we can possibly tell a universal story about how children grow.

The Same But Different Cyrille, age 9, and his brother, Dima, age 8, now try to stay safe in a bunker under a school near their home in Kharkiv, Ukraine. Understanding what is universal about children, despite their circumstances, might help families make sure their children have time to play and stick to a regular routine, despite the horrors of war.

Developmental science explains typical patterns in human development and explores why there are variations. For instance, as people grow, some predictable age-related differences occur: Most children walk around their first birthday, most 9-year-olds have a best friend, and many 14-year-olds are capable of acing algebra. This doesn't mean all of this is true for everyone. However, understanding these common patterns helps those who work with children and adolescents to know what to expect at different ages.

For instance, although Lucia is unique, she is still subject to some universal patterns of development. In other words, a 4-year-old is still a 4-year-old. Knowing the typical patterns of childhood can help her parents be prepared for the emotional, social, and even physical changes Lucia will experience as she develops.

Understanding typical patterns also helps researchers make sense of variations. For instance, scientists now understand that culture influences how babies learn how to move: Infants whose families encourage them to be active tend to learn how to walk months earlier than other babies (Adolph & Hoch, 2019). As humans, we all share many unifying characteristics, and as individuals, we exhibit our uniqueness in many areas, such as in our appearance and personality. All of these are part of the complex process of development.

Context Shapes Growth

As scientists study and document the variations and the similarities between people, it becomes abundantly clear that a person's environment has an enormous impact on how they grow. Developmental scientists use the term **context** in referring to the broad external factors that surround each of us, which includes where in *time* you live. This would be important if you were comparing the development of Lucia and her sister, Nina, for instance, with that of girls born 100 years earlier when girls were far less likely to attend school and were expected to marry and stay at home. Context also includes your **culture**, or the ideas, beliefs, and social practices that a group of people shares (Cole & Packer, 2016; García Coll et al., 2018). For instance, Lucia and Nina are growing up in a culture that believes *all* children should work hard in school and aspire to any career—whatever their gender.

Context is such a complex factor in development that theorists and researchers have developed models to keep all the details in mind. These *contextual models* include Urie Bronfenbrenner's *bioecological model*, Cynthia García Coll's *integrative model*, and Tara Yosso's *Community Cultural Wealth model*, as well as more focused investigations of the developmental impacts of money, historical moments, and culture.

Developmental scientists agree that culture and context play an important role in development, but they have different ways of describing and modeling how this works. Scientists use figures to make these models more concrete and to communicate how people interact with various parts of their environment as they grow.

Bronfenbrenner's Bioecological Model The bioecological model describes the environments that affect development as being organized into a series of nested systems, like the layers of an onion, that interact with each other (Bronfenbrenner, 1977, 2005). This model was developed by the U.S. psychologist Urie Bronfenbrenner (1917–2005), a theorist and researcher who also played an important role in founding Head Start, the early-childhood program designed to help low-income children succeed in school (Fox, 2005).

In the center of this model, shown in **Infographic 1.2**, is the *person* who interacts with the environment in their own, unique way. Around this person is a series of layers that represent the parts of their context.

Surrounding the individual is the *microsystem*, which includes the most immediate relationships and physical settings, including family, friends, school, and work. For most children around the world, family includes a wide variety of people—sometimes including biological parents, friends, their caregivers' partners, their grandparents, and half- and stepsiblings. The microsystem affects development through direct interaction.

The *mesosystem* is made up of all of the microsystems that the person interacts with and that interact with each other, like the family, child care, school, sports programs, and places of worship. For instance, family–school connections may affect children's experiences in both of those microsystems, or stresses at parents' work may influence family life. While a child may not even be sure where their parent works, their job may have important effects on the child. A raise may allow parents to pay for an afterschool program, or an irregular work schedule may make it difficult for a parent to find consistent child care.

Although the depiction of the bioecological model might suggest that children are passively trapped in the center of these overlapping spheres, developmental scientists believe that people are not entirely helpless nor powerless. People, even children, make choices, and may have an influence on what happens to them (Lerner, 2021). In addition, their unique biology—genetic makeup and health—also plays an important part in their development. The layers in this model don't rank the importance of each factor; they separate them to make them easier to analyze.

context Experiences and conditions that may shape human development, including family, community, culture, and historical moments.

culture The ideas, beliefs, customs, and social practices shared by a group of people.

What Is Your Microsystem? For some, family includes our parents, who may have time to play with blocks on the rug. Other children may be lucky enough to grow up with attention from parents, grandparents, and even great-grandparents.

Bioecological Model of Human Development

Bronfenbrenner's bioecological model is a classic model of social context. The nested circles demonstrate how there are multiple levels of the social environment that interact with each other to influence development. Researchers such as Cynthia García Coll point out that although culture is represented in the outermost level, it permeates all the layers of the system. In addition, people are not just passive recipients of the context: They influence and change their environment.

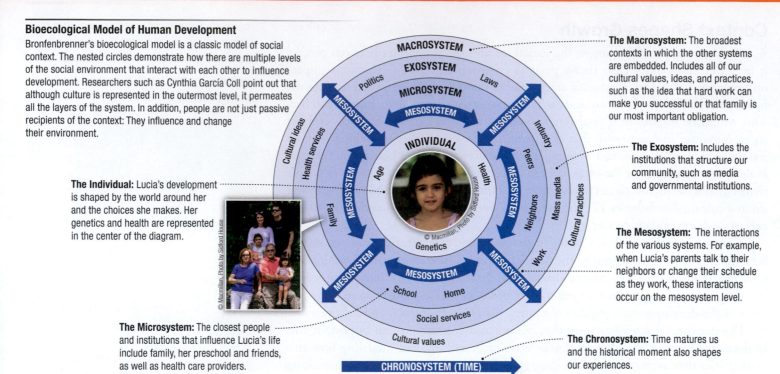

The Macrosystem: The broadest contexts in which the other systems are embedded. Includes all of our cultural values, ideas, and practices, such as the idea that hard work can make you successful or that family is our most important obligation.

The Exosystem: Includes the institutions that structure our community, such as media and governmental institutions.

The Mesosystem: The interactions of the various systems. For example, when Lucia's parents talk to their neighbors or change their schedule as they work, these interactions occur on the mesosystem level.

The Individual: Lucia's development is shaped by the world around her and the choices she makes. Her genetics and health are represented in the center of the diagram.

The Microsystem: The closest people and institutions that influence Lucia's life include family, her preschool and friends, as well as health care providers.

The Chronosystem: Time matures us and the historical moment also shapes our experiences.

Integrative Model of Human Development

The integrative model, originally developed by Cynthia García Coll and others, highlights how social position helps determine how people are affected by context and culture. Privileges are not divided equitably. Adaptive culture can help people thrive.

Experiences of discrimination or segregation may affect the goals and strategies of people in marginalized groups. Lucia's family story of immigration and prospering in new places may support her emotional development.

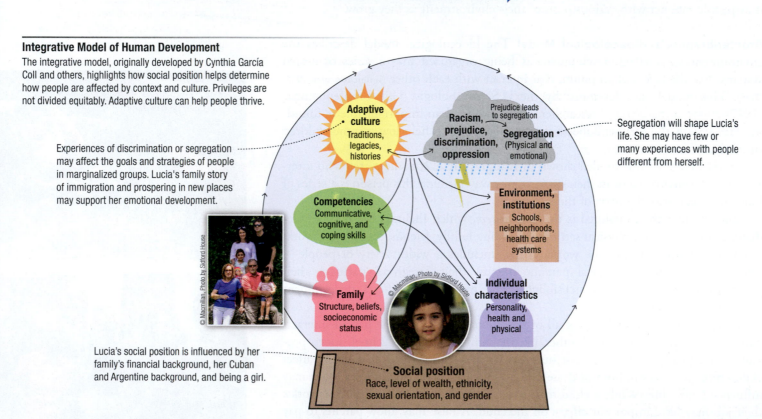

Segregation will shape Lucia's life. She may have few or many experiences with people different from herself.

Lucia's social position is influenced by her family's financial background, her Cuban and Argentine background, and being a girl.

The layer beyond the mesosystem is the *exosystem*, which includes the person's community—from their neighborhood to the local, state, and national governments and the media. A change in a school district's policies will be felt in the child's classroom experience. A change in government policy might affect a parent's ability to get a job or their likelihood of finding medical care.

Surrounding the exosystem is a more abstract level, called the *macrosystem*, which includes the culture, beliefs, and customs of a community (Bronfenbrenner, 1977). This level includes cultural attitudes about people, such as whether they are privileged in a society (as when they are born into a wealthy family) or whether they experience discrimination (perhaps because of a disability or the language they speak). This layer doesn't just hover on the outside, as it might seem to in a diagram: Beliefs and cultural practices of the macrosystem will pervade everyday life experiences and influence all the other layers, as you see in Infographic 1.2 (Rivas-Drake & Umaña-Taylor, 2019; Spencer, 2017; Vélez-Agosto et al., 2017). Permeating all the layers of the bioecological model is the impact of time, as in the changes that happen with development as well as the impact of specific historical moments, which is represented by the *chronosystem*.

Generational Change: You Can't Beat Time Development occurs over time and within a particular historical period. Your age is important—whether you are a baby, a toddler, an adolescent, or an adult. People of different ages may be treated differently depending on where they live and the culture they grow up in.

Historical time is also important. What you live through and how old you were when you experienced it will change you—whether a terrorist attack, a tornado, or a pandemic (Elder & George, 2016). For instance, in the major economic downturn of 2008, known as the Great Recession, many adults lost their jobs or were forced to get by on smaller incomes. Their children—many of whom are in college now—had less faith in the economic system, an attitude that may stay with them for a lifetime (Mortimer, 2019; Sironi, 2018). Emerging research tells us how children and adolescents of different ages were impacted by the COVID-19 pandemic: a change that some suggest was hardest on adolescents' mental health but most challenging for younger children's developing academic skills (Samji et al., 2022; UNICEF, 2022a).

Without question, significant historical events mark how young people develop (Elder & George, 2016). Experts often use major events like wars, economic crises, or natural disasters to divide groups of people into generations, or **birth cohorts** (Elder & George, 2016; Mannheim, 1970). How they divide groups often depends on communities' differing significant historical events. Chinese researchers, for instance, might look at generations in terms of how old they were when they experienced the Chinese Cultural Revolution of 1966–1976 (Jennings & Zhang, 2005). German researchers tend to divide generations in terms of the impact of the fall of the Berlin Wall in 1989 that reunited East Germany with West Germany (Liepmann, 2018). In the United States, researchers tend to divide generations by major wars—like World War II and the Vietnam War (Dimock, 2019). These generations are often referred to by nicknames (Twenge, 2020). (See **Figure 1.3**.)

birth cohorts The categories that experts use to group people from different generations.

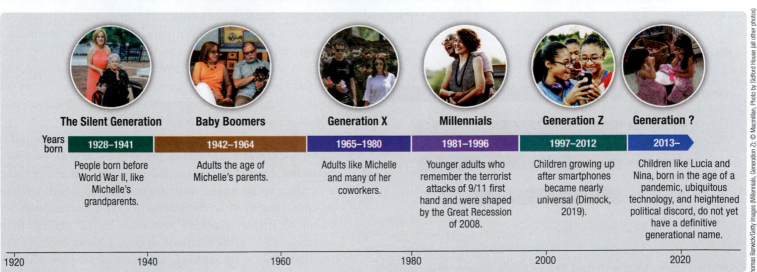

The Silent Generation	Baby Boomers	Generation X	Millennials	Generation Z	Generation ?
Years born 1928–1941	1942–1964	1965–1980	1981–1996	1997–2012	2013–
People born before World War II, like Michelle's grandparents.	Adults the age of Michelle's parents.	Adults like Michelle and many of her coworkers.	Younger adults who remember the terrorist attacks of 9/11 first hand and were shaped by the Great Recession of 2008.	Children growing up after smartphones became nearly universal (Dimock, 2019).	Children like Lucia and Nina, born in the age of a pandemic, ubiquitous technology, and heightened political discord, do not yet have a definitive generational name.

1920   1940   1960   1980   2000   2020

FIGURE 1.3 What Makes a Generation? The historical events that you experience, whether a natural disaster, a technological innovation, or a global pandemic, will shape your development. In the United States, major wars have often defined the generations, but these are not the only important historical markers. Other cultural and social changes, such as a lawsuit challenging segregated schools or a change in immigration policy, are also important events that can change lives (Vélez-Agosto et al., 2017).

John Moore/Getty Images

Looking for New Home: Must Love Dogs One of the costs of economic insecurity is losing your home. This young girl is leaving with her pet as her family is evicted from their apartment near Phoenix, Arizona.

socioeconomic status (SES) A measure of a family or individual's income and social capital.

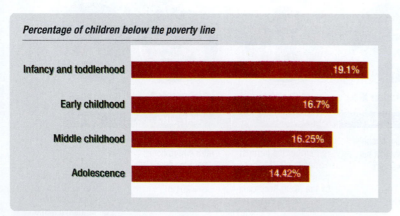

Percentage of children below the poverty line

Infancy and toddlerhood	19.1%
Early childhood	16.7%
Middle childhood	16.25%
Adolescence	14.42%

Data from U.S. Census Bureau, Current Population Survey, 2021.

FIGURE 1.4 Income in the United States by Children's Age Social scientists often assess the number of children who are low-income. The poverty line is an income threshold determined each year by the federal government and is based on current prices and household size. In 2021, it was $26,400 for a family of four.

Social Status: Money Isn't Everything Many aspects of context relate to a family's, a community's, or a country's finances. It turns out that money matters a great deal in human development. For instance, in the microsystem of the family, severe poverty, such as struggling to pay the bills and avoid eviction, can add to stress and limit the ability to provide nurturing care (Yu et al., 2020). And at the macrosystem level, if a nation is unable to provide enough food for all its people, some people are more likely to die early, like the more than 1 in 26 children around the world who die before their fifth birthday (UNICEF, 2021c).

There are several ways of analyzing how money can influence development. Some scientists look at associations between families' income or bank balance and development. As you might have guessed, your income is related to many measures of well-being (Jebb et al., 2018). High-income families and their children are likely to be healthier and happier (D'Ambrosio et al., 2020; Kim & Kim, 2018). This is not because money magically erases all challenges, but because families with higher incomes usually have other advantages that lower-income people do not. Higher-income families often experience less financial stress, less environmental pollution, fewer experiences of discrimination, and less neighborhood violence (Puterman et al., 2020; van Raalte et al., 2018).

Around the world, wealth is linked to health, and a family's economic advantages and disadvantages persist across generations. For instance, in low-income countries, children from wealthy, urban families are 30 percent more likely to live until adulthood than their rural peers (Gaigbe-Togbe, 2015). Even in an affluent country like the United States, where a child starts financially is predictive of where they end up in adulthood: More than 9 in 10 children who are born into low-income families remain low-income in adulthood (Chetty, 2021).

In the United States, experts often evaluate family income in terms such as *upper-*, *middle-*, and *lower-income* and above or below the *poverty line* (Bennett et al., 2020). In the United States, about one in six children lives below the federal poverty line of $25,500 for a family of four, and more than 4 in 10 has experienced poverty at some point in their development (Mohanty, 2021; Semega et al., 2020). (See **Figure 1.4**.)

The size of your bank account may not be the most accurate measure of the impact of economic hardship. Some experts focus instead on whether material needs are being met: Whether you have enough to eat, a stable place to live, and access to affordable health care. During childhood and adolescence, researchers have found that measuring material deprivation in addition to income may provide a more accurate understanding of a family's circumstances (Schenck-Fontaine et al., 2020).

Scientists also look at nonfinancial assets. For instance, a family might have a lot of *social capital*, or a strong network of relationships and contacts that may make it easier to find the right school system, a great babysitter, or an internship, a job, or a volunteer opportunity (Hanifan, 1916; Holland et al., 2007; Putnam, 2000).

A key measure of a family's income and social capital is called **socioeconomic status (SES)** (Entwisle & Astone, 1994). Scientists have different measures of SES that combine a family's social status with their income. Some analyze parents' education level, reasoning that someone with an advanced degree probably has more social capital than someone with a high school degree. Others look at the prestige of jobs by ranking, for instance, a supervisor or a manager above someone who is a clerk in a retail store (Duncan et al., 2015). Many researchers have found that measuring a household's SES in addition to their material income results in a more accurate understanding of differences.

As you will learn, measuring SES may be helpful, but it is far from the only factor that can impact your life.

 MAKING A DIFFERENCE
Cultural Wealth Builds Resilience

Money and social connections are not the only things that help people be happy and successful. Tara Yosso described the strength that can help us persevere in systems that can be hostile and discriminatory as **Community Cultural Wealth** (Yosso, 2006, 2020; Yosso & Solórzano, 2005).

Yosso is part of a new generation of developmental scientists and educators who identify the areas of strength and resilience that help people, particularly those who are marginalized or people of color, succeed in a discriminatory world. In the words of researcher Kris Gutiérrez, cultural values create a "grammar of hope, possibility, and resilience" in a world where being different often means you are treated as if you were deficient (Gutiérrez, 2016, p. 188). According to the Community Cultural Wealth model (Yosso, 2005, 2006), there are six forms of cultural strength that contribute to resilience:

1. *Aspirational capital* is the ability to maintain hopes and dreams, even in the face of barriers and challenges. Researchers have found that communities with high expectations and encouragement for their children's success, as with many in the Latino community, help inspire their children to persevere in school (Enriquez, 2011).
2. *Linguistic capital* refers to communication skills, often in the form of family stories or oral histories. Some researchers have suggested that the language skills developed by children who are bilingual help build cognitive strengths that last a lifetime (van den Noort et al., 2019).
3. *Familial capital* includes a sense of togetherness, caring, and connection, bringing together a community's memories and cultural knowledge. This strong sense of kinship can be protective throughout the lifespan.
4. *Social capital* includes networks of peers and other social contacts that provide support for navigating society. Community groups, faith communities, and cultural centers can help develop and sustain a sense of identity. For instance, some scientists found that first-generation college students who had stronger support from their friends were more likely to persevere through college than their peers were (Mishra, 2020).
5. *Navigational capital* includes skills for maneuvering through social institutions that were not typically created for diverse communities or have a history of structural exclusion. Many Deaf college students need to build navigational capital in order to understand how to get the most out of their education (Listman & Dingus-Eason, 2018).
6. *Resistant capital* includes knowledge and skills developed in practices that challenge inequality and subordination. People who are marginalized have always had to step up to protect themselves and their families. Some of Yosso's current work focuses on rediscovering the stories of Mexican American families who worked to desegregate California schools (García & Yosso, 2020).

Researchers suggest that it is easy for people to fall into the *deficit model* viewpoint, in which people are considered to simply be a collection of problems, rather than a complex combination of challenges and strengths. In the United States, this is particularly relevant for people of color, who have experienced multiple forms of historical and current discrimination, and whose family, community, and cultural contexts may differ from the patterns of the privileged, typically White society. Focusing on strengths helps practitioners and scholars support positive outcomes.

Community Cultural Wealth Areas of strength and resilience identified by developmental scientists that help people, particularly those who are marginalized or are people of color, succeed in a discriminatory world.

 **Share It!**

Cultural strengths can help you learn how to collaborate with other people, even with your siblings.

(Alcalá et al., 2018)

Understanding Culture

Culture is a source of strength and a critical variable in the contexts in which we develop. In developmental science, culture refers to the ideas, beliefs, and social practices that a group of people share (Cole & Packer, 2016). Culture is a critical way that human beings learn from each other and get along (Tomasello, 2016; Whiten, 2017). Sharing culture creates an easy shorthand for social interactions and helps people feel that they belong. As you will learn throughout this book, culture influences all aspects of development (Goodnow & Lawrence, 2015). It may determine what a parent eats during pregnancy, when a child starts school for the first time, or even when a person starts to feel like an adult. Culture changes our bodies, brains, how we think, and how we feel.

Scientists look at culture on multiple levels, from characterizing cultures that cross continents to cultures that extend only to a small group (Jahoda, 2012). Sometimes, culture refers to your country or community background, as when you define yourself as Egyptian American or Turkish German, also referred to as *ethnicity*. At other times, culture refers to a smaller subgroup, or a *microculture*, like the cultural community of online gamers who play *Minecraft*, people who identify as *neurodiverse*, or even a single family (Faherty & Mitra, 2020; Oyserman, 2017).

Cultural distinctions often overlap with other ways you categorize yourself, like the language you speak at home, your ethnic background, your racial identity, your religion, your gender, your physical and cognitive abilities, your romantic preferences, and even your neighborhood. All of us are part of many cultures, evident in the holidays we observe, the languages and slang that come easily, and the ways we greet each other. Scientists emphasize that it is our interpretation of these differences, rather than something essential in them, that is most important. **Intersectionality** refers to the fact that we all have multiple, intersecting cultural identities (Crenshaw, 1989; Ghavami et al., 2016). Like Lucia, we may grow up to identify as Latina, as Cuban American, as a girl, or as a Disney superfan.

How to Talk About Culture Culture may be so fundamental that it is invisible: You may not always see its impact in your own life. This may be particularly true for people who belong to the dominant or majority culture. Your culture may be something you take for granted. As one writer put it, when a young fish was once asked how he liked the water, he responded by asking, "What the hell is water?" (Wallace, 2009).

In development, understanding culture is essential to understanding the great diversity of contexts in which people can thrive. It can also help identify when people may experience cultural discrimination and it may protect them (Rivas-Drake & Umaña-Taylor, 2019). Stereotypes and assumptions about our potential begin at birth. For many, the discrimination they may encounter is intersectional: The bias they confront can be based on ethnicity, gender, family income, and physical ability, among others.

From the beginning of life to its end, discrimination based on racial and cultural differences pervades people's lives (Umaña-Taylor, 2016). For instance, in the United States, Asian American and White American babies are more likely to be born at more highly funded hospitals. But African American or Latino babies tend to be born in hospitals that serve low-income communities and typically have less access to lifesaving and life-preserving treatments. In addition, even if African American or Latino babies are born at the best hospitals, they tend to receive less intensive treatment, perhaps because as one expert noted, "biases make their way in" to medical care, putting them at twice the risk for dying in the first month of life (Horbar et al., 2019; Profit et al., 2017).

The goal of learning about culture is not necessarily to become familiar with all the cultures of the world. With more than 350 languages and more than 900 different

Scott Olson/Getty Images

Nurturing Farming Culture and Community For many families, connection to the environment and the land is part of their culture. In Marengo, Iowa, one tradition is to crown a Poultry Princess at the County Fair. Kameryn won the honors in 2018.

intersectionality A term that refers to the fact that we all have multiple, intersecting identities relating to age, gender, ability, ethnicity, nationality, romantic preferences, and so forth.

ethnic groups in the United States alone, that would never be possible within one lifetime (U.S. Census Bureau, 2015a). Becoming *culturally competent* means you are familiar with and sensitive to the diversity in cultures, a goal that may be out of reach (Berger & Miller, 2021).

Another important objective is to develop **cultural humility** (Tervalon & Murray-García, 1998), openness to cultural diversity and a self-awareness of your own cultural background with the goal of creating respectful relationships in which everyone learns from each other, and no one feels superior (Foronda et al., 2016). Cultural humility not only helps us make friends and strengthens our relationships; it also is a job skill. Cultural understanding is a core competency for many professions, from health care to education to police work.

Many of us feel awkward when talking about culture and cultural differences. In fact, we may go to great lengths to avoid talking about differences—whether religious, ethnic, or racial. This begins in childhood. In one experiment, researchers asked a diverse group of children to sort photographs of people. The children avoided using skin color to sort the paper figures, even if it made the process more time-consuming and confusing (Pauker et al., 2015).

People often believe it is impolite to talk directly, particularly to children, about differences—from gender to ability to language spoken—that may result in discrimination or stereotypes or even shame (Hilliard & Liben, 2019). Developmental science, however, tells us that talking about variations is essential to understanding their impact on people's lives and helps guard against discrimination (Fasoli & Raeff, 2021). Even more, differences can be celebrated as a source of pride.

What Does Race Tell Us? Around the world, physical and cultural differences alike have been used to categorize and divide people. Some communities separate people by ability, appearance, skin color, religion, language, or ethnicity, and being part of one or more of these groups often leads to stereotyping, bias, discrimination, and uneven opportunities.

In the United States, researchers often look at the impact of *race* and *ethnicity* on development. When scholars talk about **race**, they refer to a system of categorizing people based on their physical characteristics (Jablonski, 2021). Racial categories include those you may have checked off on a form, such as "Asian," "Native American," "White," or "Black." These physical differences are often assumed to overlap with people's geographical origins, but this is not always true. **Ethnicity** refers to groups that are based on their geographic origins and cultural heritage, like Mexican Americans or Polish Americans.

Historically, racial categories were based on appearance, like your skin color or the shape of your facial features. Although these details result from genetics—you look like your biological parents—categorizing people into groups based on appearance has no basis in biology. Genes may cause differences in skin color but are not linked to differences between groups in other, more meaningful characteristics such as personality, health, or intelligence (Nelson, 2017; Yudell et al., 2016).

Scientists have found that 99.9 percent of human genes are shared, regardless of race, ethnicity, or skin color. There are no significant genetic differences between people based on their historical geographic origins (Panofsky & Bliss, 2017; Yudell et al., 2016). When researchers look at the genes of people from different geographic origins or with different skin colors, they find that the genetic differences *within* one group are vastly larger than those *between* two groups, as you can see in **Figure 1.5** (Hunley et al., 2016). In fact, the genetic variations among the people who now live in Africa are significantly greater than those of the people who live in every other part of the world combined (Williams et al., 2021).

cultural humility An openness to cultural diversity and a self-awareness of your own cultural background that helps to create respectful relationships in which everyone learns from each other and no one feels superior.

race A system of categorizing people based on their physical characteristics. These physical differences are often assumed to overlap with people's genes or geographical origins, but this is not accurate.

ethnicity A way of referring to groups by their geographic origins and often their cultural heritage.

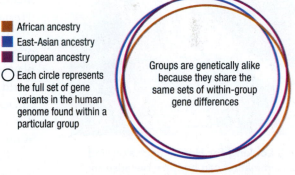

■ African ancestry
■ East-Asian ancestry
■ European ancestry
○ Each circle represents the full set of gene variants in the human genome found within a particular group

Groups are genetically alike because they share the same sets of within-group gene differences

Information from Rosenberg, 2011.

FIGURE 1.5 How Much Do Our Geographical Origins Contribute to Our Differences? When scientists measure our genes, they find that we are all 99.9 percent the same. If researchers compare the tiny 0.1 percent that accounts for all human differences, they find that the vast majority, or 95.7 percent, of these variations occur between people with similar geographical origins, and a mere 4.3 percent differ between people of different geographical origins. In other words, the overwhelming majority of what makes us unique has nothing to do with where our ancestors came from.

Thomas Nybo/UNICEF/Redux

Still Looking for Home Exclusion and discrimination can happen because of many factors, including what we look like or our cultural identity. Rohingya Muslims were driven out of Myanmar by the majority Buddhist government in 2017. Minara, shown here at age 7, was sheltering under a plastic tent after her Rohingya family fled their home in Myanmar after they were attacked during the genocide. Many are still living, like Minara, in refugee camps and are unable to return home safely.

people of color An inclusive term for people who identify as multiracial and for people who are Black, Latino, Asian American, or Native American and who have a feeling of solidarity and shared experience of marginalization.

Furthermore, the idea that our biological differences are based on where we come from is profoundly flawed: None of us live where we originated. Humans have been migrating and partnering with each other since the beginning of humanity. Being multiracial and multiethnic is a long-standing part of what it means to be human (Reich, 2018).

So, what is race? It was a historical invention, developed in the 1800s by people who adopted scientific-sounding words to justify White European domination over other people (McMahon, 2018). Indeed, racial categories have been adopted and adapted around the globe to help one group oppress another. For instance, in Romania, people from the Roma ethnic group, who many Americans would consider light-skinned White people, are considered "Black" (Grill, 2018). Racial distinctions are arbitrary and based on local history and customs (Reich, 2018). Race is a social category, not a biological reality, but nevertheless, racial group membership shapes our experiences throughout the lifespan.

In many places around the world, discriminatory categories are based on skin color (Dixon & Telles, 2017). Your skin color is based on a complicated mix of genes (Martin et al., 2017; Tang & Barsh, 2017). Darker skin and lighter skin both offer biological advantages. Darker skin protects against the dangers of too much sun exposure. Lighter skin helps people get more vitamin D from sunlight (Goodman et al., 2012). People with dark- or light-colored skin live all over the world, and where they live has changed over human history (Goodman et al., 2012; Quillen et al., 2019). For instance, until at least 8,000 years ago, many Europeans were dark-skinned (Brace et al., 2018).

But despite the complexity of skin color, in many places around the world, bias and discrimination based on color, known as *colorism*, is prevalent. Light-colored skin is often seen as a sign of wealth and success (Dixon & Telles, 2017). In the United States, color often complicates race and ethnicity-based discrimination. Discrimination based on skin color often increases the experiences of bias against darker-skinned members of Black, Latino, Native American, and Asian American communities (Hargrove, 2019; Lee & Thai, 2015).

If race is not based in biology, does this mean you should ignore it? Quite the opposite. Race, ethnicity, colorism, culture, and the experience of discrimination all play an important part in human development (Tatum, 2017). Many people around the world, particularly those from privileged groups, still endorse incorrect, racist beliefs. In fact, one in five Americans who are not Black believes that biologically based racial differences are the reason why Black Americans tend to have lower income than White Americans (Morning et al., 2019).

Race- and culture-based bias and discrimination affect how you feel about yourself, what kind of schools you have access to, what kind of job you get, how much money you earn, and even your health (Cobbinah & Lewis, 2018). Discrimination occurs in institutions, in everyday interactions between people, and in people's own beliefs, as you can see in **Figure 1.6**. Its everyday toll begins before a baby is born and extends into the end of life (Trent et al., 2019). More positive race- and culture-based pride and *positive identity* can help people thrive, serving as a protection against the harms of discrimination (Yip et al., 2019).

The United States is increasingly a nation of people of color: More than half of children identify as Latino, Black, Native American, or Asian American (Schneider, 2020). **People of color** and *Black, Indigenous, and people of color* (BIPOC) are inclusive terms for people who identify as multiracial as well as for those who are Black, Latino, Asian American, and Native American and who have a feeling of solidarity and shared experience of marginalization (Perez, 2020). As you will see, creating a positive identity often begins with the freedom to select your own label or group identity, whether that means calling yourself a person of color or another term of your choosing.

What's in a Name? Your name and how you refer to your own identity are important to how you present yourself to the world. In the United States, people identify themselves many different ways, including by their cultural origins, gender identity, immigration status, and where they live. Families may identify as having one identity, multiple intersecting identities, or a mixed identity. Or, in the words of one college student, they may just "not want to label themselves" at all (qtd. in Saulny, 2011).

Variations abound. For people who work directly with children and families, the principles of cultural humility demand you call each individual what they want to be called—and check in with families from time to time to make sure that you are still getting it right. (See **Table 1.1**.) As high school student Kiarra Spottsville, who identifies

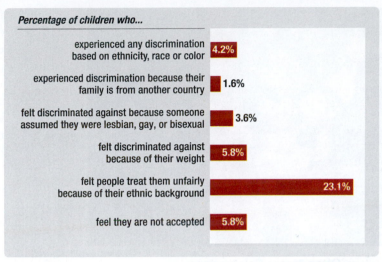

Data from Argabright et al., 2021.

TABLE 1.1 Best Practices for Referring to Identity

Identity labels refer to many ways of describing people.	Labels refer not only to gender and ethnic or cultural identity, but also to health status, ability, physical appearance, and age.
People should be called what they want to be called.	Understand common, respectful variations and confirm that you are using the right one. Sometimes individuals reappropriate labels that have been used to define them, turning their labels into identity-first points of pride. For instance, some people with autism spectrum disorder proudly refer to themselves as autistic, whereas others prefer people-first labeling (Callahan, 2018).
Many labels do not adequately convey our intersectional identities.	Scientific work often requires grouping together the data for groups of people in order to compare their experiences. Many of the terms do not match the terms families use (Taylor et al., 2012). For instance, some families choose more precise labels—such as calling themselves Syrian rather than Arab American.
Broad inclusive group labels do not always match research labels.	Group labels that are designed to be affirming and inclusive, such as BIPOC (Black, Indigenous, and people of color) and LGBTQIA+ (lesbian, gay, bisexual, transgender, questioning or queer, intersex, and agender, asexual, and/or ally), are not always consistent with the designations used in research (Baker & Harris, 2020). When we report research, we are limited to the data that we have. We cannot generalize, for instance, research findings about transgender people to the LGBTQIA+ community or about Mexican Americans to the BIPOC community.
Group labels often obscure important differences within groups.	Common designations, such as Latino, include people from many possible countries. Similarly, terms such as Asian American, African American, European American, and Native American obscure important differences within these groups. Some may include recent immigrants with different cultural identities than those who have lived in the United States for generations or even millennia (Blitvich, 2018). Some people may not identify with group labels that lump them with European Americans, such as those from the Middle East.
The terms that groups prefer are dynamic.	Community leaders may not agree on the best term to use. For instance, some Latino people, particularly those involved in research and advocacy, prefer the term *Latinx* as a gender-neutral alternative to *Latino* or *Latina* (Salinas, 2020). Many in the African American community prefer the term *Black* (Eligon, 2020). And in the Native American community, some members refer to themselves as *American Indian* or *Indigenous* (Blackhorse, 2015). Some Americans identify with their religious rather than their geographic or cultural identity, as with some Muslim or Jewish Americans.

FIGURE 1.6 Discrimination in Many Settings Discrimination occurs on a number of levels. Institutional discrimination can include bias in hiring or policing. Interpersonal discrimination can include social exclusion, rejection, or humiliation, including being harassed or called names. This graph shows results from a survey of children's experiences of discrimination based on gender, ethnic and racial identity, and LGBTQIA+ identity—only a few of the ways that we can be subjected to exclusion and bias.

Culture Often Means Celebrations.
For Liam and Raquelle, this means dressing up for their daughter Aspen's birthday. This was even more special because it was another opportunity to recognize the efforts they went through to conceive her. Liam and Raquelle were together for years before they decided the time was right to start a family. They are both transgender but stopped transitioning in order to conceive.

Culture Can Be Something That Makes You Dance. For these children participating in San Francisco's Chinese New Year celebration, culture means costumes and big grins.

developmental niche A person's cultural environment, which is subject to the specific cultural practices, material setting, and beliefs of their family.

ethnotheories Families' ideas or beliefs about development.

as Diné (an Indigenous Navajo group) and African American, explained, "It is out of respect to call us how we want to be called . . . ; it shows you care" (Blackhorse, 2015). Developmental scientists tell us that people who feel affirmed and supported in their identities tend to be happier and more creative (Austin & Pisano, 2017).

Institutions and government agencies contribute data to developmental science but are often slow to adopt new labels. For instance, the U.S. government often refers to people with Spanish-language heritage as *Hispanic*. Similarly, U.S. government data often refer to specific ethnic and racial categories, which ask people to identify themselves and their families as *American Indian*, *Asian*, *Black*, or *White*, and these terms appear in sources adapted from the U.S. Census (Brown, 2020). Professional organizations also establish standards and guidelines for group labels that further influence the terminology used in developmental science (APA, 2020; SRCD, 2021). However, within this complexity, some things are clear: Including the experiences of a wide variety of people and respecting their identities is critical to the study of development. As you will learn, studying the variations in development among different communities makes it more likely that all of us can thrive.

Are There Cultural Differences? When should an infant start walking? Is a second-grader old enough to babysit? Should teenagers be able to get married? Rethink your assumptions: Not everyone in the world agrees with you. While all communities share the challenge of raising children who will grow into adults with fulfilling, happy lives, there are distinctions among cultural communities in what families expect, how they raise children, and how people see and interact with the world (Greenfield et al., 2003; Vélez Agosto et al., 2017).

Culture influences people in ways that are specific to each individual and determined by their everyday experiences (Harkness & Super, 2021; Rogoff et al., 2018). Each of us grows up in a specific **developmental niche**, or cultural environment, subject to the specific cultural practices, material setting, and beliefs of our families (Super & Harkness, 1994). Customs, or *cultural practices*, are sometimes easy to see, like what you wear or what holidays you celebrate, but often are less obvious, like how loud you talk or how often you smile (Keller, 2020). One practice with many cultural variations is what to do with a crying baby. Should you always rush to pick up your baby, as caregivers do in the Efe community of the Congo (Morelli et al., 2017)? Should babies learn to soothe themselves, as many do in the United States?

The *material setting*, or physical place where you grow up, will also influence how you grow. For instance, if you grow up with brothers and sisters on a farm in rural Iowa, your development may be different from that of an only child growing up in urban Chicago. What your family believes about how people grow will also play an important role in how they raise you. Does your family think that people can be easily spoiled? Or that they should be creative? Experts often call families' ideas or beliefs about people's development **ethnotheories** (Harkness & Super, 2020).

Developmental scientists go beyond just listing variations in how children are raised or differences between cultures. They try to find patterns in those variations and describe their effect on people as they grow. One common variation is how much families value independence in thinking and their obligations to other people (Kagitcibasi, 2017; Keller, 2020; Miyamoto et al., 2018). Are children encouraged to express their own individuality? Or are they deeply entwined with the lives of their family and loved ones? (See **Figure 1.7**.)

In developmental science, researchers use the term *independence*, or *autonomy*, to refer to how strongly a community values individual rights (Raeff et al., 2000). Communities with an **independent** orientation might allow children to have temper tantrums out of respect for their feelings, and permit school-age children to skip out on their chores, but they also encourage individuality and personal choices (LeVine & LeVine, 2016). Communities that have strong traditions of valuing independence are often said to be **individualistic**, because they tend to value the individual over larger groups, communities, or families. Families with individualistic ethnotheories may have smaller families, enabling them to focus their attention on a few children who they hope will be able to thrive in a competitive, global world (Doepke & Zilibotti, 2019; Lareau, 2015).

In contrast, **collectivist** communities place more value on relatedness and closeness and want children to rely on other people—and to be reliable in turn (Strand et al., 2018). These communities tend to value the family or the group over the individual. Children raised in collectivist families may help out around the house, even at young ages, and are expected to take care of their siblings and even their parents without being pestered (LeVine & LeVine, 2016). Experts also call collectivist families *interdependent*, because these families value the relationships between people and the group over the individual. Interdependence is often more common in communities where families rely on children to help—whether in urban communities where children need to watch their siblings while their parents work, or in rural farming communities where children may be working in the fields (Keller, 2020).

However, researchers agree that, in every community and country, there is a mix of ethnotheories about human relationships. Ideas about how best to raise children do not apply universally (Oyserman et al., 2002; Suizzo, 2020). The differences between individual families are typically greater within a community than between cultures. Although the United States is a relatively wealthy nation, not all Americans stress independent, autonomous values in raising their children, particularly if they are from immigrant or less affluent backgrounds (Markus, 2017).

Many families are *bicultural* or *multicultural* or may have cultural values that mix autonomy, obedience, independence, and interdependence (Markus, 2017; Park & Lau, 2016). For instance, while individualistic values are at work in Lucia's family, as with their mother's concern that her daughters develop their own unique talents and identities, many collectivist values are also evident, like a commitment to their extended family in Argentina and the United States and to sticking it out together, no matter what the cost. While researchers often describe general patterns in cultural variations, individual families do not always match the statistics (Keller, 2017). Despite the diversity across communities all over the world, the most important goals that families have are strikingly similar (Lansford et al., 2021). More than anything, families want to raise children who become healthy and happy adults.

How Does Change Happen?

People change in many ways as they develop from wiggly newborns into social adults. They can learn to talk, make friends, and eventually may have children, grandchildren, and great-grandchildren of their own. Developmental researchers focus on *how* we change over time, investigating whether change is slow and steady or more rapid and irregular. They also look at what causes developmental change, examining

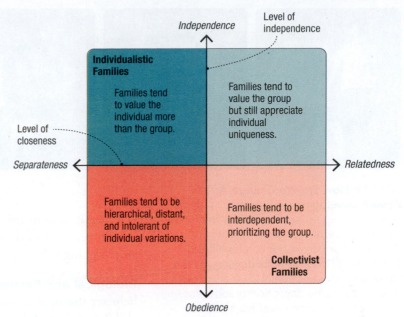

Information from Kagitcibasi, 2005.

FIGURE 1.7 Dimensions of Cultural Variation Many contemporary developmental scientists look at cultures in terms of their levels of independence and relatedness. For instance, measures of individualism might indicate how much a community values following group norms or how much a community accepts uniqueness. Measures of relatedness might indicate how much you value relating to the world as part of your group, or whether you value being on your own. This schematic diagram shows where individualistic and collectivist groups might fit on these dimensions.

Share It!

Families can help their children feel proud of their cultural identity in a process known as *ethnic* (or *racial*) *socialization*.

(Wang et al., 2020)

independent communities Societies that value individual rights. (Also known as *autonomy*.)

individualistic communities Societies that have strong traditions of valuing the individual over larger groups, communities, or families.

collectivist Communities that place more value on relatedness and closeness and tend to value the family or the group over the individual.

Zed Nelson (all photos)

FIGURE 1.8 How Do We Change As We Grow? Developmental scientists study how we change over time, along with how the pace of change contributes to the great diversity in our communities. This series of photographs documents the life of a family over nearly 25 years. Every year on the same day, photographer Zed Miller took pictures of his friends near their home in London, England, documenting their lives as their son grew into adulthood. For the young boy, now a college student studying engineering, the photographs remind him how much he's changed over the years. For his father, they are a memory of how short childhood is (Davies, 2010).

© Macmillan, Photo by Sidford House

maturation The genetically programmed growth that drives many aspects of development.

whether it is something inevitable or caused by something in the environment. Researchers also study what stays the same in individuals as they grow, like whether an easygoing baby is likely to be a mellow teenager.

Biological and Environmental Triggers Biology and the environment interact to help set the pace of maturation and aging. In the prenatal period and in much of childhood and adolescence, many aspects of development are driven by genetically programmed growth, or what developmentalists would call **maturation** (Gesell, 1928; Thelen & Adolph, 1994). As you see in **Figure 1.8**, the passage of time results in predictable developmental changes.

Throughout childhood and adolescence, the environment can accelerate or slow down your growth. For instance, inadequate nutrition during prenatal development and the first year of life can disrupt infants' early growth and make them more susceptible to diseases later in life (Barker, 2004). But warm, nurturing relationships can help children become healthier. Environmental toxins also play a role in how we mature. Physician Mona Hanna-Attisha sees the impact of this on the families she works with every day.

SCIENCE IN PRACTICE
Mona Hanna-Attisha, M.D.

One of the hallmarks of developmental science is a commitment to advocating for safer environments to help all people mature in the healthiest way possible. Dr. Mona Hanna-Attisha, a pediatrician, researcher, and public health advocate in Flint, Michigan, embodies this commitment. She was one of the first people to alert the public that families in Flint were suffering from high levels of lead in their drinking water, which was so polluted that it was damaging car parts at a nearby automotive plant. Her work helped expose a public health disaster (Hanna-Attisha et al., 2016).

The families who Dr. Hanna-Attisha served in Flint were facing challenges even before they were exposed to lead. Poverty and health challenges meant that life expectancy in Flint was nearly 15 years shorter than it was in more affluent towns nearby (Hanna-Attisha, 2019). Discrimination and racism also played a part: Nearly 60 percent of the population of Flint is Black (Hammer, 2019).

Families in Michigan are not the only ones whose growth and development are harmed by environmental pollution. More than one in four deaths around the world is caused by toxins in the environment—from respiratory infections caused by air pollution to gastrointestinal diseases caused by unsafe drinking water or dangerous chemicals in food (Prüss-Üstün et al., 2016). And marginalized communities worldwide tend to have more toxic air and water than more affluent ones have (Apergis et al., 2020).

Dr. Hanna-Attisha's study of the levels of lead in Flint began with nights spent poring over spreadsheets. She needed to confirm that changes in Flint's water supply were linked to increases in children's lead levels. Any amount of lead can be toxic to the growing brain, and in a recent representative sample in the United States, nearly half of the children had lead in their blood (Hanna-Attisha et al., 2022).

Dr. Hanna-Attisha's data showed that the average lead levels of children in Flint nearly doubled after government officials failed to install corrosion control in their water system. After Dr. Hanna-Attisha published her findings and began advocating for cleaner water, she was attacked in the media and told that she was overreacting (Hanna-Attisha, 2019).

Dr. Hanna-Attisha was prepared. Her activism began when she was a teenager in Michigan, protesting a trash incinerator that was linked to higher levels of asthma (Hanna-Attisha, 2019). Her parents, who were immigrants from Iraq, had instilled in her a commitment to science and to giving back.

Despite the attacks that Dr. Hanna-Attisha received when she first published her work, her advocacy worked. The residents of Flint now have new pipes and clean water. Families with high blood lead levels are receiving extra services to help manage their symptoms. Dr. Hanna-Attisha is still in Flint, working in her small office on the second floor of a farmer's market to make sure that families in Flint have access to fresh fruit and vegetables (Saxe-Custack et al., 2022). She still feels fortunate to be able to work with children, but more than ever, she is also certain that she needs to fight injustice. 💡

Plasticity and Its Limits The brain and body are vulnerable to the effects of lead and other toxins because of **plasticity**, which means that you can be molded, like plastic, by your experiences. Plasticity helps us adapt to the environment we live in, which means we are vulnerable to negative experiences, like toxins, but also to positive experiences, like supportive caregiving. Children and adolescents can have agency and change in order to thrive in their surroundings by learning the skills their cultures value, whether it is riding horses in Mongolia, playing Roblox in Los Angeles, or doing gymnastics in Singapore.

Scholars have found that there are certain developmental periods when change is more likely to occur, when our bodies, brains, and behaviors are more plastic and more easily shaped by the environment. These are **sensitive periods**, times when growth is particularly responsive to input from the world.

Scientists believe sensitive periods begin before birth and extend through adolescence (Blakemore & Mills, 2014; Frankenhuis & Walasek, 2020). For instance, if infants do not see anything at all because of an untreated eye disease, their brains will develop differently from other children: Brain regions typically devoted to processing visual information will be used to do other things, like process language (Lewis & Maurer, 2005). People who lose their sight later in life have different patterns of brain development (Pant et al., 2020). However, if doctors are able to reverse the visual impairment in early infancy, the brain is still relatively plastic: The body will adapt, the brain will change, and people can develop new sight.

There are more sensitive periods early in development, particularly prenatally and in the first five years of life (Frankenhuis & Walasek, 2020; Zeanah et al., 2011). But adolescence is also a sensitive period. During the teenage years, children are particularly responsive to learning how to fit in with their community, a flexibility that allows them to learn new social skills and take on adult roles specific to what their culture values (Fuhrmann et al., 2015).

While scientists believe that there is tremendous potential for children to be plastic and resilient, sensitive periods make some kinds of change more difficult than others (Nelson et al., 2020; Van IJzendoorn et al., 2007). One way that scientists learned this was to study children who have endured serious adversity, such as being abandoned in orphanages. They found that many children who were housed in institutions experienced delays in their development: They were physically smaller and more prone to sickness than other

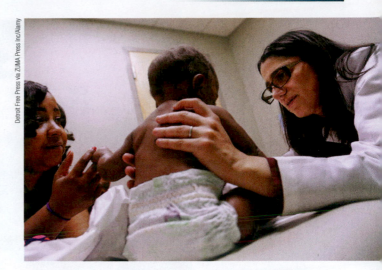

Detroit Free Press via ZUMA Press Inc/Alamy

Just Another Check-up Dr. Mona Hanna-Attisha has been all over the country spreading the word about the dangers of lead pollution. But most days, she is still in her office, checking babies and talking to families, as she is here, helping make sure Courtney's daughter, Isabella, is doing well.

Share It!

Lead is not the only environmental danger people face. Public health experts suggest that climate change will increase deaths, especially of children and older adults, as a result of undernutrition, natural disasters, and overheating.

(Watts et al., 2018)

plasticity The idea that human development is moldable, like plastic, by experiences.

sensitive periods The times in the lifespan when growth is particularly responsive to input from the world.

Courtesy Ionica Adriana (both photos)

Ionica: Then and Now Ionica spent the first months of her life in an overcrowded orphanage in Romania where food was in short supply and human attention rare. (She is the baby on the left.) She was adopted into a loving family in England as a toddler and is now a thriving young actor who also works to promote adoption around the world. Although Ionica was able to adapt and thrive despite her early challenges, not all children who have experienced similar adversity have her good fortune.

children their age were. Even if they were taken away from the orphanages and placed in nurturing homes, these children often had more difficulties with learning and with establishing strong relationships with their caregivers (Wade et al., 2020).

Children who had lived in these abusive orphanages often recovered substantially and experienced some catch-up growth once they were in a safe place, but the researchers in this study also found that there were limits to this plasticity. While some thrived after they were adopted into loving homes, most did not completely recover (Humphreys et al., 2020; Sonuga-Barke et al., 2017). Children who were removed from the abusive or neglectful situations very early in their lives, before they were 3 to 6 months old, recovered much more fully than did those who were older.

These findings tell us that people are more plastic earlier in life: It becomes more difficult to recover from stress as the years add on. Although people can build resilience, it is more difficult for an adult, for instance, to recover from stress than it is for a young child to do so (Sampedro-Piquero et al., 2018).

Can Science Predict the Future? If you look at a photograph of Lucia, you may wonder if scientists can predict what will happen to her. Is there a way to tell how the rest of her life will play out? Will fussy babies grow up to be unhappy teens? Will early walkers turn out to be athletes? Developmental science does help explain how people's pasts predict their future, but development is complex. Plenty of challenging babies grow into contented children, and inactive toddlers may turn into marathon runners in high school.

Experts describe two models of change: continuous and discontinuous growth. **Continuous** growth is relatively constant and stable. In this type of growth, "slow and steady wins the race": Bodies get bigger and skills get better, without major shifts in the type of change. Language development typically builds slowly over time until it peaks in adolescence.

Another model for how people change over time is called **discontinuous** growth. As you might guess, discontinuous growth is more irregular and unstable, happening in sprints and pauses. For instance, scientists measuring children's height found that they grow in bursts—sometimes as much as two-thirds of an inch (1.62 cm) in one day! (Lampl & Schoen, 2017).

Discontinuous growth can happen in discrete **stages**, or periods, where development changes dramatically. As we acquire a new cognitive skill, there is often an "Aha!" moment when everything becomes clear. For instance, some children walk for the first time and then never return to pulling themselves around on the furniture (Adolph et al., 2012). Many classic theories of development describe growth in terms of stagelike progressions.

continuous A model of change that is relatively constant and stable.

discontinuous A model of change that is more irregular and unstable, happening in sprints and pauses, or stages.

stage A period in which development changes dramatically.

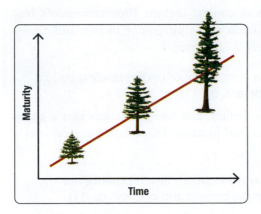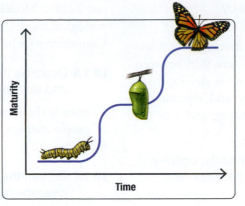

FIGURE 1.9 How Do We Change Over Time? Is change *discontinuous* and stagelike, like the separate stages in the life of a Monarch butterfly who grows from a tiny caterpillar into a beautiful butterfly? Or do humans grow more *continuously* like a redwood tree, gradually growing bigger every year little by little? Developmental scientists suggest it may be a little of both.

Some types of development, like how you acquire language, are both continuous and discontinuous. For instance, vocabulary development is continuous (it keeps getting bigger as you age) even though the rate varies. But the acquisition of *grammar*, or how you use language to communicate, is more stagelike, with qualitatively different periods as children move from cooing to babbling to eventually being able to talk back.

Many moments in development appear to be dramatic, but sudden changes have been preceded by many small developments that allowed that change to happen. Children learn to walk, for instance, after taking more than 17 falls per hour—and most continue to use their tried-and-true methods of moving around, like crawling, for a few days after they take their first steps (Adolph et al., 2012). In thinking, too, it is typical for development not to happen in a straight line: Learning a new way of counting or reasoning doesn't mean we will always use it all the time (see **Figure 1.9**). Children's development may be divided into stages, but these stages may overlap, like waves, as children grow (Siegler & Ellis, 1996).

Throughout childhood and adolescence, people go through many predictable changes as their bodies and brains mature, and their social experiences expand from their family relationships into a complex social, educational, and occupational world. Experiences can be unpredictable, too, as Lucia's family learned firsthand when her father, Patricio, was diagnosed with cancer. But people build on their past and adapt to new events.

APPLY IT!   **1.5** If you had to choose just five words, how would you identify yourself? How has your identity changed over the years?
1.6 How has your context, such as your community, your culture, or your family, changed who you are?

Wrapping It Up

LO 1.1 Define scientific thinking. (p. 2)

Science is the process of gathering knowledge in a way that is testable and reliable. Scientific thinking is based on rigorously questioning what you know, testing that information, and relying on other people to cross check what you have discovered.

LO 1.2 Define developmental science. (p. 2)

Developmental science is the systematic study of how humans grow and the underlying processes that create change over time. The goal of developmental science is to both explain and

improve the lives of children and adults. It combines scientific methodology with a commitment to the well-being of people of all ages.

LO 1.3 Describe the historical origins of developmental science. (p. 5)

People have tried to understand how to nurture development since the beginnings of humanity. Modern developmental science arose from the combination of scientific methods with advocacy for the rights of children.

LO 1.4 Analyze four key themes addressed by developmental science. (p. 11)

There are four major themes that pervade developmental science: How is development created by the interaction between each unique person and their context? How is development universal and individual? How do culture and community impact how we grow? How do we both change and stay the same?

LO 1.5 Explain the contexts of family, community, country, and historical moments in shaping development. (p. 11)

A person's environment has an enormous impact on how they grow. Context includes the time period when we live, our culture, our physical environment and financial status, and our health. Models of context include Bronfenbrenner's bio-ecological model, García Coll's integrative model, and Yosso's Community Cultural Wealth model.

LO 1.6 Describe the complexity of understanding culture and development. (p. 11)

Culture is the ideas, beliefs, and social practices that a group of people share. Cultural practices shape how we grow over a lifespan.

LO 1.7 Explain the ways in which developmentalists describe human growth and change. (p. 11)

People can change over their lifespan, but how plastic we are depends on our context. Some types of development are continuous, and others are more discontinuous, or stagelike.

KEY TERMS

resilience (p. 2)
science (p. 2)
development (p. 3)
developmental science (p. 3)
epigenetics (p. 10)
critical thinking (p. 10)
nature (p. 12)
nurture (p. 12)
context (p. 13)

culture (p. 13)
birth cohorts (p. 15)
socioeconomic status (SES) (p. 16)
Community Cultural Wealth (p. 17)
intersectionality (p. 18)
cultural humility (p. 19)
race (p. 19)

ethnicity (p. 19)
people of color (p. 20)
developmental niche (p. 22)
ethnotheories (p. 22)
independent communities (p. 23)
individualistic communities (p. 23)

collectivist (p. 23)
maturation (p. 24)
plasticity (p. 25)
sensitive periods (p. 25)
continuous (p. 26)
discontinuous (p. 26)
stage (p. 26)

CHECK YOUR LEARNING

1. At 4 months, Lucia's parents put her to bed in her own crib and let her cry for a while before she fell asleep, to help her learn to soothe herself. The belief that learning to sleep independently will keep babies from becoming spoiled and dependent is an example of a(n):
   a) mesosystem.
   b) developmental niche.
   c) ethnotheory.
   d) birth cohort.

2. Which of the following is NOT an example of a developmental context?
   a) Parenting styles
   b) Birth cohort
   c) Culture
   d) Scientific method

3. Some experiences trigger genes to be expressed or not expressed during development. This is known as:
   a) an exosystem.
   b) epigenetics.
   c) gerontology.
   d) resilience.

4. Which major period of development begins with the biological changes of puberty?
   a) Early childhood
   b) Early adulthood
   c) The prenatal period
   d) Adolescence

5. Which domain of development addresses how thinking and learning changes over time?
   a) Motor development
   b) Cognitive development
   c) Emotional development
   d) Physical development

6. The scientific method:
   a) is impossible to define.
   b) is based on the opinions of researchers.
   c) involves testing hypotheses using systematic observations.
   d) only became common in the past 50 years.

7. As scientists compare their findings and identify commonalities across multiple studies, they arrive at:
   a) diverging views.
   b) scientific consensus.
   c) scientific overload.
   d) absolute truth.

8. Which of the following is an important implication of Bronfenbrenner's bioecological model?
   a) Interventions to improve people's lives can be targeted at many different levels of their environment.
   b) Different microsystems operate independently and do not influence each other.
   c) The macrosystem is more influential than the microsystem.
   d) Biology doesn't matter in development.

9. Lucia is a member of a specific birth cohort, one who grew up with mobile devices and experienced the beginning of the COVID-19 pandemic as preschoolers. What historical events have shaped your life, and how do you think they influenced your development?

Theories and Methods of Human Development

© Macmillan, Photo by Point Studio, Inc.

Theories of Developmental Science

2.1 Identify why developmental scientists use theory to guide their work.

2.2 Explain how the biological perspective links the brain and body to developmental change.

2.3 Explain how the psychodynamic perspective links early experiences to personality development.

2.4 Explain how the behaviorist perspective focuses on how people learn.

2.5 Describe how the cognitive perspective focuses on how thinking changes as we mature.

2.6 Explain how the cultural perspective focuses on how culture shapes development.

How to Study Development

2.7 Define the steps and guiding principles of the scientific method.

2.8 Describe the ethical standards governing science and practice.

Mervlyn became part of a research study in human development while she was still in diapers. A random quirk of fate meant that Mervlyn was born as part of a scientific project that has lasted more than 50 years on the island of Kauai, in Hawaii, and continues to this day.

What did this mean for Mervlyn? Some extra doctor's visits, standardized tests, the occasional long interview with a researcher and the sense that she has contributed to something special. Mervlyn, and the tenacious team that spent decades studying her growth, helped to demonstrate that children can develop resilience: They can change, show flexibility, and bounce back from difficulties if they are given the support they need.

Mervlyn and another 697 babies born in 1955 on the Hawai'ian island of Kauai were enrolled, with the agreement of their families, in a long-term study initially designed to find out the effect of prenatal stress on newborns. But the project soon went in a different direction when a curious new researcher joined the team. This scientist, Emmy Werner, knew about stress firsthand. She had grown up malnourished in Germany, sold her own blood to pay for graduate school, and learned to speak Swahili as an adult so she could volunteer for the United Nations' Children's Fund (Werner, 2000, 2001, 2003). Emmy Werner was curious about how children thrived despite the difficulties they faced.

Mervlyn was one of those babies who experienced early stress. As she remembers, things were hard when she was little. There was fighting and violence. Her father drank too much. Her mother was "in and out of the hospital" as she tried to access the support she needed for her mental health. They had low income. Mervlyn's mother was Hawai'ian, and her father was a White man from New Jersey, a "pure haole."

Mervlyn remembers feeling different, but she acknowledges that her parents did the best they could for her, despite their own struggles.

By many in her community, Mervlyn was labeled "at risk," but she preferred to be called "a person with promise." But, Mervlyn says they did the best they could. They survived. When she became pregnant in eleventh grade, people assumed she would leave school and have a chaotic adulthood. They underestimated her and the support she would receive from the people who cared about her. While Mervlyn sometimes wonders how she survived the instability in her childhood, she knows she had many strengths. Among them was her willingness to stubbornly "dig her heels in," to work hard, and to feel a sense of responsibility and purpose in her life.

Mervlyn was the first mother to ever graduate from the school where she later worked for many years. She had the support of friends, her husband, and her family, particularly her in-laws. For more than 50 years, she and her husband, Daniel, stayed together despite the ups and downs that life threw at them. She got her college degree and then a master's degree. Daniel and Mervlyn raised seven children and now have twenty grandchildren and the respect of their family and community. Mervlyn was even voted parent of the year.

What does developmental science tell us about how Mervlyn came to be who she is? Scientists often use the term *resilience* to describe the ability to bounce back, and they might attribute Mervlyn's ability to thrive to her close relationships with people who believed in her: her husband, her grandparents, and her teachers who encouraged her to stay in school. Mervlyn benefited from caring people who made her feel like she mattered.

Developmental scientists might also be curious about how Mervlyn has both changed and stayed the same. What parts of Mervlyn stayed the same, as she grew from an infant born during a measles epidemic to a teenager walking across the graduation stage proudly parenting her toddler?

In this chapter, we will look at the questions scientists might ask about Mervlyn and how theorists might explain her resilience and her development. We will see what is unique about Mervlyn as well as what is universal about her journey.

Developmental theorists and scientists understand that development involves a complex interplay of genes, contexts, cultures, and history. Theories help to organize these ideas to create predictions about development, and the scientific method guides researchers as they build what they know. We now present major developmental theories with the goal of helping you apply your analytical skills, your ability to question what you see, and your skill in contrasting different perspectives.

Scientific American Profile

Meet Mervlyn

Learning Objectives

2.1 Identify why developmental scientists use theory to guide their work.

2.2 Explain how the biological perspective links the brain and body to developmental change.

2.3 Explain how the psychodynamic perspective links early experiences to personality development.

2.4 Explain how the behaviorist perspective focuses on how people learn.

Theories of Developmental Science

Ideas about what drives human development have been around since human beings first sought to understand why people do what they do every day. Do you already have a hunch about why Mervlyn found happiness, despite the many transitions and challenges she encountered? If so, you have formed a **theory**, which is how scientists organize their ideas and think critically about how to investigate what they observe. In developmental science, theories are explanations for how people change based on what can be observed or tested in real life. They provide a link between ideas and scientific findings by helping to generate hypotheses as well as give a lens for interpreting evidence.

Theories help direct the questions that scientists ask. For instance, researchers who adopt the biological perspective on human development might ask how Mervlyn's experiences in her church community impact her life and her ability to thrive. Theories help researchers refine their research questions and choose what to study.

Theories Lead to Critical Thinking

As you will soon learn, contemporary developmental science includes a diversity of theories and ideas about what drives development. We have highlighted five theoretical perspectives (*biological, psychodynamic, behaviorist, cognitive,* and *cultural*) and more than 12 named theories. Why so many? First, knowing these theories will help you build expertise in developmental science and make you more comfortable interpreting the research you read about in this book and throughout your life.

Second, understanding different theories of development gives you practice in critical thinking. Contrasting and comparing diverse ideas helps scientists—and all of us—think more deeply and get closer to the truth. Taking someone else's point of view helps you learn more about what you think. Being challenged by someone who disagrees with you makes it less likely that you will make a mistake.

Third, each theory and perspective gives you a different way of looking at the world around you. Developmental theories are designed to help you think carefully: This is at the heart of science. So, do not expect any one to tell the whole story. Understanding different perspectives helps us look at development from many angles.

Theories are influenced by the personalities, the history, and the beliefs of the community that created them. Many of the classic theories of developmental science were conceived of more than a hundred years ago by scholars who held values that are abhorrent to modern scientists. The first recognized theorists of developmental science were mostly White men. Many had views that were racist, sexist, ableist, and elitist: beliefs that were shared with many, but not all, of the people of their era (Allen, 2011; Yakushko, 2019). Modern developmental scientists have worked to preserve the universal and insightful aspects of their theories, while rejecting their bias, prejudice, and discrimination.

As you read about the theorists and see their old-time photographs, you might assume that they were solitary geniuses whose ideas sprang into being spontaneously (Oreskes, 2019; Shermer, 1990). This is incorrect: When the story of science is simplified, often one person gets the credit for ideas that were conceived by a team (Higgitt, 2017; Lin-Siegler et al., 2016; MacLeod, 2009). Just as they do today, scientists in the past worked with collaborators, romantic partners, students, and assistants. They were influenced by people outside the academic world, by their travels around the globe, and by their interactions with children and adults who did not share their elite, White backgrounds (King, 2019; Syed & Fish, 2018). Many of these people who inspired and collaborated on the classic theories of development remain invisible, but researchers today are eager to put them back into the narrative (García & Yosso, 2020).

The Biological Perspective

Developmentalists who take a **biological perspective** emphasize that psychological and behavioral development begin with roots in our brain, our genes, and innate or inborn instincts. Scientists who take a biological perspective might ask how development is changed by the genes we were born with and how those genes are changed by our environment. They might look at the brain to see whether there are signs that our brain development has affected who we are.

Evolutionary Theory The evolutionary perspective is, as you might guess, based on the theory of **evolution**, the idea that all life on Earth develops and changes to adapt to its environment over successive generations. Evolutionary theorists explain that over time, traits that help living beings survive are passed on to their offspring. This process, known as *natural selection*, allows some successful genes, traits, or behaviors to be replicated in the next generation (Darwin, 1872/2009). Thus, specific ways of growing or behaving were *adaptive* in allowing people to thrive—in the present or in the ancient past (Bjorklund, 2020; Ellis & Del Giudice, 2019). Developmental scientists might look at Mervlyn's life and ask how resilience helped human beings adapt to changing

2.5 Explain how the cognitive perspective focuses on how thinking changes as we mature.

2.6 Explain how the cultural perspective focuses on how culture shapes development.

theory An organized set of ideas that helps scientists think critically about what they observe.

biological perspective A perspective with an emphasis on how psychological and behavioral development begins with roots in our brain, our genes, and innate or inborn instincts.

evolution The idea that life on Earth develops and changes to adapt to the environment over successive generations.

Happiness Is in the Young. Charles Darwin and his wife, Emma, had 10 children. He is shown here with his oldest son, William. He doted on his children, telling a friend that he "cared more for them than for anything in this world" (Darwin, 1856).

and often challenging circumstances over the millennia, or how human biology and maturation support resilience (Feldman, 2020).

If you wonder whether evolution is incompatible with your religious beliefs, you are not alone (Dunk et al., 2019; Hawley & Sinatra, 2019). Even the man whose name is most closely connected with the theory of evolution, Charles Darwin, worried about whether his ideas contradicted his faith (Heiligman, 2009). Like some other religious scientists, Darwin became confident that evolutionary ideas were compatible with his faith (Collins, 2006).

Evolutionary theory continues to inspire new discoveries about how human beings have adapted to the challenges of life on Earth (Legare et al., 2018; Meehan & Crittenden, 2016). Evolutionary scholars use innovative methods, visiting people in remote communities to look for hints about the earliest human interactions as well as comparing human behavior to that of primates like chimpanzees or bonobos (de Waal, 2019). No matter where they work, developmentalists with an evolutionary approach ask provocative questions about how human behavior evolved, such as why bullying persists through the generations and the timing of puberty changes throughout human history (Hawley, 2016).

The evolutionary perspective has its critics. Some researchers caution that the theory is speculative—since it is impossible to go back in time and see how humans really developed (Downes, 2015). Others note that some of the early work in this area was hampered by gender stereotypes (Buss & von Hippel, 2018). Nevertheless, the idea that our behavioral traits are an adaptation to the environment helps scientists appreciate the wide diversity in how children develop and thrive in many environments.

Ethological Theory The theory that some human behaviors are universal and innate despite the wild diversity among humans is known as **ethology**. For instance, healthy children learn to communicate, move, and relate to the world (Bateson, 2017). Ethologists look for traits that are universal within a species, suggesting that these are part of their genetic makeup. Ethologists are trained to observe animals and human beings and might look at orangutans or birds for insights into human behavior.

Some animal behaviors appear without ever being taught—kittens do not need to be shown how to scratch in the litter box, and birds will learn how to fly even if they are raised in cages. Among some animals, even the close bond between the young and their caregivers is triggered by biology. For instance, some ducklings and goslings *imprint*, or establish a strong attachment, to the first object with eyes they see when they are a few days old—be that a parent, a human, or even a stuffed animal (Lorenz, 1981).

Human beings are not ducklings: Our complex behaviors require back-and-forth social interaction in order to develop. For instance, a baby will not learn to talk or relate to other people without human contact (Bateson, 2015). But scientists believe our complexities are supported by inborn tendencies linked to our genes.

Epigenetic Theory **Epigenetics** builds on the biological perspective by examining how our physical and inborn characteristics, including how our genes operate, are changed by our environment (Waddington, 1952). Epigenetic researchers focus on how our everyday experiences, from what we eat to how we are loved, have a cascading effect on our development (Jovanovic et al., 2017). They recognize the complicated, bidirectional interaction between our inborn tendencies and the environment (Lickliter & Witherington, 2017). Epigenetics is not just a theory: It is also a way of describing our biology, as you will learn in Chapter 3. Epigenetic changes to our genome represent how our genes are changed by our environment.

Some epigenetic theorists compare development to a series of paths taken by a marble rolling down a mountain, as you can see in **Figure 2.1**. The marble begins its journey on top of the mountain with a fixed genetic route. As it continues down the mountainside, the environment leads it to follow one of many different possible paths. Some routes are deeper and less likely to be influenced by environmental

Are You My Parent? Researcher Jessica Meir allowed a brood of baby geese to imprint on her so she could develop a close relationship with them and, eventually, learn how they fly. Humans also bond when they are young, but they do not imprint like birds.

ethology The theory that some human behaviors are universal and innate despite the wide diversity in human beings around the world.

epigenetics An area of study within the biological perspective that examines how physical and inborn characteristics, including gene activation, are changed by a person's environment.

effects, as a marble in a deep channel would not be pushed off course by a strong breeze blowing across the mountain (these are paths that have a stronger inborn component), but other paths, or variations, are also possible (Van Speybroeck, 2002; Waddington, 1952).

Epigenetic theories have inspired exciting discoveries:

- Why do some children seem to bounce back from adversity more easily than others, as Mervlyn did? Researchers have found that not all children have the same sensitivity to the environment. In a theory known as *differential susceptibility*, researchers have found that some children have genetic dispositions that are more easily changed by their life experiences. These children might be more easily changed by a positive, or negative, experience than other children (Belsky et al., 2021).
- Are your life experiences ever passed on to the next generation? It turns out that some extreme experiences, like living through a famine, will make biological changes in your genes, those of your children, and even your grandchildren (Bošković & Rando, 2018).

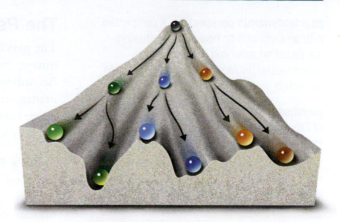

FIGURE 2.1 The Epigenetic Landscape of Development Human behavior may begin with genes, but genetic expression takes many pathways as we develop. Researchers use the analogy of a marble running down a mountain to express the many pathways we have available to use. Some of these paths, or channels, may be deeper than others (and more protected from environmental interference), and others may be the path less taken.

MAKING A DIFFERENCE
What Do We Really Need?

What do children really need to thrive? What do you need to be happy? If you are like most people, you probably expect you would be happier if you had more money, more time, and stronger relationships (Luhmann et al., 2014).

More than 80 years ago, psychologist Abraham Maslow developed a list of what motivates us, often called the *hierarchy of human needs*, that has enduring appeal (Bland & DeRobertis, 2020). He was inspired by his time spent among the Blackfoot people of Alberta, who exposed him to the idea of a hierarchy of being, from lowly fungi to the sparkling stars (Brown, 2014; Heavy Head, 2007). Maslow suggested that we have five categories of needs: (1) *physiological needs*, like the need for food, water, and the ability to breathe; (2) the need for *safety*, like knowing that you have a place to live and the resources you need to survive and not be hurt; (3) the need for *belonging* and connection to others; (4) the need for *esteem*, or respect from those around you; and finally (5) your need to be *self-actualized*, or engaged in the creative, moral, or unique work that you feel drawn to do.

Maslow suggested that most of us struggle with balancing and satisfying our needs throughout childhood and adolescence, and very few are ever able to achieve self-actualization (Maslow, 1943, 1970). Maslow was not a specialist in human development, and his ideas were based on a study of just 18 people from his own culture who he considered to be self-actualized.

In the United States, Maslow's hierarchy has become core to assessments of well-being in health care (Beccaria et al., 2018; Kaufman, 2019). Developmental researchers have criticized Maslow's hierarchy, suggesting that it is based on a single cultural perspective (Morrison et al., 2011). In many communities, including the Blackfoot nation, the goal of human development is not just one person's success but the well-being of the group, the culture, or the world (Munyaradzi et al., 2016; Winston, 2016).

Empirical research has found that, contrary to what Maslow's hierarchy might suggest, human connection is essential (Holt-Lunstad, 2017). Even if they have enough food, babies require human connection to thrive and the quality of the relationships that children develop can be more important to their future success than their income (Wade et al., 2019). The psychodynamic theorists, who we turn to next, are one reason developmentalists understand that human connection is more than "nice to have"; it is essential for growth. 🌎

Scientific American Profile

Resilience

psychodynamic perspective A perspective with an emphasis on how human behaviors are based on satisfying innate and often subconscious, biological needs for connection, protection, and love.

psychosexual stages The five stages of Freud's psychodynamic theory in which children learn how to manage different sensual and sexual energies.

The Psychodynamic Perspective

The **psychodynamic perspective** considers how our behaviors are based on satisfying innate, biological needs for connection, protection, and love (Fonagy et al., 2016). According to psychodynamic theory, much of your personality, including how you manage stress and relate to others, results from patterns that were set when you were a tiny baby (Groh et al., 2017). Psychodynamic theorists might ask how Mervlyn's earliest relationships with her family helped turn her into the person she is today.

Freud's Psychosexual Theory Psychodynamic theory began with the writings of Sigmund Freud (1856–1939), who himself was inspired by other late-nineteenth-century scientists and philosophers who examined the role of the unconscious in human development (Gay, 1998; Grayling, 2010). Like the biological theorists, Freud believed that human behavior often results from unconscious urges that arose early in human evolution to help the human species survive.

Freud was a medical doctor and researcher from Vienna, Austria, who became famous for his radical theories and his talk therapy (Gay, 1996). He was born into poverty, threatened by anti-Jewish prejudice, and addicted to cocaine (Crews, 2017). Later in life, helped by his vivid writing style and his frank discussions of human sexuality, Freud became an international celebrity (Grayling, 2010). One of his most enduring contributions came from his belief that mental illness could be treated. Freud concluded that many psychological problems stemmed from unresolved childhood issues, such as traumatic experiences with weaning, toilet-training, or being abandoned or hurt by caregivers (Gay, 1996).

Freud thought that development involved five **psychosexual stages**, in which children learned how to manage a different sensual energy, as you can see in **Table 2.1** (Freud, 2018).

Many of the terms used in Freud's stages remain alive in popular culture today, like the idea of an *oral fixation* or an *anal personality*. However, most of his theory has been discredited because it lacks empirical evidence and was informed by his limited clinical work (Grayling, 2010). Developmental scientists have also critiqued many of the degrading assumptions Freud had about girls, women, and people outside of Europe and North America (Frosh, 2013; Stoute, 2020; Tate, 1996). Despite his disparaging beliefs, Freud's emphasis on the link between the first years of life and later emotional development influenced other theorists.

Erikson's Psychosocial Theory One of the many theorists influenced by Freud was the psychoanalyst Erik Erikson (1902–1994). After high school, Erikson traveled around Europe, teaching art and searching for his life's mission. He ended up

TABLE 2.1 Freud's Stages of Psychosexual Development

Stage	Age	Characteristics
Oral	Birth to age 1	Babies learn how to manage the urge to feed and stimulate their mouth. They experience the satisfaction of being fed or sucking a pacifier, or they must cope with the disappointment of hunger or of being unable to suck.
Anal	About ages 1 to 3	Toddlers learn to balance the pleasure and challenge of controlling their elimination during toilet training.
Phallic	About ages 3 to 6	Children learn that they can derive pleasure from their genitals and adjust to society's gender roles. (Although this stage refers to the penis, Freud believed that all children have this experience.)
Latency	About ages 6 to 12	Children's sexual drives are temporarily quiet as they transfer that energy into learning and education until puberty.
Genital	About ages 12+	Adolescents can satisfy their sexual desires with romantic partners and take on adult responsibilities at work and in loving relationships.

teaching at a Montessori school in Vienna, Austria, where Freud had established his first training institute in psychoanalysis. Freud's daughter, Anna, transformed Erikson into a psychoanalyst and helped him identify his calling: helping people. Erikson never graduated from college, and in fact he said he could learn more from watching children than studying in the classroom (Erik Erikson, 1994). Erikson became a prolific writer and one of the first psychoanalytic therapists for children in the United States (Friedman, 2000).

Like Freud, Erikson focused on the role early experiences and social interaction plays in our lives and created a stage theory of *psychosocial development*. Erikson's stages are based on resolving a series of psychological crises triggered by physical maturation and society's expectations, as you can see in **Table 2.2** (Erikson, 1993).

Many of Erikson's contributions to developmental science still resonate. He embraced the complicated social context of development, describing personal growth that occurs within the family and the community (McAdams & Zapata-Gietl, 2015). In this way, Erikson's work is in line with contemporary sociocultural researchers who look at the impact of the wider world, or the *mesosystem*, on children's development (Syed & Fish, 2018).

Erikson's focus on identity development and the importance of giving back also continue to inspire researchers (Côté, 2019). However, many point out that creating a fulfilling life may not be as linear or as orderly as Erikson's stages make it seem, particularly for those who are not elite (Jordan & Tseris, 2020). Now more than ever, developmental scientists and policy makers believe that the first few years of life can create patterns of relating that last a lifetime, and that giving back to others is a necessary ingredient for life satisfaction (Becchetti & Bellucci, 2020; Shonkoff et al., 2021).

Attachment Theory Many experts in the past knew that the early years were critical to children's development, but this did not mean that children were always nurtured and cared for warmly. Sometimes experts advised just the opposite: that babies didn't have emotional needs, that parents shouldn't pick up their children when they cried, and that separating infants from their families would not harm them (van der Horst & van der Veer, 2010). As a result, until the mid-1900s, babies who were hospitalized were sometimes placed in glass cages and not held: They were kept safe and clean but not comforted. During World War II, some infants were even taken away from their families and put in overnight residential nurseries to enable their parents to keep working to contribute to the war effort (Midgley, 2007). Many argued that as long as babies were kept clean, fed, and safe, they could be resilient.

Share It!

Although he taught at Harvard, Erikson never graduated from college himself. Erikson said he preferred to be with children. He said watching a child play was like watching an artist paint.

(Erikson, 1994b)

TABLE 2.2 Erikson's Stages of Psychosocial Development

Stage	Age	Characteristics
Trust versus mistrust	Birth to about 18 months	The infant's conflict concerns whether or not the world feels safe. Infants with responsive caregivers learn that the world is a reliable place where they are likely to be cared for.
Autonomy versus shame and doubt	About 18 months to age 3	Toddlers strive to be independent, or *autonomous*, as they learn to walk, talk, and feed themselves. They may doubt themselves when they fail or cannot accept necessary limits on their behavior.
Initiative versus guilt	About ages 3 to 8	Preschoolers are eager to try new things and to be "big." Since they are unable to get everything right, they must manage their guilt at their missteps.
Industry versus inferiority	About ages 8 to 12	By middle childhood, children are ready to work at what their culture values. Children build a sense of their own industriousness and may have difficulties if they feel they are not meeting their community's expectations.
Identity versus confusion	About ages 12 to 19	Adolescents' central task is to actively discover their own identity. If they are too timid in that quest, they may be lost, confused, and unfulfilled.

manonallard/E+/Getty Images

Time Together Brought to You By Science Developmental scientists helped make this moment possible. Scientific researchers established that young children benefit from close contact with people who care about them. As a result, this man and his son, in a hospital in Quebec, are able to spend time together, which scientists believe will help them both adjust as they grow.

Not all scientists agreed. Many believed that lack of emotional contact could be destructive. Doctors noticed that infants who were separated from their caregivers tended to become listless and were more likely to die (Spitz, 1945). Some studied how isolation and separation hurt animals as well as human babies (Harlow, 1958).

It took a new theory and new scientific methods to change the practice of separating babies from their loved ones. A pioneering English medical doctor, John Bowlby (1907–1990), publicized his theory, later called **attachment theory**, maintaining that children's bonds to their caregivers were essential to their development. Like other ethological and evolutionary scholars, Bowlby believed that humans had a biological need to be attached and cared for in early life (Sroufe, 2016). Children who did not experience loving care would be more likely to have difficulties forming close relationships and could develop emotional and behavioral problems as a result (Bowlby, 2012).

Bowlby's theory gained more scientific approval after he met a Canadian psychologist, Mary Ainsworth (1913–1999), who also believed in the importance of strong early relationships (Bretherton, 1992, 2003; van Rosmalen et al., 2016). Mary Ainsworth traveled all over the world studying children—moving from Toronto, Canada, to London, England, to Kampala, Uganda, and finally settling in Baltimore, Maryland. During her travels, she developed rigorous methods for assessing early relationships through real-life observation and laboratory experiments (van Rosmalen et al., 2015). Together, Ainsworth and Bowlby developed and elaborated on attachment theory, which would help scientists understand and measure children's earliest relationships—and their effects throughout the lifespan.

Attachment theorists found that having healthy, close bonds in toddlerhood helps you to have healthy, close relationships later on (Sroufe, 2021). Like psychoanalytic theorists, attachment researchers believe that early bonds create a pattern for personality development (Mesman, 2021). Contemporary scientists agree: The value of close relationships does not end. Responsive, sensitive relationships help predict your health, your happiness, and even how long you live (Ehrlich & Cassidy, 2021).

The Behaviorist Perspective

The biological and psychodynamic perspectives tend to focus on how people feel—on their emotions, their instincts, and their early relationships. *Behaviorist* scientists point out that there is more to people than feelings and instincts: Humans do math, figure out how to get home on the bus, and how to build elaborate worlds in *Minecraft*. **Behaviorism**, or the behaviorist perspective, is a branch of psychology that is focused on things that are measurable, such as what a person *does* rather than what they think or feel (Watson, 1913). Classic forms of behaviorism focused on how human beings learn. One form, *social learning theory*, emphasized the role of social relationships in shaping behaviors.

The Theory of Behaviorism How do we learn and develop? The early behaviorists would say you should not ask someone what their motivations are, speculate on their unconscious drives, or wonder how they are feeling. Instead, you should carefully observe the events that trigger their behaviors and watch what they actually do. To a behaviorist, feelings, thoughts, and unconscious motivations are unscientific, vague, and unmeasurable.

The man who did the most to popularize behaviorism was a U.S. researcher named John Watson (1878–1958) (Harris, 2011). Watson had a troubled young life: He was a bully who was arrested twice in high school for threatening his neighbors. College did not help very much: Although he crammed for his exams, powered by

attachment theory The theory pioneered that maintains that children's emotional bonds to their caregivers are an essential part of their development.

behaviorism A branch of psychology that is focused on things that are measurable, and suggests that we learn through pairing causes and effects.

cocaine-laced Coca Cola, he graduated at the bottom of his class (Buckley, 1989). Despite his early difficulties, Watson gets credit for bringing modern scientific methods to psychology and was one of the most famous researchers of his generation.

Although Watson personally liked the ideas of psychodynamic theory, he was frustrated by the claim that inborn biology drove all human activity (Malone, 2017). In an era when many psychologists believed individual differences were based on genetics, Watson argued that they were the result of experience. He believed that all babies were born equally capable and that children learned everything they knew (Malone, 2014; Watson, 1913).

Classical Conditioning Watson believed that you learn everything—how to talk, how to walk, and even how to relate to other people—through a process called **classical conditioning**. According to this model, learning is a process of linking a *stimulus* (or experience) to a *response* (or behavior). The process of classical conditioning builds from existing automatic reflexes and works in animals (even snails) as well as in more complicated organisms like people. The principle of classical conditioning was first observed by Russian scientist Ivan Pavlov (1849–1939), who showed that dogs could "learn" to drool in response to a bell ringing, if they had practice hearing the bell while being served dinner (Pavlov, 1928). Watson, like other scientists, believed that human beings also learned this way and was one of the first to demonstrate that children could be conditioned like animals.

Watson believed that classical conditioning may help cure debilitating anxiety and fear, like the anxiety experienced by war veterans (now known as *posttraumatic stress disorder [PTSD]*) (Powell et al., 2014). But, in order to demonstrate that conditioning could cure people's fear, Watson and his team needed to show that fear itself could be conditioned. They decided to train an infant to be afraid, and they found a baby boy in a nearby hospital who became known as "Little Albert" for their experiment (Digdon, 2020).

The team was successful: By making a loud noise that terrified the baby at the same time that he saw a white rat, they conditioned Little Albert to fear white rats and other white, fluffy things, even without the loud noise. The experiment was so effective that Watson claimed that Little Albert even became terrified of Santa Claus's white beard. Little Albert had shown that human beings could learn through conditioning just like animals (Powell & Schmaltz, 2020).

Most agree that the treatment of Little Albert was unethical. Nevertheless, according to many historians, Albert never complained about what had happened to him as a child (Digdon, 2020). Later research by other behaviorists, including Mary Cover Jones, made use of Little Albert's contributions by showing that classical conditioning could also be used to *remove* fears and help people recover from trauma by pairing the fearful stimulus with a positive, comforting one (Cover Jones, 1924). Classical conditioning is used today to toilet-train newborns (see **Figure 2.2**), to help children get over their fear of dogs, and to help teenagers and adults recover from trauma (Fullana et al., 2020).

Operant Conditioning Have you ever rewarded yourself for an hour of studying or working out? Or were you told as a child that you would not get dessert if you kept misbehaving? These are behavioral principles and a form of learning described by American psychologist B. F. Skinner as **operant conditioning** (Skinner, 1938). The idea is that a behavior will be more likely to happen if it is rewarded—and less likely to occur if it is ignored or punished. In operant conditioning, rewards and punishments are used to shape behaviors.

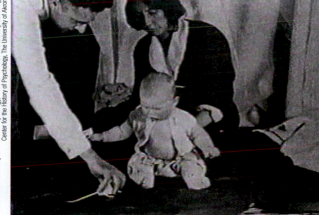

Learning to Be Afraid In this video still, the baby known as Little Albert seems to react with childish curiosity as researcher John Watson shows him a rat. John Watson showed that this curiosity could be turned into terror through classical conditioning.

classical conditioning A model of learning in which a *stimulus* (or experience) is linked to a *response* (or behavior).

operant conditioning A process of learning in which rewards and punishments are used to shape behaviors.

FIGURE 2.2 A Recipe for Classical Conditioning In the process of classical conditioning, a neutral stimulus (like whistling or bell ringing) is paired with an involuntary, reflexive response (like drooling in hunger or going to the bathroom) when it happens naturally. But gradually, after the neutral stimulus happens at the same time as the reflexive response, the stimulus alone will trigger the response. For instance, if a caregiver whistles every time a baby goes to the bathroom, the baby will eventually be triggered to go to the bathroom every time they hear the whistle.

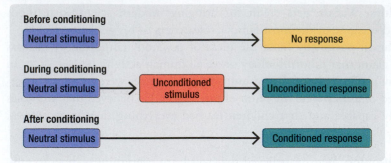

CLASSICAL CONDITIONING

Before conditioning

Neutral stimulus ────────────────→ No response

During conditioning

Neutral stimulus ──→ Unconditioned stimulus ──→ Unconditioned response

After conditioning

Neutral stimulus ────────────────→ Conditioned response

POTTY TRAINING WITH CLASSICAL CONDITIONING

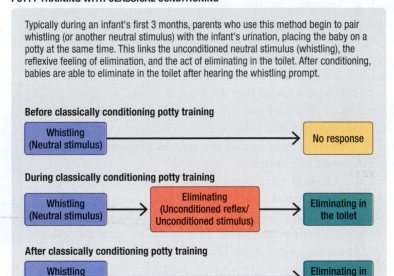

Typically during an infant's first 3 months, parents who use this method begin to pair whistling (or another neutral stimulus) with the infant's urination, placing the baby on a potty at the same time. This links the unconditioned neutral stimulus (whistling), the reflexive feeling of elimination, and the act of eliminating in the toilet. After conditioning, babies are able to eliminate in the toilet after hearing the whistling prompt.

Before classically conditioning potty training

Whistling (Neutral stimulus) ────────────────→ No response

During classically conditioning potty training

Whistling (Neutral stimulus) ──→ Eliminating (Unconditioned reflex/ Unconditioned stimulus) ──→ Eliminating in the toilet

After classically conditioning potty training

Whistling (Neutral stimulus) ────────────────→ Eliminating in the toilet

Dorling Kindersley Ltd/Alamy Stock Photo

Working Toward a Goal This little girl is using a sticker chart to mark how far she's gone toward her goals.

reinforcement Anything that strengthens a behavior, making it more likely to happen.

punishment Anything that weakens a behavior, making it less likely to happen.

Researchers like B. F. Skinner looked at animals as a model for how human beings learn, and they suggested that children, like animals, learn everything they know by a complex system of **reinforcements** and **punishments** (Skinner, 2011). A reinforcement is anything that strengthens a behavior and makes it more likely to happen. It can be a reward, like a treat after finishing a run or a smile from a teacher. A punishment, as you might imagine, is the opposite of a reinforcement and is anything that makes an activity *less* likely to happen, such as when an instructor takes away a student's phone as a consequence of their distraction.

Why shouldn't you give a screaming toddler that candy bar they are reaching for in the checkout line at the grocery store? Remember operant conditioning: If you give in this time, you are reinforcing their behavior and they are likely to scream again next time. The principles of operant conditioning are widely used in everything from training animals to health care.

Operant conditioning helps researchers understand how adolescents reinforce each other's bad behavior by laughing when a friend breaks the rules (Patterson, 2016). It is also at work in education: Skinner felt passionately that learning should be customized, responsive, and give students immediate feedback—ideas that are incorporated into many technologies today, such as the "like" button on Instagram (Skinner, 1989).

Behavioral techniques also form the core of applied behavioral analysis therapies, which are used by many families to help their children address some of the symptoms of autism spectrum disorder (Hyman et al., 2020).

Although modern scientists agree that operant conditioning is an important part of how children learn, few agree it is the only way. Other scientists have demonstrated that children also learn just from watching other people—with no reinforcement or punishment necessary.

Social Learning Theory According to **social learning theory**, learning occurs through observing and imitating others. According to social learning theorists, learning involves thinking and reasoning. People who are respected, like your parents or admired friends, are more likely to be imitated. Reinforcement may shape your learning, but it does not have to be direct. If children see someone else being rewarded or punished, that will affect their decision of whether or not to imitate their behavior.

Real-life examples of social learning can be sweet—as when a 3-year-old puts on their mother's uniform and pretends to go to work—or less so, as when your younger brother repeats the swear-words he heard you say. Researchers who take a social learning approach point out that the most important part of how people learn is often other people. Humans are social—and from birth, we are highly attuned to the facial expressions and behaviors of other people—which helps us learn from each other (Dunbar, 2020; Tomasello, 2020).

Albert Bandura (1925–2021) was a pioneering theorist who focused on the mechanics of how people learn in a social world (Bandura, 1999, 2018). He found that people *model* behavior—whether it is how to stand inside the elevator or how to sit while they are waiting for class to start. Learners pick up new behaviors through *observation*, or watching a model—as when we study a dance on TikTok. We also learn from *imitation*, or by repeating something we have observed—as when a child in the back seat mimics a hand gesture they saw in the front seat. Social learning theorists demonstrated that we can learn without direct experience, as with watching something on Zoom, watching someone else experience something, or even hearing about it thirdhand (Maccoby, 1992).

social learning theory The theory that learning occurs through observing and imitating others.

Courtesy Albert Bandura Trust

The TV Made Me Do It. In the early years of television, Albert Bandura and his team showed that children were more likely to whack an inflatable toy called a Bobo doll if they had seen another child or adult do the same thing—even if they only saw it on television. Bandura also observed that children were more likely to imitate what they saw other children get rewarded for. Imitating what you see on TV is not always harmful: Programs like Sesame Street harness children's tendency to imitate to help them learn.

Social learning theories have guided decades of scientific investigations. Researchers have found that imitation starts early: Newborns might imitate a facial expression of someone nearby, and toddlers will quickly learn how to play with a toy from someone they have just met in the laboratory (Meltzoff & Marshall, 2018; Tomasello, 2019). Studies of the impact of technology on human behavior investigate whether violent video games might teach us to be violent in real life and whether television programs can be a power for good, by preventing substance abuse and forced marriage (Anderson et al., 2017; Bandura, 2019). Social learning theory has also inspired some people to take up jobs in the classroom.

Role Model and Award Winner
Johnathon Hines is an award-winning pre-K teacher at Barack Obama Elementary School in Atlanta, Georgia, and a role model for students who want to grow up to teach and help others.

 SCIENCE IN PRACTICE
Johnathon Hines, Pre-K Teacher

Johnathon Hines says he is not be what most families expect when they sign up their children for pre-kindergarten. He's tall. He's Black. And he is a man. Hines did not expect to become a teacher, either. Like many other teenagers, he dreamed of being a basketball player. Social learning theory is why he became an award-winning pre-K teacher at Barack H. Obama Elementary Magnet School of Technology in Atlanta. Social learning theory explains that role models help us set goals, help us see what is possible, and inspire our work (Morgenroth et al., 2015).

Hines wanted to be a role model: He wanted to inspire young children and show them that being a happy, successful person could mean nurturing students and caring about school. He knew that in the United States, fewer than one in four elementary school teachers is male, and even fewer are Black (U.S. Department of Education, 2019–2020). He wanted to show children that Black men could be successful off the basketball court and in the classroom. As he puts it, he wanted to be a "hero" by showing young people how much school matters.

Empirical research supports Hines' belief: Culturally diverse teachers help students of all backgrounds succeed by reducing their biases and making them more comfortable in a diverse world (Perry, 2019). Black students who have Black teachers tend to do better in school and stay in school longer (Egalite & Kisida, 2018). One study found that Black students who had an elementary school teacher who looked like them were more than 10 percent more likely to go to college (Gershenson et al., 2018).

For Hines, being a role model is more fun than he imagined. He teaches phonics and encourages kids to wait their turn, but he enjoys his students' enthusiasm, their energy, and their love of learning.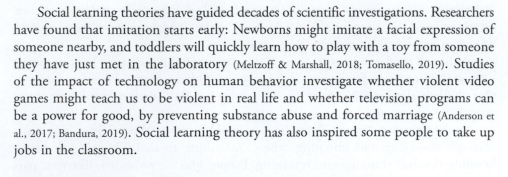

The Cognitive Perspective

Scientists who focus on cognitive development try to understand how learning shapes development—and how thinking changes through the lifespan. There are several theories about how thinking develops, including those of Jean Piaget and information-processing researchers. Along with the behaviorists, cognitive researchers brought careful laboratory techniques and observation to their work—and they made developmental science more rigorous (Anderson, 1956).

cognitive development theory The theory that growth in thinking and understanding happens as a result of active exploration of the world.

Piaget's Theory of Cognitive Development Most behavioral theories explain that learning happens in the same way for babies as it does for adults. **Cognitive development theory** takes another view: The thinking of a baby is categorically different from that of a toddler, a school-age child, and an adolescent (Flavell, 1996). In contrast to the behaviorists and social learning theorists, the revolutionary Swiss psychologist Jean Piaget (1896–1980) argued that growth happens as a result of our active exploration of the world. Children's thinking matures as they actively construct and build what they know (Piaget & Inhelder, 2019). Piaget became the most famous developmentalist of his time as he empathized with children trying to learn about the world—how to grab, suck, and talk. He believed that their thinking develops in distinct stages; that they are not capable of reasoning like adults, nor should they be expected to. But according to Piaget, their unique ways of reasoning are creative and adaptive (Miller, 2011).

Piaget had a difficult childhood and a rocky early career as a shellfish researcher before he began studying children's development. He turned the careful observation skills he had used for categorizing marine creatures to the task of studying children. While he and his wife, Valentine (also a trained psychologist), carefully observed their three children, Piaget was formulating a new theory of how children's thinking develops through breakthroughs in understanding (Fischer & Hencke, 1996; Kohler, 2014).

Piaget developed a specialized vocabulary to describe mental activities: The word **schema** refers to each bit of knowledge a person develops (Piaget, 2013). A schema can be a skill, like grabbing a rattle, or a concept, like understanding that the category of "dogs" includes your dog and others you see in the neighborhood or in a picture book. Schemas grow and become more sophisticated with development and practice, through processes of *assimilation* and *accommodation*.

Piaget's concept of **assimilation** is the expansion of an existing schema with new knowledge or experience. For instance, infants are good at sucking—they can suck a bottle or a pacifier just fine. And this sucking ability can be adapted to something else entirely, like Daddy's phone. The baby has assimilated this new, hard beeping object into their existing sucking schema that had previously just been used for soft things. As they get older, their assimilation may become more sophisticated: They may assimilate cougars into their schema for giant cats or add kale to their schema for foods.

Sometimes children's existing schemas need to be changed because new information just does not work with the old schema. **Accommodation** is the process of reorganizing knowledge when that happens. For instance, a sucking baby may realize that they cannot suck the dog (without a mouthful of fur). A toddler may realize that beach sand is not as tasty as it appears. Their schemas need to be altered to accommodate knowledge that dogs and sand are not objects to suck.

Piaget's stage theory of development described four discrete periods, or **stages**, in cognitive development, as you see in **Table 2.3**.

A Scientist and an Inventor Jean Piaget was not just good at making theories. He also made his own baby carriers, so he could take his son, Laurent, and his other children hiking in the mountains near his home in Geneva, Switzerland.

schema The word for each bit of knowledge a person develops.

assimilation The expansion of an existing schema with new knowledge or experience.

accommodation The process of reorganizing knowledge based on new experiences.

Piaget's stage theory of development The five periods of cognitive development described by Jean Piaget, in which children's thinking proceeds through qualitatively different ways of understanding the world.

stages Distinct time periods when development changes dramatically.

TABLE 2.3 Piaget's Stages of Cognitive Development

Stage	Age	Characteristics
Sensorimotor	Birth to about age 2	Infants use their senses and physical abilities to explore the world. This stage begins with involuntary movements, such as reflexes, and ends with independent movement, language, and imagination. Babies and toddlers gradually learn that there is more to the world than what they can feel or manipulate with their bodies. As they grow, they can mentally represent ideas and think about them before they happen, an achievement that marks the end of the sensorimotor period.
Preoperational	About ages 2 to 6 or 7	Young children can communicate with language, use their imagination, and think symbolically, but they cannot yet think logically and are easily tricked by appearances. A young child might believe that a costume turns someone into Captain Marvel and will have difficulty imagining things from someone else's perspective. This period is called *preoperational* because children are not yet able to perform mental operations or think through events.
Concrete operational	About ages 6 or 7 to 11 or 12	This stage is all about logic. Children can now reason through problems and examine situations from differing perspectives, as long as they are not too abstract. They can categorize things and put them in order. However, thinking is more reliable when it is linked to what can be seen, heard, or touched.
Formal operational	About age 11 through adulthood	This stage involves grasping abstract or hypothetical ideas, concepts, and scenarios. Teenagers and adults can ponder the idea of a world without money or the meaning of the word *justice*. This will enable adolescents and adults to create amazing things like new vaccines or more efficient cars—as well as more everyday insights like how to get through math class.

AP Photo/Marcio Jose Sanchez

All the Cognition He Needs to Help Others Piaget's stage theory of cognitive development suggests that we develop all the cognitive skills we need by the time we are adolescents. By eighth grade, Shubham was able to design an inexpensive machine to print Braille for people with visual impairments. It is based on an early model he made with Lego blocks for his school science fair.

Piaget's revolutionary contributions to developmental science include not just what he discovered about how children think, but how he did his work: He talked to children directly and sympathetically. When a boy told him that dreams came from his blanket, Piaget did not correct him—he just asked more questions. Piaget's description of children's thinking helped to create a whole new field of developmental science devoted to children's cognition (Flavell, 1996). His belief that children did not need to be rushed from one stage to another and that their thinking is creative within each stage continues to influence how educators work with children (Zigler & Gilman, 1991). And unsurprisingly, Piaget's stance as a curious and empathetic observer remains a model for teachers, child-care workers, and developmental scientists alike (Waite-Stupiansky, 2017).

While Piaget's stages remain a touchstone in developmental science, many have questioned how accurate they are (Carey et al., 2015). In many studies, children's cognitive development does not proceed neatly in precise periods and often depends on how much enrichment and formal schooling they receive (Busch, Watson-Jones, et al., 2020; Siegler & Ellis, 1996). Babies actually display more logical thinking and more inborn abilities than Piaget observed when he first formulated his theories (Baillargeon et al., 2016). Nevertheless, Piaget's stages of cognitive development remain a shared vocabulary within developmental science for describing cognitive growth.

Information-Processing Theory While Piaget was becoming the most prominent developmental scientist of his generation, another group of researchers was looking at the development of thinking from a perspective known as **information processing**. They studied the individual components of how you process what you perceive: how you pay attention, remember, and react to the world (Lachman et al., 1979). Inspired by computer technology, information-processing theory describes thinking and learning using the metaphor of a computer, exploring *inputs* (such as your sensation, perception, and ability to pay attention), *processing* (such as thinking and learning), *storage* and *retrieval* (memory), and *output* (your behavioral responses). (See **Figure 2.3**.)

Information-processing scientists also look at more complex thinking processes, like *executive function*, or your ability to actively regulate your thinking and behavior to accomplish a goal. Unlike Piaget, information-processing theorists do not believe that development occurs in stages, although they have observed substantial changes in people's cognitive abilities from infancy through adolescence.

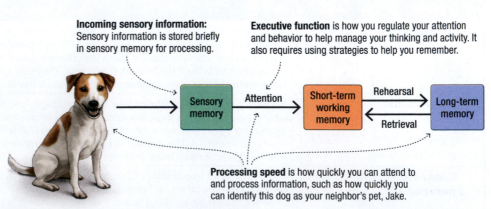

Incoming sensory information: Sensory information is stored briefly in sensory memory for processing.

Executive function is how you regulate your attention and behavior to help manage your thinking and activity. It also requires using strategies to help you remember.

Sensory memory → Attention → Short-term working memory ⇄ Rehearsal / Retrieval ⇄ Long-term memory

Processing speed is how quickly you can attend to and process information, such as how quickly you can identify this dog as your neighbor's pet, Jake.

information processing An approach that studies the development of thinking and understanding by describing how a person pays attention, remembers, and reacts to the world, similar to how a computer processes information.

FIGURE 2.3 How Do You Process "Dog"? Information-processing theorists look at the individual components of our thinking, including how we process incoming sensory information, store it in memory, and make decisions about how to regulate our attention.

The information-processing approach to development has led to important discoveries about what very young babies are capable of, how older children learn, and how puberty changes your thinking. For instance, researchers watching infants' eye movements found that at just 4 months, they expect an object that has disappeared to reappear, suggesting an early understanding of object permanence (von Hofsten & Rosander, 2018). Scientists have studied how babies use statistics to find patterns in the speech they hear, helping them learn what to focus on in language learning (Saffran, 2020).

cultural perspective A perspective that explains how culture is integrated into all of development and how cultural variations and strengths can help everyone thrive.

sociocultural theory The theory that culture plays a role in every part of development.

The Cultural Perspective

Developmental scientists' commitments to recognize the value of all people, embrace diversity, and advocate for increased tolerance and an end to discrimination means that the *cultural perspective* is one of the most prominent theories in research today (C. S. Brown et al., 2019; García Coll et al., 2018). The **cultural perspective** explains how culture is integrated into all of development and how cultural variations and strengths can help everyone thrive. Cultural theorists ask questions about the impact of culture on development, including how culture gives us strength and how discrimination can challenge us. A scientist with a cultural perspective might examine how the cultural values and sense of belonging Mervlyn found when she attended a Hawai'ian school at age 12 contributed to her resilience. Other scholars might want to learn about impact of intersectional exclusion on Mervlyn as she grew up in a world that felt prejudiced against people who came from two cultures.

Gone Too Early Lev Vygotsky was a teacher, scholar, and advocate for children and people with disabilities. Without the benefits of modern science, he died at just 37, leaving behind his wife and their two young children.

Sociocultural Theory According to **sociocultural theory,** culture plays a role in every part of human development (Packer & Cole, 2020). Cultural theorists emphasize how children's learning is based on interactions with other people in a social context (Rogoff et al., 2018). Even how you see, how you remember, and how your brain develops are influenced by culture (Wang, 2016). Rather than describing culture as the outside, or the macrosystem, of human development, sociocultural theorists see culture as embedded inside each part of how we grow (Vélez-Agosto et al., 2017).

Russian psychologist and educator Lev Vygotsky (1896–1934) was one of the first to observe how deeply culture affects how we grow. Vygotsky worked in the 1920s and 1930s, and his research was forgotten to a large extent after his early death at age 37. But in the late 1970s, Vygotsky's work was rediscovered and retranslated into English (Vygotsky & Cole, 1978; Yasnitsky & van der Veer, 2015). Vygotsky had many passions—from writing about Shakespeare to studying law—but teaching is what profoundly changed his thinking (Yasnitsky, 2018). While sick with the lung disease that later took his life, Vygotsky began to teach children with major disabilities and children who had never been exposed to the written word (Gindis, 1999). Unlike many others, Vygotsky did not overlook or dismiss the fact that these children were capable, and he argued that their differences could be strengths.

Sociocultural theorists working in Vygotsky's tradition now have three major approaches to studying culture in developmental science:

1. *Interpreting what you observe through the lens of culture helps you see more accurately.* For instance, what do you think when you see children picking grapes, as in this photograph? Are they too young to help out? Or do they feel proud

A Tradition of Helping with Harvest These girls are still in school but are taking time off to participate in the grape harvest near their home in Sicily, Italy.

Developmental scientists use theoretical models to think about and study the complex ways culture and context influence human development. How might each theoretical approach explain how Mervlyn changed and grew from an anxious second-grader to a confident and affectionate grandparent?

 Major Questions   **What is the pattern of change?**   **How do people change or grow?**   **How does this explain Mervlyn's growth?**

THE BIOLOGICAL PERSPECTIVE

 How is development triggered by our brain, our genes, and our innate or inborn instincts? How does our body influence how we grow?

Evolutionary Theory	Human behavior gradually adapts and changes over millennia through natural selection to better align with the environment.	Individual variations and diversity demonstrate how human beings can successfully adapt to their environment. Some of our variety, however, may not be a perfect adaptation to our current situation.	Some evolutionary theorists suggest that humans, like Mervlyn, may have children at a young age when they are in stressful situations.
Ethological Theory	Many human behaviors are universal and innate despite the diversity in human beings around the world.	Change is driven by inborn programming.	An ethologist might suggest that Mervlyn had an innate capability to bond with young children, including her own.
Epigenetic Theory	Inborn characteristics, including your genes, have been shaped and changed by your environment.	Each of our paths can change, but at some times our inborn tendencies or the environment can make change easier or harder than at other times.	Mervlyn was shaped by her inborn temperament and also by the cascade of life events that she experienced.

THE PSYCHODYNAMIC PERSPECTIVE

 How are human behaviors driven by our innate, biological needs for connection, protection, and love? How do our earliest experiences in our families and communities shape our developing personality?

Freud's Psychosexual Theory	We develop through five psychosexual stages, in which we learn how to manage a different sensual and sexual energy.	With positive early experiences, we address our unconscious longings and are able to live a fulfilling life.	Mervlyn is satisfying her need for love by developing close relationships with her family and students.
Erikson's Psychosocial Theory	We develop through eight psychological crises triggered by physical maturation and society's expectations. Ideally, these establish our ability to trust and relate to others.	We address and resolve crises to feel whole, trusting, and generative.	Mervlyn has discovered who she is and is giving back as an adult.
Attachment Theory	Our earliest bonds shape our future relationships with other people and with the world around us. Adult life is shaped by the pattern of relating set in early infancy.	Through supportive early attachments, we learn to trust others to love us, and to see ourselves as worthy of love.	Mervlyn developed a pattern of secure, close relationships that helped her repair the bonds that may have been less secure. Her family relationships are a continuation of a pattern that was set years before.

© Macmillan, Photo by Point Studio, Inc.

of their contribution? Researchers point out that unless you understand the cultural meaning that the child and their community attach to what they are doing, you will not understand it accurately (White & Mistry, 2016). Work can be helpful or harmful to children depending on their cultural beliefs and context.

2. *Cross-cultural research focuses on comparing human maturation around the world* (Greenfield, 2018). Understanding variations in how we grow helps researchers appreciate human beings' ability to adapt to different contexts and can broaden

THE BEHAVIORIST PERSPECTIVE

 How does learning result from an interaction between people and their environment? How can we measure who people are and how they behave, rather than simply guessing?

Behaviorist Theory	Development is a gradual, continuous process as we learn from birth until later life via classical and operant conditioning.	Learning changes us: All development is a process of linking a stimulus (or experience) with a response (or behavior). Behaviors that are reinforced happen more frequently.	Mervlyn learned to be a teacher and caring parent by accumulating skills little by little over her lifespan. Mervlyn was reinforced for caring for others, so she did it more.
Social Learning Theory	We learn through observing and imitating others. We continue to learn over the lifespan but our early role models and habits often persist.	We are likely to imitate people we admire and respect. Our role models and our community cause us to grow.	Mervlyn had role models who inspired her and taught her how to be an active, caring adult.

THE COGNITIVE PERSPECTIVE

? *How does our thinking shape our development? How does our thinking change as we get older?*

Piaget's Constructivist Theory	Children and adolescents go through four discrete stages of development as their thinking matures.	Development is driven by inborn biological maturation and by active exploration of the world as you construct and build what you know.	Mervlyn is in the stage of postformal thought, so she can think about big social values like kindness and generosity.
Information-Processing Theory	Development is a continuous process of maturation in our information-processing systems, including attention, memory, processing, and reacting to the world around you.	Many of the individual components of how we think and process information mature and age at different rates, driven by experience and biological maturation.	Mervlyn developed strong executive function skills early in her life: These allowed her to do well in school and thrive.

THE CULTURAL PERSPECTIVE

? *How does culture impact every part of development, shaping how we grow, think, and relate to one another?*

Sociocultural Theory	Growth occurs continuously over the lifespan as we mature in a specific cultural environment.	Change, growth, and learning happen through interactions with other people who pass on knowledge and skills in a cultural context.	Mervlyn learned to be a successful adult through social interactions in her community: Close family relationships are valued in her culture, and she values passing on her cultural traditions to the next generation.
Theories of Social Justice	Growth and maturation happen continuously over the lifespan and are shaped by our social status. Cultural strengths and community can help us thrive.	Change results from our interactions and our individual identity in relation with other people embedded in a hierarchical community.	Mervlyn's experiences growing up and feeling as if she did not quite fit in within her Harwaiian community give her a unique identity. She found strong ties to her Hawaiian heritage at school.

what we think of as "typical" milestones and pathways for development (Keller, 2017; Rogoff, 1990). For instance, the age when babies typically learn to sit on their own is not universal. Many babies in Cameroon sit at about 4 months—but it takes babies in the United States about two more months to achieve this milestone (Karasik et al., 2010). Common variations in development are often based on factors like whether people live in rural or urban communities or whether they live in industrialized or agricultural economies (Packer & Cole, 2020). But culture does not always mean differences—it can also mean similarities (Wang et al., 2017).

Sometimes Culture Means Sharing a Treat. These children in the Russian region of Yamalo-Nenets are celebrating their reindeer herding heritage with races, traditional costumes, and sweets.

All cultures recognize that children need responsive, loving relationships in order to thrive (Keller, 2021).

3. *Cultural research identifies variations within communities.* For instance, children experience different cultures and have different experiences depending on their social status, often based on their race, ethnicity, or income (Spencer, 2017). Researchers have even found that variations in culture can happen in different afterschool classrooms. For instance, a program held in a library developed a distinctive culture when researchers compared it to one held in a Boys-and-Girls club (and, yes, it was quieter!) (Cole, 2017).

Theories of Social Justice Scholars who focus on social justice, including those who identify as *critical race theorists*, evaluate how social inequality and discrimination affect us and how cultural identity can help us thrive (C. S. Brown et al., 2019). They point out that societies around the world have varying levels of inequality, oppression, and discrimination based on gender identity, race, age, physical and cognitive ability, sexual orientation, health, color, or culture. These communities include Indigenous Maori in New Zealand, Muslim Uighurs in China, same-sex couples and their families in Uganda, and low-income people and people of color in the United States. In the United States, critical race theorists have pointed out that discrimination based on race has been a part of government, cultural, and legal systems since early colonization (Delgado, 1995).

Discrimination is often *intersectional*, with overlapping systems of mistreatment based on ethnicity, immigration status, gender identity, religion, physical ability, income level, age, body size or appearance, and sexual orientation (Crenshaw, 1989; Ghavami et al., 2016; Velez & Spencer, 2018). People experience discrimination through systemic discrimination, everyday microaggressions, and targeted aggression and bullying (Syed, 2021). Everyday discrimination can build up and contribute to poor health and lower academic achievement (Paradies et al., 2017). But cultural identity can be protective, connecting people to their communities and giving them a feeling of meaning and belonging, and it can help children to live happier lives (Anderson & Stevenson, 2019; Park et al., 2018).

Social justice scholars have a number of research approaches:

1. *Make disparities visible.* Throughout childhood and adolescence, prejudice and inequality based on our identities contribute to stress and poor health. Quantifying and studying how and when discrimination makes an impact can lead to interventions to help children thrive.

2. *Document the development of group identity and group prejudice.* Researchers are trying to understand when prejudice and bias begin in the toddler years and whether people become fairer as they grow (Elenbaas et al., 2020). Other scholars focus on how cultural identity changes, from when babies learn that they are part of one group to how identity changes in adolescence (García Coll et al., 2018).

3. *Fix systems.* Rather than expecting individual people to display resilience so that they better fit into a system that does not treat them fairly, focus on interventions that change institutions so that they serve all people (Duchesneau, 2020).

4. *Look to strengths.* What developmental competencies do children develop as a result of living in an unequal system? From experience in advocating for yourself to enhanced executive function as a result of code-switching, many children

adapt to an unequal system and develop strengths that help them cope (Cabrera & Tamis-LeMonda, 2013; Cavanaugh et al., 2018; Rogoff et al., 2017; Yosso, 2005).

No matter what aspect of development they focus on, social justice theorists inspire questions and investigation designed to make the world fairer and more compassionate to all of us.

APPLY IT! **2.1** Erikson's theory of psychosocial development would predict that Mervlyn has developed the ability to trust and find her own identity. What signs do you see that Mervlyn has found a sense of who she is?
2.2 How would a behavioral theorist, a social learning theorist, and a sociocultural theorist explain how Mervlyn has adapted to her life? How would you describe the roles you have taken on in your family or friend group? Was it something you learned, imitated, or adapted through observation?

How to Study Development

Theories help us define questions and predictions about development. The next step is to put these questions to the test carefully and methodically.

When Emmy Werner and her team wanted to know, for instance, what factors made children like Mervlyn resilient, they met with a group of children and their families for over 60 years to pinpoint the circumstances and traits that supported positive development and those that put them at risk (Werner, 1995). The scientists found that for many children, particular protective factors helped them overcome some of the adversity they experienced. The most important element? Finding at least one adult who supported and understood them when they were small.

The Scientific Method

Science begins with the simple idea that everything needs to be tested. And tested again. And analyzed critically. The **scientific method** is a multistep process in which scientists evaluate their ideas and find out if they are accurate. As you will see in **Figure 2.4**, this process has five steps: *observation, hypothesis, data collection, analysis,* and *sharing*.

1. *Make an observation:* Science begins with curiosity, and researchers are curious people who want to know why and how come. Maybe you want to find out why some young people are able to develop resilience despite the stresses of everyday life. Maybe you noticed that some people you know who do a lot of chores around the house and community service tend to feel better than others. That might be your first observation.

2. *Form a hypothesis:* A **hypothesis** is a prediction about what researchers expect to find from the data. Many hypotheses are inspired by one or more theoretical perspectives. For instance, you may have wondered whether young people developed resilience more easily if they had the opportunity to take care of other people. Your hypothesis might be: Adolescents who spend more than one hour a week of community service or chores for their family have less depression and more resilience.

3. *Collect the data:* Gathering data is the hallmark of empirical inquiry. Scientists don't rely on their personal experiences, their friends' opinions, or stories that have been passed down. They make multiple measurements of the phenomena they are studying. Collecting data can take many forms: Researchers may conduct experiments, observe people over time, look at their brains in a scanner, sample

Learning Objectives

2.7 Define the steps and guiding principles of the scientific method.

2.8 Describe the ethical standards governing science and practice.

scientific method A multistep process in which scientists evaluate their ideas and find out if they are accurate through collecting and analyzing data.

hypothesis A prediction about what a researcher expects to find from the data.

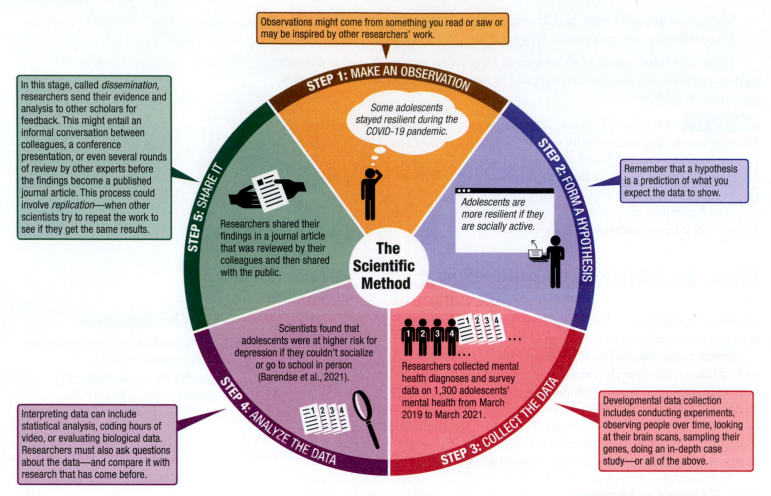

FIGURE 2.4 The Steps of the Scientific Method Developmental researchers use the scientific method to evaluate their ideas and make sure they are accurate. This process has five steps: *observation, hypothesis, data collection, analysis,* and *sharing.*

their genes, do an in-depth case study—or all of the above. For instance, to study the resilience of teenagers during the COVID-19 pandemic, one group of researchers assessed data on the mental health of an international group of more than 1,300 adolescents before and after the outbreak that began in March 2020 (Barendse et al., 2021).

4. *Analyze the data:* Making sense of data can involve formulating statistical analyses to compare how people did on tests, using powerful computers to evaluate brain imagery, or watching hours of video to code behavior. It also involves asking questions about the data—and comparing it with research that has come before. In the end, scientists need to conclude whether their hypothesis was supported by the data. When the researchers looking at adolescent mental health looked at their data, they found that sticking to a routine helped adolescents stay resilient. Adolescents were at higher risk for depression during the pandemic particularly if they were under lockdown restrictions that limited in-person schooling (Barendse et al., 2021).

5. *Share it:* The last step in the scientific process is to send your work out into the world. This is formally called *dissemination.* In this stage, researchers send their evidence and their analysis to other scientists for feedback. This step might include an informal conversation between colleagues, a conference presentation, or even several rounds of review from other experts before taking the form of a published journal article. Part of this process might involve *replication*—when other scientists test what has been done by repeating it on their own to see if they

get the same results. Often this leads to new questions and new studies—and back to the beginning of the scientific process.

Although the steps in the scientific method are common to many sciences, many of the methods that developmental scientists use are unique—because the population they study is a bit different: people of different ages. (See **Infographic 2.2.**)

Research Design

If you want to find out what strength help adolescents be resilient, you need to decide *how* you are going to test your ideas and learn more. You have to design a research study. There are a lot of options. In developmental science, common research designs include experiments, correlational studies, and descriptive research. All of these methods can be used to study people of the same age—or can be used to study changes over time.

Experimental Research In developmental science, an experiment helps to determine *why* something happens. An **experiment** tests a hypothesis that one factor is caused by another. The factors that are studied are known as **variables**, which must be measured and must vary, or differ, among different participants in the research study. Researchers check to see how one factor, called the **independent variable**, causes change in another, called the **dependent variable**. The independent variable is something that the researcher can change.

Let's describe a hypothetical experiment to make things clearer: Say you wanted to measure how adolescents' involvement in a hypothetical Zoom-based mental health project called Resilience Boosters affected their resilience. In this case, whether teenagers were randomly selected to attend the program or not would be the independent variable and mental health would be the dependent variable. If resilience is significantly higher among those who were part of the program, you will be able to conclude that the program worked. The change in the dependent variable reveals the outcome of your experiment—like whether your program worked.

In an ideal experiment, scientists control all aspects of the procedure so that they can be sure their conclusions are accurate. In the case of our experiment, part of this process involves making sure that we compare adolescents who were involved in the program, also known as the *experimental group*, with another group that did not attend Resilience Boosters, called the *control group*. Both groups should be as similar as possible—so that you know it was Resilience Boosters and not something else that caused the changes you are looking for.

Ideally, you can *randomly assign* the children to the different groups in your experiment. This means that both your experimental group and your control group are made up of the same types of children—you will not want to have all boys in one group or all girls in the other, or just tenth-graders in one group and all twelfth-graders in the other. It is important to keep as many distracting factors as you can out of the way. For instance, it would confuse the results if the teenagers in your control group all happened to be in another program on mindfulness. In a well-controlled experiment, the primary difference between the groups should be that one group was in the program and one group was not.

As you will see in **Figure 2.5**, in the hypothetical Resilience Boosters experiment, researchers randomized 100 students to either attend the program or a control group. As **Infographic 2.2** shows, the program seemed to have positive effects. The students who attended the program had less depression than those who did not attend the program.

experiment The act of testing a hypothesis that one factor is caused by another.

variables The factors that are studied in an experiment.

independent variable A factor that is tested to see if it causes change in another variable. An independent variable is something that the researcher can change.

dependent variable The factor that is measured during an experiment to determine the effect of the independent variable.

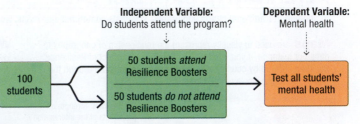

FIGURE 2.5 In the hypothetical Resilience Boosters experiments, 100 students were randomly assigned to either attend the intervention program or to attend another program. This intervention was the independent variable. The outcome was a measurement of students' mental health after the program concluded. The students' mental health was the dependent variable.

Developmental science has its own vocabulary for describing human development that includes both words and pictures. The way scientists display data has its own conventions. Learning how researchers display their results visually helps you understand the strength of their evidence. A hypothetical study of a "Resilience Boosters" intervention is used to illustrate these conventions.

HOW SCIENTISTS SHARE DATA

Bar graphs show a comparison between two groups. The groups are separated into individual bars and measured along the same continuum.

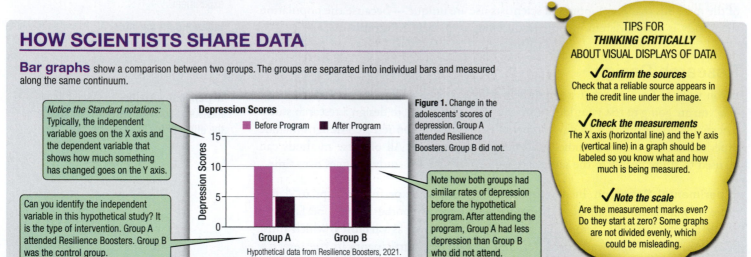

Notice the Standard notations: Typically, the independent variable goes on the X axis and the dependent variable that shows how much something has changed goes on the Y axis.

Can you identify the independent variable in this hypothetical study? It is the type of intervention. Group A attended Resilience Boosters. Group B was the control group.

Hypothetical data from Resilience Boosters, 2021.

Figure 1. Change in the adolescents' scores of depression. Group A attended Resilience Boosters. Group B did not.

Note how both groups had similar rates of depression before the hypothetical program. After attending the program, Group A had less depression than Group B who did not attend.

TIPS FOR THINKING CRITICALLY ABOUT VISUAL DISPLAYS OF DATA

✓ *Confirm the sources*
Check that a reliable source appears in the credit line under the image.

✓ *Check the measurements*
The X axis (horizontal line) and the Y axis (vertical line) in a graph should be labeled so you know what and how much is being measured.

✓ *Note the scale*
Are the measurement marks even? Do they start at zero? Some graphs are not divided evenly, which could be misleading.

Line Graphs describe the relationship between types of variables that may change together. This graph shows the relationship between participants' scores of depression and resilience in our hypothetical intervention.

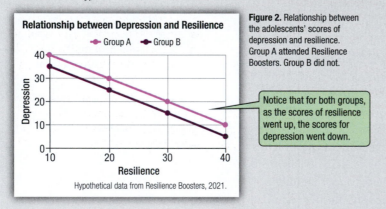

Hypothetical data from Resilience Boosters, 2021.

Figure 2. Relationship between the adolescents' scores of depression and resilience. Group A attended Resilience Boosters. Group B did not.

Notice that for both groups, as the scores of resilience went up, the scores for depression went down.

Pie Charts describe the variation in a group of people. This pie chart illustrates how many participants were in groups A and B and how many did not complete the study. Pie charts work best when the data do not represent amounts or values, which are better displayed on a numeric graph.

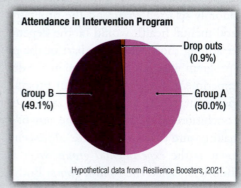

Hypothetical data from Resilience Boosters, 2021.

Figure 3. Participation in the intervention program. Group A attended Resilience Boosters. Group B did not. One person dropped out of the program before it was completed.

ALTERNATIVE DATA DISPLAYS

In addition to traditional charts and graphs, scientists sometimes use maps, word clouds, and biological images to explain their data.

Maps are used to visually represent the relationship of geography to data. For instance, if you wanted to explain how the effect of Resilience Boosters differed by country after it had been implemented around the world, you might display it on a map.

Hypothetical data from Resilience Boosters, 2021.

Figure 4. Strength of effects of the intervention program. After Resilience Boosters was offered to adolescents worldwide, the strength of the effect was compared. The key indicates the strength of the reduction in adolescent depression around the world.

Word Clouds are used to describe the relative value of words, like the frequency that they appear in documents. For instance, if you interviewed the participants in Resilience Boosters program about the value of their experience, you might display their feedback in a word cloud.

Biological Figures are used to describe changes that are happening in the body. For instance, if MRI brain scans were taken of the participants in our study, their results might look like the image below.

Callista Images/ImageSource/AGE Fotostock

In some cases, scientists want to study something that would be impossible or unethical to study in a controlled experiment—like the effect of a natural disaster, pandemic, war, or famine. However, sometimes they are able to collect data in the midst of life-changing events that are out of their control. In these *natural experiments*, researchers compare a group of people who experienced, say, an ice storm or a hurricane or a war with a group of their agemates who were not exposed—allowing the scientists to discover that natural disasters can have an impact on development (Jones et al., 2019).

Sometimes natural experiments focus on the good. In one study, researchers found that families who were unexpectedly lifted out of poverty (as a result of earnings distributed to them from a local casino) had much lower rates of significant psychological illnesses than those who remained in poverty (Akee et al., 2018). This natural experiment helped to establish that increasing families' incomes can help protect children from psychological distress.

Correlational Research Doing an experiment may not always be possible or even provide an accurate description of the phenomena scientists are studying. Say, for instance, researchers want to understand more about the economic benefits of a college education. Hypothetically, it would be possible to conduct an experiment. You might convince some high school graduates to go to college and convince others to go right to work, and then compare their salaries years later. But this may be unethical and expensive, and it will take a long time. You would therefore try another approach: a correlational study.

In a **correlational study**, a researcher gathers data and looks for relationships between variables but does not actually manipulate them. A *correlation* refers to the statistical relationship between two variables in a study. For instance, researchers conducted a correlational study that collected data about who attended college and who did not and compared their salaries. They looked for the correlation between college attendance and salary. (A correlation is *positive* if both variables tend to increase together or decrease together, *negative* if one variable tends to increase while the other decreases, or *zero* if no connection is evident.)

Unsurprisingly, the correlation between college attendance and annual salary is *very large and positive*, as you see in **Figure 2.6** (Ma et al., 2016). But studies don't always

Scientific American Profile

Participating in Research

Learn It Together

Experimental and Correlational Studies

Plan Design a study to test the hypothesis: Children's behavior is affected by eating sweets.

Engage Divide into groups. Have one group design a correlational study to evaluate this hypothesis. Have another group design an experiment to test the effect of eating sugar. What methods and measures might you use?

Reflect Compare your research plans either as a slide presentation or as a discussion. What are the strengths and weaknesses of each design?

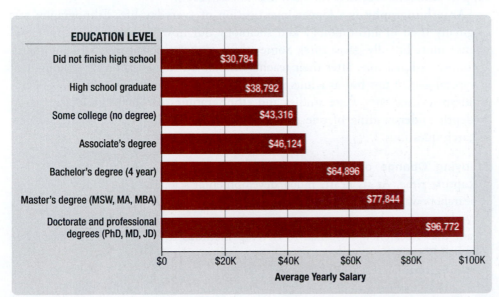

EDUCATION LEVEL

Education Level	Average Yearly Salary
Did not finish high school	$30,784
High school graduate	$38,792
Some college (no degree)	$43,316
Associate's degree	$46,124
Bachelor's degree (4 year)	$64,896
Master's degree (MSW, MA, MBA)	$77,844
Doctorate and professional degrees (PhD, MD, JD)	$96,772

Average Yearly Salary

Information from Bureau of Labor Statistics, 2020.

FIGURE 2.6 What Are the Financial Benefits of College? The number of years you stay in school correlates with your average yearly salary. So, on average, someone with a professional degree, such as a physician or a lawyer, makes more than three times as much as someone who did not complete high school.

correlational study A study in which a researcher gathers data and looks for relationships between variables but does not actually manipulate them.

case study An in-depth analysis of one child, family, or institution's experience.

ethnography A longer, richly detailed investigation of everyday life.

longitudinal research The study of the same group of people over time.

Enjoying School in Monte Alegre, Brazil Scientists often use case studies to establish how interventions work in different contexts. One research team measured the impact of early-childhood education on children's development by watching it in action in schools in Brazil.

find positive correlations—sometimes they are negative. For instance, adolescents who get better sleep take fewer risks—sleep quality is *negatively* correlated with risk-taking (Telzer et al., 2013). And some variables are not consistently related, such as whether homework is correlated with higher academic achievement (De Bruyckere et al., 2020; H. Fan et al., 2017).

Correlational studies are powerful tools for understanding how we grow, but like experiments, they also come with a caution. Just because two variables have a relationship, does not mean one variable caused the other. Experts remind us: *Correlation is not causation*. Without conducting an actual controlled experiment, we can never rule out the possibility that there is a mystery variable that links them. For instance, do popsicles cause gun violence? Statistics show that there is a positive correlation between popsicle sales and gun violence (Harper, 2013). But nothing in frozen treats leads people to become violent. The missing variable is summer: More time outside seems to be related to more opportunities for conflict—and the hot weather also leads to more popsicle sales. The false associations (and the surprisingly legitimate associations) between correlation and causation mean interpretation must be done carefully.

Case Study and Ethnographic Research In experiments and correlational studies, scientists need to study a great number of people—and often this means that they cannot spend a lot of time with any one person. Big studies provide information about groups—but not about individuals. Scientists have some alternatives when they want to understand children and adolescents in depth.

A **case study** is an in-depth analysis of one person, family, or institution's experience. If you spent a few weeks with Mervlyn, interviewing her family and her friends, you might be able to put together a case study. Scientists often use case studies to explore the development of specific people to understand, for instance, the impact of brain injury on one person's development, or to describe how someone has been able to recover from abuse. Much of the work of psychodynamic theorists was based on case studies. Case studies are also used to describe an institution's experiences—as in a case study about Brazilian preschools that implemented a successful program to help support children's executive function (Dias & Seabra, 2015).

An **ethnography** is a longer investigation of everyday life. Ethnography was originally used in anthropology and sociology but now is used in developmental science more broadly (Abebe, 2018). Some ethnographers spent time with children in a nonprofessional role, after their teachers explained they shouldn't be thought of as typical grown-ups but as adults who wanted to experience what life was like as children (Corsaro, 2017). Case studies and ethnographies can help give scientists an in-depth understanding of one particular experience and can help generate new research questions.

Studying Change over Time One challenge in developmental science is how to capture time. At its heart, much developmental science is the study of change. Researchers want to understand how language develops during infancy, how personality changes in adolescence, or how romance matures in late adulthood. This has meant that researchers have had to develop methods to measure change itself (see **Figure 2.7**).

Longitudinal research involves studying the same group of people over time. This can be a short period of time, as when researchers track babies from birth until they learn to talk or schoolchildren during one school year. Or it may be a marathon: Some notable research studies, like the one Mervlyn participates in, are tracking children from birth until the end of life. Collecting data on the same people over a long period of time allows researchers to find correlations between different experiences throughout development.

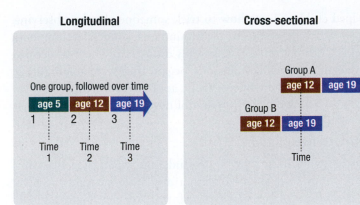

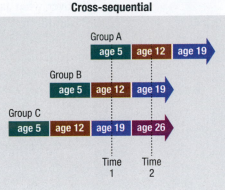

FIGURE 2.7 Age as a Variable Researchers have several ways to consider the impact of time itself on people's development. A longitudinal design requires multiple time points of data collection (noted as Time 1, 2, and 3 above) to document individuals' change over time. In a cross-sectional design, only one time point of data collection is required, as groups of people of different ages are compared. A cross-sequential design combines both aspects, conducting multiple times of study with groups of different ages. A microgenetic study engages in multiple frequent measurements, to capture the moment of developmental change when it occurs.

Longitudinal research can be a powerful tool to observe what happens over time, but it has some limitations. One of these is logistics. It is expensive and time-consuming for researchers to keep track of their research participants and convince them to stay in touch. When participants "drop out" of a longitudinal study, the results are not as strong, since researchers cannot be sure that the findings would be the same for the people who left the study as it was for the people who stayed. Time is also a limitation in longitudinal studies: What happens when historical events change the lives of your participants? Economic downturns, natural disasters, and even climate change can impact the lives of those who participate in research studies—and these big-picture changes can make interpreting data complicated (S. A. Miller, 2017).

Researchers who prefer a sprint to a marathon may try a **cross-sectional study**, which compares development in two or more groups of different ages at one point in time. For example, researchers used a cross-sectional approach to study the development of sharing behavior by comparing groups of 2- and 3-year-olds. They found that while the 2-year-olds had a sense that they should share, they very rarely shared equally. On the other hand, the 3-year-olds, with a stronger ability to divide things evenly and more experience with social situations, shared things equally nearly all the time (Tomasello, 2018). This demonstrates the advantage of cross-sectional research: Scientists can compare the behavior of children of different ages without waiting for those children to grow up. However, it is often difficult to prove that age alone causes the difference between the two age group's reactions since the groups are not precisely the same.

Another method of looking at how change happens over time is called the **cross-sequential study**. Cross-sequential studies follow two or more different age groups over time in a combination of cross-sectional and longitudinal designs. For instance, one group of researchers was curious about how the brain changes as you age (Braams et al., 2015). They collected two brain scans, two years apart, from participants aged 8 to 25. This enabled them to examine change across a 17-year period after only a two-year study period. They found that the brain was most sensitive to rewards between 15 and 20 years of age, more than both younger children and adults. The cross-sequential design enabled them not only to compare how change happened in individuals over time (the advantage of the longitudinal study) but also to compare age groups.

Microgenetic research focuses on understanding how development happens by studying change as it happens (Siegler, 2006, 2016). Researchers used this type of study to

Capturing an Ordinary Day A group of researchers in Finland gave elementary schoolchildren digital cameras as part of an ethnographic study of children's independent activities. Thea took this photo while she was swinging on the swings, capturing a piece of her afternoon.

cross-sectional study A study that compares development in two or more groups of different ages at one point in time.

cross-sequential study A study that follows two or more different age groups over time in a combination of cross-sectional and longitudinal designs.

microgenetic research Research that focuses on understanding how development happens by studying change as it happens.

discover what factors helped children learn how to trick someone else, by observing the children closely over 10 days. These scientists found that some developments happened relatively quickly: Although most 3-year-olds didn't know how to deceive someone in a game of hide-and-seek when the study began, they were able figure it out within three days (Ding et al., 2018). The microgenetic approach allowed researchers to study longitudinal change over a very short period of development.

Gathering the Evidence

Once scientists have decided who they are going to study and when they are going to study it, they turn to the question of *how*. Gathering data comes next. Scientists' mission is to collect *empirical information*, or information that is provable or verifiable.

Carsten Goerling/Getty Images

What Are They Talking About? Researchers used qualitative research methods to find out what adolescent boys felt about their friendships.

Quantitative research uses numbers to measure the topics being studied and to analyze the outcome. Scientists might interview children, observe families, or conduct experiments—but they use numbers to record and analyze their data. **Qualitative research** involves in-depth analysis, observation, and description. Scientists may observe families, conduct focus groups, or spend years living with people to better understand them. Some of the most famous theorists in developmental science, like Piaget and Erikson, conducted qualitative research involving close observation and interviews with children and adults (Erikson, 1969; Piaget, 1952).

Qualitative research is often used to explore questions about *why* and *how* people do what they do or to understand the cultural meaning that we have for our behavior. In many types of developmental science, qualitative and quantitative methods are combined in what is called *mixed-methods research* (Rojas et al., 2020; Weisner, 2020).

Observation Research often involves **observation**. Observational research occurs when scientists closely watch and record what people are doing—either in real life or in the laboratory. Scientists can record what they see on video or watch what happens live and take written notes. They can do their work behind one-way mirrors when they are not seen at all, or go undercover in the classroom. The key to observation is that it involves finding ways to record, count, or quantify behaviors. This can be done in the form of *naturalistic observation*, when researchers record behaviors in everyday life, or it can be more experimental, as when participants interact with research stimuli in a laboratory setting. Observational research can also allow researchers to get at the cultural meanings behind behaviors—by capturing the context that surrounds them (Barata & Yoshikawa, 2014).

For instance, one group of researchers in California used observation to watch what happened at parent–teacher conferences where children translated for their families. They were curious about how accurate children's translations were: Would they skip the bad parts? It took observation to find out that, in most cases, children skipped the *good* parts. Children tended not to tell their parents the nice things their teachers said about them—focusing on criticisms rather than the compliments (Orellana & Phoenix, 2017).

However, observation has its disadvantages: In many cases, the mere act of being watched can change how people behave—people tend to be on their best behavior, at least in the beginning, when they know they are being observed. Researchers may be biased in what they record or remember. Observation also takes time and lots of effort, including training observers to be reliable. Finally, there are certain things you just can't see as an observer—like a person's past or what they believe.

Surveys and Interviews In developmental research, surveys and interviews can be a fairly quick and efficient way to get information. Surveys can be powerful tools for

quantitative research Research that uses numbers to measure the topics being studied and to analyze the outcome of a study.

qualitative research Research that involves in-depth analysis, observation, and investigation.

observation When scientists closely watch and record what people are doing—either in real life or in the laboratory.

research because they often rapidly build a large data set, providing a rich source for data analysis and hypothesis testing. In today's inter-connected, mobile age, developmental scientists can ask research participants who are old enough to answer survey questions at any time of day or night on their phones (van Berkel et al., 2019). This may enable caregivers or their children to be more honest about what they are doing—and more accurately report how they are feeling or who they are with (Myin-Germeys et al., 2018).

In the longitudinal study that Mervlyn is a part of, a group of psychologists, pediatricians, and public health professionals recruited 698 children born in 1955 on the Hawai'ian island of Kauai. The study began when the parents were pregnant and was designed to track the effects of stress on development before and after birth. Mervlyn remembers first being interviewed for the study at age 18. By then, her parents had been interviewed at least five times and her medical, school, and social service records had all been collected and analyzed. A member of the research team had even talked to her teachers (Werner, 1993).

As was common at the time, the study initially incorporated a deficit perspective, focusing on links between family income and vulnerability. As it progressed, the researchers noted the resilience of most children (Werner & Smith, 1992). Their findings, widely covered in the popular media, helped shift the focus of developmental science from problems to possibility (Johnson & Wiechelt, 2004). Today the study continues, run by a new generation of researchers, many born in Hawai'i, who feel responsible for incorporating the participants' sense of their own adaptations and Indigenous Hawai'ian world views (McCubbin & Moniz, 2015).

Despite the many strengths of surveys and interviews as data collection tools, they also can come with some drawbacks. One of these is that babies are not very good at filling out forms. For young children, researchers need to rely on the reports of family members. Also, it is hard to tell whether someone is being completely truthful. As a result, researchers often supplement survey and interview data with other forms of observation.

How Do You Keep Track of How Many Words a Baby Hears? Brian and Lisa signed up to be one of the early testers of a tiny recording device that records everything. They tucked the recorder into their son Matthew's pocket and learned that he was often hearing more than 20,000 words each day.

Testing Some types of variables are measured through **assessment**—the use of a standardized tool or test. Assessments allow researchers to compare people's development—whether it is measuring how tall they are, how large their vocabulary is, or how well they get along with others.

Developmental scientists use a variety of assessments. Sometimes they use standardized tests. At other times, they develop their own tests that are designed to represent challenges people might face in real life. For instance, researchers developed the Snack Delay Task to measure how long children can wait before eating a piece of candy. Being able to wait a long time shows that preschoolers have developed self-control and are not just impulsively grabbing a Twix bar in order to gratify their impulses (Ravindran et al., 2019). Another group of researchers created fake websites to measure what makes adults susceptible to online scams (Gavett et al., 2017).

Testing allows scientists to compare their data with that of other researchers. If two researchers, for instance, are using the same assessment for evaluating self-control, they can compare their research findings more directly.

Biological Assessment Developmental assessment can also be used to measure what is going on in the body. When they were studying the 698 young people in the Kauai study Mervlyn was part of, researchers kept careful track of babies' birth

assessment The use of a standardized tool or test.

DTI	fMRI	EEG	CT

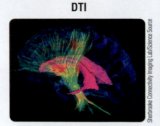 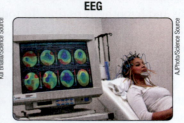 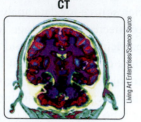

DTI, or diffusion tensor imaging, uses an MRI scanner to create a 3-D image of the white matter connections by looking at the water molecules in the brain. These scans show how the brain is interconnected.

fMRI, or functional magnetic resonance imaging, is a form of MRI that uses magnetic and radio waves to measure the amount of oxygen used by the brain in a series of images over a period of time. Because participants must stay very still, fMRI scans are difficult to use with small children. fMRI tells researchers which regions of the brain are activated during a particular activity.

EEG, or electroencephalogram, records the electrical activity in the brain from electrodes on the scalp. Researchers use a special hat that contains sensors that record electrical signals. It doesn't take very long and you can move around while it is being performed. EEG is often used to study sleep.

CT stands for computerized tomography. CT scans use X-rays to show the density of brain structures. These scans can show the size of different brain structures, but because they expose participants to radiation they are rarely used in research.

FIGURE 2.8 **Biological Assessment** New technologies have allowed scientists to look at bodies, genes, and brains in a way that they were unable to in the past. This has led to increased understanding of how connected our bodies and brains are as we grow.

weights, as well as conducted family visits and interviews and lengthy psychological tests and evaluations (Smith & Werner, 2001).

Biological assessment has a long history in developmental science. Since ancient times, researchers have measured how tall babies are in an attempt to assess their health (Weaver, 2010). Nowadays, researchers can quickly assess a person's stress level by measuring hormones from a sample of their saliva. They can send a DNA sample off to a lab to see whether it shows signs of premature aging. Or they can measure the electrical impulses in your brain while you are playing a game in an MRI scanner (see **Figure 2.8**).

Biological assessment comes with its own challenges. It is often expensive—which means that researchers are often limited to doing these assessments on a small group, who may not represent a broader range of development (Cantlon, 2020; Dahl, 2017). The nature of children, in particular, can make biological assessment difficult. For instance, most brain scans must be done on an absolutely still head. Typically, babies can be scanned while sleeping, and older children are better at controlling their bodies, but getting an accurate picture of a 4-year-old's brain is a challenge, unless they are watching a movie (Greene et al., 2018).

Is It Accurate?

After researchers have conducted observations, interviews, or testing, they need to make sure that their data are accurate. Critical thinking is an essential part of the scientific process, since every step requires reflection and interpretation against existing scientific knowledge. This often comes down to three key criteria: Is it valid, reliable, and replicable?

- *Validity* means that a measure or an assessment actually measures what it claims to measure. For instance, if a researcher investigating health habits in elementary school children asks 8-year-olds to provide a list of everything they snacked on in the past week, their reports are unlikely to be very accurate. The second-grader will probably forget what they ate (Laursen et al., 2012). The survey is not likely to be valid.

- *Reliability* means that a particular assessment stays consistent with multiple measurements. A ruler used correctly will always give the same measurement of the width of your textbook, so it is a reliable measure. In developmental science, reliable measurements often depend on the skills and training of the researchers. Some measures, like the assessments of parent–child attachment, require days of training to make sure that all observers are rating the programs in a similar way (Ainsworth et al., 2015).

- *Replicability* means that the results of your study can be confirmed or clarified by repeating it with another group of participants. Replication can reveal complexity and even contradict a study's findings. For instance, researchers in Europe and the United States were once sure that it was universally true that babies became afraid of strangers at about 8 months (Keller, 2018). That was, until other scientists tried to replicate their findings. It turns out that babies who are accustomed to interacting with new people and who are encouraged not to be fussy do not display this "universal" behavior at all (Otto et al., 2014). In this case, the *failure to replicate* explained something important: The way children express emotions is affected by their experiences. Not even fear is universal. Replication is particularly difficult in developmental science—particularly when families are affected by cultural and historical change (Greenfield, 2018).

The Importance of Inclusive Research In developmental science today, researchers make efforts to be inclusive. But too many studies are still focused on the development of relatively affluent people from White European backgrounds and are conducted by researchers from similar backgrounds (Barbot et al., 2020; Sternberg, 2017; Syed et al., 2018). This challenge is not unique to developmental science: In some medical studies, more than 98 percent of research participants are White (Hamel et al., 2016). This focus on wealthy White people is sometimes referred to (in an attempt at humor) as an overemphasis on *Western, Educated, Industrialized, Rich, and Democratic (WEIRD)* cultures (Schulz et al., 2018). Only about 12 percent of people worldwide are *WEIRD*, so focusing only on them will not give a universal or accurate picture of how most of the world develops.

For instance, about 30 percent of children in the world live in rural farming communities (Keller, 2020). Looking at the majority of the world's population, who are often low-income, sometimes rural, and often from Asia, Africa, or South America, helps scientists understand the wide diversity in human development and how culture shapes us. **Cross-cultural research** focuses specifically on comparing the development of people from diverse cultural communities (Broesch et al., 2020).

Protecting People and Science

The goal of developmental science is to improve the lives of people across the lifespan. Protecting people also happens when developmental scientists are doing their everyday jobs—when scientists conduct research, they need to make sure that they are safeguarding participants' interests. Scientists are bound by **ethical standards**, or moral guidelines, that provide principles for how to protect the public's interests and how to make sure their scientific work is honest.

Keeping Research Safe Developmental scientists are responsible for keeping research participants safe and making sure that their rights are respected when they participate in research (Fisher et al., 2015; Miller, Goyal, et al., 2015; Powell et al., 2012). Although developmental scientists work around the globe, most are bound by similar ethical principles, based on guidelines from professional organizations including the American Psychological Association, the Society for Research in Child Development,

Share It!

Diversity in science helps drive change and innovation. Ideas once considered out of the mainstream often help push science forward.

(Dietze et al., 2019)

Share It!

Communities include many cultures and subcultures. Cultures are complex and do not always align with national borders.

(Oyserman, 2017)

cross-cultural research Research that compares people from two or more different cultural communities.

ethical standards Moral guidelines for protecting the interests of research participants and making sure scientific work is as honest as it can be.

and even the United Nations (APA, 2018; Berman et al., 2016; Graham, Powell, et al., 2013; SRCD Governing Council, 2021).

One frequently used approach to keeping research consistent with safety guidelines is to bring in more voices to help researchers decide the right thing to do. Around the globe, most researchers have the benefit of an **Institutional Review Board (IRB)**, a committee that is designed to review scientific research and help make sure it is adequately protecting participants. The IRB follows several basic principles.

1. *Participants should not be harmed.* This may seem obvious, but it is often more complex. How do you define harm? Is it unfair to scare a child if you are doing a research experiment to understand how children develop fear? Is it inappropriate to ask a teenager to give a public presentation in front of strangers just to measure their level of stress? Most scientists would agree that a little bit of distress may be an acceptable part of research, particularly because being scared or having to talk in front of a group is typical of everyday life. Researchers must identify both risks and benefits to justify their plans, which is not always easy. For instance, researchers who were interviewing young people in Tanzania and Zimbabwe who had recently lost a parent to HIV/AIDS found that the participants frequently cried. Was asking about their experiences "cruel"? Or was the distress worth the insight that would be gained from understanding their shared experiences (Robson & Evans, 2013)? There are no easy answers. In this study, researchers asked the participants what they thought. They said that they wanted to share their stories, despite the tears.

2. *Participants need to be informed.* Scientists must get permission from participants before research begins. Formally this is known as *informed consent*. Young children are considered too young to understand what it means to participate in a research study, so their parents are responsible for giving permission. Adolescents, depending on their age and on local regulations, may be legally able to consent to participate in a research study on their own. Regardless of age, all participants need to be able to opt out of a research study. Getting informed consent may be difficult when researchers are studying some groups, such as adolescents and people with cognitive impairment (Biros, 2018).

3. *Participants should not be pressured to participate.* Children and their families often receive stickers, T-shirts, rides to the laboratory, or even snacks as part of research projects, but scientists should not entice people to participate in research for the money. Some populations need extra protection from coercion. For instance, college students are often invited to participate in research conducted on campus, but they should not be required to participate in exchange for a grade.

4. *Participants' personal information needs to stay private.* When researchers are conducting studies, they may have access to test scores, dating profiles, genetic information, and even pictures of a person's brain. All this information must stay confidential. But what if researchers come across information that may point to a problem? For instance, in nearly one out of every eight brain scans, scientists find an unusual brain structure—which could be entirely typical or a sign of disease—and in these cases, scientists are required to inform the participant or their family (Y. Li et al., 2021). Similarly, many researchers are also legally *mandated reporters*, who must report suspected abuse to local protection agencies.

Share It!

Understanding scientific uncertainty and consensus can build trust. Researchers are eager to understand science skepticism because people around the world have difficulty trusting the research on climate change, vaccines, and evolution.

(Rutjens et al., 2021)

Institutional Review Board (IRB) A committee that is designed to review scientific research and ensure that it is safe and adequately protects participants.

Protecting the Integrity of Science Researchers are not just required to keep people safe—they are also responsible for making sure that their science is trustworthy. More than 20 years ago, one medical researcher damaged the reputation of science and put millions of lives at risk. In 1998, Andrew Wakefield, an English surgeon, published a research paper that claimed the measles vaccine caused autism spectrum disorder (Editors of *The Lancet*, 2010; Wakefield et al., 1998; Ziv & Hotam, 2015). Wakefield became a world-traveling anti-vaccine advocate, triggering a decline in vaccination rates around the world that has accelerated since the COVID-19 pandemic (Callaghan et al., 2021). The problem: His research was fraudulent. He ultimately admitted that he had used false data. Wakefield lost his medical license; his published paper was removed, or retracted, from the journal where it was printed; and he was sued (Deer, 2020). Why? He had violated multiple standards of research ethics.

Researchers are required to follow some basic ethical guidelines:

1. *Data cannot be falsified.* This is exactly what Wakefield did in his study: He claimed that he interviewed and reviewed medical records for 12 children who developed autism spectrum disorder after receiving the measles vaccine. But this was not true. Only one child developed the disorder after receiving the measles vaccines. Eight had other developmental conditions before receiving the vaccine, and three were healthy (Deer, 2011). Furthermore, simply developing a disorder soon after a vaccination does not suggest that the vaccination was the cause. An abundance of experimental research using experimental and control groups has shown there is no link between vaccines and autism (Hviid et al., 2019).

2. *Bias needs to be avoided.* Scientists, like other people, have hunches and ideas they hope are true. Wakefield recruited children to participate in his study by working with an anti-vaccine campaign, rather than finding a representative sample (Deer, 2020).

3. *Research must be shared for replication and verification.* Researchers are encouraged to share their research data with other scientists and reviewers to help verify their claims. Wakefield was reluctant to share his sources with reviewers. He did not even share his data with the people who coauthored his paper.

4. *Possible conflicts should be reported.* Researchers are required to identify how they are funded and their possible conflicts of interest. For instance, a researcher doing experiments about the effects of video games on children would need to disclose if they were receiving payments from the makers of *World of Warcraft*. Wakefield did not disclose that his research was funded by a law firm that was suing the manufacturers of the measles vaccine. He also failed to mention that he had patented his own vaccine (Deer, 2011).

Ethical breaches as extreme as Andrew Wakefield's are extremely rare. Most scientists share the goal of learning the truth. Layers of review, critical thinking, and data sharing make it nearly impossible for a wholesale fabrication like Wakefield's to occur. More common is the misinterpretation of research findings, such as overstating the strength of the results. Critical thinking is necessary for us as consumers of research as well—the next time you see a shocking headline on your social media feed, explore more deeply.

CAN YOU BELIEVE IT?
How Do You Spot Fake Science?

How do you spot fake science? It is not always easy. Most people in the United States trust science, but we are still vulnerable to falling for something that is overhyped, particularly if it is in a field that is new to us (Funk et al., 2019). Here are three steps to help you pick out what's real from a story that might be trying to scare you, sell you something, or play to your existing biases.

1. *Learn more.* In developmental science, or any other complex field, it is hard to pick out the overhyped pseudoscience from the real breakthroughs if you are not sure what the existing science is. For instance, by the time you finish this book you will know which of these claims refers to a real scientific discovery: (1) Newborns can count; (2) online media has made teenagers more selfish; or (3) young children can understand language even before they speak their first word. Knowing the basics will help you pick out the real science from the clickbait.

   As you will learn, scientists have indeed found that infants are born with an innate sense of number: They know the difference between three and one of something. To say they can count is an exaggeration, because they cannot talk or hold up their fingers to indicate number, but this headline is based on a plausible scientific discovery (see Chapter 4; Butterworth et al., 2018). Did you guess that adolescents have become more selfish since the advent of Snapchat filters? Scientists have actually found the opposite: All that online socializing happens because teenagers are intensely interested in other people (James et al., 2017). Did you guess that very young children can understand the meaning of many words before they can even talk? (Holzen & Nazzi, 2020). If you guessed incorrectly, research may have played into one of your biases, which brings us to tip #2.

2. *Be aware of your own biases.* Many times, fake science news or pseudoscience is appealing because it supports what we think we already know, what we feel in our "gut," or what we think "intuitively" (Kenrick et al., 2018; Tangherlini et al., 2020). For instance, the idea that teenagers are self-centered and difficult is a common cultural bias. So, when you read that adolescents are selfish, you are more likely to think it is true. All of us are more likely to believe information that confirms what we already think, whether or not it is true.

3. *Be comfortable with complexity.* One sign of fake science is when someone tells you that they have found the answer to everything. When social scientists compare conspiracy theories to actual science, they find that conspiracies are simpler than the real thing, because reality is often uncomfortably complex (Tangherlini et al., 2020). Pseudoscience often gives people a chance to become an expert immediately, without getting an advanced degree or even reading a book. As you have probably already realized, developmental science experts are comfortable with detail and inconsistencies. A high level of detail helps them make sure they are making the right choices when they turn science into practice and develop interventions to improve lives. 🧑‍🔬

APPLY IT! **2.3** How would you apply the scientific method to a study of Mervlyn's life? You need to make an observation, form a hypothesis, collect some data (maybe by watching her video again), analyze what you've learned, and share it with others. You might notice that Mervlyn credits her values, her husband, and her faith for her resilience. What has contributed to your ability to bounce back in your life?

2.4 Evaluating research is a key element of scientific thinking. How would you evaluate the validity, reliability, and replicability of your observations about Mervlyn? Would you want to do another case study? Sharing your findings is an important way of checking your work. Can you share your own hypotheses and observations about your own resilience and see how the feedback you receive helps you refine your own ideas?

Wrapping It Up ⊙⊙

LO 2.1 Identify why developmental scientists use theory to guide their work. (p. 30)

In developmental science, theories provide a link between ideas and scientific findings to help explain how children change or stay the same as they develop based on what can be observed or tested. Theories generate *hypotheses* and give researchers a perspective with which to interpret evidence. Contrasting theories help scientists think critically about what they observe or believe.

LO 2.2 Explain how the biological perspective links the brain and body to developmental change. (p. 30)

Scholars who adopt the biological perspective include those who apply evolutionary theory to development. Evolutionary theorists suggest that human life, and even some human behaviors, have developed over time to help us adapt and survive. Ethology theory suggests that some human behaviors are inborn, and many ethologists study animals to look for insight into human behaviors. Epigenetic theory argues that our environment shapes how our genes are expressed, and it describes how some changes are easier to make than others.

LO 2.3 Explain how the psychodynamic perspective links early experiences to personality development. (p. 30)

Psychodynamic theory suggests that human beings have inborn needs for connection and safety and that early experiences help shape our personality development. Sigmund Freud was an early psychodynamic thinker who theorized that we advance through five psychosexual stages as we master our unconscious physical urges. Erik Erikson was a psychodynamic thinker who developed an eight-stage theory of psychosocial development. He emphasized that children need a sense of safety and acceptance of their limitations and that developing a sense of who we are is a crucial part of adolescence. Attachment theory suggests that close emotional bonds between infants and their caregivers shape our relationships and way of approaching the world throughout the lifespan.

LO 2.4 Explain how the behaviorist perspective focuses on how people learn. (p. 30)

Behaviorist theorists focus on what scientists can measure, like behavior, rather than what people think or feel, which is difficult to measure. Classical conditioning is a process of human and animal learning that links a stimulus and a response. John Watson demonstrated classical conditioning in children by conditioning Little Albert to fear white fuzzy objects. Operant conditioning is a theory of learning that explains a behavior will be more likely to happen if it is rewarded—and less likely to occur if it is ignored or punished. Social learning theory suggests that learning involves our thinking and feeling and occurs through observing and imitating others.

LO 2.5 Describe how the cognitive perspective focuses on how thinking changes as we mature. (p. 30)

Piaget's theory of cognitive development suggests that thinking matures as children actively explore the world until they reach intellectual maturity in adolescence. Piaget argued that there are four major stages of cognitive development children go through as they use their bodies and their developing thinking skills to explore the world. Information-processing theorists look at the individual components of thinking like memory, processing speed, and executive function and how they change.

LO 2.6 Explain how the cultural perspective focuses on how culture shapes development. (p. 30)

Cultural theorists explain that culture is integrated into all of development from our relationships and thinking to our biology. Sociocultural theory is inspired by the work of Lev Vygotsky, who argued that how we think and develop is shaped by our social relationships and cultural practices. Theories of social justice look at the impact of structural inequality and discrimination on development and seek to identify strengths and systemic changes that could help all people thrive.

LO 2.7 Define the steps and guiding principles of the scientific method. (p. 47)

The scientific method is a process of testing what you know to make sure it is true. This process has five steps: observation, hypothesis, data collection, analysis, and sharing. Developmental scientists have many ways of designing their research projects, including using an experiment, a correlational study, or descriptive research. Change over time can be measured using a longitudinal, cross-sectional, cross-sequential, or microgenetic research design. Data can be gathered using quantitative or qualitative research methods, which could include observation, biological assessment, surveys, or formal tests. Scientists test accuracy by making sure their data are valid, reliable, and replicable.

LO 2.8 Describe the ethical standards governing science and practice. (p. 47)

Ethical standards are designed to protect children and adolescents who are participating in research and to make sure scientific research is trustworthy. Scientists are required to be honest, avoid bias, declare their possible conflicts, and share their research.

KEY TERMS

theory (p. 30)
biological perspective
  (p. 31)
evolution (p. 31)
ethology (p. 32)
epigenetics (p. 32)
psychodynamic perspective
  (p. 34)
psychosexual stages (p. 34)
attachment theory (p. 36)
behaviorism (p. 36)
classical conditioning (p. 37)
operant conditioning (p. 37)

reinforcement (p. 38)
punishment (p. 38)
social learning theory (p. 39)
cognitive development theory
  (p. 40)
schema (p. 41)
assimilation (p. 41)
accommodation (p. 41)
Piaget's stage theory of
  development (p. 41)
stage (p. 41)
information processing
  (p. 42)

cultural perspective (p. 43)
sociocultural theory (p. 43)
scientific method (p. 47)
hypothesis (p. 47)
experiment (p. 49)
variables (p. 49)
independent variable (p. 49)
dependent variable (p. 49)
correlational study (p. 51)
case study (p. 52)
ethnography (p. 52)
longitudinal research (p. 52)

cross-sectional study (p. 53)
cross-sequential study (p. 53)
microgenetic research (p. 53)
quantitative research (p. 54)
qualitative research (p. 54)
observation (p. 54)
assessment (p. 55)
cross-cultural research
  (p. 57)
ethical standards (p. 57)
Institutional Review Board
  (IRB) (p. 58)

CHECK YOUR LEARNING

1. The biological perspective on development focuses on the impact of genetics and physical growth on development. Which of the following theoretical approaches is NOT an example of the biological perspective?

   a) Epigenetic theory   c) Ethological theory
   b) Behaviorist theory   d) Evolutionary theory

2. Three-year-old Sophia holds a baby doll up to her chest after watching her mother nurse her baby sister. Which theory would describe this behavior in terms of *modeling* and *imitation*?

   a) Erikson's psychosocial theory
   b) Piaget's constructivist theory
   c) Information-processing theory
   d) Social learning theory

3. Theories of social justice focus on:

   a) operant and classical conditioning.
   b) the impacts of discrimination on development.
   c) considering thinking in terms of the actions of a computer.
   d) assimilation and accommodation.

4. Which of these theories describes development in terms of discrete stages?

   a) Sociocultural theory
   b) Piaget's constructivist theory
   c) Erikson's psychosocial theory
   d) Freud's psychosexual theory

5. Celina is a developmental scientist interested in the experiences of children who participate in migrant work, picking crops in the United States. She spent three weeks among the workers, picking fruit with them and talking about their lives. She took extensive notes on the children's daily routines, their interactions, and the culture of the farmworker community. This type of research is known as:

   a) ethnographic research.   c) experimental research.
   b) biological assessment.   d) cross-sectional research.

6. Of these steps in the scientific method, which one typically would come FIRST?

   a) Collect data.
   b) Form a hypothesis.
   c) Analyze data.
   d) Disseminate results.

7. Which of these is an example of a *cross-sectional* study?

   a) A study that compares sleep patterns of four groups: 2-year-olds, 8-year-olds, 12-year-olds, and 18-year-olds
   b) A study that measures the correlation between sleep and anxiety
   c) A study that tracks sleep patterns of 200 participants over a 10-year period, from age 10 to age 18
   d) A study testing the effects of soothing music on the sleep patterns of babies

8. To test the effects of exercise on memory, Dr. Dolan selected 50 adolescents to participate in a three-week exercise class, and another 50 to join a cooking class. After the classes, she gave memory tests to all 100 adolescents and compared the scores of the exercise group to the scores of the cooking group. This is an example of a(n):

   a) case study.
   b) correlational study.
   c) experimental study.
   d) cross-cultural study.

9. Describe the key differences and similarities between Piaget's theory of cognitive development and Erikson's psychosocial theory.

10. Imagine you are designing a longitudinal study of children's sleep patterns and their mental health. What key ethical principles will you need to follow as you recruit participants and conduct your study?

Genetics, Prenatal Development, and Birth

© Macmillan, Photo by Sidford House

Understanding the Genome

3.1 Define key components of human genetics.

3.2 Explain basic principles of genetic transmission of traits.

3.3 Explain how the environment can affect gene expression through the epigenome.

Prenatal Development

3.4 Describe the key stages of prenatal development.

3.5 Describe the principles of prenatal risk and resilience.

Birth and the Newborn

3.6 Explain the process of vaginal childbirth and its common risks and protective factors.

3.7 Describe how newborns' senses and capabilities help them thrive.

Alizah always wanted to have a baby. She believed that when the time was right, it would happen. She was sure 2020 was going to be "the year": She was tending to her health, seeing a doctor, and taking medicine for her thyroid condition; she had a great job as a teacher in Los Angeles; and she was an active member of a creative community, mentoring students in an afterschool program on yoga, music, and social justice. So, she hoped, wished, and asked her friends to pray for her.

Alizah's partner, Spencer, was equally sure that the time was right to have a child and that Alizah was "the one." With all the challenges in the world, Spencer felt like his and Alizah's baby could make the world a brighter place. Alizah and Spencer were crazy about each other.

Not everything in Alizah and Spencer's lives was as perfect as their relationship and the lovely nursery they created for their baby. 2020 was indeed Alizah and Spencer's year to have a baby, but it was also tumultuous — the year that the COVID-19 pandemic began. Alizah was pregnant in the middle of a crisis, complicating many of her plans for the pregnancy and birth. Spencer couldn't come to many of her medical appointments. Alizah's mother was worried she could not get on a plane to help. But there were unexpected benefits: Alizah and Spencer got to spend more time together, and Alizah no longer had to commute to her job.

Most importantly, Alizah and Spencer avoided COVID-19, and so did their growing fetus. They picked a name: Courage, after the strength they hoped he would have to thrive in a difficult world. They worried about the effects of isolation during the pandemic, about getting medical care and staying safe while the baby

Scientific American Profile

▶ Meet Courage

Learning Objectives

3.1 Define key components of human genetics.

3.2 Explain basic principles of genetic transmission of traits.

3.3 Explain how the environment can affect gene expression through the epigenome.

genome The unique set of instructions that includes everything a cell might need for creating your body parts and maintaining them over the lifespan.

chromosomes The 23 pairs of long molecules of DNA containing genetic information and found in the nucleus of human cells.

deoxyribonucleic acid (DNA) A spiral-, or helix-, shaped structure made up of paired chemicals that carries the genetic code.

mitosis A type of cell division that creates two, new identical cells.

genes Sections of DNA that create particular proteins.

alleles Genes that have different forms.

was born. Alizah even worried about the effect of all that worry on her growing fetus. But both parents and baby were healthy, and Alizah was eager to show her newborn to her students on Zoom after he was born.

When Alizah's pregnancy test told her that Courage was on the way, he was just a 32-celled creature, scarcely bigger than the period at the end of this sentence. Those tiny cells contained the genetic information that would guide Courage's development. His genes will continue to shape how he grows and develops, but the environment also plays a major role. For most of us, genes are not destiny. Your genome contributes to who you are, but who you are also changes your genome.

The months fetuses spend inside the uterus also play an important role in creating who they become. Some babies are born smaller than others. Some fetuses, like Courage, have advantages that others do not. But no matter how newborns arrive, they are already remarkably capable. Like Courage, they are born ready to learn about the world and form relationships that will guide them for a lifetime.

Understanding the Genome

You often hear about genetics, perhaps as an explanation for the traits you inherited. People might tell you that you have your grandfather's smile. Or a news story may describe a genetic test that can predict the risk for breast cancer. When scientists use the term *genetics*, they mean that some of your observable characteristics are inherited and have been triggered by a chemical sequence inside your cells.

If you could take a microscope and look inside yourself, you would see that each bit of you is made up of cells. What they do is directed by the **genome**, the unique set of instructions that includes everything a cell might need for creating all of your body parts, maintaining them over the lifespan, and even telling your body, one day, how to die.

These instructions are packed in 46 **chromosomes** located inside the nucleus of each cell. Most of the time, they look like a tangled bunch of yarn, as you will see in **Infographic 3.1** (Collombet et al., 2020). But inside this crumpled mass is a precise organizational structure. Each tiny chromosome is lined up into one of 23 pairs. Inside each chromosome is a spiral, or *helix*, that can stretch out to more than two inches long and is made up of four chemicals arranged like a ladder. These chemicals are part of a molecule called **deoxyribonucleic acid**, better known as **DNA**.

The ladder-like structure of DNA allows the genetic information in each cell to be duplicated every time a new cell is created. New cells are created as people grow from a single-celled *zygote* into a 30-trillion-celled adult. In addition, the body continuously creates new cells throughout the lifespan to replace those that have worn out. DNA replicates itself each time through a mechanism known as **mitosis**. In this process, the ladder of DNA rips down the middle. Each half of the ladder rebuilds to create two new identical strands of DNA, copying genetic information into each new cell.

Genes are sections of DNA that create particular proteins. Human beings have about 22,000 genes, and each one tells the cell how to create a specific protein (Abascal et al., 2018). Not everyone has exactly the same version of each gene. Genes have different forms that are known as **alleles**.

The particular alleles you inherit can affect your individual characteristics, as well as your risks for disease. For instance, millions of people have *sickle-cell disease*, the most common single-gene disorder in the world (Kato et al., 2018). Sickle-cell disease can keep the body from getting enough oxygen—leading to painful crises and death if people cannot receive the support, possibly including gene-editing treatment that can help (Esrick et al., 2021).

Every bit of the human body grows, matures, and changes because of directions from their genome. Inside every cell are genetic instructions that tell the cell when to duplicate itself, what proteins to create, and even when to die. Some aspects of our genome are set at conception, but the way our genes are expressed over our lifespan is determined, in part, by the environment. Changes to our gene expression are made through *epigenetic marks*, chemical messengers that help turn specific genes on and off. Your own genome is known as your *genotype*, and it contributes to your unique *phenotype*.

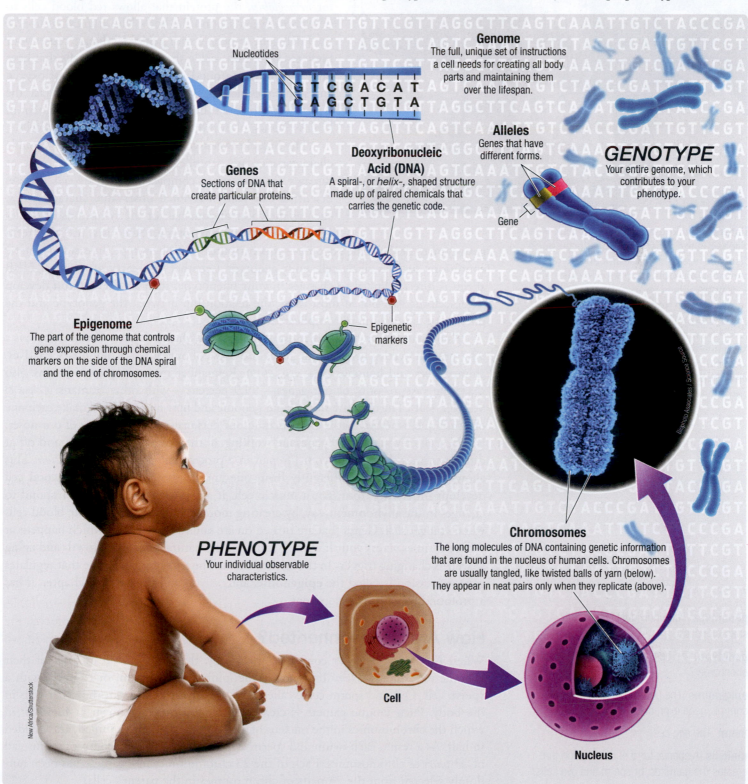

Nucleotides

Genome
The full, unique set of instructions a cell needs for creating all body parts and maintaining them over the lifespan.

GTCGACAT
CAGCTGTA

Genes
Sections of DNA that create particular proteins.

Deoxyribonucleic Acid (DNA)
A spiral-, or *helix*-, shaped structure made up of paired chemicals that carries the genetic code.

Alleles
Genes that have different forms.

Gene

GENOTYPE
Your entire genome, which contributes to your phenotype.

Epigenome
The part of the genome that controls gene expression through chemical markers on the side of the DNA spiral and the end of chromosomes.

Epigenetic markers

PHENOTYPE
Your individual observable characteristics.

Chromosomes
The long molecules of DNA containing genetic information that are found in the nucleus of human cells. Chromosomes are usually tangled, like twisted balls of yarn (below). They appear in neat pairs only when they replicate (above).

Cell

Nucleus

New Africa/Shutterstock

Biophoto Associates / Science Source

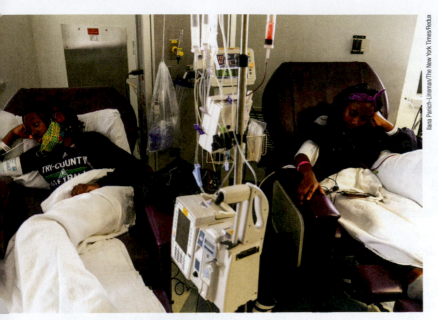

Ilana Panich-Linsman/The New York Times/Redux

Sisters in Sickness and Health Sickle cell disease is the most common single gene disorder in the world. Kami and Kyra's parents were both carriers of sickle cell, and both girls have experienced serious complications from the disease. Here, the teenagers receive blood transfusions in the hospital near their home in San Antonio, Texas. This treatment will help with the pain associated with the disease while they wait for gene therapy, a more permanent solution.

phenotype Your individual observable characteristics.

genotype The genome that contributes your phenotype.

epigenome The part of the genome that controls gene expression.

ovum The egg cell.

meiosis A special form of cell division that creates the gametes, or sperm and ova cells.

sperm The reproductive cell from a male.

zygote A new human cell typically with 46 chromosomes in 23 pairs.

As a result, globally, sickle-cell disease remains a leading cause of death for children (Oron et al., 2020).

Unlike most diseases, sickle-cell disease is genetic and is caused by a mutation in one gene, called HBB (*H*emoglobin su*B*unit *B*eta). HBB contains the instructions for *hemoglobin*, the protein that allows red blood cells to transport oxygen around the body. The atypical version of the HBB gene in people with sickle-cell disease causes your body to create thin, sickle-shaped red blood cells that have difficulty moving around your body, starving it of oxygen and sometimes clogging your blood vessels. In contrast, the typical allele for the HBB gene triggers the development of healthy hemoglobin protein and rounded red blood cells.

The links between your genome and your observable characteristics are complicated, particularly for traits or diseases that are more complex than sickle-cell disease. Scientists call your individual observable characteristics, such as the color of your hair or the symptoms of sickle-cell disease, your **phenotype**. Scientists use the term **genotype** to describe the genome that contributes your phenotype. In cases of genetic conditions such as sickle-cell, your genotype (whether you carry an atypical HBB allele) is directly linked to changes in your phenotype, such as whether you develop sickle-cell disease. But in most cases, the relationship between the genotype and the phenotype is much more complicated.

As human beings, we share most of our genes with nonhuman animals. There is a 98.7 percent overlap between our genes and those of our closest evolutionary relatives, chimpanzees and bonobos (Staes et al., 2019). Remember from Chapter 1 that we also share the vast majority of our genes—99.9 percent—with other humans (Collins & Mansoura, 2001). The tiny variations in our genome and how it is expressed make each one of us unique, whether that is differences in our personalities or the shape of our noses.

Not all of your 22,000 genes are working all the time. Genes turn on and off at different times throughout your lifespan in a process known as *gene regulation*. This allows cells to develop differently from one another, so, for instance, a blood cell develops differently from, say, a muscle cell. It also allows your body to respond to changes in the environment, say, by creating more immune-fighting white blood cells when you get sick. Genes that are turned on are said to be *expressed*, which happens at different times across your lifetime because of the natural course of growth and aging as well as changing triggers in the environment. The part of the genome that regulates gene expression is called the **epigenome**, and, as you will learn in this chapter, it has a profound effect on development.

How Are Genes Inherited?

When Alizah and Spencer conceived their baby, they each passed on part of their genome to Courage. New life involves the joining of an **ovum**, or egg cell, with a **sperm** cell. Ova and sperm cells, called *gametes*, are different from the other cells in the body. Each unique gamete is created through a process known as **meiosis**, in which the chromosomes in the nucleus of a cell are shuffled, recombined, and divided in half. As a result, each ovum and sperm cell has just 23 *single* chromosomes instead of 23 *pairs* of chromosomes. Each of the 23 chromosomes in a gamete has been randomly selected from the 23 pairs of chromosomes in the parent's cells.

When an ovum and sperm meet in the moment of conception, the 23 chromosomes from an ovum match up with 23 chromosomes from a sperm cell. This creates a new human cell with 46 chromosomes in 23 pairs, known as a **zygote**. In each of the zygote's 23 pairs of chromosomes, one chromosome comes from the ovum, and the other comes from the sperm. When you account for the random selection of chromosomes in the creation of gametes with the random selection of chromosomes in conception, the chromosomes in one zygote could be combined in one of more than 8 million possible combinations, each with half of the parent cell's genetic information! Each baby is truly one of 8 million possible siblings two people could create (Bell et al., 2022).

The Genetics of Sex

In human cells, the 23rd pair of chromosomes is unique because the pair does not always match. This pair is known as the **sex chromosomes**, which come in two main types, referred to by their shape as X or Y chromosomes. Most people who identify as men have one Y chromosome and one X chromosome, and most who identify as women have two X chromosomes. When gametes are formed, each one has only one chromosome in the 23rd position. Each ovum contains a single X, and each sperm cell will have either a single X or a single Y. Most genetically female babies inherit an X chromosome from each parent, so that their 23rd pair of chromosomes is XX, and genetically male babies inherit an X from their mother and a Y from their father, making their 23rd chromosome pair XY.

Scientists use the term **sex** to refer to the biology that relates to being female (primarily XX) and male (primarily XY) and the spectrum of biological variation beyond these binary labels. Sex can refer to your genotype and also your phenotype, which includes observable characteristics like reproductive organs and genitals. The broader term, **gender**, is used to describe the social and cultural distinctions that are linked to ideas about being male, female, and other labels, including nonbinary or genderless identities. Gender ideas often change over time. (Did you know that until the 1940s, American boys wore pink and girls wore blue? Or that nonbinary genders are not new? Ancient cultures often celebrated gender variation [Helle, 2018; Paoletti, 2012].) The term **gender identity** refers to your sense of yourself as a man, woman, or as someone not as exclusive or within the lines of these binary labels. **Gender expression** describes how you express your gender in daily life, such as how you wear makeup, style your hair, or what clothing you like.

Scientists think that almost 1 in 100 people are of a sex that is less binary than a simple distinction between XX and XY (Arboleda et al., 2014; Sandberg & Gardner, 2022). These people may use the term *intersex* to describe themselves or say that they have a gender variance or *difference of sex development (DSD)*, the term medical professionals use (Ernst et al., 2020). Many people with DSD feel comfortable in the gender they were assigned at birth, even if it does not match the XX or XY in their genotype, although they may face stigma or ongoing health complications (P. A. Lee et al., 2016). Usually, the best gauge of someone's gender is not in their chromosomes, but in what they feel.

Maria José Martínez-Patiño learned about the complexity of biological sex from experience. As the fastest hurdler in Spain, she expected to compete in the 1988 Olympics. However, a blood test administered to all female athletes at the time revealed that Maria José had an X and a Y chromosome. Maria José was told to quietly withdraw from competition, but she refused. With the support of many scientists, she argued that sex and gender were much more complicated than X and Y, and that she felt like a woman. She wrote later that she could not drop out and "pretend to be a man" (Martínez-Patiño, 2005). She fought for four years to rejoin the national team before she was allowed to return to competition.

Maria José had *androgen insensitivity*, a condition that prevents people with XY chromosomes from developing male genitals. Most people with androgen insensitivity identify as women: They have breasts and vaginas but may not have some interior reproductive organs, like ovaries. But, at that time, the Olympic Committee considered sex to be binary and based on chromosomes alone. In the years since

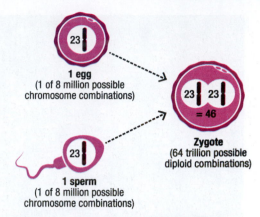

FIGURE 3.1 The Diversity of New Life When new life is formed, the 23 chromosomes from the ovum match up with 23 chromosomes from the sperm cell. This creates a new human cell with 46 chromosomes in 23 pairs, known as a zygote. When you account for the random selection of chromosomes in the creation of gametes with the random selection of chromosomes in conception, the chromosomes in one zygote represent one of more than 8 million possible combinations.

CONNECTIONS

Differences of sex development, such as being intersex, are different from being transgender or nonbinary. As you will learn in Chapter 10, children who identify as transgender or who are gender diverse do not feel comfortable with the gender they were assigned at birth.

sex chromosomes The 23rd pair of chromosomes.

sex The physical and genetic characteristics usually associated with being male, female, or a mixture.

gender The term for the social and cultural distinctions describing binary and less binary distinctions between men and women.

gender identity The term for your sense of yourself as a man, woman, or someone not as exclusively within the lines of these binary labels.

gender expression The term for how you express your gender in daily life, such as how you wear makeup, style your hair, or what clothing you like.

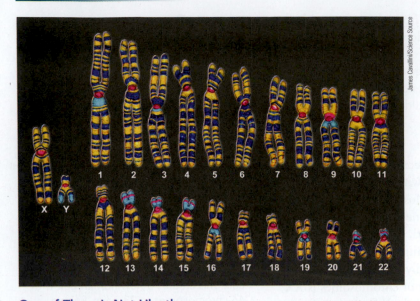

James Cavallini/Science Source

One of These Is Not Like the Others. One of these chromosomes is shown as a pair: an X and a Y. The others are shown unpaired in their duplicated form, ready for cell division. In order to visualize the chromosomes, they were chemically stained, separated, and arranged by size. This is a photograph taken through a microscope that has been enlarged about 4,000 times.

recessive inheritance pattern A type of genetic inheritance for single-gene conditions. In order to develop a recessive condition, you must have two of the disease-carrying alleles.

FIGURE 3.2 Recessive Inheritance Patterns: Transmission of Sickle-Cell Disease If both parents are carriers of the recessive sickle-cell disease allele, each of their children will have a 25 percent chance of inheriting the sickle-cell allele from both parents and getting sickle-cell disease. Each child will have a 50 percent chance of inheriting one diseased allele and being a carrier, like their parents, and a 25 percent chance of inheriting a set of typical alleles.

Maria José was forced to skip her chance at an Olympic medal, other athletes whose bodies do not conform to a narrow understanding of sex and gender have faced similar discrimination.

Maria José is among the people who are helping to change how we understand the science of gender. After her retirement from track, Maria José studied for her Ph.D. in sports science. She now works as a researcher and advises the International Olympic Committee about gender and sports (Ospina-Betancurt et al., 2021).

Single-Gene Inheritance Patterns

Some traits and conditions, like sickle-cell disease, are called *single-gene disorders* because they are linked to a single gene. In these cases, it may be possible to predict and even prevent the transmission of the disease if the gene has been found.

Sickle-cell disease is passed on through a **recessive inheritance pattern**. Remember that when a zygote is formed, it includes half of the chromosomes from the ovum and half from the sperm. The resulting child will have two versions of each gene, called *alleles*. In recessive disorders, a child must inherit the two copies of the disease-carrying allele, one from each of their parents, for the disorder to be expressed. Such conditions are called "recessive" because healthy versions of the gene are *dominant*, or more likely to be expressed, so the disease tends to *recess*, or not appear, when the dominant form of the gene is present.

In the example of sickle-cell disease, healthy hemoglobin genes are dominant, so a child must inherit disease-carrying alleles from *both* parents to have the disease. A genetic *carrier* is someone who has inherited one allele for a disease or trait, and does not express the disorder but can pass it on to their children. If two parents are carriers for sickle-cell disease, each of their children has a 50 percent chance of inheriting *one* disease-carrying allele and will be carriers, with one typical allele and one sickle-cell allele. As you can see in **Figure 3.2**, each child has a 25 percent

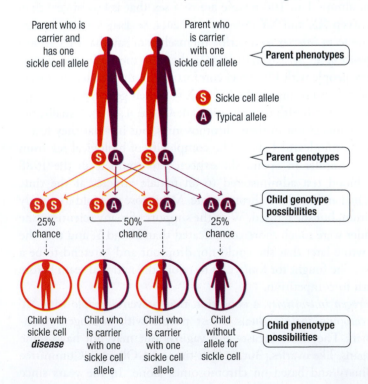

chance of inheriting two typical alleles and a 25 percent chance of inheriting two disease-carrying alleles and developing sickle-cell disorder.

Other disorders that follow a recessive inheritance pattern include *thalassemia*, a blood disorder; *cystic fibrosis*, a lung and digestive disease; and *Tay Sachs disease*, a fatal neurological syndrome. While single-gene disorders are rare, they are more common in groups that are isolated or where intermarriage within tightly knit communities is common. For instance, families from European Jewish, South Asian, and Finnish backgrounds tend to have higher rates of single-gene disorders (Nakatsuka et al., 2017).

Some single-gene disorders only require one copy of the disease-carrying allele. In these cases, even if you inherit one healthy allele and one disease-carrying allele, you will still develop the illness. These diseases are based on **dominant inheritance**, because the disease is expressed even if a single copy of the diseased allele is inherited. These diseases include *Huntington disease*, a fatal neurological illness that strikes in middle life, and *Marfan syndrome*, a chronic and sometimes fatal connective tissue disease. For dominant inheritance pattern diseases, each child born to a parent with the condition has a 50 percent chance of inheriting the affected gene and the disorder, as you can see in **Figure 3.3**.

A special form of single-gene transmission, known as *sex-linked transmission*, occurs when disorders are transmitted on the sex chromosomes. For example, some forms of *hemophilia*, a now-treatable disease that makes it difficult for blood to clot, is caused by one recessive gene located on the X chromosome (Marchesini et al., 2021). As a result, nearly all people with hemophilia are men, or people with only one X chromosome. Most women have two X chromosomes and are much more likely to inherit at least one dominant allele, but when they inherit the allele for hemophilia, most of the time they are protected by the healthy variant on the other chromosome (Ragni, 2021). Having a double copy of the X chromosome serves to protect people from the worst effects of several conditions, as it does with hemophilia: In these cases, the disease-carrying gene may be silenced or inactivated by the healthy one from the other X chromosome (Galupa & Heard, 2018).

The X chromosome can also carry genes for other conditions, although transmission of these disorders tends to be more complex. These conditions include male-pattern baldness and some forms of color-vision deficiency (Hunt & Carvalho, 2016; Yap et al., 2018). Damage to the X chromosome can lead to the development of *Turner syndrome*, which can cause infertility and other conditions in women (Kruszka et al., 2020). It can also trigger *fragile X syndrome*, which is linked to some intellectual disabilities and forms of autism spectrum disorder (Salcedo-Arellano et al., 2020). The tiny Y chromosome carries only a few disorders, most notably a risk for male infertility, but disruptions in the Y chromosomes may be one reason men are predisposed to some conditions, including Parkinson disease and high blood pressure (Lau, 2020; Signore et al., 2020).

Multiple Genes, Many Factors

Most conditions or traits, from Spencer's curls to Alizah's brown eyes, are influenced by multiple genes, which require a trigger or specific influence from the environment in order to be expressed. These traits and diseases are called **polygenic**. They are carried by a number of alleles, in a number of locations on different chromosomes, that need to be inherited and triggered at one particular time to spark the development of particular traits, or conditions.

Marfan Syndrome Maya Brown-Zimmerman (left) has Marfan syndrome, a single-gene disorder that is passed on through a dominant pattern. Marfan syndrome is a multisystem connective tissue disorder that can be painful, sometimes debilitating, and life-threatening. Maya and her husband, Mark, have four children. Her younger son, Julian, has Marfan syndrome like his mother. She says that people criticized her decision to have children. Maya says ". . . having a perfect body is not the most important thing. Even though my body is not perfect, there's a lot that I can add to the world around me. I felt that our kids would be able to do the same, even if they inherited Marfan syndrome" (Brown-Zimmerman, 2012).

dominant inheritance pattern A type of genetic inheritance for single-gene disorders. A person with a dominant condition may have just one of the disease-carrying alleles.

polygenic A type of genetic inheritance that is influenced by multiple genes acting in combination that may require influence from the environment in order to be expressed.

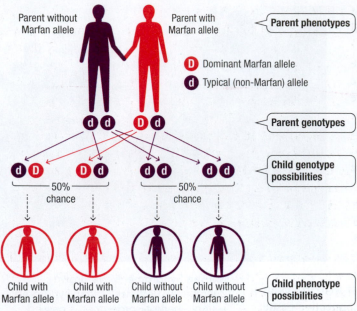

Parent without Marfan allele

Parent with Marfan allele

> Parent phenotypes

D Dominant Marfan allele

d Typical (non-Marfan) allele

d d   D d

> Parent genotypes

d D   D d   d d   d d

> Child genotype possibilities

50% chance   50% chance

Child with Marfan allele   Child with Marfan allele   Child without Marfan allele   Child without Marfan allele

> Child phenotype possibilities

FIGURE 3.3 Dominant Inheritance Patterns: Transmission of Marfan Syndrome If one parent is a carrier of the dominant Marfan syndrome allele, each of their children will have a 50 percent chance of inheriting the gene and developing the disorder.

Share It!

Would you test an embryo to find their polygenetic risk score? Some experts warn that some companies offering to evaluate a fetus's genetic risk may be promising more certainty than scientific consensus supports.

(Turley et al., 2021)

Consider eye color. In the past, many scientists thought it could be easily predicted using the rules of single-gene inheritance, but they turned out to be wrong. There are at least 16 individual genes that control whether you end up with deep brown eyes or icy blue ones (Ludwig et al., 2016). Most of the time, babies end up with brown eyes, perhaps because extra melanin in dark eyes protects you from the dangerous effects of UV light (Jablonski, 2018). The genetic complexity of eye color means that sometimes not even a geneticist can predict what color your baby's eyes will be.

In most cases, developing a disease or a particular trait requires you to inherit multiple genes, and also to be exposed to particular environmental influences. Scientists call these diseases or traits **multifactorial** because there are multiple variables that influence them (Donovan et al., 2021). For example, in order to develop a severe psychological disorder such as schizophrenia, a child who is born with multiple genes that put them at risk for the disease would also need to experience specific environmental events, which might include prenatal exposure to a virus or smoking marijuana in adolescence (Richetto & Meyer, 2021).

Researchers suggest that there are some consistent principles that guide how genes act:

1. *Your genetic map usually gives you a continuum of traits.* Most traits and disease risks are not something you either have or you do not. They exist on a continuum (Katsanis, 2016). Skin color, for instance, is one of a rainbow of possible colors. Your personality traits are also on a spectrum, as is your genetic risk for a neurocognitive disorder, such as Parkinson disease or Alzheimer disease, as you get older (Baldacci et al., 2020).

2. *The environment can change how genes are expressed.* Your epigenome helps regulate gene expression. Environmental factors, from prenatal exposure to toxins to living through childhood trauma, can trigger gene expression (Marini et al., 2020).

3. *Your genes influence your environment.* Your individual relationship with your environment can support or change your gene expression. For instance, so-called "easy" babies are often much more likely to elicit smiles from their families than babies with less flexible or interactive personalities. On the flip side, so-called "fussy" babies may stress their families, leading to more irritable responses, contributing to an ongoing cycle of stress (Austerberry & Fearon, 2021).

4. *Genes help determine how changeable you are.* The environment plays a critical role in how everyone develops. Scientists have discovered that some genes can make you more sensitive (or *plastic*) to what is around you in what is known as *differential susceptibility* (van IJzendoorn & Bakermans-Kranenburg, 2021). People with some genetic variations are more likely to be changed by life events—whether traumatic or beneficial—than others.

5. *We're all different.* With trillions of possible combinations of DNA and environments, we all have different combinations of strengths and weaknesses, risks and benefits. For instance, someone may have genes that predispose them to being sensitive to stress, but at the same time, they may also have genes that predispose them to be quick learners. As a result, creating a life that is healthy and satisfying may require something different for each genetically distinct person. Researchers take this tremendous complexity into account when designing interventions (van IJzendoorn et al., 2020).

multifactorial Traits that are influenced by multiple variables.

Chromosomal Differences

You just read about patterns of genetic inheritance, when a child's genes are passed on from their parents. However, not all genetic conditions are inherited. Sometimes, differences in DNA arise spontaneously as a result of errors in replication during mitosis or meiosis, known as *mutations*. Many of these anomalies are harmless, but at other times they may lead to serious challenges.

The most common form of DNA anomaly occurs before conception, during the maturation of ova and sperm. In about 3 out of every 10 ova, and in 2 in every 100 sperm cells, gametes contain an extra chromosome (Wartosch et al., 2021). When these cells combine, zygotes have too many chromosomes, and most do not survive. However, if the extra chromosome appears in the very small 21st chromosome, many will live.

This extra 21st chromosome causes **Down syndrome**, also known as trisomy-21. Children born with Down syndrome have differences in brain development and, sometimes, muscle tone and cardiovascular development. In comparison to typically developing children, the *cortex*, or the part of the brain that is linked to logical thought, memory, and controlling your behavior, is much smaller in children with Down syndrome. But other areas of the brain, like the subcortical structures involved in memory and emotional processing, are unaffected (Baburamani et al., 2019). As a result, children with Down syndrome have challenges with language and learning that can make independent living more difficult and worsen as they age. By age 40, nearly all people with Down syndrome show signs of early neurocognitive decline (Lott & Head, 2019).

Researchers are now making strides in understanding the complex genetics of Down syndrome and addressing some of the symptoms while fetuses are still developing (Antonarakis et al., 2020). A blood test can now detect Down syndrome in the 12th week of pregnancy to allow families time to prepare for the needs of their babies (Bull, 2020). The risk for Down syndrome is strongly connected to the age of the ovum: Young adolescents (under 15) and older parents (above 35) are at much higher risk for having ova with extra chromosomes (Wartosch et al., 2021). This means that a woman in her 40s is 20 times more likely to have a baby with Down syndrome than a woman in her 20s (Mikwar et al., 2020).

Emerging evidence links age with genetic anomalies in sperm, but these are less frequently linked to Down syndrome (Denomme et al., 2020; Thompson et al., 2019). Age may increase some genetic risks to the developing fetus, but older parents also tend to have many advantages, including more financial stability (Barbuscia et al., 2020).

The Epigenome

Genes are an important part of the genome, but they make up only 2 percent of it (Pertea et al., 2018). What is the rest? Scientists have more questions than answers, but they suspect that much of the rest of the genome is devoted to turning genes on and off and helping DNA copy itself. Remember from Infographic 3.1 that the *epigenome* is the area of the genome that is devoted to gene regulation. The epigenome controls which genes are expressed by changing the chemicals around the double helix of DNA, which are called *epigenetic marks* (O'Donnell & Meaney, 2020). Some epigenetic marks are inherited, others are created during prenatal development, and others are formed later on in the lifespan (Collins & Roth, 2021).

Dozens of factors, from parenting to nutrition, impact the epigenome (Collins & Roth, 2021). For instance, children exposed to trauma show epigenetic differences associated with stress compared to children who haven't experienced trauma (Katrinli et al., 2020). As you can see in **Figure 3.4**, epigenetic changes continue as we mature and even follow a so-called *epigenetic clock* that keeps track of the pace of aging (Li et al., 2020).

More Than Just a Pretty Smile Natty Goleniowska loves to sing along with Mamma Mia and has an extensive tiara collection. She also likes to pose in front of the camera: She was one of the first children with Down syndrome to be featured in major advertising campaigns.

Down syndrome A condition caused by an extra 21st chromosome that results in anomalies in brain development and may also impair muscle tone and cardiovascular development.

Chromosome Pairs
3-year-old twins vs. 50-year-old twins

3-year-old twins
Yellow shows where the twins have epigenetic marks in the same place.

50-year-old twins
Red and green show where the twins have epigenetic marks in different places.

FIGURE 3.4 Epigenetic Changes over Childhood and Adolescence As you see here, at age 3, monozygotic twins have very similar genomes, shown in the yellow markers on the third chromosome. When the twins are young, most of their epigenetic marks overlap and are shown as yellow. As they grow, epigenetic changes multiply. By age 50, there are many differences (Fraga et al., 2005).

monozygotic Twins with nearly identical DNA because they start off as a single zygote that separates into two in the first days after fertilization.

CONNECTIONS

Remember from Chapter 2 that the evolutionary perspective focuses on the adaptive value of genetic change. Genetic flexibility and variety allow organisms to adapt to the environment. Natural selection means that traits that allow an individual to survive and reproduce will be passed on to future generations and become more common in the population.

Which Are Monozygotic? Twins do not always look exactly alike, whether they are born from one zygote or two. Teenagers Maria and Lucy are dizygotic twins: They developed from two separate ova fertilized by two different sperm cells. They are about as alike as any set of siblings. Toddlers Amelia and Jasmine do not look exactly alike, either: They are monozygotic twins, so they developed from one ovum fertilized by one sperm cell that split early in development. However, early developmental changes helped make the girls look a little different from each other.

Epigenetic changes can be transmitted to future generations through alterations in meiosis, when egg and sperm cells are formed. For instance, the children and grandchildren of adults who survived massive famines, like those in Holland during World War II and China in the 1950s, have higher rates of physical and emotional illnesses because of damage to their parents' or grandparents' sperm and egg cells (Lassi & Teperino, 2020; Wu et al., 2017). Epigenetic changes in ova or sperm cells can also result from everyday behaviors and stresses, such as smoking cigarettes or having a unhealthy diet (Y. Wang et al., 2019). The effects of healthy behaviors can be passed on as well. For instance, fathers who exercise regularly may pass on epigenetic changes to their children that lower their risk for diseases like Parkinson disease or schizophrenia (Donkin & Barrès, 2018).

Epigenetic research is leading to more understanding and treatment of the environmental triggers for many disorders, from depression to Alzheimer disease (Cavalli & Heard, 2019). It is also helping scientists understand how epigenetic changes can be reversed: The impact of chronic stress in infants born preterm, for instance, can be overcome with the help of nurturing relationships (Kommers et al., 2016).

Evolutionary theorists point out that our flexible genome offers some benefits (Benton et al., 2021). For instance, having one copy of the sickle-cell allele (being a carrier) is protective against *malaria*, a mosquito-borne disease common in many parts of the world, including sub-Saharan Africa and parts of Asia and South America. As a result, carriers of the sickle-cell allele are less likely to die of malaria, particularly in infancy (Kariuki & Williams, 2020). Similar patterns are seen in other genetic conditions: Carriers of the neurological disorder Tay Sachs are protected against tuberculosis. The gene for cystic fibrosis is protective against typhoid and cholera (Ewald & Swain Ewald, 2019). So, generations ago, before modern medicine, some of these genetic traits may have helped us survive. Today, millions affected by these diseases are grateful for effective treatments and early intervention.

The Genetics of Twins

Sometimes, soon after ovum and sperm combine, the zygote splits in two, or more than one zygote is created. **Monozygotic** twins (or, more rarely, monozygotic triplets, quadruplets, and so on) have nearly identical DNA because they start off as a single zygote that separates into two in the first 13 days after fertilization (Jonsson et al., 2021).

Because the resulting zygotes started as a single cell, they share that original set of genes, until epigenetic changes and random mutations begin to occur.

Dizygotic twins develop when two (or more) ova are released and fertilized by separate sperm. Since they typically have the same parents, like any set of siblings, they share about half of their genetic information. It is possible for the ova to be fertilized by two different sets of sperm if a woman has different partners (Segal et al., 2020). But most of the time, when twins look very different, do not assume they have different parents. There is often a lot of natural variety between siblings or twins.

Subtle differences in the prenatal environment and the complexity of cell division mean that even monozygotic twins are never truly identical. Sometimes this results in subtle phenotypic distinctions, such as different hair or fingerprints, but others may be more profound (Jonsson et al., 2021). For example, some monozygotic twins have different eye colors because of epigenetic changes during early development or from small differences in early cell replication (Butler et al., 2016).

For some families, getting pregnant with two babies or more is a gift. But this joy may come with danger. Twins and other multiples have a higher risk of serious complications for both the babies and their families. Multiples are more likely to be born prematurely, have low birthweight, or even die before or soon after birth (Sunderam et al., 2022). Even healthy multiple babies can stress families, because parents must divide their attention and energy (Ronkin & Tone, 2020). Nevertheless, many of us are curious about twins, perhaps because, as one twin researcher points out, we secretly wish "to have someone just like us" (Nancy Segal, quoted in Muhlenkamp, 2012).

Researchers have studied twins for centuries to better understand how environment and genetics interact to make each of us unique. Many studies have found that monozygotic twins are significantly more alike than dizygotic twins. But modern research has also revealed that there are many genetic differences between monozygotic twins caused by epigenetic changes and random variations as cells duplicate over the lifespan (Vadgama et al., 2019). Indeed, studies of twins have helped researchers understand the impact of the environment on our mental and physical health and appreciate the complexity in the unpredictable interactions between our genotype and our phenotype (Lam et al., 2019).

Testing the Genome

Have you had your DNA tested? About 1 in every 25 people has, as genomic testing has become increasingly affordable and accessible (Lawton & Ifama, 2018). Genetic testing promises enormous benefits, but the science is complex, as are the possible ethical issues and concerns about gene-based discrimination (Joly et al., 2020). No tests are without risks: Getting your genetic test results creates stress and can change how you take care of your health (Turnwald et al., 2019). There are more than 50,000 distinct genetic tests that can be performed by more than 500 different laboratories to test for more than 16,000 different conditions (Regalado, 2018). What can they tell us?

Most experts and professionals do not advise getting your genome tested at home to assess your risk for a disease. Home genetic tests are not always reliable and do not usually provide the medical counseling needed to make sense of the results (Horton et al., 2019). Medical professionals and genetic counselors recommend genetic testing only when it is both *reliable* and *actionable* (Green et al., 2013). This means that a test needs to reliably and consistently diagnose the risk for a genetic disease and help you act on this information.

For example, genetic counselors would advise getting tested for a single-gene disorder like sickle-cell disease that has clear treatments and a possible cure, particularly if you have a family history of risk (Oron et al., 2020). Similarly, genetic counselors might recommend being screened if you have a family history of breast, ovarian, or

dizygotic Twins that develop when two (or more) ova are fertilized by separate sperm.

pancreatic cancer (Daly et al., 2020). While some companies offer to provide complex, polygenetic genetic scores for embryos, many experts are skeptical of their accuracy or ethics (Turley et al., 2021)

Most genetic counselors caution against testing a child or a fetus for a disease or disorder if the results are not actionable during early childhood. For instance, knowing that your fetus or child carries some genes that may increase their risk for developing a neurocognitive disorder like Alzheimer disease may only cause unnecessary worry early in life, since the relationship between these conditions and genetics is far less direct (Eid et al., 2019; NSGC, 2019).

Prenatal genetic testing can feel stressful and confusing (Parens & Applebaum, 2019). Facing the prospect that your fetus or child might have a serious genetic disease involves families' deepest-held beliefs about what makes life worthwhile. A skilled genetic counselor can help but is not always available (Clarke & Wallgren Pettersson, 2019). Culture is also relevant: Health care providers and counselors working with families who speak another language or have a different cultural background need to use cultural humility to connect with and support their clients (Ault et al., 2019; Warren, 2020).

Some forms of genetic testing promise to link you with your ancestors. Scientists advise you to take these genealogical results with a healthy dose of skepticism: They are rarely consistent when checked against those of different providers (Blell & Hunter, 2019; Grayson, 2018). In addition, most of these tests compare your DNA patterns to those of people living in other nations around the globe, but since people have moved over time, the results may never be able to tell you accurately where your ancestors lived 50 or even 200 years ago (Fullwiley, 2021; Saey, 2018). In addition, test results often oversimplify ancestry and can reinforce the idea that our genome defines who we are (Roth et al., 2020).

For many, ancestry testing brings up questions of identity. However, the science doesn't quite match up with the advertising copy and our expectations (Walajahi et al., 2019). Knowing that you are Native American, for instance, requires much more than just a genetic test match; it requires understanding a shared history and relationships within a community (Carey, 2019). Black Americans looking to pinpoint their origins in Africa often find that there are not enough data to determine where exactly they are from (Lawton et al., 2018). More than anything, ancestry testing reminds us that identity is not biology. Memories and relationships are what link people together, regardless of the genes within us.

APPLY IT! **3.1** Spencer and Alizah want baby Courage to inherit some of their traits, like Spencer's curls and Alizah's flexibility. What would you tell them about the likelihood that these characteristics are passed on through their genome?
3.2 There is much diversity in our genome and many parts of our genetic expression can be altered by the context we grow up in. How do developmental scientists explain the benefits of a complex and flexible genome?

Prenatal Development

germinal stage The first stage of prenatal development, in which the single-celled zygote divides and implants into the uterus in the first week of development.

embryonic stage The second stage of prenatal development, in weeks 2 through 8, in which the embryo develops the major parts of its body—from legs to brain.

Learning Objectives

3.4 Describe the key stages of prenatal development.
3.5 Describe the principles of prenatal risk and resilience.

Before Courage was born, Alizah and Spencer couldn't see the developing fetus: They just watched him move on fleeting ultrasounds and felt his impressive kicks. In the space of 38 weeks, a bundle of cells smaller than this "o" transforms into a squalling newborn. Scientists have a better view of what goes on inside the uterus: They use cameras and magnetic resonance imaging (MRI) to observe fetuses in the womb. They have found that learning and psychological development start before birth.

Scientists divide prenatal development into three stages (see **Infographic 3.2**). During the **germinal stage**, the single-celled zygote divides and implants into the uterus. In the **embryonic stage**, in weeks 2 through 8, the embryo develops the

Whether you measure it in stages or trimesters, prenatal development is the fastest period of growth of the lifespan, as the zygote transforms into a fetus capable of living outside of the uterus.

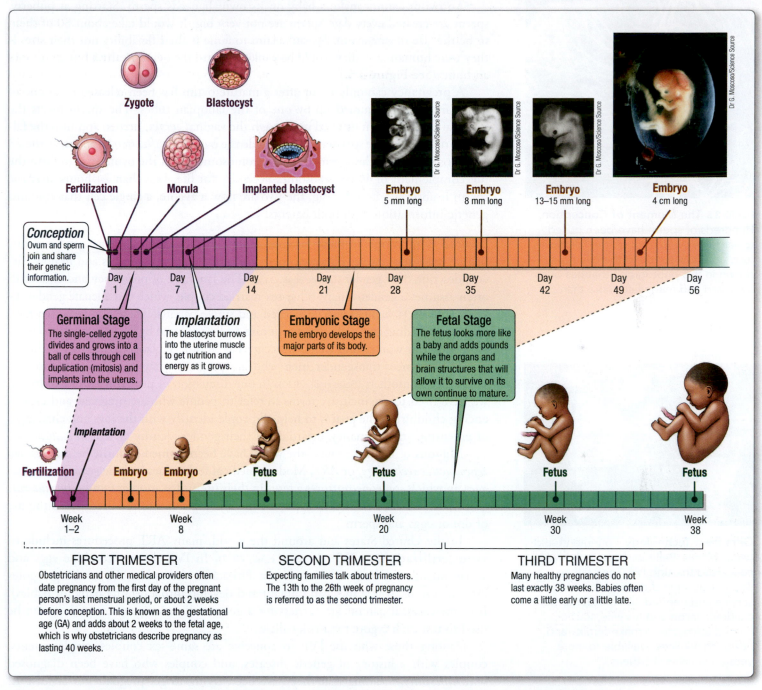

Conception
Ovum and sperm join and share their genetic information.

Zygote

Blastocyst

Fertilization

Morula

Implanted blastocyst

Embryo 5 mm long

Embryo 8 mm long

Embryo 13–15 mm long

Embryo 4 cm long

Dr. G. Moscoso/Science Source

Day 1 | Day 7 | Day 14 | Day 21 | Day 28 | Day 35 | Day 42 | Day 49 | Day 56

Germinal Stage
The single-celled zygote divides and grows into a ball of cells through cell duplication (mitosis) and implants into the uterus.

Implantation
The blastocyst burrows into the uterine muscle to get nutrition and energy as it grows.

Embryonic Stage
The embryo develops the major parts of its body.

Fetal Stage
The fetus looks more like a baby and adds pounds while the organs and brain structures that will allow it to survive on its own continue to mature.

Implantation

Fertilization

Embryo

Embryo

Fetus

Fetus

Fetus

Fetus

Week 1–2 | Week 8 | Week 20 | Week 30 | Week 38

FIRST TRIMESTER
Obstetricians and other medical providers often date pregnancy from the first day of the pregnant person's last menstrual period, or about 2 weeks before conception. This is known as the gestational age (GA) and adds about 2 weeks to the fetal age, which is why obstetricians describe pregnancy as lasting 40 weeks.

SECOND TRIMESTER
Expecting families talk about trimesters. The 13th to the 26th week of pregnancy is referred to as the second trimester.

THIRD TRIMESTER
Many healthy pregnancies do not last exactly 38 weeks. Babies often come a little early or a little late.

major parts of its body—from legs to brain. In the **fetal stage**, the fetus finally looks like a baby and adds pounds and the organs and brain structures that will allow it to survive on its own.

Conception

Did you know that you actually originated inside your mother's mother? Each of us began as one of 6 million ova created inside our mother's body when she was still a fetus developing inside of her mother's uterus. Each ovum is 10 times the size of most other cells and almost big enough to see without a magnifying glass (Alberts et al.,

fetal stage The third stage of prenatal development, weeks 9 through birth, in which the fetus begins to look like a baby and adds pounds and the organs and brain structures that will allow it to survive on its own.

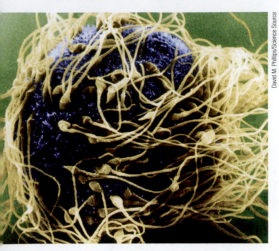

David M. Phillips/Science Source

FIGURE 3.5 The Moment of Conception
Hundreds of sperm have been pulled toward the ovum through the fallopian tube and now surround the ovum, as shown in this photograph that has been colorized and magnified more than 1,000 times.

© Valerie Mosley/The Coloradoan–USA TODAY NETWORK

Gifts from Technology Four-month-old twins, Marina Belle and Jason, Jr., were conceived through IVF. Their father, Jason, was injured during his military service and needed IVF in order to have children. Jason and his wife, Rachel, helped advocate to make fertility and adoption services available to more veteran families like theirs.

in vitro fertilization (IVF) A procedure in which doctors combine egg and sperm outside the body in a hospital laboratory and then place the resulting zygotes in the uterus, where they can implant and develop into a baby (or babies).

2002). Each includes not only the genetic code necessary to grow a new being, but also enough energy to sustain the zygote in the first days after conception.

An ovum cannot make a baby on its own: It needs sperm. Starting at puberty, sperm are created every day. Sperm are not very big: It would take about 30 of them to be the size of one ovum. Sperm's claim to fame is their flexibility not their size. If they were human-size, they would be yanked toward the ovum nearly a hundred miles an hour. (See **Figure 3.5**.)

A pregnancy can only occur after a mature ovum has been released from one of the ovaries and vacuumed up by one of the fallopian tubes. The sperm meets the ovum after it has been ushered in through the vagina, cervix, uterus, and into the fallopian tube. After the sperm is drawn inside the ovum, *fertilization* happens, as the 23 chromosomes from the sperm and 23 chromosomes from the ovum fuse to form the full complement of 46 chromosomes necessary for life. Less than 24 hours after the sperm is absorbed into the egg, the two are now a zygote, a single cell that contains genetic information from both parents.

Diverse Beginnings In many families, as in Courage's family, parents' gender identities are male and female. However, there is much diversity in families and in how parents describe their gender (Carone et al., 2020). The language of pregnancy and childbirth often assumes a gender-binary, other-sex married couple, which can alienate gender-diverse, LGBTQ+ families and unmarried and single parents. These families often have difficulties finding culturally competent care, feeling rejected by labels that refer to pregnant people as women and childbirth centers as "mothers' places" (Duckett & Ruud, 2019).

For instance, transgender men who are pregnant may not always identify as women or as mothers (Besse et al., 2020). In our discussion of pregnancy and childbirth, we have tried to use inclusive terms to refer to people who are pregnant and experiencing childbirth: The goal is to help all people identify with the joys and challenges of parenting and pregnancy, regardless of their gender identity (Moseson et al., 2020).

Millions of families around the world have been formed with the help of *assisted reproductive technology*, or *ART*. Modern medical techniques include *gestational surrogacy*, in which someone nurtures a fetus in their uterus for another family; *intrauterine insemination (IUI)*, in which a sperm is directly inserted into the uterus; and the use of donor eggs and sperm.

In the United States and around the world, many ART procedures include **in vitro fertilization**, or **IVF** (Sunderam et al., 2022). In IVF, doctors combine eggs and sperm outside the body in a laboratory. Physicians then place the resulting zygotes into the uterus, where they can implant and develop into a healthy baby (or babies). In some cases, if parents are carriers for a genetic disorder, gene technology can be used to test each zygote for a risky allele.

Among those who use IVF to conceive are same-sex couples, single parents, couples with a history of genetic diseases, and couples who have been diagnosed with *infertility*, meaning that they have been trying to get pregnant for at least 12 months without success. More than one in eight U.S. couples reports that they have trouble conceiving (Kelley et al., 2019). Rates of infertility are even higher elsewhere. In many low-income communities around the world where health care is hard to access, nearly 3 out of 10 people have difficulty getting pregnant or helping their partners get pregnant (Sun et al., 2019).

Fertility treatments can have risks. Primary among these is having more than one baby. Another is a slightly higher risk of having babies who are born small, too early, or with a disability (Luke et al., 2021). One of the biggest risks, however, is that the process will not work at all. More than one in three prospective parents who start fertility treatments are not able to have biological children (Troude et al., 2016). Many cannot afford to pursue treatment (Kelley et al., 2019). Some choose adoption in order to build a family.

FIGURE 3.6 The Germinal Stage This illustration shows the fusion of egg and sperm in a cross-section of the fallopian tube and movement of the zygote down the fallopian tube toward the uterus for implantation. Note that the zygotes and blastocysts are shown cut in half to show what they look like on the inside, since from the outside they look like a ball.

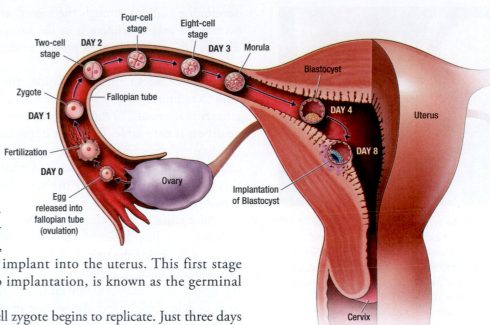

The Germinal Stage

Whether a zygote originates in a laboratory and is transferred into the body or is fertilized inside the fallopian tube, it will rapidly begin to divide and then implant into the uterus. This first stage in prenatal development, from zygote to implantation, is known as the germinal stage.

Shortly after fertilization, the single-cell zygote begins to replicate. Just three days after fertilization, this single cell has turned into a tightly packed ball of 32 cells, now called a *morula*, and has made its way down the fallopian tube toward the uterus, where it will implant. By five days after fertilization, the ball of cells has become much larger, has separated into an outer layer and an inner mass, and is more than 150 cells. It is now called a **blastocyst**. As you can tell by looking closely at **Figure 3.6**, it is no longer filled with identical cells.

In the first few days of development, the zygote contains cells that are exactly the same. But as early as two days after fertilization, genes activated in the nucleus of each cell began to direct them to specialize in a process known as *differentiation* (K. L. Moore et al., 2020). By the fourth day after fertilization, the outer layer of cells in the blastocyst have separated from the inner mass, which will become the embryo. This outer layer will form the fetus's support system: The *placenta* and the *umbilical cord*, and the inner mass will develop into the embryo.

Differentiation helps the blastocyst through its first major transition: *implantation*. This turning point in the life of the blastocyst depends on perfect timing. There are only four days in every monthly cycle when the uterus is receptive to implantation. When a blastocyst arrives at the right time, about 10 days after fertilization, it burrows deep into the fleshy inside of the uterine muscle, looking for blood vessels that will bring it nutrition and energy as it grows (Ochoa-Bernal & Fazleabas, 2020).

The Embryonic Stage

After implantation, the blastocyst begins to transform. During the *embryonic stage*, which lasts from implantation until eight weeks, cell growth accelerates. Arms and legs will appear, and the embryo begins to move. The entire body is organized around the developing nervous system, which is the embryo's first distinguishing feature.

As the blastocyst settles into the uterus, its cells begin to differentiate further into cells that will become part of the skin, brain, intestines, or the muscles. The location of cells in the blastocyst—in the middle or on the outer edge—will determine whether they end up as hair cells, heart cells, or brain cells (Moore et al., 2020).

At two weeks after fertilization, the embryo now has a support team, and its supportive structures are larger than the embryo itself. A tough, fluid-filled transparent membrane called the *amniotic sac* gives the embryo an extra layer of protection, like bubble wrap, as it bounces around inside the uterus. The **placenta** is an organ that allows energy and waste to be transferred between the parent's body and the

blastocyst The ball of cells during the germinal stage of prenatal development that becomes larger and then separates into an outer layer and an inner mass, replicating until it is more than 150 cells.

placenta An organ that allows energy and waste to be transferred between the parent's body and the developing embryo through the umbilical cord.

Building Strength and Smiles Eleven-year-old Simha was born with spina bifida. With the support of physical therapists in Jerusalem, Israel, she is gaining new skills moving on her own.

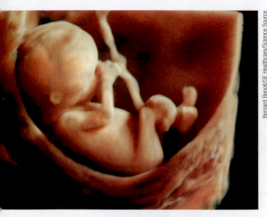

Bernard Benoit/GE Healthcare/Science Source

Curled Up to Grow This fetus was photographed with a 3D ultrasound at about 10 weeks after fertilization. Some of the support structures that help it to grow are visible, including the umbilical cord that attaches it to its parent and the amniotic sac that cushions it inside the body. The largest structure is the fetus's head.

neurons Nerve cells.

What Does a 24-Week-Old Fetus Look Like? A lot like this little baby. This child's skin looks red because it is so thin that veins are visible. The newborn has fingernails, but lung development is still not complete.

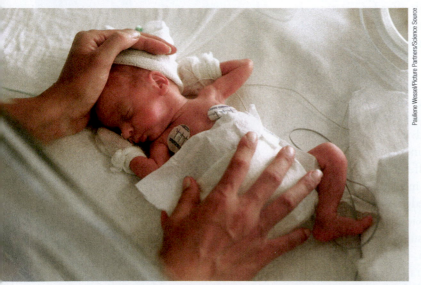

Pauliene Wessel/Picture Partners/Science Source

developing embryo through the *umbilical cord*. The developing embryo cannot eat, breathe, or excrete while it is in the uterus, so the placenta takes care of these tasks. The health of the placenta plays a critical role in the healthy development of the embryo (Bové et al., 2019).

At three weeks after fertilization, the embryo is less than a quarter of an inch long (5 millimeters) and resembles a shrimp. The embryo now has so many cells that a heart is necessary to move oxygen and nutrition around the growing body, and a heartbeat is detectable. The most important system, however, is the growing brain.

Brain development begins in the third week after fertilization. Nerve cells, called **neurons**, begin to cluster into what looks like a flat plate. In the fourth week, this plate rolls up to become the *neural tube*, which will become the brain and the spinal cord.

Anomalies in the formation of the nervous system can cause physical differences called *neural tube defects*. Some embryos diagnosed with these differences can be operated on inside the uterus, before birth (Sanz Cortes et al., 2021). Where early medical care is not available, neural tube defects can lead to severe complications. Around the world, more than 300,000 children are born every year with neural tube defects, such as spina bifida, and almost one in three dies (Blencowe et al., 2018). People living with neural tube defects may have trouble moving independently but are often able to adapt (Avagliano et al., 2019).

By the fourth week, the embryo's neural tube has turned into a factory for neurons. The pace at which neurons are produced during this period is breathtaking. More than 200,000 neurons are being created every minute!

As the embryo's brain is developing, so is the rest of its body. The embryo slowly transitions into looking like a little human. Arms appear in the third week, and fingers two weeks later. Legs begin to grow during the fourth week and toes two weeks later. By the end of week 8, the embryo is still just about one inch (27 mm) long but can be seen moving on an ultrasound.

The Fetal Period

The fetal period begins around week 9 and lasts until birth. During the next 29 weeks, the fetus will grow at an incredible rate—growing about 19 inches and putting on more than 7 pounds. The fetus will develop the ability to survive on its own. This requires maturation not only in the fetus's body—but also in its brain.

From week 9 until week 17, the fetus's organ systems are maturing rapidly. The intestines mature, although until birth, the fetus will continue to send fecal waste back into the mother's bloodstream through the umbilical cord. By 12 weeks, the kidneys have begun to work, excreting urine into the amniotic cavity. By 17 weeks, the pace of growth begins to slow as the fetus builds the fat and muscle it will need to support itself outside the uterus. However, major organ systems are not finished developing. One of the last organ systems to mature is the lungs, which are not ready to breathe air until about 26 weeks. This is one of the challenges for babies who are born early.

The reproductive organs are another slow-growing system. Male and female organs both develop from the same tissues, and these do not differentiate until late in development:

During the prenatal period, the structures of the brain form, and communication across brain structures and between the brain and body begins.

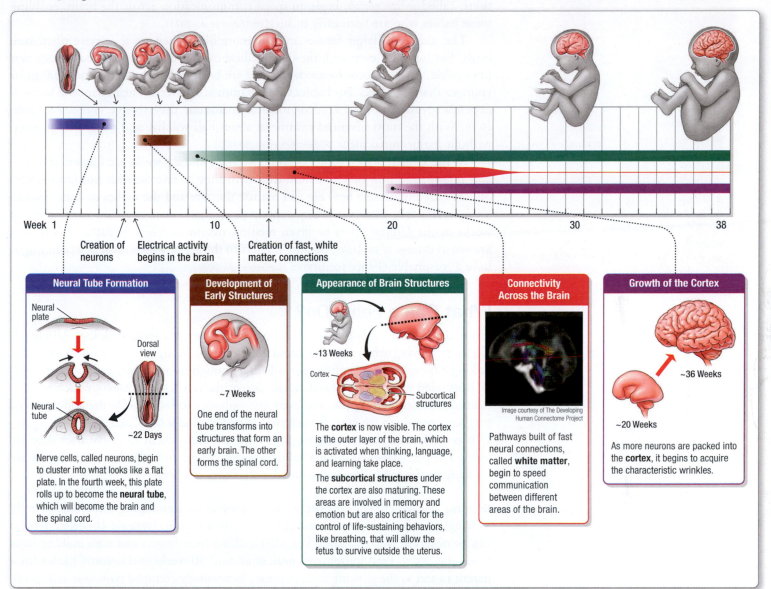

Neural Tube Formation

Neural plate

Dorsal view

Neural tube

~22 Days

Nerve cells, called neurons, begin to cluster into what looks like a flat plate. In the fourth week, this plate rolls up to become the **neural tube**, which will become the brain and the spinal cord.

Development of Early Structures

~7 Weeks

One end of the neural tube transforms into structures that form an early brain. The other forms the spinal cord.

Appearance of Brain Structures

~13 Weeks

Cortex

Subcortical structures

The **cortex** is now visible. The cortex is the outer layer of the brain, which is activated when thinking, language, and learning take place.

The **subcortical structures** under the cortex are also maturing. These areas are involved in memory and emotion but are also critical for the control of life-sustaining behaviors, like breathing, that will allow the fetus to survive outside the uterus.

Connectivity Across the Brain

Image courtesy of The Developing Human Connectome Project

Pathways built of fast neural connections, called **white matter**, begin to speed communication between different areas of the brain.

Growth of the Cortex

~36 Weeks

~20 Weeks

As more neurons are packed into the **cortex**, it begins to acquire the characteristic wrinkles.

Week 1   10   20   30   38

Creation of neurons

Electrical activity begins in the brain

Creation of fast, white matter, connections

Not until around 9 to 12 weeks can a fetus's genitals be seen on an ultrasound. Fetal testes and ovaries release hormones that cause the genital and reproductive organs to mature. By around 16 weeks, the ovaries begin to fill with immature ova. It will take until 30 weeks (and sometimes later) before the testes mature enough to leave the pelvic cavity, and it will be many years before they produce sperm.

If you have ever looked at an ultrasound image of a developing fetus, you probably noticed that its head was overly large, almost the same size as the rest of its body. Inside, millions of neurons are being created and rapidly building the brain. Many will form the *cortex*, or the outer layer of the brain, which is activated when thinking, language, and learning take place. As neurons multiply, the cortex gets bigger and more wrinkled (see **Infographic 3.3**). The *subcortical structures* under the cortex are also maturing. These areas are involved in memory and emotion but are also critical for the control of life-sustaining behaviors, like breathing, that will allow the fetus to survive outside the uterus. At the same time, pathways built of fast neural connections, called *white matter*, begin to speed communication across the brain, enabling some babies who are born early to survive (Edde et al., 2021).

The older and larger fetuses are, the more likely they are to survive premature birth. For instance, even with the best medical care, it is very unusual, although not impossible, for newborns to survive if they are born at less than a pound (400 g) or younger than 22 weeks. For babies who are born at 22 weeks, their chance of survival depends greatly on what kind of medical treatment they receive (Mercurio & Carter, 2020). With the most advanced treatment, about half will live and many will grow up without major impairment (Söderström et al., 2021).

In the United States, babies born between 20 and 25 weeks are known as *periviable infants*, and how much medical treatment they receive depends not just on how old they are but also on how big and mature they are and the wishes of their families (Rysavy et al., 2015). However, many experts recommend that any baby born after 22 weeks in the United States be given medical treatment (Lee et al., 2022). This date is known as the *age of viability*, because it refers to the age at which most newborn might have a reasonable chance to survive (Stefano et al., 2020).

What Can a Fetus Do?

From the outside, it is difficult to know exactly what a fetus is doing. Alizah felt Courage moving when she was about four months along. A few months later, his poking elbows and knees often protruded far enough to be visible, and for Spencer to be impressed with his high karate kicks. Scientists have used technology such as MRI scanners, ultrasound wands, and even microphones to look inside the abdomens of pregnant people to see what fetuses are capable of (Reid & Dunn, 2021).

In the uterus, fetuses practice skills that will allow them to thrive after they are born. The prenatal environment influences everything, from the languages babies are learning to the foods they will recognize after they are born.

Moving Movement typically begins just as soon as the developing embryo has a body to wiggle. Embryos begin to bend at 5 weeks (Hadders-Algra, 2018). At 16 weeks, fetuses can be observed with ultrasound or MRI sucking their fingers and even making faces (Ustun et al., 2022). Fetal movements peak at around 30 weeks and become harder for a parent to feel as the growing fetus becomes increasingly cramped (Verbruggen et al., 2018). Early activity helps muscles and bones mature and develop the connections in the brain that will allow newborns to control their bodies (Borsani et al., 2019).

Responding to Stress Fetuses are also learning how to respond emotionally to the world and how to regulate their physical reactions. For instance, a fetus's heart rate is in sync with their parent's, and fetuses whose parent is depressed move differently than those whose parents are not depressed (DiPietro et al., 2015; Reissland et al., 2021). As a result, pregnant parents whose heart rates mirror disorders like anxiety or depression are more likely to have babies who share their stress response patterns (O'Sullivan & Monk, 2020). Fetuses and newborns differ in how intensely they respond to stressful situations and how quickly they recover from a scare, upset, or disappointment. These differences, established prenatally, can be one of the factors that lead a child to be fussy or easy to soothe (Manczak & Gotlib, 2019).

Sensing Although you may think of fetuses as isolated from the outside world, they experience sounds, light, smells, and even tastes (see **Table 3.1**). This early experience stimulates fetuses to develop the senses they will need after birth.

TABLE 3.1 **Prenatal Development of the Senses**

Vision	It is dark inside the uterus, but starting at about 24 weeks, a fetus will move more quickly if a bright light is shone outside the abdomen. What fetuses see is very dim, lacking color and detail, but this light exposure helps set sleep schedules.
Touch and pain	The sense of touch develops early in the embryonic period. From about 20 weeks on, fetuses move when the outside of their pregnant parent's abdomen is touched. Although researchers believe that fetuses can feel pain, many suggest that they process pain differently from full-term babies because of immature brain connectivity.
Hearing	The noise of a pregnant parent's stomach and heartbeat means that the sound level in the uterus is about 90 decibels, similar to a school cafeteria or a subway train. Nevertheless, beginning at about 25 weeks, fetuses react to loud sounds with activation in their brain stem. A few weeks later, fetuses recognize sounds they hear frequently, like their parents' voices.
Smell and taste	By 26 weeks, a fetus can smell and taste and even has preferences. The taste and the smell of what their parent eats enters amniotic fluid, allowing the growing fetus to taste and smell a bit of that morning bagel.

Information from Clark-Gambelunghe & Clark, 2015; Derbyshire & Bockmann, 2020; Draganova et al., 2018; Hepper, 2015; Lee & Kisilevsky, 2014; Logan & McClung, 2019; Marx & Nagy, 2017; Ustun et al., 2022.

CAN YOU BELIEVE IT?
Does Learning Happen Before Birth?

Some families-to-be recite books and sing songs to their fetuses long before birth, hoping to make their babies more capable. Is there any evidence that this helps? While there isn't any evidence that families *should* be educating their fetuses before birth, there is ample evidence that even without special efforts, fetuses are developing their cognitive skills long before birth.

Scientists have been testing learning in fetuses for more than 100 years. In the past, researchers observed that fetuses jerked after someone blew a car horn near the pregnant parent's abdomen (Dirix et al., 2009). But after the scientists blew the horn a few times, the fetuses stopped responding. Researchers observed that fetuses had become *habituated*, or used to, the sound, and as a result, they didn't startle when they heard it again. Today, researchers test what fetuses remember and what they learn by examining their heart rate, brain activity, and movement (Reid & Dunn, 2021).

Scientists also assess prenatal learning by testing newborns to see if they remembered what they were exposed to before they were born (DeCasper & Fifer, 1980; Reissland & Kisilevsky, 2016). Researchers exposed fetuses to various sounds and noises, from nursery rhymes to jazz standards, and found that newborns reacted differently to sounds they heard in the uterus than to new sounds. Newborns appear to have habituated to the sounds they heard before, reacting more powerfully to the new sounds (Partanen & Virtala, 2017).

Using these techniques, scientists discovered, for instance, that one area of the fetus's brain is activated when a fetus hears their parents' voice, but that another is activated when they hear an unfamiliar voice (Carvalho et al., 2019). Fetuses can distinguish the tones of different languages, and the language they hear before birth even affects the way newborns cry when they are born (Manfredi et al., 2019). Researchers shining lights at a fetus have even shown that fetuses can recognize patterns before they are born, and even seem to prefer face shapes (Donovan et al., 2020; V. M. Reid et al., 2017).

Does this research mean that families need to stimulate their fetuses' brains before birth? No. However, an understanding of what fetuses learn before birth has

Scientific American Profile

Preparing for Baby

had enormous benefits for babies born prematurely. For instance, interventions that provide new babies with extra exposure to the sounds of their parents' voices can help them learn and soothe their pain (Filippa et al., 2020). 🏃

Protective and Risky Factors During Prenatal Development

Although scientists do not think that fetuses need to be read to in order to develop well, contemporary research has found that stress, disease, and environmental hazards faced by families *do* have an impact on the health of a fetus and the person it will become (Camerota & Willoughby, 2021). Research based on the theory of *fetal programming* investigates the impact of prenatal experience on lifelong health (Barker, 1995).

For instance, scientists have observed that fetal malnutrition can lead to greater risk for high blood pressure and heart disease in adulthood (Crump & Howell, 2020). Parents who experience severe trauma during pregnancy may transmit risk to their children through changes in their brain development, hormones, and epigenetic marks (Carroll et al., 2020). However, most researchers agree that although prenatal experiences may increase risks, there are ample opportunities after birth for change (Camerota & Willoughby, 2021). Pregnancy offers opportunities to build resilience and good health (Davis & Narayan, 2020).

Prenatal Care For many families, pregnancy motivates them to get healthy. Alizah says she's never eaten so many greens. She and Spencer experienced some unexpected stresses during the pregnancy, like the global pandemic, but they also enjoyed some of the key ingredients for good health during pregnancy: early prenatal care and supportive family relationships.

Around the world, medical providers are the first line of intervention for expectant parents and their fetuses. Medical care is critical in helping expectant families get the support they may need and provide intervention to prevent either serious illness or *stillbirth*, when a fetus dies after the 20th week of pregnancy. For many adults, prenatal care also serves as their first opportunity to develop long-term relationships with the health care system: relationships that may serve to improve their health over the long term. But even in the United States, prenatal care is not always easy to access, particularly for those who are low-income or who live in rural areas (National Academies of Sciences, Engineering, and Medicine, 2020a).

In the United States, *traditional prenatal care* involves regular one-on-one checkups with a medical doctor or midwife (Peahl & Howell, 2021). Around the globe, most expectant parents receive some prenatal care, but only three in five receive the minimum of four visits, which makes childbirth more dangerous for infants and expectant parents around the world (UNICEF, 2021). No matter where they live, younger, less affluent parents and those from groups that face discrimination are particularly at risk for inadequate prenatal care (Barfield, 2021; Slaughter-Acey et al., 2019).

Innovative methods of prenatal care encourage expectant families to create supportive relationships both in person and through virtual visits. In *group prenatal care* such as the Centering Pregnancy program, pregnant families provide support to each other while also receiving their regular health assessments. Group care has been found to be more effective than traditional one-on-one prenatal care, leading to fewer preterm births and more satisfied parents, particularly for those at risk of premature delivery or delivering babies with low birthweight (Buultjens et al., 2020; Mazzoni & Carter, 2017).

Other alternatives to traditional prenatal care include *home visiting*, where nurses check in on pregnant parents at home. In successful programs such as the Nurse–Family Partnership, nurses visit expectant families and build long-term relationships. Visiting nurses educate new families about healthy lifestyle choices and supportive parenting and give practical advice about education and career development. Home

Natalie Keyssar/The New York Times/Redux

Still Friends Centering Pregnancy is a group-based program of prenatal care. It gives expectant parents a chance to build social relationships with other expectant families, establishing friendships and support that help make pregnancy easier. These families in New York liked the experience so much they came back for a reunion after their babies were born.

visiting, which you will read more about in Chapter 4, has had success in preventing premature birth (Anthony et al., 2021).

Social and Family Support Whether they pester you to exercise, hold your hand during an early ultrasound, or pick up groceries after work, other people are a critical source of support during pregnancy.

The vast majority of pregnant people, like Alizah, are in a romantic relationship when they get pregnant, and more than 90 percent will have a partner when they give birth (CPS, 2021). In general, people who are in supportive relationships tend to experience less anxiety and stress during pregnancy and have lower rates of premature birth and babies with low birthweight (Shapiro et al., 2018). Even during the early months of the COVID-19 pandemic, when pregnant people were often under strain, social support helped to protect them and their growing fetuses from some of that anxiety (Provenzi et al., 2021)

Emotional support doesn't have to come from a partner: It can also come from extended social networks such as parents, siblings, coworkers, or community groups. Pregnant people who feel connected to others and have someone to rely on have lower levels of stress hormones (A. C. D. Cheadle et al., 2020). Pregnant parents who lack close personal connections or who can't access community resources are particularly at risk for complications during pregnancy.

Risks During Prenatal Development Despite the hope and excitement of bringing a new life into the world, not all babies are born healthy, and, around the world, pregnancy and childbirth are a leading cause of death in young parents and newborns (Ahn et al., 2020; Douthard et al., 2021). Some of the difficulties infants might face will be obvious on the day that they are born. Others may not appear for years, as with learning disabilities caused by prenatal alcohol exposure.

Almost 6 out of every 100 babies born around the world arrive with a major abnormality in their body or brain. These abnormalities are often called **birth defects** (WHO, 2019b). While this is the term used by the medical and public health communities, it is considered demeaning by many families and adults with disabilities because it focuses on limitations (Elliott & Evans, 2015; NCDJ, n.d.). Advocates encourage the use of terminology such as *differences*, or simply naming the specific condition.

Despite advances in fetal medicine and developmental science, doctors can only find a cause for a few major prenatal abnormalities. Some are only genetic, such as sickle-cell disease. Others are caused by **teratogens**, or factors in a parent's body or the environment that damage the fetus (Hales et al., 2018). Teratogens can include diseases like the coronavirus (COVID-19) and substances in the environment, such as lead paint or car exhaust (Taruscio et al., 2017; Woodworth et al., 2020). They also include medications or prescriptions, whether over-the-counter or prescribed, legal or illegal. Even factors like a parent's age, level of stress, depression, or anxiety can be classified as teratogens.

Scientists have discovered several underlying principles about prenatal risk:

1. *Timing is important.* If an embryo is exposed to a teratogen in the first eight weeks of pregnancy, the embryo may be so compromised that pregnancy loss, sometimes referred to as *spontaneous abortion* or *miscarriage*, may occur. Some weeks or even days are *critical periods* for the development of specific organ systems. For instance, a toxin might damage an embryo's arms if exposure occurs in the third week of development, or its legs if exposure is in the fourth week (see **Figure 3.7**; Hales et al., 2018). Other organ systems, like the brain, have longer critical periods, called *sensitive periods*. The brain can be damaged at any time during development.

2. *Dosage matters.* Exposure to a large amount of a teratogen can have more of an effect than exposure to a small amount. For instance, if a fetus is malnourished

Learn It Together

Assess the Risks of Teratogens

Alma is pregnant and planning to attend her best friend's wedding. She wonders if it is safe to have a glass of wine at the reception. Using the concepts of timing and dosage, what advice would you give her?

Plan Review the concepts of teratogens, including the importance of timing and dosage, and the timeline of prenatal development.

Engage In a small group of classmates, imagine Alma's scenario above and add some important details: Determine how far along she is in her pregnancy and how much she might drink at the wedding. How do the timing and dosage (amount of alcohol) affect your advice to her?

Reflect What was it like trying to think about applying scientific knowledge to a real-life scenario? What factors might complicate a person's decision to follow scientific advice?

birth defects Major abnormalities in the body or brain functioning present at birth.

teratogens Factors in a parent's body or the environment that damage the fetus.

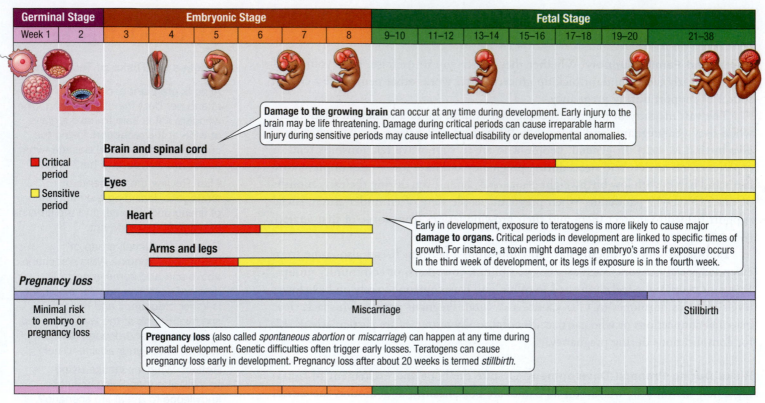

Germinal Stage		Embryonic Stage						Fetal Stage						
Week 1	2	3	4	5	6	7	8	9–10	11–12	13–14	15–16	17–18	19–20	21–38

Damage to the growing brain can occur at any time during development. Early injury to the brain may be life threatening. Damage during critical periods can cause irreparable harm Injury during sensitive periods may cause intellectual disability or developmental anomalies.

Brain and spinal cord

■ Critical period

□ Sensitive period

Eyes

Heart

Arms and legs

Early in development, exposure to teratogens is more likely to cause major **damage to organs.** Critical periods in development are linked to specific times of growth. For instance, a toxin might damage an embryo's arms if exposure occurs in the third week of development, or its legs if exposure is in the fourth week.

Pregnancy loss

Minimal risk to embryo or pregnancy loss

Miscarriage

Stillbirth

Pregnancy loss (also called *spontaneous abortion* or *miscarriage*) can happen at any time during prenatal development. Genetic difficulties often trigger early losses. Teratogens can cause pregnancy loss early in development. Pregnancy loss after about 20 weeks is termed *stillbirth*.

FIGURE 3.7 Timing Matters. Risks in early development can lead to pregnancy loss or to damage to the developing fetus. Early in development, critical periods are times when damage may not be reversible. Sensitive periods are times when development is particularly affected by the environment.

for a few days while its parent suffers from a terrible bout of morning sickness, the outcome is much less severe than if its parent suffers from significant malnutrition throughout the pregnancy (Inselman & Slikker, 2018).

3. *Individual variations make predictions difficult.* Fetuses or parents often have genetic differences that may alter the power of a teratogen (Graham, 2018). For instance, some fetuses may be more sensitive to alcohol exposure than others. Dizygotic twins (who share only about half of their genes), exposed to the same environment in uterus, do not always develop the same developmental and neurological problems because of their parent's alcohol use (Lambert, 2016).

4. *Both parents' health matters.* While the pregnant parent's health is particularly critical during the prenatal period, the biological father's health, substance use, or exposure to environmental toxins can damage sperm in ways that can be passed on to children. The psychological health of the partner is a crucial part of the pregnant parent's emotional support system (Day et al., 2016; Darwin et al., 2021).

5. *Teratogens interact in unexpected ways.* Many fetuses are exposed to multiple teratogens, which may multiply risks. For instance, a recent study of the effects of air pollution on fetal development showed that the danger caused by a pregnant parent's exposure was magnified if they had other stressors, such as living far away from social support (X. Liu et al., 2018).

Sources of Danger Around the world, some of the most common dangers for fetuses and pregnant parents come from diseases and environmental pollutants. Infectious diseases like malaria and HIV are a major cause of early birth and low birthweight around the world, with malaria the biggest cause of newborn mortality (Romero et al., 2014). Immune system changes during pregnancy make pregnant people particularly susceptible to diseases, like COVID-19, that can then be passed on to their fetuses (Chinn et al., 2021; Stock et al., 2022).

Environmental toxins in food, air, and water can harm the developing fetus and lead to miscarriage, developmental delays, or diseases. Contaminated drinking water

Share It!

Talk about risks during pregnancy without blaming parents. Expectant parents often explain that they want to hear the science, but providers need to be careful to provide humility, empathy, and respect.

(Christenson et al., 2019)

everywhere, from Bangladesh to Appalachia, and toxic fertilizers in Florida and Ecuador, invisibly poison developing embryos (Gómez-Roig et al., 2021).

Chronic and often unavoidable health conditions also may harm the health of a fetus and their parent. In many wealthy countries, researchers believe that a larger body size is a leading contributor to preterm birth and prenatal difficulties (Marchi et al., 2015). Scientists believe that too much weight can trigger inflammation and difficulties with processing sugar, which prevent the placenta from functioning as well as it should. In the end, this can lead to a higher risk for early birth and health problems later in life for the fetus. Body size is also linked to increased risk for the pregnant parent's own health, potentially doubling the risk of death during pregnancy (Catalano & Shankar, 2017; Saucedo et al., 2021; Simon et al., 2020). Other health concerns, such as high blood pressure and diabetes, are also linked to health complications for the pregnant parent and increase risk of developmental disabilities, prematurity, and high birth-weight in the newborn (Sanchez et al., 2018).

Larger body sizes are stigmatized, particularly during pregnancy (Hill & Rodriguez, 2020). As a result, conversations about weight can be awkward, even shaming and hurtful (Christenson et al., 2019; Nikolopoulos et al., 2017). Conversations about pregnancy risk often devolve into "blaming" parents, when many of these problems are linked to systemic issues like discrimination, unequal access to resources, and social status, rather than individual choices (Scott et al., 2019). In addition, healthy weight is difficult to measure during pregnancy: Scientists are developing interventions to address the risks caused by discrimination related to weight to help pregnant people protect their health, and help health care providers treat some of the risky conditions associated with larger body size (Hill, 2021; Incollingo Rodriguez et al., 2019; Saucedo et al., 2020).

Alcohol and Substances Developmental scientists have known for generations that many medications and substances, including alcohol, marijuana, nicotine, and other psychoactive drugs, can be dangerous for fetal development. Pregnant parents are advised to consult with their health care providers about any prescription and over-the-counter medication they consume, and to stop using any recreational substances. As a result, more adults abstain from drugs and alcohol during pregnancy than at any other point in the lifespan. About 8 in 10 people in the United States who use substances stop when they find out that they are pregnant (Kar et al., 2021). Stigma and criminalization of substance abuse often make families hesitant to discuss substance use with their medical providers, which can keep them from getting treatment or understanding their risks (Frazer et al., 2019).

Prenatal exposure to alcohol is linked to a cluster of disabilities called *fetal alcohol spectrum disorder (FASD)*, the most common preventable developmental disorder in the world (McQuire et al., 2020). Almost 5 in every 100 first-graders in the United States have impairments caused by fetal alcohol exposure (May et al., 2018). With large-scale studies demonstrating that even one alcoholic drink a day can triple the risk of FASD, many researchers believe that no amount of alcohol is "guaranteed to be 100% safe" (Williams et al., 2015). Stigma against FASD often keeps it from being diagnosed, but treatment and support can help reduce the symptoms, which can include learning difficulties, speech delays, and impulsive behavior (Popova et al., 2017).

Exposure to nicotine during pregnancy causes premature births, infant deaths, and prenatal birth complications around the world (Lange et al., 2018). In the United States, about 1 in 14 pregnant parents smokes cigarettes or vapes during pregnancy (Azagba et al., 2020; B. Liu et al., 2021). Nicotine is dangerous during pregnancy regardless of how you ingest it. vape pens can be nearly as dangerous to a developing fetus as a pack of cigarettes (Taylor et al., 2021).

About 1 in 20 parents uses recreational drugs while pregnant. Like many prescription medications, recreational drugs are not safe during pregnancy, and they

Anna Gorman/Kaiser Health News

Thriving After Pregnancy High blood pressure is a common complication during pregnancy and can endanger the lives of pregnant parents and their fetuses. Lara developed dangerously high blood pressure while she was pregnant with her son, Zion, and now needs to monitor her health while she's chasing her toddler around her home in California.

Love Helps. Getting help for substance abuse can be difficult during pregnancy. With support from her family, Jennifer was able to find treatment in St. Louis, Missouri, that helped her deliver a healthy baby girl, Rikki Lynn, and continue her recovery.

A Shared Stress Millions of families experienced the uncertainty and stress of pregnancy during a global pandemic, including this woman in Hong Kong. While exposure to viruses, including COVID-19, can be dangerous to pregnant people and their fetuses, social support can help build resilience.

stress The feeling of being overwhelmed.

can cause complications in pregnancy and long-term challenges in newborns. Even if babies exposed to substances prenatally look healthy, they are more likely to develop psychological or learning disorders later in life (Corsi et al., 2020). About 5 percent of parents in the United States report that they have used marijuana during their pregnancy to soothe anxiety or to manage morning sickness (Ko et al., 2020). Researchers have connected the use of marijuana to stillbirth, preterm birth, and long-term neurological and emotional problems, including difficulties with learning and attention (Kharbanda et al., 2020; Paul et al., 2021).

Sadness and Worry Most families seem to manage the daily hassles and report that they are happy during their pregnancies (DiPietro et al., 2015). But about one in four pregnant people reports feeling depressed, anxious, or overwhelmed by stress: rates that have only grown after the disruptions of the COVID-19 pandemic (Gustafsson et al., 2021; Van den Bergh et al., 2018). Expectant parents who are depressed or anxious may not be taking care of themselves, adding emotional difficulties to poor nutrition, lack of physical activity, and limited social support. As a result, researchers have found that depression or anxiety can increase the likelihood of having a baby who is low birthweight, is born prematurely, or has a higher risk of emotional problems in childhood (Borchers et al., 2021; Ghimire et al., 2021).

Partners also experience mental health problems that can impact their ability to provide emotional support and adjust to parenting. As many as one in four partners is also anxious or depressed during their partner's pregnancy (Darwin et al., 2021). If one partner has depression or anxiety, it makes it hard to support their pregnant partner, making the transition to parenthood more difficult (Pinto et al., 2020). Nevertheless, partners are often left out of the screening and intervention processes (Mayers et al., 2020).

Most studies of the mental health of families during pregnancy have focused on expectant women and their male partners rather than on same-sex, gender-diverse, or transgender couples, but the studies that have investigated same-sex couples during pregnancy have found that, like other couples, they sometimes have emotional problems. However, on top of the typical pregnancy-related stresses, gender-diverse and other-sex couples must also manage additional stigma and discrimination because of their identity (Pollitt et al., 2020).

Stress is the feeling of being overwhelmed and comes in two forms. *Chronic stress* is nonstop and occurs over a long time, such as the worry about not having enough money to pay the bills. *Episodic stress* is typically caused by a single event, as in the trauma of a death, natural disaster, or an act of violence. Like many expecting parents, Alizah and Spencer juggled multiple sources of stress during pregnancy, from worries about the pandemic to hassles with work. They even stressed about the effects of stress on the developing fetus.

Pregnant people tend to be more stressed during pregnancy because of the social and emotional changes that come with a new role, and because their bodies are particularly sensitive to stress hormones while they are carrying a fetus. The placenta creates extra stress hormones that enter the parent's body and may increase feelings of being overwhelmed (A. C. D. Cheadle et al., 2020).

A fetus exposed to *too much* stress in the uterus has a higher risk for developing problems with attention and impulsivity (Graham et al., 2019; Van den Bergh et al., 2020). On the other hand, researchers believe that *moderate* amounts of stress may actually be good for the developing brain. Moderate stress is part of a healthy, active lifestyle and will help the fetus develop a mature stress-response system to adjust to a world with everyday annoyances (DiPietro, 2015). No one can tell for sure what impact Alizah's long days teaching on Zoom had on her pregnancy: For her baby's sake, she hopes that they were manageable enough.

Chronic stressors like financial insecurity, family conflict, and racism take a much greater toll on pregnant people. Researchers link them to higher rates of preterm birth and lower birthweight (Davis, 2019). Scientists speculate that the long-term effects of racial discrimination may be a significant factor in why people who suffer discrimination, like Black American women, have a 50 percent higher rate of premature birth than White women (F. M. Jackson et al., 2020). As you'll read, this is one reason for significant income and ethnic disparities in the numbers of newborns who are born prematurely or die after birth in the United States.

Support Works. One way of helping families cope with pregnancy and childbirth is to provide them with extra support. Claire Littleton (center) benefited from the presence and expertise of her doula, Clara Sharpe (left), as she prepared for the birth of her baby.

MAKING A DIFFERENCE
Protecting Pregnant Parents from Prejudice

Kim didn't think she had any risk factors for premature birth or birth complications when she was pregnant. She had taken care of herself during her pregnancy. She was a successful lawyer working on a case she wanted to wrap up before going on leave. But her daughter had other plans: Kim went into labor unexpectedly three months before her due date. Danielle arrived weighing just 2 pounds (Adelman, 2008).

Kim had only one risk factor for pregnancy complications, but it was an important one: racism. Scientists have found that the ongoing stress of discrimination experienced by pregnant Black parents like Kim increases their risk for complications and premature birth, regardless of their education or income (Johnson et al., 2020; Slaughter-Acey et al., 2019). There are similarly high risks for other groups, including Native Americans, who experience prejudice (Janevic et al., 2017).

As Samantha, a Black mother who lost two children to premature birth, explained: "Stress leads to labor. And African American women lead a more stressful life, and so we hit preterm birth at an alarming rate" (Chatterjee & Davis, 2017). Researchers are trying to better understand how to prevent preterm births in Black parents and other groups. Currently, experts recommend that parents at risk get appropriate prenatal medical care and lots of social support, such as that provided by prenatal groups or doulas (Byerley & Haas, 2017; Kozhimannil et al., 2016; Mazzoni & Carter, 2017). Advocates and health care providers are working to reduce systemic racism and inequity in the medical system to ensure that all parents receive the best medical care they can (Scott et al., 2019). Kim hopes that her own daughter, who attended medical school, will have a chance to experience birth without the risks she endured (California Newsreel, 2008).

Missing a Brother Chrissy and her husband were expecting twins, but one of them was stillborn at just 25 weeks. Their surviving son, Cassius, was born prematurely but is now thriving. Chrissy and her husband worry that racism played a part in her health care, preventing her from getting the attention she needed to save the son she lost, whom she named Apollo. Black infants face a higher likelihood of being stillborn or arriving prematurely: Black mothers in the United States are also more likely to lose their lives during pregnancy.

APPLY IT! **3.3** Alizah and Spencer, like many expecting parents, were emotionally attached to their fetus even before birth. They gave it a pet name, and Spencer sang to it. How does prenatal experience help fetuses prepare for life after birth?

3.4 Alizah learned that she was pregnant about four weeks after conception. What can you tell Spencer and Alizah about how large the embryo was?

3.5 Alizah and Spencer worry that talking about all the things that could go wrong during a pregnancy leads parents to blame themselves and feel guilty before their baby is even born. This is a common concern. What could you tell expectant parents about the protective factors that can help make fetuses more resilient?

Birth and the Newborn

Learning Objectives

3.6 Explain the process of vaginal childbirth and its common risks and protective factors.

3.7 Explain how newborns' senses and capabilities help them thrive.

Birth is a major social and biological transition for fetuses and their families. For Alizah and Spencer, childbirth started with a remarkable sunset, a check-in with a midwife and a night of contractions and pushing. Whether it happens vaginally or surgically, delivering a baby is called *labor*, in recognition of the hard, physical work that must happen before the baby is born.

The Stages of Vaginal Childbirth

Vaginal childbirth starts when a chemical signal released by the mature fetus's lungs signals the body to begin contractions (Menon, 2019). Labor is not over when the baby is delivered. The final stage occurs *after* birth, with the delivery of the placenta that

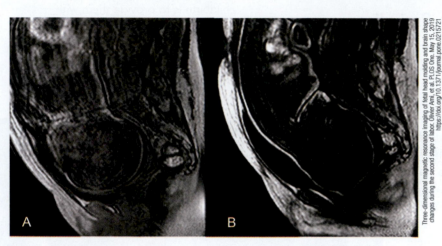

Three-dimensional magnetic resonance imaging of fetal head molding and brain shape changes during the second stage of labor. Oliver Ami, et al. PLOS One. May 15, 2019 https://doi.org/10.1371/journal.pone.0215721

has been helping to support the fetus. How long does labor take? After reviewing the typical progress of labor in thousands of women from Japan, China, Nigeria, Uganda, and the United States, researchers found that a healthy labor may progress very slowly—as long as 20 or even 30 hours (Oladapo et al., 2018).

Contractions are painful for the pregnant parent, but the fetus's journey is also dramatic. As you can see in the MRI images, fetuses' brains are compressed during a vaginal delivery as they squeeze through the cervix (Ami et al., 2019). Fetuses are shocked by a rush of hormones that mature their lungs and immune system to prepare the baby to breathe independently (Morton & Brodsky, 2016).

What a Body Can Do Amazingly, a pregnant French parent agreed to give birth in an MRI scanner. This allowed researchers to observe the transition of childbirth, including the impressive, and temporary, way the skull and brain is distorted during the final stages of childbirth.

Cultural and Social Support During Childbirth

Childbirth is an important social and cultural event. For first-time parents, it marks the beginning of parenthood. For the baby, it marks the beginning of relationships with family and community. Many cultures designate childbirth as a special, even spiritual event. In the past, when babies weren't delivered in medical facilities, some communities created a secluded, private place for childbirth. Whether a room or a hut, separate spaces gave laboring families a break from normal activities and a chance to focus on birth and recovery without the distractions of other responsibilities (DiTomasso, 2019; Sharma et al., 2016).

Around the world, as childbirth has become safer, it has become more medicalized. But cultural beliefs about what is appropriate during childbirth remain powerful. Families often want to bring their children into the world in a way that respects their traditions (Benza & Liamoputtong, 2014). Within the United States, there are many cultural variations in what families expect, how they understand labor pain, and what kind of pain relief they receive.

SelectStock/E+/Getty Images

Well-Earned Rest What does a newborn look like? A lot like this little one, resting after the journey along with their mother.

One critical part of supporting and respecting parents during labor is allowing them to have someone with them as they labor. *Continuous support* may be provided by a partner, a family member, or a paid *doula*, or birthing assistant, all of whom provide comfort and encouragement. This leads to improved health outcomes, including shortened delivery times, improvements to the newborn's health, and reduced rates of cesarean sections by as much as 20 percent (Bohren et al., 2015; Stjernholm et al., 2021). Alizah benefited from having the constant support of Spencer, along with her mother and a midwife, while she labored in the middle of the night to birth their son.

SCIENCE IN PRACTICE
Nicolle Gonzales, Certified Nurse Midwife

Nicolle Gonzales grew up on and near the Diné (also known as the Navajo) reservation in New Mexico, where she now delivers babies as a midwife. The landscape that has nurtured Nicolle since she was born is beautiful, but it hides a great deal of pain. The legacy of discrimination and inequality means that Indigenous women are over 200 percent less likely than White American women to get prenatal care and twice as likely to die after childbirth (CDC, 2021b; Petersen et al., 2019).

Gonzalez knows firsthand why many Diné women might not feel at home in a traditional medical environment. Gonzalez experienced difficulties herself during her first childbirth, which she describes as "traumatic": Her provider wouldn't answer her questions, and she was afraid she was going to die of blood loss (van Gelder, 2017). Like Gonzalez, one in six pregnant people in a recent survey complained that they felt ignored or mistreated during their labor (Vedam et al., 2019). As a result of her experiences, Gonzalez has a unique connection with her clients. As she explains, "I feel like when I visit with them one-on-one in midwifery, there's this connection because I do understand where they are coming from" (Gupta, 2015).

Gonzalez wants Indigenous women to have a role in their own prenatal care and childbirth. So, she researched traditional birthing practices and ceremonies and is working to empower Indigenous families to give birth in a way that represents their communities. Her vision is to help women feel comfortable and supported, and to get the care they need to start their families with joy and with the customs that mark the beginning of life.

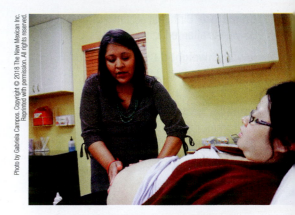

How Babies Enter the World Matters. Nicolle Gonzalez tries to provide expectant families with connections and support that will help them have healthier deliveries, babies, and lives.

Medical Support During Childbirth

Medical interventions during childbirth can help save the lives of laboring people and their newborns and alleviate the discomfort from hours of contractions. More than 800 parents and 2,700 newborns die each day during childbirth (UNICEF, 2020; WHO, 2018c). Medical help can manage expectant parents' risk of infection, bleeding, and stroke and prevent the risk that a baby will die during delivery or as a result of being born sick or preterm (UNICEF, 2019; WHO, 2019b).

Like many parents around the world, Alizah was able to give birth vaginally with the assistance of an experienced midwife. Not all parents give birth this way. Many need to give birth by **cesarean section**, or *c-section*. One of the oldest kinds of surgery, a cesarean section involves removing the baby from the body through a small cut in the uterus. In many cases, a cesarean section saves the life of an expectant parent or newborn. Nonetheless, medical professionals are concerned that it may be performed too often (Molina et al., 2015; Ye et al., 2014). Parents have a lengthier recovery time after a cesarean and a higher risk of infection and re-hospitalization.

Labor is often extremely painful, and some medical options for pain relief can be highly effective (Anim-Somuah et al., 2018; DiTomasso, 2019). Laboring people may also get relief from nonmedical approaches such as warm showers and gentle exercise (Henrique et al., 2018). In low-income countries around the world, many labor without medication, often without other measures to assuage their discomfort, like a partner or other support person (Bohren et al., 2015; Karn et al., 2016). Alizah was grateful that she not only delivered a healthy baby, she also benefited from the coaching of her mother, Spencer, and her midwife, as well as a warm bath during her hours of hard pushing. Courage was born at about 5:30 A.M.

Vulnerable Newborns

A baby's birth day is the most dangerous day in its life. More than 2 million babies around the world and more than 13,000 each year in the United States are born dead,

cesarean section A surgical birth procedure in which the baby is removed from the body through a small cut in the uterus.

premature Birth that occurs less than 35 weeks after fertilization.

low birthweight (LBW) Babies born weighing less than 2,500 grams (about 5½ pounds).

small for gestational age (SGA) Babies born smaller than expected for their level of development.

or *stillborn*, either because they do not survive childbirth or because they perished before labor began (Hoyert & Gregory, 2020; Peven et al., 2021). In the United States, about 15,000 newborns die every year (Ely & Driscoll, 2020).

More than 13 million babies are born **premature**, or less than 35 weeks after fertilization (Chawanpaiboon et al., 2019). Many of these babies, and others who are born after 35 weeks, are among the 20 million who are **low birthweight** (**LBW**), or below 2,500 grams (about 5½ pounds; Lee et al., 2022). Some babies, whether they are born at full term or prematurely, are considered **small for gestational age** (**SGA**), or smaller than expected for their level of development (Finken et al., 2018). Prematurity, LBW, and being SGA can cause immediate and long-term health crises for newborns.

Risk Factors Around the world, most babies are at risk for being premature, LBW, or SGA because their parent developed an infectious disease or has other health conditions (Chawanpaiboon et al., 2019). Some babies face challenges associated with difficulties such as a lack of oxygen, or *anoxia*, during labor (Gillam-Krakauer & Gowen, 2020). All of these risks are more common in low-income families, who tend to have poorer health due to limited access to medical care, segregated and inadequate housing and nutrition, and other unmet needs (Beck et al., 2020). (See **Figure 3.8**.)

The vast majority, or 9 out of 10, of babies born premature or LBW catch up to their peers. But some infants, particularly if they are born *very* early or *very* small, often experience long-lasting effects if they survive, including difficulties with physical coordination, learning, hearing, and vision (Bell et al., 2022; Wolke et al., 2019). Researchers suspect that a combination of genetic vulnerability plus the stresses of early birth puts these children at risk (Thomason et al., 2017).

Researchers have developed innovative treatments to help preterm and LBW babies survive. However, these lifesaving processes are often painful and stressful, with infants subjected to frequent blood draws, disrupted sleep, and separation from their families (Nist et al., 2019). Interventions designed to limit these infants' stress have helped improve their outcomes. One model program integrates families into the day-to-day care of their fragile infants by letting parents hold, soothe, and breastfeed them whenever possible (Franck & O'Brien, 2019). These practices result in immediate improvements, including faster brain maturation (Volpe, 2019).

FIGURE 3.8 Inequity in Loss Losing a baby or worrying about one born with LBW are concerns that are not shared equally. This chart shows the rate of early newborn death (in the first 28 days) and LBW in the United States for every 1,000 babies born. Risks are higher for groups that experience discrimination and lower for those whose families benefit from status, including college education.

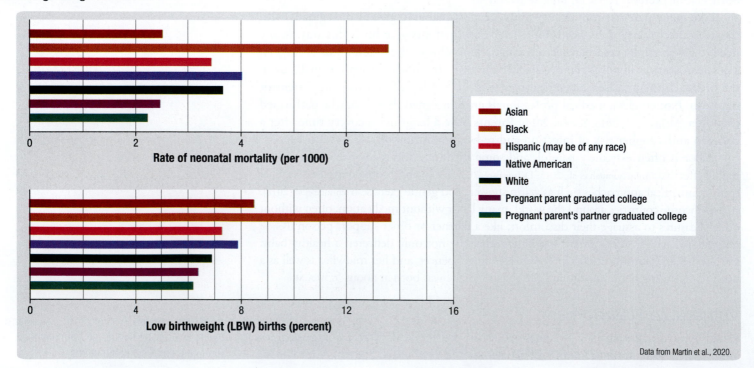

Data from Martin et al., 2020.

Although babies around the world do not always have access to high-quality care, they can all benefit from a low-tech intervention that improves LBW babies' chances of survival by more than a third. A particular form of skin-to-skin contact, called **kangaroo care**, involves continuously holding a lightly clothed newborn against a caregiver's naked chest (Boundy et al., 2016). Premature babies who receive kangaroo care have lower levels of stress hormones and accelerated brain development compared with babies who are cared for in incubators, regardless of where they are born (Wang et al., 2021). Kangaroo care has been shown to reduce infant mortality, improve parent–child relationships, and accelerate growth (Gill et al., 2021).

Meet the Newborn

Newborns aren't always cute. After a compressed journey through the cervix and vagina, they often look misshapen. They may be covered with *vernix caseosa*, a whitish layer of a waxy substance that protects the baby's skin in the uterus (Nishijima et al., 2019). Their head might seem overly large; they have hair in places you wouldn't expect—like on the tops of their shoulders—and their genitals may be swollen because of exposure to hormones during delivery. Although it may take a few weeks for newborns to grow more handsome, they come equipped with senses and social skills for their new life.

Scoring the Newborn Whether a baby is born at 23 weeks or at 41, most newborns are given an **Apgar test** immediately after birth and again five minutes later. The Apgar test is a quick medical evaluation of a newborn's breathing, activity, responsiveness, and heart rate that assesses which babies need immediate medical care (Rüdiger & Rozycki, 2020). Most healthy babies, like Courage, score 7 or higher. Babies with scores of 5 or lower are at higher risk for medical complications and may need intensive interventions.

Sensing and Moving Courage, like all babies, was born with several skills that helped him survive and thrive in the outside world. Some of these are *reflexes*, like breathing or eye blinking. Others are patterns of moving and sensing the environment. Remember that fetuses are developing all of their senses in the uterus, though they haven't practiced using them in the real world. But their senses are developed enough to help them recognize and create connections with their caregivers.

The development of fetal eye structures ends at birth, but their brains are still developing. Typical newborn vision is usually a blurry 20/400; what they see at about 20 feet away is as hazy as what an adult with good vision would see 400 feet away (Goldstein & Cacciamani, 2021). At birth, anything farther than about 10 inches is blurry to a typical newborn (Clark-Gambelunghe & Clark, 2015). Nevertheless, 10 inches is the right distance for a newborn to make out a caregiver's face, which means that despite their blurry vision, newborns can recognize that something is a face. In fact, they prefer to look at faces more than anything else (Buiatti et al., 2019). By the end of his first day of life, Courage could see his mother, grandmother, and his father and tell them apart.

Similarly, although the world becomes much quieter as newborns leave the uterus, they can already recognize the familiar voices of their caregivers as well as the characteristic sounds of the languages they speak (Moon, 2017). Alizah and Spencer are sure Courage recognized the songs they sang to him before he was born. Newborns also recognize the scent of their parents' breasts, which may smell like the amniotic fluid that they remember from inside the uterus. Scientists believe that this may help newborns orient themselves so they can nurse (Hym et al., 2021). Babies' sense of taste is closely linked to smell. Newborns recognize the flavors of breast milk and amniotic fluid, which stimulates their appetite (Muelbert et al., 2021).

A Father's Heart Sometimes low-technology solutions are the most effective. In a hospital in Colombia, Cesar holds his son, who was born prematurely, against his naked chest, providing him with warmth and calming them both as they adjust to life together.

Scientific American Profile

Becoming a Family

kangaroo care A form of skin-to-skin contact that involves holding a lightly clothed newborn against a caregiver's chest.

Apgar test A quick medical evaluation of breathing, activity, responsiveness, and heart rate that assesses which newborns need immediate medical care.

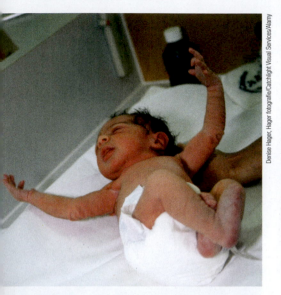

Designed to Thrive from the Beginning
In the first minutes of life, infants demonstrate developmental reflexes such as the Moro reflex, in which arms swing out, and the rooting reflex, in which a baby spontaneously turns and sucks something (like their own hand) that touches their cheek.

If you have ever watched an infant get their first shots, you likely agree that newborns feel pain. Newborns are more sensitive to pain and to other bodily sensations like skin-to-skin contact or massage than adults or older children are (Perry et al., 2018). Brief painful experiences like a shot do not seem to have any ill effects. However, researchers worry about the long-term effect of pain on newborns, such as premature babies who must undergo multiple uncomfortable procedures (Walker, 2019).

Many early movements are not under the baby's control. Most fetuses develop **reflexes**, automatic motor responses to stimuli to help them adjust to the world. These are processed in the parts of the nervous system that are the earliest to develop—the spinal cord and subcortical brain structures (Futagi et al., 2012). (Developmental reflexes are different from deep tendon reflexes, like the one in your knee, that exist lifelong.) Most developmental reflexes gradually disappear as brain maturation enables infants to have more control over their body.

Medical providers often evaluate a newborn's reflexes to make sure that their nervous system is developing as expected (see **Table 3.2**; Salandy et al., 2019). Some reflexes help a newborn learn to nurse. In the *rooting reflex*, the baby automatically turns toward a touch on the cheek, like the brush of a hand or a nipple, and opens their mouth. Others seem designed to help the baby grab on to a caregiver. In the *Moro reflex*, a baby will move their arms forward when they feel that they are falling, as if they are trying to keep from tumbling down. In the *grasping reflex*, a baby's toes or hands will curl in to automatically grab anything close to them.

Building New Relationships As you just read, newborns are responsive to the people around them. The bodies of newborns and their parents are designed to make it easier to form new relationships and even, as Spencer described it, "to be so full of gratitude."

After birth, babies are undergoing brain and hormonal changes that enable bonding. Though newborns have elevated levels of stress hormones after the birth experience, the hormone *vasopressin* helps them manage the stress of birth and also bond with their families (Evers & Wellmann, 2016). *Oxytocin* is another hormone that increases in infants during the birth process and is critical in forming social relationships, making them feel connected and loved (Kingsbury & Bilbo, 2019).

TABLE 3.2 Developmental Reflexes

Rooting reflex	If a newborn's cheek is touched, they will turn their head and open their mouth in preparation for nursing. Disappears by 2–3 months.
Moro reflex	If a newborn feels as if they are falling, their arms will swing in and out suddenly. Disappears by 5–6 months.
Palmar grasp	If you press a newborn's palm, their fingers will curl in. Disappears by 5–6 months.
Plantar grasp	If you press the sole of a newborn's foot, their toes will curl in. Disappears by 9–10 months.
Babinski reflex	If you run your finger along the sole of a newborn's foot, their toes will fan out. Disappears by 12–24 months.

reflexes Automatic motor responses to stimuli that help babies adjust to the world.

Women who are biological parents also experience a surge in oxytocin during and after birth (Olza-Fernández et al., 2014). Men who are biological parents experience hormonal changes as well, including a decline in testosterone and an increase in oxytocin (Diaz-Rojas et al., 2021; Gettler et al., 2021). Other caregivers, whether they are biologically related or not, as in adoptive or same-sex families, also experience elevated oxytocin levels (Abraham & Feldman, 2018; Bakermans-Kranenberg et al., 2019). More than 1 in 10 families is created through **adoption**. Even if adoptive parents do not meet their babies until after they appeared in the delivery room, they experience some of the same hormonal and brain changes of biological parenthood (Goldberg et al., 2013; Kreider & Lofquist, 2014).

Caregivers' brains continue to adapt after they have a newborn: They show stronger connections in brain areas connected to empathy and understanding others (Shimon-Raz et al., 2021). These connections help parents regulate their emotions as they face the new stresses of parenthood (Rutherford et al., 2020). As many as one in five new parents experiences depression, anxiety, or another *perinatal emotional disorder* after having a newborn, which can impact their functioning (Howard & Khalifeh, 2020; Philpott et al., 2020). Interventions such as family psychotherapy or medication help new parents adjust (Deligiannidis et al., 2021; O'Hara & Engeldinger, 2018).

Newborns arrive in the world after remarkable growth guided by the genes they inherited and their experiences in the womb. They are now ready to learn about the world and form relationships that will guide them through their lifetime.

 3.6 Alizah and Spencer were afraid of being separated during the birth because of restrictions imposed by the COVID-19 pandemic. Their midwife made sure that they could stay together, safely, during labor and delivery. Explain how social support gives laboring families the extra strength they need to be resilient through the biological transition of birth.

3.7 Much of the science of childbirth concerns worries about what might go wrong. Can you list three practices that help things go right?

New Beginnings Families do not always begin in the hospital. For this family, legal recognition started in a Massachusetts Courtroom, when a judge declared little Alexandra to officially be her parents' daughter.

adoption When a parent becomes a legal caregiver to a baby or child who is born to another biological parent.

Wrapping It Up

LO 3.1 Define key components of human genetics. (p. 64)

The genome includes every instruction a cell might need to create and maintain your body. These instructions are located in 46 chromosomes, each of which is made up of a helix-shaped ladder of chemicals called deoxyribonucleic acid (DNA). Genes are sections of DNA that create particular proteins and have different forms, called alleles. Genes are expressed at different times because of maturation, aging, and environmental triggers. The epigenome controls genetic expression.

LO 3.2 Explain basic principles of genetic transmission of traits. (p. 64)

Some traits and diseases can be inherited. A few disorders and traits are single-gene disorders. Some are recessive disorders, when a child must inherit the two copies of the disease-carrying allele for the disorder to be expressed. Most traits and genes are polygenetic and multifactorial and are linked to numerous individual genes and environmental factors. The genome establishes a continuum of traits, but the environment can change how genes are expressed. Your genetic makeup also influences the environment you find yourself in. Genes help determine how susceptible you are to being changed by the context.

LO 3.3 Explain how the environment can affect gene expression through the epigenome. (p. 64)

The epigenome controls which genes are expressed by changing epigenetic marks. Some epigenetic marks are inherited; others are created later in the lifespan. Twins are an illustration of the impact of epigenetics on development. Monozygotic twins have nearly identical DNA, but epigenetic changes make their genetic expression different. Dizygotic twins develop when two (or more) ova are released, and they are fertilized by separate sperm. Dizygotic twins typically share only about half of their genome.

LO 3.4 Describe the key stages of prenatal development. (p. 74)

New life involves the joining of an ovum, or egg cell, with a sperm cell. This creates a new human cell with 46 chromosomes in 23 pairs, known as a zygote. During the germinal stage, the single-celled zygote divides and implants into the uterus in the first week of development. Support structures include the amniotic sac, the placenta, and the umbilical cord. In the embryonic stage, the embryo develops the major organ systems and limbs, and the brain begins to develop. In the fetal stage, the fetus adds pounds and matures the organs and brain structures that will allow it to survive on its own. Fetuses are surprisingly capable before they are born. The prenatal period allows the fetus to practice skills, including sensing and moving, that will allow them to adapt to the world.

LO 3.5 Describe the principles of prenatal risk and resilience. (p. 74)

The context of prenatal development, including experiences of stress, disease, and environmental hazards, has an impact on fetal health. Supportive factors include prenatal care and social support. Risk factors, often called teratogens, can lead to atypical birth outcomes. Teratogens can include diseases; substances including medications, alcohol, or recreational drugs; and health conditions such as high blood pressure. Stress and depression in expectant parents can also affect the development of the fetus.

LO 3.6 Explain the process of vaginal childbirth and its common risks and protective factors. (p. 88)

Birth is a major social and biological transition. A healthy labor could take 20 or even 30 hours and can happen vaginally or through a cesarean section. Medical interventions can save the lives of pregnant people and their newborns. Some babies are born premature, or less than 35 weeks after fertilization. Some are also low birthweight (LBW), or below 2,500 grams (about 5½ pounds). Others are considered small for gestational age (SGA). Risk factors include poor health during pregnancy and trauma during childbirth itself.

LO 3.7 Describe how newborns' senses and capabilities help them thrive. (p. 88)

Newborns arrive with senses and reflexes that help them adjust to the world. They can see just as far as the face of the person holding them. They are especially attuned to faces and can hear and identify familiar voices. At birth, babies have limited control over their movement and rely on reflexes. Both new babies and their caregivers experience a rush of hormones that help them bond with each other.

KEY TERMS

genome (p. 64)

chromosomes (p. 64)

deoxyribonucleic acid (DNA) (p. 64)

mitosis (p. 64)

genes (p. 64)

alleles (p. 64)

phenotype (p. 66)

genotype (p. 66)

epigenome (p. 66)

ovum (p. 66)

sperm (p. 66)

meiosis (p. 66)

zygote (p. 66)

sex chromosomes (p. 67)

sex (p. 67)

gender (p. 67)

gender identity (p. 67)

gender expression (p. 67)

recessive inheritance pattern (p. 68)

dominant inheritance pattern (p. 69)

polygenic (p. 69)

multifactorial (p. 70)

Down syndrome (p. 71)

monozygotic (p. 72)

dizygotic (p. 73)

germinal stage (p. 74)

embryonic stage (p. 74)

fetal stage (p. 75)

in vitro fertilization (IVF) (p. 76)

blastocyst (p. 77)

placenta (p. 77)

neurons (p. 78)

birth defects (p. 83)

teratogens (p. 83)

stress (p. 86)

cesarean section (p. 89)

premature (p. 90)

low birthweight (LBW) (p. 90)

small for gestational age (SGA) (p. 90)

kangaroo care (p. 91)

Apgar test (p. 91)

reflexes (p. 92)

adoption (p. 93)

CHECK YOUR LEARNING

1. The structure of DNA is often compared to a(n):
   a) skyscraper.
   b) twisted ladder.
   c) almond.
   d) checkerboard.

2. Which of the following statements about the genetic origins of twins is TRUE?
   a) Monozygotic twins are generally conceived from two sperm joining with one ovum.
   b) Dizygotic twins occur after a single sperm and single ovum join into a zygote, which later divides into two distinct balls of cells.
   c) Monozygotic twins occur after a single sperm and single ovum join into a zygote, which later divides into two distinct balls of cells.
   d) Dizygotic twins are the result of two ova merging before conception.

3. Langston has sickle-cell disease, but both his parents are healthy. Which of the following explanations is BEST?
   a) His mother is a carrier, but his father is not.
   b) His father is a carrier, but his mother is not.
   c) Neither of his parents are carriers.
   d) Both of his parents are carriers.

4. Which of the following may contribute to a person's gender?
   a) The pattern of sex chromosomes (X and or Y) inherited from their biological parents
   b) Their body's sensitivity to hormones during prenatal development
   c) Their feelings about their identity
   d) All of the above

5. The chemicals in the epigenome that guide lasting impacts of environmental experiences on gene expression and regulation are known as:
   a) gametes.
   b) epigenetic marks.
   c) chromosomes.
   d) nuclei.

6. What marks the end of the germinal stage in prenatal development?
   a) The blastocyst implants in the wall of the uterus.
   b) The contractions of labor begin the process of childbirth.
   c) The fetal heartbeat is present.
   d) The brain and spinal cord are fully developed.

7. Which of the following statements regarding the senses of a developing fetus is TRUE?
   a) During the third trimester, a fetus is responsive to light, touch, sound, smell, and taste.
   b) Prior to birth, a fetus has no exposure to sounds.
   c) Prior to birth, a fetus has no responsivity to visual stimulation.
   d) Fetuses cannot feel pain.

8. Supportive prenatal care may include all of the following EXCEPT:
   a) social support, like a family member helping out with errands.
   b) a support group, where expectant parents share their experiences with others in their communities.
   c) a strict diet to prevent weight gain.
   d) regular visits with a medical professional to assess the growth of the fetus and health of the mother.

9. A harmful substance or experience that may impact fetal development is known as a(n):
   a) teratogen.
   b) fetal anomaly.
   c) epidural.
   d) fertilization.

10. A newborn's condition is evaluated in the moments after birth in an assessment of their breathing, heart rate, and responsiveness known as the:
    a) newborn IQ.
    b) Apgar.
    c) CPR.
    d) c-section.

Physical Development in Infancy and Toddlerhood

Growing

4.1 Explain factors promoting healthy patterns of growth and development during the first two years.

The Changing Brain

4.2 Explain the role of neurons and synapses in brain function during the first two years.

Sensing and Moving

4.3 Describe vision and hearing development in infancy.

4.4 Explain how the typical maturation of movement changes a baby's experience of the world.

© Macmillan, Photo by Point Studio, Inc.

Sam remembers his son Silas's first months of life as "very, very unicorn." Silas was born 15 weeks before his due date, at just one pound, 15 ounces, so small that his mother, Blaire, could hold him in the palm of her hand. Silas spent more than four months in the hospital before his lungs matured enough for him to go home.

Sam and Blaire greeted Silas each morning, and every evening they held him for hours. In the months they spent by his bedside, they watched him grow into a sturdy, 16-pound baby and grew certain that their son was a fighter and a survivor.

Silas has now been home for more than a year. He can run on the playground, call for his dog, Lemon, and build with blocks. Like many babies born prematurely, Silas still carries marks from his time in the hospital—a scar on his belly from his feeding tube and a pair of bright blue glasses that help give his eyes extra support. But, like other toddlers, he is growing quickly and using his senses to adapt to the world around him.

Throughout Silas's early months, as he learned to move, to eat, and to survive on his own, his family and his care team were guided by developmental science. Empirically based interventions, including skin-to-skin contact with Blair and Sam in the hospital, helped Silas thrive. An understanding of typical development patterns, such as that babies learn to control their core before they are able to walk, helped Silas's family understand what to expect as he grew.

Like many children, Silas's development was not precisely typical. His mother points out that babies, like the rest of us, grow and develop at different rates, exploding at different times just like popcorn kernels on the stove. Science helps caregivers to identify when children may need extra support.

Silas is now a 2-year-old who is nearly too heavy to carry. He has learned how to move, eat peas and pancakes, and sleep through the night. Silas's brain has gotten bigger, too, more than doubling in size and sending signals up to 100 times faster (Johnson & de Haan, 2015; Zhang, Shi, et al., 2019). Silas is now a *toddler*, a term that refers to the wobbly toddling movements of 1- to 3-year-olds.

Silas's development was powered by a nurturing environment that helped him thrive. Like him, infants and toddlers are flexible in how they adapt, whether it is crawling or walking, sleeping through the night or waking up to cuddle, or eating chili peppers or chocolate, depending on the expectations of their families and communities. The first years of life set the foundation for later health and physical development. As you will learn, there are a variety of ways to support babies as they grow.

Scientific American Profile

Meet Silas

Growing

Silas had a lot of medical visits in his first years of life, but each appointment helped his family get the support they needed to make sure he was growing as he should. Pediatricians recommend infants and toddlers get weighed and measured frequently even if they do not have conditions like Silas's, because babies grow more rapidly than at any other point in the lifespan, and their health is more fragile (BrightFutures, 2021).

By their second birthday, most babies nearly triple their birthweight and grow about a foot taller. Although Silas started out much smaller than other children, when his father charted his growth, he found that it followed a curve similar to most children. Most babies are born at around 7 pounds and weigh about 27 pounds by age 2. This trajectory for babies is common as they quickly grow muscle, bone, and brain tissue. Infants' body shape changes, too. It takes a few weeks for newborns to take on the soft, round shape we think of as babyish. Infants get lankier and leaner again around 12 months as they begin moving around (C. L. Brown et al., 2016).

Babies grow up to be adults of different heights, but they are remarkably similar in size for the first two years of life (de Onis, 2017). Genes play a long-term role in height, but they don't make a major difference for infants' size. This is why health workers around the world use the same *growth charts* that track the typical pattern of increase in babies' height and weight (see **Figure 4.1**). If babies are growing too quickly or not quickly enough, usually something in their environment or an illness is the culprit.

Around the globe, about one in five infants experiences **malnutrition**, or does not receive enough food or nutrients to support their growth (WHO et al., 2021). Researchers have found that about 7 percent of children worldwide were so seriously malnourished that they experienced **wasting** (WHO et al., 2021). Children who have growth wasting are below the 5th *percentile* in the ratio of weight to height, or lighter than 95 percent of other children their age and height.

As you can see in **Figure 4.1**, a **percentile** is a way of statistically comparing an individual to a group. Percentile tells you where a person ranks in relation to everyone else in terms of the percent of the group that falls above and below that point. For instance, if a baby's weight is in the 5th percentile for their age, they are heavier than only 5 percent of children (and lighter than 95 percent) of babies their age.

Children can experience growth wasting when they do not have enough food or develop a serious illness. For instance, a typically developing toddler is about 23 pounds (10.5 kg) at 16 months. A child with growth wasting would weigh less than

Learning Objective

4.1 Explain factors promoting healthy patterns of growth and development during the first two years.

malnutrition When someone does not have adequate nutrients to support their growth.

wasting When a child is so seriously malnourished that they are below the 5th percentile in the ratio of weight to height, or lighter for their height than 95 percent of children their age and height.

percentile A way of statistically comparing an individual to a group.

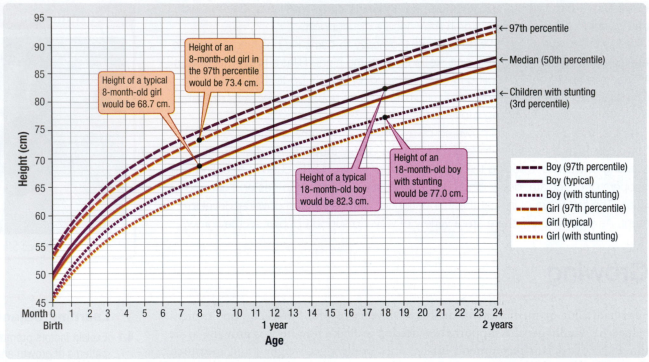

Data from World Health Organization, 2006.

FIGURE 4.1 Understanding the Growth Curve Growth charts help health professionals track individual growth. For instance, a child in 35th or 70th percentile would likely track around that same level at each checkup. Diverging from the percentile might indicate a problem, such as when an infant suddenly drops into the 25th percentile from the 70th percentile.

Checking the Garden In rural Senegal, access to fresh water for drinking and growing plants has made it easier for families to grow healthy food.

stunting When a child's growth has slowed so much that they are significantly shorter than they should be for their age.

interventions Evidence-based programs or services designed to improve health, psychological well-being, or behavior.

18½ pounds (8.5 kg). If babies are malnourished for a long period, they may also experience **stunting**, which means that their growth has slowed so much that they are significantly shorter than they should be for their age, or smaller than 98 percent of all other children (De Onis et al., 2019). For instance, at age 2, a toddler with typical growth might be 31 inches (79 cm) tall, but a toddler with stunting might be just 27 inches (69 cm) tall. About one in five children worldwide shows signs of stunted growth (WHO et al., 2021). In the United States, as in other affluent countries, very few children—fewer than 3 in every 100—develop stunted growth (Fryar et al., 2020a).

Malnutrition affects the brain as well as the body and is likely to lead to learning challenges (McCormick et al., 2020). More than half of the calories that babies take in fuel brain development. As a result, children who are malnourished may experience irregularities in their brain development that may lead to difficulties with learning if they do not receive extra support (Galler et al., 2021).

Prevention begins with improving nutrition during pregnancy and nursing, as well as making sure babies are well-nourished and avoid chronic infections early in life (Bhutta et al., 2020). Public health **interventions**—evidence-based programs or services designed to improve health, psychological well-being, or behavior—have dramatically reduced the rate of malnutrition and helped many children recover. Interventions for nutrition may happen at the population level, as when an entire community benefits from extra nutrients added to milk, or at the individual level, as when one family is offered supplemental vitamins. A generation ago, twice as many children around the world had stunted growth. Today, more children are growing to their full potential (Vaivada et al., 2020).

In the United States and in many other affluent nations, being large is more common than being too small or light (Fryar et al., 2020b). Babies who are heavier for their age and height than most other children, or above the 85th percentile on growth charts, are classified by health care professionals as having **overweight**. In the United States, about one in eight 2-year-olds has overweight (Fryar et al., 2020b).

Toddlers with a larger body size are more likely than their peers to have health difficulties later in life, including a higher rate of asthma, cardiovascular disease, and diabetes (Deal et al., 2020). This is particularly true for babies who were born prematurely and for those who gain weight very quickly in the first six months (Ou-Yang et al., 2020). Experts believe that because of early programming of their metabolism, babies who gain weight very rapidly are less likely to stay at a healthy weight in adulthood (Fall & Kumaran, 2019; Zheng et al., 2018).

At any age, talking about differences in size is difficult (Pesch et al., 2021). People with larger bodies are stigmatized in communities around the world (Puhl et al., 2021). Medical providers must explain to caregivers, without shaming them, that body size is one of many factors influencing children's health. Conversations about body size often trigger feelings of parental guilt, which make it more difficult for families to build positive attitudes about eating (Hagerman et al., 2020).

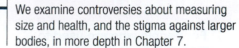

CONNECTIONS
We examine controversies about measuring size and health, and the stigma against larger bodies, in more depth in Chapter 7.

Healthy Nutrition

One of the most common questions parents have for health care providers is what they should be feeding their babies (Lavigne et al., 2017). Early foods vary. In some places, babies are not fed at all for the first days of life. In others, infants may be given special tea, honey, or formula (Chea & Asefa, 2018; O'Neil et al., 2017). Regardless of where they live, all infants must be fed frequently because their small bodies can handle only tiny servings, and they need extra nutrients to fuel their rapid growth.

Human Milk Silas's mother, Blaire, planned to nurse him as soon as he was born, but when he was in the hospital in his early weeks, he received her milk in a bottle. She got up early every morning to pump because both she and Sam believed that human milk would give Silas a healthy start. Developmental science supports this belief: Experts agree that the ideal food for babies from birth until around 6 months is human milk. From about 6 months to 2 years or longer, babies may continue to drink human milk but also begin to eat other foods (Meek & Noble, 2022). Human milk is a complex and living concoction of stem cells, immune-boosting antibodies, immune cells, and disease-fighting proteins that cannot be replicated by even the most advanced commercial formulas (Boquien, 2018).

Nursing Can Be Interesting for Siblings. . . Song Dan (shown here) helps make nursing easier on parents and their babies as a professional lactation consultant near her home in Beijing, China.

In the United States, more than 8 in 10 parents start out nursing, and about 6 and 10 are still nursing at 6 months (NIS, 2021). But producing milk and drinking it is not always easy. More than 8 in 10 nursing parents in high-income countries report difficulties with expressing milk, including difficulties with how a baby latches on, nipple pain, and worries about milk supply (ACOG, 2021). Such difficulties are more common when children have complex health conditions, like Silas, who received his breast milk through a bottle and feeding tube, and extra support to manage nursing may be needed (Hookway et al., 2021). Interventions, like professional lactation support, can make things easier.

Difficulties are also more common for adoptive or transgender parents, who *may* be able to express human milk and nurse but often lack the medical and social support to get started (Paynter, 2019; Trautner et al., 2020). You do not need to identify as

overweight When a child is heavier for their age and height than most other children, or above the 85th percentile.

a woman to produce human milk: With hormonal support, breast tissue in many people can support infant nutrition. This is why some people prefer the less gendered term *chestfeeding* to describe human milk expression (MacDonald, 2019).

CAN YOU BELIEVE IT?

Is Human Milk Magic?

You have probably heard many claims about the benefits of human milk—that it makes children smarter or saves their lives. For many caregivers, especially those who do not identify as women, those who work, and those who have certain physical conditions, expressing milk can be challenging or impossible. Some families may feel judged for not feeding their infants human milk (Penniston et al., 2021). What is the evidence for the benefits of human milk in this sometimes-sensationalized discussion (Jackson et al., 2021)?

Scientists have investigated the benefits of human milk through large observational studies of families, comparing babies who received human milk with those who did not. As you may remember from Chapter 2, these are *correlational studies*, because they look at the correlation, or the relationship, between babies' health and what and how they are fed (Azad et al., 2018). Many of these studies are also *longitudinal*, because they study children's development over time (Pereyra-Elías et al., 2022; Victora et al., 2016).

Correlational studies have found that babies who receive human milk are less likely to die early in life from intestinal or infectious diseases (Christensen et al., 2020). Some studies have found that benefits continue after infancy: Babies who were fed human milk tend to gain weight more slowly and are at lower risk for developing diabetes and cardiovascular disease when they are older (Güngör et al., 2019; Rzehak et al., 2017). Some research suggests that babies who receive human milk score slightly higher on intelligence tests later in life and may have an easier time regulating their emotions (Núñez et al., 2022; Wallenborn et al., 2021; Weaver et al., 2018). There are benefits for people who express milk, too, including lower risks for cardiovascular disease, breast and ovarian cancer, depression, and cognitive decline in later life (Fox et al., 2021; Louis-Jacques & Stuebe, 2020).

Some of the associations between human milk and children's outcomes are very large; others are smaller. For instance, babies in low-income countries are about 14 times more likely to survive to their first birthday if they receive human milk instead of formula, which is a large and meaningful difference (Horta, 2019). In fact, researchers have estimated that more than a half a million infants around the world die every year from infections that could have been prevented by nursing (Walters et al., 2019). However, babies who receive human milk have intelligence test scores that average only two-tenths of a percentage point higher than formula-fed babies, which is a statistically consistent finding, but a much smaller impact (Oster, 2019a).

Stronger evidence also comes when there is a testable explanation for *why* the relationships occur. Some studies have helped scientists establish not just that there is a relationship between nursing and children's outcomes but also *why* these outcomes may happen. Researchers have learned that there isn't just something magic in nursing. Some studies have found observable differences in the process of nursing and in human milk itself that make it beneficial. Human milk is lower in protein than formula, contains different fats, and conveys microbes that help develop intestinal bacteria: This may account for some of the health benefits (Deoni et al., 2018; Horta, 2019).

Behaviors matter, too: Families tend to interact with babies differently when they are nursing than during bottle-feeding. There is more skin-to-skin contact and back-and-forth interaction, and infants have more control over the feeding. These distinctions may contribute to later differences in babies' emotion regulation, appetite, and cognitive development (Hodges et al., 2020). There are differences in the hormones that nursing parents (and babies) release when they are nursing, which may make it easier to fight stress and establish stronger relationships (Hahn-Holbrook et al., 2013).

Remember from Chapter 2 that experiments are a gold standard for research because they seek to identify a *causal relationship* between variables. Experiments conducted in Belarus, an Eastern European country, compared the outcomes of babies who were randomly assigned to receive either human milk or formula (Singhal et al., 2004). The researchers established that babies who received human milk were healthier than those who did not receive human milk and scored slightly higher on intelligence tests, although these differences decreased over time (S. Yang et al., 2018).

As a result of these decades of correlational and experimental research, scientific consensus is that there are strong benefits for human milk, particularly when it is delivered through nursing and most crucially for families who live in low-resource settings with limited health care (Azad et al., 2018; NASEM, 2020b). However, nutrition and development are both complex: Dramatic effects due to a single variable are rarely seen. While human milk is certainly helpful, babies can thrive without it. Relationships are more central to how infants grow than micronutrients, and relationships are not built on *what* babies drink but on *how* they are fed (Hairston et al., 2019).

Around the world, fewer than half of families are able to feed their babies human milk exclusively for the first six months of life (UNICEF, 2020). In affluent countries like the United States, income and cultural differences influence how families feed their children (Beauregard et al., 2019). Parents who identify as Latina or who are immigrants to the United States are also more likely to nurse their babies than non-immigrant Black or White parents. This may be because they are more likely to have family support, particularly from mothers or grandmothers who also nursed their babies (Dennis et al., 2019). In addition, higher-income families with more years of education are more likely to provide human milk to their infants, perhaps because they can afford to stay home or have jobs that offer them more flexibility and opportunity to nurse or express milk while at work (Victora et al., 2016).

Around the world, parents who work often have difficulty sustaining nursing because they do not have adequate breaks or a place to pump. This is problematic whether they work as doctors or wait tables (Kavle et al., 2017; Melnitchouk et al., 2018). As one parent working in retail explained, "I couldn't just leave the register to pump when I needed. At first I was leaking everywhere, and then my milk supply dropped and I had to start formula" (Spencer et al., 2015, p. 979). Less than half of nursing parents report that their employer accommodates nursing (Johnson et al., 2015). But if nursing parents receive support and education, they are more likely to continue (Chetwynd et al., 2019).

Alternatives to Human Milk Babies who are not fed human milk exclusively drink commercial formulas containing a mix of cow's milk, soy or corn proteins, and a variety of nutrients. In Canada, the European Union, and the United States, all infant formulas are regulated and required to include the same basic nutrients (Harris & Pomerantz, 2020). Infant formula, unlike cow milk, provides necessary nutrition for babies in the first months of life and is convenient for multiple caregivers and those without access to human milk. Like nursing, formula-feeding comes with some challenges. One of these is cost: Many families have difficulty paying for it (Frank, 2020). In 2022, families even had difficulty finding some formulas on store shelves.

As with nursing, the mechanics of formula-feeding are not always intuitive (Kotowski et al., 2021). Families are often uncomfortable asking health care providers for advice about formula-feeding, since they perceive a stigma against families who do not nurse their babies (Dattilo et al., 2020). Pediatricians recommend holding babies while they are feeding and allowing babies to decide when they are done, practices

Westend61/Getty Images

Sharing a Moment Bottle-feeding takes patience, attention, and time. Feeding a newborn gives parents and babies time to get to know each other.

Share It!

Human milk helps protect against COVID-19, too. Children who received human milk were less likely to develop COVID-19, and parents who were vaccinated against COVID-19 passed some of their immunity to their children through their milk.

(Hall, 2021; Verd et al., 2021)

that ensure bottle-fed babies experience social interaction and learn to regulate their appetite (Kotowski et al., 2021). Babies who are bottle-propped do not get that interaction and may be at risk for overeating or suffocation. Nevertheless, 40 percent of U.S. parents put their babies to bed with a bottle, and about a quarter use a pillow or stuffed animal to prop a bottle in an infant's mouth (Perrin et al., 2014).

Moving to Solid Food Regardless of first choices caregivers make about what their little ones eat, by the time a baby is sitting up, they are probably grabbing for food. Blair and Sam had support to introduce Silas to avocado, crunchy crackers, sweet potatoes, and bananas. As babies become more mobile, solid food becomes interesting, particularly if it is something other people are enjoying. But this transition to solid food is a vulnerable time for babies' health.

Pediatricians recommend that following babies' lead is a good way to introduce infants to solid food. Between about 4 and 6 months, when babies can sit up and show that they are interested in food, caregivers are advised to let them experiment with eating solid foods (Ahluwalia, 2020; NASEM, 2020a). Pediatricians recommend introducing soft forms of a fully balanced diet, including meat, nuts, and fruits and vegetables, avoiding anything that requires a lot of chewing or that could cause choking (Chiang et al., 2020).

However, these first bites are not designed for nourishment. Typically, babies should still be nursing or taking a bottle for calories. This changes at about 6 months, when babies are big enough to obtain most of the calories and nutrients they need from "real" foods. To help infants enjoy this experience, and to avoid overfeeding, experts advise that their eating should be self-directed as much as possible, enabling babies to control how much they eat (Daniels et al., 2015). By age 1, and after a period of eating transitional foods like cereals or pureed vegetables, babies are ready to eat meals with their families (Dewey & Brown, 2003).

Solid food sets the stage for a lifetime of eating habits, and babies use many of their new skills as they are learning to eat. Watching what other people are eating requires social awareness and close attention, and picking up peas requires fine motor skills. For toddlers, eating is an opportunity to build responsive relationships, to let caregivers know what they like and do not like, and to learn to regulate their own feelings of hunger (Nix et al., 2021).

Many families are not able to provide the fruits, vegetables, and proteins their infant needs. In the United States, more than one in five babies do not eat vegetables every day (Duffy et al., 2019). Experts speculate that caregivers' food choices are often influenced by marketing and the convenience of packaged foods (Spyreli et al., 2021). Biology is working against families, as well: Infants are born with a strong preference for sweet and salty foods (Mennella et al., 2018). If given the choice, babies will always prefer cookies to kale.

Babies' focus on other people also helps them develop a preference for French fries. If babies see other people enjoying a food, they are more likely to try it (Liberman et al., 2021). Simply being exposed to foods will help babies learn to enjoy them, and these preferences will stick: Whether it is mouthed, eaten, or rubbed into the hair, early food experiences will help determine baby's tastes for the rest of their life (Switkowski et al., 2020).

Staying Healthy

Despite the best efforts of caregivers and health care providers, babies and toddlers may get sick five or six times a year (Rowland et al., 2021; Vissing et al., 2018). During the pandemic, many contracted COVID-19, but their immune systems, primed to fight new diseases, usually prevented them from developing severe physical responses to the virus (Suwanwongse & Shabarek, 2020). Babies who are in child care tend to get sick more often than other infants, because they are exposed to a greater variety of viruses.

Share It!

Small children are vulnerable to exposure to environmental toxins. Recent studies have found that many U.S. commercial foods for infants and toddlers include potentially dangerous amounts of heavy metals, including cadmium, arsenic, and lead.

(Mousavi Khaneghah et al., 2020; Radwan, 2019)

CONNECTIONS

Remember from Chapter 3 that there are striking disparities in birth outcomes by income and racial background. In the United States, babies from Black and Indigenous families are more than five times as likely as Asian or White infants to die before they are a month old.

However, by the time these toddlers reach school age, they will be ill less frequently (Ansari & Gottfried, 2020).

Disease and Mortality Around the world, nearly 4 out of every 100 babies die before their fifth birthday. Many of them die shortly after birth as a result of birth trauma, genetic disorders, prematurity, or low-birthweight (UN IGME, 2021). Older babies tend to die from diseases such as malaria and pneumonia, which are often made worse by environmental pollution and malnutrition (Heft-Neal et al., 2020; WHO, 2020a). While rates of infant and toddler mortality had been improving, experts expect that the global economic disruption caused by the COVID-19 pandemic led to an increase in deaths in recent years (Cardona et al., 2022).

Even in a technologically advanced nation like the United States, 2 out of every 1,000 children die before age 3, many of them accidentally (CDC & NCHS, 2021b). Babies are particularly vulnerable to everyday hazards like falls and car accidents and are too small and fragile to recover if they experience violence or abuse. Others die of sleep-related injuries.

Babies from low-income families and who live in rural areas tend to be at higher risk of sleep-related injuries (Ehrenthal et al., 2020; Mohamoud et al., 2021). This is not unique to the United States. In New Zealand, Indigenous Māori people, who tend to have lower incomes and experience discrimination, also have higher rates of unexplained infant death (Rutter & Walker, 2021). Many Māori babies were at higher risk before they were born, perhaps because they were premature or had low birthweight. Inequitable access to health care and the pervasive effects of discrimination contribute to such disparities (Owens-Young & Bell, 2020).

One successful intervention for preventing early mortality is to boost the social support available to new families. Home visits by nurses, social workers, or community health workers after a baby is born can help build the relationships that can keep families healthy (le Roux et al., 2020; Supplee & Duggan, 2019). These visits give caregivers extra support, including advice for soothing babies, encouragement for responsive feeding, and consultations about safe sleep. Decades of research on home visiting has demonstrated its significant success (Goodman et al., 2021). One randomized study in Memphis, Tennessee, had dramatic results: Home visits reduced the mortality rate for children and their mothers by half, with benefits that stuck with children through adolescence (Kitzman et al., 2019; Olds et al., 2014). Another randomized study in North Carolina showed that children who had received home visiting were one-third less likely to have an accident-related emergency room visit (Goodman et al., 2021).

Immunizations Shots, vaccinations, jabs—no matter what you call them, routine vaccinations are one of the biggest scientific success stories of all time, saving the lives of millions every year (Okowo-Bele, 2015). **Immunizations** protect against diseases by introducing a tiny part of an infectious virus into the body to teach it to defend itself. If you encounter the virus later, you are much less likely to get sick because your body's immune system is prepared to protect you. Around the world, disruptions caused by war and the COVID-19 pandemic meant that fewer babies were receiving their shots, but 8 in 10 still received some of their basic vaccines (WHO et al., 2021).

Despite generations of research indicating that vaccines are safe, worries are common around the world (Puri et al., 2020). Families who are hesitant about vaccination are often distrustful of the scientific community and government institutions (Salmon et al., 2015). Others are concerned, despite evidence to the contrary, that vaccines may cause developmental disorders, or that they may be unnecessary (Kempe et al., 2020).

immunization A means of protection against diseases that introduces a tiny amount of an infectious virus into the body to teach it to defend itself against that virus. If the immunized person encounters the virus later, they are less likely to get sick, because their immune system is prepared.

Extra Support Helps Families Thrive. Adjusting to life with a newborn can be easier with someone to talk to and an extra set of hands. Lorrie Arnt is a nurse with the Nurse–Family Partnership, who came to Shelby and Rafael's house in Reading, Massachusetts, to help them with their new baby, Jaden.

CONNECTIONS
Remember from Chapter 2 that reports that vaccines lead to autism spectrum disorder or other neurocognitive conditions have been discredited as an example of unethical science.

Share It!

Cultural humility helps build empathy and understanding. Vaccine hesitancy may be a result of mistrust in institutions or a result of misinformation.

(Ferdinand, 2021)

In the United States, about 9 out of 10 toddlers have received some of their basic vaccines, but only about 7 out of 10 have received all of them, including their annual flu shot (Hill et al., 2021). Many young children who haven't received all of the recommended shots are from low-income families who may not have easy access to health care (Hill et al., 2021).

In many countries, including the United States, families who chose not to vaccinate their children have contributed to outbreaks of preventable infectious diseases, such as whooping cough and measles (Dubé et al., 2021; Phadke et al., 2020). Around the world, hundreds of children still die of vaccine-preventable diseases. A recent outbreak in the Pacific nation of Samoa resulted in more than 80 measles deaths, most of them in children under 5 (A. T. Craig et al., 2020). Immunizations have been extensively tested for safety and are one of the most important ways of reducing infant mortality around the world.

SCIENCE IN PRACTICE
Sean O'Leary, M.D., M.P.H.

You might be surprised to learn that many health care providers spend time debating science in their examination rooms. This is because many families are skeptical about science and may tell their health care providers that they do not want to follow their advice about vaccinations (Lafnitzegger & Gaviria-Agudelo, 2022). Fewer than 1 in 10 children under age 5 has received a single dose of the COVID-19 vaccine (AAP, 2022).

Sean O'Leary spent four years in medical school and another three years in graduate school researching the public health innovations that help babies thrive. But for O'Leary, like many other health care providers, his years of training do not always matter in the examination room. Many parents today get their information about vaccinations (and other health topics) from social media rather than their health care providers (Clark et al., 2022).

The families O'Leary sees in his pediatric practice are like many around the world. Increasingly, parents and adults everywhere question common public health innovations (McClure et al., 2017). O'Leary has made it his mission to empower health care providers to more effectively encourage families to trust science.

One common mistake O'Leary has identified: Asking families to decide what *they* want to do about vaccines, sleep positioning, or nursing. Simply asking parents to choose implies that all the choices are equal, when science has clearly demonstrated that immunizations, back sleeping, and nursing are healthier for children. Professionals are more persuasive when they take a clear stand in favor of scientific evidence. In fact, they convince more than 80 percent of caregivers to vaccinate their children if they assume that parents plan on doing so, rather than asking them what they think. Implying that vaccination is something that everyone does appeals to families and makes them more uncomfortable about refusing vaccines.

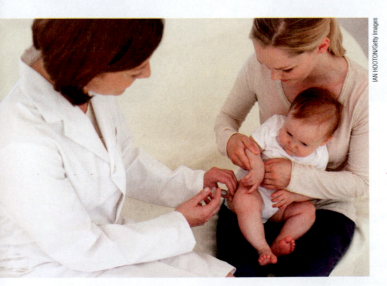
A Tiny Dose of Protection That Might Save Her Life Vaccines may hurt this infant for a moment, but they will protect her and her family and community from illnesses for years.

If parents are still skeptical of vaccines (or other common public health practices), O'Leary has found that empathy is more persuasive than a lecture. Parents who are skeptical of science are more likely to be convinced through relationships than by data. O'Leary uses a technique known as *motivational interviewing* to change minds, giving families the opportunity to share their thoughts and concerns, rather than launching into a presentation. This use of empathy works: While it is challenging to convince some people about the value of science, leading with respect is more effective in persuading families to adopt positive health practices (Braun & O'Leary, 2020; Cataldi et al., 2020).

Sleep

Like all babies, Silas spent almost half of his first two years fast asleep. In infancy, sleep is essential to rebuilding energy, growing, and recovering from illness. Babies who do not get enough tend to be more irritable and have more health conditions (Meltzer et al., 2021). Experts suggest that between 4 and 12 months, babies should be getting 12–16 hours of sleep per day, and from 12 months to 2 years, they should be getting between 11 and 14 hours (Paruthi et al., 2016b).

While infants sleep, the brain is building networks that help them remember what they have learned (Konrad & Seehagen, 2020). Even a brief nap can help babies retain information. For instance, in one study, researchers taught 15-month-olds new words, and the ones who slept after they learned the words remembered them better when tested later than did babies who skipped the nap (Werchan et al., 2021).

Infant Sleep Stages Every time you go to sleep, you experience different types of sleep. Long ago, scientists discovered that during certain times of sleep, your eyes move rapidly under your eyelids (Aserinsky, 1996; Gottesmann, 2009). These periods are called *rapid eye movement (REM) sleep.* Your brain is more active during REM sleep than during other types of sleep. Scientists believe that REM sleep is particularly important for memory development (Klinzing et al., 2019).

Infants get much more REM sleep than older children or adults—about 60 percent of their sleep time (Sadeh, 2015). Infants' REM sleep also looks different than it does in adults. While adults are nearly motionless during REM sleep, infants jerk, grimace, and smile (Guyer & Jenni, 2017). This is why REM sleep in infancy is called "active sleep."

Throughout the night, you cycle through different types of sleep several times. For babies, each sleep cycle lasts about 60 minutes, and they are sometimes completely awake between each cycle. The sequence of sleep types within each cycle changes rapidly during infants' first year. After birth, babies' sleep cycles are relatively simple. They get drowsy and fall immediately into active, REM sleep, with twitching limbs and faces. By about 3 months, infants fall into a light sleep before reaching active REM sleep. By 6 months, they have achieved the milestone of deep sleep, in which they can sleep through a car alarm (Guyer & Jenni, 2017).

Sleep Quantity Most caregivers do not consider sleep cycles until they realize that they explain the *fragmentation* of sleep in young babies. (The term "fragmentation" refers to the fact that although newborns sleep a lot, they are not doing it all at one time.) It takes months of physical maturation and exposure to the environment before babies consolidate their sleep and diversity is the rule (Jenni, 2020).

At around 4 months, a baby's **circadian rhythm**, or their internal clock for the daily cycle of rest, wake, and sleep, begins to show signs of maturation (Barry, 2021). Babies begin to show this characteristic daily rise-and-fall of activity, temperature, and hormones beginning in the first weeks of life and these cycles become more adult after 3 months (Ivars et al., 2015). It is highly influenced by the activity levels and light babies are exposed to; bright lights, movement, and noise help them learn when it is time to be awake (Yates, 2018).

Researchers who observe infants while they are sleeping see what most caregivers do not: Babies never "sleep through the night" (Adams, Master, et al., 2020; St James-Roberts et al., 2015). Neither do adults—we all have periods of wakefulness, even if we may not remember them in the morning. This short period of waking or drowsiness happens each time we transition from one cycle to another. What caregivers are really hoping for is that babies will settle themselves back to sleep without help.

Many babies can sleep for about five hours without needing a caregiver's attention by about 4 months (Barry, 2021). Yet, there is tremendous variability in when babies can rest for eight hours without needing care. While many do so by 6 months, it

circadian rhythm Your internal clock for the daily cycle of rest, wake, and sleep.

may not happen consistently and may not be a realistic expectation for many families until children are much older (Pennestri et al., 2018, 2020). By age 2, babies can typically sleep for eight hours, but most still wake up at least once every night for comfort and resettling (Paavonen et al., 2020). Three factors lead to this milestone: (1) Babies are big enough not to need to eat overnight; (2) experience with the outside world has led to the development of strong circadian rhythms; and (3) infants have learned how to settle themselves after waking.

Managing Sleep When caregivers do not get enough sleep or feel that their babies are not sleeping enough, they have difficulty functioning and are at increased risk for depression (Bai et al., 2020; N. Wilson et al., 2019). However, the ideal sleep schedule varies from family to family (Pennestri et al., 2018). In many places, caregivers put their babies to bed at the same time as they go to sleep. In the United States, bedtime is typically around 8 P.M., but in Korea, Brazil, and Italy, infants regularly go to bed around 10 P.M. (Netsi et al., 2017). How often infants are expected to wake up during the night also varies. Babies in the United States are typically only expected to wake up once nightly after 6 months, whereas babies in China, India, Finland, and Vietnam are usually expected to wake up at least twice (Q.-M. Lin et al., 2019; Mindell et al., 2010).

Keeping Sleep Safe Every year in the United States, about 3,500 babies die while they are sleeping (Bombard et al., 2018). When otherwise healthy infants pass away, their deaths are termed **sudden unexpected infant deaths (SUID)**. If investigators determine that sleep practices caused the death, as with being smothered, the death is called a *sleep-related suffocation*: These account for most of the SUID deaths in the United States (Parks et al., 2021). If the unexpected deaths are not linked to sleep practices, they are classified as *sudden infant death syndrome (SIDS)*. SIDS describes an unexpected infant death whose cause is unknown (Shapiro-Mendoza et al., 2014).

Infants who die during sleep often have three intersecting risk factors. First, they are very young, typically under 6 months. Second, even though they may appear healthy, they tend to have medical vulnerabilities, such as heart or brain irregularities or complications from being born prematurely (Cummings & Leiter, 2019; Kinney et al., 2018; Ostfeld et al., 2017). Third, they are often exposed to environmental risks, such as drugs or alcohol in their prenatal environment; exposure to nicotine, cigarette smoke, or other pollutants after they are born; an unsafe sleeping arrangement; or a minor illness like a cold (Anderson et al., 2019; Vivekanandarajah et al., 2021).

Managing sleep is often part of firmly held cultural practices. For instance, some caregivers in the Ivory Coast wake up their babies when they have visitors (Gottlieb, 2004). In other places, families prepare a separate room where their baby will sleep. In other communities, like Silas's community in Seattle, Washington, babies are kept in a quiet space while they are napping so that they avoid too much stimulation. Cultures even disagree on *where* babies should spend the night. Sam and Blaire, like many parents in North America, prepared a room where Silas settled himself down in a crib. Particularly in Asian and African communities, many caregivers *bed-share* or *co-sleep* with their babies (Rudzik & Ball, 2021). This is also true for more than half of parents in the United States (Bombard et al., 2018; Ordway et al., 2020).

Compared to other affluent countries, in the United States pediatricians have the strictest policies about sleep safety and typically admonish against bed-sharing (Doering et al., 2019). Some researchers suggest that these policies may communicate cultural insensitivity and even discourage families from seeking advice about safe sleep (Mandlik & Kamat, 2020). Caregivers can reduce risk when they are co-sleeping (see **Table 4.1**; Erck Lambert et al., 2019). Successful public health initiatives are often designed to bridge traditional practices with science, including the New Zealand program of providing families with *wahakura* bassinets that can be used to protect babies from suffocation by limiting co-sleeping (Tipene-Leach & Abel, 2019).

Courtesy National SUDI Prevention Coordination Service, Hāpai Te Hauora Tapui

Sleeping Like a Baby Public health officials in New Zealand adopted traditional woven wahakura baskets to promote safe-sleep practice. Notice that New Zealand experts allow caregivers to tuck infants in with sheets and blankets. There is limited international consensus on this practice: U.S. experts advise keeping blankets out of babies' beds.

sudden unexpected infant deaths (SUID) When an otherwise healthy infant dies. SUIDs can include *sleep-related suffocation*.

TABLE 4.1 Safe Sleep Recommendations

- Babies should be put to sleep on their backs, where they are less likely to suffocate, until age 1.
- Babies should sleep on a firm mattress in an approved surface, with no bottles, blankets, bedding, bumpers, pillows, or stuffed animals.
- Babies should not sleep on couches or recliners, or in car seats or playpens.
- Pacifiers help babies sleep and prevent sleep-related injuries.
- Families should not smoke during pregnancy and should avoid exposing babies to secondhand smoke.
- Babies should share a room (but not a bed) with their caregiver until 6 months.
- Falling asleep while feeding or soothing a baby in the middle of the night is common. It is safer to feed a baby in bed than on a recliner or a couch if the caregiver is concerned about falling asleep.
- Parents who have been drinking, using drugs or sedatives, or are extremely tired should have someone else watch the baby.
- Be extra cautious when there is a change of caregivers, sleep patterns, or sleep situations.
- Monitor babies closely at night when they are sick or have an underlying medical problem, as they may be more prone to suffocation.

Information from Möllborg et al., 2015; Moon & Hauck, 2016.

APPLY IT! **4.1** Sam and Blaire encourage Silas to eat with them and feed himself. What might Silas be learning from these experiences?

4.2 All families want to keep their babies safe in the first years when their health is fragile. How would you use principles of cultural humility to communicate the benefits of safe sleep, vaccination, and responsive feeding to new families?

The Changing Brain

The first two years are a time of major achievements: first steps, first words, first teeth. Silas is learning to scribble, negotiate for more fruit, and build with Legos. His growing brain powers all these capabilities. The experiences Silas encounters, including the hundreds of words he hears each day and the thousands of times he wiggles his fingers, shape how his brain grows.

As you will see in **Infographic 4.1**, the brain grows dramatically in the first year. Skull size in adulthood is predictive of nothing but hat size, but an infant's expanding skull actually is important. (This is why health providers measure it at every visit.) By 2 years, the brain has doubled in volume (Thompson et al., 2020). Remember from Chapter 3 that babies are born with just about all the *neurons*, or brain cells, that they will have in their life. Explosive growth is not caused by new neurons, but by new, faster connections between them (Gilmore et al., 2018). These connections help Silas learn how to control his body and also how to talk and connect with other people.

During infancy, the brain becomes customized to what babies experience, an individualization that can also have a downside. If growing infants don't have certain experiences in the first few years, like hearing language or seeing through both eyes, it may be more difficult for them to recover these skills. The young brain is particularly vulnerable, and early injuries and deprivation can have lifetime consequences (Gabard-Durnam & McLaughlin, 2020).

More Connections Make a Larger Brain

Brain growth is so critical in infancy that infants expend more calories growing the brain than growing the body (Kuzawa et al., 2014; Vasung et al., 2019). In newborns, the brain grows by 1 percent every day (Holland et al., 2014). The fastest growing area of the infant brain? The area devoted to movement and language.

Learning Objective

4.2 Explain the role of neurons and synapses in brain function during the first two years.

 Share It!

Did stress during the COVID-pandemic change infants' brain development? Some researchers think they see the signs of extra stress in brain connectivity.

(Manning et al., 2021)

THE BRAIN INCREASES DRAMATICALLY IN SIZE

The brain doubles in size between birth and age 2. Most of this explosive growth happens in the first months of life. These brain scans were taken just 90 days apart.

Photo courtesy of Dominic Holland, University of California, San Diego School of Medicine. Structural Growth Trajectories and Rates of Change in the First 3 Months of Infant Brain Development. Dominic Holland, et al. JAMA Neurol. 2014;71(10).

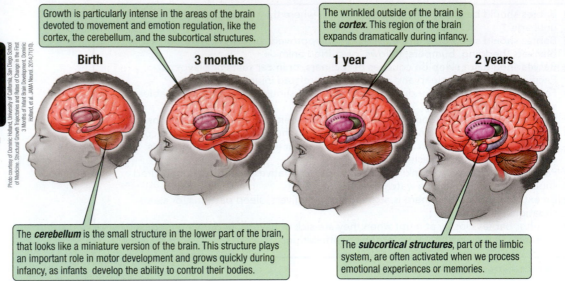

Growth is particularly intense in the areas of the brain devoted to movement and emotion regulation, like the cortex, the cerebellum, and the subcortical structures.

The wrinkled outside of the brain is the *cortex*. This region of the brain expands dramatically during infancy.

The *cerebellum* is the small structure in the lower part of the brain, that looks like a miniature version of the brain. This structure plays an important role in motor development and grows quickly during infancy, as infants develop the ability to control their bodies.

The *subcortical structures*, part of the limbic system, are often activated when we process emotional experiences or memories.

NEURONS AND CONNECTIONS GROW VIBRANTLY

Experiences shape the creation of new synapses and neural connections. The brain creates millions of new connections every second, and the network of neurons in the brain becomes denser over time.

Synaptogenesis

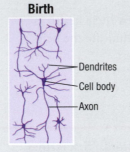

- Dendrites
- Cell body
- Axon

These drawings illustrate what a thin section of brain tissue might look like showing neurons connecting with each other.

Anatomy of a neuron

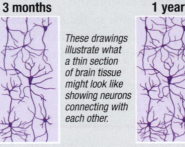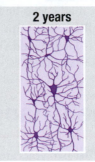

Cell body

Dendrites: The outgrowths from the body of the neuron transmit information received from other cells at synapses.

Axon: The long tail-like structure that sends information from one cell to another.

Myelin: The cholesterol-filled outer covering of an axon that helps speed messages from one neuron to another.

Synapse: Neurons communicate with other neurons through electrical impulses and chemical messages passed at synapses. Synapses can occur between dendrites, axons, and cell bodies.

EXPERIENCE SHAPES THE BRAIN THROUGH MYELINATION AND PRUNING

Neural connections that are used frequently are more likely to be myelinated. These connections become stronger and faster. They are known as white matter. Connections that are used less frequently are likely to be pruned away.

Neuron maturation

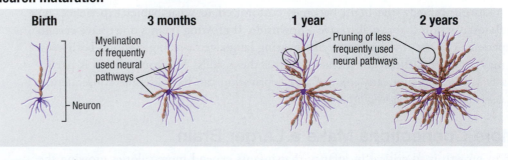

Myelination of frequently used neural pathways

Pruning of less frequently used neural pathways

Neuron

This rapid growth drives many of infants' new skills. As babies learn to control their bodies, sit without toppling over, and pull themselves up, the part of their brain known as the *cerebellum* grows and expands most quickly (Sathyanesan et al., 2019). Also fast-growing are the *subcortical structures*, which are involved in emotional processing and relationships and will help toddlers learn to connect with their parents and manage their feelings (Gilmore et al., 2018). The regions of the brain that drive communication skills grow quickly as well: The *cortex*, the outer, wrinkled part of the brain, gets thicker as children grasp more words and grammar (Gilmore et al., 2020).

More Connections The expansion of the brain is caused by changes you could only see with a high-powered microscope. Individual neurons are connecting and sending information to one another, which accounts for the extra pounds of brain Silas is carrying around (Thompson et al., 2020).

Neurons make connections through their **axon**, the long, tail-like structure attached to the cell body that transmits a chemical signal to other neurons (see **Infographic 4.1**). This communication is received by other neurons' **dendrites**, branch-like appendages that grow out of the cell body. Sometimes the message is transmitted directly to the cell body itself. Communication occurs in the *synapse*, the gap between the sending neuron's axon and the receiving neuron's dendrite, where chemical packets carry information from one neuron to another.

Each neuron's axon may connect to multiple dendrites from many different neurons (Y. Han et al., 2018). Neurons connect to as many as 7,000 other neurons, with some including as many as 30,000 synapses (Mohan et al., 2015). Each axon may be very long: The longest axons stretch from the brain way down to the bottom of the spinal cord.

Synaptogenesis, or the process of creating new synapses between neurons, begins before birth and continues throughout the lifespan. Experiences shape the creation of new synapses and neural connections. Because the brain creates millions of new connections every second, by age 2, Silas had more synaptic connections than there are grains of sand on a beach (Stiles & Jernigan, 2010). He will have 80 percent more synapses than he did at birth and far more than he will have as an adult (Sakai, 2020).

Creating Efficient Connections As babies grow, their neural connections change. The strength and density of synapses correspond to experience: The more a synapse is used, the stronger it gets. For instance, if an infant hears a lot of language, the part of the brain devoted to language will be larger as a result of increasing synaptic connections, compared to babies who don't hear as much language (Merz et al., 2019).

New connections are created every second and get stronger with experience, and the brain manages this complexity and creates efficiency by cutting back on underused synapses. This process is called **synaptic pruning**, named for the practice of pruning branches of a plant to make it stronger. Synaptic connections operate on a "use it or lose it" basis: Connections that are used are strengthened, and those that aren't die off (L. Cheadle et al., 2020). This increases speed in the brain, because neural signals travel more quickly along thicker, more robust connections.

Synaptic pruning, as with the process of creating new synapses, begins before birth and continues throughout the lifespan. It peaks between about 18 months and 2 years (Huttenlocher & Dabholkar, 1997). In many areas of the brain, half of all synapses created in infancy will gradually disappear by the end of adolescence (Stiles & Jernigan, 2010). Pruning is a delicate process and difficulties that occur in early pruning have been linked to a range of neurological conditions, including autism spectrum disorder and schizophrenia (Neniskyte & Gross, 2017).

Making Faster Connections The process of **myelination** also helps children's brains process information more quickly. Some axons in the brain are covered with **myelin**, layers of cholesterol-rich fat that insulate the axon. Just like the plastic

axon The long, tail-like structure attached to the cell body that transmits chemical signals to other neurons.

dendrite A branch-like appendage that grows out of the cell body and receives communication from other neurons.

synaptogenesis The process of creating new synapses between neurons, which begins before birth and continues throughout the lifespan.

synaptic pruning The process in which the brain cuts back on underused synapses.

myelination The lifelong process of adding myelin to axons.

myelin Layers of cholesterol-rich fat that insulate the axon, helping to speed up communication.

Specialized Development Experience-dependent brain development is not universal and relies on input from the environment. Not all babies get to push around on the grass on a toy lion, but if this infant practices every day, their brain will respond to this experience by myelinating the neural pathways that respond to the movement.

CONNECTIONS

As explained in Chapter 3, critical periods are a special type of sensitive period. Maturation that happens during a critical period operates on a "now or never" principle: If it does not happen at that time, there is no workaround. Scientists believe that critical periods happen only during prenatal development: After birth, most maturation is more flexible.

experience-expectant brain development Brain maturation that relies on nearly universal environmental inputs.

experience-dependent brain development Brain maturation that relies on the quantity or the quality of environmental input and, like all learning, continues throughout the lifespan.

covering an electrical line, myelin speeds communication by up to 100 times (Kanda et al., 2019).

Myelination is guided by both genes and experience. Axons that are used more frequently are more likely to be myelinated than those used less frequently (Rosenke et al., 2021). Individual experiences matter, as well. For instance, as a toddler learns to ride a tricycle, areas of the brain that control movement of the pedals will myelinate. A toddler who has never ridden a tricycle, however, will not show myelination in the same regions. Myelination begins prenatally, peaks during infancy, and continues through the lifespan until myelin itself begins to degrade in later life (Chapman & Hill, 2020; Dai et al., 2019). Myelination is one of the processes that helps all of us learn. For instance, if an adult learns a new motor skill, like juggling, their brain will show new areas of myelination (Steele & Zattore, 2018).

How Does Experience Change the Brain?   Neuroscientists distinguish between two ways that experience triggers changes in the brain: *experience-expectant development* and *experience-dependent development*. **Experience-expectant brain development** is brain maturation that relies on nearly universal environmental inputs (Greenough et al., 1987). These processes affect a broad range of functions, from the senses to emotional, language, and cognitive development. Experience-expectant brain development is triggered by typical, basic inputs in the environment, including nutrition, sensory stimulation, and caregiving, that are required in order for the neural circuits in the brain to develop.

Remember from Chapter 1 that *sensitive periods* are times in development when the body or brain is particularly sensitive to the environment. Infancy is a sensitive period for a few forms of experience-expectant development (Frankenhuis & Walasek, 2020). If necessary experiences do not happen at all, or at the expected time, a baby may never develop typical functioning. For instance, since brain development requires adequate nutrition, even short periods of deprivation in infancy can have lifelong effects. This was demonstrated in Israel, where, for a few weeks, some babies drank formula that lacked *thiamine*, a B vitamin, due to a manufacturing error. Since the brain requires thiamine to trigger language development, these babies' language abilities were permanently altered. Despite intensive interventions, they never caught up with their peers who received healthy formula (Harel et al., 2017).

Unlike experience-expectant brain development, **experience-dependent brain development** is not universal; it includes features that are not universal but capture individual and community differences in experiences. These processes rely on the quantity or quality of environmental input and, like all learning, continue throughout the lifespan (Fandakova & Hartley, 2020; Rosenzweig & Bennett, 1996). For instance, the ability to produce and understand language is an experience-expectant process, but the *quality* of a baby's language skills and which languages they speak are experience-dependent. Experience-dependent processes require exposure to certain experiences, as with learning to play patty-cake or fasten Velcro, but these experiences are not universally required for development.

Early Brain Injury and Stress

Some babies experience early brain injuries. For instance, in Boise, Idaho, Josiah was rushed to the emergency room when he was just 4 months old (Wootton-Greener, 2017).

Josiah had a skull fracture, which caused a *traumatic brain injury (TBI)*. A TBI occurs when an accident, a sports injury, or abuse causes a head injury, which damages the brain. Josiah is one of more than 300,000 babies in the United States who experience a TBI every year (Spies & Klevens, 2016; Peterson et al., 2019).

In the past, experts believed that young children's brains were so plastic that they would not suffer long-term damage from early brain injury (Titchner et al., 2015).

Unfortunately, the opposite appears to be true. Babies' brains are changing so rapidly that early injury can cause long-term and potentially irreversible effects that are much more harmful than similar injuries in adults. Some of the effects, such as learning delays, may not appear until much later (Miller et al., 2018).

Emergency room doctors worried that Josiah might not ever walk or even make it to his first birthday, but Josiah surprised them. Josiah, now age 3, has a nurturing environment and loving parents. He is a happy toddler who enjoys dancing to the music of *Frozen* (Wootten-Greener, 2017).

The changes to the developing brain that result from trauma are usually very different from those that are caused by everyday stress. However, chronic stress and adversity early in development can change brain development, too. For instance, an infant's earliest experiences shape the development of their brain as it adapts to the environment. If families are experiencing illness or financial strain, or are unable to provide regular interaction or nurturing care, that can change the pattern of infants' brains development (Troller-Renfree et al., 2020, 2022).

In a randomized, controlled experiment designed to evaluate whether reducing financial adversity would be linked to children's earliest brain development, researchers randomly assigned low-income families to receive either an extra $313 a month (the treatment group), or an extra $20 a month (the control group) for the first four years of their babies' lives (Noble et al., 2021). Then researchers measured the electrical activity in the infants' brains using EEG when they were about a year old (Troller-Renfree et al., 2021). (Remember from Chapter 2 that EEG uses sensors placed on the outside of a baby's skull to measure the electrical activity as neurons communicate with one another.) Scientists found that brain development was different for the infants in the treatment group whose families had received more money every month, than for the infants in the control group (Troller-Renfree et al., 2022).

How did money make a difference? Researchers are not sure, but extra income may have led to less stress. Families reported that they spent the money on baby supplies, groceries, and utility bills (Rojas et al., 2020). Having some of the basics taken care of may have given families more time to interact with their babies, leading to changes in brain development. Researchers have observed similar findings in babies whose female parents were able to take advantage of paid leave after their children were born: Less stress is often linked to healthier outcomes (Brito et al., 2022).

Principles of Early Brain Development

Over the past 30 years, scientists have observed some principles that explain the significance of early brain development (C. A. Nelson et al., 2019).

1. *Brain development is a long process that allows personalization.* Brain development begins in the embryo, but the brain isn't mature until early adulthood. It continues to change until the end of life (Walhovd & Lövdén, 2020). Slow brain development allows the brain to be shaped to experience. As a result, each baby's brain is as unique as their fingerprints.

2. *Brain development is affected by genes and the environment.* Instructions in the genome direct brain development, but genes need to be epigenetically triggered by the environment (Frith, 2019). For instance, monozygotic twins share similar genetic instructions and may even share some of the same prenatal conditions, but their experiences vary, and as a result, their brains are never exactly the same (McEwen & Bulloch, 2019).

3. *There are limits to the brain's plasticity, or ability to adjust to the environment.* The brain is always changing, as new synapses are being created and pathways myelinated, but development requires some experience-expectant experiences to happen at particular times. As the foundational structures of the brain are being built,

Walking Changes the Brain. When a group of researchers analyzed the development of the connections in children's brains, they found new networks building as the children learned to walk. At 12 months, as shown here, there was a lot of new activity in the motor cortex and in regions connecting the right and left hemispheres of the brain. Marrus, Natasha; Eggebrecht, Adam T, Walking, Gross Motor Development, and Brain Functional Connectivity in Infants and Toddlers, Cerebral cortex, February 2018, volume 28, issue 2, 750 -763, doi.org/10.1093/cercor/bhx313. Reprinted by permission of Oxford University Press, permission conveyed through Copyright Clearance Center, Inc.

CONNECTIONS

Remember from Chapter 2 that randomized controlled experiments are considered to be the highest standard for establishing causality in developmental science. When researchers conduct large-scale, randomized, controlled experiments, they feel more confident in their research findings.

trauma and extreme deprivation can cause damage that will be challenging, and perhaps impossible, to overcome (Wade, Sheridan, et al., 2020).

APPLY IT! **4.3** How does myelination and the creation of new synapses support Silas's ability to learn new skills, like how to draw with a marker?
4.4 Why do scientists think the first years of life are so important to brain development?

Sensing and Moving

Learning Objectives

4.3 Describe vision and hearing development in infancy.

4.4 Explain how the typical maturation of movement changes a baby's experience of the world.

CONNECTIONS

Remember from Chapter 3 that a baby's senses begin to develop while they are still in the uterus. At birth, newborns have remarkable abilities to see, hear, smell, taste, and feel the world around them. These early senses are shaped by prenatal experiences and help them make connections with the people in their world.

When you are picking out mangos at the grocery store, you might take for granted your ability to smell, see, and feel the mango and to hear the phone buzzing in your pocket. But you weren't born with all these skills working the way they do today and there are many individual differences in how our senses work and develop. As infants develop, real-world experience builds the connection between body and brain that helps their senses change and mature (see **Figure 4.2**). Here we focus on the typical development of two critical senses that help infants learn and connect to the world: vision and hearing. You'll also learn that the story of babies' senses is not always simple: As babies get more experience in the world, they lose something, too.

Seeing

Young babies are drawn to faces, people, and animals moving around them, and their preference for people helps propel their impressive learning abilities (Grossman, 2017; Kelly et al., 2019). Watching people, as when Silas studies his mother while she taps away at her phone, will help him learn about the world around him. Typically developing babies are able to track what the people around them are doing early in life, helping them learn how to talk, interact, and understand the world (Zubler et al., 2022).

Remember from Chapter 3 that newborns' vision is a little blurry, particularly for things that are far away, but they are able to distinguish and recognize faces from the time they are born. In their first two years, babies' vision typically improves quickly, as does their ability to move their focus from one object to another. By 3 or 4 months, infants can see a full spectrum of colors and may even have a favorite (researchers have found that most babies prefer yellow over blue) (Skelton & Franklin, 2020). Their ability to see details improves rapidly between 6 and 9 months (Goldstein & Brockmole, 2017).

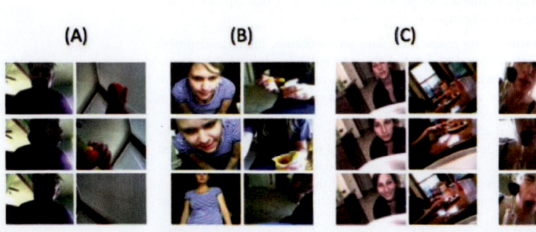

(A)   (B)   (C)   (D)

What Do Babies Look At? When researchers placed head-mounted cameras on infants, they found that babies spend a lot of time watching faces and hands. This series of video stills was taken from babies who were (left to right) about 6 weeks, 6 months, 12 months, and 2 years old.

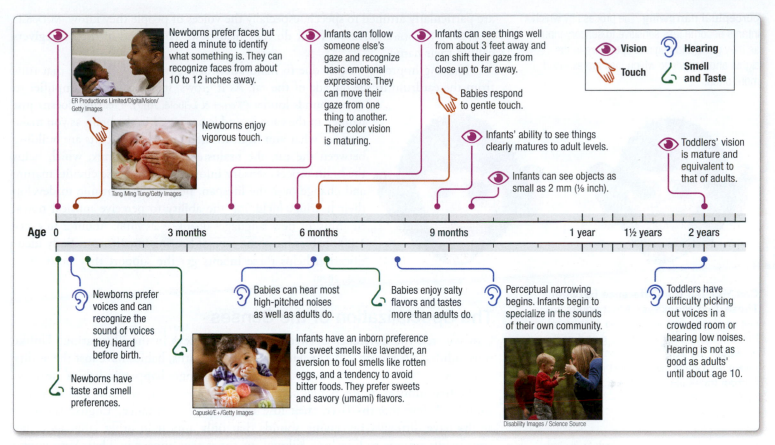

FIGURE 4.2 Highlights of Sensory Development Typically, infants are born with some sensory abilities, like the ability to recognize their caregivers close up, and some of the sounds and tastes they may have experienced before birth. But their senses are not fully developed until they are much older. Many senses show evidence of *perceptual narrowing* before a baby's first birthday, as an infant's perception begins to specialize in the sights and sounds they experience most frequently. Infants who do not display typical sensory development may benefit from additional screening and support.

When babies reach their first birthday, most can see as well as their caregivers, including all the colors of the decorations.

How do scientists know that infants will prefer yellow to blue, particularly when they cannot speak? They use the **preferential looking technique**. In this procedure, researchers harness babies' intrinsic interest in new things. Babies turn their heads to look at what they are interested in and naturally look longer at an object they haven't seen before. They also look longer at an image that interests them, such as a picture of a face as opposed to an abstract image.

Hearing

Silas has worn glasses since he was about 6 months old to help with his esotropia, a visual impairment common in infants who were born early. But his hearing, which was first tested in the hospital, has developed typically. However, like many infants, his hearing and ability to process sounds was not yet mature (Sanes & Woolley, 2011).

Even when he was in the hospital, Silas could hear voices and noises across the room. But, like most newborns, he could probably not hear whispers. (Werner & Leibold, 2017). In the first few months, typically developing babies can hear normal conversations but not whispers (Litovsky, 2015). It takes a loud noise to get infants' attention. Babies also can't make out certain sounds, particularly if they are low, like the super bass coming from a subwoofer or the growl of a dog (Litovsky, 2015). Infants (and other young children) also have a hard time ignoring background noises or distinguishing speech from background noise (Leibold & Buss, 2019). Nevertheless, babies

Scientific American Profile

Early Senses

preferential looking technique A procedure that measures what babies perceive in which researchers harness babies' intrinsic interest in new things.

perceptual narrowing The process by which infants become less sensitive to sensory input as they grow and begin to specialize in the sights and sounds to which they are exposed more often.

Can You Tell the Difference Between These Two Monkeys? Most adults are not very good at identifying monkeys, but 6-month-olds are quite good at it. However, by age 1, most babies lose this talent and have specialized in identifying human faces like their own.

FIGURE 4.3 Language Sensitivity When researchers tested babies who spoke English, Hindi, and Salish in their first year, they found that nearly all of the infants were able to perceive a variety of sounds, including the Hindi to/va/ta and the Salish ki/vs/qi in the first six months, even if they did not hear these sounds spoken in their everyday life. However, infants' sensitivity narrowed as they grew. By age 1, the English-speaking babies no longer recognized the sounds that did not appear in their language, although the Hindi- and Salish-speakers still did.

are particularly attuned to speech, especially the voices of people they know (McDonald et al., 2019; Newman et al., 2013). What do they hear best? The sound of their caregivers calling their name.

Hearing improves quickly due to maturation in the *ear canal*, the tube that runs from the eardrum to the outside of the ear. As it grows, it works like an amplifier to make sounds louder (Werner & Leibold, 2017). Hearing doesn't just happen in the ears: Sound is processed in the brain as you make sense of what you hear. In infancy, neural circuits are building between the ear, the brainstem, and the cortex, which helps the brain process sensory information. As these circuits mature and change over the lifespan, people can continue to develop their hearing, including the ability to perceive musical notes, rhythms, or new languages (Reetzke et al., 2018). About 2 in every 1,000 babies has some type of hearing impairment: Early identification helps these infants get the support they need (Bussé et al., 2020).

The Specialization of the Senses

Can you tell the difference between the two monkeys in the illustration? Unlike most adults, a 6-month-old can. However, by 9 months, babies have lost the ability (Pascalis et al., 2002; Simion & Di Giorgio, 2015). Similar changes happen in babies' hearing. In the first months of life, babies can perceive a wide variety of tones and language sounds. A few months later, they lose this skill. For instance, English-speaking adults have difficulty perceiving sounds that only appear in other languages, like consonants unique to Czech or Kikuyu, or tones that appear in Thai. Very young infants do not have this difficulty: They can perceive the sounds of all the languages of the world (Maurer & Werker, 2014). However, by age 1, their ability to hear sounds is more limited, and they no longer respond to sounds that do not occur in their own languages (Kuhl et al., 2014). Like adults, English-speaking babies will have challenges hearing tones in Thai or the difference between a *ph* and a *p* in Hindi. They will no longer be able to hear subtle differences that do not occur in their native language. (See **Figure 4.3**.)

Researchers call this phenomenon **perceptual narrowing**. At birth, infants are sensitive to distinctions in a wide variety of sensory input, whether that is features of monkey faces or the sounds of languages, but they become *less* sensitive during their first year: Babies' brains begin to specialize. Developmental processes including neural pruning and myelination make this possible; frequently used connections become faster and more efficient, and unused connections fade. As a result, babies who grow up hearing Mandarin will be good at hearing tonal differences in Mandarin. Babies who are raised among people will learn to distinguish between different people's faces and lose the ability tell the differences between monkeys.

Moving

For many families, one of the highlights of early development is movement. Babies, too, seem enthralled by their ability to control their experiences, whether that means dropping a spoon from the highchair or running to catch up to an older friend. Learning to control the body not only changes how babies see the world and relate to other people, but it also changes their brains

Percent

100
90
80
70
60
50
40
30
20
10
0

Hindi /to/vs/ta
Salish /ki/vs/qi

English-speaking Infants

English-speaking Infants

Hindi-speaking Infants

Salish-speaking Infants

English-speaking Infants

6–8 Months   8–10 Months   10–12 Months   11–12 Months

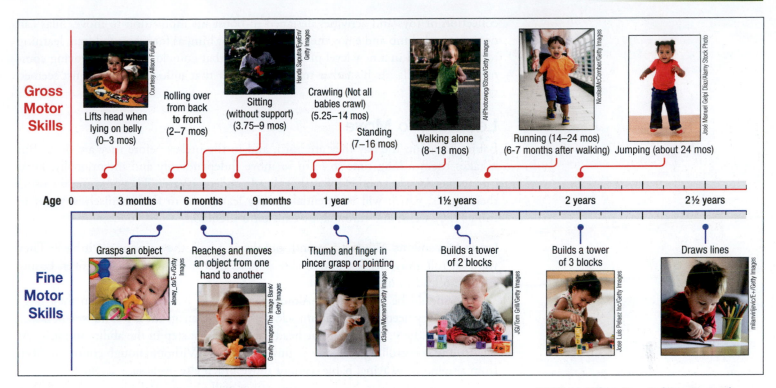

Gross Motor Skills

Lifts head when lying on belly (0–3 mos)

Rolling over from back to front (2–7 mos)

Sitting (without support) (3.75–9 mos)

Crawling (Not all babies crawl) (5.25–14 mos)

Standing (7–16 mos)

Walking alone (8–18 mos)

Running (14–24 mos) (6-7 months after walking)

Jumping (about 24 mos)

Age 0   3 months   6 months   9 months   1 year   1½ years   2 years   2½ years

Fine Motor Skills

Grasps an object

Reaches and moves an object from one hand to another

Thumb and finger in pincer grasp or pointing

Builds a tower of 2 blocks

Builds a tower of 3 blocks

Draws lines

FIGURE 4.4 What Can Babies Do with Their Bodies? No baby's development matches the precise order on a chart, but researchers have observed a common sequence for many infants and toddlers. The timing of development depends on individual and cultural factors. You will see some average ranges for typically developing children indicated in parentheses. Learning to move will change infants' thinking, relationships, and ways of responding to the world.

(Adolph & Hoch, 2020). Although babies can move in the uterus, learning to move independently after they are born takes a long time.

The development of body coordination is called **motor development**. Scientists analyze the development of bigger movements like walking, jumping, or skipping, called **gross motor development** (*gross* here means "large"). They also study the development of small movements requiring precise coordination, like picking up little objects, swallowing, or pointing, called **fine motor development** (*fine* here means "tiny"). (See **Figure 4.4**.)

Brain and Body Together

One of Silas's early challenges, and his parents' proudest moments, involved learning to move his body—learning to roll across the carpet, to cruise across the room, and, about 15 months after he left the hospital, to walk on his own. Those difficulties consumed hours of practice and many sessions of physical therapy. Remember that motor development depends on the brain. The cortex, the outer layers of the brain, is involved as you learn new skills. After you master a new activity, your cortex relays this information to subcortical structures, which remember these movements and send signals to your spinal cord that will direct your muscles to move. The effort of learning happens in the cortex and takes work, but once you have learned it, you often take it for granted (Adolph et al., 2012).

Think back to the first time you learned, for instance, to play the guitar (or another musical instrument or a sport); it took lots of effort to coordinate your fingers. Later you can play without thinking, or while thinking of something else: You aren't actually using your cortex as much anymore to focus on playing. Your subcortical structures are now doing more of the work. Similarly, when babies begin to learn how to reach, crawl, or walk, they expend a tremendous amount of cognitive effort in making new movements that one day will be automatic.

For Silas, like many babies who are born very small or very early, this process was slower: He was always gaining new skills, just not as quickly as other children. Silas's development was helped by what his family jokingly called his "boot camp," a

motor development The development of body coordination.

gross motor development The development of bigger movements like walking, jumping, or skipping.

fine motor development The development of small movements requiring precise coordination, like picking up little objects, swallowing, or pointing.

collection of toys and activities designed to boost his motivation to move. Silas can now run and climb and enjoy the playground. For him, as for many children, learning to walk ushered in a new level of independence that coincided with improving communication skills. As his father remembers, after that milestone, things just seemed to "click."

Learning to Move

Babies move on the day they are born, and in the uterus before they are born. But it takes them a long time to learn to move independently and intentionally. First, infants need to learn to control their heads and their core. They also master using their hands, which will be essential as they learn how to feed themselves, point to things they want, and throw sippy cups onto the floor.

Large Movements When a 5-month-old drops a ball, they cannot get it back. They watch it roll away, helpless and unable to grab after it without toppling over. Losing a ball can lead to utter frustration.

We should be sympathetic. Almost a quarter of babies' weight is in their large head, and they need tremendous muscle strength to manage the 2-pound weight (Bayley, 1956; Salzmann, 1943). Stabilizing the head is just the first step in the ability to move. As Silas found, controlling the body begins in the core. Without enough control to keep from tipping or swaying, babies cannot move much else (Rachwani et al., 2019).

As Silas gets older, his body proportions will change and his growth will slow down, making controlled movement easier. A 2-year-old's head is still about one-fifth the size of their body, but they aren't growing as quickly as they were as an infant (Huelke, 1998). Their bodies are also narrower, with less fat and more muscle. These new proportions make it easier to control movement (see Figure 4.4).

Babies learn to control their bodies in a **cephalocaudal**, or head-downward, pattern, beginning with the ability to support their heavy heads. By about 6 weeks, babies can hold their heads up consistently, allowing them to look at what they are interested in (Adolph & Franchak, 2017). At around 4 months, being able to roll from their back to their front or vice versa means they can now tumble off couches and are no longer safe even lying in the middle of a bed (Shoaibi et al., 2019). Sitting, which typically happens around 6 months, is another critical development. Now infants can keep themselves from toppling over and also see their hands to pick up toys and explore more of their world (Franchak, 2019).

Babies are inventive when it comes to getting from place to place. They have a variety of ways to crawl, creep, or move around, depending on their culture and their own individual tendencies. By the time babies are about 9 months old, many can typically move around on their own using both their hands and feet (Adolph & Franchak, 2017).

Babies typically walk on their own at about 1 year as a result of practice, faster neural connections, and the stronger muscles that give them more power. Nearly 100 years ago, pioneering researchers established that this milestone, like others, occurs because of a combination of physical maturation and experience (McGraw, 1943). Today, researchers point out that changes in the brain also play a role. With practice, connections are myelinated between the muscles, the spine, and the brain, and within areas of the cortex, making walking easier (Adolph, 2019; Marrus et al., 2018). But faster neural connections don't make it effortless: A typical 1-year-old baby might take more than 2,400 steps an hour and fall more than 12 times (Adolph, 2019; Han & Adolph, 2020).

The development of gross motor skills does not end with walking. By age 2, babies can typically jump and even begin to climb steps and scramble up ladders or into boats, depending on where they live. As with walking and crawling, the development of more coordinated skills like jumping or hopping takes practice (Veldman et al., 2018).

cephalocaudal Development that occurs in a head-downward pattern, beginning with a baby's ability to support their heavy head.

Controlling the Hands

While caregivers may focus on their infants' walking ability, babies are also learning how to make smaller movements. Fine motor skills require infants to coordinate many abilities: perceiving what is around them (where the Cheerio is on the table); making a plan (I want to pick up that last Cheerio); and manipulating their bodies to do their bidding (thumb and forefinger at the ready; Adolph & Franchak, 2017).

It is difficult to reach for and grab an object if your torso is swaying back and forth. Thus, babies must be able to balance their core and torso before they can control their arms and hands. This pattern of physical development, where control of movement begins in the core and expands outward, is called the **proximodistal principle**.

Babies also need to learn how to manage their strength. At birth, newborns have a powerful whole-hand grasp, called the *palmar grasp*, that would crush a blueberry. With further brain maturation and experience, they learn to be gentler: At around 10 months, they develop their *pincer grasp*, coordinating the thumb and fingers to hold small objects (Gonzalez & Sacrey, 2018). This makes it easier to eat blueberries, and also to grab little, potentially dangerous objects such as pills or batteries. By age 1, as a result of practice and brain maturation, babies are able to point, reach, and grasp small objects (Karl et al., 2019).

Fine motor dexterity also means that by age 1, babies can use basic tools such as such as spoons or markers, buttons or chopsticks (Rachwani et al., 2020). In many families, these tools also include tablets and other electronic devices, despite pediatricians' cautions against media use (Souto et al., 2020).

Culture and Motor Development

Across time and place, there are significant variations in how and when typical babies learn to move. *Ethnotheories*, or caregivers' beliefs about how children should develop, are critical. For instance, some caregivers believe that children shouldn't be pushed to walk before they are "ready," but others may encourage babies to walk so that they can be more independent (Harkness et al., 2013; Mendonça et al., 2016).

Many communities around the world, including communities in the United States, the Caribbean, India, and Africa, encourage children's mobility, beginning with infant massages and practice (Adolph & Hoch, 2020). Babies who get this exercise learn to control their bodies earlier than others. For instance, babies in Cameroon typically sit on their own at 4 months, two months earlier than babies in the United States. Similarly, babies raised in Ghana can walk holding an adult's hand at about 8½ months. On the other extreme, infants in Norway, where parents are often reluctant to "push children to perform," typically do not walk with assistance until about 10½ months (Karasik et al., 2018; WHO, 2006). There are many ways that babies may learn to walk, and *when* babies learn to walk depends on their experience. But whether they spend a lot of time sitting still or get lots of practice, most typical babies develop all the motor skills necessary for their culture (Adolph & Hoch, 2019).

Does Timing Matter? Despite the cultural and historical variations in when babies learn how to move and control their bodies, caregivers still wonder about when their children should learn how to walk (Adolph et al., 2014). What scientists have found is that motor skill development is dependent on both maturation, or nature, *and* nurture, the environment. Motor skills are an experience-expectant process. Babies are born expecting to walk, but they need specific practice, like the ability to move and opportunities to fall, in order for that to happen. Typically developing babies will learn the basic motor skills like walking, grasping, and sitting without a lot of outside support.

Cultural influences on motor development remind us that *when* children learn to walk is an experience-dependent process. But whether babies spend lots of time in

Scientific American Profile

Developing Motor Skills

Share It!

Can babies learn when parents text? Researchers watched as parents tried to teach infants a new skill while being interrupted by a text on their phones. Their babies tended to fuss while their parents were distracted but were still able to learn the new skill. Texting may not be ideal, but it does not make learning impossible.

(Konrad et al., 2021)

proximodistal principle A pattern of physical development in which control of movement begins in the core and expands outward.

Karasik LB, Tamis-LeMonda CS, Ossmy O, Adolph KE (2018) The ties that bind: Cradling in Tajikistan. PLoS ONE 13(10): e0204428. https://doi.org/10.1371/journal.pone.0204428

All Cozy and Warm Many babies in Tajikistan, a country in Central Asia, spend time during the night or during the day in a special cradle called a gahvora. While their early movements are limited, Tajik babies still grow up to run and play like other children around the world.

Hugh Scott, Sooner Magazine

How Does Movement Change the Brain? Professor Thubi Kolobe studies how infants learn to wriggle, crawl, and walk. She has also invented devices to help give extra support to babies who cannot move easily on their own, reinforcing their inborn drive to move.

affordance The term for what people can learn from objects in the world around them.

visual cliff A means of assessing what risks babies will take while crawling, in which a 2½-foot gap is covered with plexiglass that, if properly lit, appears to be an empty gap.

cradle boards, like Tajik babies who spend up to 19 hours a day lying down, or get lots of practice on their feet, healthy children all learn how to move (Karasik et al., 2018).

Learning from Moving

Silas's face lights up when he toddles across the room for the first (and second, and third, and eighteenth) time. Just as learning to move requires children to practice their perception, planning, and physical skills, moving itself also changes how children see the world (Thelen, 1995). Learning to move independently, whether crawling, walking, or pushing a toy, changes how infants experience the world (Franchak, 2020; Gibson, 1988). Moving also changes how other people relate to babies. A running child is treated much differently from an immobile infant. Movement launches a cascade of development across different parts of a baby's life.

This is one reason that pediatricians and public health experts advise caregivers to monitor how children are learning to use their bodies (Zubler et al., 2022). Movement is linked to many aspects of infants' early cognitive and emotional development. Thus, experts advise that children who are not developing their motor skills in a typical pattern receive early developmental screening or support to mitigate difficulties. Being able to move independently enables Silas, and other children, to control their own bodies and experiences. Some evidence indicates that early movement skills may encourage children's curiosity and benefits their growing cognitive and language skills: something Silas's family noticed as he became more mobile (Flensborg-Madsen & Mortensen, 2018; Ghassabian et al., 2016).

Movement helps babies learn more about the many possibilities in the physical world. For instance, a phone may be good for sucking, for tapping on, or even for throwing off a highchair. Researchers have a term for what people can make from objects in the world around them: **affordance** (Gibson, 1979, 1988). One of the basic affordances infants make about the environment is whether it is safe. For instance, what will happen if they head down the stairs?

Over the years, researchers have put babies into dozens of situations to learn how they understand what is safe. They have thrown things toward babies' heads to see if they would duck (the flying objects would never actually hit them) and found that even very small children can accurately gauge how fast a ball is moving and when to move away. They have observed how babies walk or crawl on a jiggly waterbed or over a gap in the floor. Researchers famously tested babies' willingness to take risks by watching to see if they would crawl right off a ledge, using a device called a **visual cliff** (see **Figure 4.5**) (Anderson et al., 2013; Gibson, 1988; LoBue & Adolph, 2019). Originally designed to test babies' visual depth perception (Gibson & Walk, 1960), the visual cliff is a 2½-foot gap covered with plexiglass that, if properly lit, appears to be an empty gap. Researchers have also tested babies with more extreme versions of the visual cliff, like gaps in the floor, but always with an adult close by so no one gets hurt.

This research demonstrated that it takes weeks of experience before babies learn what is safe. Experienced walkers or crawlers will stop before the edge of a dangerous situation, whether that is a big gap or a steep slope, but babies who have just learned to crawl or walk tend to make mistakes (Han & Adolph, 2020). The practical note is that babies are in more danger of making mistakes right after they have learned a new skill. They will fall off beds and tumble down stairs or slopes. Babies do not automatically learn what is safe and what is dangerous, as they master new motor skills.

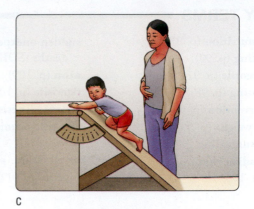

A   B   C

FIGURE 4.5 Learning from Experience
Researchers study how infants think about decisions in the laboratory by watching how they move. In panel A, you can see how a baby investigates the visual cliff, a piece of plexiglass that appears transparent. This baby seems to be an inexperienced crawler and is making a risky choice, which might result in a tumble in real life. In panel B, a new walker is taking a chance by going head-first down a steep slope. Without practice, they are likely to fall. In panel C, a more experienced walker takes the safer route and goes down the steep slope on their belly.

Babies need to re-learn rules about safety as they master each new skill. Babies need time to integrate the new movements with the sensory information they receive from the environment (Adolph, 2019).

APPLY IT! **4.5** Health providers often check infants' hearing as part of their developmental screening. Why is hearing so important to babies' development?
4.6 Practice and experience change what we can perceive. How does this support Blaire and Sam's decision to expose Silas to many new foods and sensory experiences early in development?
4.7 Babies are at risk for accidents as they learn new skills. What should families be careful of as their babies learn to move independently?
4.8 How do infants' new motor skills change how people respond to them?

Wrapping It Up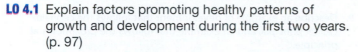

LO 4.1 Explain factors promoting healthy patterns of growth and development during the first two years. (p. 97)

Infants grow more rapidly than at any other point in the lifespan, and their health is more fragile. Infant mortality remains high around the world and is distributed inequitably. Healthy nutrition, ideally including human milk, helps set the stage for a lifetime of health. Adequate sleep, access to health care, and vaccination also help babies thrive.

LO 4.2 Explain the role of neurons and synapses in brain function during the first two years. (p. 107)

The brain doubles in volume and adds *synapses*, or connections between neurons, during the first two years. Communication in the brain is faster as a result of myelination. Pruning of underused neural connections helps make brain circuits more efficient. The brain develops in response to experience, adding synapses and myelin to regions of the brain that are frequently activated. The brain is plastic in responding to the environment, but there are limits to its ability to bounce back from traumas.

LO 4.3 Describe vision and hearing development in infancy. (p. 112)

Infants are born with a preference for faces, and their vision develops rapidly in the first years, allowing them to shift their focus and perceive details. Babies' hearing is also improving but is attuned to voices and speech. Perceptual narrowing describes how babies' senses gradually specialize in the sights and sounds they are exposed to most frequently.

LO 4.4 Explain how the typical maturation of movement changes a baby's experience of the world. (p. 112)

Babies develop independent control of their gross and fine motor systems. They tend to learn to move their bodies in a cephalocaudal pattern, as they develop the ability to move their heads. They also learn to control their core first, in proximodistal development. It takes practice for babies to learn how to move, and it often requires readjustment of how they see the world.

KEY TERMS

malnutrition (p. 97)
wasting (p. 97)
percentile (p. 97)
stunting (p. 98)
intervention (p. 98)
overweight (p. 99)
immunization (p. 103)
circadian rhythm
  (p. 105)

sudden unexpected infant
  deaths (SUID) (p. 106)
axon (p. 109)
dendrite (p. 109)
synaptogenesis (p. 109)
synaptic pruning
  (p. 109)
myelination (p. 109)
myelin (p. 109)

experience-expectant brain
  development (p. 110)
experience-dependent brain
  development (p. 110)
preferential looking
  technique (p. 113)
perceptual narrowing
  (p. 114)
motor development (p. 115)

gross motor development
  (p. 115)
fine motor development
  (p. 115)
cephalocaudal (p. 116)
proximodistal principle
  (p. 117)
affordance (p. 118)
visual cliff (p. 118)

CHECK YOUR LEARNING

1. Why is it important to identify which babies may be at risk for mal-nutrition in early life?
   a) To check for early evidence of eating disorders
   b) To make sure their bodies are getting the nutrition they need to build their brain
   c) To see if they are eating too much
   d) To evaluate their appetite

2. What is the major cause of infant mortality in the United States and around the globe?
   a) Complications from birth and prenatal development
   b) HIV/AIDS
   c) Malnutrition
   d) Sleep injury

3. At Tamara's son's 3-month pediatric checkup, the doctor said that the baby's weight is now at the 60th percentile. This means that Tamara's son:
   a) weighs more than 60 percent of other infants his age.
   b) is overweight.
   c) weighs 60 percent of what he should weigh at his age.
   d) is underweight.

4. How is infant sleep different from adult sleep?
   a) Infants' brain development and memory consolidation happen at night.
   b) Infants require assistance to get back to sleep.
   c) Infants often wake up between sleep cycles.
   d) Missing sleep affects infants' moods.

5. Which of these processes is unique to infancy?
   a) The volume of the brain increases dramatically.
   b) Myelin helps to speed neural communication.
   c) Synapses that are unused are pruned away.
   d) New synaptic connections are created.

6. Which of these is an example of experience-dependent brain development for a typically developing child?
   a) Learning to understand American Sign Language
   b) Learning to differentiate different colors
   c) Learning to communicate with language
   d) Sleeping through the night

7. During the early months of infancy, typical babies can perceive subtle differences in language sounds in languages they have never heard before. By age 1, they have begun to lose this ability. This phenomenon is known as:
   a) the visual cliff.
   b) a language deficiency.
   c) perceptual narrowing.
   d) monolingual development.

8. How does practice change babies' progress with motor development?
   a) More practice usually helps infants learn more quickly.
   b) The timing of motor milestones is entirely genetic, so practice does not matter.
   c) Practice is overwhelming to infants and is not safe.
   d) Practice destroys babies' motivation to move.

9. Describe an example of development that follows the cephalo-caudal principal, and an example that follows the proximodistal principle.

10. What is myelination, and how does it affect infant and toddler development?

Cognitive Development in Infancy and Toddlerhood

© Macmillan, Photo by Sidford House

Cognitive Development

5.1 Explain maturation in thinking during Piaget's stage of sensorimotor development.

5.2 Identify improvements in attention and memory during infancy and toddlerhood.

5.3 Describe the contributions core knowledge and cultural theorists have made to our understanding of infant cognition.

Early Learning

5.4 Describe the factors influencing learning during the first two years.

Language Development

5.5 Describe the typical pattern of language development in the first two years.

Marjorie and Dewey were excited to be parents. Before their daughter Telele arrived, they went to dozens of doctor's visits, read baby books, and picked a pediatrician. They wanted to make sure that their daughter had the best beginning possible.

Marjorie and Dewey knew that learning is important even in the first few years of life. As members of their Iñupiaq and Denaakk'e Alaskan communities, they wanted Telele to know from the beginning that she was linked to her people and their land. They wanted to welcome their daughter with the beauty of their culture: Marjorie even had Iñupiaq symbols tattooed on her legs so that they were the first images Telele saw as she was born. And the first words Telele heard were in Iñupiaq and Denaakk'e: "We love you baby. Welcome, welcome."

Marjorie and Dewey fell in love through a shared commitment to their Indigenous community, speaking their native languages and living close to the land. When they met, Dewey was teaching Denaakk'e at a Head Start center, and Marjorie was in graduate school and working as an artist. Marjorie, whose background is Iñupiaq and Kiowa, had been speaking Iñupiaq since she was a teenager. Dewey became passionate about learning and teaching Denaakk'e after he finished college.

Like many caregivers, Marjorie and Dewey have big dreams for their child. They want Telele to identify as a proud, Indigenous adult and to feel connected to their communities. They want to teach her to fish for salmon, collect berries, and bead intricate designs like her great-grandmothers. They also want to ensure that

Scientific American Profile

Meet Telele

Learning Objectives

5.1 Explain maturation in thinking during Piaget's stage of sensorimotor development.

5.2 Identify improvements in attention and memory during infancy and toddlerhood.

5.3 Describe the contributions core knowledge and cultural theorists have made to our understanding of infant cognition.

CONNECTIONS

Remember from Chapter 2 that Jean Piaget developed a stage theory of development. He believed new skills and insights (he called these *schemas*) develop day-by-day through a process of *assimilation* and *accommodation*, which propel children into each new stage.

sensorimotor Piaget's term for the cognitive stage that spans the first 18 months of a baby's life and focuses on learning through sensation and movement.

primary circular reactions The second stage of Piaget's sensorimotor period, from about 1 to 4 months, in which babies begin to adapt their reflexes to new uses and show more creative behavior.

Telele is healthy and can make her way in an English-speaking world. Therefore, Telele is learning not only Denaakk'e and Iñupiaq, but also English and a little sign language. Like one in five American children, Telele will be *multilingual*, a speaker of more than one language (ACS, 2018).

Like Telele, infants and toddlers are flexible in how they adapt, whether it is speaking one language or three, depending on the expectations of their families and communities. The first years of life set the foundation for cognitive development later on. As you will learn, there are a variety of ways to support babies as they develop the curious minds they will need to thrive.

Cognitive Development

The first two years of life involve continuous learning. For instance, Telele, like most babies, came into the world with eyes blinking, hardly able to see her surroundings. By age 2, she was confident enough in her understanding of the world that she could count her birthday candles and sing her stuffed moose to sleep with an Iñupiaq lullaby. There was certainly extensive development in Telele's ability to reason and understand the world, in her memory, and in her ability to pay attention and learn.

Piaget's Theory of Cognitive Development

Remember from Chapter 2 that Jean Piaget changed common attitudes about infant's minds, helping researchers realize that even infants are curious and inventive in their approach to understanding the world. Piaget saw young infants' early cognitive activity as a combination of their senses and their motor activities rather than real thinking (Piaget, 1952). He did not believe infants were truly capable of what we call thought or intelligence until they used language and symbols, at around 18 months (Piaget, 1952). But he did think there were important developments in learning going on before language develops. Piaget described the first 18 months of a baby's life as the **sensorimotor** period because of the focus on learning through sensation and movement. He divided this period into six substages (see **Table 5.1**).

In stage 1, called *reflexes*, from birth to about 1 month, newborns are a bundle of reflexes, like the rooting and sucking reflexes reviewed in Chapter 3 (Piaget, 1968). Newborns are not limited to reflexes for very long. They may begin by indiscriminately sucking anything that comes close to their mouths, like a finger or even a button. But babies soon begin to learn about the world. They soon learn that they cannot suck everything as they do a breast or a bottle. Infants begin to recognize and develop *schemas* about what can be sucked. This is a major accomplishment: They are remembering and developing concepts about how the world works.

Three-week-old Telele may not have looked like she was deep in thought as she sucked on her fingers, but according to Piaget, she was actually doing a lot of cognitive work. While Piaget did not consider this work "thinking," he recognized that remembering how a pacifier works and how to move your mouth in a specific way to respond to it is quite an achievement (Piaget & Inhelder, 1969).

In stage 2, called **primary circular reactions**, from about 1 to 4 months, babies begin to adapt their reflexes to new uses and show more creative behaviors (Piaget, 1952). The term *primary circular reaction* refers to an experience the baby repeats with their own body (primary), and that is repeated on purpose again and again (circular). Piaget believed babies' first adaptation to the world is to apply their basic reflexes, like sucking and grasping, to new purposes. Piaget observed this stage in his own children as they learned to suck their fingers for the joy of it (Piaget, 1952).

TABLE 5.1 Piaget's Sensorimotor Stage of Cognitive Development

Stage	Key Events	
Stage 1 Reflexes (birth to 4–6 weeks)	Babies cannot consciously control much of their bodies, but they can move nonetheless. Their hands reflexively grasp, and they suck whatever approaches their mouths. In this stage, they begin to assimilate new behaviors, like sucking their thumb, onto existing reflexes.	Thirawatana Phaisalratana/Getty Images
Stage 2 Primary Circular Reactions: Adaptation of Reflexes (1–4 months)	Infants can now adapt their movements and newborn reflexes to the world around them. They can suck a pacifier differently than a stuffed animal. They can grasp a finger differently than a rattle. In primary circular reactions, they can repeat adapted reflexes again and again.	LiuSol/iStock/Getty Images
Stage 3 Secondary Circular Reactions: Making Fun Last (4–8 months)	Infants can manipulate their bodies as well as other people or things. They enjoy not only their own movement but also its effect on something in the world. They can watch as a toy on a mobile jiggles again and again as they shake it.	Dorling Kindersley ltd/Alamy
Stage 4 Coordination of Secondary Reactions: Making a Plan for Action (8 months–1 year)	Babies can begin to make a plan and carry it out. They can anticipate what is going to happen next, like giggling with happiness as they try to put on a hat to go out into the snow.	Seth Hill/Getty Images
Stage 5 Tertiary Circular Reactions: Little Scientists Running Experiments (1 year–18 months)	Toddlers can manipulate their world to explore through trial-and-error: "What happens if I drop this toy off of my highchair?" or "What happens if I squeeze all the diaper cream out of the tube into a pile?"	Dorling Kindersley ltd/Alamy
Stage 6 Mental Combinations: Thinking Before Doing (about 1½–2 years)	Toddlers can make a plan in their mind without taking action. They can also use symbols, like language, to get what they want. They can call for their father for help or indicate that they have lost their sock.	Cavan Images/Getty Images

In stage 3, called **secondary circular reactions**, from about 4 to 8 months, babies learn to extend their activities to manipulate the world around them. Infants discover that they can use their bodies to act on an external object, which could be a toy, a person, or a pet, to get a reaction. Babies in this stage are happily interactive. Piaget described his daughter, Jacqueline, gently shaking a doll hanging from her bassinet. She clearly enjoyed her new power and, in Piaget's words, the glory of "making interesting sights last" (Piaget, 1952). She understood what the shaking would do, and when she was later lying in her bassinet for a nap, she remembered the action that led to the shaking doll and did it again.

In stage 4, *coordination of secondary circular reactions*, from about 8 to 12 months, infants are ready for new adventures. Babies can make a plan and combine separate schemas to accomplish their goals. This means they can remember activities and try to recreate them. Sometimes this new ability means they can try and avoid some activities—like crawling away when their father appears with wipes and says it is time for a diaper change.

At this age, Piaget observed that babies have discovered **object permanence**, the understanding that objects continue to exist even when they are out of sight (Piaget, 1954). Rather than appearing to ignore a hidden object, a baby who has achieved object permanence will search for it, looking around and lifting items to look underneath. This ability to keep the idea of an object in mind after it disappears from sight is an important milestone in infants' thinking. This means that Dewey could no longer trick Telele by hiding his keys out of her sight in the diaper bag.

In stage 5, *tertiary circular reactions*, between 12 and 18 months, Telele was even more clever. Sometimes, as when toddlers gleefully smear shaving cream on the bathroom floor, this stage is messy. Piaget called children this age *active experimenters* and *little scientists*. In this stage, not only are toddlers repeating activities that they enjoy, shaking a rattle, or grabbing for a toy that they like, but they are now varying and changing their activities in search for something new. They demonstrate **tertiary circular reactions**, or the ability to deliberately vary their actions to see the results. Like scientists, babies are trying to learn more about the world and the results of their actions (Piaget, 1952).

Unlike real scientists, at this age, babies do not have the ability to develop hypotheses or even imagine consequences, so they use trial-and-error to learn about the world. Toddlers may drop things in the toilet to explore the basic physics of objects sinking. This is a good time for parents to invest in toilet locks, to avoid toothbrushes, bath toys, or makeup clogging the drain. For better or worse, caregivers' frustration is no match for toddlers' drive to explore. Toddlers in stage 5 have the ability to repeat events and vary them, but their planning abilities are limited. They impulsively act and react, which may not be reassuring for the caregiver who must clean up the mess.

In stage 6, *mental combinations*, from about 18 to 24 months, toddlers can think through their plans and experiments *before* they act. The trial and error may now happen inside their head. Their improved memory means that they can now imitate behaviors they have seen, sometimes days or even weeks before. For instance, toddlers might be eager to make cookies, just like their parents. They might go right into the kitchen, push a chair toward the counter, and begin "mixing" ingredients into a bowl. Even though they make a mess, these toddlers are showing evidence of **mental representation**—the ability to think things through using internal images rather than needing to act on the environment and the first sign of true intelligence.

You can see many examples of toddlers' early ability to form mental representations in their use of language to get what they want and in their early use of make-believe. For instance, Telele might shout "qipmiq" when she is looking for her stuffed husky. She has developed the ability to use words and objects to represent things that she is not, using her senses or her body to manipulate them. This is an early

secondary circular reactions The third stage of Piaget's sensorimotor period, from about 4 to 8 months, in which babies learn to extend their activities to manipulate the world around them.

object permanence The term for the understanding that objects continue to exist even when they are out of sight.

tertiary circular reactions Babies' ability to deliberately vary their actions to see the results.

mental representation The ability to think things through using internal images rather than needing to act in the environment.

indication of the transition from the sensorimotor period to the next stage, preoperational thought. In the preoperational stage, the use of symbols and language will lead to make-believe, long stories, and the ability to learn even more about the world.

Piaget's theory is nearly 100 years old, and subsequent research has refined some of his ideas. Scientists now believe that babies are much more capable than Piaget gave them credit for: that they understand object permanence, for instance, much earlier than he thought (Carey et al., 2015; Rochat, 2018). In addition, Piaget did not write much about the influence of culture and the social world on babies' development (H. E. Davis et al., 2021). Now, through observation of babies in different contexts, researchers know that emotional and social cues are critically important for babies' cognitive development. A baby raised in a structured environment and carried much of the time, for instance, will be less of a "little scientist" than one allowed ample unstructured time and the space to practice dropping Cheerios on the floor.

Piaget's focus on the development of thought helped stimulate generations of scholars to focus on exactly how babies learn to remember, pay attention, and make connections between events. This emphasis on cognition revolutionized how we understand babies.

Building Mental Representation with Grandpa This little girl is learning to love reading and building her schemas, or mental representations, for what books mean with her grandfather at home in New Jersey.

Information Processing

In the decades since Piaget first wrote about children's thinking, many modern researchers have taken an *information-processing approach* to understand how children and adults think. Remember from Chapter 2 that this approach focuses on the individual components of thought and intelligence as they develop over time. These components include *attention*, the process of focusing on the information we take in through our senses; *memory*, how we save this information for later use; and *processing speed*, how quickly we are able to retrieve and use this information.

Paying Attention If you watch a newborn for a few minutes, you might wonder if they can pay attention. Over the course of a few minutes, they might look out into space, yawn, cry, and then nurse. Researchers closely observing how infants suck and where they look have discovered that although newborns' attention may look haphazard, they actually *can* focus (Hendry et al., 2019). Over their first year, babies get better at paying attention, whether to a toy they are playing with or to the face of someone singing them a lullaby (Abney et al., 2020).

Newborns struggle to move from looking at one thing to another, which researchers call *sticky fixation*. Once they start looking at one thing—say, the gently swaying mobile above their crib—it is hard for them to move their attention to something else (Rosander, 2020). By 4 months, as their sight improves, so does their ability to shift their attention. They become able to scan what is in front of them—which enables them to, say, pick out a particular toy from a pile. By 9 months, infants can look at things in an even more sophisticated way. They start to look at things that are interesting, rather than just fixating on whatever is in front of them (Papageorgiou et al., 2014). Babies can now hold their attention on one thing, a particular face or a picture, for longer periods of time (Reynolds & Romano, 2016).

One way that babies learn to focus is through *coordinated* or *joint attention*, the process of focusing on something with someone else (Amso & Lynn, 2017; McQuillan et al., 2020). Joint attention is at work when Dewey and Telele look at pictures in a book together, and it improves her ability to focus (Vally et al., 2015). Caregivers model and motivate babies to focus by telling a story, pointing to and explaining a new toy, or singing a silly song. This early attention training is thought to help them focus in school when they are older (Blankenship et al., 2019).

Scientific American Profile

How Caregiving Builds Cognitive Skills

autism spectrum disorder (ASD)
A cognitive and communication condition characterized by differences with communication and social interaction.

habituation A basic form of learning in which you become bored with something if you experience it repeatedly.

MAKING A DIFFERENCE
Early Screening and Intervention

Just a generation ago, health care professionals often took a "wait-and-see" approach when families were concerned about differences in their babies' early cognitive development. They suggested that children would "grow out of" any developmental differences and that early interventions would not help (Raspa et al., 2015). But that has changed. In the past decade, researchers have shown that dramatic growth happens in infants' thinking and learning in the first few years. Health care providers and scientists are now able to identify differences in cognitive development—and to intervene early when the brain is highly sensitive to environmental input (Zwaigenbaum et al., 2021). Screening for the milestones of cognitive development is now part of standard well-child visits in the United States (Committee on Practice et al., 2021).

Intervention and screening have particularly benefited children with an increased likelihood of having **autism spectrum disorder (ASD)**, a cognitive and communication condition diagnosed in about 1 in every 54 young children in the United States (Shaw et al., 2021) Some early signs of ASD include lack of eye contact and joint attention, as well as difficulty engaging in responsive back-and-forth communication such as pointing or talking (APA, 2022; Hyman et al., 2020). Young children with increased likelihood of developing ASD also may be especially reactive to sounds, lights, taste, or touch and may have passionate interests in one type of activity or toy (B. Smith et al., 2020). Early screening has helped reliably identify children as young as 12 months who may need support, and more children than ever are being identified when they are toddlers and can most benefit from intervention (Shaw et al., 2021; Zwaigenbaum et al., 2021).

Experts believe ASD is linked to genetic and brain anomalies. It is a *spectrum* disorder, which means that children with ASD have variable levels of skills and challenges. Some may require significant support: About 3 in 10 children diagnosed with ASD do not talk, and about half have intellectual developmental disorders (Hyman et al., 2020). Others may have more subtle symptoms but also benefit from support, particularly in building relationships and resilience to stigma (Kapp, 2020).

Children and adults with ASD often face challenges in a world that is not open to people who are different. They must also grapple with inaccurate stereotypes about the disorder (R. White et al., 2020). Early identification enables children with ASD to receive intervention at younger ages, boosting their communication skills (Rogers et al., 2019). Interventions also encourage responsive caregiving, acceptance of children's distinctive abilities, and understanding of the benefits of a neurodiverse world. The goal is not to eliminate the differences between children diagnosed with ASD and their peers, but to help children develop the skills—particularly communication—that will allow them to advocate for themselves and live meaningful lives (Bottema-Beutel et al., 2020; Kapp, 2020).

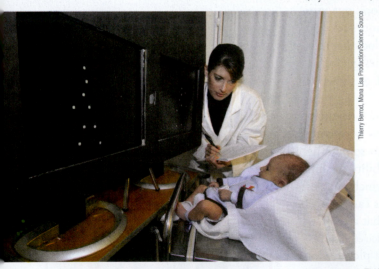

FIGURE 5.1 Which Dots Speak to You? A researcher in Grenoble, France, watches to see where this newborn is looking. Will they recognize the difference between the shapes shown on the right and the left? This experimental design can help scientists understand how long it will take babies to habituate to a stimuli and what they prefer to look at.

Memory Babies may not be able to explain what happened to them last week, but they remember more than you might think. Some babies seem to remember things at just 6 months, such as the telltale mobile at the pediatrician's office.

How do we know what babies remember? First, we react differently to things we remember. Remember from Chapter 3 that **habituation** is a basic form of learning in which you become bored with something if you experience it repeatedly. Researchers use habituation to observe whether babies notice differences between experiences or objects, called *stimuli*. If babies habituate to one object, they will begin to ignore it and look away. Given a choice of two objects, one they have seen many times and one that is new, they prefer to look at the new one. In this way, researchers can tell whether babies notice the difference between the two.

Researchers also examine how long it takes babies to become habituated. Whereas newborns typically need to look at a new stimulus, like the dots in **Figure 5.1**, a few times before they can remember it, 1-year-olds only need to look for 10 seconds before they can remember it (Hayne et al., 2015). By age 3 or 4, children only need a few seconds to be able to remember faces for months. Habituation tells us about memory, because in order to habituate to a stimulus, whether it is the smell of your burned toast or a cartoon face, you must be able to remember it. If you have forgotten it, you will react to the stimulus as if you are experiencing it for the first time.

Changes in Memory Infants are born with some unique memory strengths: They are very good at remembering people, which helps them learn new skills and processes from their caregivers, from picking up a cup to taking off their diaper. The memory for these skills and processes and the ability to habituate are referred to as **implicit memory**, which is nearly mature by 3 months (Rovee-Collier & Giles, 2010; Vöhringer et al., 2018). At the same time, they are lacking in **explicit memory**, which is the memory for facts or details (Amso & Kirkham, 2021).

Some groundbreaking studies done with a simple hanging mobile and a piece of ribbon helped researchers understand the strength of babies' early implicit memory and the fragility of their long-term memory (Cuevas & Sheya, 2019; Schneider & Ornstein, 2019). Babies as young as 2 months were introduced to a crib mobile with a ribbon hanging down from it (see **Figure 5.2**). Then researchers tied one of the baby's legs to the mobile so that the baby could move the mobile by moving their leg. After the baby realized the association between the movement of their leg and the movement of the mobile, the researchers tested the babies to see if they would remember it later on. If the baby later tried to move the mobile by kicking their leg, the researchers concluded that the baby remembered the procedure. If the baby did not move their leg at all, researchers concluded that they had forgotten.

The babies studied in this experiment, even those just a few months old, had a tremendous capacity to remember this experience. However, their memories were fragile. If something changed in the environment—for example, if the crib was decorated differently or if the room had an unusual smell—the babies were likely to forget to kick altogether (Rovee-Collier & Cuevas, 2009). As babies grew older, their memory abilities also grew stronger, despite changes in their environment.

Why do babies get better at remembering? One reason is that they have practice, but another has to do with brain development. As babies' brains mature, remembering gets easier. The areas of the brain that are involved in implicit memory (the memory for how to do something) mature long before those involved in explicit memory (memory for facts and events). Regions of the brain involved in implicit memory include the subcortical structures and some areas of the sensory and motor cortex (Gómez & Edgin, 2016; Jabès & Nelson, 2015).

The major brain structure underlying memory is the *hippocampus*, a small seahorse-shaped structure located near the center of the brain. The hippocampus matures slowly (see **Figure 5.3**). The hippocampus nearly doubles in size during infancy, and neurons continue to migrate into the hippocampus into the preschool years (Ellis et al., 2021). Connections between the hippocampus and other parts of the brain build quickly during early infancy and toddlerhood (Liu et al., 2021). These connections are one reason preschoolers, as you will learn in Chapter 8, have stronger memory skills than toddlers.

CONNECTIONS
Remember that habituation is an impulse that humans share with simpler animals like slugs. You have probably experienced this yourself if you have burned a piece of toast. When the smoke first filled the kitchen, you were annoyed by it, but after a few minutes, you stopped noticing it until your roommate came in the room and asked what happened. You became habituated to the smell, and you did not even notice it anymore.

Courtesy of Dr. Carolyn Rovee-Collier

FIGURE 5.2 Scientific Experiments Can Be Fun. Researcher Carolyn Rovee-Collier noticed that her son was happy when he could jiggle the mobile above his crib (as seems to be the case with the baby in this photograph), allowing her some time to work. She turned this observation into groundbreaking research, demonstrating that babies, like this one, have strong procedural memory very early in their lives.

implicit memory Memory of new skills and processes and ability to habituate.

explicit memory Memory of names, dates, and details.

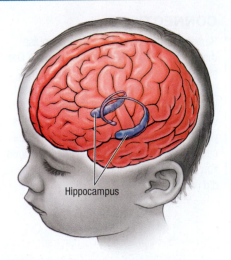

FIGURE 5.3 Memory and Brain Development
During infancy and toddlerhood, the hippocampus, a U-shaped structure deep inside the brain, grows rapidly, supporting ongoing improvements in memory.

What Do Babies Know Already?

You might not think that Telele knew very much as a newborn, but some researchers argue that babies are born with a wide range of innate knowledge about how the world works. Some researchers have focused on the language acquisition skills that infants are born with, and others look at the ways babies are predisposed to look at the world from the moment they arrive (Chomsky, 2002; Carey & Spelke, 1996). This may seem farfetched, but careful experimental work has suggested that even newborns may have more understanding than you might guess.

Researchers with a **nativist**, or *core knowledge*, **approach** investigate how much babies are born knowing. This approach represents the "nature" side of the nature–nurture continuum. For instance, even as a newborn, Telele knew that three objects cannot magically become two and that there is a difference between a living being, such as an animal, and an inanimate object, such as a coffee cup (K. A. Smith et al., 2020; Tardiff et al., 2020). Using looking paradigms and habituation methodologies to observe how babies respond to different possible and "impossible" scenarios, scientists have demonstrated that even newborns understand some basic processes, including:

- *Basic physics.* Not only do babies seem to grasp the principle of gravity, that unsupported objects should fall, but they also understand that two objects cannot take up the same physical space (Lin et al., 2021). Why do researchers believe this? Because babies tend to look longer at things that seem improbable, as if they are thinking "what?" and furrowing their eyebrows. Scientists create elaborate animations and puppet shows that seem to show objects overlapping or being supported in thin air: Infants stare at the events that violate their expectations.
- *Basic math.* Even newborns seem to have an innate sense that counting can refer to the number of things in a row, and they recognize when one item disappears (Spelke, 2017). Scientists have observed that even newborns seem to expect that counting for a long time refers to a larger number of objects than counting for a short time (Izard et al., 2009).
- *Basic biology.* Babies have some simple ideas about what makes an animal different from an inanimate object; for example, it can move on its own and it is not hollow inside (Setoh et al., 2013). Newborns will stare longer when they are shown an animation that depicts a living being that is hollow inside.
- *Basic psychology.* Even infants have a sense that people are more likely to help other people they know or who are part of their same group (Ting et al., 2020). They also assume that in a conflict, bigger players will win over smaller players (Thomsen, 2020).

Do these decades of close examinations of what infants look at with surprise mean that nativist theorists have concluded that babies are ready for college? Not at all. Instead, these scientists ask us to appreciate the tremendous capabilities that infants are born with. Awareness of what babies are born knowing can be used to design interventions that help young children learn (Dillon et al., 2017).

Born to Imitate

Nativist, or core knowledge, theorists are not the only developmental scientists who recognize newborn babies' innate genius. More than 40 years ago, when one researcher sat in front of a newborn and stuck out his tongue, he found that, with enough time and patience, the newborn will often respond with a similar facial expression in return (Meltzoff, 2020; Meltzoff & Moore, 1977). Later researchers found that newborns also imitate hand movements and even sounds (Nagy, 2011; Nagy et al., 2020).

Lisa5201/E+/Getty Images

Do As I Do. Newborn babies sometimes imitate caregivers' facial expressions. The drive to copy helps propel infants' early learning.

nativist approach A theoretical perspective that maintains that babies are born knowing a great deal about how the world works. (Also called the *core knowledge approach.*)

Imitation is yet another tool that helps infants learn and adjust to the world. Learning how to talk, for example, is much easier if a baby can watch a caregiver's mouth and mimic the same shapes with their own mouth. Understanding that someone else's body is similar to one's own is an essential part of early imitation (Nagy et al., 2020). Although babies may continue to imitate and learn (think about how easily a toddler can pick up a "bad" gesture they have seen just once), automatic imitation tends to fade in favor of more active imitation games later in life (Yu & Kushnir, 2020). How strong and robust early imitation is remains controversial, but scientists agree that copying is a crucial part of how children learn (J. Davis et al., 2021; Slaughter, 2021).

Culture, Context, and Early Cognition

Developmental scientists who study the impact of culture address how much early development is determined by culture and context, rather than by a universal genetic blueprint. They are interested in the "nurture" part of the nature–nurture continuum: Does how a baby is cared for impact how their thinking develops? Many cognitive abilities, like the abilities to learn, talk, imitate, and remember, are experience-expectant: They develop in all children who are given care, nutrition, and stimulation. However, context is also critical. Many early cognitive skills, from how children learn to their attention and memory, are experience-dependent, or contingent on the cultural context around them (Arauz et al., 2019; Legare, 2019).

One challenge in examining the impact of culture and community context on development is in finding ways of measuring development that are culturally neutral. For instance, scientists often try to study how well babies can mimic an adult's action. This imitation, a type of learning that demonstrates babies' implicit memory, happens around the world, but assessing it is often difficult. Researchers in affluent countries often test this skill by asking babies to repeat a series of actions done with toys, like pressing a button to make a train move, or using a puppet to turn on a light switch. As it turns out, prior experience with toys affects how babies perform on these tests.

For instance, when researchers compared the performance of babies in Germany who grew up with plastic toys to babies from the rural farming community of the Nso in Cameroon, who grew up playing with other children and in the natural environment, they found that that the two groups imitated quite differently. However, after studying the data a bit more, researchers realized that the difference between the two groups was in their toy skills, not in their imitation skills. When children who grew up in the Nso community were given time to familiarize themselves with the plastic toys, all the children performed similarly (Borchert et al., 2013; Kolling et al., 2016).

When developmental scientists design tests that are culturally neutral, they find there are cultural and community differences in development. For instance, as early as 1 month, babies in some cultures have longer memories and greater attention spans than those in others (Clearfield & Jedd, 2013; Werchan et al., 2019). All babies will learn to pretend and to find hidden objects, but some will do so as much as 18 months sooner than others (Callaghan, 2020; Callaghan et al., 2011). Many of these skills seem to be experience-dependent: Babies receive a lot of early practice in skills valued by their communities and, as a result, perform better at them. For instance, this enriched experience and practice builds memory capacity (Hayne et al., 2015). Toddlers who spend a lot of time talking about the past tend to remember their early experiences longer than other children.

How babies learn also depends on what families expect from children. Inspired by Vygotsky, researchers have observed that in many cultures, adults do not spend much time explicitly teaching babies one on one (Shneidman et al., 2016a, 2016b). Babies in these

CONNECTIONS
Remember from Chapter 1 that many theorists, including Lev Vygotsky, emphasize the role of culture in how children learn.

A-not-B error Inability of toddlers to keep track of a hidden object if it is moved from one location (A) to another (B), even when they see it being moved.

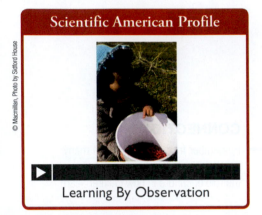

Scientific American Profile

▶ Learning By Observation

cultures learn primarily from watching, overhearing, and even helping with what is going on, called *learning through observation and pitching in* (Rosado-May et al., 2020) Developmentalists have found that babies who live in communities where observational learning is encouraged are better at learning from this teaching style than other children are. Thus, babies learn how to learn in a way that fits their culture (Shneidman et al., 2016a). For instance, Marjorie found that Telele learned from observation how to pick berries in the tundra on her own (eating a bunch as well as putting some in the bucket).

How Do Theories Help Explain Why Babies Can't Find Lost Toys? A number of theories help describe different aspects of the many changes in babies' thinking from birth to age 2, including those of Jean Piaget, information-processing theorists, cultural researchers, core knowledge thinkers, and researchers who focus on early imitation. How do these different theories explain how babies get better at finding lost toys?

When infants get their hands on something forbidden, a caregiver can easily hide the object, and the baby will act as if the object has vanished into thin air. Young infants will not persevere in trying to find the hidden object. After about 7 months, babies will try to find the object by plaintively staring at its last location or picking up a pillow to look under it. But it isn't until about age 1 that they begin to systematically and accurately locate hidden objects.

What does this tell us about how babies think and the structure of their minds? Jean Piaget devised a task to test babies' ability to find things that typically leads them to display the **A-not-B error** (see **Figure 5.4**). In this test, a baby is shown a toy that is then hidden in one place (A) several times, where it is found by the baby if the baby is around 8 months or older. Then the toy is moved, in full view of the baby, to another hiding place (B). The baby is distracted for a minute and then allowed to search for it. Babies younger than about 10 months will typically reach toward the first location (A) to find the missing toy, rather than where they saw the toy most recently hidden (B). Why do they reach toward the wrong place? Researchers have performed this task with thousands of babies (and other animals) over the decades to explore this question.

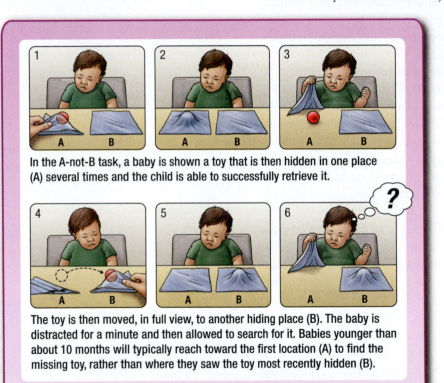

In the A-not-B task, a baby is shown a toy that is then hidden in one place (A) several times and the child is able to successfully retrieve it.

The toy is then moved, in full view, to another hiding place (B). The baby is distracted for a minute and then allowed to search for it. Babies younger than about 10 months will typically reach toward the first location (A) to find the missing toy, rather than where they saw the toy most recently hidden (B).

FIGURE 5.4 The A-Not-B Task Researchers developed the A-not-B task to assess infants' development of object permanence. They found that when a caregiver hides an object, a young infant will act as if the object has vanished. The baby will not hunt for it. After they are about 8 months old, babies will try to find the object, staring at its last location or moving a barrier to look for it. Not until 10–12 months do they begin to locate hidden objects that have been moved to a new location.

Piaget Based on his observations with his own children and others, Piaget believed that young babies do not understand that objects continue to exist when out of sight. He thought that it wasn't until infants were in sensorimotor stage 4 that they discovered *object permanence*, the understanding that objects continue to exist even when they are out of sight (Piaget, 1954). He suggested that babies who continue to look for the object in the incorrect location have not fully accomplished object permanence, and that they believe that reaching for the object itself is what makes it exist (Piaget, 1954; Wellman et al., 1986). Piaget concluded that object permanence begins to develop at around 8 months but isn't fully developed until age 18 to 24 months.

Information Processing Whereas Piaget theorized that babies' failure and eventual success on the A-not-B task were due to fundamental changes in their cognitive structure, information-processing scientists saw more discrete processes at work. One key part of the task involves waiting before looking for the toy after it is hidden in place B.

In some experiments, babies have to wait a few seconds, but in others they are made to wait a bit longer. Researchers found that younger babies failed this test more often if they were forced to wait for a longer period of time after the object was hidden in the new location. Older babies, with more robust memories and more interconnected brains, were able to remember where the object was hidden for longer (Bell et al., 2012; Diamond, 1985; Marcovitch & Zelazo, 1999).

This revealed that memory might be one key problem tapped by the task. Babies had simply forgotten where the toy was and were searching randomly. However, these researchers also found that the more times babies searched for and successfully found the toy at place A, the more difficulty they had inhibiting this impulse and looking for it in place B. They couldn't pay attention to the correct location because they were still focused on reaching toward A. Information-processing scientists believe that babies have the ability to pay attention, focus, and remember, but that these systems are underdeveloped and overwhelmed by the demands of the task. According to some of the researchers, this test measures early **executive function,** or the cognitive skills that enable you to control your thinking and focus, rather than object permanence (Diamond, 1985; Marcovitch et al., 2016; Munakata, 1998).

Nativist Theorists In the late 1980s, researcher Renee Baillargeon demonstrated that even very young babies have a sense of object permanence. Young babies may not physically be able to reach or pick up a blanket to reveal the hidden toy every time, so Baillargeon used other measures, such as watching what babies are looking at to see what they are expecting. Using looking techniques, Baillargeon found that babies as young as 3½ months old clearly recognize that hidden objects still exist, even if they are not immediately visible (Baillargeon, 1987).

Nativist, or core knowledge, theorists, like Baillargeon, suggest that babies are born with an innate sense of basic physical properties, including the fact that objects can't suddenly disappear. They suggest that babies' confusion in the A-not-B task comes from delays in the development of the ability to remember and search, rather than a lack of understanding of object permanence. Nativist theorists point out that adults often make perseverative errors, like driving to work on a Saturday morning out of habit instead of the grocery store, but that doesn't mean that they don't understand object permanence (Brace et al., 2006).

Culture Theorists Scientists who look at the impact of culture and context on human development point out that not all children perform the same way on the A-not-B task. In fact, children who are neglected or deprived make more errors on the task than children from more affluent homes (Lipina et al., 2005). Practice paying attention and managing distractions, and even practice playing with toys, impacts how well young children can find an object hidden under a blanket.

What can we learn from these different theoretical approaches? First of all, babies' thinking may be very different from adults', but it is nevertheless complex. A particular challenge with infants is how to measure what they know—a 3-month-old cannot explain why they are no longer looking for the keys that their father is hiding behind his back. What all these theoretical approaches have in common is the belief that babies are actively making sense of their world and capable of learning from their experiences (see **Infographic 5.1**).

APPLY IT! **5.1** How would Piaget explain why Telele methodically drops pieces of pear from her highchair and watches them fall?

5.2 How does Telele's memory help her learn how to pet a dog, beat a drum, and eat with a spoon, but make it difficult to memorize the alphabet?

5.3 How does the development of object permanence explain why Telele got better at searching for lost toys when she entered toddlerhood?

executive function Your ability to actively regulate your thinking and behavior to accomplish a goal.

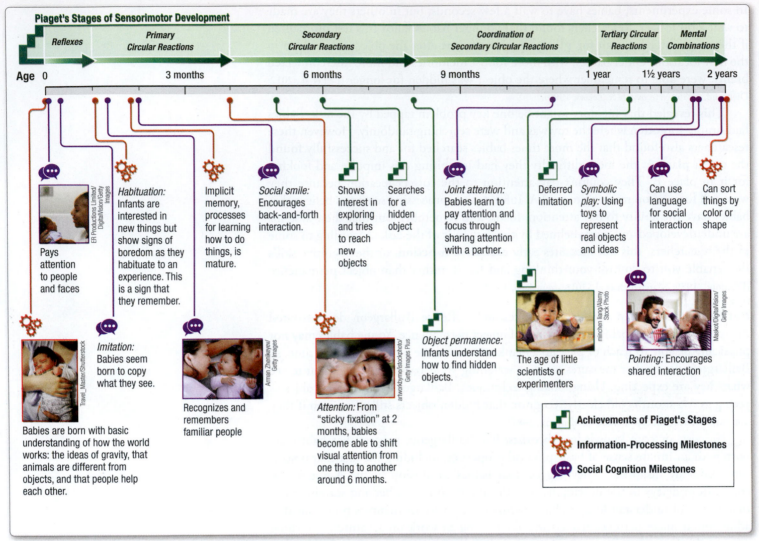

Piaget's Stages of Sensorimotor Development

| Reflexes | Primary Circular Reactions | Secondary Circular Reactions | Coordination of Secondary Circular Reactions | Tertiary Circular Reactions | Mental Combinations |

Age 0 — 3 months — 6 months — 9 months — 1 year — 1½ years — 2 years

Pays attention to people and faces

Habituation: Infants are interested in new things but show signs of boredom as they habituate to an experience. This is a sign that they remember.

Implicit memory, processes for learning how to do things, is mature.

Social smile: Encourages back-and-forth interaction.

Shows interest in exploring and tries to reach new objects

Searches for a hidden object

Joint attention: Babies learn to pay attention and focus through sharing attention with a partner.

Deferred imitation

Symbolic play: Using toys to represent real objects and ideas

Can use language for social interaction

Can sort things by color or shape

Babies are born with basic understanding of how the world works: the ideas of gravity, that animals are different from objects, and that people help each other.

Imitation: Babies seem born to copy what they see.

Recognizes and remembers familiar people

Attention: From "sticky fixation" at 2 months, babies become able to shift visual attention from one thing to another around 6 months.

Object permanence: Infants understand how to find hidden objects.

The age of little scientists or experimenters

Pointing: Encourages shared interaction

Legend:
- Achievements of Piaget's Stages
- Information-Processing Milestones
- Social Cognition Milestones

Information from Baillargeon, 1987; Brace et al., 2006; Diamond, 1985; Lipina et al., 2005; Marcovitch et al., 2016; Marcovitch & Zelazo, 1999; Piaget, 1954.

Early Learning

Learning Objective

5.4 Describe the factors influencing learning during the first two years.

At age 2, Telele has already learned a great deal. Like many babies, she benefits from lots of enrichment: Telele has been read to and sung to, and is learning four languages. She has doting parents and an extended family who are thrilled to be helping to raise the next generation.

It is challenging for researchers to measure early cognitive skills in babies. A missed nap or a growth spurt can make it difficult to know whether a baby has fallen behind or is just having a bad day (LoBue et al., 2020). However, researchers who track babies' development over time begin to see strengths and challenges in their cognitive skills even before age 2 (Betancourt et al., 2016; Johnson et al., 2016). What builds a baby's cognitive skills?

- *Good health.* As already explained, adequate nutrition before and after birth is essential for early brain development. Lack of iron, chronic infection, or exposure to toxins, even in babies who are generally healthy, can cause delays and challenges in cognitive development (Bach et al., 2022; Georgieff et al., 2018; Valentine, 2020).
- *Attention.* Babies benefit from shared, joint attention from caregivers. Whether Telele is pointing at a bird on the feeder, watching her mother unpeel a banana,

or drawing with her parents, eye contact and joint attention help babies learn to focus (Brandes-Aitken et al., 2019; Suarez-Rivera et al., 2019).

- *Responsive caregiving.* Caregivers who respond to vocalizations, movements, and gazes are encouraging their babies to explore, communicate, and learn from them. Back-and-forth, or *contingent*, interactions, where babies and caregivers share a toy, a conversation, or a clapping game, are critical to early cognitive development (King et al., 2019; McCormick et al., 2020; Rosen et al., 2020). Caregivers are more likely to be responsive when they are happy: Around the globe, babies are more likely to thrive when their caregivers have the physical and emotional energy and resources to attend to them (Sania et al., 2019).

Around the world, nearly one in three children is at risk for cognitive delays or disabilities that begin in infancy (McCann et al., 2020). The major cause is poor health, often due to malnutrition or chronic conditions like malaria (M. M. Black et al., 2020; French et al., 2020). In affluent countries like the United States, cognitive challenges are more frequently caused by neglect and adversity. Researchers have various measures for the number of *adverse experiences* a family faces during infancy, like the loss of a primary caregiver, violence, living with a family member with a serious mental health or substance use disorder, discrimination, or food or housing insecurity (Felitti et al., 1998; Hodel, 2018). The more adverse experiences an infant's family faces without enough support, the more likely the baby is to have cognitive consequences (Luby et al., 2020).

In the United States, about one in three young children has experienced at least one adverse experience, and one in five lives in a family with low income (ACS, 2020; Crouch et al., 2019). Adversity is a risk factor, not a prediction: Millions of babies whose families experience poverty, trauma, or stress do not have cognitive delays (Noble & Giebler, 2020).

Caregivers who are stressed may have less time to give infants the attention they need. Exposure to too many stress hormones can disrupt brain development. Neglect, leading to a lack of early stimulation, may cause critical neural pathways to be pruned instead of grown (Amso & Lynn, 2017). Early difficulties often stem from systemic issues in the community, rather than problems in an individual family (Shonkoff et al., 2021).

 SCIENCE IN PRACTICE

Shoneice Sconyers, B.S.W., M.S., Family Resource Partner

Shoneice describes herself as a "connector," someone who brings people together. She uses these skills and her graduate degree in social work to support children and families in need. Shoneice knows that the best way of building young children's resilience is to boost the capabilities of their families, who can give them the interaction and attention they need to grow.

One of the most serious risks to young children's developing cognitive skills is trauma, which can result from homelessness, having a caregiver with a mental illness, or having a serious illness of their own, among other difficulties. The emotional impact of trauma and other stresses, sometimes referred to as *adverse childhood experiences*, can make it more difficult for caregivers to care for their children. For instance, the emotional impact of trauma may limit back-and-forth communication, and young children's language and cognitive development may suffer as a result.

Sconyers has years of training and coursework, but she likens her job to being a "fairy godmother." Her mission: First, fill in the gaps and stop the stress when she can.

It is more difficult for caregivers to function if they are under strain, so programs like Sconyers' are designed to help connect families to housing, medical care, and employment assistance, which lessens their everyday adversity. Second, provide caregivers and their children with the therapy and coaching they need to repair their relationship. Caregivers with stronger executive function and emotion regulation will be better able to support their children's development.

Programs like Sconyers' have been shown to encourage more back-and-forth between toddlers and their caregivers, which continues even after the intervention services are over (LoRe et al., 2018). Sconyers says she loves the work, and that it "lights her up on the inside." 🎙️

Approaches to Boost Cognitive Development

Around the world, many early interventions to promote children's development focus on taking care of families' basic needs and well-being, such as making sure adults have access to parental leave, health care, and basic financial resources (Clark et al., 2020; Richter et al., 2017). Programs also focus on enhancing caregiving, so that parents, grandparents, and even older siblings can have responsive interactions with babies (Cuartas et al., 2020). Home-visiting programs, such as the Nurse–Family Partnership and ChildFirst, have shown to be effective in fostering children's early cognitive development and caregivers' well-being (Heckman et al., 2017; Molloy et al., 2021).

Another way of supporting and advancing cognitive development in young children is to make sure that they receive high-quality care outside of the home (Burchinal & Farran, 2020). High-quality child care typically has a lower ratio of children to caregivers, who have an academic background in child development and provide responsive, developmentally appropriate care. Early Head Start and Educare, a public–private partnership program, have both been shown to provide high-quality center-based child care (Yazejian et al., 2017).

Unfortunately, these government-sponsored programs are not accessible to all families: For example, Early Head Start serves fewer than half of all eligible children due to inadequate funding (NASEM, 2018). During the COVID-19 pandemic, even fewer toddlers were able to access quality out-of-home care, as many programs shut down around the world (Gilliam et al., 2021). One sign of early child care that is of poor quality is if babies and toddlers spend time in front of a screen or if caregivers are particularly stressed (Blasberg et al., 2019; Hewitt et al., 2018; Reid et al., 2021).

How Does It Work? Exploring a toy in this child care center in Tupelo, Mississippi, involves trial-and-error and engaging conversation. A caregiver's responsive, back-and-forth interactions with these toddlers will help them learn.

Adam Robison/The Northeast Mississippi Daily Journal via AP

Keeping Screens Out of Strollers

Screens are popular with families of small children, but pediatricians and developmental scientists have found that babies do not benefit from and may even be harmed by too much exposure to screen media (AAP, 2016; WHO, 2019a). For instance, the American Academy of Pediatrics (AAP) advises that babies not watch any video or screens at all until 18 months of age, and that older babies be limited to an hour a day viewed with an adult.

Developmental scientists suggest that time spent in front of a screen is time when babies are not doing things that are proven to help them develop. Infants and toddlers on screens are not engaging in responsive interaction, playing, or sleeping—activities that spur their social, cognitive, and emotional development (Madigan, McArthur, et al., 2020; Willumsen & Bull, 2020).

Despite these recommendations, many babies are exposed to more than six hours of background television and are actively watching screens for more than three hours a day (Barr et al., 2020; Chen & Adler, 2019; NSCH, 2021). The amount of screen time for babies increased dramatically after the COVID-19 pandemic in 2020 (Monteiro et al., 2021). Caregivers often use media to keep children occupied, allowing them to play a smartphone game or watch a video while a parent is on a Zoom call or washing dishes (Chen & Adler, 2019; Rideout, 2013). Babies are quieter and less disruptive when they are in front of a screen, but that helps the caregivers, not the infant.

Many caregivers, perhaps influenced by claims of the educational value of videos or apps, believe that media can accelerate cognitive development. Researchers have come to the opposite conclusion: Screens do not offer the critical back-and-forth, contingent interaction that babies need in order to learn (C. Li et al., 2017). However, babies interacting with real people through real-time video, such as a Zoom or FaceTime call, *do* pick up new words and information. As a result, developmentalists and pediatricians conclude that there is some benefit to infants who engage in video chats because they involve a responsive give-and-take (Strouse et al., 2018). So, weekly video chats with Grandma can still be beneficial because of this responsive give-and-take conversation (Myers et al., 2017).

Families may also not realize that their own media use, time spent on the phone, or the movie playing in the background, may also affect their babies. Caregivers may think that their toddler does not notice when they check their updates or take a quick call, but researchers have found that they are highly attuned to what other people do around them. Children have a harder time focusing if a caregiver is distracted or interrupted by a text or call. Toddlers learn less if their interactions are interrupted by a phone call (Reed et al., 2017).

It is not just screens and phones that interfere with responsive interactions. When researchers observe family interactions in the laboratory setting, they find that caregivers who are reading or filling out paperwork also are missing out on back-and-forth interactions (Konrad et al., 2021). However, it is not clear what kind of *ecological validity*, or application to the real world outside the laboratory, this finding offers. Babies may crave constant back-and-forth contact, but even the most devoted caregivers must balance that with caring for other children, paying the bills, and heating up lunch.

It has been clearly established that babies do not learn much from media or videos, but does this mean that it is harmful to allow babies to tap on a phone? Research has not concluded that exposure to media over time results in cognitive or language delays in babies or toddlers. Correlational research has linked hours spent watching *television* with delays in language development and difficulties sleeping, but remember that correlation does not equal causation: Television may not be the cause of these difficulties. Likewise, just because babies who watch more television and spend more time with mobile devices tend to have trouble sleeping and to develop attention difficulties does not necessarily mean that exposure to media caused those problems. There could be another factor.

Perhaps caregiving is the variable responsible for these problems. Or perhaps there is something different about the children themselves: Perhaps children who spend more time with media are different from other children. Researchers caution that there is no longitudinal research that ties toddlers' use of smartphones to their long-term development since the devices are still too new. Researchers' major concern is that spending too much time on screens reduces the important back-and-forth interaction that babies need to develop their brains (Radesky, 2021; McArthur et al., 2022).

APPLY IT! **5.4** Telele's parents are planning to send her to early child care. What qualities would you suggest they look for in a caregiver or child-care center?
5.5 What would you tell Dewey and Marjorie about the relationship between screen media and toddlers' cognitive development?

Language Development

Learning Objective

5.5 Describe the typical pattern of language development in the first two years.

From Bubbles to Babbling Blowing raspberries might not seem like communication, but it may help children practice the mouth movements that are linked to speech.

The World from a Baby's Perspective How does this baby know that his caregiver is talking about the oatmeal in the bowl? Researchers believe that babies use social cues, shared attention, and statistics. Frequently used words are more likely to be associated with frequently used objects.

For developmental scientists, the complexity of language is amazing, in part because it is unique to human beings. No other animal or machine can come close to the flexibility, versatility, and humor that humans can understand and produce. At birth, Telele can mostly just express discontent. By age 2, Telele's new language skills mean that she can now point, talk, and complain. She can ask for pears instead of cheese with dinner at 13 months and tattle on her cousin at 24 months.

By age 2, most toddlers' language skills are impressive: They are able to understand about 150 words per minute and respond in a conversation in about 200 milliseconds (Chater et al., 2016). When developmental scientists talk about language, they are not just talking about *talking*. Language is not only the words you say or read. It is a complex, rule-based system for using symbols to communicate. These symbols include spoken words, gestures, shrugs, facial expressions, finger signs, and even emojis.

Much of the brain is involved in learning language (Fedorenko & Thompson-Schill, 2014). As neuroscientists have studied the brain, they have discovered that much of the left side of the cortex is devoted to communication and that the right hemisphere is also activated in some activities, such as when babies identify their caregiver's voice (Dehaene-Lambertz, 2017). As children's brains develop, maturation in the cortex and myelination across the brain makes it faster and easier to listen and respond (Silver et al., 2021).

Steps to Talking and Understanding

Babies communicate from the moment they are born, beginning with the cry that reassures everyone that they survived childbirth. They soon begin to make other noises, such as grunts, growls, and squeals. Researchers have found that even the youngest infants make about than 5 noises every minute that they are awake (Oller et al., 2021). These noises begin to get happier over the first few months, with laughter appearing at about 3 months, and these early coos and grunts become easier to interpret as expressions of contentment or fussiness (Oller et al., 2019). Some of these early coos even sound like speech, although they are much more nasal and filled with vowels.

At the same time, babies are listening. Infants can understand language long before they are able to produce it, perhaps because they get more practice listening than they do speaking (Chater et al., 2016). By 5 months, they can recognize a few words, such as their name, from the flow of sounds that runs by them (Holzen & Nazzi, 2020). At about 6 months, they can associate words with a wide variety of things (see **Figure 5.5**).

One challenge from a baby's perspective is that there are so many words and so many things they could refer to. Researchers tracking babies' eyes have observed that they use cues such as gesture, shared attention, eye gaze, and even intonation to learn what people are talking about (L. B. Smith et al., 2018). Babies even use statistics: They notice combinations of sounds that are more common than others. Statistics also help them figure out which parts of words are frequently repeated, like endings (*-ed*, *-ing*, or *-s* in English) and function words (*of*, *to*, and *that* in English) (Saffran, 2020).

As babies begin to understand what they are hearing, they are learning how to produce new sounds. There are more than 225 different muscle combinations involved every second of spoken English (the combinations vary for other languages). Babies cannot learn to move these muscles by just looking, as most of these movements for talking are hidden inside the mouth. So, learning takes practice and experimentation (MacNeilage, 2008).

At about 5 months, infants can predictably produce sounds (Yeung & Werker, 2013). In the next few months, they begin to experiment with short sounds that sound more

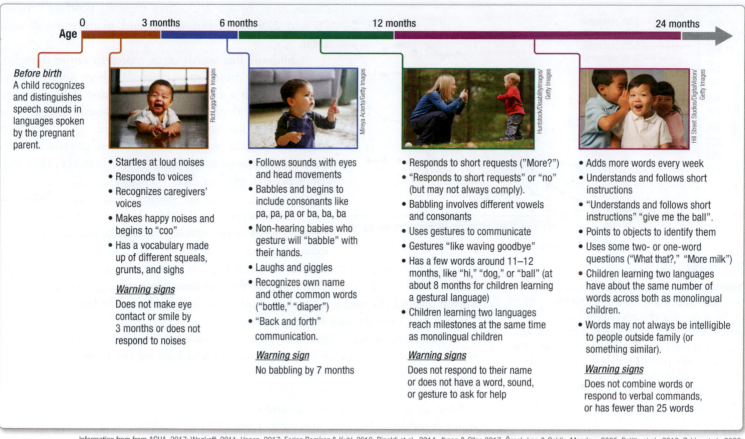

Age   0   3 months   6 months   12 months   24 months

Before birth
A child recognizes and distinguishes speech sounds in languages spoken by the pregnant parent.

- Startles at loud noises
- Responds to voices
- Recognizes caregivers' voices
- Makes happy noises and begins to "coo"
- Has a vocabulary made up of different squeals, grunts, and sighs

Warning signs

Does not make eye contact or smile by 3 months or does not respond to noises

- Follows sounds with eyes and head movements
- Babbles and begins to include consonants like pa, pa, pa or ba, ba, ba
- Non-hearing babies who gesture will "babble" with their hands.
- Laughs and giggles
- Recognizes own name and other common words ("bottle," "diaper")
- "Back and forth" communication.

Warning sign

No babbling by 7 months

- Responds to short requests ("More?")
- "Responds to short requests" or "no" (but may not always comply).
- Babbling involves different vowels and consonants
- Uses gestures to communicate
- Gestures "like waving goodbye"
- Has a few words around 11–12 months, like "hi," "dog," or "ball" (at about 8 months for children learning a gestural language)
- Children learning two languages reach milestones at the same time as monolingual children

Warning signs

Does not respond to their name or does not have a word, sound, or gesture to ask for help

- Adds more words every week
- Understands and follows short instructions
- "Understands and follows short instructions" "give me the ball".
- Points to objects to identify them
- Uses some two- or one-word questions ("What that?," "More milk")
- Children learning two languages have about the same number of words across both as monolingual children.
- Words may not always be intelligible to people outside family (or something similar).

Warning signs

Does not combine words or respond to verbal commands, or has fewer than 25 words

Information from from ASHA, 2017; Wankoff, 2011; Hanen, 2017; Ferjan Ramírez & Kuhl, 2016; Rinaldi et al., 2014; Jhang & Oller, 2017; Özçalışkan & Goldin-Meadow, 2005; Petitto et al., 2016; Zubler et al., 2022.

like language (Cychosz et al., 2020). These short, repetitive, syllable sounds, like ba-ba-ba or pa-pa-pa (in English), are called **babbling**. Babbling typically begins at about 4 months and becomes more and more speechlike by 7 months, as combinations of consonants and vowels are produced and reproduced. Babies around the world typically babble regardless of whether they are raised by talkative families or in quieter homes, whether they are babbling in speech or in gestural languages, like American Sign Language (Flaherty et al., 2021; Petitto & Marentette, 1991).

Babies babble as their brains mature and as they begin to consciously manipulate their vocal cords to make sounds using some of the same movements that they use to suck and blow bubbles. Babbling also seems to make babies happy; neuroscientists think that the brain releases more *dopamine*, the pleasure hormone, as they babble (Warlaumont & Finnegan, 2016). Babies babble in sounds from the language they are exposed to or in movements if their family uses sign language. Telele, as you might have guessed, babbled with English, Iñupiaq, and Denaakk'e sounds.

No matter where they are born, babies usually begin to produce their first words around the time of their first birthdays (MacWhinney, 2017). Babies who use gestural languages sign their first words a few months earlier (Özçalışkan & Goldin-Meadow, 2005). Around the world, caregivers report that babies' first words are about them: words like *Mama* (in English and Spanish) or *Baba* (*father* in Arabic and Marathi) (Ferguson, 1964). *Mama* and *Dada* are usually followed by other early words like *hi*, *bye*, *more*, and *no*, reminding us that toddlers use words socially (Frank et al., 2021). Telele's favorite word was, like many toddlers, "no."

While babies' vocabularies are building, their language acquisition varies dramatically (Dick et al., 2016). Some babies will show a vocabulary "burst," as you'll see in **Figure 5.6**, but others may show a slow-and-steady rise with many typical variations

FIGURE 5.5 Highlights of Language Development Language skills help infants learn and build relationships. There are many variations in how children learn to understand and produce language, but most children follow a predicable sequence. Children whose development is not quite typical may need extra support.

Share It!

Did masks affect language development? Some researchers found that babies were able to learn new words from people who wore traditional, opaque masks but had trouble learning from people who wore clear masks. Researchers suspected that the relatively unusual clear masks made it hard for babies to focus.

(Singh et al., 2021)

babbling Short, repetitive, syllable sounds, like ba-ba-ba or pa-pa-pa (in English), that begin at about 4 months and become more speechlike by 7 months.

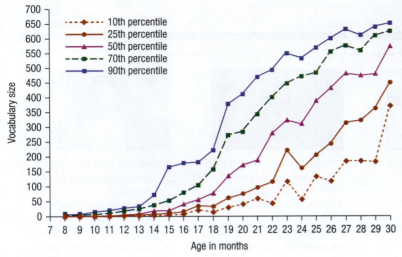

Data from Fenson et al., 1994.

FIGURE 5.6 How Many Words Do You Know? There are diverse patterns in how quickly children learn new vocabulary words. This graph shows the speed at which one group picked up new words and whether they ended up with large vocabularies, like those who were in the 90th percentile, or smaller ones, like those in the 10th percentile.

holophrases Single-word utterances by toddlers that may represent larger ideas.

telegraphic speech A short two- or three-word utterance missing grammatical filler words, such as "Go beach" to represent "I am going to the beach."

overextension An error in which a child assumes that a specific term relates to a larger category.

underextension An error in which a child insists that a word only applies to a specific member of the group, rather than the whole group itself.

fast-mapping A child's ability to quickly learn new words.

(Werker, 2018). By age 2, children typically produce between 75 and 225 words but understand many more (Rescorla, 2019).

Children's first words often represent entire thoughts. For instance, "more" may mean "is there another piece of apple," or in a different context, "more tickles." Scholars call these single words that represent bigger ideas **holophrases** (Tomasello, 2006). As children get older, they begin to combine words. Most of these phrases are very formulaic (Ambridge & Lieven, 2015). For instance, they may use repetitive phrases like "Where's _____" or "Let's _____" or "More _____" (Ibbotson, 2013). Some experts call these short phrases **telegraphic speech**. (The term comes from *telegram*, an old-fashioned communication device that transmitted words over electrical lines in the pre-cell phone era. Telegrams charged per character, so people kept communications short and sweet.) You can hear telegraphic speech when Telele putters around the house asking her mother for "more salmon" in both Iñupiaq and English, just to make sure she understands.

Researchers consider these early word combinations evidence of grammar, which refers to how we use words in a specific order and how we use tenses, prefixes, and suffixes to add meaning. For instance, "man bites dog" has a vastly different meaning from "dog bites man," even though the sentence includes the same three words. Word order is at the heart of grammar and is something children are beginning to understand as toddlers. For instance, when researchers test toddlers' understanding, babies are able to understand the difference between "the duck chasing the bunny" and "the bunny chasing the duck" before they are 2 (Tomasello, 2015).

Speaking perfectly takes quite a lot of practice. Young children may have difficulty with articulation sounds, where they may say "pisgetti" instead of "spaghetti." They also make grammatical mistakes.

This rapid vocabulary development can mean being overly rigid about what words refer to, in errors of **overextension** or **underextension**. A toddler who is overextending might assume that a specific term relates to a larger category, such as insisting that all birds are called pigeons. In a similar error, a toddler who is underextending might insist that the word *cat* only applies to their pet and never to the neighbors' cat. These errors will generally be corrected naturally as children use them in give-and-take conversations with others. Nonetheless, it is shocking how often children *don't* make errors. In one count, a researcher estimated that in English there are 24 quintillion (that is 18 zeros!) possible ways of using verbs, and only 100 of them are correct (Pinker, 1994). So, it is fairly impressive that children do as well as they do.

In addition to learning grammar, babies are building their vocabularies. By 18 months, they can learn new words almost instantaneously. For instance, if you offer a toddler a kumquat, saying: "Here, try a kumquat," they will immediately understand that the word "kumquat" refers to the tiny orange fruit (Weatherhead et al., 2021). This ability to quickly learn new words is called **fast-mapping** (Byers-Heinlein & Lew-Williams, 2018; Carey, 1978, 2010). Researchers have tested babies with nonsense words in a variety of laboratory and real-life settings. Toddlers will quickly learn new words like "wug" or "chromium" from hearing them once and even use them themselves ("pass me the wug," "the chromium tray"), with proper plurals or verb tenses. Fast-mapping, this quick adoption of new words, increases babies' vocabularies exponentially, which is why people who spend a lot of time with small children must watch what words they are using. Babies can just as easily fast-map that word you used to describe a bad driver as the name for a zoo animal.

What Helps Babies Learn to Talk?

Babies all over the world learn to communicate in one or more of 6,000 languages. How many words they learn and how fluently they use them depends on how much early language they practice. Just like learning to walk or ride a bike, learning to talk takes work. Babies who hear and use a lot of language develop larger vocabularies, which seems to help children do well later in school (Ferjan Ramírez et al., 2020).

Many adults use high-pitched, sing-songy tones and simple sentences when they talk to infants, which scholars call **infant-directed speech (IDS)**. Infant-directed speech helps babies pick out a single word in a mass of sounds and helps them focus (Byers-Heinlein et al., 2021). IDS does not have to be high-pitched baby talk or oversimplified language; its key characteristic is a responsive give-and-take, even if the child may not respond in full sentences or can only coo (Masek et al., 2021a).

In many communities, adults do not speak directly to babies and toddlers very often (Cristia et al., 2019). For instance, adults in Polynesia and Samoa believe that small children should not be spoken to until they begin to speak. The idea, as one scientist explains, is that the "child has to adapt . . . rather than the other way around" (Stoll & Lieven, 2014, p. 26). Rather than talking, families may rock, touch, or bounce their infants to entertain them. Despite this lack of early language exposure, babies in these cultures learn to talk at about the same age as babies in other places (Shneidman & Goldin-Meadow, 2012). However, the more babies are directly spoken to, the larger their vocabularies (Lopez et al., 2020; Madigan et al., 2019). The more responsive caregivers are to their babies' attempts to communicate, often called "bids" for attention, the more verbal their babies are likely to become (N. J. Anderson et al., 2021).

Within the United States, the amount of talk babies hear—and how verbally responsive their caregivers are—varies dramatically (Hart & Risley, 1995). Research that uses voice-activated recorders has shown that some families speak to their children as much as 20 times more than others (Bergelson et al., 2019). The amount of language a baby hears is correlated with the size of their vocabulary and their scores on later cognitive development tests (Madigan et al., 2019). (See **Figure 5.7**.) Does this correlation mean that quiet caregivers are the reason children might not meet the expectations for language development? That would be going too far and confusing correlation with causation. Cognitive and language development is more complex. In fact, some have suggested that identifying the differences in language exposure may stigmatize toddlers who have limited vocabulary (Adair et al., 2017; Williams, 2020). Others point out that families' interactions with their babies may reflect systemic marginalization and stress, which may be more closely linked to their children's development than their caregiving practices (Golinkoff et al., 2019).

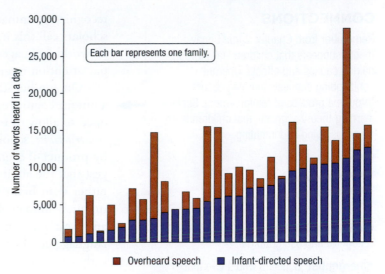

FIGURE 5.7 How Much Language Do Children Hear? There are differences in how much speech toddlers hear. In this study, researchers used tiny recording devices to record how much caregivers spoke with their 19-month-olds over a day. In one talkative family, a toddler heard 1,200 words an hour. In another family, a toddler heard only 67 words an hour. The number of words the babies heard was directly related to how well their language skills developed six months later.

Do They Mean to Be Rude? Babies learn about the world by pointing, interacting, and playing peek-a-boo with Dad.

Theories of Language Development

For many researchers, understanding how language develops comes down to a question of the environment, or nurture, versus genes, or nature (Chomsky, 1957; Friederici et al., 2017). On one side of the debate are scholars who believe that humans are typically genetically programmed to develop language (Berwick & Chomsky, 2017). They believe that all human beings are born with innate abilities designed specifically to learn language. In particular, these theorists point to babies' unique ability to

infant-directed speech (IDS) Adults' use of high-pitched, sing-songy tones and simple sentences when they talk to infants.

CONNECTIONS

Remember from Chapter 2 that behaviorist theory suggests that children learn through pairing causes and effects. Operant conditioning suggests learning occurs through a process of reinforcement. Social learning theory suggests that children learn from observing and imitating.

universal grammar A child's inborn ability to recognize and use grammar.

emergentist Scholars who argue that humans' drive to communicate and imitate and ability to recognize patterns, rather than brain processes specifically devoted to language, created the uniquely human ability to use language. (Also called *constructivist.*)

 **Learn It Together**

Reflect on Multilingual Development

Plan Analyze the benefits of multilingual language development. Review the information in this chapter about some of the benefits and challenges of learning multiple languages during the first few years of life.

Engage Divide into groups and share personal experiences or reflections from Telele's story about the cultural and cognitive benefits and potential challenges of multilingual development.

Practice Connect personal experience with research on multilingual development. How does your personal experience help support or challenge what you've learned about the research on multilingual development? Practice your skills in scientific communication by connecting the shared reflections to specific research findings and recommendations. Develop a set of "talking points" that could be used to communicate research information to parents raising multilingual children.

Reflect How should concepts of cultural humility be brought into the practice of communication with families about language development?

recognize grammatical rules without being taught them (Pinker, 1984). These nativist scholars call this inborn ability **universal grammar** (MacWhinney, 2017). They note that all world languages have grammar and argue that the infant brain is programmed to pay attention to grammar in the language they hear.

On another side of the debate are those scholars who suggest that language is not a unique cognitive process but rather is a skill that emerged as the human brain developed to allow us to think and relate to others (Bohn et al., 2019). These **emergentist**, or *constructivist*, scholars argue that human abilities to speak emerged, or appeared, as a by-product of cognitive development in a broad range of areas. For instance, they suggest that the ability to recognize patterns and the drive to communicate and imitate, rather than brain regions or processes specifically devoted to language, created the uniquely human ability to use language. Similarly, learning theories like *behaviorism* and *social learning theory* apply their basic concepts of conditioning and imitation to language development. These theorists argue that language develops because infants' early vocalizations are rewarded with praise and attention, and that children observe and imitate the language models around them.

As brain and behavioral research has expanded, most developmental scientists today adopt something close to the emergentist position. They recognize that language has both genetic *and* environmental influences. Most focus on the connections between language and other types of learning and communication. Although the complexity of language is different from other cognitive skills, it builds on many other forms of communication and thinking that toddlers demonstrate, such as their ability to imitate, think symbolically, and remember.

The Multilingual Advantage

Growing up speaking more than one language is the norm for most people around the world (Ramírez & Kuhl, 2016). In the United States, about one in five children speaks a second language (ACS, 2018).

Children raised in multilingual homes have a host of benefits. Switching from one language to another is linked to improvements in attention and communication skills and builds executive function and the self-regulation that helps them control their behavior and work toward a goal (Antoniou, 2019). For instance, babies exposed to two languages have to remember whether Grandma says "cat," or "gato" like Mom, so they must use their attention and perspective-taking skills a little more every day. These benefits are thought to last a lifetime (Bialystok, 2020).

Multilingual infants reach their early language development milestones, like babbling and first words, at about the same time as children exposed to only one language (Petitto et al., 2001). However, they tend to develop vocabularies and sophisticated grammar in each individual language more slowly than children learning just one language (Höhle et al., 2020). Children who are learning two or more languages are typically exposed to fewer words in each language, so although their combined vocabulary in both languages may be the same as that of monolingual children, their vocabulary in each separate language tends to be smaller (Lauro et al., 2020). Multilingual children may not catch up to monolingual children until they are about 10 (Hoff & Core, 2015).

What does this mean for Telele? Being fluent in multiple languages will not be her only advantage. Like all multilingual children, she will likely demonstrate more advanced executive function than monolingual children her age. In addition, Telele's languages will create a sense of identity and belonging to her community (Lynch, 2018). Language helps connect Telele and her parents to their ancestors, their land, and the sacred knowledge of their community. As Dewey and Marjorie explain, every word they teach Telele reminds them that language is "a connection to culture and a guidebook to survival," a way to "give Telele strength and a sense of who she is."

APPLY IT!   **5.6** A friend is worried that her 18-month-old makes mistakes when she speaks. For instance, she sometimes calls cats in their neighborhood "Twinkles"— the name of her pet cat. What might you say to reassure this friend about her daughter's development?

5.7 Telele is already using four languages at home with her family. What would you tell her parents about the strengths and possible challenges of being a multilingual toddler?

Scientific American Profile

How Multilingualism Boosts Cognition

Wrapping It Up

LO 5.1 Explain maturation in thinking during Piaget's stage of sensorimotor development. (p. 122)

Piaget called infancy and toddlerhood the sensorimotor period, which is divided into six stages: reflexes, primary circular reactions, secondary circular reactions, coordination of secondary circular reactions, tertiary circular reactions, and mental combinations. Infants develop object permanence and can mentally represent the results of their actions.

LO 5.2 Identify improvements in attention and memory during infancy and toddlerhood. (p. 122)

Information-processing researchers look at the components of cognition, such as attention and memory. Attention is critical to learning. Joint attention refers to the ability to share focus with someone else and is a way babies learn from others. Over the first year of life, babies develop better control of their focus and can pay attention for longer periods of time. Differences in attention appear in toddlerhood and can be one of the differences that are apparent in children with conditions such as autism spectrum disorder. Brain development, particularly in the hippocampus, and practice help babies develop memory skills. Babies have strong implicit memory skills (memory for how to do something) but are weaker at explicit memory (memory for facts).

LO 5.3 Describe the contributions core knowledge and cultural theorists have made to our understanding of infant cognition. (p. 122)

Core knowledge, or nativist, theorists focus on the knowledge babies are born with. Other researchers have found that babies are born with strong skills in imitation. Cultural theorists study how cultural expectations and caregiving change how babies think and learn.

LO 5.4 Describe the factors influencing learning during the first two years. (p. 132)

The first two years are a time of rapidly building skills. Learning depends on good health, attention from caregivers, and responsive back-and-forth stimulation. Interventions can help families build stronger, responsive relationships. Experts agree that screens and apps do not help babies learn in the first few years and take time away from more important interactions.

LO 5.5 Describe the typical pattern of language development in the first two years. (p. 136)

Babies are born attuned to language, which can include spoken words, gestures, and facial expressions. Communication typically develops through stages, from babbling, to telegraphic speech, to complex speech. Toddlers typically learn words quickly through fast-mapping and usually speak 200 words by age 2, but they understand many more. Nativist theorists suggest that language development is a unique human ability distinguished by a universal grammar. Emergentist scholars suggest that language development is more closely connected to other cognitive skills. Responsive caregiving and infant-directed speech (IDS), help build language skills. Multilingual and bilingual children tend to have stronger executive function and self-control but take longer to build their vocabularies.

KEY TERMS

sensorimotor (p. 122)
primary circular reactions
    (p. 122)
secondary circular reactions
    (p. 124)
object permanence (p. 124)
tertiary circular reactions
    (p. 124)

mental representation
    (p. 124)
autism spectrum disorder
    (ASD) (p. 126)
habituation (p. 126)
implicit memory
    (p. 127)
explicit memory (p. 127)

nativist approach (p. 128)
A-not-B error (p. 130)
executive function (p. 131)
babbling (p. 137)
holophrases (p. 138)
telegraphic speech (p. 138)
overextension (p. 138)

underextension (p. 138)
fast-mapping (p. 138)
infant-directed speech (IDS)
    (p. 139)
universal grammar (p. 140)
emergentist (p. 140)

CHECK YOUR LEARNING

1. How does responding to or interacting with infants influence their cognitive development?
   a) Infants do best without too much outside stimulation.
   b) Infants benefit from regular stimulation in most contexts.
   c) Infants' cognitive development is entirely genetic.
   d) Infants are easily stressed by extra attention.

2. When do infants begin to respond to language and communication?
   a) At 12 months
   b) At 3 months
   c) At birth
   d) At 6 months

3. According to Piaget, which behavior demonstrates a secondary circular reaction?
   a) An infant repeats the sounds "ba-ba-ba-ba" over and over.
   b) A toddler recognizes herself in a mirror.
   c) A child bangs his sippy cup on his highchair tray over and over.
   d) A toddler uses trial and error to fit together pieces of a puzzle.

4. When Telele says "Dog night-night," this is an example of:
   a) babbling.
   b) telegraphic sleep.
   c) a holophrase.
   d) a language delay.

5. Six-month-old Josue is playing with his brother's toy car. His brother takes the toy and hides it behind his back, and Josue makes a sound of disappointment but does not try to look for the hidden car. Piaget would say that Josue does not yet understand:
   a) object permanence.
   b) the A-not-B error.
   c) universal grammar.
   d) secondary circular reactions.

6. Developmental scientists who study the basic knowledge infants seem to understand from birth are known as:
   a) behaviorists.
   b) core knowledge theorists.
   c) constructivists.
   d) cultural theorists.

7. Eighteen-month-old Karina calls any female adult a "mommy." This is an example of:
   a) overextension error.
   b) underextension error.
   c) telegraphic speech.
   d) gender bias.

8. Piaget developed his theories based on close observation of his three children. This is the case study method. How did this method help Piaget develop his breakthrough ideas? Can you explain some of the limitations of this method?

9. How might culture impact toddlers' thinking? Use examples from language development and information processing.

10. Some isolated children with profound hearing impairment in Nicaragua developed their own sign language when they were grouped together in a school with no other way to communicate. Scholars rushed to Nicaragua to study the children, communicate with them, and learn their language. Can you explain what nativist or universal grammar theorists would expect to find in these children?

Social and Emotional Development in Infancy and Toddlerhood

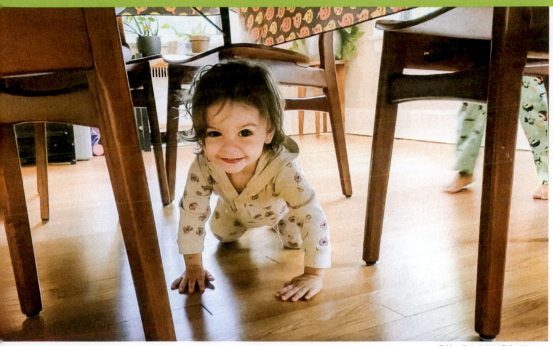

© Macmillan, photo by Sidford House

Theories of Early Emotional, Personality, and Social Development

6.1 Compare and contrast the traditional theories of emotional development.

6.2 Assess the roles of culture and context in emotional development.

Emotional Development

6.3 Describe the progress of infants' and toddlers' emotional maturation.

Personality and Temperament in the Early Years

6.4 Explain how babies begin to develop unique personalities.

Family Relationships

6.5 Describe how caregiving impacts emotional development.

6.6 Explain common variations in caregiver–child attachment relationships.

Child Care and Media in Infancy

6.7 Explain the impact of experiences outside the family on infants' emotional development.

Makena started out as a calm and quiet baby. She didn't cry; she just squeaked. Her parents, Stephanie and Jen, thought that meant she was going to be shy, the opposite of her older sister, Maya, an outgoing 3-year-old. Stephanie and Jen didn't mind the quiet: They were balancing two jobs and two children, so an easy baby was a bonus.

Stephanie and Jen's two girls had different beginnings. Both were adopted, but while Maya's biological mother was outgoing and resolved about her adoption decision, Makena's biological mother was heartbroken and conflicted about placing her daughter for adoption. Makena was quiet. Maya was loud.

Six months later, something had changed in Makena: That quiet infant had become a spunky, enthusiastic toddler. Makena is now a curious, adventurous explorer, happy to take on her sister in a tussle over sharing blocks or to dance and scream at the top of her lungs. She is capable of loud, high-energy romps around the house and also of kindness. If one of her mothers looks sad, Makena is the first to rush over with an empathetic hug and a close inspection of how she is really feeling.

As Makena grows up, Stephanie and Jen wonder which parts of her will be linked to her biological parents, prenatal experiences, and first stressful days of life, and which parts will be linked to their family. Was Makena quiet as a newborn because her biological mother was sad and worried? Would she be protected by her new parents' warm and consistent parenting? Did Makena turn out loud and mischievous because, as Jen suggests, it was the only way she could get noticed

143

Scientific American Profile

Meet Makena

around her outgoing sister, Maya? Or is it typical for children to change or become more outgoing as they grow?

In this chapter, you will read that the important achievements during the first years of life go beyond walking and talking. Emotional development, which includes learning to manage strong feelings and to trust other people, is also crucial. You will also see how infants' first relationships and inborn tendencies shape their personality and emotion regulation, and how developmental science helps explain Makena's new exuberance as well as her kindness. It can be hard to tell what a young child is feeling, but developmental science helps us understand those squeals of joy—and the bouts of tears—a little better.

Theories of Early Emotional, Personality, and Social Development

Learning Objectives

6.1 Compare and contrast the traditional theories of emotional development.

6.2 Assess the roles of culture and context in emotional development.

CONNECTIONS

You read in Chapter 1 that *ethnotheories* are a family's shared cultural beliefs about how to care for children and why children do what they do.

CONNECTIONS

Remember from Chapter 1 that communities that encourage and value independence in their children are called *individualistic cultures*. In *collectivist cultures*, the individual's needs are balanced with those of family and community.

When Jen and Stephanie talk about how they raised Makena and how she has developed, their experiences are shaped by their own upbringings and by Jen's expertise as a social worker. Informed by their own *ethnotheories* about the importance of close early bonding to development, they spent hours holding newborn Makena after they first met her in the hospital. They moved together as a family ("like a herd of sheep") from room to room.

Culture affects caregivers' *ethnotheories* about what is best for their children (Harkness & Super, 2021). All families hope their children will be successful and happy, but they often believe that success comes from different sources. For instance, German parents often tell researchers that they hope that their children will learn to express their own ideas and develop their own unique talents. Rural Cameroonian parents frequently tell scientists they hope their children will learn to respect their elders and do what they are told (Keller & Otto, 2009). Many U.S. families report that they believe their babies will be successful if they are smart and independent (Feng et al., 2020).

Adults around the world have different ideas about what drives the early social and emotional development of babies. Many, like Jen and Stephanie, believe that babies do best when they are showered with attention. Others might believe that toddlers are more like "stubborn mules" who should be dealt with strictly, because they will be spoiled if adults are too responsive (Pearl & Pearl, 2015).

Developmental science is strongly influenced by classic theories, such as those of Erikson and Freud, which established that the first years lay a critical framework for the life that follows. Contemporary approaches, influenced by breakthroughs in genetics and neuroscience, remind us that the impact of the first years is not the same for every infant. Some babies may be especially vulnerable, or they may be particularly resilient.

Traditional Theories

More than a hundred years ago, popular U.S. parenting experts advised caregivers to be strict with their children (Magai & McFadden, 1995). They recommended that babies not be held, because too much touch would turn them into "little tyrants" (Fullerton, 1911, p. 189). Other experts, like behavioral psychologist John Watson, suggested that adults "never hug and kiss" their little ones (Watson, 1928, p. 81). Psychodynamic theorists, like Sigmund Freud and, later, Erik Erikson, helped upend these traditions. They argued that children were different from adults. They also believed that the social relationships formed in a baby's first years help set the stage for their future relationships and personality.

The Legacy of Freud Sigmund Freud raised his six children in the emotionally frigid way recommended by the experts of his community. When the family met, Freud did not greet anyone with affection. As his granddaughter later recalled, "You did not hug" (Sophie Freud qtd. in Grubin, 2002). Ironically, this old-fashioned father radically changed people's cold child-rearing traditions and views.

Freud believed that many psychological challenges in adulthood stemmed from unresolved childhood issues, such as weaning or toilet training (Freud, 1977). Remember from Chapter 2 that he believed that development progressed through stages related to the mastery of a basic biological urge. During early development, babies pass through the *oral stage* and the *anal stage*. They learn how to manage the pleasure they receive from sucking, and also self-control from learning how to control their bladder and anus.

Most of Freud's stage theory has been discredited: Contemporary scholars no longer connect toilet training to later personality development (Crews, 2017). Remember from Chapter 2 that scholars also question Freud's methods of studying children, which were primarily based on his observations of adults who were remembering their childhoods rather than observing children themselves. However, Freud's ideas influenced Erik Erikson, who designed a stage theory of development that remains relevant for many who work with children today.

Erikson's Stages Erikson's developmental theory is based on the idea that all human beings develop through a series of psychological crises (see Chapter 2). In contrast to Freud, who observed stages based on biological maturation, Erikson believed that both biology and cultural expectations shape the crises in each stage.

According to Erikson, the first major crisis of development, **trust versus mistrust**, occurs during the first 18 months of life. In a successful resolution of this stage, babies learn that the world is safe and reliable. This happens when babies are nurtured responsively, and they know that they will be cared for. This trust helps babies grow into adults who feel safe in their place in the world (Erikson, 1993, 1994a).

The next crisis, **autonomy versus shame and doubt**, occurs during the toddler years. Erikson keenly appreciated the reality of young children who are not always able, or motivated, to follow the rules of the world. Young children frequently change their minds, demand to "do it themselves," and defy limits, which is why he called raising toddlers "guerrilla warfare" (Erikson, 1959, p. 66). Toddlers are building the skills to direct their own behaviors: to move around or reach for a favorite toy. Erikson believed that caregivers must sensitively manage children's early attempts at independence (autonomy), like allowing their messy attempts to feed themselves, or they will feel a sense of shame and doubt that could last a lifetime (Erikson, 1993). Erikson predicted that children who can accept the limits of the adult world without feeling ashamed of their own failures will grow up healthiest (see **Table 6.1**).

The Impact of Culture

The basic emotions of distress, happiness, fear, and anger are universal, but the expressions of emotions and their developmental progression vary depending on cultural practices and expectations (see **Figure 6.1**). Even the timing of a baby's smiles,

trust versus mistrust The first crisis in Erikson's stage theory of development in which infants learn that the world is reliable.

autonomy versus shame and doubt The second crisis in Erikson's stage theory of development in which toddlers learn to balance their desire to be independent with their limitations and frequent missteps.

How Do Ethnotheories Explain How Caregivers Get Babies to Eat Their Carrots? In Japan, parents often want to instill a strong sense of empathy. This can even be seen at the dinner table, as some researchers have observed that parents try to convince children to eat all their vegetables by begging, pleading, and asking their little ones to eat them all to please the carrot as well as the carrot farmers.

TABLE 6.1 Erikson's Stages of Psychosocial Development in Infancy and Toddlerhood

Stage	Age	Characteristics
Trust versus mistrust	Birth to 18 months	In their first year, children who have responsive caregivers learn to trust the world around them. Those who have unresponsive caregivers start to doubt that their needs will be met.
Autonomy versus shame and doubt	18 months to 3 years	At this age, children are more capable and begin to assert their *autonomy*. If caregivers respond sensitively to their attempts at independence, children develop an awareness that they can take care of themselves. If caregivers cast doubt on those attempts, children may feel ashamed and lack self-control and confidence in their ability to care for themselves.

FIGURE 6.1 Culture Shapes Emotional Development. Parents' ethnotheories about development vary around the world. Soothing and cuddling babies is universal, but how caregivers talk about and label babies' behavior is not always the same. In this study, researchers asked parents in various communities in Fiji, Kenya, and the United States when they thought babies were capable of smiling, feeling pain and pleasure, and thinking. The parents' expectations remind us that how we label babies' development may not be universal at all.

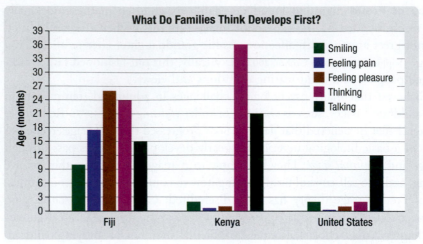

Data from Broesch et al., 2016.

tantrums, and helping behaviors are not the same around the world (Keller, 2020). From the very beginning, caregivers raise their babies in ways that align with their cultural values (Lansford & Bornstein, 2020). Babies' close contact with their caregivers gives them lots of time to learn these cultural skills and understand close connections (Rosenberg, 2021).

Remember from Chapter 1 that one way to look at the impact of culture on development is to measure families' levels of *collectivism* or *individualism*. Babies in collectivist cultures are often seen as important members of a community, who are connected to others through strong ties of respect and obligation. For instance, in Beng families in Côte d'Ivoire, this starts at birth, when newborns are expected to politely grunt in greeting to their visitors (Gottlieb, 2019). Collectivist practices encourage interdependence or relatedness (Amir & McAuliffe, 2020). Rather than encouraging a toddler's independent exploration, families who value interdependence might encourage good manners.

In collectivist cultures, families tend to use **proximal** practices, which are characterized by physical closeness. For example, caregivers in rural Kenya have been observed to hold their babies four times as much as parents in the United States (LeVine & LeVine, 2016). Families in collectivist cultures tend to soothe babies with touch and frequent nursing.

Individualistic communities and families, like many in the United States and other wealthy urban communities around the world, tend to have caregiving practices that include lots of face-to-face contact, playing with toys, and infant-directed talk (Aschemeyer et al., 2021; Little et al., 2019). These practices are termed **distal**, meaning that the caregiver and child are physically distant. Many distal caregiving practices involve joint attention, rather than physical closeness. For instance, when Makena plays on a blanket in the middle of the living room while Stephanie is making dinner, Stephanie can reassure Makena by calling across the room when she drops a favorite toy. Both proximal and distal parenting practices can be responsive and sensitive to infants' needs.

Around the world, more formally educated and affluent families tend to use individualistic parenting styles designed to build independence (Otto et al., 2017; Park & Lau, 2016). Rural, agricultural families tend to use more relational parenting styles focused on raising calm, cooperative children. However, while it may seem easy to divide the world into those who emphasize independence and those who do not, the reality is much more complex. Many immigrant communities and communities in transition mix the values of independence and interdependence in parenting. Caregivers often use both proximal and distal practices, but the balance varies. Abstract values do not easily predict what happens in real life (Röttger-Rössler, 2020).

proximal Caregiving practices that include physical closeness but not necessarily face-to-face contact.

distal Caregiving practices that are physically distant but may include joint attention and face-to-face contact.

Close in Different Ways Proximal and distal parenting are common caregiving practices. When parents use proximal practices, they are often physically close but not engaging in face-to-face contact, as when this father in Richmond, Virginia *(left)*, uses a baby carrier while he does the laundry. Distal parenting often involves face-to-face contact with less physical closeness, but for this family in Kazakhstan *(right)*, cuddling includes aspects of both distal and proximal care.

 MAKING A DIFFERENCE

How Understanding Culture Helps Soothe Babies

Some amount of distress—whether from immunizations, diaper rash, or a splash of bathwater—is inevitable in a baby's life. As a result, babies cry. Researchers have found that babies typically cry most from about 4 to 8 weeks, but how long that is depends on how their caregivers cope with it (Vermillet et al., 2022). Caregivers who have difficulty with their infant's upsets are at higher risk for depression and even child abuse, and their babies are also at higher risk for depression and behavior problems (Garratt et al., 2019).

No one likes to hear a baby cry, but parents have different ideas about what to do about it. Some cultures value emotional restraint and believe that crying should be limited. For instance, in rural Nso communities in Cameroon, in Central Africa, caregivers expect their babies to be calm and may tell their little ones "we do not cry here" (Keller & Otto, 2009, p. 1003). In other places, however, families might report that crying is inevitable or a sign of a difficult personality (Super et al., 2020).

In one classic study, scientists compared how often babies cried in rural villages in Botswana, a country in Southern Africa, with babies in more urban areas in the Netherlands, in Northern Europe. Babies in both communities got upset about the same number of times every day, but infants in Botswana were soothed much more quickly. It took about seven minutes for a caregiver in Holland to settle their 3-month-old, compared to about three minutes in Botswana (Barr et al., 1991). Over the course of a typical day, this meant that babies in the Netherlands were crying twice as long as babies in Botswana.

What caused the difference? Families in Botswana used proximal parenting techniques. They responded immediately when their babies cried, and their babies were held, carried, or breast-fed almost all the time (Devore & Konner, 2019). These results have been replicated: Babies whose caregivers use proximal techniques have shorter bouts of crying, spending half as much time upset as babies who receive distal parenting (Wolke et al., 2017). (See **Figure 6.2**.)

In multiple studies, educating new families about typical crying behavior and proximal techniques for managing it has helped caregivers better cope with their babies' distress (St. James-Roberts et al., 2019). These interventions help parents avoid depression, stress, and dangerous responses to crying, like shouting or shaking (Gilkerson et al., 2020; Wolfe & Kelly, 2019).

FIGURE 6.2 How Much Do Babies Cry Around the World? Most babies cry more at about 4 to 8 weeks than they do at other times in development, but how much they cry is shaped by how they are cared for. Babies who experience more proximal parenting practices tend to cry less. Parenting practices, particularly how often babies are held, are critically important in how much time babies spend distressed.

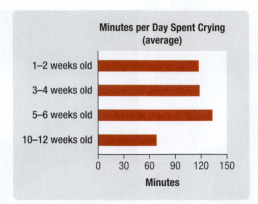

Minutes per Day Spent Crying (average)

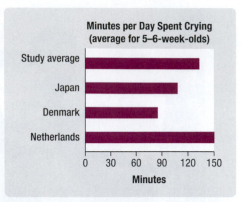

Minutes per Day Spent Crying (average for 5–6-week-olds)

Data from Wolke et al., 2017.

Displacement Can Be Frightening, Despite a Mother's Love. This mother is carrying her child in Gaza, Palestinian Territories, after they were displaced from their ancestral homes near Be'er Sheva in Southern Israel. Researchers who studied traditionally nomadic Bedouin families, like hers, before they were forced to leave their homes in the Negev desert, found that their children were becoming anxious around strangers, perhaps because of the looming threat of war, even though their parents hoped they would be friendly and outgoing.

Current Approaches to Emotion Development

Breakthroughs in the understanding of genes and the brain have added three important insights about babies' emotional development: (1) The first years of life shape brain development and genomic expression in ways that change emotions and personality; (2) not every infant responds in the same way to the environment; and (3) biological and genomic changes can often be reversed (Beijers et al., 2020).

Remember that scientists have explained that one way early experiences shape us is through the brain and the genome. The environment can change the genome by changing the chemistry of the epigenetic marks that surround DNA, causing some genes to be expressed and others to be repressed. The genome, like the brain, is particularly sensitive during the first few years of life so that infants can adapt to their surroundings (Krol, Puglia, et al., 2019; Montirosso et al., 2021).

Researchers studying children who have endured difficult experiences, such as being raised in an institution or by caregivers who are overwhelmed or unresponsive, have found signs of biological changes in their bodies. These include epigenetic changes to their genome, alterations to how their bodies manage stress and release hormones, and changes to how their brains develop (Naumova et al., 2019; Nelson et al., 2019; Shakiba et al., 2020). Does this mean that children who have grown up with adversity will not be able to have happy, meaningful lives? Not at all. As you will see, early adversity does not affect all children in the same way, and not all adversity is equal.

For instance, fear, neglect, and illness may have different effects, all of which, in turn, are dependent on when they happen and how children perceive them (Milojevich et al., 2020; Smith & Pollak, 2021). As a result, some children may have difficulties that are connected to early adversity (Colich et al., 2020). Some may develop resilience and recover from trauma, and others may even develop new strengths (Ellis et al., 2020). But adversity sometimes harms children irreversibly, which is why developmental scientists are working to develop effective interventions to help keep children safe.

Was the COVID-19 pandemic one such instance of adversity? Some researchers have studied babies who were born during the pandemic to see whether they were affected by the stress their families experienced. Several research teams, from New York City to Calgary, Alberta, have found that infants were changed by the uncertainty of the first months of the pandemic in 2020 (Manning et al., 2021; Shuffrey et al., 2022). Parents who were exposed to significant stress, like those who gave birth in New York City in early 2020, may continue to benefit from support, since they were particularly likely to have newborns in a time of social isolation.

Differential Susceptibility Researchers remind us that not all children react to adversity or to their environments in the same way (Zhang, Sayler, et al., 2021). On a global scale, children's lives are mostly improving over time due to public health achievements, as you can see from **Infographic 6.1**. However, the number of babies exposed

Every year, 140 million babies are born worldwide. Each will be shaped by the complex systems that surround them, as well as by their own individual strengths. Each baby's social structures and physical environment reflect vast inequalities and wide diversity in our capacity to thrive. Caregivers are a major source of resilience for small children, as they gradually develop the ability to regulate their own feelings and behavior.

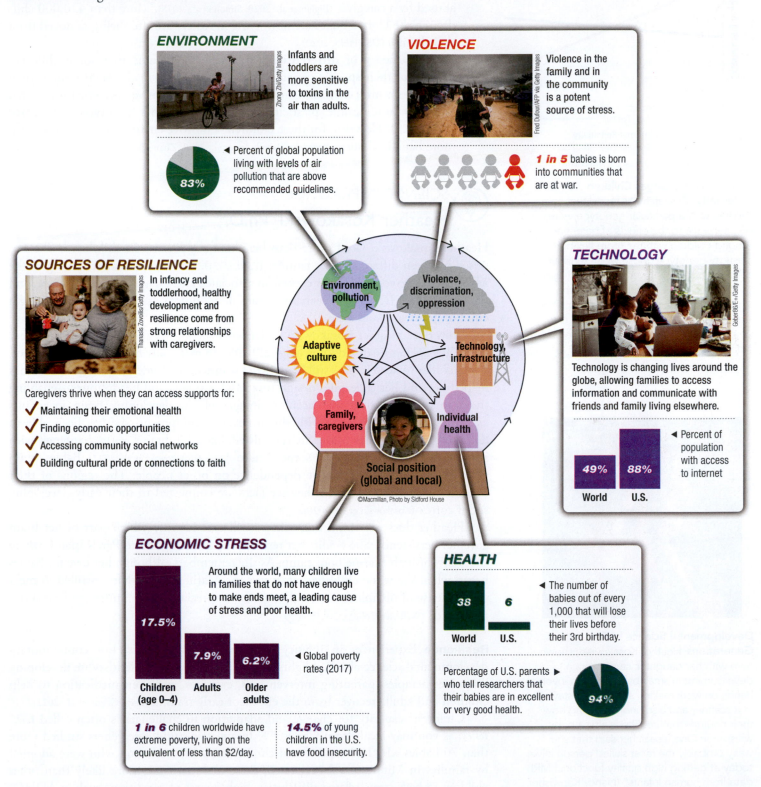

ENVIRONMENT

Infants and toddlers are more sensitive to toxins in the air than adults.

◀ Percent of global population living with levels of air pollution that are above recommended guidelines.

83%

VIOLENCE

Violence in the family and in the community is a potent source of stress.

1 in 5 babies is born into communities that are at war.

SOURCES OF RESILIENCE

In infancy and toddlerhood, healthy development and resilience come from strong relationships with caregivers.

Caregivers thrive when they can access supports for:
✓ Maintaining their emotional health
✓ Finding economic opportunities
✓ Accessing community social networks
✓ Building cultural pride or connections to faith

TECHNOLOGY

Technology is changing lives around the globe, allowing families to access information and communicate with friends and family living elsewhere.

◀ Percent of population with access to internet

49% World   88% U.S.

Environment, pollution

Violence, discrimination, oppression

Adaptive culture

Technology, infrastructure

Family, caregivers

Individual health

Social position (global and local)

©Macmillan, Photo by Sidford House

ECONOMIC STRESS

Around the world, many children live in families that do not have enough to make ends meet, a leading cause of stress and poor health.

17.5% Children (age 0–4)
7.9% Adults
6.2% Older adults

◀ Global poverty rates (2017)

1 in 6 children worldwide have extreme poverty, living on the equivalent of less than $2/day.

14.5% of young children in the U.S. have food insecurity.

HEALTH

38 World   6 U.S.

◀ The number of babies out of every 1,000 that will lose their lives before their 3rd birthday.

Percentage of U.S. parents who tell researchers that their babies are in excellent or very good health. ▶

94%

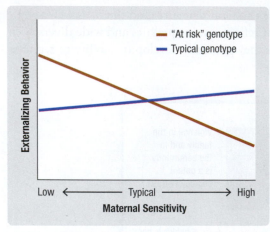

Information from Bakermans-Kranenburg & van IJzendoorn, 2015.

FIGURE 6.3 Life Changes Children Differently. Research has found that some children with a particular genotype were very sensitive to the effects of parenting. Among children with the more flexible plasticity genotype, those with "sensitive" parents had much lower rates of acting-out behavior at 18 months than those who experienced less-sensitive parenting. These findings suggest that some children may be more strongly influenced by experience than others.

Developmental Science in Two Generations Heather Kosakowski, shown here with her daughter, studies brain development in small babies, which involves hands-on work making sure infants stay still in a scanner and also understanding how their neurons mature. She is also a baby whisperer: One researcher said that she was "probably the most skilled person alive today at getting high-quality functional MRI data from human infants" (Nancy Kanwisher, qtd. in Fritts, 2021).

differential susceptibility Individual differences in how sensitive people are to the environment.

to trauma and chronic stress is mind-boggling (Finkelhor et al., 2020). Around the world, more than 140 million children grow up without families because of war or poverty (Nelson et al., 2019). In the United States, about one in eight children has been exposed to a parent's substance abuse, and 1 in 12 has been physically abused by a caregiver (Biglan et al., 2020; Simon et al., 2018). More than 420,000 children in the United States are now living in foster care after being removed from their homes (USDHHS, 2020).

The theory of **differential susceptibility** explains that some children, because of their specific genotype, are more reactive to the environment than others. A harmful environment can cause a more negative outcome for children with this more flexible, plasticity genotype than it does for a typical child (see **Figure 6.3**). However, for these children, a positive environment can have even more beneficial outcomes (van IJzendoorn et al., 2020; Zhang & Belsky, 2020).

 SCIENCE IN PRACTICE
Heather Kosakowski, Ph.D.

Heather Kosakowski faced more than her share of adversity in childhood: She was raised by seven different foster families (Fritts, 2021). Nevertheless, after serving in the Marines for five years, Heather earned an associate's and then a bachelor's degree, and now has her Ph.D. and is researching brain development at Harvard while raising a child of her own (Kosakowski, 2022).

How does Heather Kosakowski utilize what she knows about development every day? She uses her firsthand knowledge of babies to make silly faces and find lost pacifiers in order to keep infants still in an fMRI scanner. Her understanding of babies has helped her and her colleagues design tiny MRI scanners and headphones—enabling them to create detailed and accurate images of the developing brain in infants as young as 2 months old. With this innovative equipment, she has been able to demonstrate that babies' brains are specialized, like adult brains, early in infancy, with separate areas devoted to faces, scenes, and objects (Kosakowski et al., 2022). Babies' brain development reflects their close dependence on other people: The regions of their brain that are activated when they see faces are connected to their early-developing social cortex (Kosakowski et al., 2020).

Heather does not think that science will ever identify which part of her brain gave her persistence. She credits her resilience to her faith and to Parris Island, where she went through Marine boot camp. As she remembers, although her love for babies began when she was a child herself, it was the Marine Corps that "instilled in me a greater sense of discipline . . . [and] a greater appreciation and understanding about the world" (Wellesley College, 2013).

Resilience Experiences in infancy can have lifelong effects, but contemporary developmental science also highlights the ability for change. Scientists are developing intensive therapies, parenting interventions, exercises, and even medication to help children and adults recover from the effects of early trauma (Hays-Grudo et al., 2021).

Children's capacity for change and adaptation to challenges is often called *resilience*, as you may recall from Chapter 1. In a classic study, researchers studied more than 70 babies who had experienced chronic early life stress and who were adopted by families in Minnesota. As expected, these children were more likely than other children to have stress-related difficulties, higher rates of conditions such as ADHD, and even social problems like trouble making friends. Not all of the children in this study, however, had these challenges.

Two groups showed resilience. Some children, particularly those who were adopted when they were infants, had lower rates of psychological disorders. The other group had received exceptional caregiving, "supercharged" parenting that was unusually positive and emotionally supportive. Children raised by supercharged caregivers were able to make friends and avoid emotional problems; they were in many ways indistinguishable from children who had never lived in orphanages (Pitula et al., 2019).

This finding reminds us that although early challenges can have lasting effects, they are not necessarily insurmountable. While the best cure for trauma is prevention, early intervention can modify and even reverse some early difficulties. Infancy is not the only time changes can be made: As you will learn in Chapter 13, adolescence offers another sensitive period to recalibrate early social and emotional challenges (Gunnar et al., 2019).

APPLY IT! **6.1** Jen and Stephanie want to encourage Makena's *resilience*, or her ability to bounce back from stress. How do early relationships help babies such as Makena manage stress?

6.2 At age 2, Makena wants to "do it herself," whether that means getting dressed on her own or pouring her own drinks. How would Erikson's theory of psychosocial development explain this drive?

6.3 After Jen and Stephanie adopted Makena, they spent a lot of time holding her and in skin-to-skin contact. Explain how researchers think this type of proximal parenting practice might shape infants' development.

Emotional Development

At just 6 months, it was clear that Makena already had feelings. Much of the time she was filled with giggles, bringing so much laughter to her sister and her parents. At other times, like when she was trying to reach for a toy that had fallen out of reach, she was clearly frustrated.

Babies gradually move from reacting automatically to having some control over their emotions. Young infants begin the process of managing the disappointments and unexpected events in the world, such as the annoyance of being strapped into a car seat or the joy of seeing their parent again after a nap.

Measuring What Babies Are Feeling

A major challenge in understanding babies is figuring out what they are feeling. How do you know what someone is feeling if they cannot use words?

Facial expressions are not always helpful. Because they lack the motor control to make all the facial expressions adults can, young babies are good at sad faces but have a lot of difficulty smiling (Adolph & Franchak, 2017). Newborns can control their mouths

Learning Objective

6.3 Describe the progress of infants' and toddlers' emotional maturation.

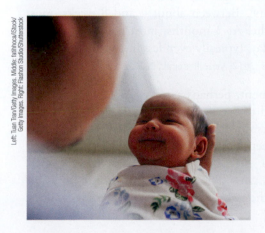

Left: Tuan Tran/Getty Images. Middle: fatihhoca/iStock/Getty Images. Right: Flashon Studio/Shutterstock

Happiness from the Very Beginning The fleeting smiles of a newborn are often random and not in their control, but by the time a baby is a year old, smiles and laughter are easy to identify. By the time a toddler is 2, they know how to grin and pose for the camera.

in order to suck but cannot use their lips to smile on purpose (Shultz et al., 2018). It takes weeks before babies master the mouth movements necessary for a smile. Not until age 3 or so do toddlers' emotional expressions approach the sophistication of adults', and even these vary by culture and are not always a precise presentation of how they are really feeling (Barrett et al., 2019; Holodynski & Seeger, 2019).

Similarly, it will take months before infants' cries communicate more than just distress. It may be a myth that caregivers can distinguish the difference between a "hunger cry" and a "pain cry." Scientists have found that even experts cannot predict why a very young infant is crying from the sounds they make (Zeifman & St. James-Roberts, 2017).

So, how do experts measure a baby's feelings? It is not easy, but technology helps. Scientists look into the baby's eyes, and they measure their hearts and their neural activity. It turns out that even at just 1 month, infants' pupils will get bigger if they are looking at something they like, such as a picture of their parent (Geangu et al., 2011). Researchers also connect babies to electrodes to measure how quickly their hearts respond or how their brain activity changes. This has helped experts understand that some babies are more reactive to emotional stimuli than others, even if they are too young to show it or talk about it (Ostlund et al., 2019).

The Basic Emotions

You can probably list a dozen emotions easily, but defining them is more difficult. **Emotions** involve your *body* (the racing heartbeat when you get scared), your *thoughts* (your awareness that you are scared), and your *behaviors* (scrambling away from a loud noise at the window). However, everyday experiences of emotion do not always include all three parts of this definition (Pollak et al., 2019). For instance, babies may not think about their pain in a logical way, but they still experience it. Adolescents may feel disappointment when a bad grade lands on their desk in front of a bunch of classmates but cover it up with a fake smile.

Which emotions do infants have? Traditional Chinese and Korean scholars believed greed and hate were core emotions (Lim, 2016). In the Philippines, families who speak Tagalog have a word for over-the-top adorableness, *gigil*, that does not exist in any other language (Cachero et al., 2017). Today, most developmentalists agree that only a few basic emotions are shared by infants (and adults) around the world. Distress, happiness, fear, and anger emerge early in infancy. As babies mature, more complex emotions like empathy, pride, and embarrassment begin to appear (see **Figure 6.4**).

Distress Infants often feel hungry, cold, and tired; unfamiliar and unpleasant feelings for newborns adjusting to new, intense sensory input and physical sensations that they did not experience in the uterus. For the first four months of life, emotions adults would identify as sadness, pain, and anger are intertwined in one general expression of *distress* (Holodynski & Seeger, 2019). Between about 4 and 8 weeks, most infants cry less and become easier to soothe. At 3 months, most babies in affluent countries are fussy for less than an hour a day, typically even less in communities that practice proximal caregiving (St. James-Roberts, 2012; Vermillet et al., 2022).

Happiness Newborns can show contentment, perhaps as they share eye contact or stare at a rotating fan. However, it is hard to see if they feel joy because they cannot smile in reaction to anything caregivers do. In their first few weeks, babies' first spontaneous smiles occur mostly during sleep, but researchers think they happen just to give facial muscles practice (Kawakami et al., 2017). At around 6 or 8 weeks, however, babies' smiles are no longer random (Camras, 2019). Babies can lock eyes and grin. This is the **social smile**, which is in reaction to the sight or sound of someone a baby likes, like a parent or a sibling.

Share It!

Hold me! Research shows that babies who receive lots of touch may differ from their peers, even as young adults: They tend to be better at perspective taking, empathic responding, and being in sync.

(Yaniv et al., 2021)

---

emotions Reactions to your thoughts or your environment that involve your body, your thoughts, and your behaviors.

social smile A smile in reaction to the sight or sound of someone an infant is connected to. These smiles may appear as early as 6 weeks, but their development is influenced by caregiving practices.

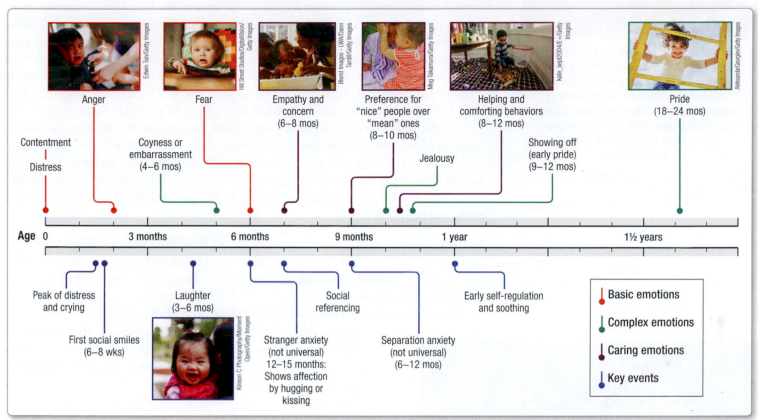

Anger

Fear

Empathy and concern (6–8 mos)

Preference for "nice" people over "mean" ones (8–10 mos)

Helping and comforting behaviors (8–12 mos)

Pride (18–24 mos)

Contentment

Distress

Coyness or embarrassment (4–6 mos)

Jealousy

Showing off (early pride) (9–12 mos)

Age 0   3 months   6 months   9 months   1 year   1½ years

Peak of distress and crying

Laughter (3–6 mos)

Social referencing

Early self-regulation and soothing

First social smiles (6–8 wks)

Stranger anxiety (not universal) 12–15 months: Shows affection by hugging or kissing

Separation anxiety (not universal) (6–12 mos)

Basic emotions
Complex emotions
Caring emotions
Key events

Information from Decety, 2015; Hammond et al., 2017; Dahl, 2015; Reddy, 2000; Hart, 2016.

FIGURE 6.4 Highlights in the Development of Emotions As infants turn into toddlers, they have more ability to express what they are feeling and more complex reactions to the world around them.

Social smiles emerge at about the same age in infants around the world, and in babies with typical development as well as those who may have visual, physical, or intellectual disabilities (Lewis, 2017). How often young babies smile depends on their caregivers. The babies of caregivers who smile a lot and who have a lot of face-to-face interactions with their babies tend to smile more (Lavelli et al., 2019).

Many European and U.S. parents tend to encourage positive, outgoing social behavior in their infants. As a result, babies in the United States tend to smile more than babies in most other places. In many cultures, parents may not focus on face-to-face interaction or outgoing emotions and may instead focus on the comfort of close physical contact. Such caregivers may not expect their babies to share social smiling until around 6 months (Wörmann et al., 2014). In Fiji, for instance, parents do not anticipate that their babies will share a smile with them until about 10 months (Broesch et al., 2016).

Smiling is quickly followed by laughing, giggling, and other signs of joy. Most infants in the United States begin to laugh before 3 months (Jhang & Oller, 2017). Babies understand simple humor, clowning, and some jokes between 3 and 5 months (Mireault et al., 2018; Reddy, 2019a).

Anger You may not think of anger as an emotional accomplishment, but it is a sign of maturity. A newborn can be upset, but it takes a few months until they express anger. By 8 weeks, babies can become angry if they do not get what they expect. Researchers are experts at measuring this using just a car seat and a toy. Strapping a baby into a car seat or taking away a toy that they had been enjoying is nearly guaranteed to produce anger (Ekas et al., 2018; Liu, Moore, et al., 2018).

Do It Again! As babies grow, smiles and laughter become more interactive and responsive. Babies who experience more face-to-face, expressive interaction tend to be more outgoing, like this little girl.

Share It!

Wait until my executive function kicks in! Executive function helps reduce tantrums and explosive behavior: Babies with strong executive function are less likely to melt down than those whose executive function is slower to develop.

(Hughes et al., 2020)

Like other emotions, anger is often in the eyes of the beholder. Culture plays an important role in whether families think their babies should get angry (Raval & Walker, 2019). For instance, some Nepalese families encourage their children to stay calm even in the face of frustration (Cole et al., 2006). On the other hand, many German and American parents expect their babies to express their feelings and show anger at 5 months (Jaramillo et al., 2017; Keller & Otto, 2009). However, U.S. parents typically find their babies' anger embarrassing, particularly in front of strangers (Keller, 2019).

By the toddler years, anger and aggression become more common (Lorber et al., 2018). In U.S. toddlers, ages 1 to 3 are among the most violent years of the lifespan. Toddlers hit, pull hair, and grab more than older children (and certainly more than adults) (Hay, 2017). Most of this aggression, however, is random or uncoordinated rather than deliberately hurtful, like pulling a sibling's braid out of curiosity or patting a dog too hard (Dahl, 2019).

Fear Newborns can be startled, but they do not remember what has frightened them long enough to show fear (Rousseau et al., 2017). As a result, babies do not show true fear until about 6 months, when their brains mature enough to remember dangers and anticipate them (Thomas et al., 2019).

Fear appears at about the same age in infants around the world. Evolutionary theorists suggest that as babies become more mobile, as they are able to sit on their own, perhaps even crawl and grab objects (some of which could hurt them), they become more sensitive to danger (Bjorklund et al., 2015). Being able to quickly learn that they should be afraid—whether it is of growling dogs or angry people—helps to keep babies safe (Frankenhuis, 2019).

Experimental research suggests that babies may be prepared to learn about certain dangers in their environment. Some things are scarier than others. When they are tested in the laboratory, infants pay special attention to some things slithering snakes, spiders, and sharp-toothed lions and tigers are at the top of the list (Bertels et al., 2020; Hoehl et al., 2017). Dangerous animals aren't the only things that are easier to fear. Infants are particularly attentive to fearful and angry faces. Just as snakes can sometimes be dangerous, so can people and poisonous plants (Aktar et al., 2018; Safar & Moulson, 2020). This perceptual sensitivity to things that may be harmful allows infants to learn quickly about dangers in their particular environment.

In many cultures, by 8 months, babies have learned to be cautious around new people, a phenomenon called **stranger anxiety** (Zubler et al., 2022). This can be embarrassing for families: Taking a photograph with the team mascot or an unfamiliar relative results in shrieks and terror as soon as they hand the baby over. Scholars call this growing unhappiness at being away from the people they care about **separation anxiety**. In many cultures, this behavior is typical for babies between around 6 and 12 months and can be a sign of their developing *attachment*, as you will learn later in this chapter. At 4 months, babies may have been content to be handed off to a visiting cousin, but a few months later, they may fuss. These anxieties peak by 12 months but may continue until age 3 (Brand et al., 2020; Van Hulle et al., 2017).

Many researchers believe the increase in babies' anxiety is a symptom of their strong preference for their usual caregivers, the people who they rely on and have come to trust. However, uneasiness around new people is far from universal (Gottlieb, 2019). In many communities, babies continue to be friendly to strangers and do not develop stranger or separation anxiety based on cultural expectations about emotional expression and their experiences being looked after by many caring people. In these places, separation anxiety may even be seen as a form of rudeness (Keller, 2018). As a

Not Yet Afraid No one is born afraid of snakes, but by 4 months, babies pay more attention to snakes (and spiders) than other creatures and may more readily develop a fear of them. This baby seems fascinated by, rather than terrified of, the python displayed at a festival in Lisbon, Portugal.

stranger anxiety Babies' demonstration of caution around new people, which emerges by about 8 months. This phenomenon is not culturally universal but is influenced by caregiving practices.

separation anxiety By about 6 months and continuing into toddlerhood, infants are upset and worried if their caregivers go away. This phenomenon is not universal but is influenced by cultural practices.

Bedouin mother living in Israel explained to a researcher, "It is desirable that the baby has relationships with many people" so "people will love him and agree to keep him when I'm not around" (Marey-Sarwan et al., 2016, p. 326).

By about 7 months, caregivers may notice that their babies check in with them when they see something new or unusual (Rochat, 2018). As Jen and Stephanie explained, raising a baby during the early months of the COVID-19 pandemic made this tendency even worse. For six months, as they raised their girls in New York City, Makena did not see anyone outside her immediate family. She responded by clinging to her mothers' legs when she first went out in public and looking closely to make sure everything was okay. This careful attention to caregivers' feelings, called **social referencing**, helps babies learn about danger. For instance, if an infant's caregiver shows fear of something, whether it is a suspicious stranger or a thunderstorm, being attentive to that response teaches babies about dangers (Elsner & Wertz, 2019).

More Complex Emotions

Now that Makena is a toddler, she seems to show many complex emotions: anger, sadness, joy, and fear, as well as jealousy and even embarrassment. As babies become more interactive, they begin to display more social emotions like embarrassment and concern (Davidov et al., 2021; Reddy, 2019b).

Self-Awareness Do babies know that they are separate beings? This is one of the philosophical questions that developmental scientists grapple with. Researchers define **self-awareness** as the understanding that you have a self that is separate from the world. Until recently, many researchers believed that babies weren't capable of this (Lewis & Brooks-Gunn, 1979; Mahler, 1974; Rochat, 2018).

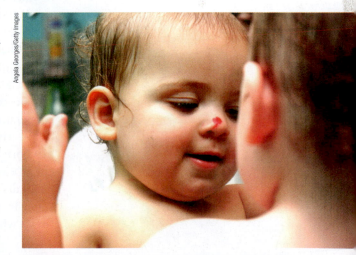

Scientists have provided a fresh analysis of a classic (and cute) measure of self-awareness called the *mirror self-recognition test* (Gallup, 1970). The experiment is simple: Without attracting any attention, researchers place a red dot on an infant's nose. Then the baby is placed in front of a mirror. If the baby shows an understanding that there is a red dot on their own nose, say, by touching or rubbing it, they are said to have self-awareness, because they recognize the image in the mirror as themselves. If babies ignore the dot, they are said to lack self-awareness.

More than 40 years ago, some pioneering psychologists found that by 18 months, most of the babies they sampled in urban and suburban North America could recognize themselves in a mirror (Amsterdam, 1972; Brooks-Gunn & Lewis, 1975). However, later researchers found that the experiment didn't work for babies outside of affluent, urban nations. In some rural communities in Kenya, Peru, and Fiji, children as old as 4 froze and stared at the mirror after a mark was placed on their faces. They did not point to the dot on their noses or try to wipe it off (Ross et al., 2017). However, these children exhibited more advanced emotions and self-awareness than other children, like empathy and caring. The profound cultural variations in babies' responses led scientists to question the usefulness of the mirror self-recognition test and develop new ways of assessing toddlers' emotional maturation (Broesch et al., 2020).

Other research suggests that infants show elements of self-awareness long before they can recognize themselves in a mirror (Lou et al., 2020). For instance, scientists using *functional near-infrared spectroscopy (FNIRS)*, which utilizes light to measure blood flow in the brain, showed that babies can distinguish themselves from other people. Different regions of their brains were activated when infants touched themselves as compared to when someone else touched them (Padilla & Lagercrantz, 2020). Also, long before they recognize themselves in the mirror, babies respond to their names, interact with others, and show social emotions like jealousy, embarrassment, and concern (Davidov et al., 2021; Grossmann & Dela Cruz, 2021; Hart, 2020).

What's That? Some researchers use the mirror self-recognition test to see if babies have self-awareness. If a baby recognizes that they have a spot on their nose, they are said to have self-awareness. Other researchers believe that this test may better assess mirror awareness or messy awareness than actual self-awareness: They suggest that babies' have self-awareness from birth.

social referencing The use of someone else's emotional response as a guide before expressing your own reaction to a new place, person, or object.

self-awareness The understanding that you have a self that is separate from others.

emotional contagion The tendency to mimic feelings we observe in others.

empathy The ability to identify with someone else's feelings.

prosocial Behaviors that are helpful or caring toward someone else.

Embarrassment   What is embarrassment? You may experience it as your cheeks flush when you do something in front of others you wish you hadn't, or when you unexpectedly become the center of attention (Nikolić et al., 2018). Before 6 months, babies show signs of self-conscious embarrassment, like turning their heads or looking away when they get too much attention (Colonnesi et al., 2020). After 6 months, babies begin to show embarrassment when they make a mistake, like spilling cereal. Embarrassment may be uncomfortable at any age, but showing regret for something you have done or discomfort with being the center of attention signals that you care what other people think (Grossmann, 2020). This concern helps create close relationships.

By 18 months, scientists found that nearly 9 in 10 babies show signs of embarrassment if they are overpraised. What triggers this embarrassment? Researchers told toddlers that they were going to share their photos so their "friends can see how cute [they] are!" (Eggum-Wilkens et al., 2015).

Concern for Others   From the time they are born, infants show some awareness of the feelings of others. For instance, in a hospital nursery, newborns will begin to cry after they hear another baby's wail, which researchers call **emotional contagion** (Palagi et al., 2020; Ruffman et al., 2017). (You have experienced this if you have ever felt the urge to yawn after seeing someone else do it.)

Babies are born with the capacity for **empathy**, the ability to identify with someone else's feelings (Tomasello, 2020). As one researcher explained, typically developing babies have a "basic tendency to be nice" (Sebastián-Enesco et al., 2013, p. 186). Scientists believe that they even prefer to look at kind, helpful people over those who are unfair (Margoni & Surian, 2018). As they grow, they become more capable of behaving **prosocially**, or helpfully, acting in ways that help other people, such as sharing or cooperating.

A critical part of empathy is the ability to sense what others are feeling. Although newborns can sense big upsets, like screaming, they cannot pick up on more subtle cues (Decety & Steinbeis, 2020). But by the time they are a few months old, babies respond to adults' emotional expressions and tend to mirror what they observe (Lavelli et al., 2019). In other words, infants are likely to smile when their caregiver is smiling or frown when their caregiver is upset (Wass et al., 2019; Waters et al., 2017).

A few months later, babies start trying to be helpful. This is their first prosocial achievement. By 6 or 8 months, babies will pat someone who is upset (Davidov et al., 2021). If they see someone trying to grab an object that is out of reach, they will push it toward them (Tomasello, 2021). By age 2, many toddlers are even willing to give up a favorite toy to comfort someone else (Cowell & Decety, 2015).

Babies may begin helping out around the house, perhaps by putting their toys away, before age 1 (Dahl & Brownell, 2019). Many communities expect toddlers to pitch in by doing small tasks, such as carrying food to the table. As you might expect, in places where this behavior is expected of children, babies tend to be helpful at earlier ages (Köster & Kärtner, 2019). In urban families in the United States, babies who are not quite 1 often help out in everyday activities, especially with encouragement from parents (Dahl, 2019). Even if babies do not have chores, they can help their caregivers change their diaper or put on their hat. Babies can be cooperative, but they are not very reliable. Toddlers tend to be unreliable as when they are asked to put away their toys or put on their shirt, until they are about 2½ (Hammond & Brownell, 2018; Kärtner et al., 2021).

Does an early capacity to be nice mean that toddlers share eagerly? Far from it (Waugh & Brownell, 2017). The most difficult prosocial behavior for toddlers is sharing, and may require frequent reminders until children are about age 4 (Poelker &

Born to Be Nice Some researchers suggest that babies are born with a basic tendency to be kind. Six-month-olds will try and comfort someone who is upset, and older children, like these girls, are often willing to share with a friend.

Gibbons, 2019). Toddlers may be willing to share a cookie, but most will not give up the toy they were playing with. However, just because sharing is difficult for toddlers does not mean that caregivers should stop encouraging it. Caregivers who encourage sharing are helping toddlers learn to get along with other children and allowing them to experience the good feelings that come from generosity (Song, Broekjuizen, et al., 2020).

Managing Emotions

When Makena fussed when she was 6 months old, Jen and Stephanie did not mind. That behavior is quite different in a 2-year-old. As infants grow into toddlers and then into little kids, adults increasingly expect them to manage their emotions. As they gain experience in the world and as their brains develop, babies can better control their feelings and emotional responses. But this process does not always go smoothly.

Emotion regulation is the ability to manage emotions in a way that is appropriate for the cultural context. In many cases, this means that caregivers expect children to calm themselves down or minimize the expression of negative emotions like frustration or sadness. Emotion regulation also involves positive feelings. For instance, at a birthday party, Jen and Stephanie hope that Makena will be able to smile, clap, and sing along with other guests, but not be too loud.

Infants are not capable of calming themselves and depend on caregivers to help soothe them. As babies mature, they develop behaviors and brain connections that help them avoid emotional extremes without as much help. Scientists believe that infancy is a sensitive period for infants to develop emotion regulation and learn about what feelings are acceptable in their unique cultural and family context (Gee, 2020).

The *still-face procedure* is one way that researchers have measured infants' ability to manage their feelings (Tronick et al., 1978). This short test is designed to upset a baby and then measure how easily they can be soothed. What is guaranteed to upset a baby? Being ignored. In this procedure, a caregiver is asked to be unresponsive and keep a "still face."

Researchers using this procedure and others have found that over the first two years, babies develop the ability to tolerate upsetting events and to calm themselves (Gago Galvagno et al., 2019). By age 1, infants anticipate that a caregiver will help them feel better, and so the sound of an approaching caregiver will quiet a wailing baby (Brownell et al., 2015). Toddlers also learn independent ways of coping with their feelings: They may pick up a distracting toy, look away, or suck their thumb (Bozicevic et al., 2021; Planalp & Braungart-Rieker, 2015).

Although most toddlers have fewer ups and downs than younger babies, they are far from even-tempered. In many communities around the world, families struggle with a new form of dysregulation as babies become toddlers—the *meltdown*, or temper tantrum. A meltdown is typically a moment of upset that begins as anger and transitions into hysterical sadness. Toddlers may collapse, kick, scream, or even hold their breath. More than 9 in 10 2-year-olds in U.S. communities have one meltdown every week (B. L. Manning et al., 2019). What triggers a meltdown? New limits and expectations. Toddlers' new abilities, such as talking and walking, often lead to higher adult expectations. In addition, many families have difficulty soothing upset toddlers. They no longer use the calming methods, like nursing or rocking, that worked for younger children, and verbal methods that work for older children, like logical reasoning, are often ineffective (Deichmann & Ahnert, 2021; Kopp, 1989).

emotion regulation The ability to manage your feelings in a way that is appropriate to your community circumstances.

Lovett Stories + Strategies

Not the Still Face Again! In the still-face procedure, caregivers are asked to maintain a neutral expression for just two minutes. In this video still from Dr. Edward Tronick's laboratory at the University of Massachusetts, a baby reacts with characteristic upset while their parent tries to remain unreactive. Don't worry: The baby was easily consoled after the procedure, which mimics what might happen when a caregiver is temporarily distracted or unavailable in real life.

Share It!

Check your universals. Researchers have found that infants' reactions to the still-face procedure are not universal: This test, like many others, is most useful in communities with distal parenting. In communities where babies are held close most of the time, like those in rural Bolivia, for instance, infants react differently in the procedure.

(Broesch et al., 2022)

 **Share It!**

Don't worry about the mask. Researchers studying whether wearing an opaque mask upset babies found that it did not worry them like the still-face procedure.

(Tronick & Snidman, 2021).

APPLY IT! **6.4** Makena starts to look sad and cry when Stephanie picks up her phone to check a text, but Makena recovers in a minute. How is this experience similar to the still-face procedure?

6.5 Families with young children often have different ethnotheories about sharing. How might you explain the science of sharing and caring to Jen and Stephanie, who wonder whether they should expect Makena to share with Maya?

Personality and Temperament in the Early Years

Learning Objective

6.4 Explain how babies begin to develop unique personalities.

Jen and Stephanie thought Makena was going to grow up to be shy and quiet when she was a newborn. But as she grew, she became an outgoing, goofy, loud, and affectionate toddler. Like Makena, some babies are a little hesitant about new people, while others have an easy smile for strangers in the checkout line. Even the intensity of babies' responses to the world varies. Some seem to have mild responses, whether to an immunization or a new person. Others are more intense. Are Jen and Stephanie right to think that Makena's outgoing attitude to the world is something she learned from her equally exuberant big sister, Maya? How have Jen and Stephanie's parenting and Makena's own biology influenced her personality?

Researchers are fascinated by these questions. They are trying to understand **personality**, or the individual differences in emotions, thinking, and behaviors that make each of us unique. Early patterns of feelings and reactions in infants and toddlers are known as **temperament**, a precursor to personality (Shiner, 2017).

What Are the Dimensions of Temperament?

In the 1950s, pioneering child psychiatrists Alexander Thomas and Stella Chess developed a way of analyzing temperament in small children. They wanted to understand why babies were so different and why some were out of sync with their caregivers (Chess et al., 1963; Thomas & Chess, 1957). Thomas and Chess identified three basic temperamental categories: **easy**, **slow-to-warm-up**, and **difficult** (Thomas & Chess, 1977). Easy babies, about 40 percent of the sample in Thomas and Chess's work, were flexible in new situations and usually happier than other babies. Slow-to-warm-up babies, about 15 percent of the group, were shyer than other children and slower to adjust to new circumstances, but they were not intense in their reactions. The 10 percent of children classified as difficult were easily frustrated, slow to adapt to change, and tended to react intensely.

Did you notice that those percentages do not add up to 100 percent? Thomas and Chess were aware of this, too: Their classification system was not designed to exactly match the complexity of all children (Thomas et al., 1970). In the years since Thomas and Chess's groundbreaking work, many researchers have moved empirically beyond those temperamental categories. For instance, many now suggest that Thomas and Chess's terminology, including the word *difficult*, stigmatizes babies. Whereas Thomas and Chess were quite candid about the challenges of intense and explosive behavior in babies, many contemporary researchers prefer more neutral and person-first terms, referring to such behavior as "undercontrolled" or "challenging" (Super et al., 2020).

Instead of fitting all babies into three basic categories, many contemporary researchers think of early temperament as a set of traits that are displayed on a continuum of intensity (Putnam et al., 2019). Researchers focus on three major elements of early personality: *effortful control*, *negative affect*, and *extraversion*. The ability to focus attention and control behavior is called effortful control. Some babies are always looking for something new and have trouble controlling their focus for a long time.

personality Habits of emotionally relating and responding to people and events in our lives.

temperament An early pattern of personality in infants and toddlers.

easy In Thomas and Chess's dimensional approach to temperament, babies who are flexible and usually content.

slow-to-warm-up In Thomas and Chess's dimensional approach to temperament, these babies tend to be shy and slower to adjust to new circumstances, but not intense in their responses.

difficult In Thomas and Chess's dimensional approach to temperament, babies who are easily frustrated, are slow to adapt to change, and react intensely. This term is no longer preferred, outside of scholarly research.

Babies who are higher in effortful control may be content to play with one toy for a long time.

The second major factor in personality is how often and how strongly babies display their negative feelings, often called negative affect. Some babies are just more irritable than others, easily scared by new things, or more likely to be frustrated by a late lunch or missed nap. Others, like Makena, are more flexible.

The third element is the baby's level of extraversion, or how outgoing they are. In babies, being physically active and approaching new things happily is often seen as a sign of extraversion. An active explorer like Makena is considered high in extraversion.

Other scientists have described additional elements of personality beyond these three categories (Planalp & Goldsmith, 2020). Some focus on a baby's level of fear or shyness in new situations, often called *inhibition* (Kagan, 2018). Others look at a baby's level of *agreeableness*, or their level of openness to new experiences (Cloninger et al., 2019). No matter what researchers focus on, they find that the early years lay the foundation for personality.

CAN YOU BELIEVE IT?
Is Personality Something You Are Born With?

Is your personality something set in your DNA? Or is it something you learn as you grow? Many families attribute babies' early temperament to genes. They may blame an intense mother for an aggressive toddler's behavior or attribute an easygoing baby's personality to being "just like their dad" (Stover et al., 2015). Researchers suggest that this thinking might be misguided: Makena's development, it turns out, is not completely shaped by the tendencies she inherited from her biological parents, her prenatal experience, or the hours she's spent running around the house with her spunky big sister. Personality, like so much of development, is complicated, and genes do not hold all the answers.

Personality development is an example of how the environment and genetics work together epigenetically (Shiner, 2017). It is also an example of how children's characteristics can shape their environment just as the environment shapes them. Genes play a role in what kind of person babies become, but they are far from the only answer (Beam & Turkheimer, 2017; Kandler et al., 2021).

The first few years of life are a time when early personality is molded by the environment: More genes related to personality are activated during the first three years than at any other point in the lifespan (Conradt, 2017). What causes these genes to be activated or not? The environment, including prenatal exposure to hormones, early health, and, perhaps most importantly, early parenting (Gartstein & Skinner, 2018; Jones & Sloan, 2018; Miguel et al., 2019). Caregivers influence their baby's ability to manage strong feelings and to focus, as well as how positive they are. For instance, babies whose parents are depressed, stressed, or have a mental illness are more likely to be emotionally reactive than those whose caregivers are more stable (Brooker et al., 2020; Martinez-Torteya et al., 2018). Supportive parenting can help moderate challenging personality characteristics, such as extreme shyness or high energy (Augustine & Stiller, 2019; Planalp & Goldsmith, 2020).

Blaming (or crediting) the environment for babies' personalities does not give a complete picture of who we are. It turns out that caregiving is also influenced by a baby's temperament (Ayoub et al., 2019). Infants who are difficult to soothe and frequently upset are more challenging for parents than other babies; their behavior stresses the relationship, and as a result, they may receive less-sensitive caretaking (Freund et al., 2019).

Personality development doesn't end in toddlerhood. Personality can change. A baby who seems overly irritable or easily frustrated is more likely to become even-tempered two years later than at any other time during the lifespan (Parade et al., 2018). And personality continues to develop: A new school, new job, divorce, or hurricane are all events that can change personality over the lifespan (Turkheimer et al., 2014).

goodness of fit The idea that babies benefit from a good match between their personalities and their caregivers.

Managing Early Personality

Thomas and Chess coined the term **goodness of fit** to highlight the fact that everyone, particularly small children, benefits from caregivers who meet the needs of their unique personalities (Chess & Thomas, 1991). For instance, babies who tend to be anxious may have more difficulty adjusting to new circumstances and may need a few days of gentle adjustment when being dropped off at a new child-care center. As Chess and Thomas pointed out, this does not mean anything is *wrong* with these children; being anxious is just a variation. Chess and Thomas advised that caregivers, parents, teachers, and health care providers should use their understanding of early personality to adjust their expectations of babies' needs (Chess & Thomas, 1996).

Over the past decades, researchers studying infant–caregiver interactions have generally supported Thomas and Chess's conclusions. All children benefit from strong relationships. Children with more challenging temperaments, typically those who have a lot of energy, lack effortful control, or are particularly fearful, show more intense benefits from strong, understanding connections with caregivers (Gartstein et al., 2018; Wittig & Rodriguez, 2019).

The Impact of Culture

Jen and Stephanie are smitten with Makena's laughter and the energetic way she chases her sister around the house, but other adults might be horrified. Culture plays an important role in how we understand babies' behavior, and these expectations, as researchers have found, can shape an infant's early temperament. Parents in Italy, for instance, tend to prize the flexibility of babies who easily adapt to different social settings, but caregivers in Holland tend to place more value on cheerfulness (Chen, 2018). Babies in Finland tend to smile more than babies in the United States. Chinese babies tend to be shyer (Slobodskaya et al., 2018). (See **Figure 6.5**.)

Researchers have found that U.S. parents, on average, prefer their babies to be outgoing and energetic, and babies in the United States typically are rated accordingly (Sung et al., 2015). This extraversion seems to arise because U.S. parents tend to encourage their children to be bold and outgoing and discourage fear or anger (Gartstein & Putnam, 2018). Some scientists suggest that children are more likely to be outgoing in

FIGURE 6.5 Where Are the Happiest Babies in the World? Researchers in 14 countries asked families to describe their babies' temperaments and found that families often described their toddlers in ways that reflected their cultural values. These scientists used temperamental categories to look at their data: Babies with high energy are said to be energetic and outgoing and have lots of positive emotions. Those with high scores for negative affect have families that report that they are more likely to be distressed, perhaps reflecting ethnotheories that are more accepting of fussiness. Those with high effortful control are said to be flexible and better able to control their behavior to match expectations. If you were looking for babies who were rarely distressed and showed outgoing, positive emotions, you might find them in Finland.

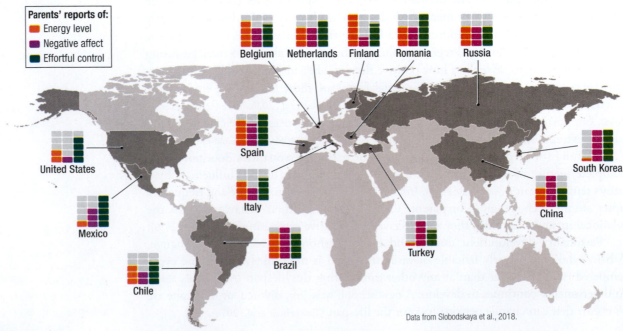

Parents' reports of:
- Energy level
- Negative affect
- Effortful control

Belgium　Netherlands　Finland　Romania　Russia

United States

Spain

Italy

Mexico

Chile

Brazil

Turkey

China

South Korea

Data from Slobodskaya et al., 2018.

communities that are individualistic, like those in the United States, where children must advocate for themselves in a competitive world. In contrast, in cultures that are more collectivist, families tend to encourage children to control their impulses, and to be less outgoing and more reserved so they will get along better with others (Chen, 2018).

It is important to point out that these are general patterns and not predictions of what will be true in any given family. The United States, like other countries, represents many cultural traditions. For instance, the expectation that families in less individualistic cultures are more likely to appreciate shyness in their children does not necessarily predict how one family will feel about their reserved toddler (Chen, 2019). Parents raising their children in a diverse community may worry about how their shy child will succeed in a dominant culture that values extraversion. Understanding the impact of culture on early personality is important, and very complex.

APPLY IT! **6.6** Stephanie and Jen worry that Makena's experience growing up during a pandemic might increase her risk for emotional difficulties later in life. What does developmental science say about risk in early development and the power of caregiving?

6.7 Based on what you know about Makena, a good sleeper who had mild reactions to most everyday experiences as a baby, what temperament do you think she has?

Family Relationships

Jen and Stephanie are juggling busy schedules but they work hard to stay close to family. They want their daughters to remain in touch with their cousins, grandparents, and birth mothers, who still connect with Makena and her sister online. Dozens of people make up Makena's family, created by bonds of love. Developmental scientists believe that a child's relationships with close caregivers in the first years of life create patterns of relating to others that last a lifetime.

What Makes a Family?

Consider the family members on Jen's FaceTime list or in your "favorites" on your phone. What defines family varies from person to person (Cavanagh & Fomby, 2019). In the United States, about 9 in 10 babies come home from the hospital with their birth parent and their partner, but by the time they are toddlers, about 1 in 12 has experienced a family transition, like a divorce, remarriage, or repartnering (Declercq et al., 2013). Families in the United States are often complex, comprised of parents and their married or unmarried partners, along with other siblings, who may or may not be biologically related. Around the world, babies are often raised by their biological parents, but siblings, grandparents, and neighbors also play a critical role. The idea that one or even two adults provide all the care a baby needs is not typical of most communities across the world (Abraham & Feldman, 2018; Sear, 2021).

Close relationships between an infant and a caregiver can be formed regardless of the biological or legal relationship or the identity of the caregiver. Parents with any gender identity or relationship status, adoptive parents, and caregiving siblings or grandparents can all help babies thrive (Golombok, 2017). Research on caregiving in developmental science has historically tended to focus on female caregivers and often neglected both male caregivers and children's extended family. However, most evidence suggests that the basic principles of sensitive parenting are similar no matter what the identity of the caregiver (Cabrera et al., 2018; Gettler et al., 2020; Schoppe-Sullivan & Fagan, 2020). As you will see, it is the specific caregiving practices and the quality of the relationship, rather than the caregiver themselves, that are important.

Learning Objectives

6.5 Describe how caregiving impacts emotional development.

6.6 Explain common variations in caregiver–child attachment relationships.

Caregiving Comes in Different Sizes. Sometimes love, and help with a runny nose, comes from a big brother and not an adult. Siblings often provide caregiving in families around the world.

responsiveness The idea that a caregiver should acknowledge and react to an infant's bids for attention.

Scientific American Profile

Supportive Parenting and Responsiveness

Measuring Caregiving in Infancy and Toddlerhood

Much of what caregivers do with babies is unique to each family or community. Parents have different values about caregiving and how they want their children to turn out (Harkness & Super, 2021). Across cultures, however, caregivers who are responsive and supportive with their babies seem to have better-adjusted children, even though specific parenting practices may differ.

Supportive Parenting Despite cultural variations, all caregivers engage in some of the same practices. They all tend to their upset babies, teach them to communicate and move, and keep them clean. When researchers ask parents around the world what makes an ideal parent, they agree on some core ideas: responsiveness, sensitivity, and positivity (Lansford, Rothenberg, et al., 2021).

Responsiveness is the idea that a caregiver should promptly respond to a baby's signals, whether they are cries of distress or giggles of happiness (Bornstein, 1989, 2019). There are many cultural variations in how adults respond. For example, when Stephanie hears Makena fussing, she sometimes turns on a video to keep her occupied. In other families, adults may attend to fussy babies by nursing them, patting them, or picking them up. The critical element in responsiveness is establishing the back-and-forth relationship between caregiver and child (Mesman et al., 2018). Responsiveness helps babies learn their caregivers are reliable and helps infants regulate their feelings (see **Figure 6.6**).

Supportive caregiving can also be characterized as *sensitive*. Sensitive caregivers accurately interpret their child's signals (Mesman, 2021). When Jen expertly redirects Makena after the baby puts her hands in Jen's eyes, she understands that Makena is just trying to be close. She is interested in Makena's point of view but still manages to convince her to keep her fingers out of her eye sockets. When researchers examine these kinds of back-and-forth interactions, they often see their movements, facial expressions, and even sounds aligning. Scientists call this close coordination of responses *synchrony* (DePasquale, 2020). Caregivers and infants who are in sync share energy levels, patterns of brain activity, heart rates, and may even show a boost in *oxytocin*, the hormone associated with close attachments (Azhari et al., 2019; Levy et al., 2021).

Another aspect of supportive caregiving is that it is *positive*. Stephanie and Jen clearly enjoy being with Makena, even when she is challenging. Caregiving is undoubtedly hard, and families are frequently forced to impose limits on curious toddlers. However, parents who enjoy being with their children and who can communicate affection develop more positive relationships and foster their children's emotion regulation more easily (Planalp et al., 2017).

Babies who do not experience supportive parenting are at risk. Sometimes parents are stressed, depressed, or perhaps just unaware of how critical it is to be responsive to their child. Less commonly, infants may live in institutions where caregivers are too busy to be attentive (Humphreys et al., 2018). Two styles of caregiving are particularly harmful in the early years: *detachment*, when a caregiver is unresponsive and inattentive, and *harshness*, when a caregiver is consistently negative, angry, or frightening.

FIGURE 6.6 Sensitive Parenting Around the World When researchers asked families around the world to rank what caregivers should (and should not do) with their babies, some ideas were universal.

Families Around the World Ranked What Caregivers Should and Should Not Do:

Caregivers should...	Caregivers should not...
1. Demonstrate they care by touch.	1. Act negatively or critically to the child.
2. Show that the child makes them happy.	2. Ignore and be unresponsive to the child.
3. Share praise with the child.	3. Behave as if the child is inanimate or inhuman.
4. Encourage the child to try new things.	4. Get annoyed if the child wants to sit close to them.
5. Be happy around the child.	5. Ignore the infant's smiles or sounds.

Information from Mesman et al., 2016.

Infants who lack supportive parenting may later have trouble making friends and establishing close relationships and have learning, behavioral, or emotional problems (Crouch et al., 2017; Wu & Feng, 2020).

Attachment

Stephanie gets misty-eyed when she talks about Makena: "She's just brought so much joy to our family." Both Jen and Stephanie admit to worrying initially about bonding with their adopted babies, but they found that their love for their girls came naturally and bountifully. Jen and Stephanie may refer to their relationship with Makena as "love," but developmental scientists call this bond **attachment**. Attachment is a close, ongoing relationship between a child and their caregiver.

Jen, Stephanie, and Makena have built a relationship that makes Makena feel safe but also allows her to grow and explore. In times of stress, whether that is a new person in the room or just naptime, babies seek out their attachment figures. Researchers call this **proximity seeking**. Babies may seek attachment by climbing into an adult's lap or by clinging to their arms. Animals show this behavior as well, as demonstrated in the research of Harry Harlow: Monkeys raised in a laboratory with inanimate caregivers would seek comfort from these figures if they were soft and cuddly, even if they did not provide physical nourishment (Harlow, 1958).

Attachment figures also help children investigate the world by providing a **secure base**, or a safe haven for them to return to when they feel nervous or worried. For instance, when a new babysitter comes to the house, Makena checks in with her parents, but it doesn't take long for her to scoot over to meet them. Her parents act as a secure base for her exploration, allowing her to make new friends.

The patterns set in their first relationships will be taken into babies' future relationships. Researchers call this memory an **internal working model** (Bowlby, 1980; Bretherton & Munholland, 2016). Internal working models are not all positive: Attachment happens regardless of the quality of the bond. Babies can be attached to caregivers who are supportive but also to those who are neglectful or abusive (Perry et al., 2017). However, infants who have positive and responsive early relationships are more likely to develop internal working models that help them form better and stronger friendships (Sroufe, 2021).

The first years of life is a sensitive period for the development of attachment (Groh et al., 2017; Roisman & Groh, 2021). Attachment does not end in infancy; adults are attached, too, to romantic partners, friends, and their own parents. Even in adulthood, we continue to rely on our attachment figures for comfort. (Perhaps you have been known to call your parents when times get tough.)

Measuring Attachment Remember from Chapter 2 that it was a young doctor, John Bowlby, who helped develop attachment theory (Bowlby, 1951; Bowlby et al., 1952). At that time, many experts believed it was safer for sick babies to be cared for in a sterile hospital ward without their families, but Bowlby believed that children could not thrive in such isolation (Bowlby, 1969). He was one of many scientists who emphasized the importance of early relationships in creating emotional resilience across the lifespan and who looked to animals as a model for human behavior (Harlow, 1958). This approach remains at the forefront of developmental science today (Mikulincer & Shaver, 2019; Schuengel et al., 2021).

Bowlby's colleague, Canadian scientist Mary Ainsworth, explored individual differences in attachment and developed a categorization of attachment styles that continues to be influential today (Ainsworth & Bowlby, 1991; Bretherton, 1992). After studying children from Uganda, Canada, England, and the United States, Ainsworth created a test to assess how children investigated the world around them and how they responded in times of stress. Ainsworth discovered that briefly separating and reuniting babies with their caregivers could measure attachment behaviors (Ainsworth et al., 2015). Her experimental procedure became known as the **Strange Situation**,

attachment An emotional bond in a close relationship. Attachment begins with the relationship between infants and their caregivers and may not always be positive.

proximity seeking The tendency for children (and adults) to seek comfort by being physically close to someone they are attached to.

secure base In attachment theory, a safe haven for children to return to when they may feel anxious.

internal working model In attachment theory, the idea that our early habits of relating to our caregivers create a pattern of relating that we will use later on in our lives.

Strange Situation An empirical method developed by Mary Ainsworth for evaluating the attachment status of toddlers.

secure attachment In attachment theory, children who have a sense of trust in their caregivers that allows them to explore their environment.

insecure attachment In attachment theory, children who have not established a sense of trust in their caregivers to soothe them when they are upset.

insecure-resistant attachment In attachment theory, a form of insecure attachment characterized babies' angry and hostile responses to their caregiver who they perceive as inconsistent and unreliable.

insecure-avoidant attachment In attachment theory, a form of insecure attachment characterized by babies' emotional distance from their caregivers who they perceive as being unable to soothe them.

disorganized attachment In attachment theory, children who have unusual responses in the Strange Situation procedure and who may be afraid of their caregivers.

Are You My Mommy? The Strange Situation is designed to temporarily stress toddlers to assess how they react to their caregivers and how they regulate their emotions in a new situation. In this video still, a baby adjusts to a new caregiver (the Stranger) after their parent has left the room.

because it tested how toddlers reacted when separated from their caregivers in an unfamiliar place. In a span of 20 minutes, a toddler between 12 and 20 months was separated from their caregiver, watched by a friendly stranger, briefly left alone, and then reunited with their caregiver.

Types of Attachment Researchers who study toddlers' reactions in the Strange Situation find that they fall into four different types, called attachment styles or statuses. In **secure attachments**, toddlers feel comfortable exploring the laboratory and playing on their own but might show some distress when separated from their caregiver. They are also happy to see their caregivers when they return and are comforted by their caregivers when they are upset. Securely attached babies trust that their caregivers will be there when they need them; this gives them confidence and security to explore the world (Ainsworth et al., 2015). Warm, sensitive relationships between parents and children produce secure attachments.

Most studies of families around the world estimate that about 60 percent of toddlers are securely attached (Mesman et al., 2016). This means that about 40 percent of children are not. Ainsworth called these children **insecurely attached** and theorized that such toddlers have not developed trust in someone to take care of them when they are upset (Ainsworth et al., 2015).

Ainsworth and subsequent researchers described three varieties of insecure attachment. During the Strange Situation, toddlers who have an **insecure-resistant attachment** are upset when their caregivers leave and return, but they react with mixed or angry feelings and are difficult to calm (Ainsworth et al., 2015). These children feel insecure about separation and do not trust that their caregivers will return. They may not feel comfortable exploring the environment even when their caregiver is present and may be clingy. Researchers believe this pattern of attachment stems from an inconsistent parenting style (Leerkes & Zhou, 2018). In many communities, about 15 percent of babies exhibit this type of attachment (Mesman et al., 2016).

Children who display **insecure-avoidant attachment** do not appear to react when their caregivers leave the room. Instead, they tend to focus on objects in the room. When their caregivers return, they do not attempt to reconnect (Ainsworth et al., 2015). Researchers believe that these children may actually be upset by the Strange Situation but hide their feelings because they do not expect to be soothed. Children with insecure-avoidant attachment styles tend to have caregivers who are less attentive, so they learn to adapt by no longer expecting to be nurtured (Szepsenwol & Simpson, 2021). About 15 percent of toddlers in the United States are classified as insecure-avoidant. This type of attachment is much less common in communities where infants are not often separated from their caregivers, as some studies from South Korea and Israel have found (Jin et al., 2011; Zreik et al., 2017).

Children with the last type of insecure attachment, **disorganized attachment**, exhibit unusual behaviors in the Strange Situation (Main & Solomon, 1986). They might freeze, stare off into space, or seem afraid of their caregiver. These reactions are more frequently seen in children who have experienced serious trauma or whose caregivers are frightening. In many communities around the world, about 10 to 15 percent of children fall into this category (Granqvist et al., 2017).

After studying children in the Strange Situation, researchers determined that children with different attachment styles tended to have different life experiences when they grew up. No matter what type of early personality children had, those who showed secure attachment in the Strange Situation were more likely to get along with their peers and develop good friendships, perhaps because they had learned successful ways of relating to others in infancy. On the other hand, children with insecure or disorganized attachment types were more likely to have difficulty making friends. Children who had developed an insecure-avoidant or a disorganized attachment style were also more likely to have emotional difficulties such as a lack of emotion regulation (Groh et al., 2017).

Critiques of the Strange Situation Researchers generally agree that attachment is a universal human need, but they also remind us that attachment looks different in different cultures. The Strange Situation in particular has been often criticized, even by Ainsworth herself, for oversimplifying the complexities of real life (Ainsworth & Marvin, 1995; Keller, 2018; Vicedo, 2017).

In some cases, attachment theory has been used in legal settings in ways that theorists never intended. Elements of the Strange Situation itself, meant to be a research assessment, have been inappropriately used to measure caregiving in divorce and child welfare proceedings, and even to justify removing children from their families (Forslund et al., 2021). Indigenous families in North America, Australia, and New Zealand have been particularly concerned about misuse of attachment theory to justify the separation of children from their ancestral communities (Choate et al., 2019, 2020).

One concern about attachment theory is that in most families, babies have attachments to multiple caregivers and may show different patterns of relating to them (Keller, 2018). For instance, in the Central African Republic, researchers observed that babies in one close-knit village were attached to six people on average (Meehan & Hawks, 2013). The Strange Situation focuses on a single relationship, which may not provide an accurate measure of how a baby will relate to others or how sensitive any one caregiver is. Researchers have found that combining the patterns of babies' attachment to all of their caregivers may be more accurate than just focusing on one relationship (Dagan & Sagi-Schwartz, 2018).

In addition, the Strange Situation test does not take cultural variations into account. In some communities where babies are very unused to being cared for by new people, the procedure was extremely stressful. In others, it was not stressful at all. For instance, in some experiments with German families in the 1980s, about half of the babies were classified as having an insecure-avoidant attachment status, nearly double what researchers expected. What happened? The German babies had been raised to be very independent, to soothe themselves, and to expect less comfort when they were stressed (Grossmann et al., 1985; LeVine & LeVine, 2016). On the other hand, in South Korea and Japan, researchers observed that very few babies had developed the independence and the ability to explore that would lead to a designation of secure attachment (Jin & Rounds, 2012). These babies were not used to being separated from their families at all, and the situation itself was too stressful for them. Many researchers now use measures of caregiving quality that avoid the stresses of the Strange Situation (Mesman, 2021).

Although the Strange Situation is not a perfect measure, few researchers question the importance of early relationships. While it remains difficult to accurately measure the bond between caregivers and children, experts agree that forming strong, enduring relationships is critical to healthy development (Keller, 2018).

The Biology of Early Family Relationships

Whereas Ainsworth tried to measure attachment using observation, some contemporary developmental scientists use brain-imaging technology and hormone tests to assess the biological bases of early relationships. Scientists have found that early caregiving programs babies' hormonal stress systems and brain connectivity (Gee, 2020;

Scientific American Profile

Building New Attachments

Building Attachment Children form attachments with all their caregivers, whether they are family or, like Patricia Adams, child care professionals. After serving in the Navy and raising three children, Patricia Adams now runs day care centers in Detroit, Michigan, where she builds relationships and shares a love of Dr. Seuss with young children.

Nelson et al., 2019). These researchers believe that since caregivers soothe and suppress babies' responses to acute stress in cases of trauma, sensitive caregiving protects them from the long-term effects of too much exposure to stress hormones like cortisol (Gunnar, 2020).

For babies without supportive caregiving, early stress may epigenetically program the stress system to respond with more or less powerful stress responses in the future. For instance, less-attentive parenting seems to cause higher levels of stress hormones in babies, which may suppress their stress responses later in life (Wu & Feng, 2020). Infants under more acute stress experience a more extreme phenomenon: Babies and toddlers who receive neglectful care, like those in institutions or orphanages, can become unresponsive to normal stressors, which prevents them from responding flexibly to their environment (Gunnar, 2020).

Cortisol is not the only hormone that is affected by early caregiving; oxytocin plays an important role as well (Krol, Puglia, et al., 2019). Caregivers with higher levels of oxytocin tend to be more attentive to their newborns and exhibit higher levels of synchrony (Feldman & Bakermans-Kranenburg, 2017). Caregivers with depression, on the other hand, often have lower levels of oxytocin (Ellis et al., 2021). Much of this biological research has focused on the relationship between babies and their female caregivers. However, researchers have also found that men's hormone levels change as they parent: Men, too, have higher levels of oxytocin when they do hands-on caregiving (Bakermans-Kranenburg et al., 2019; Dijk et al., 2020; T. Li et al., 2017).

Neuroscientists theorize that early baby–caregiver relationships do not just change hormones—they actually shape the neural networks in the brains of caregivers and babies. As you may remember, the circuits connecting the subcortical structures that process emotion, such as the amygdala, and the prefrontal cortex, where more thinking and planning take place, help babies control and manage their feelings. Supportive caregiving *delays* the development of these brain networks. Babies with caregivers who soothe them and reduce their stress rely on their caregivers to manage their strong feelings while their brains are still maturing (Gunnar, 2020).

In contrast, these circuits mature early in babies who are neglected (Tottenham, 2020). You might think that accelerated development is a good thing, but in this case, early maturation brings challenges. These babies' brains adapted to help them survive in neglectful environments, making it difficult for them to adapt to a world in which they need to develop healthy relationships and learn social skills. Children who have been neglected often have difficulties managing their feelings and accurately responding to the feelings of those around them.

Does this mean that babies should never experience any stress? Actually, researchers say mild stresses help train the brain to handle everyday stresses in the future. What you experience in infancy gives you practice and training for life to come: Some stress is actually a good thing (Gee, 2020; Gunnar, 2020). Concerns arise not with mild everyday stressors, but with acute trauma and long-term neglect.

Challenges in Early Parenting

Not everyone's experience with early parenting is easy. One young parent in Vancouver, British Columbia, experienced depression when her daughters were newborns. She remembered "falling apart" in the aisles of Costco, struggling to smile back at her daughter, and not knowing what to say when her toddler asked, "Mommy, are you happy?" (Goyette, 2016). She was diagnosed with depression, like almost one in five new mothers and one in eight new fathers around the world (Da Costa et al., 2019; Granat et al., 2017). Depression is not the only challenge faced by new parents. Nearly one in two U.S. families with infants and toddlers has financial difficulties, with more than one in six experiencing food insecurity (Coleman-Jensen et al., 2019; Jiang et al., 2015).

Early treatment for mental health challenges is critical. Depression or overwhelming stress can make it difficult to give children the responsive back-and-forth that is essential for infants as they develop emotion regulation and social skills (Granat et al., 2017). Depression in women has gotten the most attention from researchers and health care providers, but all parents, including men and people who are nonbinary, are also susceptible (Charter et al., 2021). Depressed partners not only have difficulty responding to their babies, but their depression is also more likely to strain their relationship with the other parent (Da Costa et al., 2019). Relationship conflicts, from bickering to breakups, can also stress young families (Zhou et al., 2017).

Nearly one in seven U.S. families with an infant includes a caregiver who uses alcohol or other substances in an unhealthy way, or has substance use disorder (SUD) (Clemans-Cope et al., 2019; Finkelhor, 2020; Kuppens et al., 2020). Babies in families marked by SUD are more likely to be fussy, irritable, and at higher risk for neglect and abuse and for developing emotional and behavioral problems later in life (Kuppens et al., 2020).

Infants and toddlers who have parents with SUD are also more likely to end up in the foster-care system, as a result of the criminalization of substance use disorder in many communities (Meinhofer & Angleró-Díaz, 2019). Interventions often take a family-focused approach, treating the caregivers' mental health issues while coaching them to be more responsive, supportive, and patient with their children (Barlow et al., 2019; Smith et al., 2016).

Whitney Curtis for The Washington Post via Getty Images

Staying Close No Matter What
Christine and her two-month-old daughter, Isabelle, are allowed to stay together even though Christine is temporarily incarcerated in a correctional center in Illinois. They have benefited from a program that helps new parents maintain custody of their infants while they are incarcerated.

APPLY IT! **6.8** When Makena met the babysitter for the first time, she initially clung to Stephanie before venturing out to meet the new person. How is this an example of using her parent as a secure base?

6.9 Infants are often attached to their caregivers, even if they are subjected to neglect and abuse. How does attachment theory explain this?

Child Care and Media in Infancy

Around the globe, babies spend time in child care. Even when they are cared for at home, many babies spend time in front of screens and on devices, contrary to the advice of experts. Both child care and screen time can have profound effects on babies' developing social and emotional skills.

Learning Objective

6.7 Explain the impact of experiences outside the family on infants' emotional development.

How Does Media Affect Emotional Development?

Like many caregivers, Jen and Stephanie's screen time rules are not always consistent: particularly at times when they are both trying to work from home. Without a video, they could not return phone calls and get work done. As you may recall from Chapter 4, experts recommend that babies avoid screens, except for video calls, until about 18 months, at which point their screen use should be limited to less than an hour a day (AAP, 2016). However, like Jen and Stephanie, many caregivers use media to entertain their children, and the amount of time small children spent on screens skyrocketed during the COVID-19 pandemic (Parents Together, 2020). Many caregivers feel, as Jen and Stephanie do, that the recommendations about screen use are unworkable and unrealistic: Screens are often on, and nearly every caregiver has a cell phone (Barr et al., 2020; Radesky, 2019).

New parents report that they are distracted by their phones or by the television at least 30 percent of the time that they are feeding their infants (Ventura et al., 2019). Caregivers who use media in this way tend to have fewer back-and-forth interactions with their children and are less attentive (Stockdale et al., 2020; Wan et al., 2021). However,

How Does It Work? Whether in Spain, like this toddler, or elsewhere in the world, phones are fascinating to children. Researchers caution that too much screen time may keep children from having responsive, real-life interactions.

 Learn It Together

The Transition to Child Care

Plan Imagine your cousin has been a stay-at-home father to his 9-month-old since the baby's birth, and they have a warm emotional bond. Now, he is thinking about going back to work, but is worried about how this will affect his relationship with the baby, and whether being with a child-care provider will be stressful for his daughter. Using your understanding of attachment theory and sensitive caregiving, give him your expert advice. Review information about attachment security, including factors that help promote secure attachment and information about attachment to multiple caregivers.

Engage Working with a few classmates, discuss the factors to consider relating to infant care. How does the baby's age, 9 months, impact how she might respond to a new caregiver? What features should your cousin look for in a child-care provider? What features should he avoid? Should he be worried about his own relationship with his daughter?

Reflect Do you have any personal experience with this issue? Do you know anyone who has recently made a decision regarding infant care? Has learning about attachment security changed how you think about child care in the early years?

whether parents are interrupted by a text or by needing to fill out forms by hand, some evidence indicates that both babies and their families are able to bounce back from the interruptions (Konrad et al., 2021).

What about when babies use media by themselves? Babies exposed to technology for long periods of time, whether that is sitting in front of the television or spending hours with a hand-held device are at greater risk for emotional problems are for falling behind in their physical or cognitive development. However, researcher are not sure whether it is their family circumstances or the media exposure that is the culprit (Lin et al., 2020; McHarg et al., 2020; Supanitayanon et al., 2020). In addition, because mobile and online media use in infants and toddlers is relatively new, researchers have not had time to study its effects in children over time.

Scientists have found that parents of infants and toddlers who see their children as difficult expose them to more media (McDaniel & Radesky, 2020; Munzer et al., 2018). However, it is not clear why this happens: Do parents of challenging children put them in front of a television or mobile device so they can get a break? Or do parents with limited skills in managing their children allow too much screen time, which exacerbates their children's difficult behavior? There is evidence for both theories. In either case, parents who rely on media to quiet their children may benefit from extra support from friends or family. Others may benefit from professional help to learn how to better manage their children's behavior and how to have responsive, back-and-forth interactions that will help their children flourish.

Early Child Care

Like many other working parents, Jen and Stephanie struggle to balance caring for two young children with their job responsibilities. Around the world, working parents rely on help from family members and from paid caregivers to balance their jobs and the needs of their young children. However, finding high-quality and affordable infant and toddler care is difficult (R. Malik et al., 2020). This is one of the reasons many parents take a leave from work when they have small children (Dotti Sani & Scherer, 2018). But in some places, affordable child care is subsidized by the community. Quality child care is one of the reasons families in Denmark, for instance, are able to continue to work after their children are born. The local government pays more than three-quarters of child-care costs (BBC, 2016). In other countries, including the United States, infant child care is expensive and difficult to find (Banghart et al., 2020; OECD, 2020).

In the United States, infants and toddlers are not likely to attend a child-care center. More than 97 percent of child care in the United States is provided in private homes, and most child-care providers for infants and toddlers are informal and unpaid (Paschall & Trout, 2018). Many of these home-based child-care providers are friends or neighbors who have agreed to watch the baby as a favor (National Survey of Early Care and Education, 2016). Others are more formal arrangements. Parents tend to choose child care based on advice from family members and friends and look for a provider who can work with their budget and their schedule and who understands their culture (Forry, 2015; Forry et al., 2013; Gordon et al., 2008).

Remember from Chapter 5 that research has shown that early child care can provide many cognitive benefits. Being able to work also relieves families from economic strain. In addition, mothers who work are less likely to experience depression, in part because work offers important social support (B. A. Lewis et al., 2017). Babies and toddlers benefit from developing supportive relationships with their care providers (Ereky-Stevens et al., 2018).

High-quality infant-care programs nurture the attachment between babies and caregivers in a supportive environment (McMullen, 2018). Programs that foster warm relationships share three key features:

1. They provide continuity of care—a consistent relationship between one caregiver and an infant, rather than a changing roster of caregivers (Bratsch-Hines et al., 2020).

2. They have low infant-to-caregiver ratios, which enable caregivers to individually attend to infants' needs. Most experts advise that one provider be responsible for fewer than four infants under 15 months old and fewer than six toddlers (NAEYC, 2018).

3. They hire caregivers who understand typical infant development, are positive, and do not feel overwhelmed by spending all day with babies (NAEYC, 2019).

Unfortunately, much infant and toddler care in the United States does not meet these standards (Burchinal, 2018). Like parents, many child-care providers are overstressed, exhausted, and depressed (Kwon et al., 2019). Caregivers tend to be underpaid and underprepared for their challenging work (Kwon et al., 2020). Many programs are unable to provide continuity of care and move babies between providers every six months or every year (Ruprecht et al., 2016). What does this mean for babies? Some reports suggest that babies who spend a lot of time in poor-quality child care may be at risk for emotional or behavioral problems (Brownell & Drummond, 2020; Donoghue et al., 2017). Babies who have access to high-quality care do well; Jen and Stephanie count their daughters among the lucky ones.

APPLY IT! **6.10** Jen and Stephanie, like many parents, are worried about the recommendations for small children and screen media. What advice can you give them about managing their children's media exposure?

6.11 Jen and Stephanie want to find a new child-care situation for their daughters. What should they look for?

> ### Share It!
>
> It happens fast: Even when child-care providers are nurturing multiple children, being able to respond quickly helps create a secure bond. Scientists have found that some caregivers were able to respond in as little as **3 seconds.**
>
> (Ahnert, 2021)

Wrapping It Up

LO 6.1 Compare and contrast the traditional theories of emotional development. (p. 144)

Classic theories of emotional development, including those of Erikson and Freud, established that the social relationships formed in a baby's first years help set the stage for their future relationships and personality. There are two major crises of development in Erikson's theory of psychosocial development: trust versus mistrust and autonomy versus shame and doubt. Erikson believed children need to learn to trust and develop confidence in their ability to take care of themselves.

LO 6.2 Assess the roles of culture and context in emotional development. (p. 144)

Emotional maturation is shaped by cultural expectations and practices. The timing and expression of basic emotions varies around the world. Families may adopt proximal or distal parenting practices, or a mix of the two. Families' ethnotheories may emphasize collectivist or individualistic values. Contemporary research emphasizes the negative impact of early adversity on infants' development and their differential susceptibility to trauma and stress.

LO 6.3 Describe the progress of infants' and toddlers' emotional maturation. (p. 151)

Babies gradually develop some control over their emotions. Measuring infants' emotions is difficult: Their facial expressions, vocalizations, and physiology all give researchers clues about how they might be feeling. Small infants are capable of contentment and distress but as they grow older, more complex emotions appear, depending on cultural expectations, including anger, fear, and empathy. Even babies are capable of *prosocial*, or helpful, behaviors.

LO 6.4 Explain how babies begin to develop unique personalities. (p. 158)

Early patterns of reactions in infants and toddlers are known as *temperament*, a precursor to personality. Thomas and Chess described infant temperament in three broad categories: easy, slow-to-warm-up, and difficult. Other researchers examine babies' effortful control, agreeableness, or level of shyness. Children's personalities are a result of genetics, early prenatal experience, and early caregiving. Cultures vary in the personality traits they appreciate, but all children benefit from *goodness of fit*, a mutually supportive match between caregivers and their babies.

LO 6.5 Describe how caregiving impacts emotional development. (p. 161)

Babies can thrive in a variety of family configurations. Developmental scientists believe that a child's relationships with close caregivers in the first years of life create patterns of relating to others that last a lifetime. Across cultures, caregivers who are responsive and supportive with their babies seem to have better-adjusted children, even though specific parenting practices may differ.

LO 6.6 Explain common variations in caregiver–child attachment relationships. (p. 161)

The theory of attachment describes how caregivers can act as a secure base for the infants, allowing them to explore their environment. Based on the theoretical and empirical work of Bowlby and Ainsworth, some researchers describe four attachment styles: secure, insecure-resistant, insecure-avoidant, and disorganized attachment. Attachment can be measured through the Strange Situation. Scientists concur on the value of close relationships between caregivers and babies but do not always agree on how to measure it.

LO 6.7 Explain the impact of experiences outside the family on infants' emotional development. (p. 167)

Early child care can benefit infant and toddlers' development if it is of high quality. High-quality early child-care supports early relationships. Many families have difficulty finding high-quality early child care. Many infants and toddlers are exposed to media in their early years, which can interrupt the development of responsive relationships.

KEY TERMS

trust versus mistrust (p. 145)
autonomy versus shame and doubt (p. 145)
proximal (p. 146)
distal (p. 146)
differential susceptibility (p. 150)
emotions (p. 152)
social smile (p. 152)
stranger anxiety (p. 154)

separation anxiety (p. 154)
social referencing (p. 155)
self-awareness (p. 155)
emotional contagion (p. 156)
empathy (p. 156)
prosocial (p. 156)
emotion regulation (p. 157)
personality (p. 158)
temperament (p. 158)

easy (p. 158)
slow-to-warm-up (p. 158)
difficult (p. 158)
goodness of fit (p. 160)
responsiveness (p. 162)
attachment (p. 163)
proximity seeking (p. 163)
secure base (p. 163)
internal working model (p. 163)

Strange Situation (p. 163)
secure attachments (p. 164)
insecure attachment (p. 164)
insecure-resistant attachment (p. 164)
insecure-avoidant attachment (p. 164)
disorganized attachment (p. 164)

CHECK YOUR LEARNING

1. At 18 months, Makena wanted to hold her own spoon when eating cereal. Most of the cereal and milk went onto her lap, on the table, and in her hair. Thinking about Erikson's stage of autonomy versus shame and doubt, what advice would you give her parents?
   a) Her attempts should be encouraged, even though she is not very coordinated yet.
   b) She should be taught that it is not okay to make a mess.
   c) Her parents should take over the feeding to save time and show her the proper way to use a spoon.
   d) She may have a developmental disorder.

2. Cultural differences in adults' expectations for their infants' emotional expressions are known as:
   a) collectivism.
   b) ethnotheories.
   c) social exclusion.
   d) attachment.

3. Which of these is an example of a proximal parenting practice?
   a) Providing a variety of toys for the baby to play with on a blanket
   b) Holding an infant in a carrier strapped to the parent's body while folding laundry
   c) Playing music and singing songs with the baby
   d) Allowing the baby to practice putting on her own hat

4. Although early experiences of stress and trauma can negatively impact infants' brain development, some children have more severe reactions than others due to their particular genotype. This variation is known as:
   a) hyperplasticity.
   b) nonreactivity.
   c) head-sparing.
   d) differential susceptibility.

5. Which of these emotions is typically NOT expressed by a 7-month-old?
   a) Pride
   b) Distress
   c) Happiness
   d) Fear

6. The still-face procedure is designed to demonstrate infants' emotional reactions to a violation of their expectations by:
   a) forcing babies to keep their own faces motionless.
   b) instructing caregivers to look unresponsively at their infants.
   c) showing babies pictures of clown faces.
   d) teaching babies a simple form of "freeze-tag."

7. Individual differences in babies' patterns of emotional responsiveness that seem to be present soon after birth are known as:
   a) temperament.
   b) resilience.
   c) personality disorder.
   d) meltdowns.

8. Supportive parenting includes all of these EXCEPT:
   a) sensitivity.
   b) punishment.
   c) responsiveness.
   d) positivity.

9. How is a securely attached 14-month-old likely to react when her grandmother drops her off with a new babysitter?
   a) She may cry when Grandma leaves and will look for a reassuring cuddle with Grandma when she returns.
   b) She will feel confident to explore the new space and will not cry when Grandma leaves.
   c) She will cry when Grandma leaves and continue to feel angry after Grandma returns.
   d) She will react with anger when Grandma returns and cling to the babysitter for comfort.

10. How can the concept of *goodness of fit* be applied to advice for a parent coping with an irritable infant?

11. Why are patterns of secure and insecure attachment using the Strange Situation assessment different in countries like South Korea when compared to countries like Germany? What are some cultural explanations for these variations?

7 Physical Development in Early Childhood

© Macmillan, Photo by Point Studio, Inc.

Growing Bodies and Brains

7.1 Describe typical growth in height and weight from age 2½ to 6.

7.2 Identify the areas of the brain that are changing rapidly in early childhood.

Controlling the Body

7.3 Explain the connection between the development of motor skills and children's feelings of competence.

Staying Healthy

7.4 Describe common health challenges during early childhood.

7.5 Assess the risks of accidents and injuries prevalent during early childhood.

Sebastian and Theodore are nearly always together. They sleep in the same room and follow each other around the house, the yard, and the playground at preschool. Sebastian and Theodore are monozygotic twins, born at the same time nearly three years ago at the beginning of the COVID-19 pandemic. The twins are still nearly identical in size: about 3 feet (90 cm) tall and 33 pounds (15 kg).

Like many twins, they have reached many of their developmental milestones at the same time but are developing their own unique ways of responding to the world. Both boys are chatty and love monster trucks, but one tends to be more talkative. They are close companions, which was a source of comfort to their parents particularly during the isolating early period of the pandemic. It is clear that they love each other dearly, but this attachment comes with limits: They occasionally push each other, and "no" is a favorite word.

Sebastian and Theodore still require a watchful eye, but they are more capable now that they are almost 3. They are no longer babies or toddlers; they have more independent skills than younger children as they enter the stage of early childhood. Both Sebastian and Theodore can get around on their own without tripping or falling, communicate in both Korean and English, and learn how to use the bathroom and draw dinosaurs.

early childhood The period between ages 2½ and 6. It typically begins as toddlers develop language and movement skills and ends as they develop more abstract thinking and independent living skills and, in many communities, start formal schooling.

Like other children in early childhood, Sebastian and Theodore love to move, dancing in the kitchen or chasing a ball or bubble in the yard. They like to walk around the neighborhood with their parents, pushing their cart or their toy lawnmower. They are also developing fine motor skills such as the ability to scoop up noodles at dinnertime or scribble at the kitchen table. Their new independence means that childproofing has taken on a new dimension: Their parents are less worried they will bump into something and more concerned about traffic in their Los Angeles neighborhood. Keeping the boys safe now means that someone has to watch them at all times, whether that is their parents, their grandmother, or their teachers.

The COVID-19 pandemic was accompanied by sometimes alarming news and scientific reports about young children's development. Their robust immune systems protected most young children from the most serious effects of the virus (Yoshida et al., 2022). However, some researchers suggested that the early isolation caused by the pandemic may have led some children to be delayed in their development of some physical skills (González et al, 2022). Theodore and Sebastian show no signs of any negative effects from the early pandemic, although they still think all small machines are hand sanitizer dispensers.

Theodore and Sebastian's parents are working to make sure they grasp of all the skills the boys will need as they prepare for kindergarten in a few years (P. G. Williams et al., 2019). They spend time every day reading to the boys, practicing handwriting skills, and making sure they know how to follow directions and help out where they can—like putting their trash away and cleaning up their toys.

Most of Sebastian and Theodore's time is spent playing—throwing balls, chasing each other, or putting on a fire helmet and dreaming of being a firefighter. Developmental scientists understand now more than ever how crucial play is to early childhood as children's bodies and brains mature.

Early childhood is the period between about ages 2½ to 6. It typically begins as toddlers develop the language and movement skills that drive their independent exploration. It ends as preschoolers develop more abstract thinking and independent living skills and, in many communities, start formal schooling. Early childhood is also when children's bodies and brains are creating the foundation for the developments that follow. Much of this growth is shaped by children's early experiences: from exposure to pollution to enjoyment on the playground.

From this glimpse of Sebastian and Theodore's lives, you will learn about the physical advances of early childhood. You will read about how important it is for young children to get enough healthy food and to be active and play. You will also learn about the many interventions that have improved the lives of young children around the world.

Scientific American Profile

Meet Sebastian and Theodore

Growing Bodies and Brains

Learning Objectives

7.1   Describe typical growth in height and weight from age 2½ to 6.

7.2   Identify the areas of the brain that are changing rapidly in early childhood.

Theodore and Sebastian are like many preschool children: They sometimes spill and fuss at school dropoff. But, they are closer to being "big kids": Their growing bodies and brains enable them to learn more about the world. Children in other families may be learning gardening or gymnastics rather than playing with bubbles in the yard, but young children everywhere are developing the ability to acquire new skills, powered by their bigger bodies and brains.

Changing Body

Over the years of early childhood, children often grow about 9 inches (23 cm) and gain about 20 pounds (9 kg). Sebastian and Theodore will turn from chubby-cheeked toddlers into longer and leaner little boys. At around age 5, children typically have the least amount of body fat of the lifespan, giving them a more grown-up appearance (Gallagher et al., 2020). Theodore and Sebastian's growing bodies will enable more challenging physical activities but will also lead adults to expect more mature behavior.

Monitoring physical growth continues to be a measure of children's health. If illness or malnutrition slows growth, brain development may also falter (Galler et al., 2021). Children around the world have similar patterns of maturation in early childhood: Most are roughly similar in height until around age 5 (Karra et al., 2017). As you might recall from Chapter 4, some children who were profoundly malnourished in their first few years of life have growth that is *stunted* and are shorter for their age. While these children may get heavier, most will continue to be smaller than their peers (Leroy et al., 2020).

After their fifth birthday, as children's long bones begin to grow, inborn genetic differences begin to show (Lampl & Schoen, 2017). Some children, particularly those with tall parents, will begin to grow noticeably taller than their preschool classmates. Others may stay relatively petite. When children grow up in an ideal setting, with a stable environment, the necessary nutrition, and adequate health care, their physical growth reflects the genetic predispositions they were born with. Sebastian and Theodore, who are monozygotic (or so-called identical) twins, are precisely the same height and weight, which may reflect that they share not only the same environment but also a similar genome.

Growing Brain

The brain continues to grow during early childhood, but at a slower pace than in infancy. By age 6, Tito's brain will be about 95 percent of adult size (Gilmore et al., 2018). Early childhood is a period of intensive growth of the circuits that connect different parts of the brain, a process that will continue throughout childhood and adolescence (Haynes et al., 2020). Early childhood is also a sensitive period for brain development, particularly for learning skills that will help children thrive in school. Many new abilities are powered by the network of neural connections in the brain, known as the *connectome*. Controlling behavior becomes easier in early childhood with maturation in the cortex, particularly in the **prefrontal cortex**, the area at the front of the brain behind the forehead, critical to thinking logically.

While overall brain size does not increase dramatically, the number of connections between neurons and the complexity of the *cortex* (the surface area on the outside of the brain) increase. There are about a quadrillion synapses in the brain during early childhood (that is 15 zeros!) (Zelazo & Lee, 2010). The surface area of the cortex increases and thickens, resulting in more prominent wrinkles as these new dendrites squeeze into the skull (Norbom et al., 2021).

Increasing Connectivity During early childhood, neurons in the brain continue to add *myelin*, the fatty insulating layer that helps speed communication between them. The biggest tract of myelin covers a large set of neural connections called the *corpus callosum*, which connects the right and left hemispheres of the brain (Danielsen et al., 2020). This bridge helps young children coordinate their movements, using both sides of their bodies, and will contribute to more complex thinking.

Breakthroughs in brain-scanning technology have helped scientists visualize the growth of networks in the brain made of myelinated synaptic connections known as the **connectome** (Ciarrusta et al., 2021; Howell et al., 2019). When scientists study the connectome using DTI imaging, they find it looks a little like a road map. The connectome map shows the connections between different parts of the brain. Sometimes,

Share It!

Protect young brains (and all brains) from air pollution. Some researchers in Mexico have found that young people who have been exposed to the particulates in smog are more likely to develop brain-damaging proteins that are linked to neurocognitive disorders later in life.

(Calderón-Garcidueñas et al., 2018)

CONNECTIONS

Remember from Chapter 2 that *DTI*, or *diffusion tensor imaging*, is a form of MRI scanning in which the movement of water in the brain creates images of the pattern of myelinated axons in the brain.

prefrontal cortex The area at the front of the brain behind the forehead that is critical to logical thinking and controlling behavior.

connectome Each individual's unique pattern of connections in the brain.

INCREASING CONNECTIVITY

During early childhood, the body spends most of its energy building the brain. Much of this is creating new connections between neurons and myelinating them to make them faster and more efficient. Images of a cross section of the brain taken with MRI scans show it becoming progressively whiter, a sign of the buildup of white matter.

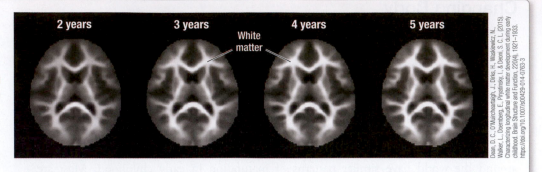

Dean, D. C., O'Muircheartaigh, J., Dirks, H., Waskiewicz, N., Walker, L., Doernberg, E., Piryatinsky, I., & Deoni, S. C. L. (2015). Characterizing longitudinal white matter development during early childhood. Brain Structure and Function, 220(4), 1921–1933. https://doi.org/10.1007/s00429-014-0763-3

MATURATION IN THE CORTEX

There are different ways to look at the growing brain: from the outside, from the top, or with a scanning device to visualize a slice through the middle. Each way allows researchers to see different structures. During early childhood, maturation in the cortex helps young children control their behavior and learn new skills.

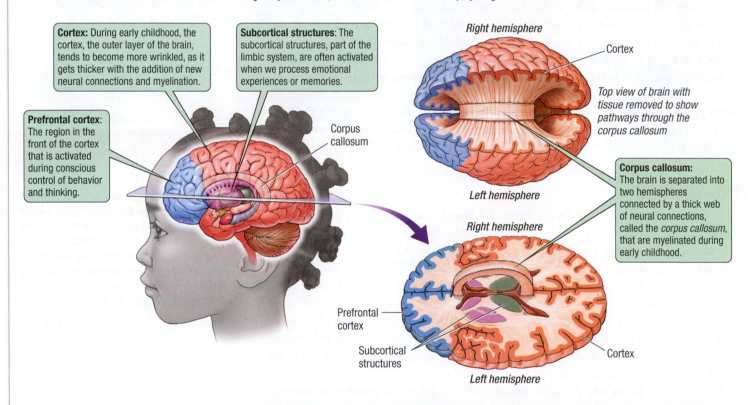

Cortex: During early childhood, the cortex, the outer layer of the brain, tends to become more wrinkled, as it gets thicker with the addition of new neural connections and myelination.

Subcortical structures: The subcortical structures, part of the limbic system, are often activated when we process emotional experiences or memories.

Prefrontal cortex: The region in the front of the cortex that is activated during conscious control of behavior and thinking.

Corpus callosum

Right hemisphere

Cortex

Top view of brain with tissue removed to show pathways through the corpus callosum

Left hemisphere

Corpus callosum: The brain is separated into two hemispheres connected by a thick web of neural connections, called the *corpus callosum*, that are myelinated during early childhood.

Right hemisphere

Prefrontal cortex

Subcortical structures

Cortex

Left hemisphere

Individualized Connectome

There are some universal patterns in brain development, but life experiences give each child a different network of white matter connections reflecting ongoing myelination. Each one of us has a slightly different connectome, as distinct as a fingerprint, that represents our individual neural circuitry. This is a DTI image showing the pattern of white matter development in the brain of one 4½-year-old girl who was able to sit very still in an MRI.

The individual connectome of one 4-year-old

Catherine Lebel and Curtis Ostertag

White matter pathways of the whole brain

Four isolated white matter pathways

White matter pathways of a cross section through the brain

these connections are thicker, faster, and more robust, like super-highways going from one part of the brain to another. At other times, the brain connections are smaller and slower, like local streets. Scientists also look at the overall structure of where brain connections begin, merge, and end.

Scientists believe that the foundation for this network of brain connections is set in the first year of life, but it continues to develop into adulthood (Stephens et al., 2020). During early childhood, increasing connections between the cortex and other regions of the brain reflect children's stronger control of their feelings, increasing ability to coordinate their bodies, and expanding cognitive and language skills (Reynolds et al., 2019). As children grow, they build more long-range connections, particularly between the subcortical structures and cortex. This helps the brain work more quickly and allows different areas of the brain to specialize in different tasks while still working together. Researchers believe that these faster connections help children better control their behavior (Haynes et al., 2020).

Each one of us has a slightly different connectome, as distinct as a fingerprint, that represents our individual neural circuitry. Despite this diversity, scientists have found some patterns. For instance, children's connectomes change in consistent ways over time as they learn to read or their memory matures (Lebel et al., 2019). Similarly, some shared neural circuits are found in people who have experienced similar psychological disorders or environmental stresses (Gilchrist et al., 2022; Johnson et al., 2021).

The Prefrontal Cortex As you will learn in Chapter 8, the major cognitive advances of early childhood include improvements in attention and memory as well as *executive function*, the ability to control your behavior, and *theory of mind*, the ability to understand other people's perspectives (Goddings et al., 2021; Grosse Wiesmann et al., 2020). Myelination, increasing connectivity, *and* maturation in the cortex make these cognitive gains possible.

The cortex increases and thickens during early childhood and blood flow to the cortex is at its peak (Norbom et al., 2021; Paniukov et al., 2020). A preschool-age child's cortex uses twice as much energy as an adult's cortex, as it is rapidly maturing (Dienel, 2019). This growth allows children to better control their behavior, improve their memory, and think more logically.

The prefrontal cortex is activated during logical thought and planning. It allows children to think about what they are doing and, as it matures, to better plan ahead and consider the consequences of their actions. During early childhood, the prefrontal cortex typically becomes more active, as it increasingly connects to other regions of the brain (Fiske & Holmboe, 2019).

The rapid growth of the cortex and the proliferation of the connections to it are two reasons why early childhood is a sensitive period for the development of many skills, such as executive function, attention, and language (OECD, 2017). Remember that early in life, the brain is easily shaped. Experiences such as being read to, having positive relationships, and being injured by accidents or even pollution all contribute to unique patterns of brain maturation (Hyde et al., 2020; Hutton et al., 2020a, 2020b).

The links between what a preschooler experiences and their brain development are complex: Families, communities, and a child's own strengths and the genome they were born with all help contribute to how they grow (Boyce et al., 2021; Hyde et al., 2020). The brain remains resilient and changeable, but early experiences may leave a mark (Kraaijenvanger et al., 2020). For instance, researchers found anomalies in the brain development of children who experienced profound deprivation when they lived their early lives in orphanages in Romania, even after they had been adopted by warm, caring families (Mackes et al., 2020).

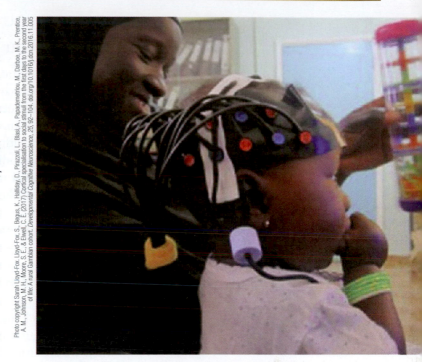

Can You See Her Cortex Growing? Tremendous development occurs in cortex during the early years. Researchers in Keneba, Gambia, in western Africa, measured brain maturation using *functional near infrared spectroscopy (fNIRS)*. In fNIRS, children wear a special head covering that enables scientists to use light to measure the blood flow and oxygen levels in the cortex. An advantage of fNIRS is that once children have put the cap on, they can move naturally, allowing scientists to visualize their brain in action.

 Share It!

Be aware of the signs of brain injury in young children. Preschoolers may have trouble identifying what is wrong when they have experienced a concussion. But that does not mean they are not hurting: They may be particularly tired or need more cuddling than usual. Protect their brains by getting early intervention to find out whether they have experienced an injury.

(Dupont et al., 2022)

CAN YOU BELIEVE IT?

Can You Use Just One Side of the Brain?

You may have heard people say that they are a "right-brain" or a "left-brain" person. Or perhaps you may have heard that what hand you write with may mean you have different brain structures or ways of thinking. Maybe you have heard that lefties are more creative. Is there any science behind these ideas?

Let's begin with the basics: The brain has two sides, or hemispheres. Many areas of the brain, including the cortex and the cerebellum, are divided into two halves. A thick bundle of myelinated fibers known as the *corpus callosum* is what connects the two sides of the cortex. In many ways, the two hemispheres of the brain look symmetrical, but they are not quite identical.

Beginning in early fetal development, regions of the brain begin to specialize in different tasks. Specialization in the brain makes it more efficient: Information does not need to travel far across the brain if activation is clustered in one area. Some cognitive tasks tend to be performed by regions in the left side of the brain and others to by those in the right (Gazzaniga, 2005; Sha et al., 2021). This division of activation into hemispheres is known as **lateralization**.

Early researchers discovered that the left side of the brain tends to be activated when we are using language skills. They also found that the right side of the brain tends to be activated when we use spatial skills, such as locating where something is on a table. Even controlling the body tends to be divided between the sides of our brain. For instance, the area of the cortex that controls movement, the *motor cortex*, crosses both halves of the brain. The areas of the cortex that control the right side of the body are located in the motor cortex on the left side of the brain and vice-versa (Corballis, 2019). As a result, a prenatal brain injury to the motor cortex in the right hemisphere may lead to childhood difficulties in moving the left side of the body (Ferre et al., 2020).

Much of what we do, however, involves activation in multiple areas across the brain: While language may be processed primarily in regions of the left side of the brain in many people, that is not the only area of the brain that is activated when we are listening or communicating: Other regions in both hemispheres in the cortex and in the subcortical structures are also active (Bartha-Doering et al., 2021). Similarly, when you use your right hand, you use both sides of your brain as you plan for what to do with your hand and picture where it is in space (Mutha et al., 2012). Nearly every behavior we perform involves interconnected activity coordinated in multiple areas of the brain.

With the advent of modern neuroimaging technology, researchers have also discovered that there is much more variability in the brain than they had realized. This variability extends to lateralization: Not everyone's brain specializes in exactly the same way. For instance, about one in every four people has specialized language regions on the right side of the brain, rather than the left (Guadalupe et al., 2021). Similarly, not everyone uses their right hand. Perhaps as many as one in five people is not exclusively right-handed (Papadatou-Pastou et al., 2020).

Brain lateralization and handedness are complex traits that are influenced by our genes and earliest environmental influences, including how fetuses lay in the uterus as they grow (Michel et al., 2018; Sha et al., 2021). Young children tend to demonstrate their dominant hand by about age 1; this is the hand they will scribble and eat with. This development depends on children's earliest experiences, genomes, and their community's expectations. Culture plays an important role in handedness (Kushner, 2017). Many communities discourage children from using their left hands (Yang et al., 2018).

No matter whether children are left- or right-handed, or how their brain is lateralized, all of us use multiple regions of the brain all of the time. It is a myth that

lateralization The process of brain development in which certain functions become located in one hemisphere of the brain.

some people are "right dominant" and therefore more creative, or "left dominant" and therefore more logical (Corballis, 2019; McManus, 2019). There is no association between personality traits and brain lateralization or handedness for typically developing children. However, children with autism spectrum disorder and some other intellectual developmental disorders may also have anomalies in their patterns of brain lateralization (Floris et al., 2021).

Experts believe that children should be allowed to use whatever hand comes naturally to them. Lefties can benefit from some support—like special scissors—but they shouldn't be forced to be righties. Being a "lefty" is also not an impediment to success: Five of the past nine U.S. presidents were left-handed (Selden, 2019).

APPLY IT! **7.1** Many caregivers report that people expect more of children when they begin to look more like little kids than toddlers. How can you explain to others why preschooler's brains are still not like an adult's?

7.2 Describe two aspects of brain maturation that support Sebastian and Theodore's learning during early childhood.

Controlling the Body

Theodore and Sebastian are so coordinated that they can chase each other across the playground and go down the slide the right way. They can also draw (preferably dinosaurs). Thus, it may not surprise you that researchers say that 4-year-olds display the same level of coordination and balance as adults do (Gabel & Scheller, 2013).

Theodore and Sebastian have done more than excel at *gross motor skills* such as dancing and jumping; they have also developed some *fine motor skills*. They can sit still to color and feed themselves (although chopsticks remain difficult). At the same time, the twins clearly need help with some motor skills: It takes a village of caregivers to help all the children in their preschool to get their rain gear on correctly.

Motor-skill development does not happen automatically as children mature; it requires practice (Haga et al., 2018). The skills Sebastian and Theodore are learning are specific to their family: They are playing with monster trucks in the yard and drawing with markers in the kitchen because their family and community value these activities. Children around the world learn the motor skills important to their culture, from writing their names, to threading a loom, to tap dancing. Unlike many of the motor achievements of infancy and toddlerhood, the motor advances of early childhood and beyond are far from universal. Even a basic advance, like learning to walk up stairs, depends on the environment. Children who have access to stairs learn to walk up them by themselves at earlier ages than children who do not (Berger et al., 2007).

Motor skills give children a feeling of competence that can help them to better interact with friends and do schoolwork (Cameron et al., 2016). Practicing physical skills strengthens children's brains as well as their bodies, improving their executive function and their ability to control their behavior (McClelland & Cameron, 2019; Hudson et al., 2021).

Gross Motor Skills In infancy, most babies reach some nearly universal motor milestones, regardless of how they are raised, but there are no globally accepted milestones in early childhood (Adolph et al., 2014). In early childhood and throughout the lifespan, motor development is influenced by opportunity as well as biological maturation (Feitoza et al., 2018). Even within a single country, differences in children's environments may affect when they develop typical skills.

For example, researchers in Myanmar found that 5-year-olds from rural areas were more likely to hop and leap than those who grew up in cities, perhaps because they had more open space to play in. On the other hand, children from urban areas were

Learning Objective

7.3 Explain the connection between the development of motor skills and children's feelings of competence.

CONNECTIONS

Remember from Chapter 4 that gross motor skills refer to big body skills like running, jumping, and throwing a ball. Fine motor skills refer to small movements that require eye-hand coordination and control over the muscles in your fingers and hands to draw, write letters and words, double-click on a tablet, or play a musical instrument.

🗣 Share It!

Thank your big brother or sister for your sports skills! Having an older sibling to play with often helps preschoolers develop more advanced motor skills.

(Kwon & O'Neill, 2020)

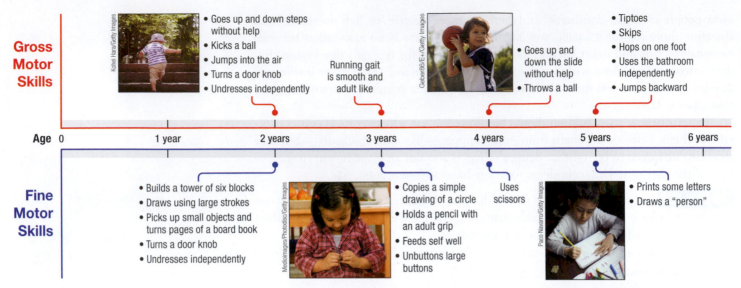

Gross Motor Skills
- Goes up and down steps without help
- Kicks a ball
- Jumps into the air
- Turns a door knob
- Undresses independently

Running gait is smooth and adult like

- Goes up and down the slide without help
- Throws a ball

- Tiptoes
- Skips
- Hops on one foot
- Uses the bathroom independently
- Jumps backward

Age   0   1 year   2 years   3 years   4 years   5 years   6 years

Fine Motor Skills
- Builds a tower of six blocks
- Draws using large strokes
- Picks up small objects and turns pages of a board book
- Turns a door knob
- Undresses independently

- Copies a simple drawing of a circle
- Holds a pencil with an adult grip
- Feeds self well
- Unbuttons large buttons

Uses scissors

- Prints some letters
- Draws a "person"

FIGURE 7.1 Progression of Motor-Skill Development in Early Childhood These are some common skills many children learn in the United States. They are based on cultural norms, rather than physical or neurological development: If children are never allowed to use scissors, they will not automatically learn how to use them at age 4. Similarly, many children can ride a tricycle at age 3, but if they do not have a tricycle or access to a slide, or if they are not allowed to walk up stairs on their own, they will not develop these capabilities.

Love My Patchwork Elephant? Drawing helps build fine motor skills, enabling children to practice controlling their hands, sitting still, and concentrating—skills that will come in handy at school.

better at playing with a ball (kicking, throwing, catching), probably because they had more instruction in and time to play organized games (Aye et al., 2017). In communities around the world, the environment is critical to the motor skills children develop (Tomaz et al., 2019).

Understanding community expectations for motor-skill development can help educators and health care providers identify children who may need extra help meeting those expectations (Hulteen et al., 2020). Since motor skills take practice, more participation in physical activity generally leads to more advanced skills (Wick et al., 2017; see **Figure 7.1**).

It may not be as fun as learning to play soccer or tap dance, but toilet training, like dressing and undressing, is helpful to children's growing independence (de Carvalho Mrad et al., 2021). In many affluent countries, children typically begin toilet training before they are enrolled in pre-kindergarten. However, more than 1 in 10 still have toileting accidents when they enter kindergarten at age 5 (M. L. Jackson et al., 2020).

Pediatricians in the United States usually recommend against toilet training until children show interest in using the bathroom and awareness of their own elimination, which can occur anytime between age 18 months and 4 years. Many U.S. children are trained before they are 3 (Sejkora et al., 2021). In many other countries, including China, Nigeria, and Vietnam, children are trained much earlier, often before their first birthdays (Rouse et al., 2017; Solarin et al., 2017).

Successful toilet training requires the coordination of body awareness, the language to talk about it, the ability to plan when to get to the bathroom, and the motor skills to get dressed and undressed (Baird et al., 2019). Children who are trained very early, before these skills have fully developed, require extra support and flexibility (Bender et al., 2021). However, children who start later may be less interested in learning to use the bathroom and less flexible about new routines (Van Aggelpoel et al., 2019).

Fine Motor Skills In early childhood, young children develop more control over their hands, enabled by increasing connections in the brain. By kindergarten, they are expected to be able to draw a person and write their name with a marker. How well children control their hands in preschool often predicts how they will do in kindergarten and even in elementary school (Cadoret et al., 2018; Suggate et al., 2018). This is because 4-year-olds who have developed strong fine motor skills are likely better able to focus, sit still, and control their behavior.

Indeed, many children with strong fine motor skills also have more mature executive function (Hudson et al., 2020; McClelland & Cameron, 2019). The brain networks activated when young children are controlling themselves are very similar to those that they use when practicing fine motor skills (Kim et al., 2018).

APPLY IT!   **7.3** Theodore and Sebastian have terrific coordination on the playground and love to draw with markers. How might their ability to control their bodies help them adjust to kindergarten?

Staying Healthy

Although preschoolers are developing minds of their own and the ability to excel on the playground, they are still dependent on the adults around them to keep them healthy. The things children do every day—moving, eating, and getting rest—foster healthy bodies, brains, and relationships. The habits that adults teach children, from loving plantains to enjoying running on the playground, can last a lifetime.

In early childhood, children's bodies are sturdier and less vulnerable to infectious diseases and illnesses. But this is not true for everyone: Some young children show signs of chronic conditions that may take a toll on their health later in life. During early childhood, children are susceptible to the dangers of pollution and toxins in their environment, and also to injury as they explore their world more independently and sometimes fearlessly.

Sleep in Early Childhood

Sebastian and Theodore's parents are serious about sleep. Before 8:00 P.M., the boys are in their room, often sleeping until 7 the next morning. Sometimes they wake each other up fussing in the night, but mostly they enjoy settling down and getting rest. Getting enough sleep is essential for brain development; without it, preschoolers can have difficulties with emotion regulation and learning (Hoyniak et al., 2019; R. C. Williams et al., 2019).

Most preschoolers get the recommended 10–13 hours of sleep, but about one in four families has conflicts with their children about getting to bed (Newton et al., 2020; Paruthi et al., 2016b). About one in three U.S. preschoolers is not getting enough sleep, and most do not have a consistent sleep schedule (Wheaton & Claussen, 2021). Families with consistent routines have an easier time getting their children to bed (Covington et al., 2019). Consistency is not the only answer, however. Children who are on screens or watch television as part of their bedtime routine may have trouble sleeping through the night (Janssen et al., 2020). Throughout our lives, screen time before bedtime is a risk factor for sleep problems (Buxton et al., 2015).

One major transition for U.S. families is giving up the afternoon nap. However, in many countries, including Australia, Japan, and China, children continue to take a daily nap into their school years (Jeon et al., 2021). Children in the United States generally stop napping by age 5, most likely because U.S. families tend to find naps difficult to schedule and are eager to consolidate sleep (Staton et al., 2020). However, many 3- and 4-year-olds are not ready to go all day without a rest, and naps continue to have emotional and cognitive benefits for older children (Horváth & Plunkett, 2018). Children outgrow naptime at different ages, often leaving parents to guess and child-care providers to manage multiple children with varying napping needs (Thorpe et al., 2020).

Learning Objectives

7.4 Describe common health challenges during early childhood.

7.5 Assess the risks of accidents and injuries prevalent during early childhood.

Scientific American Profile

Developing Fine Motor Skills

© Macmillan, Photo by Point Studio, Inc.

Naptime in Kabul An after-lunch rest is common in day-care centers around the world. These children are napping at a child-care center in Afghanistan. Sleep is essential for brain development and emotion regulation in early childhood.

Not getting enough sleep during childhood is linked to increased risks for a number of conditions, including depression, acting out, and difficulties developing language and memory skills (Hoyniak et al., 2020; Sivertsen et al., 2021; Zheng et al., 2021). Children who are not sleeping enough typically face other difficulties, such as living in families stressed by conflict, poverty, or chaotic daily routines (Hoyniak et al., 2022; Wheaton & Claussen, 2021). Like other correlational research, it is not clear whether lack of sleep causes developmental difficulties in children, or whether it is part of a group of risk factors that are linked to poorer health and well-being.

Researchers know that sleep is important in improving mood and helping children learn, but they aren't sure whether sleep problems are the cause of emotional challenges or whether children with emotional challenges tend to sleep less than other children (Sivertsen et al., 2015). Either way, getting enough sleep is a goal to help preschool-age children avoid the long-term risks to health during a critical period for growth.

Staying Active

Early childhood is one of the most physically active periods of childhood. If you visit a preschool, you will see children racing around the playground and dashing down the corridors. In early childhood, this physical activity is often called *gross motor play*, or *big body play* (Carlson, 2011). Children's physical activity is sometimes adult-organized and directed, as in Tito's soccer program. More frequently, it is child-directed and free form, such as when the children from Tito's preschool stream out into the playground to slide down the slides and scamper up the monkey bars. Both types of physical activity have critical benefits in early childhood.

Some of the benefits of active play are not surprising. Preschoolers who are very physically active are more likely to stay healthy and develop strong muscles and better coordination (Wiersma et al., 2020). Other correlations that scientists have connected to active play are less obvious: Active children tend to have an easier time planning and controlling their behavior (Cook et al., 2019). Physically active children may also be less likely to act out or to be depressed (Dale et al., 2019; McNeill et al., 2018).

Physical activity is good for the brain; moving your body releases "feel-good" hormones and neurotransmitters, helps move nutrients into your brain, and accelerates the growth of your neurons (Lubans et al., 2016; Meijer et al., 2020). In early childhood, physical activity usually means that preschoolers are playing, which spurs cognitive, social, and emotional development. Finally, remember that being physically active can build executive function. Waiting in line to kick the ball or learning complicated

The Best Playground in the World? It is probably the one you are playing in. Whether children are enjoying water play in a public playground in Singapore or climbing on monkey bars in Mumbai, they are getting the physical activity they need to stay healthy.

dance routines trains the mind to manage behavior (Liu et al., 2020; Willoughby et al., 2021a). It also builds emotional resilience: Scientists suggest that being stuck inside without enough time to move was one reason young children's mental health deteriorated during the early part of the COVID-19 pandemic (W. Li et al., 2021).

Experts recommend that preschool-age children get about three hours of physical activity a day (USDHHS, 2018; WHO, 2019a). Unfortunately, not all U.S. children get that much (Tulchin-Francis et al., 2021; Webster et al., 2019). Researchers have identified several reasons why children stay still. First, some preschools emphasize academic skills rather than play, so children may not have enough time on the playground (Ellis et al., 2017). Time spent in groups, like when Tito sits on the rug while his teacher talks to the class, tends to be the least active part of the school day (Schenkelberg et al., 2020). Even when children *do* have time to play at preschool, teachers (and the parents of their students) may worry that outdoor play is unsafe, too hot, or too cold, and almost always too dirty (Ezeugwu et al., 2021; Kandemir & Sevimli-Celik, 2021; Sandseter et al., 2021).

Furthermore, when at home, many children spend more time in *sedentary*, or seated, activities, such as watching television or playing with tablets or phones, than running around (Madigan, Racine, et al., 2020; Wadsworth et al., 2020). Friendly neighborhoods with plenty of playmates make it more likely that families will be able to get their children on the playground (Boxberger & Reimers, 2019; Yoon & Lee, 2019). But outside play-time is often hard to come by: Rural children may live too far from playmates (Wende et al., 2020). Suburban and city children may live close to other children but stay home because adults, like those in many communities, lack the time to supervise them on the playground (Finkelstein et al., 2017; Hoyos-Quintero & García-Perdomo, 2019).

What is the solution? Children need safe, supervised spaces to play both at home and in school, although these are not always available in many neighborhoods (Christian et al., 2015). Young children tend to move around more when they have opportunities for free, open play: Most preschoolers are more active when they can be self-directed than when they are following an adults' lead in a game (Schenkelberg et al., 2020). Ideally, this safe space should be outside: Most children move more outside than inside (Tandon et al., 2013). However, children also need indoor spaces for play on days when the weather does not permit outside play (Boyle et al., 2022; Neshteruk et al., 2018). Getting adequate movement indoors may require ample space and adult flexibility when furniture occasionally is upended.

Having access to a safe play facility is not always enough to encourage active play. Caregivers need to believe that play matters, and it helps if they are active themselves (Boxberger & Reimers, 2019; Lee et al., 2021; Pereira et al., 2021). Many interventions focus on promoting physical activity and limiting screen time among families, but many have not been effective (Morgan et al., 2020; Oh et al., 2022). Finding opportunities to be active can be difficult for many busy families who may have to travel to find a green space or an indoor playground, but the benefits of activity extend to the entire family. For instance, being outside can renew everyone's energy and mood (Collado & Staats, 2016). Sebastian and Theodore are lucky to get a lot of active time. They have tried formal swimming lessons and sometimes focus on learning to hit a ball or flying a kite, but most of their active time is spent playing.

Eating for Health

Like all preschoolers, Sebastian and Theodore need sufficient calories to make it through the day. Their mother, Christine, has tried to make sure they eat healthily, mostly traditional Korean food, but they have also learned to love ice cream.

During early childhood, families can help young children establish eating patterns that reduce health risks in the long-term (Nix et al., 2021). Healthy eating in early childhood (and throughout development) means a balanced, nutrient-rich diet. However, in more than two out of three families, preschoolers are not eating meals that meet

Scientific American Profile

Staying Active in Early Childhood

CONNECTIONS

Remember from Chapters 3 and 4 that during the prenatal period and the first two years, taste preferences develop that will last a lifetime. Babies who gain weight very quickly establish metabolic and immune responses that may make a healthy weight harder to maintain later on.

selective eating The phenomenon common during early childhood when young children become more resistant to trying new foods or develop picky eating practices.

Share It!

Give it another chance! Researchers have found that it takes multiple exposures, sometimes more than 10 tries before children will happily eat a new food.

(Appleton et al., 2018)

CONNECTIONS

Remember from Chapter 4 that health professionals often use a standardized growth chart or the body mass index (BMI) to evaluate weight. These measures are imperfect but continue to be used as a convenient starting point for evaluating health, particularly when evaluating the health of large populations rather than deciding what is ideal for one child.

healthy diet guidelines. U.S. preschoolers typically eat only half the vegetables they should (NCHS, 2021). By snacking on cookies and sugary drinks, such as chocolate milk and juice, young children are getting more of their calories from sugar than they should (NCHS, 2021). However, compared to other age groups, preschoolers eat more fruits and vegetables: In fact, most eat fruit every day (Hoy et al., 2020). The average preschooler in the United States eats more healthily than most teenagers (Wambogo et al., 2020).

Changing what children eat is difficult. Preschoolers' taste preferences are based on years of experience. Researchers have had the most success in convincing children to try new foods by offering them (and expecting them to be rejected) many times. For some new foods, it may take 10 tries before children to learn to accept a new taste. Sneaking new tastes in, extoling their virtues, or bribing children to eat them does not seem to be effective (Nekitsing et al., 2018). Pressuring children and turning eating into a chore can backfire (Zucker & Hughes, 2020). This is why it is difficult to convince parents to change what they feed their families. It takes patience, enthusiasm, and a certain amount of waste to alter taste preferences (Hodder et al., 2020).

Selective Eating   Many young children have some curious eating habits: They may separate their food on the plate so that it does not touch. As you read in Chapter 4, infants and toddlers tend to be somewhat flexible eaters. Everything is new to them, and they are often curious about new foods. However, even the most flexible toddler eaters tend to become picky in early childhood (Zucker & Hughes, 2020). Half of preschoolers around the world are *picky* or **selective eaters** (Chao, 2018; Taylor & Emmett, 2019).

Researchers have an evolutionary explanation for this vexing behavior: Children generally become more selective at about the same time that they can find food on their own (Ahlstrom et al., 2017). Pickiness may have protected our ancestors from eating unsafe foods, like poisonous berries or rotten meat, and may have been adaptive when children were able to forage on their own. Today, selective eating is challenging for preschool teachers who are trying to serve cantaloupe to a group of disgusted 4-year-olds and for families who want to get through dinnertime without tears (Schuster et al., 2019; Taylor & Emmett, 2019). For most preschoolers, picky eating is a phase that will end without any ill effects by kindergarten, but about one in six children will remain choosy about what they eat (Fernandez et al., 2020).

The Impact of Body Image   Young children are not only observant about what their food looks like: They are also already absorbing messages about their body size (Stanford & Kyle, 2018). Scientists have found that children as young as 3 respond

TABLE 7.1   Making Healthy Eating Easier

- Do not expect children to eat everything or clean their plates.
- Involve children in growing food, shopping for food, cooking, and cleaning up. Feeling responsible and capable about food helps create positive attitudes toward eating.
- Offer a range of vegetables and fruits, dairy products, grains, and proteins.
- Expose children to different foods and expect that it will take at least 8–10 tries before they will eat them.
- Keep the pressure off and make eating fun; eating should not be stressful.
- Set up consistent routines for eating regular meals and snacks as a group.
- Avoid high-calorie, nutrient-light foods, such as sweets or high-fat snacks.
- Avoid artificial sweeteners. Even though they may not have calories, they can still train a child to crave sweets.
- Try not to use food as a reward (e.g., offering dessert if you finish your green beans).
- Being too restrictive or controlling of what children eat can backfire: Food should not be a fight. The best solution may be not to have the food in the house.
- Model healthy eating. Children notice adults' eating patterns.

Information from Hoelscher et al., 2022; Knobl et al., 2022; Nekitsing et al., 2018.

to stigma about what they look like. As a result, experts recommend talking with sensitivity about children's bodies (Pont et al., 2017). Language matters: Using terms like "larger body" to refer to a person's size is preferred to terms like *overweight* and *obesity*, even though these medical terms are still used in research and when talking about group differences (Rubino et al., 2020; J. D. Smith et al., 2020).

Determining healthy weight is not a simple calculation: Individual variations, like a family history of diabetes or high blood pressure, bone mass, or a lot of physical activity, make it difficult to predict exactly how big a particular child should be (Strings, 2019; Vanderwall et al., 2018). Children, like the rest of us, come in a variety of healthy shapes and sizes. However, there is scientific consensus that some heavier bodies are associated with health risks in later life. Children whose weight is higher than the 97.5th percentile on a standardized growth chart are considered to have *obesity*. They may not experience any immediate health consequences but are likely to continue to have larger bodies than their peers, which may increase their risk of developing diabetes and cardiovascular disease, among other conditions, later in life (Delvecchio et al., 2020).

In the United States, about one in seven preschool children is classified as having obesity, a rate similar to other high-income countries (de Bont et al., 2020; Stierman et al., 2021). Around the world, more children and adults develop a larger body size because of what researchers call a *nutrition transition*, and in many countries, larger bodies have become typical (Ronto et al., 2018). Families are transitioning from a diet filled with traditional fruits and vegetables to more processed, convenient, high-calorie foods that have more sugar and salt and fewer nutrients (Jaacks et al., 2019). For many of us, stress is often connected to eating more high-calorie foods and treats: Extra stress is one reason experts think young children became heavier during the first year of the COVID-19 pandemic (Lange et al., 2021).

Children who are larger than their peers may be targets for bullying or exclusion, even in preschool: They may need adults to stand up for them (Donkor et al., 2021; Rex-Lear et al., 2019). Caregivers and other adults can model kindness and inclusion of all children to help prevent the harms that can come from peers and other adults.

A major risk factor for children's health is family income: Good nutrition is expensive. Young children are often wasteful, either through pickiness or clumsiness. In addition, they are likely to demand the convenient and tasty foods marketed to them (Cornwell et al., 2020). About 1 in 10 U.S. families with young children is *food insecure*, meaning that they may be skipping meals or running out of groceries because of the cost (Ullmann et al., 2021). Children whose families worry about affording food are more likely to be at an unhealthy weight than other families, particularly as they grow older (Ontai et al., 2019). Researchers suspect that financial stress and limited availability of nutritious food contribute to children's larger body size (Na et al., 2021; Vargas et al., 2017).

Interventions to Improve Nutrition Helping children with nutritional problems, whether caused by food insecurity or by other factors, often means addressing the needs not just of the children, but of the entire family (J. D. Smith et al., 2020). Any intervention must reduce the stigma around weight, normalize the challenge of maintaining a healthy weight when the environment makes it hard to do so, and support a family's strengths. Interventions designed to improve children's nutrition are not always successful: Some increase poor body image and stigma (Dietz, 2019; Richmond et al., 2021).

Families play a critical role in managing taste preferences and establishing healthy eating patterns. The most powerful predictor of what a child eats is the food adults offer them: If caregivers do not provide sugary drinks or high-calorie snacks, children will not eat them (Rex et al., 2021). This does not mean being excessively restrictive: Caregivers

Daniela Linares/Anzenberger/Redux

Do It Yourself. One way to improve nutrition and provide food security is to grow your own. This little girl is showing the squashes she has grown in her family's garden in Jinotega, Nicaragua.

with too many rules about food often see them backfire. Food should be fun rather than a fight (Adams, Caccavale, et al., 2020).

Common Hazards

Like the rest of us, children are susceptible to colds and the occasional gastrointestinal illness. During the recent COVID-19 pandemic, however, they typically benefited from a strong immune system in combating the virus (Marks et al., 2022). As a result, young children were less likely to develop serious COVID-related complications, even though, like other viruses, it traveled widely through child-care centers and preschools (Bhopal et al., 2021; C. Kim et al., 2021).

Young children may have been spared the worst of the pandemic, but they feel the effects of other infectious diseases (Dawood et al., 2020; WHO, 2020). The easiest way to prevent many of these, whether it is the common cold or the stomach flu, is by doing something you have probably been told a million times: Wash your hands. Scientists have found that doing so can reduce gastrointestinal infections in early-childhood centers by about 30 percent and respiratory infections by 20 percent (van Beeck et al., 2016).

In the United States, young children who go to day care are sick enough to stay home at least four times every year: Many experience a runny nose or a simple cold nearly for more than a month every year (National Health Interview Survey, 2015; Vissing et al., 2018). Even a minor illness can be a substantial strain on families, particularly when parents cannot take time off from work or lack backup care to take care of a sick child (CS Mott Children's Hospital, 2017).

MAKING A DIFFERENCE
Making Room for a Little Dirt

In recent decades, there has been an increase in the number of children diagnosed with immune-related illnesses, such as food allergies and asthma. In the United States, about 13 percent of children have been diagnosed with a skin allergy or eczema, 6 percent with food allergies, and 9 percent with asthma (NCHS, 2022). One in six U.S. children with allergies and asthma visits the emergency room every year (CDC, 2018). Managing allergies and asthma adds stress to the lives of children and their families (Segura Moreno & Diaz Heredia, 2021; Westwell-Roper et al., 2022).

In communities around the world, air pollution is a major trigger for allergies and asthma (Trikamjee et al., 2022). Pollution is a major contributor to asthma for many U.S. children as well, but scientists also believe that some of our lifestyle may also play a part in making us susceptible to asthma and allergies. Our emphasis on staying clean and avoiding dirt may be damaging some of the bacteria that protect us from immune diseases, known as our **microbiome**. Bacterial cells in our bodies outnumber our own cells: We have about 1.25 bacterial cells for each of our own cells. (Although that may seem like a lot, the tiny bacteria only contribute about a half a pound to our overall size [Sender et al., 2016].)

Our microbiome is essential to our health and helps protect our bodies from harmful microbes that may make us sick (Brodin, 2022). This colony of microbes and bacteria develops in our early life, maturing by about age 3 (Laue et al., 2022). As a baby is exposed to microbes through childbirth, early feeding, and interacting with their surroundings, bacteria begin to find a home in their intestines and throughout their body, protecting them and training their immune system (Ronan et al., 2021).

The **hygiene hypothesis** proposes that our modern lifestyle may be preventing many children from developing the balance of beneficial bacteria needed to build a healthy microbiome and immune system. Without a healthy microbiome, children are at higher risk for allergies and asthma as well as, some researchers suggest, for other conditions such as depression and cardiovascular disease (Brodin, 2022).

microbiome The collection of beneficial bacteria that live in our bodies that work with our immune system to help protect us from disease. A healthy balance of bacteria is linked to some early life experiences like breastfeeding and vaginal delivery.

hygiene hypothesis A theory suggesting that regular exposure to a variety of microbes helps people develop a robust microbiome, protecting them from some allergies, asthma, and immune-related conditions.

This hypothesis began with an observation by some scientists that only-children had a much greater chance of developing common respiratory allergies than those from larger families (Strachan, 1989). Other researchers observed similar patterns. The more microbes and bacteria children were exposed to early on, the lower their rate of allergies.

For example, children who grew up on Amish farms in Indiana, where they were exposed to horses, played outside, and drank unpasteurized milk, had lower rates of allergy-related diseases like asthma and eczema than their relatives without a rural Amish lifestyle (Holbreich et al., 2012). One study even found that children whose pacifiers were not washed after they were dropped on the ground were less susceptible to allergies (Hesselmar et al., 2013). Researchers conducting large, correlational studies found that children with an atypical balance of microbes in their intestines were more likely to have both allergies and conditions such as depression and autism spectrum disorder (Laue et al., 2021; Sbihi et al., 2021).

Scientists found that the strongest correlations with a healthy immune system came from factors that may not be changeable or under a family's control. The strongest links between a healthy immune system and microbiome include being born vaginally, nursing, avoiding antibiotics in the first years of life, growing up on a farm, and having older siblings (Scudellari, 2017).

Early experiments aimed at exposing children to more microbes have not been definitive, particularly among children who are healthy. However, a healthier balance of bacteria can be particularly important to children who are already unwell: Scientists found that supplementing the food of children with acute malnutrition in Bangladesh with beneficial bacteria promoted growth (Barratt et al., 2022). Without a clear consensus on what actions individual families can play in developing a healthy microbiome, what do scientists suggest families can do to help children stay healthy?

- Get dirty. Children who play outside in the elements are building a healthy immune system (Finlay & Arrieta, 2017).
- Adopt a pet. All that mess, drool, and hair strengthens the immune system and may reduce the chances that a child develops allergies or asthma (Finlay & Arrieta, 2017).
- Wash your hands with soap. Building a healthy microbiome is important, but that does not mean you want an extra dose of pathogens or viruses (Scudellari, 2017).

So, as it turns out, you can keep on cleaning. Sweeping and vacuuming do not change the bacteria and the microbes that live in your house; they just reduce dust (Weber et al., 2015). On the other hand, getting dirty on the playground may be good for everyone. 🌍

Dangers in the Environment Children can be sickened by their environment. Around the world, more than one in four deaths in children under age 5 are linked to pollution: either respiratory infections caused by air pollution, gastrointestinal diseases caused by unsafe drinking water, or dangerous chemicals or toxins in food (Prüss-Üstün et al., 2016). Young children are particularly sensitive to environmental toxins, because the doses of chemicals or pollutants are disproportionately likely to cause immediate or long-term consequences in their tiny bodies, including cognitive disorders and even death (Costa et al., 2021; Landrigan et al., 2019).

In the United States and around the world, the toll of environmental pollution often falls heavily on marginalized, low-income communities (Nigra, 2020). Remember from Chapter 1 that during the 2015 drinking water crisis in Flint, Michigan, 18 months of drinking corrosive, polluted water, doubled the lead levels in the blood of children living in Flint (Hanna-Attisha, 2019).

Once commonly used in paint and gasoline, lead is an environmental toxin that can affect learning, thinking, and self-control. It is one of the most common and

Time Outside Comes with Invisible Benefits. These two boys live in an Amish community in Lancaster County, Pennsylvania. Researchers have found that children who live on farms are less likely to develop allergies and asthma, perhaps because they have developed beneficial bacteria early in life.

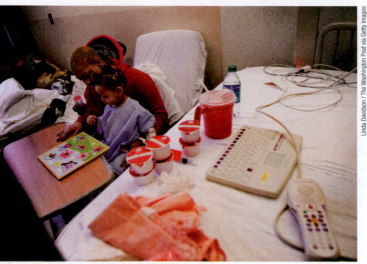

Beginning Recovery Like about 2 in every 100 U.S. children, Heavenz was exposed to lead in her home. Lead exposure is often not in families' control: in Heavenz's case, her mother believes that the landlord did not adequately test her home for lead.

Swimming Is Fun and Keeps You Safe. Drowning is a leading cause of death in young children around the world, particularly in communities with open water, rivers, and pools. These young children are learning to swim in a pond in Bangladesh.

preventable causes of brain damage in young children in the United States and around the world: Studies have shown that the brains of adults who were exposed to lead as children are smaller than those of other adults. Lead also damages the kidneys and the cardiovascular system, but nearly half of U.S. adults were exposed to lead as children and may continue to experience the consequences (Grandjean & Landrigan, 2014; Landrigan et al., 2019; McFarland et al., 2022).

Rural children and children of color are more than twice as likely to be exposed to lead as their city-dwelling, more affluent peers, frequently due to poor-quality water sources in rural homes (J. M. Gibson et al., 2020). Lead toxins do not just come through water. Children can be exposed to lead through dust from old, peeling paint, from broken or improperly disposed of electronic devices, or even from unregulated remedies, such as some kinds of skin lighteners or even colic treatments (Brown & Longoria, 2010; Ori & Larsen, 2018; UNICEF & Pure Earth, 2020).

Compared to many cities around the country, the rates of lead exposure in Flint, Michigan, were actually low. For example, in Allentown, Pennsylvania, almost one in four young children has elevated levels of lead in their blood, compared to only one in eight in Flint (Hanna-Attisha et al., 2016; Frostenson, 2016). Whereas fewer than 2 in every 100 children in the United States have high levels of lead, more than one in three around the world show signs of lead exposure (Egan et al., 2021; UNICEF & Pure Earth, 2020). In the United States, lead-based paint has been banned since 1977, but millions of older homes are still contaminated (Benfer, 2017). Lead-based paint is still used in more than 60 percent of the nations in the world, including countries like India, Indonesia, and Nigeria, and children in these countries are exposed to lead every day (UNEP, 2020).

Accidents and Injuries Young children are healthier than babies, but they face a new danger: accidental injury, a leading cause of death for preschoolers around the world (NCHS National Vital Statistics System, 2021; WHO, 2020). Such deaths are tragic: Preschoolers struck by cars while in strollers, drowned in swimming pools, or consumed by house fires. Accidents are also a leading cause of nonfatal injury: In the United States, one in eight preschoolers each year goes to the emergency room because of an accidental injury (Albert & McCaig, 2014).

Children are particularly vulnerable during early childhood because their developing motor skills may lead them to take physical risks they are not ready for (Damashek & Kuhn, 2014). Young children act quickly and often unexpectedly, which leads to accidents. Preschoolers who typically have more difficulty than others following directions and controlling their impulses are at more risk for injury, perhaps because they forget or do not heed warnings about safety. (Damashek et al., 2021; Morrongiello, 2018). Researchers estimate that more than 90 percent of injuries can be prevented by safer environments and more supervision.

The rate of accidental injury in the United States is twice that of other high-income countries (Morrongiello, 2018). The culprit? Unequal access to safe living environments (Thakrar et al., 2018). The number of children in hazardous living conditions, such as housing with overloaded electrical systems, scalding hot water, or windows without safety guards, is double that of other affluent countries (Pressman, 2017; Slemaker et al., 2017; Tilburg, 2017). Children may live in neighborhoods lacking streetlights and crosswalks to protect pedestrians, or without fences around pools and ponds to prevent drownings (Frank et al., 2019).

Child-proofing homes and neighborhoods can prevent injuries, but paying attention is another form of prevention. Children who are not closely watched have a risk five times higher for serious injuries (Schnitzer et al., 2015). Forty percent of all injuries from accidents, like scalding, poisoning, or strangulation, are related to inadequate supervision (Damashek & Kuhn, 2014). What counts as supervision? Although adults cannot keep their eyes on children every second of the day, children are safer when they are in view. However, many children spend as many as one in five of their waking hours out of earshot or out of sight of an adult (Morrongiello, 2018).

At the same time, experts caution that all activities include some risk, and that children must experience some of the consequences of risky behaviors to learn how to be safe. Children need to be allowed to explore even if it means climbing a tree or all the way to the top of a play set (Morrongiello, 2018).

SCIENCE IN PRACTICE
Ashley Causey-Golden, M.A., School Director and Advocate

Ashley Causey-Golden is the part-owner and director, along with her friend and colleague Shelby Stone-Steel, of an outdoor, forest-based school called Gather near Atlanta, Georgia. Gather is an outdoor program for children aged 3 to 10 inspired by Montessori and Waldorf teaching principles that is particularly focused on creating an inclusive, welcoming space for Black families. Gather is rooted in academic research about child development and Causey-Golden's years of practice making sure children feel seen, uplifted, and connected to what they are learning.

Yes, "forest-based school" really means forest-based. The children are out-of-doors five mornings a week, in all weather, which in Georgia could mean 92 degrees in September or freezing rain in January. Outdoor school means allowing children to take risks as they engage with the outdoors: jumping (and falling) over logs, investigating toads (and sometimes being bitten by bugs), and building houses out of pine needles (and sometimes getting splinters).

Outdoor school is thrilling: Causey-Golden sometimes lights a fire to make warm tea for the children, and they have seen animals (mostly squirrels) approach during rest time. Many adults worry that spending time outdoors, particularly in school, might just be too risky for young children (Button & Wilde, 2019). Children could wander off or could hurt themselves. But experts note that taking healthy risks, including being near open fires, slippery rocks, and wild insects, actually helps children learn about what is safe and what is not (Brussoni et al., 2015).

Causey-Golden points out that being outside in nature has benefits beyond just encouraging exciting outdoor play: She thinks (and research supports this) that being in nature is less stressful and rushed than a typical preschool classroom and helps children learn to pay attention and regulate their behavior. It also helps children stay active and develop control over their bodies in a place where big physical activity, including jumping and running, is more feasible (Kuo et al., 2019).

Causey-Golden finds that being outside is rejuvenating for her as well, making it easier to support children, help them find joy, and help them get along in the world. ◉

APPLY IT! **7.4** Families are responsible for encouraging healthy habits in early childhood, but they may have different ethnotheories about safety. How would you apply the principle of cultural humility when talking to a family about establishing healthy routines with their preschooler?

7.5 Sebastian and Theodore's family is proud of their physical skills. How would you explain the benefits of physical activity to their caregivers? Which types of accidental injuries might they worry about?

Wrapping It Up

LO 7.1 Describe typical growth in height and weight from age 2½ to 6. (p. 172)

During early childhood, children typically begin with the softer, rounder body of a toddler and grow longer and leaner, with more adult body proportions.

LO 7.2 Identify the areas of the brain that are changing rapidly in early childhood. (p. 172)

The brain continues to grow, but at a slower pace than in infancy. This is a period of intensive growth of the faster, myelinated connections that link different parts of the brain, called the connectome. In addition, the cortex continues to mature in early childhood, particularly the prefrontal cortex, an area at the front of the brain that is critical to logical thinking and controlling behavior.

LO 7.3 Explain the connection between the development of motor skills and children's feelings of competence. (p. 177)

Motor-skill development in early childhood requires practice. Children learn the skills that their communities and cultures support, whether tricycle riding or ballet dancing. Motor skills help children feel competent and build executive function skills and self-control. During early childhood, if not before, most children learn to manage their own toileting and develop fine motor skills, allowing them to be more independent and adjust to formal school.

LO 7.4 Describe common health challenges during early childhood. (p. 179)

Sleep continues to be important to health in early childhood. In many U.S. communities, children give up daytime naps at this age. Many children have sleep difficulties, which may be linked to media use. Physical activity and nutritious foods are important to health, but many children do not get enough. Even in preschool, children are aware of the stigma around body size, so adults must be careful about how they talk about weight. Most young children were protected from the worst effects of the COVID-19 pandemic, but infectious diseases still take a toll on preschoolers around the world.

LO 7.5 Assess the risks of accidents and injuries prevalent during early childhood. (p. 179)

Children are particularly susceptible to environmental dangers, like lead. Accidents are a leading cause of death and injury as children are better able to explore but have trouble making safe choices.

KEY TERMS

early childhood (p. 172)   **connectome** (p. 173)   **selective eaters** (p. 182)   **hygiene hypothesis** (p. 184)

prefrontal cortex (p. 173)   **lateralization** (p. 176)   **microbiome** (p. 184)

CHECK YOUR LEARNING

1. During early childhood, the band of neurons connecting the brain's two hemispheres becomes increasingly myelinated. This connective brain structure is known as:
   a) gray matter.
   b) the cell nucleus.
   c) the corpus callosum.
   d) synaptic pruning.

2. The unique pattern of myelinated pathways between areas in the cortex and structures inside the brain is known as a person's:
   a) microbiome.
   b) lateralization.
   c) ethnotheory.
   d) connectome.

3. Increasing lateralization of brain functions during early childhood support young children's increasing skills in all of these EXCEPT:
   a) fine motor skills.
   b) executive function.
   c) picky eating.
   d) handedness.

4. Which of these is an example of a gross motor skill that may develop during early childhood?
   a) Jumping
   b) Folding origami
   c) Eye blinking
   d) Using chopsticks

5. During early childhood, which of these issues may affect eating and nutrition?
   a) High risk of developing food allergies
   b) Selective eating
   c) Greatly increased appetite
   d) Inability to distinguish sweet and salty flavors

6. Which of these may be effective in preventing young children from developing an unhealthy weight?
   a) Limiting the amount of time looking at screens (phones, tablets, computers, and TV)
   b) Increasing families' access to fresh fruits and vegetables
   c) Creating safe spaces in the community for active outdoor play
   d) All of the above

7. According to the hygiene hypothesis, children may be less likely to develop allergies if:
   a) their parents have asthma.
   b) they are exposed to a variety of bacteria and viruses in daily life.
   c) their sleeping and eating areas are carefully sterilized three times per day.
   d) they are only children.

8. Which of these statements about illness in early childhood is TRUE?

   a) Preschool-age children have high levels of immunity and are rarely infected with viruses.

   b) Exposure to environmental toxins has similar impacts on preschoolers as it does on adults.

   c) Handwashing is effective at minimizing the spread of infectious illnesses in preschool settings.

   d) Early childhood is the age period with the highest level of vulnerability to gastrointestinal illnesses.

9. Describe the role of culture in motor development. Are the gross motor skills and fine motor skills developed during early childhood universal?

10. What are some of the key features of young children's physical and brain development in early childhood that make them particularly susceptible to accidents and injuries?

8 Cognitive Development in Early Childhood

© Macmillan, Photo by Sidford House

They call Aidan the mayor. His city: the playground near his apartment in New York City. Aidan knows everyone's name, even the ones his father cannot remember, and he greets everyone. At age 5, play is Aidan's favorite thing to do: outside in the park, blanket forts, Spider-Man and Star Wars with his 7-year-old sister, Dylan, or games on the tablet.

Like many parents, Alex and Sinead want to make sure Aidan is ready for kindergarten. He has attended preschool for years, which he loves: His favorite part is serving pretend drinks to his classmates from the play kitchen. However, Aidan's parents imagine that kindergarten will be more serious and are not sure he is looking forward to it. Although he can already count, write his name, and read simple words, sitting down to do schoolwork is not so fun.

Like many young children, Aidan would rather run around, pretend, or draw than do a worksheet or flashcards. He procrastinates when his parents set aside time for him to do academic work. Sometimes he even complains that he is "having a breakdown" and tries to negotiate his way out of it: His parents sometimes worry that this may be unusual immaturity, but according to developmental science, Aidan is not immature for his age at all: He is just not grown up yet.

In early childhood, the way children think and how they use language is changing, as they are better able to pay attention and focus on what they are doing. This is an important period for the development of many cognitive and language skills that children will draw on later in life. Young children are eager to learn, whether in school or out, but most of that learning comes easiest if it is integrated with the social and physical activities that children enjoy — like play.

In this chapter, you will learn about Aidan's accomplishments during early childhood, such as the ability to tell long stories about superheroes, count to 100, and make an airplane out of construction paper. You will also learn about the other cognitive markers of early childhood. Finally, you will read about the importance of play for young children and about the many interventions that have improved the opportunities for preschoolers around the world.

Scientific American Profile

Meet Aidan

Cognitive Development

Despite Aidan's hard work in learning his numbers and letters, aspects of his thinking are still characteristic of the curiosity and energy of younger children. He has a lot to say, and his ideas are wide ranging. Aidan has ideas about the past and the future: putting wings on superheroes and supervising a match-up between Green Lantern and Batman. How is Aidan's thinking different from both an infant and a more mature first-grader?

Developmental scientists like Jean Piaget developed theories to explain the characteristics of thought that make early childhood unique. Other researchers, like Lev Vygotsky, explained how children learn and how the way they learn shapes their cognitive skills. Young children's advances—pretending, talking, and learning—are powered by brain maturation and a better ability to pay attention, remember, and process information. The observations of these researchers clarify some of the interesting inconsistencies in children's thinking in early childhood, such as why Aidan might still believe in the Tooth Fairy and why it may be impossible to teach him algebra right now (see **Infographic 8.1**).

Learning Objectives

8.1 Identify the key features of Piaget's preoperational stage.

8.2 Apply Vygotsky's theory of development to young children's thinking.

8.3 Describe advances in information-processing skills during early childhood.

Piaget's Theory of Preoperational Thought

When Aidan insists that he is Batman, he is being a typical 5-year-old. Piaget's classic research drew attention to the inventiveness of children's thinking during early childhood. Although Aidan's ideas are magical, they actually have a certain kind of logic to them. When he argues that Batman can "overpower Green Lantern," he is not just showing his impressive and growing vocabulary and his fascination with superheroes, he is also demonstrating that he knows something about how cause-and-effect works: that even pretend powers follow some kind of rules. Piaget's work helps us understand that there is a special kind of intelligence behind his thinking.

Preoperational thought is the second stage in children's thinking and spans ages 2 to 7. In Piaget's view, young children in the preoperational stage are capable of *symbolic*, but not quite logical, thought (see **Table 8.1**). For instance, children can use language and their imaginative ideas to talk about things they cannot see and to play make-believe. However, children are still "preoperational" since they cannot perform logical mental operations, like reversing or undoing something that just happened or considering multiple perspectives on a problem. During early childhood, preschoolers even struggle with basic logical ideas like "more than" or "less than."

Symbolic Thought One of the hallmarks of the preoperational stage is the imagination that Aidan shows while he throws spider webs out of his fingertips. During early childhood, children show more symbolic thinking. Remember that during the sensorimotor period, toddlers begin to demonstrate *some* symbolic thought, as they learn to use words as symbols to represent objects that are not there. Preschoolers take

Symbolic Thinking in Two Dimensions The sun doesn't really look like a circle with rays coming out from it, but we all understand that this preschooler's drawing shows the sun. Similarly, human arms and legs are thicker than the single lines used here to represent arms and legs, but we know that these figures represent people.

preoperational thought The second stage in Piaget's theory of children's cognitive development, spanning about ages 2 to 7, in which young children are capable of symbolic, but not quite logical, thought.

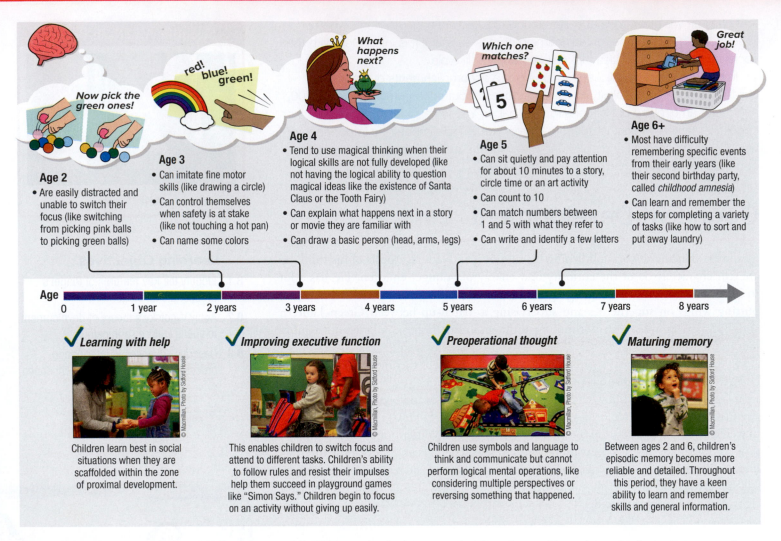

Age 2
• Are easily distracted and unable to switch their focus (like switching from picking pink balls to picking green balls)

Age 3
• Can imitate fine motor skills (like drawing a circle)
• Can control themselves when safety is at stake (like not touching a hot pan)
• Can name some colors

Age 4
• Tend to use magical thinking when their logical skills are not fully developed (like not having the logical ability to question magical ideas like the existence of Santa Claus or the Tooth Fairy)
• Can explain what happens next in a story or movie they are familiar with
• Can draw a basic person (head, arms, legs)

Age 5
• Can sit quietly and pay attention for about 10 minutes to a story, circle time or an art activity
• Can count to 10
• Can match numbers between 1 and 5 with what they refer to
• Can write and identify a few letters

Age 6+
• Most have difficulty remembering specific events from their early years (like their second birthday party, called *childhood amnesia*)
• Can learn and remember the steps for completing a variety of tasks (like how to sort and put away laundry)

Age
0   1 year   2 years   3 years   4 years   5 years   6 years   7 years   8 years

✓ **Learning with help**

Children learn best in social situations when they are scaffolded within the zone of proximal development.

✓ **Improving executive function**

This enables children to switch focus and attend to different tasks. Children's ability to follow rules and resist their impulses help them succeed in playground games like "Simon Says." Children begin to focus on an activity without giving up easily.

✓ **Preoperational thought**

Children use symbols and language to think and communicate but cannot perform logical mental operations, like considering multiple perspectives or reversing something that happened.

✓ **Maturing memory**

Between ages 2 and 6, children's episodic memory becomes more reliable and detailed. Throughout this period, they have a keen ability to learn and remember skills and general information.

Highlights of Cognitive Development in Early Childhood Researchers use insights from Piaget, Vygotsky, and information-processing theorists to describe the maturation of children's thinking as they grow.

symbolic play further. They can play with others and adopt adult roles, becoming a "chef" in a play kitchen or Mr. Incredible on the swings. They even use drawings to symbolically represent the world they see, which can be a mixture of the real and the metaphorical (Piaget & Inhelder, 1969).

Children differ in how imaginative they are—and how they display their creativity (Barbot et al., 2016). Many preschool-age children display **animism**, describing nonliving things as if they are alive and have human feelings or motives. Animism can help young children explain their world, even if their explanations seem illogical. Children may wonder whether the sun goes down because it is tired, or if trees can talk. They may even assign human feelings to machines—which may be a strategy to explain a world they do not quite understand. When a group of experimenters talked to children about how a robot solves problems, younger children were more likely to explain that a robot had feelings (Druga et al., 2018). By age 8, most children no longer thought that robots have feelings, or get hungry.

Piaget saw animism as a sign of developmental immaturity, but other researchers disagree. For many of us, animism lasts well into adulthood. Many adults talk lovingly to their pets, and nearly half of U.S. adults believe in ghosts (Ballard, 2019). Certainly, most have us have complained that our phones, our cars, or our computers "won't let us" do something from time to time.

animism The tendency to describe nonliving things as if they are alive and have human feelings or motives.

TABLE 8.1 Characteristics of Piaget's Period of Preoperational Thought

Symbolic thought	Children use objects to stand in for, or symbolize, another object. A block can become a rocket ship; the space under the table can be a house.	Images by Jodie Hanna/Getty Images
Intuitive thought	This is the stage of "why?" Children begin to have a more logical sense of how the world works but still display some limitations.	Peoplemages/iStock/E+/Getty Images
Centration	Children focus on one feature of a problem (like how wide a glass is) to the exclusion of other features.	©Macmillan
Magical thinking	Children often come up with illogical or magical explanations for events they do not fully understand.	d3sign/Moment/Getty Images

SCIENCE IN PRACTICE
Randi Williams, Robot Developer

When Randi Williams introduces herself to children and explains that she is an engineer, she is often asked what kind of train she drives. (Some children think engineers drive steam engines.) Randi, however, develops robots for young children. And, she knows that many people fear the impact that robots and "smart" devices like Alexa, Google Home, or Siri may have on small children (Madrigal, 2017). Williams does not share this fear. In fact, she designs robots that will help young children learn to program on their own. She hopes this will help them develop a critical understanding of robots and also inspire a new generation of engineers.

Courtesy Randi Williams, photo by Halli Chen

Courtesy Randi Williams

Science in Action Randi Williams studies how children interact with robots to understand how children think and how to use robots to help them learn. Here she shows off some of the robots she uses with young children to help them learn how to program.

Williams has discovered that, as Piaget might have predicted, young children have animistic beliefs about robots. According to most children, you should be nice to Alexa or Siri lest their feelings get hurt (Druga et al., 2017, 2018). Her studies have shown that children ask robots concrete questions to test how real they are, such as "What is your favorite color?" and "How old are you?" One favorite: "Can I eat you?" (Druga et al., 2017). In Williams's work technology inspires children's creativity and gives children and researchers insights into how these smart devices actually work (Williams, Biscaro, et al., 2019).

conservation tasks Piaget's hands-on tasks that measure how preschoolers' logical thinking develops. Each involves asking children what has happened to an object or a set of objects that is rearranged or manipulated in front of them to look different. Preschoolers struggle to logically complete the conservation tasks, but over time, their abilities improve.

Share It!

Preoperational thought can make medical procedures frightening for children, but play can help. Children who watched a doll go through a difficult medical procedure (having a cast removed) were less anxious than those who did not get to play.

(Wong et al., 2018)

Limitations of Logic in Early Childhood A 4-year-old is likely to believe in magic (Subbotsky, 2014). As children grow older, however, fewer resort to fantastical explanations. Thus, without exceptional intervention, fewer 6-year-olds than 3-year-olds will believe in Santa Claus or the Tooth Fairy (Kapitány et al., 2020).

Young children's creative thinking and reliance on magical explanations often conceal their limited understanding of cause and effect and the logic of the world around them. Remember that Piaget described their thinking as *preoperational thought*, which means that children are unable to perform true mental *operations*. A mental operation is the ability to logically think through something in your head. Preschoolers have tremendous difficulty with many mental operations, such as the idea that some events are reversible or that matter cannot just disappear. Preschool-age children tend to be focused on their perceptions of their surroundings, rather than looking at a problem from different perspectives to think it through logically. Piaget called children's focus on their own perspective *egocentrism*, a perspective that can keep children from seeing the big picture or even someone else's point of view (Piaget, 1968).

For instance, young children often have difficulty with the idea of *reversibility*. This is part of what makes masks so scary for preschoolers: They are truly afraid that the act of putting on a mask is permanent and cannot be reversed. In a classic study, a researcher brought her very patient cat into a preschool and put a rabbit mask on it. She was able to convince a group of 3- and 4-year-olds that the cat had magically turned into a rabbit (de Vries, 1969). Researchers interpret children's inability to conceive that actions may be reversible as a sign of their inability to perform mental operations.

Piaget created a number of hands-on tasks to measure how preschooler's logical thinking develops. One classic series of measures is known as the **conservation tasks** (Piaget, 1952). Each involves asking children what has happened to an object or a set of objects that is rearranged or manipulated to look different right in front of them. For instance, one ball of clay may be squished down while the other is rolled into a long form. Are children able to mentally reverse this operation and understand that the amount of the clay has not changed even though its appearance has? Preschoolers struggle to logically complete the conservation tasks, but over time, their abilities improve.

For instance, in conservation-of-number tasks, children are shown two rows of coins of equal number and length lined up next to each other (see **Figure 8.1**). Then, the experimenter rearranges one row so that the ten coins in this row are more spread

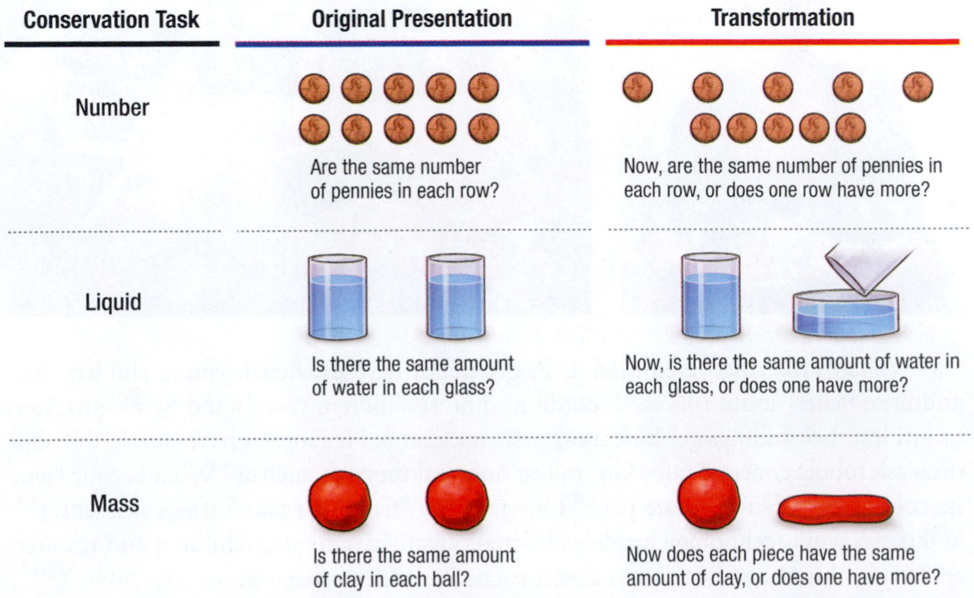

FIGURE 8.1 Piaget's Conservation Tasks: Mass, Number, and Liquid As they get older, children develop experiences and strategies that enable them to understand that number, liquid, and mass are conserved. Children in the preoperational stage are easily confused and typically have difficulty with these tasks, because they focus on one feature of the problem rather than the whole. For instance, a preschooler might argue that there are more objects in a longer row of pennies than a shorter one or more play dough in a flat shape than in a round one.

out and longer than those in the other. Children are asked which row has "more" coins. Younger children will typically explain that the longer row has more. Rather than counting the coins, younger children focus on one aspect of the problem, the length of the row. As children have more practice counting, they are often able to demonstrate conservation on this task by painstakingly counting each of the coins in order to be sure that there are the same number in both rows (Clements, 1984).

In the classic conservation-of-liquid task, an experimenter pours equal amounts of liquid into two identical glasses. Next, the experimenter pours one glass of liquid into a container of a different shape, either taller and thinner or shorter and wider. The child is then asked which container has "more" of the liquid. Preschool-age children tend to focus on the height of the glasses rather than the amount of liquid, an error known as *centration*, or they may believe that the amount has magically changed (Piaget & Inhelder, 1969).

Most children develop a sense of conservation over time, achieving conservation in these tasks by about age 8 (Lozada & Carro, 2016). Practice and experience can contribute to typical variations. Children who spend a lot of time playing with clay, for instance, will have a sense of the conservation of mass earlier than those without hands-on experience with clay (Price-Williams et al., 1969). Children who are allowed to pour the water themselves are often better able to display logical reasoning than are those who are passive observers (Lozada & Carro, 2016).

The Role of the Prefrontal Cortex in Logical Thinking Brain development plays an important role in how children understand the conservation task. Remember from Chapter 7 that the prefrontal cortex and the connections between the prefrontal cortex and other areas of the brain are rapidly maturing during early childhood. Neuroscientists who observed preschoolers in fMRI scanners solving conservation tasks have learned that children who achieve the conservation task are using more of their prefrontal cortex when making their choices (Houdé & Borst, 2014).

Why does engaging more of the prefrontal cortex help solve the conservation task? Children's initial instincts when they see water poured into a tall glass are to focus on a basic rule that they've used many times before—taller usually means more. (This is a rule that also applies in adult life: The large drink is always taller than the small one, right?) In order to correctly complete the task, children need to override their instinct to focus on height and think about volume (Poirel et al., 2012). Children who can correctly solve the conservation task engage their prefrontal cortex and the brain systems involved in self-control, *executive function*, and logical thinking, rather than brain systems activated by more intuitive decision-making (Houdé et al., 2011). Children who can't solve the conservation task are using more intuitive, automatic parts of the brain, unlike older children who are able to switch off this system and turn to more logical thinking.

Egocentrism In addition to the conservation tasks, Piaget devised ways to assess whether children can consider someone else's point of view. Piaget's **three mountains task** tests how well children can imagine how someone else would see the world. In this problem, Piaget and his team constructed a diorama of three mountains. This three-dimensional model included alpine peaks of different shapes and sizes with landmarks nestled among the hills (see **Figure 8.2**). Piaget and his colleagues asked children what objects a doll across the room would see (Piaget & Inhelder, 1956). Children had great difficulty consistently predicting what someone else would see until they were about 8. Younger children consistently guessed that someone else would see the scene as they did, an error Piaget called **egocentrism**.

three mountains task Piaget's test of how well children can imagine how someone else would see the world.

egocentrism In the Piagetian sense, children's inability to see the world from other people's point of view.

FIGURE 8.2 What Do You See? In Piaget's three mountains task, children are asked to imagine a scene from someone else's point of view: What would the doll see if she looked at this mountain scene? Would the little girl be able to understand that the doll saw things differently?

Learn It Together

Classic Conservation Tasks

In this activity, you will observe a young child engaging in a classic task that is commonly used to illustrate thinking during early childhood.

Plan Review some of the key characteristics of preoperational thinking, such as egocentrism, centration, and irreversibility. Then search Achieve or other internet sources for a video of one of the following:

- Conservation task
- Three mountains task
- False-belief task

Engage In a small group, review the video and analyze the task:

- What did the child have to do?
- What cognitive ability was being demonstrated?

Reflect Analyze the child's performance:

- What was the child's response?
- Did the child provide the expected age-typical response?
- What does this task and the child's reaction to it illustrate about thinking during early childhood?

You can see this error in everyday life. In a game of hide-and-seek, 4-year-olds may hide with their head hidden but their feet showing. A 3-year-old may nod her head when talking to Grandma on the phone, unable to understand that Grandma cannot see her. When scholars use the term *egocentrism* in the Piagetian sense, they mean children are unable to see the world from other people's point of view. In this stage, children assume that everyone *literally* sees everything the way they do. They are not yet able to perform the mental operation of imagining something from a different perspective. But Piaget did not mean that children were self-centered in the emotional or social sense of the word. In fact, he even began to move away from using the term *egocentrism* because he was concerned that it made children seem selfish (Piaget, 1968).

More contemporary researchers have critiqued the three mountains task itself. They point out that very young children often realize that other people see the world differently than they do, but that they struggle to mentally rotate the mountains in the task itself (Frick et al., 2014).

Challenges to Piaget Piaget helped educators and scientists appreciate the unique strengths of young children's thinking. He believed that early childhood was a special time that should be protected, and that play was an essential way that young children make sense of the world (Piaget & Inhelder, 1969). He argued that development was best seen as a "spontaneous process" that is driven by the child's own internal timetable and cautioned against trying to accelerate it (Piaget, 1954). Rushing children could do more harm than good (Hall, 1970). Piaget believed that children learn best when they are actively engaged in their environment and can construct their own knowledge through their experiences with objects and people (Piaget, 1968). Contemporary scholars agree that children's creativity is triggered by what is around them. Some research indicates that more open, natural environments encourage children to be more imaginative and playful than ones that are more structured or filled with toys (Zamani, 2016).

Other researchers, however, have challenged many of the details of Piaget's theory. For instance, scientists have found evidence that children's development of conservation and perspective-taking do not always happen according to Piaget's timetables (Dasen, 1994; Gelman, 1973). Critics have pointed out that children who have not been to school and who do not have experience playing with objects like those used in the conservation tasks generally show delayed development on the tasks. However, if these children are tested with tools from their own communities, they pass the conservation tasks earlier (Cole, 1990; Greenfield, 2012; Piaget, 1970).

Many contemporary researchers believe that one reason why some children fail the conservation tasks is because logical reasoning does not develop all at once. Children, just like adults, may use strategies of logical reasoning at some times but not others (Siegler, 1999). Many scientists now believe that development occurs not in strict stages, but in starts and stops, more like overlapping waves than discrete steps. Piaget himself acknowledged that the ages that applied to the development of preoperational thought (and his other stages of cognitive reasoning) were somewhat arbitrary (Piaget, 1970). Piaget emphasized the value of pretend play, something that is not fostered in all families. As a result, in some communities symbolic play does not appear as early as it did in the Swiss children studied by Piaget (Callaghan et al., 2011).

Despite these critiques, developmental science remains indebted to Piaget for valuing the thinking that children display before they fully understand logic.

Vygotsky's Theory of Children's Learning

Like Piaget, the Russian developmental theorist Lev Vygotsky appreciated the creativity and playfulness of preschool children's thinking (Vygotsky, 1933/2016). Unlike Piaget, Vygotsky did not believe cognitive development occurred in universal stages. Instead, he felt that social and cultural factors shaped cognitive development. Remember from

Chapter 2 that Vygotsky believed that cognitive maturation is the result of a complex, social interaction between children and their environment that begins on the day that they are born (Vygotsky & Cole, 1978).

Like many contemporary developmental scientists, Vygotsky believed that the building blocks of cognition, like attention and memory, are skills learned through interaction with other people (Vygotsky & Cole, 1978). Vygotsky's ideas about learning have influenced education around the world and helped researchers articulate how children learn and use strategies, like language, to build their understanding. Researchers who examine the cultural context of human development are often inspired by the theoretical insights of Vygotsky (Cole, 2018; Greenfield, 2018; Hruschka et al., 2018).

Learning in the Zone When you think about learning, you probably picture sitting at a desk in school or reading a textbook like this. Vygotsky believed that learning also happens outside of school. Children learn important skills, like turn-taking or language skills, through play, whether they are pretending a stick is a galloping horse or building a river in the sandbox (Vygotsky & Cole, 1978). The way children learn changes their thinking for a lifetime. For instance, if children have lots of opportunities to learn by observing adults around them as they do everyday activities, they will develop close observational skills. If they grow up accustomed to being formally taught, they may be used to the high stimulation and the back-and-forth question-and-answer format that happens in school (Rogoff, 2016).

Vygotsky believed that teaching happens in a variety of contexts, but that it works best when a sensitive partner individually targets a child's capabilities. Do you ever have trouble focusing in class? Perhaps that is because you simply do not find what you are learning to be meaningful (Hulleman et al., 2016). According to Vygotsky and researchers inspired by his work, children are motivated by sensitive teaching that engages them by considering their interests and individual abilities (Vygotsky & Cole, 1978). This teaching can be done by formal teachers, but also by friends, peers, or family members. Researchers term this sensitive, one-on-one, guidance **scaffolding** (Wood et al., 1976). Just as builders use scaffolding to support their work in a building under construction, allowing them to reach greater heights, teachers use the process of scaffolding to help children learn things that they couldn't achieve on their own. Individualized scaffolding keeps children focused and also helps them avoid frustration (Wood et al., 1976).

Vygotsky used the term **zone of proximal development (ZPD)** to describe the range of what students can learn with help (Margolis, 2020; Vygotsky & Cole, 1978). Your zone of proximal development is not what you know right now, but what you are capable of if you are scaffolded. Many educators describe tasks that are in the ZPD as having a "perfect balance" between being too boring and too hard. Children in the ZPD feel both challenged and engaged at the same time.

For instance, a sensitive gymnastic coach might start Aidan out on a balance beam close to the ground, hovering over him a bit. The low beam is in his ZPD. The high beam and a flipped dismount are beyond his capability. Not all coaches know Vygotsky by name, but as expert teachers, they know to keep instruction within the ZPD.

Vygotsky was a hands-on educator who worked with many different children, some with serious disabilities and others living in extreme poverty. He knew that formal assessments could not give an accurate reading on these children's potential or intelligence. Children's ability to learn when sensitively scaffolded was a better measure of their capabilities than a traditional test. For example, if a teacher tests preschoolers to see if they can count to 10, one 4-year-old may not be capable of keeping their numbers straight. If the same

scaffolding A term for teaching, whether by formal teachers, friends, peers, or family members, that engages children by considering their interests and individual abilities.

zone of proximal development (ZPD) Vygotsky's term for the range of what students can learn with adult help.

Cooking with Help Following a recipe is one way young children can learn math in the real world. If parents engage their children's interest in counting and math during a simple cooking activity, their children may find basic counting and math easier when they get to school.

4-year-old is sensitively scaffolded, with prompting or pointing, they may be able to count to 10 or even 100 (Beller et al., 2018).

Vygotsky's insights about how to help children learn have tremendous results in the classroom. Collaborative and sensitive scaffolding can change children's feelings about school and make early education more successful (Rogoff, 1990). Scaffolding need not come from an adult: Children, including siblings and friends, are capable of teaching (Howe et al., 2016). The process of teaching can help both the young learner and the young teacher develop a deeper knowledge and understanding, whether it is how to play a new game or how to brush the dog (Rogoff, 1990, 1998).

Learning comes with different expectations depending on families' cultural backgrounds. In many communities around the world, children learn basic tasks like laundry, cooking, and cleaning by observing and helping the adults around them. Remember from Chapter 2 that the phrase *learning by observing and pitching in* describes this process (Rogoff, 2016; Rogoff et al., 2016). When children are integrated into family work, they are not explicitly taught how to fold napkins, for instance, but instead learn while doing.

In contrast, in other families, children are explicitly taught by being verbally instructed and even rewarded. In these families, children's focus and motivation are managed by adults (Paradise et al., 2014). In many cultures, scaffolding may include storytelling and direct experience with nature and the outdoor world. One study found that rural Turkana children in Kenya learned science concepts from their national curriculum through observational and hands-on scaffolding from parents and the narratives of their elders (Ng'asike, 2011).

Children who learn by doing may fold napkins exactly the same way as children who are taught through explicit instruction, but both groups of children have learned more than just how to fold napkins; they have learned different ways of learning. When children learn by observing and pitching in, they manage their own attention. Children who are used to this type of teaching are often used to sitting quietly and helping out without being prodded (Coppens et al., 2018).

When Aidan draws, he isn't quiet. "The Batman has pointy ears like a bat," he says to himself as he draws his favorite superhero. Vygotsky would say that Aidan's muttering is an important cognitive skill. Vygotsky theorized that thinking is made up of various mental tools or strategies. One key tool is language. Vygotsky called the language children use when they talk to themselves **private speech** (Vygotsky, 1962). Both private speech and the speech children use with others can help children focus. Private speech helps children develop self-control and executive function; children with strong executive function also tend to have strong language skills and higher scores on cognitive assessments (Aro et al., 2015; Mulvihill et al., 2021). You may hear preschoolers using private speech to coach themselves when they get upset or face a challenging task. Private speech can also help preschool-age children scaffold their own learning. Over time, children internalize private speech as *inner speech*, or silent thinking.

Reading in the Zone Sometimes the zone of proximal development happens when you get a chance to share a book with a friend, as Ricki reads to her friend Destiny in a child-care center in Ontario, Canada.

private speech Vygotsky's term for the language children use when they talk to themselves.

Information-Processing Advances

Adults expect preschoolers to develop the maturity to sit still long enough to scrawl their names, get dressed on their own, and explain what happened during their day. How does a 5-year-old become capable of taking the bus to school and telling long stories about a day at kindergarten? Remember that the information-processing approach looks at the components of thinking and provides new insights about how children mature. During this period, children's memory and attention advance, as do the executive function skills that will enable them to sit still at school.

Developing Stronger Memory Skills

A key part of children's cognitive growth involves improvements in the ability to remember. In preschool, children learn to remember the letters in their name and the rules for circle time. At the same time, children may sometimes struggle to keep track of what they are supposed to do, and even to recall what happened during the day. During early childhood, children's memory changes rapidly.

Episodic Memory Different types of memory serve different functions. One type of memory involves your long-term memory, such as your memory of a birthday party or a first date. Scientists call this long-term memory for specific events **episodic memory**. Episodic memory allows you to remember the who, what, and when of something that happened in the past, like the cupcakes, piñata, and sudden fire alarm at your fifth birthday party.

Is there a reason Aidan, like many other preschoolers, has a blank expression when his father asks him what he did that day? By preschool, children are only just beginning to develop episodic memories. At age 2 and a half, Aidan may have been able to tell his father that he went to the pool that day, but his memories lacked detail compared to his memories at age 4, when he could offer specifics about the kind of ice cream he had after lunch and that he played with his sister at the playground. By the time Aidan is 6, his memories will be even more detailed (Hudson & Mayhew, 2009; Nelson, 2018).

Episodic memory improves rapidly due to improving language skills, practice with telling stories, and maturity in the parts of the brain that process memory, like the *hippocampus*, a set of seahorse-shaped brain structures located under the cortex (Ngo et al., 2017; Riggins et al., 2018). Children's memory improves as new connections between the hippocampus and the cortex form and strengthen. By kindergarten, if properly motivated, children generally will be able to provide a detailed description of their day. Talking about past events helps children learn how to remember and retain their memories (Fivush, 2014). The preschoolers with the best memories in the world are said to be from Maori families in New Zealand, who have a rich storytelling tradition. Maori families often reminisce in great detail with their small children about the past (Reese & Neha, 2015). This helps some Maori children develop the ability to remember and talk about the past years before children from many other communities.

It is unusual for adults to remember their first day of kindergarten in detail. Children, however, are able to remember significant events from infancy, even from as early as 6 months, although these memories are usually forgotten as they get older in what is sometimes called *childhood amnesia*. (Mullally & Maguire, 2014). It isn't until between ages 7 and 9 that children will have the same ability to store and retain their memories as adults (Bauer & Larkina, 2014).

Although children's memory improves, they are not yet ready to memorize their multiplication tables. Remembering facts, lists, and dates of unrelated information, or *semantic memory*, is difficult for young children. Children need years of practice before they can remember bits of information well, particularly if this information is not personally relevant (Bauer, 2015).

Working Memory One type of short-term memory that does not last long but is essential to learning and to controlling behavior is called **working memory**. Children's episodic memory gradually reaches adult levels by middle childhood, but working memory is not mature until adolescence. Whereas episodic memory is dependent on the hippocampus and neural circuits that run to it, working memory depends on circuits in the late-developing cortex (Bathelt et al., 2018).

Working memory is crucial for developing the academic skills children will need in kindergarten (Jones et al., 2020). It enables children to remember parts of a basic math

CONNECTIONS

Remember from Chapter 5 that there are different types of memory. Infants have impressive *implicit memory* that allows them to quickly learn how to walk, talk, and relate to their environment. *Explicit memory* is the ability to recall specific events and develops later. In this chapter, we focus on the development of *episodic memory*, a type of explicit memory, and *working memory*.

davidf/E+/Getty Images

Tell Me Another! This little girl from the Maori community in New Zealand is whispering into her father's ear. Telling stories helps children build their long-term memory, and Maori children have some of the most impressive memories in the world.

episodic memory Long-term memory for specific events.

working memory A type of short-term memory that is essential to learning and to problem solving.

Hands-on Learning Can Happen Anywhere. Children's cognitive development is shaped by their environment. These preschool children spend every school morning in the middle of a forest near their home in rural Marsac, France, learning from and observing nature (and friendly dogs).

Share It!

What would a superhero do? Sometimes children can quickly boost their executive function by imagining what someone else would do in the same situation.

(White & Carlson, 2016)

executive function A group of thinking skills that allow you to control your behavior, suppress impulsive actions, and implement long-term plans.

problem (Purpura et al., 2017). For instance, in order to calculate the answer to "2 + 3," children need to be able to keep the *2* and the *3* in mind. Children learning how to read must hold letter sounds in working memory to decode even simple words. Over the preschool years, children's working memory becomes more efficient and reliable, allowing them to remember more complicated instructions and even begin to learn basic academic skills (Perlman et al., 2016).

Attention and Executive Function

If you observe a story hour at the library, you will find that most preschoolers have difficulty sitting still. They whisper. They may stare into the distance or at the ceiling. The librarian may say "eyes on me," but within a minute, most eyes will drift away. This is all typical for preschoolers.

Young children are slowly developing the ability to pay attention and control their behavior, but this does not mean they can happily sit for hours to take tests or sit quietly in a restaurant (Ristic & Enns, 2015). Remember from Chapter 5 that *attention* allows you to focus, shut out distractions, and keep your mind from wandering. **Executive function** refers to a group of thinking skills that allow you to suppress impulsive actions and implement long-term plans. Both skills are works in progress during early childhood, as the prefrontal cortex matures and strengthens connections with other parts of the brain.

Children who have stronger executive function skills are better prepared to learn and succeed in school (Morgan et al., 2019; Moriguchi et al., 2016). Early learning requires being able to quickly and flexibly switch between one thing and another and remember what to do next. Children who have difficulties with attention and executive function also tend to have difficulty managing their relationships and emotions, in addition to learning, as you will read in Chapter 10 (Zelazo, 2020). Children with strong executive function can manage their impulses most of the time and focus when they need to, making it easier to listen to a friend's ideas or to a teacher trying to explain how to make a perfect number 5.

Scientists see dramatic maturation in attention skills during early childhood. A 5-year-old's focus is much more reliable than that of a toddler. In fact, by the time they are seven, most young children perform as well as adults on laboratory tests of attention (Ristic & Enns, 2015; Rueda et al., 2004). Children's other executive function skills, such as planning, take much longer to develop and will not be fully mature until late adolescence (Doebel, 2020). Many first-graders forget to bring their coats to school, and many fourth-graders may forget their coats on the bus, both age-typical behaviors.

You can see children's fast-developing executive function skills at work in the game Simon Says. Preschool-age children have great difficulty controlling their impulses, which is precisely why Simon Says is so exciting for them but easy and thus boring for older children. Scientists created the "head-toes-knees-shoulders" task, a game that is similar to Simon Says, in which children must first imitate and then do the opposite of what an adult tells them to do. Accomplishing this task requires children to stop themselves from imitating what the adult says and does, remember the rules, and focus their attention. The game is challenging for 3-year-olds; half of them cannot follow the directions at all (Ponitz et al., 2008). Children's performance is three times as accurate by the time they are in first grade (von Suchodoletz et al., 2013).

A number of factors influence whether young children will use their attention or executive function at any given time (Zelazo, 2020). Too much excitement may make it difficult for children to focus, and what motivates one child may bore another. For instance, in one experiment, preschool boys tended to perform better on some tests of executive function because they were less excited than the girls about the reward they would receive for participating: glittery stickers (Garon et al., 2012). Emotional involvement can also sometimes help children focus. As experienced teachers will remind you, effective learning means that children are emotionally engaged in what they are learning, like listening to stories they enjoy rather than those that bore them (Lennox, 2013).

Motivation plays a critical role in attention and executive function. Both intrinsic and extrinsic motivation foster executive function. Scientists have found that children who think they are going to receive a reward tend to pay more attention than those who aren't expecting a reward (Anderson et al., 2011; Gmeindl et al., 2016).

The development of self-control and attention is partially driven by brain maturation. Remember that the prefrontal cortex, the region linked to logical thought, matures and becomes more connected to other parts of the brain during the preschool years, allowing children to better control their behavior. As the prefrontal cortex matures, it also becomes more connected to other parts of the brain, giving it a faster and stronger influence on children's behaviors (Posner et al., 2016). However, the circuits that connect the prefrontal cortex to the subcortical structures of the brain, such as the amygdala, where emotion is processed, are slow in maturing. The late development of these circuits makes it challenging for children to control their impulses in emotional or stressful circumstances (Perone et al., 2018; Zelazo & Carlson, 2020).

The development of executive function is also shaped by experience, practice, and context. Early childhood is a critical period for children to learn these skills (Diamond & Ling, 2016). Children who spend a lot of time engaging in pretend play and who have opportunities to make choices on their own often display well-developed executive function skills, although it is not clear whether this is a cause-and-effect relationship or is simply a correlation (Munakata & Michaelson, 2021). Children with more sophisticated language skills, including the use of private speech, also tend to have stronger executive function skills (Gooch et al., 2016).

Early environments that are chaotic, unpredictable, and stressful may make it difficult for children to practice and improve their executive function skills. Health difficulties such as exposure to pollution can contribute to difficulties with executive function (Gatzke-Kopp et al., 2021). Caregivers who have strong executive function skills themselves can help children build their executive function abilities (Chen et al., 2020).

Early-intervention programs and formal school can help children who have difficulties with executive function (Zhang, Wang et al., 2019). Some interventions teach mindfulness and prompt children to reflect on their behaviors (Semenov et al., 2020). Others encourage executive function through physical activities like Tae Kwon Do or basketball. Some programs boost focus within relationships both at home and at school.

In one intervention called Tools of the Mind, children work on self-control through group play and make-believe. The focus is on helping children be intentional and reflective, by encouraging them to make "play plans" before engaging in an activity. Based on Vygotsky's theory of learning, activities are designed to engage children where they are in their learning, in their zone of proximal development. At home, parents encourage impulse control and the ability to follow directions. In one evaluation of this program, children with executive function delays were able to catch up with their peers after just one year (Diamond & Ling, 2016).

Challenges to Attention and Self-Control Preschoolers are full of energy. However, this worries some families: Nearly half of all parents believe that their preschool children have trouble with attention (Fiks et al., 2016; Jacobson et al., 2018).

In the United States, about 1 out of every 10 children has been diagnosed with **attention-deficit/hyperactivity disorder (ADHD)**, which is characterized by consistent inattention, hyperactivity, or impulsivity that prevents them from functioning

attention-deficit/hyperactivity disorder (ADHD) A condition in which children have challenges with focusing or controlling themselves, that make it difficult to function without extra support at home or in school.

Checking Her Plan In interventions like Tools of the Mind, children are encouraged to plan their play, building their planning skills, fine motor skills, and executive function while having fun in the process.

at school and at home (APA, 2013; Wong & Landes, 2021). While the name of the disorder refers to attention, children with ADHD also have difficulties with executive function that are more profound than what most preschoolers typically experience and that are likely to persist (Nigg et al., 2020). Untreated, children with ADHD are at high risk for academic difficulties and may continue to have trouble functioning as they grow older: Only about 1 in 10 people with ADHD outgrow their symptoms (Hinshaw, 2018; Sibley et al., 2022).

Researchers suspect that ADHD is linked to both genetic and environmental factors. Some neuroscientists suggest that there are differences in the brain structure and connectivity of children who are diagnosed with the disorder compared with more typically developing preschoolers (Guo et al., 2020; Jacobson et al., 2018). However, it is not clear that these differences cause the symptoms of ADHD or if they are a side effect. Some experts also suggest that early stresses and difficulties with early caregiving can contribute to developing ADHD (Hinshaw, 2018; Miller and Hastings, 2019).

Effective treatments are available for ADHD (Wolraich et al., 2019). Some scientists have found that if preschoolers who are at risk receive behavioral and family therapy, including advice about establishing regular routines and supportive disciplinary practices, one in five will no longer meet the criteria for the diagnosis as they grow up (Murray et al., 2021; Sudre et al., 2018). The most common and effective intervention for children with ADHD is medication, such as Ritalin or Adderall (Harstad et al., 2021). Some researchers believe that these treatments may work because they increase levels of dopamine, which activates the reward system in the brain, making it a bit easier for children to do things that may have seemed tedious, like waiting their turn (Schrantee et al., 2016).

Diagnoses of ADHD can be controversial. Some suggest that the disorder might be misdiagnosed or overdiagnosed in some children (Kazda et al., 2021). Others worry that schools and teachers might be too intolerant of children's age-typical levels of energy and exuberance. These researchers point out that every child has a hard time sitting still once in a while, and that diagnoses rise when the demands of school are mismatched with children's age-typical maturity (Caye et al., 2020; Hinshaw, 2018). Still others are concerned that ADHD may be *underdiagnosed* in children who have neurocognitive differences but are treated as if they have a discipline problem (Simoni, 2021).

There are significant gender and ethnic differences in ADHD diagnoses in the United States. Teachers tend to be more likely to identify Black children's behavior as ADHD than similar behavior in a White child (Accavitti & Williford, 2020; Kang & Harvey, 2020). Affluent families tend to be more comfortable with a medical explanation for their children's behavior than less-affluent families, resulting in fewer ADHD diagnoses in low-income children (Owens, 2021; Simoni, 2021). Researchers find that gender plays a role in the patterns observed in ADHD: Girls tend to differ from boys in their symptoms, such as being overly talkative rather than having difficulty sitting still (DuPaul et al., 2020).

Even with treatment, children with ADHD still face difficulties: They are more likely to be expelled from preschools and pre-K programs than their peers (Zeng et al., 2021). One challenge is that teachers and other adults often stigmatize children with ADHD *and* their families, blaming the children and their parents instead of differences in their brain functioning (Metzger & Hamilton, 2021; Nguyen & Hinshaw, 2020).

CAN YOU BELIEVE IT?
Does Waiting to Eat a Marshmallow Mean You'll Be Successful?

Whether experts call it grit, perseverance, or self-control, there is a substantial body of research and popular media attention devoted to helping children (and adults) exert more self-control (Claro et al., 2016; Duckworth & Seligman, 2017). In early childhood,

Waiting for a Treat In the original studies, Mischel did not just use marshmallows to evaluate children's ability to delay gratification. Some were lucky enough to be tested with Oreos, and a few only got pretzels.

self-control means being able to listen in school and pay attention, even when the day seems long.

Researchers have devised multiple ways to measure children's developing self-control, including what is informally known as the "marshmallow test" (Mischel, 2015; Mischel et al., 1989). This task focuses on the *delay of gratification*, or how long children can wait to get something they want—a skill that helps us throughout the lifespan.

Noted social psychologist Walter Mischel developed the marshmallow test in the 1960s in an affluent preschool on the campus of Stanford University (Mischel, 2015; Mischel & Ebbesen, 1970). Children were asked to sit facing a plate with one marshmallow on it and told that they could eat it immediately, or they could wait a little while and get to eat *two* marshmallows. Then, the researchers left the room, telling the children they would be back in a bit and that they could ring a bell if they couldn't wait any longer. Some children were able to wait longer than 17 minutes before ringing the bell. Others grabbed the marshmallow even before the researcher was out of the room. Most waited about six minutes (Mischel, 2015).

Years later, Mischel and his colleagues followed up with the children and found that the children who were able to postpone gratification and wait for two marshmallows were more socially and academically successful when they grew up. Children who were unable to wait very long did not do as well as their peers: They were more likely to develop substance use disorder and less likely to finish college (Mischel, 2015; Shoda et al., 1990). Of course, these results were only a correlation; many factors could have contributed to these long-term results.

Researchers found that children with exceptional cognitive abilities and well-developed executive function skills tended to perform better on the tasks, perhaps because they know how to distract themselves during the long wait (Diamond, 2013). Cognitive skills are not the only factors that lead to success in this task: Social relationships also play a part. Children who are securely attached with sensitive parents have an easier time developing self-control (Dindo et al., 2017). Children who are doing the task with a friend (even one who is in a different room) tend to be able to wait longer than those doing it by themselves (Koomen et al., 2020).

While some researchers and policy makers inspired by Mischel's research went on to design interventions to help children ace the marshmallow test and develop more self-control, other scientists raised some serious questions about the marshmallow task (Mischel, 2015). They replicated the test with different groups and questioned how accurately it predicted the children's future. They found:

- A lack of self-control is not the only reason children might reach for the marshmallow right away. If children saw the experimenter treat another adult unkindly or did not trust the experimenter for some other reason, they were more likely to eat the marshmallow quickly: They may not have thought they could trust the experimenter to keep their word (Michaelson & Munakata, 2020).
- When Mischel's study was repeated with more diverse groups of children, the results were not as conclusive, particularly over time. In these samples, being able to exert self-control alone was not predictive of academic or social outcomes. Among these children, self-control mattered to their success, but it was less important than their performance on cognitive tests or their behavior in school (Watts, Duncan, et al., 2018). Culture matters, too: U.S. children are more accustomed to waiting to receive a present, but Japanese children are better at waiting for food (Yanaoka et al., 2022).

To sum it up, researchers agree that self-control is important, but the difficulties contemporary researchers face in replicating Mischel's work remind us that measuring development is complex. As Vygotsky suggested nearly a century ago, one test cannot represent all of what any preschooler (or adult) can do (Vygotsky & Cole, 1978). And the

Scientific American Profile

Delaying Gratification

theory of mind The ability to understand that other people have different beliefs, ideas, and desires.

best test of science and scientific interventions designed to help children is to make sure they are replicated. 👤

Theory of Mind

Preschool-age children are beginning to understand that not everyone thinks quite the same way they do. They know that Daddy's favorite color is green and that their sister's favorite color is purple. These developments are a sign of preschoolers' growing **theory of mind**, which is the ability to understand that other people have different beliefs, ideas, and desires (Astington et al., 1988; Peterson & Wellman, 2019).

Macmillan Publishers

Researchers test theory of mind with elaborate tricks. In one classic test, they presented children with what appeared to be a box of candy. The child was excited to open it up, only to find that the experimenter had replaced the candies with pencils. The interesting part of the experiment was not that the 3-year-old was disappointed; it was that the 3-year-old was sure that a friend would not be tricked by the box of "candy." Like most 3-year-olds in the experiment, they assumed that everyone else knew what they now knew—that there were pencils in the box (Astington & Gopnik, 1988; Wimmer & Perner, 1983).

Children quickly grow out of this limitation: By age 4 or 5, children have developed a much more robust understanding of other people's minds (Wellman, 2018). They will happily tell an experimenter that someone else would also be tricked by the pencils-in-the-box experiment. They no longer assume that everyone else can read their minds, and they understand that other people often have different perceptions than they do.

What Is Inside That Box? What do you think this 4-year-old will say is inside the crayon box? After he finds out that this box is filled with M&Ms, will he think his mother, who was in the other room, will know that the box is filled with M&Ms? Children who have developed a "theory of mind" will be able to understand that not everyone knows what they know: and that their mother will not guess that a treat hides inside the crayon box.

Theory of mind opens up a new world for children. Once they understand that other people can have different beliefs than they do, they can lie. This is why a 2-year-old is unlikely to fib about eating the last cookie, but a 5-year-old could do so easily (Lavoie et al., 2017).

Not all children develop a theory of mind, or are able to pass the tests that researchers use to measure it, at age 4 or 5. Those who develop it a bit early tend to have more social skills, perhaps because they understand other people better, that others think differently than they do (Hughes & Devine, 2015; Slaughter et al., 2015). Children who are bilingual, and children who have a lot of social interaction with other people (for instance, they have siblings or friends at school), tend to develop a theory of mind earlier (Hou et al., 2020; Hughes, Devine, et al., 2018). Children who have limited early conversational experience, as with babies born with hearing impairment to hearing parents who have not yet learned alternative forms of communication, tend to be delayed in developing theory of mind (Peterson & Wellman, 2019).

In many communities around the world, children generally pass theory of mind tasks between ages 4 and 5, although there are some differences. Children who do not start school until age 6, as in Japan and Italy, tend to pass tests measuring their theory of mind a little later (Hughes et al., 2014). Children who are seldom tested by outsiders, as with children from the remote South Pacific nation of Vanuatu, are often unable to pass the task until early adolescence (Dixson et al., 2018).

CONNECTIONS

Remember from Chapter 5 that autism spectrum disorder (ASD) is a condition that affects cognitive and communication skills. Symptoms include difficulties with social interaction, repetitive behaviors, and obsessive interests.

Children who are diagnosed with *autism spectrum disorder (ASD)* also may also have differences with tests of theory of mind, which may mean they need additional support in understanding other people's social motivations (Jones et al., 2018). In one recent study, only 4 percent of children with ASD had typical responses to assessments of theory of mind (Peterson et al., 2016). Inability to understand other people's motivations can make it difficult for young people with autism to learn from other people—or engage in imaginary play (Kang et al., 2016). Typically, theory of mind builds through experiences with others who have different understandings or beliefs, as occurs in early childhood during interactive play, storytelling, and problem solving, but for children with ASD, differences in brain development may make this challenging (White & Carlson, 2021).

APPLY IT!   **8.1** Like many preschoolers, Aidan is easily confused by the classic cognitive tasks of early childhood. He can sit still, follow directions, and talk about the conservation of liquid, but he may not be able to explain that the amount of liquid remains the same, whether it is in a tall, thin glass or a shorter, squatter one. What logical capabilities would Piaget say Aidan is missing?

8.2 How would you explain to the family of a preschooler the cognitive strengths of early childhood according to Piaget, Vygotsky, and information-processing theorists?

Developing Language in Early Childhood

If you listen to Aidan chattering to his sister, it is startlingly apparent how quickly his language skills have developed. Now, Aidan and Dylan can have a real conversation and take turns speaking. Between ages 2 and 6, children's use of language blossoms (see **Figure 8.3**). Most 2-year-olds can only speak a few hundred words in short sentences. By age 6, most English-speaking children use about 6,000 words and can understand about 14,000 (Carey, 2010; Templin, 1957). For about one in four children in the United States, this language experience is enriched by learning more than one language (U.S. Census Bureau, 2015).

Growth in Vocabulary and Complexity

Children use a number of strategies to build their vocabularies. Most preschoolers only need to hear a new word once before they remember it for weeks or months (Carey & Bartlett, 1978; Kan, 2014). Remember from Chapter 5 that children continue to use their *fast-mapping* skills to quickly learn new words. Attention and social skills

Learning Objective

8.4 Discuss vocabulary and grammar development during early childhood.

FIGURE 8.3 Achievements in Language Development During Early Childhood Language development allows young children to better communicate and express themselves and forms a foundation for success in school. Understanding typical development helps identify children who need extra support.

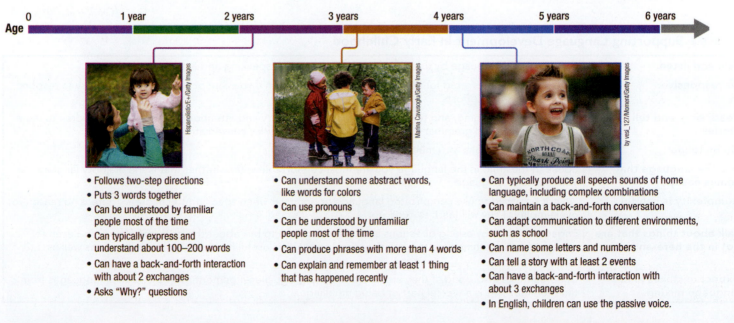

| Age | 0 | 1 year | 2 years | 3 years | 4 years | 5 years | 6 years |

- Follows two-step directions
- Puts 3 words together
- Can be understood by familiar people most of the time
- Can typically express and understand about 100–200 words
- Can have a back-and-forth interaction with about 2 exchanges
- Asks "Why?" questions

- Can understand some abstract words, like words for colors
- Can use pronouns
- Can be understood by unfamiliar people most of the time
- Can produce phrases with more than 4 words
- Can explain and remember at least 1 thing that has happened recently

- Can typically produce all speech sounds of home language, including complex combinations
- Can maintain a back-and-forth conversation
- Can adapt communication to different environments, such as school
- Can name some letters and numbers
- Can tell a story with at least 2 events
- Can have a back-and-forth interaction with about 3 exchanges
- In English, children can use the passive voice.

help preschoolers observe what other people are looking at when they hear new terms (Baldwin & Meyer, 2007).

Children's understanding of grammar is evident as they slowly move from short two-word combinations ("more cookie") into more complicated, sophisticated forms by age 6. Developing more complex language skills often leads to errors. In languages with irregular verb forms, such as English, children often confuse unfamiliar forms, saying "I drinked it" rather than "I drank it." But more familiar irregular forms, such as "ran" rather than "runned," tend to be acquired more quickly (Ambridge et al., 2015).

Many first sentences use basic forms like "No drink, no water, no milk" or "What that?" (Mayor & Plunkett, 2014). As children grow, they begin to grasp more complex grammar and sentence construction, including the passive voice, which adults use less than 1 percent of the time in English. (The passive voice occurs in sentences like "the dog was let out," as opposed to the more common active voice, "she let the dog out.") However infrequently they hear it, most children can use the passive voice in English by the time they are 4 or 5 (Ambridge et al., 2015; Bidgood et al., 2020).

Communicating with other people helps children build their grammar, vocabulary, and articulation skills (Masek et al., 2021a). But the quantity of children's language exposure is not the only important piece: Quality also matters (Masek et al., 2021b). If a preschooler is surrounded by an endless monologue or is just overhearing conversation, they may struggle to acquire new words or more sophisticated grammar. Preschoolers learn more if they are engaged by adults who ask questions such as "why," "when," or "how" (Rowe et al., 2017). Children learn to talk by talking and responding, not just by listening (Ribot et al., 2018).

Families and teachers can help expand children's language skills by extending conversations and gently recasting errors or mispronunciations (see **Table 8.2**) (Alper et al., 2021). Many conversations with children miss opportunities to engage and extend the content and sophistication of their talk (Cabell et al., 2015). This is partly because talking to children takes time. Children can take almost 10 times as long as adults to answer a question, as they work out what to say (Casillas et al., 2016).

Despite this, conversations with preschoolers can be complex, as in this back-and-forth observed while a teacher and a preschooler worked with play dough:

CHILD: My dinosaur is bigger than yours.
TEACHER: Yeah, but mine has got a horn on its head. . . .
CHILD: Mine too. Mine is bigger than yours. Mine is bigger than yours.
TEACHER: Mine has got a big mouth and it's got a sharp horn.

[Cabell et al., 2015, p. 90]

TABLE 8.2 Supporting Language Development in Early Childhood

Talk *and* listen.	Children build language by using it; they need to practice speaking and listening.
Be responsive.	When a child makes a bid for attention or reaches out (even if you cannot quite understand), try to respond to encourage their efforts.
Read, sing, and tell stories.	Reading aloud, singing, and telling stories builds vocabulary and attention and introduces children to more complex words and grammar than they might hear in everyday conversation.
Go on longer.	Aim for conversations with multiple back-and-forths or turns.
Use the language that comes easily.	Speak to the child in the language you are most comfortable with, whether that is the majority language or your heritage language.
Complexity is helpful.	Do not be afraid to use complicated language or grammar when speaking to children. There is no reason to oversimplify: They will learn to keep up.
Talk about things that are not in the here-and-now.	Engage children by asking questions and using language to talk about the past, the future, and even to speculate on why things are the way they are. Language is useful for building thinking skills as well as vocabulary.
Expect mistakes and language mixing.	Children make errors and, if they are raised in a multilingual environment, will mix up their languages from time to time. This is a typical part of being multilingual.

The quality of language skills, such as vocabulary size and level of sophistication, often correlates with children's success in school and in their social relationships (Golinkoff et al., 2019; Suggate et al., 2018). In communities that value extroverted verbal skills, being able to easily articulate yourself is a benefit. Children's language skills tend to build on themselves: Adults tend to talk more with children who have larger vocabularies than with those with smaller ones (Marklund et al., 2015).

About 1 in 10 kindergarteners has trouble with communication, including difficulty with speech articulation or with expressing or understanding language, that may be diagnosed as a *speech-language disorder* (Norbury et al., 2017). Global communication disorders, such as difficulty understanding and expressing language, tend to be more persistent than problems with articulation, such as mispronouncing your *r*s (Fernald & Marchman, 2012; Määttä et al., 2014). Speech-language interventions during early childhood are aimed at supporting children's early language skills while they are still developing rapidly (Norbury & Sonuga-Barke, 2017).

Multilingual Language Development

Most children around the world grow up learning more than one language, which gives them cognitive advantages in addition to the joy of being able to talk to more people (Barac et al., 2014; Hartanto et al., 2019). Early childhood is an important time for multilanguage learners: Children may be more motivated and less self-conscious about learning a new language than they will be when they are older (Oliver & Nguyen, 2018). Young children can pick up a new language through play and immersion with less difficulty than older children can. For children who have never learned a second language, this is the ideal time to begin learning one.

Young children typically have stronger language skills in their home language than in their second language, simply because they have more opportunities for practice (Unsworth, 2016). In Belgium, for instance, where Flemish and French are both spoken, many children's language abilities are weaker in their second language than in their home language (De Houwer, 2020). Similarly, in the United States, many *dual language learners (DLLs)* have stronger language skills in their home language, like Spanish, Mandarin, or Tagalog, than they do in English when they enter preschool, even if they have learned both (Barrow & Markman-Pithers, 2016). Around the world, children with strong language skills in more than one language benefit from extra opportunities to hear and practice their language skills: Maintaining your language skills takes effort (Unsworth, 2016).

In the United States, many DLLs tend to have more limited language development in *both* their home and their second language (Hoff, 2018; Lewis et al., 2016). This may make the transition to kindergarten difficult, but bilingualism itself is not the reason. Many DLLs also have other experiences associated with academic difficulties, like limited opportunities to practice language skills, living in low-income neighborhoods, or lack of access to high-quality early-childhood education (Ansari & Crosnoe, 2018). In other countries, being bilingual is linked to higher academic achievement. For instance, in Singapore, most children enter kindergarten speaking English and a home language such as Mandarin Chinese, Tamil, or Tagalog, and these children score better than their monolingual peers on achievement tests (Sun & Yin, 2020).

Across contexts, researchers have found that children who have strong skills in their home language, large vocabularies, and facility with complex grammar learn a second language more easily, particularly as they move into the dominant language of the culture, like English, in elementary school (Lewis et al., 2016; Ramírez-Esparza et al., 2020).

Quality early education can help narrow the gap for low-income DLLs. When early education is provided in children's home language, it

Share It!

Early childhood is not your last chance to learn a language. Adolescents and adults can still develop the skills they need to develop the proficiency of a native speaker, although immersion, rather than classes, is the most effective method.

(Hartshorne et al., 2018)

CONNECTIONS

Remember from Chapter 5 that people who grow up speaking more than one language are building their executive function and self-regulation skills. Often called *dual language learners (DLLs)*, children who speak multiple languages are not just learning cognitive and language skills, they are also maintaining an important cultural connection.

Sounding It Out in a New Language
Tommy is working on his reading in a preschool in Singapore, where most preschools are multilingual in the official languages of Singapore—English, Chinese, Malay, and Tamil—and children receive daily 45-minute lessons in their heritage language in addition to English (He et al., 2020).

supports language development in both the home language and the second language and contributes to later academic success (Park et al., 2017). Preschool education in children's home language may be ideal, but high-quality preschool in any language can help DLLs become more successful academically later on (Yazejian et al., 2015).

APPLY IT!   **8.3** Aidan's parents are considering sending him to a dual-language kindergarten. What would you tell them about the advantages of learning more than one language in the early years?

8.4 Like most 5-year-olds, Aidan talks differently than many adults. What advice would you give to his pre-K teacher in facilitating responsive conversation with him?

Supporting Early Learning

In an apartment building in Accra, Ghana, 5-year-old Herbert practices his reading with his father, reviewing flashcards and going over his letters before bedtime. His father, Herman, is also focused on making sure that Herbert starts kindergarten ready to learn, so that Herbert can grow up to do "whatever he wants to do" (Aizenman & Warner, 2018). Many longitudinal studies of children's academic performance support Herman's goals. Preschool can build a foundation for children's developing academic skills (OECD, 2017).

Developmental scientists agree that the foundation for learning that happens during these early childhood years is critical, but effective foundations can be built in many ways. Whether children are at home or in school, effective learning experiences harness the energy and imagination of young children and prepare them for the demands of formal schooling.

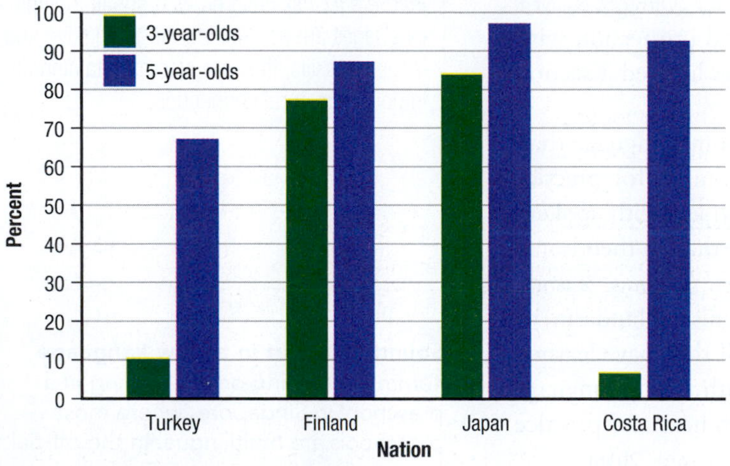

Early Childhood Education

Like Herbert and Aidan, most children around the world begin formal schooling at the end of early childhood, at about age 6 (see **Figure 8.4**). However, the majority are cared for outside of the home at a much earlier age in informal preschools, child-care centers, or kindergartens (Crosnoe et al., 2016). In the United States, where many communities do not have public preschool or pre-K programs, children who attend preschool are from relatively affluent families (NIEER, 2019). In other places in the world where child care and preschool are well supported by the government, such as Finland and Italy, more children attend preschool, and early child care is considered a human right (OECD, 2017). Aidan benefited from going to a community preschool for much of his early childhood and then transitioned to the pre-K program at a nearby public school in New York City. Some of Aidan's preschool experience was disrupted by the COVID-19 pandemic. As his family learned, preschool is difficult to move online, and many communities found that there were concerns about the quality and the equity of the educational materials that were provided (Hashikawa et al., 2020; Timmons et al., 2021).

FIGURE 8.4 Who Goes to Preschool?
About 6 out of 10 preschool-age children in the United States attend some preschool, most commonly a year of pre-K before starting kindergarten at age 5. Parents with more education and higher incomes are much more likely to enroll their children in preschool. Fewer children in the United States attend preschool than in other affluent countries, but the rate of preschool attendance is rising dramatically around the world.

Boosting Skills

Many preschoolers arrive at school filled with a love of learning and desire to acquire skills they think are "fun" (Eccles & Wigfield, 2020). Preschoolers tend to have abundant **intrinsic motivation** to learn. Intrinsic motivation refers to the drive to do something because it is its own reward, whereas **extrinsic motivation** refers to doing something for a tangible reward, for example, more time on the tablet in exchange for

intrinsic motivation The drive to do something because it is its own reward and just doing it feels rewarding.

extrinsic motivation The drive to do something because you are hoping for a reward.

setting the table. In early childhood, intrinsic motivation is critical in helping children succeed in school, because children need to be able to motivate themselves to learn reading, writing, and math (Wigfield et al., 2015). Research shows that many preschoolers are enthusiastic. They love school. Intrinsic motivation is more powerful at driving children's learning than extrinsic rewards are (Alvarez & Booth, 2014). Early childhood educators try to harness children's intrinsic motivation to learn, because it will help keep them engaged throughout their school career (van der Aalsvoort & Broadhead, 2016; Wigfield et al., 2016).

Around the world, research has shown that high-quality preschool experiences boost children's academic skills (Gray-Lobe et al., 2021; OECD, 2017). Early education can help develop *emergent literacy*, or the early reading skills that help children learn how to decode text and write stories. Learning how to read begins with *phonemic awareness*, or being aware of the individual sounds that make up words (Castles et al., 2018). However, literacy goes beyond memorizing sounds and the letters of the alphabet: One big predictor of children's later reading skills is how much time they spend with books and practicing reading and writing. This practice includes being read to, writing letters, or simply flipping through the pages of a board book (Carroll et al., 2019; Grolig et al., 2020).

Also critical to later school success are early math skills, which involve a basic awareness of numbers (see **Table 8.3**). For instance, children should have a sense of *ordinality*, or counting in order, like first, second, third, fourth, and so on. Over time they will also develop the concept of *seriation*, or the ability to order things, such as by size. When children in a preschool classroom order blocks by size, or meticulously count popsicle sticks, they are not just playing, they are actually working on their math concepts.

Many families read to their children, but few practice math. Parents often explain that they are anxious about incorporating math into everyday life (Berkowitz et al., 2015). Asking children to count the number of plates at the table or socks in the hamper can help build math concepts (Hanner et al., 2019). This enables preschoolers to meet the higher expectations many kindergarten teachers have for their students. Many of these teachers tell researchers that they expect their students to be able to count to 100 and write a sentence (Mader, 2020).

Preschool has particular advantages for children whose parents are less affluent or less formally educated or do not speak the majority language; however, these children are often less likely to be enrolled (Gupta & Simonsen, 2016; NCES, 2022; Yazejian et al., 2015). For instance, a year in Head Start, a federal early-education program in the United States

Learning Through Play Around the world, educators engage young children through relationships and fun. In Ghana, in western Africa, this kindergarten has implemented a play-based curriculum that prepares children for learning by boosting their academic and social skills through responsive, playful interactions.

Scientific American Profile

Creativity and Intrinsic Motivation

TABLE 8.3 **What Does It Take to Be Ready for School?**

Self-regulation skills	Can you follow simple instructions? Can you keep working on a task until it is done? Can you settle down after being upset or overexcited?
Social and emotional skills	Are you able to recover from frustration or disappointment most of the time? Can you be caring and empathetic to other people? Can you make a friend? Can you play with other children?
Health	Do you receive any needed health care and other supports to be able to go to school and attend regularly?
Early academic skills	Do you recognize the letters of the alphabet? Can you link sounds to letters? Can you name common shapes and colors? Can you count to 20?

Information from Paschall et al., 2020.

Early Learning Around the World Outdoor time and tricycles are part of universal pre-K in San Antonio, Texas (*left*), where Samantha and her older sister, Addison, enjoy the playground. In London, England (*right*), learning is hands- and goggles-on. Hands-on work is a characteristic of Montessori education, as in this classroom: Hammering helps build fine motor skills and concentration.

that serves low-income families, accelerates children's language skills by an extra six months and their general cognitive skills by three months (Yoshikawa et al., 2016).

Quality Practices

On a playground in San Antonio, Texas, 4-year-olds build castles and cottages in a Lego construction contest (McNeel, 2018). These children are part of San Antonio's ambitious pre-K program that builds their attention, executive function, and social skills through hands-on learning, creative play, and collaboration, rather than an emphasis on reading. The children spend a lot of time outside, growing their own food and stomping in mud puddles (Lieberman, 2019). The effort has paid off: Even though they do not focus on testing, children in the program tend to outperform those from other pre-K programs.

Three thousand miles away, in a classroom in London, England, the scene is calm and orderly. Working by herself, a little girl carefully pours water from one pitcher into another. Another child painstakingly hammers a nail into a tree trunk. These children are part of a preschool program based on the work of Maria Montessori, an Italian physician and teacher who believed children learn best through independent exploration and hands-on practice. Montessori classrooms encourage children to work on their own using specially prepared materials, such as counting beads and wooden blocks, designed to build fine motor, cognitive, and language skills (Lillard, 2016).

The London and San Antonio programs look very different, but they demonstrate some elements common to successful preschools. Experts describe these universal features as *developmentally appropriate practices* (Bredekamp, 1992; NAEYC, 2020). They include:

1. Building warm communities. Children are social learners, so preschools need to build supportive relationships in a safe environment. These responsive bonds are formed not only between teachers and children, but also between children and their peers.
2. Individualized guidance. Children have unique ways of learning, so teaching should be customized to meet their needs.
3. Establishing goals. While successful schools may have different curricula or theories about learning, they all have explicit objectives that guide learning and aspire to build children's skills.

4. Assessment. Keeping track of how children are learning and developing helps educators evaluate the effectiveness of their programs.

5. Supporting families. Preschool programs need to work with families to support their children's learning, whether that means ensuring that caregivers feel that they belong or helping them get extra community support when needed.

High-quality programs often demonstrate the influence of Piaget and Vygotsky by emphasizing children's active engagement in learning. Allowing children to pour water and manipulate blocks in a Montessori classroom inspires them to experiment on their own as Piaget may have appreciated. Sensitive preschool teachers, like those supporting building with Lego blocks in San Antonio, encourage 4-year-olds to move beyond what they have achieved on their own by trying to build higher, more complex structures. In many classrooms, teachers elaborate on children's pretend play, encouraging play dinosaurs to roar together and fly to a meteor. Rather than lecturing in front of the classroom, most preschool teachers can be found on the floor, mentoring children.

Most high-quality preschools harness children's intrinsic motivation and playfulness, rather than drilling them with facts. Experts agree that flashcards and memorization are not developmentally appropriate for 4-year-olds, whose bodies and brains are best prepared to learn when they can move their bodies and manipulate objects to learn about them. In fact, much research indicates that children learn more when they engage in *child-directed* activities rather than *teacher-directed* activities or direct instruction (McCoy & Wolf, 2018). One research study in Accra, Ghana, where Herbert went to preschool, showed that programs that encourage hands-on learning in which children have some choice or autonomy in what they do, like "cooking" in a pretend kitchen, actually develop more academic skills than programs that emphasize memorization and lecture (McCoy & Wolf, 2018).

Programs that balance child-directed work with some structured, teacher-directed activity tend to lead to stronger language and cognitive outcomes (Fuligni et al., 2012; Skene et al., 2022). Emerging research, for instance, suggests that in some programs children may spend twice as much time lining up as they do playing or being physically active. These programs, like one model pre-K program in Tennessee, have been linked to poorer longer-term outcomes, like increased rates of discipline problems and lower test scores (Durkin et al., 2022; Farran, 2016). More balanced programs with more time to play than time spent in transitions, like one in Boston, have been linked to better long-term outcomes, including higher rates of college attendance (Gray-Lobe et al., 2021).

 MAKING A DIFFERENCE
Play Is Work for Preschoolers

Many families will tell you that children should work hard in preschool (Kabay et al., 2017). They are often surprised to hear that drills and workbooks are not the most effective ways to help young children learn (McCoy & Wolf, 2018). Educators also often worry about balancing learning and play in preschool (Rentzou et al., 2019). However, researchers have found when children play, they are learning (Hirsh-Pasek, 2021).

Piaget and Vygotsky valued pretend play in early childhood because it helps children develop cognitive skills such as theory of mind and abstract thinking (Piaget, 1952; Vygotsky, 2016). Make-believe allows children to practice their emotion regulation skills by pretending to be afraid or angry (Slot et al., 2017). Dressing up and working together in a play kitchen or an imaginary spaceship can be so engaging that children are unaware they are building their social, language, and executive function skills (Thibodeau et al., 2016).

Share It!

Playing at home can build skills. Preschoolers stuck at home during the COVID-19 pandemic showed better executive function if they spent more time in open-ended creative play than in more structured or screen-based activities.

(Stucke et al., 2022)

Dressing up as Spider-Man or serving pretend pancakes does not overtly teach children reading or math. Experts have found that *teacher-guided play,* in which a teacher works within the framework of children's play to build academic skills, is typically more effective than direct instruction (Weisberg et al., 2016). Guided play incorporates children's creativity, imagination, and motivation with guidance from an adult to connect it to learning. For instance, in one classroom a teacher writes down students' creative stories and has them act them out. This helps the children build language skills while having fun pretending to be monsters (Nicolopoulou et al., 2015). This teacher is meeting children at their developmental level and using creative play to help them grow academically.

Encouraging Learning at Home

Halfpoint/iStock/Getty Images

A Little Math Before Bed Responsive communication is important to young children's development and can even include a little counting practice, as this father tries with his little one at home Slovakia.

Children who do not attend a preschool program can nonetheless prepare for formal schooling. Parents can help by reading with their children, engaging them in conversation, and doing simple math problems (Loeb, 2016; York et al., 2019). They can also encourage play that builds executive function and fine motor skills, from dress-up to arts and crafts (LaForett & Mendez, 2017). Families can cultivate their children's social and emotional skills by adopting positive disciplinary practices and maintaining high expectations (MacPhee et al., 2018).

Children from high-income families tend to develop academic skills earlier than children from lower-income families in the United States. However, thanks to increasing enrollment in preschool, these gaps are narrowing (Bassok et al., 2016). Researchers believe the gaps occur because high-income families have more financial resources to spend on cultural or educational activities and more time for intensive, one-on-one play and instruction (Reardon & Portilla, 2016). Systemic challenges are the primary cause for the differences. However, while developmental scientists advocate for institutional changes to help boost the academic readiness for young children, they also point to ways individual families can help their children succeed. These include encouraging parents to believe they can shape their children's cognitive development through back-and-forth responsive communication, time for open-ended play, and regular routines (Alper et al., 2021; Doebel & Lillard, 2021; Moore et al., 2020). Ideally this enrichment happens as an easy add-on to families' existing routines: Researchers have had success encouraging families to see writing the grocery list, setting the table (and counting the plates), and including children in meal-time conversations as ways of boosting their thinking (Leyva et al., 2022).

Researchers have found that resilient families have particular social and emotional strengths, such as knowing when and how to take care of themselves: Caregivers who are depressed or stressed have more difficulty providing children with cognitive stimulation (Pratt et al., 2016). Relationships also matter. Even in families who experience adversity, strong parent–child relationships promote cognitive resilience and school success (Anderson, 2018).

APPLY IT! **8.5** During the COVID-19 pandemic, there were weeks when Aidan could not attend in-person school. What activities or practices would you have recommended to his family to encourage cognitive growth at home?

8.6 Aidan's family is not sure what to look for in a quality after-school program. What would you recommend they look for?

Wrapping It Up ⊙⊙

LO 8.1 Identify the key features of Piaget's preoperational stage. (p. 191)

Piaget's stage of preoperational thought spans the period of about ages 2 to 7. Young children's thinking is now symbolic but not quite logical. Most children can use language and their imagination to talk about things they cannot see, but they cannot perform logical mental operations, like mentally reversing or undoing something that just happened or considering multiple perspectives on a problem. Classic Piagetian tasks, like the conservation and three mountains tasks, illuminate the gaps in children's thinking.

LO 8.2 Apply Vygotsky's theory of development to young children's thinking. (p. 191)

Vygotsky believed that children's cognitive maturation results from social interaction and is best when customized to the needs of the individual learner. Vygotskian researchers suggest that children learn best with sensitive guidance, or scaffolding, in the zone of proximal development (ZPD). Children may talk to themselves, or use private speech, to help direct their own thinking or activity.

LO 8.3 Describe advances in information-processing skills during early childhood. (p. 191)

During early childhood, memory and attention advance, as well as the executive function that will enable children to sit still at school. Episodic memory improves dramatically due to brain maturation and practice, but semantic memory remains immature. Improvements in working memory help children learn to read, count, and follow directions. Their attention and executive function are still developing, but they are increasingly able to focus and regulate their own behavior. Children at this age are also developing *theory of mind*, the ability to see things from other people's perspective.

LO 8.4 Discuss vocabulary and grammar development during early childhood. (p. 205)

Children's language grows dramatically between ages 2 and 6. By age 6, most English-speaking children use about 6,000 words and can understand about 14,000 words. Many children speak more than one language. Children's grammar becomes more sophisticated. Language growth happens through high-quality, responsive conversations. Most children typically have stronger language skills in their home language than in their second language, because they have more opportunities for practice.

LO 8.5 Explain developmentally appropriate early education. (p. 208)

Early education, in preschool or at home, develops children's early academic skills. Quality preschools come in many different forms, but they all nurture strong relationships and harness children's intrinsic motivation to learn. Play can help children learn in and out of school. Building children's executive function and cognitive skills can also happen at home or at school, through arts and crafts, pretend play, or engaging conversations.

KEY TERMS

preoperational thought (p. 191)
animism (p. 192)
conservation tasks (p. 194)
three mountains task (p. 195)

egocentrism (p. 195)
scaffolding (p. 197)
zone of proximal development (ZPD) (p. 197)
private speech (p. 198)

episodic memory (p. 199)
working memory (p. 199)
executive function (p. 200)
attention-deficit/ hyperactivity disorder (ADHD) (p. 201)

theory of mind (p. 204)
intrinsic motivation (p. 208)
extrinsic motivation (p. 208)

CHECK YOUR LEARNING

1. According to Piaget's constructivist theory, which stage of cognitive development in early childhood includes symbolic thought but limitations to logic?
   a) Concrete operations
   b) Sensorimotor
   c) Preoperational
   d) Formal operations

2. Which of these helps explain the risks of accidental injury in early childhood?
   a) Preschoolers lack the physical coordination and the ability to think through the possible consequences of their actions.
   b) Preschoolers cannot feel pain, so they do not mind falling off the monkey bars.

   c) Young children cannot learn from their experiences, so they tend to repeat dangerous behaviors.
   d) Young children need some painful experiences in order to learn how to be safe in the world.

3. When applied to the thinking of early childhood, *egocentrism* means that:
   a) young children do not care about other people.
   b) young children have difficulty seeing the world from others' point of view.
   c) young children want all the attention to be on them at all times.
   d) young children's brains are growing from the center outward.

4. Which skill is developed as young children's executive function improves?
   a) Excelling at the game Simon Says
   b) Being able to climb a ladder
   c) Long-distance vision
   d) Speaking four-word sentences

5. Which statement about learning and speaking more than one language in early childhood is FALSE?
   a) A majority of children around the world learn more than one language.
   b) Children are likely to become confused if learning more than one language at the same time.
   c) Children learning two languages may show smaller vocabulary in each language during the early childhood years.
   d) Children learning two languages show some stronger executive function skills than children learning only one language.

6. A preschool child who is practicing skills like building a block tower in a specific order and learning to pour liquids may be in which type of preschool program?
   a) Developmentally inappropriate
   b) Academically focused
   c) Vygotskian
   d) Montessori

7. What are some key features of Vygotsky's sociocultural theory, and how can they be applied to providing developmentally appropriate practices in preschool classrooms?

Social and Emotional Development in Early Childhood

© Macmillan, Photo by Sidford House

Olivia has a ready smile and dances to any song she hears (even if she is unsure of the words). Now almost 4, she was a miracle baby, born prematurely and weighing just 3 pounds after her mother, Brionnah, developed dangerously high blood pressure midway through her pregnancy. Fortunately, Brionnah's health improved after Olivia was born, and Olivia was an "easy baby": Her mother recalls that even in the hospital, she was quiet and content. But as she has grown, Olivia has become an outgoing, empathetic child who can always make her mother laugh. She is sweet to other children, always the first to congratulate a friend for getting something right or to hug someone who is having a bad day.

Olivia is not just learning about other people's feelings and how to be kind, she is also learning about her own emotions and ideas. Olivia's parents have encouraged this, respecting Olivia's emerging ability to say what she wants. They even set up their apartment so Olivia can reach the snacks she wants and find the toys she loves on lower shelves. As developmental theorists would suggest, Olivia is filled with the capability and initiative of early childhood, ready to explore the world.

Like many children, Olivia transitioned from a cozy life at home with her mother, father, and the occasional babysitter, to life at preschool. There, Olivia faced a new routine of required morning circle time, assigned cubbies, lining up for recess, and waiting until she was called upon to share her ideas. Preschool is not always a perfect fit for the exuberant initiative that is characteristic of children this age. Olivia's parents and her good-natured teacher, Jennifer, needed to strategize about

215

how to support Olivia's adjustment. Three- and four-year-olds have no shortage of creative ideas and dance routines, but they are not always ready for the more controlled behavior expected by teachers managing a classroom of children.

Many children have to work hard to control their strong feelings when things do not go their way. Emotions can be overwhelming in early childhood, and meltdowns are sometimes unavoidable. Developmental scientists point out that many adults, even parents and teachers, often overestimate the capabilities of young children, who may be able to talk and walk and play but are not experts in self-control. Providing understanding caregiving, like the warmth and empathy shown by Olivia's parents, and consistent expectations, make the adjustment easier.

In this chapter, you will read about the hallmarks of social and emotional development during early childhood. Preschoolers' emotion regulation and self-control are more mature than in the toddler years, but these are still peak years for hitting, crying, and melting down. Young children make mistakes, messes, and even enemies on the playground. Nevertheless, with guidance, they can learn to be kind and develop an early sense of identity.

For Olivia, life at school got easier. She got used to the routine, and her mother observes that Olivia now feels even more competent and confident. Both Olivia and her family are excited about the future.

Development of Self

© Macmillan, Photo by Sidford House

Scientific American Profile

Meet Olivia

Learning Objectives

9.1 Analyze advances in emotional expression and regulation during Erikson's stage of initiative versus guilt.

9.2 Describe features of young children's understanding of their identity or self-concept.

A typical 2-year-old knows their name and may be able to tell you about their big brother or baby sister. By the time that toddler turns 6, they will be able to describe what they are good at (almost everything) and manage feelings that may have reduced them to tears or tantrums when they were younger. In early childhood, children develop emotion regulation and a sense of who they are that will help them succeed in the years to come (Robson et al., 2020). Developing these skills is not something that happens magically: It takes practice and patience.

Erikson's Theory of Early Childhood Development

If you watch preschoolers on the playground, you might be impressed by their willingness to try new things. Most of the time, young children are confident enough to "go for it," jumping off the monkey bars even if they might scratch a knee. Erik Erikson describes this enthusiasm as *initiative*. Remember from Chapter 2 that each of Erikson's eight stages of human development involves a unique psychological crisis. The third stage, which occurs between ages 3 and 5, is known as **initiative versus guilt** (Erikson, 1950/1993; see **Table 9.1**).

initiative versus guilt Erikson's third stage of development, which occurs between ages 3 and 5 and involves the conflict between children's enthusiasm to try new things independently and their remorse when they get things wrong.

TABLE 9.1 Erikson's Stage of Initiative Versus Guilt

Stage	Age	Characteristics
Initiative versus guilt	3–5 years	Children have abundant *initiative*, or enthusiasm, to try new things and do them independently. They are also often disappointed when they do things incorrectly. Some *guilt*, or remorse about getting things wrong, ensures that children learn to be careful with other people's feelings and to work toward getting things right. Healthy development requires children to preserve their initiative without feeling too much guilt about making mistakes.

Initiative is abundant in preschoolers' play. They are anxious to be like "big kids" and grown-ups, whether that means buckling their car seat by themselves or pretending to be a parent while doing make believe. This drive is accompanied by the risk of failure. In early childhood, milk is spilled. It is hard to settle down when it is bedtime or when a teacher says it is time to stop playing and join circle time. Feelings of guilt emerge as preschoolers recognize these shortcomings, which can become amplified when someone responds insensitively.

Erikson's insight was that healthy development requires a balance between preschoolers' initiative and guilt. Shame or guilt may arise if adults respond with too much anger or frustration over children's mistakes. This might lead to a hesitancy to take healthy risks later in life. On the other hand, if children are not given limits and protections, they may never learn to take responsibility and follow the rules. In Erikson's view, caregivers and teachers can help children successfully navigate the crisis of early childhood by protecting them with limits, while allowing them to preserve their imaginative dreams.

For Olivia, both her preschool and family try to respect her enthusiasm by combining predictable structure with choices she can make on her own. When Olivia gets home from school, she knows she can choose between reading a story or doing some art, and she knows where to find the markers and paper that are just for her. Her family supports Olivia's initiative while decreasing the likelihood that she will be frustrated because she cannot watch TV all afternoon.

On Her Way to Third Paulina is playing tee-ball near her home in Las Cruces, New Mexico. Like other activities, learning how to play a sport requires emotion regulation and initiative—the courage to try something new even if it may not work out.

Emotion Regulation in Early Childhood

As toddlers grow into preschoolers, adults expect them to control their behavior and their feelings. Children who are successful in developing *emotion regulation* have an easier time adjusting to the world as they grow (Denham, 2019; Harrington et al., 2020). Brain maturation and cognitive development help preschoolers learn to control their emotions (Grabell et al., 2022). Emotional maturation also happens in a social context: Children learn different ways of expressing their feelings from their communities, differences that in turn will shape how their brain and bodies respond to the world around them (Kitayama & Salvador, 2017).

Advances in Self-Regulation During early childhood, children become more *self-regulated* when it comes to managing their feelings, rather than depending on others to help calm them down. Toddlers may cling and wail when dropped off at day care, but children who are Olivia's age are expected to arrive at school and say goodbye without too much upset, although that does not always happen. Preschoolers are even expected to modulate their positive feelings: When Olivia is excited about getting to play outside during recess, her teachers remind her to use her "inside voice."

There are cultural and individual differences in families' expectations for their children, such as whether children are expected to be happy and friendly in public, or whether an occasional bout of jealousy is acceptable or hidden (Ding et al., 2021). However, preschoolers around the world are expected to grow more independent and more capable of managing their feelings. This does not mean that 3-year-olds do this as well as adults: Preschoolers have many ups and downs and meltdowns. Younger children are particularly prone to bouts of upset, tantrums, and separation anxiety, which resolve but do not completely disappear as they get older (Battaglia et al., 2017; Wakschlag et al., 2018).

Caregivers often have unrealistic expectations of their preschoolers' capabilities (Zero to Three, 2016c). For instance, most think that preschool-age children should be

CONNECTIONS

Remember from Chapter 6 that *emotion regulation* refers to the ability to manage emotions appropriately to the situation.

Share It!

Blame it on the game. How do you guarantee frustration in a preschooler? When researchers are studying emotion regulation, they use specially designed video games that show the player failing and disappointing people again and again.

(Grabell et al., 2022)

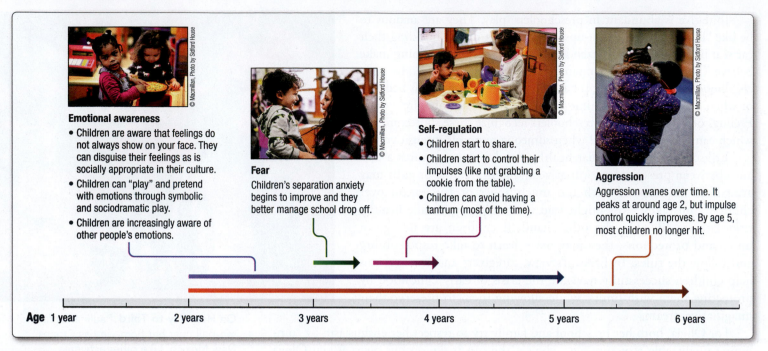

Emotional awareness
- Children are aware that feelings do not always show on your face. They can disguise their feelings as is socially appropriate in their culture.
- Children can "play" and pretend with emotions through symbolic and sociodramatic play.
- Children are increasingly aware of other people's emotions.

Fear
Children's separation anxiety begins to improve and they better manage school drop off.

Self-regulation
- Children start to share.
- Children start to control their impulses (like not grabbing a cookie from the table).
- Children can avoid having a tantrum (most of the time).

Aggression
Aggression wanes over time. It peaks at around age 2, but impulse control quickly improves. By age 5, most children no longer hit.

Age 1 year   2 years   3 years   4 years   5 years   6 years

FIGURE 9.1 Emotion Regulation in Early Childhood As children grow, they are better able to manage their feelings on their own in the ways that their communities expect. During early childhood, children still need help and encouragement to manage big feelings, but meltdowns typically become less frequent.

CONNECTIONS

Recall from Chapter 8 that as many as 1 in 10 children in the United States will be diagnosed with ADHD.

psychological disorders Disruptions in feelings, thinking, or behavior that interfere with a person's ability to function in everyday life.

able to share and to avoid tantrums when they are just 2½. However, most developmental scientists think most children are not capable of these accomplishments until at least age 4, and even then they should not be expected to control themselves consistently (see **Figure 9.1**).

Difficulties with Emotion Regulation Some young children struggle more than others with emotion regulation. **Psychological disorders** can occur when disruptions in children's feelings, thinking, or behavior interfere with their ability to function in everyday life. It is estimated that if all preschoolers were screened, one in five would meet the diagnosis for a psychological disorder: a number that increased during the early part of the COVID-19 pandemic (Panchal et al., 2021; Whalen et al., 2017). Such children might get overly upset at being separated from their families or experience atypical fears or phobias (Mian & Gray, 2019). Some acquire skills to manage these challenges, but those who continue to have emotional difficulties benefit from treatment (Finsaas et al., 2020).

Developmental scientists have identified some early warning signs for emotion regulation conditions that are not age-typical. For instance, children who get upset very quickly and frequently, or who hurt people or damage property when they are distraught, may not outgrow their difficulties without intervention (Wakschlag et al., 2018). Children whose anxiety does not improve may also need extra help (Battaglia et al., 2017). Preschoolers who have trouble managing their feelings need encouragement, modeling, and reinforcement (Dunst & Espe-Sherwindt, 2017).

Some children have trouble regulating their emotions because of early trauma, such as witnessing family or community violence or being seriously injured (Bartlett, 2021). More than one in four children will experience early trauma and are at higher risk to develop psychological conditions such as PTSD, anxiety, and depression (Copeland et al., 2018). Family therapy can build resilience after adversity by fostering and reinforcing strong relationships. Teachers help by providing *trauma-informed care*, in which consistent, warm relationships nurture strong attachments and scaffold children's ability to regulate their feelings (Loomis, 2018). As you will read, first responders are also trying to keep children protected, so they are less likely to develop traumatic responses.

SCIENCE IN PRACTICE
Sgt. Osvaldo Garcia, Advocate of Trauma-Informed Policing

Osvaldo Garcia is a muscular police officer who has worked in New Haven, Connecticut, for many years. He is also an expert at mindful breathing and working with small children. He has some firsthand experience, and extra patience, from raising three of his own, but he has also worked closely with researchers to learn how to protect young children who are in crisis.

As a police officer, he has been first on the scene with children in traumatic situations more times than he can count: He has intervened in cases of family violence and interviewed children who witnessed shootings in their neighborhoods.

To help these children, Sgt. Garcia became an expert in mindful breathing and trauma-informed policing (de la Fontaine et al., 2021). He teamed up with mental health professionals and spent days in the classroom trying to understand how to apply developmental science to his police work. He has even become a trainer, explaining to fellow officers how important it is to protect children in times of crisis.

Sgt. Garcia has learned that experiencing trauma will change children. He explains that these situations will change their daily lives and that their minds may constantly replay what has happened. He understands that children under stress might respond in any number of ways that are age appropriate: They might giggle, stare off into space, or just cry and be clingy, even to a parent who has just been violent (Marans & Hahn, 2017).

Parents and other adults might not want to accept that children have experienced a crisis: They might believe that children slept through it or were distracted by the TV. Sgt. Garcia tells them the truth: that children pick up on more than adults realize, and in addition to the other stresses people in crisis need to manage, caregivers must address children's reactions to difficult experiences.

Sgt. Garcia is aware that interacting with police can often be a source of trauma itself: Many children are afraid of the police. His job is to avoid exposing children to trauma whenever possible: avoiding making arrests in front of children and ensuring that they always have someone safe to take care of them. Since Sgt. Garcia is often the first person a child sees after something horrible has happened, he must be honest, reassure them that he is there to protect them, and address their worries, even if that means checking under the bed and in closets.

He also offers these children some techniques to cope with stress, because even preschoolers can calm themselves down. He teaches them to breathe quietly, to do something with their hands to distract themselves, like color, and to make sure they have a safety plan and a safety person in case something scary happens again. His dream is that making children feel safe will help them do a little better in the future.

Brain Maturation for Self-Regulation Brain development and new cognitive strategies help young children better manage their feelings. Olivia is developing her own strategies, including deep breaths, yoga poses, using her words to talk about her frustration, and distracting herself by thinking about something she likes (like snack!).

Young children, as well as the rest of us, process emotions through networks connecting the *subcortical* parts of the brain with the more logical prefrontal cortex. These circuits mature over a long time, beginning before birth and continuing into early adulthood. That long period of maturation allows experiences and environment to shape our emotional expression (Tottenham, 2020). Emotion-regulating networks become more robust around age 4 or 5, at which point the prefrontal cortex can help children to control impulsive actions and to calm upset feelings (Gee, 2016; Zelazo, 2020).

However, these networks do not develop identically in all children. Major adversity can alter them, resulting in and reflecting anomalies in emotion regulation

(Van Tieghem et al., 2021). These networks need to be "just right": Difficulties in early care-giving experiences or too much stress may make subcortical structures too sensitive or not sensitive enough. For instance, children who have difficulty regulating emotions may be overly sensitive and may overreact to new or scary events. On the other hand, children who are not sensitive enough may be unimpressed by a teacher's command to stop and listen. Just because children *can* control their behavior does not mean that they will always be able to do so; they may not know that it is necessary or may be tired, hungry, or overexcited.

One way scientists study children's growing emotional maturity is to ask them what they would do if they received a disappointing gift, in what is called the *disappointing gift task* (Saarni, 1984). By age 6, most children can mask their true feelings if they receive a gift that is not quite right with a polite smile or other appropriate behavior (Cole & Jacobs, 2018; Ip et al., 2021). They may be able to use their developing cognitive skills, like their theory of mind or perspective-taking ability, to control how they display their emotions. Remember, children can lie by this age, and they may use this new cognitive skill to avoid hurting a gift giver's feelings (Demedardi et al., 2021). This is a sign of emotional maturity and a form of kindness. How many times have you told someone their new haircut looked great?

Culture and Socializing Emotions *Emotional socialization* is the process of learning how to express feelings in a way that is appropriate for your culture (Eisenberg, 2020). Sometimes children are explicitly taught how to express emotions, such as when Olivia's teacher, Jennifer, tells Olivia to talk about what she feels. At other times, children learn by watching others express their emotions. Families' *ethnotheories*, or beliefs about why emotions happen and how to display them, are a crucial part of emotional socialization (García Coll et al., 1996; Liu, Harkness, et al., 2020).

How children display their feelings is far from universal. For instance, many communities, including some in the United States, value being emotionally expressive. In these families, intense emotional behavior, like tantrums or howls of joy, may be expected and even appreciated (Perez Rivera & Dunsmore, 2011; Raval & Walker, 2019). In some U.S. studies, families who identified as Black or White were more likely than parents who identified as Latino or Asian to believe that "kids will be kids" and tended to have more acceptance of their children's expressions of their feelings and even their misbehavior (Labella, 2018; Parker et al., 2012).

Other communities' ethnotheories value emotional restraint. For instance, in the United States, Mexican American mothers are less likely to talk about emotions with their preschoolers than White American mothers (Eisenberg, 1999; Lugo-Candelas et al., 2015). Preschoolers in nations like India, Japan, Korea, and China tend to be less emotionally expressive and more self-controlled (Grabell et al., 2015; Yang & Wang, 2019). Emotional restraint even extends to picture books (Ding et al., 2021). Researchers found that in U.S. picture books, children were often depicted with big, outgoing smiles. In Taiwanese books, however, the smiles were calmer and less exaggerated (Tsai et al., 2007).

Families' emotion-regulation strategies often reflect cultural values (Halberstadt et al., 2020). Many U.S. families value independence and expect that even young children will learn to manage their strong feelings on their own (Corapci et al., 2018). (See **Figure 9.2**.)

Despite the variations in emotion socialization, some practices have been found to foster preschoolers' emotion regulation across diverse communities. *Emotion-coaching* involves adults strategizing or problem solving with their children about how to manage feelings while setting limits (Gottman, 2011; Katz et al., 2020). Other supportive techniques include empathic listening or physical comfort, like hugs (Bergnehr & Cekaite, 2018). Talking about feelings also tends to help build stronger emotion regulation skills (Curtis et al., 2020). Some practices, such as responding with dismissiveness, disdain, or anger, are associated with developmental challenges (Hooper et al., 2018; Marçal, 2021).

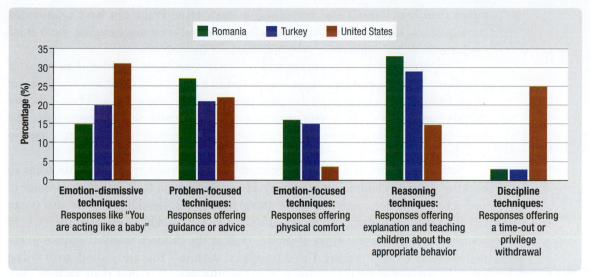

Data from Corapci et al., 2018.

Developing a Sense of Self

If you talk to a group of 4-year-olds, they will tell you that they are going to be celebrities, inventors, presidents, and NBA stars. This is because, as Erikson predicted, young children display a great deal of initiative and confidence as they develop a sense of who they are, called a *self-concept* (Harter, 2015). Preschoolers' self-concept is typically more positive than at any other time during the lifespan (Dweck, 2019; Wigfield & Eccles, 2020).

As children grow, their understanding of who they are becomes more complex. In early childhood, self-concept is initially limited by children's concrete thinking and tends to be based on very tangible characteristics, such as "I like pizza" or "I have red hair" (Pesu et al., 2016). As they grow, children are building an early physical self-concept, or *body image* (Rodgers et al., 2017). Even in preschool, children may have a sense of how they do in school, an early *academic self-concept* (Compagnoni & Losenno, 2020). By age 4 or 5, children can describe themselves and their self-worth using more general, abstract terms (Cimpian et al., 2017). This is closely tied to *self-esteem*, or how they feel about themselves generally (Harter, 1993; Rosenberg, 1963).

Preschoolers' self-esteem tends to stick: Young children who think they are capable tend to do better in school and are more motivated to succeed (Marsh et al., 2019; Orth et al., 2018). Children who feel negatively about themselves are at higher risk of experiencing difficulties in school and with friends and developing emotional disorders like depression (Keane & Loades, 2017).

Community expectations differ in terms of how young children should express their self-concepts. In Olivia's classroom, her teacher, Jennifer, enthusiastically cheers when a child does something good, like staying seated during circle time. Her encouragement of positive self-concept and appreciation of pride is neither unusual nor universal (Raval & Walker, 2019). When researchers observed how preschoolers in Japan and the United States reacted to success on a game, they noticed that U.S. children expressed pride when they had been successful. Japanese preschoolers were much less likely to express pride at their successes and much more likely to express embarrassment at their failures (Lewis et al., 2010).

FIGURE 9.2 How Do Families Respond If a Preschooler Has a Tantrum? Practices for managing emotion regulation vary around the world. Researchers asked families in three different countries—Romania, Turkey, and the United States—how they might manage a preschooler's meltdowns. U.S. parents were much less likely to use emotion-focused comforting techniques, like holding or hugging a child, than parents from Romania or Turkey were. U.S. parents were also more likely to use emotionally dismissive techniques and to manage outbursts with time-outs.

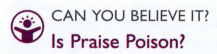

CAN YOU BELIEVE IT?

Is Praise Poison?

If you spend time in a preschool classroom, you will likely hear "Great job!" or "You're the best!" many times throughout the day. Does telling a 5-year-old that they did a great job actually help them work harder? Researchers have found that it may hurt rather than help (Cimpian et al., 2007; Zentall & Morris, 2010). Praise can have unintended consequences, like reducing children's self-esteem and even discouraging them from working hard (Brummelman et al., 2016; Brummelman & Dweck, 2020).

First, preschoolers' self-concept and self-esteem are more sensitive than many of us realize. As young children begin school and face new social situations and pressure to perform, their self-concepts become more fragile (Cimpian, 2017). Their concrete thinking may lead them to misconstrue a comment about something specific, like how they wrote their name, to be an overall commentary on them as a person (Muenks et al., 2018).

Second, decades of research have revealed that certain types of praise seem to backfire, sapping children's motivation, discouraging them from trying their hardest, and actually making them feel worse about themselves. Shockingly, these effects can last for years. In a classic study, scientists tested 4-year-olds to see how they would react to hearing different types of praise. Half of the children received generic praise that focused on their personal characteristics, such as "You are a good artist." The other group was given praise that focused on the process, rather than ability: They were told that they "did a good job drawing."

These slight differences in wording made a big difference. If children had trouble making a drawing, the children who received generic praise were more likely to react emotionally. In fact, they told experimenters that they might just walk away after making a mistake. On the other hand, children who received process-oriented praise had an easier time recovering from mistakes (Cimpian et al., 2007). Over the years, studies with older children and different types of praise have reinforced this finding: Warm encouragement—like a high five—boosts motivation, but telling children they are smart does not (Morris & Zentall, 2014). Too much praise that emphasizes personal characteristics tends to lead to struggles when children encounter inevitable setbacks.

Praise affects children's achievement as well as their motivation. Process-oriented praise helps them to understand that social and academic success happen through hard work and dedication, rather than inborn talent. Indeed, children who receive process-oriented praise seem to be more dedicated to their studies and score higher in tests of reading and math (Gunderson, Sorhagen, et al., 2018).

So, does this mean that adults need to stop being positive? No. But praising the process keeps the focus on effort. Kind words about a preschooler's hard work will enable them to fail gracefully and learn from their mistakes, as they continue to grow.

APPLY IT! **9.1** Olivia wants to "do it by herself." How would Erikson explain her drive to be independent?

9.2 Olivia's teacher encourages her students to talk about their feelings and manage them with yoga and mindfulness. How might these approaches be shaped by culture and community expectations?

Creating an Identity

Learning Objectives

9.3 Discuss the major theoretical viewpoints on gender development in early childhood.

9.4 Describe the development of stereotypes in early childhood.

Preschoolers may still sit in car seats, but they have already developed complex ways of comparing themselves to other people. Young children are quickly learning, imitating, and even overimitating the adults and peers in their lives (Hoehl et al., 2019). Children at this age tend to be more inflexible about labels than people are at other times of life. For instance, young children may rigidly assert that only boys can be firemen or only girls can dance (Poulin-Dubois et al., 2002). Preschoolers' ideas about gender, ethnicity, and other social categories develop along with other aspects of cognition (Wang, Fong, et al., 2021). While most of these ideas become more flexible with time, some biases may persist (Baron & Banaji, 2006; Rhodes & Baron, 2019).

Gender Development

Gender is an important part of the way many children and adults define themselves. In early childhood, children are beginning to develop their *gender identity*, or their sense of themselves as boys, girls, or another less binary or more fluid label (Diamond, 2020). Culture, family, and biology play important parts in helping children understand these social roles.

In early childhood, and across the lifespan, there is diversity in how people express their gender. Many communities are moving away from rigid stereotypes about social roles (Charlesworth & Banaji, 2021). For instance, in some schools in Sweden, teachers and children actively avoid gender labels, revising nursery rhymes to avoid stereotypes and even using gender-neutral pronouns for all children (Shutts et al., 2017). But many families remain more enthusiastic about gender stereotypes (Halim et al., 2018; Parker et al., 2017).

Perspectives on Gender Development Across human history, people have observed that gender distinctions go beyond the binary division of "boys' toys" and "girls' toys" that you will find in the aisles of a big box store. For instance, ancient Chinese medicine taught that all beings included a balance of male and female energy (Furth, 1988). Traditional cultures around the world often incorporated ideas about people who belonged to less binary genders, like the *kitesha* of the Bala people in Zaire, the *bakla* in the Philippines, or the gender-bending Greek god Dionysus (David & Cruz, 2018; Merriam, 1971).

The repercussions of gender stereotypes go far beyond whether parents buy a pink glitter tutu or a football jersey for their 4-year-old. Gender roles are linked to power and social status. For instance, in some communities in India, preschool girls are more likely to get sick than preschool boys, in part because they are less likely to receive vaccinations (Chaudhuri, 2015). On the other hand, in the United States, many families tend to prefer to have girls, and if they have a daughter they will not continue to try for a son (Blau et al., 2020). In many U.S. and European communities, children who do not conform to gender stereotypes, and particularly those who tend to be more feminine, are at higher risk for bullying and may need protection from social rejection (Sullivan et al., 2018; Warren et al., 2019).

Social Learning Theories of Gender In developmental science, the discussion of gender often goes back to Sigmund Freud. Like many thinkers of his time, Freud had some shocking ideas about gender, including a profound belief in women's inferiority (Freud, 1927, 1968a, 1968b; Sauerteig, 2012). But while his more outlandish ideas have been rejected, some of his theoretical ideas continue to be influential (Bell, 2018; Zakin, 2011).

Freud argued that gender is something that children learn as they grow, rather than something they are born with (Freud, 1917/1989). He also believed that children develop a gender identity through *identification*, or modeling their own identity on their same-sex parent (Freud, 1899/1964). Most developmental psychologists still agree that gender roles are learned: Researchers who adopt a *social learning theory* describe the process of learning about gender as occurring through *modeling* and *reinforcement* (Bussey & Bandura, 1999; Mischel, 1966).

From the color of their bedding, to the books they are read, to the toys they play with, children are surrounded by gender messages (MacPhee & Prendergast, 2019). How many of us have seen T-shirts for toddlers printed with gender stereotypes like "Does this diaper make my butt look big?" or "Lock up your daughters" (Barbara, 2019). In families worldwide, gender changes how people treat children. Boys tend to be taken to

Room for Everyone in the Kitchen At this preschool in Stockholm, Sweden, children are encouraged to play together in diverse groups, regardless of their gender identity. Teachers try to avoid stereotypes and make sure everyone has a turn at the play stove.

Jessica Nelson/Getty Images

Stereotypes Versus the Weather
Sometimes the power of stereotypes can defy the weather report. It is not unusual for young children to fall in love with clothes that are inappropriate for the forecast. Children are particularly rigid about categories during the preschool years, which can make them more likely to choose clothing that expresses a strong gender stereotype, even if it means getting cold.

gender roles The social and cultural ideas a person holds about appropriate behaviors or roles of people based on their gender.

gender schema A framework for understanding the world in terms of cultural expectations related to gender identity.

play outside more than girls, and they also receive harsher, more physical punishment (Bornstein et al., 2016).

Researchers call the embedding of gender stereotypes in children's environments—and even their personalities—*gender-typing* (Kollmayer et al., 2018). Children are often expected to adhere to a binary distinction between boys and girls. Boys are expected to be strong, aggressive, and often naughty, whereas girls are assumed to be nurturing, beautiful, and obedient (Halim et al., 2017). Adults may not be aware of their own stereotypes, but they often unconsciously display them. They may frown with disapproval if their son picks up a Barbie or discourage their daughter from dressing as a ninja (Bussey & Bandura, 1999; Endendijk et al., 2019).

Adults and children are much more open to girls who break gender stereotypes than they are to boys. For instance, girls who play sports are often seen as "strong" or "independent," but boys who do ballet are received less warmly (Parker et al., 2017). Boys who do not adhere to stereotypes often face social ostracism and bullying (Leaper & Brown, 2018). Many adults believe boys who are less masculine are gay, and homophobic prejudices amplify the pressure on boys to conform (Skočajić et al., 2020; Sullivan et al., 2018).

Adults and children also *model* ideas about gender (Bussey & Bandura, 1999). **Gender roles** refer to social and cultural ideas about appropriate behaviors or roles of people often based on binary ideas about gender. For instance, in many other-sex, two-parent families, people who identify as women are more likely to be the primary caregivers for children and to do more household chores like cooking and cleaning (Saguy et al., 2021). People who identify as men are more likely to work outside the home full time and do household chores like outdoor work and home repairs.

Young children pick up on ideas about gender by observing the adults in their families and communities (Halpern & Perry-Jenkins, 2016; Sinno et al., 2017). Children who grow up in families where men do more hands-on caregiving tend to have fewer gender stereotypes (Dawson et al., 2015). Some studies have found that, in families with gay and lesbian parents, children often have more flexible stereotypes about gender but tend not to differ from their peers in their sense of their own gender identity (Carone, Lingiardi, et al., 2020; Farr et al., 2018; Sumontha et al., 2017).

Cognitive Theories of Gender Remember from Chapter 8 that preschoolers are rapidly developing the ability to think and assimilate new information but often struggle with logic. These cognitive strengths and limitations are reflected in their thinking about gender categories (Ruble et al., 2007).

In communities around the world, children become aware of social ideas and categories about gender very early in development. For instance, even as toddlers, children identify themselves using gendered labels (Campbell et al., 2002). But between ages 3 and 5, children begin to develop *gender stereotypes*, with the most rigid ones appearing at around age 5 (Martinez et al., 2019). Most preschool-age children, whether they are transgender or identify with their gender assigned at birth, tend to have very fixed and often binary ideas about gender (Gülgöz et al., 2021). This is the age children may clamor for gender-typed clothing.

Young children are often unclear about the relationship between anatomical distinctions and the social categories that refer to gender. Researcher Sandra Bem, who encouraged flexibility about social roles in her own children, recalled the reaction her son received when he wore barrettes to school (Golden & McHugh, 2017). One child suggested that barrettes would turn him, perhaps permanently, into a girl. Another, perhaps demonstrating the egocentrism Piaget might have predicted in a preschooler, along with a characteristic rigidity about gender categories insisted, "Everybody has a penis; only girls wear barrettes" (Bem, 1989, p. 662).

Cognitive theorists suggest that rigid social categories about gender develop as a result of children's use of **gender schemas** (Bem, 1981; Martin & Halverson, 1981). By the time they are toddlers, children organize their world by gender, becoming "gender detectives" to figure out what applies to which gender (Halim et al., 2017). For instance, a 3-year-old girl may look at a screwdriver and think "not for me" and at a pair of sparkly shoes and think "for me." Preschoolers are integrating a vast amount of new information about the world. Although schemas help them assimilate and adapt much of this information quickly, they make children vulnerable to stereotyping of all kinds (Cimpian, 2016).

During early childhood, children typically show an awareness of social groups, and a preference for the gender they identify with (Martin & Ruble, 2010). As a result, social divisions may appear on the playground that reflect the adult social roles children see (Lew-Levy et al., 2020). Children who identify as boys and those who identify as girls often split off and play separately, in what is called *gender segregation* (Maccoby & Jacklin, 1987). As they approach kindergarten age, children become more flexible in their understanding of social categories. This will help them try new things and play with children who are different from themselves (Halim, 2016).

Biological Research on Gender Many people assume that biology, rather than culture, helps to create gender identity in children: This idea is often linked to an insistence that gender is binary and unchangeable (Saguy et al., 2021). Many scientists, as you have seen, point to culture and social expectations, rather than biology, as the main drivers of gender development. Most scientific consensus rejects the idea that there are unchangeable, binary distinctions between genders. In fact, scientists point out that there is no "boy" brain and no "girl" brain: Brain characteristics, like the rest of gender, exist on a continuum rather than a binary divide (Zhang, Luo, et al., 2021). Additionally, neuroscientists are not sure whether any of the minute differences, estimated at just 1 percent, found between the brains of various groups are a function of social experiences or innate distinctions (Eliot et al., 2021; Rippon et al., 2021).

Researchers have found that even though differences in the brain may be small, biology still plays a role in children's gender development. Biology can change how sensitive children are to social messages about gender (Hines, 2020). Prenatal experience may make children more flexible about stereotypes than their peers. For instance, some researchers found that preschoolers who identified as girls and who had been exposed to more testosterone prenatally were more likely to play with toys typically oriented toward another gender than other girls, perhaps because they were less sensitive than their peers to social stereotypes that told them what they "ought" to do (Spencer et al., 2021). However, while biology and life experience both contribute to identity, even in these studies, the absolute differences in ability and brain development between children who identify as boys, girls, or other gender labels are very small (Forger, 2018; Rouse & Hamilton, 2021).

The Influence of the Media on Gender in Early Childhood The people children know in real life are not the only influence on their ideas about gender. Spider-Man, Doc McStuffins, and Barbie may be even more important. Despite recommendations from experts, young children spend nearly three hours on media every day—much of it spent absorbing stereotypes about gender (Chen & Adler, 2019; Rideout & Robb, 2019).

Researchers have found that the more time girls spend watching princess movies, the more likely they are to be drawn to feminine toys. They are also more likely to believe that being beautiful is important and that working hard is not feminine (Coyne et al., 2016). Similarly, boys who spend more time watching superhero movies are more likely to engage in more masculine play like play-fighting than boys who watch more neutral shows do (Coyne et al., 2014). Other research suggests that media also communicates messages about power and gender (Golden & Jacoby,

CONNECTIONS

Remember from Chapter 2 that developmental psychologists like Piaget use the term *schema* to describe how you sort and categorize information as you learn new things.

CONNECTIONS

The biology of sex begins in your genome (see Chapter 3). Zygotes typically have either two X chromosomes (XX) and female reproductive anatomy or an X and a Y chromosome (XY) and male reproductive anatomy. Remember that the biology of gender may be more complex than a simple X and Y. *Gender identity*, or the gender people feel they are, is often less binary than the distinction between boys and girls.

Sometimes Changing the World Requires Strings. In 2017, puppeteer Mansoora Sherzad showed children a puppet from the Afghan version of *Sesame Street*. The puppet, a 6-year-old girl named Zari, is spunky and energetic and loves school. The show's producers hoped that their program would encourage young girls to go to school in a time when schools in Afghanistan were open to all.

2018; Walsh & Leaper, 2020; Ward & Grower, 2020). Many shows feature active, powerful male characters and passive female characters. As a result, the more television children watch, the more likely they are to believe that boys are more powerful and capable than girls, a belief that may stick with children for a lifetime (Halim et al., 2013).

Gender Questioning and Conformity As children grow, most integrate stereotypically male and female interests and characteristics into who they are. Many stay flexible about gender roles, which can be a good thing. Children who are more flexible in terms of interests and stereotypes, and who have more positive attitudes about children who are different from them tend to get along with others better than their peers do (Xiao et al., 2021).

Nikki Kahn/The Washington Post via Getty Images

At some time or another, about one in four preschool-age children feels uncomfortable with the gender they have been assigned: Many are simply dissatisfied with the gender stereotypes or systems they are surrounded by (Halim et al., 2013). Other children may have gender expression that is *nonconforming*, or outside the binary gender stereotypes, but may not identify as *transgender* (Rae et al., 2019). According to most experts, about 1 in 100 children is transgender (Fast & Olson, 2018; Rafferty et al., 2018). Children who identify as **transgender** consistently feel that their gender identity does not match the sex they were assigned at birth. Preschoolers usually begin to verbalize their feelings about their preferred gender between the ages of 2 and 5 (Gülgöz et al., 2019).

For transgender children, the feeling of being in the wrong body is neither a "phase" nor the result of willfulness or unusual parenting. Transgender children's dissatisfaction with the sex assigned to them at birth is very different from the feeling many children report of wanting to break free of gender stereotypes. Experts advise that children's expressed gender identity should be supported (Rafferty et al., 2018). Researchers who have studied children who have transitioned or been affirmed in their new gender find them well adjusted and with stable gender identities similar to those of other children (Fast & Olson, 2018).

Tyler, the Way He Wants to Be Tyler began to explain that he was a boy when he was in preschool. With his family's support, he publicly transitioned to a new name and gender identity when he started kindergarten. Like many children his age, he loves soccer, Spider-Man, and riding his bike.

The Impact of Ethnicity

Young children do not just observe and form stereotypes about gender: They are also keenly observant of other social categories, such as age, beauty, and wealth (Perszyk et al., 2019; Shutts, 2015; Vermeir & Sompel, 2017). By early childhood, children begin to articulate preferences and prejudices about ethnicity and are more aware of discrimination (Banerjee & Eccles, 2019). Without intervention, the effects of these stereotypes can persist (Qian et al., 2017).

Many preschoolers have developed ethnic preferences, frequently favoring their own group but often favoring another, more socially dominant group. Children may internalize the prejudice they experience. In the 1930s, pioneering Black psychologists Mamie and Kenneth Clark asked Black preschoolers if they would rather play with a dark-skinned doll or a light-skinned doll (Clark & Clark, 1939, 1940). The children chose the light-skinned doll and said that the dark-skinned doll was probably bad. In the 1950s, the Clarks' research was pivotal in the famous U.S. Supreme Court case, *Brown v. Board of Education*, which helped to overturn legal segregated public schools in the United States. The Supreme Court agreed with the Clarks that segregation had made Black children feel inferior and that desegregating schools was one way to help repair their self-esteem.

Some scientists have replicated the Clarks' results with children raised in more contemporary communities. For instance, in one study, researchers asked preschool children to plan a birthday party for a group of dolls. White girls preferred to invite White dolls, and so did Black girls (Kurtz-Costes et al., 2011). However, other studies have found that

transgender A gender identity in which someone consistently feels that their gender identity does not match the sex they were assigned at birth.

Black children no longer seem to prefer light-skinned dolls (Davis, 2005; Hraba & Grant, 1970; Jarrett, 2016; Spencer, 2010).

Preschoolers' ethnic preferences and exposure to discrimination occur in communities around the world: In multiethnic societies, as in the United States, it is not unusual for children to prefer a higher status or the majority ethnic group over the others, even at the expense of their own group (Newheiser et al., 2014; Setoh et al., 2019). It is also not unusual for adults, even teachers who care for children, to harbor discriminatory attitudes (see **Figure 9.3**) (Gilliam, 2016).

Children pick up on the prejudices around them, and their innate sense of categorization helps perpetuate this phenomenon. Preschoolers automatically categorize people, as they do objects, and they tend to prefer things they see frequently, such as familiar faces (Qian et al., 2021; Skinner & Meltzoff, 2019). Many children grow out of their ethnic preferences as they do their rigid ideas about gender, but some do not (Lee, Quinn, et al., 2017). Children who are exposed to people from diverse backgrounds are less likely to dislike new or different people. In one research study, children from China who had limited exposure to people who were not Han Chinese learned to differentiate and accept people from other ethnic groups once they were exposed to them (Qian et al., 2019). Similarly, in the United States, children who were exposed to a diverse group of children in preschool had less racial bias later in life and developed more diverse friendships (Gaias et al., 2018; Qian et al., 2017).

In the United States, many preschool teachers and White parents feel that preschoolers are too young to talk to openly about ethnicity or prejudice (Farago et al., 2019). Scientists suggest the opposite: Helping children develop a sense of pride in their background can build resilience in a prejudicial world (Dunbar et al., 2017; Wang, Degol, et al., 2020). White American families rarely talk with their kindergartners about their cultural heritage, but these conversations are common among Black, Latino, and Asian American, and other multiethnic families (Vittrup, 2018). One Black mother explained that she felt that her 3-year-old was not too young to learn about her background: "She needs to understand her heritage, where she comes from and how society is going to react to her as a strong Black female" (Suizzo et al., 2008, p. 298).

APPLY IT!   **9.3** Olivia says she wants to grow up to be "just like Mommy." Freud would describe this comment as an example of what kind of process?

9.4 A preschool teacher with a diverse classroom wonders whether his students are too young to understand social categories and ethnic differences. What would you explain about the current research about children's understanding of social categories?

Why Is She Nice? Documentary filmmaker Kiri Laurelle Davis replicated Mamie and Kenneth Clark's famous 1930s doll test while studying *Brown v. Board of Education* during high school. She showed 4- and 5-year-old children in New York City Black and White baby dolls and asked them to show her the "nice doll." This little boy (like 15 out of the 21 other children) picked up the White doll. "And why is that the nice doll?," Davis then asked. "Because she's White." More than 70 years after the Clarks' pioneering work, this film demonstrated that young children still showed signs of internalized bias.

FIGURE 9.3 Bias in Preschool Which child is acting up? When scientists asked teachers to look at a photograph similar to this one and identify which children were causing trouble, 43 percent identified a Black child. In reality, none of the children was doing anything wrong. How do you combat this conscious or unconscious prejudice in the classroom? Some scientists suggest educating teachers about bias, combating teachers' classroom stress, training to identify true behavioral challenges, and alternative methods for managing disruptions (Gilliam et al., 2016).

Family Relationships in Early Childhood

Learning Objective

9.5 Describe variations in parenting practices and styles and how they affect children's development.

Spend any amount of time with a parent of a preschooler and you will likely hear a similar mix of joy, optimism, and a little guilt that we heard from Olivia's parents. As Brionnah explained to us, she finds "so much joy" in being Olivia's mother. Olivia's big grin can make Brionnah's day. Nevertheless, Brionnah still sometimes worries about the future—about kindergarten and whether she is preparing Olivia for what she will face next. Indeed, developmental scientists argue that although family is critical in early childhood, many factors in development are not within a family's control (Lansford & Bornstein, 2020; Teti et al., 2017). For instance, Brionnah's challenges getting through college as a working parent and finding an affordable apartment have much more to do with systemic societal issues than with her parenting skills.

Parental Beliefs

During early childhood, families build on the foundation set in infancy to create habits of relating that can impact children's development for a lifetime (Groh et al., 2017; Sroufe, 2016). However, parenting preschool-age children is often difficult. The years between ages 2 and 4 are some of the most stressful for parents, as their children demand time, patience, and attention (Olson et al., 2017; Weaver et al., 2015). Caregivers who feel competent and capable, who have positive beliefs about their preschoolers, and who believe that their parenting makes a difference tend to have an easier time (Bornstein, 2015). (See **Infographic 9.1**.) Brionnah, for instance, takes a lot of responsibility for her daughter's behavior.

Like Brionnah, caregivers from Black and Latino backgrounds are more likely to agree that their children's successes or struggles are due to parenting. This can be a good thing: Parents who feel that they have a lot of control over their children's outcomes are more likely to invest in their children and, like Brionnah, to offer more effective, supportive caregiving (Bornstein et al., 2011). However, not all families agree that their children's success depends on the quality of their parenting: Only about half of U.S. caregivers believe that their children's successes are due to their parenting skills, rather than their child's inborn strengths (Parker & Horowitz, 2015; see **Figure 9.4**).

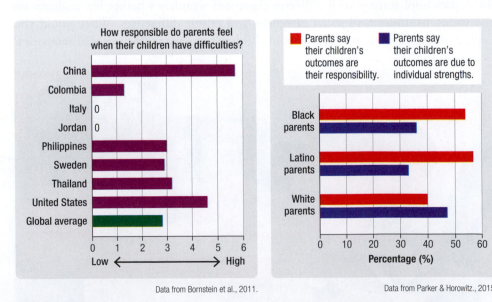

Data from Bornstein et al., 2011.   Data from Parker & Horowitz., 2015.

FIGURE 9.4 Parental Beliefs How important is parenting to children's development? Researchers believe that the work parents do to nurture their children is critical to healthy development, but parents are not always sure that it will have an impact.

Each young child is shaped by both the complex systems surrounding them and their individual strengths. The social structures and physical environment children grow up in illustrate the vast inequalities around the world, as well as the great diversity in our capacity for resilience. In early childhood, resilience develops through relationships with caregivers inside and outside the home.

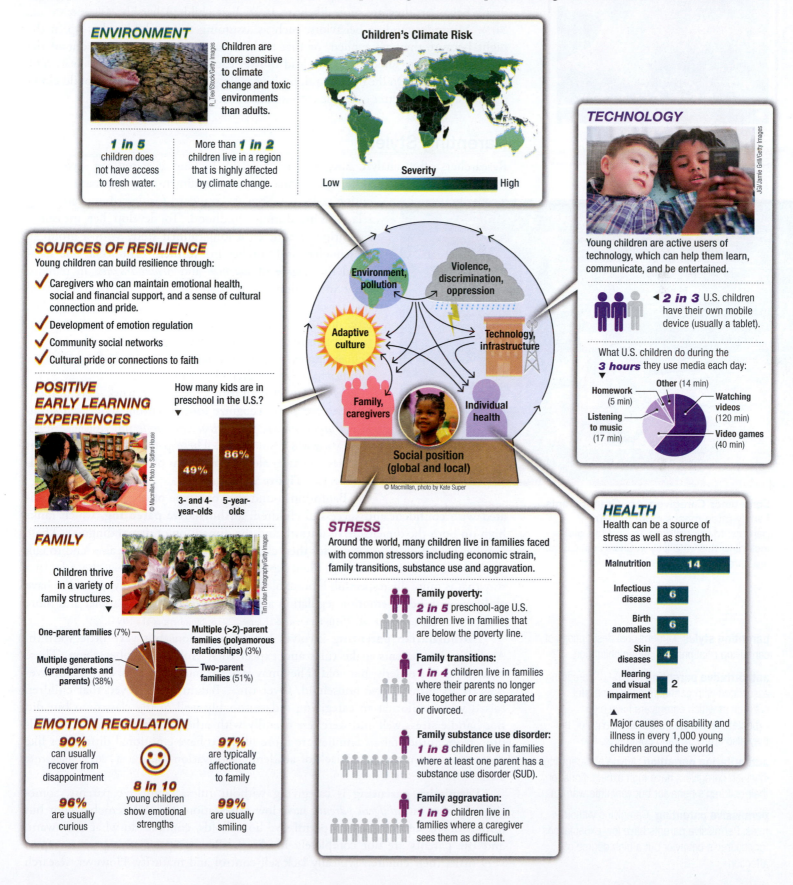

ENVIRONMENT

Children are more sensitive to climate change and toxic environments than adults.

1 in 5 children does not have access to fresh water.

More than **1 in 2** children live in a region that is highly affected by climate change.

Children's Climate Risk

Severity: Low — High

TECHNOLOGY

Young children are active users of technology, which can help them learn, communicate, and be entertained.

◄ **2 in 3** U.S. children have their own mobile device (usually a tablet).

What U.S. children do during the **3 hours** they use media each day:

- Homework (5 min)
- Other (14 min)
- Watching videos (120 min)
- Listening to music (17 min)
- Video games (40 min)

SOURCES OF RESILIENCE

Young children can build resilience through:

✔ Caregivers who can maintain emotional health, social and financial support, and a sense of cultural connection and pride.

✔ Development of emotion regulation

✔ Community social networks

✔ Cultural pride or connections to faith

POSITIVE EARLY LEARNING EXPERIENCES

How many kids are in preschool in the U.S.?

- 49% — 3- and 4-year-olds
- 86% — 5-year-olds

FAMILY

Children thrive in a variety of family structures.

- One-parent families (7%)
- Multiple (>2)-parent families (polyamorous relationships) (3%)
- Multiple generations (grandparents and parents) (38%)
- Two-parent families (51%)

EMOTION REGULATION

90% can usually recover from disappointment

97% are typically affectionate to family

8 in 10 young children show emotional strengths

96% are usually curious

99% are usually smiling

Environment, pollution

Violence, discrimination, oppression

Adaptive culture

Technology, infrastructure

Family, caregivers

Individual health

Social position (global and local)

© Macmillan, photo by Kate Super

STRESS

Around the world, many children live in families faced with common stressors including economic strain, family transitions, substance use and aggravation.

Family poverty: **2 in 5** preschool-age U.S. children live in families that are below the poverty line.

Family transitions: **1 in 4** children live in families where their parents no longer live together or are separated or divorced.

Family substance use disorder: **1 in 8** children live in families where at least one parent has a substance use disorder (SUD).

Family aggravation: **1 in 9** children live in families where a caregiver sees them as difficult.

HEALTH

Health can be a source of stress as well as strength.

- Malnutrition: 14
- Infectious disease: 6
- Birth anomalies: 6
- Skin diseases: 4
- Hearing and visual impairment: 2

▲ Major causes of disability and illness in every 1,000 young children around the world

Parental Aspirations for their Children

Sometimes Caregivers Are Grandparents.
Family often means more than just parents: Many children around the globe, including this little boy in Shanghai, China, are cared for by their extended family.

parenting styles Dimensional descriptions of caregiving relationships during childhood.

authoritative parenting A type of caregiving associated with confident and successful children in which caregivers have high expectations for their children's behavior, but they also are warm and communicative.

authoritarian parenting A type of caregiving in which caregivers have high expectations for their children's behavior but very little warmth.

permissive parenting Caregiving without rules. Permissive parents have low expectations for children's behavior but a high degree of affection.

Families around the world overestimate what preschoolers are capable of (Durrant et al., 2017). Realistic expectations help parents react more warmly to their children's behavior (NASEM, 2016). When parents attribute hostility or willfulness to young children's behavior, they are more likely to treat their children harshly (Milner & Crouch, 2013). Misunderstanding behaviors, such as assuming that a child wakes up in the night because they are spoiled, or that a child has dumped everything out of the kitchen cabinet to annoy you, can lead to overreaction or abuse (Beckerman et al., 2018; Durrant et al., 2017). On the other hand, positive beliefs about parenting help build closer relationships and better outcomes (Bornstein et al., 2018).

Parenting Styles

Researchers often analyze caregiving practices by looking at **parenting styles**. For more than 50 years, psychologist Diana Baumrind's dimensional approach to parenting styles has been the standard for describing caregiving relationships during childhood. To develop her measures, Baumrind conducted a longitudinal study with a group of preschoolers and families in Northern California. She measured the degree of *warmth* and *demandingness* in parents' daily interactions with their children and then observed them over time (Baumrind, 1971, 2013; Baumrind & Black, 1967). The level of warmth in Baumrind's typology refers to how sensitive, responsive, and supportive caregivers are. The level of demandingness, or control, refers to the type of expectations families have for children's behavior.

As a result of Baumrind's pioneering work, developmental scientists now recognize four parenting styles: *authoritative, authoritarian, permissive,* and *neglectful* (Baumrind, 1989, 1991; Maccoby & Martin, 1983). These parenting styles represent families' practices along dimensions of warmth and demandingness (see **Figure 9.5**).

Baumrind found that one type of caregiving was associated with confident and successful children: **authoritative parenting**, which ranks high on both the dimension of warmth and the dimension of demandingness. These families have high expectations for their children's behavior, but they also tend to talk things over with their children. They expect that their children follow the rules in a way that is mutually respectful. Households with authoritative caregivers tend to have children with better emotion regulation and self-control, who are happier and more independent (Baumrind et al., 2010; Pinquart & Kauser, 2018; Steinberg et al., 1994).

Authoritarian parenting involves high expectations but very little warmth. Authoritarian parents make rules and expect their children to obey them. These households are orderly, but cold: They may lack the laughter, hugs, and responsiveness of an authoritative household. Over time, Baumrind observed that children raised with authoritarian caregiving did reasonably well in the classroom but did not handle stress well and were less friendly with other children. As a result, children from authoritarian families are more likely to have emotional difficulties like depression, acting out, and lack of academic motivation (Braza et al., 2015; Pinquart & Kauser, 2018).

Permissive parenting is caregiving without rules. Permissive parents, sometimes known as *indulgent parents*, have low expectations for children's behavior but a high degree of affection. In permissive households, children do what they want, and the parents are not completely in charge. Because permissive parents expect very little, their children typically lack self-control and maturity. However, research on the outcomes of permissive parenting has been inconsistent: Children raised by permissive parents tend to have strong social skills but may have difficulty following directions (Baumrind et al., 2010; Steinberg et al., 1994).

Neglectful parenting is caregiving without warmth or expectations (Baumrind, 1989, 1991; Maccoby & Martin, 1983). Neglectful parents do not focus much on their children, perhaps because they are occupied with their own challenges and, as a result, may fail to keep children safe. Children from neglectful families are at high risk for emotional and behavioral difficulties as they grow up, from serious disciplinary problems in school to academic struggles and substance abuse (Pinquart, 2017; Steinberg et al., 1994).

In the many years since Baumrind originally made her observations, scientists have continued to find that the combination of caring and control characteristic of the authoritative parenting style is linked to more successful and emotionally healthy children in a variety of circumstances, families, and cultures around the world (Pinquart & Kauser, 2018; Smetena, 2017). Children whose caregivers are harsh and use emotionally manipulative techniques to manage their children's behavior—like shame, embarrassment, or rejection—are more likely to act out in school and to develop other emotional problems. Children whose caregivers are warm and who manage their children's behavior while respecting their developing independence have stronger social relationships and lower risks for emotional disorders or academic challenges (Pinquart, 2017; Smetana, 2017).

Despite the influence of Baumrind's dimensional parenting styles on developmental science, parts of her work remain controversial. Contemporary researchers have argued that Baumrind's parenting styles do not give enough weight to the roles culture, the community environment, and children themselves play in caregiving (Wittig & Rodriguez, 2019; Zamir et al., 2020).

Evaluating parenting styles can be challenging, particularly when comparing families from different cultures and ethnotheories (Pinquart & Kauser, 2018; Sorkhabi & Mandara, 2013). Warmth and control may be expressed in different ways in different communities across the globe, since the specific parenting practices families adopt are often vastly different. For instance, in Japan, preschoolers often sleep with their parents, but in the United States, experts recommend that children sleep independently (LeVine & LeVine, 2016). Does this mean that Japanese parents are permissive? Many scholars would say no. Researchers suggest using the principle of *cultural humility* when comparing parenting practices across communities, recognizing that behaviors are shaped by cultural contexts and remaining open to learning from different cultures (Williams, Biscaro, et al., 2019).

Over the years, researchers and parents have taken exception with the rule that authoritative parenting works, but those claims rarely pan out. For instance, one Chinese American parent argued that cold "tiger parenting" was essential for Chinese American children to be successful (Chua, 2011). Researchers (and other Chinese American families) objected to this, stating that there is little truth in the assertion that being tough leads to happier or more successful children (Chuang et al., 2018). To the contrary, studies in the United States and in China have found that preschool children who have authoritative parents have fewer emotional problems and are more successful in school than those with authoritarian ones are (Doan et al., 2017; Pomerantz & Wang, 2009).

In the past, some scholars argued that Black families were also an exception to the recommendation for authoritative caregiving. Researchers suggested that a harsher parenting style might be adaptive for families who are in situations of high stress, like

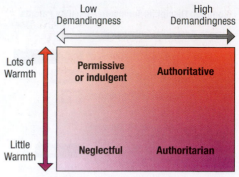

FatCamera/E+/Getty Images

Information from Baumrind, 1971; Maccoby & Martin, 1983.

FIGURE 9.5 Parenting Styles In Baumrind's classic dimensional approach to parenting styles, caregiving relationships are analyzed in terms of how warm or demanding they are. Four categories—permissive, authoritative, authoritarian, and neglectful—represent common variations.

You Can't Go Wrong with Warmth. Families communicate affection in different ways depending on their cultural ethnotheories. Some may prefer hugs and kisses, as in this family in Canada. Others may be more reserved, but young children thrive no matter how care is communicated.

neglectful parenting Caregiving without warmth or expectations. Children from neglectful families are at high risk for emotional and behavioral difficulties as they grow up.

Common Discipline Techniques Used By Parents

Power-Assertive Techniques

Time-out   72%
Taking something away   34%
Removal of privileges   23%

Inductive-Reasoning Techniques

Talking about what happened   50%

Physical Punishment

Any physical punishment
(spanking, hand slapping)   44%

Other

Yelling   7%
Ignoring behavior   12%
Counting to 3   12%
Threatening   2%

Data from Thompson et al., 2017.

FIGURE 9.6 How Do Parents Describe Their Disciplinary Practices? There may be no easy answer: Warmth and high expectations work in the long run, but in practice, parents often struggle with finding methods to help children manage their emotions and behave appropriately. Common forms of discipline in the United States include power-assertive techniques and inductive discipline. Harsh and rejecting practices are destructive and harmful. Growing up takes time and patience for both caregivers and children.

discipline Caregiving practices or strategies used to teach children how to behave by setting rules, encouraging good behavior, and discouraging missteps.

power-assertive techniques Disciplinary strategies that rely on parents' control.

inductive reasoning A disciplinary approach that relies on motivating children to change their behavior through talk.

poverty and systematic racism (Baumrind, 1972). Scientists working with one group of Black families from rural southeastern United States found that some families who were stricter than typical authoritative parents had children who were more successful on some measures than those raised in traditionally authoritative families. These families were not quite authoritarian: They were slightly stricter than typical authoritative families but just as warm, so they were given a new label: *no-nonsense parents* (Brody & Flor, 1998).

Subsequent researchers studying other families found that this style of parenting did not always translate to other contexts. In fact, researchers have found that the strictness of no-nonsense parenting can create additional risks for children in many communities (Anton et al., 2015; Querido et al., 2002). Most researchers have found that despite the context, parenting that balances warmth and high expectations without harshness works best for most children around the world.

Discipline: Helping Children to Get Along

While parenting styles describe the overall pattern of how parents interact with their children on a day-to-day basis, the specific practices parents use to shape children's behavior come down to **discipline**, which is any strategy used to teach children how to behave by setting rules, encouraging good behavior, and discouraging missteps (Grusec et al., 2017). (See **Figure 9.6**.)

More than half of all parents in the United States admit that they struggle with finding effective ways to manage their preschoolers' behavior (Zero to Three, 2016c). As a mother in Chicago explained, "Lately, I've been so frustrated I'm screaming like a banshee most of the time . . . [then] I will hear them playing, and then my daughter . . . will be screaming at her brother in exactly the same tone of voice" (Zero to Three, 2016b). As this mother discovered, some forms of discipline have negative consequences.

Developmental scientists divide disciplinary practices into *power-assertive* and *inductive-reasoning* techniques (Lansford, 2017). Strategies that rely on parents' control are called **power-assertive techniques** and have a number of benefits (Baumrind, 2012). Power assertion is often immediately effective, as with immediately picking up a 3-year-old who is running into traffic rather than having a long discussion about the dangers it poses. Other common forms of power assertion include the *time-out*, counting to three, rewards for good behavior, and removing privileges (like taking away a video game). Research indicates that these forms of discipline are effective if used consistently and positively (Kazdin et al., 2018).

However, as researchers and Brionnah have found, talking things out often fosters better long-term relationships and better behavior (Grusec et al., 2017; Lansford et al., 2018). Brionnah explains that disciplining Olivia by slowing things down and taking time to talk about why Olivia is upset, no matter what the cause, makes things easier. This approach to discipline, called **inductive reasoning**, relies on motivating children to change their behavior through talk. Caregivers who use inductive reasoning explain their reasoning and listen to the child's perspective (Hoffman, 1977). Children in families that use this approach are more likely to develop strong self-regulation skills and to behave kindly and prosocially (Eisenberg et al., 2015). They are less likely to act out and more likely to be socially successful later in life (Choe et al., 2013).

Some practices, such as physical punishment and shaming, are destructive (Sege et al., 2018). Children who experience these are more likely to act out and have emotional conditions like depression (Lansford et al., 2021). Emotional rejection, like when a parent tells a child, "I can't believe I have to put up with such a brat," is harmful. Physical punishment also has unintended consequences, as you will learn (Sege et al., 2018).

MAKING A DIFFERENCE
The Science Against Spanking

What happens when children push the limits too far? In about two in three families in the United States, the consequence is spanking (Thompson et al., 2017). Nearly 8 in 10 U.S. adults believe that physical punishment is sometimes necessary to get children to behave (Lansford et al., 2015; Perrin et al., 2017). Nineteen states allow spanking in public preschool and pre-kindergarten programs (Gershoff et al., 2019).

However, beliefs about spanking are changing. Scientific consensus supports the finding that physical punishment is not effective and can hurt children in the long run (Gershoff & Grogan-Kaylor, 2016). Parents are using physical discipline less than they used to, even when they are under stress (Finkelhor et al., 2019). In recent years, developmental scientists and pediatricians in the United States have joined those from around the world to advocate against physical punishment (Sege et al., 2018).

Parents often explain that they spank because their children were not doing what they were told to do. When researchers track what children were doing before a spanking, many of them were making fairly minor mistakes: eating improperly or getting out of a chair without permission. They were not hurting someone or willfully destroying something. According to observational reports, families turn to spanking just 30 seconds after a child has misbehaved (Holden et al., 2014).

No matter what sparks a spanking, it simply does not work. In the short term, children who are spanked are no more likely to sit still, eat their carrots, or stop talking back. In fact, when researchers recorded what happened when parents disciplined their preschoolers, they observed that, within 10 minutes of a spanking, most children repeated the behavior (Holden et al., 2014). As Laura, a mother in Illinois put it, "We gave him a spanking and then he just laughs in our face" (Zero to Three, 2016a).

Scientists have also found that children who are spanked have more, rather than fewer, conflicts with their caregivers (Alampay et al., 2017). They tend to act out more after parents start spanking (Gershoff et al., 2019). Families who use physical discipline are also more likely to escalate their interactions with their children into something more aggressive and abusive (Sege et al., 2018). As a result, pediatricians and scientists now caution against spanking in all cases.

Maltreatment and Violence in the Family

Around the world, more than three in four children are regularly exposed to violence in their homes (UNICEF, 2020). In the United States, about one in five families reports that they are currently experiencing the effects of family violence and abuse (Breiding, 2014). Children may not just see violence: They may be its victim. In the United States, more than 15 in 1,000 preschoolers are the victims of abuse (USDHHS, 2021).

Scientists use the words *maltreatment*, *abuse*, and *neglect* to describe the wide range of harm that can come to children. While these terms are often used interchangeably, they also have legal definitions that vary regionally (Stoltenborgh et al., 2015). **Maltreatment** is the general term scholars use to describe the many types of abuse and neglect of children by adults who are responsible for them. In the United States, **abuse** is the legal term used to describe the most serious types of harm to children (Child Welfare Information Gateway, 2019).

Maltreatment may involve *physical abuse*, which involves harm to a child's body, as when a child is beaten or bruised. It can also include *emotional abuse*, when a child's emotional well-being is chronically

maltreatment The general term scholars use to describe the many types of abuse and neglect of children by adults who are responsible for them.

abuse The legal term used to describe the most serious types of harm to children, which can be physical, emotional, sexual, or neglectful.

Share It!

Keeping it positive helps them brush their teeth. Scientists observed how families convinced their preschoolers to clean their teeth. They wanted to understand which practices actually worked. They found that praise was most effective. So, more smiles, fewer warnings about germs and gingivitis.

(Leonard et al., 2022)

No Nonsense About Spanking Stacey Patton is a historian, journalist, and child advocate working to change beliefs about parenting and discipline. Dr. Patton has worked to change attitudes about harsh physical violence, including appearing on television and radio shows. As she argues, "Disciplining children shouldn't hurt."

Courtesy Stacey Patton, sparethekids.com

FIGURE 9.7 Reports of Maltreatment in the United States Maltreatment and family violence are difficult to measure. Community expectations help define what abuse is, and it is often hidden or described as punishment. When researchers survey families, parents are much more likely to volunteer information about harsh physical discipline than abuse. The extent of children's exposure to violence is not clear, particularly for children who are too young to explain what has happened to them.

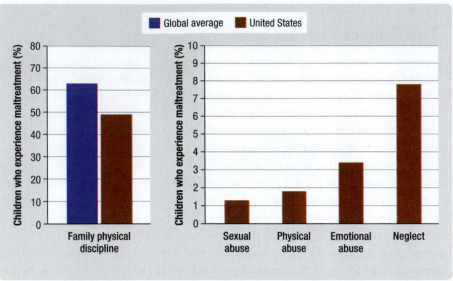

Data from Finkelhor et al., 2013; Finkelhor et al., 2019; Gewirtz-Meydan & Finkelhor, 2020; UNICEF, 2017; Vanderminden et al., 2019.

threatened, as when a child is repeatedly belittled, rejected, or frightened (English et al., 2015). *Sexual abuse* involves any intimate activity affecting a child including sexual touch between an adult and a child, child pornography, and human trafficking. *Neglect* occurs when adults fail to take care of the basic physical, emotional, educational, and medical needs of children for whom they are responsible (Children's Bureau, 2019). Neglect may not be intentional, and can be caused by poverty, by substance use within the family, or by an inability to access the medical or educational resources available in a community. (See **Figure 9.7**.)

During early childhood, many instances of physical and emotional abuse arise from overreaction to typical preschooler behaviors, like separation anxiety, slip-ups when learning to use the bathroom, or unwillingness to follow directions (Christian & Committee on Child Abuse and Neglect, 2015; Flaherty et al., 2010). As one mother explained, "Our beating is out of love. We can't help carrying out beating for the child's good" (Qiao & Xie, 2017, p. 214). Children who act out, who have high energy, and who have developmental disabilities face increased risk for maltreatment (Christian & Committee on Child Abuse and Neglect, 2015).

Some parents do not think it is wrong to use physical violence, but developmental scientists and pediatricians disagree (Lansford et al., 2018; Sege et al., 2018). Children may feel the consequences of maltreatment for the rest of their lives, with higher rates of emotional disorders, substance abuse, and health conditions such as diabetes and heart disease. Like other forms of trauma, maltreatment changes the brain, causing structural and functional changes that may be difficult to alter (Teicher & Samson, 2016). In kindergarten, children who have experienced trauma and abuse tend to have a harder time controlling themselves and focusing, which affects their classroom performance (Jimenez et al., 2016).

Supporting Positive Relationships

Maintaining positive, supportive relationships during early childhood is critical to children's emotional health, teaches them right from wrong, and helps them learn to relate to others (Kochanska et al., 2019). Scientists have observed that supportive relationships in early childhood are characterized by closeness, warmth, and positivity (Esposito et al., 2017; Pastorelli et al., 2016).

Caregivers' ability to regulate their own emotions is critical to healthy relationships (Belsky, 1984). Adults need to be able to stay positive and consistent in the face of preschoolers' often-challenging behavior (Hajal et al., 2015; Morris et al., 2017). Parents with poor emotion regulation are also more likely to be harsh, demeaning, or negative with their children, making it more likely that their children will have trouble making friends or develop externalizing disorders (Smith, Dishion, et al., 2014).

Caregivers' goal is to communicate affection and warmth. This is usually done through loving interchanges, like cuddling or hugging, praise, or nicknames (Lee et al., 2013). When parents and children interact with warmth, whether through fist-bumps or a crazy dance, children are more likely to accept their parents' direction, develop self-regulation skills, and get along with others (Kochanska et al., 2019).

One goal of families is to convince children to do what they are told. In the laboratory, researchers measure this by watching what happens when they ask families to pick up toys after they have played with them (Matas et al., 1978). Children are typically capable of being compliant and cleaning up as young toddlers (Kochanska, 2002; Kochanska et al., 2019). However, this does not mean that children will actually do what they are asked. Many children in U.S. studies will refuse to help, at least initially, until they are about 7 (Huang & Lamb, 2014). Parents who are successful at convincing their children to help out are teaching them to control themselves and get along with others (Eisenberg et al., 2015).

During early childhood, *parent-training* programs help caregivers adopt more constructive beliefs about caregiving and more effective parenting practices. Caregiving practices that are reviewed in *evidence-based* programs help families increase healthy interactions with their children, avoid harsh patterns, and understand developmental norms. A few weeks of classes can help caregivers better manage their stress and be more responsive (Barlow et al., 2014; Mingebach et al., 2018). Helping parents helps children: Children are less likely to act out after their parents have participated in a parent-training program (Nystrand et al., 2019).

Sometimes Daddy Is Just on Screen. About 8 in every 100 children have a parent who is incarcerated: But families still manage to maintain bonds, even if they only happen virtually. Here Edna tries to make sure her 4-year-old son is able to keep in touch with his father while he is incarcerated through video-visitation near their home in Texas.

Sibling Relationships

One thing Brionnah has not given Olivia, despite her hints, is a little brother or sister. For now, Olivia is an only child, as is true for about 1 in 10 children in the United States (Kotecki, 2018). For many families, early childhood is the time when a new baby arrives, typically when the first child is about 3 or 4 (Copen et al., 2015). Siblings can help children learn how to share, be helpful, and care for someone else (Hughes, McHarg, et al., 2018).

Many people believe that the birth of a sibling creates a crisis for the older child, but current research indicates that this is not necessarily the case (Volling, 2012). The first few weeks of having a new baby in the house are typically filled with jealousy, readjustment, and excitement, but not trauma (Volling et al., 2014). How children react to a new baby depends on existing relationships, individual personalities, and how parents manage the transition (Yaremych & Volling, 2020). For instance, in families where first children were securely attached before their sibling was born, most adjust positively. However, if children have an insecure attachment style, their relationships with their parents and the new baby could be more conflictual (Volling et al., 2014).

The sibling relationship plays an important role in how children will interact not just with brothers and sisters, but also with peers. Relationships between siblings are often filled with conflict, but this does not mean that bullying in families is healthy (Dirks et al., 2019). In one survey, siblings fought once every 10 minutes during the preschool years (Dirks et al., 2015). About 4 in 10

Sibling Love Learning to care for a brother or sister can help create a model for future relationships. Supportive, warm bonds between siblings can be a source of strength across development.

sibling pairs have an extremely difficult relationship, which can escalate into bullying (Dantchev & Wolke, 2019; Oh et al., 2015). But families can encourage their children to solve their conflicts with less aggression and with more warmth. These skills provide good training for building the friendships outside the family that will sustain children as they grow.

APPLY IT! **9.5** Olivia's parents have adopted regular routines and show her lots of affection. Which parenting styles and ethnotheories does this reflect?

9.6 Parenting styles do not just apply to families. Some researchers use them to evaluate caregiving at school. How might a preschool teacher show characteristics of warmth and demandingness?

Getting Along with Peers

Learning Objective

9.6 Describe the features of play and their role in learning and development.

Learning to get along with other children is a central challenge in early childhood. Most of the time, it is also a time of joyful play. If you watch children on the playground pretending to be Black Panther and Wolverine, or selling each other "ice cream," or endlessly chasing around the swings, it may be hard to imagine that for some children, this part of development does not come easily. Learning how to socialize taps into—and helps build—children's rapidly growing emotional and cognitive skills.

Play

In Olivia's preschool, like many in the United States, children can choose to spend time at a number of stations, including a pretend kitchen, a block area, and a dress-up corner filled with firefighter's hats and sparkly tiaras. Olivia's school made space for play because it helps children learn skills in self-regulation, executive function, and forming social relationships (Howe & Leach, 2018; Rubin et al., 2015).

Early childhood is a peak time for play. Between the ages of 2½ and 5, children spend more time playing than they ever will again (Weisberg, 2015). Play is certainly fun, but it also involves a lot of learning about language, symbolic thinking, and problem solving (Lillard, 2017). When children are playing, they typically show more maturity, focus, and creativity than they do in their everyday life (Gray, 2017). As Vygotsky explained, "In play a child is always above his average age, above his daily behavior; in play it is as though he were a head taller than himself" (Vygotsky, 2016, p. 102).

Scientists define play as an enjoyable activity that children choose to do for its own sake (Burghardt, 2010). Children twirling pretending to be fairies while waiting in line to go to the cafeteria for lunch, are playing, but children waiting patiently, staring into space, are not. Play takes different forms depending on children's level of maturity and the constraints of the environment around them.

Social and Cognitive Components of Play Developmental scientists analyze play based on the level of social and cognitive sophistication it reveals. As children grow, their play becomes more social, but the development of play is not a progression from one stage to another (Coplan et al., 2006; Parten, 1932). Toddlers begin playing by themselves in what is known as *solitary play*, for example, acting out a scene with stuffed animals or building a block tower. They may also engage in *onlooker play*, where a preschooler observes other children playing but is not engaged in the play. For example, one child may watch intently from the sidelines, reluctant to join in, as a group of children plays with trains.

Alex Chan Tsz Yuk/SOPA Images/LightRocket via Getty Images

Play Even When You Are Underground. Children find time to play and need to play even in the most stressful circumstances. These children are playing in an underground shelter in Zaporizhia, where their families found refuge during the war in Ukraine.

When children play physically close together but are not working on a shared project, they are engaged in **parallel play**. For instance, two children may be sitting together at a table working with play dough and may even look up from time to time to see what their friend is doing or share tools, but they are not playing together. Truly **cooperative play**, or playing together on a joint project, takes a while for preschoolers to grasp; it may not be until they are 4 or 5 before they can play well together. Consider all the skills it takes for a group of preschoolers to play superhero chase on the playground, taking turns being Spider-Man and analyzing each other's web-throwing skills: They are taking turns, listening to each other's ideas, and sharing a vision of what Spider-Man and web-throwing looks and sounds like.

Types of Play Play becomes more cognitively complex as children grow. Babies engage in a lot of **functional play**, repeating an action over and over again just for the joy of it. Toddlers and preschoolers also enjoy functional play, which defines most types of gross motor play. Swinging on the swing, hopping, or yelling in the bathroom to hear the echo of your voice against the tiles are all forms of functional play.

As children grow older, functional play is likely to become more complex and turn into *games with rules*, like hopscotch, Simon Says, hide-and-seek, or something of their own invention. Games with rules become more popular as children get older and can focus their attention for longer periods of time (Rubin et al., 2015). **Constructive play** includes all forms of creativity, from making a fort out of couch pillows to cutting shapes out of construction paper. **Sociodramatic play** involves pretending to be something you are not and requires symbolic thought and theory of mind. In this type of play, children need to keep track of what everyone knows about the game they are playing, whether it is pretending to take a pet to the vet's office or playing "house" (Lillard, 2017).

One of the hallmarks of early childhood, sociodramatic play helps children build cognitive and social skills (Lillard et al., 2013; Weisberg, 2015). Some families provide children with dress-up materials, read them fairy tales, and show them movies that provide fodder for the imagination (Haight, 2006). In other communities, families discourage pretend play because of religious concerns or because they prefer their children focus on other skills, like getting ready for school or helping out around the house (Roopnarine & Davidson, 2015; Weisberg, 2015). Sociodramatic play is particularly popular in the United States, where many families value building social skills and encouraging imagination (Singer et al., 2009).

Another common but sometimes controversial form of play is **rough-and-tumble play**, or the physically active play where children chase, play fight, and wrestle (Howe & Leach, 2018). This type of play is also common in other young animals from kittens to orangutans (Lillard, 2017; Pellegrini & Smith, 1998). Rough-and-tumble play can sometimes look violent or involve play swords, superheroes, and fire-breathing zombies, but most researchers agree that it is helpful (Hart & Tannock, 2019; Levin & Carlsson-Page, 2005). In fact, when play guns or violent fantasy play is forbidden, it often "goes underground," as children turn blocks into weapons and juice box straws into shooters (Yanık & Yasar, 2018).

Friendship

As children play together, they develop close relationships and learn how to be friends. Even children as young as age 3 want to have friends and are aware of who has social status within the group. Children who make friends easily tend to be those with stronger social and language skills who can navigate their way around the playground. However, this is not always easy.

Even in preschool, children are anxious about finding friends and keeping them. "You didn't sit next to me," Pinar, a little girl in a Turkish preschool said to her friend.

---

parallel play When children play physically close together but are not working on a shared project.

cooperative play Playing together on a joint project.

functional play Repeating an action over and over again just for the joy of it.

constructive play Play that involves all forms of creativity.

sociodramatic play Play that involves pretending to be something you are not and requires symbolic thought and theory of mind.

rough-and-tumble play Physically active play where children chase, play fight, and wrestle.

 Learn It Together

Play in Early Childhood

Your classmate is looking for a preschool for her 4-year-old child. She visited the neighborhood child development center, but was concerned because when she visited, "the children were just playing all day." Given what you have learned about physical, cognitive, and social development during early childhood, what advice can you give her about the role of play in early childhood development?

Prepare Review the key features of development for typical 4-year-olds. Consider cognitive and language development, physical and motor development, and what you have learned in this chapter about Erikson's stage of initiative versus guilt, the development of self-regulation, play, and relationships.

Engage In a small group of classmates, discuss how play during early childhood may play a role in each domain of development described above. Develop a set of "talking points" you could use to explain how play in the preschool setting may influence development.

Reflect Consider the connections you have made between different domains of development. Did this activity help you to see ways that the growing brain and body are involved in advancing cognitive, language, and social development?

bullying A pattern of physical and/or social aggression by a child with social power against a child with less social acceptance.

"You're [still] my friend, aren't you?" (Yanık & Yasar, 2018, p. 492). Throughout childhood, the ability to make friends and be accepted by the group are important measures of social success. Children who have friends are better at managing relationships of all kinds and tend to be better at managing conflict and communicating, and more likely to be generous. Building friendships gives children practice in resolving problems and taking turns but also gives them the delight of sharing interests (Hartup, 1996).

In early childhood, friendships tend to be built around shared interests and activities (Selman, 1980). Children are aware of social distinctions such as income level and ethnicity, and they tend to associate with children who they see as "like them" (Rubin et al., 2015). These early friendships are generally long-lasting; more than two in three preschoolers can maintain a friendship for more than six months (Gottman & Graziano, 1983).

About one in eight children has a hard time making friends. Some of these children struggle with emotion regulation and aggression; others are anxious or shy and may have difficulties interacting and learning to play with others. Some children may experience rejection from others based on differences in race, ability, or other characteristics. In general, children with strong, securely attached relationships with their parents and who are better at managing their emotions have an easier time finding friends (Rubin et al., 2015).

Peer Pressure in Preschool Preschoolers are cute, but they are not always kind: Preschool is not too soon for peer pressure and **bullying**. Children, like all of us, are acutely sensitive to what their friends and peers think of them (Haun & Tomasello, 2011). It is not unusual for preschool children to exclude and reject other children (Swit & Slater, 2021). Since they are still developing an understanding of the world and learning about categories and identity, preschoolers can be even *more* rigid about categories than older children. This makes them more likely than older children to exclude others who are not following the social rules (Köymen et al., 2014; Toppe, 2020).

When one group of researchers observed preschool children on the playground, they found that social exclusion happened about every 6.5 seconds. One 4-year-old approaching a group in the sandbox heard: "Go away! You're not our friend." Another group of children schemed: "I'm not inviting her to my birthday" (Fanger et al., 2012). Experiencing repeated exclusion is particularly damaging early in life and may set the stage for later victimization (Godleski et al., 2015). Even if young children are not the direct victims of rejection or aggression, ostracism can poison the school climate for all (Marinović & Träuble, 2021). Teachers and other caregivers can help try to create a more welcoming and inclusive classroom by identifying potential biases, recognizing unkind behavior when it happens, and encouraging children to defend and comfort their friends who have been ostracized (Allen et al., 2021; Smith-Bonahue et al., 2015).

APPLY IT! **9.7** A parent asks why preschools allow children to spend so much time playing. How would you explain the value of play in early childhood?
9.8 Despite her teacher's best efforts, Olivia has witnessed some rejecting behaviors in her classroom. Is she too young to understand what is going on? How would you explain bullying to a preschooler?

Getting Along in the World: Moral Development

Learning Objective

9.7 Describe aggressive and prosocial behaviors in early childhood.

During early childhood, children learn how to maintain relationships, understand the difference between right and wrong, and figure out how to put these ideas into practice. This is not always easy. For the most part, young children get along, but they are also learning new ways to hurt each other. During early childhood, preschoolers acquire a sense of *morality*, or an understanding of how people should treat one another (Dahl & Killen, 2018). They also become more able to behave in a kind, or *prosocial*, way.

Children's social emotions, such as empathy and guilt, encourage them to be kind. These emotions take advantage of children's perspective-taking and theory-of-mind skills, which make it more painful to hurt someone and, after the fact, create a potent memory of how badly it felt (Davidov et al., 2016; Malti & Dys, 2018). Sometimes, however, feelings can be overwhelming. For instance, a child could be so distressed by their friend's tears that they are unable to get help or even give a hug. Or, a child could be so overwhelmed by guilt after breaking something that they may not be able to apologize or help repair it (Vaish & Hepach, 2020). As children are better able to regulate their emotions, they are more likely to be responsive to others.

Getting along with others not only helps children make friends in preschool; it will also help them get along with others later in life (Scrimgeour et al., 2016). Acting out is common in early childhood, but becoming kind and managing aggression are aspects of the self-regulation children need as they grow up. Longitudinal research reveals that the social skills that children have when they enter kindergarten often influence how successful they are later on in school (Jones, Greenberg, et al., 2015).

Hurting Others

New cognitive and social skills make it possible for young children to hurt each other in new ways—through words and relationships. Many researchers describe the toddler years and early childhood as the most violent time of the lifespan (Côté et al., 2006; Lorber et al., 2018). But physical violence decreases quickly as children learn to control their bodies and replace kicks with criticisms.

Developmental science has many ways of describing how children hurt each other (Sukhodolsky et al., 2016). Preschoolers can be *physically aggressive*, for example, when an angry 3-year-old throws a toy across the room. They can also be **relationally aggressive**, or use their words and relationships to hurt another person socially or emotionally (Crick & Grotpeter, 1996).

Both physical and relational aggression can be *reactive* or *proactive*. **Reactive aggression** is a hostile action out of frustration or anger in an immediate reaction to something that has just happened. **Proactive aggression**, sometimes called *instrumental aggression*, is aggression that is planned and executed on purpose to gain personal advantage (Rieffe et al., 2016). This may include knocking another child down to grab candy out of their hand or tattling on another child to gain social status in the classroom.

As children develop the ability to control themselves, the ways they hurt each other change. Two-year-olds kick, shove, pull hair, and grab toys out of other children's hands at a shocking rate (Alink et al., 2008). For instance, about seven in ten 2-year-olds have hit someone in the last week, but by age 4, only about one in five has (NICHD, 2004). However, many young children do not hit out of a desire to harm (Dahl, 2016; Hay, 2017; Hay et al., 2021). In fact, for many young children, hitting may be a mishandled attempt to engage in rough-and-tumble play. For children who struggle with controlling their aggression, acting out that continues after preschool can trigger a cascade of problems, from stresses in the family to troubles in school that can last throughout childhood and adolescence (Hay et al., 2021; Olson et al., 2017).

Physical aggression tends to decline, but relational aggression increases. Children who employ relational aggression often have poorer social skills than their classmates and lack empathy (Camodeca & Coppola, 2016). The victims of bullying may be children who also lack social skills, or they may be chosen at random (Huitsing & Monks, 2018). Some children are able to defend their peers against bullies. These defenders often

relationally aggressive Using words and relationships to hurt another person socially or emotionally.

reactive aggression A hostile action out of frustration or anger in an immediate reaction to something that has just happened.

proactive aggression Aggression that is planned and executed on purpose to gain personal advantage (sometimes called *instrumental aggression*).

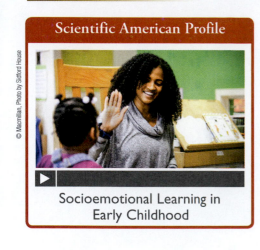

Scientific American Profile

Socioemotional Learning in Early Childhood

have stronger social skills than their peers and keen abilities to understand and empathize with other people's emotions.

Becoming Kind

When many caregivers in the United States think about kindness in children, they think about manners. They tell interviewers that they want children who can say "please" and "thank you." They see these skills as more important than more abstract concepts like developing empathy (Sesame Workshop, 2016). Developmental scientists point out that having good manners does not always mean that children are kind. They suggest that prosocial behavior can go beyond politeness: Prosocial behavior is what Olivia shows when she hugs a classmate who bursts into tears, reassures her mother that everything will be okay when they are running late, or helps out by putting her socks into the hamper.

When children are just 2 or 3, they already prefer kind people over those who are cruel or unfair (Cowell et al., 2017; Dahl & Killen, 2018). For instance, in research studies, 3-year-olds will complain about someone who tears up someone's drawing and are less likely to help an adult who has been unhelpful (Vaish & Hepach, 2020). Young children can also distinguish between breaking the rules and being truly unkind: for example, being "naughty" by making a mess as opposed to being "mean" by kicking a friend (Dahl & Kim, 2014).

Children's increased emotional and cognitive maturity helps them think and talk about moral issues in a more sophisticated way in early childhood (see **Figure 9.8**), however they are not always able to do the right thing in the heat of the moment. Conflicts over toys, treats, and trinkets are common (Smetana, 2015). In fact, when researchers asked 4-year-olds how they would feel after stealing a toy from a friend, some admitted knowing that it was wrong, but many said that they would probably feel happy about it (Arsenio, 2014). Children have difficulty balancing their understanding of their own anticipated happiness at getting a toy in their hands with their ability to understand their friend's perspective. This makes it easier for children to forgive their own mistakes than someone else's (Smetana, 2015). However, as they get older, children begin to anticipate the guilt they would feel from doing wrong, which helps prevent them from swiping a friend's toy.

Preschoolers face similar challenges with sharing. They are very sensitive to being treated unfairly and can explain that a dozen pieces of candy should be equally shared between two hypothetical children (Malti & Dys, 2018; Rochat et al., 2009). In real life, however, they often give themselves a little extra (Smith et al., 2013). They are also more likely to share fairly with people they are friendly with than with people they do not

FIGURE 9.8 Moral Development in Early Childhood As children grow, their ability to control their behavior and understand both the expectations of their community and the feelings of other people help them behave more prosocially. Researchers believe that even toddlers are capable of empathy and care, but mistakes still happen: Sharing and kindness are difficult skills to learn.

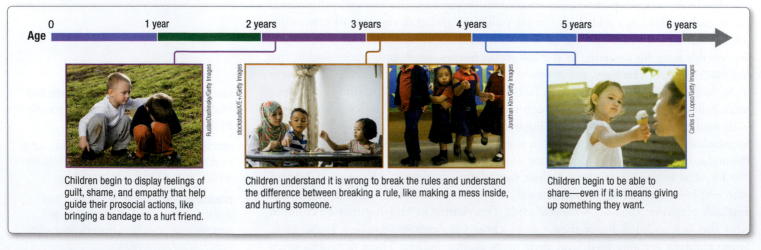

Children begin to display feelings of guilt, shame, and empathy that help guide their prosocial actions, like bringing a bandage to a hurt friend.

Children understand it is wrong to break the rules and understand the difference between breaking a rule, like making a mess inside, and hurting someone.

Children begin to be able to share—even if it is means giving up something they want.

like or know very well (Smetana, 2015). Expectations about sharing differ in communities around the world. For instance, many U.S. and Chinese children are taught that sharing equally is an important form of kindness at an early age, but there is less emphasis on sharing in some other communities, such as those in Turkey and South Africa (Cowell et al., 2017).

Family and community expectations certainly play an important part in helping children share (House, 2018). If children are not encouraged to do it, they are less likely to do so (Cowell et al., 2017; Huppert et al., 2019). Sharing is often overwhelming for children, pitting their desires against their still developing self-control, theory of mind, empathy, and counting ability (Chernyak et al., 2020). In addition, children often have social preferences and beliefs about who to share with and when, that may make handing over a favorite truck difficult (Smetana, 2015).

Despite these challenges, experts recommend that adults keep on encouraging children to be kind. Does it matter if someone says they are sorry? Researchers have found that 4-year-olds report that they think people who apologize are nicer than those who do not, and they understand that saying sorry can make people feel better. While only about half of all preschoolers' apologies are unprompted by an adult, practicing can help children learn to be kind (Smith et al., 2017).

Families who develop warm, supportive relationships are more likely to have children who are kind (Davidov et al., 2016; Kochanska et al., 2015). While practice helps, simply being told what to do will not help children develop the internal conscience that helps them do the right thing (see **Table 9.2**). Preschoolers fare better when they follow an adult's example and suggestions, rather than when caregivers use power assertion to impose kindness (Killen & Smetana, 2015).

Talking is another way to promote kindness. Children who talk a lot with their families—about right and wrong, "bad guys" and "good guys," being nice and being mean—have better social and prosocial skills (Conte et al., 2018; Salmon & Reese, 2016). Preschoolers who acquire better communication skills can use words to figure out solutions to their social challenges. These skills will help children as they move on to their next adventure: middle childhood and a world of more opportunities and responsibility as they enter formal school.

Share It!

Experiencing adversity might have a (small) upside: It may make children kinder, at least temporarily. Researchers studying sharing in Sichuan, China, found that experiencing an earthquake firsthand made children more likely to be generous.

(Li et al., 2013)

Practicing Kindness Being generous and caring to other people is a skill preschoolers are learning. Some families encourage children to be expressive (and work on their handwriting) by giving handmade gifts.

TABLE 9.2 Best Practices for Prosocial Development

Be a coach. Acknowledge, name, and help to problem-solve big feelings. This can help children learn to calm down and learn to be kinder in the heat of the moment.
Talk about it. Discussing feelings can model empathy and concern. Remind children that how we feel when we are upset is often different from how we feel when we have calmed down. Ask them to think big in tough situations: What would a grown-up or a superhero do in the same situation?
Start early. Do not shy away from talking about moral choices. Young children often want to talk about "good guys" and "bad guys." Do not be afraid to talk about the moral choices that they face every day, such as how to share fairly or whom to include in play.
Talk about differences. Children are aware enough to know that not everyone is the same, and it is not too early to talk about prejudice, racism, and exclusion. Make sure they know it is wrong to exclude.
Expect kindness. If you want children to combat unkindness, do not just tell them not to do it: Give them a job to do. Remind children that they can stand up for each other, defend each other, and comfort people who are hurt.
Help repair mistakes. Everyone makes mistakes and hurts people from time to time. Work with children to go beyond saying "I'm sorry" and help them make amends.

APPLY IT!   **9.9** Unkind behavior is common in preschoolers. How would you explain to a caregiver why this typical behavior should not be ignored?

9.10 Brionnah often talks to Olivia about the importance of "doing the right thing" even when sharing or saying sorry might feel awkward. How does her practice reflect the research finding that learning kindness takes both practice and good examples who also show caring, thoughtful behaviors?

Wrapping It Up ⬤⬤⬤

LO 9.1 Analyze advances in emotional expression and regulation during Erikson's stage of initiative versus guilt. (p. 216)

Erikson believed the crisis of the third stage, between ages 3 and 5, was a conflict between initiative and guilt. Children have enthusiasm to try new things and do them independently but are often unable to do things quite right. Some remorse over mistakes ensures that children become careful about other people's feelings and learn to work hard to accomplish tasks. During early childhood, children are expected to develop more emotion regulation. Brain development and cognitive maturity help young children have an easier time managing their feelings. Emotional maturation also happens in a social and cultural context: Children learn different ways of managing their feelings from their communities. Caregivers often expect children to be able to control their big feelings, but this is unrealistic.

LO 9.2 Describe features of young children's understanding of their identity or self-concept. (p. 216)

Your sense of who you are in the world is known as your *self-concept*. Your general feelings about yourself are known as your *self-esteem*. Preschoolers tend to have a more positive self-concept than older children, but it tends to be very concrete and built on visible characteristics. They are beginning to build a sense of their body image and academic self-concept. Feeling good about themselves helps children's adjustment, but not all communities encourage boasting about successes. Praise and overinflated flattery can backfire and make children feel confused or even badly about themselves.

LO 9.3 Discuss the major theoretical viewpoints on gender development in early childhood. (p. 222)

In early childhood, children develop their *gender identity*, or their sense of themselves as boys, girls, or another less binary gender label. Young children tend to be rigid and overly concrete about categories and stereotypes, including those of gender. Children who do not conform to gender stereotypes can be vulnerable to bullying. Freud argued children learned gender through identification with their parents. Social learning theorists believe that gender is learned through a process of modeling and reinforcement. Cognitive theorists point out that children's

thinking about gender, like other forms of logical thought, is often limited. Biological research suggests that all children, regardless of their gender identity, are very similar. Media plays a role in enforcing gender stereotypes. Some emerging research suggests that biology may play a role in making children more or less sensitive to social stereotypes. Scientific consensus supports affirming children's expressed gender identity.

LO 9.4 Describe the development of stereotypes in early childhood. (p. 222)

Young children are aware of many social categories, including those relating to ethnicity. They have preferences and prejudices about ethnicity and are more aware of discrimination. Many children have preferences for higher-status social groups. Talking to children about social categories is a helpful way of building pride and protecting them from some of the effects of discrimination.

LO 9.5 Describe variations in parenting practices and styles and how they affect children's development. (p. 228)

Families' relationships build on the foundation set in infancy to create habits of relating that can impact children for a lifetime. They are affected by the context, like cultural issues and economic conditions, and by individual factors, like a parent's personality. Parenting during early childhood is often challenging for parents. Families may not have accurate understanding of what small children are capable of. Parenting styles, including authoritative, authoritarian, permissive, and neglectful, describe caregiving based on levels of warmth and demandingness. *Discipline* refers to caregiving practices that help shape children's behavior. There are variations in parenting practices around the world, but children everywhere thrive when their caregivers express warmth and have consistent expectations. Scientific consensus opposes physical punishment and spanking. Neglectful, abusive, and shaming parenting harms children. Interventions can help improve caregiving.

LO 9.6 Describe the features of play and their role in learning and development. (p. 236)

Children play more during early childhood than they will again. Play gives children an opportunity to learn about relationships and build language and cognitive skills. Researchers describe different types of play, including solitary and onlooker play, parallel play, cooperative play, functional play, constructive play, sociodramatic play, and rough-and-tumble play. Communities vary in how much they encourage some forms of play.

LO 9.7 Describe aggressive and prosocial behaviors in early childhood. (p. 238)

In early childhood, children become more aware of morality, or right and wrong, and have more ability to behave in a kind,

or prosocial, way. Children's feelings, like empathy and guilt, influence how they treat other people. During early childhood, children begin to develop a sense of morality, or an understanding of how people should treat one another. Children can also hurt other children, either through physical aggression or through relational aggression. Aggression can be planned, or proactive, or impulsive and reactive. Children may not always behave prosocially and may have difficulty sharing, but adult encouragement helps.

KEY TERMS

initiative versus guilt (p. 216)
psychological disorders
  (p. 218)
gender roles (p. 224)
gender schema (p. 224)
transgender (p. 226)
parenting styles (p. 230)
authoritative parenting
  (p. 230)

authoritarian parenting
  (p. 230)
permissive parenting
  (p. 230)
neglectful parenting
  (p. 231)
discipline (p. 232)
power-assertive techniques
  (p. 232)

inductive reasoning (p. 232)
maltreatment (p. 233)
abuse (p. 233)
parallel play (p. 237)
cooperative play (p. 237)
functional play (p. 237)
constructive play (p. 237)
sociodramatic play
  (p. 237)

rough-and-tumble play
  (p. 237)
bullying (p. 238)
relationally aggressive
  (p. 239)
reactive aggression
  (p. 239)
proactive aggression
  (p. 239)

CHECK YOUR LEARNING

1. When 5-year-old Capri grabbed her classmate Jacob's crayons, Jacob cried for a minute, but soon recovered. This developing ability to control emotional reactions is known as:
   a) trauma.
   b) emotion regulation.
   c) a subcortical structure.
   d) self-concept.

2. According to Erik Erikson's psychosocial stage theory, the period of early childhood involves a conflict of:
   a) trust versus mistrust.
   b) autonomy versus shame.
   c) initiative versus guilt.
   d) industry versus inferiority.

3. A 4-year-old's self-concept may include which of these?
   a) I have two dogs, and I like soccer.
   b) I am not very good at writing my name.
   c) I am trustworthy and patient.
   d) I am optimistic.

4. The authoritative parenting style described by developmental scientist Diana Baumrind is characterized by:
   a) high warmth and high demandingness.
   b) high permissiveness.
   c) high warmth and low demandingness.
   d) low warmth and low communication.

5. Tara adores her three children. She thinks it is funny when the kids jump on the sofa and rarely asks the children to put away their toys. Which parenting style BEST describes Tara?
   a) Authoritative
   b) Authoritarian
   c) Dismissive
   d) Permissive

6. Which discipline technique is MOST likely to help children develop their own self-regulation?
   a) Power assertion
   b) Spanking
   c) Inductive discipline
   d) No-nonsense parenting

7. What do most developmental experts recommend regarding the use of spanking?
   a) It is okay before the age of 7.
   b) It can be effective at immediately stopping a behavior but may lead to more misbehavior later.
   c) It is illegal.
   d) It is okay after the age of 7.

8. Which of these is NOT a possible outcome of children's experiences of trauma or maltreatment?
   a) Altered stress responses to traumatic events
   b) Difficulty with self-regulation
   c) Advanced executive function
   d) Difficulty focusing attention

9. Which of these examples represents sociodramatic play commonly seen in early childhood?
   a) A group of children playing a made-up game of "superheroes and dragons"
   b) A group of children playing Simon Says
   c) A child playing alone with a jigsaw puzzle
   d) Two children riding tricycles

10. Which of these statements about young children's exposure to media and television is TRUE?
   a) Many shows depict gender stereotypes.
   b) Watching screens is harmful for developing vision.
   c) Children cannot understand what they see on television.
   d) Most children do not watch enough television or other media.

11. Alisha and Kamal are preschool classmates. While building a block tower together, Kamal got frustrated and knocked down the tower. Alisha responded by throwing a block at Kamal. Alisha's behavior is BEST described as:
   a) proactive aggression.
   b) reactive aggression.
   c) instrumental aggression.
   d) bullying aggression.

10 Physical Development in Middle Childhood

Growth in Body and Brain

10.1 Describe variations in growth, motor development, and maturation in the brain during middle childhood.

Challenges to Health

10.2 Identify common health conditions during middle childhood.

Building Health

10.3 Discuss protective health habits in middle childhood.

© Macmillan, Photo by Point Studio, Inc.

Victor started learning his family tradition at age 2. Now that he is 8, he has skills on a horse and with a rope that amaze audiences. Victor is the third generation in a talented family of *charreada*, or Mexican rodeo, performers. He has already developed his family's gift for floreo de reata, or rope tricks.

Victor can twirl a rope horizontally and vertically, jump in and out of it with agility, and lasso a bull while on horseback. For fun, he chases and lassos his 4-year-old brother in the yard while on his bike. He is proud to learn the skills that will allow him to join family as an entertainer, artist, and athlete.

Other children may dream of horses or performing in front of huge audiences, but Victor is doing both. He often practices six days a week—spinning his rope, riding horses, and chasing after bulls. He is proud to be joining his family in their tradition, and his mother, Cristal Michelle, believes that he is also learning to concentrate from all that practice. Performing helps Victor to be more outgoing, but it still makes him nervous to be in front of a crowd.

Victor not only practices for the *charrería*; he also works hard learning geography and math in school and enjoys playing with his brother and cousins on the play set in the back yard. His little brother is learning rodeo tricks, too, although he is more interested in bull riding than lasso for now.

Victor is developing skills that are unusual for many children — competing in front of big crowds and developing coordination that most adults could never match — but like many children his age, he is learning the skills that his family values and performing at an expert level. Many children his age confine their adventures to tree climbing, monkey bars, or virtual worlds, but the opportunity to be independent is something many aspire to during middle childhood.

Victor has a few inches and more than 10 pounds on his little brother, but the impressive difference between an 8-year-old and a preschooler is in their coordination and ability to focus. Like Victor, most children have tremendous capacity for growth and change during **middle childhood**, the years from about 6 to 11. This stage begins as children develop the independence and self-regulation to take on new responsibilities, such as starting elementary school, doing chores, and watching younger siblings (Rogoff et al., 1975). Middle childhood ends as children begin *adolescence*, a period marked by the outward signs of the physical maturation of puberty. The skills Victor is developing, from jumping over his riata to emptying the dishwasher, may be unique to his culture and his family, but children everywhere are learning to take care of themselves (Grove & Lancy, 2018).

This chapter covers the hallmarks of physical development during middle childhood. As you will see, the changes of puberty begin long before adolescence, in the early years of middle childhood. These changes help children develop skills, whether on horseback or in school, allowing them to become more capable and develop new interests and even crushes. In middle childhood, as across development, health shapes children's development. Children with serious health conditions may miss school or need additional support. Around the world, the years just before adolescence are the healthiest in the lifespan (WHO, 2019a). Physical activity can give children a sense of competence and also help build an identity. Even if they are not trick-roping champions, movement helps children develop skills and interests that will last a lifetime.

As you peek into Victor's world, you will learn more about the things he loves: his dog, his family, and the traditions of Mexican dance and rodeo. You will also read about the hallmarks of health and physical development in childhood, as children's bodies and brains are shaped by their genes, hormones, and the world they live in.

middle childhood The period spanning ages 6 to 11 that begins as children develop the independence and self-regulation to take on new responsibilities.

Scientific American Profile
Meet Victor

Growth in Body and Brain

In middle childhood, children's physical growth slows from the frantic pace of early childhood, as much of their energy is diverted from body development to brain development (Bogin, 1997). They are focused on learning, whether jumping over a lasso, programming robots, adding and subtracting, or making new friends (Kuzawa & Blair, 2019). This learning leads to the reshaping of children's *cortex*, the outer layer of the brain that helps children better control their behavior and think more efficiently (Hong et al., 2021).

Learning Objective

10.1 Describe variations in growth, motor development, and maturation in the brain during middle childhood.

Physical Growth

In the United States, children typically gain about 5 pounds (2 kilograms) and more than 2 inches (5 centimeters) each year during middle childhood (Section on Endocrinology, 2014). Typically, 6-year-olds are about 45 pounds (20 kilograms) and 45 inches (110 centimeters) tall; by age 12, they are nearly 85 pounds (45 kilograms) and 5 feet (145 centimeters) tall (NCHS, 2000). Children are slowly growing stronger, gaining the muscle that will allow them to throw a ball through a basketball hoop or carry a heavy backpack (Yamato et al., 2018).

Because of hormonal changes, most children start to add more body fat and muscle mass and begin a rapid *growth spurt* at the end of middle childhood. For most girls, this growth spurt typically begins at around age 10, and for boys, it begins about two years later (Sanders et al., 2017). As a result, by the end of elementary school, girls often tower over boys. (See **Figure 10.1**.)

FIGURE 10.1 Rate of Growth in Middle Childhood During middle childhood, the pace of growth tends to slow, until the rapid growth spurt that is an early sign of puberty.

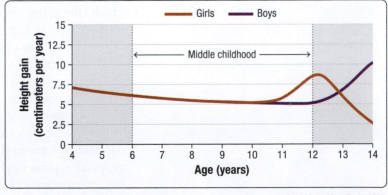

Data adapted from Bogin, 1997.

During middle childhood, differences in size become more apparent, which can affect a child's developing body image and even lead to social exclusion (De Coen et al., 2021; Nabors et al., 2019). Some children are taller or heavier than others. For well-nourished children, height is highly influenced by genes, which also dictate the timing of their growth spurts. However, in many communities around the globe where children experience chronic infections, malnutrition, or disease, size is more closely related to children's health than to their genome (Jelenkovic et al., 2020).

Around the world, children and their families often care a great deal about how tall they are (Murano et al., 2020). Height is often correlated with a host of social benefits beyond just being big enough to enjoy the rides at the amusement park; taller children tend to get their way more frequently and are more likely to be socially dominant (Desmichel & Rucker, 2022; Quitmann et al., 2016). Children in some communities hold negative stereotypes about their smaller peers, and may be more likely to bully those who are smaller (Backeljauw et al., 2021).

Learning to Sit Still One of the hallmarks of middle childhood is an increased ability to control the body. In this classroom in Canada, this includes practicing sitting still and doing yoga.

Motor Skill Development

In middle childhood, children can perform complex physical activities: Many can hit a ball with a bat or write a neat paragraph. Their bodies are still not as strong or fast as adults', even adjusting for their smaller size, but anyone who has chased a 7-year-old around the playground knows that children have more energy than many adults. In fact, when experts measure children's aerobic capacity and ability to recover from exertion, they find that the average child rivals a trained triathlete (Bontemps et al., 2019).

During middle childhood, children typically acquire the motor skills that will foster independence, academic success, and a sense of competence among their friends. At this age, they are generally expected to be self-sufficient in everyday self-care: Most 7-year-olds can dress themselves and stay dry through the night (Vaziri Flais et al., 2018). Children at this age also need fine motor skills for academic success: Difficulty with writing often leads to academic difficulties later on (Gaul & Issartel, 2016).

Much of what children do in school involves fine motor skills, whether that means clicking on a chat box in a Zoom class, writing numbers clearly, or constructing a diorama about bats. As many as one in four children around the world struggles with fine motor skills like handwriting (Coker & Kim, 2018; Rosenblum, 2018). Messy or slow writing may seem like an old-fashioned concern, particularly in an era of keyboards and smartphones, but children who have trouble with the motor coordination involved in writing also tend to have difficulties with getting their ideas down clearly (Limpo & Graham, 2020). The solution that works for most? More practice. Handwriting requires integrating visual perception, motor coordination, and planning skills, which, for many children, just take more practice to develop (McClelland & Cameron, 2019; Ose Askvik et al., 2020). Once children can write fluidly by hand, they can put more of their energy into deeper thinking.

Many physical education experts hope that children also develop gross motor skills during middle childhood, such as doing sit-ups, throwing and catching a ball, or walking on a balance beam. However, formal athletic skills like these require practice and opportunity—putting them out of reach of many children. Most children in the United States and in other countries around the world do not meet the ideal standards for motor development: They are not quite able to hop, sit up, or pull up as sports experts might hope (Aubert et al., 2021; Barnett et al., 2016). Children who have less access to sports programming outside of school and less time devoted to physical education in school, typically because they come from lower-income neighborhoods and families, are the least likely to develop strong motor skills (Logan et al., 2019; Ré et al., 2020).

Children whose motor skills are less developed in preschool are also likely to have difficulties keeping up in elementary school (Gu et al., 2021). If a child is not able to excel at the playground equipment in kindergarten, they are less likely to be able to run around the track, throw and catch a ball, and do push-ups in fourth grade. Researchers suggest that these children may have difficulty developing the motivation to try, perhaps because they feel that they are already far behind or that athletic activity is too hard for them. Whatever activities a community values, feeling physically competent increases the likelihood that children will do better in school and stay active and healthier later in life (Barnett et al., 2020).

Practice Builds the Brain

The physical skills that children acquire during middle childhood can be complex; in addition to moving muscles, children need to be able to plan and execute that jump, spin, or twist (Van der Fels et al., 2015). Along with larger muscles and bones and lots of practice, changes in the maturing brain help children learn these physical skills faster (Magallon et al., 2016). Stronger muscles and bigger bodies make it easier to throw a basket or paint a rainbow, but the most important body part in motor skill development is the *brain*.

Children use their executive function skills like attention, memory, and planning that developed during early childhood to help them learn new and complex motor skills. These skills are supported by gradual maturation in the brain networks that control movement (as you will see in **Infographic 10.1** on page 252). These networks connect the cortex with subcortical structures, such as the *basal ganglia* and *cerebellum*. The basal ganglia is involved in controlling movement, but it also plays a role in emotion and decision-making. The cerebellum is the structure in the back of the brain that is shaped like a miniature brain and is essential for balance and motor coordination.

Growth in the brain's neural networks means that children can begin to achieve complex skills between the ages of 6 and 9; however, they will not pick these skills up as quickly as adults or teenagers. Preadolescent children may struggle with the decision-making, timing, and social input it takes to succeed in complex sports, such as soccer or rodeo: They may not be ready for the level of competition and intensity that many sports require (Logan et al., 2019).

Achieving skills such as horseback riding, reading, or playing a musical instrument requires that our skills become *automatic*, or happen quickly, without our conscious awareness (Magallon et al., 2016). In a process formally known as *automatization*, you become able to perform a skill without consciously paying attention, so you can focus on other things at the same time. Automatization, whether in sports, music, or reading, changes the structure of the brain (Habibi et al., 2017; Ozernov-Palchik et al., 2021; Zuk & Gaab, 2018). Depending on the activity and the intensity with which children practice, physical activity accelerates neural pruning, increases connectivity and myelination, and enlarges parts of the brain, including the motor cortex (Kim et al., 2016; López-Vincente et al., 2017).

CAN YOU BELIEVE IT?

Do Sports Make You Smarter?

In the United States, after-school sports are among the most common after-school activities children participate in, with about 4 in 10 U.S. children having participated in some kind of sports team or class (Aspen Institute, 2021). Parents often explain that

Share It!

Don't burst their bubble. Children are not very realistic in assessing how good they are at sports, but that does not seem to hurt. Children still benefit from being active even if they don't know how good they are.

(Barnett et al., 2020)

Working to Make Things Automatic Practice may never make things perfect, but it can help build skills. Dribbling, catching, and throwing the ball are motor skills that can be automatized over time.

they sign their children up for sports to keep them busy after school and to help them develop social skills (Holt et al., 2011; Kroshus et al., 2021). Children are often motivated to join a team because sports can be fun, or because they bolster youthful dreams about being a professional athlete (Project Play, 2020). Some experts suggest that playing sports can boost children's cognitive skills. What is the evidence?

There is ample scientific consensus that, across the lifespan, being physically active is beneficial to the brain and the body. Researchers suspect that there are biological explanations for this: Being active increases the amount of oxygen and hormones available in the brain and may even encourage growth in brain structures, like the hippocampus, that are activated when we are learning (Gorham & Barch, 2020; Valkenborghs et al., 2019). Scientists also suspect that there are social and cognitive reasons sports can be beneficial: Playing sports requires focus, teamwork, and self-control, skills that benefit children and adults.

Many correlational studies have found that young people who participate in sports or are physically active are different from those who do not. Exercise is associated with lower rates of depression and may help children be more outgoing, more persistent, and less reactive (Bruner et al., 2021; Conley et al., 2020; Logan et al., 2019). Athletic activities also help children learn new motor skills and develop new relationships and a social identity that can persist into adulthood (Aumètre & Poulin, 2018).

However, there is some scientific controversy about exactly *how* physical activity and sports change children. There are strong correlations between children's cognitive functioning and their level of physical activity, such as the link between sports participation and higher scores in tests of executive function (Biddle et al., 2019; Koepp & Gershoff, 2022). However, there are often other differences between children who participate in sports and who are physically active and those who are not: Sports often require a lot of parental time and money. Children who can participate in sports often have other privileges, including more motivated and affluent families (Aspen Institute, 2021).

To determine whether physical activity *causes* improved executive function, researchers have conducted randomized controlled experiments to establish a link. In these programs, they typically randomly assign one group of children to participate in an intensive after-school sports program while another group (the control group) participates in another, more sedentary, activity or just goes on with their lives as usual. These trials have found strong links between sports activity and higher scores in executive function and increased brain activation in tests requiring cognitive control (Hillman et al., 2014). When researchers analyze all randomized controlled trials that have been conducted, many find strong connections between regular athletic activities and improved executive function (Meijer et al., 2020; Xue et al., 2019).

But questions remain: For instance, does it matter whether children are doing cognitively demanding workouts, like playing basketball or learning Tae Kwan Do, or whether they are just running on a treadmill? An influential group of scientists suggests that to be maximally effective, exercise needs to be "mindful" and not simply "mindless" (Diamond & Ling, 2016; Schmidt et al., 2015). Other researchers have found strong connections between children's overall level of fitness and their executive function, regardless of how intellectually demanding the activity might be (Hillman et al., 2018; Hsieh et al., 2020).

Researchers also caution that sports are not always welcoming to all children. Some children do not enjoy sports. Others may have difficulty participating, particularly if they have disabilities and are not welcomed or supported. It is important to remember that sports are not the *only* way to boost executive function and well-being. Participating in after-school activities like music groups or even classes designed to teach executive function training can be helpful (Darcy et al., 2020; Ilari, 2020; Schmidt et al., 2020; Tomporowski & Pesce, 2019). The most important thing to remember? No matter what the method, cognitive skills and executive function are changeable. 🌀

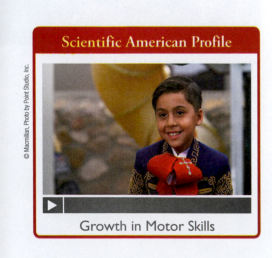

Scientific American Profile

Growth in Motor Skills

Brain Development

Children's brains are maturing during middle childhood, which gives them greater control over their thoughts, emotions, and bodies. This is why many children can keep smiling even if they lose a championship and can remember how to spell "friend" (most of the time). These changes are supported by two major developments in the brain: First, maturation in the cortex speeds up children's thinking, improving skills such as reading, math, and planning ahead (Butterworth & Walsh, 2011; Ronan et al., 2020; Thiebaut de Schotten et al., 2014). Second, increasing connectivity in the brain helps children learn to manage their emotions, master new social relationships, and develop unique personalities and ways of responding to the world (Kopala-Sibley et al., 2020; Tottenham & Gabard-Durnam, 2017).

Faster Connections and Pruning in the Cortex As described in Chapter 4, your brain develops according to a use-it-or-lose-it principle. Synaptic connections that are used frequently get stronger; those used less frequently tend to fade away. This is particularly true during middle childhood, when children are learning a great deal—building new synaptic connections and automatizing the skills they have acquired. Remember from Chapter 4 that the neurons involved in pathways that are used more often become *myelinated*, or insulated with a substance called myelin, which speeds up transmission and turns the cells into *white matter*. During middle childhood, myelination occurs throughout the cortex, building more white matter (Natu et al., 2019).

Remember that myelinated white matter connections make up the fast, long-range synaptic connections that create what neuroscientists refer to as the *connectome*, or the network that links regions of the brain (Kim et al., 2019). These improved connections enhance the motor coordination, executive function, attention, and memory skills that children need to control their behavior, do long division, and remember their login passwords (Piccolo et al., 2019).

As frequently used synaptic connections become myelinated, unused synapses and dendrites are gradually *pruned*, or fade away. As you may remember, unmyelinated connections are referred to as *gray matter*. During middle childhood, pruning continues in the cortex, and gray matter is pruned so much that the cortex itself becomes thinner as unnecessary connections disappear (Tamnes & Mills, 2020; Walhovd et al., 2017). This thinner, smaller cortex has more longer, faster myelinated connections, or *white matter*, which also changes shape over time: The surface of the cortex continues to fold in on itself, deepening the characteristic wrinkles and whorls, known as *sulci* and *gyri*, visible on the outside (Garcia et al., 2018).

Variations in the pace of cortical thinning are common during middle childhood, when the cortex is particularly plastic because of the experiences that are constantly shaping children's brains (Tooley et al., 2021). Remember that children's bodies and brains often show accelerated development as a response to stress in the environment or prenatal injuries. This is believed to be the case with cortical thinning (Alnæs et al., 2020). Children who have significant cognitive gains build more synapses in the cortex, leading to a slower rate of cortical thinning or even to cortical thickening (Estrada et al., 2019).

This is not always true of children who are exposed to significant adversity: Children who are frequently afraid, feel unsafe, or lack opportunities for learning may have a faster rate of cortical thinning and accelerated maturation of neural circuits (Colich et al., 2020; Smith & Pollak, 2021). Earlier cortical thinning means that the period of plasticity in brain development is shortened. Fewer opportunities for cognitive stimulation and more exposure to stress hormones may shape children's memory and attention skills and adapting to their circumstances. While adversity is never ideal,

CONNECTIONS

Remember the principles of brain development (see Chapter 4): Experiences create new synaptic connections; connections that are used become faster through myelination; and, as children grow, shorter, localized connections are replaced with more efficient, long-range connections across regions of the brain.

Share It!

Could there be benefits to stress? Children adapt to stressful circumstances. Some researchers suggest that this may give them unique strengths: better procedural memory (which helps them learn new skills) and a greater ability to perceive changes in their environment.

(Frankenhuis & Nettle, 2020)

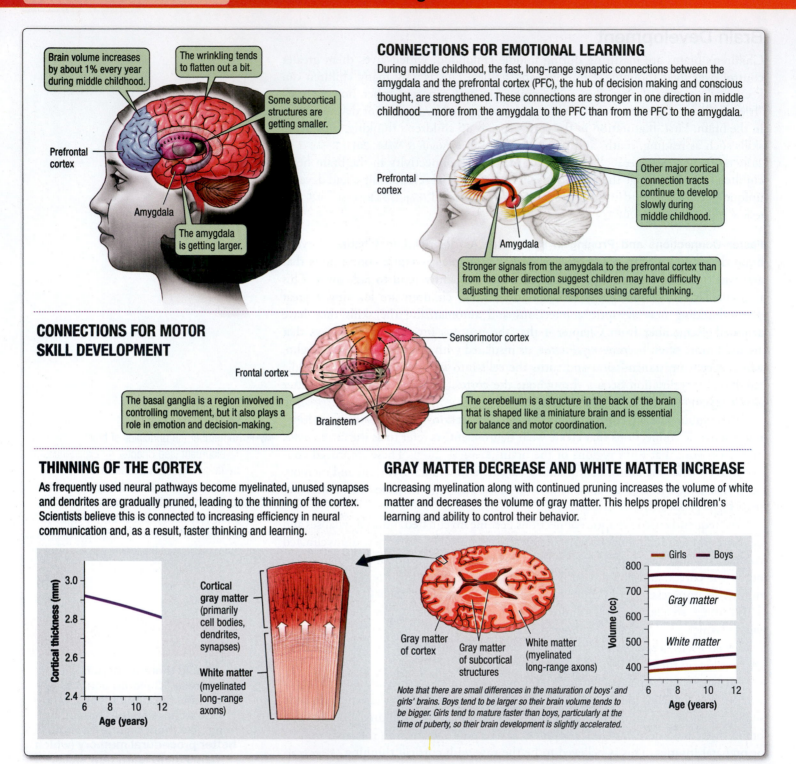

CONNECTIONS FOR EMOTIONAL LEARNING

During middle childhood, the fast, long-range synaptic connections between the amygdala and the prefrontal cortex (PFC), the hub of decision making and conscious thought, are strengthened. These connections are stronger in one direction in middle childhood—more from the amygdala to the PFC than from the PFC to the amygdala.

Brain volume increases by about 1% every year during middle childhood.

The wrinkling tends to flatten out a bit.

Some subcortical structures are getting smaller.

Prefrontal cortex

Amygdala

The amygdala is getting larger.

Prefrontal cortex

Other major cortical connection tracts continue to develop slowly during middle childhood.

Amygdala

Stronger signals from the amygdala to the prefrontal cortex than from the other direction suggest children may have difficulty adjusting their emotional responses using careful thinking.

CONNECTIONS FOR MOTOR SKILL DEVELOPMENT

Sensorimotor cortex

Frontal cortex

The basal ganglia is a region involved in controlling movement, but it also plays a role in emotion and decision-making.

Brainstem

The cerebellum is a structure in the back of the brain that is shaped like a miniature brain and is essential for balance and motor coordination.

THINNING OF THE CORTEX

As frequently used neural pathways become myelinated, unused synapses and dendrites are gradually pruned, leading to the thinning of the cortex. Scientists believe this is connected to increasing efficiency in neural communication and, as a result, faster thinking and learning.

Cortical thickness (mm)

3.0
2.8
2.6
2.4

6 8 10 12

Age (years)

Cortical gray matter (primarily cell bodies, dendrites, synapses)

White matter (myelinated long-range axons)

GRAY MATTER DECREASE AND WHITE MATTER INCREASE

Increasing myelination along with continued pruning increases the volume of white matter and decreases the volume of gray matter. This helps propel children's learning and ability to control their behavior.

Gray matter of cortex

Gray matter of subcortical structures

White matter (myelinated long-range axons)

Note that there are small differences in the maturation of boys' and girls' brains. Boys tend to be larger so their brain volume tends to be bigger. Girls tend to mature faster than boys, particularly at the time of puberty, so their brain development is slightly accelerated.

Girls Boys

Volume (cc)

800
700
600
500
400

Gray matter

White matter

6 8 10 12

Age (years)

exposure to stress has been shown to lead to some unique strengths, like enhanced ability to pick up on new information in the environment (Chad-Friedman et al., 2021; Ellis, Cliff, et al., 2017).

Connections for Emotion Learning Children learn a great deal during middle childhood, whether out with friends or at home, but some of their most important learning involves managing their feelings. Researchers are particularly interested in how brain development reflects children's emotional maturity (Kopala-Sibley et al., 2020).

Remember from Chapter 6 that emotions are processed deep in the brain's subcortical structures, particularly in the *amygdala*. During middle childhood, the fast, long-range synaptic connections between the subcortical structures and the *prefrontal cortex* (PFC), the hub of decision-making and conscious thought, are strengthened. These connections influence children's personalities, their emotion regulation, and their ways of relating (Callaghan & Tottenham, 2016). These connections are stronger in one direction in middle childhood—more activation occurs in pathways from the amygdala to the PFC than from the PFC to the amygdala. Pathways are stronger in the opposite direction during adolescence and adulthood, when the PFC starts to manage and inhibit input from the amygdala (Cohodes et al., 2021). In essence, during middle childhood, children's emotional experiences shape how they think and make decisions (Tottenham, 2020).

The neural changes just described help explain the typical challenges children have with emotion regulation. Although they are much less prone to tantrums than preschoolers, school-age children are still less emotionally mature than teenagers. They still rely on their caregivers for comfort and have an easier time tackling new challenges—like starting at a new school or getting a flu shot—if family members come along (Tan et al., 2020). Their brains do not yet have strong connections between the PFC (the "thinking" part) and the amygdala (the "fear" part), so they cannot use thinking to change how they feel. Therefore, children need to use other methods to manage their feelings, like reaching out for support or avoiding upsetting situations altogether. Whereas children might cover their eyes or hide during the scary parts of a movie, adults can remind themselves that it's "just a movie" (Silvers et al., 2019).

Adrenarche and the Early Signs of Puberty

If you look at the group of elementary-age schoolchildren in Victor's class, you might believe that they are far from adolescence. However, inside their bodies, new hormones are triggering maturation (Rosenfield, 2021). Most of this happens because the *adrenal glands*, two thumb-sized structures on the top of your kidneys, begin to secrete higher levels of hormones such as dehydroepiandrosterone (DHEA) between the ages of 5 and 9 (Goddings et al., 2021; Keestra et al., 2021). This process, which prepares the body for puberty and initiates physical maturation, is called **adrenarche**.

Adrenarche triggers the appearance of some **secondary sex characteristics**, the physical markers that are associated with adult appearance, including pubic hair, facial hair, the Adam's apple, and breasts. (**Primary sex characteristics** are the reproductive organs that babies are typically born with, like genitals.) (See **Figure 10.2**.) By age 8, one in five typical girls may have some pubic hair (Kaplowitz et al., 2016; Stein et al., 2019). By age 10, children may need deodorant and have acne breakouts. Children at this age often begin to have romantic or sexual desires, like crushes, although their sexual identity often takes a few more years to develop (Bishop et al., 2020; Fortenberry, 2014).

As you will learn in Chapter 13, puberty is triggered by a different set of hormones than adrenarche. Ovarian hormones trigger some early signs of puberty, including the beginnings of breast development, at around age 9 (Greenspan, 2017; Kaplowitz et al., 2016). Changes triggered by puberty begin a few years later for children with testes, but they may begin to put on weight in advance of a growth spurt that begins around age 12 (Sanders et al., 2017). Children who are transgender or identify as nonbinary may need to prepare for some of these physical changes: Their families may consider beginning hormone treatments to postpone maturation (Shumer & Araya, 2019). But for all children, understanding adrenarche and the early signs of puberty can reassure children that there is nothing unusual about what they are going through.

adrenarche The first hormonal changes preparing the body for puberty, typically occurring between ages 5 and 9.

secondary sex characteristics The physical markers of what makes people look like adults after puberty. Secondary sex characteristics include pubic hair, facial hair, the Adam's apple, and breasts.

primary sex characteristics The reproductive organs that babies are typically born with, like genitals.

FIGURE 10.2 The Changes of Adrenarche Between the ages of about 5 and 9, hormonal changes triggered by the adrenal glands mark the beginning of adrenarche, a hormonal process driven by the adrenal glands. Adrenarche leads to the development of some secondary sex characteristics, including changes in smell, skin, and hair growth. During this time, children may also experience the early signs of puberty, a process driven by the ovaries and testes.

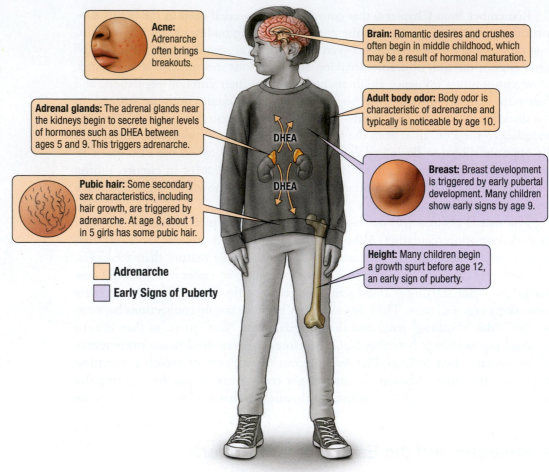

Acne: Adrenarche often brings breakouts.

Brain: Romantic desires and crushes often begin in middle childhood, which may be a result of hormonal maturation.

Adrenal glands: The adrenal glands near the kidneys begin to secrete higher levels of hormones such as DHEA between ages 5 and 9. This triggers adrenarche.

Adult body odor: Body odor is characteristic of adrenarche and typically is noticeable by age 10.

DHEA

DHEA

Breast: Breast development is triggered by early pubertal development. Many children show early signs by age 9.

Pubic hair: Some secondary sex characteristics, including hair growth, are triggered by adrenarche. At age 8, about 1 in 5 girls has some pubic hair.

Height: Many children begin a growth spurt before age 12, an early sign of puberty.

■ Adrenarche

■ Early Signs of Puberty

APPLY IT! **10.1** Victor's family has encouraged him to learn some specialized physical skills, including rope tricks, not just chasing his dog and his brother through the yard. How does the development of culturally valued motor skills benefit Victor and other young children?

10.2 Victor has never heard of adrenarche. What are the three things he might want to be prepared for before he turns 10?

Challenges to Health

Learning Objective

10.2 Identify common health conditions during middle childhood.

Share It!

Healthy teeth are more than a pretty smile: They also mean you are more likely to be in school. Cavities and tooth decay hurt, and pain keeps children out of school.

(Rebelo et al., 2019)

Like Victor, most children in the United States are thriving during middle childhood. In recent surveys, nearly 98 percent of U.S. families reported that their children's health was good or excellent (NCHS, 2021). However, health statistics reveal that the overall picture is not quite as rosy. Like other periods in development, the school years come with health risks. Unsupported health conditions not only impact children's bodies; they also can have cognitive and social consequences (Allison et al., 2019). Children who are not well and lack support are more likely to miss school, which can mean missed opportunities for learning and making friends (Ansari & Gottfried, 2021; Bundy et al., 2018).

Most children's health troubles are minor during middle childhood. But some can be more severe, like a cancer diagnosis, a car crash, or a traumatic accident with a firearm. Other children live with impairments that may be less visible, such as cavities, visual impairments, or the chronic effects of environmental pollution. In addition, unsupported emotional, cognitive, and behavioral disorders are a leading cause of children's disability around the world (Patel et al., 2018; Whitney & Peterson, 2019).

Childhood Illnesses

In the United States, about one in five children has a chronic physical health condition, like asthma or diabetes, that impacts their everyday life (Blackwell et al., 2019). In low-income countries, middle childhood is more perilous: About 6 of every 1,000 children lose their lives because of chronic disease or malnutrition (Bundy et al., 2017; UN IGME, 2020). In such places, infectious diseases continue to be the leading cause of death in young children.

Children become healthier as they get older and are better able to handle the stresses of common illnesses. As a result, it is not until after age 10 that children are strong enough to reliably recover from common infectious diseases, particularly if they have underlying malnutrition or chronic illness (Bundy et al., 2017; see **Figure 10.3**). One of these common diseaes is malaria. More than half of the children around the world are at risk to develop malaria, primarily in sub-Saharan Africa, the Indian subcontinent, and South America. Malaria is often untreated or undertreated in children, because their symptoms may appear less severe than those in adults (Cohee et al., 2020). However, undertreated malaria is linked to anemia, brain injuries, and cognitive delays (Ssemata et al., 2020). Children who have malaria miss school, often for months, which can make it difficult or impossible to fully catch up (Halliday et al., 2020). Preventive treatments, including a vaccine, exist but are often unavailable in low-income communities (Ashley & Poespoprodjo, 2020; WHO, 2022b).

As noted in Chapter 6, active immune systems protect most children from the worst effects of COVID-19, although they can still pass the virus on to other people (Bhopal et al., 2021). Elementary-age schoolchildren also benefited from early access to COVID-19 vaccinations. Children who already had a serious condition, such as a chronic lung disease, neurological condition, or diabetes, were at higher risk from the virus (Shi et al., 2022; Woodruff et al., 2021). But even amid the COVID-19 pandemic, in affluent countries, the death of a young child is a rare event (Cunningham et al., 2018; Dorney et al., 2020).

Protected for First Grade Like about 4 in 10 children her age, 6-year-old Calista is vaccinated to protect herself and her community from the COVID-19 virus. Here she receives her second COVID-19 vaccine near her home in San Francisco, California.

CONNECTIONS

Remember from Chapter 4 that malaria is a mosquito-borne disease that is a leading cause of death in infants and young children around the globe. Malaria can be prevented through the use of bed nets and mosquito eradication along with vaccination.

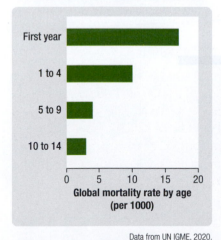

GLOBAL MORTALITY IMPROVES WITH AGE

First year | 1 to 4 | 5 to 9 | 10 to 14

Global mortality rate by age (per 1000)

Data from UN IGME, 2020.

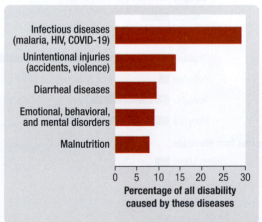

LEADING CAUSES OF DISABILITY IN CHILDREN AROUND THE WORLD

Infectious diseases (malaria, HIV, COVID-19)
Unintentional injuries (accidents, violence)
Diarrheal diseases
Emotional, behavioral, and mental disorders
Malnutrition

Percentage of all disability caused by these diseases

Data from WHO, 2020.

LEADING CAUSES OF DEATH IN CHILDREN IN THE UNITED STATES

Accidents
Cancer
Gun-related injuries (may include other categories)
Suicide
Homicide

Leading causes of death in children 5–14 (cases per year)

Data from CDC Wonder, 2022.

FIGURE 10.3 How Healthy Are Children Around the World? Bigger, sturdier bodies mean that children are healthier during middle childhood than they are during earlier periods in development. Around the globe, infectious diseases continue to be a leading cause of illness in younger children. In the United States, more than one in five children need support with a chronic emotional, behavioral, or health condition, and many leading causes of death are linked to accidents and gun violence.

Share It!

Keep them securely stored: Children are naturally inquisitive. Guns are involved in one in four accidental deaths in children in the United States.

(Cohen et al., 2021)

CONNECTIONS

Remember from Chapter 7 that accidental injuries such as drowning or electrical fires are a major cause of death in early childhood. Preventing injuries and accidents involves increased adult attention and making the environment safer.

The leading cause of death in children in high-income countries including the United States is accidents, primarily traffic fatalities (CDC Wonder, 2022; UN IGME, 2021). The rate of motor vehicle fatalities in the United States is nearly double that of other affluent countries, primarily because of low rates of seatbelt use and high rates of alcohol and substance-impaired driving (Sauber-Schatz et al., 2016). Many children who die in accidents were not wearing seatbelts or were not properly strapped into booster seats (Findlay et al., 2019; Lee et al., 2015; Missikpode et al., 2021). For every one of the more than 600 U.S. children who die each year in car accidents, 250 more are treated for nonfatal injuries (CDC Wonder, 2022; Sauber-Schatz et al., 2015). However, public health experts see car accidents as a success story: The number of children dying in car accidents has dropped by more than two-thirds in recent years due to improved vehicle safety and use of car seats (Sauber-Schatz et al., 2014).

One area that has not improved in recent years is children's risk of violent death. U.S. children are at higher risk than children in other affluent countries are for dying violently, particularly as a result of suicides or homicides, many of them linked to firearms (Andrews et al., 2022; Grinshteyn & Hemenway, 2019). Rates of child and adolescent deaths due to homicide, suicide, and firearm accidents are more than two times higher in the U.S. than in other affluent nations (Grinshteyn & Hemenway, 2019). Researchers link violent death to unsecured firearms, which make suicide easier, and to an increase in serious emotional conditions in children (Curtin & Heron, 2019; Grinshteyn & Hemenway, 2019). Other scientists link family difficulties to young children's deaths, pointing out that both suicide and homicide are higher in families with chronic levels of conflict. One in five homicides of children results from ongoing family violence (Adhia et al., 2019; DeVille et al., 2020). The rest are typically the result of a criminal assault (Taylor et al., 2021). (See **Figure 10.4**.)

Violence is not the only unexpected and uncontrollable danger that children may face. Nearly 800 U.S. children lose their lives every year to cancer, typically leukemia or brain cancers, along with an additional 142,000 children in other countries (Force

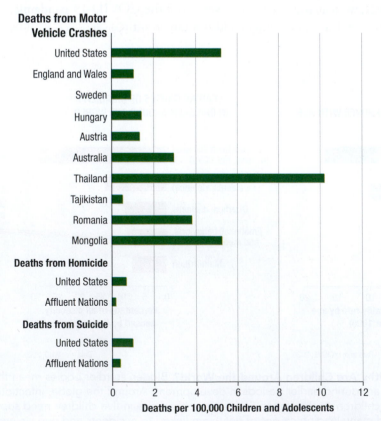

FIGURE 10.4 Comparative Risks The leading cause of death for children in the United States and many other high-income nations is motor vehicle accidents, but the risks vary depending on the communities in which the children live. Violence and suicide are also leading causes of death in young children: Rates in the United States are higher than in other affluent countries.

Data from Grinshteyn & Hemenway, 2019.

et al., 2019; Siegel et al., 2022). In high-income countries, more than 80 percent of children recover from cancer. In low-income countries where treatment is less accessible, about 50 percent of children recover (Force et al., 2019). Even in affluent countries like the United States, there are disparities in how cancer affects children. Some children, particularly if they are from low-income families or are from groups that experience marginalization, are more likely to get cancer and are less likely to survive. For some types of cancers, this may increase children's risk of dying by nearly 50 percent (Kehm et al., 2018; Zavala et al., 2021).

Researchers suspect that family income plays the most important role in these risks. Environmental pollution, families' exposure to life stresses, and the impact of discrimination faced by families of color may also play a part. Even if children survive cancer, the treatments result in time missed from friends and schoolwork, weeks of pain, ongoing feelings of trauma, and increased risk for health complications (Hudson et al., 2021; Sharp et al., 2022; Tsimicalis et al., 2018). As you will learn, caring for children who are ill requires families and health care providers to be imaginative and sensitive to their developmental needs (Law et al., 2019).

SCIENCE IN PRACTICE
Camille Frasier, Child Life Specialist

Camille Fraser doesn't remember the name of the woman who changed her life. Diagnosed with cancer as a teenager, Camille was terrified of needles but needed a tube inserted in her chest to enable physicians to administer her medication and take blood. When Camille felt too panicked to allow them close to her, a *child life specialist* showed her exactly what the doctors were going to do, soothing Camille and helping her get through the procedure. This kindness led Camille to a mission: After recovering from cancer, Camille decided to become a child life specialist herself, so she could help children who were experiencing similar difficulties.

Child life specialists are health care providers with a background in child development, including an undergraduate and sometimes a master's degree, who undergo intensive hands-on training to support children with various conditions and their families. They work in hospitals to prepare children for invasive procedures or to help reduce the pain or anxiety they may have about their illnesses.

Camille spent weeks in the hospital over the course of her treatment, but she left committed to turning her experience into an opportunity to help other children. Thirteen years later, Camille became certified as a child life specialist, a job she loves. From her own experience as a patient, she remembers "what it feels like to be stuck in your room for long periods of time. . . . I know what it means to be a part of a family that is dealing with a very difficult diagnosis" (Echegaray, 2017). Now she works with children with heart disease, sometimes pulling out her puppet friend, Hank, who makes young children smile as he "explains" the details of a complicated medical procedure.

Children may not understand why they are at the hospital or what is wrong with them. Child life specialists explain what is happening and help children who may be coping with loneliness or separation from family, sometimes for the first time. Child life specialists have been known to pull out candy and marshmallows to explain leukemia. They might explain that IV fluids will be cold and that the alcohol used to clean children's skin may have a strong smell. Specialists can coax a child to watch a movie on an iPad to keep them still for an MRI.

Children who have worked with child life specialists recover more quickly from serious illnesses and short procedures like IV placement or a trip to the emergency room, with less pain and less emotional upset (Committee on Hospital Care, 2014; Pillai, 2020; Romito et al., 2021). For Camille, it is a dream job. She feels honored to make a difference and return the empathy that helped her in her own recovery.

Raising Money for Her Friends Caroline was diagnosed with leukemia when she was just a toddler. After more than two years of treatment, she is now in remission and raises money for cancer treatment by selling lemonade, in conjunction with a charity known as Alex's Lemonade Stand, near her home in St. Petersburg, Florida.

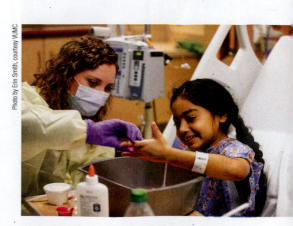

Slime Helps Child life specialists understand that although they may be sick, children are still children even in the hospital. Here, a child life specialist at Vanderbilt University Medical Center helps explain science and brings a little joy by making slime in a hospital bed.

Chronic Health Conditions

In affluent countries, deadly illnesses and accidents are rare, but chronic conditions and illnesses are not (Pulcini et al., 2017). They are often linked to structural and environmental conditions that are beyond the control of children and their families. In the United States, as many as one in five children has been diagnosed with a condition like asthma, allergies, or dental issues that interferes with school and increases their likelihood for health complications later in life (Ullah & Kaelber, 2021).

An increasing number of children in affluent countries have challenges linked to diet and weight that may affect their physical development and health in later years (Sahota et al., 2020; Tagi & Chiarelli, 2020; Wühl, 2019). Public health experts suggest about one in five children around the globe may be too heavy and that, for some, this weight may trigger changes in their metabolism and cardiovascular system that result in diabetes, liver disease, and heart disease (Caprio et al., 2020; Smith, Fu, et al., 2020; UNICEF, 2021b). Stigma and bias against children who are heavy may also be linked to their increased risk for metabolic and cardiovascular complications. In communities that allow children and adults to exclude others based on their appearance, children who are bigger than their peers are more likely to experience bullying, poor body image, and depression, an additional stress that can undermine their health (Killedar et al., 2020; Morales et al., 2019).

Systems beyond children's control can make it difficult to maintain a healthy weight: Genetics, early metabolic programming, and biology lead school-age children to prefer sweets and salty snacks to fruits and vegetables (Beckerman et al., 2017; Kansra et al., 2020). In many nations, processed foods are less expensive than fresh fruits and vegetables, and families are often overwhelmed by marketing that promotes unhealthy diets (Fischer et al., 2021; Headey & Alderman, 2019).

Dental cavities are the most common chronic disease among young children in the United States and around the world, affecting more than one in four U.S. kindergarteners and more than half of the children around the world every year (Folayan et al., 2020; Pitts et al., 2017; Ramos-Gomez et al., 2020). Rates of dental cavities are increasing around the world, as children eat sugary treats and are not able to keep their teeth clean, use fluoride regularly, or get regular dental care (Folayan et al., 2020).

Cavities can be more than an annoyance. Without treatment, they can cause pain and infection and keep children home from school (Chou et al., 2021). Dental problems are often stigmatized, and if untreated they can often last into adulthood and can make it difficult for adults to find work (Isiekwe et al., 2016). Around the world, dental treatment is often unavailable or expensive and is not well integrated into medical care systems (Ramos-Gomez et al., 2020; Watt et al., 2019). In many U.S. communities, low-income children and those from marginalized communities are particularly likely to experience untreated dental conditions (Northridge et al., 2020). Interventions to expand access to pediatric dentistry for low-income children have helped to improve children's dental health in recent years, but gaps still remain (Gargano et al., 2019).

Emotional Disorders

For many children, a trip to an amusement park is exciting, but for others it can be terrifying. One family shared the experience of their son, Erik, with researchers. He was afraid of the rides at the park, being left alone, and being kidnapped. Erik had a long list of worries: the dentist, asking for help in a store, walking to the bus stop alone (Lundkvist-Houndoumadi & Thastum, 2013). He had been anxious and shy as a toddler, and by the fifth grade, he often had stomach pains and panicked at the thought of going to school or running errands with his mother. Like about 1 in 12 children in

Robert A. Reeder/The Washington Post via Getty Images

Waiting For a Turn Kwajuh and Amiah are waiting for their chance to be seen by dental hygienist Nellie Carey, once she finishes checking Dejanae's teeth in a dental clinic in Washington, D.C. Dental health is linked to well-being in childhood and across the lifespan.

the United States, Erik was diagnosed with an *anxiety disorder*, a state of constant worry that made it challenging for him to learn in school, make friends, and live a full life (Bitsko et al., 2022; Ghandour et al., 2019).

Surveys have found that at least one in eight children around the world meets the criteria to be diagnosed with a *psychological disorder*, a pattern of feelings or behaviors that causes distress and makes it difficult to function (see **Figure 10.5**) (Danielson et al., 2021; Vasileva et al., 2021). Children with psychological conditions may have difficulty learning, being understood, and getting along with family members and friends (Baranne & Falissard, 2018). Diagnosing a psychological disorder in a child is often challenging. Many adults might think children are too young to have an emotional disorder, may stigmatize mental health conditions, or may consider children's behavior to be under their control (UNICEF, 2021b; Villatoro et al., 2018). Children may not see themselves as having any unusual difficulties (Lewis, 2014). Behavioral challenges are part of learning to get along in the world and are typical as we grow, but when difficulties are severe, persistent, and damaging to the child's well-being, they are considered to be a disorder (Costello, 2016).

Researchers often organize emotional conditions in children into two major categories. In **internalizing disorders**, children's emotions are focused inward, and they experience overwhelming feelings of sadness (e.g., *depression*) or worry (e.g., *anxiety*). Since children often lack the vocabulary or opportunity to talk about these feelings, their anxiety and depression frequently emerge as physical complaints, such as headaches, stomachaches, or difficulty sleeping (Mullen, 2018; Shanahan et al., 2015). In contrast, **externalizing disorders** are characterized by problematic behaviors that affect others, such as acting out or severe aggression. Externalizing disorders include disruptive behavior disorders such as *oppositional defiant disorder (ODD)* and *conduct disorder (CD)* (Achenbach & McConaughy, 1992; Olson et al., 2017). Children with ODD are prone to unusual irritability and angry outbursts and have difficulty following rules and doing what they are told by authority figures like teachers or other adults (APA, 2022; Burke & Romano-Verthelyi, 2018). A diagnosis of CD or ODD indicates that a child's difficulty goes beyond bad moods and disrupts their daily life.

Whereas all children sometimes disobey a caregiver or teacher, children with ODD exhibit a persistent and severe pattern of oppositional behavior at home and at school that is keeping them from thriving. Conduct disorder, a much more severe and uncommon behavioral disorder, is characterized by violence and disregard for other people. Children with CD might steal or fight with other children, hurt animals, or set fires, often without remorse (APA, 2022; Fairchild et al., 2019).

Researchers point out that trauma often plays a role in diagnoses of CD and ODD: Children tend to be more reactive after they have experienced significant adversity and have difficulty managing their emotions (Beltrán et al., 2021). ODD and CD are often stigmatizing diagnoses: Evidence suggests that children with behavioral difficulties who are Black or Latino are more likely to be diagnosed with ODD than White children with similar behavior (Fadus et al., 2020). Many adults think that the behaviors associated with CD or ODD are best treated with strict discipline, but experts advise that harsh caregiving can make things worse: Children with these disorders often need intense professional help to help their families coach them toward more adaptive behavior with warmth, consistent limits, and acceptance (Booker et al., 2020). Ideally, a diagnosis of ODD or CD should be a way for children to access extra support to help them build the skills they need to get along.

Any psychological disorder results from a complicated mix of vulnerabilities, beginning with genetic risk, brain maturation, and prenatal development, often coupled with environmental stress (Cicchetti, 2018; McQuillan et al., 2018). Emotional

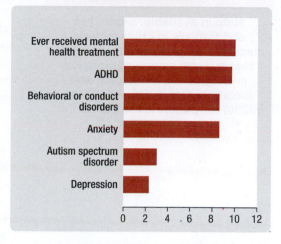

PSYCHOLOGICAL CONDITIONS IN MIDDLE CHILDHOOD

Data from Bitsko et al., 2022.

FIGURE 10.5 Psychological Conditions in the United States About one in eight children have been diagnosed with a psychological disorder, but more may benefit from extra support or treatment. During middle childhood, succeeding at school often requires increased awareness of children's difficulties getting along with others and thriving in groups.

Share It!

Does your tummy hurt? Stomach upset is often a way that children express their feelings. Researchers suggest this may be because stress changes our intestinal microbiome.

(Callaghan et al., 2020)

internalizing disorders Psychological conditions in which children's emotions are focused inward, manifesting as overwhelming feelings of sadness (depression) or worry (anxiety).

externalizing disorders Psychological conditions characterized by difficult behaviors that affect others, such as acting out or severe aggression. Externalizing disorders include disruptive behavior disorders such as oppositional defiant disorder (ODD) and conduct disorder (CD).

conditions are often a family affair: Children's difficulties often trigger more difficulties in their parents, and parents' emotional difficulties are linked to children's mental health (Wilkinson et al., 2021; Yan et al., 2021). Trauma, stress, and adversity can all contribute to children's emotional difficulties. Family stress, discrimination and poverty, and other adverse experiences all make it more likely that children will need support (Bitsko et al., 2022; Ghandour et al., 2019; Hutchins et al., 2022). However, the environment can also be a source of resilience: Strong social relationships with family, friends, and community can help reduce children's risk for disorders like depression (Fritz et al., 2018).

For many children, difficulties can escalate as conflicts develop with friends and teachers at school (Costello, 2016). Fortunately, there are treatments that can help, although they may be difficult to access in many communities, particularly for children who need in-patient or crisis care (Cutler et al., 2022). Help often comes from supporting families as well as children themselves. Exposure therapy helped Erik, the boy who was afraid of the amusement park and leaving the house, to practice going into the situations that scared him with help of a supportive therapist. This helped him feel more confident in school and make new friends (Lundkvist-Houndoumadi, 2013).

Thriving with Disabilities

Some children have physical and emotional conditions that are serious enough to require treatment to help them to function and fully participate in the world. Experts refer to children with health concerns that require treatment as having a *disability* (Graham et al., 2017). The term disability does not refer to the challenges the child faces, but to the mismatch between a child's needs and their environments (WHO, 2011). **Disability** is any interaction between people with impairments and the environment where barriers keep people from being able to fully participate (CRPD, 2006).

Around the world, it is hard to assess how frequently children experience disability because of differences in how local recordkeepers define and track it (Simeonsson & Lee, 2017). In fact, only a small portion of children with a disability have challenges with mobility. Most U.S. children who have a disability have been diagnosed with conditions related to learning or communicating (Young, 2021). Children with disabilities often experience stigma and discrimination. In addition, children with health impairments are at risk for sexual and physical abuse, and they are often unable to advocate for themselves (Byrne, 2018). Around the world, children with disabilities are much less likely to go to school, and in many low-income countries, fewer than half finish the fifth grade (Male & Wodon, 2017). The United States has long been a model for inclusive education: Most U.S. children with disabilities go to school, as you will read in Chapter 11 (Schwartz et al., 2021; Winter, 2020).

Which One Is Your Favorite? Amal (*right*) is 9 and loves the seesaw best. She is playing with her friends Hala and Tasneem at the school playground near her home in the Za'atari Refugee Camp in Jordan.

disability A mismatch between a person's physical, cognitive, or emotional condition and the support provided in the environment, which impairs the ability to participate in daily life.

Environmental Impacts on Health

More than 90 percent of the world's children breathe toxic air every day, the result of traffic, of industry, or of burning fuels like wood and kerosene for cooking (WHO, 2018b). Children's developing bodies and brains are particularly sensitive to pollution and stresses caused by natural disasters (Helldén et al., 2021). Air pollution causes respiratory infections in children and can lead to cognitive difficulties and cancer (Brumberg et al., 2021; Landrigan et al., 2019).

Children are also vulnerable to the effects of climate change, which has led to an increase in global temperatures and extreme weather. Climate change is expected to increase air pollution, transmission of infectious diseases, and serious weather events such as hurricanes, droughts, and winter storms (Helldén et al., 2021). Children are more easily impacted by environmental stresses, from the overpopulation of disease-bearing ticks to heat-stroke from high temperatures (Stanberry et al., 2018).

Even a few days of hot weather can have unexpected effects. For instance, students in schools without air conditioning have difficulty concentrating when the weather gets hot. In one study of children in New York City, students who took their exams in a classroom with no air conditioning on a hot day scored 15 points lower than those who sat for exams on a cooler day (Heal & Park, 2015). Most children can tolerate a few days of heat, but for the children around the world who already experience daily adversity, the effects of climate change may be more stressful and, ultimately, more deadly (Clark et al., 2020).

APPLY IT! **10.3** A friend suggests that elementary-age schoolchildren are too young to worry about their teeth or their mental health. Can you explain why they may be mistaken?

10.4 There are variations around the world in the rate of serious health conditions in childhood. What are contextual factors that are linked to rates of illness in children?

Children Making Change Children are more sensitive than adults to toxins in the air and water. Mari Copeny tried to do something about it: She raised thousands of dollars to provide free, safe water to her neighbors in Flint, Michigan. Here, Mari and her cousin, Ivory Moon, help load vehicles with water donations.

Building Health

How can families and communities foster health in young children amid a host of challenges, including the COVID-19 pandemic, the allure of TikTok, and easy access to sweets? Experts recommend four behavioral practices to build physical resilience in children: sufficient sleep, nutrition, activity, and play.

Learning Objective

10.3 Discuss protective health habits in middle childhood.

Sleep

Remember that sleep is essential for brain development, helping children consolidate their learning and better control their behavior (Cheng et al., 2020). Experts recommend that children aged 6–12 get between 9 and 12 hours of sleep a night, but many children fall short of this goal (Paruthi et al., 2016a). Parents report that as many as 3 in 10 children have sleep-related difficulties, from resistance to bedtime to chronic daytime sleepiness (Bathory & Tomopoulos, 2017). Children who are missing out on rest are more likely to experience depression and have different patterns of brain maturation than those who get enough rest (Yang et al., 2022).

Bedtime battles may have their origins in biology. Natural circadian rhythms cause all of us to have a period of alertness in the evening, or a "second wind," and for children this often occurs before bedtime, making it particularly difficult to settle down (Bruni & Novelli, 2010). Another challenge comes from technology: Children who are on phones or play video games before bed often have difficulty falling asleep. The excitement of playing combined with the brain-stimulating blue light emitted by screens interfere with children's sleep (LeBourgeois et al., 2017; Przybylski et al., 2019). Elementary school-age children are more sensitive to light than adults, since their eyes are still developing (Turner & Mainster, 2008). Although the research on factors impacting children's sleep suggests many factors such as family contexts, health, and life stressors play a role, limiting exposure to the light and stimulation of screens at bedtime could help children maintain a healthy sleep schedule.

Eating for Health

A nutritious diet is essential to good health in children (and adults). Undernutrition and food insecurity can make it difficult for children to learn. Eating too much or

Scientific American Profile

Building Health in Middle Childhood

Snacks with Friends School lunches are a public health success story, providing healthy nutrition to children. Yadier and Samantha *(left)* are digging into lunch in Old Havana, Cuba, including chicken, taro, and pea soup. During the height of the COVID-19 pandemic, children in Shanghai *(right)* ate rice, too, but were separated by plastic partitions to protect them from disease.

missing out on essential nutrients like iron and zinc also harm brain development (Black, Trude, et al., 2020).

You may not have fond memories of your school lunches, but whether it is green bean casserole in the United States, polenta and beans in Zimbabwe, or sushi in Japan, cafeteria lunches provide nearly half of a child's daily calories and sustain more than 368 million children around the world (Cohee et al., 2020). In affluent countries, most children get their midday meals at school (and often breakfast, too), enabling them to eat lunch without having to pack a sandwich. In low-income countries, school lunch programs are more limited but are important in fighting malnutrition (Downs & Demmler, 2020).

Improving school lunch means not only offering healthier foods but also making sure children actually eat them (Kessler, 2016). In the United States, simple interventions, such as lengthening the lunch period, lead to more fruit and vegetable consumption (Cohen et al., 2020). Other efforts connect schools with community gardening programs or change the menu altogether. Farm-to-school efforts encouraging children to eat more vegetables are now underway in more than 4 in 10 schools around the United States (National Farm to School Network, 2022). In Barrow County, Georgia, this means planting collard greens and radishes to encourage children to try new vegetables (Moss, 2019). New menu options and chef-designed meals also improve children's diets (Cohen et al., 2015). In Wisconsin, this means introducing traditional indigenous foods like wild rice and bison into menus (McLeod & Winter, 2022). The goal of these innovations is to convince children to eat more whole foods, fruits, and vegetables and perhaps even to love school lunch.

Children's diets at home are also crucial for getting the healthy nutrition they need. Poor nutrition is more common among families in low-income communities, which are more likely to be *food deserts* (neighborhoods without supermarkets), or *food swamps* (neighborhoods with an overabundance of fast-food restaurants) (Bell et al., 2019). Limited access to food—whether it is unaffordable or just not locally available—reflects widespread social inequalities. Low-income families have less access to healthy food (Lacko et al., 2021; Monsivais et al., 2021). Prepared foods, sugary drinks, and high-calorie snacks often fill the void, because they cost less, last for a long time, and immediately satisfy hungry children (Moran et al., 2019).

A Dose of Sunshine Before School Silvia, Henry, and Rosario are walking to school in Metalio, El Salvador, with their mother, Nuya. In the United States, only 1 in 10 children walks or bikes to school. Around the world, it is common for children to walk to school, providing sunshine and physical activity before school begins.

Staying Active

Some parents invest in exercise trackers to see how much their children are moving each day. Victor's parents have not gone that far: Most experts advise that detailed tracking is not necessary. Like Victor, most children are motivated by the fun of running on the beach, not by a reminder to get their steps in, and they tend to be more active than adults. (Experts recommend children her age get between 12,000 and 16,000 steps each day; most adults get only 5,000 [Tudor-Locke et al., 2011a, 2011b]).

Moving the body builds strong bones and prevents cardiovascular disease (Physical Activity Guidelines Advisory Committee, 2018). Regular physical activity may even improve cognition (Álvarez-Bueno et al., 2020; Ishihara et al., 2018). Exercise often requires children to practice executive function skills, which stimulates the creation of neurons, strengthens myelinated connections in the brain, and supports the growth of brain structures that facilitate memory and thinking (Meijer et al., 2020; Valkenborghs et al., 2019). Researchers agree that, in the words of one neuroscientist, "exercise is like Miracle-Gro for your brain" (Ratey & Hageman, 2013).

One key reason many children do not get enough physical activity is that they are in school. Once children begin kindergarten, they spend much of their time sitting. Children may have breaks for recess, physical education, or gym, but most of their time is what researchers call *sedentary*: sitting or standing still in a classroom. Most elementary-age schoolchildren in the United States have access to recess during the school day, but once children are in middle school (or about age 11), those breaks for physical activity are typically eliminated (CDC, 2022).

During middle childhood, children increasingly focus on screens rather than on active play when they are not at school, doing an adult-supervised activity, or working on homework. Screens give children who are unable to socialize with other children after school the opportunity to do so remotely or to catch up on the games and apps everyone talks about at school. However, this screen time often takes away from more beneficial in-person activities (McArthur et al., 2021). In the United States, most children spend nearly five hours a day using their screens for entertainment (Rideout & Robb, 2019). After the start of the COVID-19 pandemic, online and screen time increased. Early reports indicated that children's recreational screen time with Roblox and TikTok increased (Fischer, 2021).

Recess may not seem like an essential part of the school day, but experts suggest that having a break to move and play helps keep children learning (Council on School Health et al., 2013). Quality recess time is linked to physical and psychological health: Children control their behavior better at school, get along with each other more easily, and have an easier time staying focused when they are given a break to move around (Massey et al., 2021). Quality recess occurs when children are supervised enough to make sure that they are not being aggressive to each other and encouraged to play cooperatively (London, 2019a). Like other opportunities, access to recess is often unequitable: Children in lower-funded schools tend to have less (London, 2019b).

Some researchers have even suggested that children need more breaks for physical activity during the school day, which can help them learn in school. Danish researchers who conducted a randomized, controlled trial found that children learned more math when their classes were broken up by physical activity: Their math scores went up compared to their peers who were in the control group (Have et al., 2018). However, these findings have not been consistently replicated (Norris et al., 2020). For instance, an attempt in the Netherlands to intersperse learning the multiplication tables with juggling lessons or dance succeeded in improving students' class enjoyment but not their math skills (van den Berg et al., 2019a, 2019b).

Children often rely on school-based interventions for physical activity because they are not getting enough activity outside of school as part of their everyday life, whether walking to school, to the market, or to a friend's house on the weekend. In the United States, only one in six children walks or bikes to school (Omura et al., 2019). A change in physical activity has happened in only one generation: Just 20 years ago,

Share It!

How are children staying active in the United States? Basketball, biking, and baseball are still the top forms of physical activity, but soccer is gaining. Individual sports like golf and tennis are growing in popularity in the wake of the pandemic.

(Aspen Institute, 2021)

Enjoying Being Active Sometimes having fun and being active during recess takes a boost from adults. These children benefit from the support of a team from Playworks, an organization that encouraged them to try new things (including hula hooping).

Experiences Change the Brain. Learning to juggle takes time, practice, and focus.

Finding Joy on the Ice Jade, a fourth-grader, excels at figure skating in an after-school program near her home in New York City. She has not only learned how to do a difficult spiral; she has also built up her self-confidence and made new friends, and she feels a sense of freedom and joy when she spins on the ice.

more than 70 percent of school-age children in the United States walked or rode their bicycles to and from school. Today, nearly all children are supervised on their way to school and back, primarily because of concerns about crime and safety (Jones & Sliwa, 2016).

Similar changes have occurred in some other affluent countries, including Canada, New Zealand, and the United Kingdom (Loebach & Gilliland, 2019; Shoeppe et al., 2015; Witten et al., 2013). But concerns about children's safety and independence are not universal. In Japan, for instance, nearly all children walk to school on their own (Hino et al., 2021). In the United States, public health interventions to encourage children to walk to school have included traffic calming and the national walk to school day (Kontou et al., 2020).

Children who get enough physical activity tend to exercise outside of school. They may walk to school or the bus, or practice poses in jiujitsu. Many play organized sports, which has its own benefits (Conley et al., 2020; Gorham & Barch, 2020). What may be most important about physical activity is that it is enjoyable (Logan et al., 2019). Children, and adults, are more likely to stick with something because they love it than because it is good for them: Activity needs to be fun (Dietz et al., 2019). Nevertheless, most U.S. children stop playing sports before they are in middle school and drop out before they are 11. Many explain that team sports are too intense and no longer as fun (Aspen Institute, 2021).

Intense dedication to a sport can come with consequences. Sports injuries are on the rise in children, and pediatricians often attribute these injuries to overtraining and a focus on a single sport, rather than multiple activities at an early age (Bell et al., 2018). Most sports medicine researchers suggest that there is limited benefit to committing to a single sport before adolescence and that children should try out a variety of activities to avoid the risks of injury and burnout (Post et al., 2020). Experts also remind families to make sure their children are wearing protective gear and following the rules, avoiding "heading" the ball in soccer and "checking" in hockey to stay safe (Herriman et al., 2019).

Children and their families often harbor dreams of making it big playing sports. For most, these dreams are unrealistic: A mere half of 1 percent of children will grow up to play sports professionally (Myer et al., 2015). Learning to play a sport to stay active and make friends is a more realistic goal than hoping to make it as a professional. That does not mean that Victor is abandoning his dreams. He is committed to contining his family's traditions by being the third generation to excel in charrería. Research shows that he has one thing going for him: Parents who were both professional-level athletes and who can encourage his skills. Children whose parents are elite athletes have a much better shot at turning professional (Myer et al., 2015). With luck, this will help Victor continue to develop his roping skills—entertaining audiences and amazing his friends.

MAKING A DIFFERENCE
Children Need More Freedom to Play

It is true that technology, the cost of organized sports, and school keep children from being active, but there is another major factor: Many children simply have much less unsupervised free time than their parents or grandparents did (Hofferth, 2009; Lee et al., 2021). They are not outside playing tag or street hockey, or climbing trees. Children spend at least 25 percent less time playing than they did 20 years ago (Gray, 2020; Loebach & Gilliland, 2019; Mullan, 2019). Some estimates indicate that children spend as few as seven minutes a day in free play (Sobchuk et al., 2019).

Play has been curtailed for a variety of reasons. Some families keep their children indoors and in supervised activities because they worry their children will be injured or become the victims of a crime (Rixon et al., 2019). Changes in neighborhood dynamics and in work schedules have meant many families are less connected to their neighbors, and fewer adults are available to keep an eye out for children playing outside (Ross et al., 2020). Other families feel pressure to engage their children in activities that will help them in school (Pynn et al., 2019). Much of this reflects a parenting strategy, often called *intensive parenting* or *concerted cultivation*, that is focused on achievement and adult supervision (Lareau, 2011; Weininger et al., 2015).

Developmental scientists are confident that children benefit from unstructured play, in which they can make their own choices about what to do and how to do it (Nijhof et al., 2018). It helps children develop social skills and relationships, encourages evaluating acceptable physical risks, and spurs creativity (Farmer et al., 2017; Louv, 2008; Sobchuk et al., 2019). Free play builds cognition: Children who engage in self-directed play, like fort building or a spontaneous round of capture the flag, have stronger executive function (Barker et al., 2014).

Developmental scientists suggest that children need opportunities to guide their own play and do some problem solving on their own, with adults available to help only when needed. 🌐

APPLY IT! **10.5** Victor likes to ride horses, practice his roping skills, and play soccer. How would you explain the benefits of free, active play to adults who might not remember how fun it was?

10.6 How does nutrition help children grow?

Outdoor Play Free play can take place in adventure playgrounds, like this one in London. In an adventure playground, children are allowed to build their own structures using hammers and nails, encouraging physical activity, independent play, and problem solving, despite the occasional bruised thumb.

Wrapping It Up

LO 10.1 Describe variations in growth, motor development, and maturation in the brain during middle childhood. (p. 245)

During middle childhood, children typically gain about 40 pounds (25 kilograms) and about a foot (35 centimeters). The hormonal changes of adrenarche trigger a growth spurt at about age 10 for girls and age 12 for boys. Children have a tremendous amount of energy for motor skill development, but which skills they learn depends on cultural and community values. During middle childhood, the cortex continues to mature, building more fast, myelinated connections and gradually pruning underused gray matter. Increasing connectivity between the subcortical region and the cortex helps children develop emotion regulation. Children's experiences help shape how their brain matures.

LO 10.2 Identify common health conditions during middle childhood. (p. 252)

Most children in affluent countries are healthy during middle childhood, but some have chronic conditions such as asthma, hypertension, or difficulties with emotional health. Environmental pollution can trigger poor health. Rising rates of diabetes and hypertension may be linked to weight and weight-related stress.

LO 10.3 Discuss protective health habits in middle childhood. (p. 259)

Getting enough sleep helps children stay healthy and learn. A healthy diet can help children grow: School lunch programs are one of the best ways of preventing malnutrition around the globe. Moving is one of the best ways to build resilience: Physical activity stimulates brain growth and builds stronger bones and muscles. For children, being active often comes through physical play.

KEY TERMS

middle childhood
(p. 245)

adrenarche (p. 251)

secondary sex characteristics
(p. 251)

primary sex characteristics
(p. 251)

internalizing disorders
(p. 257)

externalizing disorders
(p. 257)

disability (p. 258)

CHECK YOUR LEARNING

1. The period of middle childhood ends with the onset of the physical changes of:
   a) infancy.
   b) myelination.
   c) puberty.
   d) dementia.

2. Children's ultimate height is primarily influenced by _____ if they are healthy and well-nourished.
   a) genes
   b) environment
   c) ethnicity
   d) parenting

3. Which of these fine motor skill achievements is associated with increased academic success in elementary or primary school?
   a) Buttoning a shirt
   b) Writing by hand
   c) Typing on a keyboard
   d) Sewing

4. The coating of neurons with myelin creates brain tissue often described as:
   a) pruning.
   b) cortex.
   c) gray matter.
   d) white matter.

5. Cortical thinning in middle childhood is an indication of:
   a) child maltreatment.
   b) maturation.
   c) chromosomes.
   d) synaptic exuberance.

6. The hormonal changes during middle childhood that begin to prepare the body for puberty are known as:
   a) menopause.
   b) amygdala.
   c) teratogens.
   d) adrenarche.

7. Which of these statements about sleep in middle childhood is TRUE?
   a) Since children no longer need a nap, their sleep needs are the same as adults.
   b) Most children get much more sleep than they need.
   c) The recommended amount of sleep for healthy development is 9–12 hours per night.
   d) The recommended amount of sleep for healthy development is 12–14 hours per night.

8. Which of these is NOT a benefit of unstructured play during middle childhood?
   a) Specialized training in organized sports
   b) Practice evaluating acceptable physical risks
   c) Increased creativity and problem-solving skills
   d) Enhanced social relationships

9. A psychological condition associated with intense or debilitating feelings of sadness or worry is known as:
   a) externalizing disorder.
   b) internalizing disorder.
   c) oppositional defiant disorder (ODD).
   d) attention-deficit/hyperactivity disorder (ADHD).

10. Describe the structural and community factors that may influence children's access to nutritious and fresh foods.

© Macmillan, Photo by Sidford House

Cognitive Development

11.1 Explain the key features of Piaget's concrete operational stage.

11.2 Discuss why Vygotsky believed that learning comes from social interaction.

11.3 Describe the typical cognitive improvements during middle childhood.

Language Development

11.4 Explain how language advances support children's learning.

Learning In and Out of School

11.5 Explain how schools influence achievement during middle childhood.

Things can change quickly when you are 10. In fourth grade, this became true for Logan. There was a global pandemic, but he was also learning long division and the French defense in chess. Logan had been homeschooling long before COVID-19 became a worry. So, while many children had difficulty adjusting to virtual school, Logan continued to enjoy it, because it gave him extra time to hang out with his aging dog and to go to the beach. Fourth grade ended up being a wonderful experience for Logan. One of the best parts: meeting new friends who also loved to play chess, playing video games, and planning his future career as a Twitch creator and YouTube influencer.

Logan's family and his chess coach, Tom, helped him find solace from the pandemic through chess and learning. Chess helps Logan relax and focus, and it gives him something predictable and memorizable. It also gives him the challenge of trying to predict his opponent's next move. Logan dreams about chess, visualizes it to calm himself down, and memorizes opening moves in his spare time. He receives guidance from Coach Tom, who is understanding, kind, and funny. He "gets" Logan and inspires him to show up and compete under pressure.

Not everything is as easy as chess for Logan: He still unravels from time to time. He recently lost his video game privileges. But chess is something he can fall back on. It enables him to practice the skills that will help him in other parts of his life: accepting losses, preparing to face new situations and competitors, and showing up to work hard.

265

Scientific American Profile

Meet Logan

Learning Objectives

11.1 Explain the key features of Piaget's concrete operational stage.

11.2 Discuss why Vygotsky believed that learning comes from social interaction.

11.3 Describe the typical cognitive improvements during middle childhood.

Like Logan, most children have tremendous capacity for learning during middle childhood. You will read about several approaches to understanding thinking and communicating during childhood, including Piaget's theory of children's reasoning, Vygotsky's emphasis on the sociocultural context, and newer theories that focus on information processing and executive function. You will also learn how scientists investigate how children can connect with learning in school: Part of Logan's pandemic success occurred when his curious, adventurous thinking was linked with guidance that inspired him to work harder than he ever had before.

Cognitive Development

When Logan was asked what makes someone good at chess, instead of listing memory skills or even the ability to think ahead, he said it came down to focus and imagination. These are talents that Logan has in abundance. Most children's core cognitive skills blossom during middle childhood, including their reasoning ability, executive function, problem solving, and abilitiy to focus. Two qualities reflect the unique thinking of children and also fuel the imagination that Logan suggests makes someone good at chess: curiosity and flexibility.

The Benefits of Thinking Like a Child

If you talk with a school-age child, even a very capable one like Logan, you may notice how much they do not know. So much is new to them. Developmental scientists, however, point out that children have a number of cognitive strengths and that their thinking can be even more creative than adults' (Gopnik, 2020; Schulz et al., 2019).

In a transition some developmental scientists term the *5 to 7 shift*, children's ability to manage their own thinking and behavior matures dramatically as children begin school (Sameroff & Haith, 1996). Around the world, children begin to take on new responsibilities at about age 6. Families expect that by this age children have developed the skills to control themselves (Burrage et al., 2008; Lancy, 2021). Wiggling and distracted kindergartners develop into self-regulated first-graders who can focus long enough to sound out words and write down the date (Morrison et al., 2019).

This burst of reasoning ability is a result of brain maturation triggered by experience. One group of neuroscientists conducted a clever study to show how a year of first grade makes a difference in how children use their brain (see **Figure 11.1**) (Brod et al., 2017). Researchers compared two groups of children very close in age. One group included children who were just old enough to start first grade, and the other group was slightly younger. They found that children who completed the first grade used their brains differently than children who stayed in kindergarten, even though their ages were only a month or so apart.

When the children were asked to perform executive function tasks, like pressing a button for "dog" and not "cat," regions in their cortex were activated in both the kindergartners and first-graders. (Remember that the cortex is the outside region of the brain.) However, there was a difference in how the two groups used their cortices. Many more areas of the cortex were activated in kindergartners than in first-graders. The more limited activation in the first-graders' brains, primarily in two regions connected to executive function, indicated that these tasks no longer required as much effort. In effect, the first-graders' brains had become more efficient, developing brain regions that specialized in following directions and boosted executive function (Brod et al., 2017). Similar studies have replicated this finding: Formal schooling, whether it starts in kindergarten or first grade, shapes children's functioning (M. H. Kim et al., 2021).

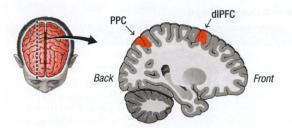

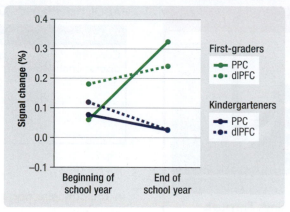

Data from Brod et al., 2017.

FIGURE 11.1 Practice in First Grade Creates Changes in the Brain Researchers compared fMRI scans of children who had been through a year of first grade (*green lines*) with children who did not make the age cutoff for first grade (*blue lines*). When the two groups of children were asked to perform tests of executive function, fMRI scans showed that they used their brains differently. Children who had been through first grade showed more activation in their cortex related to executive functioning, like the regions known as the posterior parietal cortex (PPC) and the dorsolateral prefrontal cortex (dlPFC). In contrast, the children who had not been to first grade used broader, less specialized regions of their cortex. The researchers' explanation was that those first-grade children had more practice using their executive function skills. A year's experience in first grade taught them to focus and follow directions. As a result, their brains were activated more efficiently: These skills no longer required as much cortical activation and conscious control.

Scholars consistently observe a similar phenomenon across middle childhood: As children develop, the brain becomes more efficient. Throughout development, regions in the cortex are activated when children need to use lots of conscious effort, focus, and thinking. In early childhood, the cortex and particularly the *prefrontal cortex (PFC)* are activated much of the time when children need to control their behavior or do something that requires conscious thought. As children grow and acquire new tasks, larger regions no longer need to be as involved. Following basic directions or remembering to raise their hand in class, or playing a G on the violin, no longer requires as much activation. Instead, more specialized areas of the brain manage these jobs (Putkinen & Saarikivi, 2018).

During middle childhood, advances in executive function combined with children's inexperience in the world make them amazing learners. School-age children are hungry for learning and are more flexible, creative, and curious in their thinking than younger children or adults (Schulz et al., 2019). Indeed, children's inexperience often spurs them to create innovative and interesting solutions to challenges. When scientists test children and adults in the laboratory, they find that children are not afraid to come up with new suggestions or explanations for phenomena. Adults tend to target their efforts, but children attend to everything, which gives them a broader awareness and more creativity (Blanco & Sloutsky, 2019). Children

Piaget's Stage of Concrete Operations

Remember that developmental theorist Jean Piaget devised practical, hands-on ways of testing children to investigate what they understood and thought about the world. Piaget called middle childhood the stage of **concrete operations** (Piaget & Inhelder, 1969). He believed that children's logical thinking abilities gradually improve throughout middle childhood, as they work their way through understanding problems of greater complexity. The term *concrete operations* refers to children's ability to perform logical operations, or transformations, in their minds and apply them to concrete or real-life situations. In the concrete operational stage, children's thinking becomes more logical and flexible, enabling them to follow more complex rules and avoid the logical mistakes common in the *preoperational* period. Children

Children's Curiosity Can Spark Science. With support from their school, a visiting scientist, and a devoted teacher, a group of children in Blackawton, England, published a peer-reviewed paper on bees. The children did not know how to present a scientific study, but they had other strengths: They were able to come up with new ideas. They discovered that bees use both color and space to choose which flowers to pollinate, and they concluded that "science is cool and fun because you get to do stuff that no one has ever done before" (Blackawton et al., 2011, p. 1).

concrete operations Piaget's stage of cognitive development occurring in middle childhood in which children's logical thinking abilities gradually improve as they begin to understand problems of greater complexity.

Scientific American Profile

Thinking Things Through

CONNECTIONS

Remember from Chapter 8 that early childhood is Piaget's period of preoperational thought in which children are able to think symbolically (and do make-believe) but have challenges with logical operations.

FIGURE 11.2 The Classification Task Are there more red beads or more wooden beads? In order to correctly answer this question, children must attend to multiple categories, like what color the beads are and what they are made of.

classification The categorization and grouping of objects according to multiple dimensions.

seriation The ordering of objects in a series according to an abstract rule.

TABLE 11.1 Piaget's Concrete Operational Stage

Stage	Age	Characteristics
Concrete operational	About age 6 to 12	The breakthroughs in this age are all about logic. Children can now reason through problems and examine situations from differing perspectives, as long as the problem is not too abstract. They can put things into categories and order them. However, their thinking is still relatively concrete, and is more reliable when it is linked to what can be seen, heard, or touched.

in the concrete operational stage can look at problems from multiple perspectives (Piaget, 1971).

The Logic of Concrete Operations With age, children begin to consider multiple aspects of a simple problem and are less susceptible to being tricked by appearances, as demonstrated by the conservation task described in Chapter 8. By age 8, most children are able to explain that there is no magic involved when you pour liquid from one container to another. Children in the concrete operational stage are more flexible thinkers; they can reverse events in their minds and shift their focus (Houdé et al., 2011). They can explain that although one glass of juice is taller, another one is wider, demonstrating their ability to avoid centration on just one aspect of the situation. They are also able to activate networks in the brain that inhibit instinctive and emotional responses to produce more logical decisions. These breakthroughs occur because of brain maturation as well as practice answering questions and focusing in school (Inhelder & Piaget, 1964).

Children's developing flexible thinking allows them to apply categories more accurately and logically. They can now more reliably complete **classification** tasks, in which they must categorize objects and group them according to multiple dimensions (Inhelder & Piaget, 1964). (See **Figure 11.2.**) For instance, in one classic Piagetian task, children are presented with a row of flowers that includes eight roses and two daffodils and are asked: "Are there more roses or more flowers?" In order to correctly answer this question, they need to remember that roses and daffodils are flowers and that something can belong to more than one category at once. Being able to attend to multiple categories is a powerful cognitive tool that enables Logan to organize Lego bricks by color and by shape.

Children's ability to think about categories also allows them to organize objects in a series according to an abstract rule, which Piaget referred to as **seriation**. For instance, school-age children can order a group of rods in order of size or put a collection of blocks in rainbow order (Inhelder & Piaget, 1964).

Piaget believed that children's reasoning in middle childhood has major strengths, but that it is not fully mature. He pointed out that it is most accurate when applied to concrete objects. As children get older, they can apply their logical thinking skills to more abstract ideas, from geometric proofs and algebraic equations to ideas about war and peace.

Lessons from Piaget Contemporary researchers agree that children's thinking changes dramatically between ages 5 and 7, but they have refined Piaget's observations. They point out that children tend to be unpredictable, and their development does not always move forward in a straight line.

Remember from Chapter 1 that there is an ongoing debate in developmental science about whether maturation is continuous or stagelike. Many researchers argue that children's development is based on specific improvements in discrete areas that add up over time, rather than on an overarching, global jump in skills (Siegler & Ellis, 1996). They may take a skills-based look at children's thinking, focusing on children's maturity in specific areas of thinking like executive function, memory, or spatial skills (Carey et al., 2015; Viarouge et al., 2019).

Piaget believed that children do not display concrete reasoning until between ages 6 and 8, but later researchers identified signs of logical thought much earlier. Children may even show signs of their reasoning ability before they are able to articulate it in words, for example, by showing with gestures that they know which one is "more" even if they are not verbalizing it (Goldin-Meadow, 2015). Nevertheless, Piaget's theory remains extremely popular with many educators. A skilled observer of children, Piaget was captivated by and respectful of children's creative thinking. His argument that it should be motivated by curiosity and not be hurried along continues to inspire (Flavell, 1996; Ponticorvo et al., 2020).

Hands-On Science These third-graders from Montville, Connecticut, are collecting ocean data through Project Oceanology in New York's Long Island sound. They are taking samples to measure the ocean water's temperature and saltiness. When they are off the boat, they learn how to sort their findings and even display their data graphically according to multiple dimensions.

Vygotsky and the Sociocultural Approach to Children's Thinking

Whereas Piaget's ideas about children's thinking changed developmental science in the 1970s and 1980s, Lev Vygotsky's ideas revolutionized the science of education in the 1990s and early 2000s (Davydov, 1995; Gauvain, 2020).

Vygotsky and the sociocultural theorists inspired by his work established that children's cognitive skills build on their relationships and the cultural activities they do every day (Gauvain & Nicolaides, 2015; Rogoff, 2003; Vygotsky, 1962; Vygotsky & Cole, 1978). They argue that there is no universal "right way" of thinking (Greenfield, 1997). Instead, they recognize that children often develop different cognitive strengths because of the diversity in cultures and communities around the world (Qi & Roberts, 2019; Saxe & de Kirby, 2014). For instance, researchers found that children from Indigenous communities in Australia develop strong spatial reasoning skills from their daily activities that help them to solve arithmetic problems (Kearins, 1981). Similarly, children who buy and sell items, whether in a farmer's market or on the street, develop sophisticated understanding of ratios in order to compute their profit (Saxe, 1988).

Vygotsky argued that children's thinking is most apparent not in their results on standardized tests, but when they are working with another person in their *zone of proximal development (ZPD)* (Gauvain & Perez, 2015; Vygotsky & Cole, 1978). Targeting learning at children's individual ZPD rather than generically teaching a group, classroom, or reading level helps children learn more quickly and effectively (Connor et al., 2013).

Vygotsky's impact on educational psychology and on classrooms around the world cannot be overstated (Davydov, 1995). How many times have you been encouraged to work in a group? Have you engaged in hands-on active learning? Have you ever had to verbalize your reasoning? Vygotsky is one of the theorists you have to thank for these educational innovations (Moll, 2013). His optimistic belief that "there is no right way to think," his argument that social interactions build thinking, and his advocacy for diversity and an end to inequity echo throughout current scholarship on how to improve school.

CONNECTIONS

Unlike Piaget, Vygotsky believed that children's thinking is shaped by social interactions (see Chapter 2). Piaget believed that children's thinking progresses through a sequence of stages, but Vygotsky believed development was continuous.

CONNECTIONS

Remember from Chapter 8 that the zone of proximal development (ZPD) refers to the range of children's capabilities that includes what children can do on their own and what they can do with help.

What You Do Every Day Changes Your Thinking. Selling eggs at this farmer's market in Santa Barbara might have a benefit beyond just dollars. Researchers have found that making change and figuring out how to earn a profit build cognitive skills that help with formal math.

CONNECTIONS

Remember that executive function refers to the ability to control attention and thinking through planning, focus, and memory.

 Share It!

What do you want? Some research indicates that allowing children to make choices supports children's executive function skills.

(Castelo et al., 2022)

Learning with Others Motivation for Ricky Rodriguez has meant playing Scrabble. Appreciating his love for words has enabled Ricky to build new relationships with other Scrabble players, like his friend Pat Griffith.

Improvements in Information Processing

When Logan meets with a group for a chess match, there are moments of laughter and other moments of quiet punctuated with the clicking of pieces. This level of effort would have been impossible a few years before, when they were distractible kindergartners. In middle childhood, children develop an impressive array of thinking skills that help them excel at chess and manage school's increasing demands. Remember from Chapter 2 that researchers who take an *information-processing perspective* look at the components of thinking, including executive function, memory, and the ability to think about and use these new cognitive strategies. These advances are supported by brain maturation and new environmental demands, such as school.

Executive Function Throughout middle childhood, children refine their executive function skills, which helps them to succeed in school (Zelazo & Carlson, 2020). Executive function is particularly important in the early grades, as children learn skills such as reading, writing, and basic math that serve as a base for their academic performance later in school (Ahmed et al., 2019).

As children grow, the components of executive function, including working memory, selective attention, inhibition, and planning, become easier to measure and evaluate (Zelazo & Carlson, 2020). Children's *working memory*, or the mental workspace that allows them to remember things in the short term, develops incrementally (Fiske & Holmboe, 2019). If children are tested to see how many numbers they can repeat back immediately, most will have difficulties remembering all 7 or 10 numbers in a typical phone number and will only be able to remember about 5 numbers, a few less than the typical adult (Dehn, 2011). Even if not fully developed, working memory allows children to learn to sound out words as they learn how to read, as well as remember which numbers they are carrying as they practice arithmetic (Diamond, 2013; Downes et al., 2017).

Children's *selective attention*, or their ability to control their focus, improves dramatically over middle childhood, but it is still not at adult levels (Turoman et al., 2021). Scientists estimate that children are asked to focus for long periods of time in school (about 17 minutes at a stretch), and most are not paying attention at least 25 percent of the time (Godwin et al., 2016, 2021). Young children are often easily distracted by visually enticing classroom displays, animations, or something happening in another window on their laptop. Many children have difficulties focusing when there is a lot of background noise, whether it is a friend tapping their pen or a sibling yelling in the other room (Fisher et al., 2014). Most elementary school classrooms have a noise level of about 72 decibels, higher than that in your neighborhood coffee shop. These background conversations, scraping desks and tapping pens, can distract children and make it difficult for them to learn, unless they have strong attention skills (Massonnie et al., 2019).

Noise is not the only part of the environment that can hurt children's focusing abilities: Researchers have found that trauma, including exposure to violence, can change children's focus, as well as their test scores (Laurito et al., 2019). Stress, whether it is episodic or chronic, can make it harder for children to concentrate (Roos et al., 2020). School requires children to pay attention, complete assignments under time pressure and adjust to inevitable difficulties without becoming overwhelmed. All of these require attention that works in tandem with children's stress response system, which may be too sensitive or not quite sensitive enough in situations when children are under strain (Obradović & Armstrong-Carter, 2020).

Working in school also requires controlling or inhibiting impulses. Sometimes this means switching from multiplication to addition on the same worksheet or not blurting out the first thing that comes to mind without raising your hand first.

Researchers measure *inhibition* by giving children tasks that require them to repress their initial impulses, like saying "day" when shown a picture of a moon or "night" when shown a picture of the sun (De Haan, 2015). Practice and brain maturation help children inhibit their impulses throughout middle childhood.

Executive function helps children to remember to get on the correct bus after school and to do their homework (Moffett & Morrison, 2020). Planning for both short- and long-term goals becomes more important, as children take on more responsibility with their own learning and with tasks at home, like doing chores and even watching younger siblings. Planning builds on children's skills in memory, inhibition, and attention (Gauvain et al., 2018). Scientists test children's planning skills by asking them to solve puzzles, such as the pyramid puzzle (see **Figure 11.3**).

In middle childhood, supportive relationships with family, school community, and teachers help children build their executive function (Huizinga et al., 2018; Roebers, 2017). Stress and adversity may make it harder for children to develop executive function (Merz et al., 2019). Interventions are often designed to help children build their resilience, or their ability to maintain their executive function, despite the stresses of trauma, everyday adversity, or discrimination. The ideal way to protect children's skills is to make sure they grow up with positive connections and environments that are safe and free from adversity. Getting enough sleep, avoiding too much screen time, and participating in extracurricular activities like sports or arts programming have all been shown to help boost cognitive resilience (Kirlic et al., 2021). While researchers and families may not always be able to address the larger, seemingly intractable stresses that impact children's lives, interventions can help boost resilience.

Another way to build executive function is through building mindfulness skills, now popular in some schools as a way of developing children's awareness of their own thinking and feelings (Greenberg & Harris, 2012; Zelazo, 2020). *Mindfulness* is a meditative practice of focusing on thoughts and perceptions in the moment and letting go of them. In a major Canadian study, a mindfulness-based intervention program improved students' cognitive skills and their ability to bounce back from stress and get along better with other children (Schonert-Reichl et al., 2015).

Other techniques to improve executive function, such as digital training programs or apps designed to help children build their working memory capacity, have had mixed results (Kassai et al., 2019; Jones et al., 2020; Sala & Gobet, 2020). In some studies, some children with strong self-control and personality traits of effortful control built skills that they were able to transfer from the training to real life, but other children did not. In some experiments, time spent building memory skills actually led to declines in children's academic performance (Roberts et al., 2016; Studer-Luethi et al., 2016).

 Share It!

Feeling like you belong to a community matters. While trauma and violence can make it difficult for children to concentrate, feeling connected can help them be resilient. Scientists found that children in New York City schools who felt a sense of community did not have the same drop in test scores after neighborhood violence as their peers who did not feel they were part of the group.

(Laurito et al., 2019)

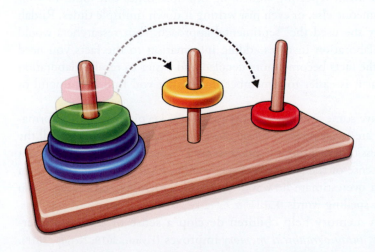

FIGURE 11.3 Pyramid Puzzle Can you solve this puzzle? The goal is to move the tower of discs from one tower to another by moving only one disc at a time and never placing a larger disc on a smaller one. In a three-disc game, you should be able to solve the puzzle in just seven moves.

Andrew H. Walker/Tribeca Film Festival/Getty Images

Amazing Feats of Memory Rifdah Rasheed came in third in the International Qur'an Competition held in Cairo, Egypt, impressing the audience with her style and beautiful voice. She is from an island in the Maldives, in the Indian Ocean, where she had the support of her parents in memorizing and reciting the Qur'an.

semantic memory The mental storage for facts and information.

rehearsal A memorization technique that involves repetition, either out loud, in your head, in front of someone else, or on paper.

elaboration Adding information to the facts you need to remember so that they become more detailed and easier to recall.

metamemory The awareness of the process of remembering.

Memory Young children are capable of amazing feats of memory. For instance, every year, hundreds of elementary schoolchildren participate in international Qur'an competitions held in major cities like Cairo, Egypt, and Doha, Qatar. All of them have memorized the entire Qur'an, the Muslim holy book, which takes more than 15 hours to recite. One young girl, Rifdah Rasheed, won third prize in the competition at age 10 after spending three years memorizing. She returned home to the Maldives with enough money to buy her family a new house. Ordinary children as well as elite memorizers, like those who participate in Qur'an competitions, spelling bees, and memory Olympiads, are capable of impressive recall (R. Black et al., 2020).

When children are reciting the Qur'an or solving an arithmetic problem like 6×7, they use a specific form of explicit memory known as **semantic memory**, or the mental storage for facts and information. When children tell their families about their field trip or remember how they felt when their dog died, they are using their *autobiographical memory*, or their memory about their own past. Both semantic and autobiographical memory mature during middle childhood and are essential for developing a sense of self and for learning about the world.

Children's new memory skills develop because of maturation of the *hippocampus*, the brain structure central to memory storage, and the PFC, which both mature slowly during childhood and adolescence. The leisurely pace of the development of the hippocampus means that, even in middle childhood, children are best at remembering the general overview of a situation or a concept and at looking for repeating patterns rather than focusing on the details (Keresztes et al., 2017).

Expert memorizers like Rifdah may appear to be born with a special talent, but actually, what makes Rifdah different from the rest of us is practice. It takes years of practice to learn to remember bits of information, particularly if it is not personally meaningful (Stenson et al., 2019). Around the world, children acquire and remember semantic information, although their memory skills may differ depending on what their community values. Some communities, like Rifdah's, may value memorizing religious texts, while others value memorizing the multiplication tables (Rogoff & Mistry, 1985).

Memorization skills are critical to school success, and focusing in school helps build memory skills (Blankenship et al., 2018; Peng & Kievit, 2020). Even in the era of being able to look everything up online, children who have strong understanding of math and reading facts are more successful in school. Learning information so well that it becomes *automatized*, or reflexively remembered, helps children tackle complex tasks more easily (Magallón et al., 2016).

Strategies to encode information into memory include rehearsal, elaboration, organization, and visualization. **Rehearsal** is a memorizing technique that involves repetition. This could mean repeating something multiple times out loud, in your head, or in front of someone else, or even just writing it down multiple times. Rifdah called another strategy she used the "sentimental approach," but researchers would call it **elaboration**. Elaboration involves adding information to the facts you need to remember so that the facts become more detailed and easier to recall. Elaboration builds on the fact that it is easier to remember things that you find meaningful or emotional.

Many children have some awareness of the process of keeping track of information by the time they are in elementary school (Simons et al., 2020). Researchers call the awareness of the process of remembering **metamemory** (Flavell, 1979). Children do not always have a strong sense of the accuracy of their memories (Fandakova et al., 2018). In school, children often overestimate how well they will remember something, from lines in a play to their spelling words (Karably & Zabrucky, 2009).

Improvements in memory help children develop a sense of their own personal history as their *autobiographical memory* improves (Fivush, 2019; Nelson, 2018).

As children grow, it will become easier for them to remember and keep track of details about their lives (Bauer et al., 2019). By about age 7, their hippocampus, the brain structure involved in memory, has matured enough so that they are no longer subject to *childhood amnesia*, or the forgetting of childhood experiences (Riggins et al., 2020). Children begin to build memories that may stick with them for a lifetime, helping what they are learning in school to stick with them (although children's memories, like adults', can still erode and become less reliable over time (Brubacher et al., 2019).

Around the world, children are sometimes the only witnesses in serious criminal cases, including war crimes and abuse, and prosecutors rely on them to deliver justice (Amani & Khalfaoui, 2019; Pantell et al., 2017). But are children's memories reliable? Like adults, children can be *suggestible*, or vulnerable to having their memories influenced (Ceci & Bruck, 1993). Some studies have shown that because children are respectful of adults and authority figures, they can be more suggestible than adults and more likely to form false memories (Otgaar et al., 2018). Unlike adults, children often do not know what is expected of them and do not necessarily have preconceived biases about what adults want to hear. As a result, they are *less* likely than adults to form spontaneous false memories and are more likely to accurately report their memories (Otgaar et al., 2018).

Thinking About Thinking When asked how he memorizes new chess strategies or spelling words, Logan has trouble explaining exactly how the magic happens. Talking about thinking can be a little awkward. But Logan knows when he is doing focused or creative work, and he pays attention to when he feels "brain tired" and needs a break (or a chess game to refresh his thinking). Developmental scientists call this **metacognition**, or awareness of how you are thinking and reflecting on it, which can maximize your learning and productivity (Bayard et al., 2021; Flavell, 1979).

Children do not usually learn how to think about thinking on their own. They benefit when teachers and other adults help scaffold and strategize with them about how to build awareness of their thinking (Simons et al., 2020). One metacognitive technique is just the awareness of how hard you are working. Children are often aware if they are expending what researchers call *cognitive effort*, or hard mental work, on a project (Chevalier, 2018).

Motivation plays a major role in whether children can regulate their own thinking. Metacognitive strategies often come more easily to children who are already doing well in school and who have had some success. Metacognition helps such children jump even further ahead of their peers (Connor, 2016).

CAN YOU BELIEVE IT?
Can Online Games Change Your Brain?

Around the world, children are spending much of their time on screens. In the United States, children are on screens for fun—including television, phones, and gaming devices—for about five hours a day, whether they are watching videos on YouTube, playing with filters on Snapchat, or playing games. In 2021, U.S. children typically spent about an hour and a half each day playing games online or on their phones (Rideout et al., 2022). How do all these hours playing *Minecraft* or *Splatoon* affect the developing brain?

Gaming, like other screen media use, is controversial and complex. Some researchers suggest that the overstimulation caused by gaming is associated with attention difficulties such as ADHD or behavioral challenges such as acting out (Beyens & Valkenburg, 2022; Eirich et al., 2022). Other experts worry that video games can be addictive, particularly for children and adolescents (Bender et al., 2020).

XiXinXing/Shutterstock

Talking About Learning Reflecting on what they are learning, which utilizes cognitive skills such as metamemory, is helping these fifth-graders become more efficient students.

metacognition The act of thinking and reflecting on your own thinking processes.

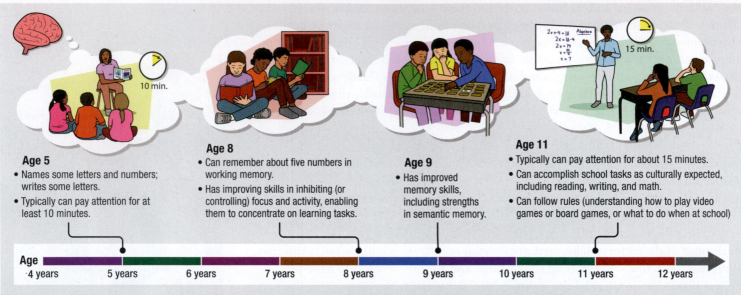

Age 5
- Names some letters and numbers; writes some letters.
- Typically can pay attention for at least 10 minutes.

Age 8
- Can remember about five numbers in working memory.
- Has improving skills in inhibiting (or controlling) focus and activity, enabling them to concentrate on learning tasks.

Age 9
- Has improved memory skills, including strengths in semantic memory.

Age 11
- Typically can pay attention for about 15 minutes.
- Can accomplish school tasks as culturally expected, including reading, writing, and math.
- Can follow rules (understanding how to play video games or board games, or what to do when at school)

Age								
4 years	5 years	6 years	7 years	8 years	9 years	10 years	11 years	12 years

Major Features of Cognitive Development in Middle Childhood
Can You Identify The Major Theoretical Perspectives?

The 5–7 shift: Children are better able to manage their thinking and behavior as they begin school.

The benefits of childhood cognition: Children's thinking tends to be more flexible and creative than adults. Inexperience means they may see solutions that experienced adults may miss.

Increased efficiency in brain activation: Studies of the brain have shown that fewer regions are activated when children are reasoning or concentrating as they gain more experience and practice in controlling their behavior.

Concrete operations: Piaget's stage of concrete operations refers to the growth in children's logical reasoning abilities. They can now follow more complex rules (including those for playing soccer), reason in their minds, and avoid logical mistakes, although tasks are still easier if they are concrete.

Learning in context: Vygotsky and sociocultural theorists point out that learning and cognitive development is always connected to culture. Learning is most effective when it is personalized to a child's zone of proximal development (ZPD). Children develop skills in how to learn depending on the expectations of their community.

Executive function: Executive function (EF) skills include the ability to control behavior and focus attention. EF skills will help children focus on schoolwork (or household chores) and develop problem-solving and reasoning abilities.

Memory: Children's semantic and autobiographical memory improve. Children are no longer subject to childhood amnesia.

Metacognition: Children's ability to control and monitor their own thinking, learning and memory skills are known as metacognitive abilities. Metacognitive abilities are often tied to school achievement.

CONNECTIONS

Remember from Chapter 2 that theorists who use *social learning theory,* like Albert Bandura, suggest that children learn how to behave from models. Bandura's Bobo doll experiment showed that children were likely to imitate violence they had watched on television in real life.

One area of dispute is whether watching violence makes children aggressive. Some researchers and social learning theorists have long cautioned that seeing violence on screens may make children aggressive in real life (Bandura et al., 1963; Calvert et al., 2017; Christakis et al., 2016). Current scientific consensus suggests that the relationship between violent media is more complex (Ferguson et al., 2022). Most researchers find that playing violent games may make children *desensitized,* or unreactive, to images of violence, but that it cannot be blamed for making children aggressive or hurtful to other people (APA, 2020; Ferguson et al., 2020; Kühn et al., 2019). However, spending less time playing violent games may be helpful for children who have difficulties getting along with others. Interventions suggest that children's behavior often becomes easier to manage after they spend less time playing violent games (Hasan et al., 2014).

How do video games effect children's cognitive skills? Large correlational studies conducted in the United States and Europe have found that time spent playing video games does not dull children's thinking abilities (Gnambs et al., 2020). In fact, some studies have found that playing some video games may build some cognitive skills like executive function or specific attention or spatial skills (Blumberg et al., 2019). A few educational games have been shown to help boost children's cognitive skills, although those may not be the apps most children are playing for fun every day (Kim et al., 2021; Ramani et al., 2020).

As you might expect, playing video games, like any other experience changes your brain (Kühn et al., 2022). For instance, in an experiment requiring adult participants to play *Super Mario Bros.* for hours, scientists observed on fMRI scans that there were changes in their brains after game play. New neural connections were created, particularly in areas of the brain related to navigation and planning (Kühn et al., 2014). It is not ethically feasible to conduct an experiment requiring children to play video games for hours each day, but some correlational studies have shown that children who play video games also tend to have stronger connections in brain areas devoted to processing visual information along with planning, navigation, and movement (Pujol et al., 2016). The relationships between brain structure and thinking are complex: Researchers suspect that brain changes are linked to the types of games children play, how long they play them, and what other activities (including school work) they are engaged in (Paulus et al., 2019).

Is playing video games actually good for children, then? Most researchers would not go that far. There may be some benefits, particularly when children are playing social, interactive games (Gray, 2018; Markey et al., 2020). There appear to be few cognitive risks for most children whose gaming is not taking away from their other activities—particularly sleep, physical activity, and homework (AAP, 2016; Bediou et al., 2020). However, when time online takes away from making friends, keeping healthy, or doing homework, children's learning and cognitive development might be at risk (Gnambs et al., 2020).

Learning on Screen Children are on screens in and out of school: Many schools, like this one in Groton, Connecticut, have adopted learning technology to provide students with customized learning experiences. Fifth- grader Ashlynn is using her device to practice math.

The Quest to Measure Intelligence

What makes someone "smart"? For many, the idea of **intelligence** is often complicated by stereotypes and cultural expectations. When developmental scientists use the term *intelligence*, they are referring to the abilities to learn and to apply what has been learned (Niu, 2020). However, how these abilities are measured depends on who is doing the measuring (Greenfield, 1998).

Understanding Differences Scholars and policy makers around the world have been trying to define who is smart for millennia, whether it was to pick priests in ancient Egypt or find capable civil servants in China (Higgins & Xiang, 2009; Van der Horst, 1987). In the United States and Europe, intelligence testing began in earnest in the 1800s as researchers tried to use science to predict who would be successful in school and at work (White, 2006).

French scientists created the first intelligence test that reliably recorded differences in children's cognitive capabilities. They wanted to identify which children needed help so they could be given extra support. The researchers believed that an objective test would eliminate biases from teachers, parents, and school administrators who might be motivated to exaggerate or minimize children's talents or difficulties (Siegler, 1992). The early test was adapted in 1916 at Stanford University in California and took the name *Stanford-Binet*. This test still exists today, although it has been adapted greatly over the years. The Stanford-Binet was followed by a U.S. test developed for children by David Wechsler in the 1940s. Weschler's test is now known as the *WISC*, or the *Wechsler Intelligence Scale for Children* (Weschler, 2014).

One feature of intelligence tests is that they provide scores on a standardized scale that is easy to understand. The scores on these tests are known as the **IQ**, or *intelligence quotient*. The "typical" or average range on the test is between 85 and 115, meaning that more than two in three people score in that range. Most people who take the test score in the "typical range" with relatively fewer in the extremes. People

intelligence The ability to learn and apply what has been learned.

IQ A person's score on a standardized intelligence test which, for most people, is between 85 and 115.

FIGURE 11.4 The Range of Intelligence This is a graphical depiction, known as a *bell curve*, of how people score on intelligence tests. Most people score in the average range, or in the big hump in the middle of the bell. Fewer fall in the extremely high or low ends of the spectrum. People who fall at the extremely low end of the distribution are likely to have an intellectual disability. Those at the extremely high end of the distribution may benefit from specialized education.

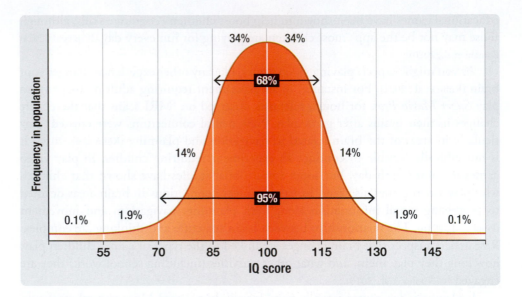

who fall in the extremely high end of the spectrum are said to have exceptional abilities, while those in the lower end are likely to have *intellectual developmental disorders (IDDs)*. If you plot these scores graphically, you will see that they fall into a bell shape (see **Figure 11.4**). This type of statistical distribution, with most people falling into the middle and with relatively fewer at the extremes, is often called a *bell curve*.

Early intelligence tests designed to identify children with IDDs were soon put to a more sinister purpose (Stough, 2015). Many early scientists used intelligence tests to promote the idea that some people are inherently superior to others—an incorrect belief that informed *eugenics*, which was a popular social movement in many parts of the world (Bashford & Levine, 2010). Eugenicists thought that they could improve society by preventing those they deemed less intelligent from having children or getting an education. By lavishing resources on those they thought were capable, eugenicists believed they could increase the overall "intelligence" of the population (Galton, 1883; Stoskopf, 2012; Terman, 1916).

Many early intelligence tests were biased: Elite and educated people often scored high, but less educated, lower-income people often received lower scores. Intelligence testing was used to discriminate against people by keeping them out of school, sterilizing them, and even institutionalizing them (Reddy, 2007). After the horrors of racial and ethnic hatred during World War II, support for eugenics decreased in the scientific community in the United States, although discrimination and stigma persist. Intelligence tests have been revised to reduce bias (Black, 2012; Stern, 2015; Weschler, 2014).

Group differences remain in intelligence test scores. Typically, children whose parents are more educated and have higher income score higher on the tests (Kaufman et al., 2015). Traditional intelligence tests are not the most reliable predictor of academic success; children's ability to control themselves and their motivation is more influential (Braaten & Norman, 2006). Intelligence tests, however, are a helpful way to screen children for learning disabilities, brain injuries, and exceptional abilities (Giofrè et al., 2017). They must be administered in a child's first language by a professional who understands the child's background and culture (Chen & Lindo, 2018).

Test results around the world have revealed that as communities become healthier and more affluent, and as more children attend school for longer periods of time, the general population tends to score higher on intelligence tests (Bratsberg & Rogeberg, 2018). This trend for population's average IQ test scores to rise over time is termed the *Flynn effect*, after the researcher from New Zealand who first documented it (J. R. Flynn, 2020).

Other Models of Intelligence Traditional intelligence assessments have many critics. Many argue that they do not predict success in the way some of their adherents promised (Sternberg, 2021). Others believe that the tests measure the wrong kind of intelligence, that being smart is a broader set of talents than traditional tests measure (Gardner, 2011; Sternberg, 2021).

Howard Gardner, a neuroscientist who loves the arts and plays the piano, is one such critic. He does not believe that traditional IQ tests recognize the bigger potential inside everyone (Gardner, 2011). In his **theory of multiple intelligences**, Gardner set out his idea that intelligence is a broad set of discrete abilities. He differentiated between different types of thinking, such as *linguistic skills* (language and communicating), *spatial skills* (understanding maps and geometry), and *musical skills*, to name a few. Gardner has suggested that all children have components of all these intelligences (Gardner, 1999). He has argued that schools should nurture and build abilities beyond math and verbal skills and assess students' skills in less traditional ways (Gardner, 2011).

The theory of multiple intelligences has appeal because it validates the intuitive idea that we all have different strengths and weaknesses. This theory, however, is not as popular among developmental scientists (Kaufman et al., 2015). Multiple intelligences are difficult to evaluate, and many attempts to accurately identify them in large groups of children have been inconclusive (Visser et al., 2006).

Another critic of traditional intelligence testing was himself once considered a failure on an intelligence test (Sternberg, 2015). Robert Sternberg spent the next 60 years proving that assessment wrong while working in a variety of positions at some of the most prestigious universities in the United States. Sternberg's **theory of successful intelligence** (formerly known as the *triarchic theory of intelligence*) argues that intelligence can best be measured by how you create a successful life through three types of intelligence (Sternberg, 1985, 2018a). *Analytic intelligence* involves thinking abstractly and solving problems. *Creative intelligence* involves the generation of new ideas. *Practical intelligence* involves applying ideas to real life, or common sense (Sternberg, 1997, 2018b). In addition to these components, Sternberg has suggested that people who are high in successful intelligence also have wisdom, moral understanding, and the ability to change (Sternberg, 2015, 2021).

Myths About Intelligence Despite the value of measuring intelligence, particularly for children with learning disabilities or brain injuries, myths abound. Let's look critically at some of these myths:

- *Is intelligence your destiny?* Many studies support the idea that children who perform well on intelligence tests are more successful later in life. They do better in school, are more likely to be promoted at work, and live longer (Halpern-Manners et al., 2020). However, scholars caution that this may be a *correlation*, not an indication of a causal relationship between testing well and doing well. Intelligence test scores are not the best or only predictor of success. According to developmental scientists, other factors may better predict lifetime achievement: physical and mental health, strong relationship skills and attachment, metacognition, personality, and cognitive traits such as self-control and conscientiousness (Dixson et al., 2016; Ohtani & Hisasaka, 2018).

- *Is intelligence fixed for life?* Scores on intelligence tests are more changeable early in life, but change is possible across the lifespan. (IQ scores can be affected by prenatal and early life factors, such as the health of the pregnant parent, stress, early education, and nutrition [Nisbett et al., 2012; Protzko, 2017].) During middle childhood, good health, a balanced diet, afterschool activities, and playing a musical instrument have all been identified as ways to boost intelligence test scores (Kirlic et al., 2021; Protzko, 2017). Educational interventions are also effective for children with low IQ scores (Colbert et al., 2018).

theory of multiple intelligences Gardner's idea that intelligence is a broad set of discrete abilities and that all children have components of all these intelligences.

theory of successful intelligence Sternberg's idea that intelligence can best be measured by how you create a successful life through three types of intelligence.

- *Is intelligence only genetic?* Some developmental scientists argue that genetics plays an important role in how we think (Plomin & von Stumm, 2018), but no single gene or group of genes has been identified as responsible for intelligence test scores. Scientists believe that some aspects of cognitive function are influenced by genes, but the relationship is complex, epigenetic, and highly influenced by the environment (Kong et al., 2018). For instance, in some studies children's intelligence test scores are more closely tied to those of their adopted families than their biological ones, indicating the importance of environment to cognitive development (Nisbett et al., 2012).

APPLY IT!   **11.1** Logan told us that he has several strategies for remembering, like writing down his spelling words and reciting his multiplication tables. How might his use of these strategies help him in school?

11.2 Logan says he learns best when he can focus on what he is interested in with other people at hand to coach him. How does this idea support Vygotsky's view of how children learn?

Language Development

Learning Objective

11.4 Explain how language advances support children's learning.

During middle childhood, children's use of language continues to expand, sometimes dramatically, and they develop the more complex ways of communicating that they will use at school. Children's vocabulary and grammar become more advanced. For most children around the world, this means using more than one language both at school and at home. Language acquisition—of one or many—is a skill that will help children succeed at school and in their relationships (Lee, 2010; Westrupp et al., 2020).

More Words

Children's vocabularies increase as they enter school. These new words are linked to school success, allowing children to communicate and write with more precision and accuracy. Some children learn 3,000 new words every year, and others pick up nearly 5,000 (Anderson & Nagy, 1993). Scholars believe that some schools and teachers are more effective at teaching vocabulary—a challenging undertaking—than others (Marulis & Neuman, 2010). It is often a lower priority than phonics and math skills (Snow & Matthews, 2016). Some promising interventions come from play-oriented classrooms that build vocabulary through acting out stories (Flint, 2020).

Individual differences also affect the speed at which children's vocabularies grow. Children with larger vocabularies learn more words more quickly than those with smaller vocabularies, and these differences increase as children begin to read (C. T. Stanley et al., 2018; Suggate et al., 2018). As children progress through elementary school, one of the biggest predictors of the size of their vocabulary is how much they read, especially printed books (Sullivan & Brown, 2015; Torppa et al., 2020). Environmental factors such as family stress and the parents' educational achievement continue to influence children's language development (Song et al., 2015).

One of the goals of school is to familiarize children with *academic language*, a formal way of communicating that allows students to learn details about content and that will become critical to their academic success (Cummins, 1984; Uccelli et al., 2019). Children who can use academic language effectively have had a lot of practice having conversations about things that go beyond the concrete present. Talking about the future and the past, telling stories using abstract ideas helps children gain these language skills that will help them tackle more complex content in school (Demir et al., 2015; Uccelli et al., 2019). Similarly, guiding children to develop more self-awareness about how they speak and write and the functions of language,

Reading with Family Although reading aloud may seem like something children outgrow, like footed pajamas, shared reading continues to help children build vocabulary and abstract thinking skills even after they have started school.

pixelheadphoto digitalskillet/Shutterstock

or **metalinguistic awareness**, will also help them build high-level language skills (Tunmer et al., 1984; Wijnands et al., 2021).

Using Language to Communicate

Children use language not only to ace tests or write book reports, but also to gossip, taunt each other, and make each other laugh. In addition to using his vocabulary to plan chess moves and write poetry, Logan uses language to socialize. Scholars call this ability to shift language styles **pragmatics**, which involves knowing how to talk with other people, what is appropriate to talk about, and how to interpret tone of voice, gestures, and other cues to keep a conversation going (Toe et al., 2020).

Effective use of pragmatics does not come easily to all children. Some children need support in order to read social cues and understand how to take turns in conversations. A few children with communication difficulties may need intervention in order to make friends and function well at school, and some of them may be diagnosed with a social communication disorder or autism spectrum disorder (Simms & Jin, 2015; Adams, 2021).

As children get older, there are greater demands for them to use language appropriately as they make friends and develop relationships with adults outside their families (Fujiki & Brinton, 2017). Younger children may have just grasped the difference between indoor voices and outdoor voices, but older children must understand when to change the subject when talking to a friend about a sensitive subject (Locke & Bogin, 2006).

Culture profoundly influences the pragmatics of language (DeCapua & Wintergerst, 2016). Children who act as *language brokers*, or informal translators, for their families or friends, often develop sophisticated and detailed understanding of social pragmatics, which benefits them into adulthood (Garcia-Sanchez, 2018; Guan et al., 2014). Logan adjusts his pragmatics as he interacts with adults, speaking much more casually with his brother than he does with his teachers and parents. In many languages, children even use a formal pronoun, like *usted* in Spanish, to respectfully address their elders.

Acquiring Multiple Languages

In the United States, about one in six elementary schoolchildren is an *English learner (EL)*, the term most schools use to refer to someone who is learning English in addition to another language or languages. Remember from Chapter 8 that speaking more than one language has cognitive benefits, such as improved executive function, and substantial economic benefits, including higher income and greater employability in adulthood (Bialystock et al., 2022; Gándara, 2018).

As a group, ELs bring important strengths to their school experience: Typically, are often more emotionally well-adjusted and socially competent than their peers (Gándara, 2017). Nevertheless, they often score less well than their peers on achievement tests and may have other academic difficulties (Takanishi & Le Menestrel, 2017). One reason is that many ELs are from low-income families who must navigate a U.S. education system that gives lackluster support to new immigrants (Ansari & Crosnoe, 2018; Sorenson Duncan & Paradis, 2020). Another reason is that they are learning core academic subjects in a language that they do not yet fully understand (Collier & Thomas, 2017; MacSwan et al., 2017). Finally, ELs are more likely to attend under-resourced schools and less likely to feel accepted by their school community (Bialystock, 2018; Echevarria et al., 2015).

Policy makers, parents, and educators often disagree about how best to help ELs succeed. Developmental scientists studying the outcomes of thousands of children have found repeatedly that those who enter school without strong English skills benefit from being taught core academic subjects in their home languages, while also learning English (MacSwan et al., 2017; Takanishi & Le Menestrel, 2017). They suggest that learning core skills is nearly impossible if children do not understand the language

metalinguistic awareness The ability to think about the features of language, such as the sounds that make up words and the way words go together to make meaning.

pragmatics Knowing how to talk with other people, including what is appropriate to talk about, and how to interpret tone of voice, gestures, and other cues.

CONNECTIONS

Autism spectrum disorder (ASD) is a developmental disorder typically diagnosed in toddlers and young children (see Chapter 5). Children with ASD often have sensory sensitivities and often have difficulties communicating and an insistence on routine. Treatments for ASD can help children and families manage their symptoms and teach them how to communicate with others.

Learn It Together

Supporting English Learners in School

Your neighborhood elementary school is interested in learning more about the best practices for supporting their students whose home language is not English. They have asked your class for some expert advice.

Prepare Review information about language development, bilingual development, and learning in elementary school. What are some of the strengths and challenges for students whose home language doesn't match the majority language at school?

Engage Have a conversation with a few of your classmates about personal experiences with learning English. Did everyone in your group learn English at home? If not, when did you begin to learn English, and what was your schooling experience like? Apply the information from the textbook to identify the key messages you would want to communicate to the elementary school principal.

Reflect As you thought about the best, science-based approaches to support English learners in elementary school, did you think of any barriers? What might make it difficult for schools to follow your recommendations, and how could you address those barriers?

of instruction. In addition, when schools support children's home language, children benefit from being dual- or multiple-language speakers, including improved executive function, strong self-esteem, and a sense of connection with their families and cultural identity. In fact, children who remain connected to their heritage and their home language may be protected from some risks, such as leaving school early (López et al., 2021).

APPLY IT!   **11.3** Logan speaks differently depending on whether he is hanging out with his family or responding to a teacher online. Why is learning pragmatics important in middle childhood?

11.4 What are benefits of speaking a second (or third) language in middle childhood?

Learning In and Out of School

Learning Objective

11.5 Explain how schools influence achievement during middle childhood.

Middle childhood provides children with the opportunity to build a foundation for learning that will help them as they grow. Education, whether in or outside of school, can link children to their communities, help them make friends, and establish skills that will help them making meaningful contributions and work in adulthood.

Variations in Schools

Around the world, nearly 9 in 10 children attend elementary school, but what school looks like and how children learn differ around the world (UNICEF, 2022c). In some countries, like Ireland, children may attend elementary schools run by religious institutions. In others, like Chile, most children attend private schools. In Finland, all children follow a rigorous, standardized curriculum, and the vast majority attend public schools (García et al., 2021). In many countries, children are taught the basics of reading, writing, and mathematics but also local history and customs (Seixas, 2018). The United States has a strong tradition of local control over schools and respect for parental choice in making educational decisions. As a result, what students learn in U.S. schools varies depending on the community (Thompson & Thompson, 2018).

Around the world, schools vary based on the affluence of the communities where they are located. Families with financial means tend to be able to provide their children with higher-quality education, no matter where they live (Chmielewski, 2019). Countries around the globe have gaps in the quality of children's schools based on family income, but the United States stands out among affluent countries for its

Eyes on Me Whether they are wearing uniforms, as in the Catholic school in Wales (*left*) or in casual wear, as in this science classroom in th United States (*right*), children's relationships with teachers help motivate and connect them to school.

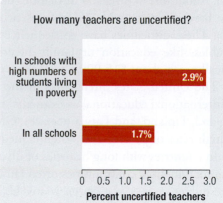
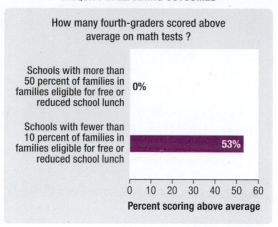

INEQUITABLE ACCESS

How many U.S. children had access to the internet and a computer at home during 2020?

In families with incomes less than $25,000 — 83%

In families with incomes over $150,000 — 97%

Percent (0 20 40 60 80 100)

Data from U.S. Department of Commerce, 2020.

INEQUITY IN TEACHER PREPARATION

How many teachers are uncertified?

In schools with high numbers of students living in poverty — 2.9%

In all schools — 1.7%

Percent uncertified teachers (0 0.5 1.0 1.5 2.0 2.5 3.0)

Data from U.S. Department of Education, 2016.

INEQUITY IN LEARNING OUTCOMES

How many fourth-graders scored above average on math tests?

Schools with more than 50 percent of families in families eligible for free or reduced school lunch — 0%

Schools with fewer than 10 percent of families in families eligible for free or reduced school lunch — 53%

Percent scoring above average (0 10 20 30 40 50 60)

Data from TIMSS, 2019.

FIGURE 11.5 Inequity in Education in the United States In the United States, schools are managed locally, which often means schools in low-income neighborhoods cannot offer the access to resources like computers, internet access, or highly qualified teachers that schools in more affluent neighborhoods can. The inequities are often linked to learning outcomes: Students who attend more highly resourced schools are more likely to score above average on tests.

level of inequity in school achievement and quality based on family income (Chzhen et al., 2018). In recent years, the achievement gap between high- and low-income U.S. students has been closing because of new investments in early education (Hanushek et al., 2019).

In the United States, as in many other countries, where children go to school is determined by where families live (Owens, 2018; see **Figure 11.5**). This results in schools that are vastly different. Children in low-income neighborhoods are more likely to have crowded classrooms and enjoy fewer after-school programs than those in more affluent neighborhoods (Jang & Reardon, 2019). The wealthiest districts in the United States, most of them suburban and White, spend nearly three times as much money per student as those in the least affluent districts (Kelly, 2020).

However, statistics do not tell the entire story. Schools are made up of people, and many teachers have an impact beyond what funding levels might predict. Children can be academically resilient even if they are learning in schools that are under-resourced. Researchers have found that supportive, positive schools with high expectations where students believe higher education will help them succeed are linked to children's academic performance, no matter what economic difficulties they may face (Agasisti et al., 2021; Erberber et al., 2015).

Variations in Achievement

Achievement test scores are a measure of what educators think children and adults should know. Researchers use them to compare children's learning and to compare the effectiveness of schools around the world. Unlike intelligence tests, which are designed to measure how children think, achievement tests measure what children have learned, including reading comprehension and math and science skills.

Many adults and children do not reach the markers set by common achievement tests. Around the world, only about half of all 10-year-olds can read and write at a basic level in their own languages (World Bank et al., 2022). In the United States, both children and adults have difficulty meeting the standards for reading and writing skills: Only one in three 10-year-olds meets the standards for reading, and only 4 in 10 meet the standards for math (U.S. Department of Education, 2019). About one in eight U.S. adults has difficulty with sixth-grade reading and writing skills, meaning that they have difficulties making inferences and doing comparisons (Mamedova & Pawlowski, 2019). About one in three has difficulties doing math at the sixth-grade level, meaning they have difficulty with percentages or estimating numbers (Mamedova & Pawlowski, 2020). These difficulties have consequences: Even when researchers control for other variables, like education or family income, people with stronger academic skills typically earn about $15,000 a year more than their peers (Rothwell, 2020).

The United States often ranks in the average or lower tier of affluent countries on international educational assessments, ranking below countries such as Singapore, England, Finland, and Latvia (Carr, 2017). Many researchers blame U.S. performance on high rates of poverty and systemic inequities (Yu & Cantor, 2016).

In countries with long histories of discrimination like the United States, children from marginalized communities often fall behind in school because of unequal access to resources (S. Meek et al., 2020). Many U.S. children live in neighborhoods that are segregated by race or ethnicity. Since funding for schools is highly localized, children of color, whose families are typically less affluent, are more likely than White children to attend schools in districts with lower levels of funding for books, teacher salaries, and art supplies (Reardon et al., 2019).

Additionally, children from marginalized groups are often stigmatized and discriminated against by their peers and even their teachers (Johnston-Goodstar & VeLure Roholt, 2017). This increases anxiety, saps motivation, and impedes learning (Killen, 2019; Verkuyten et al., 2019). In the United States, immigrant children, as well as Black, Native American, and Latino children, often feel disconnected from their schools and may not consider themselves high achievers. A sense of belonging can be strongly protective, leading to higher achievement (DeNicolo et al., 2017; Gillen-O'Neel & Fuligni, 2013). Ethnic pride is also protective, increasing self-esteem and, in turn, academic performance (Hernández et al., 2017; Rivas-Drake et al., 2014).

The COVID-19 pandemic, which closed schools and increased stress for families, children, and their teachers, had dramatic effects on children's learning around the world (Azevedo et al., 2021). U.S. children did not learn as much during the pandemic as they did before, although many children seemed to catch up once they were back in school in person (Kuhfeld & Lewis, 2022). The lingering effects of the pandemic have not been erased: It may take as many as five years for most children to catch up. The effects of the pandemic were particularly significant for children who were just learning to read when the pandemic began and for middle schoolers, particularly in math. The impact of the pandemic was not equitable: Younger children from lower-income

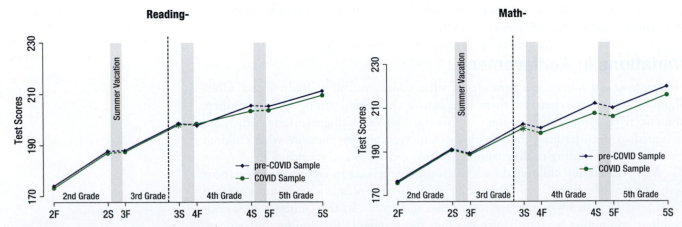

FIGURE 11.6 Changes in Achievement Scores After the Pandemic These graphs show the typical growth in achievement between second and fifth grades as measured by the NWEA with the blue lines. The green lines show results of early analyses of the children who were in third grade when the COVID-19 pandemic disrupted schooling. These results suggest that children's growth dipped during early months of the pandemic (after the dotted line), and children's scores continued to be slightly lower over the next year, particularly in math.

schools and from marginalized groups, including Black and Latino families, saw the most dramatic losses in learning during the pandemic, perhaps as a result of their schools' limited ability to adapt to remote schooling (Kuhfeld & Lewis, 2022).

 MAKING A DIFFERENCE
Bringing Fairness to School

All children have moments when they misbehave in school. Sometimes sitting in your seat, staying in line on the way to lunch, or being quiet during snack is difficult. But sometimes misbehavior is more serious, as when children get in a playground fight or lash out at an adult.

For some, the punishment for acting out is being handcuffed, confined in a locked box, paddled, or even sent to jail overnight. For one 11-year-old, kicking a trash can in the school lunchroom in Virginia led to juvenile court (Ferriss, 2015). For about 70,000 children every year in 19 states across the United States, getting in trouble has led to physical punishment, such as being spanked or hit by their teachers (Mathewson, 2022). About one in three children faces exclusionary discipline, like expulsion, suspension, or in-school detention, during the course of their school career (Rosenbaum, 2020).

Physical and exclusionary discipline are linked to an escalating pattern of difficulties for children who are likely be suspended again, in a process that some call the *school-to-prison pipeline* (Gilliam, 2016; J. L. Yang et al., 2018). This type of harsh discipline falls disproportionately on children with disabilities and children from Black, Native American, and Latino backgrounds. Children from these groups are disciplined two to three times more often than their peers (Ahranjani, 2020; Gershoff & Font, 2016; Liu et al., 2022; Mallett, 2016; Welsh & Little, 2018; Whitaker & Losen, 2019).

Why are such children at risk? Experimental and correlational research has found that educators often stereotype children's behavior. For instance, teachers are more likely to recommend discipline for Black boys who act up than for White boys who act up (Okonofua & Eberhardt, 2015; Okonofua et al., 2016). And because Black boys and girls are often perceived to be older than their classmates, they are perceived as more threatening if they misbehave and are often held to higher standards (Epstein et al., 2017; Goff et al., 2014). Children with behavioral disabilities like ADHD are often thought to be intentionally disruptive, sometimes triggering harsh responses from teachers eager to keep classrooms calm (Miller & Meyers, 2015; Ramey, 2015). However, no child benefits from harsh discipline.

The solution? First, educators and families must learn more about how to support children with disabilities and chronic conditions, acknowledge their own biases, and have more empathy for their students (Gregory & Fergus, 2017; S. Meek et al., 2020). Second, families and educators can reduce factors that lead to disciplinary problems by boosting the children's social and emotional regulation and making sure they have access to mental health resources, particularly those designed to treat trauma (Dutil, 2020). Third, teachers and schools can use proactive routines and high expectations, rather than reactive punishment to organizing classrooms and keeping children focused on learning (Blazar & Pollard, 2022). Finally, when difficulties arise, restorative, relationship-based interventions help teachers, children, and communities get along better and keep schools safer for everyone (Ahranjani, 2020; Darling-Hammond et al., 2020).

Skills for School

Unlike walking and talking, learning to read and write are not skills that children naturally develop on their own. Scholars call reading and writing skills **literacy** and the ability to manipulate numbers and do arithmetic **numeracy**. Building literacy

Strategy, Creativity, Achievement Chess uses many of children's cognitive skills. Here James is just relaxing with a game of chess in the park near his home in Brooklyn, New York, but at school, he led his team to the win at the national Junior High School Chess championships.

Share It!

Not so many excuses. Tough, discipline-focused charter schools known as "no excuses" schools have become much less popular. A recent analysis found that fewer of these schools are opening in communities around the United States.

(National Association of Charter School Authorizers [NACSA], 2019)

literacy Reading and writing skills.

numeracy The ability to manipulate numbers and do arithmetic.

Advancing Language Skills

Reading Is Her Superpower. In Georgia, Cicely Lewis, a school librarian, builds children's motivation to read through her program "Read Woke."

phonics-based instruction Instruction that builds children's reading skills by reinforcing the links between letters and their sounds.

whole-language approach Instruction that is based on the idea that children will learn how to read more effectively in an environment that weaves literacy into everything they do.

and numeracy takes lots of practice and leads to brain development as the skills are acquired (Bathelt et al., 2018; Hyde, 2021).

Building Literacy Learning to read builds on children's existing language skills but also requires new ones. Children need to build their *phonemic awareness*, the ability to identify the sounds in words. Then they need practice sounding out words and to understand what they are reading in order to build their reading comprehension (Christopher et al., 2015). Learning how to read builds new neural connections between brain areas that relate to processing visual information and language (Chyl et al., 2021).

Best practices for teaching children to read can be a controversial research area with passionate advocates on both sides. **Phonics-based instruction** builds reading skills by reinforcing the links between letters and their sounds. Phonics-based instruction is designed to build phonemic awareness and is considered by researchers to be the most effective way to teach early reading (Castles et al., 2018). However, some teachers worry that phonics takes the joy out of reading and saps students' motivation with its focus on repetition and memorization. As a result, many teachers are often unprepared to teach phonics (Drake & Walsh, 2020). However, more districts in the United States are moving toward phonics-enriched curricula (Goldstein, 2022).

Much reading instruction in the United States relies on the **whole-language approach**, which is based on the idea that children will learn how to read naturally in an environment that weaves literacy into everything they do (Gunderson, 2013; Krashen, 1999). In a whole-language classroom, books and written words are visible everywhere, and children are encouraged to tell stories and practice "writing" even before they learn all the rules of print and spelling. Despite the popularity of the whole-language approach, some researchers believe that more phonics instruction would reduce the number of children who struggle with reading by two-thirds (Putnam & Walsh, 2021).

However, whole-language approaches can build students' love of reading, which may be more important now than in the past. Elementary schoolchildren around the world are reading less than they did in previous generations (Parsons et al., 2018). Many are less motivated to read, and when they do read, they choose less-challenging books (Schaeffer, 2021). What can reverse this trend? Allowing children to choose their own books and develop their own interests, perhaps with the help of an expert school librarian (Wigfield et al., 2016).

Building Numeracy Most Americans understand the importance of teaching children to read well, but a surprising number believe that math is no longer necessary (Budd, 2015). However, even in an era of smartphone calculators, numeracy is essential to help children and adults think critically about the numbers that surround them. At a higher level, mathematical knowledge is important for building a career in the sciences, for evaluating evidence, and even for everyday life skills. How much math children know in second grade is one good predictor of how successful they will be at work 30 years later, regardless of their affluence, reading scores, or IQ (Ritchie & Bates, 2013; Zacharopoulos et al., 2021).

The goal of most elementary school teachers is to build a sense of numbers and their magnitude, place value, and basic arithmetic functions, such as addition and subtraction (Aunio & Räsänen, 2016). Many children struggle with early skills like counting and understanding the relative size of numbers: for example, whether 571 is bigger than 517 (Clark et al., 2013).

As children build their math skills, they use strategies for solving and understanding math problems such as counting with their bodies, which makes computation easier by reducing the demands on working memory (Friso-van den Bos et al., 2018; Siegler

& Braithwaite, 2017). Most children use their fingers to keep track of numbers until at least age 8 (De Chambrier et al., 2018). As children become more experienced with numbers, basic skills become automated, and they rely less on their bodies (Butterworth & Varma, 2013). But staying active continues to help children learn. Researchers suggest that effective math teaching happens when children are working actively, figuring things out in a group, using manipulatives, or otherwise doing more than pencil-on-worksheet tasks (Blazar & Pollard, 2022).

Improving Learning in School

From Coach Tom's chess tutoring to project-based learning, there are thousands of ideas for improving student learning in schools. Interventions based on developmental science apply theories of development to classroom practices.

Teach the whole child. A central theme of developmental science is that children's development is made up of interlocking domains: Being ready to learn means children need to be supported physically *and* emotionally. Successful interventions support children's physical needs by making sure that children have access to free breakfast to keep them focused and to school nurses to help coordinate their medical needs (Best et al., 2021; Frisvold, 2015; Kolbe, 2019). More than two in three children in school worldwide and one in two in the United States have experienced at least one traumatic or adverse experience, such as a serious illness, loss of a parent, or a natural disaster. Without support, children who are emotionally upset can have difficulties focusing in the classroom (Carlson et al., 2020; Porche et al., 2016). In-school mental health services and **socioemotional learning** designed to educate students to develop emotion regulation, establish their goals, and cultivate caring relationships have been linked to improving children's well-being and achievement (Mahoney et al., 2021; Taylor et al., 2017).

Relationships matter. The responsive relationships that children develop in early-education programs help them in elementary school. However, once children enter elementary school, many teachers focus more on learning than on building connections (Rucinski et al., 2018). When students and teachers get to know each other, children develop a stronger sense of belonging in school, which can lead to higher test scores (Walton & Brady, 2020; Wang, Degol, et al., 2020). This can be particularly important for students of color, who may not feel connected and understood in a classroom with White teachers (Gehlbach et al., 2016; Gray et al., 2018).

Building a growth mindset. Researchers refer to children's beliefs about learning as their *mindsets*. They distinguish between students with a *growth mindset*, who believe that their abilities can change over time, and those with a *fixed mindset*, who believe that talents and intelligence are set and cannot be changed. Scientists have shown that it is possible to change children's mindsets so that they understand that working hard, and the occasional mistake, are essential to learning (Dweck & Yeager, 2019).

Growing motivation. What makes Logan stay focused on his chess game for hours? Some developmental scientists would call it *motivation*. As children move through elementary school, their motivation and excitement about school typically diminishes (Scherrer & Preckel, 2019; Wigfield et al., 2015). School becomes "boring" and "irrelevant" at the same time it often becomes harder. Harnessing students' intrinsic motivation can start with encouraging them to work on things they are interested in, thereby respecting their growing independence and need for autonomy over their learning (Guthrie et al., 2006).

Other scholars study how motivation is sparked by a sense of **self-efficacy**, or the belief in one's own ability to make a change or have an impact (Bandura, 1999, 2019).

Fingers Help. Counting on your fingers can make things easier as children learn math.

How Would It Feel to Be an Ant? Teacher Craig Muzzy is reading a book about empathy and perspective-taking to students in New Britain, Connecticut, as part of an attempt to build friendships in school and decrease isolation.

CONNECTIONS

Remember from Chapter 8 that there are two types of motivation. *Intrinsic motivation* is the joy you get from learning about something you care about or that is meaningful to you. *Extrinsic motivation* is when you are working to earn a reward, such as a paycheck or a grade.

socioemotional learning Curriculum that focuses on teaching students skills for understanding and regulating their emotions and building caring relationships.

self-efficacy The belief in one's ability to make a change or have an impact.

Jackie Mader/The Hechinger Report

Project-Based Learning Can Boost Students' Motivation. These children in Michigan worked with their second-grade teacher to investigate safety problems at a local park. Here they work on the poster they presented to a local city councilperson. The children learned an important civics lesson and helped improve their community; their motivation was credited with helping them do better on achievement tests (Barshay, 2018).

Yunghi Kim/Contact Press Images

Love Has No Label. Bonnie has intellectual disabilities and her daughter, Myra, is in gifted education. Myra says that her mom is a "good parent and just because [she is] disabled doesn't mean [she does] anything less for me."

grit The ability to persevere in order to achieve a long-term goal.

specific learning disorders Difficulties with language development, reading, or arithmetic that lead to problems functioning in school or at home.

intellectual developmental disorder Difficulties with academics, practical skills, or social relationships.

Students with a stronger sense of self-efficacy use self-regulation to focus harder, plan out their work, and increase awareness of what they need to do. Building self-efficacy can come from repeated small successes and from working collaboratively with peers (Høigaard et al., 2015; Schunk & DiBenedetto, 2016).

Some researchers have suggested that a key factor in school success is self-control, or a closely related concept called *grit* (Duckworth & Gross, 2014; Mischel, 2014). **Grit** refers to the ability to persevere in order to achieve a long term-goal. Impulse control, like putting off watching a movie to study for a science test or turning off your phone to read a book, is often part of becoming successful.

However, critics caution that children need more than characteristics of self-efficacy, motivation, and grit to succeed (Generett & Olson, 2020; Lam & Zhou, 2022). As you will learn, this is particularly true for children with learning differences who need expert support (He et al., 2021).

Reaching All Learners

In any classroom, some children may take longer to understand something while learning comes easily to others. Myra Brown is one of those children for whom things came easily: She has been in gifted-and-talented classes since elementary school (Simon, 2013). But she knows firsthand that not everyone has this experience. Her mother, Bonnie, who has an intellectual developmental disorder, raised Myra as a single parent. Like Myra and her mother, there are many children in classrooms around the world who learn differently (see **Figure 11.7**).

Learning Disabilities Experts believe that about one in eight children have *learning disabilities*, including difficulty with language development, ADHD, or **specific learning disorders**, which include ongoing difficulty learning skills such as reading, writing, or math (Schaeffer, 2021; U.S. Department of Education, 2020b). Advocates for learning disabilities suggest as many as one in five children may have a learning disability and just not have the diagnosis (Horowitz et al., 2017). Two common learning disabilities are *dyslexia*, an impairment related to reading and spelling, and *dyscalculia*, an impaired ability to understand and manipulate numbers. About 2 in 100 students experience broad challenges with learning that interfere with their everyday functioning (McKenzie et al., 2019). These children may have an **intellectual developmental disorder (IDD)**, which means they not only have difficulty with academics but also with practical skills and social relationships (Tasse, 2016). Children who have an IDD or a specific learning disability may also be diagnosed with a traumatic brain injury, autism spectrum disorder (ASD), ADHD, or a genetic condition such as fragile X or Down syndrome.

About 5 percent of students in the United States have been diagnosed with a specific learning disability, but scholars suggest that the number should be much higher. Many children who have academic difficulties may never have been screened or diagnosed, preventing them from getting the extra help they need (Morgan et al., 2017, 2021). Children from low-income families who attend stressed and under-resourced schools are particularly likely to miss out on early-intervention services that address learning difficulties.

SCIENCE IN PRACTICE
Rodrigo Enciso, M.A., L.E.P., San Diego, California

Rodrigo Enciso is a school psychologist in San Diego, California. He thinks of himself as a problem solver: a wise resource, a fresh set of eyes, and a compassionate and creative thinker when children or their teachers need support. Like other school psychologists, Enciso is a professional who works with students, families, teachers, and administrators. School psychologists provide creative interventions and solutions when

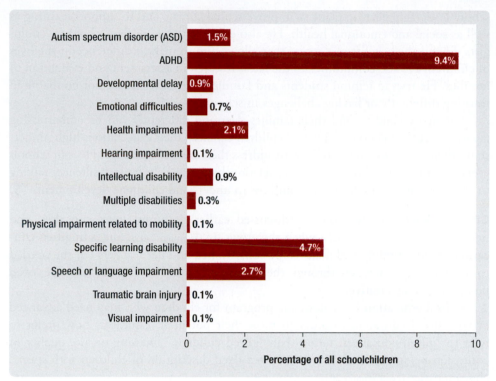

Data from U.S. Department of Education, 2020; Danielson et al., 2018.

FIGURE 11.7 **Types and Prevalence of Learning Differences in the United States** About one in eight students has been diagnosed with some type of learning difference, from autism spectrum disorder (ASD) to visual impairment. Researchers suggest that the number who are diagnosed with a specific learning disability, like dyslexia or dyscalculia, is actually too low: More students could benefit from extra support to build their reading, writing, and math skills.

young people are experiencing a behavioral, learning, or emotional challenge at school. In any given day, school psychologists might coach a teacher about how to engage a student who seems disconnected, strategize with administrators about how to improve the overall school climate, reach out to families to find out why their children are not coming to school, or provide one-on-one counseling, coaching, and assessment for individual students. Enciso brings many skills to school every day. These include a graduate degree, research expertise, comfort with numbers and statistics, hands-on experience raising five children of his own, as well as language and cultural skills. Enciso grew up in Mexico and is bilingual, allowing him to connect with many of the students in his community who are Spanish speaking (National Association of School Psychologists, 2017). Perhaps most important is Enciso's practice of empathy: for listening to children and his colleagues with understanding and respect.

Enciso's experience and scientific training enable him to develop solutions to help young people learn, get along with others, and enjoy being in school—a process that for many school psychologists has become even more challenging as schools and children adjust after the disruptions of the COVID-19 pandemic (Mathews et al., 2022). Enciso's language skills give him insight in understanding the achievement and adjustment of English learners in a state where about one in eight children receives special education services (Petek, 2019).

One area of Enciso's expertise is in providing the culturally and linguistically appropriate assessment that ELs need, understanding that every child is a little different. Some students may have strong language and reading skills in their heritage language but need more help in English. Others may need support to understand the cultural expectations in their new community (Ortiz, 2019). Assessing these young people requires language development in English and other languages. Some languages, including Spanish, are more phonetic than English, and students may have different patterns of reading skills in each language. Early assessment is used to ensure that students receive services that will make a difference, enabling them to develop the foundational skills that will help them thrive in school (Ortiz & Wong, 2022).

In the years that Enciso has been working as a school psychologist, he has developed special expertise in communicating with his colleagues and peers: He helps

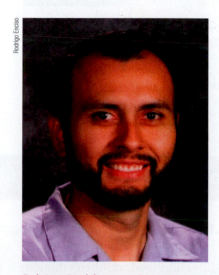

Solving Problems in San Diego Rodrigo Enciso is a school psychologist, bringing research expertise, empathy, and compassion to elementary schools. School psychologists use their understanding of developmental science to support students, teachers, and administrators.

gifted education An academic program for children who may need enriched or specialized education in order to meet their potential.

Share It!

Are you an Einstein? Some children (like the famous physicist Albert Einstein) may benefit from both gifted education and extra support for learning disabilities. Some analyses suggest that children with learning disabilities are more likely to have exceptional promise than their peers.

(Toffalini et al., 2017)

Extra-Curiosity Education Gifted education provides extra support and stimulation—and sometimes more hands-on experimentation. These children in Montgomery County, Maryland, are receiving extra excitement and enrichment in science.

school leadership develop plans to improve school climate and to support learning as well as social and emotional health. He also explains the work that school psychologists do and the benefits of a career that allows him to make a difference in the lives of children. He also communicates the latest research in assessment and evaluation to families. He tries to remind students and families that there should not be shame in learning differently or having challenges in school.

For many children and their families, learning differently can be embarrassing (Mitter et al., 2019). Enciso explains that children can keep their expectations high, understand their strengths, and learn how to address their areas of challenge. He is in schools every day helping to build the caring relationships that help build resilience, talking to children and other educators about how to understand children's development. 🎧

Gifted Education Myra Brown (discussed earlier) is funny, loves cupcakes, and hopes to be a marine biologist when she grows up (Fleming, 2009). She is in gifted education because reading and math come easily to her, and her teachers felt she needed to be challenged. She flew through the material she was learning in class: She loved books and being creative.

Gifted education is an academic program for children who may need advanced or specialized education in order to meet their potential. Educators now prefer to refer to "gifted education" rather than "gifted children," focusing on the quality of education being provided rather than on a fixed description of children with special characteristics (Lo & Porath, 2017).

Historically, there has been a profoundly unequal distribution of children in gifted-and-talented programs in public schools (Peters et al., 2019). In the United States, gifted-and-talented slots at public schools are more likely to go to affluent White children than those from Black, Native American, or Latino backgrounds, like Myra (Peters, 2021).

One reason for this may be bias in the identification of children who would benefit from gifted programs. Most nominations for gifted programs come from teachers, and these teacher reports have been found to be susceptible to stereotypes. For instance, White teachers are likely to underestimate the talents of their Black students: Black children were four times less likely to be recommended for gifted education if their teacher was White than if their teacher was Black (Grissom & Redding, 2016).

As children grow, whether they are in gifted education or in the typical track, their advances in thinking, learning, and communicating also create opportunities for more complex emotions and relationships.

APPLY IT! **11.5** Logan has thrived in virtual school, which has given him the freedom to pursue his own interests. How has this contributed to his motivation? **11.6** A friend of Logan's is being evaluated for learning disabilities. How would you explain the value of identifying learning differences?

Wrapping It Up ⭕⭕⭕

LO 11.1 Explain the key features of Piaget's concrete operational stage. (p. 266)

In middle childhood, children's thinking is flexible and curious. Piaget described this stage as concrete operations: Children can work through a problem logically and even reverse an action in their head. During this stage, children can pass typical conservation tasks and look at problems from multiple perspectives. They can perform tasks that require seriation or classification.

LO 11.2 Discuss why Vygotsky believed that learning comes from social interaction. (p. 266)

Vygotsky observed that children learn in a rich cultural context: They learn what is valued in their communities, and how they learn and think is also influenced by where they live. It is best when learning happens in your individual zone of proximal development and is scaffolded by a sensitive social partner.

LO 11.3 Describe the typical cognitive improvements during middle childhood. (p. 266)

Maturation involves dramatic improvements in children's executive function. Children's selective attention and memory also improve. Maturation in the brain, particularly in the hippocampus, helps make this possible, but so does practice. Metacognitive techniques enable students to manage their own learning. Intelligence testing is a way of comparing children's cognitive functioning, which may help identify children with learning or intellectual disabilities.

LO 11.4 Explain how language advances support children's learning. (p. 278)

Children's vocabulary, grammar, and pragmatics improve, allowing them to interact appropriately in a variety of contexts. Children who are learning more than one language have a number of strengths, but many attend under-resourced schools and may have academic difficulties.

LO11.5 Explain how schools influence achievement during middle childhood. (p. 280)

Children's achievement depends on where they go to school. Schools vary around the world, and children do not have equitable access to education. In the United States, schools are often segregated by family income: Higher-income neighborhoods have more highly resourced schools. Some children face discrimination from teachers and peers, making it more difficult to learn. Learning to read, write, and do math takes time and practice. Learning often benefits from strong relationships, growth mindset, grit, a sense of self-efficacy, and motivation. About one in eight students has learning difficulties that benefit from intervention. Some students have access to gifted education, which is designed to motivate capable students.

KEY TERMS

concrete operations (p. 267)
classification (p. 268)
seriation (p. 268)
semantic memory (p. 272)
rehearsal (p. 272)
elaboration (p. 272)
metamemory (p. 272)
metacognition (p. 273)

intelligence (p. 275)
IQ (p. 275)
theory of multiple intelligences (p. 277)
theory of successful intelligence (p. 277)
metalinguistic awareness (p. 279)

pragmatics (p. 279)
literacy (p. 283)
numeracy (p. 283)
phonics-based instruction (p. 284)
whole-language approach (p. 284)
socioemotional learning (p. 285)

self-efficacy (p. 285)
grit (p. 286)
specific learning disorders (p. 286)
intellectual developmental disorder (p. 286)
gifted education (p. 288)

CHECK YOUR LEARNING

1. During the concrete operations period of cognitive development, Piaget noted that children's thinking is:
   a) more logical and flexible than in early childhood.
   b) constrained by logical errors, such as irreversibility.
   c) based purely on imagination and magical thinking.
   d) highly abstract and theoretical.

2. Improvements in executive function during middle childhood are NOT associated with the ability to:
   a) succeed at games like Simon Says.
   b) recover more quickly from emotional outbursts.
   c) do 10 sit-ups in a row.
   d) sit still for several minutes to practice writing.

3. Which of these statements about Vygotsky's views of learning during middle childhood is TRUE?
   a) Children's learning follows a distinct set of stages.
   b) Children learn the same concepts in all cultures around the world.
   c) Children learn through independent exploration of the environment.
   d) Children learn the tools and skills of their culture through interacting with others.

4. Improvements in several forms of information processing during middle childhood make children much better at memorizing information than they were earlier. Explain the role of memory strategies like rehearsal, elaboration, and metamemory in supporting children's memorization.

5. What is the key difference between achievement tests and intelligence tests?
   a) Intelligence tests are used for children and achievement tests are used for adults.
   b) Achievement tests assess what has been learned, whereas intelligence tests assess the way people think and learn.
   c) Intelligence tests are not biased.
   d) There is no difference; these terms refer to the same thing.

6. An instructional approach that focuses on providing a literacy-rich environment and allowing children to practice writing stories before they have learned all the rules of print and spelling is known as:
   a) phonics-based instruction.
   b) phonemic awareness.
   c) metamemory.
   d) a whole-language approach.

7. Which of these is NOT associated with more learning in elementary school?
   a) Decontextualized memorization
   b) Motivation
   c) Growth mindset
   d) Strong teacher–child relationships

8. A diagnosis that involves difficulty with academics, social relationships. and practical skills is:
   a) intellectual developmental disorder.
   b) dyscalculia.
   c) dyslexia.
   d) oppositional defiance disorder.

9. Describe the recommended approach for educating children who are English learners (ELs).

Social and Emotional Development in Middle Childhood

© Macmillan, Photo by Sidford House

Ten-year-old Amara loves TikTok, *Roblox*, and drawing. When she grows up, she wants to be a doctor, but before that she wants to be an activist, a singer, and maybe have a YouTube channel. She has some time before medical school but is already an activist, her mission since kindergarten. Her inspiration comes in equal parts from her mother, Martin Luther King Jr., and the after-school program she is part of that encourages her advocacy efforts.

Many of us might feel awkward about making TikToks, dancing on camera, or rapping in front of a crowd. We might wish the world was different but never actually try to do something about it. Amara, on the other hand, can look into the camera and sing about police brutality, stereotyping, and the class bully.

Amara's mother says she has always been kind and outgoing, but the rest of the world didn't know it until Amara ended up in an afterschool program that encouraged her work. Now, thousands of people around the world have watched Amara's videos. She is coauthoring a book for children and is writing a rap about Black history.

Schoolchildren can accomplish big things. For example, Amara has created dozens of videos, writes songs, and has helped to write a book — all while getting through fourth grade on Zoom. Children everywhere know how to help their families and develop new talents, whether that means taking care of a younger sibling after school or performing in the school talent show. More mature emotions, bodies, and cognition help make this possible.

Nevertheless, children are not yet adults. Caregivers may not be as nearby as they once were, but relationships continue to be essential to healthy development.

Children benefit from increasingly diverse relationships, with friends, family, teachers, and even first crushes.

In this chapter, you will read about social and emotional development during middle childhood, which means many things around the world. Children may be stacking wood to help their families or practicing their TikTok dances, but from ages 6 to 12, all children are developing the emotion regulation and personality characteristics that will shape them as they move toward adulthood. They may not rap or advocate as Amara does, but all children are trying to find their place in the world, supported by the people in their lives.

Scientific American Profile

Meet Amara

Building Emotional Maturity

During middle childhood, children are expected to better control their feelings and impulses and manage their relationships without a lot of adult help. There is much variation in how they do this: Experiencing adversity requires some children to grow up more quickly than others. Children spend more of their waking hours with their friends and classmates than with their parents, and these relationships become critical to their happiness. But the emotional expectations and habits formed at home are still at the core of how they learn to manage feelings and relationships.

Learning Objective

12.1 Explain the goals of emotion regulation during middle childhood.

Growing Up Quickly

Despite the universal idea that children need special protections, millions of children around the world are in situations that force them to navigate the world as an adult. More than 14 million children worldwide live on their own, without parents or other adults in the home (Ntuli et al., 2020). For example, Sarita and Bipani (see photo) live with their siblings in the village of Puranguan, Nepal. They have raised themselves and their younger brother and sisters for the past five years since their parents left home to find work as migrant laborers (Aryal, 2016).

Researchers estimate that one in every eight young children around the globe is forced to take on adult roles, such as head of the family, soldier, or worker, before they are adolescents (ILO/UNICEF, 2021). Growing up quickly may be the only way children like Sarita and Bipani can survive in the short term, but taking on adult roles too early can have lasting effects on mental and physical health (Agorastos et al., 2019; McLaughlin et al., 2019). Children who have grown up on their own or endured significant adversity often have higher rates of emotional disorders and poor health in adulthood: Some scientists even see signs of accelerated aging in their cells (Colich et al., 2020; Marini et al., 2020).

In many communities, *who* is considered a child differs depending on their appearance and background (Priest et al., 2018). Adults often think of children as less innocent if they are from a group that is different from them, particularly if they are lower in social status. These discriminatory perceptions can affect immigrant children living in the Netherlands, Roma children living in Hungary, or children of color in the United States (Bruneau et al., 2020; D'hondt et al., 2021). In the United States, researchers have found that adults often rate young Black boys and girls as less innocent-looking than their White peers (Goff et al., 2014; Thiem et al., 2019; Todd et al., 2016). In effect, prejudice forces some children to grow up before their time. Nevertheless, warm social relationships can help children build resilience and health despite their adult responsibilities or the stress induced by discrimination that might age them beyond their years.

On Their Own Sarita, age 13, Reema, age 6, Deepa, age 8, and Bipani, age 10, work on their homework at their home in the village of Puranguan, Nepal. The two older sisters care for their younger siblings, the house, and their goats and cattle. Deepa and Reema are in school, and every day all four of them spend time on their studies.

Building Resilience

Most children can bounce back from acute stressors like sudden illness or a natural disaster, but not all navigate adversity and stress in the same way (Galatzer-Levy et al., 2018; Zhou & Wu, 2021). Remember from Chapter 1 that *resilience* refers to the ability to recover from stressors and challenges, even traumatic or chronic ones (Masten et al., 2021). It is a process that can be fostered as children grow (Garmezy & Rutter, 1983; Werner, 1989).

Resilience is built on social connections (Denckla et al., 2020; Luthar & Eisenberg, 2017). Positive early attachment, warm parenting, and strong friendships in middle childhood can help children heal from many traumas, including illness, loss, or disaster, and even maltreatment within their own families (Gach et al., 2018). Sometimes even just one loving, caring person can make a difference for a child who is experiencing adversity.

Children who develop strong early relationships are also more likely to build other skills like intelligence and emotion regulation that will protect them over the long run (Luthar & Eisenberg, 2017; Rodman et al., 2019). Those who encounter adversity, such as childhood cancer or the loss of a parent, draw from positive relationships to find meaning in their experiences and respond to their trauma with a sense of purpose (Hamby et al., 2020). Researchers hope that these children are able not only to bounce back but also to find a way to thrive and feel optimistic about the future (Non et al., 2020).

Human beings have tremendous ability to be *plastic*, or to change, but nevertheless, chronic adversity, trauma, and stress can impair children's health and development. Cumulative stress inevitably takes a toll and is unequally distributed (Masten et al., 2021). Adversity is often driven by inequality in communities and rooted in exclusion and discrimination based on ethnicity, immigration status, race, or gender identity (Liu et al., 2022).

One of the best ways to help a child who is experiencing adversity is early intervention to shield them from further trauma and stress. Lifting families out of poverty, reducing the everyday burden of low income, can reduce overall stress. For instance, when a group of researchers monitored a group of low-income families, they found that the rate of emotional problems dropped by more than half after their family incomes went up by about $5,000. These improvements in well-being continued as the children grew into adults (Costello et al., 2003; Copeland et al., 2022). Simply having more money reduced family stress and allowed more children to thrive.

While too much stress can lead to strains, some adversity is inevitable. With support, disappointments, failures, and hardship allow children to practice their coping skills and build emotional maturity that will help them grow (Masten & Cicchetti, 2016).

Erikson's Stage of Industry Versus Inferiority

During middle childhood, children are typically expected to progress from playful preschoolers to more responsible schoolchildren who can get down to work. This could mean measuring ocean warming in a laboratory in the Great Barrier Reef, a long morning of achievement testing in Alabama, or keeping track of reindeer on the tundra in Norway.

Remember from Chapter 2 that Erik Erikson described eight stages of human development. He shared many ideas about middle childhood with Sigmund Freud. Freud described middle childhood as a period of *latency*, when major sensual and sexual drives are "sleeping" or only active in the background (Freud, 1905/2000). Both Freud and Erikson believed the task of middle childhood was for children to learn how to tame their passions and imaginations to become more independent and dutiful learners (Erikson, 1950/1993; Freud, 1905/2000).

Erikson called the crisis of the fourth stage of development **industry versus inferiority** (Erikson, 1950/1993). This conflict is successfully resolved when children

industry versus inferiority The fourth stage of Erikson's theory in which children are challenged to build their sense of themselves as capable and avoid feeling inadequate.

TABLE 12.1 Erikson's Stages of Psychosocial Development: Middle Childhood

Stage	Age	Characteristics
Industry versus inferiority	5–12 years	Children need to resolve a conflict between a sense of competence and a sense of failure. If children feel that they are capable and can accomplish something, they will take that feeling of their own resourcefulness with them into adulthood.

develop a sense of their own *industriousness*, or their ability to be productive (see **Table 12.1**). Children can feel inferior if the pressure to learn new skills makes them feel inadequate or discouraged by a mismatch between their abilities and their community's expectations. Children who have academic difficulties might experience inferiority, as could children whose families have unrealistic expectations for their behavior (Trinidad, 2019).

Erikson was confident that encouraging children's interests during this stage is critical to developing a sense of identity as competent adults. Children who are not allowed to try something new, Erikson argued, may never learn that they can take the risks necessary to grow (Erikson, 1950/1993).

Contemporary researchers have found that many of Erikson's observations still ring true today. Remember from Chapter 11 that researchers believe that children's commitment to learning new skills helps them grow into successful adults, although they rarely use Erikson's term *industry* to refer to this tendency. Instead, researchers use a variety of terms like *grit*, *conscientiousness*, or *achievement motivation* (Conger et al., 2021; Duckworth, 2016; Ponnock et al., 2020).

Regardless of the terminology, children who adopt these habits are more likely to use them in adulthood. The drive to work hard is a trait found in many successful children and adults (Blatný et al., 2015). As you will see, children who feel productive and successful when they learn new skills also are more likely to develop a positive self-concept and a sense of *self-efficacy*, or confidence in their own capabilities.

Ironically, as children enter school, it is typical for the buoyant self-confidence of preschool to falter. Their stronger social awareness forces them to become more realistic about their abilities (Wigfield & Eccles, 2020). Some declines in confidence may be inevitable, as Erikson predicted, but serious feelings of inadequacy or failure can lead to mental health problems (Ghandour et al., 2019). One way for children to feel competent is to give them a chance to help.

FIGURE 12.1 What Do You Want to Be When You Grow Up? As Erikson would have predicted, most children gradually abandon their fanciful plans to be superheroes and begin to think about careers that their community values. By elementary school, most children adopt slightly more realistic goals, such as becoming doctors or teachers, although many still have the optimistic goal of becoming a professional athlete.

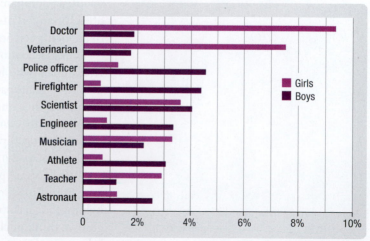

Top 3 Professions by Age

Age (years)	1st	2nd	3rd
1–2	Don't know	Doctor	Animal
2–3	Doctor	Parent	Firefighter
3–4	Super hero	Doctor	Parent
4–5	Veterinarian	Scientist	Doctor
5–6	Doctor	Firefighter	Athlete
6–7	Athlete	Doctor	Police Officer
7–8	Athlete	Engineer	Veterinarian
8–9	Video game designer	Teacher	Doctor
9–10	Athlete	Doctor	Video game designer
10+	Athlete	Chef/baker	Veterinarian

Top 10 Professions by Gender (all ages)

Doctor, Veterinarian, Police officer, Firefighter, Scientist, Engineer, Musician, Athlete, Teacher, Astronaut

Girls / Boys

0 2% 4% 6% 8% 10%

Data from Fatherly, 2015, 2017.

Pitching In Whether they are watching the reindeer in Tsagaan Nuur, Mongolia, or bathing a baby sister in San Basilio de Palenque, Colombia, children who help out can build confidence in their own capabilities, or what Erikson called industriousness.

MAKING A DIFFERENCE
The Benefits of Helping Out

Work outside of the classroom is the reality for many children around the globe (Lancy, 2020). More than 1 in 10 children worldwide works outside the home, selling things on the street or harvesting on a farm (ILO/UNICEF, 2021). Children help out at home, too, by watching younger siblings, cooking, or doing laundry (Lew-Levy et al., 2017). As Erikson may have predicted, developmental scientists have observed that work can be beneficial for children's development. It can make them feel valued and connected to their families and builds their industriousness (Coppens et al., 2018; Gallois et al., 2015; Orellana, 2001).

In the United States, however, many families report that chores are too stressful to assign, since their children are unwilling to help. Only about 3 in 10 children under 11 have regular chores, and fewer than 1 in 100 have paid jobs, mostly on farms (Mercer, 2013; Wallace, 2015).

In the United States, higher-income parents often expect that their children will be too busy with schoolwork and activities to do chores. Helping is more common in lower-income households and immigrant families (Klein et al., 2009; Rende, 2015). One research group found that children in lower-income families spent nearly twice as much time assisting their families as children in wealthier ones did (Coppens et al., 2018).

When researchers compared children who do chores with those who do not, they found that children who were expected to help had greater self-confidence and self-efficacy and had an easier time following the rules (White et al., 2019). One group of scientists compared children who helped their families by translating in the doctor's office or at parent–teacher conferences and found that the child-translators did better than their peers in school (Dorner et al., 2007).

Children who work with their parents outside of the home can also gain benefits. Researchers who have spent time with such children have found that work, whether helping a grandparent or pitching in at a family business, did not seem oppressive to them. On the contrary, working often made them feel important, helpful, and valued (Grugel & Ferreira, 2012). Working created stronger bonds with their families and built social relationships that helped them find work in adulthood (Estrada, 2019; Estrada & Hondagneu-Sotelo, 2011).

While some paid work may be risky to children, particularly if they are working long hours, missing school, using fertilizers or pesticides, or operating heavy machinery, helping out has many benefits (Bourdillon et al., 2019; ILO/UNICEF, 2021). Researchers suggest we think of chores not as a distraction from school but as a way of caring for each other (Rende, 2015). The payoff will be children who feel capable and competent.

Emotion Regulation

Amara wants you to know that being a fourth-grader in the middle of a pandemic was not easy. Keeping her cool when the internet went down in the middle of a test and her mother had to drive to find a place to log on was tough. She missed school, the friends she sang and danced with, Ms. Silver, who ran her afterschool program, and performing in front of live audiences. Nevertheless, she had much to look forward to. The California weather meant that she could meet her friends outside, and, when all else failed, she could have a game night with her mother.

Amara's efforts to keep her cool despite the stress of the pandemic are not unique: During middle childhood, all children take on the task of learning how to manage their feelings in a way that their community expects. Children in middle childhood still occasionally melt down, cry, and snap at their siblings, but it happens less often than in early childhood (National Survey of Children's Health, 2019). Families' strategies for managing emotions vary, but children are more likely to thrive when they can react to frustrations with some degree of calm and stay optimistic and motivated to do the hard work of learning that comes with middle childhood (R. A. Thompson, 2019). Being both persistent and curious are particularly linked to children's ability to persevere in school (OECD, 2021b).

The ability to manage emotions is critical to children's academic and social success alike (Distefano et al., 2021; Schlesier et al., 2019). Their developing cognitive skills help them with emotion regulation: Remember from Chapter 11 that children at this age have increased awareness of their own thinking, and this extends to their emotions (Raval & Walker, 2019). In many cultures, by middle childhood, children are adept at using words to describe how they are feeling, and many can understand how negative and positive thoughts affect their moods (Lagattuta et al., 2015; Raval & Green, 2018). They are also aware of how other people perceive them and how to manage their feelings in a complex social environment (Domitrovich et al., 2017; Saarni, 1999). These skills will help them throughout their lives.

Communities and families around the globe socialize emotional expression in different ways, as you may recall from Chapter 6 (Raval & Green, 2018). Children everywhere are expected to regulate their own feelings more independently as they grow, but what it means to be emotionally mature varies (Weis et al., 2016). Some communities value calmness and emotional restraint, and others value self-expression and outward displays of emotion (Raval & Walker, 2019). For instance, many families, including those from Mapuche communities in Chile, socialize their children to minimize fear, encouraging them to be "brave" and not overly anxious about thunder, wild animals, or other typical childhood worries (Halberstadt et al., 2020). Some communities, such as many in the United States, encourage pride when children are recognized for their accomplishments, but children from communities in Japan may be embarrassed by the attention (Furukawa et al., 2012).

 **Share It!**

Does your tummy hurt? Stomach upset is often a way that children express their feelings of upset: Researchers suggest that may be because stress changes our intestinal microbiome.

(Callaghan et al., 2020)

CONNECTIONS

Remember that cultural values can be *collectivist* or *individualist*. Collectivist orientations mean that people value the group and interdependent relationships over individual desires and accomplishments (see Chapter 1). Individualistic orientations value the individual's autonomy and independence over the good of the larger group. Families and cultures often have a mix of these values.

How many kids have trouble with getting along with others, managing emotions, or concentrating?

No difficulties — 78.9%
Some difficulties — 15.5%
Severe difficulties — 5.6%

Data from NSCH, 2011–2012.

How often can children stay calm when faced with a challenge?

Always — 22.5%
Usually — 38.8%
Sometimes — 38.7%

Data from NSCH, 2011–2012.

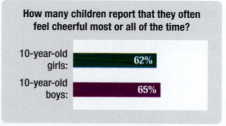

How many children report that they often feel cheerful most or all of the time?

10-year-old girls: 62%
10-year-old boys: 65%

Data from OECD, 2021b.

FIGURE 12.2 Emotional Development During Middle Childhood Most U.S. families report that their children can get along with others or manage their feelings, but that does not mean that they always stay calm when they experience frustration. During childhood, developing emotion regulation is an important skill, but maturity takes a long time.

Learning That Is Designed to Be Fun
In this school in Bihar, India, teachers encourage students to feel comfortable with their teachers and their peers by encouraging students to be playful. School leaders believe that students who feel emotionally comfortable in the classroom will have an easier time learning.

Have you ever heard an adult remind a child to "use their words?" In North America and Europe, children are often encouraged to articulate and share their feelings, even those of anger or frustration (De Leersnyder et al., 2020). This emphasis on self-expression is far from universal (Ip et al., 2021; Jaramillo et al., 2017). For instance, researchers have found that children in some collectivist communities in India are discouraged from sharing feelings of sadness and anger, because doing so is considered impolite and damaging to interpersonal relationships (Raval & Green, 2018). More individualistic communities encourage children to freely express their feelings. In doing so, families may be sending the message that expressing your individual feelings is more important than making sure everyone is comfortable. Differences in emotional socialization reflect varying cultural values about the value of the individual versus the group.

Regardless of which culture they live in, children's emotion regulation is tied to their relationships. Parents who have strong emotion regulation skills and who have positive bonds with their children are more likely to have children who more easily manage their feelings. Relationship quality is the biggest predictor of children's emotional health, regardless of the specific practices that parents use to socialize their children (Cook et al., 2019; Raval & Walker, 2019).

The parenting practices that adults use to help children with their emotions are diverse. Some are common in the United States, such as asking children to name and talk about their feelings (Garrett-Peters et al., 2017). Other practices include offering comfort when children are upset; empathizing with their feelings; and coaching and problem solving through difficult situations (Eisenberg et al., 1998; Gottman et al., 1996; Morris et al., 2017). Some practices are clearly unhealthy: Dismissing or being contemptuous of children's feelings is problematic in every community (England-Mason et al., 2020).

Families are not the only place where children learn about feelings: They also learn how to manage their feelings at school. Large analyses have found that socio-emotional learning curriculums can boost children's social skills and emotional well-being—and improve their academic achievement at the same time (Durlak et al., 2011; Mahoney et al., 2021).

APPLY IT!   **12.1** Erikson described middle childhood as a time when children should develop a sense of their own capabilities or industriousness. What are some ways that Amara is able to feel industrious?

12.2 Amara benefits from strong relationships with her mother and teacher. How else is she building resilience?

Developing a Sense of Self

Learning Objective

12.2 Describe advances in self-concept and the role of social comparison in self-esteem during middle childhood.

During middle childhood, children develop a clearer sense of who they are. School and the world outside the family sometimes provide a harsh reality check for children: They may not do well in the spelling bee, they may get picked last for basketball, or they may feel that they do not fit in. Children's developing cognitive skills make much more sophisticated social comparisons possible (Lapan & Boseovski, 2017). As a result, children's self-concept, self-esteem, and feelings of general well-being often dip in middle childhood, although most continue to feel good about themselves (Casas & González-Carrasco, 2019; Wigfield & Eccles, 2020).

Self-Understanding in a World of Peers

In school, children are constantly compared to each other. Sometimes this is subtle, as when reading comes easily to one friend and another has a hard time grasping long division. As children mature, their social comparison skills improve dramatically because of practice and cognitive abilities that make it easier to navigate complexity (Lapan & Boseovski, 2017).

Researchers seeking to measure self-esteem often ask children whether they like themselves (Harris et al., 2018). The answers to this question can have important consequences. For many, how they feel about themselves predicts how well they will do in school, how they get along with other children, and even how healthy and successful they will be as adults (Magnusson & Nermo, 2018; Zheng et al., 2020). Children with chronically low self-esteem are at risk for depression and other emotional disorders as they get older (Brummelman & Sedikides, 2020).

Self-esteem is built on a legacy of relating to others that began in early childhood. Children who have warm, securely attached relationships with their parents tend to have higher self-esteem (M. A. Harris et al., 2017). By the time children are in school, their friendships and their sense of how they compare to other children also begin to affect their self-esteem (Newland et al., 2019).

Self-concept also develops quickly once children start elementary school. Remember, self-concept refers to how children perceive themselves in various domains, such as how good they are at math, playing soccer, or even making friends (Harter, 2006; Shavelson et al., 1976). These distinctions will begin to form the basis for their identity or their sense of who they are (Oyserman et al., 2012).

When most children start elementary school, they have a positive self-concept and abundant enthusiasm for the new experience. They expect great things from themselves and are sure they will be great readers, doctors, or astronauts (Muenks et al., 2018). As mentioned, while children progress through school, reality sinks in, and often their beliefs in their abilities decline (Thomaes et al., 2017). (See **Figure 12.3**.) Families and teachers can help children develop a healthy self-concept by giving them opportunities to improve their skills and by expressing positive beliefs about what they can accomplish (Koenka, 2020; Muenks et al., 2018).

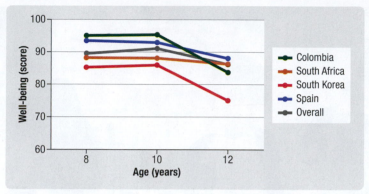

Data from Casas & González-Carrasco, 2019.

FIGURE 12.3 Life Gets Less Rosy over Time. Maturity often means that children are better able to compare their lives with others'. For many, growing up provides a reality check. When researchers asked children from 18 nations whether they felt their lives were going well or if their lives were "just right," fewer were completely positive as they got older.

Personality Development

Do you think Amara, outspoken and determined, will be the same kind of person as an adult as she is as a fourth-grader? Will her persistence help her in her journey to adulthood? These questions relate to the study of *personality*, or the individual differences that make each of us unique. As children move through middle childhood, their personalities tend to become more stable in ways that will stay with them through adulthood (Mõttus et al., 2019; Shiner, 2021). Some of these individual patterns, like Amara's bravery and determination, will be an easy match to their communities' expectations and benefit children as they grow up, while others may cause difficulties (Conger et al., 2021; Stallings & Neppl, 2021).

Researchers measure personality in middle childhood using the same components as they do for adults, the *five-factor model*. These five parts of personality include *extraversion*, or how outgoing someone is; *agreeableness*, or how a child gets along with others; *conscientiousness*, or how diligent or hardworking a child is; *neuroticism*, or emotional stability; and *openness*, or imagination or curiosity about new experiences (Shiner, 2021). As children mature, researchers find that they typically become more conscientious and agreeable, and a little less curious and imaginative, as they prepare for the transition to adolescence (Brandes et al., 2020).

Culture affects how families react to children's emerging personalities. In the United States, many White and Black parents expect their children to be extraverted and outgoing rather than shy. Children are expected to show some initiative, such as being able to order by themselves at a restaurant. This preference for outgoing children is not universal; Latino and Asian American parents are more comfortable with shy children

CONNECTIONS

Remember from Chapter 6 that researchers who measure personality in babies refer to differences in *temperament*. The Thomas and Chess model categorizes babies as *easy*, *slow-to-warm-up*, and *difficult*. Other models measure babies' level of *effortful control*, *negative affect*, and *extraversion*.

CONNECTIONS

Remember that developmentalists believe that children's early personalities are a complex interaction of genes and the environment. Genes play a part in personality, but environmental factors like health, environmental toxins, family stress, and friendships are also influential. Remember from Chapter 2 that the theory of *differential susceptibility* reminds us that children do not all respond in the same way to life experiences.

A Little Shy to Meet You Personalities come in many different shapes and sizes. Some children are a little nervous in new situations, while others may be a bit more bold. Cultural expectations play a role in how accepting adults may be of the diversity in how children approach the world.

CONNECTIONS

Remember from Chapter 9 that preschoolers tend to be very rigid about their ideas about gender, as they are with other categories, but that not all young children identify with stereotypes or binary gender categories. As children develop *concrete operational thought* and more flexibility in thinking, their ideas about gender become more flexible.

Share It!

Stigma and bullying are not inevitable: Adults can help. Encouraging children to be friends with children who may have different identity markers can help all children feel that they belong.

(Halim et al., 2021)

(Chen, 2018). The preference for extraverted children is common to many affluent countries around the world (Latham & Von Stumm, 2017). However, attitudes about what types of emotional displays are appropriate often change over time. For instance, over the past 20 years, as China has become more urban, some city parents are less accepting of shyness than they were in the past (Ding et al., 2020).

Warm parenting is closely associated with agreeable personalities, and parents who feel competent are more likely to raise children who are conscientious (Egberts et al., 2015). Other personality traits change because of experiences outside the home (N. D. Brandt et al., 2019). For instance, doing a lot of homework can make children more persistent and conscientious (Göllner et al., 2017). But some personality changes may be caused by random events that affect children differently, depending on their genetic makeup and personal history (Tucker-Drob, 2017). For instance, the success of Amara's online videos will probably expose her to more opportunities for public speaking and outreach, which may make her even more outgoing than she was before. Another child, with a different genome and set of life experiences, may respond to this type of notoriety differently.

Personality alone does not determine what will happen later in children's lives, but in many communities, some personality traits may make it easier for children to succeed (Kajonius & Carlander, 2017; Nave et al., 2017). Children who are conscientious and open to new things generally do well at school, and this success is likely to continue later in their lives (Israel et al., 2021; Soto & Tackett, 2015). On the other hand, children who have difficulty regulating their emotions, becoming conscientious, and being understood by and understanding of others are more likely to break rules and act out (Tetzner et al., 2020).

Gender Development

If you compare the colors of elementary schoolchildren's clothing with those of preschoolers' clothing, you will likely notice some stark differences, such as less pink on the older children (Martinez et al., 2019). One outcome of the new cognitive flexibility of middle childhood is that children's gender categories become less rigid as they learn to separate appearance from gender identity (Rogers, 2020). However, even as children become more flexible in their thinking, they are acquiring new stereotypes, attitudes, and ideas about what it means to identify as a boy or a girl, or as another gender identity. As you will learn, some of these are more serious than what colors you wear.

Although children in elementary school are willing to give up some of their very literal rules about gender, ideas about what is "for boys" and what is "for girls" are still limiting. About one in four girls tells researchers that she likes what are considered typical "boy" activities, such as robotics or football. Fewer boys admit to enjoying "girl" pursuits, and those who do may face more social consequences (Coyle et al., 2016; Rogers, 2020). Children who do not adhere to gender stereotypes, such as a boy who loves sewing, are at higher risk for being harassed or bullied by their peers (Ioverno et al., 2021; Zosuls et al., 2016). Children who identify as gender nonconforming, transgender, or lesbian, gay, or bisexual are at even greater risk (Kwan et al., 2020; MacMullin et al., 2021; Martin-Storey & Fish, 2019).

As children mature, they become more aware of the stereotypes and attitudes about gender that surround them (Rogers & Meltzoff, 2017). Most children think that girls are more likely to be "good" or "nice" than boys are. But they also believe that boys have higher social status than girls (Hammond & Cimpian, 2021; Leaper & Brown, 2018). By the fourth grade, more than three in four boys and girls tell researchers that they are aware of gender discrimination (Brown et al., 2011). As one girl explained, "People say that boys can do more things than girls. I do not believe that at all" (Rogers, 2020, p. 188).

Children are even aware of complex stereotypes. For instance, most children are aware that girls are not "supposed" to be good at math or science (Bian et al., 2017). They also assume that boys are likely to be "trouble" (Chu, 2014). One fourth-grader explained that boys "always get into fights, always talking bad about other people, getting in trouble in class for talking back to the teacher . . . talking in class, being on their phones" (Rogers, 2020, p. 185).

Stereotypes about gender impact children's achievement in school. Girls tend to earn higher grades and test scores than boys, but stereotypes about girls' talent for math and science can make them feel that they do not belong in STEM fields (Bian et al., 2017; Leaper & Brown, 2018). Gender stereotypes likely have even more of an impact on boys than many realize. Boys often tell researchers that men are not supposed to talk about their feelings, ask for help, or work hard. These stereotypical attitudes about masculinity may be one reason boys begin to fall behind girls in achievement in school in many countries around the world (Leaper & Brown, 2018; O'Dea et al., 2018).

Just a Bunch of Children Playing Games in Austin, Texas Whether you are trans (like some of these children) or not, growing up includes deciding how to express your gender identity, and maybe how to make it to the next level on Mario.

 ### SCIENCE IN PRACTICE
Justine Ang Fonte, M.P.H., M.ED., Health Educator

Most adults around the world agree that elementary schoolchildren are too young for romance. In fact, school districts around the United States have gone so far as to ban romantic relationships from elementary schools (Kobin, 2019). However, researchers point out that banning romance may be impossible, and that children should begin having comprehensive education about gender, sexuality, and romance in elementary school (Cacciatore et al., 2019; Fisher et al., 2015; Pound et al., 2017).

Justine Ang Fonte has been teaching for almost 20 years and educates elementary schoolchildren about gender identity, sexuality, stereotypes, and, yes, consent. She says that people sometimes freak out when they find out she talks to first-graders about sex (Safronova, 2021). But Fonte points out that hiding information from kids does not help them be healthy. Fonte talks to young children about stereotypes about gender, what makes people different biologically, what it is to have *agency*, or a sense of control, over your body, and what it means to be emotionally and physically ready for intimacy.

Developmental scientists have found that talking to children about biology, gender identity, sexuality, and relationships does not encourage children to have sex. In fact, it seems to decrease rates of sexual activity and may even reduce rates of bullying and discrimination (Hilliard & Liben, 2020; Robinson et al., 2017). This kind of education can also help children who are victims of sexual abuse find a safe place to heal (Tutty et al., 2020). Fonte comes prepared with two graduate degrees (in education and public health) and a career that started with teaching math.

What has changed the most in Fonte's work during the past several years? The internet. Many children in the United States have already learned about gender stereotypes and sex from images they have seen online or on their phones. More than 9 in 10 children have seen pornography online by the time they enter adolescence (Davis et al., 2019; Rothman et al., 2017).

Since access to images online is not going to disappear, Fonte takes another approach. It starts with talking about gender, agency, and sexuality to children who may be years away from puberty. She believes in educating children about media literacy—including what is real, what is fake, and how images stereotype and shock, along with what real relationships look like. She hopes that sitting down with kids, listening to what they have experienced and what they think, will make them more

Surfer, Tennis Player, and Health Educator Justine Ang Fonte talks to children and adults about how to be healthy: not just physically, but also emotionally and socially. In middle childhood, children are ready to think about how to be empathetic and kind to each other in romantic relationships and how to talk about what they want.

resilient to the power of the images and stereotypes they will inevitably encounter, either online or off. 🔍

Ethnic and Racial Identity

Many children feel awkward talking about gender identity, but discussing ethnicity, race, or religious differences is sometimes even tougher (Rogers & Meltzoff, 2017; Verkuyten, 2016). If researchers ask children to label pictures of other children, they are comfortable dividing them by gender, but children from many backgrounds have difficulty talking about the ethnic or racial differences between them (Pauker et al., 2015).

Researchers suspect this is because for many families, particularly those in privileged groups, talking about differences in cultural background, appearance, or ethnicity is considered impolite or unnecessary (Abaied & Perry, 2021; Pahlke et al., 2012; Zucker & Patterson, 2018). This "colorblindness" keeps children from understanding the impact of discrimination, privilege, and stereotypes (Yogeeswaran et al., 2018). Colorblindness does not make children more comfortable with peers who are from a different background (Scott et al., 2020). It also does not help children who are the target of negative stereotypes or discrimination counter bias and build healthy ethnic and racial identities (Umaña-Taylor & Hill, 2020).

Even if children are discouraged from talking about ethnic differences, they still pick up on stereotypes. By elementary school, children have already been exposed to stigmatizing stereotypes about ethnicity and race, among many others. (See **Figure 12.4**.) Children who grow up in communities with histories of ethnic, religious, or racial discrimination are aware of stereotypes and bias earlier than those in other communities (Verkuyten, 2016). For instance, when researchers compared children who grew up in integrated, multiethnic Hawaii with those who lived in more segregated Massachusetts, they found that the children in Hawaii generally held fewer negative stereotypes about children who were not like them than did those who grew up in Massachusetts (Pauker et al., 2016).

Like Amara, many U.S. children growing up in the wake of the Black Lives Matter movement understand that race and racism are an unavoidable "thing." Some scientists suggest that awareness of structural discrimination has become more explicit among children of all backgrounds (Rogers et al., 2021). This awareness may help to build pride and buffer some of discrimination's effects. Negative stereotypes can be powerful; they can make children feel excluded and anxious. Children who report being the victims of discrimination and stigma often have lower grades and higher rates of mental health difficulties such as depression (Cave et al., 2020; Gillen-O'Neel et al., 2021; Shepherd et al., 2017).

Children from Latino, Black, Native American, and Asian American backgrounds in the United States experience discrimination in school and in the community (Delgado et al., 2019; Nagata et al., 2021; Umaña-Taylor, 2016). When researchers interview adults, including those who work closely with children, such as pediatricians and teachers, they find that many harbor negative stereotypes about children of color, particularly about Black and Latino children (Johnson et al., 2017; Priest et al., 2018; Thiem et al., 2019).

What can boost children's resilience in the face of such stressors? Social connections, family ties, and pride in their identity can protect children from some of the corrosive effects of discrimination on their achievement and mental health (Barton & Brody, 2018; Marcelo & Yates, 2019; Umaña-Taylor & Hill, 2020). Remember from Chapter 9 that children who have a strong sense of their ethnic, religious, or racial identity are more likely to feel good about themselves (Huguley et al., 2019). Parents who encourage this are

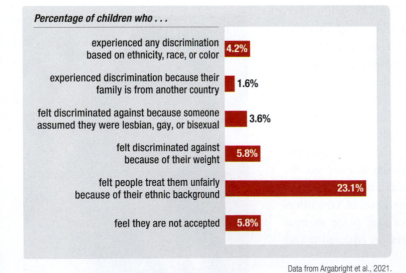

Percentage of children who . . .

experienced any discrimination based on ethnicity, race, or color	4.2%
experienced discrimination because their family is from another country	1.6%
felt discriminated against because someone assumed they were lesbian, gay, or bisexual	3.6%
felt discriminated against because of their weight	5.8%
felt people treat them unfairly because of their ethnic background	23.1%
feel they are not accepted	5.8%

Data from Argabright et al., 2021.

FIGURE 12.4 How Many Children Feel the Effects of Discrimination? Elementary schoolchildren are not too young to experience discrimination. When researchers ask children whether they have ever experienced unfair treatment, name calling, or bullying based on their ethnicity or racial identity, children across the country report that this is part of their everyday lives. Discrimination can hurt children's sense of belonging and damage their self-esteem.

often trying to prepare children to experience and cope with discrimination. Families and communities can also reduce stigma and bias by encouraging friendships between children from diverse backgrounds and by openly talking about ethnicity, rather than pretending discrimination and bias do not exist (Gillen-O'Neel et al., 2021).

APPLY IT! 12.3 Amara's activism has helped her make friends and feel capable in a world filled with stereotypes and stigma. How would you explain the value of community pride to families who may not want their children involved in potentially divisive political conversations?

12.4 Amara is outspoken and energetic—characteristics her family and her community value. What are other personality traits that communities may admire?

Family During Middle Childhood

Children are more capable and self-reliant in middle childhood than they were in preschool, but they still need their families. Warm family relationships, between parents and children, between siblings, and across generations, protect children from adversity, help boost their achievement in school, and promote mental health (Collins & Madsen, 2019). However, during middle childhood, families are often changing as parents separate, divorce, or begin new relationships (Raley & Sweeney, 2020). (See **Figure 12.5**.) As you will see, this common experience can amplify children's stress.

Relationships

Children in many parts of the world spend about half as much time with their families as they did in preschool, but parents provide the same amount of emotional support and help as before; it is just compressed into less time (Collins & Madsen, 2019). Further, the characteristics of this support change in middle childhood: Parents provide more homework help and fewer hugs. This does not mean that parents become impersonal when their children start elementary school. When they are responsive and attentive, they teach their children to cope with the effects of stress outside the

Learning Objective

12.3 Describe the importance of family relationships in middle childhood.

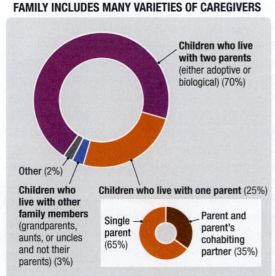

FAMILY INCLUDES MANY VARIETIES OF CAREGIVERS

Children who live with two parents (either adoptive or biological) (70%)

Children who live with one parent (25%)

Other (2%)

Children who live with other family members (grandparents, aunts, or uncles and not their parents) (3%)

Single parent (65%)

Parent and parent's cohabiting partner (35%)

Data from U.S. Census, 2021; Livingston, 2018.

CHILDREN'S HOUSEHOLDS

1 in 7 children live with a parent(s) and a grandparent or other extended family

1 in 5 children live with a parent(s) and someone who is not a relative, like a parent's roommate or partner

Data from Pilkauskas & Cross, 2018.

CHANGES IN FAMILIES

5 average number of changes in children's families

1.2 parent relationships (separation, new partner)

1.7 sibling relationships (new sibling, sibling moves out)

0.7 grandparent relationships (grandparent moves in/out)

1.3 other extended family relationships (aunt, uncle, or cousin moves in/out)

0.9 friend/partner relationships (parents' partner, friend, or roommate moves in/out)

Average number of family changes

Data from Raley et al., 2019.

FIGURE 12.5 Family Structures and Transitions During Middle Childhood Children live in many types of family structures. Researchers studying U.S. families have found that change is common, with at least five changes in family structure during childhood.

home (E. Chen et al., 2017). During middle childhood, parents are still critically important in shaping children's success in school and giving them a strong foundation for their future (Rothenberg et al., 2021).

Patterns of Caregiving

Amara and her mother, Crystal, have a close relationship: Some of Amara's favorite times are when she and Crystal get a treat at Starbucks or play a board game together. Amara says her mother is her biggest role model, someone who has taught her to look out for other people. Despite their closeness, Amara does not take her mother's advice about everything, like what to wear to school or how much time to spend online. During middle childhood, relationships between parents and children inevitably change as children become more independent.

Healthy Relating As discussed, at this age, caregivers spend less time with their children and hug them less often. Nevertheless, researchers find that attachment, security, and authoritative parenting remain as critical to caregiving as they were in earlier stages of development.

In middle childhood, families are an emotional resource for children as they navigate peers and school. In securely attached families, children feel supported by their caregivers, and families provide a secure base for children to return to. Securely attached caregivers may be around less than they were when children were younger, but they need to be available when their children face stress, such as not getting invited to a birthday party, being cut from the soccer team, or failing a math test. Securely attached children understand that their families are not always nearby but that their caregivers will prioritize supporting them in times of need (Bosmans & Kerns, 2015). For most families, attachment patterns set in infancy and early childhood continue in middle childhood (Jewell et al., 2019; Waters et al., 2019). Not all children have secure attachments: Children with insecure patterns of attachment may feel rejected by their families or worry about whether their parents will be there for them (Bosmans & Kerns, 2015).

One way that families maintain control of their children's behavior is through **monitoring**, or keeping track of what children are doing (Dishion & McMahon, 1998). Monitoring is a form of caregiving that is focused on children's widening exploration of the world outside of home. Families are monitoring their children when they ask how the math test went, if there were tryouts for the soccer team, or who they are friends with on *Roblox* or another online game.

Monitoring happens in real life and online. For instance, families that set limits on what children watch and play online tend to have healthier children who get more sleep and get along better with others (Collier et al., 2016; Gentile et al., 2014). However, many parents report having daily negotiations with their children about media use (Mollborn et al., 2022). Monitoring helps keep children safe; families know where their children are and what they are doing, and it also helps cement relationships.

Monitoring is a two-way interaction, because it requires that children be open and disclosing to their parents about what they are doing (Kerr et al., 2008). In strong relationships, adults and children share information so that families can figure out what happened at school, and children feel that their families care to hear the answer.

Setting boundaries and tracking children's activities can go too far. Researchers have found that parents who are too controlling of their children's behavior can negatively impact their mental health (Barber et al., 2005). Parents who are overly intrusive, or who try to control their children's feelings with guilt or shame, may put their children at risk for anxiety and depression (Chen-Bouck et al., 2019; Marusak et al., 2018; Pomerantz et al., 2014).

Relationships at Risk Children are better able to regulate themselves during middle childhood, but caregiving can still be difficult at times (Collins & Madsen, 2019).

Share It!

Love can fight colds: Researchers found that children who reported close bonds with their family had stronger immune systems and were better able to fight off the common cold, even if they had grown up with some disadvantages.

(Cohen et al., 2020)

Celebrating Friendship Peers and friends become increasingly important in middle childhood. These girls are enjoying time together and competing in a dance competition in the Gathering of Nations Powwow in Albuquerque, New Mexico.

monitoring When caregivers keep track of what their children are doing.

Misbehavior may be harder to manage once children are too big to be physically removed from a challenging situation. Caregivers can develop harsh, rejecting, or disengaged relationship patterns that may damage children's mental and physical health. These cycles are particularly common for families under stress (Elder, 1998; Gard et al., 2020; Schenck-Fontaine et al., 2020; Suh & Luthar, 2020; Vreeland et al., 2019).

Harsh caregiving occurs when adults are consistently negative, angry, or disappointed in their children. This pattern may include screaming or using physical punishment. The adults' behavior often derives more from their inability to manage their own feelings than from their desire to harm the child (Hajal & Paley, 2020; Schofield et al., 2017). Harsh parenting is detrimental to physical and emotional development (Bauer et al., 2021).

Rejecting caregiving happens when adults demean their children or communicate that they disapprove of or dislike them (Rowe et al., 2015). Children who do not adhere to typical gender stereotypes or have an intellectual or physical disability are at particular risk for parental rejection (Grossman et al., 2021; Mills-Koonce et al., 2018). If children grow up feeling that their families do not like or accept them, they risk depression, acting out, and profound social and academic difficulties (Putnick et al., 2015).

Disengaged parenting occurs when caregivers emotionally separate from their children, ignoring their requests for attention or responding in a perfunctory or hollow way. Families may disengage as a result of extreme stress, their own emotional problems, or a cycle of difficult interactions with their child (Lunkenheimer et al., 2016; Vreeland et al., 2019). Children whose caregivers have disengaged are more likely to act out and exhibit aggressive and oppositional behavior with friends and at school (Roskam, 2019).

Caregivers may disengage and reject their children, or they may escalate their discipline into progressively harsher punishments because they have fallen into what researchers call a *coercive cycle* (Patterson, 1982, 2016). A coercive cycle happens when children and parents behave in a harsh or unpleasant way but get what they want because the other person does not want to experience the unpleasantness anymore. For instance, an adult may ask a child to go to bed, and their child may react with a screaming fit. If the parent gives up, desperate to stop the yelling, and allows their child to stay up later, a coercive cycle may have begun.

Parents can also initiate the cycle. For instance, a child may seek attention, perhaps by asking for help with homework, and their parent reacts by saying they are too busy and telling them to "go away." If the child gives up because the rejection was too painful, the child may stop trying to receive help and a coercive cycle continues (Patterson, 1982, 2016). Families stuck in coercive cycles experience higher levels of violence than other families, and their children are at risk for developing externalizing disorders like CD or ODD and for engaging in criminal activity and substance abuse in adulthood (Chang & Shaw, 2016).

Unsupportive parenting has damaging effects on children's bodies and brains. Children with unsupportive families have higher rates of depression and externalizing disorders and also show signs of physical damage, such as high blood pressure and early signs of cardiovascular disease caused by the long-term effects of exposure to stress hormones (Brody et al., 2016). Family stress, like other forms of chronic adversity, including exposure to discrimination, creates epigenetic changes in children's DNA, causing what is called "weathering," or premature aging (Schofield et al., 2017).

Interventions to help boost supportive caregiving during middle childhood focus on boosting adults' mental health and teaching positive relationship skills (see **Table 12.2**). Programs such as the Family Check-Up offer skills training and one-on-one assessment to assist families (Berkel et al., 2021; Shelleby et al., 2018). The Family Check-Up focuses on families' strengths and helps them set their own goals, with positive impacts on family interactions and children's behavior. In the Strong African American Families Project (SAAF), a successful program that began in the rural Southeastern United States, families learn about being emotionally supportive,

Share It!

Some things get better: Children are more protected than they were in the past: Scientists report that children today are less likely to witness violence at home and to be subject to physical abuse than they were 20 years ago.

(Finkelhor, 2020)

Share It!

Normalize hard work: As kids get older, they are more likely to think that having to work hard means there is something wrong with them. Praise for effort is important with older children, who tend to get more criticism than kudos for their schoolwork.

(Gunderson et al., 2018)

Weathering Change with the Help of Family More than a million children around the world have lost a caregiver to the COVID-19 pandemic. Outside of Kathmandu, Nepal, Raj, just 21, is now raising his younger sister after their parents died during the pandemic.

TABLE 12.2 Protective Parenting in Middle Childhood

Building resilience starts with getting along. Strong family relationships help children bounce back after adversity. Feeling understood and establishing secure attachments can help children weather everyday stresses and traumas. Acknowledging, naming, and problem-solving big feelings encourages children to calm down and be kinder in the heat of the moment.
Encourage strong friendships. Relationships with adults and children outside the home become important during middle childhood and can be a source of strength and, sometimes, stress. Social exclusion, discrimination, and rejection are part of life for many children: Relationships with teachers, extended family, and other children help buffer their effects.
Scaffold emotion regulation. Remember that children are more capable of managing their ups and downs during middle childhood, but that does not mean that they can always do it themselves. Everyone sometimes needs a shoulder to cry on or someone to celebrate the big win with. Children develop individual personality strengths and habits of coping.
Appreciate the new opportunities. Caregiving during middle childhood is not as time intensive as in earlier years, but it now requires families to manage education, play dates, and after-school activities. Understanding academic expectations and helping children find their way in more complex social groups has long-term benefits.
Get support. Parents and children can both benefit from extra help when there is too much stress or an emotional disorder.
Work to improve the context. Systems that are outside the family play an important role in how children develop, but caregivers sometimes need support to improve schools, neighborhoods, or the environment.
Build pride and a sense of belonging. Connections to something outside of the family and to the greater community, whether that is a faith group, a cultural organization, or a shared commitment to a hobby, can help boost pride.

Information from National Academies of Sciences, Engineering, and Medicine, 2016.

keeping a close eye on their children and the importance of having a sense of family and ethnic pride (Brody et al., 2004, 2019).

Families and Achievement

Many families have big dreams for their children. Parents' beliefs about their children's abilities can be a powerful predictor of children's success. If families do not believe their children are competent, even when teachers or the children themselves believe otherwise, the children are more likely to struggle (Putnick et al., 2020). However, just believing is not enough. When parents communicate to their children that achievement is a process and support their efforts, rather than telling them that success is based on an inborn ability, children have more academic success (Haimovitz & Dweck, 2016).

Parents' expectations also influence their children's success. Families who believe their children will score well in reading, or who expect their children to go to college, are likely to transmit those hopes to their children (Pinquart & Ebeling, 2020). However, parents who have overly high aspirations, such as expecting a child who has difficulties with math to become an engineer, or a shy child to become class president, may actually undermine their child's success (Murayama et al., 2016).

Parents' beliefs about their children's potential may not be as powerful as what supports are available to enrich their children's learning. For example, there is an achievement gap between children of highly educated parents with high income and children whose parents lack these privileges (Egalite, 2016; see Chapter 8). This is due to variation in school quality (Darling-Hammond et al., 2017). Another factor is unequal access to often expensive enrichment activities and after-school programs that boost children's learning—an investment that often pays off with better grades (Hastings & Schneider, 2021; Knifsend et al., 2018). Well-educated and well-off families also have more time to spend with their children to help them with homework or drive them to afterschool activities (Doepke & Zilibotti, 2019).

Family Transitions and Stress

Families change over time. In the United States, by age 12, most children experience a parent leaving the home, a formal separation, divorce, or a parental deployment, incarceration, or even death (Cavanagh & Fomby, 2019; Raley & Sweeney, 2020). Family transitions are common around the world: Scholars have found that most children, including in India, Peru, and Vietnam, experience family structure changes as they grow up (Cakouros & Reynolds, 2022). Transition is common, but how children respond depends on how the changes fit into the bigger picture of their lives. Children and families can manage some change and adversity, but too much may lead to a cascade of difficulties.

Change Happens Family transitions are actually less common in the United States today than they were in the early 2000s (Fomby & Johnson, 2022). However, in most communities, they are still a regular part of children's lives. Lower-income families, who are already managing the stress of poverty, are likely to experience more family transitions, and lower-income mothers are more likely to be parenting on their own (Cavanagh & Fomby, 2019). Similarly, lower-income children more commonly live in blended or complex families with half-siblings or stepsiblings (Fomby & Osborne, 2017).

What are the effects of family instability? Family transitions that involve adjusting to a new apartment or missing a loved parent or a close sibling can be hard for children, particularly in the short term. Their grades may suffer, or they may feel a sense of loss or sadness (Bastaits & Mortelmans, 2016). Adults who are coping with relationship conflict or transition may parent with less patience and more harshness than usual (Amato, 2010; van Dijk et al., 2020). In the long term, however, most children adjust to their new circumstances (Härkönen et al., 2017; Lansford, 2009). For some children, like those from families stressed by substance use, violence, or constant conflict, transitions can even bring relief (Amato, 2010; Demo & Fine, 2010).

Culture influences what happens after parents break up. In countries with strong traditions of gender equity, such as Sweden and Holland, parents typically share custody equally (Bergström et al., 2018). However, despite experts' recommendations that children share time with both parents, particularly in cases where conflict is low, joint custody is less common in the United States (Mahrer et al., 2018; Steinbach, 2019). Parents who have separated are not necessarily less invested in their children's lives: Some researchers have found that fathers who do not live with their children full time actually spend more hands-on time with their children than other dads (Jones & Mosher, 2013). Maintaining contact with a variety of caregivers provides children with an opportunity to experience a wide variety of relationships (Cabrera et al., 2018).

What helps children thrive during and after a family transition? Remember that the theory of resilience reminds us that people are our important asset. Positive, warm relationships with any caregivers, stepparents, extended family, or any combination help children recover from stress and avoid emotional hurt (Modecki et al., 2015; Nielsen, 2017). Helping families adjust often involves coaching adults to develop better strategies for co-parenting, addressing emotional challenges like depression, and training everyone to be positive and warm despite the increased challenges (Becher et al., 2019; Lamela et al., 2016; Weaver & Schofield, 2015).

Share It!

Stress matters more than structure. Children thrive in all sorts of families. Researchers studying children raised in single-mother and two-parent families found that family strain, not family structure, was linked to children's risk for developing emotional difficulties.

(Golombok et al., 2021)

Josh Edelson/AFP/Getty Images

Landscape of Loss There may be no silver lining when you lose your home to a fire, as these children did in Redding, California. But children can recover from stress: Strong relationships can help children bounce back. For many, however, the effects of cumulative stresses may add up, making it harder to heal.

In middle childhood, resilience can be fostered through strong relationships at home, supportive friends, and relationships with adults at school and in the community. The environment can make things difficult for some children: Difficulties with health, finances, and the environment, along with poorly funded schools and stressed families, make growing up harder.

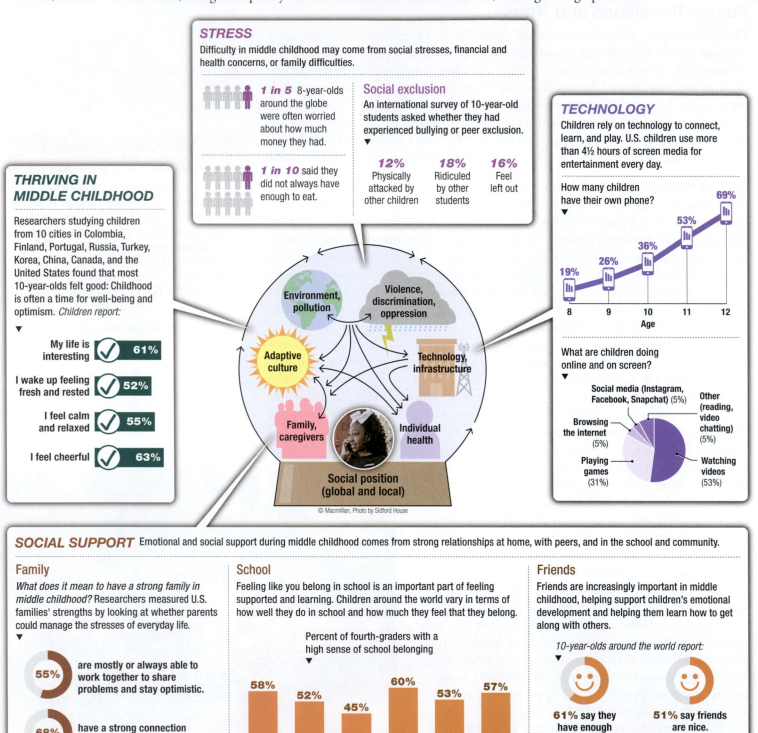

STRESS

Difficulty in middle childhood may come from social stresses, financial and health concerns, or family difficulties.

1 in 5 8-year-olds around the globe were often worried about how much money they had.

1 in 10 said they did not always have enough to eat.

Social exclusion

An international survey of 10-year-old students asked whether they had experienced bullying or peer exclusion.

12% Physically attacked by other children

18% Ridiculed by other students

16% Feel left out

THRIVING IN MIDDLE CHILDHOOD

Researchers studying children from 10 cities in Colombia, Finland, Portugal, Russia, Turkey, Korea, China, Canada, and the United States found that most 10-year-olds felt good: Childhood is often a time for well-being and optimism. *Children report:*

My life is interesting — **61%**

I wake up feeling fresh and rested — **52%**

I feel calm and relaxed — **55%**

I feel cheerful — **63%**

TECHNOLOGY

Children rely on technology to connect, learn, and play. U.S. children use more than 4½ hours of screen media for entertainment every day.

How many children have their own phone?

Age	8	9	10	11	12
	19%	26%	36%	53%	69%

What are children doing online and on screen?

- Social media (Instagram, Facebook, Snapchat) (5%)
- Other (reading, video chatting) (5%)
- Browsing the internet (5%)
- Playing games (31%)
- Watching videos (53%)

Environment, pollution

Violence, discrimination, oppression

Adaptive culture

Technology, infrastructure

Family, caregivers

Individual health

Social position (global and local)

© Macmillan, Photo by Sidford House

SOCIAL SUPPORT
Emotional and social support during middle childhood comes from strong relationships at home, with peers, and in the school and community.

Family

What does it mean to have a strong family in middle childhood? Researchers measured U.S. families' strengths by looking at whether parents could manage the stresses of everyday life.

55% are mostly or always able to work together to share problems and stay optimistic.

68% have a strong connection with their children.

66% cope with parenting very well.

School

Feeling like you belong in school is an important part of feeling supported and learning. Children around the world vary in terms of how well they do in school and how much they feel that they belong.

Percent of fourth-graders with a high sense of school belonging

Global average	United States	Singapore	Finland	Canada	Chile
58%	52%	45%	60%	53%	57%

Friends

Friends are increasingly important in middle childhood, helping support children's emotional development and helping them learn how to get along with others.

10-year-olds around the world report:

61% say they have enough friends.

51% say friends are nice.

61% say friends are supportive.

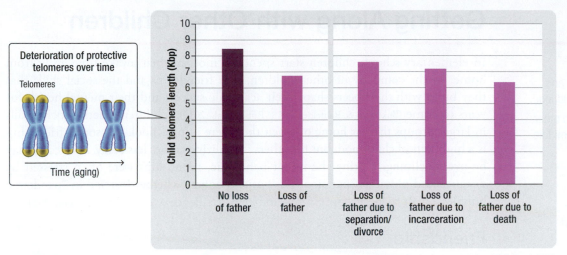

Deterioration of protective telomeres over time

Telomeres

Time (aging)

FIGURE 12.6 The Biological Impact of Stress Researchers measured changes in children's telomeres, the protective end-caps at the end of their chromosomes, over time. Telomeres usually wear away as we age, but the pace of the change is often related to life experiences. Researchers found that the telomeres tended to be shorter (as measured in base pairs) in children who had experienced separation from one of their parents, including if they had lost their father to death, relationship transitions, or incarceration.

Cumulative Stress For some children, however, a transition like a divorce, remarriage, or separation may be just one of many stresses that they face (see **Infographic 12.1**). The impact of the recent COVID-19 pandemic was another added stressor, requiring children to adjust to remote school, grieve lost family members, and worry about family finances. These stressors were often experienced disproportionately by low-income children and families of color (Fraiman et al., 2021; Merrick et al., 2018). Some family structures are more likely to be subject to discrimination and prejudice than others, including single-mother led and same-sex families (Cross et al., 2022; Patterson, 2019). For instance, nearly one in two Americans tells pollsters that they believe single mothers are "bad for society" (Hurst, 2022).

Remember that stress has a cumulative effect on children. For children already at risk, such as those living in poverty or who have emotional problems, the impact of family transition or other stressors is much greater (Härkönen et al., 2017). Repeated breakups and changes in living situations increase the likelihood that children will develop emotional difficulties that they express by acting out (Fomby & Osborne, 2017). Similarly, children from families with long histories of conflict prior to the transition tend to have higher rates of emotional disorders and report less satisfaction later in their lives (Amato & Anthony, 2014; Murphy et al., 2017; Wallerstein, 1987). The long-term consequences of stress and adversity before and after the transition, rather than the transition itself, is the likely cause of these challenges (Härkönen et al., 2017; Seijo et al., 2016).

The cumulative effect of stress means that family transitions, like other types of chronic stress, can take a toll on children's bodies and minds. For instance, scientists analyzed the chromosomes of children who had lost a parent to incarceration, separation, or death and found that this loss was reflected in their genes, particularly if families experienced additional adversity through loss of income. Children showed signs of epigenetic changes to their chromosomes. Their *telomeres*, or the endcaps on chromosomes that protect them, were dramatically shortened, as if the children had aged dramatically (see **Figure 12.6**) (Mitchell et al., 2017).

Stress may be damaging, but it does not have to be permanent. Just as the body can show signs of damage from chronic stress, it can also show signs of recovery (Raffington et al., 2021). Short telomeres can lengthen, and children can build resilience (Cowell et al., 2021).

APPLY IT! **12.5** Amara and her mother have abundant mutual admiration. What are three other signs of positive parenting in middle childhood?
12.6 What are ways that families can build resilience in the face of common stressors like financial strain or family transition?

CONNECTIONS

Remember from Chapter 3 that chromosomes are in the nucleus of every cell and direct cell replication throughout the lifespan. As telomeres degrade, errors in replication become more common, creating more risk for disease.

Extra Hands to Love Children thrive in all kinds of families, but having more than one parent to love you, like Sophia and Ava, might mean you get extra attention and time for tickles.

Getting Along with Other Children

Learning Objectives

12.4 Describe the role of friendships and peer relationships in middle childhood.

12.5 Define the role of popularity and other social status categories during middle childhood.

 **Learn It Together**

Themes of Middle Childhood in Television

Plan What lessons do elementary-age children obtain from television shows that target their age group? How do these messages correspond with what you have learned about social and emotional development? In this activity, you will watch a television show geared toward children aged 7–11 and give it a "grade" for how well it addresses a developmental concept for this age group.

Prepare Before class, identify a single episode of a show designed for the target age group (hint: look for shows that have a "family friendly" rating or description). Agree with your group members to all watch the same episode before class and take notes on the main storyline, messages, images, and themes that you notice. Some common themes may have to do with moral development (getting into trouble, doing the "right thing"), gender stereotypes (fitting in, not fitting in), social acceptance (bullying, popularity, being excluded from the group), or family themes (family conflicts, stresses).

Engage In class, meet with your group to share your insights. What connections can you make to topics from the chapter? Did you see examples of children displaying prosocial behavior or being challenged by social exclusion? Make note of specific developmental topics and terminology that relate to this episode.

Reflect As a team, write a summary of your observations in the form of an "evaluation" from the perspective of a developmental expert. Let the media executives know what important topics they portrayed or what they might have missed. Did the show do a good job of depicting important concepts for children of this age?

In elementary school, children start spending most of their awake time away from home, in the company of other children. The friendships and the social skills that they build with their peers shape their academic success and their mental health for years to come (Bukowski & Raufelder, 2018; Rubin et al., 2015). Children practice social skills in larger groups than at home or when they were in preschool. For some, friendship is a highlight of childhood, but for others, socializing comes less easily, and recess may be overwhelming. During the recent pandemic, friendships were often stressed by distance and physical separation, but positive bonds, whether fostered in "pandemic bubbles" or in friend groups, were a source of resilience (Cameron & Tenenbaum, 2021).

Friendship

What makes someone a friend? By elementary school, children have the cognitive skills and emotion regulation to develop sophisticated ideas about maintaining friendships (Parker & Asher, 1993). Children in middle childhood can talk about their feelings, take other people's perspectives, and learn how to manage their emotions during conflicts. One young girl described her friend to researchers this way: "A best friend is somebody I can depend on. When I need you I can call you, and you come out here to see what's wrong. . . . You'll have my back." This girl describes her "true friend" as someone she really understands: "We got a real close connection. . . . I know what she's like. . . . It's so deep" (Chan Tack & Small, 2017, p. 240).

Friendships can be life-changing for children; they are a source of comfort in times of difficulty and teach habits of relating that will last into adulthood. Biologically, children's positive friendships protect their bodies by reducing stress hormone levels (Doom et al., 2017). Friendships can even reduce some of the risks from difficult early family relationships or personality traits (Buhs et al., 2018; Ladd, 1999). Perhaps most importantly, friends are fun: They do things with you, keep you company, and play with you at recess (Maunder & Monks, 2019).

Most studies find that between 60 and 80 percent of children have a friend (Rubin et al., 2015). Researchers test this not just by asking children if they have a friend, but by making sure that when children say someone is a friend that the feeling is truly reciprocal (it is not always). Remember from Chapter 9 that, like adults, children tend to form friendships with people they perceive to be like them in fairly superficial ways. Children tend to follow the principle of *homophily*, or looking for friends who seem "like me." This means that most of the time, children end up with friends who mirror their age, gender identity, first language, ethnicity, behavior in school, and even athletic ability or academic achievement (Laninga-Wijnen et al., 2018; Mulvey et al., 2018).

Once children hit it off, the characteristics of a good relationship in elementary school are much the same as any good relationship across the lifespan. Friends care about each other and can manage the inevitable conflicts. Friends are there for help and even protection. They share secrets. And they have good times (Parker & Asher, 1993). Children's friendships are not fleeting: More than half of children's friendships last the entire school year (Rubin et al., 2015).

In their close relationships, children practice skills that they will use with friends and romantic partners over their lifetime. Those who start with secure, positive relationships with their parents and siblings are likely to establish warm friendships in elementary school (Furman & Rose, 2015). Children who do not learn at home how to be kind to other people or how to comfort someone who is upset will struggle with these skills in their friendships (Glick & Rose, 2011; S. E. Miller et al., 2020). Friendship gives these children a chance to develop new skills. Whether they are sharing a game of *Minecraft* or playing on the playground, friendships enable children to practice relationship skills such as managing conflict and asserting oneself without being mean (Rubin et al., 2015).

Children may struggle to make and keep friendships if they are very shy (Rubin et al., 2018). Shy or withdrawn children have difficulty speaking up in class or meeting someone new (Fredstrom et al., 2012). Their lack of experience with other children may also lead to trouble understanding others' points of view, such as what they need and want in a friendship (Penela et al., 2015). They may have a hard time understanding the social rules of friendships and opening up with their friends (Rubin et al., 2018). If they do not have an understanding friend, their social troubles may escalate, leading to more withdrawal, anxiety, and even depression (Penela et al., 2015).

Aggressive children, on the other hand, also have challenges navigating close relationships. They may be overreactive and misinterpret a harmless comment as threatening. If they are used to getting their way through physical or emotional aggression, many of their relationships may not be reciprocal and trusting (Rubin et al., 2015).

CAN YOU BELIEVE IT?
Can Time Online Be Play?

Play is at the core of children's relationships. Children squeeze in time for fun, whether it is in the lunch line, on the basketball court, or on the bus (Howard et al., 2017). In many communities around the world, fun during middle childhood now often involves clicking and looking at screens. The vast majority of U.S. and European children ages 6 to 12 play online or video games (Adachi & Willoughby, 2017; Smahel et al., 2020). For instance, more than half of children in the United States report having played *Roblox*, an interactive multiplayer game that, in one of its most popular versions, involves adopting virtual pets (Puleo, 2020; Richtel, 2021). One in five U.S. children spends time on social media such as Snapchat or Instagram each day, connecting with friends and following celebrities (Rideout et al., 2022).

Remember from Chapter 10 that media use in childhood is often controversial. The occasional headlines warn that screen time is "digital heroin" that will "turn kids into psychotic junkies." However, many developmental scientists argue that playing games online is just play, and that, in moderation, it can help children build social skills and make friends (Granic et al., 2014; Kardaras, 2016; Richtel, 2021; Twenge & Campbell, 2018). Many parents agree, suggesting that playing online games will help children develop digital skills that will enable them to be successful as adults (Mollborn et al., 2022).

Most of the games children play online are not solitary: The most popular games, including *Roblox* and *Minecraft*, require cooperation and social interaction (Adachi & Willoughby, 2017). Even in war games, children collaborate on how to achieve victory. Researchers have found that in communities where most children play online games, the children who do not play may be socially isolated. When researchers compared a group of children in Norway who played online games with a group who did not, they found that playing video games did not hurt social skills such as the ability to share, listen to each other, and pick up on nonverbal cues (Hygen et al., 2020).

There is less consensus among developmental scientists about the amount of time children spend on social media. While children under 13 are often prohibited from officially signing up for social media accounts, their use of platforms such as Snapchat or Instagram to connect with friends exploded during the early months of the COVID-19 pandemic. Now, nearly half of children report that they have social media accounts, although fewer check them regularly (Dillon, 2022; Rideout et al., 2022). Some experts, citing internal research from social media providers, warn that too much time online is linked to body dissatisfaction, particularly for girls (Wells et al., 2021). However, some point out that children who use social media when they are still

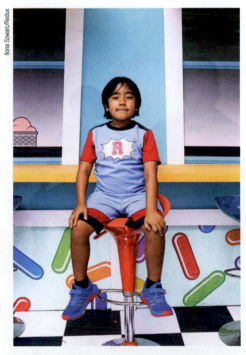

Popularity Measured in Millions Ryan Kaji is still in elementary school but is one of the most popular YouTube stars in any age group. Together with his family, including his younger sisters, he posts nearly every day, and his videos have been seen by billions all over the world.

in elementary school tend to use it for positive purposes, including to learn about politics and community activism (Charmaraman et al., 2022).

While scientists have had years to research social media use in adolescents, there has not been time to establish a clear understanding of all the impacts of social media on younger children. Scientists do agree that there are benefits of online interaction for young children. Online friendships can be particularly important sources of support when children have limited opportunities for in-person interaction, as occurred during the pandemic (Maheux et al., 2021). Online friends may also be helpful to children who have difficulties making friends in person, perhaps because they face rejection in their real-life communities (Lenhart et al., 2015; Massing-Schaffer et al., 2022). Nonetheless, children who spend too much time online may be missing out on the support they need to keep from feeling isolated in real life (Hygen et al., 2020; Lobel et al., 2017). 🖐️

Spending Time in Groups

Pandemic restrictions notwithstanding, when children are at school, on the playground, or practicing sports, they spend most of their time in big groups. As they grow older, much of this time is away from the close supervision of adults who increasingly trust children to follow the rules and stay safe. This gives children the opportunity to develop their independence, but it also increases the likelihood that children will hurt each other or learn dangerous behaviors from other children.

Measuring Popularity In middle childhood, children use their stronger cognitive skills to compare and rank their popularity with their peers. In fact, if researchers ask children to rate whether they like or dislike the other children in a group, they find that children's descriptions of each other fall into predictable categories (Cillessen & Bukowski, 2018).

Most children are generally well-liked or **popular**, meaning that many in their class say they "like them" or that they are their friends (Newcomb et al., 1993). Some are **rejected**, or actively disliked by most children in the class. Another category of children is **neglected**, either forgotten altogether or not rated by children in their class. **Controversial** children receive mixed ratings, strongly disliked by some and strongly liked by others. Other children are just **average**, or fall around the middle of being liked and disliked, not quite making it into the other categories (Cillessen & Bukowski, 2018).

There are two types of popular children in any group. Likeable children have good social skills; they know how to show empathy, they can regulate their emotions to manage difficult situations, and they can assert themselves from time to time (Rubin et al., 2015; van den Berg et al., 2017). Children who have strong *perceived popularity* are dominant, whether that means they are captains of the kickball team or decide who sits where at lunch. These children may not be prosocial or kind. They may be socially aggressive or even bullying, and they may use manipulation, threats, and exclusion to gain social power (Laninga-Wijnen et al., 2019; Rubin et al., 2015).

Rejected children are described by their peers as unlikeable and actively excluded from the group. In some cases, they may be extremely shy or withdrawn. Others may be aggressive or mean. Researchers find that they tend to have trouble playing group games, are too shy to speak up, or are too volatile to play with (Rubin et al., 2015). Children often justify excluding them by explaining that they are too difficult, do not follow the rules, or are not fun (Rutland & Killen, 2015). Children are also rejected because they are different from their peers in some way: They may speak a different language, have a disability, or belong to a different racial or ethnic group (Juvonen et al., 2019).

Children who are controversial or neglected do not fit neatly into any other categories. They may receive mixed ratings from their peers or be forgotten altogether. Controversial children may include the class clown or bully, who displays more aggression or is prone to emotional outbursts. Neglected children are typically quiet,

popular Children who are liked or perceived to be socially successful by many of their peers.

rejected Children who are actively disliked by most of their peers.

neglected Children who are unconsidered or forgotten altogether by their peers.

controversial Children who receive mixed ratings by their peers, strongly disliked by some and strongly liked by others.

average social acceptance Children who fall around the middle of being liked and disliked, not quite making it into the other categories.

Grins All Around Whether in Canada or in South Africa, fun with friends helps children learn how to get along with other people and learn to thrive in larger social groups.

shy children who are forgotten by their peers. They are isolated from social activity, but their peers do not have a negative view of them (Kulawiak & Wilbert, 2020; Rytioja et al., 2019; van Der Wilt et al., 2019).

Tracking the Costs of Exclusion   Being excluded in elementary school can hurt children in the short and long term. In the long term, repeated exclusion can damage children's sense of belonging and their emotional health (Schacter, 2021). Social neuroscientists scanning children's brains have found that being rejected or excluded really does hurt: Children who are excluded show signs of activity in cortical areas where the brain processes physical pain (Eisenberger et al., 2003; Lieberman & Eisenberger, 2015).

Repeated experiences of rejection affect the brain just like other repeated stressful experiences. When children are consistently left out, excluded from play, or picked last for a team, negative emotional pathways in their brains are activated and strengthened, making them more readily available for processing future experiences. These networks influence how children process their social experiences for years to come (Guyer & Jarcho, 2018; Quinlan et al., 2020).

Children do not "get used to" being excluded. When researchers observe children over time, they find that for many the pain intensifies. They become likely to assume the worst, to overreact, and have more difficulty calming themselves down (Guyer & Jarcho, 2018; Will et al., 2016). This can lead to academic difficulties, not because the excluded children are cognitively incapable, but because they feel they just do not belong. They may experience depression or anxiety, or start acting out and behaving aggressively toward other children (Will et al., 2016). As they grow older, this emotional pain may increase their likelihood to experience bullying, emotional difficulties, substance abuse, and even criminal behavior.

Bullying

Bullying happens in all cultures around the world and has been documented since the earliest human civilizations (Nguyen et al., 2020; Richardson & Hiu, 2018; Savahl et al., 2019). Remember from Chapter 9 that *bullying* is any physical and/or social aggression between a child who is perceived as socially powerful and another with less social power (Olweus, 1978). Bullying can include physical violence or involve *relational aggression*, such as spreading rumors, social exclusion, and online attacks (*cyberbullying*).

In many communities, children who seem "different" or who do not "fit in" are targeted by bullies. Researchers call this *bias-related bullying*, and depending on the community, children who are from a different ethnic group or economic background,

CONNECTIONS

Remember from Chapter 9 that peer victimization is not unique to middle childhood: Signs of social exclusion appear in preschool. Social aggression actually gets worse before it gets better (see Chapter 15) and reaches a peak in early adolescence.

Scientific American Profile

Standing Up to Bullying

have a larger body size or a disability, or do not adhere to gender stereotypes may be targeted (Palmer & Abbott, 2018). Estimating just how many children are involved is challenging because victims do not always understand that what is happening to them is worth reporting. Only half of children who are bullied tell someone (Hawley, 2015). Researchers believe that about one in three children are involved in bullying during middle childhood, either as victims or as aggressors (Camerini et al., 2020; Zych et al., 2019).

Bullying typically happens in front of other children and adults, but the victims often feel invisible (Mazzone et al., 2021). Typically, recess monitors or teachers notice only 10 percent of playground bullying incidents and fewer than 20 percent of classroom incidents (Hawley, 2015). Other children may be passive bystanders, failing to intervene or, in some circumstances, even supporting the bully. But not all children are passive. Those who are both empathetic and socially confident are able to step in to defend a victim of bullying (Kärnä et al., 2013; Mazzone et al., 2016; van der Ploeg et al., 2020).

Children who are the victims of bullying and ostracism may carry the consequences with them into adulthood. Victims often have signs of stress and accelerated aging in their epigenome (Mulder et al., 2020). Chronic exclusion is particularly harmful if it reinforces discrimination children face outside of school (Palmer & Abbott, 2018). Particularly if children lack the protection of a close friend or a nurturing family, the stress of social aggression can damage physical and mental health. Children may struggle in school and have higher rates of depression and anxiety (McDougall & Vaillancourt, 2015; Meter & Bauman, 2018). One child explained that victims take the effects of bullying "home with them at night. It lives inside them and eats away at them. It never ends. So neither should our struggle to end it" (Hymel & Swearer, 2015, p. 296).

Developmental scientists are working to end bullying. Interventions designed to combat social aggression try to turn children from passive bystanders into active defenders. Children who feel empowered to intervene can help change the school environment to make all children feel safer and more included (Herkama et al., 2017; Waasdorp et al., 2021).

APPLY IT! 12.7 Amara stood up for a friend who was targeted by other students at school for being taller than her peers. What are ways strong friendships can help children bounce back from social exclusion?

12.8 Social rankings happen outside of elementary school, including on college campuses and in the workplace. How would you use the ways scientists measure popularity in the classroom to look at social dynamics in your community?

Moral Development

Amara was bullied when she first started school. She does not like to talk about it, because she is sure that the children who made her cry didn't know what they were doing. "It wasn't anything," she says. "Kids hurt each other sometimes." Amara knows the importance of speaking up. Her friend was bullied because she is tall; Amara confronted her tormenters. Was she afraid? "No," she says. "You can't be afraid. Or even if you are, you still have to do it." That isn't the only nice thing that Amara has done lately. In fact, her mother keeps a list of the kind things Amara likes to do for people: for example, helping her grandmother by running an errand or washing the dishes. Amara wants to be a doctor when she grows up so she can continue to help those in need.

How does Amara understand the importance of helping out? When do children know how to be nice? Most adults around the world do not think children are fully responsible for their actions during middle childhood (Lancy, 2018). However, most schools, families, and even other children expect that children will be able to treat each other *prosocially*, or kindly, during middle childhood. Children are expected to respect each other, to temper their outbursts, and to follow the rules. For many—but not all—children, this comes easily over time.

Thinking About Right and Wrong

When many people, including psychologists, think about right and wrong, they think about following rules (Haidt, 2009). Some scientists, beginning with Piaget, believed that children's development of moral behavior is a consequence of their improving ability to understand these rules (Piaget, 1965). Piaget believed that one way children learn to behave morally is by playing increasingly complex rule-based games with other children. As children move from playing tag to playing kickball, they learn the consequences and the rewards of following directions. Like some other researchers, Piaget believed that children naturally learn to follow rules from their peers and do not need to be directly taught.

Psychologist Lawrence Kohlberg adapted Piaget's theories of cognitive development in his stage theory of children's moral reasoning (Kohlberg, 1978; Kohlberg & Kramer, 1969). For Kohlberg, moral decisions were not abstract, but deeply personal. Like so many others who served during World War II, Kohlberg wanted to understand why some people became killers, some sacrificed themselves, and others stood by (Snarey, 2012). To develop his stage theory, he posed moral dilemmas to children and observed how their moral reasoning became more complex as they grew older. He noted how children gradually moved from making decisions based on concrete factors, such as avoiding punishment, to thinking more abstractly about right and wrong (Kohlberg, 1981).

Kohlberg used a story called *Heinz's dilemma* to illustrate the development of moral reasoning. He asked children whether it would be okay for a sick woman's husband, named Heinz, to steal a medication that he could not afford in order to save her life. Did saving his partner's life justify the burglary? How children answered this dilemma depended on their level of cognitive development and moral reasoning. Kohlberg was interested in more than the children's answers: He wanted to know how children made sense of the moral problem. Could they understand that people might have different perspectives? Could they balance the man's desire to obey the law with the woman's desire to live? What about the perspective of the pharmacist who owned the medication? Or the police? Based on their answers to Heinz's dilemma, Kohlberg theorized there were three stages in children's moral development: *preconventional*, *conventional*, and *postconventional* moral reasoning (see **Table 12.3**).

Children in the **preconventional** stage of moral reasoning tend to use concrete and self-centered (*egocentric*) reasoning, as you might expect from children in Piaget's preoperational stage of cognitive development. Children at this stage are focused on the concrete effects of Heinz's choices. They say Heinz should not steal the medicine, because he will go to jail. Alternatively, they say that he should steal because if his wife dies, he will be sad and lonely.

In the next stage, **conventional** moral reasoning, children think more abstractly about what is right and wrong. They may talk about "rules" or "laws" that govern behavior, and they tend to have more sense of the consequences of breaking the law. Despite this, they will still show some empathy for Heinz and his family. A child in this stage might say something like, "Heinz may have been disappointed that the drug was so expensive, but we need to have laws to make everything work." They might suggest that Heinz should have investigated other possibilities rather than breaking the law.

Many people remain in the conventional stage of moral reasoning, but Kohlberg believed that a small number of people, capable of deep perspective taking and empathy, move into the **postconventional** stage of moral reasoning. People who reach this stage can think abstractly and about right and wrong as something that supersedes rules and laws. Kohlberg viewed people such as Martin Luther King Jr. as a moral

preconventional stage of moral reasoning Kohlberg's stage of moral reasoning in which children use concrete and self-centered (egocentric) reasoning.

conventional stage of moral reasoning Kohlberg's stage of moral reasoning in which children think more abstractly about what is right and wrong.

postconventional stage of moral reasoning Kohlberg's stage of moral reasoning in which people can think abstractly and about right and wrong as something that supersedes rules and laws.

TABLE 12.3 Kohlberg's Stages of Moral Reasoning

Stage	Age	Characteristics
Preconventional	Typically at about the age of Piaget's preconventional reasoning, or until about ages 8–10.	Children are motivated by not getting in trouble. They follow rules so as not to get punished by a parent, a teacher, or the police, not because of any internalized sense of right and wrong.
Conventional	Typically children reach this stage at around the same time as they gain the ability to consider multiple perspectives and reach Piaget's concrete operational thought stage, or during middle childhood. Many people spend the rest of their lives in this stage.	Children begin to think about the abstract values of being "good" or "bad" and want other people to think of them as "good." They may throw out their trash because "only bad kids litter." They begin to take on other people's perspectives when making moral decisions and to think about values like "laws" or religious commandments that control their behavior.
Postconventional	Not all adults or children reach this stage, but those who do have acquired the ability for complex abstract thought, typically only possible in adolescence and beyond.	Individuals put moral actions above their own self-interest and the laws of their community. They stand up for what they believe is right, even if that means breaking the law. In this stage, individuals have internalized a sense that a community is bound together through a social contract, a commitment that humans are committed to work together for the good of the many.

Courtesy Melissa Shang

Sometimes a Doll Is Not Just a Doll. Sometimes a doll inspires social action. Melissa Shang is a student, a writer, and an advocate for people with disabilities who has tried to convince manufacturers to create dolls that reflect the experiences of all children.

exemplar because they engaged in civil disobedience, breaking the law in pursuit of a higher, more just goal (Kohlberg, 1978).

In the many years since Kohlberg developed his theory of moral reasoning, its universality and relevance have been questioned by many critics (Goldschmidt et al., 2021; Haidt, 2009). Scholar Carol Gilligan pointed out that for many people, particularly women and girls in the United States, caring for other people is more important than following abstract rules, an orientation she called the *ethics of care*. Like others, she challenged Kohlberg's idea that being able to grapple with ideas like "justice" meant that people were more caring in real life (Brown & Gilligan, 1993; Gilligan, 1977, 1993). Many critics joined Gilligan in questioning whether Kohlberg's stages were actually as universal as Piaget's (Goldschmidt et al., 2021). Around the world, families believe that there is more to becoming a good person than being able to reason (Xu, 2019). In other cultures, many people value adherence to religious traditions or value the well-being of the group over being able to reason about what is best for one person, like Heinz's wife (Killen & Smetana, 2015).

The universality and relevance of Kohlberg's stages have also been questioned by researchers who discovered that children do not think that all moral choices are equivalent (Nucci & Turiel, 1978; Turiel, 1983; Turiel & Dahl, 2019). Even kindergarteners see that that not all rules are the same. They distinguish between *moral choices*, such as whether it is okay to hurt someone, *conventional rules*, such as not running in the hall, and *personal choices*, such as whether it is okay to dye your hair pink.

Doing Good

Children are capable of incredible acts of bravery and kindness. Melissa Shang made herself internet famous when she was just 10 years old by trying to convince the American Girl doll company to make a doll who had a visible disability. She started an online petition, pointing out that more than one in five Americans, including herself, has a disability. Melissa had more than 150,000 supporters, but the American Girl doll company was not convinced. Melissa is still working to accomplish big things: She is now writing a novel.

Scientists have found that many children, like Melissa, are good at thinking about the greater good. For instance, most adults tell scientists that they would spend lottery winnings on themselves, but children say they would spend their money on gifts and charity, particularly for their family (Kiang et al., 2016). Even if they are not spending weekends in social activism or handing out food at a food pantry, children act pro-socially when doing everyday tasks and chores, like sharing with a friend or clearing the table. Children's maturing abilities to think about the world from other people's perspectives and control their behavior, help them do more for other people. There are individual and community variations in children's prosocial behavior, but the benefits of helping are profound (Aknin et al., 2018). Helping not only helps the receiver, but also gives the helper a sense of mission and meaning in their life.

Scientists have found that children are capable of extremely complex thinking when it comes to deciding how to share, including the consideration of who is worthy of sharing with and what is fair (House & Tomasello, 2018). For instance, around the world, most preschoolers would agree that the best way to share is to be precisely equal no matter what. For them, equal is fair, and each friend should get exactly the same number of coins (Huppert et al., 2019). But as children get older, their ideas about what is fair become more complex (Almas et al., 2015). Children's sharing reflects their developing ability to think abstractly and how well they have internalized the particular social rules of their community (Almas et al., 2015).

When researchers test children around the world to see how they share and with whom, they discover some surprising results. It turns out that U.S. children are actually very good at sharing compared to children from other communities, perhaps because being a "good sharer" is something that is emphasized in schools (Cowell et al., 2017; Rao & Stewart, 1999). U.S. children also tend to develop very complicated ideas about how to share fairly at earlier ages than children from other countries, perhaps because they are aware of more inequity than other children (Cowell et al., 2017; Huppert et al., 2019). If researchers compare how children share around the world, they find that all children gradually share more with peers who are hardworking, poor, or hurt, as they get older and break away from a strict idea of equality. But children from individualistic cultures, where inequity is more common, develop ideas about who deserves generosity at earlier ages. In contrast, those from more collectivist communities, hold on for longer to the idea that everyone deserves an equal share (Huppert et al., 2019).

Whenever it happens, prosocial behavior, like sharing, gives children something more than the momentary rush of good feelings. Helping others benefits children in the long term by strengthening their relationships and connections with other people (Aknin et al., 2018; Miller & Hastings, 2019). Scientists have found that being prosocial even changes children's bodies, making them increasingly more flexible in their responses to stress and anxiety: Children who shared with others responded to stress more flexibly and were better able to manage their anxiety, a difference that remained when the researchers checked on the children again two years later (Miller, 2018). This suggests that children who can connect and respond to others in need with empathy and kindness will develop healthier reactions to anxiety and stress of their own. Helping others trains children's nervous system to manage anxiety in a healthier way (Miller, 2018; Miller et al., 2015).

As you will see in the next chapters, children's ability to help others only gets stronger as they get older. As children move into adolescence, they become even more

Sarah L. Voisin/The Washington Post via Getty Images

Creating a Memory Aaliyah, age 8, and her little sister, Emma, remember the classmates and soccer teammates she lost in the May 2022 shootings at Robb Elementary School in Uvalde, Texas. Participating in memorials, while upsetting, can help children over the long term by boosting their connections with their community.

©Macmillan, Photo by Sidford House

Scientific American Profile

Engaging with the World

industrious, and their prosocial behaviors become more visible and valued by their communities. Like Amara, they can think about how to solve problems in their community or advocate for something they believe in. Giving of themselves, which results in stronger social connections and a sense of their own competence, can continue to help children build resilience (Fuligni, 2019).

APPLY IT!   **12.9** Amara's mother has raised her to value being compassionate and helping other people in need. Her ethnotheories emphasize the values of kindness and advocacy. What ethnotheories about morality do you recognize in your own family? **12.10** Amara thinks abstractly about social issues. Where do you think she might fit in Kohlberg's stages of moral reasoning?

Wrapping It Up

LO 12.1 Explain the goals of emotion regulation during middle childhood. (p. 291)

Children are expected to control their feelings more independently during middle childhood. Some are forced by adversity to grow up more quickly than others. In middle childhood, resilience is based on secure attachments, warm caregiving, and friendships. Erikson described middle childhood as a conflict between *industry versus inferiority*, a concept supported by contemporary researchers. Children learn how to manage their feelings in ways that are specific to their communities. Strong relationships help build strong emotion regulation. Some children develop psychological disorders, such as *internalizing disorders* like depression and anxiety and *externalizing disorders* like ADHD, oppositional defiant disorder, and conduct disorder. Disorders are caused by a complex mix of genes, brain development, and stress.

LO 12.2 Describe advances in self-concept and the role of social comparison in self-esteem during middle childhood. (p. 296)

Children develop a stronger sense of who they are and how they compare to other children in middle childhood. Scientists analyze personality in middle childhood (and beyond) using the *five-factor model*. Children tend to become more agreeable and conscientious as they get older. Culture affects children's personality development. Children continue to have stereotypes about gender and to develop a sense of their racial and ethnic identity. Many children experience discrimination; a sense of solidarity and pride can help buffer its effects.

LO 12.3 Describe the importance of family relationships in middle childhood. (p. 301)

Children are much more independent than in the preschool years but still benefit from strong, supportive family relationships. Warm caregiving supports secure attachments and includes monitoring children's behavior without being too controlling. Harsh, rejecting, and disengaged parenting can be harmful to children. Some families are caught in a coercive cycle of acting out. Families' beliefs and their resources can help children's school achievement. Many families are in transition and under stress. Cumulative stress can hurt children, but families can build resilience.

LO 12.4 Describe the role of friendships and peer relationships in middle childhood. (p. 308)

Friendships help children build social skills. Elementary-age children have a better understanding of what makes a friend, and these patterns of relating will stick with children as they develop relationships later in life. Some children have difficulty finding and making friends, particularly if they are shy.

LO 12.5 Define the role of popularity and other social status categories during middle childhood. (p. 308)

Children spend much of their time in big groups. Scientists observe and categorize how children relate to each other and identify *popular*, *rejected*, *neglected*, *controversial*, and *average* children. Children in groups frequently exclude and bully others, which can lead to difficulties. Interventions are aimed at building a sense of belonging and empowering everyone in a community to intervene and stop exclusion and bullying.

LO 12.6 Describe the development of moral reasoning and moral behavior in middle childhood. (p. 312)

Children are capable of kindness and understand how to follow moral rules. Kohlberg described children's moral development as a series of increasingly complex stages modeled on Piaget's stages of cognitive development. He used a hypothetical scenario called *Heinz's dilemma* to evaluate children's moral reasoning. Kohlberg's critics have pointed out that morality is influenced by culture and that caring is often interpersonal, rather than based on abstract reasoning. Children are capable of very complex thinking about sharing and equality, which is also influenced by cultural values. Giving helps children build resilience, relationships, empathy, and a sense of competence.

KEY TERMS

industry versus inferiority (p. 292)

monitoring (p. 302)

popular (p. 310)

rejected (p. 310)

neglected (p. 310)

controversial (p. 310)

average social acceptance (p. 310)

preconventional stage of moral reasoning (p. 313)

conventional stage of moral reasoning (p. 313)

postconventional stage of moral reasoning (p. 313)

CHECK YOUR LEARNING

1. According to Erikson, successful psychological development in middle childhood involves:
   a) tackling subconscious aggressive tendencies.
   b) developing a strict sense of gender identity.
   c) learning universal human concepts.
   d) navigating the expectations of school and social relationships.

2. Elementary-age children who do not feel successful in school may experience what Erikson described as:
   a) inferiority.
   b) mistrust.
   c) shame.
   d) role confusion.

3. Which of these statements is FALSE?
   a) Helping out is correlated with positive outcomes like self-confidence and self-efficacy.
   b) Most children resent having to do chores around the house.
   c) Children's participation in household chores or helping with other family work is more common among low-income U.S. families.
   d) Engaging in helpful activities at home is a form of industriousness.

4. The improving ability during middle childhood to control strong reactions like temper tantrums and to display responses appropriate in social settings is known as:
   a) cumulative stress.
   b) emotion regulation.
   c) latency.
   d) secure attachment.

5. Boys' tendency to participate and persist more than girls in STEM activities during middle childhood is partially explained by:
   a) boys' higher achievement throughout school.
   b) stereotypes about the appropriateness of STEM for boys rather than girls.
   c) hormonal differences that make boys more interested in STEM.
   d) girls' lower grades in math and science.

6. Supportive parenting includes all of these EXCEPT:
   a) monitoring behavior when children are away from home.
   b) warm emotional interactions.
   c) coercive cycles.
   d) two-way communication.

7. Nine-year-old Dilan frequently leaves a mess in the kitchen when he makes his own after-school snack. When his father reprimands him and demands he clean it up, Dilan makes a dramatic show of his resentment and does a poor job cleaning. Despite wanting Dilan to take responsibility for his own mess, his father tends to finish the cleaning himself. This repeated pattern of family interaction is an example of:
   a) a coercive cycle.
   b) secure-base behavior.
   c) ADHD.
   d) neglectful parenting.

8. Which of these statements about friendships during middle childhood is TRUE?
   a) Children form friendships with whomever they spend the most time with, regardless of individual characteristics.
   b) Children's stereotypes disappear in middle childhood and they tend to befriend children very different from them in gender, ethnicity, and interests.
   c) Children tend to form friendships with others who share their cultural experiences and interests.
   d) Most children's friendships last only a week or so.

9. Fourth-grader Cody has a goofy sense of humor and is somewhat of a "class clown." Some of his classmates admire him, but several others find him to be a little mean. Cody is likely:
   a) popular.
   b) rejected.
   c) neglected.
   d) controversial.

10. What approaches can adults use for supporting positive ethnic and racial identity among elementary-age children?

11. What is cumulative stress, and how does it impact development?

12. What is the difference between preconventional and conventional moral reasoning?

Physical Development in Adolescence

What Is Adolescence?

13.1 Define adolescence.

Changing Body

13.2 Identify the biological changes of puberty.

13.3 Explain healthy sexual development during adolescence.

Developing Healthy Habits

13.4 Explain the best ways for adolescents to maintain positive health.

© Macmillan, Photo by Sidford House

Sisters Ruby and Rosie spend a lot of time together, going back and forth between their mother's and father's houses each week. For most of the COVID-19 pandemic, they even sat side-by-side in front of their laptops for remote school. They think the world of each other. Rosie admires her older sister for being talented and fun, and for making the best oatmeal cookies. Ruby admires her little sister for her energy and her creativity.

Having a sister at home meant they each had someone to turn to during the isolated months of the pandemic. They worked hard to keep up with their friendships through occasional meetups in the front yard and on Zoom, all the while wondering what relationships would be left after in-person school resumed.

Both girls experienced the COVID-19 pandemic in the middle of big transitions in their lives. Rosie is 11 and just starting middle school. Ruby is two years older and about to start high school. These changes scare them both a little: They love their teachers and have gotten used to the routines at school. Their new schools are bigger and filled with unknowns.

The girls are a lot alike in many ways: They are responsible and can be trusted to keep up with their schoolwork without much of a hassle. They also help with dishwashing and cooking. They are not identical, though: Rosie is more active and would rather swing from a tree than read in a hammock like her sister. Ruby likes school, wants to learn about science, and maybe will be a psychologist when she grows up.

Their bodies have also changed during the past year: While Rosie still looks a lot like she did in fourth grade, Ruby has gone through a growth spurt and is

318

taller than her friends. She looks more like a grown-up. She stays up later, sleeps later, and spends hours reading about science on the internet: Chromosomes, synapses, and dendrites are exciting to her (as are fancy cakes). Rosie would still rather have a dance party and play video games.

As you will learn, even when they are not navigating a global pandemic, adolescents are prepared to face and adapt to change, whether that is attending a new high school or learning how to multiply exponents. Developmental scientists have found that the biological and cognitive maturation of puberty helps adolescents like Rosie and Ruby prepare for new challenges with optimism as they begin the transition to adulthood.

Scientific American Profile

Meet Ruby and Rosie

What Is Adolescence?

Most cultures over time and around the world recognize a special period between childhood and adulthood in which we are no longer children but are not quite adults (Kinney, 2004; Schlegel, 1995, 2015; Schlegel & Barry, 1991). Developmental scientists call this period of transition **adolescence**. This life stage begins with the biological changes of puberty and ends when young people are recognized as adults.

How long adolescence takes and what marks its end are determined by culture and history. For instance, in Classical China and among the Maya of ancient Mexico, some elite boys were considered adults at around 19 after years of learning laws, language, and religious beliefs, whereas girls were considered adults a few years earlier when they began to take on more household responsibilities (Kinney, 2004; Scherer, 2015). In England and the United States during the Industrial Revolution, children often took jobs in factories to support their families: For them, the period between childhood and adulthood was likely shorter (Modell & Goodman, 1990).

Today, adolescence in most affluent societies is generally considered to begin with the major biological milestones of puberty occurring as early as age 9 or 10 and end when teenagers reach the age of legal majority or adulthood, at about age 18. However, given the rising number of young people attending college and the fact that many privileges like drinking alcohol or renting a car are not granted until later, some experts argue that contemporary adolescence may last until age 25 (Patton et al., 2018)!

APPLY IT! **13.1** When did you first feel like an adolescent? Did you look forward to being a teenager with excitement or was it something you dreaded?
13.2 What markers of adulthood do you think signify the end of adolescence?

Changing Body

Puberty is the process that transforms children into adults who are typically able to have children of their own. Puberty includes maturation of the reproductive organs, development of secondary sex characteristics, and a growth spurt (Witchel & Topaloglu, 2019). (See **Infographic 13.1**.) This process will also trigger social and emotional changes like increased sexual desire and increased sensitivity to stress (Sisk & Romeo, 2020).

Learning Objective
13.1 Define adolescence.

Changing the World One brushstroke at a time, Jessica helps to beautify her neighborhood in Milwaukee, Wisconsin, by participating in a community art project. Adolescents have more skills and independence, enabling them to make bigger and more meaningful contributions to their communities.

adolescence The life stage that begins with the biological changes of puberty and ends when young people are recognized as adults.

puberty The process that transforms children into adults who are typically able to reproduce and have children of their own.

Learning Objectives
13.2 Identify the biological changes of puberty.
13.3 Explain healthy sexual development during adolescence.

TIMELINE OF PUBERTY

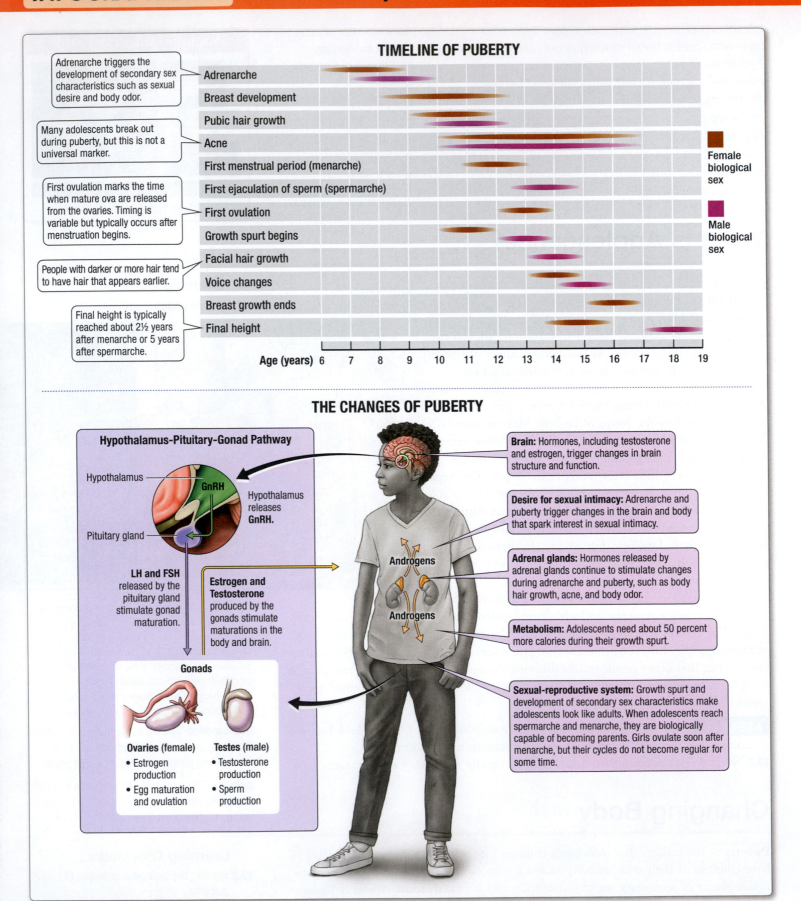

Adrenarche triggers the development of secondary sex characteristics such as sexual desire and body odor.

Many adolescents break out during puberty, but this is not a universal marker.

First ovulation marks the time when mature ova are released from the ovaries. Timing is variable but typically occurs after menstruation begins.

People with darker or more hair tend to have hair that appears earlier.

Final height is typically reached about 2½ years after menarche or 5 years after spermarche.

Adrenarche
Breast development
Pubic hair growth
Acne
First menstrual period (menarche)
First ejaculation of sperm (spermarche)
First ovulation
Growth spurt begins
Facial hair growth
Voice changes
Breast growth ends
Final height

Age (years)   6   7   8   9   10   11   12   13   14   15   16   17   18   19

Female biological sex

Male biological sex

THE CHANGES OF PUBERTY

Hypothalamus-Pituitary-Gonad Pathway

Hypothalamus

GnRH

Pituitary gland

Hypothalamus releases **GnRH.**

LH and FSH released by the pituitary gland stimulate gonad maturation.

Estrogen and Testosterone produced by the gonads stimulate maturations in the body and brain.

Gonads

Ovaries (female)
• Estrogen production
• Egg maturation and ovulation

Testes (male)
• Testosterone production
• Sperm production

Androgens

Androgens

Brain: Hormones, including testosterone and estrogen, trigger changes in brain structure and function.

Desire for sexual intimacy: Adrenarche and puberty trigger changes in the brain and body that spark interest in sexual intimacy.

Adrenal glands: Hormones released by adrenal glands continue to stimulate changes during adrenarche and puberty, such as body hair growth, acne, and body odor.

Metabolism: Adolescents need about 50 percent more calories during their growth spurt.

Sexual-reproductive system: Growth spurt and development of secondary sex characteristics make adolescents look like adults. When adolescents reach spermarche and menarche, they are biologically capable of becoming parents. Girls ovulate soon after menarche, but their cycles do not become regular for some time.

Remember from Chapter 10 that *adrenarche* begins between the ages of 5 and 9. During adrenarche, the adrenal glands begin secreting hormones that prepare the body for puberty, usually triggering body odor and launching the development of some *secondary sex characteristics* such as hair growth. Puberty is a more visible transformation than adrenarche: A different set of hormones triggers the development of additional secondary sex characteristics, like breasts and deeper voices, as well as changes to primary sex characteristics that make pregnancy possible.

Unlike some other developmental processes, many stages of puberty are experienced differently depending on children's hormones and reproductive organs at birth. Regardless of a child's gender identity, the genes and hormones that drive the pubertal transition depend on maturation of the *ovaries* or *testes*, the reproductive organs that are responsible for conception. Pubertal maturation is not completely binary, however: Whatever their anatomy, all adolescents have parallel hormonal and physical changes, although the visible signs of that maturation happen at different times (DuBois & Shattuck-Heidorn, 2020).

Typically, puberty begins as the ovaries and testes mature (between ages 8 and 13 and ages 9 and 14, respectively). There are many healthy variations in pubertal timing, and the process is often gradual, spanning five years or longer (Mendle et al., 2019; Wolf & Long, 2016).

The HPG Axis Matures

Puberty is triggered by the development of a set of glands in the **HPG axis** (Aylwin et al., 2019). These glands include the *hypothalamus* (a pea-sized structure in the center of the brain at the back of the nose); the *pituitary gland* (a tiny pencil-eraser-sized structure at the base of the brain); and the *gonads* (testes and ovaries). (If you need a mnemonic to help you remember the HPG axis, try Helping People Grow.)

Puberty is driven by the expression of hundreds of genes that trigger the activity in the HPG axis (Witchel & Topaloglu, 2019). This gene expression is also sensitive to epigenetic signals, one reason its timing is responsive to factors like health, environmental toxins, and social stress (Worthman et al., 2019).

Maturation of the testes and ovaries stimulates the production of a number of hormones, including **testosterone** and **estrogen**. All adolescents secrete both hormones at relatively the same levels before puberty, but the testes typically secrete more testosterone, and the ovaries more estrogen, during puberty. Both testosterone and estrogen reorganize neural circuits in the brain, and they help reshape the body in distinct ways. Testosterone is connected to many parts of maturation, including wider jaws, ovulation, increased sexual desire, and increased interest in risk-taking (Berli & Plemons, 2020; Jordan-Young & Karkazis, 2019). Estrogen levels fluctuate, making it difficult to study, but researchers believe it is connected to brain development that alters emotion regulation (Chung et al., 2019; Dai & Scherf, 2019; Goddings et al., 2019). Estrogen also triggers bone growth and breast development (DuBois & Shattuck-Heidorn, 2020).

The First Signs of Puberty

Although there are variations around the world, in most highly resourced countries, early signs of puberty begin before children are in middle school. By age 9, breast development has begun in many children (Eckert-Lind et al., 2020). Breasts begin to change and grow in most children who are biologically female and in nearly half of typically developing children who are biologically male (Lorek et al., 2019). Typically by about age 9 or 10, children may also experience the emergence of pubic hair, along with changes in the size of the testicles and penis (Wolf & Long, 2016).

The awakening of the glands in the HPG axis also triggers a **growth spurt**—a very rapid increase in height and size—that begins at about age 10 in children with

CONNECTIONS

Remember from Chapter 10 that secondary sex characteristics are physical markers such as pubic hair, breasts, and facial hair. They differ from primary sex characteristics, which include the genitals and the sex organs, like ovaries and testicles.

HPG axis A set of glands that trigger puberty, including the hypothalamus, pituitary gland, and gonads (testes and ovaries).

testosterone A hormone produced by the gonads that is linked to reproduction, maturation, brain development, and sexual function. Testosterone levels are higher in adolescents with testes but are important to typical functioning in both those with ovaries and those with testes.

estrogen A hormone that is linked to reproduction, maturation, brain development, and sexual function in both males and females. Estrogen levels are higher in biological females but are important to typical functioning in both males and females.

growth spurt A very rapid increase in height and size that begins at about age 10 in girls and age 12 in boys.

CONNECTIONS

Remember from Chapter 3 that biological differences, such as having ovaries or testes, do not always align with our *gender identity*, or how we identify as men, women, or another less binary category. Language such as "children with testes" is designed to be inclusive and refer to the biology, rather than to the identity, of children.

ovaries and about age 12 in those with testes (Kozieł & Malina, 2018; Malina et al., 2020). The peak of growth for children with ovaries is about age 12, and for other children it is nearly two years later, making most children with ovaries taller than their peers at about age 13 (Gardstedt et al., 2019; Kozieł & Malina, 2018). During the peak of growth, adolescents may grow more than 3 inches in a year, evident when a child grows two shoe sizes over a summer or needs a new pair of jeans before the first pair has worn out. Around the world, improvements in health and nutrition mean that by age 19, adolescents are taller than they have ever been: The tallest are in the Netherlands (Rodriguez-Martinez et al., 2020).

Menarche and Spermarche

The key biological event of puberty for most children is when the biological changes associated with reproduction occur. A first menstrual period, known as **menarche**, and a first ejaculation of sperm, or **spermarche**, signify young people's developing ability to have children of their own. These milestones typically occur several years after gonadal hormones have begun to flow through the body. There are variations around the world, but in the United States, as in many other highly resourced countries, menarche typically occurs at around age 12 and spermarche at around age 14 (Biro et al., 2018; Pyra & Schwarz, 2019; Tinggaard et al., 2012).

Menstruation is the monthly regular bleeding that occurs as the body expels the endometrial lining coating the uterus. Remember from Chapter 2 that *ova*, or egg cells, begin to develop before a baby is born. However, these cells are not mature until puberty. During *ovulation*, about once a month, an ovum matures and is released from the ovaries. If these eggs are not fertilized and implanted in the endometrial lining, that lining is discharged from the body. In young people, menstruation is often irregular and, for more than half, painful or uncomfortable. First ovulation, marking the time when reproduction is possible, typically happens a few months or years after *menarche*, the first menstrual period (Gunn et al., 2018).

Adolescents experience menarche in different ways depending on their families' cultural beliefs (Marván & Alcalá-Herrera, 2019). In some communities, there is stigma attached to getting your period (Johnston-Robledo & Chrisler, 2013). But in many others, it is becoming less taboo. This major biological change is often described as an "annoying" but not traumatic part of growing up (Marván & Alcalá-Herrera, 2019; Ruble & Brooks-Gunn, 1982).

In some communities around the world, however, children lack basic understanding of menstruation, which can make them feel embarrassed and even scared (Chandra-Mouli & Patel, 2020; Coast et al., 2019; Hebert-Beirne et al., 2017; Herbert et al., 2017). The cost of tampons or pads and the hassle of managing them can make it difficult for adolescents to attend school or participate in sports (Schmitt et al., 2021). Interventions include providing children with low-cost sanitary pads, washable menstrual underwear, and educational programs that battle menstruation-related discrimination (Chandra-Mouli et al., 2019; Hennegan et al., 2019; Plesons et al., 2021).

Maturation of the testes is formally marked by *spermarche*, the first ejaculation of sperm. Most children will be unaware of this event, since it is obvious only with the help of a microscope to locate the tiny sperm cells. Spermarche is not typically an adolescent's first ejaculation, since children can ejaculate and orgasm prior to spermarche without expressing semen (Chad, 2020). Early ejaculation can take adolescents by surprise, with some reporting that they feel confused by what is happening to their bodies (Gaddis & Brooks-Gunn, 1985). Families and even pediatricians are often more uncomfortable talking about spermarche than they are about

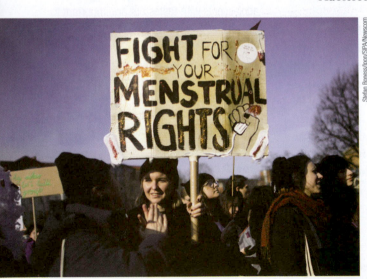

Stefan Boness/Ipon/SIPA/Newscom

Celebrating the Body Talking about menstruation can lessen the stigma. These campaigners are advocating for menstrual rights at a woman's equality rally in Berlin, Germany.

menarche The first menstrual period.

spermarche The first ejaculation of sperm.

menstruation, but being straightforward about ejaculation and sperm production can help children feel more comfortable (Grubb et al., 2020; Marván & Alcalá-Herrera, 2019).

For children who identify as transgender or nonbinary, puberty can require them to confront the biological characteristics of a gender they may not identify with (Kimberly et al., 2018). This is a time when adolescents and their families may choose gender-confirming or puberty-delaying hormone treatments, which may continue into adulthood (Notini et al., 2021; Panagiotakopoulos et al., 2020). Gender-diverse teenagers are frequently rejected by their communities and families and, as a result, have higher rates of emotional and mental health problems than their peers (Grossman et al., 2021). Allowing transgender and gender-questioning teenagers extra time to go through puberty, and hormonally transitioning them to the gender with which they identify, is linked to positive mental health outcomes such as lower rates of depression (Rafferty et al., 2018; Turban et al., 2020).

Variations in Timing

Around the globe, puberty depends partly upon a population's health. For instance, until the late 1800s in the United States and much of Europe and in the early 2000s in less-resourced regions, most adolescents did not reach puberty until their mid- to late teens. However, because of widespread improvements in public health and nutrition, adolescents in most countries today reach menarche and spermarche at about age 12 or 13, five to six years earlier than their counterparts years ago (Kaplowitz et al., 2016; Moodie et al., 2020; Tijani et al., 2019). For instance, just 20 years ago, girls in Nepal did not reach puberty until about 16, but now they typically experience menarche at around 12½ (Chalise et al., 2018; Parent et al., 2003; Thomas et al., 2001). Other signs of maturation, like breast development, also occur earlier around the world than they once did, although puberty often proceeds slowly, particularly in countries with limited resources (Campisi et al., 2020; Eckert-Lind et al., 2020).

Developmental scientists call this gradual, long-term progression toward earlier puberty a **secular trend**. Most experts believe that the tendency to reach puberty at younger ages is a result of improvements in health, since in the past, infectious diseases and malnutrition may have prevented young people from gaining the weight and body fat necessary to trigger puberty (Papadimitriou, 2016). (See **Figure 13.1**.)

secular trend The term developmental scientists use to describe the gradual, long-term progression toward earlier puberty.

FIGURE 13.1 The Secular Trend in Puberty In many nations, the age of menarche has declined as population health has improved. The major markers of puberty are stabilizing at around age 12 or 13.

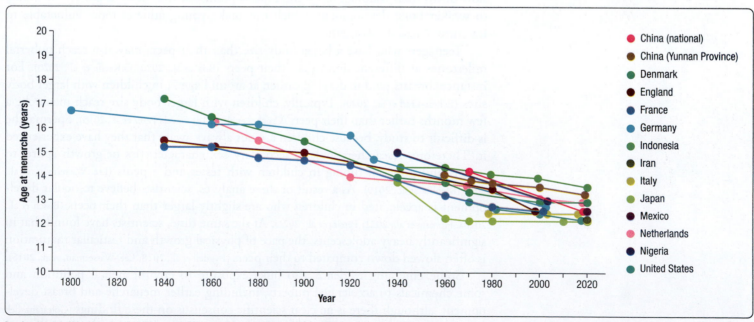

Data from Liu et al., 2021; Meng et al., 2017; Garenne, 2021; Wyshak & Frisch, 1982; Lalys & Pineau, 2014; Bau et al., 2009; Whincup et al., 2001; Biro et al., 2018; Herman-Giddens, 2006; Helm & Grønlund, 1998; Talma et al., 2013; Wahab et al., 2020; Hosokawa et al., 2012; Piras et al., 2020.

David Grossman/Alamy

Puberty in the Real World Variations in the timing of puberty are common, as in this group practicing for a choir performance in New York City.

Common Variations in Pubertal Timing If you look at a line of middle school students waiting for the bus, you can see that puberty does not happen at the same time for everyone. Some adolescents experience the major hallmarks of puberty earlier or later than their peers: This diversity is typical, since puberty is driven by a number of factors, including children's health, their environment, their genes, and their life experience (Worthman et al., 2019). While typically developing children could start puberty any time between ages 9 and 16, adolescents often are treated differently if they reach major milestones at a different age than their communities expect (Seaton & Carter, 2019).

Scientists have found that the HPG axis is tightly entangled with the hormones and chemicals that regulate metabolism. The physical maturation of puberty requires a tremendous amount of energy and results in significant changes in how children burn calories and store energy (Manfredi-Lozano et al., 2018). Hormones released in the gastrointestinal system, nerve cells in the hypothalamus, and even the balance of bacteria in the microbiome help regulate the timing of puberty (Navarro, 2020; Worthman et al., 2019).

Two hormones, *leptin* and *ghrelin*, are involved in regulating hunger, weight, and metabolism. A certain amount of leptin, which is stored in body fat and gives you a "full" feeling, needs to be available in the body in sufficient amounts in order to launch puberty. Scientists believe that leptin levels signal to the body that it has enough body fat to sustain the intense growth connected with puberty. Throughout development, leptin affects hormone balance and reproduction. For instance, without enough leptin, people are likely to miss their menstrual period (Childs et al., 2020). Ghrelin, which makes you feel hungry, can also delay puberty or slow its progress (Rodríguez-Vázquez et al., 2020). As a result, children who do not get enough to eat or who do not have sufficient body fat may have delays in maturation (Richmond & Rogol, 2016).

In affluent communities, delays in puberty are particularly common for children who are extremely athletic (Logue et al., 2018). For instance, teenagers who participate in sports in which intensive exercise is combined with a preference for a thin frame, such as distance running, gymnastics, or wrestling, may experience delayed menarche or growth spurts (Huhmann, 2020; Roemmich & Sinning, 1997). Most will catch up when they slow down their training, but some experts point out that delayed puberty is linked to weaker bone development, which can make young athletes more vulnerable to fractures (Farpour-Lambert, 2020).

Teenagers who have a larger body size than their peers may also reach pubertal milestones at different times than their peers (Brix et al., 2020; O'Keeffe et al., 2020). For instance, breasts tend to develop earlier, at around age 7, in children with larger body sizes (Eckert-Lind et al., 2020). Typically, children with larger body size reach menarche a few months earlier than their peers (Crocker et al., 2014; Gavela Pérez et al., 2015). Spermarche is difficult to study, because children are not always aware that they have experienced it. Therefore, researchers look to secondary sex characteristics or growth spurts to understand pubertal timing in children with testes and a penis (Lee, Wasserman, et al., 2016; Mendle et al., 2019). As a result of these analyses, scientists believe testicular development is accelerated in children who are slightly larger than their peers (Busch et al., 2020a; Herting et al., 2021; Pereira et al., 2021). At the same time, scientists have found that in significantly heavy adolescents, the pace of physical growth and testicular maturation is often slowed down compared to their peers (Bygdell et al., 2018; Lee, Wasserman, et al., 2016).

Some emerging evidence also links exposure to environmental pollution and some chemicals to accelerated puberty, including earlier menarche and breast development, although there is no clear scientific consensus on these findings (Golestanzadeh et al., 2020; Harley et al., 2019). Children who are from Black or Latino communities, and children from any background who live in low-income neighborhoods, are more likely to be exposed to these environmental toxins, which may contribute to a higher likelihood of early puberty (Attina et al., 2019; Galvez et al., 2018).

The Impact of Genetics and Life Stress If Rosie asked her pediatrician when she would start her growth spurt, her doctor would probably ask if she knew when her own parents experienced puberty. This is because one of the strongest predictors of when children reach puberty is their genome (Busch et al., 2020b; Horvath et al., 2020; Wohlfahrt-Veje et al., 2016). Most children, if they are healthy, typically reach menarche or spermarche at about the same time as their parents did, and in Rosie's case, she will probably reach her milestones at about the same time as her big sister, Ruby. So now is probably not the time to stock up on new clothes: A growth spurt is coming.

For some genetically susceptible children, *life stress* may trigger puberty to come a little early (Belsky, 2019; Sun et al., 2020). Researchers have found that children tend to reach puberty a bit sooner if they have felt threatened or experienced significant fear, as with a natural disaster, family trauma, discrimination, or harsh parenting (Colich et al., 2020; Deardorff et al., 2019). These adverse experiences are thought to create chronic stress responses that can stimulate the biological changes associated with puberty (Deardorff et al., 2019).

Evolutionary or *life history theory* suggests that in the past, these biological responses to early life stress may have offered an advantage (Belsky, 2019). For instance, children who mature earlier tend to be able to have children earlier, which would have been beneficial at times during human evolution when there was a high risk of dying young (Ellis & Del Giudice, 2019).

The Consequences of Pubertal Timing In the past, many researchers believed that early puberty granted teenagers certain advantages, particularly for children who identified as boys. For instance, reaching puberty early may allow boys to excel in sports and be more dominant because of their larger size (Deardorff et al., 2019; Huddleston & Ge, 2003). However, contemporary researchers often worry that early development may be less beneficial (Mendle et al., 2019). Children who look "older than their age" may be treated like adults before they are emotionally ready (Carter et al., 2018a).

Looking older also puts adolescents at risk for exclusion by their peers, particularly if they lack the social skills to navigate their new identities (Carter et al., 2018a). Perhaps as a result, some researchers have found that adolescents who develop early tend to join new friend groups, with teenagers who are older but not necessarily wiser.

There are different risks related to pubertal timing depending on adolescents' gender identity: Scientists have found that children who identify as boys who are more physically mature than their peers are more likely to be victims of violent crime. They are also more likely to be diagnosed with behavioral or emotional disorders such as conduct disorder and depression than their peers (Dimler & Natsuaki, 2015; Hamlat et al., 2020; Mendle & Ferrero, 2012). However, late-developing children who identify as boys also report some stresses: They often feel self-conscious about being smaller than their peers, and they, too, may be more likely to develop depression (Gaysina et al., 2015; Huddleston & Ge, 2003).

For adolescents who identify as girls, developing early often makes them more vulnerable to abuse by older partners (Chen, Rothman, et al., 2017; Javdani et al., 2019). They can feel isolated and are more likely to experience psychological disorders such as depression, substance abuse, and eating disorders (Pfeifer & Allen, 2021; Wang et al., 2016). These difficulties may be exacerbated by the stereotypes adults, including teachers, hold about early developers. Some researchers have found that teachers expect young girls who are early developers, particularly if they are Black, to have more problems at school and with friends than other children, creating a cycle of low expectations that may be hard to break (Carter et al., 2018b).

Over the lifespan, some research suggests that the health impact of early puberty can be significant. Being an early developer has been linked to increased risk of heart disease and diabetes and to the development of breast cancer (Magnus et al., 2020).

Share It!

Natural disasters may accelerate puberty. Some researchers found that living through an earthquake (and its frightening and chaotic aftermath) hurried puberty for young children, particularly those who were preschoolers at the time of the disaster.

(Lian et al., 2018)

CONNECTIONS

Remember from Chapter 2 that *evolutionary*, or *life history*, *theory* focuses on how diversity in development may result from ancient adaptations to the environment.

Learn It Together

Puberty Can Be Surprising

Plan Review the factors that influence when adolescents go through puberty.

Engage Choose two factors that are very surprising to you and that you did not know before. Pick a partner and share your surprises with one another, talking about why you were surprised and how this has changed how you think about puberty.

Reflect Does this make you think more about how biology and the environment interact to shape development? How would you explain the complexity of puberty to your family or friends?

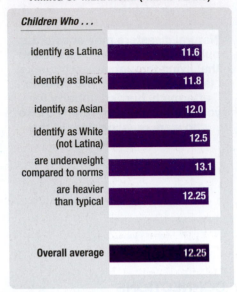

TIMING OF MENARCHE (AGE IN YEARS)

Children Who . . .

identify as Latina	11.6
identify as Black	11.8
identify as Asian	12.0
identify as White (not Latina)	12.5
are underweight compared to norms	13.1
are heavier than typical	12.25
Overall average	12.25

Data from Biro et al., 2018.

FIGURE 13.2 Variations in the Timing of Puberty In the United States, researchers have often linked group differences in the timing of puberty to ethnic differences, but the timing of development often varies depending on children's size and their family income. Many researchers study variations in the timing of menarche because it is easier to determine than the timing of spermarche.

However, it is difficult to conclude that early puberty truly *causes* these outcomes. The findings are *correlations*, and many of the worrisome health associations are connected to risk factors that predate puberty or the social stresses that result from it, rather than to pubertal timing itself (Bell et al., 2018).

Many of the challenges faced by early developers improve with time. For instance, the association of early puberty with acting out behavior seems to dissipate by the time adolescents reach their late 20s (Dimler & Natsuaki, 2015). As with so much else in development, social and family context makes an enormous difference. Supportive family and friends can buffer many of the challenges early developers may face (Deardorff et al., 2019).

CAN YOU BELIEVE IT?
Why Are There Group Differences in the Timing of Puberty?

In diverse countries like the United States, researchers, families, and pediatricians have noticed some common variations in the timing of puberty (see **Figure 13.2**). For instance, in the United States, many adolescents from Asian American backgrounds reach puberty later than those from other communities (Biro et al., 2018; Lee, Wasserman, et al., 2016). In countries around the world, group differences often emerge as children mature. But these differences are not always aligned to ethnic identity.

The triggers for puberty are complex. In some contexts, extreme adversity leads to *later* puberty, when young people may lack adequate nutrition for puberty to start (Campisi et al., 2020). For instance, in China, high-income, urban children tend to reach puberty before rural children, who have more limited health care and access to nutrition (Sun et al., 2012).

In other situations, social stresses or chronic adversity may contribute to trigger *earlier* puberty. In Australia, as in the United States, where most children have enough to eat, family income makes a difference. Having low income often increases stress, and as a result, children who are low income are more likely to reach puberty early (Sun et al., 2017). In the United States, for instance, menarche happens nearly a year earlier in teenagers from low-income families than in those from more privileged backgrounds (James-Todd et al., 2010). The everyday unfair treatment, hostility, and sense of threat associated with racism adds to stress, so adolescents from groups that experience discrimination are more likely to reach puberty early (Kelly et al., 2017; Suglia, Chen, et al., 2020; Trent et al., 2019).

Because of the tremendous diversity in when adolescents reach puberty, scientists caution against assigning a genetic explanation for group differences (Deardorff et al., 2019). Remember from Chapter 2 that ethnic and racial labels do not accurately reflect differences in our genomes. Researchers suggest that group differences in the timing of puberty in the United States are linked to differences in environmental exposures to toxins, trauma, birth size, poor health, and the stress of racism, not genetics (Herting et al., 2021; James-Todd et al., 2016).

These data remind us that ethnic labels are not an ideal way to describe differences between groups. The unequal circumstances children grow up in affect their development and biology. Puberty is yet another demonstration of how the social environment shapes children's development in complex ways.

Sexuality

Ruby and Rosie's mother, Jill, raises her eyebrows when we ask about dating. She has talked to her girls about dating, but maybe, she admits, not *enough*. Indeed, adults are not usually in a hurry to talk to adolescents about sex (Ashcraft & Murray, 2017; Astle et al., 2021).

Despite the awkwardness, changing brains and bodies spark a new interest in sexuality that starts before middle school (Suleiman et al., 2017). Sex also surrounds teenagers: They live in a world that is saturated with sexualized content, from billboard advertising to online pornography (Collins et al., 2017). Yet, despite their heightened interest in sex and the ubiquity of sexualized material, adolescents do not talk much with adults or each other about sexuality (Weissbourd et al., 2017).

Young people might be embarrassed to talk about it, but developmental scientists are not. As many researchers have discovered, sexual desire and behavior—at the right time, with the right person, and with the right protection—can be a healthy and positive part of adolescent life (Golden et al., 2016; Harden, 2014; Verbeek et al., 2020).

Despite the focus of many parents and the media on hookups and intercourse, sexuality emerges gradually and in many forms during the adolescent years. The hormonal changes of puberty help to create feelings of desire that adolescents—employing their increasingly mature cognitive and social abilities—explore by themselves and in their social relationships.

The Origins of Desire Remember from Chapter 10 that many researchers believe that sexual desire begins with the first hormonal stirrings of adrenarche. Children as young as 9 or 10 have crushes and feel sexual attraction (McClintock & Herdt, 1996; Mustanski et al., 2014). By the time they are 14, most adolescents have fantasized about sex (Fortenberry, 2014).

Desire is triggered by the release of hormones, such as the adrenal hormone DHEA, estrogen, and testosterone during adrenarche and puberty. Interest in sex and romance are also set off by maturity in brain systems that help us feel pleasure and enjoy new experiences. Dopamine becomes prevalent in the subcortical structures involved in the *reward system*, and adolescents' cortex is activated when they think about romantic relationships (Suleiman & Harden, et al., 2016).

A Variety of Sexual Experiences In most places around the world, cultural ethnotheories make sexual activity taboo in early adolescence. As a result, very few teenagers have sex before they are 15, and the rate of sexual activity in young people is declining (Liang et al., 2019; Starrs et al., 2018). In the United States, only about half of teenagers have oral sex or penetrative intercourse before age 18 (Astle et al., 2021; Underwood et al., 2020). This is a significant change from the 1990s and 2000s: Fewer ninth- and tenth-graders today are sexually active than young people were in their parents' generation (Lei & South, 2021). Many developmental scientists believe waiting may be protective: Older teenagers are more likely to make safer decisions about how and when to become intimate and usually have more positive experiences (Ethier et al., 2018; Janis et al., 2019; Lara & Abdo, 2016; Vasilenko et al., 2016).

Just because more teenagers are putting off intercourse does not mean that adolescents are not experimenting with their sexuality: Many adolescents participate in a variety of intimate activities, including solo masturbation and mutual touching. By the time they are 19, most have experimented with penetrative and oral sex (Astle et al., 2021). However, when young people become romantically involved, how they move from exchanging texts to physical intimacy, and what that entails, varies widely.

Around the world, teenagers' sexual identities and behaviors are more flexible than previous generations: For instance, about 4 in 100 identify as transgender or another nonbinary identity (Boyon & Silverstein, 2021). Young people are often nervous about answering questions about their sexual identity, but about 1 in 10 U.S. high school students polled in one survey indicated that they identified as gay, lesbian, or bisexual (see **Figure 13.3**) (YRBS, 2019). Adolescents' romantic partners and sexual identities do not always align or adhere to strict labels (Diamond, 2020; Watson et al., 2020). In addition, it is common for romantic and sexual preferences to change over time (Li & Davis, 2019; Stewart et al., 2019; Ybarra et al., 2019).

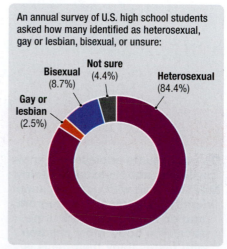

An annual survey of U.S. high school students asked how many identified as heterosexual, gay or lesbian, bisexual, or unsure:

Not sure (4.4%)
Bisexual (8.7%)
Heterosexual (84.4%)
Gay or lesbian (2.5%)

Data from YRBS, 2019.

FIGURE 13.3 Sexual Identity in Adolescence An increasing number of young people are comfortable saying that they are lesbian, gay, bisexual, or another category.

Researchers have found that nearly half of teenagers who identify as lesbian or gay are likely to have had an other-sex partner. Adolescents who are attracted to another sex may fall in love or become intimate with a same-sex partner (Ybarra et al., 2019). For some, these sexual experiences will form their sexual identity. For others, they are part of a continuum of sexual behavior that may include a variety of relationships (Diamond et al., 2015; Li & Davis, 2019).

The Social Context of Sexuality

Although adolescents' hormonal and brain development may trigger their sexual interest, adolescent sexuality takes place within a larger social context of close relationships, families, and communities. Many U.S. adolescents tell researchers that they think sex should happen in serious relationships, after they have said "I love you" (Choukas-Bradley et al., 2015).

Families have a crucial influence on when adolescents begin to have sex and the health of their relationships (Nogueira Avelar e Silva et al., 2016). Teenagers from closer and supportive families tend to postpone sex until they are older, and they use protection more regularly (Astle et al., 2019; Cadely et al., 2020; Suleiman & Harden, et al., 2016). Friends and peer groups also set expectations for adolescents' sexual activity (Van de Bongardt et al., 2015).

Cultural values about sex are an important factor in whether adolescents become sexually active, and expectations for romance vary widely. For instance, in a recent survey, more than two in three adolescents in cities in Indonesia reported that they had been in love, but only 1 in 10 adolescents in Kinshasa, Democratic Republic of the Congo, said they had been in love (Blum et al., 2021). In Bhutan, many young people do not have sex until they are in their 20s, but in the United States, nearly half have been intimate by the time they leave high school (GSSHS, 2016; Martinez & Abma, 2020).

In the United States, some young people delay sexual activity, but not always romance, if they have religious beliefs or cultural taboos about adolescent sexuality (Haglund & Fehring, 2010; Vasilenko & Espinosa-Hernández, 2019). Immigrant youth, particularly if they come from families with more conservative views on sexuality, also tend to have lower rates of sexual activity (Tsai et al., 2017). However, researchers caution that community values do not always reflect community practices. Adolescents from communities that value abstinence may not be abstinent themselves (Abboud et al., 2020; Munro-Kramer et al., 2016).

Healthy Sexual Practices

Developmental researchers suggest that for many adolescents, sexual relationships can be positive, particularly for teenagers who put off sex until their late teens and have positive emotional bonds to their partner (Golden et al., 2016; Shulman et al., 2020). Researchers suggest that healthy sexual practices occur when sex is consensual, respectful, and enjoyable, and when teenagers are protected from risks of pregnancy or infection (Harden, 2014; UNESCO, 2018). Adolescents are better able to make safe sex choices if they are able to manage the romantic aspects of sexuality, know how to talk about sex with a partner, and know how to prevent sexually transmitted diseases, unplanned pregnancies, and coercive sexual contact (Widman et al., 2014).

Sex Education Around the world, teenagers learn about sex in a variety of ways: at home, in school, and on their own. For instance, schools in the Netherlands are often held up as a model for offering frank, relationship-oriented sexual education that involves discussions of desire, pleasure, and sexual diversity (Baams et al., 2017; van der Doef & Reinders, 2018).

Many developmental scientists have found that school-based, *comprehensive sexual education* can improve the sexual well-being of young people: promoting health, reducing stigma about sexual diversity, and fostering healthier relationships

 **Share It!**

Do not assume adolescents know the basics about sexual anatomy. Most children with ovaries cannot identify the vagina on a diagram and do not know where urine leaves the body. Most children with testes think their penis is undersized. Sex education needs to start simple.

(Hebert-Beirne et al., 2017; Rothman et al., 2021)

(Goldfarb & Lieberman, 2021). In the United States, families, educators, policy makers, and adolescents do not always share the same goals for sexual education or agree on where it should happen. As a result, school-based sexual education often focuses on abstinence and prevention of sexually transmitted infections and is ineffective at encouraging healthy sexual behaviors (Denford et al., 2017). In the United States, more than 90 percent of young people learn about sexually transmitted infections from their schools or their families, but much fewer learn about preventing pregnancy, and even fewer feel prepared for the emotional and social aspects of sexuality (Garceau & Ronis, 2019; Kantor & Lindberg, 2020; Weissbourd et al., 2017). Adolescents often report to researchers that the message they receive about sex at school is that it is dangerous, risky, and even shameful (Stewart et al., 2021).

Most U.S. teenagers learn about sex from their friends and online (Nikkelen et al., 2020; Rothman et al., 2021). Some of the online resources used by young people contain factual information and may offer a needed and safe space for LGBTQIA+ youth to explore their sexuality (McInroy et al., 2019). Not many resources, however, provide much in terms of education about sexual feelings and communication (Simon & Daneback, 2013). For some youth, online pornography forms the basis of their sexual education and may contribute to poor body image and confusion about appropriate sexual gender roles (Bőthe et al., 2019; Coyne et al., 2019; Grubbs & Kraus, 2021).

Sex education seems to be most effective if it starts at home (Guilamo-Ramos et al., 2020; Widman et al., 2019). Young people who can communicate with their partners and understand their own desire typically learn these skills from parents and friends with whom they have close relationships (Mastro & Zimmer-Gembeck, 2015). It is perhaps not surprising, then, that young people who talk to their families about sex tend to have more positive experiences (Vasilenko et al., 2014; Widman et al., 2014; Wright et al., 2020).

Staying Protected Knowing about sex and how to talk about it increases the likelihood that young people will take measures that protect their physical and emotional health. Safer sex includes *barrier methods* that protect against sexually transmitted infections, such as the internal or external condom, and, for partners who can get pregnant, *long-acting reversible contraception*, such as implants, intrauterine devices (IUDs), or hormone shots (Francis & Gold, 2017).

Sexually transmitted infections, or **STIs**, is the term health care providers use to describe diseases that can be passed from one person to another through intimate contact. STIs include viruses, bacterial infections, and parasites that can be harmful whether or not someone shows symptoms. Many providers use the term *STI* instead of *STD (sexually transmitted disease)* in order to reduce the stigma around these conditions, although the terms are often used interchangeably (Lederer & Laing, 2017).

Around the globe, *human immunodeficiency virus (HIV)* continues to be a leading cause of death in young people. HIV can be transmitted sexually but can also be acquired through blood transfusions and prenatally. It can lead to *acquired immune deficiency syndrome (AIDS)*, which can keep the body from fighting infection. Effective treatments, including preventative ones, exist for HIV, but not all adolescents know they carry the disease or have access to treatment. An estimated 29,000 teenagers worldwide died from complications of HIV in 2020 (UNICEF, 2022b). The virus continues to infect adolescents in the United States, who account for about one in five new infections (CDC, 2020).

In the United States, the rates of HIV are low, but nearly one in four adolescents has an STI (Shannon & Klausner, 2018). Common STIs among young people include *chlamydia, herpes simplex virus, trichomoniasis,* and *human papilloma virus (HPV)* (Kreisel et al., 2021). Experts predict that *MPX,* a virus that can be spread through intimate contact, may emerge as another transmissible STI among young people. MPX generally causes fevers and uncomfortable rashes that can be contagious for weeks but does not generally lead to hospitalization (Thornhill et al., 2022).

sexually transmitted infection (STI) The term health care providers use to describe diseases that can be passed from one person to another through intimate contact.

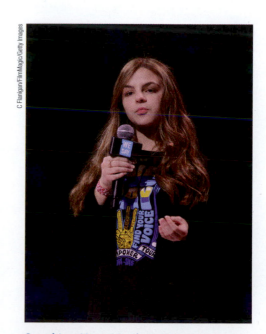

C Flanigan/FilmMagic/Getty Images

Speaking Up to Reduce Stigma
Canadian activist Ashley Rose Murphy has been speaking up on behalf of young people with HIV since she was 10. She explains that HIV can be treated and prevented and that all people, regardless of their health conditions, should be treated with kindness.

Share It!

Do you need to tell your family about that? In the United States, adolescents do not need parental consent to receive testing or treatment for an STI. However, in 18 states, health care professionals may share medical information with parents without a child's consent.

(Guttmacher Institute, 2022)

Developmental scientists believe that U.S. adolescents have high rates of STIs because they engage in unprotected sex in higher numbers than adults do, particularly when they are very young or they are using alcohol or substances (Kessler et al., 2020). In the United States, only about half of teenagers used barrier protection when they last had penetrative sexual contact (Szucs et al., 2020). In addition, young people are more prone to infections because their bodies are still biologically immature (Shannon & Klausner, 2018).

The biggest predictor of the use of barrier protection is whether young people feel comfortable talking about sex with their partners, which can be difficult for adolescents, especially when they are very young (Vasilenko et al., 2015; Widman et al., 2014). The ability to talk openly with their partners may also help young people identify and avoid coercive or abusive sexual relationships (Boislard et al., 2016). Some studies have shown that more than one in five young people have been in a relationship in which their partner used verbal or physical threats or abused them: Rates were higher in same-sex-attracted young people and transgender youth, who may be particularly isolated (Katz et al., 2019; Miller, Jones, et al., 2018).

Pregnancy Around the world, more than 16 million teenagers give birth every year, and many of these young parents and their babies experience some difficulties in their transition to parenthood. Babies born to adolescents are at high risk for complications, including being born early and too small. Pregnancy is a leading cause of death in young people around the globe (Chandra-Mouli et al., 2019; WHO, 2022a).

In the United States, rates of teenage parenthood are at an all-time low, but they are still higher than in any other wealthy country (OECD, 2021a). Developmental scientists attribute this to widespread *economic inequality*, or the gap between financially well-off families and those who are poor, which has been linked to early pregnancy worldwide (Santelli et al., 2017). In the United States, rates of adolescent pregnancy are highest in rural counties and communities with pervasive inequality, and among low-income youth (Kearney & Levine, 2015; Sutton et al., 2019).

About 17 of every 1,000 teenagers with ovaries in the United States has had a baby (Maddow-Zimet & Kost, 2021; Martin et al., 2021). Researchers are unsure how many teenagers with testes become parents, but estimates are about 5 in every 1,000 (Bamishigbin et al., 2019; U.S. DHHS, 2021). Income is typically one of young families' major hurdles, but young parents are also likely to have a history of trauma (Flaviano & Harville, 2021; Ott et al., 2020). Being a young parent comes with stigma, as well. Adolescent parents often report feeling judged by adults, who question their ability to be competent caregivers (Conn et al., 2018; SmithBattle, 2020).

Although most adolescent pregnancies are unplanned, many are met with excitement (Finer & Zolna, 2016; Kost et al., 2017). Expectant young people often report feeling that their pregnancy was inevitable, or something that was "meant to be" (Borrero et al., 2015). Many express ambivalence about what was often a surprise, but they may also show some of the characteristic optimism of adolescents (Cashdollar, 2018). Nevertheless, balancing school, work, and an infant is challenging for parents of any age.

Emotional Strains

As with many behaviors that adolescents are learning, sexual activity can involve risk, particularly if it happens when participants are not ready or are unwilling (Harden, 2014). While sexual relationships can be one of the joys of growing up, they can also be a source of strain, adding to children's overall stress, harming their well-being, and distracting them from their schoolwork (Golden et al., 2016; Rossi et al., 2021).

Being sexually active at a younger age tends to increase the stresses associated with sex, from unplanned pregnancy and STIs to the use of substances during intimate encounters, and may increase the risk of future emotional challenges, including substance use disorder (Baiden et al., 2021; Epstein et al., 2018; Kahn & Halpern, 2018). Both in the

United States and around the world, adolescents who are sexually active before age 16 also tend to face greater risk of sexual coercion and sexual violence, which can add further emotional stress (Hawks et al., 2019; Howard et al., 2021; Lindberg et al., 2019). Most U.S. adolescents delay intimacy, but about 3 percent have sex before age 13 (CDC, 2019). Young adolescents may not yet have developed the social skills to manage complex relationships, which may be one reason sexual activity can sometimes add stress.

Abusive sexual behavior occurs across the lifespan but is more prevalent in adolescence. The rates of sexual victimization, which includes a spectrum of behaviors from sexual harassment to rape, double after puberty. However, because sexual abuse is such a private, hidden, and painful act, accurate data are hard to obtain: Most children do not report it to their families or to legal authorities (Gewirtz-Meydan & Finkelhor, 2020).

In the United States and in many places around the world, about one in four adolescents who identify as girls and 1 in 20 who identify as boys report having been the victim of sexual abuse before age 18 (Letourneau et al., 2018). Rates are much higher among children with intellectual developmental disorders and children who identify as LGBTQIA+ (Caputi et al., 2020; Johns et al., 2020; Norris & Orchowski, 2020; Walters & Gray, 2018). In adolescence, much of this abuse comes from peers: In some studies, as many as one in three adolescents who identify as boys and one in two who identify as girls report having been the victim of sexual harassment, unwanted physical contact, or coercive sex (Morrison-Beedy & Grove, 2018; Ngo et al., 2018).

Even sexual behavior that is consensual may be uncomfortable or painful. Only about half of adolescents report that sex is "quite" or "extremely" pleasurable (Beckmeyer et al., 2021). However, even when young people report that sex is painful, they may continue to engage in it (Fortenberry, 2014; Jones & Furman, 2011; Meier & Allen, 2009).

Young people who are inexperienced with intimacy may have difficulty communicating with their partners about what sexual behaviors they want to try and when. The risk of coercion and a lack of clarity around consent is common in adolescent relationships: Adolescents are not sure how to be sure their partners are interested (Righi et al., 2021). While some experts recommend what is called *affirmative consent*, where partners verbally consent to any sexual activity, adolescents are often unsure about how this works in practice, particularly in established relationships (Javidi et al., 2020; Richards et al., 2022). In some studies, nearly 40 percent of young people have been in a relationship where their partner used threats to convince them to have sex (Collibee & Furman, 2014; Katz et al., 2019). Interventions designed to address intimate partner violence among adolescents have been most successful when they have involved families, rather than just the young people themselves, in helping create more supportive relationships (Piolanti & Foran, 2021; see **Table 13.1**).

TABLE 13.1 **Best Practices for Intervening in Cases of Intimate Partner Violence**

- Addressing stress and adversity in adolescence often involves family-based, rather than individual interventions.
- Violence can happen to anyone: If you are worried about a family member, friend, student, or acquaintance, reach out and explain that violence and abuse happen to many people. This can help reduce the shame that survivors often face.
- Bystanders can help. Classmates, acquaintances, coworkers, and teachers can prevent violence by addressing it when they become aware of it.
- Speaking up is hard. You may have to ask more than once. The goal is not just disclosure: It is to connect the affected person to supportive resources in the community.
- Remind them that trauma and violence have consequences, for their health and their family's health and well-being.
- Reassure them that safe spaces do exist. Many people in abusive relationships worry about their online and social reputation in their school community.
- Find community resources that advocate in culturally appropriate ways, such as an LGBTQIA+ organization or support services in the affected person's home language.

APPLY IT!   **13.3** Ruby's mother, Jill, wonders whether her daughter's growth spurts came too early. How might you reassure her that there is a wide variety of natural variation in the timing of puberty?

13.4 If you had to teach a group of children Rosie's age about puberty, what would be the first three things you would tell them?

13.5 Communities vary in their ethnotheories about adolescent sexuality. How would the principles of *cultural humility* dictate how you might talk to adolescents and their families about sex?

13.6 Talking about sex is often the hardest part of positive sexual development. How might you explain to young adolescents how to put feelings into words?

Developing Healthy Habits

Learning Objective

13.4 Explain the best ways for adolescents to maintain positive health.

For many, adolescence is a time when teenagers begin to take control of their own health choices, whether they begin adolescence with chronic conditions or with the blessing of good health. Rosie and Ruby are starting to keep track of their physical activity and how much they sleep, and they both know how to find snacks when they are hungry.

Eating on Their Own

Unlike younger children, adolescents can make more of their own decisions about where, when, and what they eat. Rosie and Ruby, for instance, bake on their own, although even Ruby is a bit intimidated by the responsibility of making dinner. Mostly they like to make cake. All that cooking helps them get the calories they need to build bones and muscles: Teenagers need more food than they will at any other time of their lifespan. During the peak of the growth spurt, adolescents need between 2,200 and about 2,800 calories a day (Das et al., 2018).

Most U.S. adolescents are eating enough, but the vast majority are not following healthy dietary guidelines: Their diets are too high in sugar and too low in micronutrients, fruits, and vegetables. Adolescents tend to get too many of their calories from sweetened sports drinks instead of vegetables and fruits (Merlo et al., 2020). Researchers are not the only ones who understand that the habits adolescents are building may last a lifetime: Intensive food-marketing efforts focused on teenagers are designed to foster loyalty to sweetened drinks and processed foods (Abarca-Gómez et al., 2017).

Developmental scientists have found that nagging adolescents to choose healthier habits does not work: Many teenagers do not want to be told what to do. Instead, one group of researchers educates young people about how food marketing aims to convince them that convenience foods are "cool." Adolescents told researchers that this awareness made them want to fight back and eat more healthily in the process (Bryan et al., 2019). The lesson? Adolescents want to be independent and respected: Intervention programs designed to harness their own decision-making powers may be more successful than those that do not recognize their capabilities.

Challenges of Body Size

Big picture social structures make it difficult for many teenagers around the world to maintain a healthy size. Physical activity is often something that gets squeezed into an already-busy day, instead of being integrated into everyday routines like walking to school. Food that is high in sugars, fats, and refined carbohydrates is often inexpensive, convenient, and highly advertised (Shultz et al., 2020). Global stigma, particularly the belief that people with unhealthy weight lack self-control, also make it more difficult to maintain a healthy size (Puhl et al., 2021; Reinka et al., 2021).

Share It!

Micronutrients are not something to skip out on. Low iron levels can tire you out. Experts estimate that as many as 1 in 10 adolescents who menstruate have low iron levels.

(Sekhar et al., 2017; Sun & Weaver, 2021)

Taking the "Cool" Out of Junk Food In one intervention program, teenagers were encouraged to mark up popular advertisements that encouraged them to eat unhealthily.

Remember from Chapter 7 that, while fewer children are undernourished around the globe, the numbers of children with heavier bodies are increasing worldwide because of a universal transition from traditional diets to processed foods high in fat and refined carbohydrates (Ameye & Swinnen, 2019; Popkin, 2021). Remember that researchers often use BMI and growth charts as rough measures of body size for populations, although how well those measures evaluate the health of people on the individual level has been questioned. This is particularly true during adolescence, when puberty can change body size quickly (Bomberg et al., 2021).

In looking at population health, there is scientific consensus on the correlation between *obesity*, which is defined as a BMI above 30 or a weight that is higher than about 97.5 percent of the median on a growth chart, and cardiovascular health complications (Twig et al., 2019; Wühl, 2019). By these measures, about one in five U.S. adolescents has obesity, along with about 6 out of every 100 adolescents worldwide (Bryan et al., 2021; Abarca-Gómez et al, 2017). Despite the imprecision of measuring body size, having a high weight in adolescence increases the likelihood of adverse outcomes, including diabetes and high blood pressure (Abarca-Gómez et al., 2017; Havers et al., 2021).

Being larger has an increased stigma in adolescence, as teenagers become more focused on their appearance and social relationships, and body size continues to result in exclusion, particularly for those who identify as girls (Farhat, 2015; Koyanagi et al., 2020; Martin-Storey et al., 2015; Morrissey et al., 2020). As a result of this stigma and exclusion, adolescents of larger size may experience depression and stress, and even get less sleep than their peers (Lacroix et al., 2020; Rao et al., 2020).

If adolescents and their families are concerned that their size poses a health risk, one way to help adolescents build a healthy weight is to enlist the help of the entire family (Roberts et al., 2021). *Family-based treatment*, in which an entire family works together to increase activity and eat a healthier diet, can be an effective way for adolescents to reach a healthier size (Cardel et al., 2020; Spruijt-Metz, 2011). Pediatricians recommend adopting small, incremental changes and a positive approach to body image and overall health, rather than harmful alternatives like dieting, which are typically ineffective and damaging to body image (Golden et al., 2016). Regardless of their size, adolescents need support to protect against teasing and to build self-acceptance in a world that often stigmatizes people who do not match media ideals (Lacroix et al., 2020).

Unhealthy Eating

As children move toward adulthood, their **body image**, or how they feel about their bodies, is closely tied to how they feel about themselves (Andrew et al., 2016). Teenagers often compare themselves to media images, such as photos of their friends on Instagram or famous actors in movies (Marengo et al., 2018; Salomon & Brown, 2019). The more time young people spend looking at idealized versions of the human body online, even if they know the images are manipulated, filtered, or enhanced, the more likely they are to feel badly about themselves (Vandenbosch et al., 2022). The people adolescents know in real life, including their peers, also make a difference: Being teased about your appearance is particularly likely to make adolescents feel badly about what they look like (Lacroix et al., 2022).

Particularly in early adolescence, and for those who identify as girls, as many as half of all teenagers are disappointed in how they look (Lacroix et al., 2020; Nelson et al., 2018). Adolescents' high standards for their appearance tend to appear across cultural communities (Blum et al., 2021). In affluent communities around the world, few adolescents are immune to poor body image or unhealthy eating habits (Espinoza et al., 2019; Hornberger et al., 2021).

The pressure to be attractive in adolescence and across the lifespan reflects common prejudices, sometimes referred to as *lookism*. In adolescence, people deemed

CONNECTIONS

Remember from Chapter 7 that the term *obesity* is stigmatizing even though it is used by scientists and health care providers. Scientists often prefer terms like *larger body size* when referring to people whose weight is in the high range, even though that language is often imprecise.

Share It!

Fighting body shame may begin with gratitude for the bodies we have. Researchers in Qatar found that writing thank-you notes to their bodies helped some young people build a healthier body image.

(O'Hara et al., 2021)

body image The feelings and ideas you have about your body.

CONNECTIONS

Psychological conditions often develop through an epigenetic process in which genetic vulnerabilities are triggered by environmental factors. Adolescents are particularly vulnerable to psychological conditions, as you will learn in Chapter 15. Psychological disorders also emerge in childhood, as you may remember from Chapters 9 and 12.

eating disorders Psychological conditions that are marked by long-term, unhealthy patterns of eating, obsessions with food, and poor body image that cause problems with the ability to function.

binge-eating disorder The most prevalent eating disorder in adolescents, marked by episodes of compulsive, excessive eating that make you feel out of control, ashamed, or upset.

bulimia nervosa A consistent pattern of disordered eating that involves overeating compensated by throwing up, excessive exercise, or abusing laxatives.

anorexia nervosa A consistent pattern of disordered eating that may involve extreme calorie restriction, purging, excessive exercise, and a distorted belief that one's body is overly heavy.

attractive tend to be perceived as more popular and even tend to do better in school (Gordon et al., 2013; Hamermesh et al., 2019; Pivnick et al., 2021). This "bias for the beautiful" continues into adulthood. Adults who are perceived as having socially desirable appearances tend to be more socially successful and earn more income over their lifetimes (Monk et al., 2021).

In the United States, almost 40 percent of teenagers who identify as girls and 15 percent of those who identify as boys engage in *disordered eating*, a broad category of behaviors that could range from regularly skipping meals, to making themselves throw up, to extreme dietary restrictions (Solmi, Sharpe, et al., 2021; YRBS, 2019). Adolescents who are larger than their peers and those who are transgender have a higher likelihood for disordered eating, in part because of the stigma and exclusion they face (Hornberger et al., 2021).

While disordered eating is fairly common, eating disorders are more serious and unusual. **Eating disorders** are psychological conditions marked by long-term, unhealthy patterns of eating, obsessions with food, and poor body image that cause problems with teenagers' ability to function in everyday life (APA, 2022; Hornberger et al., 2021). The social stresses of adolescence and cultures that value thinness make young people susceptible to eating disorders (Ferguson et al., 2014). As with most conditions, both genetic and environmental factors contribute to eating disorders (Bakalar et al., 2015; Culbert et al., 2015; Munn-Chernoff et al., 2021).

The most commonly diagnosed eating disorders in adolescence are *binge-eating disorder*, *bulimia nervosa*, and *anorexia nervosa*. Around the world, **binge-eating disorder** is the most prevalent eating disorder in adolescents, affecting as many as 5 in every 100 adolescents (Marzilli et al., 2018). It is marked by episodes of compulsive, excessive eating that make the person feel out of control, ashamed, or upset (APA, 2022).

Bulimia nervosa and **anorexia nervosa** occur in fewer than 1 percent of adolescents (Brodzki et al., 2018). Bulimia is a consistent pattern of disordered eating that involves behaviors like overeating compensated by throwing up, excessive exercise, or abusing laxatives (APA, 2022). Anorexia can involve similar extremes along with extreme calorie or food restriction and excessive exercise. Adolescents with anorexia diet to an unhealthy weight, yet still believe they are too heavy (APA, 2022). Those who have bulimia or anorexia are consumed with their weight and what they look like to the point that they can no longer function in their everyday lives in a healthy, productive way.

An eating disorder makes it difficult to enjoy and accomplish the important tasks of adolescence. The cost can be significant. Teenagers who have eating disorders are at higher risk for suicide and may continue to have difficulties with disordered eating as they grow up (Hornberger et al., 2021). Developmental researchers suggest that for most, family-based treatments are the most effective ways of building social support and treating eating disorders (Dalle Grave et al., 2021).

Staying Active

One way to improve body image and eating habits is to stay active (Mulgrew, 2020). For many teenagers, this often means finding time to exercise. By the time they reach early adolescence, children no longer run around for the joy of it. Fifth-graders play tag, whereas eighth-graders stand in circles talking. By the time adolescents get to high school, they are unlikely to have any recess time at all, which means even less activity.

In most parts of the world, adolescents become less active as they reach puberty (Trang et al., 2012; Van Hecke et al., 2016). The time they used to spend on the swings is now increasingly spent doing homework, working, visiting with friends, and clicking on

Swimming for Joy (and the Win) Paris (*center*) swims competitively near her home in Chicago and is even thinking of training for a triathlon. Working out with others on a team often helps young people stay active.

AP Photo/M. Spencer Green

their phones. Ruby and Rosie provide a dramatic example of this: Rosie has trouble staying still during school and is ready to dash outside as soon as she gets a break. But her older sister is happy to stay sedentary, for hours reading and clicking online.

To stay healthy, pediatricians recommend that adolescents get about 60 minutes of exercise every day (WHO, 2020a). However, fewer than 30 percent of adolescents in highly resourced countries, including the United States, get enough activity (Guthold et al., 2020; Steene-Johannessen et al., 2020). High-income teenagers and those who identify as boys are more likely to be getting their hour in every day, but lower-income adolescents who identify as girls are likely to be missing out, typically getting less than half the recommended time (Armstrong et al., 2018).

In adolescence, being active helps prevent depression and anxiety and boosts brain development (Belcher et al., 2021; Biddle et al., 2019). Exercise sharpens attention and focus and can even improve academic achievement (Belcher et al., 2021; Reigal et al., 2020). Staying active takes time and is easier if it is part of an everyday routine, whether that means biking to school or mowing lawns in the afternoon.

For many adolescents, regular activity comes in the form of organized exercise (UNICEF, 2019). Not all adolescents, however, have the opportunity to play. Some schools do not offer any athletic programs. Other schools may not have spots for all students or may charge fees that are unaffordable for some (NPAPA, 2018). For instance, one in three high schools located in high-poverty neighborhoods in the United States offers no sports at all, as compared to just one in six low-poverty neighborhood schools (Veliz et al., 2019).

Getting Enough Sleep

If you asked many adolescents what they could do to be happier, do better in school, and get along better at home, they would never guess that one thing is to simply get enough sleep. Most young people are trying to cram more things into their day, which prevents them from getting adequate sleep.

Adolescents function best with about 8 to 10 hours of sleep every night. But more than two in three U.S. high school students get fewer than eight hours a night (Park et al., 2019; Wheaton et al., 2018). Lack of sleep is a problem around the world (Gariepy et al., 2020). Indeed, in affluent communities in East Asia, nearly 9 out of 10 adolescents do not get enough sleep (Ong et al., 2019; Yeo et al., 2019). Sleep deprivation puts teenagers at risk: Sleep is important for the development of the adolescent brain and for overall physical and emotional health (Booth et al., 2021; Galván, 2020; Troxel & Wolfson, 2016). Simply getting enough rest makes it easier to manage the inevitable ups and downs of teenage life, from social stresses to community discrimination (Wang & Yip, 2020).

Developmental scientists have found that lack of sleep is associated with a long list of problems, including heightened anxiety, attention difficulties, and lower grades (Crowley et al., 2018; Gillen-O'Neel et al., 2013). Sleep deprivation is also linked to trouble with learning, higher levels of depression, trouble getting along with peers, emotion regulation difficulties, and even criminal behavior (Carskadon & Barker, 2020; McMakin et al., 2016; Telzer et al., 2013).

Adolescents have trouble with sleep because of what some researchers call a "perfect storm," in which their biology, which makes their sleep more flexible, collides with a culture that overloads, overschedules, and overstimulates them (Carskadon, 2011; Carskadon & Barker, 2020; Crowley et al., 2018; Leonard et al., 2021). At the beginning of puberty, adolescents' **circadian rhythm**, or their daily sleep-and-wake cycle, shifts so that they want to stay up later at night and sleep later in the morning. This is incompatible with school start times, which move earlier in the morning during middle and high school.

circadian rhythm A person's daily sleep-and-wake cycle.

Sometimes a Dirt Road Is Enough for Recreation. These teenagers have the week off to help with the potato harvest near their home in Aroostook County, Maine. As you can see here, they get physical activity from more than just digging potatoes.

Scientific American Profile

Sleep Changes

Up Too Early? Many young people still need to get on the school bus before dawn in order to get to class. Experts suggest that moving school start times later would improve their sleep, well-being, and grades.

One solution would be for high schools to start later, after 8:30 A.M., as required by a law that went into effect in the state of California in 2022 (Troxel & Wolfson, 2016). Students in schools that have moved to later start times enjoy better academic performance, higher quality sleep, and greater well-being (Berry et al., 2021). However, few schools have adopted later start times, and for many, even starting school at 8:30 might not give them enough sleep.

Experts recommend some simple interventions to help teenagers get more rest (Bonnar et al., 2015; Tarokh et al., 2016):

- Go to bed and wake up at the same time every day on weekdays *and* on weekends.
- Get some sunshine or bright light early in the morning to reset your internal clock.
- Avoid too much excitement, physical activity, bright light, and screen time an hour before bedtime.
- Leave electronic devices off to make sleeping through the night more likely.

 13.7 Ruby and Rosie are becoming better sleepers: They try to get at least nine hours of sleep a night. What are some of the benefits of this extra rest?

13.8 Some experts worry that an emphasis on appearance and the constant pressure of being connected on image-oriented social media makes it more likely for adolescents to feel badly about how they look. What are some solutions you might suggest to teenagers who want to feel better about themselves?

Wrapping It Up

LO 13.1 Define adolescence. (p. 319)

Adolescence is the transition that begins with the changes of puberty and ends when youth are recognized as adults. How long adolescence lasts is determined by the cultural context. In modern times, puberty often begins at age 9, and adolescence is said to end at around 18, but some argue that it may last until the mid-20s.

LO 13.2 Identify the biological changes of puberty. (p. 319)

Puberty is the biological process that transforms children into adults who can have children. It includes maturation of the reproductive organs, including the milestones of menarche and spermarche, development of secondary sex characteristics, and a growth spurt. Puberty is triggered by maturation in the ovaries and testes between ages 8 and 13 in children with ovaries and ages 9 and 14 in children with testes. It is triggered by hormones released by the HPG axis. In what is known as the secular trend, the age of menarche has gradually stabilized at around age 12. Common variations in pubertal timing are linked to genetics, environmental stress, pollution, and health. Stigma and prejudice based on appearance mean that some children who reach puberty early or late may face exclusion or social stresses.

LO 13.3 Explain healthy sexual development during adolescence. (p. 319)

Sexual desire begins with adrenarche and grows during puberty. Positive sexual practices include knowing how to communicate about sex and how to manage the risk of pregnancy and STI. In the United States, many teenagers have limited sex education. Many participate in a variety of sexual activities. Adolescents have high rates of STIs in part because they have difficulty talking with their partners about sexual practices.

LO 13.4 Explain the best ways for adolescents to maintain positive health. (p. 332)

Adolescents are building the ability to maintain their own health independently. They need extra nutrition to power their growth spurt. Stigma about body size is on the rise in adolescence, and many teenagers have poor body image. A few are diagnosed with eating disorders. Adolescents tend to be less active than younger children, but their physical and mental development benefits from getting about 60 minutes of exercise a day. Teenagers need 8 to 10 hours of sleep every night, but many are sleep-deprived, which can trigger a cascade of difficulties with growth, emotion regulation, and learning.

KEY TERMS

adolescence (p. 319)

puberty (p. 319)

HPG axis (p. 321)

testosterone (p. 321)

estrogen (p. 321)

growth spurt (p. 321)

menarche (p. 322)

spermarche (p. 322)

secular trend (p. 323)

sexually transmitted infection (STI) (p. 329)

body image (p. 333)

eating disorders (p. 334)

binge-eating disorder (p. 334)

bulimia nervosa (p. 334)

anorexia nervosa (p. 334)

circadian rhythm (p. 335)

CHECK YOUR LEARNING

1. Which of these is a marker for the end of adolescence?
   a) When teenagers get their drivers' license
   b) When adolescents move out of their parents' house
   c) When teenagers graduate high school
   d) When adolescents are recognized as adults by their community

2. What is the BEST way that families can prepare children for puberty?
   a) Consider hormone treatments if puberty seems late.
   b) Ignore the signs of puberty in their child.
   c) Make sure their child is making friends and knows what to expect.
   d) Tell their child they are now ready for adult responsibilities.

3. Difficulties with sleep during adolescence are caused by:
   a) lack of self-control and emotion regulation.
   b) genetic differences.
   c) cultural expectations and biological flexibility.
   d) poor parenting practices.

4. Which skill BEST helps adolescents develop positive sexual health?
   a) Strong communication skills
   b) Knowing how to abstain from sexual activity
   c) Avoiding online media
   d) Awareness of the dangers of STIs

5. Which tendency shapes adolescents' health habits as they mature?
   a) Stronger motivation to follow adults' health advice
   b) More mature ability to manage their own health habits
   c) Less interest in what health practices their friends and peers follow
   d) Declining interest in staying healthy

6. Many adolescents are sleep-deprived. How much sleep should adolescents plan to get each night?
   a) 6–7 hours
   b) 8–10 hours
   c) 10–12 hours
   d) There is no scientific consensus.

7. How is the timing of puberty shaped by biological, environmental, and genetic factors in many adolescents?

8. What are some possible impacts of pubertal timing for young adolescents? How is this an example of scientific consensus changing over time?

14 Cognitive Development in Adolescence

Brain and Cognitive Development

14.1 Identify important elements of brain maturation during adolescence.

14.2 Describe the fundamental changes in cognition during adolescence.

Learning In and Out of School

14.3 Describe strengths and challenges in secondary education.

14.4 Analyze group differences in academic achievement.

© Macmillan, Photo by Point Studio, Inc.

Akira is an award-winning high school debater from Boston, Massachusetts, who also loves to read mystery novels, play volleyball, and watch movies on Netflix. Akira's life is full. She is often busy with homework, debate preparation, and volleyball practice, but she still makes time to get pizza with friends after a tournament and to walk her dog.

Debate has helped Akira strengthen her speaking and analytical skills. A bigger vocabulary and greater stamina for a discussion makes her quite convincing in an argument, something that has impressed her mother. She is not afraid to share her opinions about homework, police brutality, and reproductive rights.

Akira says that debate inspired her to think about a career as a lawyer. She joined the debate team in sixth grade and quickly learned how to communicate effectively. While Akira credits debate for her ability to create a persuasive argument, developmental scientists may also credit adolescence itself.

Whether teenagers are programming video games or just playing them, they are learning new things and taking risks that enable them to thrive as more independent adults. Their brains are undergoing major refinement as the prefrontal cortex enters its final period of maturation, making thinking faster and more complex. The regions of the brain that process social and emotional information, including the reward system and cortical regions across the frontal, temporal, and parietal areas are also maturing, helping to make adolescents passionate about what they learn and intrigued by the social world around them.

As you will read, school is not the only place that prepares teenagers for adulthood. Relationships and opportunities outside of school, like Akira's experience in debate, also motivate teenagers to achieve the skills they need to become capable and competent adults, whether that is designing roller coasters, learning how to weld, or passing social studies.

Brain Development

From the outside, the changes in the brain during adolescence may not seem very dramatic. For instance, if you could view Akira's brain while she is studying history, it would not look very different at age 15 than when she was in middle school. In fact, her brain might even weigh a little bit less (Lenroot et al., 2007; Mills et al., 2016). However, on a microscopic level, Akira's brain is undergoing significant transformation.

Three major changes characterize brain development during adolescence: maturation of the prefrontal cortex, heightened activation of subcortical regions and systems, and enhanced connectivity between these subcortical systems and the prefrontal cortex. Together, these changes make the adolescent brain more *plastic*, or able to change and adapt as a function of life experience, than during adulthood (Guyer et al., 2018; Laube et al., 2020). This brain development helps make adolescence a sensitive period for learning, enabling adolescents to learn a tremendous amount as they prepare for what comes next (Fandakova & Hartley, 2020).

Developing Prefrontal Cortex

Adolescents can manage abstractions, solve chemical equations, and define the word *justice*. Akira can explain inequality and plan a presentation for her English class. Maturation in the cortex makes these cognitive skills easier to grasp in adolescence than they were in childhood (Dong et al., 2021; Knoll et al., 2015).

Remember that at the level of the neuron, brain maturation consists of three interconnected processes. First, *synaptogenesis* involves the creation of synapses, which connect neurons to each other. Second, *synaptic pruning* is the removal or pruning of underused synapses. Maturation also includes *myelination*, the growth of the fatty sheath that accelerates the signaling of neurons. Together, these processes allow for faster and more efficient signaling within the developing brain. In the teenage years, all three processes are supercharged as the brain is reshaped, leading to the increased cognitive abilities of adolescents (Ismail et al., 2017).

Some of the most significant reshaping of the brain happens in the *prefrontal cortex (PFC)*—the region linked to conscious control of our behavior and thinking (Ando et al., 2021; Corrigan et al., 2021). Triggered by puberty, nearly half of an adolescents' synaptic connections will be replaced by millions of new, faster, myelinated ones (Selemon, 2013; Vijayakumar et al., 2021a). Faster connections mean quicker processing and learning and that the amount of *white matter*, or the myelinated axons of brain cells, increases dramatically. At the same time, the amount of *gray matter*, including brain cell bodies and synapses, decreases as unused connections are pruned away (Vijayakumar et al., 2018; see **Infographic 14.1**). Both pruning and myelination make the brain more efficient as communication becomes faster and more direct. These processes are one reason adolescents can develop such impressive memory, problem-solving, abstract reasoning, and planning skills (Fuhrmann et al., 2015).

The timing of puberty affects how and when the brain matures: The hormones that are active during puberty shape brain maturation. This means, for instance, that teenagers who experience hormonal changes more quickly tend to show characteristic cortical pruning and subcortical development more quickly as well (Vijayakumar et al., 2021a, 2021b). Individual life experiences also shape the brain, as they do across the lifespan: Adverse experiences and stress seem to accelerate brain development, particularly in early adolescence (Rakesh et al., 2021).

Learning Objectives

14.1 Identify important elements of brain maturation during adolescence.

14.2 Describe the fundamental changes in cognition during adolescence.

CONNECTIONS

Remember from Chapters 10 and 13 that hormones, including DHEA, estrogen, and testosterone, are secreted in larger amounts during adrenarche and puberty and help to reshape neural circuits in the brain and help mature the body.

Three major changes characterize brain development during adolescence: maturation of the prefrontal cortex, heightened activation of the subcortical regions and systems, and enhanced connectivity between these subcortical systems and the prefrontal cortex. The brain is particularly flexible during adolescence, helping to power adolescents' ability to learn and adjust to the adult world.

SCULPTING THE CORTEX

During adolescence, myelination and growth continue in the prefrontal cortex (PFC), and thinning continues in the brain, particularly in the other sections of the cortex, such as the parietal lobe.

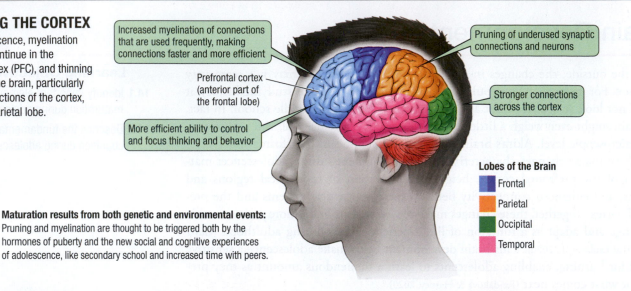

Increased myelination of connections that are used frequently, making connections faster and more efficient

Pruning of underused synaptic connections and neurons

Prefrontal cortex (anterior part of the frontal lobe)

Stronger connections across the cortex

More efficient ability to control and focus thinking and behavior

Lobes of the Brain
- Frontal
- Parietal
- Occipital
- Temporal

Maturation results from both genetic and environmental events: Pruning and myelination are thought to be triggered both by the hormones of puberty and the new social and cognitive experiences of adolescence, like secondary school and increased time with peers.

INCREASED ACTIVITY IN SUBCORTICAL SYSTEMS

During adolescence, maturation continues in the subcortical structures. The reward circuit matures and is particularly sensitive to and filled with higher levels of dopamine, the neurotransmitter associated with learning and reward. These developments allow young people to develop better emotion regulation, social skills, and an increased likelihood to be motivated by social experiences.

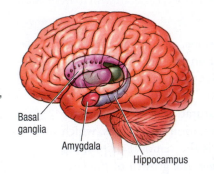

Basal ganglia
Amygdala
Hippocampus

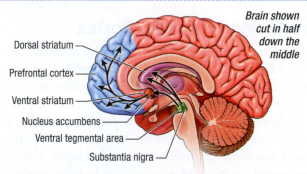

Brain shown cut in half down the middle

Dorsal striatum
Prefrontal cortex
Ventral striatum
Nucleus accumbens
Ventral tegmental area
Substantia nigra

The Reward Circuit (also known as the dopamine system) links many regions of the brain, including the dorsal and ventral striatum in the basal ganglia, with other regions, including the ventral tegmental area in the midbrain. The nucleus accumbens, a component of the ventral striatum, is linked to decision making about behaviors that tend to lead to pleasure and rewards.

MATURING CONNECTIONS ACROSS THE BRAIN

Connections continue to mature between the prefrontal cortex and subcortical structures of the social-emotional brain, such as the amygdala. These stronger connections allow more control and regulation of emotions.

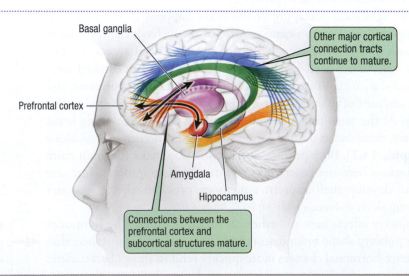

Basal ganglia

Other major cortical connection tracts continue to mature.

Prefrontal cortex

Amygdala

Hippocampus

Connections between the prefrontal cortex and subcortical structures mature.

Active Subcortical Structures

Brain development is not just about the changes that make Akira's thinking sophisticated enough to understand algebra or pick up nuances in *The Bluest Eye*. In adolescence, changes in the brain are also linked to how teenagers manage their emotions and develop social skills. The hormones of puberty trigger new activity, growth, and increased responsiveness in the subcortical structures of the brain that are devoted to processing emotion, motivation, and rewards (Casey et al., 2019; Shulman et al., 2016).

Changes in these structures help explain some of the characteristics of many adolescents. Young people tend to have more intense emotions than younger children do; teenagers' emotions are often linked to their social world; and they are motivated to learn and try new things (McLaughlin et al., 2015; van Hoorn et al., 2019). Neuroscientists believe the maturation of adolescents' subcortical structures helps adolescents develop the social skills, motivation, and emotion regulation they need for adulthood. In turn, these skills and the brain structures that support the skills are also shaped by teenagers' life experiences as they mature (Dahl et al., 2018).

One region in the subcortical brain activated during adolescence is the *reward system* or *circuit* (Galván, 2013; Schreuders et al., 2018). The reward system connects brain regions including the *dorsal* and *ventral striatum*, small structures inside the basal ganglia (see **Infographic 14.1**). This set of tiny structures is what is activated when we think about pleasure, whether it is winning a video game or enjoying ice cream afterward. Scientists have observed that this region tends to be activated when we are making decisions about behaviors that are likely to lead to pleasure and other rewards (Floresco, 2015). Scientists studying adolescents in the laboratory find that what motivates or excites teenagers is different than for younger children. Unsurprisingly, teenagers are more interested in social rewards, like winning a game or impressing their friends, or even getting "likes" on social media, than younger children are (Galván, 2013; Sherman et al., 2018).

The responsiveness of the reward system has to do with the neurotransmitter *dopamine*, which plays a role in feeling pleasure and in more intangible things that make you feel good, such as likes on your Instagram post or a deposit in your bank account (Galván, 2017). Adolescents have more dopamine in their reward systems than adults or children do, up to seven times more than children according to some estimates (Spear, 2013). They are also more responsive to the dopamine they have (Baker & Galván, 2020). So, when Akira is excited thinking about an upcoming tournament, she probably feels more excitement and pleasure than her mother would.

What *Can't* an Adolescent Brain Do? Adolescents working together can be amazing. One team of girls from Afghanistan won a silver medal in a robotics competition in 2017, defying gender stereotypes. A group of high school students from Carl Hayden Community High School in West Phoenix, Arizona, beat a team of college students in another competition—even though they had only $800 to build their project (as compared to more than $11,000 for the other team).

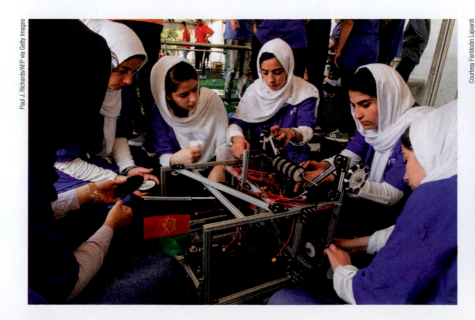

exploratory learning Trying out different ways to solve a problem before deciding on the best solution.

concussion A form of traumatic brain injury (TBI) caused by a blow to the head.

The maturation of the reward circuit intensifies adolescents' motivation to learn and solve problems. Teenagers are motivated to try new things and explore alternatives because these activities bring them pleasure (Davidow et al., 2018). Studies have suggested that teenagers are better than both children and adults at what is called **exploratory learning**, or trying out different ways to solve a problem before deciding on the best solution (Davidow et al., 2016; Somerville et al., 2017). By trying different options and making mistakes early, teenagers can find the best solution more easily than adults can.

Maturing Brain Networks

Although it is sometimes helpful to think about structures or circuits in the brain individually, none of these function in isolation from one another. Remember from Chapter 7 that the brain is an interconnected system of networks called the *connectome*. Scientists are particularly interested in the maturation of the connections between our subcortical structures and the prefrontal cortex during adolescence, because they are linked to our emotion regulation and decision-making skills (Galván, 2017). These networks link the conscious, logical processing in the brain with the regions devoted to emotional processing, shaping how we react to emotional experiences and how our experiences trigger our emotional reactions. The maturation of these networks is a long process and is not complete until our mid- or even late-20s (Casey et al., 2019; Romer et al., 2017; Steinberg & Icenogle, 2019).

Remember from Chapter 10 that, as these networks mature during middle childhood, neural signals primarily run from the subcortical structures to the PFC, allowing children's emotions to shape their decision-making while also contributing to some of children's typical difficulties with emotion regulation (Kopala-Sibley et al., 2020; Thijssen et al., 2017). During adolescence, the direction shifts: Neural connections begin to run between the PFC to the subcortical structures. In essence, the PFC starts to manage the information it is receiving from the subcortical structures (Casey et al., 2019; Gee et al., 2014; Tottenham & Gabard-Durnam, 2017). This allows the PFC to both respond to and guide how feelings are processed, enabling adolescents to use cognitive strategies to reframe their emotions, control their motivation, and focus on long-term pleasures.

MAKING A DIFFERENCE
Protecting Adolescents from Brain Injury

Madeline Uretsky considered herself strong and capable. She played soccer, ice hockey, and two seasons of track, but all of this changed during one soccer game.

Passing the Help Along Madeline is still recovering from the effects of concussions she had as an adolescent but is now working to help other young people recover from the impact of head injuries.

Madeline cannot remember that day very well. Her friends told her she tumbled to the ground, and her head whiplashed, swinging back and forth hard. It soon became apparent that Madeline had experienced a severe concussion. For months she had terrible headaches, dizziness, sensitivity to noise, bright lights hurt her eyes, and she couldn't keep track of what day it was. Ten years later, there are still times when she doesn't feel quite right; Madeline has to bring sunglasses wherever she goes to keep her headaches at bay, she has attention difficulties and changes in the weather cause extreme fatigue (Uretsky, 2021; Weintraub, 2013).

In the United States, nearly one in four adolescents, like Madeline, report that they have experienced a **concussion**, a form of *traumatic brain injury (TBI)* caused by a blow to the head (Veliz et al., 2021). A few decades ago, pediatricians and scientists believed that brain injuries during adolescence were not very serious and that concussions would not cause long-term challenges for most (Martini et al., 2017; Redelmeier & Raza, 2016). However, developmental scientists have helped demonstrate that concussions and other TBIs can cause lasting challenges for teenagers, including problems with executive function, emotion regulation, and attention (Christensen et al., 2021).

The rapid development of the adolescent brain makes it more vulnerable to trauma and injury. A TBI can derail development, since the brain has to spend energy on repair rather than on building new neural connections (Brett et al., 2020; Taylor et al., 2018). Adolescent concussions have been linked to greater risk for degenerative diseases like multiple sclerosis, amyotrophic lateral sclerosis (ALS), and *chronic traumatic encephalopathy (CTE)*, a debilitating condition that can result in significant mood changes and cognitive problems (Caffey & Dalecki, 2021; Hornbeck et al., 2017; Povolo et al., 2021).

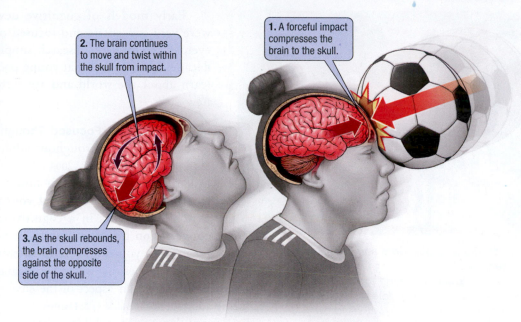

FIGURE 14.1 Brain Injury, Step by Step A concussion is the term for a mild brain injury caused by a blow to the head. Our brains may be able to recover, but injuries can cause long-term difficulties, particularly during a time of rapid development like adolescence.

Concussions cause breakages in the cell walls of individual neurons as the entire brain is rocked, rotated, or rushed from side to side, and cause widespread inflammation (see **Figure 14.1**). For instance, Madeline's brain was injured both at the point of impact (when her head hit the ground) and also on its opposite side (when it was bruised as it banged against the back of her skull). The immediate effects of a concussion, like feeling spacey or dizzy, typically resolve within a few weeks, but about one in four teenagers does not get better right away (Lima Santos et al., 2021).

As was the case for Madeline, many head injuries come from sports, but concussions often also result from car accidents or assaults (Dufour et al., 2020; Haarbauer-Krupa et al., 2018). Some experts have suggested that young people avoid high-risk sports or change the rules to make them less dangerous (Hornbeck et al., 2017; Piedade et al., 2021). Particularly dangerous sports include football, hockey, martial arts, boxing, field hockey, and soccer (Halstead et al., 2018). Some evidence indicates that young women, like Madeline, may be particularly susceptible to brain injuries because of variations in neck strength or hormones (Sanderson, 2021).

Adolescents who experience a brain injury often face a long recovery. After months of rehab, Madeline was finally able to leave her darkened room, go back to school, and, step by step, start rebuilding her life. Her experience with concussions ignited her interest in neuroscience, and she wants to help prevent and treat head trauma in young athletes (Uretsky, 2021).

Cognitive Development

Maturation of the brain, as well as years of practice, brings dramatic enhancements to teenagers' cognitive abilities, including faster thinking and an improved ability to focus. Adolescents are now able to grasp abstractions and make wise decisions in everyday life, which is why they can be trusted to drive a car or babysit overnight. Reasoning ability becomes more logical, meaning that adolescents can more easily work through a problem using formal operational thought and make decisions using analytic problem-solving skills.

Steven St.John; Spaceport America

Credit Goes to Boredom and Teenage Ingenuity. Joshua (holding the rocket) had a summer without enough to do, so he connected with other adolescents online. The result: Joshua, along with Andrew (kneeling) and Saad (standing), built a rocket that they launched at a facility in New Mexico called Spaceport America.

Share It!

Skip the marijuana for the sake of your information processing. Scientific consensus agrees that cannabis will not help your learning abilities or your processing speed.

(Lorenzetti et al., 2020)

formal operational thought Piaget's stage of cognitive development that begins in early adolescence and lasts into adulthood and is both logical and abstract.

Early models of cognitive development suggested that adolescents were very egocentric and focused on their own selves (Elkind, 1967). However, little empirical research supported this. Research over the past two decades has revealed that young people are very sophisticated in how they learn about the world and are extremely motivated to explore and learn new tasks.

Faster and More Focused Thought The ability to process information quickly increases throughout adolescence and into early adulthood (Kail & Ferrer, 2007; Luna et al., 2004). Remember from Chapter 5 that researchers call this *processing speed*, or how rapidly you can respond to something, whether that is the sound of your name being called across the room or matching patterns in a cognitive test. In school or even in a dynamic conversation between friends, being able to process information quickly means that you can keep up when new material is presented.

Remember that in developmental science, *attention* refers to the ability to focus on one particular aspect of the environment. For many, this ability improves during adolescence (Fandakova & Hartley, 2020; Kuhn, 2009). Teenagers are better at ignoring distractions than younger children. It is easier for them to pay attention to one sound in a sea of noise, like a teacher's voice in a crowded auditorium filled with coughs, whispers, and cell phone vibrations (Karns et al., 2015).

Working memory, or the ability to keep track of what you can quickly hold in your mind before storing it long-term memory, improves throughout adolescence (Andre et al., 2016; Embury et al., 2019; Linares et al., 2016). Adolescents have stronger memory skills than younger children, although their sensitivity to social cues may sometimes interfere in social situations. Some studies have even shown that teenagers have trouble remembering something as simple as a three-digit number if they are stressed or excited by a social situation (Mills et al., 2015).

Formal Operational Thought Remember that developmental scientists like Jean Piaget view cognitive development as a series of discrete periods. In adolescence, Piaget focused on adolescents' ability to think abstractly about big, hard-to-define topics such as peace, love, or fate, and to go a step further and imagine not just a single abstraction, but what one abstraction could do to another. Piaget called the stage that begins in early adolescence and continues into adulthood **formal operational thought** (Inhelder & Piaget, 1958). The key characteristics of formal operational thinking are that it is both logical *and* abstract (see **Table 14.1**).

Piaget used a practical device to measure the changes in adolescents' thinking: a balance scale (see **Figure 14.2**). Before every grocery store had a scanner, post offices and fruit sellers used balance scales to measure the weight of packages or produce. With his colleague Bärbel Inhelder, Piaget used this balance scale to assess if adolescents could make hypotheses and logically test them out.

To balance a scale, the weights on both sides need to be equal. However, you can also balance the scale by adjusting the weights so that the heavier weights are

TABLE 14.1 Piaget's Stage of Formal Operational Thought

Stage	Age	Characteristics
Formal operational thought	About 11 through adulthood	Children and adults can think abstractly and apply logical concepts to other logical concepts.

aer

Chapter 14 • Cognitive Development in Adolescence   345

farther away from the center of the scale, or the *fulcrum*, and the lighter weights are closer.

Younger children are unable to systematically figure out how the scale works, but older children and adolescents begin to figure out how to solve the problem. Some, particularly those in the concrete operational stage, may use trial-and-error in their reasoning by randomly placing the weights at various points on the scale. But adolescents in the formal operational stage will be systematic in figuring out the balance scale: They can make predictions, test them out, and use words or symbols to explain their thinking. Piaget predicted that most children would be able to figure out how the balance scale works by age 12.

Despite Piaget's predictions, many adults and teenagers do not use formal operational thought and have difficulty explaining how a balance scale works (Capon & Kuhn, 1982; Flynn & Shayer, 2018; Shayer & Ginsburg, 2009). Scientists now believe that achieving formal operational thought and using it all the time require significant motivation and a particular type of education (Commons & Davidson, 2015). Most adults make everyday decisions, like what kind of snack to buy or even who to vote for, by habit and impulse rather than with their logical thinking skills. As a result, many developmentalists believe that although reasoning ability *can* become more sophisticated in adolescence, people will not always use it consistently or think analytically or abstractly outside laboratory or classroom settings (Kokis et al., 2002; Siegler, 2016).

Analytical and Heuristic Thought Piaget was not the only developmental scientist who noticed adolescents' thinking becoming more logical. Other researchers noticed that there are multiple components to teenagers' reasoning abilities. For instance, adolescents working on an algebraic equation to solve the balance-scale problem are using **analytic thinking**, a type of thinking that is logical, weighing evidence and making a decision that requires conscious thought. (See **Infographic 14.2**.) Researchers also identified an additional type of advanced reasoning that we use across the lifespan: **heuristic thinking**, which is the automatic thinking that you do outside of consciousness (Herbert, 2010). Heuristic thinking can be useful, as when you walk to your bus stop without consciously thinking about how to get there or driving to work without paying close attention to street names. In some ways, this represents the beginning of what may be called "wisdom" in adults much older: Adolescents' accumulation of experience helps them make quicker and more informed decisions (Romer et al., 2017).

When researchers ask adolescents to solve complex problems, older adolescents are more likely to use analytical thinking than are younger ones, who are more likely to use more impulsive, heuristic thinking (Felmban & Klaczynski, 2019; Klaczynski, 2014; Kokis et al., 2002). These analytical skills will be useful in school. Students who are able to think analytically perform better on the logical and abstract thinking tasks that school requires, from understanding all the reasons for the Civil War to completing biology.

But heuristic thinking is not without its benefits. Sometimes analytical thinking cannot help you with a problem, as when you are trying to figure out what advice to give a friend who is upset or decide what you want to do with your life. Adolescents, like adults, tend to switch to heuristic thinking particularly when they are in emotional or social situations, such as when they are upset or when they are with peers (Crone & Dahl, 2012; Somerville et al., 2010). As adolescents gain more experience in the world, they get better at finding the essence of real-life questions and getting to the "gist" of things (Reyna & Panagiotopoulos, 2020).

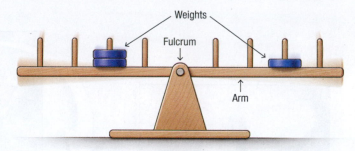

FIGURE 14.2 Can You Balance the Scale? A younger child might experiment randomly, but as children use formal operational thought, they are increasingly able to use abstract ideas to describe the relationship between distance and weight that is necessary to balance the scale.

analytic thinking A type of thinking that is logical, weighing evidence and making a decision that requires conscious thought.

heuristic thinking A type of advanced reasoning, which is automatic thinking that you do outside of consciousness.

1. Cognitive Development Is Linked to Brain Development
Heightened plasticity is influenced by the timing and hormones of puberty. It is driven by 1) maturation of the prefrontal cortex; 2) increased activation of subcortical regions and systems responsible for emotional processing; and 3) enhanced connectivity between these subcortical systems and the prefrontal cortex.

Adolescents are motivated to learn, and their learning is shaped by social and emotional experiences.

Timing of puberty influences brain maturation.

6. Culture and Environmental Context for Cognitive Development
In adolescence, as across the lifespan, how we think is shaped by environmental influences ranging from our health to what we do every day. Cultural practices and opportunities shape adolescents' thinking skills.

2. Analytic and Heuristic Thinking
Adolescents can use analytic thinking, logical based on conscious thought, or heuristic thinking, the automatic thinking that occurs outside of conscious awareness. They learn how to use their analytic thinking in context, such as at school, when it is appropriate for problem-solving.

5. The Impact of School
School is a major context for building analytic and formal operational skills. School typically helps to foster logical thinking but works most effectively when it is tied to the unique ways adolescents learn, allowing them autonomy, strong relationships, and a sense of purpose and meaning.

3. Formal Operations
Piaget's stage of formal operations is the final stage in his theory of cognitive development. The key characteristics of formal operational thinking are that it is both logical and abstract.

Cognitive development is typically tied to young people accomplishing the tasks expected of their culture.

4. Information Processing
Adolescents typically have faster processing speed, more focused attention skills, and stronger working memory than younger children. Their information processing and executive function skills are highly linked to their social and emotional environment.

Adolescents typically have the ability to follow complex rules, whether for a video game or how to behave in school.

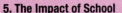

APPLY IT! **14.1** Scientists call adolescence a sensitive period for brain development. How does brain development help teenagers as they grow into adult roles?
14.2 How are teenagers' brains more sensitive to reward and emotional input than adults' brains are?
14.3 Akira is preparing for a debate about U.S. foreign policy in Ukraine. How does this abstract work represent Piaget's stage of formal operational thought?
14.4 Akira feels that she is more efficient at learning than she used to be. How does this reflect gains in information-processing skills?

Learning In and Out of School

Brain development and cognitive maturation make adolescence a particularly sensitive time for learning: It is now easier and more efficient to learn new skills (Romer et al., 2017). What teenagers learn in adolescence, whether it is how to navigate friendships, how to concentrate, or how to write a five-paragraph essay, will shape them and provide a foundation for their development for years to come. You may think of learning as something that happens in school, but formal education is just one way that adolescents build their capabilities.

Learning Objectives

14.3 Describe strengths and challenges in secondary education.

14.4 Analyze group differences in academic achievement.

The Growth of Secondary Schools

From the beginning of written history, some adolescents, mostly wealthy boys, had the opportunity to spend their adolescent years in formal education. Around the world, these elite teenagers practiced their writing skills and studied law, religion, or even astrology (Kinney, 2004; Scherer, 2015). *Secondary school* is the formal name for middle and high schools designed for young people who have finished elementary or primary school at about age 11 or 12. For communities around the world, secondary schools help to create an educated workforce and are linked to economic growth (Goldin, 1998). But secondary schools are not just beneficial to communities: They are also good for the adolescents who attend them.

Universal high schools are a relatively recent U.S. invention. In the early twentieth century, fewer than 1 in 10 teenagers attended high schools in the United States; most were boys, and all were wealthy. High school was designed to teach them the specialized skills, like fluency in ancient Greek, that they would need to study in universities (Goldin, 1998). Less privileged adolescents were likely to leave school in their early teens and enter the workforce. Some may have been lucky enough to secure an apprenticeship to learn a skilled trade. Others might have joined the legions of less formally trained farmers and factory workers. Most girls left school to work at home, helping raise their siblings or beginning a family of their own (Mintz, 2004).

It was not until the 1950s that more than half of all U.S. teenagers graduated from high school (Goldin, 1998). This idea soon took hold elsewhere (Goldin & Katz, 1997). After World War II, many affluent nations in Europe and around the world also began to require that adolescents stay in school until they were in their late teens, a prospect designed to build workers who could thrive in a more challenging job environment. Today, high school education has become the norm worldwide. Low-income countries still lag wealthier countries in high school enrollment but

AP Photo/The Huntsville Times, Glenn Baeske

Getting Ready for Space These students from Col. Nuestra Señora del Perpetuo Socorro High School in Puerto Rico created their own self-propelled rover, designed to use in space. They rode it and came in second, to another team from Puerto Rico, in an international competition in Huntsville, Alabama.

now more than three in four adolescents are enrolled in some kind of secondary school (UNESCO, 2022).

Secondary education has been linked to a host of benefits for communities. High schools create an educated workforce and are linked to economic growth. Researchers credit the early drive for secondary education in the United States for its establishment as a superpower in the twentieth century (Goldin, 1998). Contemporary researchers link the rise in secondary school enrollments in nations such as Japan, Korea, and Singapore with their strengthening economies in the last generation (Fukao, 2021).

Secondary schools typically benefit adolescents, too. Going to high school is associated with boosting cognitive skills, postponing family formation, and improving financial potential (Rasmussen et al., 2019; Sheehan et al., 2017). School also helps build social connections: The longer adolescents stay in school, the more likely they are as adults to have strong friendships, someone to rely on in an emergency, and a place to volunteer in their communities (OECD, 2021b). Researchers suggest that encouraging more teenagers to stay in school may be the best investment in improving the well-being of adolescents and adults around the world (Chalasani et al., 2019; Sheehan et al., 2017).

Varieties of Secondary Schools

Secondary schools around the world have diverse curricula that reflect local values. Some focus on preparing adolescents for college; many are more focused on preparing young people for work. Variations abound. For instance, schools may include religious training, such as in Saudi Arabia, or military training, such as in Eritrea (Human Rights Watch, 2019; Omar, 2020).

Secondary education in the United States is typically divided into *middle schools,* which serve students from about sixth through eighth grades, and *high schools,* which serve children from ninth through twelfth grades. Most U.S. students attend **comprehensive high schools**, a form of secondary education that serves a broad range of adolescents, regardless of their academic ability and future plans. Comprehensive high schools offer four years of broad-ranging education in math, history, English, and science. They are designed to help prepare adolescents for adult work that requires them to write clearly, read a technical manual, and know how diseases are transmitted. Acquiring this wide range of skills will help teenagers succeed in a wide variety of careers in manufacturing, health care, and the service sector (Goldin & Katz, 2008; NASEM, 2019).

The U.S. commitment to comprehensive universal high school is relatively unique. In many other affluent countries in Europe and Asia, students are *tracked,* or separated early in their academic careers by their interests and abilities, and attend schools focused on either academic preparation for college or career training. Many of these career-oriented schools offer high-quality **career and technical education (CTE)**, often called *vocational education* in the United States. In Europe and Asia, CTE is highly prized, and more than 4 in 10 students choose a vocational track because it often leads to earnings that are similar to those of an academic track (OECD, 2021b). Globally, access to CTE is limited: In areas of South Asia and sub-Saharan Africa, only 1 in every 100 has access to formal vocational education (UNESCO, 2022).

Interest in career and technical education is having a resurgence in the United States (Jacob, 2017; Rosen et al., 2018). Policy makers agree that the idea that all adolescents should go to college has not served everyone well, particularly those who do not graduate from college, end up saddled with burdensome student loans, or have difficulties finding high-paying jobs (Jacob, 2017). The CTE high schools that are becoming

Building Digital Literacy Around the world, understanding how to work with computers, online information, and the internet is an essential part of becoming a successful adult. These adolescents in Butare, Rwanda, are getting a head start by learning about computers in school.

comprehensive high schools Traditional high schools that are designed to meet the needs of adolescents who plan on attending college and those who do not, including a broad variety of academic courses and a limited selection of vocational courses.

career and technical education (CTE) Education that focuses on preparation for a trade, technical, or professional career. (Often called *vocational education* in the United States.)

more common in the United States are different from the vocational schools of the past. Their academic *and* technical standards are higher, giving students better preparation for a changing economy whether they choose to go to a four-year college, get a two-year degree, or seek more technical training.

These programs often require substantial investment from the community: They often have a lower student-to-teacher ratio than typical high schools and are filled with up-to-date technological equipment (Dougherty & Smith, 2022). However, when researchers have tracked students over time, they have found that these schools are more likely to help students find well-paying work after they leave high school (Afranie & Clagett, 2020). In some cases, CTE high schools even encourage more students to go to college, particularly if they are planning on going into fields like education or health care (Ecton & Dougherty, 2021).

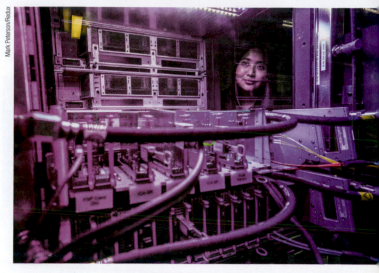

Measuring Effectiveness

While more students have access to secondary schooling than they did in the past, only about 4 in 10 adolescents around the globe have acquired the reading, writing, math, and digital literacy skills experts believe are necessary for adult achievement in a world that requires young people to read, write, and have some digital literacy (The Education Commission & UNICEF, 2022). Young adults with these skills tend to live in high-income countries or communities, including the United States.

Most young people in the United States read books that are in about the sixth-grade level, meaning that they can comprehend a novel like those in the Harry Potter series but may not be able to perform complicated analyses on texts or comfortably read Shakespeare or college textbooks like this one (Renaissance Learning, 2022). Most can do basic addition and subtraction but have difficulty with fractions, percentages, and statistics. This means that the many U.S. high school students (and adults) do not read or do math on what educators consider grade level (Rothwell, 2020). On tests of reading and math, about 4 in 10 U.S. high school seniors are not performing at the basic level in math, and 3 in 10 are not performing at the basic level in reading (U.S. Department of Education, 2020a).

Over the past few years, researchers have found that there is an increasing divide in student achievement in the United States. On the one hand, more students are taking advanced classes, like Advanced Placement English, than they were in the past (College Board, 2022; U.S. Department of Education, 2019a). The scores of students who are in the top 10 percent of high school students are higher than they were in the past. However, there are also more who are performing below expectations—and their scores are dropping (U.S. Department of Education, 2020a). The COVID-19 pandemic exacerbated these trends: Early reports suggest that U.S. adolescents' test scores have fallen as a result of the pandemic, particularly in math (Kuhfeld & Lewis, 2022). Adolescents with disabilities and mental health conditions, those who were caregiving for family members, and those who were low-income or English learners were most likely to fall behind in their learning as a result of the COVID-19 pandemic, particularly if they attended school remotely (Goldhaber et al., 2022). These scores may concern experts, but adolescents themselves remain positive and hopeful. In the United States, most were not worried about the academic impact of the pandemic, although many of them preferred learning in person to the isolation of being remote (Anderson et al., 2022).

Remember from Chapter 11 that schools around the world are commonly compared in terms of how their students perform on achievement tests. On

CTE Works. Suriana Rodriguez graduated high school in Newburgh, New York, with a high school diploma, an associate's degree, and a full-time job at a technology company. Her CTE program allowed her to combine high school and technical education.

Share It!

Being able to read this is privilege. Most young people around the globe can read in at least one language, but in low-income countries, one in four adolescents has not yet learned to read.

(ICFE, 2021)

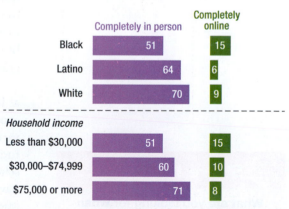

Information from Anderson et al., 2022.

FIGURE 14.3 Online or Remote? In the United States, most adolescents preferred to go to school in person, although there were significant disparities based on income and ethnicity in some surveys, including this one from 2022. Young people from communities that were more adversely affected by the pandemic appeared to be more concerned about returning to in-person school.

FIGURE 14.4 Comparing Student Learning In selected schools around the globe, 15-year-olds take a test known as the *Program For International Student Assessment (PISA)*. Their performance on tests of reading, math and science, is used to compare student achievement between nations and communities around the globe. This figure shows the performance of North American students in 2018, along with those from a variety of other high- and middle-income nations.

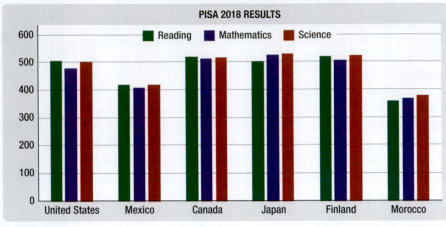

Data from OECD, 2020.

international tests, U.S. secondary school students typically score in the average or lower-average range, often behind other wealthy nations like Japan, the Netherlands, and Canada, as you can see in **Figure 14.4** (OECD, 2021c; Whitehurst, 2018). However, these averages mask the great diversity in student outcomes within the United States. For instance, teenagers in the relatively affluent state of Massachusetts are some of the highest scorers in the world, but adolescents in lower-income states tend to score much lower (OECD, 2015). Many researchers have connected lagging U.S. scores to high levels of poverty and inequality and unequal funding of schools: Low-income students in the United States tend to attend different schools than their high-income peers, in what is often referred to as economic segregation (Jang & Reardon, 2019; Rowley et al., 2020; Workman, 2022).

Achievement in high school and test scores, in the United States and across the globe, tend to relate to students' economic success in adulthood: Students who get higher scores on academic achievement tests are more likely to find work and are better paid as adults, whether they go to college or directly into the workforce (Goldhaber & Özek, 2019). Students who score higher on achievement tests are more likely to go on to college, as do about 7 in 10 U.S. students, and to graduate from college with a degree (Petrilli, 2016; U.S. Department of Education, 2020a). These associations are correlations, however: Young people's success in finding work and a stable adult life is often linked to other factors, including their family's economic status, more than simple achievement test scores (Carnevale et al., 2019). Feeling like you belong in school and are accepted by your community also affect how well students do both in school and after you graduate (Allen et al., 2018).

Schools vary in their effectiveness in helping students score well on tests as well as in other measures, like whether young people find work, delay starting a family, or avoid interactions with the criminal justice system (Jackson, 2021). Researchers have used various methods to study how effective schools can be. Some have conducted longitudinal studies that track students over time, looking for correlations between the schools they have attended and their adult well-being (Beuermann & Jackson, 2022). Others have watched what happens when students are randomly assigned to schools, after tracking students who were assigned by a lottery (Angrist et al., 2016; Deming et al., 2014).

These studies have found that schools do matter: One study of students randomized to attend charter schools in Boston found that some schools increased the number of students going to four-year colleges by more than 17 percent (Angrist et al., 2016). Researchers looking at random assignments within the Chicago public schools found significant variation in whether students graduated high school, went to college, and interacted with the criminal justice system, effects that were particularly powerful for students who tended to have lower test scores (Jackson et al., 2020).

CONNECTIONS

Remember from Chapter 1 that the *ecological fallacy* reminds us that what is true for a large group is not always true for an individual (Piantadosi et al., 1988). Group differences often mask tremendous individual variation.

Share It!

What are you looking for when you choose a high school? In regions with school choice, families often focus first on who else is signed up — before looking at test scores, college enrollments, or graduation rates.

(Abdulkadiroğlu et al., 2020)

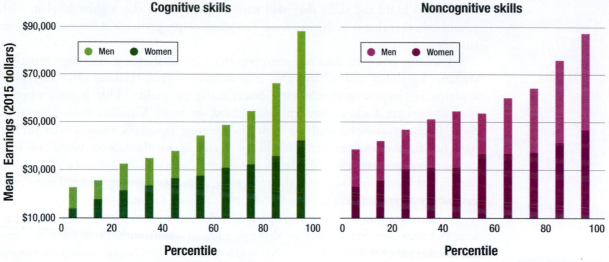

Data from Schanzenbach et al., 2016.

Traditional achievement tests measure students' academic and cognitive skills, but some developmental scientists suggest that these do not account for everything students will need for success. Contemporary researchers suggest that in our global, automated economy, *soft skills,* or social and emotional skills such as the ability to communicate, persevere through difficulties, and work in a group, may matter as much as traditional cognitive ones (see **Figure 14.5**) (Napolitano et al., 2021; Chernyshenko et al., 2018).

Challenges with Secondary Schools

Despite the potential of secondary schools around the world, policy makers and scientists worry that middle and high schools are not as effective as they could be (ICFE, 2021). Around the globe, many students are not attending secondary schools, and many are not learning as much as experts hope. Nearly half of U.S. students need extra academic support after they arrive at college (Chen et al., 2020). Despite the opportunities for learning in adolescence, many students have difficulties staying motivated in school: Around the world, student engagement in school tends to dip as students get older (see **Figure 14.6**) (Hodges, 2018).

Tracking One unsettled controversy in research about secondary school education comes from the observation that many students have disparate experiences: They may attend the same school but never attend the same classes as their peers. More than 80 percent of U.S. high school students and 75 percent of U.S. middle school students attend schools with some sort of **tracking** system (Loveless, 2016; Rui, 2009). Tracking typically involves grouping together students with similar achievement and test scores and offering them a curriculum that matches both their interests and abilities.

Tracking is common in school systems around the world, where students might be tracked into vocational education at age 10 (as in Germany) or age 16 (as in Finland). Tracking may happen as the result of a major test or may happen more subtly, as with a student's choice to sign up for a third language or with qualifying for advanced math in seventh grade (Skopek et al., 2019).

Tracking is designed to provide students to have learning that is customized to their needs, a process also known as institutionalized *differentiated instruction* (Smale-Jacobse et al., 2019). Ideally, this means that students have classes that are motivating and engaging to them and that those with greater academic potential have a more challenging curriculum. In the United States, this might enable promising young

FIGURE 14.5 Getting Along and Being Conscientious Matter in the Long Run. When researchers looked at young people's scores on the Armed Forces Qualification Test (AFQT), they found that both cognitive skills and soft skills mattered to young people's outcomes. The higher people scored (the higher their percentile compared to their peers), the higher their incomes, an effect that was particularly strong for men.

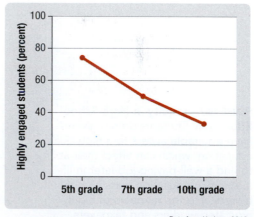

Data from Hodges, 2018.

FIGURE 14.6 Student Engagement Declines Young people spend hours each day on schoolwork, but it becomes less interesting and inspiring as they get older. Researchers suggest that allowing students to make more choices about what they learn and strengthening their relationships with their peers and teachers could help reverse the trend.

tracking The practice of grouping together students with similar achievement and test scores and offering them a more customized school curriculum.

students to build the skills they will need to perform at the highest level in high school, whether that is in *International Baccalaureate* programs or *Advanced Placement* courses (Loveless, 2016).

Tracking, however, does not seem beneficial for all students. Although grouping students by ability and achievement may sound sensible, tracking often segregates students by income and ethnicity, exacerbating inequality. This is true whether observations are made in Sweden, Switzerland, or South Carolina (Smale-Jacobse et al., 2019). In many schools, students with low income, especially those whose parents have not finished college, are more likely to end up on the less-academic and less-rigorous tracks regardless of grades or test scores (Cullen et al., 2013; Parker et al., 2016). In the United States, such students also tend to be disproportionately Black, Latino, and English-language learners (Crosnoe & Muller, 2014; Kanno & Kangas, 2014).

Adolescents who end up in less rigorous tracks not only score lower on achievement tests but may also feel inferior or shamed, and are significantly more likely to leave school altogether (Francis et al., 2020; McGillicuddy & Devine, 2020). Some researchers suggest that tracking should happen later in high school to offer students more equal opportunities for longer periods of time. Others suggest that students be permitted to choose their tracks for themselves, so that more rigorous tracks are open to all striving teenagers (Card & Giuliano, 2016; Loveless, 2016). Accelerated and advanced coursework can have a larger impact on low-income and Black and Latino children, raising their test scores substantially, particularly if it begins in middle school (Card & Giuliano, 2016; Cohodes, 2020).

Funding Inequalities In the United States and many affluent nations, secondary school is available without charge to all young people, but around the globe, 4 in 10 adolescents leave school early, primarily because their families cannot afford the school fees for tuition, uniforms, or books. Low-income children and those with disabilities are particularly at risk (Human Rights Watch, 2016).

The United States has a commitment to universal secondary education, but students' opportunities may be vastly different depending on where they attend school. Remember from Chapter 11 that, unlike many other high-income countries, public school funding in the United States is largely dependent on the wealth of the local community.

As a result of funding formulas in the United States, affluent communities spend more per pupil than do less affluent communities, resulting in inequitable quality of secondary education in the United States (NASEM, 2019; Schanzenbach et al., 2016). (See **Figure 14.7**.) Secondary schools in lower-income communities tend to have teachers with fewer years of experience, more limited access to Advanced Placement courses, and more decayed physical environments (NASEM, 2019). Lower-income schools are more likely to have peeling paint, broken bathroom doors, and defective air conditioners

FIGURE 14.7 Inequity in High School Education Students do not always have equitable access to a high-quality education, which can affect their ability to find a well-paying job later in life. Inequity in education hurts communities by reducing the numbers of highly educated workers and taxpayers.

STUDENTS DO NOT HAVE EQUITABLE ACCESS TO HIGH-QUALITY EDUCATION.

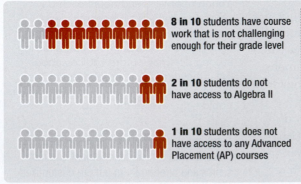

8 in 10 students have course work that is not challenging enough for their grade level

2 in 10 students do not have access to Algebra II

1 in 10 students does not have access to any Advanced Placement (AP) courses

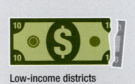

Low-income districts receive only **9.3 dollars for every 10 dollars** received by high-income districts.

Data from U.S. Department of Education, 2018; TNTP, 2018.

WHAT STUDENTS LEARN IN SCHOOL AFFECTS THEIR FUTURE.

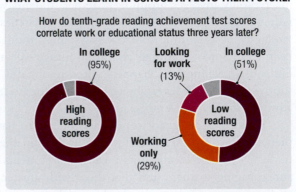

How do tenth-grade reading achievement test scores correlate work or educational status three years later?

High reading scores
- In college (95%)
- Looking for work (13%)

Low reading scores
- In college (51%)
- Working only (29%)

Data from Mamedova et al., 2021.

(Cullen et al., 2013). These schools are disproportionately likely to serve students who are from rural and/or Black and Latino communities (NASEM, 2019). Regardless of cultural or ethnic background, being low-income and attending under-resourced schools increase adolescents' risk for academic difficulties: Students who go to under-resourced schools are more likely to leave high school early, less likely to complete college, and more likely to be underemployed as adults (Means et al., 2019; NASEM, 2019).

Discrimination Some disparities in school quality and student performance are linked to an unequal starting point: Living in low-income neighborhoods brings a host of challenges for teenagers, not only under-resourced schools, but also exposure to neighborhood violence and discrimination (Gordon & Cui, 2018). Discrimination affects students' learning in schools around the world. For adolescents who are from marginalized groups, name-calling in the hallway, disparities in discipline from administrators, harassment by police on the way to school, and low expectations from teachers can all profoundly affect academic performance (Benner et al., 2018; Bryan et al., 2018; Liu et al., 2022; Schmader & Forbes, 2017; Spencer et al., 2016; Zeiders et al., 2021). In the Philippines, discriminatory behavior may target LGBTQ+ students; in India it might target children from the Ghasiya groups; in China it might target the children of rural migrants; and in the United States, it might target children who are heavier than their peers (Hill & Zhou, 2021; Lessard & Puhl, 2021; Martínez, 2016; Thoreson, 2017).

A Sense of Belonging Can Help. In a school in San Francisco, California, Teresa, Noor, and Ahya take time to support each other in the cafeteria as part of their school's Muslim Culture Club.

While exclusion is dangerous at any age, discrimination seems to happen more often to older children, and socially sensitive teenagers are particularly discouraged when they feel excluded or unsafe (Morris et al., 2020; SPLC, 2019). Such students are likely to have difficulty concentrating and to feel anxious, unsafe, and stressed. Exclusion and discrimination can happen to students based on their ethnic background, gender identity, sexual orientation, language, ability, or body size (NASEM, 2019).

In the United States, one in three high school students report that they have experienced racism in school, including more than half of all Asian and Black students (Mpofu et al., 2022). Two in three teachers report that they have witnessed an incident of hate speech, bias, or discrimination at schools, although many were never reported (SPLC, 2019). Teachers tend to have lower expectations for children they consider to be different—whether that means Eastern European immigrants in Great Britain or the children of immigrants in Boston or San Francisco (Dabach et al., 2018; Tereshchenko et al., 2019).

CONNECTIONS

Social exclusion and the effects of racism and sexism impact children throughout development. The stress of racism can even affect fetal development (Chapter 3), and preschoolers already have stereotyped beliefs that shape their development (Chapter 9).

One way students experience discrimination is through *stereotypes*, the shorthand assumptions we hold about other people based on characteristics such as appearance, ethnicity, body size, gender, sexual orientation, ability, or income level. **Stereotype threat** occurs when you feel judged in an area where there are common stereotypes about your group, and the resulting anxiety negatively affects your performance (Protzko & Aronson, 2016; Steele & Aronson, 1995). For instance, if children believe that they are from a group that "isn't good at math," and their membership to that group is pointed out, they perform poorly on tasks as basic as remembering a list of numbers. This finding has been replicated in a variety of groups ranging from children who have a larger body size, children of color, and girls and boys alike (Guardabassi & Tomasetto, 2020; Hartley & Sutton, 2013; McKowen & Strambler, 2009; Wasserberg, 2014).

Stereotypes are not always negative, but even stereotypes that are "positive" can be damaging. For instance, many people believe that Asian Americans are "good at math" and better than students from other ethnicities. This belief can hurt the math performance of adolescents who are not Asian, but it can also present difficulties for Asian students who have to live up to the stereotype (Cvencek et al., 2015).

stereotype threat The phenomenon that occurs when you feel judged in an area where there are common stereotypes about your group, and the resulting anxiety negatively affects your performance.

CONNECTIONS

Remember from Chapter 1 that researchers refer to *community cultural wealth* as six types of cultural strengths: aspirational capital (such as high expectations and dreams), linguistic capital (such as being able to speak more than one language); familial capital (such as close ties with family); social capital (such as strong links with the broader community), navigational capital (such as understanding how institutions like schools work), and resistant capital (such as understanding how to make change in social systems).

Achievement of Immigrants Families move around the world in search of new beginnings, better jobs, and safer schools for their children. Global instability has meant that millions of children all over the world are going to secondary school in a country that is new to their family, whether they are Syrian immigrants in Jordan, Congolese immigrants in the United States, or Ukrainian immigrants in Spain. In affluent countries around the globe, about one in every six young people comes from a family of immigrants (OECD, 2022). About one in four teenagers attending U.S. schools is a child of immigrants or an immigrant themselves (MPI, 2022). Their origins may be in Mexico, China, or India, or they may have arrived as refugees from Syria or Democratic Republic of the Congo (MPI, 2022).

Around the world, children from immigrant families face difficulties — including learning a new community's cultural expectations, language, and school system. Some children may have experienced trauma as they escaped war, violence, or adversity on their way to their new homes (Fazel & Betancourt, 2018). Immigrants are more likely to live in lower-income neighborhoods and to be segregated into under-resourced schools where they experience bullying, exclusion, and discrimination (Finch et al., 2021). It is therefore unsurprising that in many nations, children from immigrant families do not perform as well on achievement tests as their peers do (Karakus et al., 2022). Researchers have found that resilience is more likely if students are in better-resourced schools and feel a sense of belonging and acceptance in their community (OECD, 2022; Rodríguez et al., 2020).

For many immigrant young people, having a fresh start means a burst of hope and higher expectations for their children's future (Cebolla-Boado et al., 2021). In the United States, 9 in 10 immigrant families expect that their children will go on to college, as compared to just 7 in 10 of other families. In general, immigrant families report that their children get better grades, are less likely than their peers to have discipline problems in school, leave high school early, or even be suspended (Feliciano & Lanuza, 2017; Tilley et al., 2021; U.S. Department of Education, 2016).

Some researchers suggest that this resilience can be seen as an *immigrant paradox*, or an "immigrant advantage" (Feliciano & Lanuza, 2017; Tilley et al., 2021). Many immigrant families benefit from *community cultural wealth* (Pérez et al., 2021; Yosso, 2005). Some may have connections with community members that can help them navigate new school systems, find afterschool programs, and make new friends (Zhou & Gonzales, 2019). Immigrant families often benefit from cultural traditions of interdependence and connectedness, sometimes called *familism*. These ties often boost young people's achievement by giving them a sense of community and support in times of stress (Suárez-Orozco et al., 2018). Pride in children's heritage can also bolster their achievement, whether it is feeling proud of being Roma in Romania, bicultural in Korea, or Latino in the United States (Cobb et al., 2019; Dimitrova et al., 2018; Lee et al., 2018).

Immigrant families, like all families in the United States, are diverse: When researchers have analyzed the academic achievement of immigrant families more closely, they have found that the educational backgrounds of immigrant parents are strongly associated with their children's academic success. Immigrant families who arrive in the United States from countries with strong education systems, such as China and India, often have high expectations for their children's academic success and have experience in navigating complex educational systems. Other immigrant families may not have been to college themselves and may be more likely to have difficulties navigating the U.S. educational system (Zhou & Bankston, 2020; Zhou & Gonzales, 2019). Children and families who are undocumented face the unique stress of living without access to social safety net programs and the ever-present threat of deportation and family separation, which are linked to mental health diagnoses and learning difficulties (Sánchez et al., 2022; Suárez-Orozco et al., 2021).

Programs designed to help young people growing up in immigrant families need to address concerns at multiple levels: changing anti-immigrant policies and sentiment at the national level, cultivating a sense of belonging and pride in both heritage and new communities, and offering services designed to support the financial, emotional, and health care needs of adolescents (Bajaj & Suresh, 2018; Hopkins et al., 2021). These interventions build on the individual strengths of immigrant families, who have shown flexibility and courage in starting again and whose children often feel a sense of obligation for years of risk and sacrifice on their behalf. As one young man from a Mexican immigrant family explained: "They [his parents] did so much for us, especially my dad. They worked so hard just to get us where we are and I really appreciate that. And, . . . the way I can pay them back right now is to get good grades" (Fuligni & Fuligni, 2009, p. 238).

Leaving School Early   Around the globe, more students left school early during the COVID-19 pandemic than in earlier years, particularly in low-income countries where remote schooling was difficult to access, to care for their families in a time of increased financial uncertainty (Moscoviz & Evans, 2022). In the United States, early reports suggest that fewer students were able to graduate in 2021 than in previous years as a result of disruptions caused by the pandemic (Barnum et al., 2022).

Although the United States invented the idea of comprehensive high school, it no longer leads the world in high school completion. In fact, it ranks a bit below the average for European and other high-income countries (OECD, 2019b). In the United States, one in six ninth-graders will not graduate from high school in four years, although most will persevere, and more than 95 percent will eventually earn a high school diploma or *General Education Development (GED)* by age 24 (NCES, 2021a). Students who do not graduate with a traditional high school diploma remain at a disadvantage, even with a GED. They are significantly less likely to find a well-paying job or finish college (Jepsen et al., 2017).

Researchers point out that while teenagers who leave school may not be making an ideal decision in terms of their long-term earnings potential, their decisions may seem logical in terms of their experiences. Students experiencing a negative, hostile school environment may prefer to leave school to avoid the negativity (Elmore, 2009). Most young people who leave school have experienced school-based stresses, like feeling that they do not belong or that school is chaotic or unsafe (Peguero et al., 2019). They may have recently experienced an acute life stress, such as a death in the family, failing a class, or breaking up with a romantic partner, or have watched as a friend left school (Dupéré et al., 2018, 2021).

Many students who leave school early also experience long-term stresses, like low income, discrimination, childhood adversity, abuse, and unsupported disabilities (McFarland et al., 2018; Morrow & Vilodas, 2018). Students are particularly likely to drop out when they believe that there is little chance that a degree will help them improve their lives, as is the case in communities with high levels of poverty and income inequality (Kearney & Levine, 2017). Researchers suggest that interventions can be effective if students receive more support years before they graduate (in elementary school), or if teachers, families, and administrators work to improve the environment of high school itself (Lee-St. John et al., 2018; McDermott et al., 2019).

Opportunities to Improve Secondary Schools

Research suggests that secondary schools could be more effective and encourage more students to stay in school longer if they incorporated what is known about how adolescents learn best: strong relationships and opportunity for autonomy. This is what helped Jamie stay motivated at school and on the debate team: He loves the opportunity to work on his own. With no one looking over his shoulder or telling him what to do, he finally has a chance to dive deep into things. Additionally, Jamie feels like his coaches truly care about him: They take time to check in on him, and

Sharing Passion Strong relationships and a shared motivation to excel can help adolescents thrive in secondary school. In a high school in Astoria, New York, Shannon, Kiara, Nabila, and Masbah work on a media project in a program designed to boost leadership and STEM skills in young women.

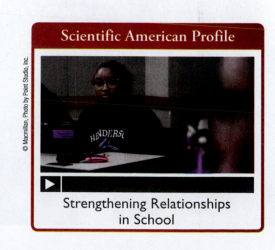

Scientific American Profile

Strengthening Relationships in School

they appreciate his passion and his curiosity. He is also surrounded by peers who share his excitement and feed his passion.

Young people's motivation to learn the skills that they will need to thrive in adulthood makes adolescence a perfect time for making changes in school performance. Researchers have found that teenagers are able to make major alterations to their academic trajectories in middle and high school, allowing them to catch up or move beyond what they had expected of themselves and set themselves up for more success in adulthood (Guryan et al., 2021).

Strengthening Relationships Developmental scientists have established that teenagers are highly motivated by positive relationships, with their peers and teachers alike. Establishing a feeling of trust, community, and belonging is an effective way to build a positive learning environment (Gray et al., 2018; Wang et al., 2020; Yeager et al., 2018). Teenagers who feel closer to a teacher are more likely to perform better in school than are children who lack that connection (Battistich et al., 2004; García-Moya et al., 2019). Programs like *looping*, in which students stay with one teacher for more than one year, are designed to promote teacher–student relationships (Rutledge et al., 2020).

Other programs have seen success in improving relationships *and* student outcomes by changing how teachers communicate with students and encouraging more empathetic, respectful communication. In one randomized trial, teachers who provided positive, or so-called "wise" feedback on student papers, such as "I'm giving you these comments because I have high expectations and know you can reach them" were able to convince 72 percent of their students to revise essays, as compared to just 17 percent of students who received standard feedback (Yeager et al., 2014).

Strong connections may be one reason why smaller school size is often linked to school success (Werblow & Duesbery, 2009). Around the world, middle and high schools tend to be larger than grade schools, which often comes at a cost in terms of personal connections (NCES, 2020). At large schools, students often report feeling unsure that their teachers care about them and whether they belong (Eccles & Midgley, 1989; Elmore, 2009).

Improving classroom climate means helping students get along better, with each other and with teachers. In many schools, discipline is unequitable and marked by consistent biases based on race, income, and ethnic background: Black and Latino students tend to face harsher disciplinary consequences than their White peers do (Liu et al., 2022; Welsh & Little, 2018). In high school, getting in trouble has serious consequences: Suspensions do not help adolescents. In fact, they increase the likelihood that young people will have difficulty finding work or attending college after high school, especially for people who experience racism (Davison et al., 2022). Restorative disciplinary practices, designed to improve relationships and build respect, have shown some promise in reducing disciplinary disparities (Rainbolt et al., 2019). Other approaches include early interventions for children who have difficulties getting along and teacher education to reduce biases and build understanding of children with disabilities (Quereshi & Okonofua, 2018; Carter et al., 2017). While school violence in high school gets much attention in the news media, teachers report that the rate of violence and abuse actually lessens as children get older: In the United States, elementary school students, who are young and often impulsive, are much more likely to yell or hurt their teachers (McMahon et al., 2022).

Peer relationships are also important: Young people who have strong friendships are likely to have an easier transition to high school if they keep the friends they had in middle school (Lessard & Juvonen, 2022). New and old friends alike help ease the strain of school and provide young people with the support they need (Wentzel et al., 2018). Relationships with peers as well as with teachers suffered when students attended school remotely during the COVID-19 pandemic. Researchers suspect that social isolation was one

Persevering for the Win Eleventh-graders India Skinner, Mikayla Sharrieff, and Bria Snell from Washington, D.C., created a plan for purifying lead-contaminated water for an online competition. They encountered discrimination and harassment, but they did not let it stop them. They are still determined to study science in college.

reason many adolescents had difficulties emotionally and academically during the pandemic (Duckworth et al., 2021; Orben et al., 2020). Many students reported that they felt more distant from their teachers over Zoom than they did in real life (Lessard & Puhl, 2021). For many, returning to in-person school was an opportunity to build and strengthen bonds.

Increased Autonomy and Agency Adolescents are capable of having more independence than younger children are, and they thrive when provided with respect, opportunities for exploration, independence, and a sense that what they are doing matters. However, many school environments put a premium on following the rules, limit students' independence, and reward obedience rather than encouraging exploration and choice (NASEM, 2019). Scientists call this a poor **stage–environment fit** (Eccles & Roeser, 2011).

Surprisingly, schoolwork can become *less* challenging for students as they grow older. For many, middle school is easier than elementary school. Increased use of worksheets and rote memorization at a time when adolescents are cognitively capable of quicker and more advanced learning leads to boredom, disengagement, and tuning out (Chase et al., 2014; Salmela-Aro et al., 2021). Strategies to avoid this decline in engagement include focusing on *project-based learning*, in which students develop skills by working together to respond to a challenge or address a real-world problem. Project-based learning not only boosts student motivation but also helps students retain material—and analyses have found that it is highly effective (Chen & Yang, 2019).

Individualized Learning Adolescence is an ideal time to reinvigorate students' interest in learning: Teenagers are not too old to connect with school. Interventions to help improve students' engagement through mentoring, tutoring, and individualized projects can be effective in helping students connect with schools and catch up with their peers (Guryan et al., 2021).

Students arrive in secondary schools with a mix of individual talents (Cascio & Staiger, 2012). Individualized instruction is designed to motivate students by reaching them where they are, rather than using a one-size-fits-all model. Many researchers suggest that personalized classroom instruction, rather than a uniform curriculum or set of courses, will help more students reach their goals (NASEM, 2019).

Schools that emphasize responsive teaching may offer intensive tutoring, one-on-one courses or accelerated programs depending on students' abilities. Some schools, like Harlem's Promise Academy, a charter high school in New York City, help students make remarkable improvements in their academic abilities by offering intensive tutoring and teaching customized to each student's learning needs. In one entering-middle school class at Promise Academy, only 10 percent of students were able to meet the standards for math, whereas three years later, 40 percent of them were on target—an impressive improvement (Dobbie & Fryer, 2011; Hanson, 2013). Successful middle and high schools have different approaches, but they share similarities that researchers say characterize great schools: close relationships between students, families and staff and individualized, high expectations for academic success for each student (Crosnoe & Benner, 2016).

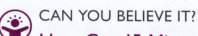

CAN YOU BELIEVE IT?
How Can 15 Minutes Boost Achievement?

What are your core values (Cohen & Sherman, 2014)? Do you value your job, your family, making music, your community, your faith, or something else? Can you believe that taking 15 minutes to write about what is important to you can really make a difference in your life?

Staying Connected Using multiple devices, this high school student in Naples, Italy, tried to stay in the loop with her teachers and friends during the COVID-19 pandemic in 2020.

Share It!

Family still matters: One randomized intervention that texted parents when their middle and high school children missed their homework assignments raised adolescents' grades and achievement significantly.

(Bergman, 2021)

stage–environment fit The idea that we do better when the world matches our developmental needs.

Learn It Together

Designing High Schools for Success

Plan Review the three opportunities to improve secondary schools for adolescents

Engage Gather with two other students. Each of you pick a different opportunity and discuss a concrete way that you could apply it in high school organization, practices, or teaching.

Reflect How easy or difficult would it be to introduce what you suggest? How could you overcome barriers to introducing it?

Share It!

Reflecting on your values can help keep you off your phone. Is all that time on Twitch and Instagram in line with your values? Researchers found that asking young people to reflect on how social media use aligned with their own personal values helped them control how much time they spent on social media sites.

(Galla et al., 2021)

Scientific American Profile

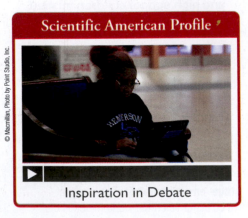

Inspiration in Debate

Researchers have found that taking the time to jot down what is important to you, often called a *values affirmation*, can help students who are stressed or face discrimination or prejudice do better in school and even reverse the effects of stereotype threat (Cohen et al., 2009; Goyer, Garcia, et al., 2017; Miyake et al., 2010). It does not seem to matter if your values are skateboarding or serving others: Simply reflecting on what is important to you works. Thinking about core values can encourage adolescents to apply to college or help adults adopt healthier diets (Fotuhi et al., 2022; Logel et al., 2019).

In a set of classic studies, researchers found that asking middle school students to write a values affirmation led to dramatic improvements in their grades (Cohen et al., 2006; Cohen et al., 2009; Goyer et al., 2017). In fact, the number of students who failed courses declined by more than half. This effect was particularly significant for Black students who experienced stereotype threat in school. These findings have been replicated in other studies with groups, including women in male-dominated engineering courses and first-generation college students (Goyer et al., 2017; Tibbetts et al., 2016).

What makes this quick intervention work? Researchers theorized that thinking about core values changes adolescents' *mindset* by making them feel like they belong to something bigger than themselves and builds *resilience* by connecting them to other people (Cook et al., 2012; Walton & Wilson, 2018). Thinking about core values changes how people perceive a difficult situation, such as school, by asking them to take a bigger, more meaningful perspective (Walton & Wilson, 2018). Values affirmations boost relationships by making adolescents more likely to approach other people positively, which will result in stronger connections and a greater sense of belonging to the group (Walton & Brady, 2017).

Despite the potential of these interventions, they are not—as researchers point out—a "magic" or a "silver bullet" to all of adolescents' challenges (Cohen qtd in Stanford, 2012; Yeager & Walton, 2011). These interventions are not enough to make up for underfunded schools, mental health difficulties, or anxiety caused by discrimination (Hecht et al., 2021). Nevertheless, they can be a step toward helping young people find meaning and the feeling that they belong.

Out-of-School Activities

What teenagers do outside of school, from afterschool programs to mentorship opportunities, can make a difference in helping them stay in school and excel. Some teenagers may spend their time doing schoolwork or sports, learning new video games, or practicing a kickflip on a skateboard. Others do family chores and watch younger siblings. Many volunteer in their communities, feeding people at soup kitchens, cleaning harbors, or organizing for political work.

Extracurricular Activities Students who spend time in formal activities, such as sports, debate, or volunteering, tend to do better in school and have better mental health (Oberle et al., 2020; Vandell et al., 2019). Activities can give teenagers a sense of purpose, supervision, and skill development outside of school—and keep them from focusing too much on their social life (Tjaden et al., 2019).

Organized programs enable teenagers to develop closer relationships with adults outside the family, such as coaches or teachers. Organized activities and mentoring programs also help adolescents develop new skills that they can apply in future careers (Zarrett et al., 2020). The importance of relationships is underlined by the success of one-on-one mentoring programs, such as Big Brother/Big Sister, that have been shown to improve students' school performance and later success (Raposa et al., 2019; Tolan et al., 2020). It is also shown in an innovative program in New York City that puts teenagers on stage, and changes their lives.

SCIENCE IN PRACTICE
Alex Batres, Artistic Director, The Possibility Project

Alex Batres says that rapping saved his life (Batres, 2012). Before he started making music and finding himself as an artist, he had difficulty envisioning his future. But when he was in high school, he found his voice on stage and has been making music and performing poetry across New York City ever since. His goal is to be an entertainer, and he recently released his first EP under the name the Free Mind. Currently, he coaches New York City teenagers, many of whom have been affected by the criminal justice system, on writing, producing, and performing their own musicals, videos, and podcasts. He works with a nonprofit community theater group called The Possibility Project that provides mentorship and *social and emotional learning (SEL)*. Batres's expertise is in music, but he is applying developmental science in his job every day.

Batres doesn't miss a thing. If a student is on their phone instead of paying attention, he finds a way to bring them back into focus. He communicates high expectations and provides individualized instruction.

Batres is not only a creative coach; he is also training young people in skills that will help them succeed. Social and emotional skills, the *soft skills*, which include the ability to communicate, persevere, and work in a group, may matter as much as traditional ones that achievement tests measure (Gordon & Cui, 2018; Schanzenbach et al., 2016).

Batres makes sure his participants feel safe and respected and that they share control over what they are doing. Some of the students with whom he works do not have permanent housing. Most have long histories of trauma. They often face stigma and feel like outsiders in their high schools. At The Possibility Project, he holds them to high standards, but these standards come with a nod of understanding and the reassurance that Alex values them and believes they can succeed. He makes it possible for students to share their stories, to feel understood and part of something bigger than themselves.

Adults like Batres are able to build connections and trust with young people through high expectations and lots of warmth (Gregory & Weinstein, 2008; Lepper & Woolverton, 2002). These connections outside of school and their families help students achieve more, in addition to helping them feel good about themselves. At The Possibility Project, achieving more means finishing producing a movie and writing music. Researchers studying The Possibility Project have found that students in the program are more likely to stay in school, get higher grades, and continue on to college. The students have built skills in empathy and conflict resolution, in part by the sense that they are a member of a new, shared community (Hanson, 2020). And, of course, the core belief of The Possibility Project is "possibility": Developmental science that reminds us that all adolescents can build resilience and change.

Employment Adolescents may meet mentors not only in afterschool programs but also at work. While teenage employment has been declining in the United States over the past two decades, about half of high school seniors has had a job over the summer months (U.S. Bureau of Labor Statistics, 2022). Most say they enjoy the independence of working, even though their jobs—most are working in food service or retail—are often dreary (Mortimer, 2020). The skills students learn in entry-level jobs may not be the most exciting, but they help prepare them for the transition to independence (Martin et al., 2014; Vuolo et al., 2014).

Credible Messenger Alex Batres is a rapper, teacher, and role model. He also thinks of himself as a "credible messenger," because his varied life experiences help him connect with other young people and build empathy and trust.

Tasting the Gelato Can Be a Benefit of Working. But even if they are not scooping ice cream, adolescents like this one in Singapore can gain a sense of autonomy from their jobs.

Jim West/Alamy

Serving More Than Casserole
Community service can help young people, like these teenagers from California serving a meal in Colorado, feel that they are contributing to others.

However, working too much can mean missing out on school. About 10 percent of teenagers put in more than 26 hours every week on the job (Staff et al., 2020). This intensive work may be too much: Some begin to struggle to keep up with their course work and may end up spending their money on social activities (Staff et al., 2020). However, other scientists have noted that teenagers from low-income families who work, particularly to save for college or help their families with everyday expenses do not seem to experience negative consequences from their jobs (McLoyd & Hallman, 2020). In fact, for these adolescents, working may even be a way of transitioning into the full-time workforce (Lee et al., 2018).

Community Service   For the many teenagers who participate, community service and volunteering can be life changing (Sparks, 2018). Service seems to be effective in helping adolescents think beyond themselves, particularly if they are asked to reflect on what they have done by sharing the experience or writing about it (Van Goethem et al., 2014). This ability to think beyond themselves helps adolescents excel in all aspects of their own lives, from doing better in school to finding happiness outside of it (Ballard et al., 2019, 2021).

Involvement in public work or leadership as a teenager—whether it is public speaking at a synagogue or political activity—predicts public involvement as an adult, such as voting, following current events, or participating in community activities (Flanagan & Gallay, 2014). Many young people become less involved with their community organizations as they get older and become more involved with their peers, but many find a source of connection, pride, and purpose when they connect with service (Fuligni et al., 2021; Wray-Lake et al., 2020). However, opportunities to serve are often difficult to find, and many interventions focus on making it easier for young people to make a difference and have the sense of purpose and meaning that volunteering can offer (Fuligni, 2020).

This ability will, as we will learn in the next chapter, help them tackle the social and emotional transitions of the teenage years.

APPLY IT!   **14.4** How might you explain to a younger friend that adolescence is a time of opportunity for growth?

14.5 Virtual school was challenging for teenagers around the world, particularly those who did not have access to the internet or had limited opportunity for online classes. How did this reflect more general inequalities in secondary education around the world?

Wrapping It Up

LO 14.1 Identify important elements of brain maturation during adolescence. (p. 339)

The brain is more plastic during adolescence as teenagers build the skills they will need to be independent in adulthood. Adolescence is a sensitive period for brain development. Highlights of brain development include: (1) maturation of the prefrontal cortex (PFC); (2) heightened activation of subcortical regions and systems; and (3) enhanced connectivity between these subcortical systems and the prefrontal cortex. Adolescents' subcortical regions and systems, including the reward circuit, are activated, contributing to adolescents' emotional intensity and their focus on social relationships. The connections between the PFC and the subcortical systems are strengthening, and the PFC increasingly shapes communication to the subcortical structures, allowing teenagers to have more emotional control.

LO 14.2 Describe the fundamental changes in cognition during adolescence. (p. 339)

Maturation in the brain helps contribute to adolescents' improving cognitive skills, including faster processing speed, stronger focus, and improved working memory. Jean Piaget described adolescence as the time of *formal operational thought*, or the ability to think logically about abstractions and even use logical reasoning about abstractions. Subsequent researchers have found that development of formal operational thought depends on education rather than just on simple maturation. Other researchers describe the development of heuristic and analytical thought during adolescence.

LO 14.3 Describe strengths and challenges in secondary education. (p. 347)

More students are enrolled in secondary schools than ever before. The quality of those schools is variable and often inequitable. Efforts to reform education in the United States often focus on incorporating more career and technical education and helping schools better match students' need for autonomy and strong personal relationships.

LO 14.4 Analyze group differences in academic achievement. (p. 347)

In the United States and around the world, there is inequity in access to well-resourced secondary education and inequality in students' achievement. Students who experience discrimination and those who do not have access to well-resourced schools are more likely to have difficulty finishing school and to perform more poorly on achievement tests than are students who do not experience discrimination and do have access.

KEY TERMS

exploratory learning (p. 342)

concussion (p. 342)

formal operational thought (p. 344)

analytic thinking (p. 345)

heuristic thinking (p. 345)

comprehensive high schools (p. 348)

career and technical education (CTE) (p. 348)

tracking (p. 351)

stereotype threat (p. 353)

stage–environment fit (p. 357)

CHECK YOUR LEARNING

1. Adolescence is a time of maturation of the prefrontal cortex (PFC) and the:
   a) subcortical structures.
   b) hippocampus.
   c) cerebellum.
   d) spinal cord.

2. The brain system that helps regulate our feeling of pleasure and helps us understand our motivation is known as the:
   a) punishment cortex.
   b) reward circuit.
   c) achievement triangle.
   d) refreshment circuit.

3. Why do scientists think adolescence is a sensitive period for brain development?
   a) The brain stops changing after adolescence.
   b) The brain grows larger and more quickly during adolescence than at any other point in the lifespan.
   c) The brain has heightened ability to change and is more plastic.
   d) Teenagers are self-centered and sensitive.

4. The type of reasoning that is more subconscious, intuitive, and more efficient at solving problems is called:
   a) heuristic thinking.
   b) formal operational thought.
   c) logical thinking.
   d) analytical thinking.

5. Piaget developed his theories of development based on close observation of young people in a highly resourced school in Switzerland. How might this group have influenced his idea that all children enter the stage of formal operational thought?

6. One challenge faced by secondary schools is that:
   a) adolescence is too late for school to make a difference.
   b) schools often stifle autonomy in an example of poor stage–environment fit.
   c) students learn more outside of school than in it.
   d) school does not make a difference in children's success.

7. Why do researchers suggest that achievement test may not measure adolescents' potential?

15 Social and Emotional Development in Adolescence

© Macmillan, Photo by Sidford House

Jesús has things to do, and he is getting them done. In the last year, he starred in his school's production of *Hamilton*, volunteered at his community center, painted murals, and planted a pollinator garden for monarch butterflies. He loves animals, acting, and art. He is immensely proud of his Mayan and Purépecha Indigenous Mexican heritage but also makes time to play handball and gossip over Instagram with his friends. Perhaps most impressively, Jesús is only 16.

Jesús wants to make a difference in the world, and now that his age affords him the skills to plan and follow through, he is doing just that. He leads classes about animal welfare and helps younger children with their homework. He harnesses his artistic talent to decorate his home and his neighborhood and draws pictures to make people happy (smiling dogs are always a hit). He also shares his pride in his Indigenous heritage with anyone who will listen, posting drawings of traditional dancers online and helping to organize cultural festivals.

Like many teenagers, Jesús is figuring out who he is as he grows up. That means asking his parents questions about who they are, where his family comes from (other than their bungalow in Los Angeles), and why they eat the food they eat and celebrate Mexican Independence Day. It also means looking different: not just getting taller, but also wearing the clothes that make him feel good.

What emboldens Jesús to speak out? Jesús's parents will tell you that he is a special teenager, and he certainly is, but his optimism, creativity, and energy is typical of adolescents, as you will learn. He is energized by his friends and his family, including his parents, Jesús Senior and Martha, who are behind him 100 percent.

More than any other time, adolescence is when young people are motivated to take risks and to connect to the social world. Adolescents have enough brain maturation to learn things quickly, and enough flexibility to be profoundly changed by what they learn (Suleiman & Dahl, 2019). This may help them to take the risk of learning to drive, asking someone to prom, or starting a new school.

As is true for Jesús, feeling useful, having a sense of purpose, and helping other people boosts resilience (Tashjian et al., 2021). Whether they are starting a new school during a pandemic, trying to make a new friend, or deciding what kind of adult they want to become, adolescents benefit from support and resilience as they grow.

Scientific American Profile

Meet Jesús

Family Relationships

Many people have inaccurate ideas or mixed feelings about the relationship between teenagers and grown-ups. But Jesús, like most teenagers, gets along with his family. As he has gotten older, he has come to cherish them even more. He appreciates the hours his father spends driving him to a high school at the Los Angeles Zoo where he can study animals, and the way his mother has always championed his art and never disguises how proud she is of him. As he says, "They have always made me feel beloved."

Decades of research demonstrates that families remain important for adolescents as they create the foundation for their adult lives (Liu & Wang, 2021; Morris et al., 2013). Supportive families, like Jesús's, can help adolescents perform better in school and avoid antisocial and criminal behavior, depression, and substance abuse—all strengths that will help teenagers transition into their adult lives (Chen & Harris, 2019; Vagos et al., 2021).

Taking on Responsibility

One of the perks of growing up is being able to make your own decisions and having your own voice. Adolescents are eager to decide everything, from having that extra cookie to staying out later. They may also look forward to their ideas—about politics, dress codes, or even what phone to buy—having more impact. This is all a part of the adolescent quest for **autonomy**, or independence. Teenagers want to express their own *agency*, or control over their behavior. Having autonomy does not mean that teenagers are not connected to other people, but rather that they increasingly have more responsibility as they take on adult roles. Their growing sense of themselves, and of their own ideas and perspectives, plays a larger role in their lives than it did earlier in childhood (Benito-Gomez et al., 2020).

Adolescents often strive for more decision-making power, a type of autonomy sometimes called *behavioral autonomy* that refers to everyday choices, such as what kind of snack to pick up on the way home, which apps to download, or who to be friends with. Unsurprisingly, this type of agency can be a source of disagreement between caregivers and their children as they navigate what exactly can be a private decision (Chen-Gaddini et al., 2020; Smetana & Rote, 2019). Teenagers tend to be granted autonomy over their appearance, such as their hairstyle and clothing, before they are allowed to make independent choices about romantic partners or what high school courses to take. While it may seem superficial, choosing what you look like seems to be a universal first freedom (Romo et al., 2014). Jesús explains that he, too, makes decisions about what to wear, heading out most days in the huarache sandals and guayabera pullover that represent his heritage. His parents have given him the space to make these decisions, as they trust him to become his own person in the world.

Learning Objectives

15.1 Explain the development of autonomy during adolescence.

15.2 Describe variations in parent–adolescent relationships.

 Share It!

More than 5 million young people in the United States have primary responsibility for a family member. Typically, these adolescents are assisting a parent or grandparent with their everyday needs.

(Armstrong-Carter et al., 2021)

autonomy Taking responsibility, having greater agency, and making more decisions.

Choosing What You Wear Around the world, young people express themselves by making choices about what they look like. In some cultures, being able to choose what you wear is an important part of becoming an adult; whereas, in others, adolescents are expected to respect cultural expectations about what to wear. These young women in London are expressing their autonomy and their grownup looks.

Adolescents often believe that who they are friends with, or who they date, is in their personal domain before their parents are ready to give up this control (Soenens & Vansteenkiste, 2020). However, this does not mean that adolescents disagree with or disrespect their families' limits. As one teenager explained to a researcher: "They're your parents; you got to respect them. You got to do what they say" (qtd. in Villalobos Solís et al., 2017, p. 11). Autonomy development is a give-and-take process between adolescents and their parents. Teenagers who feel that they are respected and have a voice are less likely to *act out*, or have externalizing behavior, over time (Ravindran et al., 2020; Vrolijk et al., 2020).

Culture impacts how and when adolescents display their autonomy (Benito-Gomez et al., 2020; Tran & Raffaelli, 2020). Families differ in their expectations or ethnotheories about what timing is appropriate for various milestones, such as whether adolescents are old enough to commute home alone from school, go on a date, or get their own cell phone (Jensen & Dost-Gözkan, 2015; Silbereisen & Schmitt-Rodermund, 2020). Some U.S. families, such as those from some Latino or Asian American backgrounds or from immigrant communities, tend to have later timetables for certain markers of independence (Fuligni et al., 2009; Roche et al., 2014). In most cultures and communities around the world, however, there is a general trend toward increased behavioral autonomy as adolescence progresses (Lansford, Rothenberg, et al., 2021).

Getting Along Most of the Time

Contrary to some stereotypes, most teenagers and their parents get along. If you could peek into homes around the world and watch families with teenagers preparing dinner, you would see mostly scenes of domestic tranquility. As Martha and Jesús Senior explain, they feel blessed to have Jesús in the house. They are grateful to have him as a son and are his biggest fans. He makes them laugh, and they debate politics at dinner in the spirit of what Martha describes as "trust and openness."

Researchers who have surveyed or texted adolescents at different times of day, asked families to keep daily diaries, and interviewed caregivers and children together and apart have shown that most teenagers do get along with their parents as much as they did as children (Laursen et al., 1998). However, because they spend less time together, some parents feel that there is more conflict. When researchers ask families about their level of parenting stress, they often find it is highest during the adolescent years (Luthar & Ciciolla, 2016; Meier et al., 2018). Disagreements are often easily solved but are more irritating, as families and teenagers (who have become better arguers) try to navigate new responsibilities and routines. High-intensity conflict that involves screaming, for example, is *not* typical and may be a sign of deeper difficulties (Fosco et al., 2021; LoBraico et al., 2020; Weymouth et al., 2016).

When it does occur, parent–adolescent conflict often reflects cultural values about arguing and family roles. For instance, families may interpret children's disagreement as disrespectful or "talking back," as some Latino or Black families report (Buehler, 2020; Juang & Cookston, 2009). In immigrant families, everyday conflicts may also reflect a generational disconnect (Juang et al., 2012). As one Latina mother explained, "Our son, who was born here, he has different customs; he is not like us . . . although we [my husband and I] have raised him. Americans do things differently . . . This is part of the stress we face when our children become adolescents" (Roblyer et al., 2015, p. 13).

Close in a Different Way

Adolescents spend half as much time with, and feel less close to, their families than they did in elementary school (see **Figure 15.1**) (Fuligni, 1998). These changes have much to do with their involvement in things outside of the home and with the increased importance of peers. Adolescents hang out after school with friends,

Making It Work Like this mother–daughter duo in Norfolk, Virginia, most parents and children support and appreciate each other during adolescence.

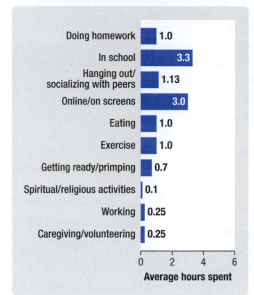

WHAT ARE ADOLESCENTS DOING ALL DAY?

Activity	Average hours spent
Doing homework	1.0
In school	3.3
Hanging out/socializing with peers	1.13
Online/on screens	3.0
Eating	1.0
Exercise	1.0
Getting ready/primping	0.7
Spiritual/religious activities	0.1
Working	0.25
Caregiving/volunteering	0.25

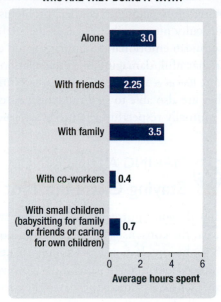

WHO ARE THEY DOING IT WITH?

	Average hours spent
Alone	3.0
With friends	2.25
With family	3.5
With co-workers	0.4
With small children (babysitting for family or friends or caring for own children)	0.7

Data from Ortiz-Ospina, 2020; U.S. Bureau of Labor Statistics, 2021.

FIGURE 15.1 What Are Adolescents Doing All Day? In the United States, adolescents spend less time at home with their families than they did in elementary school, but they still spend more time with their families than with their friends (at least in person). Much of adolescents' time online or on screens is spent communicating with their peers. These data are from before the COVID-19 pandemic: Many experts suggest that time online has increased since 2020.

participate in afterschool programs, and have jobs (Lam et al., 2014; Larson et al., 1996). They increasingly depend on friends for advice and for fun (Allen & Tan, 2016; Rosenthal & Kobak, 2010).

Teenagers around the globe still turn to their caregivers in a crisis, consider them the most important people in their lives, and feel loved by them on a daily basis (Coffey et al., 2020). Young people generally are closest to their mothers but typically maintain good relationships with other family members, including their fathers and stepparents (King et al., 2018). Over time, a continuing feeling of closeness, support, and attachment with parents seems to protect teenagers: Adolescents who report this are more likely to say they are happy and are even more likely to attend college (Janssen et al., 2021; King et al., 2020). Young people who are not close with their family, or feel that they cannot trust them, may need extra support. As a group, they are at increased risk for depression and for dangerous behavior such as substance use and law-breaking (Gault-Sherman, 2012; Mak et al., 2021).

Building Effective Relationships

Some parents tell researchers that they believe there is nothing they can do to help their children once they are teenagers (Lenhart, 2015). But scientific consensus agrees that adolescents are not too old to benefit from their families' help: Adolescents are particularly *plastic* and able to change. Adolescence is a time when relationships have a great impact (Shirtcliff et al., 2017; Suleiman & Dahl, 2019).

Parenting practices adapt as children get older: Caregivers may stop checking homework and start to set curfews. Like Jesús's parents, older teenagers may be granted more space to make their own decisions and come and go as they wish. Nevertheless, researchers have observed that the parenting style that works with teenagers is the same one that works with younger children (Baumrind, 2013; Horvath & Lee, 2015; Morris et al., 2013). *Authoritative* parenting, combining warmth with high expectations, continues to be associated with better outcomes. Children with authoritative caregivers tend to have higher grades and test scores, better self-esteem, and closer friendships, and they are less likely to use substances or develop depression (Martinez et al., 2021; Meisel & Colder, 2021; Szkody et al., 2020).

CONNECTIONS

Remember from Chapter 12 that families come in all different shapes and sizes and change over time. In the United States, two in three adolescents lives with two parents, and about one in three lives with one parent (typically their mother). About 8 in 10 have siblings, and 1 in 20 also lives with a grandparent (Pearce et al., 2018).

Scientific American Profile

Family Relationships

parental monitoring The process of caregivers observing and keeping track of what children are doing.

CONNECTIONS

Remember from Chapter 9 that the parenting styles framework measures the balance of warmth and expectations (also called *demandingness*) in the parent–child relationship. There are four parenting styles: *authoritative*, *authoritarian*, *neglectful*, and *permissive*.

Families with warm, close relationships encourage their children, help them feel better after talking over their problems, and enable them to weather criticism and difficulty more easily (Butterfield et al., 2021; Rodríguez et al., 2014). Emotional closeness does not mean emotional manipulation and control, however: Guilt and emotional threats are harmful, damaging both the relationship and children's sense of themselves (Meeus, 2016; Romm et al., 2020; Scharf & Goldner, 2018). Authoritative parents are not only close; they are also able to set limits for their children, whether on screen time or chores, in a mutually respectful way (Henry & Hubbs-Tait, 2013).

MAKING A DIFFERENCE
Staying Close but Not Controlling

How do you improve the lives of teenagers and keep them out of trouble? For many years, the consensus of scientists, and of many policy makers, was that parents were the solution: If families would just keep a closer eye on their children, teenagers would stay out of harm's way. However, when a new generation of developmental scientists studied the data, they found that this seemingly good advice might actually be harmful.

What happened? For many years, researchers have noticed a strong *correlation* between **parental monitoring** and children's behavior (see **Figure 15.2**) (Boyd-Ball et al., 2014; Patterson & Dishion, 1985). In communities around the globe, parents who know what their teenagers are doing—who their friends are, what they are doing, and where they are—tend to have children who are more successful, with lower rates of emotional disorders, better grades, and less criminal behavior (Kapetanovic et al., 2020; Smetana & Rote, 2019). Increasing parental monitoring became a mantra for policy makers eager to improve the lives of adolescents, but this idea also fed into negative stereotypes: Parents, rather than schools or other institutions, were blamed when teenagers had difficulties. Adolescents were stereotyped as being dangerous troublemakers, which can foster even more unproductive behavior (Dishion & McMahon, 1998; Qu et al., 2016).

In addition, researchers found that telling parents to monitor their children simply did not work. Teenagers are open with parents who they trust and get along with, and who care about them and "get" them (Baudat et al., 2020; Kerr & Stattin, 2000; Liu, Chen, et al., 2020). In the absence of such a relationship, prodding a teenager for information may result in blank stares or evasiveness. Overreaching may even backfire and encourage an authoritarian parenting style (Flanagan et al., 2019). Parents may damage their relationships by undermining trust, respect, and adolescents' sense of autonomy (Kobak et al., 2017; Lansford et al., 2014).

Parents who are too controlling and whose children feel disrespected may even be more likely to break rules, lie, use substances, and get into trouble with the law (Barber et al., 2012; Baudat et al., 2020; Tilton-Weaver et al., 2010). In one study of Swedish teenagers, children who felt their parents were too controlling were more likely to steal, drink alcohol, get into fights, or skip school (Tilton-Weaver et al., 2013).

When researchers observed that children whose parents knew a lot about them did not get into as much trouble as children whose parents were less aware, they mistook *correlation* for *causation*. They thought that monitoring led to better outcomes, but the critical factor was the quality of the relationship, not monitoring itself. With teenagers, the secret weapon is support, not just supervision (Mowen & Schroeder, 2018).

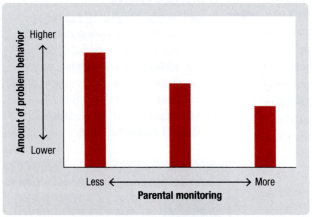

RELATIONSHIP OF PARENTAL MONITORING WITH PROBLEM BEHAVIOR

Information from Fosco et al., 2012.

FIGURE 15.2 Is This Correlation Faulty? In this study, children whose parents kept track of where they were in sixth grade and who they were with exhibited lower rates of problematic behavior than other children in eighth grade. But was there another variable in the mix? Just because parents who knew where their children were—and who they were with—had children who got into less trouble did not mean that asking was the key to raising safe children. There may have been other variables: the quality of the relationships in the family or the child's own level of functioning. The correlation between parental knowledge or monitoring and children's behavior did not mean that one variable led to the other. In fact, as other research demonstrated, too much parental monitoring might actually lead to the opposite effect.

Feeling understood, accepted, and respected, while still being held to high expectations, helps adolescents get along with their caregivers. 🌍

Learning About Culture in the Family For many young people, getting older means that they become more interested in their own heritage and cultural background (Hughes et al., 2016b). For Jesús, this means learning about traditional Indigenous dancing, reading about the history of colonialism, and painting murals of colorful flowers and lowriders.

Developmental scientists use the term **cultural socialization** to describe how families teach their children about their culture (Umaña-Taylor & Hill, 2020). As explained in Chapter 1, families may find a shared culture in cultural heritage, as in Jesús's Indigenous background, or in shared physical abilities, ethnicity, or race, or in any *intersectional* or *bicultural* combination (Safa & Umaña-Taylor, 2021). Remember that culture is not a genetic or a geographic link but a sense of togetherness in a community. In adolescence, families may encourage teenagers to celebrate their culture by learning a heritage language such as Chinese, cooking biryani, playing the bagpipes, or building a sweat lodge (Cross et al., 2020; Harding et al., 2017; Wang, Henry, et al., 2020).

A sense of cultural pride is both powerful and protective. In many studies of families from various backgrounds, including Indigenous, Latino, Black, and Asian American, the children of parents who talked with them about their culture had lower rates of depression, better grades, and higher self-esteem than children from otherwise similar families (Hughes, Del Toro, et al., 2016; Pasco et al., 2021; Wheeler et al., 2017; Xie et al., 2021; Yasui et al., 2015). For instance, a study of Asian American teenagers in the southeastern United States found that when families discussed their ethnic background and conveyed pride about their Asian roots, the teenagers were less likely to feel depressed and more likely to have high self-esteem years later (Gartner et al., 2014).

Families from European backgrounds also display a sense of cultural pride, often around religious or ethnic heritage communities, although White families often avoid talking directly about racial differences (Grossman & Charmaraman, 2009; Loyd & Gaither, 2018). As a young woman named Alysse explained, "I grew up understanding that my ethnicity was Italian and that was something I was extremely proud to be . . . all about talking with my hands, loving the hell out of my family, dressing gaudy and glamorous and never apologizing for who you are" (Dalessandro, 2015).

Remember from Chapter 1 that some cultures are said hold *interdependent* or *collectivist* values, which emphasize a shared commitment to each other and respect for older members of the community. Many Latin American communities, for instance, value taking care of the family as a group, a concept often called **familism** (Fuligni et al., 1999; Knight et al., 2018; Padilla et al., 2020). In Muslim American communities, it is common for parents to share the value of respect for elders with their children (Carolan et al., 2000). In many families, cultural socialization includes a mix of values and cultural practices, like food. One young woman from Chicago explained to a researcher that her cultural identity combined the encouragement to succeed with cuisine: "Eating rice almost every single meal—that is Asian" (Yoon et al., 2017, p. 71).

Among the cultural values common in many communities is the belief that, as adolescents become more independent, they have more of an obligation to help their family (Elder & Conger, 2014; Fuligni & Tsai, 2015). This may involve doing chores, working on a farm or at a family restaurant, taking care of younger siblings, or doing laundry (Hernández & Bámaca-Colbert, 2016). For many, helping out at home is linked to generosity with friends and even positive experiences at school: a cycle of giving (Armstrong-Carter & Telzer, 2021). Julio, who used his English skills to interpret for his Spanish-speaking family, reported: "I translated as I was asked. [It made me feel]

cultural socialization The way children learn about their heritage or the community to which they belong, typically in their families.

familism The concept of responsibility of the family as a group.

Helping Out Whether they are harvesting vegetables in Palmer, Alaska, or selling crepes in Paris, France, adolescents are more capable of work that builds their skills, supports their families, and enables them to feel useful and capable.

empowered, proud, frustrated at times, [but] understanding of my parents' struggle" (Guan et al., 2014, p. 332).

Too many family obligations can overburden teenagers and take time away from school and peer activities (Telzer & Fuligni, 2009). Still, there are benefits. In addition to sustaining close relationships with their families, helping out makes adolescents feel good about themselves, gives them a sense of accomplishment, and encourages family bonding and empathy (Armstrong-Carter et al., 2020; Estrada, 2019; Kiang & Fuligni, 2010).

Cultural socialization also prepares youth for the possibility that they will be mistreated by others because of their background (Priest et al., 2014). For many families like Jesús's, this may involve talking frankly to their children about the discrimination and abuse they may face from other children and institutions, including police officers and immigration officials (Cross et al., 2020; Whitaker & Snell, 2016). Discussing how to handle discrimination can help children cope—and even improve their achievement in school (McDermott et al., 2018).

For instance, Martha and Jesús Senior helped Jesús prepare for the transition to a new school in a different part of their city where, as they recalled, "he would be one of only a few Brown-skinned students." Jesús would need to understand how to find the balance between being respectful and not backing down in the face of discrimination. This helped Jesús anticipate and know how to respond to classmates who might make fun of his shoes and his outfits.

Many families worry about dangerous interactions with law enforcement officers: Black families, for instance, are more than four times as likely as White families to fear violence at the hands of police officers (Graham et al., 2020). This worry can have lasting consequences: Living in fear and distrusting the world around you, even when it is justified, can present challenges to your mental health (Cross et al., 2020).

APPLY IT! **15.1** Martha and Jesús Senior have a close relationship with their son. How do they illustrate the value of the support that families can give their growing children as they reach adolescence?

15.2 Some young people are not sure what their ethnic or cultural heritage might be. Perhaps they are adopted or from a multicultural family. How can family culture, whether it is a love of macaroni and cheese or the NBA, help build resilience?

15.3 Not all adolescents are as fortunate as Jesús: Some teenagers are rejected or estranged from their families. Building on what you have learned, how can these teenagers be supported as they grow?

Friends and Peers

Adults try to prepare young people for the world, but teenagers also learn life lessons from their friends. As children progress from middle school to high school, one constant is their new orientation toward classmates. Whether researchers are observing adolescents' brain activity or interviewing young people face-to-face, they find that friends and peers inspire more response and emotional intensity during adolescence than at any other time (Güroğlu, 2021; Somerville et al., 2013). This is a time for learning social skills, and adolescents learn many of them from friends (Ellis et al., 2012).

An eighth-grader may have TikTok followers, YouTube subscribers, or friends they play video games with, but if you ask them who their true friends are, they likely met them in real life and can count them on one hand (Lenhart, 2015). Researchers have found that adolescents typically have between one and about five close friends (Flynn et al., 2017; Hartl et al., 2015). These friendships often change, particularly as teenagers go through school transitions, which can be painful. However, most adolescents can recover and build new, often deeper relationships (Nielson et al., 2020a). Young people begin to feel that their friends care about them and that they will "be there for them" in difficult times (Meeus, 2016). Adolescents with good friendships do better in school, feel better about themselves, and have fewer psychological challenges than other teens (Pinquart & Pfeiffer, 2020; Schwartz-Mette et al., 2020).

Making Friends

Who are middle and high school students making friends with? Many adolescents' friends are determined by social status, ethnicity, academic success, hobbies, or sports. Teenagers typically befriend people who are similar to them, a powerful tendency known as **homophily**, which is Greek for "love of the same" (Furman & Rose, 2015). Whether they are put together with strangers by scientists in a laboratory or thrown into a new group in a school cafeteria, adolescents are motivated to befriend people who are like them. They find friends who like the same type of music, or enjoy the same activities, but do not necessarily have the same personalities (Hartl et al., 2015). Jesús, for instance, had an instant friendship with his bestie, Juan, because they both loved handball. Young people want friends who love what they love.

Adolescents with good social skills and good relationships with their families have more positive friendships (Furman & Rose, 2015; Oh et al., 2021; Staats et al., 2018). As one researcher described it, the "rich get richer" when it comes to friendship (Flynn et al., 2017, p. 21). Teenagers with healthy relationships keep developing healthy relationships. One reason may be that these young people are building on their existing social skills. Adolescents who can assert themselves, express their warmth, and back off in times of conflict tend to have better and closer relationships in the future (Allen et al., 2020; Flynn et al., 2018; Van Doorn et al., 2011).

Friendships give teenagers the chance to support each other and be supported in turn. Jesús and his friends will sacrifice and be there for each other, whether that means sharing money to buy a burger, or talking about their frustrations about school. They will spend a lot of time together, whether it is playing handball or making art. Caring for others through the ups and downs of teenage life can have benefits of its own, giving adolescents the opportunity to feel useful and competent as caregivers (Armstrong-Carter & Telzer, 2021).

They Share More Than Friendship. What makes these two click? We don't know what it was on the phone that made these teenage friends in London, England, laugh, but we can guess that, like many adolescents, they have much in common.

homophily The tendency to like and associate with people we perceive as being like us.

Learning Objectives

15.3 Explain how adolescents make friends.

15.4 Analyze how peer groups influence adolescents.

Finding a Friend Jackie and Mason find some extra support at a transgender support group near their home in Syracuse, New York.

Gender Differences in Friendship

Most of the time, teenagers find friends who share their gender identity. This is particularly true early in middle school and seems common in communities around the globe (Al-Attar et al., 2017; Nielson et al., 2020b). By the end of high school, more diverse friendships are more common (Arndorfer & Stormshak, 2008).

Throughout adolescence, friendships and peer relationships serve as a way that adolescents practice the roles and communication styles that they have come to associate with their gender (Kågesten et al., 2016; Rose & Smith, 2018). For instance, teenagers who identify as girls often have more emotionally intense relationships earlier than do those who identify as boys (Borowski & Zeman, 2018; Costello et al., 2020). These relationships may dwell too much on feelings, which can exacerbate a cycle of stress and drama. Scientists use the term **rumination** to refer to this tendency to repetitively and obsessively focus on what is wrong (Rose et al., 2017).

Anyone can ruminate, and, in fact, relationships that include rumination tend to be more supportive, on average, than other friendships (Hruska et al., 2015). Sometimes, though, too much rumination can encourage negativity and catastrophizing rather than healthy problem solving. Some researchers connect ruminating in friendships to depression, which becomes more common during adolescence, particularly in people who identify as girls (Bastin et al., 2021; DiGiovanni et al., 2021; Stone & Gibb, 2015).

Teenagers who identify as boys may not ruminate as often as other teenagers, but this can be problematic as well. Many contemporary researchers worry that adolescents' beliefs about traditional masculinity can be damaging to young people who identify as male, preventing their friendships from being supportive. Male adolescents often explain that talking about their emotions with their friends will make them seem "effeminate" or "less of a man" (Way, 2019). As Kyle, a high school student, explained: "You're not supposed to be scared or you're not supposed to be worried about something. That I believe is kind of dumb, because emotions are normal" (Way et al., 2014, p. 245). Emerging research links these traditional ideas about masculinity, including admiring toughness and avoiding feelings, to mental health challenges and even externalizing behaviors (Amin et al., 2018; Exner-Cortens et al., 2021). However, not all adolescents who identify as male are reluctant to discuss their feelings and endorse the stereotypes about their gender: Many, like Jesús, are able to maintain close friendships (Rogers & Way, 2018).

Adolescents in Groups

In adolescence, friendships exist within larger social networks with less intimate relationships. Teenagers have friends, acquaintances, peers from the school bus, Instagram followers, and people they may only know from gaming. The overall number of people in social networks grows dramatically during adolescence, peaking in many groups in the beginning of high school (Felmlee et al., 2018; Wrzus et al., 2013).

Cliques and Crowds Typically, a **clique** is a small "friend group" who share interests and activities. Cliques may include the people with whom teenagers do things on a daily basis, such as having lunch together or hanging out after school. Cliques are subgroups of **crowds**, which are larger, looser collections of adolescents from the school or neighborhood. Crowds often have distinct identities, such as skaters, popular kids, athletes, music kids, nerds, rebels, and so on (Rubin et al., 2015). Crowd labels differ across schools and decades but tend to form along some predictable dimensions, such as academic success, athletic ability, economic status, popularity, substance use, and even aggression (Crabbe et al., 2019; Echols & Graham, 2013).

> ### Share It!
>
> **Break the stereotypes if you want to get along. Teenagers who believe in traditionally masculine gender roles are more likely to manage conflict in their relationships in unhealthy ways: They are more likely to be coercive and less likely to understand how to negotiate both partners' needs.**
>
> (Rogers et al., 2020)

rumination The tendency to repetitively and obsessively focus on what is wrong.

clique A small "friend group" that shares interests and activities.

crowds Larger, looser collections of adolescents within the school or neighborhood.

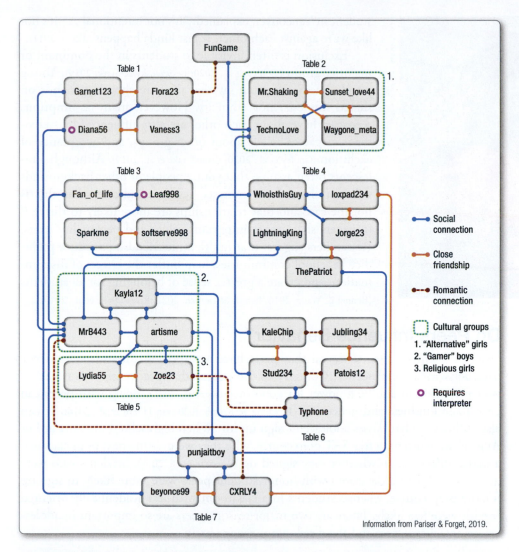

FIGURE 15.3 **Visualizing Social Relationships** This sociogram was adapted from the notes taken by an art teacher in Montreal, Quebec, who noted the groups of students in class and how they interacted online. Three major cliques emerged: "alternative" girls, "gamer" boys, and religious girls.

These groups can be complex and overlapping, as you can see in **Figure 15.3** (McFarland et al., 2014).

Young people often are motivated to join a crowd to make friends and to feel like they belong to a group in the complicated social environment of middle and high school (Lachman et al., 2013). Adolescents, like adults, can also be assigned to a crowd by their peers even if they do not see themselves that way. Stereotyping and social reputations can pigeonhole people into groups without their even being aware of it.

The Role of Ethnicity in Crowds Much of the world is ethnically diverse, but peer groups on- and offline are often segregated (Leszczensky & Pink, 2019; Smith, 2018). In 1997, psychologist Beverly Tatum observed that adolescents ate at separate tables in the school cafeteria according to their ethnicity in her classic book, *Why Are All the Black Kids Sitting Together in the Cafeteria?* (Tatum, 1997). Segregation is still evident in lunchrooms around the globe (Crosnoe, 2012; Leszczensky & Stark, 2019). In Vancouver, for instance, one reporter noticed that the Asian Canadian high school students spent their free time in the cafeteria, and the French-speaking students ate by their lockers (Lum, 2011). The adolescents themselves reported that these choices were not conscious. Sarah, a high school

Learn It Together

Peer Crowds in High School

Plan Review the definition of crowds in high school and how they form.

Engage Gather a group of five classmates and come up with a list of the types of crowds that existed in your high schools. In addition to the names of the crowds, discuss any similarities across high schools and whether they were defined by common factors such as academic success, athletic participation, and ethnicity or economic background.

Reflect How do crowds shape the lives of high school students by guiding them toward some experiences and away from others?

Courtesy Football United, footballunited.org.au

Coming Together Researchers studied the Football United program in Sydney, Australia. Football United uses the magic of the world game (a.k.a. soccer) to promote social inclusion, bringing together refugee youth from places like Iraq and Sierra Leone with other Australians. One boy reported that the soccer program changed his life: "Everyone started playing and started talking and try and make a friend, which is good stuff" (Nathan et al., 2013). A shared passion launched new friendships and benefited the entire community, with long-lasting positive impacts.

Share It!

7½ hours a day. That is not how long teenagers sleep; it is how many hours some researchers have found that they consume screen media, when averaged year-round, for entertainment and socialization (not counting schoolwork).

(Rideout & Robb, 2019)

age-segregated Grouped with other people of the same age.

social status A person's social rank within the larger group.

student in Vancouver, explained: "It's not intentional . . . it's not like we're against each other. It just kinda happens" (Lum, 2011).

Exclusion is often invisible to students in the dominant or majority group (Cooley et al., 2020; Leszczensky & Stark, 2019). Young people like Sarah often say that they are choosing friends on shared interests, not ethnicity. However, many assumptions teenagers have about each other are also influenced by stereotypes, negative beliefs about other groups, and acceptance of exclusion (Cooley et al., 2020; Rivas-Drake et al., 2019). Although adolescents often assume that young people of other backgrounds will not share their interests, research indicates that this is not the case and that relationships are more likely to thrive if teenagers share more important values and personality traits. Researchers suggest that multiethnic friendships reduce prejudice in school communities, help buffer the effects of discrimination, and create a greater sense of belonging for all students (Benner & Wang, 2016; Echols & Ivanich, 2021; Rivas-Drake et al., 2019).

Do Peers Influence Behavior?

Years of scientific research reveal that peers have a surprising amount of influence over behavior in adolescence. Contrary to the notion that peer pressure is negative, peer pressure can also be a power for good (Andrews et al., 2021). Being with peers can encourage kindness and generosity (Busching & Krahé, 2020; van Hoorn et al., 2016). It can also influence what classes adolescents sign up for: When high school students in Los Angeles were offered a free SAT prep course, who they were sitting next to in class was a major influence on whether they signed up (Bursztyn et al., 2019). Students who were given the offer in a classroom with honor-student peers were more likely to sign up for the prep course, whereas students in a classroom with less academically oriented friends were less likely. There are two major reasons peers are so important in adolescence: social structure and the developing teenage brain.

A Social Context that Magnifies the Power of Peers Several decades ago, Margaret Mead, a well-known anthropologist, suggested that peers become particularly important influences on children in societies that undergo rapid changes, like the transformations happening in our increasingly technological, global world (Mead, 1975). Parents remain significant, but peers gain in importance because they know things about the changing world that parents do not. Additionally, adolescents in most affluent, industrialized societies spend a great deal of their time with other adolescents, whether in or out of school.

Adolescents are indeed more **age-segregated**—that is, grouped with other children of the same age—than they were as children (Schlegel, 2015). Researchers believe that when teenagers are separated from other age groups, they become more preoccupied with creating their own social structure and establishing **social status**, or their social rank within the larger group (Allen & Loeb, 2015). Peers become more influential, because adolescents are surrounded by them so much of the time and are anxious to fit into the group.

Margaret Mead did not anticipate the internet and social media, but these advances also serve to enhance the impact of peers. Within many technology-rich contemporary societies, online social networks amplify the power of peers in adolescence, allowing teenagers to superficially monitor and maintain connections with hundreds of people. They are efficient, if imperfect, vehicles for managing lots of complicated, intersecting relationships. This may explain why many young people spend hours every day checking updates, liking, and following others on social media (K. Davis et al., 2020; Sherman et al., 2018).

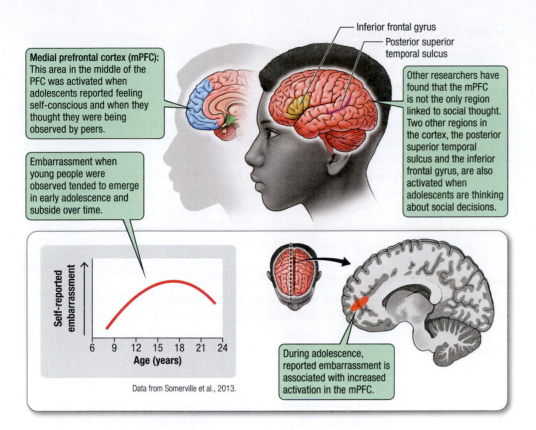

Medial prefrontal cortex (mPFC): This area in the middle of the PFC was activated when adolescents reported feeling self-conscious and when they thought they were being observed by peers.

Embarrassment when young people were observed tended to emerge in early adolescence and subside over time.

Inferior frontal gyrus
Posterior superior temporal sulcus

Other researchers have found that the mPFC is not the only region linked to social thought. Two other regions in the cortex, the posterior superior temporal sulcus and the inferior frontal gyrus, are also activated when adolescents are thinking about social decisions.

During adolescence, reported embarrassment is associated with increased activation in the mPFC.

Data from Somerville et al., 2013.

Self-reported embarrassment

Age (years): 6 9 12 15 18 21 24

FIGURE 15.4 Adolescents' Social Brain When researchers told adolescents they were being observed over video by a peer while their brains were scanned in an fMRI, their brains reacted differently than those of children or adults. Adolescents said that they were embarrassed, and researchers believed that they were particularly sensitive to being observed. The key areas of activation were in the social brain networks in the cortex, including the medial prefrontal cortex (mPFC), particularly regions involved in thinking about other people's feelings, watching their faces, and interpreting their movements.

A Brain that Magnifies the Power of Peers Along with social contexts, brain development shapes the power of peers. The reward system is active when teenagers are with their friends—more active than it is for children and adults (Andrews et al., 2021; Crone & Konijn, 2018; E. P. Shulman et al., 2016). At the same time, the **social brain**—neural networks associated with understanding the views and intentions of other people—undergoes significant development during adolescence (see **Figure 15.4**) (Andrews et al., 2021; Crone & Fuligni, 2020). Adolescents become more perceptive of the facial expressions, perspectives, and motivations of other people. Their perceptions are better coordinated with the reward system, making it more rewarding when they are accepted by their peers and more painful when they are excluded (Bos et al., 2020; Somerville et al., 2019; Tomova et al., 2021). Together, these developments appear to be linked with adolescents' tendency to pay more attention to the opinions and influence of their age-mates, particularly during early adolescence (Ahmed et al., 2020).

Researchers have examined the role of the brain in peer influence in a number of creative ways (van Hoorn et al., 2019). In one study, they scanned the brains of teenagers while they were viewing how many "likes" different posts received on Instagram. When adolescents see popular posts—those with more "likes" from other teenagers—there is greater activity in the brain's reward system than when they see posts with fewer "likes" (Sherman et al., 2018).

In another set of studies, scientists created a simulated driving game that required players to decide whether to go through yellow lights in order to reach their destination more quickly (Smith et al., 2014). They found that young people were more likely to drive through yellow lights when they thought that their peers were watching than when they thought that they were being observed by adults. This was not true of younger children or adults, who tended to play the same way regardless of whether peers were looking on (Albert et al., 2013; Smith et al., 2014). When the researchers imaged the youths' brains in an MRI machine, they found that the reward system was more active in teenagers than in children or adults when their friends were watching them play the game.

social brain Neural networks associated with understanding the views and intentions of other people.

Peer Victimization

Adolescents' sensitivity to their peers makes being with friends more exciting, but it can also make the feeling of exclusion even more painful, as when someone is kept off group chats, not invited to parties, or "ghosted." Social exclusion is most common during the middle school years. About 1 in 10 adolescents report having been harassed or victimized by another teen in any given year. Almost 30 percent report having been a victim of social aggression, and about 1 in 20 admits to having hurt someone on purpose (Juvonen & Graham, 2014; Lebrun-Harris et al., 2019).

Teenagers may be hurt, put down, or rejected by their peers but do not feel that the term *bullying* describes their experience. Being a victim is embarrassing and stigmatizing, and young people may not want to admit to it (Lai & Kao, 2018). Peer aggression in adolescence, as at other times in the lifespan, often targets people whose identity stands out: Young people are likely to experience peer aggression based on their gender expression, sexual orientation, size, physical abilities, or, in some schools, ethnicity or race (Jackman et al., 2020; Lessard & Juvonen, 2020).

Adolescents are particularly sensitive to social victimization: They want to be accepted by their peers and to feel that they are successful in their social world (Blakemore, 2018; Forbes et al., 2019). Teenagers who experience exclusion repeatedly may have long-term problems with depression and anxiety, which may be one reason they tend to miss school and see their grades slip (Juvonen & Schacter, 2018). Some international researchers suggest that exclusion, bullying, and discrimination in school is a leading context for adolescent mortality, because it is linked to poor mental health and dangerous risk taking (Ismail et al., 2021). Feeling excluded wears on the body, boosting inflammation in ways that could impact later health (Schacter, 2021; Scott & Manczak, 2021).

The targets of peer aggression are not its only victims: Those who witness bullying also feel more anxious and negative about school (Midgett & Doumas, 2019; Werth et al., 2015). For the aggressors themselves, this behavior is not something that they outgrow. In adulthood, those who as children excluded or victimized others report having trouble in their relationships, using substances more frequently, and having higher rates of depression and criminal behavior than other adults do (Copeland et al., 2013; Hysing et al., 2019).

Social aggression is a global problem, but it occurs less frequently in some schools. Schools with more nurturing and positive social climates, where students and teachers feel content, tend to have lower rates of bullying whether researchers study them in Kenya or Peru or in the United States (Cornell et al., 2015; Miranda et al., 2019; Mucherah et al., 2018). Students in classrooms where bullies are confronted about their behavior show fewer of the negative effects of experiencing or witnessing victimization (Yun & Juvonen, 2020).

Fortunately, school climate can be changed. Intervention efforts have had some success in reducing bullying (Earnshaw et al., 2018; Fraguas et al., 2021). Many successful programs are based on the work of pioneering Norwegian psychologist Dan Olweus, and focus on increasing awareness, supervising students, and identifying aggressors and victims (Olweus, 1993; Olweus et al., 2019). Newer interventions designed to involve the entire school community include the KiVa program, first established in Finland, whose success stems from encouraging peers to speak up when they witness victimization (Johander et al., 2021; Juvonen et al., 2016). In general, interventions that take a whole-school approach, provide information for parents, and include informal peer involvement tend to have the most success (Gaffney et al., 2021).

Standing Up for Bravery Egypt Ify Ufele is a teenage fashion designer, entrepreneur, and the founder of the anti-bullying organization Bullychasers, all based in her family's home in Queens, New York.

APPLY IT! **15.4** Jesús is close to his friends: They support and sacrifice for each other. How does this emotional closeness contrast with traditional gender roles researchers have found in some friendships in adolescence?

15.5 Boosting resilience for teenagers who have experienced exclusion or victimization can come from finding a friend, a mentor, or a support person. What kind of interventions could you imagine might support the resilience of adolescents who have experienced victimization?

Romantic Relationships

From first crushes to first dates, romantic relationships are one of the hallmarks of adolescence. In the United States, more than 8 in 10 middle-schoolers hope to be in a romantic relationship, and more than 7 in 10 have been in a relationship by the time they turn 18 (Suleiman & Deardorff, 2015). Adolescents with healthy romantic experiences benefit from the extra support and care: They are less likely to act out and to experience depression, and they have longer and happier relationships in adulthood (Beckmeyer & Weybright, 2020; Kansky & Allen, 2018). Romantic relationships can help adolescents practice social skills outside the family, and often become a central and positive relationship in a teenager's life (Furman, 2018; Gómez-López et al., 2019). As 19-year-old Ty put it: "A girlfriend is something that you work on . . . You develop trust and different things. . . . You definitely gotta have responsibility. And just being there just to listen. Just to love" (Towner et al., 2015).

In most places around the world, feelings of attraction transform into romantic relationships in mid to late adolescence, at about age 16, as the result of a combination of a changing social world, a changing brain, and hormonal activity. Neuroscientists even see that the reward circuit is activated when teenagers think about romance, much as it is when they might think about chocolate, a new car, or anything else that brings them pleasure (Telzer et al., 2015).

From Peers to Partners

Scientists observe that many teenagers progress through four stages of romantic development (Furman, 2018). In the first stage, socializing often happens in groups (Dunphy, 1963, 1969), evident in the large groups of 11- or 12-year-olds you see at a mall. In the second stage, adolescents develop crushes. They may trade anxious texts to find out if their crush even knows they exist or develop intense feelings about celebrities. In the third stage, romantic relationships are in their early phases; rather than spend a lot of time alone, couples go out in larger groups. In the fourth and final stage, older adolescents move to exclusive romantic relationships. These relationships last longer and exhibit some of the emotional intimacy of adult partnerships, such as sharing feelings and secrets, offering mutual support, and feeling loved and connected (Xia et al., 2018).

Although researchers often observe that the development of romantic relationships occurs in stages, this is not completely universal. Many adolescents, like Jesús, are happy without partners, believing that this is something that can wait until later, when they have more of their life figured out. In addition, cultural expectations and stigma against certain types of relationships may alter romantic development, particularly for young people who are gender nonbinary, gender fluid, lesbian, gay, bisexual, asexual, or another identity label (Araya et al., 2021; Savin-Williams & Cohen, 2015). Ongoing stigma often forces these teenagers to delay "coming out," affirming their gender identity, or starting a relationship (Araya et al., 2021; Bishop et al., 2020; Martos et al., 2015). Nevertheless, romantic relationships can provide teenagers with a buffer against the stress around them (Araya et al., 2021; Whitton et al., 2018).

Variations in Romance

Cultures around the world have varying expectations for teenage romance. Most discourage dating. For instance, many families in India, Indonesia, and Mexico try to dissuade adolescents from starting romantic relationships until their 20s (van de Bongardt et al., 2015). However, in some rural communities including some in China, Niger, Georgia, and Pakistan, it is common for much younger adolescents, particularly those

Learning Objective

15.5 Identify the changes in romantic relationships during adolescence.

Share It!

"Hotness" may not help you. You may have guessed this already, but being seen as physically attractive in high school is not connected to your long-term life satisfaction or the quality of your relationships later on.

(Allen et al., 2020)

Will You Be Mine? This was Marie's fifth prom and the second time her boyfriend of three years, Caleb, was crowned prom king. This couple from Gorham, Maine, share a love of Pizza Hut, romantic movies, and, like many couples, kissing.

Ben McCanna/Portland Press Herald via Getty Images

CONNECTIONS

Remember from Chapter 13 that ethnotheories also vary in terms of how they condone sexual activity, which is often part of adolescent romance.

Crushes from Afar Sometimes adolescent romance involves crushes on celebrities. These young people are excited to see K-pop stars at a convention in New Jersey.

CONNECTIONS

Remember from Chapter 13 that young people may not know how to spot physical and emotional abuse in relationships, a topic not often broached with families or peers, or within sex education programs (Francis & Pearson, 2019).

Learning Objective

15.6 Explain how identity develops during adolescence.

identity A person's sense of who they are and how they fit into the social groups of the world.

from low-income families, to get married as they advance toward adulthood (Bremer, 2018; Efevbera & Bhabha, 2020; Nasrullah et al., 2017). For adolescents in affluent nations, cultural variations also dictate what kind of romance is acceptable. In some families, teenagers pledge to remain abstinent until marriage, but in others, relationships are encouraged.

The dominant culture in North America and Europe allows and often encourages teenage relationships, with high school dances, movies, television series, and popular music that idealize romance (Sanchez et al., 2017). Parents and children may even see youthful relationships as a training ground for adult relationships. However, the acceptance of adolescent dating is far from universal (Connolly & McDonald, 2020). This may be true of a variety of cultural, religious, or ethnic backgrounds, from evangelical Christians and conservative Muslims to immigrant Catholic Mexican Americans (Raffaelli et al., 2012). Such parents are typically worried that romantic entanglements could derail their children's education, lead to unexpected pregnancy, or force teenagers to assume adult roles before they are ready (Yoon et al., 2017).

Some of these concerns are supported by research: Certain types of early intimate relationships can have risks (Kansky & Allen, 2018). For instance, some researchers have found that young people who have churning, short-term romantic relationships that start in the early teens may benefit from some extra support, because they are more likely to develop depression, use drugs, or do poorly in school. This may be because they have difficulty managing the stresses of romance, or because they had preexisting vulnerabilities (Kansky & Allen, 2018; Loeb et al., 2020).

Almost 1 in 10 U.S. teenagers reports having been physically hurt or emotionally abused in a relationship, the highest rate across the lifespan (Espelage et al., 2020). Other risks of adolescent relationships include excessive jealousy, harassment, or abuse, particularly online and by text (Cava et al., 2020; Francis & Pearson, 2019; Ha et al., 2019). Nevertheless, many adolescent relationships can help teenagers grow and find a source of emotional support as they discover what is important to them (Kansky & Allen, 2018).

APPLY IT! **15.6** Adolescent relationships may come, like all relationships, with heartbreak or happiness. What would you advise your younger self about what they might learn from romantic relationships?

15.7 What ethnotheories about romantic relationships do you see in the media or in your family community culture?

Finding Yourself: Identity Development

From posting a new picture to their Snapchat story to selecting classes, adolescents are surrounded by choices. Who are they? Who do they want to be? Do they want to be religious like their mothers or get into electronica like their friends? These choices help them define their **identity**, or their sense of who they are and how they fit into the social groups of the world.

Committing to their choices and creating an identity helps adolescents feel settled, mature, and happy (Beyers & Luyckx, 2016; Christiaens et al., 2021). For instance, Jesús feels that he has a strong sense of who he is as a person: He is an artist, is a proud Indigenous Mexican, and is committed to service. This commitment helps keep him focused and connects him with opportunities to work with other people who appreciate him, whether he is sharing his art on Instagram or helping younger people draw a perfect giraffe.

Erikson's Identity Framework

As young people contemplate becoming adults, they discover that there are many roles open to them. Erik Erikson believed that the key task for adolescents is to resolve the **identity crisis**—the conflict in deciding between the possible roles they could play and the possible selves they could be—by creating a stable identity. He called this the stage of **identity versus role confusion** (Erikson, 1968; see **Table 15.1**). Erikson believed that exploration is necessary as young people prepare for adulthood, but acknowledged that identity continues to develop and change throughout the lifespan (Erikson, 1950/1993, 1968).

Erikson's theories were not tested in the field until Canadian psychologist James Marcia gathered empirical data to establish four identity statuses: diffusion, moratorium, foreclosure, and achievement. These identity statuses, which were based on Erikson's theory, are determined according to adolescents' *exploration* of different identity options and their *commitment* to adopting specific identities.

- **Diffusion status** occurs when young people are not exploring or putting any effort toward creating an identity. This may be because they feel ambivalent about their choices or because they have difficulty making a plan (Becht et al., 2019; van Doeselaar et al., 2018). Diffusion is typical for young adolescents (and children), but remaining in this status can lead to long-term complications, such as academic underachievement, unemployment, mental illness, or substance abuse (Côté, 2018a).
- **Moratorium status** occurs when young people are actively exploring their options but have not committed to an identity quite yet. These adolescents are fully involved in the process of finding out who they are. They may be changing their profile photos, taking a broad range of college classes, or trying to decide whether to join the military or become a doctor (Côté, 2018b; Wood et al., 2016). Moratorium is a time of instability, and adolescents in this status tend to be more anxious than other young people (Meeus, 2011).
- **Foreclosure status** happens when young people have committed to an identity but have not done much exploration. For example, when someone quickly adopts their parents' political values without investigating the options, they are in foreclosure status. Many adolescents choose this path of early commitment, in part because making a choice, even if it may not be "perfect," leads to contentment (Crocetti, 2017).
- **Achievement status** occurs when young people have done a significant amount of exploration and have made a firm commitment. Because they have learned about themselves and discovered their path, as well as shown commitment to what they believe in, adolescents in this status tend to be more vocationally and personally successful than those in other identity statuses (Kroger & Marcia, 2011).

As you see in **Figure 15.5**, most young people tend to enter committed statuses in late adolescence and in their 20s (Kroger et al., 2010). Many do not go in a set order, say, from diffusion to moratorium to achievement (Meeus, 2011). Most adolescents (and adults) go through a period of exploration and identity experimentation before they develop a consistent sense of who they are (Crocetti, 2017). Some young people have a strong sense of who they are, but it is common and can be healthy for people to

TABLE 15.1 Erikson's Stages of Psychosocial Development: Adolescence

Age	Stage	Characteristics
Adolescence	Identity versus confusion	The key struggle of adolescence is finding something to be committed to as an adult and finding your role in the world.

CONNECTIONS

The identity crisis is the fifth of Erikson's eight stages of development. Remember that he observed that infants resolve the crisis of *trust versus mistrust*, and that toddlers navigate the crisis of *autonomy versus shame and doubt* (see Chapter 6). The preschool years are characterized by the crisis of *initiative versus guilt* (Chapter 9), and in elementary school, children strive to develop a sense of competence, or *industry*, rather than *inferiority* (Chapter 12).

identity crisis The conflict in deciding between the possible roles a person could play and the possible selves they could be.

identity versus role confusion In Erikson's theory of lifespan development, the crisis of adolescent development that is resolved when youth understand themselves and their role in the world.

diffusion status In Marcia's theory, this identity status occurs when adolescents are not exploring or committed to an identity.

moratorium status In Marcia's theory, this identity status occurs when adolescents have postponed committing to an identity and are exploring options.

foreclosure status In Marcia's theory, this identity status occurs when adolescents have committed to a path or identity without exploration.

achievement status In Marcia's theory, this identity status occurs when adolescents have explored and committed to a path.

FIGURE 15.5 How Does Identity Status Change over Adolescence and the Transition to Adulthood? Researchers who tracked identity development longitudinally, over many years, found identity is not fixed by the time adolescents graduate from high school or even enter their 20s.

Data from Kroger et al., 2010.

continue seeking their purpose into their 20s or later (Hatano & Sugimura, 2017; Schwartz et al., 2012).

Marcia's identity statuses do not apply to all cultures around the world. In many places, young people commonly do not experience moratorium or identity achievement at all (Schwartz et al., 2012). Moratorium, the prolonged and healthy period of exploration, may be somewhat unique to North America and Europe, particularly in affluent communities. In communities where young people lack the opportunity to explore in high school or college, they may need to quickly commit to an adult identity.

Multiple Identities

There are many pieces that make up your identity. Jesús, for instance, is not just an artist or an Indigenous Mexican. He is also a man, a son, a Catholic, and a handball player. Having many facets to their identity means that adolescents must figure out who they are in a variety of arenas, which may include work, gender, ethnicity, sexuality, family, and religion. Remember from Chapter 1 that the term *intersectionality* refers to the fact that we all have multiple, intersecting identities (Moffitt et al., 2020).

Ethnic and Cultural Identity For many young people, developing a deeper **ethnic identity** becomes critical as they move outside of the family. In longitudinal studies, multiple scientists have surveyed and interviewed adolescents from a variety of backgrounds about their ethnic and cultural identities (Williams et al., 2020). They repeatedly found that when adolescents take pride in their heritage, they have higher self-esteem, face fewer challenges, such as depression or even criminal behavior, and perform better in school (Fuligni et al., 2005; Rivas-Drake et al., 2014). For instance, Mexican American boys perform better in high school if they report that they are proud of their Mexican roots (Umaña-Taylor et al., 2012).

For many young people like Jesús, feeling positive about their ethnic, racial, or cultural identity can protect them from the corrosive effects of discrimination (Rivas-Drake et al., 2014; Wantchekon & Umaña-Taylor, 2021; Yip, 2014). Adolescents may encounter teasing from peers, unfair treatment from teachers, and harassment from police (Hughes et al., 2016; Huynh & Fuligni, 2010). This increases the risk of many difficulties, from poor health to criminal behavior to academic strains (Gibbons et al., 2020; Zeiders et al., 2021). The toll is even evident in teenagers' bodies. In one study, young people who reported more everyday discrimination had higher markers of stress such as higher levels of the hormone cortisol (Huynh et al., 2016).

Scientific American Profile

WARNING GENIUS AT WORK

Cultural Identity

© Macmillan. Photo by Sidford House

Share It!

More than one in seven young people identify as multiracial. Like other young people, they benefit from a sense of pride in their background but may have their identity challenged by people who have rigid ideas about who belongs.

(Jones & Rogers, 2022; Jones et al., 2021)

ethnic identity A sense of yourself as belonging to a particular ethnic group or community.

Establishing an identity can help build resilience. Indigenous adolescents from a rural community in Oregon who learned about their heritage and how to manage discrimination in an intervention program reported lower levels of depression (Yasui et al., 2015). Feeling connected to something greater than themselves, such as tribe, culture, or community, can be a powerful source of support when adolescents face challenges.

More than one in five U.S. adolescents is an immigrant (Passel, 2011). Researchers use the term **acculturation** to describe the process of adapting to cultural change, which happens as immigrants move from one culture to another (Berry & Vedder, 2016). As they adapt to their new communities, immigrants may adopt aspects of their new culture while remaining linked to their heritage (Nguyen & Benet-Martínez, 2013).

For example, Sami, an adolescent living in Washington, D.C., speaks English fluently, participates in three afterschool clubs, and plays on a soccer team in his multiethnic school. But he has also maintained a connection to his family's culture of origin, speaks Spanish with his grandparents, eats traditional Mexican food, and celebrates Jewish holidays with his family's traditional Mexican silverware. Researchers call this a *bicultural*, or *multicultural*, identity (Nguyen & Benet-Martínez, 2013). Sami's flexibility and his ability to navigate multiple cultures may be an ideal way of adapting as an immigrant (Berry & Vedder, 2016). His ability to assimilate in some ways, such as with his English skills, makes it easier for him to be successful in his new country. But, his continued embrace of his heritage helps him feel linked to his family.

What Is Your Identity? Like many adolescents, Sami, shown here with his younger brother, Juju, has more than one ethnic and cultural identity. His mother is from Mexico City. His father is from Dallas, Texas. So, like many adolescents, Sami can use many identity labels, as Mexican American, Jewish, and a little bit Texan, even though he now lives in Washington, D.C.

Gender Identity Remember from Chapter 13 that, as adolescents begin to develop more adult bodies, their *gender identity* and gender expression, become more complex. For many adolescents, gender expression may intensify during early adolescence, which can bring new challenges and added discrimination (Johns et al., 2019; Lowry et al., 2018; Parker et al., 2018).

In a world that bombards young people with macho archetypes, those who identify as male may feel pressure to conform to a rigid idea of what it means to be a man (Nielson et al., 2020b; Perry & Pauletti, 2011). This rigidity is shared with their peers: Teenagers who identify as boys tend to be more popular if they conform to stereotypes of masculinity, particularly in middle school (Jewell & Brown, 2014). However, research suggests that in the long term, teenagers who resist these stereotypes and, in particular, reject the idea that they should not share their emotions, tend to be more successful academically and feel better about themselves (Exner-Cortens et al., 2021; McFadden et al., 2020).

Many communities are more flexible about feminine identity and gender expression. For instance, adolescents who identify as girls can be popular with their peers in high school even if they do not conform precisely to a gender stereotype, as with girls who are athletic or independent. However, adhering to traditional gender stereotypes tends to foster more peer popularity. And what traditional roles do people think are for girls? Researchers are frequently told that girls are supposed to be easygoing and attractive (Jewell & Brown, 2014). However, adopting feminine stereotypes may only bring popularity in the short term. Preoccupation with traditionally feminine gender expression can be harmful, increasing risks for poor body image and depression (Calogero et al., 2017).

Remember that researchers estimate that about 2 percent of young people currently identify as transgender, nonbinary, or another label, but these numbers are increasing as public acceptance increases (Johns et al., 2019). Transgender and nonbinary teenagers still face peer aggression and discrimination (Norris & Orchowski, 2020). Communities and schools are finding ways to be welcoming and safe for all teenagers, whether they are transgender or identify as gender nonconforming, gender fluid, or questioning (Day et al., 2018).

CONNECTIONS

Adolescence is not the first time that children recognize themselves as boys, girls, or another gender identity. Even young children begin to develop a sense of gender (see Chapter 9). Children who identify as *gender nonconforming* or *transgender* typically begin to explore alternate gender roles, expectations, and identities long before they reach puberty (see Chapter 12). Remember that gender expression refers to the outward displays of your gender. Your gender identity refers to your internal sense of yourself as a man, woman, or a nonbinary label.

acculturation The process of adapting to some of the traditions and expectations of a cultural community.

Monica Almeida/The New York Times/Redux

What Makes You Feel Grown Up? For Zarifeh, 17, it was finding the right glittery dress to celebrate being prom queen at Summit High School in Fontana, California. She found this dress in a family friend's closet, and the hijab belongs to her grandmother. Like many teenagers, Zarifeh is trying to figure out how to be a woman while balancing that with her other identities.

Learning Objectives

15.7 Describe how emotions and feelings change during adolescence.

15.8 Identify the psychological and behavioral challenges of adolescence.

 **Share It!**

Do not believe the hype: Stereotypes of adolescents can hurt them. Teenagers who believe that adolescence is filled with stress and that teenagers are irresponsible are themselves more likely to be irresponsible and stressed.

(Qu et al., 2020a, 2020b)

moodiness Emotional changeability, often leaning toward negative feelings like irritability.

Sexual Orientation During adolescence, adolescents often begin to express their *sexual orientation*, or their sense of themselves as being queer, straight, asexual, lesbian, gay, bisexual, or another label (Bishop et al., 2020). It is increasingly common for young people to report that they do not know or that their sexual orientation is fluid, in-between, or undefined by existing categories. Teenagers who feel their identity is accepted tend to feel more stable, particularly for those who are bisexual, who may feel in-between and less accepted (Diamond, 2016; Savin-Williams, 2016; Watson et al., 2020). Adolescents' sexual orientation identities are often multidimensional: One term may not always cover their romantic attraction, sexual behaviors, or outward identity (Calzo et al., 2017).

Many adolescents are able to "come out" with their gay, lesbian, or bisexual identity in high school; for others, especially in communities unwelcoming of such relationships, this process may be delayed until early adulthood (Martos et al., 2015). The reaction of families can be critical as children establish their adult identity (McConnell et al., 2016; Ryan et al., 2015). Family support also helps build adolescents' resilience in the face of exclusion and discrimination, reducing the chances that they will develop long-term emotional challenges or turn to substance abuse (Magette et al., 2018; McConnell et al., 2016). As you will read, learning to manage stress is important for all teenagers.

APPLY IT! **15.8** Not all adolescents know what they want to be. What questions might you ask a young person to better understand how they are exploring their identity? **15.9** What about you? How do you define yourself and your own journey to understand your own identity? If you had to put yourself in one of Marcia's statuses, which would you choose?

Changing Feelings and Sense of Self

Stereotypes suggest that teenagers are rife with drama and emotion or, in the words of an early psychologist, "storm and stress" (Hall, 1904). But the reality is more complicated. Adolescents generally feel good about themselves, but their emotions are changing. They are not as happy-go-lucky as they may have been in elementary school. They are more sensitive to stress and drawn to adventure. Like Jesús, they may be more aware of the realities and complexities of the world than when they were younger.

Despite the physical and social changes of early adolescence, most teenagers feel good about themselves, a trend that continues as they move into adulthood (see **Figure 15.6**) (Orth et al., 2018). Remember from Chapter 9 that *self-esteem* describes how you feel about yourself and includes the thoughts and beliefs you have about your capabilities in a variety of areas, from your body to your social relationships (Harter, 2012). As adolescents exercise more independence and take on adult roles, they often experience an increase in self-esteem.

Changes in Emotion

Teenagers may feel good about themselves, but they are not always cheerful. Researchers note that although adolescents' self-esteem increases, they are actually less happy than they were in childhood (Griffith et al., 2021; Larson et al., 2002). When researchers ask adolescents to report on their moods by logging them every night, responding to surveys, or replying to random alerts, they find that young adolescents experience more extremes of happiness and upset than they did in elementary school. This emotional changeability, often leaning toward negative feelings like irritability, is called **moodiness**. Moodiness tends to level off by the time adolescents adjust to high school, in about tenth grade (Maciejewski et al., 2015).

Does this mean that adolescents are generally unhappy? On a scale from "very happy" to "very unhappy," they still rate themselves as "happy" almost all the time (Larson et al., 2002).

More Sensitive to Stress

One reason adolescents' emotions are changing is because their brains are more reactive to stress, which increases emotional intensity. (See **Figure 15.7**.) Remember that the body secretes the hormone *cortisol* in response to stress. Teenagers produce more cortisol than children and adults in typical situations, and even higher levels when they are under stress (Doom et al., 2017). What triggers stress in adolescence is different than in childhood: Social situations, particularly with people their own age, are more likely to increase their levels of cortisol (Hostinar et al., 2014).

These short-term doses of cortisol can be helpful, supplying energy to push us to study harder, submit a job application, or muscle through a few more pull-ups in boot camp. Cortisol may also help teenagers react more quickly to challenging life transitions, like a new classroom, a new teacher, or glances from strangers at the bus stop. Unfortunately, this extra jolt of energy can come with a cost. For some, this stress sensitivity may contribute to the higher levels of depression and other emotional problems during these years (Anniko et al., 2019; Spear, 2009).

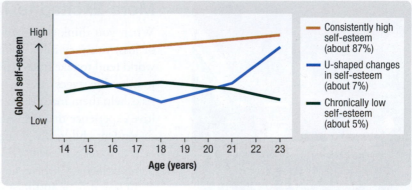

Data from Birkeland et al., 2012.

FIGURE 15.6 Life Keeps Getting Better. For many teenagers, self-esteem just keeps getting better. However, not everyone follows this trend. As you see, self-esteem stays low over time for about 5 percent of adolescents. For another 7 percent, self-esteem dips and then improves over time.

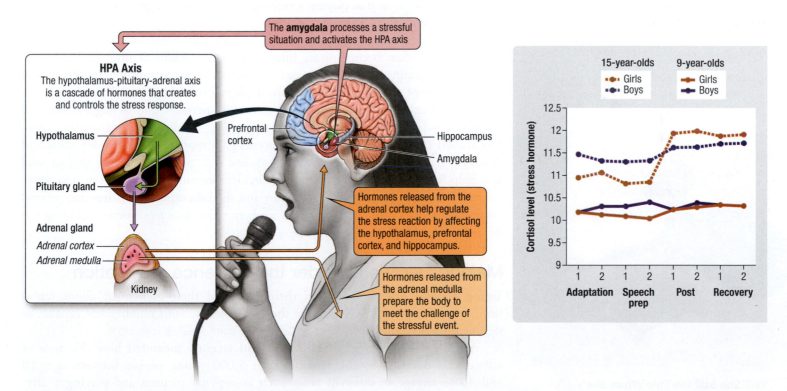

FIGURE 15.7 Stress in Adolescence When the brain detects threat, a coordinated physiological response is activated. The HPA axis involves regions of the hypothalamus, pituitary gland, and the adrenal glands. The hypothalamus releases hormones that trigger the pituitary gland to secrete hormones that in turn initiate the adrenal glands to release hormones, delivering a potent mix of hormones to the body. This allows the body to react quickly in times of crisis, whether at the sight of a disturbing online update or a menacing python. This axis is often triggered by the amygdala, which processes fear and other strong emotional events. The prefrontal cortex can work to help reset the HPA axis and return it to normal levels. Scientists sometimes examine cortisol levels by asking people to give a speech, typically a stressful experience for most people. In this study, researchers observed that adolescents had higher levels of cortisol and were more sensitive to stress than children; their stress levels were slower to return to normal. All the children's cortisol levels rose as they were asked to speak, but the younger children's levels recovered after the task was over.

Adolescent Risk-Taking Can Be Heroic. For Lily, taking a risk meant intervening when she saw smoke coming out of a window when she was walking her dog, Isobel. She returned to the fire with a ladder from home (after calling the fire department) and helped the three people inside evacuate.

Will She Still Do This When She's Older? Poppy Olsen has been skateboarding since she was 8. Will taking risks on the board be something she outgrows, or a profession she will stick with into middle age?

sensation-seeking The drive for excitement and the thrill of doing something a bit scary.

More Excited to Take Risks

When you think about *risk-taking*, or any activity that may have a potential downside or loss, you may think about bungee jumping or drag racing. Teenagers all around the world tend to take risks—from drinking to driving too fast—at higher rates than people in other life stages (Duell et al., 2018). But not all the risks teenagers take are harmful. Many risks help them mature and take on adult roles. For most adolescents, risk-taking is a positive experience that helps them explore what the world has to offer and transition from dependent children to young adults able to manage their own needs independently (Ellis et al., 2012; Romer et al., 2017). Even helping others—such as intervening when a classmate is being bullied—involves an element of risk-taking (Duell & Steinberg, 2020).

How does a 400-foot drop at 120 miles an hour sound to you? Not your thing? You will want to skip the Kingda Ka roller coaster at Six Flags Great Adventure in New Jersey, then, although the line is often hours long during the summer. Who is waiting in line? Lots of teenagers. Researchers are unsurprised: They agree that the drive to try something new and exciting increases during adolescence (Meeus et al., 2021). This is **sensation-seeking**, or the drive for excitement and the thrill of doing something a bit scary, like a 400-foot drop (Spielberg et al., 2014).

Teenagers' sensation-seeking increases after puberty and declines in late adolescence (Khurana et al., 2018; Quevedo et al., 2009; Romer, 2010; Steinberg, 2008). When researchers measure sensation-seeking, they ask adolescents how much they like excitement, such as whether they "like to do 'crazy' things for fun." They might also measure adolescents' heart rates or patterns of brain activation when they are in potentially exciting situations, such as playing a video game or looking at pictures of sharks or of threatening people (Quevedo et al., 2009; Steinberg, 2008).

Experimenters who studied adolescents longitudinally over the course of puberty found that children become more interested in excitement around the time their bodies are activating the HPG axis and the hormonal changes of puberty. Again, the reward circuit of the adolescent brain likely plays a role. As you read in Chapter 13, greater responsivity of the systems to rewards—perhaps due to higher levels of dopamine—is a key reason for young people's sensation-seeking (Galván, 2013). Researchers suspect that, with age, adolescents gain more experiences with the world that help temper this sensation-seeking (Khurana et al., 2018). Brain development may also help limit the power of the reward circuit. Remember that, as teenagers grow, connections between the prefrontal cortex and the subcortical structures that process emotions tend to grow stronger, enabling better emotion regulation, including the desire for excitement (Casey, 2015; Shulman et al., 2016).

Making Decisions Under the Influence of Emotion

Young people's ability to control themselves and their excitement about sensation-seeking increases over time. By their early teens, most children are capable of significantly better impulse control (Galván et al., 2007; Steinberg et al., 2017).

A team of researchers around the world recently measured how this type of self-control develops by asking more than 5,000 young people between ages 10 and 30 to engage in different tasks, such as copying pictures and playing a driving game (Steinberg et al., 2017). As shown in **Figure 15.8**, young people's interest in sensation-seeking increases much more rapidly than their ability to control themselves, especially in early adolescence. Younger adolescents have lots of interest in exciting things, but less ability to control their impulses when they are in a highly emotional state. This imbalance between sensation-seeking and self-control explains why adolescents sometimes take dangerous risks.

As you recall from Chapter 14, the prefrontal cortex does not fully mature until young people reach their mid to late 20s (Steinberg et al., 2017). In addition, the

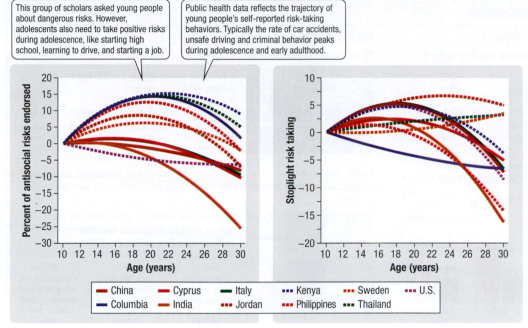

This group of scholars asked young people about dangerous risks. However, adolescents also need to take positive risks during adolescence, like starting high school, learning to drive, and starting a job.

Public health data reflects the trajectory of young people's self-reported risk-taking behaviors. Typically the rate of car accidents, unsafe driving and criminal behavior peaks during adolescence and early adulthood.

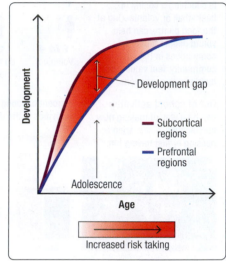

Data from Duell et al., 2018.

FIGURE 15.8 Risk-Taking During Adolescence A group of scholars examined more than 5,000 young people from over 11 countries in a study of risk-taking. As shown in the left panel, they observed that many young people were more willing to take some negative risks, like vandalism or fighting, in mid-adolescence. The middle panel shows the results of the researchers' experimental test of young people in a driving simulation. They found that in many countries, young people were more willing to take chances driving, such as running a red light or speeding, in mid-adolescence. The last panel shows a schematic of the relationship of brain development to risk-taking. The researchers suggest that differences in the timing of brain maturity contribute to risk-taking. The subcortical brain regions connected to motivations for rewards and attention to social input mature more quickly than the prefrontal regions that help to logically control behavior.

connections between the prefrontal cortex and the subcortical structures are gradually strengthened and become faster, making it easier to control emotional impulses (Casey et al., 2019; Liston et al., 2009). For most adolescents, a little emotional impulsivity does not cause serious difficulties and may even help them adapt to the challenges of becoming an adult, but for some it may contribute to behavioral challenges (Khurana et al., 2018).

When Adolescents Need Support

Most adolescents gracefully navigate the transition from childhood to adulthood, but for some, this can be a difficult time in a world that may not always give them the support they need. Rates of psychological disorders and adverse experiences increase in adolescence, approaching adult levels (see **Infographic 15.1**) (SAMHSA, 2020). The combination of brain development, increases in hormones, and the realities of adjusting to a new social world with fewer supports poses risks for many adolescents. For some young people additional stressors in the environment, such as family transitions, violence, or economic instability, add to the mix (Guyer et al., 2016; Pfeifer & Allen, 2021; Shulman & Scharf, 2018). High rates of anxiety, depression, substance abuse, and externalizing behaviors in adolescence continue into young adulthood (Samek et al., 2017). Rates of psychological disorders in children and teenagers have been increasing in the past decades, but the increased stress and instability caused by the COVID-19 pandemic has been linked to even higher rates of emotional difficulties in young people around the globe, particularly those who experience discrimination, poverty, and disconnection (Racine et al., 2021; Rico et al., 2022).

Emotional Disorders and Suicide Adolescents, like adults and children, may experience a cascade of brain, hormonal, and social stresses that may make them unable to function in their everyday life, and they may be diagnosed with a *psychological disorder*.

Share It!

What is your major stress? For 4 in 10 U.S. teenagers, it is not having enough money. Family income is a source of anxiety across the lifespan.

(Desilver, 2019)

BUILDING RESILIENCE IN ADOLESCENCE

CONNECTION AND CONTRIBUTION TO THE COMMUNITY

Helping others, whether it is coaching a sibling in basketball or volunteering at the food pantry, can help young people find new connections in the community, feel valued and build positive emotions.

How many young people volunteer in the U.S.?

1 in 4
Volunteer

1 in 3
do favors for neighbors

1 in 5
regularly participate in civic organizations

Out of school activities can be a way of making new connections, discovering a passion or just having fun.

SDI Productions/E+/Getty Images

Percent of young people in extracurricular activities in the United States, by family income.

■ Low income
■ Higher income

- Sports: 32% / 57%
- Clubs: 19% / 37%
- Tutoring and lessons: 20% / 40%

RELATIONSHIPS

Friendships are a crucial source of support in adolescence.

Maskot/Getty Images

How many adolescents in the U.S. report having strong friendships?

98% have one or more good friends

78% have 2 to 5 good friends

20% 6 or more good friends

2% have no close friends

Family continues to be a source of support and guidance as adolescents grow up: although relationships tend to change as young people develop their own autonomy and agency.

Boogich/E+/Getty Images

Most families in the U.S. report that they are able to share ideas and talk about meaningful subjects with their adolescent children.

60% say they are very good at talking about things that matter

33% say they are somewhat good at talking about things that matter

6% say they are not doing very well at talking about things that matter

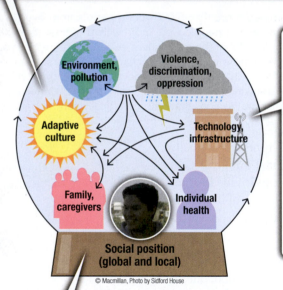

- Environment, pollution
- Violence, discrimination, oppression
- Adaptive culture
- Technology, infrastructure
- Family, caregivers
- Individual health
- Social position (global and local)

© Macmillan, Photo by Sidford House

TECHNOLOGY

gawrav/E+/Getty Images

Adolescents use technology to learn, create, make friends and entertain themselves. In the U.S., young people use screen-media for entertainment and socializing for about 7 hours a day.

Teenagers report that on average they are spending that screen time:

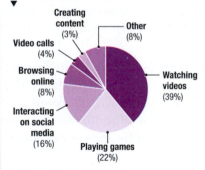

- Creating content (3%)
- Other (8%)
- Video calls (4%)
- Browsing online (8%)
- Watching videos (39%)
- Interacting on social media (16%)
- Playing games (22%)

SOURCES OF STRESS

ADVERSE EXPERIENCES IN ADOLESCENCE
Adverse experiences in adolescence (per 100 children)

- 9.4 Witnessed family violence
- 4.8 Witnessed shooting
- 33 Witnessed assault in community
- 11.3 Injured in an assault
- 17 Experienced bias-related harassment

- 4.5 Harassed online or on the phone
- 8 Experienced parent's divorce or separation
- 7 Experienced physical abuse at home
- 7 Experienced neglect at home
- 15.7 Experienced emotional abuse at home

- 21 Experienced bullying
- 5.1 *Boys*
- 26 *Girls*
Sexually assaulted

ADOLESCENTS WHO NEED SUPPORT
Psychological disorders in adolescence (per 100 children)

- 18.7 Any psychological disorder
- 4.5 Substance use disorder
- 10.5 Anxiety disorder
- 6.1 Depression
- 7.5 Behavioral or conduct disorder

- 2.8 Eating disorders
- 2.4 Autism Spectrum Disorder
- 12 Attention Deficit Hyperactivity Disorder (ADHD)
- 2.5 Serious suicide attempt requiring medical treatment

For instance, the social sensitivity that makes spending time with peers particularly enjoyable can also make social rejection more painful and make going to school more anxiety provoking (Costello et al., 2011; Rapee et al., 2019). Because the developing adolescent brain leads to increased interest in risk-taking, teenagers may behave in impulsive ways that could end in self-harm or suicide (Ho et al., 2021).

Almost one in three adolescents has received an anxiety disorder or trauma-related diagnosis at some point (APA, 2013; SAMHSA, 2020). **Anxiety disorders** are characterized by excessive fear and worry that make it impossible to carry out everyday activities, whether that is making friends or going to school. They include a broad range of psychological difficulties, from generalized anxiety to specific fears like that of public speaking, and are often related to *posttraumatic stress disorder (PTSD)* (Siegel & Dickstein, 2012). Teenagers who experience anxiety disorders or PTSD may have been exposed to abuse or trauma or may have struggled with worry since childhood. Adolescents who are anxious may not even describe themselves as being anxious; instead, they may describe physical rather than emotional symptoms and complain about stomachaches or headaches. Their families may report that their children have become irritable, worried, or nervous.

Rates of depression also increase dramatically during the teenage years. Clinical **depression** is diagnosed when you feel so unhappy and disconnected from your life that you lose interest in things that once brought you joy, and you can no longer function at home and at school (APA, 2013). Almost 1 in 10 U.S. adolescents has been diagnosed with depression, and many more report feeling sad or depressed (see **Infographic 15.1**; Mojtabai et al., 2016). Such teenagers look fine on the outside but feel miserable inside. Or, they show more noticeable signs, such as spending a lot of time alone or being excessively tearful or touchy.

Thinking of suicide is uncomfortably common in adolescence, with almost one in five adolescents reporting suicidal thoughts (Ivey-Stephenson et al., 2020). Although most do not hurt themselves, more than 2,500 die by their own hands in the United States every year (Miron et al., 2019; Nock et al., 2013). Around the world, more than 35,000 adolescents die by suicide every year, more than in terrorist attacks or war (WHO, 2021). Suicide is not the only way adolescents hurt themselves. Nearly one in six teenagers has injured themselves, a behavior formally called *nonsuicidal self-injury* (NSSI; Millner & Nock, 2020; Nock, 2009). (See **Table 15.2** for warning signs.)

Effective, empirically based treatments can help. Many of these treatments are distinct from those that work for children or adults (Kazdin, 2003; Weisz et al., 2013). Most teenagers who have emotional disorders are also helped by talk therapies that may involve their families and communities, building a sense of community and family support that aid recovery (Weisz et al., 2013). Some treatments for adolescents at risk for suicide, for instance, encourage a sense of pride

Share It!

What do you want to be when you grow up? Asking young people about their goals can be a nonthreatening way to get to know them better. Having a lofty goal is usually a good sign. Young people who have ambitious careers in mind, whether that is being a physician or an aircraft mechanic, tend to feel better about themselves than do those who have more limited ambitions.

(Dudovitz et al., 2017)

Finding Hope These teenagers are working with a coach to identify sources of social and emotional support in their community.

TABLE 15.2 Showing Support When You Worry About Suicide

— Always ask. Asking someone whether they are thinking of harming themselves may feel awkward or rude, but it also shows that you care.
— Listen, empathize, and reflect back. Listening and helping people feel genuinely heard can help people calm down.
— Worry when someone is talking about or threatening to hurt themselves, or looking for a means of hurting themselves, or writing or talking about dying in a way that is new to them.
— Be concerned if someone tells you they have no reason to keep going and feel hopeless and even withdraw from the people they care about.
— Check on someone if they are using substances more than usual.
— Look for help if someone is particularly anxious or depressed or if their mood seems different.
— Let them know that there is support out there if they are acting particularly angry, impulsive, or anxious for revenge. Sometimes people act out and hurt themselves.

anxiety disorders A clinical diagnosis based on a pattern of excessive worry or fear that keeps children, adolescents, or adults from fully functioning in their lives.

depression A clinical diagnosis based on a pattern of sadness and lack of energy that impairs your ability to function.

and community that can protect young people from social stress and discrimination, recognizing the importance of identity development to adolescents (Brody et al., 2021). One such treatment program, the Western Athabaskan Natural Helpers Program, reduced the rate of suicide attempts by more than half in high-risk communities in New Mexico and Canada (Goldston et al., 2008; May et al., 2005).

CAN YOU BELIEVE IT?
Is Social Media to Blame for Adolescent Depression?

You have probably seen headlines about how much time teenagers spend on social media and their smartphones. Some developmental scientists have argued that new technologies are responsible for an epidemic of adolescent depression, loneliness, and retreat from the adult world (Twenge, 2017). This may ring true to anyone who has felt envious scrolling through the perfect-looking photos on someone's Instagram, disappointed about having someone ghost them, or hurt when a partner looked at their phone during an intimate conversation. New technology clearly has some downsides (Appel et al., 2016; Kross et al., 2013; McDaniel & Coyne, 2016). But, does social media harm adolescents? Is it truly "ruining a generation" (Twenge, 2017, 2019)? Let us look at the evidence.

- Large surveys of adolescents in the United States have consistently shown that rates of reported depression and other mental health challenges, as well as suicide, have risen by at least 10 percent in the past 10 to 20 years (Costello et al., 2005; Mojtabai et al., 2016; Twenge et al., 2018a; Weinberger et al., 2018).
- Over the same time period, adolescents (and adults) have embraced new technology, from smartphones to personal computers, for fun and schoolwork. Many teenagers now spend nearly 7½ hours a day on recreational technology (Rideout & Robb, 2019).

Is there a correlation between increased time spent online and the increase in mental health problems? Some researchers have found a connection between teenagers' media use and their rates of depression and observed that there is a correlation: Teenagers who use technology the most, particularly those who identify as girls, are indeed at greater risk of depression and other psychological disorders (Twenge et al., 2018a, 2018b). Others, however, have found somewhat different results (Daly, 2018). When researchers looked at the amount of time teenagers spend on their phones or social media, they found that moderate use is not correlated with depression at all. Only those who spent more than 40 hours a week are more likely to develop depression (Daly, 2018; Twenge, 2019; Twenge et al., 2018b).

In general, the findings are inconsistent and collectively do not point to social media as a critical factor in mental health (Kreski et al., 2021; Odgers et al., 2020). Why did these studies produce different results? First, they may have confused correlation with causation. They may have also forgotten about the theory of *differential susceptibility*: Not all children share the same risk factors, and it is unlikely that one element of the environment would affect all of them in exactly the same way (Ellis et al., 2011).

The data showed that depression increased over the past 10 to 20 years, along with media use, but there was no proof that the media use *caused* depression. As some scholars pointed out, the causal factor may have been something completely different, such as the economic recession that occurred in 2008 (Daly, 2018). Or perhaps another third variable, such as economic inequality, discrimination, school performance anxiety, parent distraction with technology, or even not enough time spent being active, was the culprit (Daly, 2018; N. Goldman et al., 2018).

Social Media for Good Adolescents are often derided for spending too much time online. But 19-year-old Mohammad is using his phone to share the stories of people in his community, a camp for more than 1 million Rohingya refugees in Kutupalong, Bangladesh, with followers all of the world, raising awareness and building community.

More recent studies that have examined smaller groups of teenagers over time have found that, in many cases, the relationship between media use and mental health is much more complex than the headlines indicate. For some teenagers, depression comes first and leads to more time spent online, perhaps exacerbating social isolation (Heffer et al., 2019). For adolescents at risk for depression or who are depressed, spending a lot of time online does not make them feel better (Boers et al., 2019). However, keep in mind that these associations are not universal and do not apply to all mental health challenges (George et al., 2018).

Does this mean that adolescents can click away on their phones without worry? Most experts do not go that far (Odgers, 2018). Too much time spent on your phone does seem to be problematic, particularly if it displaces healthy behaviors like getting enough sleep, completing homework, and exercising (Hawi & Samaha, 2016; Kenney & Gortmaker, 2017; Lemola et al., 2015; Toh et al., 2019).

Using and Abusing Substances Although it is illegal for teenagers in the United States, experimenting with alcohol and marijuana is not uncommon. Before graduating from high school, more than 6 in 10 U.S. teenagers report that they have tried alcohol, and nearly half report having tried marijuana (Miech et al., 2021). U.S. teenagers have some of the highest rates of binge-drinking and marijuana use in the world, but adolescents around the globe experiment with, use, and abuse substances—typically alcohol, tobacco, and marijuana (Currie et al., 2012; Degenhardt et al., 2016). For many, using these substances is a way to bond with friends and signals a new form of independence (Schulenberg et al., 2014). For others, alcohol and other substances put their lives into disarray.

Rates of teenage substance use are lower than they have been for generations, but some adolescents use substances in an unhealthy and dangerous way (Miech et al., 2021). The risks of adolescent substance use range from brain damage after using MDMA to lung diseases from vaping marijuana (Dharmapuri et al., 2020; Mustafa et al., 2020). One study in the United States found that nearly one in six young people engaged in **binge drinking**, or consuming more than five drinks at one time, in the past month (Miech et al., 2021). Researchers are concerned that the heavy use of marijuana in adolescents may put them at risk for anomalies in brain development that may be linked to emotional and memory problems in later life (Albaugh et al., 2021; Scheier & Griffin, 2021; Willford et al., 2021). Around 4 percent of adolescents develop a **substance use disorder** (SUD), which is diagnosed when someone's use of substances prevents them from functioning or causes some kind of impairment in their life (SAMHSA, 2021). For teenagers, "impairment" means not keeping up with schoolwork, family obligations, or friendships. SUDs can lead to increasingly worse problems, such as lost friendships and failing grades, as well as criminal activity and death.

Family or individual therapy is the most effective treatment for substance use disorders. Family therapy involves the entire family to address the sources of stress and conflict that may contribute to the adolescent's substance use, to help the teenager get back to an active, productive life as quickly as possible (Fadus et al., 2019; Tanner-Smith et al., 2013). For all adolescents, building resilience in the face of the stresses of growing up is often easier if they receive support, including help in building stronger and more positive relationships, boosting their emotion regulation skills, and understanding the potential harms of alcohol and substance use (Skeen et al., 2019).

Breaking Rules and Hurting Others Although many adolescents break the law in some way before they turn 18, most of these crimes are relatively minor: speeding, drinking alcohol, sneaking into a movie theater without paying for a ticket, or shoplifting a lipstick from a drugstore (NRC, 2013). Others are far more serious. Every year in the United States, teenagers are responsible for about 20 percent of violent crimes, which include assault, rape, and murder. About 1 in 10 teenagers has committed a violent crime, although not all of these crimes are reported (Oudekerk & Morgan, 2016).

binge drinking Consuming more than five drinks at one time.

substance use disorder A clinical diagnosis based on a pattern of substance use that is causing someone functional difficulties in their everyday life.

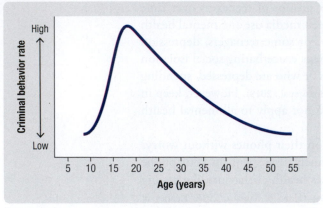
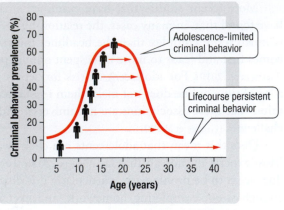

Information from U.S. Department of Justice, 2019.   Information from Moffitt, 1993.

FIGURE 15.9 Criminal Behavior in Adolescence Many teenagers have broken the law in minor ways, whether by speeding or underage drinking. Most grow up and begin to follow the rules. A few have difficulties that continue, which is known as lifecourse-persistent behavior.

Fewer than one in four adolescent boys and about one in five adolescent girls have been arrested, mostly for offenses such as fighting, robbery, or substance use (Brame et al., 2014; Puzzanchera, 2021). However, adolescents and young adults tend to break the law and get arrested more than older adults do (see **Figure 15.9**).

Most teenagers who break the law become rule-abiding adults (NRC, 2013). Some have **adolescent-limited** criminal activity, only breaking the law during adolescence. Typically, adolescent-limited activity happens when adolescents break the law for social reasons, such as to gain their friends' approval or to prove their independence (Moffitt, 1993, 2006). However, about 10 percent of teenagers who are arrested become adults with lengthy histories of criminal behavior (Steinberg, 2014). **Lifecourse-persistent** criminal activity often begins when people commit crimes such as petty theft or property destruction at young ages and continue doing similar or more serious acts into adulthood (Piquero & Moffitt, 2010).

Many adolescents with lifecourse-persistent criminal activity have *conduct disorder*, which involves aggressive behaviors such as hurting people and animals and damaging property without remorse (Fairchild et al., 2019). In adolescence, these problems become more severe; children have more difficulty getting along with others, and their parents may even be afraid of them (Condry & Miles, 2014). Researchers suggest the best way to help children control their aggression and impulses is to intervene early. Intensive interventions can help at-risk young people develop the necessary skills to resist externalizing behaviors (Boisjoli et al., 2007; Conduct Problems Prevention Research Group, 2011; McMahon & Frick, 2019).

The vast majority of teenagers who run into trouble with the law, whether it is a violent offense or something less harmful, will grow out of that behavior and adapt to the adult world. Researchers suggest that the best approach for teenagers with adolescent-limited criminal behaviors is to help them make amends to their communities and ensure that their lives are not derailed by a criminal record (Steinberg, 2014). As one youth activist explained, "What changes people is relationships. Somebody willing to walk through the shadow of the valley of adolescence with them" (Bill Milliken qtd. in Sonlight, 2017).

SCIENCE IN PRACTICE
Noé Romo, M.D.

A busy emergency room at a major trauma center may be an unlikely place for developmental science in action, but this is where Dr. Noé Romo applies lessons learned from life and scientific research to stop gun violence (Romo, 2019). He developed a

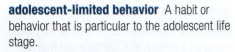

adolescent-limited behavior A habit or behavior that is particular to the adolescent life stage.

lifecourse-persistent behavior A habit or behavior that is consistent across the lifespan.

community violence prevention program in the Bronx, New York, that has reduced gun injuries by about 60 percent (Kim, 2021). His initiative, called Stand Up to Violence, treats assault as a disease that can be eradicated.

Even though he is a pediatrician, his program goes way beyond the hospital walls. With the help of partners within the community, including social workers, a pastor, and trusted outreach volunteers, he makes sure that every teenager who ends up in the emergency room as a result of violence leaves with a mentor: an adult who will follow up with them and help them develop strategies for avoiding retaliation and stopping the cycle of violent gang activity. Relationships and cultural humility are at the core of Stand Up to Violence, concepts Dr. Romo understands from scientific literature and from his own life.

Dr. Romo grew up in a low-income neighborhood in Los Angeles that was marked by community violence and discrimination. As a teenager, Dr. Romo was once told that medical school was not for him because children from his neighborhood were unlikely to become doctors. He proved them wrong, graduating from medical school and becoming a researcher, activist, and pediatrician. His work as a pediatrician was what inspired him to start his program. Dr. Romo explains that the hopeless grief from seeing a 16-year-old die from a gunshot wound spreads from the hospital staff to the child's families, friends, and neighbors and lasts for a long time (Romo, 2019).

In Action in Front of the Cameras Whether he is in the emergency room or in front of the cameras, Dr. Noe Romo is trying to prevent young people from hurting themselves, and each other, by helping them find stronger, healthier relationships.

About 1 in every 20 U.S. teenagers reports that they regularly carry a gun (Carey & Coley, 2022). Across the United States, gun violence is now the most common cause of death among teenagers (other leading causes are car accidents and suicide) (Goldstick et al., 2022). This is 35 times higher than in other affluent countries around the world, where guns are more restricted, and criminal violence is not as prevalent (Cunningham et al., 2018). Researchers like Dr. Romo suggest that young adolescents are particularly susceptible to gun violence because their peers are so important to them: Experiences of exclusion and a desire to be socially successful increase teenagers' likelihood to get involved with criminal groups and turn to violence (Estrada et al., 2018; Shelley & Peterson, 2019). These risks are especially potent in low-income neighborhoods where criminal activity is prevalent (Beardslee et al., 2019).

Dr. Romo has seen firsthand that relationships can determine whether a teenager ends up in jail or dead. One strength of his program is that he, and the other adults who work with the adolescents, understand the community they serve and respect the challenges these teenagers face. They are also motivated by their understanding that a bullet not only destroys a teenager's body; it also destroys communities. Stand Up to Violence helps adolescents build new relationships with adults who link them to activities that provide an alternative to dangerous peer groups: volunteering at a church, finding a part-time job, or buckling down with homework.

APPLY IT! **15.10** Jesús identifies as an artist, as Indigenous, and as a community activist. How would you define yourself in three words or less? How has your identity changed over time?

15.11 Connecting with a community and feeling like you belong can be sources of resilience in adolescence and across the lifespan. Jesús connects with his church, his heritage community, and his local neighborhood. How have communities supported your development?

15.12 We need support at any age, but development plays a role in what support we need and what types of interventions are effective. Which characteristics of adolescents may make them need extra support?

15.13 How might you design a program to boost the strengths of young people who were at risk for acting out in adolescence?

Wrapping It Up

LO 15.1 Explain the development of autonomy during adolescence. (p. 363)

As adolescents mature and prepare for adult roles, they take on more responsibility. This includes taking on more autonomy. Autonomy does not mean you are completely independent; rather, it means that your own ideas play a larger role in your decisions. Teenagers often assert behavioral autonomy, or the ability to make decisions about things they consider personal, like what they wear and who they are friends with. Families and cultures often differ in the accepted milestones of autonomy, like when teenagers get their first phone or when they are ready to date.

LO 15.2 Describe variations in parent–adolescent relationships. (p. 363)

Most adolescents and their families get along. Conflicts arise between teenagers and their family as they do in any relationship, but they may seem more common than with younger children because teenagers are better at articulating themselves and do not spend as much time with the family. Teenagers are still emotionally close to their families but are also developing stronger emotional attachments with their friends. Strong family support can help adolescents grow up healthier and do better in school. Researchers describe authoritative parenting, which includes lots of warmth and high expectations, as an ideal parenting style during adolescence. Adolescents benefit from building relationships with their family that are based on trust, understanding, and mutual respect, rather than control. Families teach their children about culture in adolescence: Cultural pride can help build resilience.

LO 15.3 Explain how adolescents make friends. (p. 369)

Adolescents learn social skills from their peers. Their peer groups often change as they move from middle to high school. Friendships are often based on homophily, or the idea that we befriend people we think are like us. Friends begin to provide support, and adolescents learn to support their friends. Friendships often include gendered communication styles: Teenagers who identify as girls are more likely to ruminate. Adolescents who identify as boys need to manage social norms that often suggest that men do not share their feelings.

LO 15.4 Analyze how peer groups influence adolescents. (p. 369)

Adolescents live inside complex social networks made up of cliques and crowds, which are based on identity characteristics and, in many schools, are ethnically and racially segregated. Diverse friendships and crowds help build a sense of belonging for all students. Age-segregated environments make peers more influential on adolescent behavior. Brain development makes teenagers more sensitive to their friends and makes it more rewarding to be accepted by them. These developments also make social exclusion and peer aggression more painful.

LO 15.5 Identify the changes in romantic relationships during adolescence. (p. 375)

Many adolescents begin romantic relationships, which can be a source of emotional support as well as instruction for social skills. Many adolescents move toward exclusive paired relationships through a series of stages: from socializing in nonromantic larger groups to smaller ones as they get older. Adolescents who are not gender binary, who are transgender, or who are attracted to the same sex may face discrimination as they become interested in romance. Cultures around the world differ in how accepting they are of adolescent romance. As it does across the lifespan, teenage romance comes with risks, including heartbreak and abuse.

LO 15.6 Explain how identity develops during adolescence. (p. 376)

Erikson described the crisis between identity and confusion, observing that adolescents need to explore possible options of who to be and what they believe in as they grow. Marcia described the process of identity development in terms of four identity statuses: diffusion, moratorium, foreclosure, and achievement. Most adolescents do not progress through these statuses as stages, but it is typical for teenagers to experiment with who they are. Developing a sense of purpose and identity helps boost mental health and well-being. Many young people have multiple, intersectional identities or identify as bicultural or multicultural. During adolescence, teenagers develop a sense of their ethnic or racial identity, their gender expression and identity, and their sexual orientation. A sense of community pride can boost resilience in teenagers who may be subject to discrimination.

LO 15.7 Describe how emotions and feelings change during adolescence. (p. 380)

Adolescents' emotions are more changeable than they were in childhood, but most teenagers are still generally content, and their self-esteem is rising as they become more capable. Teenagers are more sensitive to stress, particularly related to social pressures. Adolescents are braver about risk-taking, which helps them take on adult roles and try new things in order to develop their adult capabilities. Teenagers are more interested in sensation-seeking after puberty. Younger teenagers may have limited ability to control their feelings in exciting situations and may be more impulsive, which helps them tackle their new roles and responsibilities.

LO 15.8 Identify the psychological and behavioral challenges of adolescence. (p. 380)

Rates of psychological disorders, including substance use disorder and externalizing disorders increase during adolescence. This is a result of hormonal and brain development, a changing and often less supportive social world, and a stressful environment. Empirical treatments can support adolescents' resilience. Most teenagers in the United States experiment with marijuana and alcohol, but only a few are diagnosed with a substance use disorder. Many teenagers break the rules in minor ways, but some are involved in criminal activity, some of which is adolescent-limited.

KEY TERMS

autonomy (p. 363)
parental monitoring (p. 366)
cultural socialization (p. 367)
familism (p. 367)
homophily (p. 369)
rumination (p. 370)
clique (p. 370)

crowds (p. 370)
age-segregated (p. 372)
social status (p. 372)
social brain (p. 373)
identity (p. 376)
identity crisis (p. 377)
identity versus role confusion (p. 377)

diffusion status (p. 377)
moratorium status (p. 377)
foreclosure status (p. 377)
achievement status (p. 377)
ethnic identity (p. 378)
acculturation (p. 379)
moodiness (p. 380)

sensation-seeking (p. 382)
anxiety disorders (p. 385)
depression (p. 385)
binge drinking (p. 387)
substance use disorder (p. 387)
adolescent-limited (p. 388)
lifecourse-persistent (p. 388)

CHECK YOUR LEARNING

1. In adolescence, gaining more autonomy and agency typically includes all of these EXCEPT:
   a) becoming more selfish and individualistic.
   b) expecting to take on more responsibility for chores.
   c) deciding what clothes to wear.
   d) having more of a say in everyday life.

2. Jesús has a friend who tells him that all he does with his parents is fight. What should Jesús tell him?
   a) This is just a typical relationship between teenagers and parents.
   b) He should seek some support from another adult, mentor, teacher, or health care provider.
   c) He is probably expecting too much from his parents.
   d) He does not need his parents anymore.

3. Jesús met his good friend, Juan, in their physical education class, and they had an instant friendship: They both loved handball and identified as Indigenous. This is an example of:
   a) adolescent sensation-seeking.
   b) homophily.
   c) adolescent stress sensitivity.
   d) puberty.

4. Is peer victimization an inevitable part of adolescence?
   a) Yes, because adolescents are always going to hurt each other.
   b) No, because the rates of bullying vary between schools and nations.
   c) Yes, because some people are always going to be victims.
   d) Yes, because hormones drive adolescents to attack each other.

5. How do scientists characterize romantic relationships in adolescents?
   a) Romantic relationships can allow teenagers to expand their network of support.
   b) Romantic relationships are mostly dangerous in adolescence.
   c) Romantic relationships are not important during adolescence.
   d) Romantic relationships should be avoided during adolescence.

6. Jesús's friend Paul is not sure what he wants to do with his life; he is taking advanced math in high school and trying out the drums and the guitar. What identity status BEST matches his experience?
   a) Identity achievement
   b) Identity moratorium
   c) Identity foreclosure
   d) Identity diffusion

7. Why do researchers think that developing your own identity may happen differently depending on your culture's ethnotheories and opportunities?

8. Which of these is NOT a reason why researchers think adolescents are more susceptible to psychological disorders?
   a) A brain that is more sensitive to stress
   b) Increasing adversity in the environment
   c) Inadequate social support
   d) Lack of self-control and hard work

9. What unique strengths help make adolescence a time of positive risk-taking and opportunity?

10. Which of these statements about adolescent emotional development is TRUE?
    a) Adolescents are usually unhappy.
    b) Adolescents usually feel poorly about themselves.
    c) Adolescents are likely to feel more deeply happy or sad than children or adults.
    d) Adolescents are capable of adult levels of emotional self-regulation.

The Transition to Adulthood

© Macmillan, Photo by Sidford House

"What makes you feel like an adult?," we ask Haruki. Is it that she is a "dog momma" with a puppy of her own? Is it her age (25)? Or that she has her own apartment, graduated college, or works full time as a school counselor? Or is it that she just married her partner, Marvin?

Haruki might be smiley and youthful looking, but she is clearly not a kid. Like many young people, it still surprises her to discover that *she* is the adult in the room — the one her students turn to when they want advice about where to go to college, where to find a good doctor, or how to get an oil change. Haruki cares for herself, pays her own bills, and chooses what to have for dinner and where to get health insurance. Although she has a lot of strengths — her close relationship with her mother, her Peruvian relatives, her partner, a satisfying job — she says being adult comes with a lot of pressure. Some days it is easier than others.

Right now, Haruki's focus is on taking care of herself so she can care for her students and her family. She wants to make sure that she and Marvin are in good health so that they are ready for whatever comes next. Learning is at the top of her list: She wants to learn Pashtu so she can better connect with her immigrant students, and perhaps some Japanese to complement her Spanish so she can build stronger relationships with relatives in Peru and Japan.

Marvin is adjusting to his move to the United States from El Salvador: He and Haruki have a lot to learn about the immigration process as Marvin improves his English skills and considers training as an electrician. They are far from their adult dreams of having their own home and maybe having children. As Haruki says, everyone has their own timeline: There are inevitable bumps in the road and different ways to become the person you are meant to be.

At age 25, Haruki is in the life stage many developmental scientists refer to as **early adulthood**, or young adulthood. Early adulthood is a culturally defined period that typically ranges between ages 18 and 30 and is marked by tremendous individual flexibility and potential but less structure and assistance than many adolescents receive.

Although many young adults, like Haruki, have adult responsibilities and roles, they are not quite the same as older people and certainly differ from the teenagers they once were. Human bodies and brains are still maturing into the 20s. This enables young adults to adapt to their changing circumstances and acquire new skills, whether it is learning a third language or adjusting to full-time work.

In young adulthood, this impressive potential is combined with a decreasing amount of structure. The days of compulsory schooling are over, and although young people remain tied to their families and communities, there is no longer one path for everyone. Young adults are particularly sensitive to the long-term effects of social changes beyond their control, such as the impact of a global recession or the COVID-19 pandemic (Recksiedler & Settersten, 2020; Settersten et al., 2020). Social inequality means that young people do not begin adulthood on the same starting line. However, armed with cognitive flexibility and the ability to learn, they can develop the skills they need to thrive.

early adulthood A culturally defined period typically ranging between ages 18 and 30 that is marked by individual flexibility but less support.

Scientific American Profile

Meet Haruki

What Is Adulthood?

Like Haruki, many young people are unsure about what exactly makes you an adult and when, although they often feel adult responsibilities acutely. Unlike adolescence, which has a clear biological beginning in the unmistakable physical changes of puberty, the markers of adulthood are flexible to match the changing expectations of each culture, time, and place.

In past centuries, people were considered adults at any time from about age 15 to 40. Historians note that although people in the past tended to have children earlier than many today, they were not necessarily considered ready for all responsibilities of adult life, like financial independence or political office, until they were older (Mintz, 2015). The legal markers of adulthood today remain highly variable. Anthropologists note that, in ancient human societies and among many rural communities today, most young adults are not independent: It often takes several years to become proficient at survival skills like hunting, foraging, or agriculture (Hochberg & Konner, 2020).

Despite these variations, researchers caution that it is always more respectful to treat someone as an adult. Young adults often feel discriminated against at work and in the community simply for being young (Bratt et al., 2020; Chasteen et al., 2020).

Markers of Adulthood

Scholars identify five aspirational *external* markers that mark adulthood in many communities today. These include: (1) finishing school; (2) establishing a household (which means taking responsibility to rent or buy a dwelling); (3) finding work; (4) committing to a long-term relationship; and (5) having children (Cepa & Furstenberg, 2021; Settersten et al., 2015). Other scholars point to *internal* markers, like the self-recognition of being emotionally mature or adult (Arnett & Mitra, 2020).

Many of us never reach all of these markers—many adults may be happily single or in college in their 40s, and well-paying jobs and a feeling of maturity are

Learning Objective

EP.1 Identify the key historical markers and common variations in adulthood.

both hard to find. Nonethless, these markers continue to affect how adults judge themselves (Settersten et al., 2015). Adults who have achieved these markers, particularly those who have finished their education, found a job, and set up a household, are more likely to say they feel competent, accomplished, and satisfied (Cepa & Furstenberg, 2021; Culatta & Clay-Warner, 2021; Sharon, 2016). In some communities, particularly in the economic boom years of the 1950s and 1960s in the United States, these hallmarks were easier to reach than they are today. Many young people in that period graduated from high school, married, and found a well-paying job before age 22 (Mintz, 2015). In low-income countries, this timeline still matches many young people's experiences. In most, nearly half of all women have children and a long-term partnership before age 25 (Pesando et al., 2021).

In most affluent countries today, fewer young people have jobs or have set up a home of their own (Gagné et al., 2021a). Researchers estimate that fewer than 25 percent of young adults in the United States meet even four of these markers before age 35 (Vespa, 2017) (see **Infographic EP.1**). The reason? The economy, which has made it harder to find a stable, high-paying job in a globalized world. As a result, it now takes longer for most young people to save the money to start a family and set up an independent household. If they seek a committed relationship and a household of their own, they often wait until their late 20s.

There is also more variety in how people start families: Adults may have children before they have finished their education or before they are married, or they may be happily partnerless or childless (Rybińska & Morgan, 2019; Tillman et al., 2019). Others may not maintain a separate household until their late 20s. Contemporary young adults are forced to be flexible, particularly those who do not have the resources to achieve their dreams right away or those who were transitioning into adulthood during the pandemic era (Dalessandro, 2019; McCue, 2021).

Is Emerging Adulthood for Everyone?

emerging adulthood A term used by some scholars to describe the period between about ages 18 and about 29 in which young people consciously postpone some of the milestones of adulthood to explore their identity.

Some scholars use the term **emerging adulthood** to describe the period between ages 18 and about 29 (Arnett, 2000; Nelson, 2021). They suggest that a new label is needed to describe a period when young people are consciously postponing some of the milestones of adulthood, like committing to a partner or becoming responsible for children. These young adults are exploring their identity in an in-between stage rather than setting down roots (Arnett & Mitra, 2020).

Marking Adulthood with Rituals Some communities ceremonially mark the transition to adulthood. In Seoul, South Korea, young men participate in a traditional ceremony to mark their 20th birthdays. In Waterloo, Iowa, young women celebrate growing up at a debutante cotillion.

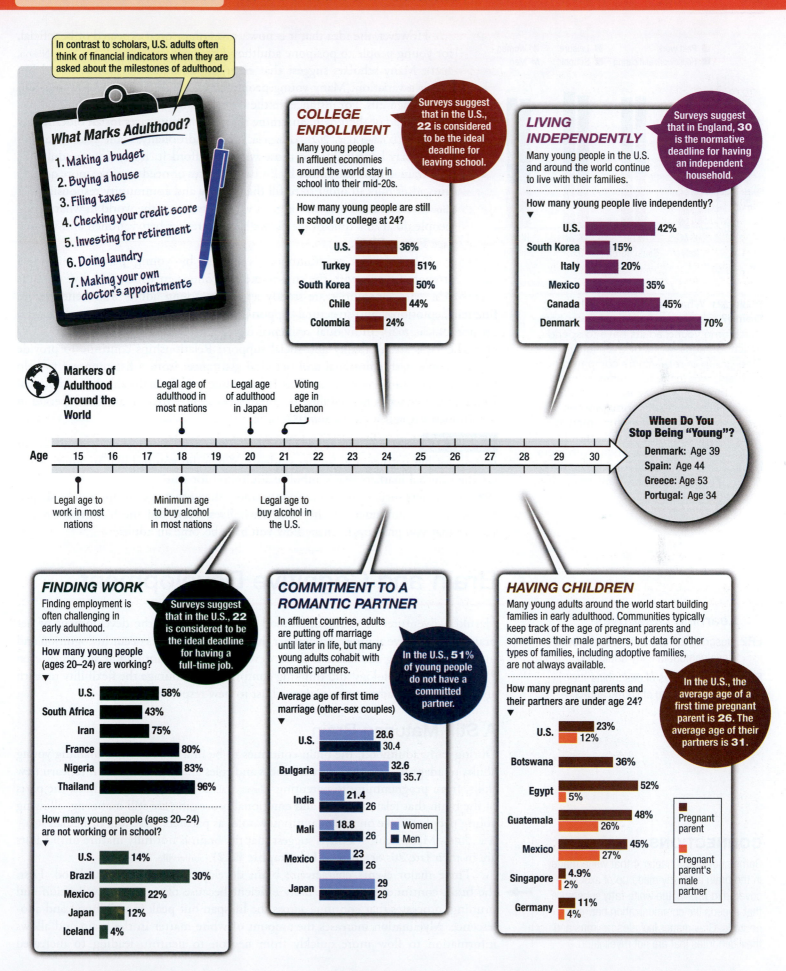

In contrast to scholars, U.S. adults often think of financial indicators when they are asked about the milestones of adulthood.

What Marks Adulthood?
1. Making a budget
2. Buying a house
3. Filing taxes
4. Checking your credit score
5. Investing for retirement
6. Doing laundry
7. Making your own doctor's appointments

COLLEGE ENROLLMENT

Many young people in affluent economies around the world stay in school into their mid-20s.

Surveys suggest that in the U.S., **22** is considered to be the ideal deadline for leaving school.

How many young people are still in school or college at 24?

U.S.	36%
Turkey	51%
South Korea	50%
Chile	44%
Colombia	24%

LIVING INDEPENDENTLY

Many young people in the U.S. and around the world continue to live with their families.

Surveys suggest that in England, **30** is the normative deadline for having an independent household.

How many young people live independently?

U.S.	42%
South Korea	15%
Italy	20%
Mexico	35%
Canada	45%
Denmark	70%

Markers of Adulthood Around the World

Legal age of adulthood in most nations — 18
Legal age of adulthood in Japan — 20
Voting age in Lebanon — 21

Age: 15 16 17 18 19 20 21 22 23 24 25 26 27 28 29 30

Legal age to work in most nations — 15
Minimum age to buy alcohol in most nations — 18
Legal age to buy alcohol in the U.S. — 21

When Do You Stop Being "Young"?
Denmark: Age 39
Spain: Age 44
Greece: Age 53
Portugal: Age 34

FINDING WORK

Finding employment is often challenging in early adulthood.

Surveys suggest that in the U.S., **22** is considered to be the ideal deadline for having a full-time job.

How many young people (ages 20–24) are working?

U.S.	58%
South Africa	43%
Iran	75%
France	80%
Nigeria	83%
Thailand	96%

How many young people (ages 20–24) are not working or in school?

U.S.	14%
Brazil	30%
Mexico	22%
Japan	12%
Iceland	4%

COMMITMENT TO A ROMANTIC PARTNER

In affluent countries, adults are putting off marriage until later in life, but many young adults cohabit with romantic partners.

In the U.S., **51%** of young people do not have a committed partner.

Average age of first time marriage (other-sex couples)

	Women	Men
U.S.	28.6	30.4
Bulgaria	32.6	35.7
India	21.4	26
Mali	18.8	26
Mexico	23	26
Japan	29	29

HAVING CHILDREN

Many young adults around the world start building families in early adulthood. Communities typically keep track of the age of pregnant parents and sometimes their male partners, but data for other types of families, including adoptive families, are not always available.

In the U.S., the average age of a first time pregnant parent is **26**. The average age of their partners is **31**.

How many pregnant parents and their partners are under age 24?

	Pregnant parent	Pregnant parent's male partner
U.S.	23%	12%
Botswana	36%	
Egypt	52%	5%
Guatemala	48%	26%
Mexico	45%	27%
Singapore	4.9%	2%
Germany	11%	4%

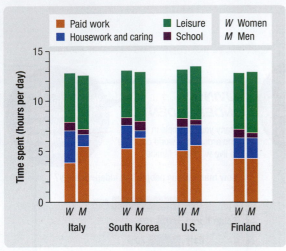

Data from Craig et al., 2019.

FIGURE EP.1 **What Are Young Adults Doing?** Community support affects how much time young adults have to spend in school, housework, or even leisure. One group of researchers compared how men and women in four different nations spent their everyday time. They found that, in nearly every country, women tend to spend more time than men in housework, caring tasks, and school. Young people in some nations with more community support for youth, such as Finland, had more leisure time than those in other countries.

However, the idea that it is now universal, or even expected or beneficial, for young people to postpone adulthood has been criticized (Côté, 2014; Nelson, 2021). Many scholars suggest that emerging adulthood is not universal but rather a variation. Many young people do take on considerable responsibilities in their 20s. For instance, in the United States, about half of young adults have a child of their own, and more than one in four cares for an older family member (D'Amen et al., 2021; Livingston, 2018). Additionally, while years of exploration may be valuable for those who can afford it, many young adults are constrained from adventure by limited finances or need to move more quickly into adult roles in order to fulfill their family and community responsibilities (Bowen et al., 2021). There also is great variability across the world in what young people do at this time of life, as well as differences between men and women (see **Figure EP.1**).

The journey to adulthood is shaped by young people's individual strengths, along with the environmental context in which they live (Shanahan et al., 2016). Inequities are starkly apparent: Young adults who benefit from financial, emotional, and structural supports are more likely to thrive than those who do not (Nelson, 2021). Individual resilience can help ease the transition. One source of resilience is strong family and social support: Relationships continue to provide young people with emotional and practical assistance, from a listening ear to help with the rent (Hartnett et al., 2018). This helps young people maintain their emotional health at a time when mental illnesses are more common than in any other period in the lifespan (Gagné et al., 2021b; SAMHSA, 2020).

APPLY IT! **EP.1** Haruki knows she is an adult because she feels responsible — for herself, for her partner, and for her students. When did you feel like an adult? What are the external markers that symbolize adulthood for you?
EP.2 Researchers suggest that young adults, more than other age groups, can be shaped by external circumstances as they start their lives. How did the historical circumstances that you grew up in shape how you have become an adult?

Brain and Cognitive Development

Learning Objectives

EP.2 Describe the characteristics of brain development in early adulthood.

EP.3 List three ways of describing the flexible thinking of young adults.

Haruki's adventures in young adulthood are supported by the development of her brain and cognitive abilities. Remember that dramatic changes occur in cognition and in the brain during adolescence. Brain development does not end at age 18 or even 25. Young adults' biology and thinking continues to encourage the flexibility to learn and adapt to new adventures as they adjust to new responsibilities.

A Still-Maturing Brain

During early adulthood, the brain continues to be in a state of flux, enabling young adults to adapt to changing circumstances and roles and powering them to learn new skills, from programming to parenting (Guyer et al., 2018). In younger adults, the parts of the brain that relate to social and emotional processing are still maturing, allowing young people to take on and adapt to new roles as partners or school principals (Casey et al., 2019). Many neuroscientists suggest that the brain is not fully mature until adults are in their late 20s or 30s (see **Infographic EP.2**) (Somerville, 2016).

Three major events characterize brain development in early adulthood. First, the brain continues to become more efficient because of ongoing myelination and pruning, processes that continue across the lifespan but peak in childhood and adolescence. Myelination increases the amount of white matter in the brain and allows information to flow more quickly from neuron to neuron, leading to increased

CONNECTIONS

Remember from Chapter 4 that white matter in the brain is mostly made up of axons covered in *myelin*, the white fatty substance that speeds the communication between neurons. Gray matter includes neurons and their dendrites that are not myelinated.

MATURATION OF THE BRAIN WITH CONTINUED INCREASE IN EFFICIENCY

Brain connections continue to increase in efficiency as young people enter adulthood, leveling off as they approach their mid-20s. Pruning continues, resulting in fewer, but more efficient connections in the frontal cortex.

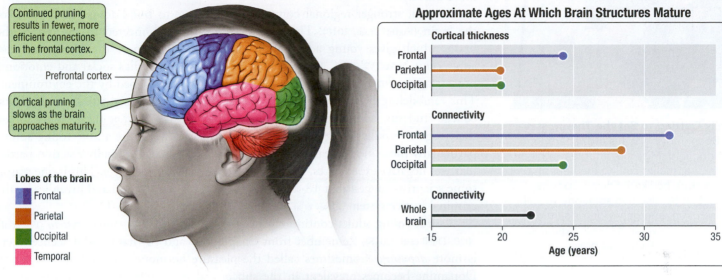

Continued pruning results in fewer, more efficient connections in the frontal cortex.

Prefrontal cortex

Cortical pruning slows as the brain approaches maturity.

Lobes of the brain
- Frontal
- Parietal
- Occipital
- Temporal

Approximate Ages At Which Brain Structures Mature

Cortical thickness — Frontal, Parietal, Occipital

Connectivity — Frontal, Parietal, Occipital

Connectivity — Whole brain

Age (years) — 15, 20, 25, 30, 35

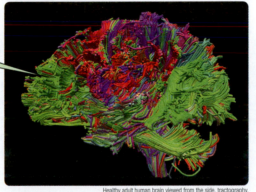

As the brain reaches the peak of speed and efficiency, the rate of myelination of slows.

Maturation of brain white matter tracts
This computer model shows the neural tracts of a young adult. Neurons in different parts of the brain use these pathways to share information with each other. These pathways continue to increase in efficiency into early adulthood.

Healthy adult human brain viewed from the side, tractography.
Henrietta Howells, NatBrainLab. Attribution 4.0 International (CC BY 4.0)

MATURATION OF COGNITIVE CAPACITY

Cognitive capacity reaches levels of adult maturity by mid-adolescence.

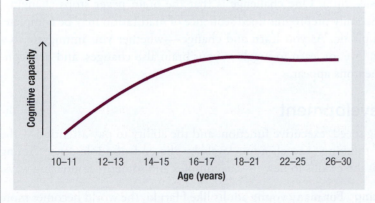

Cognitive capacity

Age (years) — 10–11, 12–13, 14–15, 16–17, 18–21, 22–25, 26–30

PSYCHOSOCIAL MATURITY

Psychosocial maturity continues through adolescence and early adulthood.

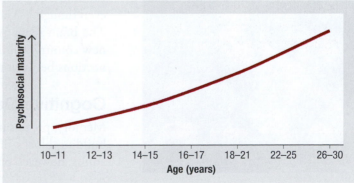

Psychosocial maturity

Age (years) — 10–11, 12–13, 14–15, 16–17, 18–21, 22–25, 26–30

Finally Getting to Set the Thermostat
For Boen, moving to his own apartment in Springfield, Missouri, after leaving foster care, meant setting the heat at a temperature he liked. Social supports meant that he also had someone to call in case of an emergency or for a little extra help, like when he wasn't quite sure how to make biscuits and gravy.

Medical School Utilizes Your Cognitive Skills. These young medical students in Riverside, California, are learning new skills and vocabulary. They are taking advantage of their peak levels of processing speed, executive function, and attention.

efficiency, particularly in the prefrontal cortex (PFC)—the area of the brain activated during logical thinking, self-control, and decision-making (Mills et al., 2016; Vanes et al., 2020). Researchers suggest that pruning and myelination allow young adults to process information faster, have more control over their behavior, and learn things more quickly.

Second, stronger regional connections continue to build across the regions of the brain (Faghiri et al., 2018). The PFC becomes more connected to the rest of the brain, which gives young adults more cognitive control over their behavior than adolescents have (Váša et al., 2020). This means that young adult's social and emotional processing continues to be particularly plastic and easily shaped by the environment. This remodeling helps young people adjust to their new social roles: as caregivers, college students, and colleagues. However, this also means that their ability to use their cognitive skills to regulate their emotions is still not quite adult: Young adults, particularly those in their early 20s, continue to be more emotionally reactive, particularly to negative experiences, than older adults are (Casey et al., 2019). This is one reason some scientists suggest that 18- to 21-year-olds should be considered juveniles by the criminal justice system (Casey et al., 2022).

Third, young adults continue to benefit from a sensitive *reward system* (Bos et al., 2020; Duell et al., 2018). Remember from Chapters 13 and 15 that in adolescence, there is more *dopamine* (sometimes called the pleasure hormone) available in the brain. Dopamine becomes prevalent in the subcortical structures involved in the reward system and when we think about pleasurable experiences, whether that is a romantic event or a video game win.

Some researchers suggest that this pattern of brain development may be one reason young adults are more adaptable to new circumstances and able to take on healthy risks such as starting new jobs, taking new classes, and meeting new people. However, this may also be one reason many need support, or be at risk of hurting themselves. Around the globe, young adults are more likely than younger people—and older ones—to die as a result of violence, accidents, and suicide (Masquelier et al., 2021). In the United States and in many other nations, young people also have higher rates of potentially dangerous behaviors, such as substance use and reckless driving (Willoughby et al., 2021b).

So, when is the brain done growing? Neuroscientists do not agree on exactly when maturation ends, only that it does not happen at 18. Some argue that the brain is adult in the mid-20s (Scott et al., 2016). Others suggest that it is not fully mature until the mid-30s (Somerville, 2016). One challenge is that the brain never stops changing, even though its genetically preprogrammed sequence of maturation may be complete. The brain remains plastic. As you learn and change—whether you immigrate to a new country, fall in love, or learn to juggle—your brain also changes, and new connections between neurons appear.

Cognitive Development

Memory, processing speed, executive function, and the ability to pay attention—the building blocks of thinking—reach adult levels by the end of adolescence. Young adults, however, put these skills to new uses in complex and sometimes amazing ways.

Relativistic Thinking   For many young adults like Haruki, the world becomes more complex after high school. Decisions are not simple, and choices become less clear. Some of the decisions of adulthood are important, and some just *feel* important, as Haruki tells us. She describes overthinking many choices she has had to make. As she has learned, one part of adulthood is accepting that there is not just one right answer, and that you may have to ask for support.

When Haruki says that there is no single right answer, she is embracing **relativistic thinking** (Sinnott et al., 2015). This way of thinking acknowledges that there is no absolute truth, but rather a collection of different perspectives. Instead of assuming there is one right answer to life's problems, relativistic thinkers are aware that their assumptions are biased and subjective. For example, Haruki has learned to accept that, for her, extra adult responsibility sometimes comes with a need for more support.

Dialectical Thinking Relativistic thinking is not the only new way young adults approach problems. **Dialectical thinking** is the ability to look at the opposing sides to a problem, explore the contradictions between them, and accept that the solution may lie somewhere in between. Dialectical thinkers know that "every coin has two sides," and that few problems have perfect solutions (Pang et al., 2017). Young adults who use dialectical thinking tend to be creative and flexible in determining solutions. For example, Haruki saw the complexity of her decision to get married, informed by her understanding of the complexity of relationships, especially long-distance romances, as well as by her bond with Marvin. Dialectical reasoning helps us understand that no choice is ever perfect or will ever satisfy all the people who give you advice.

Postformal Thought Some researchers believe that flexible thinking marks a new stage of cognitive development that follows Piaget's adolescent stage of formal operational thought. This stage, called **postformal thought**, allows young adults to think through complex issues by reviewing different viewpoints and considering emotional, contextual, and interpersonal factors (Labouvie-Vief, 1980, 2015; Sinnott, 1998, 2002). Although Piaget did not include postformal thought in his core stages of cognitive development, researchers Gisela Labouvie-Vief and Jean Sinnott used some of his methods—observation and interviews—to investigate how young adults think. They found that young people who use postformal reasoning can see things from a variety of perspectives and understand that many challenges have multiple solutions (Galupo, 2009). Postformal thought can help adults be more flexible in their thinking and break beyond the binary choices that are commonplace in politics or in everyday life (Sinnott, 2021; Sinnott et al., 2020).

SCIENCE IN PRACTICE
Susan Salcido, Community Outreach Worker

Susan Salcido put in many hours on her feet every day during the early months of the COVID-19 pandemic. Salcido was on the streets and in community centers around Los Angeles, trying to educate her community about how they can protect themselves and their families during the pandemic. One of her missions was to fix the mistrust in health care. A few of the people she met were skeptical about the vaccine, but most were simply nervous. These are the people who are often eager to talk (Shalby, 2021).

Developmental scientists have found that many people took a wait-and-see approach to the COVID-19 vaccine (Adams et al., 2021). In fact, younger people tend to be more mistrustful than older people are of vaccines and of health care, whether for themselves or for their young children (Funk et al., 2019; Grant et al., 2021; Shih et al., 2021; Tram et al., 2021).

Is there something in young adults' cognition that makes them vulnerable to mistrust? Some researchers have pointed out that health care decisions, particularly during a stressful time like a global pandemic, tend to be more *heuristic* and intuitive than *analytical* (Jennings et al., 2021). People who are nervous about vaccines, for instance, tend to be making heuristic judgments: perhaps putting off the side effects

Scientific American Profile

▶ Dialectical Reasoning and Life Decisions

CONNECTIONS

Remember from Chapter 14 that Jean Piaget believed that *formal operational thought*, the ability to think abstractly and systematically about the world, emerges in adolescence.

relativistic thinking A type of thinking that acknowledges there is no absolute truth, but rather a collection of different perspectives. Instead of assuming there is one right answer to life's problems, relativistic thinkers understand that their assumptions are biased and subjective.

dialectical thinking The ability to look at the opposing sides to a problem, explore the contradictions between them, and accept that the solution may lie somewhere in between.

postformal thought A stage of thinking that allows young adults to think through complex issues by reviewing different viewpoints, considering emotional, contextual, and interpersonal factors.

or the uncertainty about the vaccine and mistrusting the risks of getting COVID-19 (Bronstein et al., 2019).

Young people often have complex reasons for why they are nervous about vaccines or other health interventions. Compared to other age groups, young people are more likely to say that they have experienced bias in health care, and they are often more aware of historical discrimination within the health system (Benkert et al., 2019; Nong et al., 2020). Discrimination and mistrust go hand in hand: Both are at high levels in many groups of young people, including Black Americans, women, low-income adults, and those who identify as transgender, lesbian, gay, bisexual, or queer (Adams et al., 2021; Dean et al., 2021; Human Rights Campaign Foundation, 2018).

Susan Salcido worked to hand out masks and set up vaccine appointments, but more than anything she put in her time and her empathy to help rebuild trust. Research supports what she is doing: Getting to know people and giving them time to get to know you is one way to build trust in the medical system (NORC, 2021). Salcido is tackling that, one conversation at a time. 🔍

Building Relationships One Conversation at a Time Susan Salcido (*left*) is a community outreach worker in Los Angeles who educates her community about the importance of getting vaccinated for COVID-19 and, at the same time, tries to foster their confidence in the health care system.

APPLY IT! EP.3 Haruki has learned to be more understanding of the complexity of adult decision-making. Choices are not always clear. Have you been able to appreciate the complexity of decisions in your own adult life?

EP.4 Haruki is adapting to a new job as a high school counselor and a new role as a live-in partner. How does young-adult brain development help her adapt to these new roles?

EP.5 Haruki is planning on studying a third language, Pashtu, and maybe also Japanese, in the coming year. What are strategies that can be applied to learning in or out of school during early adulthood?

Education After High School

Learning Objective

EP.4 Describe the benefits of college and challenges to success in college.

In earlier generations, a college degree was not necessary to find a well-paying job. Today, two in three jobs in the United States require at least some college education. This trend extends around the world: Well-paying jobs now require at least some post–high school coursework or certification (Marshall & Symonds, 2021; Symonds et al., 2011).

From Albania to Australia, more young people are in college than ever before (UNESCO, 2020). The United States is a world leader in college enrollment. Even though enrollment has decreased since the COVID-19 pandemic, more than 6 in 10 young people attend either community or four-year colleges (BLS, 2021; NSCRC, 2022). Less than a quarter of U.S. college students attend college full time and live on campus (Irwin et al., 2021). Most are juggling school, work, and family, which can be overwhelming.

Benefits of College

For the almost 20 million U.S. college students, the investment may be worth it, particularly if they make it to graduation (Kim & Tamborini, 2019). When economists analyze adult incomes, they typically find that completing even a few college courses is linked to higher incomes than for those who have only received a high school diploma (Ma et al., 2020).

There are strong correlations between attending college and other measures of well-being. For instance, the children of college graduates are more likely to be affluent than those whose parents did not graduate from college (OECD, 2021d). College graduates also tend to have more romantic stability. They are more likely to be married and are 60 percent less likely to get divorced (Trostel, 2015). After graduation, young people report more job satisfaction and more happiness. They even tend to be

Share It!

Hungry in class? College students may have higher salaries once they graduate, but while they are in school, they face high rates of food and housing insecurity: More than one in five are food insecure and about 1 in 10 is housing insecure.

(Broton & Goldrick-Rab, 2018; Freudenberg et al., 2019)

healthier—smoking less and exercising more—and typically live longer than adults who do not complete college (Hong et al., 2020; Ma et al., 2020; Trostel, 2015).

Challenges of College

Although graduating from college is linked to better earnings and overall health, getting through college and paying for it can be complex and stressful. Millions of young people in the United States optimistically enroll in college, but not all of them graduate. In fact, compared to other affluent countries, the United States leads the pack in the number of students who leave college without a degree (Sarrico et al., 2017). Only about one in three students at two-year colleges graduates after three years, and only about 4 in 10 students at four-year colleges graduate after four years (Marcus, 2021; McFarland et al., 2017).

Students leave school for many reasons, including financial difficulties, academic strain, the stress of juggling college with work and family responsibilities, and feeling excluded from campus culture (Gopalan & Brady, 2020; NASEM, 2017; Sanchez & Kolodner, 2021). Some policy makers suggest that colleges could offer students more support to make graduating more achievable. They recommend making financial aid more comprehensive and transparent, so that it covers all the costs of college (including lab fees) and necessities like child care, and ensuring that college students are not excluded from programs that provide food, housing, and income support (Balzer Carr & London, 2020; Chaplot et al., 2015).

Student support programs that provide this financial support along with social and emotional supports like one-on-one advising and a closer sense of community have had impressive success. One program at the City University of New York nearly doubled the number of students who received their degrees (Weiss et al., 2019). Another in Fort Worth, Texas, nearly tripled the number of women who received their associate's degrees (Evans et al., 2020).

Some scholars believe that the culture on some campuses can be particularly alienating to less affluent and *first-generation college students*, those whose parents did not attend college. When compared with peers from similar income backgrounds, first-generation college students are 60 percent less likely to graduate (Wilbur & Roscigno, 2016). For these students, as well as for young people who are transgender, disabled, or from other marginalized backgrounds, an unwelcoming campus culture may be the culprit (Goldberg et al., 2019; Hernandez et al., 2021; Warnock & Hurst, 2016).

Institutions can help change their culture, but in many cases, young adults may need to build on their own sense of pride and community to help boost their achievement. Students who recognize their own strengths and the grit they drew on to get them into college are more likely to succeed (Hernandez et al., 2021).

How to Succeed in College Many markers associated with whether young adults have an easy time in college are already in place before they set foot on campus or may be out of our individual control. A major factor in student success in college is what came before: Not surprisingly, the more academically rigorous their high school experience and the better their grades, the more successful young adults tend to be in college (Allensworth & Clark, 2020).

But many students have difficulty adjusting to the pressures of college no matter their preparation. We have all been told what will help us succeed in college—getting the right course materials, showing up for class, doing the homework, and studying regularly (instead of cramming). What else matters? Building a support network, asking for help, spending time on assignments, and taking the right classes at the right time can all help you succeed.

- Build relationships and ask for support. Peers, family, or mentors can advise about college majors or how to track down an advisor who is missing during office hours and not answering e-mails (Hamilton, 2016). A helpful instructor or administrator can be a great resource for information about college majors, internships, or career

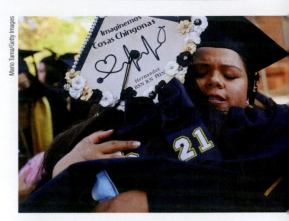

Persevering for the Win Graduation is always sweet, but it may be even more so for young adults who are balancing many commitments, like Macris. She is a parent and veteran who is celebrating her graduation from California State University, Los Angeles.

Waiting for Mommy to Finish Kristi is reading for her psychology class while her 3-year-old Kasiti watches a little television with friends. They all live on campus together at a college in Chambersburg, Pennsylvania, that offers housing and on-site day care for parents with young children.

Recruiting Apprentices D.J. is explaining the benefits of apprenticeship and careers in the pipe trades to students in Oshkosh, Wisconsin.

paths (Means & Pyne, 2017). Peers can help you find support on campus. Feeling that you belong is an essential part of the college experience: Seek out community to help you feel that you fit in (Broda et al., 2018).

- Recognize your own strengths. Reflect the strengths that got you where you are today: persistence, dedication to a long-term goal, and hard work. Sometimes these can pick you up when things seem daunting (Hernandez et al., 2021). Feeling pride in your own identity and values can remind you of something greater than yourself that can sometimes ease stress (Harackiewicz & Priniski, 2018).

- Befriend people who are ambitious. If your peers are studying, you are more likely to hit the books (Conley et al., 2015). And that time studying does pay off. Most students spend less than four hours a day, or less than 15 hours a week on classwork (and about the same time in leisure activities; Babcock & Marks, 2010).

- Do not be intimidated by your instructors. Developing relationships with people who can be role models and mentors is one of the transformative aspects of college, but you may need to persevere to make those relationships happen. Persistent students are often the ones who get attention from faculty (Means & Pyne, 2017; Schwartz et al., 2016).

- Make sure your school is the right fit for you. More than one in three students transfer to a different college (Shapiro et al., 2018). Some research indicates that students are more successful in schools with smaller classes, more motivated instructors, and engaging pedagogical methods (Brand et al., 2014; Kalogrides & Grodsky, 2011). A school-to-work or vocational program may be a better fit for those who want the financial benefits of a college degree but are worn out by academics (Jerrim, 2014).

School to Work

Some scholars point out that education is often more effective when it directly links to your future career. In fact, students enrolled in preprofessional tracks like health or pre-law are less likely to leave school without a degree than are those enrolled in general studies programs (Baum et al., 2013). For some students, programs that link education more closely to employment, called *career and technical education (CTE) programs*, are valuable alternatives to traditional college programs.

Gaining Skills through Job Corps Mandy is a student at the Job Corps program in Astoria, Oregon, where she had the opportunity to learn cooking techniques on a Coast Guard boat stationed nearby.

Critics of U.S. higher education often suggest that college does not cultivate enough of the work-related skills students need to succeed in their careers (Hanushek et al., 2020). They point to technical and school-to-work programs, often inspired by those in Europe, as models (Barnow et al., 2021; Bonvillian & Sarma, 2021). Remember from Chapter 13 that in many European countries, more than half of high school students enroll in work-related educational programs (Kris, 2016). While these European vocational programs are often technically demanding, they are effective in preparing students for the highly automated jobs of the current economy (Billett, 2014; Hanushek et al., 2017).

The United States offers a school-to-work program in Job Corps, a residential program serving about 60,000 young people every year. The program focuses on helping young people earn a GED and gain practical skills. Although about 7 in 10 Job Corps participants find work after participating in the program, their wages and long-term prospects are only modestly higher than those of young people who do not participate in the program (Blanco et al., 2013; Schochet, 2018). Unlike European programs, Job Corps is a small, relatively short-term intervention that may not always help graduates develop the technical skills they need for top-paying trades or careers (Fahrenthold, 2014).

APPLY IT! **EP.6** College is an investment of time and money that often takes much longer than young people plan. Haruki wishes she had been able to build more relationships in college. What has helped you identify your own college goals?

EP.7 "College for all" is a mantra in many U.S. high schools. Based on what you have learned in this chapter, what do you see as the strengths and risks of this strategy?

Succeeding on the Job

For many young adults, work is not only where they spend most of their time; it is also an important source of identity. Work is a way to support yourself and be connected to your community. For those who are fortunate enough, it can also be a source of meaning. Haruki finds meaning in going to work every day, building relationships, and helping younger people find their way through high school.

Who Is Working in Young Adulthood?

Most young adults in the United States are employed (U.S. Bureau of Labor Statistics, 2021). (See **Figure EP.2**.) Others are able to focus on unpaid opportunities, like internships or volunteering, during early adulthood. About one in eight young people is in neither the formal workforce nor in college (NCES, 2021b). In the United States and in most affluent countries, youth unemployment has been high since the recession of 2008 and continues to stagnate, in part because of the COVID-19 pandemic (ILO, 2021; Ross & Showalter, 2020).

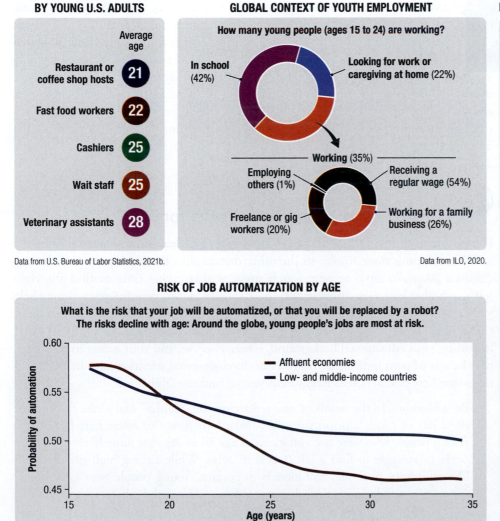

JOBS MOST COMMONLY HELD BY YOUNG U.S. ADULTS

	Average age
Restaurant or coffee shop hosts	21
Fast food workers	22
Cashiers	25
Wait staff	25
Veterinary assistants	28

Data from U.S. Bureau of Labor Statistics, 2021b.

GLOBAL CONTEXT OF YOUTH EMPLOYMENT

How many young people (ages 15 to 24) are working?

In school (42%)
Looking for work or caregiving at home (22%)
Working (35%)

Employing others (1%)
Receiving a regular wage (54%)
Freelance or gig workers (20%)
Working for a family business (26%)

Data from ILO, 2020.

PROJECTED JOB GROWTH ACROSS THE U.S. ECONOMY

3%
• Health care aides, care workers, and technicians
• STEM professionals
• Health professionals

1%
• Business or legal professionals
• Creative, advertising, and arts professionals
• Transportation or property services

0%
• Education
• Construction
• Skilled trades
• Farming

-1%
• Warehousing

-8%
• Office support
• Customer service and sales

Data from McKinsey, 2021.

RISK OF JOB AUTOMATIZATION BY AGE

What is the risk that your job will be automatized, or that you will be replaced by a robot? The risks decline with age: Around the globe, young people's jobs are most at risk.

— Affluent economies
— Low- and middle-income countries

Probability of automation (y-axis: 0.45 to 0.60)
Age (years) (x-axis: 15 to 35)

Data from ILO, 2020.

FIGURE EP.2 How Many Young People Are Working? Young people are working in jobs across the economy, but careers in health care and technology are booming.

Some young people who are not working are excluded from these unemployment numbers because they are not looking for formal work. Economists and sociologists suspect that many of these people are working, but in informal gig work (Venkatesh, 2006). Even young people who are working are more likely to be cobbling together a living from various part-time and freelance jobs (Katz & Kreuger, 2016). Researchers warn that gig work is likely to be unstable, temporary, and part time (Staff et al., 2015). This may suit some people's independent spirit and allow them to find more work–family balance, but experts worry that it causes additional stress and can erode mental health (Macmillan & Shanahan, 2021).

There is significant inequality based on identity, family income, ethnicity, culture, and physical and cognitive disability in whether young people are in the workforce, what kinds of jobs they find, and how they succeed at work (Khatiwada & Sum, 2016). Discrimination in hiring is persistent and widespread around the globe. It can be based on appearance, ethnicity, and as for about 1 in every 100 young people, a history of involvement with the justice system (Booker, 2016; Carnevale et al., 2019; Quillian et al., 2017; Wanberg et al., 2020). Inequality also impacts young people, as with those in rural areas, who may live too far from employment opportunities that meet their skills (Brooks, 2019).

Perhaps because so many jobs in our economy require college or technical education, it is taking young people longer to find jobs with a good salary than it did in past generations (Carnavale et al., 2013). And once young adults find work, it may be unstable: Young people now tend to have about eight employers over the course of early adulthood, and only 1 in 10 say that their current job is their "career" (Bureau of Labor Statistics, 2021). Even if young people find a career, jobs can transform quickly. Some opportunities have moved outside of North America, with accountants, radiologists, or web developers elsewhere in the world responding to clients in the United States (Sako, 2014). Industrialization and advances in robotics mean that machines now do many jobs that humans were once paid well to perform (Carnevale et al., 2018b).

Hoping for a Better Opportunity
Michelle is protesting for paid sick leave and a higher minimum wage in Denver, Colorado. Like other young workers, she is looking for stable, well-paying work.

MAKING A DIFFERENCE
How to Land a Job That Works for You

For many young adults, finding a job is crucial to establishing an adult identity and is a stepping stone similar to the other dreams, like finding a partner or having children (Mortimer, 2015). Some research suggests that taking time to find the right job—whether by trying different careers or staying true to your interests—may help you end up in a better-paying and more satisfying career years later (Chow et al., 2017; Gervais et al., 2016). Many of the factors that shape your ability to find meaningful work, including your educational background, where you live, and your access to resources, may be out of your individual control, but developmental scientists have helped identify some best practices that might help you to find the "right" job.

- Be ambitious. In the words of one researcher: Be "planful" and make finding the right job or career a priority (Clausen, 1991). One group of researchers found that young people who were not ambitious at age 16 or 26 were more likely than their peers to struggle to find a job (Staff et al., 2010). While aiming high often sounds like an empty platitude, ambition is important. Young people who have higher expectations and stick to their dreams tend to end up with higher-paying and more satisfying jobs than their peers do (Mortimer et al., 2014).
- Explore. Go to career days, volunteer, and ask for help. Young people who actively research careers are more likely to find jobs that are fulfilling and

On-the-Job Training Senior Airman Christina Phillips, like many young adults, found a career in the military, the largest employer in the United States. Here, she shows off her technical skills at Nellis Air Force Base in Nevada.

well-paying (Mortimer et al., 2014). College students may be able to access career centers for help in finding internships and learning about college majors and future careers. Young people who are ready for a job right out of high school are often at a disadvantage in finding job leads, because the pathway to work is often not clear and high schools are not always set up to help you find work (Mortimer et al., 2002, 2014).

- Evaluate your own strengths. Your interests and personality are only two things that can contribute to your success at work, but they are a great place to start. Are you good with children? Do you love to write? Are you an avid gamer? Thinking about what you are good at and enjoy may lead you to a vocational path.
- Consider your values. Focusing on the intrinsic values of work—that it is something you like and that feels meaningful—tends to pay off in the long run. If you enjoy your work, you will most likely be successful, which will typically lead, in the end, to job satisfaction and more money (Chow et al., 2017).
- Develop "soft" job skills. Employers look for communication skills, time management, punctuality, reliability, and creative problem solving (Chernyshenko et al., 2018; Lippman et al., 2015).
- Expect some transition pains. Work culture is different from the high school or college environment, and the transition can be challenging. New workers are not evaluated regularly, they are often isolated and surrounded by colleagues who are different—many new employees do not feel that they belong (Wendlandt & Rochlen, 2008).
- Stick with it. Jobs are often routine, boring, and sometimes lonely. Young people are often disappointed with the lack of supervision and help from supervisors and by how little responsibility they are given (Wendlandt & Rochlen, 2008). Persistence in the face of such challenges can lead to greater success in the future (Duckworth & Gross, 2014; Rowan-Kenyon et al., 2017). 🌐

APPLY IT! **EP.8** Haruki has found a job that makes her feel useful in a community where she feels that she belongs. She's been able to combine her interest in people with a job that gives her purpose. Do you have a sense of purpose or meaning in your life that helps drive your career aspirations?

EP.9 Employment structures are often unequitable, often segregated by family income, education, gender, and ethnicity (among other variables). How do scholars suggest that individuals can persevere to find meaningful work?

intimacy versus isolation Erikson's stage of human development that occurs in young adulthood. In his view, the successful resolution of the crisis is finding love.

Scientific American Profile

Life Transitions

What Is This Thing Called Love?

Theoretical Approaches to Romantic Love

For many, one of the hallmarks of young adulthood is the capability to create new romantic relationships like the one between Haruki and Marvin. A challenge is to figure out who and how to love.

Intimacy Versus Isolation Erik Erikson's theory describes a key conflict of young adulthood as the struggle of **intimacy versus isolation**. In his view, the successful resolution of this developmental stage is finding love, which entails not only physical intimacy but also a joint commitment to "significant sacrifices and compromises" and to making a new life together. To Erikson, who spent almost 65 years working, writing, and raising four children with his wife, Joan, the ideal life is built on the foundation of a close adult relationship. The antithesis of this *intimacy* was, in his mind, *isolation*, a life spent separate and uncommitted.

Learning Objective

EP.6 Describe major theories of love in young adulthood.

CONNECTIONS

Intimacy versus isolation is the conflict described in Erikson's sixth stage, early adulthood. Chapter 15 reviewed the stage of identity versus role confusion: The quest for identity often continues into early adulthood.

Welcome Home Sgt. Johnathan Link was welcomed home by his girlfriend, Christine, after he served nine months in Afghanistan. Scientists sometimes study couples reuniting to understand their attachment styles.

CONNECTIONS

Remember that attachment theory was developed by John Bowlby and others (see Chapter 2). Refer to Chapter 6 for a refresher on the theory of attachment in infancy, including the attachment styles based on the work of Mary Ainsworth, which classifies caregiving relationships as secure or insecure.

Erikson recognized that being in a relationship does not necessarily mean that one has achieved intimacy: He witnessed many young adults suffering in relationships that were merely joint isolation. The successful resolution of this stage, according to Erikson, requires companionship in which each partner creates a better life together: not because they are afraid of being alone, but because they have learned how to make a commitment (Erikson & Erikson, 1998).

In contrast with Erikson, many contemporary researchers point out that adults can be fulfilled without commitment or romance. Adults can build closeness in friendships, in family, or in shared meaningful work (DePaulo, 2017). Having a partner in early adulthood (or across the lifespan) does not mean that you are healthier or more "typical" than others: In fact, most young adults are not partnered, and being partnered is no guarantee of psychological health (van den Berg & Verbakel, 2021). In addition, whereas Erikson optimistically assumed that development was linear, and that adults moved from establishing an identity to finding a partner as they grew, many contemporary scholars suggest that many young adults are still discovering who they are: a process of identity development and personality change that continues throughout early adulthood (Landberg et al., 2018).

The Attachment Approach Attachment theorists, as explained in Chapter 2, believe that adults' habits of relating—even if they trust their partners and want to be close—are formed over a lifetime by other relationships, including their relationships with their caregivers as infants and their friendships and caregiving experiences later in childhood and adolescence (Fraley & Roisman, 2019; Hazan & Shaver, 1987; Mikulincer & Shaver, 2021).

Recall from Chapter 6 that researchers measure infant–caregiver relationships in terms of attachment styles, categorized as *secure, anxious, avoidant,* and *disorganized.* Adult attachment researchers measure romantic relationships in a similar way: They look at how well romantic partners interact with their partners when they are stressed and how well they comfort each other (Fraley, 2019; George et al., 1985; Main et al., 1985). As a result of this work, scientists have found that attachment continues to describe how adults relate. Some young adults have a *secure relationship style*: They are confident that their partners are available and supportive of them. Others are less so.

Researchers find that there are two key dimensions of attachment insecurity—*anxiety* and *avoidance*. They suggest we often take these habits of relating with us from childhood into new relationships (Chopik et al., 2021; Mikulincer & Shaver, 2021). People who have an *anxious relationship style* are unsure whether their partner will be there for them and need a lot of reassurance about their affection. People who have an *avoidant relationship style* believe that their partner will be unable to offer comfort and disengage as a result. They tend to be less open, intimate, and connected with their partners, believing it is safer to manage their feelings on their own.

IDEAL CHARACTERISTICS

1.	**Funny**
2.	**Intelligent**
3.	**Honest**
4.	**Attractive**
5.	**Kind**
6.	**Understanding**
7.	**Ambitious**
8.	**Loyal**
9.	**Caring**
10.	**Trustworthy**

Information from Sparks et al., 2020.

UNCONSCIOUS BIAS IN DATING

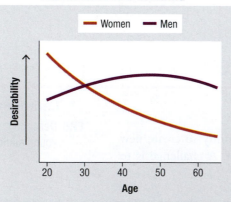

Information from Bruch & Newman, 2018.

FIGURE EP.3 What Are You Looking for in a Partner? Scientists have found that what you think you like does not always predict who you will end up with in real life: Most adults report they are looking for a partner who is funny and intelligent. But when scientists observe who is perceived as desirable by analyzing who clicks online, they find that contact is often driven by demographic factors like age, a bias that often favors older men.

Finding a Partner

Many young adults are not terribly interested in what we know about the theories of love. Many want to know how to find the right person (see **Figure EP.3**). Researchers are interested in how young adults find each other, not necessarily because they want to help young people find "the one" (or ones), but because romance has an outsized impact on our life. For instance, romance often leads to starting a family and sharing a home and finances, practices that shape communities and our life course. In addition, romance is often shaped by the social structures and institutions around us.

Finding Romance There are about 6 million people on Tinder, another 5 million on Grindr, and another 10 million on the Chinese dating app Jiayuan, but most will likely end up with people who live near them and who share similar backgrounds (Haandrikman, 2019; Huber & Malhotra, 2017; Iqbal, 2021; Thomala, 2021). Even when couples meet online, our tendency to like people who we think are similar to us, called *homophily*, plays an important role in finding a partner, just as it does in making a friend in fourth grade. People tend to match with people who share their politics and even use the same words in their dating profiles (Huber & Malhotra, 2017; Maldeniya et al., 2017). In this way, romance can perpetuate group differences and segregation (Mijs & Roe, 2021).

Young adults in the United States and in other affluent countries are more accepting of some kinds of diverse partnerships than they were in the recent past (Choi & Goldberg, 2020). Same-sex, gender-diverse, interethnic, interreligious, and interracial relationships are at an all-time high in the United States. Today, one in six weddings occurs between people with different ethnic backgrounds (Livingston & Brown, 2017). Young same-sex couples tend to be even more open-minded about whom they live with or marry, with nearly one in five gay men living with someone from a different ethnic group (Ciscato et al., 2020; Lundquist & Lin, 2015).

However, young people today are less likely than previous generations to date people from different educational and occupational backgrounds. College-educated young adults in same- and other-sex partnerships tend to marry each other. People with high-status jobs tend to marry other people with high-status jobs: Doctors marry other doctors, and lawyers marry other lawyers (Schwartz et al., 2021). This trend is strongest for other-sex couples and for lesbian couples; men tend to be more open-minded about their partner's educational and job background when they seriously date or marry other men (Ciscato et al., 2020).

Sexual Orientation One of the variables young people select when looking for a partner is gender. Increasingly, young adults are fluid in terms of their gender identity and to whom they are attracted, and their gender identity expression and their sexual attraction may continue to develop and change as they go through their 20s and beyond (Diamond, 2016; Kaestle, 2019; Kuper et al., 2018).

An increasing number of young adults now feel comfortable identifying as transgender or nonbinary. Recent surveys of young people in the United States and more than 27 other affluent countries found that about 3 in every 100 do not identify with gender-binary labels (Boyon & Silverstein, 2021; Harris Poll, 2017; Ipsos, 2021). Many young people in the United States, about 20 to 25 percent, depending on the survey, identify as having a sexual orientation other than "completely heterosexual" (Ipsos, 2021; Jones, 2021). This is similar to the estimate of about 30 percent of adults who identify as LGBTQIA+ in many other affluent countries (Boyon & Silverstein, 2021). (See **Figure EP.4**.) The language that younger adults use to describe their gender identity and sexual orientation often differs from that of older adults: They may prefer modern terminology like *queer*, *pansexual*, or *agender* to older labels that reflect more fixed, exclusive, and binary identities (Bishop et al., 2020; McCormack & Savin-Williams, 2018).

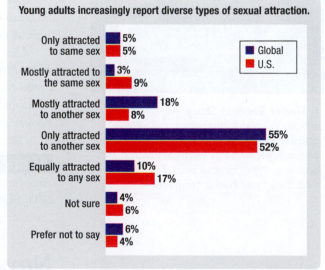

Young adults increasingly report diverse types of sexual attraction.

	Global	U.S.
Only attracted to same sex	5%	5%
Mostly attracted to the same sex	3%	9%
Mostly attracted to another sex	18%	8%
Only attracted to another sex	55%	52%
Equally attracted to any sex	10%	17%
Not sure	4%	6%
Prefer not to say	6%	4%

Data from Ipsos, 2021.

FIGURE EP.4 Increasing Diversity in Sexual Attraction Around the globe, researchers have found that nearly half of young people report being attracted to people of the same sex or of any sex.

As you read in Chapter 15, some people begin to identify as gay, lesbian, bisexual, or another label during adolescence, and some children express a gender-diverse identity in childhood. But, gender and sexual identity may not develop in a fixed series of stages (Pullen Sansfaçon et al., 2020). Expressing your identity often depends on family and community expectations. Many wait to come out or express a gender-diverse identity until they are more independent (Kuper et al., 2018; Medico et al., 2020). In general, young people come out earlier in more accepting communities and at younger ages than in previous generations, but many still face prejudice and rejection from their families (Bishop et al., 2020; van Bergen et al., 2021).

CAN YOU BELIEVE IT?
Has Swiping Changed Dating?

Technology has changed how young people meet their romantic partners. Most U.S. couples now meet online (Rosenfeld et al., 2019). Online dating is popular worldwide: It is even more popular in Russia, Brazil, and China than in the United States (Boxall, 2017).

The relationships young people begin online are not particularly different from those that start through blind dates or introductions from friends-of-friends. In general, they tend to have a similar chance of success and of breakup (Cacioppo et al., 2013; Rosenfeld, 2017).

Online dating tends not to be very different from the world outside of it. For some, including people who were too shy to meet up in real life, identify as non-binary, queer, or disabled, or belong to certain religious groups, online dating has opened up new possibilities for finding partners (Lundquist & Curington, 2019; Porter et al., 2017; Rochadiat et al., 2018; Rosenfeld & Thomas, 2012).

Unfortunately, toxic behavior is common online, with frequent reports of harassment and abuse (Anderson et al., 2020). Exclusion based on race, size, and ability pervades interactions and even the apps' algorithms and filters (Wade & Harper, 2020). Users often feel that their preferences are not under their conscious control, justifying their attractions or rejections and, sometimes, their degrading or stereotypical comments (Anderson et al., 2020; Hutson et al., 2018). Social norms also often encourage online dating to be treated as a casual game when, for many, it is extensively curated and emotionally serious (Berkowitz et al., 2021).

One challenge is that many of us believe we know what we are looking for and what type of partner will work for us. But most people are just not very good at predicting the spark of chemistry or the long-term compatibility that will make a relationship work (Sparks et al., 2020). Relationship success often comes down to how people get along, rather than the qualities that brought the two people together (Joel et al., 2017, 2020).

APPLY IT! **EP.10** How would you explain the benefits of understanding the science behind romantic love?

EP.11 Have you ever been in love? Can you analyze your experience using Erikson's crisis or attachment theory?

New Family Relationships

Haruki took a big leap when she was in her 20s and got on a plane to El Salvador to meet a man she had only talked to online. She was introduced to Marvin by her aunt, but they had never met in real life before she landed in San Salvador. However, she already thought that he might be the one: They had a connection, he understood her, and they talked for hours on the phone. Now 25, Haruki and Marvin are married

Share It!

Who is losing out online? Some research suggests that as a group, men are likely to feel rejected online: They tend to get much less interest than they expect.

(Anderson et al., 2020)

A Tinder Success Story At least that is how Wilmarie describes it: She is a graphic designer in Johannesburg, South Africa, who met her partner, Zakithi, an online analyst, on the app. They found that they "just had a connection."

Learning Objective

EP.7 Describe common variations in family and parenting relationships during young adulthood.

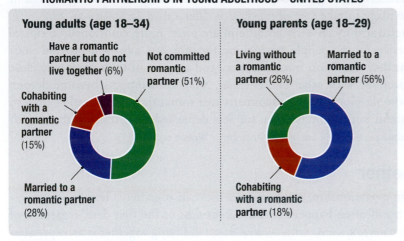

ROMANTIC PARTNERSHIPS IN YOUNG ADULTHOOD—UNITED STATES

Young adults (age 18–34)

Have a romantic partner but do not live together (6%)

Not committed romantic partner (51%)

Cohabiting with a romantic partner (15%)

Married to a romantic partner (28%)

Young parents (age 18–29)

Living without a romantic partner (26%)

Married to a romantic partner (56%)

Cohabiting with a romantic partner (18%)

Data from General Social Survey, 2018.   Data from U.S. Census Bureau, 2020b.

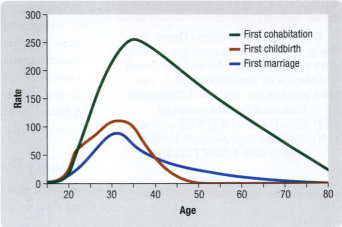

FAMILY TRANSITIONS IN YOUNG ADULTHOOD—UNITED STATES

- First cohabitation
- First childbirth
- First marriage

Data from Manning, 2020.

FIGURE EP.5 Family Relationships in Early Adulthood Relationships and families are diverse in early adulthood in the United States. However, many young adults are cohabitating for the first time or are not currently committed.

and living together, as are about one in three young adults in the United States. Like Haruki, about 8 in 10 young people want to be in a long-term relationship, but many, unlike Haruki, have not yet found their person (see **Figure EP.5**) (Manning et al., 2019; Smock & Schwartz, 2020).

Happily Single

Singlehood is typical in young adulthood in the United States, even though it is often stigmatized in communities that see being paired off as normative (Zhang & Ang, 2020). Researchers estimate that more than half of young people in the United States are not actively seeing anyone, which is broadly consistent with other affluent nations (Fry & Parker, 2021). Some young adults postpone relationships until they are married; others are waiting until they have accumulated the education and wealth that it takes to be independent (Shulman & Connolly, 2013).

Casual Relationships

Most romances during early adulthood do not lead to committed relationships. In the years after high school and in the early 20s, short-term, intimate relationships are common (Lyons et al., 2015). For many, short-term relationships are a way of beginning more emotionally intimate, long-term relationships (Eastwick et al., 2021; Watson et al., 2017). For others, casual relationships are mostly just about fun (Olmstead et al., 2021).

In young adulthood, sex outside of a committed relationship may not be in the context of a committed relationship, but it does not necessarily mean "sex with strangers." In fact, people who have sex but do not consider themselves committed may actually have long-term, close relationships with their partners (Eastwick et al., 2021; Lyons et al., 2014). Nearly 9 in 10 sexually active young adults had a stable, ongoing relationship with their last sexual partner, and many report having romance, rather than just intimacy on their minds (Tillman et al., 2019; Weitbrecht & Whitton, 2020).

Unabashedly Single Bollywood actress Sayani Gupta is not married and (when this picture was taken) not dating anyone. She has been outspoken in destigmatizing singlehood in India.

Committed Relationships

Throughout the lifespan, supportive, warm relationships are beneficial. Good relationships are linked with well-being partly because people who are mentally healthy and who have strong attachments tend to be in couples. In addition, close relationships themselves can give people an emotional boost by reducing stress and making us more likely to take care of our health (Allen et al., 2020; Meeus et al., 2007).

Romantic relationships in early adulthood are often more emotionally intimate than in adolescence: Young people are looking for someone who will provide emotional support as they transition from the safety and support of their parents to close emotional connections with other adults (Sassler, 2010). Attachments become deeper. Young people who develop secure attachments to a romantic partner, rather than to a friend or a parent, tend to be happier and less depressed than those without such relationships (Lehnart et al., 2010; Luciano & Orth, 2017; Wagner et al., 2015).

Living Together

At some point in a relationship, many couples move in together. There is no universal time frame, but it often happens within six months of the first date, regardless of gender (Orth & Rosenfeld, 2018; Sassler et al., 2018). Living together is an expression of closeness, symbolized by sharing a bed, a roof, and dirty dishes.

When romantic partners live together full time, they are *cohabiting*. **Cohabitation** is now more common than marriage among young adults (Manning et al., 2019). Other young adults choose to stay committed but *live apart together (LAT)*, living together on weekends or a few days a week but not sharing the rent or mortgage (Tillman et al., 2019). Most U.S. women have lived with someone before their 30th birthday, but LAT relationships tend to be more common among those who have the financial means to maintain separate homes (Manning, 2020).

Cohabiting is common among same-sex and other-sex couples (Frost et al., 2015; Joyner et al., 2017). Cohabiting relationships in other parts of the world, such as Norway, France, or the Philippines, tend to be longer lasting, perhaps because they are more accepted as an alternative to marriage (Hiekel et al., 2014; Manning, 2020; Perelli-Harris et al., 2014; Schwanitz & Mulder, 2015).

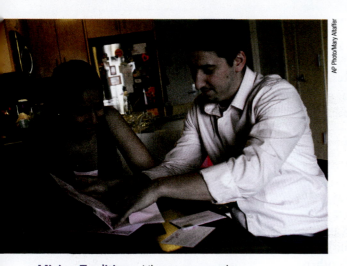

Mixing Traditions Like many couples, Catherine and Max grew up in different faith communities. Catherine identifies as Roman Catholic and Max as Jewish. For their wedding in New York, they plan to blend religious traditions from both of their faiths.

Marriage

A generation ago, most young adults in the United States were married before age 25. Now, Haruki is a little younger than most brides. The median age for a first marriage in the United States is about 28 for women and 30 for men (U.S. Census, 2020). Similar trends are happening around the world—couples are getting married later, and there is more diversity in family forms (Zaidi & Morgan, 2017).

Researchers have observed that four major factors have shifted the timeline for marriage from the late teens to the late 20s. First, a changing and challenging economy makes it difficult for many young adults to gain financial stability before their late 20s (Zaidi & Morgan, 2017). Second, the roles of partners have changed. In many marriages, both partners now expect to establish independent identities and pursue careers, as well as share child care and domestic tasks (Mintz, 2015). Third, many adults no longer feel that marriage should come before children: Young adults who have children are much more likely to be unmarried (Annie E. Casey, 2018). Fourth, expectations of marriage have changed (Finkel, 2019). Many couples now believe that marriage is something that you enter into once you have your life together, rather than a journey that you embark on together (Coontz, 2016).

Even though many young adults put off marriage, many U.S. couples do get married in their early 20s. This is more common in communities that are religiously or culturally conservative (Denton & Uecker, 2018; Uecker, 2014; Zhang & Ang, 2020). Many young people, like Haruki, are aware of the social stigma sometimes associated with early marriage, yet nearly one in four young adults decides to tie the knot before age 30 (Tevington, 2018; Uecker, 2014).

cohabitation Sharing a home with a romantic partner.

APPLY IT! **EP 12** Most young adults are single, but there are many cultural expectations for being partnered. How would you explain the benefits and possible risks of commitment in early adulthood?

Community Engagement

As young people move into adulthood, they take on new roles in the broader community. They may organize lunches in a soup kitchen, coach soccer, or direct after-school programs. Whether it is volunteer work, organizing, or simply showing up in the voting booth, engagement with and service to the community is known as **civic engagement** (Delli Carpini, 2000).

For many young people, community engagement means being involved with politics. This can take different forms: voting, attending rallies and marches, following political leaders, organizers, and movements on Twitter, or reading Instagram updates. Interest in politics, voting, and political action increases from age 18 to 24 (Wray-Lake et al., 2020). Young adults are more politically active than they were in the past, particularly online: 7 in 10 get political information online and 4 in 10 post, tag, or otherwise share political information on social media (Booth et al., 2020; Harvard Kennedy School, 2021).

For today's generation of young people, online political involvement often leads to offline participation, with high numbers of young people signing petitions, joining boycotts, and protesting. Nearly one in three young people participated in protests in the United States in 2020 (CIRCLE, 2018; Holbein et al., 2021). This participation can have individual as well as community benefits. For instance, young people who managed to stay politically active during the pandemic tended to report feeling more optimistic than their peers did (Lundberg, 2021).

However passionate they are, many young people are not participating in the formal political process by voting or running for political office. In the United States and around the world, many people in their 20s feel unconnected to traditional political parties and even excluded from traditional political institutions (Deal, 2019; Weiss, 2020). In the United States, Europe, and many nations in Africa, young adults have the lowest rates of voting of any age group (United Nations, 2016). Although more U.S. young people voted in the 2020 presidential election than in years past, only half of all young adults went to the polls (CIRCLE, 2021).

Although young people may not be voting in large numbers, many are actively making a difference in their communities. In college and high school, young people are connecting to their communities by teaching, serving food at soup kitchens, and coaching (Hill & den Dulk, 2013). One in four U.S. young adults frequently volunteers with schools or community organizations, and one in three regularly does favors for their neighbors (CNCS, 2018). Outside of college, programs like AmeriCorps and City Year, funded by the U.S. federal government, offer stipends to help young people participate in public service when they may not be able to afford to do so on their own. One goal of intervention efforts is to make sure that all young people feel that they can give back to their communities.

Religious Participation

Many young people who volunteer do so through a religious organization, whether it is a food pantry at a local church or a tutoring program at a neighborhood synagogue. However, many do not attend services as regularly as they did in high school

Learning Objective

EP.8 Describe patterns of civic engagement among young people.

Share It!

Hope is at an all-time high: Young people tell pollsters that they feel hopeful that the world is getting better.

(Harvard Kennedy School, 2021)

Michael Macor/The San Francisco Chronicle via Getty Images

Making a Difference with Sticks Volunteer coach Jon Yip takes time to offer younger students some lacrosse tips. Scholars suggest that volunteering helps the volunteers as well as those they serve.

civic engagement Working to make a difference in the community in a variety of ways, including volunteering, organizing, and voting.

FatCamera/E+/Getty Images

Making Time for Faith The unsettled years of early adulthood often make attending services difficult, but young people often hold onto the faith that they grew up with.

(Chan et al., 2015). For most young people, this seems to be more a reflection of their generally unsettled lifestyle than a rejection of the values or faith they grew up with. It is particularly true for young people who have not made their religion a central part of their identity, who describe themselves as "spiritual, but not religious" (Barry & Abo-Zena, 2014).

For some, however, young adulthood is a time to commit to their religion or to explore new spiritual practices, particularly if they have children (Denton & Uecker, 2018; Negru-Subtirica et al., 2017). More than 7 in 10 U.S. young people report that their faith is an important part of their lives (Ryberg et al., 2018). For many, faith and connection to the broader community will continue to be a source of support as they navigate the transition to middle life.

APPLY IT! EP.13 Have you ever wanted to volunteer? Many students want to help others, but may not have the time or find an organization that feels like a good fit. What ideas do you have to design interventions to make service more accessible?

Wrapping It Up

LO EP.1 Identify the key historical markers and common variations in adulthood. (p. 393)

The markers of adulthood are flexible to match the changing expectations of each culture, time, and place. Biological maturation is variable. There are five aspirational markers of adulthood: finishing school; establishing an independent household; finding work; finding a romantic partner; and having children. Most young adults do not reach all of these markers because of changing cultural expectations and economic strains. Some scholars suggest that there is a new life stage called *emerging adulthood*, in which young people in their 20s explore who they are. Other scholars suggest that this exploration may be a privilege. Young adults are more profoundly shaped by historical events than other age groups are.

LO EP.2 Describe the characteristics of brain development in early adulthood. (p. 396)

The brain is not fully mature until adults are in their mid-20s or mid-30s. The brain is very plastic and easily shaped by the environment as adults adapt to new roles. The areas of the brain devoted to social and emotional processing mature during early adulthood. Connections between the subcortical structures that process emotion and the more logical prefrontal cortex are still not quite mature, allowing young adults to be more emotionally reactive and more optimistic about taking risks than adults.

LO EP.3 List three ways of describing the flexible thinking of young adults. (p. 396)

Scholars observe that young adults' thinking tends to become more relativistic as they grow. Dialectical thinking acknowledges that there are different viewpoints, and that the ideal solution may be found from a hybrid position. A stage of thinking called *postformal thought* is inspired by Piaget's stages and suggests that adult thought is flexible, nonbinary, and more aware of the human variability in real-life decisions.

LO EP.4 Describe the benefits of college and challenges to success in college. (p. 400)

In affluent countries around the world, schooling often continues long into early adulthood. College has many benefits to health, social relationships, and employment but is not always an easy fit for young people. Many take a long time to graduate and may not complete their degree. Students who are low-income and who do not feel connected to campus community tend to have more difficulties in college. Scholars suggest that students need support to succeed. College programs that connect school to work can provide good opportunities.

LO EP.5 Analyze recent changes in employment and ways young people can identify their interests and employment strengths. (p. 403)

A globalized, technological economy means that work is often less permanent than it was in generations past. Many well-paying jobs require some college education or post-high school training. Young people often change jobs frequently. Finding a job that gives you a sense of purpose and meaning can boost your well-being.

LO EP.6 Describe major theories of love in young adulthood. (p. 405)

Young adults often begin serious romantic relationships. Researchers have developed theories to describe love. Erikson's theory suggests that early adulthood involves the crisis between intimacy and isolation. Attachment theorists suggest that adult relationships are shaped based on habits of relating that began in childhood and can be described in terms of secure or insecure attachment styles.

LO EP.7 Describe common variations in family and parenting relationships during young adulthood. (p. 408)

Most young adults are single, but some are also dating casually, cohabiting, or married. Increasingly, young adults put off getting married until they are in their late 20s. Cohabiting relationships tend to be more short term in the United States than in other nations.

LO EP.8 Describe patterns of civic engagement among young people. (p. 411)

Young people are more enthusiastic about making a difference in their community than they have been in many years. Volunteering and civic participation can help them connect and create a sense of generativity that benefits both young people and their communities. Young people are typically less connected to formal forms of civic participation, like voting, than older adults are, but are more active online and on the streets. Volunteer work and connections to faith communities continue to give young people a sense of belonging.

KEY TERMS

early adulthood (p. 393)
emerging adulthood (p. 394)
relativistic thinking (p. 399)
dialectical thinking (p. 399)
postformal thought (p. 399)
intimacy versus isolation (p. 405)
cohabitation (p. 410)
civic engagement (p. 411)

CHECK YOUR LEARNING

1. Which of these is a marker for the beginning of adulthood?
   a) When your body has finished maturing
   b) When you stop going to school
   c) When you take on adult responsibilities
   d) When you are recognized as an adult by your community

2. What are the possible advantages of a brain that is continuing to mature into early adulthood?
   a) It can be more easily damaged by head injuries.
   b) It is more susceptible to poor decision-making.
   c) It is more flexible as the individual adapts to new roles.
   d) It drains more energy from physical growth.

3. The type of reasoning that evaluates both sides of a problem is called:
   a) dialectical reasoning.
   b) formal operational thought.
   c) analytical thinking.
   d) heuristic thinking.

4. One challenge faced by students in college is that:
   a) young adults are too old to learn.
   b) college is no longer necessary for success.
   c) students often do not have the financial or social supports they need to succeed.
   d) students are not mature enough to take advantage of what college has to offer.

5. How has employment changed over the past 20 years?
   a) More automatization and use of robotics in many jobs
   b) Increased globalization of employment
   c) More short-term, gig work
   d) All of these are correct.

6. All of these are forms of civic engagement EXCEPT:
   a) sharing voting information with friends on Snapchat.
   b) volunteering as a poll worker.
   c) joining a rally.
   d) tutoring your younger brother.

GLOSSARY

A-not-B error Inability of toddlers to keep track of a hidden object if it is moved from one location (A) to another (B), even when they see it being moved. (p. 130)

abuse The legal term used to describe the most serious types of harm to children, which can be physical, emotional, sexual, or neglectful. (p. 233)

accommodation The process of reorganizing knowledge based on new experiences. (p. 41)

acculturation The process of adapting to some of the traditions and expectations of a cultural community. (p. 381)

achievement status In Marcia's theory, this identity status occurs when adolescents have explored and committed to a path. (p. 379)

adolescence The life stage that begins with the biological changes of puberty and ends when young people are recognized as adults. (p. 321)

adolescent-limited behavior A habit or behavior that is particular to the adolescent life stage. (p. 390)

adoption When a parent becomes a legal caregiver to a baby or child who is born to another biological parent. (p. 93)

adrenarche The first hormonal changes preparing the body for puberty, typically occurring between ages 5 and 9. (p. 251)

affordance The term for what people can learn from objects in the world around them. (p. 118)

age-segregated Grouped with other people of the same age. (p. 374)

alleles Genes that have different forms. (p. 64)

analytic thinking A type of thinking that is logical, weighing evidence and making a decision that requires conscious thought. (p. 347)

animism The tendency to describe nonliving things as if they are alive and have human feelings or motives. (p. 192)

anorexia nervosa A consistent pattern of disordered eating that may involve extreme calorie restriction, purging, excessive exercise, and a distorted belief that one's body is overly heavy. (p. 336)

anxiety disorders A clinical diagnosis based on a pattern of excessive worry or fear that keeps children, adolescents, or adults from fully functioning in their lives. (p. 387)

Apgar test A quick medical evaluation of breathing, activity, responsiveness, and heart rate that assesses which newborns need immediate medical care. (p. 91)

assessment The use of a standardized tool or test. (p. 55)

assimilation The expansion of an existing schema with new knowledge or experience. (p. 41)

attachment An emotional bond in a close relationship. Attachment begins with the relationship between infants and their caregivers and may not always be positive. (p. 163)

attachment theory The theory pioneered that maintains that children's emotional bonds to their caregivers are an essential part of their development. (p. 36)

attention-deficit/hyperactivity disorder (ADHD) A condition in which children have challenges with focusing or controlling themselves, that make it difficult to function without extra support at home or in school. (p. 201)

authoritarian parenting A type of caregiving in which caregivers have high expectations for their children's behavior but very little warmth. Authoritarian parents make rules and expect their children to obey them. (p. 230)

authoritative parenting A type of caregiving associated with confident and successful children in which caregivers have high expectations for their children's behavior, but they also are warm and communicative. (p. 230)

autism spectrum disorder (ASD) A cognitive and communication condition characterized by differences with communication and social interaction. (p. 126)

autonomy Taking responsibility, having greater agency, and making more decisions. (p. 365)

autonomy versus shame and doubt The second crisis in Erikson's stage theory of development in which toddlers learn to balance their desire to be independent with their limitations and frequent missteps. (p. 145)

average social acceptance Children who fall around the middle of being liked and disliked, not quite making it into the other categories. (p. 312)

axon The long, tail-like structure attached to the cell body that transmits chemical signals to other neurons. (p. 109)

babbling Short, repetitive, syllable sounds, like ba-ba-ba or pa-pa-pa (in English), that begin at about 4 months and become more speechlike by 7 months. (p. 137)

behaviorism A branch of psychology that is focused on things that are measurable, and suggests that we learn through pairing causes and effects. (p. 36)

binge drinking Consuming more than five drinks at one time. (p. 389)

binge-eating disorder The most prevalent eating disorder in adolescents, marked by episodes of compulsive, excessive eating that make you feel out of control, ashamed, or upset. (p. 336)

biological perspective A perspective with an emphasis on how psychological and behavioral development begins with roots in our brain, our genes, and innate or inborn instincts. (p. 31)

birth cohorts The categories that experts use to group people from different generations. (p. 15)

birth defects Major abnormalities in the body or brain functioning present at birth. (p. 83)

blastocyst The ball of cells during the germinal stage of prenatal development that becomes larger and then separates into an outer layer and an inner mass, replicating until it is more than 150 cells. (p. 77)

body image The feelings and ideas you have about your body. (p. 335)

bulimia nervosa A consistent pattern of disordered eating that involves overeating compensated by throwing up, excessive exercise, or abusing laxatives. (p. 336)

bullying A pattern of physical and/or social aggression by a child with social power against a child with less social acceptance. (p. 238)

career and technical education (CTE) Education that focuses on preparation for a trade, technical, or professional career. (Often called *vocational education* in the United States.) (p. 350)

case study An in-depth analysis of one child, family, or institution's experience. (p. 52)

cephalocaudal Development that occurs in a head-downward pattern, beginning with a baby's ability to support their heavy head. (p. 116)

cesarean section A surgical birth procedure in which the baby is removed from the body through a small cut in the uterus. (p. 89)

chromosomes The 23 pairs of long molecules of DNA containing genetic information and found in the nucleus of human cells. (p. 64)

circadian rhythm Your internal clock for the daily cycle of rest, wake, and sleep. (p. 105)

civic engagement Working to make a difference in the community in a variety of ways, including volunteering, organizing, and voting. (p. 411)

classical conditioning A model of learning in which a *stimulus* (or experience) is linked to a *response* (or behavior). (p. 37)

classification The categorization and grouping of objects according to multiple dimensions. (p. 270)

clique A small "friend group" that shares interests and activities. (p. 372)

cognitive development theory The theory that growth in thinking and understanding happens as a result of active exploration of the world. (p. 40)

cohabitation Sharing a home with a romantic partner. (p. 410)

collectivist Communities that place more value on relatedness and closeness and tend to value the family or the group over the individual. (p. 23)

Community Cultural Wealth Areas of strength and resilience identified by developmental scientists that help people, particularly those who are marginalized or are people of color, succeed in a discriminatory world. (p. 17)

comprehensive high schools Traditional high schools that are designed to meet the needs of adolescents who plan on attending college and those who do not, including a broad variety of academic courses and a limited selection of vocational courses. (p. 350)

concrete operations Piaget's stage of cognitive development occurring in middle childhood in which children's logical thinking abilities gradually improve as they begin to understand problems of greater complexity. (p. 269)

concussion A form of traumatic brain injury (TBI) caused by a blow to the head. (p. 344)

connectome Each individual's unique pattern of connections in the brain. (p. 173)

conservation tasks Piaget's hands-on tasks that measure how preschoolers' logical thinking develops. Each involves asking children what has happened to an object or a set of objects that is rearranged or manipulated in front of them to look different. Preschoolers struggle to logically complete the conservation tasks, but over time, their abilities improve. (p. 194)

constructive play Play that involves all forms of creativity. (p. 237)

context Experiences and conditions that may shape human development, including family, community, culture, and historical moments. (p. 13)

continuous A model of change that is relatively constant and stable. (p. 26)

controversial Children who receive mixed ratings by their peers, strongly disliked by some and strongly liked by others. (p. 312)

conventional stage of moral reasoning Kohlberg's stage of moral reasoning in which children think more abstractly about what is right and wrong. (p. 315)

cooperative play Playing together on a joint project. (p. 237)

correlational study A study in which a researcher gathers data and looks for relationships between variables but does not actually manipulate them. (p. 51)

critical thinking The ability to thoughtfully question what you believe or what other people believe. (p. 10)

cross-cultural research Research that compares people from two or more different cultural communities. (p. 57)

cross-sectional study A study that compares development in two or more groups of different ages at one point in time. (p. 53)

cross-sequential study A study that follows two or more different age groups over time in a combination of cross-sectional and longitudinal designs. (p. 53)

crowds Larger, looser collections of adolescents within the school or neighborhood. (p. 372)

cultural humility An openness to cultural diversity and a self-awareness of your own cultural background that helps to create respectful relationships in which everyone learns from each other and no one feels superior. (p. 19)

cultural perspective A perspective that explains how culture is integrated into all of development and how cultural variations and strengths can help everyone thrive. (p. 43)

cultural socialization The way children learn about their heritage or the community to which they belong, typically in their families. (p. 369)

culture The ideas, beliefs, customs, and social practices shared by a group of people. (p. 13)

dendrite A branch-like appendage that grows out of the cell body and receives communication from other neurons. (p. 109)

deoxyribonucleic acid (DNA) A spiral-, or helix-, shaped structure made up of paired chemicals that carries the genetic code. (p. 64)

dependent variable The factor that is measured during an experiment to determine the effect of the independent variable. (p. 49)

depression A clinical diagnosis based on a pattern of sadness and lack of energy that impairs your ability to function. (p. 387)

development The pattern of changes and stability in individuals that happens as we grow. It is also the study of what in the environment and in our genes make each of us unique. (p. 3)

developmental niche A person's cultural environment, which is subject to the specific cultural practices, material setting, and beliefs of their family. (p. 22)

developmental science The systematic study of how humans grow and the underlying processes that create change and stability over time. (p. 3)

dialectical thinking The ability to look at the opposing sides to a problem, explore the contradictions between them, and accept that the solution may lie somewhere in between. (p. 399)

differential susceptibility Individual differences in how sensitive people are to the environment effects. (p. 150)

difficult In Thomas and Chess's dimensional approach to temperament, babies who are easily frustrated, are slow to adapt to change, and react intensely. This term is no longer preferred, outside of scholarly research. (p. 158)

diffusion status In Marcia's theory, this identity status occurs when adolescents are not exploring or committed to an identity. (p. 379)

disability A mismatch between a person's physical, cognitive, or emotional condition and the support provided in the environmental, which impairs the ability to participate in daily life. (p. 258)

discipline Caregiving practices or strategies used to teach children how to behave by setting rules, encouraging good behavior, and discouraging missteps. (p. 232)

discontinuous A model of change that is more irregular and unstable, happening in sprints and pauses, or stages. (p. 26)

disorganized attachment In attachment theory, children who have unusual responses in the Strange Situation procedure and who may be afraid of their caregivers. (p. 164)

distal Caregiving practices that are physically distant but may include joint attention and face-to-face contact. (p. 146)

dizygotic Twins that develop when two (or more) ova are fertilized by separate sperm. (p. 73)

dominant inheritance pattern A type of genetic inheritance for single-gene disorders. A person with a dominant condition may have just one of the disease-carrying alleles. (p. 69)

Down syndrome A condition caused by an extra 21st chromosome that results in anomalies in brain development and may also impair muscle tone and cardiovascular development. (p. 71)

early adulthood A culturally defined period typically ranging between ages 18 and 30 that is marked by individual flexibility and potential but less support. (p. 393)

early childhood The period between ages 2½ and 6. It typically begins as toddlers develop language and movement skills and ends as they develop more abstract thinking and independent living skills and, in many communities, start formal schooling. (p. 172)

easy In Thomas and Chess's dimensional approach to temperament, babies who are flexible and usually content. (p. 158)

eating disorders Psychological conditions that are marked by long-term, unhealthy patterns of eating, obsessions with food, and poor body image that cause problems with the ability to function. (p. 336)

egocentrism In the Piagetian sense, children's inability to see the world from other people's point of view. (p. 195)

elaboration Adding information to the facts you need to remember so that they become more detailed and easier to recall. (p. 274)

embryonic stage The second stage of prenatal development, in weeks 2 through 8, in which the embryo develops the major parts of its body—from legs to brain. (p. 74)

emergentist Scholars who argue that humans' drive to communicate and imitate and ability to recognize patterns, rather than brain processes specifically devoted to language, created the uniquely human ability to use language. (Also called *constructivist*.) (p. 140)

emerging adulthood A term used by some scholars to describe the period between about ages 18 and about 29 in which young people consciously postpone some of the milestones of adulthood to explore their identity. (p. 394)

emotion regulation The ability to manage your feelings in a way that is appropriate to your community circumstances. (p. 157)

emotional contagion The tendency to mimic feelings we observe in others. (p. 156)

emotions Reactions to your thoughts or your environment that involve your body, your thoughts, and your behaviors. (p. 152)

empathy The ability to identify with someone else's feelings. (p. 156)

epigenetics An area of study within the biological perspective that examines how physical and inborn characteristics, including gene activation, are changed by a person's environment. (pp. 10, 32)

epigenome The part of the genome that controls gene expression. (p. 66)

episodic memory Long-term memory for specific events. (p. 199)

estrogen A hormone that is linked to reproduction, maturation, brain development, and sexual function in both males and females. Estrogen levels are higher in biological females but are important to typical functioning in both males and females. (p. 323)

ethical standards Moral guidelines for protecting the interests of research participants and making sure scientific work is as honest as it can be. (p. 57)

ethnic identity A sense of yourself as belonging to a particular ethnic group or community. (p. 380)

ethnicity A way of referring to groups by their geographic origins and often their cultural heritage. (p. 19)

ethnography A longer, richly detailed investigation of everyday life. (p. 52)

ethnotheories Families' ideas or beliefs about development. (p. 22)

ethology The theory that some human behaviors are universal and innate despite the wide diversity in human beings around the world. (p. 32)

evolution The idea that life on Earth develops and changes to adapt to the environment over successive generations. (p. 31)

executive function Your ability to actively regulate your thinking and behavior to accomplish a goal. (p. 131)

experience-dependent brain development Brain maturation that relies on the quantity or the quality of environmental input and, like all learning, continues throughout the lifespan. (p. 110)

experience-expectant brain development Brain maturation that relies on nearly universal environmental inputs. (p. 110)

experiment The act of testing a hypothesis that one factor is caused by another. (p. 49)

explicit memory Memory of names, dates, and details. (p. 127)

exploratory learning Trying out different ways to solve a problem before deciding on the best solution. (p. 344)

externalizing disorders Psychological disorders characterized by difficult behaviors that affect others, such as acting out or severe aggression. Externalizing disorders include disruptive behavior disorders such as oppositional defiant disorder (ODD) and conduct disorder (CD). (p. 257)

extrinsic motivation The drive to do something because you are hoping for a reward. (p. 208)

familism The concept of responsibility of the family as a group. (p. 369)

fast-mapping A child's ability to quickly learn new words. (p. 138)

fetal stage The third stage of prenatal development, weeks 9 through birth, in which the fetus begins to look like a baby and adds pounds and the organs and brain structures that will allow it to survive on its own. (p. 75)

fine motor development The development of small movements requiring precise coordination, like picking up little objects, swallowing, or pointing. (p. 115)

foreclosure status In Marcia's theory, this identity status occurs when adolescents have committed to a path or identity without exploration. (p. 379)

formal operational thought Piaget's stage of cognitive development that begins in early adolescence and lasts into adulthood and is both logical and abstract. (p. 346)

functional play Repeating an action over and over again just for the joy of it. (p. 237)

gender The term for the social and cultural distinctions describing binary and less binary distinctions between men and women. (p. 67)

gender expression The term for how you express your gender in daily life, such as how you wear makeup, style your hair, or what clothing you like. (p. 67)

gender identity The term for your sense of yourself as a man, woman, or someone not as exclusively within the lines of these binary labels. (p. 67)

gender roles The social and cultural ideas a person holds about appropriate behaviors or roles of people based on their gender. (p. 224)

gender schema A framework for understanding the world in terms of cultural expectations related to gender identity. (p. 224)

genes Sections of DNA that create particular proteins. (p. 64)

genome The unique set of instructions that includes everything a cell might need for creating your body parts and maintaining them over the lifespan. (p. 64)

genotype The genome that contributes your phenotype. (p. 66)

germinal stage The first stage of prenatal development, in which the single-celled zygote divides and implants into the uterus in the first week of development. (p. 74)

gifted education An academic program for children who may need enriched or specialized education in order to meet their potential. (p. 290)

goodness of fit The idea that babies benefit from a good match between their personalities and their caregivers. (p. 160)

grit The ability to persevere in order to achieve a long-term goal. (p. 288)

gross motor development The development of bigger movements like walking, jumping, or skipping. (p. 115)

growth spurt A very rapid increase in height and size that begins at about age 10 in girls and age 12 in boys. (p. 323)

habituation A basic form of learning in which you become bored with something if you experience it repeatedly. (p. 126)

heuristic thinking A type of advanced reasoning, which is automatic thinking that you do outside of consciousness. (p. 347)

holophrases Single-word utterances by toddlers that may represent larger ideas. (p. 138)

homophily The tendency to like and associate with people we perceive as being like us. (p. 371)

HPG axis A set of glands that trigger puberty, including the hypothalamus, pituitary gland, and gonads (testes and ovaries). (p. 323)

hygiene hypothesis A theory suggesting that regular exposure to a variety of microbes helps people develop a robust microbiome, protecting them from some allergies, asthma, and immune-related conditions. (p. 184)

hypothesis A prediction about what a researcher expects to find from the data. (p. 47)

identity A person's sense of who they are and how they fit into the social groups of the world. (p. 378)

identity crisis The conflict in deciding between the possible roles a person could play and the possible selves they could be. (p. 379)

identity versus role confusion In Erikson's theory of lifespan development, the crisis of adolescent development that is resolved when youth understand themselves and their role in the world. (p. 379)

immunization A means of protection against diseases that introduces a tiny amount of an infectious virus into the body to teach it to defend itself against that virus. If the immunized person encounters the virus later, they are less likely to get sick, because their immune system is prepared. (p. 103)

implicit memory Memory of new skills and processes and ability to habituate. (p. 127)

in vitro fertilization (IVF) A procedure in which doctors combine egg and sperm outside the body in a hospital laboratory and then place the resulting zygotes in the uterus, where they can implant and develop into a baby (or babies). (p. 76)

independent communities Societies that value individual rights. (Also known as *autonomy*.) (p. 23)

independent variable A factor that is tested to see if it causes change in another variable. An independent variable is something that the researcher can change. (p. 49)

individualistic communities Societies that have strong traditions of valuing the individual over larger groups, communities, or families. (p. 23)

inductive reasoning A disciplinary approach that relies on motivating children to change their behavior through talk. (p. 233)

industry versus inferiority The fourth crisis of Erikson's theory in which children are challenged to build their sense of themselves as capable and avoid feeling inadequate. (p. 294)

infant-directed speech (IDS) Adults' use of high-pitched, sing-songy tones and simple sentences when they talk to infants. (p. 139)

information processing An approach that studies the development of thinking and understanding by describing how a person pays attention, remembers, and reacts to the world, similar to how a computer processes information. (p. 42)

initiative versus guilt Erikson's third stage of development, which occurs between ages 3 and 5 and involves the conflict between children's enthusiasm to try new things independently and their remorse when they get things wrong. (p. 216)

insecure attachment In attachment theory, children who have not established a sense of trust in their caregivers to soothe them when they are upset. (p. 164)

insecure-avoidant attachment In attachment theory, a form of insecure attachment characterized by babies' emotional distance from their caregivers who they perceive as being unable to soothe them. (p. 164)

insecure-resistant attachment In attachment theory, a form of insecure attachment characterized by babies' angry and hostile responses to their caregiver who they perceive as inconsistent and unreliable. (p. 164)

Institutional Review Board (IRB) A committee that is designed to review scientific research and ensure that it is safe and adequately protects participants. (p. 58)

intellectual developmental disorder Difficulties with academics, practical skills, or social relationships. (p. 288)

intelligence The ability to learn and apply what has been learned. (p. 277)

internal working model In attachment theory, the idea that our early habits of relating to our caregivers create a pattern of relating that we will use later on in our lives. (p. 163)

internalizing disorders Psychological disorders in which children's emotions are focused inward, manifesting as overwhelming feelings of sadness (depression) or worry (anxiety). (p. 257)

intersectionality A term that refers to the fact that we all have multiple, intersecting identities relating to age, gender, ability, ethnicity, nationality, romantic preferences, and so forth. (p. 18)

interventions Evidence-based programs or services designed to improve health, psychological well-being, or behavior. (p. 98)

intimacy versus isolation Erikson's stage of human development that occurs in young adulthood. In his view, the successful resolution of the crisis is finding love. (p. 405)

intrinsic motivation The drive to do something because it is its own reward and just doing it feels rewarding. (p. 208)

IQ A person's score on a standardized intelligence test which, for most people, is between 85 and 115. (p. 277)

kangaroo care A form of skin-to-skin contact that involves holding a lightly clothed newborn against a caregiver's chest. (p. 91)

lateralization The process of brain development in which certain functions become located in one hemisphere of the brain. (p. 176)

lifecourse-persistent behavior A habit or behavior that is consistent across the lifespan. (p. 390)

literacy Reading and writing skills. (p. 285)

longitudinal research The study of the same group of people over time. (p. 52)

low birthweight (LBW) Babies born weighing less than 2,500 grams (about 5½ pounds). (p. 90)

malnutrition When someone does not have adequate nutrients to support their growth. (p. 97)

maltreatment The general term scholars use to describe the many types of abuse and neglect of children by adults who are responsible for them. (p. 233)

maturation The genetically programmed growth that drives many aspects of development. (p. 24)

meiosis A special form of cell division that creates the gametes, or sperm and ova cells. (p. 66)

menarche The term for the first menstrual period. (p. 324)

mental representation The ability to think things through using internal images rather than needing to act in the environment. (p. 124)

metacognition The act of thinking and reflecting on your own thinking processes. (p. 273)

metalinguistic awareness The ability to think about the features of language, such as the sounds that make up words and the way words go together to make meaning. (p. 279)

metamemory The awareness of the process of remembering. (p. 274)

microbiome The collection of beneficial bacteria that live in our bodies that work with our immune system to help protect us from disease. A healthy balance of bacteria is linked to some early life experiences like breastfeeding and vaginal delivery. (p. 184)

microgenetic research Research that focuses on understanding how development happens by studying change as it happens. (p. 53)

middle childhood The period spanning ages 6 to 11 that begins as children develop the independence and self-regulation to take on new responsibilities. (p. 245)

mitosis A type of cell division that creates two, new identical cells. (p. 64)

monitoring When caregivers keep track of what their children are doing. (p. 304)

monozygotic Twins with nearly identical DNA because they start off as a single zygote that separates into two in the first days after fertilization. (p. 72)

moodiness Emotional changeability, often leaning toward negative feelings like irritability. (p. 383)

moratorium status In Marcia's theory, this identity status occurs when adolescents have postponed committing to an identity and are exploring options. (p. 379)

motor development The development of body coordination. (p. 115)

multifactorial Traits that are influenced by multiple variables. (p. 70)

myelin Layers of cholesterol-rich fat that insulate the axon, helping to speed up communication. (p. 109)

myelination The lifelong process of adding myelin to axons. (p. 109)

nativist approach A theoretical perspective that maintains that babies are born knowing a great deal about how the world works. (Also called the *core knowledge approach*.) (p. 128)

nature The influence of genetics on development. (p. 12)

neglected Children who are unconsidered or forgotten altogether by their peers. (p. 312)

neglectful parenting Caregiving without warmth or expectations. Children from neglectful families are at high risk for emotional and behavioral difficulties as they grow up. (p. 231)

neurons Nerve cells. (p. 78)

numeracy The ability to manipulate numbers and do arithmetic. (p. 285)

nurture The influence of experience on development. (p. 12)

object permanence The term for the understanding that objects continue to exist even when they are out of sight. (p. 124)

observation When scientists closely watch and record what people are doing—either in real life or in the laboratory. (p. 54)

operant conditioning A process of learning in which rewards and punishments are used to shape behaviors. (p. 37)

overextension An error in which a child assumes that a specific term relates to a larger category. (p. 138)

overweight When a child is heavier for their age and height than most other children, or above the 85th percentile. (p. 99)

ovum The egg cell. (p. 66)

parallel play When children play physically close together but are not working on a shared project. (p. 237)

parental monitoring The process of caregivers observing and keeping track of what children are doing. (p. 368)

parenting styles Dimensional descriptions of caregiving relationships during childhood. (p. 230)

people of color An inclusive term for people who identify as multiracial and for people who are Black, Latino, Asian American, or Native American and who have a feeling of solidarity and shared experience of marginalization. (p. 20)

percentile A way of statistically comparing an individual to a group. (p. 97)

perceptual narrowing The process by which infants become less sensitive to sensory input as they grow and begin to specialize in the sights and sounds to which they are exposed more often. (p. 114)

permissive parenting Caregiving without rules. Permissive parents have low expectations for children's behavior but a high degree of affection. (p. 230)

personality Habits of emotionally relating and responding to people and events in our lives. (p. 158)

phenotype Your individual observable characteristics. (p. 66)

phonics-based instruction Instruction that builds children's reading skills by reinforcing the links between letters and their sounds. (p. 286)

Piaget's stage theory of development The five periods of cognitive development described by Jean Piaget, in which children's thinking proceeds through qualitatively different ways of understanding the world. (p. 41)

placenta An organ that allows energy and waste to be transferred between the parent's body and the developing embryo through the umbilical cord. (p. 77)

plasticity The idea that human development is moldable, like plastic, by experiences. (p. 25)

polygenic A type of genetic inheritance that is influenced by multiple genes acting in combination that may require influence from the environment in order to be expressed. (p. 69)

popular Children who are liked or perceived to be socially successful by many of their peers. (p. 312)

postconventional stage of moral reasoning Kohlberg's stage of moral reasoning in which people can think abstractly and about right and wrong as something that supersedes rules and laws. (p. 315)

postformal thought A stage of thinking that allows young adults to think through complex issues by reviewing different viewpoints, considering emotional, contextual, and interpersonal factors. (p. 399)

power-assertive techniques Disciplinary strategies that rely on parents' control. (p. 232)

pragmatics Knowing how to talk with other people, including what is appropriate to talk about, and how to interpret tone of voice, gestures, and other cues. (p. 281)

preconventional stage of moral reasoning Kohlberg's stage of moral reasoning in which children use concrete and self-centered (egocentric) reasoning. (p. 315)

preferential looking technique A procedure that measures what babies perceive in which researchers harness babies' intrinsic interest in new things. (p. 113)

prefrontal cortex The area at the front of the brain behind the forehead that is critical to logical thinking and controlling behavior. (p. 173)

premature Birth that occurs less than 35 weeks after fertilization. (p. 90)

preoperational thought The second stage in Piaget's theory of children's cognitive development, spanning about ages 2 to 7, in which young children are capable of symbolic, but not quite logical, thought. (p. 191)

primary circular reactions The second stage of Piaget's sensorimotor period, from about 1 to 4 months, in which babies begin to adapt their reflexes to new uses and show more creative behavior. (p. 122)

primary sex characteristics The reproductive organs that babies are typically born with, like genitals. (p. 251)

private speech Vygotsky's term for the language children use when they talk to themselves. (p. 198)

proactive aggression Aggression that is planned and executed on purpose to gain personal advantage (sometimes called *instrumental aggression*). (p. 239)

prosocial Behaviors that are helpful or caring toward someone else. (p. 156)

proximal Caregiving practices that include physical closeness but not necessarily face-to-face contact. (p. 146)

proximity seeking The tendency for children (and adults) to seek comfort by being physically close to someone they are attached to. (p. 163)

proximodistal principle A pattern of physical development in which control of movement begins in the core and expands outward. (p. 117)

psychodynamic perspective A perspective with an emphasis on how human behaviors are based on satisfying innate and often subconscious, biological needs for connection, protection, and love. (p. 34)

psychological disorders Disruptions in feelings, thinking, or behavior that interfere with a person's ability to function in everyday life. (p. 218)

psychosexual stages The five stages of Freud's psychodynamic theory in which children learn how to manage different sensual and sexual energies. (p. 34)

puberty The process that transforms children into adults who are typically able to reproduce and have children of their own. (p. 321)

punishment Anything that weakens a behavior, making it less likely to happen. (p. 38)

qualitative research Research that involves in-depth analysis, observation, and investigation. (p. 54)

quantitative research Research that uses numbers to measure the topics being studied and to analyze the outcome of a study. (p. 54)

race A system of categorizing people based on their physical characteristics. These physical differences are often assumed to overlap with people's genes or geographical origins, but this is not accurate. (p. 19)

reactive aggression A hostile action out of frustration or anger in an immediate reaction to something that has just happened. (p. 239)

recessive inheritance pattern A type of genetic inheritance for single-gene conditions. In order to develop a recessive condition, you must have two of the disease-carrying alleles. (p. 68)

reflexes Automatic motor responses to stimuli that help babies adjust to the world. (p. 92)

rehearsal A memorization technique that involves repetition, either out loud, in your head, in front of someone else, or on paper. (p. 274)

reinforcement Anything that strengthens a behavior, making it more likely to happen. (p. 38)

rejected Children who are actively disliked by most of their peers. (p. 312)

relationally aggressive Using words and relationships to hurt another person socially or emotionally. (p. 239)

relativistic thinking A type of thinking that acknowledges there is no absolute truth, but rather a collection of different perspectives. Instead of assuming there is one right answer to life's problems, relativistic thinkers understand that their assumptions are biased and subjective. (p. 399)

resilience The ability to bounce back and recover despite difficult life circumstances. (p. 2)

responsiveness The idea that a caregiver should acknowledge and react to an infant's bids for attention. (p. 162)

rough-and-tumble play Physically active play where children chase, play fight, and wrestle. (p. 237)

rumination The tendency to repetitively and obsessively focus on what is wrong. (p. 372)

scaffolding A term for teaching, whether by formal teachers, friends, peers, or family members, that engages children by considering their interests and individual abilities. (p. 197)

schema The word for each bit of knowledge a person develops. (p. 41)

science A process of gathering and organizing knowledge about the world in a way that is testable and reliable. (p. 2)

scientific method A multistep process in which scientists evaluate their ideas and find out if they are accurate through collecting and analyzing data. (p. 47)

secondary circular reactions The third stage of Piaget's sensorimotor period, from about 4 to 8 months, in which babies learn to extend their activities to manipulate the world around them. (p. 124)

secondary sex characteristics The physical markers of what makes people look like adult males or females after puberty. Secondary sex characteristics include pubic hair, facial hair, the Adam's apple, and breasts. (p. 251)

secular trend The term developmental scientists use to describe the gradual, long-term progression toward earlier puberty. (p. 325)

secure attachment In attachment theory, children who have a sense of trust in their caregivers that allows them to explore their environment. (p. 164)

secure base In attachment theory, a safe haven for children to return to when they may feel anxious. (p. 163)

selective eating The phenomenon common during early childhood when young children become more resistant to trying new foods or develop picky eating practices. (p. 182)

self-awareness The understanding that you have a self that is separate from others. (p. 155)

self-efficacy The belief in one's ability to make a change or have an impact. (p. 287)

semantic memory The mental storage for facts and information. (p. 274)

sensation-seeking The drive for excitement and the thrill of doing something a bit scary. (p. 384)

sensitive periods The times in the lifespan when growth is particularly responsive to input from the world. (p. 25)

sensorimotor Piaget's term for the cognitive stage that spans the first 18 months of a baby's life and focuses on learning through sensation and movement. (p. 122)

separation anxiety By about 6 months and continuing into toddlerhood, infants are upset and worried if their caregivers go away. This phenomenon is not universal but is influenced by cultural practices. (p. 154)

seriation The ordering of objects in a series according to an abstract rule. (p. 270)

sex The physical and genetic characteristics usually associated with being male, female, or a mixture. (p. 67)

sex chromosomes The 23rd pair of chromosomes. (p. 67)

sexually transmitted infection (STI) The term health care providers use to describe diseases that can be passed from one person to another through intimate contact. (p. 331)

slow-to-warm-up In Thomas and Chess's dimensional approach to temperament, these babies tend to be shy and slower to adjust to new circumstances, but not intense in their responses. (p. 158)

small for gestational age (SGA) Babies born smaller than expected for their level of development. (p. 90)

social brain Neural networks associated with understanding the views and intentions of other people. (p. 375)

social learning theory The theory that learning occurs through observing and imitating others. (p. 39)

social referencing The use of someone else's emotional response as a guide before expressing your own reaction to a new place, person, or object. (p. 155)

social smile A smile in reaction to the sight or sound of someone an infant is connected to. These smiles may appear as early as 6 weeks, but their development is influenced by caregiving practices. (p. 152)

social status A person's social rank within the larger group. (p. 374)

sociocultural theory The theory that culture plays a role in every part of development. (p. 43)

sociodramatic play Play that involves pretending to be something you are not and requires symbolic thought and theory of mind. (p. 237)

socioeconomic status (SES) A measure of a family or individual's income and social capital. (p. 16)

socioemotional learning Curriculum that focuses on teaching students skills for understanding and regulating their emotions and building caring relationships. (p. 285)

specific learning disorders Difficulties with language development, reading, or arithmetic that lead to problems functioning in school or at home. (p. 288)

sperm The reproductive cell from a male. (p. 66)

spermarche The first ejaculation of sperm. (p. 324)

stage A period in which development changes dramatically. (p. 26)

stage–environment fit The idea that we do better when the world matches our developmental needs. (p. 359)

stages Distinct time periods when development changes dramatically. (p. 41)

stereotype threat The phenomenon that occurs when you feel judged in an area where there are common stereotypes about your group, and the resulting anxiety negatively affects your performance. (p. 355)

Strange Situation An empirical method developed by Mary Ainsworth for evaluating the attachment status of toddlers. (p. 163)

stranger anxiety Babies' demonstration of caution around new people, which emerges by about 8 months. This phenomenon is not culturally universal but is influenced by caregiving practices. (p. 154)

stress The feeling of being overwhelmed. (p. 86)

stunting When a child's growth has slowed so much that they are significantly shorter than they should be for their age. (p. 98)

substance use disorder A clinical diagnosis based on a pattern of substance use that is causing someone functional difficulties in their everyday life. (p. 389)

sudden unexpected infant death (SUID) When an otherwise healthy infant dies. SUIDs can include *sleep-related suffocation*. (p. 106)

synaptic pruning The process in which the brain cuts back on underused synapses. (p. 109)

synaptogenesis The process of creating new synapses between neurons, which begins before birth and continues throughout the lifespan. (p. 109)

telegraphic speech A short two- or three-word utterance missing grammatical filler words, such as "Go beach" to represent "I am going to the beach." (p. 138)

temperament An early pattern of personality in infants and toddlers. (p. 158)

teratogens Factors in a parent's body or the environment that damage the fetus. (p. 83)

tertiary circular reactions Babies' ability to deliberately vary their actions to see the results. (p. 124)

testosterone A hormone produced by the gonads that is linked to reproduction, maturation, brain development, and sexual function. Testosterone levels are higher in adolescents with testes but are important to typical functioning in both those with ovaries and those with testes. (p. 323)

theory An organized set of ideas that helps scientists think critically about what they observe. (p. 31)

theory of mind The ability to understand that other people have different beliefs, ideas, and desires. (p. 204)

theory of multiple intelligences Gardner's idea that intelligence is a broad set of discrete abilities and that all children have components of all these intelligences. (p. 279)

theory of successful intelligence Sternberg's idea that intelligence can best be measured by how you create a successful life through three types of intelligence. (p. 279)

three mountains task Piaget's test of how well children can imagine how someone else would see the world. (p. 195)

tracking The practice of grouping together students with similar achievement and test scores and offering them a more customized school curriculum. (p. 353)

transgender A gender identity in which someone consistently feels that their gender identity does not match the sex they were assigned at birth. (p. 226)

trust versus mistrust The first crisis in Erikson's stage theory of development in which infants learn that the world is reliable. (p. 145)

underextension An error in which a child insists that a word only applies to a specific member of the group, rather than the whole group itself. (p. 138)

universal grammar A child's inborn ability to recognize and use grammar. (p. 140)

variables The factors that are studied in an experiment. (p. 49)

visual cliff A means of assessing what risks babies will take while crawling, in which a 2½-foot gap is covered with plexiglass that, if properly lit, appears to be an empty gap. (p. 118)

wasting When a child is so seriously malnourished that they are below the 5th percentile in the ratio of weight to height, or lighter for their height than 95 percent of children their age and height. (p. 97)

whole-language approach Instruction that is based on the idea that children will learn how to read more effectively in an environment that weaves literacy into everything they do. (p. 286)

working memory A type of short-term memory that is essential to learning and to problem solving. (p. 199)

zone of proximal development (ZPD) Vygotsky's term for the range of what students can learn with adult help. (p. 197)

zygote A new human cell typically with 46 chromosomes in 23 pairs. (p. 66)

REFERENCES

Abaied, J. L., & Perry, S. P. (2021). Socialization of racial ideology by White parents. *Cultural Diversity and Ethnic Minority Psychology, 27*(3), 431–440. https://doi.org/10.1037/cdp0000454

Abarca-Gómez, L., Abdeen, Z. A., Hamid, Z. A., Abu-Rmeileh, N. M., Acosta-Cazares, B., Acuin, C., Adams, R. J., Aekplakorn, W., Afsana, K., Aguilar-Salinas, C. A., Agyemang, C., Ahmadvand, A., Ahrens, W., Ajlouni, K., Akhtaeva, N., Al-Hazzaa, H. M., Al-Othman, A. R., Al-Raddadi, R., Buhairan, F. A., . . . Ezzati, M. (2017). Worldwide trends in body-mass index, underweight, overweight, and obesity from 1975 to 2016: A pooled analysis of 2416 population-based measurement studies in 128·9 million children, adolescents, and adults. *The Lancet, 390*(10113), 2627–2642. https://doi.org/10.1016/S0140-6736(17)32129-3

Abascal, F., Juan, D., Jungreis, I., Martinez, L., Rigau, M., Rodriguez, J. M., Vazquez, J., & Tress, M. L. (2018). Loose ends: Almost one in five human genes still have unresolved coding status. *Nucleic Acids Research, 46*(14), 7070–7084. https://doi.org/10.1093/nar/gky587

Abbott, D. M., Pelc, N., & Mercier, C. (2019). Cultural humility and the teaching of psychology. *Scholarship of Teaching and Learning in Psychology, 5*(2), 169–181. https://doi.org/10.1037/stl0000144

Abboud, S., Flores, D., Redmond, L., Brawner, B. M., & Sommers, M. S. (2020). Sexual attitudes and behaviours among Arab American young adults in the USA. *Culture, Health & Sexuality*, 1–17.

Abdulkadiroğlu, A., Pathak, P. A., Schellenberg, J., & Walters, C. R. (2020). Do parents value school effectiveness? *American Economic Review, 110*(5), 1502–1539. https://doi.org/10.1257/aer.20172040

Abebe, T. (2018). *A plea for participatory ethics and knowledge production with children in Africa* (CODESIRA Policy Briefs No. 1). Council for the Development of Social Science Research in Africa.

Abney, D. H., Suanda, S. H., Smith, L. B., & Yu, C. (2020). What are the building blocks of parent–infant coordinated attention in free-flowing interaction? *Infancy, 25*(6), 871–887. https://doi.org/10.1111/infa.12365

Abraham, E., & Feldman, R. (2018). The neurobiology of human allomaternal care; Implications for fathering, coparenting, and children's social development. *Physiology & Behavior, 193*, 25–34. https://doi.org/10.1016/j.physbeh.2017.12.034

Aburto, J. M., Scholey, J., Zhang, L., Kashnitsky, I., Rahal, C., Missov, T. I., Mills, M. C., Dowd, J. B., & Kashyap, R. (2021). Quantifying impacts of the COVID-19 pandemic through life expectancy losses. *MedRxiv*, 2021.03.02.21252772. https://doi.org/10.1101/2021.03.02.21252772

Accavitti, M. R., & Williford, A. P. (2020). Teacher perceptions of externalizing behaviour subtypes in preschool: Considering racial factors. *Early Child Development and Care*, 1–15. https://doi.org/10.1080/03004430.2020.1825405

Achenbach, T. M., & McConaughy, S. H. (1992). Taxonomy of internalizing disorders of childhood and adolescence. In W. M. Reynolds (Ed.), *Internalizing disorders in children and adolescents* (pp. 19–60). Wiley.

Adachi, P. J., & Willoughby, T. (2017). The link between playing video games and positive youth outcomes. *Child Development Perspectives, 11*(3), 202–206.

Adair, J. K., Colegrove, K. S.-S., & McManus, M. E. (2017). How the word gap argument negatively impacts young children of Latinx immigrants' conceptualizations of learning. *Harvard Educational Review, 87*(3), 309–334. https://doi.org/10.17763/1943-5045-87.3.309

Adams, C. (2021). Pragmatic language impairment. In *Encyclopedia of autism spectrum disorders* (pp. 3602–3608). Cham: Springer International Publishing.

Adams, E. L., Caccavale, L. J., Smith, D., & Bean, M. K. (2020). Food insecurity, the home food environment, and parent feeding practices in the era of COVID-19. *Obesity, 28*(11), 2056–2063. https://doi.org/10.1002/oby.22996

Adams, E. L., Master, L., Buxton, O. M., & Savage, J. S. (2020). Patterns of infant-only wake bouts and night feeds during early infancy: An exploratory study using actigraphy in mother-father-infant triads. *Pediatric Obesity, 15*(10), e12640. https://doi.org/10.1111/ijpo.12640

Adams, S. H., Schaub, J. P., Nagata, J. M., Park, M. J., Brindis, C. D., & Irwin, C. E. (2021). Young adult perspectives on COVID-19 vaccinations. *The Journal of Adolescent Health, 69*(3), P511–P514. https://doi.org/10.1016/j.jadohealth.2021.06.003

Adelman, L. (2008). When the bough breaks. *Unnatural Causes* (Episode 2). https://unnaturalcauses.org/episode_descriptions.php?page=2

Adhia, A., Austin, S. B., Fitzmaurice, G. M., & Hemenway, D. (2019). The role of intimate partner violence in homicides of children Aged 2–14 years. *American Journal of Preventive Medicine, 56*(1), 38–46. https://doi.org/10.1016/j.amepre.2018.08.028

Adolph, K. E. (2019). An ecological approach to learning in (not and) development. *Human Development, 63*(3–4), 180–201. https://doi.org/10.1159/000503823

Adolph, K. E., Cole, W. G., & Vereijken, B. (2014). Intraindividual variability in the development of motor skills in childhood. *Handbook of Intraindividual Variability Across the Life Span*, 79–103.

Adolph, K. E., Cole, W. G., Komati, M., Garciaguirre, J. S., Badaly, D., Lingeman, J. M., Chan, G., & Sotsky, R. B. (2012). How do you learn to walk? Thousands of steps and dozens of falls per day. *Psychological Science, 23*(11), 1387–1394. https://doi.org/10.1177/0956797612446346

Adolph, K. E., & Franchak, J. M. (2017). The development of motor behavior. *Wiley Interdisciplinary Reviews. Cognitive Science, 8*(1–2), e1430. https://doi.org/10.1002/wcs.1430

Adolph, K. E., & Hoch, J. E. (2019). Motor development: Embodied, embedded, enculturated, and enabling. *Annual Review of Psychology, 70*(1), 141–164. https://doi.org/10.1146/annurev-psych-010418-102836

Adolph, K. E., & Hoch, J. E. (2020). The importance of motor skills for development. In M. M. Black, A. Singhal, & C. H. Hillman (Eds.), *Building future health and well-being of thriving toddlers and young children* (Nestlé Nutrition Institute Workshop Series, Vol. 95, pp. 136–144). Karger. https://doi.org/10.1159/000511511

Adolph, K. E., Karasik, L. B., & Tamis-Lemonda, and C. S. (2014, June 3). Motor skill. *Handbook of Cultural Developmental Science*. https://doi.org/10.4324/9780203805497-11

Afranie, A., & Clagett, M. G. (2020). *Preparing opportunity youth for the future of work*. Jobs for the Future (JFF). https://www.jff.org/resources/preparing-opportunity-youth-future-work/

Agasisti, T., Avvisati, F., Borgonovi, F., & Longobardi, S. (2021). What school factors are associated with the success of socio-economically disadvantaged students? An empirical investigation using PISA data. *Social Indicators Research, 157*(2), 749–781. https://doi.org/10.1007/s11205-021-02668-w

Agorastos, A., Pervanidou, P., Chrousos, G. P., & Baker, D. G. (2019). Developmental trajectories of early life stress and trauma: A narrative review on neurobiological aspects beyond stress system dysregulation. *Frontiers in Psychiatry, 10*, 118. https://doi.org/10.3389/fpsyt.2019.00118

Ahlstrom, B., Dinh, T., Haselton, M. G., & Tomiyama, A. J. (2017). Understanding eating interventions through an evolutionary lens. *Health Psychology Review, 11*(1), 72–88. https://doi.org/10.1080/17437199.2016.1260489

Ahluwalia, N. (2020). Nutrition monitoring of children aged birth to 24 mo (B-24): Data collection and findings from the NHANES. *Advances in Nutrition, 11*(1), 113–127. https://doi.org/10.1093/advances/nmz077

Ahmed, S. F., Tang, S., Waters, N. E., & Davis-Kean, P. (2019). Executive function and academic achievement: Longitudinal relations from early childhood to adolescence. *Journal of Educational Psychology, 111*(3), 446.

Ahmed, S., Foulkes, L., Leung, J. T., Griffin, C., Sakhardande, A., Bennett, M., Dunning, D. L., Griffiths, K., Parker, J., Kuyken, W., Williams, J. M. G., Dalgleish, T., & Blakemore, S. J. (2020). Susceptibility to prosocial and antisocial influence in adolescence. *Journal of Adolescence, 84*, 56–68. https://doi.org/10.1016/j.adolescence.2020.07.012

Ahn, R., Gonzalez, G. P., Anderson, B., Vladutiu, C. J., Fowler, E. R., & Manning, L. (2020). Initiatives to reduce maternal mortality and severe maternal morbidity in the United States. *Annals of Internal Medicine, 173*(11_Supplement), S3–S10. https://doi.org/10.7326/M19-3258

Ahnert, L. (2021). Attachment to Child Care Providers. In *Attachment: The Fundamental Questions*. Guilford Publications.

Ahranjani, M. (2020). School "safety" measures jump constitutional guardrails. *Seattle University Law Review, 44*, 273.

Ainsworth, M. D. S., Blehar, M. C., Waters, E., & Wall, S. N. (2015). *Patterns of attachment: A psychological study of the strange situation*. Psychology Press. (Original work published 1978)

Ainsworth, M. D. S., & Bowlby, J. (1991). An ethological approach to personality development. *American Psychologist, 46*(4), 333–341. https://doi.org/10.1037/0003-066X.46.4.333

Ainsworth, M. D. S., & Marvin, R. S. (1995). On the shaping of attachment theory and research: An interview with Mary D. S. Ainsworth (Fall 1994). *Monographs of the Society for Research in Child Development, 60*(2–3), 3–21. https://doi.org/10.1111/j.1540-5834.1995.tb00200.x

Aizenman, N., & Warner, G. (2018). What can we learn from Ghana's obsession with preschool. *National Public Radio*.

Akee, R., Copeland, W., Costello, E. J., & Simeonova, E. (2018). How does household income affect child personality traits and behaviors? *American Economic Review, 108*(3), 775–827. https://doi.org/10.1257/aer.20160133

Aknin, L. B., Van de Vondervoort, J. W., & Hamlin, J. K. (2018). Positive feelings reward and promote prosocial behavior. *Current Opinion in Psychology, 20*, 55–59.

Aktar, E., Mandell, D. J., de Vente, W., Majdandžić, M., Oort, F. J., van Renswoude, D. R., Raijmakers, M. E. J., & Bögels, S. M. (2018). Parental negative emotions are related to behavioral and pupillary correlates of infants' attention to facial expressions of emotion. *Infant Behavior and Development, 53*, 101–111. https://doi.org/10.1016/j.infbeh.2018.07.004

Alampay, L. P., Godwin, J., Lansford, J. E., Bombi, A. S., Bornstein, M. H., Chang, L., Deater-Deckard, K., Di Giunta, L., Dodge, K. A., Malone, P. S., Oburu, P., Pastorelli, C., Skinner, A. T., Sorbring, E., Tapanya, S., Uribe Tirado, L. M., Zelli, A., Al-Hassan, S., & Bacchini, D. (2017). Severity and justness do not moderate the relation between corporal punishment and negative child outcomes: A multicultural and longitudinal study. *International Journal of Behavioral Development, 41*(4), 491–502. https://doi.org/10.1177/0165025417697852

Al-Attar, G., De Meyer, S., El-Gibaly, O., Michielsen, K., Animosa, L. H., & Mmari, K. (2017). "A boy would be friends with boys . . . and a girl . . . with girls": Gender norms in early adolescent friendships in Egypt and Belgium. *Journal of Adolescent Health, 61*(4, Supplement), S30–S34. https://doi.org/10.1016/j.jadohealth.2017.03.013

Albaugh, M. D., Ottino-Gonzalez, J., Sidwell, A., Lepage, C., Juliano, A., Owens, M. M., Chaarani, B., Spechler, P., Fontaine, N., Rioux, P., Lewis, L., Jeon, S., Evans, A., D'Souza, D., Radhakrishnan, R., Banaschewski, T., Bokde, A. L. W., Quinlan, E. B., Conrod, P., . . . IMAGEN Consortium. (2021). Association of cannabis use during adolescence with neurodevelopment. *JAMA Psychiatry, 78*(9), 1031–1040. https://doi.org/10.1001/jamapsychiatry.2021.1258

Albert, D., Chein, J., & Steinberg, L. (2013). Peer influences on adolescent decision making. *Current Directions in Psychological Science, 22*(2), 114–120. https://doi.org/10.1177/0963721412471347

Albert, M., & McCaig, L. F. (2014). *Injury-related emergency department visits by children and adolescents: United States, 2009–2010.* U.S. Department of Health and Human Services, Centers for Disease Control and Prevention, National Center for Health Statistics.

Alberts, B., Johnson, A., Lewis, J., Raff, M., Roberts, K., & Walter, P. (2002). Eggs. In B. Alberts, A. Johnson, & J. Lewis (Eds.), *Molecular biology of the cell* (4th ed.). Garland Science. https://www.ncbi.nlm.nih.gov/books/NBK26842/

Alcalá, L., Rogoff, B., & López Fraire, A. (2018). Sophisticated collaboration is common among Mexican-heritage US children. *Proceedings of the National Academy of Sciences, 115*(45), 11377–11384.

Alink, L. R. A., van Ijzendoorn, M. H., Bakermans-Kranenburg, M. J., Mesman, J., Juffer, R., & Koot, H. M. (2008). Cortisol and externalizing behavior in children and adolescents: Mixed meta-analytic evidence for the inverse relation of basal cortisol and cortisol reactivity with externalizing behavior. *Developmental Psychobiology, 50*, 427–450. https://doi.org/10.1002/dev.20300

Allen, G. E. (2011). Eugenics and modern biology: Critiques of eugenics, 1910–1945. *Annals of Human Genetics, 75*(3), 314–325. https://doi.org/10.1111/j.1469-1809.2011.00649.x

Allen, J. P., & Loeb, E. L. (2015). The autonomy-connection challenge in adolescent peer relationships. *Child Development Perspectives, 9*(2), 101–105. https://doi.org/10.1111/cdep.12111

Allen, J. P., & Tan, J. S. (2016). The multiple facets of attachment in adolescence. In J. Cassidy & P. R. Shaver (Eds.), *Handbook of attachment: Theory, research, and clinical applications* (pp. 399–415). Guilford.

Allen, J. P., Narr, R. K., Kansky, J., & Szwedo, D. E. (2020). Adolescent peer relationship qualities as predictors of long-term romantic life satisfaction. *Child Development, 91*(1), 327–340. https://doi.org/10.1111/cdev.13193

Allen, K., Kern, M. L., Vella-Brodrick, D., Hattie, J., & Waters, L. (2018). What schools need to know about fostering school belonging: A meta-analysis. *Educational Psychology Review, 30*(1), 1–34. https://doi.org/10.1007/s10648-016-9389-8

Allen, R., Shapland, D. L., Neitzel, J., & Iruka, I. U. (2021). Viewpoint: Creating anti-racist early childhood spaces. *Young Children, 76*(2).

Allensworth, E. M., & Clark, K. (2020). High school GPAs and ACT scores as predictors of college completion: Examining assumptions about consistency across high schools. *Educational Researcher, 49*(3), 198–211. https://doi.org/10.3102/0013189X20902110

Allison, M. A., Attisha, E., & Council on School Health. (2019). The link between school attendance and good health. *Pediatrics, 143*(2), e20183648. https://doi.org/10.1542/peds.2018-3648

Almas, A. N., Degnan, K. A., Walker, O. L., Radulescu, A., Nelson, C. A., Zeanah, C. H., & Fox, N. A. (2015). The effects of early institutionalization and foster care intervention on children's social behaviors at the age of eight. *Social Development, 24*(2), 225–239.

Alnæs, D., Kaufmann, T., Marquand, A. F., Smith, S. M., & Westlye, L. T. (2020). Patterns of sociocognitive stratification and perinatal risk in the child brain. *Proceedings of the National Academy of Sciences, 117*(22), 12419–12427.

Alper, R. M., Beiting, M., Luo, R., Jaen, J., Peel, M., Levi, O., Robinson, C., & Hirsh-Pasek, K. (2021). Change the things you can: Modifiable parent characteristics predict high-quality early language interaction within socioeconomic status. *Journal of Speech, Language, and Hearing Research, 64*(6), 1992–2004. https://doi.org/10.1044/2021_JSLHR-20-00412

Alvarez, A. L., & Booth, A. E. (2014). Motivated by meaning: Testing the effect of knowledge-infused rewards on preschoolers' persistence. *Child Development, 85*(2), 783–791.

Álvarez-Bueno, C., Hillman, C. H., Cavero-Redondo, I., Sánchez-López, M., Pozuelo-Carrascosa, D. P., & Martínez-Vizcaíno, V. (2020). Aerobic fitness and academic achievement: A systematic review and meta-analysis. *Journal of Sports Sciences, 38*(5), 582–589. https://doi.org/10.1080/02640414.2020.1720496

Amani, M. K., & Khalfaoui, A. (2019, March 28). Congolese warlord convicted of war crimes with the help of ABA ROLI. *ABA Journal.* https://www.abajournal.com/news/article/warlord-habarugira-drc-aba-abroad

Amato, P. R. (2010). Research on divorce: Continuing trends and new developments. *Journal of Marriage and Family, 72*(3), 650–666.

Amato, P. R., & Anthony, C. J. (2014). Estimating the effects of parental divorce and death with fixed effects models. *Journal of Marriage and Family, 76*(2), 370–386.

Ambridge, B., Kidd, E., Rowland, C. F., & Theakston, A. L. (2015). The ubiquity of frequency effects in first language acquisition. *Journal of Child Language, 42*(2), 239–273.

American Academy of Pediatrics. (2022). Children and COVID-19 Vaccination Trends. American Academy of Pediatrics. https://www.aap.org/en/pages/2019-novel-coronavirus-covid-19-infections/children-and-covid-19-vaccination-trends/

American Academy of Pediatrics, Council on Communications and Media (AAP). (2016). Media and young minds. *Pediatrics, 138*(5), e20162591. https://doi.org/10.1542/peds.2016-2591

American College of Obstetrics and Gynecology (ACOG). (2021). Breastfeeding challenges. ACOG Committee Opinion, Number 820. *Obstetrics and Gynecology, 137*(2), e42–e53.

American Community Survey (ACS), U.S. Census Bureau. (2018). *Detailed languages spoken at home and ability to speak English for the population 5 years and over: 2009–2013 American Community Survey.* https://www.census.gov/data/tables/2018/demo/2009-2018-lang-tables.html

American Community Survey (ACS). (2020). *Population Reference Bureau, analysis of data from the U.S. Census Bureau, Census 2000 Supplementary Survey, 2001 Supplementary Survey, 2002 through 2019* (CS table B17001).

American Psychiatric Association (APA). (2013). *Diagnostic and statistical manual of mental disorders* (5th ed.) (*DSM-5*). American Psychiatric Association Publishing. https://doi.org/10.1176/appi.books.9780890425596

American Psychiatric Association (APA). (2022). *Diagnostic and statistical manual of mental disorders* (5th ed., text rev.) (*DSM-5-TR*). American Psychiatric Association Publishing.

American Psychological Association. (2020). *Publication manual of the American Psychological Association* (7th ed.).

American Speech and Hearing Association (ASHA). (2017). *How does your child hear and talk?*

Ameye, H., & Swinnen, J. (2019). Obesity, income and gender: The changing global relationship. *Global Food Security, 23*, 267–281. https://doi.org/10.1016/j.gfs.2019.09.003

Ami, O., Maran, J. C., Gabor, P., Whitacre, E. B., Musset, D., Dubray, C., Mage, G., & Boyer, L. (2019). Three-dimensional magnetic resonance imaging of fetal head molding and brain shape changes during the second stage of labor. *PLOS ONE, 14*(5), e0215721. https://doi.org/10.1371/journal.pone.0215721

Amin, A., Kågesten, A., Adebayo, E., & Chandra-Mouli, V. (2018). Addressing gender socialization and masculinity norms among adolescent boys: Policy and programmatic implications. *Journal of Adolescent Health, 62*(3), S3–S5. https://doi.org/10.1016/j.jadohealth.2017.06.022

Amir, D., & McAuliffe, K. (2020). Cross-cultural, developmental psychology: Integrating approaches and key insights. *Evolution and Human Behavior, 41*(5), 430–444.

Amso, D., & Kirkham, N. (2021). A multiple-memory systems framework for examining attention and memory interactions in infancy. *Child Development Perspectives, 15*(2), 132–138. https://doi.org/10.1111/cdep.12410

Amso, D., & Lynn, A. (2017). Distinctive mechanisms of adversity and socioeconomic inequality in child development: A review and recommendations for evidence-based policy. *Policy Insights from the Behavioral and Brain Sciences, 4*(2), 139–146. https://doi.org/10.1177/2372732217721933

Amsterdam, B. (1972). Mirror self-image reactions before age two. *Developmental Psychobiology, 5*(4), 297–305. https://doi.org/10.1002/dev.420050403

Anderson, B. A., Laurent, P. A., & Yantis, S. (2011). Learned value magnifies salience-based attentional capture. *PLOS ONE, 6*(11), e27926. https://doi.org/10.1371/journal.pone.0027926

Anderson, C. A., Bushman, B. J., Bartholow, B. D., Cantor, J., Christakis, D., Coyne, S. M., Donnerstein, E., Brockmyer, J. F., Gentile, D. A., Green, C. S., Huesmann, R., Hummer, T., Krahé, B., Strasburger, V. C., Warburton, W., Wilson, B. J., & Ybarra, M. (2017). Screen violence and youth behavior. *Pediatrics, 140*(Suppl. 2), S142–S147. https://doi.org/10.1542/peds.2016-1758T

Anderson, D. I., Campos, J. J., Witherington, D. C., Dahl, A., Rivera, M., He, M., Uchiyama, I., & Barbu-Roth, M. (2013). The role of locomotion in psychological development. *Frontiers in Psychology, 4*, 440. https://doi.org/10.3389/fpsyg.2013.00440

Anderson, J. E. (1956). Child development: An historical perspective. *Child Development, 27*(2), 181–196. https://doi.org/10.2307/1126088

Anderson, M., Faverio, M., & Mcclain, C. (2022, June 2). How teens navigate school during COVID-19. *Pew Research Center: Internet, Science & Tech.* https://www.pewresearch.org/internet/2022/06/02/how-teens-navigate-school-during-covid-19/

Anderson, M., Vogels, E. A., & Turner, E. (2020). *The virtues and downsides of online dating.* Pew Research Center.

Anderson, N. J., Graham, S. A., Prime, H., Jenkins, J. M., & Madigan, S. (2021). Linking quality and quantity of parental linguistic input to child language skills: A meta-analysis. *Child Development, 92*(2), 484–501. https://doi.org/10.1111/cdev.13508

Anderson, R., & Nagy, W. (1993). *The vocabulary conundrum* (No. 57). Center for the Study of Reading Technical Report.

Anderson, R. E. (2018). And still WE rise: Parent–child relationships, resilience, and school readiness in low-income urban Black families. *Journal of Family Psychology, 32*(1), 60–70.

Anderson, R. E., & Stevenson, H. C. (2019). RECASTing racial stress and trauma: Theorizing the healing potential of racial socialization in families. *American Psychologist, 74*(1), 63.

Anderson, T. M., Ferres, J. M. L., Ren, S. Y., Moon, R. Y., Goldstein, R. D., Ramirez, J.-M., & Mitchell, E. A. (2019). Maternal smoking before and during pregnancy and the risk of sudden unexpected infant death. *Pediatrics, 143*(4), e20183325. https://doi.org/10.1542/peds.2018-3325

Ando, A., Parzer, P., Kaess, M., Schell, S., Henze, R., Delorme, S., Stieltjes, B., Resch, F., Brunner, R., & Koenig, J. (2021). Calendar age and puberty-related development of regional gray matter volume and white matter tracts during adolescence. *Brain Structure & Function, 226*(3), 927–937. https://doi.org/10.1007/s00429-020-02208-1

Andre, J., Picchioni, M., Zhang, R., & Toulopoulou, T. (2016). Working memory circuit as a function of increasing age in healthy adolescence: A systematic review and meta-analyses. *NeuroImage: Clinical, 12*, 940–948.

Andrew, R., Tiggemann, M., & Clark, L. (2016). Predictors and health-related outcomes of positive body image in adolescent girls: A prospective study. *Developmental Psychology, 52*(3), 463.

Andrews, A. L., Killings, X., Oddo, E. R., Gastineau, K. A. B., & Hink, A. B. (2022). Pediatric firearm injury mortality epidemiology. *Pediatrics,* 149(3), e2021052739. https://doi.org/10.1542/peds.2021-052739

Andrews, J. L., Ahmed, S. P., & Blakemore, S.-J. (2021). Navigating the social environment in adolescence: The role of social brain development. *Biological Psychiatry, 89*(2), 109–118.

Angrist, J. D., Cohodes, S. R., Dynarski, S. M., Pathak, P. A., & Walters, C. R. (2016). Stand and deliver: Effects of Boston's charter high schools on college preparation, entry, and choice. *Journal of Labor Economics, 34*(2), 275–318. https://doi.org/10.1086/683665

Anim-Somuah, M., Smyth, R. M., Cyna, A. M., & Cuthbert, A. (2018). Epidural versus non-epidural or no analgesia for pain management in labour. *The Cochrane Database of Systematic Reviews, 5*, CD000331–CD000331. https://doi.org/10.1002/14651858.CD000331.pub4

Annie E. Casey Foundation. (2018). *Opening doors for young parents* (Policy Report: Kids Count).

Anniko, M. K., Boersma, K., & Tillfors, M. (2019). Sources of stress and worry in the development of stress-related mental health problems: A longitudinal investigation from early- to mid-adolescence. *Anxiety, Stress, & Coping, 32*(2), 155–167. https://doi.org/10.1080/10615806.2018.1549657

Ansari, A., & Crosnoe, R. (2018). The transition into kindergarten for English language learners. In A. J. Mashburn, J. LoCasale-Crouch, & K. C. Pears (Eds.), *Kindergarten transition and readiness: Promoting cognitive, social-emotional, and self-regulatory development* (pp. 185–204). Springer International Publishing. https://doi.org/10.1007/978-3-319-90200-5_8

Ansari, A., & Gottfried, M. A. (2020). Early childhood educational experiences and preschool absenteeism. *The Elementary School Journal, 121*(1), 34–51. https://doi.org/10.1086/709832

Ansari, A., & Gottfried, M. A. (2021). The grade-level and cumulative outcomes of absenteeism. *Child Development, 92*(4), e548–e564. https://doi.org/10.1111/cdev.13555

Anthony, E. R., Cho, Y., Fischer, R. L., & Matthews, L. (2021). Examining the causal impact of prenatal home visiting on birth outcomes: A propensity score analysis. *Maternal and Child Health Journal.* https://doi.org/10.1007/s10995-020-03054-7

Anton, M. T., Jones, D. J., & Youngstrom, E. A. (2015). Socioeconomic status, parenting, and externalizing problems in African American single-mother homes: A person-oriented approach. *Journal of Family Psychology, 29*(3), 405.

Antonarakis, S. E., Skotko, B. G., Rafii, M. S., Strydom, A., Pape, S. E., Bianchi, D. W., Sherman, S. L., & Reeves, R. H. (2020). Down syndrome. *Nature Reviews Disease Primers, 6*(1), 1–20.

Antoniou, M. (2019). The advantages of bilingualism debate. *Annual Review of Linguistics, 5*(1), 395–415. https://doi.org/10.1146/annurev-linguistics-011718-011820

APA Ethics Committee Rules and Procedures. (2018). *Ethical principles of psychologists and code of conduct.* American Psychological Association. https://www.apa.org/ethics/code

Apergis, N., Bhattacharya, M., & Hadhri, W. (2020). Health care expenditure and environmental pollution: A cross-country comparison across different income groups. *Environmental Science and Pollution Research, 27*(8), 8142–8156. https://doi.org/10.1007/s11356-019-07457-0

Appel, H., Gerlach, A. L., & Crusius, J. (2016). The interplay between Facebook use, social comparison, envy, and depression. *Current Opinion in Psychology, 9*, 44–49.

Appleton, K. M., Hemingway, A., Rajska, J., & Hartwell, H. (2018). Repeated exposure and conditioning strategies for increasing vegetable liking and intake: Systematic review and meta-analyses of the published literature. *The American Journal of Clinical Nutrition, 108*(4), 842–856. https://doi.org/10.1093/ajcn/nqy143

Arauz, R. M., Dexter, A. L., Rogoff, B., & Aceves-Azuara, I. (2019). Children's management of attention as cultural practice. In T. Tulviste, D. L. Best, & J. L. Gibbons (Eds.), *Children's social worlds in cultural context* (pp. 23–39). Springer International Publishing. https://doi.org/10.1007/978-3-030-27033-9_3

Araya, A. C., Warwick, R., Shumer, D., & Selkie, E. (2021). Romantic relationships in transgender adolescents: A qualitative study. *Pediatrics, 147*(2), e2020007906. https://doi.org/10.1542/peds.2020-007906

Arboleda, V. A., Sandberg, D. E., & Vilain, E. (2014). DSDs: Genetics, underlying pathologies and psychosexual differentiation. *Nature Reviews: Endocrinology, 10*(10), 603–615. https://doi.org/10.1038/nrendo.2014.130

Argabright, S. T., Visoki, E., Moore, T. M., Ryan, D. T., DiDomenico, G. E., Njoroge, W. F. M., Taylor, J. H., Guloksuz, S., Gur, R. C., Gur, R. E., Benton, T. D., & Barzilay, R. (2021). Association Between Discrimination Stress and Suicidality in Preadolescent Children. *Journal of the American Academy of Child & Adolescent Psychiatry, 0*(0). https://doi.org/10.1016/j.jaac.2021.08.011

Armstrong, S., Wong, C. A., Perrin, E., Page, S., Sibley, L., & Skinner, A. (2018). Association of physical activity with income, race/ethnicity, and sex among adolescents and young adults in the United States: findings from the National Health and Nutrition Examination Survey, 2007–2016. *Jama Pediatrics, 172*(8), 732–740.

Armstrong-Carter, E., & Telzer, E. H. (2021). Family assistance spills over into prosocial behaviors toward friends and positive academic behaviors. *Journal of Research on Adolescence, 31*(4), 1188–1201. https://doi.org/10.1111/jora.12629

Armstrong-Carter, E., Ivory, S., Lin, L. C., Muscatell, K. A., & Telzer, E. H. (2020). Role fulfillment mediates the association between daily family assistance and cortisol awakening response in adolescents. *Child Development, 91*(3), 754–768. https://doi.org/10.1111/cdev.13213

Armstrong-Carter, E., Johnson, C., Belkowitz, J., Siskowski, C., & Olson, E. (2021). The United States should recognize and support caregiving youth. *Social Policy Report, 34*(2), 1–24. https://doi.org/10.1002/sop2.14

Arndorfer, C. L., & Stormshak, E. A. (2008). Same-sex versus other-sex best friendship in early adolescence: Longitudinal predictors of antisocial behavior throughout adolescence. *Journal of Youth and Adolescence, 37*(9), 1059–1070. https://doi.org/10.1007/s10964-008-9311-x

Arnett, J. J. (2000). Emerging adulthood: A theory of development from the late teens through the twenties. *American Psychologist, 55*(5), 469–480. http://doi.org/10.1037/0003-066X.55.5.469

Arnett, J. J. (2006). G. Stanley Hall's *Adolescence*: Brilliance and nonsense. *History of Psychology, 9* (3), 186–197. https://doi.org/10.1037/1093-4510.9.3.186

Arnett, J. J., & Mitra, D. (2020). Are the features of emerging adulthood developmentally distinctive? A comparison of ages 18–60 in the United States. *Emerging Adulthood, 8*(5), 412–419. https://doi.org/10.1177/2167696818810073

Aro, T., Poikkeus, A. M., Laakso, M. L., Tolvanen, A., & Ahonen, T. (2015). Associations between private speech, behavioral self-regulation, and cognitive abilities. *International Journal of Behavioral Development, 39*(6), 508–518.

Arsenio, W. (2014). Moral emotion attributions and aggression. In M. Killen & J. G. Smetana (Eds.), *Handbook of moral development* (pp. 235–255). Psychology Press.

Aryal, M. (2016, April 21). *A child-headed household perseveres a year after the Nepal earthquake.* https://www.unicef.org/stories/child-headed-household-perseveres-year-after-nepal-earthquake

Aschemeyer, F., Rosabal-Coto, M., Storm, S., & Keller, H. (2021). The role of culture and caregivers' formal education for babies' learning environments: The case of two Costa Rican Communities. *Journal of Cross-Cultural Psychology, 52*(2), 103–128. https://doi.org/10.1177/0022022120981715

Aserinsky, E. (1996). Memories of famous neuropsychologists: The discovery of REM sleep. *Journal of the History of the Neurosciences, 5*(3), 213–227. https://doi.org/10.1080/09647049609525671

Ashcraft, A. M., & Murray, P. J. (2017). Talking to parents about adolescent sexuality. *Pediatric Clinics of North America, 64*(2), 305–320. https://doi.org/10.1016/j.pcl.2016.11.002

Ashley, E. A., & Poespoprodjo, J. R. (2020). Treatment and prevention of malaria in children. *The Lancet Child & Adolescent Health, 4*(10), 775–789. https://doi.org/10.1016/S2352-4642(20)30127-9

Aspen Institute. (2021). *Project Play: State of Play, 2021.* Aspen Institute.

Astington, J. W., & Gopnik, A. (1988). Knowing you've changed your mind: Children's understanding of representational change. In J. W. Astington, P. L. Harris, & D. R. Olson (Eds.), *Developing theories of mind* (pp. 193–206). Cambridge University Press.

Astington, J. W., Harris, P. L., & Olson, D. R. (1988). *Developing theories of mind.* Cambridge University Press.

Astle, S., Leonhardt, N., & Willoughby, B. (2019). Home base: Family of origin factors and the debut of vaginal sex, anal sex, oral sex, masturbation, and pornography use in a national sample of adolescents. *The Journal of Sex Research, 57*(9), 1089–1099. https://doi.org/10.1080/00224499.2019.1691140

Astle, S., Toews, M., Topham, G., & Vennum, A. (2021). To talk or not to talk: An analysis of parents' intentions to talk with children about different sexual topics using the theory of planned behavior. *Sexuality Research and Social Policy.* https://doi.org/10.1007/s13178-021-00587-6

Attina, T. M., Malits, J., Naidu, M., & Trasande, L. (2019). Racial/ethnic disparities in disease burden and costs related to exposure to endocrine disrupting chemicals in the US: An exploratory analysis. *Journal of Clinical Epidemiology, 108*, 34–43. https://doi.org/10.1016/j.jclinepi.2018.11.024

Aubert, S., Brazo-Sayavera, J., González, S. A., Janssen, I., Manyanga, T., Oyeyemi, A. L., Picard, P., Sherar, L. B., Turner, E., & Tremblay, M. S. (2021). Global prevalence of physical activity for children and adolescents; inconsistencies, research gaps, and recommendations: A narrative review. *International Journal of Behavioral Nutrition and Physical Activity, 18*(1), 1–11.

Augustine, M. E., & Stiller, C. A. (2019). Children's behavioral self-regulation and conscience: Roles of child temperament, parenting, and parenting context. *Journal of Applied Developmental Psychology, 63*, 54–64. https://doi.org/10.1016/j.appdev.2019.05.008

Ault, R., Morales, A., Ault, R., Spitale, A., & Martinez, G. A. (2019). Communication pitfalls in interpreted genetic counseling sessions. *Journal of Genetic Counseling, 28*(4), 897–907. https://doi.org/10.1002/jgc4.1132

Aumètre, F., & Poulin, F. (2018). Academic and behavioral outcomes associated with organized activity participation trajectories during childhood. *Journal of Applied Developmental Psychology, 54*, 33–41. https://doi.org/10.1016/j.appdev.2017.11.003

Aunio, P., & Räsänen, P. (2016). Core numerical skills for learning mathematics in children aged five to eight years—A working model for educators. *European Early Childhood Education Research Journal, 24*(5), 684–704. https://doi.org/10.1080/1350293X.2014.996424

Austerberry, C., & Fearon, P. (2021). Chapter 3—An overview of developmental behavioral genetics. In L. Provenzi & R. Montirosso (Eds.), *Developmental human behavioral epigenetics* (Vol. 23, pp. 59–80). Academic Press. https://doi.org/10.1016/B978-0-12-819262-7.00003-9

Austin, R. D., & Pisano, G. P. (2017, May–June). Neurodiversity as a competitive advantage. *Harvard Business Review, 96*–103. https://hbr.org/2017/05/neurodiversity-as-a-competitive-advantage

Avagliano, L., Massa, V., George, T. M., Qureshy, S., Bulfamante, G., & Finnell, R. H. (2019). Overview on neural tube defects: From development to physical characteristics. *Birth Defects Research, 111*(19), 1455–1467. https://doi.org/10.1002/bdr2.1380

Aye, T., Oo, K. S., Khin, M. T., Kuramoto-Ahuja, T., & Maruyama, H. (2017). Gross motor skill development of 5-year-old kindergarten children in Myanmar. *Journal of Physical Therapy Science, 29*(10), 1772–1778. https://doi.org/10.1589/jpts.29.1772

Aylwin, C. F., Toro, C. A., Shirtcliff, E., & Lomniczi, A. (2019). Emerging genetic and epigenetic mechanisms underlying pubertal maturation in adolescence. *Journal of Research on Adolescence, 29*(1), 54–79. https://doi.org/10.1111/jora.12385

Ayoub, M., Briley, D. A., Grotzinger, A., Patterson, M. W., Engelhardt, L. E., Tackett, J. L., Harden, K. P., & Tucker-Drob, E. M. (2019). Genetic and environmental associations between child personality and parenting. *Social Psychological and Personality Science, 10*(6), 711–721. https://doi.org/10.1177/1948550618784890

Azad, M. B., Vehling, L., Chan, D., Klopp, A., Nickel, N. C., McGavock, J. M., Becker, A. B., Mandhane, P. J., Turvey, S. E., Moraes, T. J., Taylor, M. S., Lefebvre, D. L., Sears, M. R., Subbarao, P., & Investigators, on behalf of the CHILD Study Investigators. (2018). Infant feeding and weight gain: Separating breast milk from breastfeeding and formula from food. *Pediatrics, 142*(4), e20181092. https://doi.org/10.1542/peds.2018-1092

Azagba, S., Manzione, L., Shan, L., & King, J. (2020). Trends in smoking during pregnancy by socioeconomic characteristics in the United States, 2010–2017. *BMC Pregnancy and Childbirth, 20*(1), 52. https://doi.org/10.1186/s12884-020-2748-y

Azevedo, J. P. W. D., Rogers, F. H., Ahlgren, S. E., Cloutier, M. H., Chakroun, B., Chang, G. C., Mizunoya, S., Reuge, N. J., Brossard, M., & Bergmann, J. L. (2021). The state of the global education crisis: A path to recovery (English). UNESCO, UNICEF and the World Bank Group. https://documents.worldbank.org/curated/en/416991638768297704/The-State-of-the-Global-Education-Crisis-A-Path-to-Recovery

Azhari, A., Leck, W. Q., Gabrieli, G., Bizzego, A., Rigo, P., Setoh, P., Bornstein, M. H., & Esposito, G. (2019). Parenting stress undermines mother-child brain-to-brain synchrony: A hyperscanning study. *Scientific Reports, 9*(1), 11407. https://doi.org/10.1038/s41598-019-47810-4

Baams, L., Dubas, J. S., & Van Aken, M. A. (2017). Comprehensive sexuality education as a longitudinal predictor of LGBTQ name-calling and perceived willingness to intervene in school. *Journal of Youth and Adolescence, 46*(5), 931–942.

Babcock, P., & Marks, M. (2010). The falling time cost of college: Evidence from half a century of time use data. *The Review of Economics and Statistics, 93*(2), 468–478. https://doi.org/10.1162/REST_a_00093

Baburamani, A. A., Patkee, P. A., Arichi, T., & Rutherford, M. A. (2019). New approaches to studying early brain development in Down syndrome. *Developmental Medicine & Child Neurology, 61*(8), 867–879. https://doi.org/10.1111/dmcn.14260

Bach, A. M., Xie, W., Piazzoli, L., Jensen, S. K. G., Afreen, S., Haque, R., Petri, W. A., & Nelson, C. A. (2022). Systemic inflammation during the first year of life is associated with brain functional connectivity and future cognitive outcomes. *Developmental Cognitive Neuroscience, 53*, 101041. https://doi.org/10.1016/j.dcn.2021.101041

Backeljauw, P., Cappa, M., Kiess, W., Law, L., Cookson, C., Sert, C., Whalen, J., & Dattani, M. T. (2021). Impact of short stature on quality of life: A systematic literature review. *Growth Hormone & IGF Research, 57–58*, 101392. https://doi.org/10.1016/j.ghir.2021.101392

Bai, L., Whitesell, C. J., & Teti, D. M. (2020). Maternal sleep patterns and parenting quality during infants' first 6 months. *Journal of Family Psychology, 34*(3), 291–300. https://doi.org/10.1037/fam0000608

Baiden, P., Panisch, L. S., Kim, Y. J., LaBrenz, C. A., Kim, Y., & Onyeaka, H. K. (2021). Association between first sexual intercourse and sexual violence victimization, symptoms of depression, and suicidal behaviors among adolescents in the United States: Findings from 2017 and 2019 National Youth Risk Behavior Survey. *International Journal of Environmental Research and Public Health, 18*(15), 7922. https://doi.org/10.3390/ijerph18157922

Baillargeon, R. (1987). Young infants' reasoning about the physical and spatial properties of a hidden object. *Cognitive Development, 2*(3), 179–200. https://doi.org/10.1016/S0885-2014(87)90043-8

Baillargeon, R., Scott, R. M., & Bian, L. (2016). Psychological reasoning in infancy. *Annual Review of Psychology, 67*(1), 159–186. https://doi.org/10.1146/annurev-psych-010213-115033

Baird, D., Bybel, M., & Kowalski, A. W. (2019). Toilet training: Common questions and answers. *American Family Physician, 100*(8), 468–474.

Bajaj, M., & Suresh, S. (2018). The "warm embrace" of a newcomer school for immigrant & refugee youth. *Theory Into Practice, 57*(2), 91–98.

Bakalar, J. L., Shank, L. M., Vannucci, A., Radin, R. M., & Tanofsky-Kraff, M. (2015). Recent advances in developmental and risk factor research on eating disorders. *Current Psychiatry Reports, 17*(6), 42. https://doi.org/10.1007/s11920-015-0585-x

Baker, A. E., & Galván, A. (2020). Threat or thrill? The neural mechanisms underlying the development of anxiety and risk taking in adolescence. *Developmental Cognitive Neuroscience, 45*, 100841.

Baker, K. E., & Harris, A. C. (2020). Terminology should accurately reflect complexities of sexual orientation and identity. *American Journal of Public Health, 110*(11), 1668–1669.

Bakermans-Kranenburg, M. J., Lotz, A., Dijk, K. A., & Van IJzendoorn, M. (2019). Birth of a father: Fathering in the first 1,000 days. *Child Development Perspectives, 13*(4), 247–253. https://doi.org/10.1111/cdep.12347

Bakermans-Kranenburg, M. J., & Van Ijzendoorn, M. H. (2015). The hidden efficacy of interventions: Gene× environment experiments from a differential susceptibility perspective. *Annual review of psychology, 66*, 381–409.

Baldacci, F., Mazzucchi, S., Della Vecchia, A., Giampietri, L., Giannini, N., Koronyo-Hamaoui, M., Ceravolo, R., Siciliano, G., Bonuccelli, U., Elahi, F. M., Vergallo, A., Lista, S., & Giorgi, F. S. (2020). The path to biomarker-based diagnostic criteria for the spectrum of neurodegenerative diseases. *Expert Review of Molecular Diagnostics, 20*(4), 421–441. https://doi.org/10.1080/14737159.2020.1731306

Baldwin, D., & Meyer, M. (2007). How inherently social is language? In E. Hoff & M. Shatz (Eds.), *Blackwell handbook of language development* (pp. 87–106). Blackwell Publishing.

Ballard, P. J., Daniel, S. S., Anderson, G., Nicolotti, L., Caballero Quinones, E., Lee, M., & Koehler, A. N. (2021). Incorporating volunteering into treatment for depression among adolescents: Developmental and clinical considerations. *Frontiers in Psychology, 12*, 1581.

Ballard, P. J., Hoyt, L. T., & Pachucki, M. C. (2019). Impacts of adolescent and young adult civic engagement on health and socioeconomic status in adulthood. *Child Development, 90*(4), 1138–1154.

Balzer Carr, B., & London, R. A. (2020). Healthy, housed, and well-fed: Exploring basic needs support programming in the context of university student success. *AERA Open, 6*(4), 2332858420972619. https://doi.org/10.1177/2332858420972619

Bamishigbin, O. N., Dunkel Schetter, C., & Stanton, A. L. (2019). The antecedents and consequences of adolescent fatherhood: A systematic review. *Social Science & Medicine, 232*, 106–119. https://doi.org/10.1016/j.socscimed.2019.04.031

Bandura, A. (1999). *Self-efficacy: The exercise of control.* W. H. Freeman.

Bandura, A. (2018). Toward a psychology of human agency: Pathways and reflections. *Perspectives on Psychological Science, 13*(2), 130–136. https://doi.org/10.1177/1745691617699280

Bandura, A. (2019). Applying theory for human betterment. *Perspectives on Psychological Science, 14*(1), 12–15. https://doi.org/10.1177/1745691618815165

Bandura, A., Ross, D., & Ross, S. A. (1963). Imitation of film-mediated aggressive models. *The Journal of Abnormal and Social Psychology, 66*(1), 3.

Banerjee, M., & Eccles, J. S. (2019). Perceived racial discrimination as a context for parenting in African American and European American youth. In H. E. Fitzgerald, D. J. Johnson, D. B. Qin, F. A. Villarruel, & J. Norder (Eds.), *Handbook of children and prejudice: Integrating research, practice, and policy* (pp. 233–247). Springer International Publishing. https://doi.org/10.1007/978-3-030-12228-7_13

Banghart, P., Halle, T., Bamdad, T., Cook, M., Redd, Z., Cox, A., Carlson, J., & Zaslow, M. (2020). *A review of the literature on access to high quality care for infants and toddlers.* Child Trends.

Barac, R., Bialystok, E., Castro, D. C., & Sanchez, M. (2014). The cognitive development of young dual language learners: A critical review. *Early Childhood Research Quarterly, 29*(4), 699–714. https://doi.org/10.1016/j.ecresq.2014.02.003

Baranne, M. L., & Falissard, B. (2018). Global burden of mental disorders among children aged 5–14 years. *Child and Adolescent Psychiatry and Mental Health, 12*(1), 19.

Barata, M. C., & Yoshikawa, H. (2014). Mixed methods in research on child well-being. In A. Ben-Arieh, F. C. Frønes, & J. E. Korbin (Eds.), *Handbook of child well-being: Theories, methods and policies in global perspective* (pp. 2879–2893). Springer Netherlands. https://nyuscholars.nyu.edu/en/publications/mixed-methods-in-research-on-child-well-being

Barbara, V. (2019, January 16). Opinion | I put my baby daughter in dinosaur overalls. Am I an anarchist? *The New York Times.* https://www.nytimes.com/2019/01/16/opinion/brazil-gender-alves.html

Barber, B. K., Stolz, H. E., Olsen, J. A., Collins, W. A., & Burchinal, M. (2005). Parental support, psychological control, and behavioral control: Assessing relevance across time, culture, and method. *Monographs of the Society for Research in Child Development, 70*(4), i–147.

Barber, B. K., Xia, M., Olsen, J. A., McNeely, C. A., & Bose, K. (2012). Feeling disrespected by parents: Refining the measurement and understanding of psychological control. *Journal of Adolescence, 35*(2), 273–287. https://doi.org/10.1016/j.adolescence.2011.09.010

Barbot, B., Hein, S., Trentacosta, C., Beckmann, J. F., Bick, J., Crocetti, E., Liu, Y., Rao, S. F., Liew, J., Overbeek, G., Ponguta, L. A., Scheithauer, H., Super, C., Arnett, J., Bukowski, W., Cook, T. D., Côté, J., Eccles, J. S., Eid, M., . . . IJzendoorn, M. H. van. (2020). Manifesto for new directions in developmental science. *New Directions for Child and Adolescent Development, 2020*(172), 135–149. https://doi.org/10.1002/cad.20359

Barbuscia, A., Martikainen, P., Myrskylä, M., Remes, H., Somigliana, E., Klemetti, R., & Goisis, A. (2020). Maternal age and risk of low birth weight and premature birth in children conceived through medically assisted reproduction. Evidence from Finnish population registers. *Human Reproduction, 35*(1), 212–220. https://doi.org/10.1093/humrep/dez275

Bardanzellu, F., Fanos, V., & Reali, A. (2017). "Omics" in human colostrum and mature milk: Looking to old data with new eyes. *Nutrients, 9*(8), 843. https://doi.org/10.3390/nu9080843

Barendse, M., Flannery, J., Cavanagh, C., Aristizabal, M., Becker, S. P., Berger, E., Breaux, R., Campione-Barr, N., Church, J. A., Crone, E., Dahl, R., Dennis-Tiwary, T. A., Dvorsky, M., Dziura, S., Ho, T., Killoren, S. E., Langberg, J., Larguinho, T., Magis-Weinberg, L., . . . Pfeifer, J. (2021). Longitudinal change in adolescent depression and anxiety symptoms from before to during the COVID-19 pandemic: An international collaborative of 12 samples. *PsyArXiv.* https://doi.org/10.31234/osf.io/hn7us

Barfield, W. D. (2021). Social disadvantage and its effect on maternal and newborn health. *Seminars in Perinatology,* 151407. https://doi.org/10.1016/j.semperi.2021.151407

Barker, D. J. (1995). Fetal origins of coronary heart disease. *BMJ, 311*(6998), 171–174.

Barker, D. J. P. (2004). The developmental origins of chronic adult disease. *Acta Paediatrica, 93*(s446), 26–33. https://doi.org/10.1111/j.1651-2227.2004.tb00236.x

Barker, J. E., Semenov, A. D., Michaelson, L., Provan, L. S., Snyder, H. R., & Munakata, Y. (2014). Less-structured time in children's daily lives predicts self-directed executive functioning. *Frontiers in Psychology, 5*, 593. https://doi.org/10.3389/fpsyg.2014.00593

Barlow, J., Sembi, S., Parsons, H., Kim, S., Petrou, S., Harnett, P., & Dawe, S. (2019). A randomized controlled trial and economic evaluation of the parents under pressure program for parents in substance abuse treatment. *Drug and Alcohol Dependence, 194*, 184–194. https://doi.org/10.1016/j.drugalcdep.2018.08.044

Barlow, J., Smailagic, N., Huband, N., Roloff, V., & Bennett, C. (2014). Group-based parent training programmes for improving parental psychosocial health. *Cochrane Database of Systematic Reviews,* (5), CD002020. https://doi.org/10.1002/14651858.CD002020.pub4

Barnett, L. M., Lai, S. K., Veldman, S. L., Hardy, L. L., Cliff, D. P., Morgan, P. J., Zask, A., Lubans, D. R., Shultz, S. P., Ridgers, N. D., Rush, E., Brown, H. L., & Okely, A. D. (2016). Correlates of gross motor competence in children and adolescents: A systematic review and meta-analysis. *Sports Medicine, 46*(11), 1663–1688.

Barnett, L. M., Stodden, D. F., Hulteen, R. M., & Sacko, R. S. (2020). Motor competence assessment. In T. Brusseau, S. Fairclough, & D. Lubans (Eds.), *The Routledge handbook of youth physical activity* (pp. 1–25). Routledge.

Barnow, B. S., Miller, L. M., & Smith, J. A. (2021). Workforce entry including career and technical education and training. *The Annals of the American Academy of Political and Social Science, 695*(1), 260–274. https://doi.org/10.1177/00027162211031811

Barnum, M., Kelsha, K., & Wilburn, T. (2022, January 24). Graduation rates dip across U.S. as pandemic stalls progress. *Chalkbeat.* https://www.chalkbeat.org/2022/1/24/22895461/2021-graduation-rates-decrease-pandemic

Baron, A. S., & Banaji, M. R. (2006). The development of implicit attitudes: Evidence of race evaluations from ages 6 and 10 and adulthood. *Psychological Science, 17*(1), 53–58.

Barr, R. G., Kirkorian, H., Radesky, J., Coyne, S., Nichols, D., Blanchfield, O., Rusnak, S., Stockdale, L., Ribner, A., Durnez, J., Epstein, M., Heimann, M., Koch, F.-S., Sundqvist, A., Birberg-Thornberg, U., Konrad, C., Slussareff, M., Bus, A., Bellagamba, F., & Fitzpatrick, caroline on behalf of CAFE Consortium Key Investigators. (2020). Beyond screen time: A synergistic approach to a more comprehensive assessment of family media exposure during early childhood. *Frontiers in Psychology, 11*, 1283. https://doi.org/10.3389/fpsyg.2020.01283

Barr, R. G., Konner, M., Bakeman, R., & Adamson, L. (1991). Crying in !Kung San infants: A test of the cultural specificity hypothesis. *Developmental Medicine & Child Neurology, 33*(7), 601–610. https://doi.org/10.1111/j.1469-8749.1991.tb14930.x

Barratt, M. J., Nuzhat, S., Ahsan, K., Frese, S. A., Arzamasov, A. A., Sarker, S. A., Islam, M. M., Palit, P., Islam, M. R., Hibberd, M. C., Nakshatri, S., Cowardin, C. A., Guruge, J. L., Byrne, A. E., Venkatesh, S., Sundaresan, V., Henrick, B., Duar, R. M., Mitchell, R. D., . . . Gordon, J. I. (2022). Bifidobacterium infantis treatment promotes weight gain in Bangladeshi infants with severe acute malnutrition. *Science Translational Medicine, 14*(640), eabk1107. https://doi.org/10.1126/scitranslmed.abk1107

Barrett, L. F., Adolphs, R., Marsella, S., Martinez, A. M., & Pollak, S. D. (2019). Emotional expressions reconsidered: Challenges to inferring emotion from human facial movements. *Psychological Science in the Public Interest, 20*(1), 1–68.

Barrow, L., & Markman-Pithers, L. (2016). Supporting young English learners in the United States. *The Future of Children, 26*(2), 159–183.

Barry, C. M., & Abo-Zena, M. M. (2014). *Emerging adults' religiousness and spirituality: Meaning-making in an age of transition.* Oxford University Press.

Barry, E. S. (2021). What is "normal" infant sleep? Why we still do not know. *Psychological Reports, 124*(2), 651–692.

Barshay, J. (2018, August 27). *A study finds promise in project-based learning for young low-income children.* The Hechinger Report. http://hechingerreport.org/a-study-finds-promise-in-project-based-learning-for-young-low-income-children/

Bartha-Doering, L., Kollndorfer, K., Schwartz, E., Fischmeister, F. Ph. S., Alexopoulos, J., Langs, G., Prayer, D., Kasprian, G., & Seidl, R. (2021). The role of the corpus callosum in lan-guage network connectivity in children. Developmental *Science, 24*(2), e13031. https://doi.org/10.1111/desc.13031

Bartlett, J. D. (2021). Trauma-informed practices in early childhood education. *Zero to Three, 41*(3), 24–34.

Barton, A. W., & Brody, G. H. (2018). Parenting as a buffer that deters discrimination and race-related stressors from "getting under the skin": Theories, findings, and future directions. In B. Major, J. F. Dovidio, & B. G. Link (Eds.), *The Oxford handbook of stigma, discrimination, and health* (pp. 335–354). Oxford University Press.

Bashford, A., & Levine, P. (Eds.). (2010). *The Oxford handbook of the history of eugenics.* Oxford University Press.

Bassok, D., Finch, J. E., Lee, R., Reardon, S. F., & Waldfogel, J. (2016). Socioeconomic gaps in early childhood experiences: 1998 to 2010. *Aera Open, 2*(3), 2332858416653924.

Bastaits, K., & Mortelmans, D. (2016). Parenting as mediator between post-divorce family structure and children's well-being. *Journal of Child and Family Studies, 25*(7), 2178–2188.

Bastin, M., Luyckx, K., Raes, F., & Bijttebier, P. (2021). Co-rumination and depressive symptoms in adolescence: Prospective associations and the mediating role of brooding rumination. *Journal of Youth and Adolescence, 50*(5), 1003–1016. https://doi.org/10.1007/s10964-021-01412-4

Bateson, P. (2015). Ethology and human development. In *Handbook of child psychology and developmental science* (pp. 1–36). Wiley. https://doi.org/10.1002/9781118963418.childpsy106

Bateson, P. (2017). Adaptability and evolution. *Interface Focus, 7*(5), 20160126. https://doi.org/10.1098/rsfs.2016.0126

Bathelt, J., Gathercole, S. E., Butterfield, S., & Astle, D. E. (2018). Children's academic attainment is linked to the global organization of the white matter connectome. *Developmental Science, 21*(5), e12662. https://doi.org/10.1111/desc.12662

Bathory, E., & Tomopoulos, S. (2017). Sleep regulation, physiology and development, sleep duration and patterns, and sleep hygiene in infants, toddlers, and pre-school-age children. *Current Problems in Pediatric and Adolescent Health Care, 47*(2), 29–42. https://doi.org/10.1016/j.cppeds.2016.12.001

Batres, A. (2012, July 9). Alumni profile: Alejandro "Alex" Batres (Saturday cast, 2010–2012). *The Possibility Project Summer 2012 News.*

Battaglia, M., Garon-Carrier, G., Côté, S. M., Dionne, G., Touchette, E., Vitaro, F., Tremblay, R. E., & Boivin, M. (2017). Early childhood trajectories of separation anxiety: Bearing on mental health, academic achievement, and physical health from mid-childhood to preadolescence. *Depression and Anxiety, 34*(10), 918–927. https://doi.org/10.1002/da.22674

Battistich, V., Schaps, E., & Wilson, N. (2004). Effects of an elementary school intervention on students' "connectedness" to school and social adjustment during middle school. *Journal of Primary Prevention, 24*(3), 243–262.

Bau, A. M., Ernert, A., Schenk, L., Wiegand, S., Martus, P., Grüters, A., & Krude, H. (2009). Is there a further acceleration in the age at onset of menarche? A cross-sectional study in 1840 school children focusing on age and bodyweight at the onset of menarche. *European Journal of Endocrinology, 160*(1), 107–113. https://doi.org/10.1530/EJE-08-0594

Baudat, S., Van Petegem, S., Antonietti, J.-P., Sznitman, G. A., & Zimmermann, G. (2020). Developmental changes in secrecy during middle adolescence: Links with alcohol use and perceived controlling parenting. *Journal of Youth and Adolescence, 49*(8), 1583–1600. https://doi.org/10.1007/s10964-020-01281-3

Bauer, A., Fairchild, G., Halligan, S. L., Hammerton, G., Murray, J., Santos, I. S., Munhoz, T. N., Barros, A. J. D., Barros, F. C., & Matijasevich, A. (2021). Harsh parenting and child conduct and emotional problems: Parent- and child-effects in the 2004 Pelotas Birth Cohort. *European Child & Adolescent Psychiatry*, 1–11.

Bauer, P. J. (2015). Development of episodic and autobiographical memory: The importance of remembering forgetting. *Developmental Review, 38*, 146–166. https://doi.org/10.1016/j.dr.2015.07.011

Bauer, P. J., Dugan, J. A., Varga, N. L., & Riggins, T. (2019). Relations between neural structures and children's self-derivation of new knowledge through memory integration. *Developmental Cognitive Neuroscience, 36*, 100611.

Bauer, P. J., & Larkina, M. (2014). The onset of childhood amnesia in childhood: A prospective investigation of the course and determinants of forgetting of early-life events. *Memory, 22*(8), 907–924. https://doi.org/10.1080/09658211.2013.854806

Baum, S., Ma, J., & Payea, K. (2013). *Education pays 2013.* The College Board. http://www.rilin.state.ri.us/Special/ses15/commdocs/Education%20Pays,%20The%20College%20Board.pdf

Baumrind, D. (1971). Current patterns of parental authority. *Developmental Psychology, 4*(1, Pt. 2), 1–103. https://doi.org/10.1037/h0030372

Baumrind, D. (1972). An exploratory study of socialization effects on black children: Some black-white comparisons. *Child Development, 43*(1), 261–267.

Baumrind, D. (1989). Rearing competent children. In W. Damon (Ed.), *Child development today and tomorrow* (pp. 349–378). Jossey-Bass/Wiley.

Baumrind, D. (1991). The influence of parenting style on adolescent competence and substance use. *The Journal of Early Adolescence, 11*(1), 56–95. https://doi.org/10.1177/0272431691111004

Baumrind, D. (2012). Differentiating between confrontive and coercive kinds of parental power-assertive disciplinary practices. *Human Development, 55*(2), 35–51.

Baumrind, D. (2013). Authoritative parenting revisited: History and current status. In R. E. Larzelere, A. S. Morris, & A. W. Harrist (Eds.), *Authoritative parenting: Synthesizing nurturance and discipline for optimal child development* (pp. 11–34). American Psychological Association. https://doi.org/10.1037/13948-002

Baumrind, D., & Black, A. E. (1967). Socialization practices associated with dimensions of competence in preschool boys and girls. *Child Development, 38*(2), 291–327.

Baumrind, D., Larzelere, R. E., & Owens, E. B. (2010). Effects of preschool parents' power assertive patterns and practices on adolescent development. *Parenting: Science and Practice, 10*(3), 157–201.

Bayard, N. S., van Loon, M. H., Steiner, M., & Roebers, C. M. (2021). Developmental improvements and persisting difficulties in children's metacognitive monitoring and control skills: Cross-sectional and longitudinal perspectives. *Child Development, 92*(3), 1118–1136.

Bayley, N. (1956). Individual patterns of development. *Child Development, 27*(1), 45–74. https://doi.org/10.2307/1126330

BBC. (2016, December 30). Can Denmark's generous childcare system survive? *BBC News.* https://www.bbc.com/news/business-38254474

Beam, C. R., & Turkheimer, E. (2017). Gene–environment correlation as a source of stability and diversity in development. In P. H. Tolan & B. L. Leventhal (Eds.), *Gene-environment transactions in developmental psychopathology: The role in intervention research* (pp. 111–130). Springer International Publishing. https://doi.org/10.1007/978-3-319-49227-8_6

Beardslee, J., Docherty, M., Mulvey, E., & Pardini, D. (2019). The direct and indirect associations between childhood socioeconomic disadvantage and adolescent gun violence. *Journal of Clinical Child & Adolescent Psychology, 50*(3), 326–336. https://doi.org/10.1080/15374416.2019.1644646

Beauregard, J. L., Hamner, H. C., Chen, J., Avila-Rodriguez, W., Elam-Evans, L. D., & Perrine, C. G. (2019). Racial disparities in breastfeeding initiation and duration among U.S. infants born in 2015. *Morbidity and Mortality Weekly Report, 68*(34), 745–748. https://doi.org/10.15585/mmwr.mm6834a3

Beccaria, L., Kek, M. Y. C. A., & Huijser, H. (2018). Exploring nursing educators' use of theory and methods in search for evidence based credibility in nursing education. *Nurse Education Today, 65*, 60–66. https://doi.org/10.1016/j.nedt.2018.02.032

Becchetti, L., & Bellucci, D. (2020). Generativity, aging and subjective well-being. *International Review of Economics, 68, 1411–84.* https://doi.org/10.1007/s12232-020-00358-6

Becher, E. H., Kim, H., Cronin, S. E., Deenanath, V., McGuire, J. K., McCann, E. M., & Powell, S. (2019). Positive parenting and parental conflict: Contributions to resilient coparenting during divorce. *Family Relations, 68*(1), 150–164.

Becht, A. I., Luyckx, K., Nelemans, S. A., Goossens, L., Branje, S. J. T., Vollebergh, W. A. M., & Meeus, W. H. J. (2019). Linking identity and depressive symptoms across adolescence: A multisample longitudinal study testing within-person effects. *Developmental Psychology, 55*(8), 1733–1742. https://doi.org/10.1037/dev0000742

Beck, A. F., Edwards, E. M., Horbar, J. D., Howell, E. A., McCormick, M. C., & Pursley, D. M. (2020). The color of health: How racism, segregation, and inequality affect the health and well-being of preterm infants and their families. *Pediatric Research, 87*(2), 227–234. https://doi.org/10.1038/s41390-019-0513-6

Beckerman, J. P., Alike, Q., Lovin, E., Tamez, M., & Mattei, J. (2017). The development and public health implications of food preferences in children. *Frontiers in Nutrition, 4*, 66. https://doi.org/10.3389/fnut.2017.00066

Beckerman, M., van Berkel, S. R., Mesman, J., & Alink, L. R. A. (2018). Negative parental attributions mediate associations between risk factors and dysfunctional parenting: A replication and extension. *Child Abuse & Neglect, 81*, 249–258. https://doi.org/10.1016/j.chiabu.2018.05.001

Beckmeyer, J. J., & Weybright, E. H. (2020). Exploring the associations between middle adolescent romantic activity and positive youth development. *Journal of Adolescence, 80,* 214–219. https://doi.org /10.1016/j.adolescence.2020.03.002

Beckmeyer, J. J., Herbenick, D., Fu, T.-C., Dodge, B., & Fortenberry, J. D. (2021). Pleasure during adolescents' most recent partnered sexual experience: Findings from a U.S. probability survey. *Archives of Sexual Behavior, 50*(6), 2423–2434. https://doi.org/10.1007 /s10508-021-02026-4

Bediou, B., Rich, M., & Bavelier, D. (2020). Digital media and cognitive development. In *Education in the Digital Age: Healthy and Happy Children.* OECD Publishing. https://read.oecd-ilibrary.org/education /education-in-the-digital-age_3b071e13-en

Beijers, R., Hartman, S., Shalev, I., Hastings, W., Mattern, B. C., de Weerth, C., & Belsky, J. (2020). Testing three hypotheses about effects of sensitive–insensitive parenting on telomeres. *Developmental Psychology, 56*(2), 237–250. https://doi.org/10.1037 /dev0000879

Belcher, B. R., Zink, J., Azad, A., Campbell, C. E., Chakravartti, S. P., & Herting, M. M. (2021). The roles of physical activity, exercise, and fitness in promoting resilience during adolescence: Effects on mental well-being and brain development. *Biological Psychiatry. Cognitive Neuroscience and Neuroimaging, 6*(2), 225–237. https://do.org/10.1016/j.bpsc.2020.08.005

Bell, C. N., Kerr, J., & Young, J. L. (2019). Associations between obesity, obesogenic environments, and structural racism vary by county-level racial composition. *International Journal of Environmental Research and Public Health, 16*(5), 861. https://doi.org/10.3390 /ijerph16050861

Bell, D. R., Post, E. G., Biese, K., Bay, C., & Valovich McLeod, T. (2018). Sport specialization and risk of overuse injuries: A systematic review with meta-analysis. *Pediatrics, 142*(3).

Bell, E. F., Hintz, S. R., Hansen, N. I., Bann, C. M., Wyckoff, M. H., DeMauro, S. B., Walsh, M. C., Vohr, B. R., Stoll, B. J., Carlo, W. A., Van Meurs, K. P., Rysavy, M. A., Patel, R. M., Merhar, S. L., Sánchez, P. J., Laptook, A. R., Hibbs, A. M., Cotten, C. M., D'Angio, C. T., . . . Eunice Kennedy Shriver National Institute of Child Health and Human Development Neonatal Research Network. (2022). Mortality, in-hospital morbidity, care practices, and 2-year outcomes for extremely preterm infants in the US, 2013–2018. *JAMA, 327*(3), 248–263. https://doi.org /10.1001/jama.2021.23580

Bell, J. A., Carslake, D., Wade, K. H., Richmond, R. C., Langdon, R. J., Vincent, E. E., Holmes, M. V., Timpson, N. J., & Smith, G. D. (2018). Influence of puberty timing on adiposity and cardiometabolic traits: A Mendelian randomisation study. *PLOS Medicine, 15*(8), e1002641. https://doi.org/10.1371/journal.pmed.1002641

Bell, L. (2018). Psychoanalytic theories of gender. In N. K. Dess, J. Marecek, & L. C. Bell (Eds.), *Gender, sex, and sexualities: Psychological perspectives* (pp. 195–217). Oxford University Press.

Bell, M. A. (2012). A psychobiological perspective on working memory performance at 8 months of age. *Child Development, 83*(1), 251–265.

Beller, S., Bender, A., Chrisomalis, S., Jordan, F. M., Overmann, K. A., Saxe, G. B., & Schlimm, D. (2018). The cultural challenge in mathematical cognition. *Journal of Numerical Cognition, 4*(2), 448–463. https://doi .org/10.5964/jnc.v4i2.137

Belsky, J. (1984). The determinants of parenting: A process model. *Child Development, 55*(1), 83–96.

Belsky, J. (2019). Early-life adversity accelerates child and adolescent development. *Current Directions in Psychological Science, 28*(3), 241–246. https://doi .org/10.1177/0963721419837670

Belsky, J., Zhang, X., & Sayler, K. (2021). Differential susceptibility 2.0: Are the same children affected by different experiences and exposures? *Development and Psychopathology,* 1–9. https://doi.org/10.1017 /S0954579420002205

Beltrán, S., Sit, L., & Ginsburg, K. R. (2021). A call to revise the diagnosis of oppositional defiant disorder — Diagnoses are for helping, not harming. *JAMA Psychiatry.* https://doi.org/10.1001 /jamapsychiatry.2021.2127

Bem, S. L. (1981). Gender schema theory: A cognitive account of sex typing. *Psychological Review, 88*(4), 354–364. https://doi.org/10.1037/0033-295X.88.4.354

Bem, S. L. (1989). Genital knowledge and gender constancy in preschool children. *Child Development, 60*(3), 649–662. https://doi.org/10.2307/1130730

Bender, J. M., Lee, Y., Ryoo, J. H., Boucke, L., Sun, M., Ball, T. S., Rugolotto, S., & She, R. C. (2021). A longitudinal study of assisted infant toilet training during the first year of life. *Journal of Developmental & Behavioral Pediatrics, 42*(8), 648–655.

Bender, P. K., Kim, E. L., & Gentile, D. A. (2020). Gaming disorder in children and adolescents: Risk factors and preventive approaches. *Current Addiction Reports, 7*(4), 553–560.

Benfer, E. A. (2017). Contaminated childhood: How the United States failed to prevent the chronic lead poisoning of low-income children and communities of color. *Harvard Environmental Law Review, 41,* 493.

Benito-Gomez, M., Williams, K. N., McCurdy, A., & Fletcher, A. C. (2020). Autonomy-supportive parenting in adolescence: Cultural variability in the contemporary United States. *Journal of Family Theory & Review, 12*(1), 7–26. https://doi.org/10.1111/jftr.12362

Benkert, R., Cuevas, A., Thompson, H. S., Dove-Meadows, E., & Knuckles, D. (2019). Ubiquitous yet unclear: A systematic review of medical mistrust. *Behavioral Medicine, 45*(2), 86–101. https://doi.org/10 .1080/08964289.2019.1588220

Benner, A. D., & Wang, Y. (2016). Racial/ethnic discrimination and adolescents' well-being: The role of cross-ethnic friendships and friends' experiences of discrimination. *Child Development, 88*(2), 493–504. https://doi.org/10.1111/cdev.12606

Benner, A. D., Wang, Y., Shen, Y., Boyle, A. E., Polk, R., & Cheng, Y. P. (2018). Racial/ethnic discrimination and well-being during adolescence: A meta-analytic review. *American Psychologist, 73*(7), 855.

Bennett, J., Fry, R., & Kochhar, R. (2020, July 23). *Are you in the American middle class? Find out with our income calculator.* Pew Research Center. https://www.pewresearch.org/fact-tank/2020/07/23 /are-you-in-the-american-middle-class/

Benton, M. L., Abraham, A., LaBella, A. L., Abbot, P., Rokas, A., & Capra, J. A. (2021). The influence of evolutionary history on human health and disease. *Nature Reviews Genetics, 22*(5), 269–283. https://doi.org /10.1038/s41576-020-00305-9

Benza, S., & Liamputtong, P. (2014). Pregnancy, childbirth and motherhood: A meta-synthesis of the lived experiences of immigrant women. *Midwifery, 30*(6), 575–584. https://doi.org/10.1016/j.midw.2014.03.005

Bergelson, E., Casillas, M., Soderstrom, M., Seidl, A., Warlaumont, A. S., & Amatuni, A. (2019). What do North American babies hear? A large-scale cross-corpus analysis. *Developmental Science, 22*(1), e12724. https:// doi.org/10.1111/desc.12724

Berger, J. T., & Miller, D. R. (2021). Health disparities, systemic racism, and failures of cultural competence. *The American Journal of Bioethics, 21*(9), 4–10. https:// doi.org/10.1080/15265161.2021.1915411

Berger, S. E., Theuring, C., & Adolph, K. E. (2007). How and when infants learn to climb stairs. *Infant Behavior and Development, 30*(1), 36–49. https://doi .org/10.1016/j.infbeh.2006.11.002

Bergman, P. (2021). Parent-child information frictions and human capital investment: Evidence from a field experiment. *Journal of Political Economy, 129*(1), 286–322.

Bergnehr, D., & Cekaite, A. (2018). Adult-initiated touch and its functions at a Swedish preschool: Controlling, affectionate, assisting and educative haptic conduct. *International Journal of Early Years Education, 26*(3), 312–331. https://doi.org/10.1080/09669760.2017.1414690

Bergström, M., Fransson, E., Fabian, H., Hjern, A., Sarkadi, A., & Salari, R. (2018). Preschool children living in joint physical custody arrangements show less psychological symptoms than those living mostly or only with one parent. *Acta Paediatrica, 107*(2), 294–300.

Berkel, C., Fu, E., Carroll, A. J., Wilson, C., Tovar-Huffman, A., Mauricio, A., Rudo-Stern, J., Grimm, K. J., Dishion, T. J., & Smith, J. D. (2021). Effects of the Family Check-Up 4 Health on Parenting and Child Behavioral Health: A Randomized Clinical Trial in Primary Care. *Prevention Science, 22*(4), 464–474.

Berkowitz, D., Tinkler, J., Peck, A., & Coto, L. (2021). Tinder: A game with gendered rules and consequences. *Social Currents, 8*(5), 491–509. https:// doi.org/10.1177/23294965211019486

Berkowitz, T., Schaeffer, M. W., Maloney, E. A., Peterson, L., Gregor, C., Levine, S. C., & Beilock, S. L. (2015). Math at home adds up to achievement in school. *Science, 350*(6257), 196–198.

Berli, J. U., & Plemons, E. (2020). The importance of facial gender confirmation surgery. In L. S. Schechter (Ed.), *Gender confirmation surgery* (pp. 91–97). Springer.

Berman, G., Hart, J., O'Mathúna, D., Mattellone, E., Potts, A., O'Kane, C., Shusterman, J., & Tanner, T. (2016, June 30). *What we know about ethical research involving children in humanitarian settings: An overview of principles, the literature and case studies* (Innocenti Working Papers No. 2016/18). UNICEF Innocenti Research Centre. https://doi.org/10.18356/ce5b9789-en

Berry, J. W., & Vedder, P. (2016). Adaptation of immigrant children, adolescents, and their families. In U. P. Gielen & J. L. Roopnarine (Eds.), *Childhood and adolescence: Cross-cultural perspectives and applications* (pp. 321–346). Praeger/ABC-CLIO.

Berry, K. M., Erickson, D. J., Berger, A. T., Wahlstrom, K., Iber, C., Full, K. M., Redline, S., & Widome, R. (2021). Association of delaying school start time with sleep–wake behaviors among adolescents. *Journal of Adolescent Health.* https://doi.org/10.1016/j .jadohealth.2021.04.030

Bertels, J., Bourguignon, M., de Heering, A., Chetail, F., De Tiège, X., Cleeremans, A., & Destrebecqz, A. (2020). Snakes elicit specific neural responses in the human infant brain. *Scientific Reports, 10*(1), 7443. https://doi.org/10.1038/s41598-020-63619-y

Berwick, R. C., & Chomsky, N. (2017). Why only us: Recent questions and answers. *Journal of Neurolinguistics, 43,* 166–177. https://doi.org/10.1016/j.jneuroling.2016.12.002

Besse, M., Lampe, N. M., & Mann, E. S. (2020). Experiences with achieving pregnancy and giving birth among transgender men: A narrative literature review. *The Yale Journal of Biology and Medicine, 93*(4), 517–528.

Best, N. C., Nichols, A. O., Waller, A. E., Zomorodi, M., Pierre-Louis, B., Oppewal, S., & Travers, D. (2021). Impact of school nurse ratios and health services on selected student health and education outcomes: North Carolina, 2011–2016. *Journal of School Health, 91*(6), 473–481. https://doi.org/10.1111/josh.13025

Betancourt, L. M., Avants, B., Farah, M. J., Brodsky, N. L., Wu, J., Ashtari, M., & Hurt, H. (2016). Effect of socioeconomic status (SES) disparity on neural development in female African-American infants at age 1 month. *Developmental Science, 19*(6), 947–956. https://doi.org/10.1111/desc.12344

Beuermann, D. W., & Jackson, C. K. (2022). The short- and long-run effects of attending the schools that parents prefer. *Journal of Human Resources, 57*(3), 725–746.

Beyens, I., & Valkenburg, P. M. (2022). Children's Media Use and its Relation to Attention, Hyperactivity, and Impulsivity. In *The Routledge International Handbook of Children, Adolescents, and Media* (pp. 202–210). Routledge.

Beyers, W., & Luyckx, K. (2016). Ruminative exploration and reconsideration of commitment as risk factors for suboptimal identity development in adolescence and emerging adulthood. *Journal of Adolescence, 47,* 169–178. https://doi.org/10.1016/j.adolescence.2015.10.018

Bhopal, S. S., Bagaria, J., Olabi, B., & Bhopal, R. (2021). Children and young people remain at low risk of COVID-19 mortality. *The Lancet Child & Adolescent Health, 5*(5), e12–e13. https://doi.org/10.1016/S2352-4642(21)00066-3

Bhutta, Z. A., Akseer, N., Keats, E. C., Vaivada, T., Baker, S., Horton, S. E., Katz, J., Menon, P., Piwoz, E., Shekar, M., Victora, C., & Black, R. (2020). How countries can reduce child stunting at scale: Lessons from exemplar countries. *The American Journal of Clinical Nutrition, 112*(Supplement_2), 894S–904S. https://doi.org/10.1093/ajcn/nqaa153

Bialystok, E. (2018). Bilingual education for young children: Review of the effects and consequences. *International Journal of Bilingual Education and Bilingualism, 21*(6), 666–679. https://doi.org/10.1080/13670050.2016.1203859

Bialystok, E. (2020). Bilingual effects on cognition in children. In *Oxford research encyclopedia of education.* https://doi.org/10.1093/acrefore/9780190264093.013.962

Bialystok, E., Hawrylewicz, K., Grundy, J. G., & Chung-Fat-Yim, A. (2022). The swerve: How childhood bilingualism changed from liability to benefit. *Developmental Psychology, 58*(8), 1429–1440. https://doi.org/10.1037/dev0001376

Bian, L., Leslie, S.-J., & Cimpian, A. (2017). Gender stereotypes about intellectual ability emerge early and influence children's interests. *Science, 355*(6323), 389–391.

Biddle, S. J. H., Ciaccioni, S., Thomas, G., & Vergeer, I. (2019). Physical activity and mental health in children and adolescents: An updated review of reviews and an analysis of causality. *Psychology of Sport and Exercise, 42,* 146–155. https://doi.org/10.1016/j.psychsport.2018.08.011

Biddle, S. J., Ciaccioni, S., Thomas, G., & Vergeer, I. (2019). Physical activity and mental health in children and adolescents: An updated review of reviews and an analysis of causality. *Psychology of Sport and Exercise, 42,* 146–155.

Bidgood, A., Pine, J. M., Rowland, C. F., & Ambridge, B. (2020). Syntactic representations are both abstract and semantically constrained: Evidence from children's and adults' comprehension and production/priming of the English passive. *Cognitive Science, 44*(9), e12892. https://doi.org/10.1111/cogs.12892

Biglan, A., Elfner, K., Garbacz, S. A., Komro, K., Prinz, R. J., Weist, M. D., Wilson, D. K., & Zarling, A. (2020). A strategic plan for strengthening America's families: A brief from the coalition of behavioral science organizations. *Clinical Child and Family Psychology Review, 23*(2), 153–175. https://doi.org/10.1007/s10567-020-00318-0

Billett, S. (2014). The standing of vocational education: Sources of its societal esteem and implications for its enactment. *Journal of Vocational Education & Training, 66*(1), 1–21.

Binning, K. R., Kaufmann, N., McGreevy, E. M., Fotuhi, O., Chen, S., Marshman, E., Kalender, Z. Y., Limeri, L., Betancur, L., & Singh, C. (2020). Changing social contexts to foster equity in college science courses: An ecological-belonging intervention. *Psychological Science, 31*(9), 1059–1070.

Birkeland, M. S., Melkevik, O., Holsen, I., & Wold, B. (2012). Trajectories of global self-esteem development during adolescence. *Journal of adolescence, 35*(1), 43–54.

Biro, F. M., Pajak, A., Wolff, M. S., Pinney, S. M., Windham, G. C., Galvez, M. P., Greenspan, L. C., Kushi, L. H., & Teitelbaum, S. L. (2018). Age of menarche in a longitudinal US cohort. *Journal of Pediatric and Adolescent Gynecology, 31*(4), 339–345. https://doi.org/10.1016/j.jpag.2018.05.002

Biros, M. (2018). Capacity, vulnerability, and informed consent for research. *The Journal of Law, Medicine & Ethics, 46*(1), 72–78. https://doi.org/10.1177/1073110518766021

Bishop, M. D., Fish, J. N., Hammack, P. L., & Russell, S. T. (2020). Sexual identity development milestones in three generations of sexual minority people: A national probability sample. *Developmental Psychology, 56*(11), 2177–2193. https://doi.org/10.1037/dev0001105

Bitsko, R. H., Claussen, A. H., Lichstein, J., Black, L. I., Jones, S. E., Danielson, M. L., Hoenig, J. M., Davis Jack, S. P., Brody, D. J., Gyawali, S., Maenner, M. J., Warner, M., Holland, K. M., Perou, R., Crosby, A. E., Blumberg, S. J., Avenevoli, S., Kaminski, J. W., Ghandour, R. M., & Meyer, L. N. (2022). Mental health surveillance among children — United States, 2013–2019. *MMWR Supplements, 71*(2), 1–42. https://doi.org/10.15585/mmwr.su7102a1

Bjorklund, D. F. (2020). *Child development in evolutionary perspective.* Cambridge University Press.

Bjorklund, D. F., Blasi, C. H., & Ellis, B. J. (2015). Evolutionary developmental psychology. In D. M. Buss (Ed.), *The handbook of evolutionary psychology* (pp. 1–21). American Cancer Society. https://doi.org/10.1002/9781119125563.evpsych238

Black, E. (2012). *War against the weak: Eugenics and America's campaign to create a master race.* Dialog Press.

Black, M. M., Trude, A. C. B., & Lutter, C. K. (2020). All children thrive: Integration of nutrition and early childhood development. *Annual Review of Nutrition, 40*(1), 375–406. https://doi.org/10.1146/annurev-nutr-120219-023757

Black, R., Mushtaq, F., Baddeley, A., & Kapur, N. (2020). Does learning the Qur'an improve memory capacity? Practical and theoretical implications. *Memory, 28*(8), 1014–1023.

Blackawton, P. S., Airzee, S., Allen, A., Baker, S., Berrow, A., Blair, C., Churchill, M., Coles, J., Cumming, R. F.-J., Fraquelli, L., Hackford, C., Hinton Mellor, A., Hutchcroft, M., Ireland, B., Jewsbury, D., Littlejohns, A., Littlejohns, G. M., Lotto, M., McKeown, J., . . . Lotto, R. B. (2011). Blackawton bees. *Biology Letters, 7*(2), 168–172. https://doi.org/10.1098/rsbl.2010.1056

Blackhorse, A. (2015, July 2). "Native American" 1 or "American Indian" 1? 5 more Native voices respond. *Indian Country Today.* https://indiancountrytoday.com/archive/blackhorse-native-american-or-american-indian-5-more-native-voices-respond?redir=1

Blackwell, C. K., Elliott, A. J., Ganiban, J., Herbstman, J., Hunt, K., Forrest, C. B., Camargo, C. A., & on behalf of program collaborators for Environmental influences on Child Health Outcomes. (2019). General health and life satisfaction in children with chronic illness. *Pediatrics, 143*(6), e20182988. https://doi.org/10.1542/peds.2018-2988

Blakemore, S.-J. (2018). Avoiding social risk in adolescence. *Current Directions in Psychological Science, 27*(2), 116–122. https://doi.org/10.1177/0963721417738144

Blakemore, S.-J., & Mills, K. L. (2014). Is adolescence a sensitive period for sociocultural processing? *Annual Review of Psychology, 65*(1), 187–207. https://doi.org/10.1146/annurev-psych-010213-115202

Blanco, G., Flores, C. A., & Flores-Lagunes, A. (2013). Bounds on average and quantile treatment effects of Job Corps training on wages. *Journal of Human Resources, 48*(3), 659–701.

Blanco, N. J., & Sloutsky, V. M. (2019). Adaptive flexibility in category learning? Young children exhibit smaller costs of selective attention than adults. *Developmental Psychology, 55*(10), 2060.

Bland, A. M., & DeRobertis, E. M. (2020). Maslow's unacknowledged contributions to developmental psychology. *Journal of Humanistic Psychology, 60*(6), 934–958. https://doi.org/10.1177/0022167817739732

Blankenship, T. L., Keith, K., Calkins, S. D., & Bell, M. A. (2018). Behavioral performance and neural areas associated with memory processes contribute to math and reading achievement in 6-year-old children. *Cognitive Development, 45,* 141–151.

Blankenship, T. L., Slough, M. A., Calkins, S. D., Deater-Deckard, K., Kim-Spoon, J., & Bell, M. A. (2019). Attention and executive functioning in infancy: Links to childhood executive function and reading achievement. *Developmental Science, 22*(6), e12824. https://doi.org/10.1111/desc.12824

Blasberg, A., Bromer, J., Nugent, C., Porter, T., Shivers, E. M., Tonyan, H., Tout, K., & Weber, B. (2019). A conceptual model for quality in home-based child care. *OPRE Report, 37.*

Blatný, M., Millová, K., Jelínek, M., & Osecká, T. (2015). Personality predictors of successful development: Toddler temperament and adolescent personality traits predict well-being and career stability in middle adulthood. *PLOS ONE, 10*(4), e0126032.

Blau, F. D., Kahn, L. M., Brummund, P., Cook, J., & Larson-Koester, M. (2020). Is there still son preference in the United States? *Journal of Population Economics, 33*(3), 709–750. https://doi.org/10.1007/s00148-019-00760-7

Blazar, D., & Pollard, C. (2022). *Challenges and tradeoffs of "good" teaching: The pursuit of multiple educational outcomes* (Ed Working Paper No. 22–591). Annenberg Institute, Brown University.

Blell, M., & Hunter, M. A. (2019). Direct-to-consumer genetic testing's red herring: "Genetic ancestry" and personalized medicine. *Frontiers in Medicine, 6*. https://doi .org/10.3389/fmed.2019.00048

Blencowe, H., Kancherla, V., Moorthie, S., Darlison, M. W., & Modell, B. (2018). Estimates of global and regional prevalence of neural tube defects for 2015: A systematic analysis. *Annals of the New York Academy of Sciences, 1414*(1), 31–46.

Blitvich, P. G.-C. (2018). Globalization, transnational identities, and conflict talk: The superdiversity and complexity of the Latino identity. *Journal of Pragmatics, 134*, 120–133. https://doi.org/10.1016/j .pragma.2018.02.001

Blum, R. W., Li, M., Choiriyyah, I., Barnette, Q., Michielson, K., & Mmari, K. (2021). Body satisfaction in early adolescence: A multisite comparison. *Journal of Adolescent Health, 69*(1, Supplement), S39–S46. https:// doi.org/10.1016/j.jadohealth.2021.03.009

Blumberg, F. C., Deater-Deckard, K., Calvert, S. L., Flynn, R. M., Green, C. S., Arnold, D., & Brooks, P. J. (2019). Digital games as a context for children's cognitive development: Research recommendations and policy considerations. *Social Policy Report, 32*(1), 1–33.

Boddice, R. (2019). *A history of feelings*. Reaktion Books.

Boers, E., Afzali, M. H., Newton, N., & Conrod, P. (2019). Association of screen time and depression in adolescence. *JAMA Pediatrics, 173*(9), 853–859. https:// doi.org/10.1001/jamapediatrics.2019.1759

Bogin, B. (1997). Evolutionary hypotheses for human childhood. *American Journal of Physical Anthropology, 104*(S25).

Bohn, M., Kachel, G., & Tomasello, M. (2019). Young children spontaneously recreate core properties of language in a new modality. *Proceedings of the National Academy of Sciences, 116*(51), 26072–26077. https:// doi.org/10.1073/pnas.1904871116

Bohren, M. A., Vogel, J. P., Hunter, E. C., Lutsiv, O., Makh, S. K., Souza, J. P., Aguiar, C., Coneglian, F. S., Diniz, A. L. A., Tunçalp, Ö., Javadi, D., Oladapo, O. T., Khosla, R., Hindin, M. J., & Gülmezoglu, A. M. (2015). The mistreatment of women during childbirth in health facilities globally: A mixed-methods systematic review. *PLOS Medicine, 12*(6), e1001847. https://doi.org/10.1371/journal.pmed.1001847

Boisjoli, R., Vitaro, F., Lacourse, É., Barker, E. D., & Tremblay, R. E. (2007). Impact and clinical significance of a preventive intervention for disruptive boys: 15-year follow-up. *The British Journal of Psychiatry, 191*(5), 415–419.

Boislard, M.-A., van de Bongardt, D., & Blais, M. (2016). Sexuality (and lack thereof) in adolescence and early adulthood: A review of the literature. *Behavioral Sciences, 6*(1). https://doi.org/10.3390/bs6010008

Bombard, J. M., Kortsmit, K., Warner, L., Shapiro-Mendoza, C. K., Cox, S., Kroelinger, C. D., Parks, S. E., Dee, D. L., D'Angelo, D. V., Smith, R. A., Burley, K., Morrow, B., Olson, C. K., Shulman, H. B., Harrison, L., Cottengim, C., & Barfield, W. D. (2018). Vital signs: Trends and disparities in infant safe sleep practices — United States, 2009–2015. *Morbidity and Mortality Weekly Report, 67*(1), 39–46. https://doi .org/10.15585/mmwr.mm6701e1

Bomberg, E. M., Addo, O. Y., Sarafoglou, K., & Miller, B. S. (2021). Adjusting for Pubertal Status Reduces Overweight and Obesity Prevalence in the United States. *The Journal of Pediatrics, 231*, 200–206. e1. https://doi.org/10.1016/j.jpeds.2020.12.038

Bonnar, D., Gradisar, M., Moseley, L., Coughlin, A.-M., Cain, N., & Short, M. A. (2015). Evaluation of novel school-based interventions for adolescent sleep problems: Does parental involvement and bright light improve outcomes? *Sleep Health: Journal of the National Sleep Foundation, 1*(1), 66–74. https://doi .org/10.1016/j.sleh.2014.11.002

Bontemps, B., Piponnier, E., Chalchat, E., Blazevich, A. J., Julian, V., Bocock, O., Duclos, M., Martin, V., & Ratel, S. (2019). Children exhibit a more comparable neuromuscular fatigue profile to endurance athletes than untrained adults. *Frontiers in Physiology, 10*, 119. https://doi.org/10.3389/fphys.2019.00119

Bonvillian, W. B., & Sarma, S. E. (2021). *Workforce education: A new roadmap*. MIT Press.

Booker, J. A., Capriola-Hall, N. N., Greene, R. W., & Ollendick, T. H. (2020). The parent-child relationship and post-treatment child outcomes across two treatments for oppositional defiant disorder. *Journal of Clinical Child & Adolescent Psychology, 49*(3), 405–419. https://doi.org/10.1080/15374416.2018.1555761

Booker, M. (2016). *BJS data shows graying of prisons*. Prison Policy Initiative.

Booth, R. B., Tombaugh, E., Kiesa, A., Lundberg, K., & Cohen, A. (2020). *Young people turn to online political engagement during COVID-19* (CIRCLE / Tisch College 2020 Pre-Election Youth Poll). Tufts University.

Booth, S. A., Carskadon, M. A., Young, R., & Short, M. A. (2021). Sleep duration and mood in adolescents: An experimental study. *Sleep, 44*(5), zsaa253. https:// doi.org/10.1093/sleep/zsaa253

Boquien, C.-Y. (2018). Human milk: An ideal food for nutrition of preterm newborn. *Frontiers in Pediatrics, 6*, 295. https://doi.org/10.3389/fped.2018.00295

Borchers, L. R., Dennis, E. L., King, L. S., Humphreys, K. L., & Gotlib, I. H. (2021). Prenatal and postnatal depressive symptoms, infant white matter, and toddler behavioral problems. *Journal of Affective Disorders, 282*, 465–471. https://doi.org/10.1016/j .jad.2020.12.075

Borchert, S., Lamm, B., Graf, F., & Knopf, M. (2013). Deferred imitation in 18-month-olds from two cultural contexts: The case of Cameroonian Nso farmer and German-middle class infants. *Infant Behavior and Development, 36*(4), 717–727.

Bornstein, M. H. (1989). *Maternal responsiveness: Characteristics and consequences*. Jossey-Bass.

Bornstein, M. H. (2015). Culture, parenting, and zero-to-threes. *Zero to Three, 35*(4), 2–9.

Bornstein, M. H. (2019). Parenting infants. In M. H. Bornstein (Ed.), *Handbook of parenting* (pp. 3–55). Routledge.

Bornstein, M. H., Putnick, D. L., & Lansford, J. E. (2011). Parenting attributions and attitudes in cross-cultural perspective. *Parenting, Science and Practice, 11*(2–3), 214–237. https://doi.org/10.1080/15295192 .2011.585568

Bornstein, M. H., Putnick, D. L., & Suwalsky, J. T. D. (2016). Infant–Mother and Infant–Caregiver Emotional Relationships: Process Analyses of Interactions in Three Contemporary Childcare Arrangements. *Infancy: The Official Journal of the International Society on Infant Studies, 21*(1), 8–36.

Bornstein, M. H., Putnick, D. L., & Suwalsky, J. T. D. (2018). Parenting cognitions → parenting practices → child adjustment? The standard model. *Development and Psychopathology, 30*(2), 399–416. https://doi .org/10.1017/S0954579417000931

Borowski, S. K., & Zeman, J. (2018). Emotional competencies relate to co-rumination: Implications for emotion socialization within adolescent friendships. *Social Development, 27*(4), 808–825. https://doi .org/10.1111/sode.12293

Borrero, S., Nikolajski, C., Steinberg, J. R., Freedman, L., Akers, A. Y., Ibrahim, S., & Schwarz, E. B. (2015). "It just happens": A qualitative study exploring low-income women's perspectives on pregnancy intention and planning. *Contraception, 91*(2), 150–156.

Borsani, E., Della Vedova, A. M., Rezzani, R., Rodella, L. F., & Cristini, C. (2019). Correlation between human nervous system development and acquisition of fetal skills: An overview. *Brain and Development, 41*(3), 225–233. https://doi.org/10.1016/j .braindev.2018.10.009

Bos, D. J., Dreyfuss, M., Tottenham, N., Hare, T. A., Galván, A., Casey, B. J., & Jones, R. M. (2020). Distinct and similar patterns of emotional development in adolescents and young adults. *Developmental Psychobiology, 62*(5), 591–599. https://doi.org/10.1002 /dev.21942

Bošković, A., & Rando, O. J. (2018). Transgenerational epigenetic inheritance. *Annual Review of Genetics, 52*(1), 21–41. https://doi.org/10.1146/ annurev-genet-120417-031404

Bosmans, G., & Kerns, K. A. (2015). Attachment in middle childhood: Progress and prospects. *New Directions for Child and Adolescent Development, 2015*(148), 1–14.

Bőthe, B., Vaillancourt-Morel, M. P., Bergeron, S., & Demetrovics, Z. (2019). Problematic and non-problematic pornography use among LGBTQ adolescents: A systematic literature review. *Current Addiction Reports, 6*(4), 478–494.

Bottema-Beutel, K., Kapp, S. K., Lester, J. N., Sasson, N. J., & Hand, B. N. (2020). Avoiding ableist language: Suggestions for autism researchers. *Autism in Adulthood, 3*(1), 18–29. https://doi.org/10.1089/ aut.2020.0014

Boundy, E. O., Dastjerdi, R., Spiegelman, D., Fawzi, W. W., Missmer, S. A., Lieberman, E., Kajeepeta, S., Wall, S., & Chan, G. J. (2016). Kangaroo mother care and neonatal outcomes: A meta-analysis. *Pediatrics, 137*(1). https://doi.org/10.1542/peds.2015-2238

Bourdillon, M. (2019). "Child labour" and children's lives. In A. T.-D. Imoh, M. Bourdillon, & S. Meichsner (Eds.), *Global childhoods beyond the North-South divide* (pp. 35–55). Palgrave Macmillan.

Bouza, J., Camacho-Thompson, D. E., Carlo, G., Franco, X., Garcia Coll, C., Halgunseth, L. C., Marks, A., Livas Stein, G., Suarez-Orozco, C., & White, R. M. B. (2018). *The science is clear: Separating families has long-term damaging psychological and health consequences for children, families, and communities*. Society for Research in Child Development (SRCD). https://www .srcd.org/briefs-fact-sheets/the-science-is-clear

Bové, H., Bongaerts, E., Slenders, E., Bijnens, E. M., Saenen, N. D., Gyselaers, W., Van Eyken, P., Plusquin, M., Roeffaers, M. B. J., Ameloot, M., & Nawrot, T. S. (2019). Ambient black carbon particles reach the fetal side of human placenta. *Nature Communications, 10*(1), 3866. https://doi.org/10.1038/s41467-019-11654-3

Bowen, E., Ball, A., Jones, A. S., & Miller, B. (2021). Toward many emerging adulthoods: A theory-based examination of the features of emerging adulthood for cross-systems youth. *Emerging Adulthood, 9*(3), 189–201. https://doi.org/10.1177/2167696821989123

Bowlby, J. (1951). *Maternal care and mental health* (Vol. 2). World Health Organization.

Bowlby, J. (1969). *Attachment*. Basic Books.

Bowlby, J. (1980). *Attachment and loss*. Basic Books.

Bowlby, J. (2008). *Attachment*. Basic Books.

Bowlby, J. (2012). *The making and breaking of affectional bonds*. Routledge.

Bowlby, J., Robertson, J., & Rosenbluth, D. (1952). A two-year-old goes to hospital. *The Psychoanalytic Study of the Child, 7*(1), 82–94.

Boxall, A. (2017, February 16). *Russia loves its dating apps, tops the charts for download numbers*. Business of Apps. https://www.businessofapps.com/news/russia-loves-dating-apps-tops-charts-download-numbers/

Boxberger, K., & Reimers, A. K. (2019). Parental correlates of outdoor play in boys and girls aged 0 to 12—A systematic review. *International Journal of Environmental Research and Public Health, 16*(2), 190. https://doi.org/10.3390/ijerph16020190

Boyce, W. T., Levitt, P., Martinez, F. D., McEwen, B. S., & Shonkoff, J. P. (2021). Genes, environments, and time: The biology of adversity and resilience. *Pediatrics, 147*(2). https://doi.org/10.1542/peds.2020-1651

Boyd-Ball, A. J., Véronneau, M.-H., Dishion, T. J., & Kavanagh, K. (2014). Monitoring and peer influences as predictors of increases in alcohol use among American Indian youth. *Prevention Science, 15*(4), 526–535. https://doi.org/10.1007/s11121-013-0399-1

Boyle, M. H., Olsho, L. E., Mendelson, M. R., Stidsen, C. M., Logan, C. W., Witt, M. B., Gola, A. A. H., & Copeland, K. A. (2022). Physical activity opportunities in US early child care programs. *Pediatrics, 149*(6).

Boyle, P. A., Wang, T., Yu, L., Barnes, L. L., Wilson, R. S., & Bennett, D. A. (2021). Purpose in life may delay adverse health outcomes in old age. *The American Journal of Geriatric Psychiatry*. https://doi.org/10.1016/j.jagp.2021.05.007

Boyon, N., & Silverstein, K. (2021). *LGBT+ Pride 2021 Global Survey points to a generation gap around gender identity and sexual attraction*. Ipsos. https://www.ipsos.com/en-us/news-polls/ipsos-lgbt-pride-2021-global-survey

Bozicevic, L., De Pascalis, L., Montirosso, R., Ferrari, P. F., Giusti, L., Cooper, P. J., & Murray, L. (2021). Sculpting culture: Early maternal responsiveness and child emotion regulation—A UK-Italy comparison. *Journal of Cross-Cultural Psychology, 52*(1), 22–42. https://doi.org/10.1177/0022022120971353

Braams, B. R., van Duijvenvoorde, A. C., Peper, J. S., & Crone, E. A. (2015). Longitudinal changes in adolescent risk-taking: A comprehensive study of neural responses to rewards, pubertal development, and risk-taking behavior. *Journal of Neuroscience, 35*(18), 7226–7238.

Braaten, E. B., & Norman, D. (2006). Intelligence (IQ) testing. *Pediatrics in Review, 27*(11), 403.

Brace, J. J., Morton, J. B., & Munakata, Y. (2006). When actions speak louder than words: Improving children's flexibility in a card-sorting task. *Psychological Science, 17*(8), 665–669.

Brace, S., Diekmann, Y., Booth, T. J., Faltyskova, Z., Rohland, N., Mallick, S., Ferry, M., Michel, M., Oppenheimer, J., Broomandkhoshbacht, N., Stewardson, K., Walsh, S., Kayser, M., Schulting, R., Craig, O. E., Sheridan, A., Pearson, M. P., Stringer, C., Reich, D., . . . Barnes, I. (2018). Population replacement in Early Neolithic Britain. *BioRxiv*, 267443. https://doi.org/10.1101/267443

Brame, R., Bushway, S. D., Paternoster, R., & Turner, M. G. (2014). Demographic patterns of cumulative arrest prevalence by ages 18 and 23. *Crime & Delinquency, 60*(3), 471–486.

Brand, J. E., Pfeffer, F. T., & Goldrick-Rab, S. (2014). The community college effect revisited: The importance of attending to heterogeneity and complex counterfactuals. *Sociological Science, 1*, 448–465.

Brand, R. J., Escobar, K., & Patrick, A. M. (2020). Coincidence or cascade? The temporal relation between locomotor behaviors and the emergence of stranger anxiety. *Infant Behavior and Development, 58*. https://doi.org/10.1016/j.infbeh.2020.101423

Brandes, C. M., Kushner, S. C., Herzhoff, K., & Tackett, J. L. (2020). Facet-level personality development in the transition to adolescence: Maturity, disruption, and gender differences. *Journal of Personality and Social Psychology, 121*(5), 1095–1111. https://doi.org/10.1037/pspp0000367

Brandes-Aitken, A., Braren, S., Swingler, M., Voegtline, K., & Blair, C. (2019). Sustained attention in infancy: A foundation for the development of multiple aspects of self-regulation for children in poverty. *Journal of Experimental Child Psychology, 184*, 192–209. https://doi.org/10.1016/j.jecp.2019.04.006

Brandt, N. D., Mike, A., & Jackson, J. J. (2019). Do school-related experiences impact personality? Selection and socialization effects of impulse control. *Developmental Psychology, 55*(12), 2561–2574. https://doi.org/10.1037/dev0000817

Bratsberg, B., & Rogeberg, O. (2018). Flynn effect and its reversal are both environmentally caused. *Proceedings of the National Academy of Sciences, 115*(26), 6674–6678.

Bratsch-Hines, M. E., Zgourou, E., Vernon-Feagans, L., Carr, R., & Willoughby, M. (2020). Infant and toddler child-care quality and stability in relation to proximal and distal academic and social outcomes. *Child Development, 91*(6), 1854–1864. https://doi.org/10.1111/cdev.13389

Bratt, C., Abrams, D., & Swift, H. J. (2020). Supporting the old but neglecting the young? The two faces of ageism. *Developmental Psychology, 56*(5), 1029.

Braun, C., & O'Leary, S. T. (2020). Recent advances in addressing vaccine hesitancy. *Current Opinion in Pediatrics, 32*(4), 601–609. https://doi.org/10.1097/MOP.0000000000000929

Braza, P., Carreras, R., Muñoz, J. M., Braza, F., Azurmendi, A., Pascual-Sagastizábal, E., Cardas, J., & Sánchez-Martín, J. R. (2015). Negative maternal and paternal parenting styles as predictors of children's behavioral problems: Moderating effects of the child's sex. *Journal of Child and Family Studies, 24*(4), 847–856.

Bredekamp, S. (1992). What is "developmentally appropriate" and why is it important? *Journal of Physical Education, Recreation & Dance, 63*(6), 31–32. https://doi.org/10.1080/07303084.1992.10606612

Breiding, M. J. (2014). Prevalence and characteristics of sexual violence, stalking, and intimate partner violence victimization—National Intimate Partner and Sexual Violence Survey, United States, 2011. *Morbidity and Mortality Weekly Report. Surveillance Summaries, 63*(8), 1–18.

Bremer, G. (2018). Giving girls a chance: Ending child marriage and promoting education in Georgia and Niger. *Global Majority E-Journal, 9*(2), 59–70.

Bretherton, I. (1992). The origins of attachment theory: John Bowlby and Mary Ainsworth. *Developmental Psychology, 28*(5), 759–775.

Bretherton, I. (2003). Mary Ainsworth: Insightful observer and courageous theoretician. In G. A. Kimble & M. Wertheimer (Eds.), *Portraits of pioneers in psychology* (Vol. 5, pp. 317–331). Erlbaum.

Bretherton, I., & Munholland, K. A. (2016). The internal working model construct in light of contemporary neuroimaging research. In J. Cassidy & P. R. Shaver (Eds.), *Handbook of attachment: Theory, research, and clinical application* (pp. 63–88). Guilford.

Brett, B. L., Savitz, J., Nitta, M., España, L., Teague, T. K., Nelson, L. D., McCrea, M. A., & Meier, T. B. (2020). Systemic inflammation moderates the association of prior concussion with hippocampal volume and episodic memory in high school and collegiate athletes. *Brain, Behavior, and Immunity, 89*, 380–388. https://doi.org/10.1016/j.bbi.2020.07.024

Bribiescas, R. G. (2020). Aging, life history, and human evolution. *Annual Review of Anthropology, 49*(1), 101–121. https://doi.org/10.1146/annurev-anthro-010220-074148

BrightFutures / American Academy of Pediatrics. (2021). *Recommendations for preventative pediatric health care*. American Academy of Pediatrics.

Brito, N. H., Werchan, D., Brandes-Aitken, A., Yoshikawa, H., Greaves, A., & Zhang, M. (2022, April 4). Paid maternal leave is associated with infant brain function at 3 months of age. *Child Development*. https://doi.org/10.1111/cdev.13765

Brix, N., Ernst, A., Lauridsen, L. L. B., Parner, E. T., Arah, O. A., Olsen, J., Henriksen, T. B., & Ramlau-Hansen, C. H. (2020). Childhood overweight and obesity and timing of puberty in boys and girls: Cohort and sibling-matched analyses. *International Journal of Epidemiology, 49*(3), 834–844. https://doi.org/10.1093/ije/dyaa056

Brod, G., Bunge, S. A., & Shing, Y. L. (2017). Does one year of schooling improve children's cognitive control and alter associated brain activation? *Psychological Science, 28*(7), 967–978. https://doi.org/10.1177/0956797617699838

Broda, M., Yun, J., Schneider, B., Yeager, D. S., Walton, G. M., & Diemer, M. (2018). Reducing inequality in academic success for incoming college students: A randomized trial of growth mindset and belonging interventions. *Journal of Research on Educational Effectiveness, 11*(3), 317–338. https://doi.org/10.1080/19345747.2018.1429037

Brodin, P. (2022). Immune-microbe interactions early in life: A determinant of health and disease long term. *Science, 376*(6596), 945–950. https://doi.org/10.1126/science.abk2189

Brody, G. H., & Flor, D. L. (1998). Maternal resources, parenting practices, and child competence in rural, single-parent African American families. *Child Development, 69*(3), 803–816.

Brody, G. H., Murry, V. M., Gerrard, M., Gibbons, F. X., Molgaard, V., McNair, L., Brown, A. C., Wills, T. A., Spoth, R. L., Luo, Z., Chen, Y.-F., & Neubaum-Carlan, E. (2004). The strong African American families program: Translating research into prevention programming. *Child Development, 75*(3), 900–917.

Brody, G. H., Yu, T., Chen, E., Beach, S. R. H., & Miller, G. E. (2016). Family-centered prevention ameliorates the longitudinal association between risky family processes and epigenetic aging. *Journal of Child Psychology and Psychiatry, and Allied Disciplines, 57*(5), 566–574. https://doi.org/10.1111/jcpp.12495

Brody, G. H., Yu, T., Chen, E., Miller, G. E., Barton, A. W., & Kogan, S. M. (2021). Family-centered prevention effects on the association between racial discrimination and mental health in black adolescents: Secondary analysis of 2 randomized clinical trials. *JAMA Network Open, 4*(3), e211964. https://doi.org/10.1001/jamanetworkopen.2021.1964

Brody, G. H., Yu, T., Miller, G. E., Ehrlich, K. B., & Chen, E. (2019). Preventive parenting intervention during childhood and young black adults' unhealthful behaviors: A randomized controlled trial. *Journal of Child Psychology and Psychiatry, 60*(1), 63–71.

Brodzki, I., Huryk, K. M., Casasnovas, A. F., Sanders, L., & Loeb, K. L. (2018). Eating disorders. In S. G. Forman & J. D. Shahidullah (Eds.), *Handbook of pediatric behavioral healthcare: An interdisciplinary collaborative approach* (pp. 229–241). Springer International Publishing. https://doi.org/10.1007/978-3-030-00791-1_17

Broesch, T., Crittenden, A. N., Beheim, B. A., Blackwell, A. D., Bunce, J. A., Colleran, H., Hagel, K., Kline, M., McElreath, R., Nelson, R. G., Pisor, A. C., Prall, S., Pretelli, I., Purzycki, B., Quinn, E. A., Ross, C., Scelza, B., Starkweather, K., Stieglitz, J., & Mulder, M. B. (2020). Navigating cross-cultural research: Methodological and ethical considerations. *Proceedings of the Royal Society B: Biological Sciences, 287*(1935), 20201245. https://doi.org/10.1098/rspb.2020.1245

Broesch, T., Little, E. E., Carver, L. J., & Legare, C. H. (2022). Still-face redux: Infant responses to a classic and modified still-face paradigm in proximal and distal care cultures. *Infant Behavior and Development, 68,* 101732.

Broesch, T., Rochat, P., Olah, K., Broesch, J., & Henrich, J. (2016). Similarities and differences in maternal responsiveness in three societies: Evidence from Fiji, Kenya, and the United States. *Child Development, 87*(3), 700–711.

Bronfenbrenner, U. (1977). Toward an experimental ecology of human development. *American Psychologist, 32*(7), 513–531. https://doi.org/10.1037/0003-066X.32.7.513

Bronfenbrenner, U. (2005). *Making human beings human: Bioecological perspectives on human development.* Sage.

Bronstein, M. V., Pennycook, G., Bear, A., Rand, D. G., & Cannon, T. D. (2019). Belief in fake news is associated with delusionality, dogmatism, religious fundamentalism, and reduced analytic thinking. *Journal of Applied Research in Memory and Cognition, 8*(1), 108–117. https://doi.org/10.1016/j.jarmac.2018.09.005

Brooker, R. J., Kiel, E. J., MacNamara, A., Nyman, T., John-Henderson, N. A., Van Lieshout, R., & Schmidt, L. A. (2020). Maternal neural reactivity during pregnancy predicts infant temperament. *Infancy: The Official Journal of the International Society on Infant Studies, 25*(1), 46–66. https://doi.org/10.1111/infa.12316

Brooks, M. (2019). The uneven perils of unemployment and underemployment: The role of employment structure in explaining rural-urban poverty differences, 1970–2018 [Unpublished paper].

Brooks-Gunn, J., & Lewis, M. (1975). Mirror-image and self-recognition in infancy. In *Biennial Meeting of the Society for Research in Child Development, Denver, CO* (ERIC Document Reproduction No. ED 114 193).

Broton, K. M., & Goldrick-Rab, S. (2018). Going without: An exploration of food and housing insecurity among undergraduates. *Educational Researcher, 47*(2), 121–133. https://doi.org/10.3102/0013189X17741303

Brown, A. (2020, February 25). *The changing categories the U.S. Census has used to measure race.* Pew Research Center. https://www.pewresearch.org/fact-tank/2020/02/25/the-changing-categories-the-u-s-has-used-to-measure-race/

Brown, C. L., Skinner, A. C., Yin, H. S., Rothman, R. L., Sanders, L. M., Delamater, A. M., Ravanbakht, S.

N., & Perrin, E. M. (2016). Parental perceptions of weight during the first year of life. *Academic Pediatrics, 16*(6), 558–564. https://doi.org/10.1016/j.acap.2016.03.005

Brown, C. S., Alabi, B. O., Huynh, V. W., & Masten, C. L. (2011). Ethnicity and gender in late childhood and early adolescence: Group identity and awareness of bias. *Developmental Psychology, 47*(2), 463.

Brown, C. S., Mistry, R. S., & Yip, T. (2019). Moving from the margins to the mainstream: Equity and justice as key considerations for developmental science. *Child Development Perspectives, 13*(4), 235–240.

Brown, L. M., & Gilligan, C. (1993). Meeting at the crossroads: Women's psychology and girls' development. *Feminism & Psychology, 3*(1), 11–35.

Brown, R. W., & Longoria, T. (2010). Multiple risk factors for lead poisoning in Hispanic sub-populations: A review. *Journal of Immigrant and Minority Health, 12*(5), 715–725.

Brown, S. S. (2014). *Transformation beyond greed: Native self-actualization.* Sidney Stone Brown.

Brownell, C. A., & Drummond, J. (2020). Early child-care and family experiences predict development of prosocial behaviour in first grade. *Early Child Development and Care, 190*(5), 712–737. https://doi.org/10.1080/03004430.2018.1489382

Brownell, C. A., Lemerise, E. A., Pelphrey, K. A., & Roisman, G. I. (2015). Measuring socioemotional development. In M. E. Lamb & R. M. Lerner (Eds.), *Handbook of child psychology and developmental science: Socioemotional processes* (pp. 11–56). John Wiley & Sons. https://doi.org/10.1002/9781118963418.childpsy302

Brown-Zimmerman, M. (2012, November 14). What Marfan means to Maya. *The LDS Women Project.* http://ldswomenproject.com/interview/what-marfan-means-to-maya/

Brubacher, S. P., Peterson, C., La Rooy, D., Dickinson, J. J., & Poole, D. A. (2019). How children talk about events: Implications for eliciting and analyzing eyewitness reports. *Developmental Review, 51,* 70–89.

Bruch, E. E., & Newman, M. E. J. (2018). Aspirational pursuit of mates in online dating markets. *Science Advances, 4*(8), eaap9815.

Brumberg, H. L., Karr, C. J., & Council on Environmental Health. (2021). Ambient air pollution: Health hazards to children. *Pediatrics, 147*(6), e2021051484. https://doi.org/10.1542/peds.2021-051484

Brummelman, E., & Dweck, C. S. (2020). Paradoxical effects of praise: A transactional model. In *Psychological perspectives on praise* (pp. 55–64). Routledge.

Brummelman, E., & Sedikides, C. (2020). Raising children with high self-esteem (but not narcissism). *Child Development Perspectives, 14*(2), 83–89. https://doi.org/10.1111/cdep.12362

Brummelman, E., Crocker, J., & Bushman, B. J. (2016). The praise paradox: When and why praise back-fires in children with low self-esteem. *Child Development Perspectives, 10*(2), 111–115. https://doi.org/10.1111/cdep.12171

Bruneau, E., Szekeres, H., Kteily, N., Tropp, L. R., & Kende, A. (2020). Beyond dislike: Blatant dehumanization predicts teacher discrimination. *Group Processes & Intergroup Relations, 23*(4), 560–577. https://doi.org/10.1177/1368430219845462

Bruner, M. W., McLaren, C. D., Sutcliffe, J. T., Gardner, L. A., Lubans, D. R., Smith, J. J., & Vella, S. A. (2021). The effect of sport-based interventions on positive youth development: A systematic review and meta-analysis. *International Review of Sport and*

Exercise Psychology, 1–28. https://doi.org/10.1080/1750984X.2021.1875496

Bruni, O., & Novelli, L. (2010). Sleep disorders in children. *BMJ Clinical Evidence, 2010,* 2304.

Brussoni, M., Brunelle, S., Pike, I., Sandseter, E. B. H., Herrington, S., Turner, H., Belair, S., Logan, L., Fuselli, P., & Ball, D. J. (2015). Can child injury prevention include healthy risk promotion? *Injury Prevention, 21*(5), 344–347. https://doi.org/10.1136/injuryprev-2014-041241

Bryan, C. J., Yeager, D. S., & Hinojosa, C. P. (2019). A values-alignment intervention protects adolescents from the effects of food marketing. *Nature Human Behaviour, 3*(6), 596–603. https://doi.org/10.1038/s41562-019-0586-6

Bryan, J., Williams, J. M., Kim, J., Morrison, S. S., & Caldwell, C. H. (2018). Perceived teacher discrimination and academic achievement among urban Caribbean Black and African American youth: School bonding and family support as protective factors. Urban Education. https://doi.org/10.1177/0042085918806959

Bryan, S., Afful, J., Carroll, M., Te-Ching, C., Orlando, D., Fink, S., & Fryar, C. (2021). *NHSR 158. National Health and Nutrition Examination Survey 2017–March 2020 Pre-pandemic Data Files.* U.S. National Center for Health Statistics. https://doi.org/10.15620/cdc:106273

Buckley, K. W. (1989). *Mechanical man: John Broadus Watson and the beginnings of behaviorism.* Guilford.

Budd, C. J. (2015). Promoting maths to the general public. In R. C. Kadosh & A. Dowker (Eds.), *Oxford handbook of numerical cognition.* Oxford University Press.

Buehler, C. (2020). Family processes and children's and adolescents' well-being. *Journal of Marriage and Family, 82*(1), 145–174. https://doi.org/10.1111/jomf.12637

Buhs, E. S., Koziol, N. A., Rudasill, K. M., & Crockett, L. J. (2018). Early temperament and middle school engagement: School social relationships as mediating processes. *Journal of Educational Psychology, 110*(3), 338.

Buiatti, M., Giorgio, E. D., Piazza, M., Polloni, C., Menna, G., Taddei, F., Baldo, E., & Vallortigara, G. (2019). Cortical route for facelike pattern processing in human newborns. *Proceedings of the National Academy of Sciences, 116*(10), 4625–4630. https://doi.org/10.1073/pnas.1812419116

Bukowski, W. M., & Raufelder, D. (2018). Peers and the self. In W. M. Bukowski, B. Laursen, & K. H. Rubin (Eds.), *Handbook of peer interactions, relationships, and groups* (pp. 141–156). Guilford.

Bull, M. J. (2020). Down sSyndrome. *New England Journal of Medicine, 382*(24), 2344–2352. https://doi.org/10.1056/NEJMra1706537

Bundy, D. A. P., de Silva, N., Horton, S., Patton, G. C., Schultz, L., & Jamison, D. T. (2017). Child and adolescent health and development: Realizing neglected potential. In D. A. P. Bundy, N. de Silva, S. Horton, D. T. Jamison, & G. C. Patton (Eds.), *Disease control priorities: Vol. 8. Child and adolescent health and development* (3rd ed., pp. 1–24). The World Bank. https://doi.org/10.1596/978-1-4648-0423-6_ch1

Bundy, D. A. P., de Silva, N., Horton, S., Patton, G. C., Schultz, L., Jamison, D. T., Abubakara, A., Ahuja, A., Alderman, H., Allen, N., Appleby, L., Aurino, E., Azzopardi, P., Baird, S., Banham, L., Behrman, J., Benzian, H., Bhalotra, S., Bhutta, Z., . . . Sawyer, S. M. (2018). Investment in child and adolescent health and development: Key messages from disease control priorities, 3rd Edition. *The Lancet, 391*(10121), 687–699. https://doi.org/10.1016/S0140-6736(17)32417-0

Burchinal, M. (2018). Measuring early care and education quality. *Child Development Perspectives, 12*(1), 3–9. https://doi.org/10.1111/cdep.12260

Burchinal, M. R., & Farran, D. C. (2020). What does research tell us about ECE programs? In *Getting it right: Using implementation research to improve outcomes in early care and education* (pp. 13–36). Foundation for Child Development.

Burghardt, G. M. (2010). Defining and recognizing play. In P. Nathan & A. D. Pellegrini (Eds.), *The Oxford handbook of the development of play*. https://doi.org/10.1093/oxfordhb/9780195393002.013.0002

Burke, J. D., & Romano-Verthelyi, A. M. (2018). Oppositional defiant disorder. In M. M. Martel (Ed.), *Developmental pathways to disruptive, impulse-control and conduct disorders* (pp. 21–52). Academic Press. https://doi.org/10.1016/B978-0-12-811323-3.00002-X

Burrage, M. S., Ponitz, C. C., McCready, E. A., Shah, P., Sims, B. C., Jewkes, A. M., & Morrison, F. J. (2008). Age- and schooling-related effects on executive functions in young children: A natural experiment. *Child Neuropsychology, 14*(6), 510–524. https://doi.org/10.1080/09297040701756917

Bursztyn, L., Egorov, G., & Jensen, R. (2019). Cool to be smart or smart to be cool? Understanding peer pressure in education. *The Review of Economic Studies, 86*(4), 1487–1526. https://doi.org/10.1093/restud/rdy026

Busch, A. S., Hagen, C. P., & Juul, A. (2020a). Heritability of pubertal timing: Detailed evaluation of specific milestones in healthy boys and girls. *European Journal of Endocrinology, 183*(1), 13–20. https://doi.org/10.1530/EJE-20-0023

Busch, A. S., Højgaard, B., Hagen, C. P., & Teilmann, G. (2020b). Obesity is associated with earlier pubertal onset in boys. *The Journal of Clinical Endocrinology and Metabolism, 105*(4), dgz222. https://doi.org/10.1210/clinem/dgz222

Busch, J. T. A., Watson-Jones, R. E., & Legare, C. H. (2020). Cultural variation in the development of beliefs about conservation. *Cognitive Science, 44*(10), e12909. https://doi.org/10.1111/cogs.12909

Busching, R., & Krahé, B. (2020). With a little help from their peers: The impact of classmates on adolescents' development of prosocial behavior. *Journal of Youth and Adolescence, 49*(9), 1849–1863. https://doi.org/10.1007/s10964-020-01260-8

Buss, D. M., & von Hippel, W. (2018). Psychological barriers to evolutionary psychology: Ideological bias and coalitional adaptations. *Archives of Scientific Psychology, 6*(1), 148. https://doi.org/10.1037/arc0000049

Bussé, A. M. L., Hoeve, H. L. J., Nasserinejad, K., Mackey, A. R., Simonsz, H. J., & Goedegebure, A. (2020). Prevalence of permanent neonatal hearing impairment: Systematic review and Bayesian meta-analysis. *International Journal of Audiology, 59*(6), 475–485. https://doi.org/10.1080/14992027.2020.1716087

Bussey, K., & Bandura, A. (1999). Social cognitive theory of gender development and differentiation. *Psychological Review, 106*(4), 676.

Butler, G. H., Flood, K., Doyle, E., Geary, M. P., Betts, D. R., Foran, A., O'Marcaigh, A., & Cotter, M. (2016). Similar but different: Identical pathology with differing outcome in 'Not-so-identical' twins. *British Journal of Haematology, 178*(1), 152–153. https://doi.org/10.1111/bjh.14117

Butler, R., & Katona, C. (2019). *Seminars in old age psychiatry*. Cambridge University Press.

Butterworth, B., Gallistel, C. R., & Vallortigara, G. (2018). Introduction: The origins of numerical abilities. *Philosophical Transactions of the Royal Society B: Biological Sciences, 373*(1740). https://doi.org/10.1098/rstb.2016.0507

Butterfield, R. D., Silk, J. S., Lee, K. H., Siegle, G. S., Dahl, R. E., Forbes, E. E., Ryan, N. D., Hooley, J. M., & Ladouceur, C. D. (2021). Parents still matter! Parental warmth predicts adolescent brain function and anxiety and depressive symptoms 2 years later. *Development and Psychopathology, 33*(1), 226–239. https://doi.org/10.1017/S0954579419001718

Butterworth, B., & Varma, S. (2013). Mathematical development. In D. Mareschal, B. Butterworth, & A. Tolmie (Eds.), *Educational neuroscience* (Chap. 8). John Wiley & Sons.

Butterworth, B., & Walsh, V. (2011). Neural basis of mathematical cognition. *Current Biology, 21*(16), R618–R621. https://doi.org/10.1016/j.cub.2011.07.005

Button, J., & Wilde, A. (2019). Exploring practitioners' perceptions of risk when delivering Forest School for 3- to 5-year-old children. *International Journal of Play, 8*(1), 25–38. https://doi.org/10.1080/21594937.2019.1580334

Buultjens, M., Farouque, A., Karimi, L., Whitby, L., Milgrom, J., & Erbas, B. (2020). The contribution of group prenatal care to maternal psychological health outcomes: A systematic review. *Women and Birth*. https://doi.org/10.1016/j.wombi.2020.12.004

Buxton, O. M., Chang, A.-M., Spilsbury, J. C., Bos, T., Emsellem, H., & Knutson, K. L. (2015). Sleep in the modern family: Protective family routines for child and adolescent sleep. *Sleep Health, 1*(1), 15–27. https://doi.org/10.1016/j.sleh.2014.12.002

Byerley, B. M., & Haas, D. M. (2017). A systematic overview of the literature regarding group prenatal care for high-risk pregnant women. *BMC Pregnancy and Childbirth, 17*(1), 329. https://doi.org/10.1186/s12884-017-1522-2

Byers-Heinlein, K., & Lew-Williams, C. (2018). Language comprehension in monolingual and bilingual children. In E. M. Fernández & H. S. Cairns (Eds.), *The Handbook of Psycholinguistics* (pp. 516–535). Wiley.

Byers-Heinlein, K., Tsui, A. S. M., Bergmann, C., Black, A. K., Brown, A., Carbajal, M. J., Durrant, S., Fennell, C. T., Fiévet, A.-C., Frank, M. C., Gampe, A., Gervain, J., Gonzalez-Gomez, N., Hamlin, J. K., Havron, N., Hernik, M., Kerr, S., Killam, H., Klassen, K., . . . Wermelinger, S. (2021). A multilab study of bilingual infants: Exploring the preference for infant-directed speech. *Advances in Methods and Practices in Psychological Science, 4*(1), 2515245920974622. https://doi.org/10.1177/2515245920974622

Bygdell, M., Kindblom, J. M., Celind, J., Nethander, M., & Ohlsson, C. (2018). Childhood BMI is inversely associated with pubertal timing in normal-weight but not overweight boys. *The American Journal of Clinical Nutrition, 108*(6), 1259–1263. https://doi.org/10.1093/ajcn/nqy201

Byrd, C. M. (2016). Does culturally relevant teaching work? An examination from student perspectives. *SAGE Open, 6*(3), 2158244016660744. https://doi.org/10.1177/2158244016660744

Byrne, B. (2018). Dis-equality: Exploring the juxtaposition of disability and equality. *Social Inclusion, 6*(1), 9–17.

Cabell, S. Q., Justice, L. M., McGinty, A. S., DeCoster, J., & Forston, L. D. (2015). Teacher–child conversations in preschool classrooms: Contributions to children's vocabulary development. *Early Childhood Research Quarterly, 30*, 80–92.

Cabrera, N. J., & Tamis-LeMonda, C. S. (2013). *Handbook of father involvement: Multidisciplinary perspectives*. Routledge.

Cabrera, N. J., Volling, B. L., & Barr, R. (2018). Fathers are parents, too! Widening the lens on parenting for children's development. *Child Development Perspectives, 12*(3), 152–157. https://doi.org/10.1111/cdep.12275

Cacciatore, R., Korteniemi-Poikela, E., & Kaltiala, R. (2019). The steps of sexuality—A developmental, emotion-focused, child-centered model of sexual development and sexuality education from birth to adulthood. *International Journal of Sexual Health, 31*(3), 319–338. https://doi.org/10.1080/19317611.2019.1645783

Cachero, P., Edgett, K., & Tsur, S. (2017, July 21). An untranslatable word for pure joy. *BBC*. https://www.bbc.com/culture/article/20170714-an-untranslatable-word-for-pure-joy

Cacioppo, S., Couto, B., Bolmont, M., Sedeno, L., Frum, C., Lewis, J. W., Manes, F., Ibanez, A., & Cacioppo, J. T. (2013). Selective decision-making deficit in love following damage to the anterior insula. *Current Trends in Neurology, 7*, 15–19.

Cadely, H. S. E., Finnegan, V., Spears, E. C., & Kerpelman, J. L. (2020). Adolescents and sexual risk-taking: The interplay of constraining relationship beliefs, healthy sex attitudes, and romantic attachment insecurity. *Journal of Adolescence, 84*, 136–148.

Cadoret, G., Bigras, N., Duval, S., Lemay, L., Tremblay, T., & Lemire, J. (2018). The mediating role of cognitive ability on the relationship between motor proficiency and early academic achievement in children. *Human Movement Science, 57*, 149–157. https://doi.org/10.1016/j.humov.2017.12.002

Caffey, A. L., & Dalecki, M. (2021). Evidence of residual cognitive deficits in young adults with a concussion history from adolescence. *Brain Research, 1768*, 147570.

Cakouros, B., & Reynolds, S. (2022). Household structure across childhood in four lower- and middle-income countries. *Demographic Research, 47*(6), 143–160. https://doi.org/10.4054/DemRes.2022.47.6

Calderón-Garcidueñas, L., Gónzalez-Maciel, A., Reynoso-Robles, R., Delgado-Chávez, R., Mukherjee, P. S., Kulesza, R. J., Torres-Jardón, R., Ávila-Ramírez, J., & Villarreal-Ríos, R. (2018). Hallmarks of Alzheimer disease are evolving relent-lessly in Metropolitan Mexico City infants, children and young adults. APOE4 carriers have higher suicide risk and higher odds of reaching NFT stage V at ≤ 40 years of age. *Environmental Research, 164*, 475–487.

California Newsreel. (2008). News about people and communities appearing in the series. *Unnatural Causes*. https://unnaturalcauses.org/series_updates.php

Callaghan, B. L., & Tottenham, N. (2016). The stress acceleration hypothesis: Effects of early-life adversity on emotion circuits and behavior. *Current Opinion in Behavioral Sciences, 7*(Supplement C), 76–81. https://doi.org/10.1016/j.cobeha.2015.11.018

Callaghan, B. L., Fields, A., Gee, D. G., Gabard-Durnam, L., Caldera, C., Humphreys, K. L., Goff, B., Flannery, J., Telzer, E. H., Shapiro, M., & Tottenham, N. (2020). Mind and gut: Associations between mood and gastrointestinal distress in children exposed to adversity. *Development and Psychopathology, 32*(1), 309–328. https://doi.org/10.1017/S0954579419000087

Callaghan, T. (2020). The origins and development of a symbolic mind: The case of pictorial symbols. *Interchange, 51*(1), 53–64. https://doi.org/10.1007/s10780-020-09396-z

Callaghan, T., Moghtaderi, A., Lueck, J. A., Hotez, P., Strych, U., Dor, A., Fowler, E. F., & Motta, M. (2021). Correlates and disparities of intention to vaccinate against COVID-19. *Social Science & Medicine (1982), 272*, 113638. https://doi.org/10.1016/j.socscimed.2020.113638

Callaghan, T., Moll, H., Rakoczy, H., Warneken, F., Liszkowski, U., Behne, T., Tomasello, M., & Collins, W. A. (2011). *Early social cognition in three cultural contexts*. Wiley-Blackwell.

Callahan, M. (2018, July 12). "Autistic person" or "person with autism": Is there a right way to identify people? *News@Northeastern.* https://news.northeastern.edu/2018/07/12/unpacking-the-debate-over-person-first-vs-identity-first-language-in-the-autism-community/

Calogero, R. M., Tylka, T. L., Donnelly, L. C., McGetrick, A., & Leger, A. M. (2017). Trappings of femininity: A test of the "beauty as currency" hypothesis in shaping college women's gender activism. *Body Image, 21*, 66–70. http://www.sciencedirect.com/science/article/pii/S1740144516305034

Calvert, S. L., Appelbaum, M., Dodge, K. A., Graham, S., Nagayama Hall, G. C., Hamby, S., Fasig-Caldwell, L. G., Citkowitz, M., Galloway, D. P., & Hedges, L. V. (2017). The American Psychological Association Task Force assessment of violent video games: Science in the service of public interest. *American Psychologist, 72*(2), 126.

Calzo, J. P., Masyn, K. E., Austin, S. B., Jun, H.-J., & Corliss, H. L. (2017). Developmental latent patterns of identification as mostly heterosexual vs. lesbian, gay, and bisexual. *Journal of Research on Adolescence, 27*(1), 246–253. https://doi.org/10.1111/jora.12266

Camerini, A. L., Marciano, L., Carrara, A., & Schulz, P. J. (2020). Cyberbullying perpetration and victimization among children and adolescents: A systematic review of longitudinal studies. *Telematics and Informatics, 49*, 101362.

Cameron, C. E., Cottone, E. A., Murrah, W. M., & Grissmer, D. W. (2016). How are motor skills linked to children's school performance and academic achievement? *Child Development Perspectives, 10*(2), 93–98.

Cameron, L., & Tenenbaum, H. R. (2021). Lessons from developmental science to mitigate the effects of the COVID-19 restrictions on social development. *Group Processes & Intergroup Relations, 24*(2), 231–236. https://doi.org/10.1177/1368430220984236

Camerota, M., & Willoughby, M. T. (2021). Applying interdisciplinary frameworks to study prenatal influences on child development. *Child Development Perspectives, 15*(1), 24–30.

Camodeca, M., & Coppola, G. (2016). Bullying, empathic concern, and internalization of rules among preschool children: The role of emotion understanding. *International Journal of Behavioral Development, 40*(5), 459–465.

Campbell, A., Shirley, L., & Caygill, L. (2002). Sex-typed preferences in three domains: Do two-year-olds need cognitive variables? *British Journal of Psychology, 93*(2), 203–217. https://doi.org/10.1348/000712602162544

Campisi, S. C., Humayun, K. N., Rizvi, A., Lou, W., Söder, O., & Bhutta, Z. A. (2020). Later puberty onset among chronically undernourished adolescents living in a Karachi slum, Pakistan. *Acta Paediatrica, 109*(5), 1019–1025. https://doi.org/10.1111/apa.15053

Camras, L. A. (2019). Facial expressions across the life span. In V. LoBue, K. Pérez-Edgar, & K. A. Buss (Eds.), *Handbook of emotional development* (pp. 83–103).

Springer International Publishing. https://doi.org/10.1007/978-3-030-17332-6_5

Cantlon, J. F. (2020). The balance of rigor and reality in developmental neuroscience. *NeuroImage, 216*, 116464. https://doi.org/10.1016/j.neuroimage.2019.116464

Capon, N., & Kuhn, D. (1982). Can consumers calculate best buys? *Journal of Consumer Research, 8*(4), 449–453. http://www.jstor.org/stable/2489032

Caprio, S., Santoro, N., & Weiss, R. (2020). Childhood obesity and the associated rise in cardiometabolic complications. *Nature Metabolism, 2*(3), 223–232. https://doi.org/10.1038/s42255-020-0183-z

Caputi, T. L., Shover, C. L., & Watson, R. J. (2020). Physical and sexual violence among gay, lesbian, bisexual, and questioning adolescents. *JAMA Pediatrics, 174*(8), 791–793. https://doi.org/10.1001/jamapediatrics.2019.6291

Card, D., & Giuliano, L. (2016). Can tracking raise the test scores of high-ability minority students? *American Economic Review, 106*(10), 2783–2816. https://doi.org/10.1257/aer.20150484

Cardel, M. I., Atkinson, M. A., Taveras, E. M., Holm, J.-C., & Kelly, A. S. (2020). Obesity treatment among adolescents: A review of current evidence and future directions. *JAMA Pediatrics, 174*(6), 609–617. https://doi.org/10.1001/jamapediatrics.2020.0085

Cardona, M., Millward, J., Gemmill, A., Yoo, K. J., & Bishai, D. M. (2022). Estimated impact of the 2020 economic downturn on under-5 mortality for 129 countries. *PLOS ONE, 17*(2), e0263245. https://doi.org/10.1371/journal.pone.0263245

Carey, N., & Coley, R. L. (2022). Prevalence of adolescent handgun carriage: 2002–2019. *Pediatrics, 149*(5), e2021054472. https://doi.org/10.1542/peds.2021-054472

Carey, S. (1978). The child as word learner. Linguistic theory and psychological reality In M. Halle, J. Bresnan, & G. A. Miller (Eds.), *Linguistic theory and psychological reality* (pp. 264–293). MIT Press.

Carey, S. (2010). Beyond fast mapping. *Language Learning and Development: The Official Journal of the Society for Language Development, 6*(3), 184–205. https://doi.org/10.1080/15475441.2010.484379

Carey, S., & Bartlett, E. (1978). Acquiring a single new word. *Papers and Reports on Child Language Development, 15*, 17–29.

Carey, S., & Spelke, E. (1996). Science and core knowledge. *Philosophy of Science, 63*(4), 515–533

Carey, S., Zaitchik, D., & Bascandziev, I. (2015). Theories of development: In dialog with Jean Piaget. *Developmental Review, 38*, 36–54. https://doi.org/10.1016/j.dr.2015.07.003

Carey, T. L. (2019, May 9). *DNA tests stand on shaky ground to define Native American identity*. National Human Genome Research Institute.

Carlson, F. M. (2011). Rough play: One of the most challenging behaviors. *Young Children, 66*(4), 18.

Carlson, J. S., Yohannan, J., Darr, C. L., Turley, M. R., Larez, N. A., & Perfect, M. M. (2020). Prevalence of adverse childhood experiences in school-aged youth: A systematic review (1990–2015). *International Journal of School & Educational Psychology, 8*(sup1), 2–23.

Carnevale, A. P., Fasules, M. L., Quinn, M. C., & Campbell, K. P. (2019). *Born to win, schooled to lose*. Georgetown University Center on Education and the Workforce.

Carnevale, A. P., Hanson, A. R., & Gulish, A. (2013). *Failure to launch: Structural shift and the new lost generation*. Georgetown University Center on Education and the Workforce. http://eric.ed.gov/?id=ED558185

Carnevale, A. P., Strohl, J., Gulish, A., Van Der Werf, M., & Peltier Campbell, K. (2019). *The unequal race for good jobs: How Whites made outsized gains in education and good jobs compared to Blacks and Latinos*. Georgetown University Center on Education and the Workforce.

Carnevale, A. P., Strohl, J., Ridley, N., & Gulish, A. (2018b). *Three educational pathways to good jobs: High school, middle skills, and bachelor's degree*. Georgetown University Center on Education and the Workforce.

Carolan, M. T., Bagherinia, G., Juhari, R., Himelright, J., & Mouton-Sanders, M. (2000). Contemporary Muslim families: Research and practice. *Contemporary Family Therapy, 22*(1), 67–79.

Carone, N., Lingiardi, V., Tanzilli, A., Bos, H. M. W., & Baiocco, R. (2020). Gender development in children with gay, lesbian, and heterosexual parents: Associations with family type and child gender. *Journal of Developmental & Behavioral Pediatrics, 41*(1), 38–47. https://doi.org/10.1097/DBP.0000000000000726

Carr, P. G. (2017). *Commissioner's remarks-NCES Statement on PIRLS 2016-December 5, 2017*. National Center for Education Statistics. https://nces.ed.gov/whatsnew/commissioner/remarks2017/12_05_2017.asp

Carroll, J. E., Mahrer, N. E., Shalowitz, M., Ramey, S., & Dunkel Schetter, C. (2020). Prenatal maternal stress prospectively relates to shorter child buccal cell telomere length. *Psychoneuroendocrinology, 121*, 104841. https://doi.org/10.1016/j.psyneuen.2020.104841

Carroll, J. M., Holliman, A. J., Weir, F., & Baroody, A. E. (2019). Literacy interest, home literacy environment and emergent literacy skills in preschoolers. *Journal of Research in Reading, 42*(1), 150–161.

Carskadon, M. A. (2011). Sleep in adolescents: The perfect storm. *Pediatric Clinics of North America, 58*(3), 637.

Carskadon, M. A., & Barker, D. H. (2020). Editorial perspective: Adolescents' fragile sleep—shining light on a time of risk to mental health. *Journal of Child Psychology and Psychiatry, 61*(10), 1058–1060.

Carter, P. L., Skiba, R., Arredondo, M. I., & Pollock, M. (2017). You can't fix what you don't look at: Acknowledging race in addressing racial discipline disparities. *Urban Education, 52*(2), 207–235.

Carter, R., Halawah, A., & Trinh, S. L. (2018a). Peer exclusion during the pubertal transition: The role of social competence. *Journal of Youth and Adolescence, 47*(1), 121–134. https://doi.org/10.1007/s10964-017-0682-8

Carter, R., Mustafaa, F. N., & Leath, S. (2018b). Teachers' expectations of girls' classroom performance and behavior: Effects of girls' race and pubertal timing. *The Journal of Early Adolescence, 38*(7), 885–907. https://doi.org/10.1177/0272431617699947

Carvalho, M. E. S., de Miranda Justo, J. M. R., Gratier, M., & da Silva, H. M. F. R. (2019). The impact of maternal voice on the fetus: A systematic review. *Current Women's Health Reviews, 15*(3), 196–206. https://doi.org/10.2174/1573404814666181026094419

Casas, F., & González-Carrasco, M. (2019). Subjective well-being decreasing with age: New research on children over 8. *Child Development, 90*(2), 375–394.

Cascio, E. U., & Staiger, D. O. (2012). *Knowledge, tests, and fadeout in educational interventions* (No. w18038). National Bureau of Economic Research.

Casey, B. J. (2015). Beyond simple models of self-control to circuit-based accounts of adolescent behavior. *Annual Review of Psychology, 66*(1), 295–319. https://doi.org/10.1146/annurev-psych-010814-015156

Casey, B. J., Heller, A. S., Gee, D. G., & Cohen, A. O. (2019). Development of the emotional brain.

Neuroscience Letters, 693, 29–34. https://doi.org /10.1016/j.neulet.2017.11.055

Casey, B. J., Simmons, C., Somerville, L. H., & Baskin-Sommers, A. (2022). Making the sentencing case: Psychological and neuroscientific evidence for expanding the age of youthful offenders. *Annual Review of Criminology, 5*(1), 321–343.

Cashdollar, S. E. (2018). Neither accidental nor intended: Pregnancy as an adolescent identity project among Hispanic teenage mothers in Doña Ana County, New Mexico. *Journal of Adolescent Research, 33*(5), 598–622. https://doi.org/10.1177/0743558417712014

Casillas, M., Bobb, S. C., & Clark, E. V. (2016). Turn taking, timing, and planning in early language acquisition. *Journal of Child Language, 43,* 1310–1337.

Caspari, R., & Lee, S.-H. (2004). Older age becomes common late in human evolution. *Proceedings of the National Academy of Sciences, 101*(30), 10895–10900. https://doi.org/10.1073/pnas.0402857101

Castelo, R. J., Meuwissen, A. S., Distefano, R., McClelland, M. M., Galinsky, E., Zelazo, P. D., & Carlson, S. M. (2022). Parent Provision of Choice Is a Key Component of Autonomy Support in Predicting Child Executive Function Skills. *Frontiers in psychology, 12,* 6324.

Castles, A., Rastle, K., & Nation, K. (2018). Ending the reading wars: Reading acquisition from novice to expert. *Psychological Science in the Public Interest, 19*(1), 5–51. https://doi.org/10.1177/1529100618772271

Cat, C. D., Gusnanto, A., & Serratrice, L. (2018). Identifying a threshold for the executive function advantage in bilingual children. *Studies in Second Language Acquisition, 40*(1), 119–151. https://doi.org/10.1017 /S0272263116000486

Catalano, P. M., & Shankar, K. (2017). Obesity and pregnancy: Mechanisms of short term and long term adverse consequences for mother and child. *BMJ, 356.* https://doi.org/10.1136/bmj.j1

Cataldi, J. R., Kerns, M. E., & O'Leary, S. T. (2020). Evidence-based strategies to increase vaccination uptake: A review. *Current Opinion in Pediatrics, 32*(1), 151–159.

Catillon, M., Cutler, D., & Getzen, T. (2018). *Two hundred years of health and medical care: The importance of medical care for life expectancy gains* (No. w25330). National Bureau of Economic Research. https://doi.org/10.3386/w25330

Cava, M.-J., Martínez-Ferrer, B., Buelga, S., & Carrascosa, L. (2020). Sexist attitudes, romantic myths, and offline dating violence as predictors of cyber dating violence perpetration in adolescents. *Computers in Human Behavior, 111,* 106449. https://doi.org /10.1016/j.chb.2020.106449

Cavalli, G., & Heard, E. (2019). Advances in epigenetics link genetics to the environment and disease. *Nature, 571*(7766), 489–499. https://doi.org/10.1038 /s41586-019-1411-0

Cavanagh, S. E., & Fomby, P. (2019). Family instability in the lives of American children. *Annual Review of Sociology, 45*(1), 493–513. https://doi.org/10.1146 /annurev-soc-073018-022633

Cavanaugh, A. M., Stein, G. L., Supple, A. J., Gonzalez, L. M., & Kiang, L. (2018). Protective and promotive effects of Latino early adolescents' cultural assets against multiple types of discrimination. *Journal of Research on Adolescence, 28*(2), 310–326. https://doi.org/10.1111/jora.12331

Cave, L., Cooper, M. N., Zubrick, S. R., & Shepherd, C. C. (2020). Racial discrimination and child and adolescent health in longitudinal studies: A systematic review. *Social Science & Medicine, 250,* 112864.

Caye, A., Petresco, S., de Barros, A. J. D., Bressan, R. A., Gadelha, A., Gonçalves, H., & Rohde, L. A.
(2020). Relative age and attention-deficit/hyperactivity disorder: Data from three epidemiological cohorts and a meta-analysis. *Journal of the American Academy of Child & Adolescent Psychiatry, 59*(8), 990–997.

Cebolla-Boado, H., González Ferrer, A., & Nuhoğlu Soysal, Y. (2021). It is all about "hope": Evidence on the immigrant optimism paradox. *Ethnic and Racial Studies, 44*(2), 252–271. https://doi.org/10.1080/01419870.20 20.1745254

Ceci, S. J., & Bruck, M. (1993). Suggestibility of the child witness: A historical review and synthesis. *Psychological Bulletin, 113*(3), 403.

Centers for Disease Control and Prevention (CDC). (2018). *Asthma in children (CDC Vital Signs).* Centers for Disease Control and Prevention.

Centers for Disease Control and Prevention (CDC). (2019). *2019 High School Youth Risk Behavior Survey Data: High school sexual behaviors.* http://yrbs-explorer .services.cdc.gov/

Centers for Disease Control and Prevention (CDC). (2020). HIV surveillance report, 2018 (Updated; Vol. 31). http://www.cdc.gov/hiv/library/reports /hiv-surveillance.html

Centers for Disease Control and Prevention (CDC). (2021a). *Health United States, 2019* (table 9). https:// www.cdc.gov/nchs/data/hus/2019/009-508.pdf

Centers for Disease Control and Prevention, National Center for Health Statistics. (2021b). National Vital Statistics System, Mortality 1999-2020. CDC WONDER Online Database. http://wonder.cdc.gov /ucd-icd10.html

Centers for Disease Control and Prevention (CDC), National Center for Health Statistics. (2021c). *Underlying cause of death 1999–2020 on CDC WONDER Online Database, released in 2021.* http:// wonder.cdc.gov/natality-expanded-current.html

Centers for Disease Control and Prevention, WONDER Online Database. (2022). National Vital Statistics System, Mortality 2018–2020, multiple cause of death files, 2018–2020. National Center for Health Statistics. http://wonder.cdc.gov/mcd-icd10-expanded.html

Cepa, K., & Furstenberg, F. F. (2021). Reaching adulthood: Persistent beliefs about the importance and timing of adult milestones. *Journal of Family Issues, 42*(1), 27–57. https://doi.org/10.1177/0192513X20918612

Chad, J. A. (2020). The first ejaculation: A male pubertal milestone comparable to menarche? *Journal of Sex Research, 57*(2), 213–221. https://doi.org/10.1080/002 24499.2018.1543643

Chad-Friedman, E., Botdorf, M., Riggins, T., & Dougherty, L. R. (2021). Early childhood cumulative risk is associated with decreased global brain measures, cortical thickness, and cognitive functioning in school-age children. *Developmental Psychobiology, 63*(2), 192–205. https://doi.org/10.1002/dev.21956

Chalasani, S., Engel, D., Friedman, H. S., Knutsson, A., Mahon, J., Patton, G., & Sawyer, S. M. (2019). An investment case to guarantee the rights of adolescents. *Journal of Adolescent Health, 65*(1), S3–S7. https://doi .org/10.1016/j.jadohealth.2019.04.015

Chalise, U., Pradhan, A., Lama, C. P., Panta, P. P., & Dhungel, S. (2018). Age at menarche among the school going children of Jorpati, Kathmandu. *Journal of College of Medical Science—Nepal, 14*(3), 142–146.

Chan, M., Tsai, K. M., & Fuligni, A. J. (2015). Changes in religiosity across the transition to young adulthood. *Journal of Youth and Adolescence, 44*(8), 1555–1566.

Chan Tack, A. M., & Small, M. L. (2017). Making friends in violent neighborhoods: Strategies among
elementary school children. *Sociological Science, 4,* 224–248.

Chandra-Mouli, V., & Patel, S. V. (2020). Mapping the knowledge and understanding of menarche, menstrual hygiene and menstrual health among adolescent girls in low- and middle-income countries. In C. Bobel, I. T. Winkler, B. Fahs, K. A. Hasson, E. A. Kissling, & T.-A. Roberts (Eds.), *The Palgrave handbook of critical menstruation studies* (pp. 609–636). Palgrave.

Chandra-Mouli, V., Ferguson, B. J., Plesons, M., Paul, M., Chalasani, S., Amin, A., Pallitto, C., Sommers, M., Avila, R., Eceéce Biaukula, K. V., Husain, S., Janušonytė, E., Mukherji, A., Nergiz, A. I., Phaladi, G., Porter, C., Sauvarin, J., Camacho-Huber, A. V., Mehra, S., . . . Engel, D. M. C. (2019). The political, research, programmatic, and social responses to adolescent sexual and reproductive health and rights in the 25 years since the international conference on population and development. *Journal of Adolescent Health, 65*(6, Supplement), S16–S40. https:// doi.org/10.1016/j.jadohealth.2019.09.011

Chang, H., & Shaw, D. S. (2016). The emergence of parent-child coercive processes in toddlerhood. *Child Psychiatry and Human Development, 47*(2), 226–235. https://doi.org/10.1007/s10578-015-0559-6

Chao, H.-C. (2018). Association of picky eating with growth, nutritional status, development, physical activity, and health in preschool children. *Frontiers in Pediatrics, 6,* 22. https://doi.org/10.3389 /fped.2018.00022

Chaplot, P., Cooper, D., Johnstone, R., & Karandjeff, K. (2015). *Beyond financial aid: How colleges can strengthen the financial stability of low-income students and improve student outcomes.* http://www.luminafoundation.org /files/resources/beyond-financial-aid.pdf

Chapman, T. W., & Hill, R. A. (2020). Myelin plasticity in adulthood and aging. *Neuroscience Letters, 715,* 134645. https://doi.org/10.1016/j.neulet.2019.134645

Charlesworth, T. E. S., & Banaji, M. R. (2021). Patterns of implicit and explicit stereotypes III: Long-term change in gender stereotypes. *Social Psychological and Personality Science,* 1948550620988425. https://doi.org /10.1177/1948550620988425

Charmaraman, L., Lynch, A. D., Richer, A. M., & Grossman, J. M. (2022). Associations of early social media initiation on digital behaviors and the moderating role of limiting use. *Computers in Human Behavior, 127,* 107053. https://doi.org/10.1016/j.chb.2021.107053

Charter, R., Ussher, J., Perz, J., & Robinson, K. (2021). Negotiating mental health amongst transgender parents in Australia. *International Journal of Transgender Health,* 1–13. https://doi.org/10.1080/26895269.2021 .1875951

Chase, P. A., Hilliard, L. J., Geldhof, G. J., Warren, D. J., & Lerner, R. M. (2014). Academic achievement in the high school years: The changing role of school engagement. *Journal of Youth and Adolescence, 43*(6), 884–896.

Chasteen, A. L., Horhota, M., & Crumley-Branyon, J. J. (2020). Overlooked and underestimated: Experiences of ageism in young, middle-aged, and older adults. *The Journals of Gerontology: Series B, 76*(7), 1323–1328. https://doi.org/10.1093/geronb/gbaa043

Chater, N., McCauley, S. M., & Christiansen, M. H. (2016). Language as skill: Intertwining comprehension and production. *Journal of Memory and Language, 89,* 244–254.

Chatterjee, R., & Davis, R. (2017, December 20). How racism may cause black mothers to suffer the death of their infants. *Morning Edition.* National Public Radio.

Chaudhuri, S. (2015). Excess female infant mortality and the gender gap in infant care in Bihar, India. *Feminist Economics, 21*(2), 131–161. https://doi.org/10.1080/13545701.2014.999007

Chawanpaiboon, S., Vogel, J. P., Moller, A.-B., Lumbiganon, P., Petzold, M., Hogan, D., Landoulsi, S., Jampathong, N., Kongwattanakul, K., Laopaiboon, M., Lewis, C., Rattanakanokchai, S., Teng, D. N., Thinkhamrop, J., Watananirun, K., Zhang, J., Zhou, W., & Gülmezoglu, A. M. (2019). Global, regional, and national estimates of levels of preterm birth in 2014: A systematic review and modelling analysis. *The Lancet Global Health, 7*(1), e37–e46. https://doi.org/10.1016/S2214-109X(18)30451-0

Chea, N., & Asefa, A. (2018). Prelacteal feeding and associated factors among newborns in rural Sidama, south Ethiopia: A community based cross-sectional survey. *International Breastfeeding Journal, 13*(1), 7. https://doi.org/10.1186/s13006-018-0149-x

Cheadle, A. C. D., Ramos, I. F., & Schetter, C. D. (2020). Stress and resilience in pregnancy. In *The Wiley encyclopedia of health psychology* (pp. 717–723). John Wiley & Sons. https://doi.org/10.1002/9781119057840.ch124

Cheadle, L., Rivera, S. A., Phelps, J. S., Ennis, K. A., Stevens, B., Burkly, L. C., Lee, W.-C. A., & Greenberg, M. E. (2020). Sensory experience engages microglia to shape neural connectivity through a non-phagocytic mechanism. *Neuron, 108*(3), 451–468.e9. https://doi.org/10.1016/j.neuron.2020.08.002

Chen, C.-H., & Yang, Y.-C. (2019). Revisiting the effects of project-based learning on students' academic achievement: A meta-analysis investigating moderators. *Educational Research Review, 26*, 71–81. https://doi.org/10.1016/j.edurev.2018.11.001

Chen, C. R., & Lindo, E. J. (2018). Culturally responsive practices in special education evaluations: A review of literature. *Dialog: Journal of the Texas Educational Diagnosticians Association, 47*(2), 9–13.

Chen, E., Brody, G. H., & Miller, G. E. (2017). Childhood close family relationships and health. *American Psychologist, 72*(6), 555.

Chen, F. R., Rothman, E. F., & Jaffee, S. R. (2017). Early puberty, friendship group characteristics, and dating abuse in US girls. *Pediatrics, 139*(6), e20162847. https://doi.org/10.1542/peds.2016-2847

Chen, P., & Harris, K. M. (2019). Association of positive family relationships with mental health trajectories from adolescence to midlife. *JAMA Pediatrics, 173*(12), e193336. https://doi.org/10.1001/jamapediatrics.2019.3336

Chen, S. H., Cohodes, E., Bush, N. R., & Lieberman, A. F. (2020). Child and caregiver executive function in trauma-exposed families: Relations with children's behavioral and cognitive functioning. *Journal of Experimental Child Psychology, 200*, 104946. https://doi.org/10.1016/j.jecp.2020.104946

Chen, W., & Adler, J. L. (2019). Assessment of screen exposure in young children, 1997 to 2014. *JAMA Pediatrics, 173*(4), 391–393. https://doi.org/10.1001/jamapediatrics.2018.5546

Chen, X. (2018). Culture, temperament, and social and psychological adjustment. *Developmental Review, 50*, 42–53. https://doi.org/10.1016/j.dr.2018.03.004

Chen, X. (2019). Culture and shyness in childhood and adolescence. *New Ideas in Psychology, 53*, 58–66. https://doi.org/10.1016/j.newideapsych.2018.04.007

Chen, X., Caves, L. R., Pretlow, J., Caperton, S. A., Bryan, M., & Cooney, D. (2020). Courses taken, credits earned, and time to degree: A first look at the postsecondary transcripts of 2011–12 beginning postsecondary students (NCES 2020-501). U.S. Department of Education. Washington, DC: National Center for Education Statistics. https://nces.ed.gov/pubsearch/pubsinfo.asp?pubid=2020501.

Chen-Bouck, L., Patterson, M. M., & Chen, J. (2019). Relations of collectivism socialization goals and training beliefs to Chinese parenting. *Journal of Cross-Cultural Psychology, 50*(3), 396–418.

Cheng, W., Rolls, E., Gong, W., Du, J., Zhang, J., Zhang, X.-Y., Li, F., & Feng, J. (2020). Sleep duration, brain structure, and psychiatric and cognitive problems in children. *Molecular Psychiatry*, 1–12. https://doi.org/10.1038/s41380-020-0663-2

Chen-Gaddini, M., Liu, J., & Nucci, L. (2020). "It's my own business!": Parental control over personal issues in the context of everyday adolescent–parent conflicts and internalizing disorders among urban Chinese adolescents. *Developmental Psychology, 56*(9), 1775–1786. https://doi.org/10.1037/dev0001053

Chernyak, N., Turnbull, V., Gordon, R., Harris, P. L., & Cordes, S. (2020). Counting promotes proportional moral evaluation in preschool-aged children. *Cognitive Development, 56*, 100969.

Chernyshenko, O. S., Kankaraš, M., & Drasgow, F. (2018). Social and emotional skills for student success and well-being: Conceptual framework for the OECD study on social and emotional skills.

Chess, S., & Thomas, A. (1991). Temperament and the concept of goodness of fit. In J. Strelau & A. Angleitner (Eds.), *Explorations in temperament: International perspectives on theory and measurement* (pp. 15–28). Springer US. https://doi.org/10.1007/978-1-4899-0643-4_2

Chess, S., & Thomas, A. (1996). *Temperament: Theory and practice*. Brunner/Mazel.

Chess, S., Thomas, A., Rutter, M., & Birch, H. G. (1963). Interaction of temperament and environment in the production of behavioral disturbances in children. *American Journal of Psychiatry, 120*(2), 142–148. https://doi.org/10.1176/ajp.120.2.142

Chetty, R. (2021). Improving equality of opportunity: New insights from big data. *Contemporary Economic Policy, 39*(1), 7–41. https://doi.org/10.1111/coep.12478

Chetwynd, E. M., Wasser, H. M., & Poole, C. (2019). Breastfeeding support interventions by international board certified lactation consultants: A systemic review and meta-analysis. *Journal of Human Lactation, 35*(3), 424–440. https://doi.org/10.1177/0890334419851482

Chevalier, N. (2018). Willing to think hard? The subjective value of cognitive effort in children. *Child Development, 89*(4), 1283–1295.

Chiang, K. V., Hamner, H. C., Li, R., & Perrine, C. G. (2020). Timing of introduction of complementary foods—United States, 2016–2018. *Morbidity and Mortality Weekly Report, 69*(47), 1787.

Child Welfare Information Gateway. (2019). *Definitions of child abuse and neglect*. U.S. Department of Health and Human Services, Children's Bureau.

Children's Bureau. (2019). *What is child abuse and neglect? Recognizing the signs and symptoms* [Fact sheet].

Childs, G. V., Odle, A. K., MacNicol, M. C., & MacNicol, A. M. (2020). The importance of leptin to reproduction. *Endocrinology, 162*(2), bqaa204. https://doi.org/10.1210/endocr/bqaa204

Chinn, J., Sedighim, S., Kirby, K. A., Hohmann, S., Hameed, A. B., Jolley, J., & Nguyen, N. T. (2021). Characteristics and outcomes of women with COVID-19 giving birth at US academic centers during the COVID-19 pandemic. *JAMA Network Open, 4*(8), e2120456. https://doi.org/10.1001/jamanetworkopen.2021.20456

Chmielewski, A. K. (2019). The global increase in the socioeconomic achievement gap, 1964 to 2015. *American Sociological Review, 84*(3), 517–544. https://doi.org/10.1177/0003122419847165

Choate, P. W., CrazyBull, B., Lindstrom, D., & Lindstrom, G. (2020). Where do we go from here? Ongoing colonialism from attachment theory. *Aotearoa New Zealand Social Work, 32*(1), 32–44.

Choate, P. W., Kohler, T., Cloete, F., CrazyBull, B., Lindstrom, D., & Tatoulis, P. (2019). Rethinking *Racine v Woods* from a decolonizing perspective: Challenging the applicability of attachment theory to indigenous families involved with child protection. *Canadian Journal of Law and Society/La Revue Canadienne Droit et Société, 34*(1), 55–78. https://doi.org/10.1017/cls.2019.8

Choe, D. E., Olson, S. L., & Sameroff, A. J. (2013). Effects of early maternal distress and parenting on the development of children's self-regulation and externalizing behavior. *Development and Psychopathology, 25*(2), 437–453.

Choi, K. H., & Goldberg, R. E. (2020). The social significance of interracial cohabitation: Inferences based on fertility behavior. *Demography, 57*(5), 1727–1751. https://doi.org/10.1007/s13524-020-00904-5

Chomsky, N. (1957). Logical structures in language. *American Documentation, 8*(4), 284.

Chomsky, N. (2002). *On nature and language*. Cambridge University Press.

Chopik, W. J., Nuttall, A. K., & Oh, J. (2021). Relationship-specific satisfaction and adjustment in emerging adulthood: The moderating role of adult attachment orientation. *Journal of Adult Development*. https://doi.org/10.1007/s10804-021-09380-6

Chou, R., Pappas, M., Dana, T., Selph, S., Hart, E., & Schwarz, E. (2021). Screening and prevention of dental caries in children younger than five years of age: A systematic review for the US Preventive Services Task Force. Evidence Synthesis No. 210. Agency for Healthcare Research and Quality Publication 21-05279-EF-1.

Choukas-Bradley, S., Goldberg, S. K., Widman, L., Reese, B. M., & Halpern, C. T. (2015). Demographic and developmental differences in the content and sequence of adolescents' ideal romantic relationship behaviors. *Journal of Adolescence, 45*, 112–126.

Chow, A., Galambos, N. L., & Krahn, H. J. (2017). Work values during the transition to adulthood and mid-life satisfaction: Cascading effects across 25 years. *International Journal of Behavioral Development, 41*(1), 105–114. https://doi.org/10.1177/0165025415608518

Christakis, D., Hill, D., Ameenuddin, N., Chassiakos, Y. L. R., Corss, C., Fagbuyi, D., Hutchinson, J., Levine, A., McCarthy, C., Mendelson, R., Moreno, M., & Swanson, W. S. (2016). Virtual violence. *Pediatrics* 138(2), e20161298.

Christensen, J., Eyolfson, E., Salberg, S., & Mychasiuk, R. (2021). Traumatic brain injury in adolescence: A review of the neurobiological and behavioural underpinnings and outcomes. *Developmental Review, 59*, 100943. https://doi.org/10.1016/j.dr.2020.100943

Christensen, N., Bruun, S., Søndergaard, J., Christesen, H. T., Fisker, N., Zachariassen, G., Sangild, P. T., & Husby, S. (2020). Breastfeeding and infections in early childhood: A cohort study. *Pediatrics, 146*(5), e20191892.

Christenson, A., Johansson, E., Reynisdottir, S., Torgerson, J., & Hemmingsson, E. (2019). ". . . Or else I close my ears": How women with obesity want to be approached and treated regarding gestational weight management: A qualitative interview study. *PLOS ONE, 14*(9), e0222543. https://doi.org/10.1371/journal.pone.0222543

Christiaens, A. H. T., Nelemans, S. A., Meeus, W. H. J., & Branje, S. (2021). Identity development across the transition from secondary to tertiary education: A 9-wave longitudinal study. *Journal of Adolescence.* https://doi.org/10.1016/j.adolescence.2021.03.007

Christian, C. W., & Committee on Child Abuse and Neglect. (2015). The evaluation of suspected child physical abuse. *Pediatrics, 135*(5), e1337–e1354. https://doi.org/10.1542/peds.2015-0356

Christopher, M. E., Hulslander, J., Byrne, B., Samuelsson, S., Keenan, J. M., Pennington, B., & Olson, R. K. (2015). Genetic and environmental etiologies of the longitudinal relations between prereading skills and reading. *Child Development, 86*(2), 342–361.

Chu, J. Y. (2014). *When boys become boys: Development, relationships, and masculinity.* New York University Press. https://www.degruyter.com/document/doi/10.18574/9780814724859/html

Chua, A. (2011). *Battle hymn of the tiger mother.* Penguin.

Chuang, S. S., Glozman, J., Green, D. S., & Rasmi, S. (2018). Parenting and family relationships in Chinese families: A critical ecological approach. *Journal of Family Theory & Review, 10*(2), 367–383. https://doi.org/10.1111/jftr.12257

Chung, H. Y., Kim, D. H., Lee, E. K., Chung, K. W., Chung, S., Lee, B., Seo, A. Y., Chung, J. H., Jung, Y. S., Im, E., Lee, J., Kim, N. D., Choi, Y. J., Im, D. S., & Yu, B. P. (2019). Redefining chronic inflammation in aging and age-related diseases: Proposal of the senoinflammation concept. *Aging and Disease, 10*(2), 367–382. https://doi.org/10.14336/AD.2018.0324

Chyl, K., Fraga-González, G., Brem, S., & Jednoróg, K. (2021). Brain dynamics of (a)typical reading development—A review of longitudinal studies. *NPJ Science of Learning, 6*(1), 1–9. https://doi.org/10.1038/s41539-020-00081-5

Chzhen, Y., Rees, G., Gromada, A., Cuesta, J., & Bruckauf, Z. (2018). *An unfair start: Inequality in children's education in rich countries* (Innocenti Report Card No. 15). UNICEF Office of Research.

Ciarrusta, J., Christiaens, D., Fitzgibbon, S. P., Dimitrova, R., Hutter, J., Hughes, E., Duff, E., Price, A. N., Cordero-Grande, L., Tournier, J.-D., Rueckert, D., Hajnal, J. V., Arichi, T., McAlonan, G., Edwards, A. D., & Batalle, D. (2021). The developing brain structural and functional connectome fingerprint. *BioRxiv,* 2021.03.08.434357. https://doi.org/10.1101/2021.03.08.434357

Cicchetti, D. (2018). A multilevel developmental approach to the prevention of psychopathology in children and adolescents. In J. N. Butcher & P. C. Kendall (Eds.), *APA handbook of psychopathology: Child and adolescent psychopathology* (pp. 37–53). American Psychological Association. https://doi.org/10.1037/0000065-003

Cillessen, A. H. N., & Bukowski, W. M. (2018). Sociometric perspectives. In W. M. Bukowski, B. Laursen, & K. H. Rubin (Eds.), *Handbook of peer interactions, relationships, and groups* (pp. 64–83). Guilford.

Cimpian, A. (2016). The privileged status of category representations in early development. *Child Development Perspectives, 10*(2), 99–104. https://doi.org/10.1111/cdep.12166

Cimpian, A. (2017). Early reasoning about competence is not irrationally optimistic, nor does it stem from inadequate cognitive representations. In A. J. Elliot, C. S. Dweck, & D. S. Yeager (Eds.), *Handbook of competence and motivation: Theory and application* (pp. 387–407). Guilford.

Cimpian, A., Arce, H.-M. C., Markman, E. M., & Dweck, C. S. (2007). Subtle linguistic cues affect children's motivation. *Psychological Science, 18*(4), 314–316. https://doi.org/10.1111/j.1467-9280.2007.01896.x

Cimpian, A., Hammond, M. D., Mazza, G., & Corry, G. (2017). Young children's self-concepts include representations of abstract traits and the global self. *Child Development, 88*(6), 1786–1798. https://doi.org/10.1111/cdev.12925

CIRCLE. (2018). *So much for "slacktivism": Youth translate online engagement to offline political action* (CIRCLE / Tisch College 2018 Pre-Election Youth Poll). Tufts University.

CIRCLE. (2021, April 29). *Half of youth voted in 2020, an 11-point increase from 2016.* https://circle.tufts.edu/latest-research/half-youth-voted-2020-11-point-increase-2016

Ciscato, E., Galichon, A., & Goussé, M. (2020). Like attract like? A structural comparison of homogamy across same-sex and different-sex households. *Journal of Political Economy, 128*(2), 740–781. https://doi.org/10.1086/704611

Clark, C. A., Sheffield, T. D., Wiebe, S. A., & Espy, K. A. (2013). Longitudinal associations between executive control and developing mathematical competence in preschool boys and girls. *Child Development, 84*(2), 662–677.

Clark, H., Coll-Seck, A. M., Banerjee, A., Peterson, S., Dalglish, S. L., Ameratunga, S., Balabnova, D., Bhan, M. K., Bhutta, Z. A., Borrazzo, J., Claeson, M., Doherty, T., El-Jardali, F., George, A. S., Gichaga, A., Gram, L., Hipgrave, D. B., Kwamie, A., Meng, Q., . . . Costello, A. (2020). A future for the world's children? A WHO–UNICEF–Lancet Commission. *The Lancet, 395*(10224), 605–658.

Clark, K. B., & Clark, M. K. (1939). The development of consciousness of self and the emergence of racial identification in Negro preschool children. *The Journal of Social Psychology, 10*(4), 591–599. https://doi.org/10.1080/00224545.1939.9713394

Clark, K. B., & Clark, M. K. (1940). Skin color as a factor in racial identification of Negro preschool children. *The Journal of Social Psychology, 11* (1), 159–169. https://doi.org/10.1080/00224545.1940.9918741

Clark, S. E., Bledsoe, M. C., & Harrison, C. J. (2022). The role of social media in promoting vaccine hesitancy. *Current opinion in pediatrics, 34*(2), 156–162.

Clarke, A. J., & Wallgren-Pettersson, C. (2019). Ethics in genetic counselling. *Journal of Community Genetics, 10*(1), 3–33. https://doi.org/10.1007/s12687-018-0371-7

Clark-Gambelunghe, M. B., & Clark, D. A. (2015). Sensory development. *Pediatric Clinics, 62*(2), 367–384.

Claro, S., Paunesku, D., & Dweck, C. S. (2016). Growth mindset tempers the effects of poverty on academic achievement. *Proceedings of the National Academy of Sciences, 113*(31), 8664–8668.

Clausen, J. S. (1991). Adolescent competence and the shaping of the life course. *American Journal of Sociology, 96*(4), 805–842.

Clearfield, M. W., & Jedd, K. E. (2013). The effects of socio-economic status on infant attention. *Infant and Child Development, 22*(1), 53–67. https://doi.org/10.1002/icd.1770

Clemans-Cope, L., Lynch, V., Epstein, M., & Kenney, G. M. (2019). Opioid and substance use disorder and receipt of treatment among parents living with children in the United States, 2015–2017. *The Annals of Family Medicine, 17*(3), 207–211. https://doi.org/10.1370/afm.2389

Clements, D. H. (1984). Training effects on the development and generalization of Piagetian logical operations and knowledge of number. *Journal of Educational Psychology, 76*(5), 766.

Cloninger, C. R., Cloninger, K. M., Zwir, I., & Keltikangas-Järvinen, L. (2019). The complex genetics and biology of human temperament: A review of traditional concepts in relation to new molecular findings. *Translational Psychiatry, 9*(1), 1–21. https://doi.org/10.1038/s41398-019-0621-4

Coast, E., Lattof, S. R., & Strong, J. (2019). Puberty and menstruation knowledge among young adolescents in low- and middle-income countries: A scoping review. *International Journal of Public Health, 64*(2), 293–304. https://doi.org/10.1007/s00038-019-01209-0

Cobb, C. L., Branscombe, N. R., Meca, A., Schwartz, S. J., Xie, D., Zea, M. C., Molina, L. E, & Martinez Jr., C. R. (2019). Toward a positive psychology of immigrants. *Perspectives on Psychological Science, 14*(4), 619–632.

Cobbinah, S. S., & Lewis, J. (2018). Racism & health: A public health perspective on racial discrimination. *Journal of Evaluation in Clinical Practice, 24*(5), 995–998. https://doi.org/10.1111/jep.12894

Coffey, J. K., Xia, M., & Fosco, G. M. (2020). When do adolescents feel loved? A daily within-person study of parent–adolescent relations. *Emotion.* https://doi.org/10.1037/emo0000767

Cohee, L. M., Opondo, C., Clarke, S. E., Halliday, K. E., Cano, J., Shipper, A. G., Barger-Kamate, B., Djimde, A., Diarra, S., Dokras, A., Kamya, M. R., Lutumba, P., Ly, A. B., Nankabirwa, J. I., Njagi, J. K., Maiga, H., Maiteki-Sebuguzi, C., Matangila, J., Okello, G., . . . Chico, R. M. (2020). Preventive malaria treatment among school-aged children in sub-Saharan Africa: A systematic review and meta-analyses. *The Lancet Global Health, 8*(12), e1499–e1511.

Cohen, G. L., Garcia, J., Apfel, N., & Master, A. (2006). A self-affirmation intervention to reduce the racial achievement gap. *Science, 313*, 1307–1310.

Cohen, G. L., Garcia, J., Purdie-Vaughns, V., Apfel, N., & Brzustoski, P. (2009). Recursive processes in self-affirmation: Intervening to close the minority achievement gap. *Science, 324*(5925), 400–403. https://doi.org/10.1126/science.1170769

Cohen, G. L., & Sherman, D. K. (2014). The psychology of change: Self-affirmation and social psychological intervention. *Annual Review of Psychology, 65*, 333–371.

Cohen, J. F., Richardson, S. A., Cluggish, S. A., Parker, E., Catalano, P. J., & Rimm, E. B. (2015). Effects of choice architecture and chef-enhanced meals on the selection and consumption of healthier school foods: A randomized clinical trial. *JAMA Pediatrics, 169*(5), 431–437.

Cohen, J. S., Donnelly, K., Patel, S. J., Badolato, G. M., Boyle, M. D., McCarter, R., & Goyal, M. K. (2021). Firearms injuries involving young children in the United States during the COVID-19 pandemic. *Pediatrics, 148*(1), e2020042697. https://doi.org/10.1542/peds.2020-042697

Cohen, S., Chiang, J. J., Janicki-Deverts, D., & Miller, G. E. (2020). Good relationships with parents during childhood as buffers of the association between childhood disadvantage and adult susceptibility to the common cold. *Psychosomatic Medicine, 82*(6), 538–547. https://doi.org/10.1097/PSY.0000000000000818

Cohodes, E. M., Kitt, E. R., Baskin-Sommers, A., & Gee, D. G. (2021). Influences of early-life stress on frontolimbic circuitry: Harnessing a dimensional approach to elucidate the effects of heterogeneity in stress exposure. *Developmental Psychobiology, 63*(2), 153–172. https://doi.org/10.1002/dev.21969

Cohodes, S. R. (2020). The long-run impacts of specialized programming for high-achieving students. *American Economic Journal: Economic Policy, 12*(1), 127–166. https://doi.org/10.1257/pol.20180315

Coker, D. L., Jr., & Kim, Y. S. G. (2018). Critical issues in the understanding of young elementary school students at risk for problems in written expression: Introduction to the special series. *Journal of Learning Disabilities, 51*(4), 315–319.

Colbert, D., Tyndall, I., Roche, B., & Cassidy, S. (2018). Can SMART training really increase intelligence? A replication study. *Journal of Behavioral Education, 27*(4), 509–531. https://doi.org/10.1007/s10864-018-9302-2

Cole, M. (1990). Cognitive development and formal schooling: The evidence from cross-cultural research. In L. C. Moll (Ed.), *Vygotsky and education: Instructional implications and applications of sociohistorical psychology* (pp. 89–110). Cambridge University Press.

Cole, M. (2017). Idiocultural design as a tool of cultural psychology. *Perspectives on Psychological Science, 12*(5), 772–781. https://doi.org/10.1177/1745691617708623

Cole, M. (2018). Special section: Luria's legacy in cultural-historical psychology. *Psychology in Russia: State of the Art, 2.*

Cole, M., & Packer, M. (2016). A bio-cultural-historical approach to the study of development. In M. J. Gelfand, C. Chiu, & Y. Hong (Eds.), *Handbook of advances in culture and psychology* (Vol. 6, pp. 1–76). Oxford University Press. https://doi.org/10.1093/acprof:oso/9780190458850.003.0001

Cole, P. M., & Jacobs, A. E. (2018). From children's expressive control to emotion regulation: Looking back, looking ahead. *The European Journal of Developmental Psychology, 15*(6), 658–677. https://doi.org/10.1080/17405629.2018.1438888

Cole, P. M., Tamang, B. L., & Shrestha, S. (2006). Cultural variations in the socialization of young children's anger and shame. *Child Development, 77*(5), 1237–1251.

Coleman-Jensen, A., Rabbitt, M. P., Gregory, C. A., & Singh, A. (2019). *Household food security in the United States in 2018.* USDA. http://www.ers.usda.gov/publications/pub-details/?pubid=94848

Colich, N. L., Rosen, M. L., Williams, E. S., & McLaughlin, K. A. (2020). Biological aging in childhood and adolescence following experiences of threat and deprivation: A systematic review and meta-analysis. *Psychological Bulletin, 146*(9), 721–764. https://doi.org/10.1037/bul0000270

Collado, S., & Staats, H. (2016). Contact with nature and children's restorative experiences: An eye to the future. *Frontiers in Psychology, 7*, 1885.

College Board. (2022). *AP Program Results: Class of 2021.* https://reports.collegeboard.org/ap-program-results/2021

Collibee, C., & Furman, W. (2014). Impact of sexual coercion on romantic experiences of adolescents and young adults. *Archives of Sexual Behavior, 43*(7), 1431–1441.

Collier, K. M., Coyne, S. M., Rasmussen, E. E., Hawkins, A. J., Padilla-Walker, L. M., Erickson, S. E., & Memmott-Elison, M. K. (2016). Does parental mediation of media influence child outcomes? A meta-analysis on media time, aggression, substance use, and sexual behavior. *Developmental Psychology, 52*(5), 798.

Collier, V. P., & Thomas, W. P. (2017). Validating the power of bilingual schooling: Thirty-two years of large-scale, longitudinal research. *Annual Review of Applied Linguistics, 37*, 203–217.

Collins, F. S. (2006). *The language of God: A scientist presents evidence for belief.* Simon & Schuster.

Collins, F. S., & Mansoura, M. K. (2001). The Human Genome Project. *Cancer, 91*(S1), 221–225. https://doi.org/10.1002/1097-0142(20010101)91:1+<221::AID-CNCR8>3.0.CO;2-9

Collins, N., & Roth, T. L. (2021). Chapter 7 — Intergenerational transmission of stress-related epigenetic regulation. In L. Provenzi & R. Montirosso (Eds.), *Developmental human behavioral epigenetics* (Vol. 23, pp. 119–141). Academic Press. https://doi.org/10.1016/B978-0-12-819262-7.00007-6

Collins, R. L., Strasburger, V. C., Brown, J. D., Donnerstein, E., Lenhart, A., & Ward, L. M. (2017). Sexual media and childhood well-being and health. *Pediatrics, 140*(Supplement 2), S162–S166. https://doi.org/10.1542/peds.2016-1758X

Collins, W. A., & Madsen, S. D. (2019). Parenting during middle childhood. In M. H. Bornstein (Ed.), *Handbook of parenting: Children and parenting* (3rd ed., Vol. 1, pp. 81–110). Routledge.

Collombet, S., Ranisavljevic, N., Nagano, T., Varnai, C., Shisode, T., Leung, W., Piolot, T., Galupa, R., Borensztein, M., Servant, N., Fraser, P., Ancelin, K., & Heard, E. (2020). Parental-to-embryo switch of chromosome organization in early embryogenesis. *Nature, 580*(7801), 142–146. https://doi.org/10.1038/s41586-020-2125-z

Colonnesi, C., Nikolić, M., & Bögels, S. M. (2020). Development and psychophysiological correlates of positive shyness from infancy to childhood. In L. A. Schmidt & K. L. Poole (Eds.), *Adaptive shyness: Multiple perspectives on behavior and development* (pp. 41–61). Springer International Publishing. https://doi.org/10.1007/978-3-030-38877-5_3

Committee on Hospital Care and Child Life Council. (2014). Child life services. *Pediatrics, 133*(5), e1471–e1478. https://doi.org/10.1542/peds.2014-0556 (Reprinted February 2018).

Committee on Practice and Ambulatory Medicine, Hackell, J. M., Abularrage, J. J., Almendarez, Y. M., Boudreau, A. D. A., Berhane, A. M., Cantrell, P. E., Kafer, L. M., Schafer, K. S., Skatrud, A., Warner, R., Hagan, J. F. Jr., Kemper, A. R., & Shaw, J. S. (2021). 2021 Recommendations for Preventive Pediatric Health Care. *Pediatrics, 147*(3). https://doi.org/10.1542/peds.2020-049776

Commons, M. L., & Davidson, M. N. (2015). The sufficiency of reinforcing problem solutions for transition to the formal stage. *Behavioral Development Bulletin, 20*(1), 114–130. https://doi.org/10.1037/h0101033

Compagnoni, M., & Losenno, K. M. (2020). "I'm the best! Or am I?": Academic self-concepts and self-regulation in kindergarten. *Frontline Learning Research, 8*(2), 131–152.

Condry, R., & Miles, C. (2014). Adolescent to parent violence: Framing and mapping a hidden problem. *Criminology & Criminal Justice, 14*(3), 257–275. https://doi.org/10.1177/1748895813500155

Conduct Problems Prevention Research Group. (2011). The effects of the Fast Track preventive intervention on the development of conduct disorder across childhood. *Child Development, 82*(1), 331–345.

Conger, R. D., Martin, M. J., & Masarik, A. S. (2021). Dynamic associations among socioeconomic status (SES), parenting investments, and conscientiousness across time and generations. *Developmental Psychology, 57*(2), 147–163. https://doi.org/10.1037/dev0000463

Conley, M. I., Hindley, I., Baskin-Sommers, A., Gee, D. G., Casey, B. J., & Rosenberg, M. D. (2020). The importance of social factors in the association between physical activity and depression in children. *Child and Adolescent Psychiatry and Mental Health, 14*(1), 1–15.

Conley, T., Mehta, N., Stinebrickner, R., & Stinebrickner, T. (2015). *Social interactions, mechanisms, and equilibrium: Evidence from a model of study time and academic achievement* (No. w21418). National Bureau of Economic Research.

Conn, B. M., de Figueiredo, S., Sherer, S., Mankerian, M., & Iverson, E. (2018). "Our lives aren't over": A strengths-based perspective on stigma, discrimination, and coping among young parents. *Journal of Adolescence, 66*, 91–100. https://doi.org/10.1016/j.adolescence.2018.05.005

Connolly, J., & McDonald, K. P. (2020). Cross-cultural perspectives on dating and marriage. In S. Hupp & J. D. Jewell (Eds.), *The encyclopedia of child and adolescent development* (pp. 1–13). American Cancer Society. https://doi.org/10.1002/9781119171492.wecad486

Connor, C. (2016). Using cognitive development research to inform literacy instruction and improve practice in the classroom. In C. M. Connor (Ed.), *The cognitive development of reading and reading comprehension* (pp. 166–185). Routledge.

Connor, C. M., Morrison, F. J., Fishman, B., Crowe, E. C., Al Otaiba, S., & Schatschneider, C. (2013). A longitudinal cluster-randomized controlled study on the accumulating effects of individualized literacy instruction on students' reading from first through third grade. *Psychological Science, 24*(8), 1408.

Conradt, E. (2017). Using principles of behavioral epigenetics to advance research on early-life stress. *Child Development Perspectives, 11*(2), 107–112. https://doi.org/10.1111/cdep.12219

Conte, E., Grazzani, I., & Pepe, A. (2018). Social cognition, language, and prosocial behaviors: A multitrait mixed-methods study in early childhood. *Early Education and Development, 29*(6), 814–830.

Cook, C. J., Howard, S. J., Scerif, G., Twine, R., Kahn, K., Norris, S. A., & Draper, C. E. (2019). Associations of physical activity and gross motor skills with executive function in preschool children from low-income South African settings. *Developmental Science, 22*(5), e12820. https://doi.org/10.1111/desc.12820

Cook, J. E., Purdie-Vaughns, V., Garcia, J., & Cohen, G. L. (2012). Chronic threat and contingent belonging: protective benefits of values affirmation on identity development. *Journal of Personality and Social Psychology, 102*(3), 479.

Cooley, S., Burkholder, A. R., & Killen, M. (2019). Social inclusion and exclusion in same-race and interracial peer encounters. *Developmental Psychology, 55*(11), 2440–2450. https://doi.org/10.1037/dev0000810

Coontz, S. (2016). *The social origins of private life: A history of American families, 1600–1900.* Verso Books.

Cooper, S. M., Hurd, N., & Loyd, A. B. (2022). Advancing scholarship on anti-racism within developmental science. *Child Development.* https://doi.org/10.1111/cdev.13783

Copeland, W. E., Angold, A., Costello, E. J., & Egger, H. (2013). Prevalence, comorbidity, and correlates of

DSM-5 proposed disruptive mood dysregulation disorder. *American Journal of Psychiatry, 170*(2), 173–179. https://doi.org/10.1176/appi.ajp.2012.12010132

Copeland, W. E., Shanahan, L., Hinesley, J., Chan, R. F., Aberg, K. A., Fairbank, J. A., van den Oord, E. J. C. G., & Costello, E. J. (2018). Association of childhood trauma exposure with adult psychiatric disorders and functional outcomes. *JAMA Network Open, 1*(7), e184493–e184493. https://doi.org/10.1001/jamanetworkopen.2018.4493

Copeland, W. E., Tong, G., Gaydosh, L., Hill, S. N., Godwin, J., Shanahan, L., & Costello, E. J. (2022). Long-term outcomes of childhood family income supplements on adult functioning. *JAMA Pediatrics, 176*(10), 1020–1026..

Copen, C. E., Thoma, M. E., Kirmeyer, S. (2015). Interpregnancy intervals in the United States: Data from the birth certificate and the national survey of family growth. *National Vital Statistics Reports, 64*, 1–10.

Coplan, R. J., Rubin, K. H., & Findlay, L. C. (2006). Social and nonsocial play. In D. P. Fromberg & D. Bergen (Eds.), *Play from birth to twelve: Contexts, perspectives, and meanings* (pp. 75–86). Routledge.

Coppens, A. D., Alcalá, L., Rogoff, B., & Mejía-Arauz, R. (2018). Children's contributions in family work: Two cultural paradigms. In S. Punch & R. M. Vanderbeck (Eds.), *Families, intergenerationality, and peer group relations* (pp. 187–213). Springer Singapore. https://doi.org/10.1007/978-981-287-026-1_11

Corapci, F., Friedlmeier, W., Benga, O., Strauss, C., Pitica, I., & Susa, G. (2018). Cultural socialization of toddlers in emotionally charged situations. *Social Development, 27*(2), 262–278. https://doi.org/10.1111/sode.12272

Corballis, M. C. (2019). Chapter 7 — Evolution of cerebral asymmetry. In M. A. Hofman (Ed.), *Progress in brain research* (Vol. 250, pp. 153–178). Elsevier. https://doi.org/10.1016/bs.pbr.2019.04.041

Cornell, D., Shukla, K., & Konold, T. (2015). Peer victimization and authoritative school climate: A multilevel approach. *Journal of Educational Psychology, 107*(4), 1186–1201. https://doi.org/10.1037/edu0000038

Cornwell, T. B., Setten, E., Paik, S.-H. W., & Pappu, R. (2020). Parents, products, and the development of preferences: Child palate and food choice in an obesogenic environment. *Journal of Public Policy & Marketing, 40*(3), 429–446. https://doi.org/10.1177/0743915620939581.

Corporation for National and Community Service (CNCS). (2018). *Volunteering in America.*

Corrigan, N. M., Yarnykh, V. L., Hippe, D. S., Owen, J. P., Huber, E., Zhao, T. C., & Kuhl, P. K. (2021). Myelin development in cerebral gray and white matter during adolescence and late childhood. *NeuroImage, 227*, 117678. https://doi.org/10.1016/j.neuroimage.2020.117678

Corsaro, W. A. (2017). *The sociology of childhood.* Sage.

Corsi, D. J., Donelle, J., Sucha, E., Hawken, S., Hsu, H., El-Chaâr, D., Bisnaire, L., Fell, D., Wen, S. W., & Walker, M. (2020). Maternal cannabis use in pregnancy and child neurodevelopmental outcomes. *Nature Medicine, 26*(10), 1536–1540. https://doi.org/10.1038/s41591-020-1002-5

Costa, L. G., Cole, T. B., Dao, K., Chang, Y.-C., Coburn, J., & Garrick, J. M. (2020). Effects of air pollution on the nervous system and its possible role in neurodevelopmental and neurodegenerative disorders. *Pharmacology & Therapeutics, 210*, 107523. https://doi.org/10.1016/j.pharmthera.2020.107523

Costello, E. J. (2016). Early detection and prevention of mental health problems: Developmental epidemiology and systems of support. *Journal of Clinical Child & Adolescent Psychology, 45*(6), 710–717. https://doi.org/10.1080/15374416.2016.1236728

Costello, E. J., Compton, S. N., Keeler, G., & Angold, A. (2003). Relationships between poverty and psychopathology: A natural experiment. *JAMA, 290*(15), 2023–2029.

Costello, E. J., Copeland, W., & Angold, A. (2011). Trends in psychopathology across the adolescent years: What changes when children become adolescents, and when adolescents become adults? *Journal of Child Psychology and Psychiatry, and Allied Disciplines, 52*(10), 1015–1025. https://doi.org/10.1111/j.1469-7610.2011.02446.x

Costello, E. J., Egger, H., & Angold, A. (2005). 10-year research update review: The epidemiology of child and adolescent psychiatric disorders: I. Methods and public health burden. *Journal of the American Academy of Child and Adolescent Psychiatry, 44*(10), 972–986. https://doi.org/10.1097/01.chi.0000172552.41596.6f

Costello, M. A., Narr, R. K., Tan, J. S., & Allen, J. P. (2020). The intensity effect in adolescent close friendships: Implications for aggressive and depressive symptomatology. *Journal of Research on Adolescence, 30*(1), 158–169. https://doi.org/10.1111/jora.12508

Côté, J. E. (2014). The dangerous myth of emerging adulthood: An evidence-based critique of a flawed developmental theory. *Applied Developmental Science, 18*(4), 177–188. https://doi.org/10.1080/10888691.2014.954451

Côté, J. E. (2018a). The enduring usefulness of Erikson's concept of the identity crisis in the 21st century: An analysis of student mental health concerns. *Identity, 18*(4), 251–263.

Côté, J. E. (2018b). *Youth development in identity societies: Paradoxes of purpose.* Routledge. https://doi.org/10.4324/9780429433856

Côté, J. E. (2019). *Youth development in identity societies: Paradoxes of purpose.* Routledge.

Côté, S., Vaillancourt, T., LeBlanc, J. C., Nagin, D. S., & Tremblay, R. E. (2006). The development of physical aggression from toddlerhood to pre-adolescence: A nation wide longitudinal study of Canadian children. *Journal of Abnormal Child Psychology, 34*(1), 68–82. https://doi.org/10.1007/s10802-005-9001-z

Council on School Health, Murray, R., Ramstetter, C., Devore, C., Allison, M., Ancona, R., Barnett, S., Gunther, R., Holman, B. W., Lamont, J., Minier, M., Okamoto, J., Wheeler, L., & Young, T. (2013). The crucial role of recess in school. *Pediatrics, 131*(1), 183–188.

Cover Jones, M. (1924). A laboratory study of fear: The case of Peter. *The Journal of Genetic Psychology, 31*, 308—315.

Covington, L. B., Rogers, V. E., Armstrong, B., Storr, C. L., & Black, M. M. (2019). Toddler bedtime routines and associations with nighttime sleep duration and maternal and household factors. *Journal of Clinical Sleep Medicine, 15*(6), 865–871. https://doi.org/10.5664/jcsm.7838

Cowell, J. M., & Decety, J. (2015). Precursors to morality in development as a complex interplay between neural, socioenvironmental, and behavioral facets. *Proceedings of the National Academy of Sciences, 112*(41), 12657–12662. https://doi.org/10.1073/pnas.1508832112

Cowell, J. M., Lee, K., Malcolm-Smith, S., Selcuk, B., Zhou, X., & Decety, J. (2017). The development of generosity and moral cognition across five cultures. *Developmental Science, 20*(4), e12403. https://doi.org/10.1111/desc.12403

Cowell, W., Tang, D., Yu, J., Guo, J., Wang, S., Baccarelli, A. A., Perera, F., & Herbstman, J. B. (2021). Telomere dynamics across the early life course: Findings from a longitudinal study in children. *Psychoneuroendocrinology, 129*, 105270. https://doi.org/10.1016/j.psyneuen.2021.105270

Coyle, E. F., Fulcher, M., & Trübutschek, D. (2016). Sissies, mama's boys, and tomboys: Is children's gender nonconformity more acceptable when nonconforming traits are positive? *Archives of Sexual Behavior, 45*(7), 1827–1838.

Coyne, S. M., Linder, J. R., Rasmussen, E. E., Nelson, D. A., & Birkbeck, V. (2016). Pretty as a princess: Longitudinal effects of engagement with Disney Princesses on gender stereotypes, body esteem, and prosocial behavior in children. *Child Development, 87*(6), 1909–1925. https://doi.org/10.1111/cdev.12569

Coyne, S. M., Linder, J. R., Rasmussen, E. E., Nelson, D. A., & Collier, K. M. (2014). It's a bird! It's a plane! It's a gender stereotype!: Longitudinal associations between superhero viewing and gender stereotyped play. *Sex Roles, 70*(9), 416–430. https://doi.org/10.1007/s11199-014-0374-8

Coyne, S. M., Ward, L. M., Kroff, S. L., Davis, E. J., Holmgren, H. G., Jensen, A. C., Erickson, S. E., & Essig, L. W. (2019). Contributions of mainstream sexual media exposure to sexual attitudes, perceived peer norms, and sexual behavior: A meta-analysis. *Journal of Adolescent Health, 64*(4), 430–436. https://doi.org/10.1016/j.jadohealth.2018.11.016

Crabbe, R., Pivnick, L. K., Bates, J., Gordon, R. A., & Crosnoe, R. (2019). Contemporary college students' reflections on their high school peer crowds. *Journal of Adolescent Research, 34*(5), 563–596. https://doi.org/10.1177/0743558418809537

Craig, A. T., Heywood, A. E., & Worth, H. (2020). Measles epidemic in Samoa and other Pacific islands. *The Lancet Infectious Diseases, 20*(3), 273–275.

Craig, L., Churchill, B., & van Tienoven, T. P. (2019). Young people's daily activity in a globalized world: A cross-national comparison using time use data. *Journal of Youth Studies, 23*, 1–22. https://doi.org/10.1080/13676261.2019.1659941

Crawford, S., Hadley, D., & Shepherd, G. (2018). *The Oxford handbook of the archaeology of childhood.* Oxford University Press.

Crenshaw, K. (1989). Demarginalizing the intersection of race and sex: A Black feminist critique of antidiscrimination doctrine, feminist theory and antiracist politics. *University of Chicago Legal Forum, 1989*, 139.

Crews, F. (2017). *Freud: The making of an illusion.* Metropolitan Books.

Crick, N. R., & Grotpeter, J. K. (1996). Children's treatment by peers: Victims of relational and overt aggression. *Development and Psychopathology, 8*(2), 367–380.

Cristia, A., Dupoux, E., Gurven, M., & Stieglitz, J. (2019). Child-directed speech is infrequent in a forager-farmer population: A time allocation study. *Child Development, 90*(3), 759–773. https://doi.org/10.1111/cdev.12974

Crocetti, E. (2017). Identity formation in adolescence: The dynamic of forming and consolidating identity commitments. *Child Development Perspectives, 11*(2), 145–150. https://doi.org/10.1111/cdep.12226

Crocker, M. K., Stern, E. A., Sedaka, N. M., Shomaker, L. B., Brady, S. M., Ali, A. H., Shawker, T. H., Hubbard, V. S., & Yanovski, J. A. (2014). Sexual dimorphisms in the associations of BMI and body fat with indices of pubertal development in girls and boys. *The Journal of Clinical Endocrinology & Metabolism, 99*(8), E1519–E1529.

Crone, E. A., & Dahl, R. E. (2012). Understanding adolescence as a period of social–affective engagement and goal flexibility. *Nature Reviews Neuroscience, 13*(9), 636–650. https://doi.org/10.1038/nrn3313

Crone, E. A., & Fuligni, A. J. (2020). Self and others in adolescence. *Annual Review of Psychology, 71*(1), 447–469. https://doi.org/10.1146/annurev-psych-010419-050937

Crone, E. A., & Konijn, E. A. (2018). Media use and brain development during adolescence. *Nature Communications, 9*(1), 588. https://doi.org/10.1038/s41467-018-03126-x

Crosnoe, R. (2012). *Fitting in, standing out: Navigating the social challenges of high school to get an education.* Cambridge University Press.

Crosnoe, R., & Benner, A. D. (2016). Educational pathways. In *Handbook of the life course* (pp. 179–200). Springer, Cham.

Crosnoe, R., & Muller, C. (2014). Family socioeconomic status, peers, and the path to college. *Social Problems, 61*(4), 602–624. https://doi.org/10.1525/sp.2014.12255

Crosnoe, R., Purtell, K. M., Davis-Kean, P., Ansari, A., & Benner, A. D. (2016). The selection of children from low-income families into preschool. *Developmental Psychology, 52*(4), 599–612. https://doi.org/10.1037/dev0000101

Cross, C. J., Fomby, P., & Letiecq, B. (2022). Interlinking structural racism and heteropatriarchy: Rethinking family structure's effects on child outcomes in a racialized, unequal society. *Journal of Family Theory & Review.* https://doi.org/10.1111/jftr.12458

Cross, F. L., Agi, A., Montoro, J. P., Medina, M. A., Miller-Tejada, S., Pinetta, B. J., Tran-Dubongco, M., & Rivas-Drake, D. (2020). Illuminating ethnic-racial socialization among undocumented Latinx parents and its implications for adolescent psychosocial functioning. *Developmental Psychology, 56*(8), 1458–1474. https://doi.org/10.1037/dev0000826

Crouch, E., Probst, J. C., Radcliff, E., Bennett, K. J., & McKinney, S. H. (2019). Prevalence of adverse childhood experiences (ACEs) among US children. *Child Abuse & Neglect, 92*, 209–218.

Crouch, J. L., Irwin, L. M., Milner, J. S., Skowronski, J. J., Rutledge, E., & Davila, A. L. (2017). Do hostile attributions and negative affect explain the association between authoritarian beliefs and harsh parenting? *Child Abuse & Neglect, 67*, 13–21. https://doi.org/10.1016/j.chiabu.2017.02.019

Crowley, S. J., Wolfson, A. R., Tarokh, L., & Carskadon, M. A. (2018). An update on adolescent sleep: New evidence informing the perfect storm model. *Journal of Adolescence, 67*, 55–65.

Crump, C., & Howell, E. A. (2020). Perinatal origins of cardiovascular health disparities across the life course. *JAMA Pediatrics, 174*(2), 113–114. https://doi.org/10.1001/jamapediatrics.2019.4616

CS Mott Children's Hospital. (2017). *Parents struggle with when to keep sick kids home from school* (National Poll on Children's Health, Vol. 28, Issue 3). https://mottpoll.org/reports-surveys/parents-struggle-when-keep-sick-kids-home-school

Cuartas, J., Jeong, J., Rey-Guerra, C., McCoy, D. C., & Yoshikawa, H. (2020). Maternal, paternal, and other caregivers' stimulation in low- and- middle-income countries. *PLOS One, 15*(7), e0236107. https://doi.org/10.1371/journal.pone.0236107

Cuevas, K., & Sheya, A. (2019). Ontogenesis of learning and memory: Biopsychosocial and dynamical systems perspectives. *Developmental Psychobiology, 61*(3), 402–415. https://doi.org/10.1002/dev.21817

Culatta, E., & Clay-Warner, J. (2021). Falling behind and feeling bad: Unmet expectations and mental health during the transition to adulthood. *Society and Mental Health.* https://doi.org/10.1177/2156869321991892

Culbert, K. M., Racine, S. E., & Klump, K. L. (2015). Research review: What we have learned about the causes of eating disorders — a synthesis of sociocultural, psychological, and biological research. *Journal of Child Psychology and Psychiatry, 56*(11), 1141–1164. https://doi.org/10.1111/jcpp.12441

Cullen, J. B., Levitt, S. D., Robertson, E., & Sadoff, S. (2013). What can be done to improve struggling high schools? *The Journal of Economic Perspectives, 27*(2), 133–152. http://www.ingentaconnect.com/contentone/aea/jep/2013/00000027/00000002/art00007

Cummings, K. J., & Leiter, J. C. (2019). Take a deep breath and wake up: The protean role of serotonin in preventing sudden death in infancy. *Experimental Neurology, 326*, 113165. https://doi.org/10.1016/j.expneurol.2019.113165

Cummins, J. (1984). Wanted: A theoretical framework for relating language proficiency to academic achievement among bilingual students.. *Selected Papers of the Language Proficiency Assessment Symposium,* Warrenton, VA, March 14–18,Vol. 400, p. 21.

Cunningham, R. M., Walton, M. A., & Carter, P. M. (2018). The major causes of death in children and adolescents in the United States. *New England Journal of Medicine, 379*(25), 2468–2475. https://doi.org/10.1056/NEJMsr1804754

Current Population Survey Annual Social and Economic Supplement (CPS). (2021). *America's families and living arrangements: 2017.* Table C1. Household relationships and family status of children under 18 years, by age and sex: 2019. U.S. Census Bureau.

Currie, C., Zanotti, C., Morgan, A., Currie, D., De Looze, M., Roberts, C., Samdal, O., Smith, O. R. F., & Barnekow, V. (2012). *Social determinants of health and well-being among young people. Health behaviour in school-aged children (HBSC) study: International report from the 2009/2010 survey* (Health Policy for Children and Adolescents). WHO Regional Office for Europe.

Curtin, S. C., & Heron, M. P. (2019, October). Death rates due to suicide and homicide among persons aged 10–24: United States, 2000–2017. *NCHS Data Briefing, 352*, 1–8.

Curtis, K., Zhou, Q., & Tao, A. (2020). Emotion talk in Chinese American immigrant families and longitudinal links to children's socioemotional competence. *Developmental Psychology, 56*(3), 475–488. https://doi.org/10.1037/dev0000806

Cutler, G. J., Bergmann, K. R., Doupnik, S. K., Hoffmann, J. A., Neuman, M. I., Rodean, J., Zagel, A. L., & & Zima, B. T. (2022). Pediatric mental health emergency department visits and access to inpatient care: A crisis worsened by the CoViD-19 pandemic. *Academic Pediatrics, 22*(6), 889–891.

Cvencek, D., Nasir, N. I. S., O'Connor, K., Wischnia, S., & Meltzoff, A. N. (2015). The development of math–race stereotypes: "They say Chinese people are the best at math." *Journal of Research on Adolescence, 25*(4), 630–637.

Cychosz, M., Cristia, A., Bergelson, E., Casillas, M., Baudet, G., Warlaumont, A. S., & Seidl, A. (2020). Canonical babble development in a large-scale crosslinguistic corpus. *PsyArXiv.*

D'Ambrosio, C., Jantti, M., & Lepinteur, A. (2020). Money and happiness: Income, wealth and subjective well-being. *Social Indicators Research, 148*(1), 47–66. https://doi.org/10.1007/s11205-019-02186-w

D'Amen, B., Socci, M., & Santini, S. (2021). Intergenerational caring: A systematic literature review on young and young adult caregivers of older people. *BMC Geriatrics, 21*(1), 105. https://doi.org/10.1186/s12877-020-01976-z

D'hondt, F., Maene, C., Vervaet, R., Van Houtte, M., & Stevens, P. A. (2021). Ethnic discrimination in secondary education: Does the solution lie in multicultural education and the ethnic school composition? *Social Psychology of Education,* 1–28.

Da Costa, D., Danieli, C., Abrahamowicz, M., Dasgupta, K., Sewitch, M., Lowensteyn, I., & Zelkowitz, P. (2019). A prospective study of postnatal depressive symptoms and associated risk factors in first-time fathers. *Journal of Affective Disorders, 249*, 371–377. https://doi.org/10.1016/j.jad.2019.02.033

Dabach, D. B., Suárez-Orozco, C., Hernandez, S. J., & Brooks, M. D. (2018). Future perfect?: Teachers' expectations and explanations of their Latino immigrant students' postsecondary futures. *Journal of Latinos and Education, 17*(1), 38–52. https://doi.org/10.1080/15348431.2017.1281809

Dagan, O., & Sagi-Schwartz, A. (2018). Early attachment network with mother and father: An unsettled issue. *Child Development Perspectives, 12*(2), 115–121. https://doi.org/10.1111/cdep.12272

Dahl, A. (2015). The developing social context of infant helping in two U.S. samples. *Child Development, 86*(4), 1080–1093. https://doi.org/10.1111/cdev.12361

Dahl, A. (2016). Infants' unprovoked acts of force toward others. *Developmental Science, 19*(6), 1049–1057.

Dahl, A. (2017). Ecological commitments: Why developmental science needs naturalistic methods. *Child Development Perspectives, 11*(2), 79–84. https://doi.org/10.1111/cdep.12217

Dahl, A. (2019). The science of early moral development: On defining, constructing, and studying morality from birth. In J. B. Benson (Ed.), *Advances in child development and behavior* (Vol. 56, pp. 1–35). JAI. https://doi.org/10.1016/bs.acdb.2018.11.001

Dahl, A., & Brownell, C. A. (2019). The social origins of human prosociality. *Current Directions in Psychological Science, 28*(3), 274–279. https://doi.org/10.1177/0963721419830386

Dahl, A., & Killen, M. (2018). Moral reasoning: Theory and research in developmental science. In E. A. Phelps & L. Davachi (Vol. Eds.), *Stevens' handbook of experimental psychology and cognitive neuroscience* (Vol. 4, pp. 323–353). Wiley New York.

Dahl, A., & Kim, L. (2014). Why is it bad to make a mess? Preschoolers' conceptions of pragmatic norms. *Cognitive Development, 32*, 12–22.

Dai, J., & Scherf, K. S. (2019). Puberty and functional brain development in humans: Convergence in findings? *Developmental Cognitive Neuroscience, 39*, 100690.

Dai, X., Müller, H.-G., Wang, J.-L., & Deoni, S. C. (2019). Age-dynamic networks and functional correlation for early white matter myelination. *Brain Structure &*

Function, 224(2), 535–551. https://doi.org/10.1007/s00429-018-1785-z

Dale, L. P., Vanderloo, L., Moore, S., & Faulkner, G. (2019). Physical activity and depression, anxiety, and self-esteem in children and youth: An umbrella systematic review. *Mental Health and Physical Activity, 16*, 66–79. https://doi.org/10.1016/j.mhpa.2018.12.001

Dalessandro, A. (2015, October 8). *I'm not your snooki.* Ready To Stare. https://www.readytostare.com/im-not-your-snooki/

Dalessandro, C. (2019). "It's a lifestyle": Social class, flexibility, and young adults' stories about defining adulthood. *Sociological Spectrum, 39*(4), 250–263. https://doi.org/10.1080/02732173.2019.1669239

Dalle Grave, R., Sartirana, M., Sermattei, S., & Calugi, S. (2021). Treatment of eating disorders in adults versus adolescents: Similarities and differences. *Clinical Therapeutics, 43*(1), 70–84. https://doi.org/10.1016/j.clinthera.2020.10.015

Daly, M. (2018). Social-media use may explain little of the recent rise in depressive symptoms among adolescent girls. *Clinical Psychological Science, 6*(3), 295.

Daly, M. B., Pilarski, R., Yurgelun, M. B., Berry, M. P., Buys, S. S., Dickson, P., Domchek, S. M., Elkhanany, A., Friedman, S., Garber, J. E., Goggins, M., Hutton, M. L., Khan, S., Klein, C., Kohlmann, W., Kurian, A. W., Laronga, C., Litton, J. K., Mak, J. S., . . . Darlow, S. D. (2020). NCCN Guidelines insights: Genetic/familial high-risk assessment: Breast, ovarian, and pancreatic, Version 1.2020: Featured updates to the NCCN Guidelines. *Journal of the National Comprehensive Cancer Network, 18*(4), 380–391. https://doi.org/10.6004/jnccn.2020.0017

Damashek, A., & Kuhn, J. (2014). Promise and challenges: Interventions for the prevention of unintentional injuries among young children. *Clinical Practice in Pediatric Psychology, 2*(3), 250–262.

Damashek, A., Morrongiello, B., Diaz, F., Prokos, S., & Arbour, E. (2021). Tailoring a child injury prevention program for low-income U.S. families. *Clinical Practice in Pediatric Psychology.* https://doi.org/10.1037/cpp0000421

Daniels, L., Heath, A. L. M., Williams, S. M., Cameron, S. L., Fleming, E. A., Taylor, B. J., Wheeler, B. J., Gibson, R. S., & Taylor, R. W. (2015). Baby-Led Introduction to SolidS (BLISS) study: A randomised controlled trial of a baby-led approach to complementary feeding. *BMC Pediatrics, 15*(1), 1–15.

Danielsen, V. M., Vidal-Piñeiro, D., Mowinckel, A. M., Sederevicius, D., Fjell, A. M., Walhovd, K. B., & Westerhausen, R. (2020). Lifespan trajectories of relative corpus callosum thickness: Regional differences and cognitive relevance. *Cortex, 130*, 127–141. https://doi.org/10.1016/j.cortex.2020.05.020

Danielson, M. L., Bitsko, R. H., Ghandour, R. M., Holbrook, J. R., Kogan, M. D., & Blumberg, S. J. (2018). Prevalence of Parent-Reported ADHD Diagnosis and Associated Treatment Among U.S. Children and Adolescents, 2016. *Journal of Clinical Child and Adolescent Psychology: The Official Journal for the Society of Clinical Child and Adolescent Psychology, American Psychological Association, Division 53, 47*(2), 199–212. https://doi.org/10.1080/15374416.2017.1417860

Danielson, M. L., Bitsko, R. H., Holbrook, J. R., Charania, S. N., Claussen, A. H., McKeown, R. E., Cuffe, S. P., Owens, J. S., Evans, S. W., Kubicek, L., & Flory, K. (2021). Community-based prevalence of externalizing and internalizing disorders among school-aged children and adolescents in four geographically dispersed school districts in the United States. *Child Psychiatry & Human Development, 52*(3), 500–514. https://doi.org/10.1007/s10578-020-01027-z

Dantchev, S., & Wolke, D. (2019). Trouble in the nest: Antecedents of sibling bullying victimization and perpetration. *Developmental Psychology, 55*(5), 1059.

Darcy, S., Ollerton, J., & Grabowski, S. (2020). "Why can't I play?": Transdisciplinary learnings for children with disability's sport participation. *Social Inclusion, 8*(3), 209–223.

Darling-Hammond, L., Burns, D., Campbell, C., Goodwin, A. L., & Low, E. L. (2017). International lessons in teacher education. In M. Akiba & G. K. LeTendre (Eds.), *International handbook of teacher quality and policy* (pp. 336–349). Routledge.

Darling-Hammond, S., Fronius, T. A., Sutherland, H., Guckenburg, S., Petrosino, A., & Hurley, N. (2020). Effectiveness of restorative justice in US K-12 schools: A review of quantitative research. *Contemporary School Psychology, 24*, 295–308.

Darwin, C. (1856, March 9). *To Syms Covington* [Letter]. https://www.darwinproject.ac.uk/letter/DCP-LETT-1840.xml

Darwin, C. (2009). *The origin of species by means of natural selection: Or, the preservation of favored races in the struggle for life.* A. L. Burt. (Original work published 1872)

Darwin, Z., Domoney, J., Iles, J., Bristow, F., Siew, J., & Sethna, V. (2021). Assessing the mental health of fathers, other co-parents, and partners in the perinatal period: Mixed methods evidence synthesis. *Frontiers in Psychiatry, 11*, 585479. https://doi.org/10.3389/fpsyt.2020.585479

Das, J. K., Lassi, Z. S., Hoodbhoy, Z., & Salam, R. A. (2018). Nutrition for the next generation: Older children and adolescents. *Annals of Nutrition and Metabolism, 72*(3), 56–64. https://doi.org/10.1159/000487385

Dasen, P. (1994). Culture and cognitive development from a Piagetian perspective. In W. J. Lonner & R. S. Malpass (Eds.), *Psychology and culture* (pp. 145–149). Allyn & Bacon.

Dattilo, A. M., Carvalho, R. S., Feferbaum, R., Forsyth, S., & Zhao, A. (2020). Hidden realities of infant feeding: Systematic review of qualitative findings from parents. *Behavioral Sciences, 10*(5), 83. https://doi.org/10.3390/bs10050083

David, E., & Cruz, C. J. P. (2018). Big, *bakla*, and beautiful: Transformations on a Manila pageant stage. *Women's Studies Quarterly, 46*(1/2), 29–45.

Davidov, M., Paz, Y., Roth-Hanania, R., Uzefovsky, F., Orlitsky, T., Mankuta, D., & Zahn-Waxler, C. (2021). Caring babies: Concern for others in distress during infancy. *Developmental Science, 24*(2), e13016. https://doi.org/10.1111/desc.13016

Davidov, M., Vaish, A., Knafo-Noam, A., & Hastings, P. D. (2016). The motivational foundations of prosocial behavior from a developmental perspective–evolutionary roots and key psychological mechanisms: Introduction to the special section. *Child Development, 87*(6), 1655–1667.

Davidow, J. Y., Foerde, K., Galván, A., & Shohamy, D. (2016). An upside to reward sensitivity: The hippocampus supports enhanced reinforcement learning in adolescence. *Neuron, 92*(1), 93–99. https://doi.org/10.1016/j.neuron.2016.08.031

Davidow, J. Y., Insel, C., & Somerville, L. H. (2018). Adolescent development of value-guided goal pursuit. *Trends in Cognitive Sciences, 22*(8), 725–736.

Davies, B. (2010, October 29). Life in a snapshot: Amazing year-by-year sequence of the changing face of one British family. *Mail Online.* https://www.dailymail.co.uk/news/article-1325006/Year-year-changing-face-British-family.html

Davis, A. C., Wright, C., Curtis, M., Hellard, M. E., Lim, M. S. C., & Temple-Smith, M. J. (2019). "Not my child": Parenting, pornography, and views on education. *Journal of Family Studies*, 1–16. https://doi.org/10.1080/13229400.2019.1657929

Davis, D.-A. (2019). *Reproductive injustice: Racism, pregnancy, and premature birth.* New York University Press.

Davis, E. P., & Narayan, A. J. (2020). Pregnancy as a period of risk, adaptation, and resilience for mothers and infants. *Development and Psychopathology, 32*(5), 1625–1639. https://doi.org/10.1017/S0954579420001121

Davis, H. E., Crittenden, A. N., & Scalise Sugiyama, M. (2021). Ecological and developmental perspectives on social learning. *Human Nature.* https://doi.org/10.1007/s12110-021-09394-9

Davis, J., Redshaw, J., Suddendorf, T., Nielsen, M., Kennedy-Costantini, S., Oostenbroek, J., & Slaughter, V. (2021). Does neonatal imitation exist? Insights from a meta-analysis of 336 effect sizes. *Perspectives on Psychological Science.* https://doi.org/10.1177/1745691620959834

Davis, K. (2005). *A girl like me* [Short film].

Davis, K., Charmaraman, L., & Weinstein, E. (2020). Introduction to special issue: Adolescent and emerging adult development in an age of social media. *Journal of Adolescent Research, 35*(1), 3–15. https://doi.org/10.1177/0743558419886392

Davison, M., Penner, A. M., Penner, E. K., Pharris-Ciurej, N., Porter, S. R., Rose, E. K., Shem-Tov, Y., & Yoo, P. (2022). School discipline and racial disparities in early adulthood. *Educational Researcher, 51*(3), 231–234. https://doi.org/10.3102/0013189X211061732

Davydov, V. V. (1995). The influence of LS Vygotsky on education theory, research, and practice. *Educational Researcher, 24*(3), 12–21.

Dawood, F. S., Chung, J. R., Kim, S. S., Zimmerman, R. K., Nowalk, M. P., Jackson, M. L., Jackson, L. A., Monto, A. S., Martin, E. T., Belongia, E. A., McLean, H. Q., Gaglani, M., Dunnigan, K., Foust, A., Sessions, W., DaSilva, J., Le, S., Stark, T., Kondor, R. J., . . . Flannery, B. (2020). Interim estimates of 2019–20 seasonal influenza vaccine effectiveness — United States, February 2020. *Morbidity and Mortality Weekly Report, 69*(7), 177–182. https://doi.org/10.15585/mmwr.mm6907a1

Dawson, A., Pike, A., & Bird, L. (2015). Parental division of household labour and sibling relationship quality: Family relationship mediators. *Infant and Child Development, 24*(4), 379–393. https://doi.org/10.1002/icd.1890

Day, J. K., Perez-Brumer, A., & Russell, S. T. (2018). Safe schools? Transgender youth's school experiences and perceptions of school climate. *Journal of Youth and Adolescence, 47*(8), 1731–1742.

Day, J., Savani, S., Krempley, B. D., Nguyen, M., & Kitlinska, J. B. (2016). Influence of paternal preconception exposures on their offspring: Through epigenetics to phenotype. *American Journal of Stem Cells, 5*(1), 11–18.

de Bont, J., Díaz, Y., Casas, M., García-Gil, M., Vrijheid, M., & Duarte-Salles, T. (2020). Time trends and sociodemographic factors associated with overweight and obesity in children and adolescents in Spain. *JAMA Network Open, 3*(3), e201171. https://doi.org/10.1001/jamanetworkopen.2020.1171

De Bruyckere, P., Kirschner, P. A., & Hulshof, C. (2020). *More urban myths about learning and education: Challenging eduquacks, extraordinary claims, and alternative facts.* Routledge.

de Carvalho Mrad, F. C., da Silva, M. E., de Oliveira Lima, E., Bessa, A. L., de Bessa Junior, J., Netto, J. M. B., & de Almeida Vasconcelos, M. M. (2021). Toilet training methods in children with normal neuropsychomotor development: A systematic review. *Journal of Pediatric Urology.* https://doi.org/10.1016/j.jpurol.2021.05.010

de Chambrier, A.-F., & Zesiger, P. (2018). Is a fact retrieval deficit the main characteristic of children with mathematical learning disabilities? *Acta Psychologica, 190,* 95–102.

De Coen, J., Verbeken, S., & Goossens, L. (2021). Media influence components as predictors of children's body image and eating problems: A longitudinal study of boys and girls during middle childhood. *Body Image, 37,* 204–213. https://doi.org/10.1016/j.bodyim.2021.03.001

De Haan, M. (2015). Neuroscientific methods in children. In W. Overton & P. Molenaar (Eds.), *Handbook of child psychology* (pp. 102–140). John Wiley & Sons.

De Houwer, A. (2020). Harmonious bilingualism: Well-being for families in bilingual settings. In A. C. Schalley & S. A. Eisenchlas (Eds.), *Handbook of home language maintenance and development: Social and affective factors* (pp. 63–83). De Gruyter Mouton.

de la Fontaine, N., Hahn, H., Stover, C. S., & Marans, S. (2021). Extending law enforcement reach to children exposed to violence: Police training evaluation. *Journal of Police and Criminal Psychology.* https://doi.org/10.1007/s11896-021-09448-9

De Leersnyder, J., Mesquita, B., & Boiger, M. (2020). What has culture got to do with emotions? A lot. In M. J. Gelfand, C.-Y. Chiu, & Y.-Y. Hong (Eds.), *Handbook of advances in culture and psychology* (Vol. 8, pp. 62–119). Oxford University Press.

de Onis, M. (2017). Child growth and development. In S. de Pee, D. Taren, & M. W. Bloem (Eds.), *Nutrition and health in a developing world* (pp. 119–141). Springer International Publishing. https://doi.org/10.1007/978-3-319-43739-2_6

de Onis, M., Borghi, E., Arimond, M., Webb, P., Croft, T., Saha, K., De-Regil, L. M., Thuita, F., Heidkamp, R., & Krasevec, J. (2019). Prevalence thresholds for wasting, overweight and stunting in children under 5 years. *Public Health Nutrition, 22*(1), 175–179. https://doi.org/10.1017/S1368980018002434

de Vries, R. (1969). Constancy of generic identity in the years three to six. *Monographs of the Society for Research in Child Development, 34*(3), iii–67. https://doi.org/10.2307/1165683

de Waal, F. (2019). *Mama's last hug: Animal emotions and what they tell us about ourselves.* W. W. Norton.

Deal, B. J., Huffman, M. D., Binns, H., & Stone, N. J. (2020). Perspective: Childhood obesity requires new strategies for prevention. *Advances in Nutrition, 11*(5), 1071–1078. https://doi.org/10.1093/advances/nmaa040

Deal, J. (2019, November 4). Youth political engagement and hope ahead of the 2020 election. *Harvard Political Review.* https://harvardpolitics.com/youth-political-engagement-and-hope-ahead-of-the-2020-election/

Dean, L. T., Greene, N., Adams, M. A., Geffen, S. R., Malone, J., Tredway, K., & Poteat, T. (2021). Beyond Black and White: Race and sexual identity as contributors to healthcare system distrust after breast cancer screening among US women. *Psycho-Oncology, 30*(7), 1145–1150. https://doi.org/10.1002/pon.5670

Dear, P. (2008). *The intelligibility of nature: How science makes sense of the world.* University of Chicago Press.

Deardorff, J., Hoyt, L. T., Carter, R., & Shirtcliff, E. A. (2019). Next steps in puberty research: Broadening the lens toward understudied populations. *Journal of Research on Adolescence, 29*(1), 133–154. https://doi.org/10.1111/jora.12402

DeCapua, A., & Wintergerst, A. C. (2016). *Crossing cultures in the language classroom.* University of Michigan Press.

DeCasper, A. J., & Fifer, W. P. (1980). Of human bonding: Newborns prefer their mothers' voices. *Science, 208*(4448), 1174–1176. https://doi.org/10.1126/science.7375928

Decety, J. (2015). The neural pathways, development and functions of empathy. *Current Opinion in Behavioral Sciences, 3,* 1–6.

Decety, J., & Steinbeis, N. (2020). Multiple mechanisms of prosocial development. In J. Decety (Ed.), *The social brain: A developmental perspective* (pp. 219–246). MIT Press.

Declercq, E. R., Sakala, C., Corry, M. P., Applebaum, S., & Herrlich, A. (2013). *Listening to mothers sm III. New mothers speak out.* Childbirth Connection.

Deer, B. (2011). How the case against the MMR vaccine was fixed. BMJ, 342, c5347. https://doi.org/10.1136/bmj.c5347

Deer, B. (2020). *The doctor who fooled the world: Science, deception, and the war on vaccines.* JHU Press.

Degenhardt, L., Stockings, E., Patton, G., Hall, W. D., & Lynskey, M. (2016). The increasing global health priority of substance use in young people. *The Lancet Psychiatry, 3*(3), 251–264. https://doi.org/10.1016/S2215-0366(15)00508-8

Dehaene-Lambertz, G. (2017). The human infant brain: A neural architecture able to learn language. *Psychonomic Bulletin & Review, 24*(1), 48–55. https://doi.org/10.3758/s13423-016-1156-9

Dehn, M. J. (2011). *Working memory and academic learning: Assessment and intervention.* Wiley.

Deichmann, F., & Ahnert, L. (2021). The terrible twos: How children cope with frustration and tantrums and the effect of maternal and paternal behaviors. *Infancy, 26*(3), 469–493. https://doi.org/10.1111/infa.12389

Delgado, M. Y., Nair, R. L., Zeiders, K. H., & Jones, S. K. (2019). Latino adolescents' experiences with ethnic discrimination: Moderating factors and mediating mechanisms. In H. E. Fitzgerald, D. J. Johnson, D. B. Qin, F. A. Villarruel, & J. Norder (Eds.), *Handbook of children and prejudice: Integrating research, practice, and policy* (pp. 515–531). Springer International Publishing. https://doi.org/10.1007/978-3-030-12228-7_29

Delgado, R. (1995). *Critical race theory.* Temple University Press.

Deligiannidis, K. M., Meltzer-Brody, S., Gunduz-Bruce, H., Doherty, J., Jonas, J., Li, S., Sankoh, A. J., Silber, C., Campbell, A. D., Werneburg, B., Kanes, S. J., & Lasser, R. (2021). Effect of Zuranolone vs placebo in postpartum depression: A randomized clinical trial. *JAMA Psychiatry, 78*(9), 951–959. https://doi.org/10.1001/jamapsychiatry.2021.1559

Delli Carpini, M. X. (2000). Gen.com: Youth, civic engagement, and the new information environment. *Political Communication, 17*(4), 341–349.

Delvecchio, M., Pastore, C., Valente, F., & Giordano, P. (2020). Cardiovascular implications in idiopathic and syndromic obesity in childhood: An update. *Frontiers in Endocrinology, 11.* https://www.frontiersin.org/article/10.3389/fendo.2020.00330

Demedardi, M.-J., Brechet, C., Gentaz, E., & Monnier, C. (2021). Prosocial lying in children between 4 and 11 years of age: The role of emotional understanding and empathy. *Journal of Experimental Child Psychology, 203,* 105045. https://doi.org/10.1016/j.jecp.2020.105045

Deming, D. J., Hastings, J. S., Kane, T. J., & Staiger, D. O. (2014). School choice, school quality, and postsecondary attainment. *American Economic Review, 104*(3), 991–1013.

Demir, Ö. E., Rowe, M. L., Heller, G., Goldin-Meadow, S., & Levine, S. C. (2015). Vocabulary, syntax, and narrative development in typically developing children and children with early unilateral brain injury: Early parental talk about the there-and-then matters. *Developmental Psychology, 51*(2), 161–175. https://doi.org/10.1037/a0038476

Demo, D. H., & Fine, M. A. (2010). *Beyond the average divorce.* Sage.

Denckla, C. A., Cicchetti, D., Kubzansky, L. D., Seedat, S., Teicher, M. H., Williams, D. R., & Koenen, K. C. (2020). Psychological resilience: An update on definitions, a critical appraisal, and research recommendations. *European Journal of Psychotraumatology, 11*(1), 1822064.

Denford, S., Abraham, C., Campbell, R., & Busse, H. (2017). A comprehensive review of reviews of school-based interventions to improve sexual-health. *Health Psychology Review, 11*(1), 33–52. https://doi.org/10.1080/17437199.2016.1240625

Denham, S. A. (2019). Emotional competence during childhood and adolescence. In V. LoBue, K. Pérez-Edgar, & K. A. Buss (Eds.), *Handbook of emotional development* (pp. 493–541). Springer International Publishing. https://doi.org/10.1007/978-3-030-17332-6_20

DeNicolo, C. P., Yu, M., Crowley, C. B., & Gabel, S. L. (2017). Reimagining critical care and problematizing sense of school belonging as a response to inequality for immigrants and children of immigrants. *Review of Research in Education, 41*(1), 500–530. https://doi.org/10.3102/0091732X17690498

Dennis, C.-L., Shiri, R., Brown, H. K., Santos, H. P., Schmied, V., & Falah-Hassani, K. (2019). Breastfeeding rates in immigrant and non-immigrant women: A systematic review and meta-analysis. *Maternal & Child Nutrition, 15*(3), e12809. https://doi.org/10.1111/mcn.12809

Denomme, M. M., Haywood, M. E., Parks, J. C., Schoolcraft, W. B., & Katz-Jaffe, M. G. (2020). The inherited methylome landscape is directly altered with paternal aging and associated with offspring neurodevelopmental disorders. *Aging Cell, 19*(8), e13178. https://doi.org/10.1111/acel.13178

Denton, M. L., & Uecker, J. E. (2018). What God has joined together: Family formation and religion among young adults. *Review of Religious Research, 60*(1), 1–22. https://doi.org/10.1007/s13644-017-0308-3

Deoni, S. (2022). Impact of the COVID-19 Pandemic Environment on Early Child Brain and Cognitive Development. *Biological Psychiatry, 91*(9), S26. https://doi.org/10.1016/j.biopsych.2022.02.082

Deoni, S. C., Beauchemin, J., Volpe, A., Dâ Sa, V., & RESONANCE Consortium. (2021). Impact of the COVID-19 pandemic on early child cognitive development: Initial findings in a longitudinal observational study of child health. *MedRxiv: The Preprint Server for Health Sciences,* 2021.08.10.21261846. https://doi.org/10.1101/2021.08.10.21261846

Deoni, S., Dean, D., Joelson, S., O'Regan, J., & Schneider, N. (2018). Early nutrition influences developmental myelination and cognition in infants and young children. *NeuroImage, 178*, 649–659. https://doi.org/10.1016/j.neuroimage.2017.12.056

DePasquale, C. E. (2020). A systematic review of caregiver–child physiological synchrony across systems: Associations with behavior and child functioning. *Development and Psychopathology, 32*(5), 1754–1777. https://doi.org/10.1017/S0954579420001236

DePaulo, B. (2017). Toward a positive psychology of single life. In D. S. Dunn (Ed.), *Positive psychology: Established and emerging issues* (pp. 251–275). Routledge.

Derbyshire, S. W., & Bockmann, J. C. (2020). Reconsidering fetal pain. *Journal of Medical Ethics, 46*(1), 3–6. https://doi.org/10.1136/medethics-2019-105701

Desilver, D. (2019, February 26). The concerns and challenges of being a U.S. teen: What the data show. *Pew Research Center.* https://www.pewresearch.org/fact-tank/2019/02/26/the-concerns-and-challenges-of-being-a-u-s-teen-what-the-data-show/

Desmichel, P., & Rucker, D. D. (2022). Social-rank cues: Decoding rank from physical characteristics, behaviors, and possessions. *Current Opinion in Psychology, 43*, 79–84. https://doi.org/10.1016/j.copsyc.2021.06.012

Desmond, C., Watt, K., Saha, A., Huang, J., & Lu, C. (2020). Prevalence and number of children living in institutional care: Global, regional, and country estimates. *The Lancet Child & Adolescent Health, 4*(5), 370–377. https://doi.org/10.1016/S2352-4642(20)30022-5

DeVille, D. C., Whalen, D., Breslin, F. J., Morris, A. S., Khalsa, S. S., Paulus, M. P., & Barch, D. M. (2020). Prevalence and family-related factors associated with suicidal ideation, suicide attempts, and self-injury in children aged 9 to 10 years. *JAMA Network Open, 3*(2), e1920956. https://doi.org/10.1001/jamanetworkopen.2019.20956

Devore, I., & Konner, M. J. (2019). 6. Infancy in hunter-gatherer life: An ethological perspective. In N. F. White (Ed.), *Ethology and psychiatry* (pp. 113–141). University of Toronto Press. https://www.degruyter.com/document/doi/10.3138/9781487575663-009/html

Dewey, K. G., & Brown, K. H. (2003). Update on technical issues concerning complementary feeding of young children in developing countries and implications for intervention programs. *Food and Nutrition Bulletin, 24*(1), 5–28.

Dharmapuri, S., Miller, K., & Klein, J. D. (2020). Marijuana and the pediatric population. *Pediatrics, 146*(2).

Di Ventra, M. (2018). *The scientific method: Reflections from a practitioner.* Oxford University Press.

Diamond, A. (1985). Development of the ability to use recall to guide action, as indicated by infants' performance on AB. *Child Development,* 868–883.

Diamond, A. (2013). Executive functions. *Annual Review of Psychology, 64*(1), 135–168. https://doi.org/10.1146/annurev-psych-113011-143750

Diamond, A., & Ling, D. S. (2016). Conclusions about interventions, programs, and approaches for improving executive functions that appear justified and those that, despite much hype, do not. *Developmental Cognitive Neuroscience, 18*(Supplement C), 34–48. https://doi.org/10.1016/j.dcn.2015.11.005

Diamond, L. M. (2016). Sexual fluidity in male and females. *Current Sexual Health Reports, 8*(4), 249–256. https://doi.org/10.1007/s11930-016-0092-z

Diamond, L. M. (2020). Gender fluidity and nonbinary gender identities among children and adolescents.

Child Development Perspectives, 14(2), 110–115. https://doi.org/10.1111/cdep.12366

Diamond, L. M., Bonner, S. B., & Dickenson, J. (2015). The development of sexuality. In M. E. Lamb & R. M. Lerner (Eds.), *Handbook of child psychology and developmental science: Socioemotional processes* (pp. 888–931). Wiley.

Dias, N. M., & Seabra, A. G. (2015). Is it possible to promote executive functions in preschoolers? A case study in Brazil. *International Journal of Child Care and Education Policy, 9*(1), 6. https://doi.org/10.1186/s40723-015-0010-2

Diaz-Rojas, F., Matsunaga, M., Tanaka, Y., Kikusui, T., Mogi, K., Nagasawa, M., Asano, K., Abe, N., & Myowa, M. (2021). Development of the paternal brain in expectant fathers during early pregnancy. *NeuroImage, 225*, 117527. https://doi.org/10.1016/j.neuroimage.2020.117527

Dick, F., Krishnan, S., Leech, R., & Curtin, S. (2016). Language development. In G. Hickok & S. L. Small (Eds.), *Neurobiology of language* (pp. 373–388). Academic Press. https://doi.org/10.1016/B978-0-12-407794-2.00031-6

Dienel, G. A. (2019). Brain glucose metabolism: Integration of energetics with function. *Physiological Reviews, 99*(1), 949–1045.

Dietz, W. H. (2019). We need a new approach to prevent obesity in low-income minority populations. *Pediatrics, 143*(6), e20190839. https://doi.org/10.1542/peds.2019-0839

Dietze, P., Gantman, A., Nam, H. H., Niemi, L., & Marginalia Science. (2019). Marginalised ideas are key to scientific progress. *Nature Human Behaviour, 3*(10), 1024–1024. https://doi.org/10.1038/s41562-019-0699-y

Digdon, N. (2020). The Little Albert controversy: Intuition, confirmation bias, and logic. *History of Psychology, 23*(2), 122.

DiGiovanni, A. M., Vannucci, A., Ohannessian, C. M., & Bolger, N. (2021). Modeling heterogeneity in the simultaneous emotional costs and social benefits of co-rumination. *PsyArXiv.* https://doi.org/10.31234/osf.io/gmjvk

Dijk, K. A., Thijssen, S., van 't Veer, A., Buisman, R. S. M., van IJzendoorn, M. H., & Bakermans-Kranenburg, M. (2020). Exploring the transition into fatherhood: Behavioral, hormonal, and neural underpinnings of responses to infant crying. *PsyArXiv.* https://doi.org/10.31234/osf.io/5bxk9

Dillon, M. R., Kannan, H., Dean, J. T., Spelke, E. S., & Duflo, E. (2017). Cognitive science in the field: A preschool intervention durably enhances intuitive but not formal mathematics. *Science, 357*(6346), 47–55. https://doi.org/10.1126/science.aal4724

Dillon, R. M. (2022, August 9). Snapchat's new parental controls try to mimic real-life parenting, minus the hovering. *NPR.* https://www.npr.org/2022/08/09/1116385906/snapchat-parental-controls

Dimitrova, R., Johnson, D. J., & van de Vijver, F. J. R. (2018). Ethnic socialization, ethnic identity, life satisfaction and school achievement of Roma ethnic minority youth. *Journal of Adolescence, 62*, 175–183. https://doi.org/10.1016/j.adolescence.2017.06.003

Dimler, L. M., & Natsuaki, M. N. (2015). The effects of pubertal timing on externalizing behaviors in adolescence and early adulthood: A meta-analytic review. *Journal of Adolescence, 45*, 160–170.

Dimock, M. (2019, January 17). *Defining generations: Where Millennials end and Generation Z begins.* Pew Research Center. https://www.pewresearch.org/fact-tank/2019/01/17/where-millennials-end-and-generation-z-begins/

Dindo, L., Brock, R. L., Aksan, N., Gamez, W., Kochanska, G., & Clark, L. A. (2017). Attachment and effortful control in toddlerhood predict academic achievement over a decade later. *Psychological Science, 28*(12), 1786–1795.

Ding, R., He, W., & Wang, Q. (2021). A comparative analysis of emotion-related cultural norms in popular American and Chinese storybooks. *Journal of Cross-Cultural Psychology, 52*(2), 209–226. https://doi.org/10.1177/0022022120988900

Ding, X., Chen, X., Fu, R., Li, D., & Liu, J. (2020). Relations of shyness and unsociability with adjustment in migrant and non-migrant children in urban China. *Journal of Abnormal Child Psychology, 48*(2), 289–300. https://doi.org/10.1007/s10802-019-00583-w

Ding, X. P., Heyman, G. D., Fu, G., Zhu, B., & Lee, K. (2018). Young children discover how to deceive in 10 days: A microgenetic study. *Developmental Science, 21*(3), e12566. https://doi.org/10.1111/desc.12566

DiPietro, J. A., Costigan, K. A., & Voegtline, K. M. (2015). Studies in fetal behavior: Revisited, renewed, and reimagined. *Monographs of the Society for Research in Child Development, 80*(3), vii, 1–151. https://doi.org/10.1111/mono.v80.3

Dirix, C. E. H., Nijhuis, J. G., Jongsma, H. W., & Hornstra, G. (2009). Aspects of fetal learning and memory. *Child Development, 80*(4), 1251–1258.

Dirks, M. A., Persram, R., Recchia, H. E., & Howe, N. (2015). Sibling relationships as sources of risk and resilience in the development and maintenance of internalizing and externalizing problems during childhood and adolescence. *Clinical Psychology Review, 42*, 145–155. https://doi.org/10.1016/j.cpr.2015.07.003

Dirks, M. A., Recchia, H. E., Estabrook, R., Howe, N., Petitclerc, A., Burns, J. L., Briggs-Gowan, M. J., & Wakschlag, L. S. (2019). Differentiating typical from atypical perpetration of sibling-directed aggression during the preschool years. *Journal of Child Psychology and Psychiatry, 60*(3), 267–276. https://doi.org/10.1111/jcpp.12939

Dishion, T. J., & McMahon, R. J. (1998). Parental monitoring and the prevention of child and adolescent problem behavior: A conceptual and empirical formulation. *Clinical Child and Family Psychology Review, 1*(1), 61–75.

Distefano, R., Grenell, A., Palmer, A. R., Houlihan, K., Masten, A. S., & Carlson, S. M. (2021). Self-regulation as promotive for academic achievement in young children across risk contexts. *Cognitive Development, 58*, 101050.

DiTomasso, D. (2019). Bearing the pain: A historic review exploring the impact of science and culture on pain management for childbirth in the United States. *The Journal of Perinatal & Neonatal Nursing, 33*(4), 322. https://doi.org/10.1097/JPN.0000000000000407

Dixon, A. R., & Telles, E. E. (2017). Skin color and colorism: Global research, concepts, and measurement. *Annual Review of Sociology, 43*(1), 405–424. https://doi.org/10.1146/annurev-soc-060116-053315

Dixson, D. D., Worrell, F. C., Olszewski-Kubilius, P., & Subotnik, R. F. (2016). Beyond perceived ability: The contribution of psychosocial factors to academic performance. *Annals of the New York Academy of Sciences, 1377*(1), 67–77.

Dixson, H. G., Komugabe-Dixson, A. F., Dixson, B. J., & Low, J. (2018). Scaling theory of mind in a small-scale society: A case study from Vanuatu. *Child Development, 89*(6), 2157–2175.

Doan, S. N., Tardif, T., Miller, A., Olson, S., Kessler, D., Felt, B., & Wang, L. (2017). Consequences of 'tiger' parenting: A cross-cultural study of maternal psychological control and children's cortisol stress response. *Developmental Science, 20*(3), e12404.

Dobbie, W., & Fryer Jr, R. G. (2011). Are high-quality schools enough to increase achievement among the poor? Evidence from the Harlem Children's Zone. *American Economic Journal: Applied Economics, 3*(3), 158–187.

Doebel, S. (2020). Rethinking executive function and its development. *Perspectives on Psychological Science, 15*(4), 942–956.

Doebel, S., & Lillard, A. (2021). *How does play support learning? A new executive function perspective.*

Doepke, M., & Zilibotti, F. (Eds.). (2019). *Love, money, and parenting: How economics explains the way we raise our kids.* Princeton University Press. https://doi.org/10.1515/9780691184210

Doering, J. J., Salm Ward, T. C., Strook, S., & Campbell, J. K. (2019). A comparison of infant sleep safety guidelines in nine industrialized countries. *Journal of Community Health, 44*(1), 81–87.

Domitrovich, C. E., Durlak, J. A., Staley, K. C., & Weissberg, R. P. (2017). Social-emotional competence: An essential factor for promoting positive adjustment and reducing risk in school children. *Child Development, 88*(2), 408–416.

Dong, H.-M., Margulies, D. S., Zuo, X.-N., & Holmes, A. J. (2021). Shifting gradients of macroscale cortical organization mark the transition from childhood to adolescence. *Proceedings of the National Academy of Sciences, 118*(28), e2024448118. https://doi.org/10.1073/pnas.2024448118

Donkin, I., & Barrès, R. (2018). Sperm epigenetics and influence of environmental factors. *Molecular Metabolism, 14*, 1–11. https://doi.org/10.1016/j.molmet.2018.02.006

Donkor, H. M., Toxe, H., Hurum, J., Bjerknes, R., Eide, G. E., Juliusson, P., & Markestad, T. (2021). Psychological health in preschool children with underweight, overweight or obesity: A regional cohort study. *BMJ Paediatrics Open, 5*(1), e000881. https://doi.org/10.1136/bmjpo-2020-000881

Donoghue, E. A., & Council on Early Childhood, American Academy of Pediatrics. (2017). Quality early education and child care from birth to kindergarten. *Pediatrics, 140*(2), e20171488. https://doi.org/10.1542/peds.2017-1488

Donovan, B. M., Weindling, M., Salazar, B., Duncan, A., Stuhlsatz, M., & Keck, P. (2021). Genomics literacy matters: Supporting the development of genomics literacy through genetics education could reduce the prevalence of genetic essentialism. *Journal of Research in Science Teaching, 58*(4), 520–550. https://doi.org/10.1002/tea.21670

Donovan, T., Dunn, K., Penman, A., Young, R. J., & Reid, V. M. (2020). Fetal eye movements in response to a visual stimulus. *Brain and Behavior, 10*(8), e01676. https://doi.org/10.1002/brb3.1676

Doom, J. R., Doyle, C. M., & Gunnar, M. R. (2017). Social stress buffering by friends in childhood and adolescence: Effects on HPA and oxytocin activity. *Social Neuroscience, 12*(1), 8–21. https://doi.org/10.1080/17470919.2016.1149095

Doom, J. R., Mason, S. M., Suglia, S. F., & Clark, C. J. (2017). Pathways between childhood/adolescent adversity, adolescent socioeconomic status, and long-term cardiovascular disease risk in young adulthood. *Social Science & Medicine, 188*, 166–175.

Dorner, L. M., Orellana, M. F., & Li-Grining, C. P. (2007). "I helped my mom," and it helped me: Translating the skills of language brokers into improved standardized test scores. *American Journal of Education, 113*(3), 451–478.

Dorney, K., Dodington, J. M., Rees, C. A., Farrell, C. A., Hanson, H. R., Lyons, T. W., & Lee, L. K. (2020). Preventing injuries must be a priority to prevent disease in the twenty-first century. *Pediatric Research, 87*(2), 282–292. https://doi.org/10.1038/s41390-019-0549-7

Dotti Sani, G. M., & Scherer, S. (2018). Maternal employment: Enabling factors in context. *Work, Employment and Society, 32*(1), 75–92.

Dougherty, S. M., & Smith, M. M. (2022). At what cost?: Is technical education worth the investment?. (EdWorkingPaper: 22-640). Annenberg Institute at Brown University: https://doi.org/10.26300/h3g8-tp62

Douthard, R. A., Martin, I. K., Chapple-McGruder, T., Langer, A., & Chang, S. (2021). U.S. maternal mortality within a global context: Historical trends, current state, and future directions. *Journal of Women's Health, 30*(2), 168–177. https://doi.org/10.1089/jwh.2020.8863

Downes, M., Bathelt, J., & Haan, M. D. (2017). Event-related potential measures of executive functioning from preschool to adolescence. *Developmental Medicine & Child Neurology, 59*(6), 581–590. https://doi.org/10.1111/dmcn.13395

Downes, S. M. (2015). Evolutionary psychology, adaptation and design. In T. Heams, P. Huneman, G. Lecointre, & M. Silberstein (Eds.), *Handbook of evolutionary thinking in the sciences* (pp. 659–673). Springer.

Downs, S., & Demmler, K. M. (2020). Food environment interventions targeting children and adolescents: A scoping review. *Global Food Security, 27*, 100403. https://doi.org/10.1016/j.gfs.2020.100403

Draganova, R., Schollbach, A., Schleger, F., Braendle, J., Brucker, S., Abele, H., Kagan, K. O., Wallwiener, D., Fritsche, A., Eswaran, H., & Preissl, H. (2018). Fetal auditory evoked responses to onset of amplitude modulated sounds: A fetal magnetoencephalography (fMEG) study. *Hearing Research, 363*, 70–77. https://doi.org/10.1016/j.heares.2018.03.005

Drake, G., & Walsh, K. (2020). *2020 Teacher prep review: Program performance in early reading instruction: Teacher preparation to teach reading: Summary of findings on NCTQ's Early Reading Standard.* National Center for Teacher Quality.

Druga, S., Williams, R., Breazeal, C., & Resnick, M. (2017). "Hey Google is it ok if I eat you?" Initial explorations in child-agent interaction. In *Proceedings of the 2017 Conference on Interaction Design and Children* (pp. 595–600).

Druga, S., Williams, R., Park, H. W., & Breazeal, C. (2018). How smart are the smart toys? Children and parents' agent interaction and intelligence attribution. In *Proceedings of the 17th ACM Conference on Interaction Design and Children* (pp. 231–240).

Dubé, È., Ward, J. K., Verger, P., & MacDonald, N. E. (2021). Vaccine hesitancy, acceptance, and anti-vaccination: Trends and future prospects for public health. *Annual Review of Public Health, 42*, 175–191.

DuBois, L. Z., & Shattuck-Heidorn, H. (2020). Challenging the binary: Gender/sex and the bio-logics of normalcy. *American Journal of Human Biology,* e23623. https://doi.org/10.1002/ajhb.23623

Duchesneau, N. (2020). *Social, emotional, and academic development through an equity lens.* Education Trust. https://eric.ed.gov/?id=ED607298

Duckett, L. J., & Ruud, M. (2019). Affirming language use when providing health care for and writing about childbearing families who identify as LGBTQI+. *Journal of Human Lactation, 35*(2), 227–232. https://doi.org/10.1177/0890334419830985

Duckworth, A. (2016). *Grit: The power of passion and perseverance.* Ebury Publishing.

Duckworth, A. L., & Seligman, M. E. P. (2017). The science and practice of self-control. *Perspectives on Psychological Science, 12*(5), 715–718. https://doi.org/10.1177/1745691617690880

Duckworth, A., & Gross, J. J. (2014). Self-control and grit: Related but separable determinants of success. *Current Directions in Psychological Science, 23*(5), 319–325. https://doi.org/10.1177/0963721414541462

Duckworth, A., Kautz, T., Defnet, A., Satlof-Bedrick, E., Talamas, S. N., Luttges, B. L., & Steinberg, L. (2021). Students attending school remotely suffer socially, emotionally, and academically. PsyArXiv. https://doi.org/10.31234/osf.io/rpz7h

Dudovitz, R. N., Chung, P. J., Nelson, B. B., & Wong, M. D. (2017). What do you want to be when you grow up? Career aspirations as a marker for adolescent well-being. *Academic Pediatrics, 17*(2), 153–160. https://doi.org/10.1016/j.acap.2016.08.006

Duell, N., & Steinberg, L. (2020). Differential correlates of positive and negative risk taking in adolescence. *Journal of Youth and Adolescence, 49*(6), 1162–1178. https://doi.org/10.1007/s10964-020-01237-7

Duell, N., Steinberg, L., Icenogle, G., Chein, J., Chaudhary, N., Giunta, L. D., Dodge, K. A., Fanti, K. A., Lansford, J. E., Oburu, P., Pastorelli, C., Skinner, A. T., Sorbring, E., Tapanya, S., Tirado, L. M. U., Alampay, L. P., Al-Hassan, S. M., Takash, H. M. S., Bacchini, D., & Chang, L. (2018). Age patterns in risk taking across the world. *Journal of Youth and Adolescence, 47*(5), 1052–1072. https://doi.org/10.1007/s10964-017-0752-y

Duffy, E. W., Kay, M. C., Jacquier, E. F., Catellier, D., Hampton, J., Anater, A. S., & Story, M. (2019). Trends in food consumption patterns of US infants and toddlers from Feeding Infants and Toddlers Studies (FITS) in 2002, 2008, 2016. *Nutrients, 11*(11), 2807. https://doi.org/10.3390/nu11112807

Dufour, S. C., Adams, R. S., Brody, D. L., Puente, A. N., & Gray, J. C. (2020). Prevalence and correlates of concussion in children: Data from the adolescent brain cognitive development study. *Cortex, 131*, 237–250.

Dunbar, A. S., Leerkes, E. M., Coard, S. I., Supple, A. J., & Calkins, S. (2017). An integrative conceptual model of parental racial/ethnic and emotion socialization and links to children's social-emotional development among African American families. *Child Development Perspectives, 11*(1), 16–22. https://doi.org/10.1111/cdep.12218

Dunbar, R. I. M. (2020). Structure and function in human and primate social networks: Implications for diffusion, network stability and health. *Proceedings of the Royal Society A, 476*(2240), 20200446.

Duncan, G. J., Magnuson, K., & Votruba-Drzal, E. (2015). Children and socioeconomic status. In *Handbook of child psychology and developmental science* (pp. 1–40). Wiley. https://doi.org/10.1002/9781118963418.childpsy414

Dunk, R. D. P., Barnes, M. E., Reiss, M. J., Alters, B., Asghar, A., Carter, B. E., Cotner, S., Glaze, A. L., Hawley, P. H., Jensen, J. L., Mead, L. S., Nadelson, L. S., Nelson, C. E., Pobiner, B., Scott, E. C., Shtulman, A., Sinatra, G. M., Southerland, S. A., Walter, E. M., . . . Wiles, J. R. (2019). Evolution education is a complex landscape. *Nature Ecology & Evolution, 3*(3), 327–329. https://doi.org/10.1038/s41559-019-0802-9

Dunphy, D. C. (1963). The social structure of urban adolescent peer groups. *Sociometry,* 230–246.

Dunphy, D. C. (1969). *Cliques, crowds & gangs: Group life of Sydney adolescents*. Melbourne: Cheshire.

Dunst, C. J., & Espe-Sherwindt, M. (2017). Contemporary early intervention models, research, and practice for infants and toddlers with disabilities and delays. In J. M. Kauffman, D. P. Hallahan, & P. C. Pullen (Eds.), *Handbook of special education* (2nd ed., pp. 831–849). Routledge.

DuPaul, G. J., Fu, Q., Anastopoulos, A. D., Reid, R., & Power, T. J. (2020). ADHD parent and teacher symptom ratings: Differential item functioning across gender, age, race, and ethnicity. *Journal of Abnormal Child Psychology, 48*(5), 679–691. https://doi.org/10.1007/s10802-020-00618-7

Dupéré, V., Dion, E., Cantin, S., Archambault, I., & Lacourse, E. (2021). Social contagion and high school dropout: The role of friends, romantic partners, and siblings. *Journal of Educational Psychology, 113*(3), 572.

Dupéré, V., Dion, E., Leventhal, T., Archambault, I., Crosnoe, R., & Janosz, M. (2018). High school dropout in proximal context: The triggering role of stressful life events. *Child Development, 89*(2), e107–e122. https://doi.org/10.1111/cdev.12792

Dupont, D., Beaudoin, C., Désiré, N., Tran, M., Gagnon, I., & Beauchamp, M. H. (2022). Report of early childhood traumatic injury observations & symptoms: Preliminary validation of an observational measure of postconcussive symptoms. *The Journal of Head Trauma Rehabilitation, 37*(2), E102. https://doi.org/10.1097/HTR.0000000000000691

Durkin, K., Lipsey, M. W., Farran, D. C., & Wiesen, S. E. (2022). Effects of a statewide pre-kindergarten program on children's achievement and behavior through sixth grade. *Developmental Psychology.*

Durlak, J. A., Weissberg, R. P., Dymnicki, A. B., Taylor, R. D., & Schellinger, K. B. (2011). The impact of enhancing students' social and emotional learning: A meta-analysis of school-based universal interventions. *Child Development, 82*(1), 405–432.

Durrant, J., Plateau, D. P., Ateah, C. A., Holden, G. W., Barker, L. A., Stewart-Tufescu, A., Jones, A. D., Ly, G., & Ahmed, R. (2017). Parents' views of the relevance of a violence prevention program in high, medium, and low human development contexts. *International Journal of Behavioral Development, 41*(4), 523–531. https://doi.org/10.1177/0165025416687415

Dutil, S. (2020). Dismantling the school-to-prison pipeline: A trauma-informed, critical race perspective on school discipline. *Children & Schools, 42*(3), 171–178. https://doi.org/10.1093/cs/cdaa016

Dweck, C. S., & Yeager, D. S. (2019). Mindsets: A view from two eras. *Perspectives on Psychological Science, 14*(3), 481–496. https://doi.org/10.1177/1745691618804166

Earnshaw, V. A., Reisner, S. L., Menino, D. D., Poteat, V. P., Bogart, L. M., Barnes, T. N., & Schuster, M. A. (2018). Stigma-based bullying interventions: A systematic review. *Developmental Review, 48*, 178–200. https://doi.org/10.1016/j.dr.2018.02.001

Eastwick, P. W., Joel, S., Molden, D. C., Finkel, E., & Carswell, K. L. (2021, March 8). Predicting romantic interest during early relationship development: A preregistered investigation using machine learning. *OSF Preprints*. https://doi.org/10.31219/osf.io/sh7ja

Eberhard, D. M., Simons, G. F., & Finnig, C. D. (Eds.). (2022). *Ethnologue: Languages of the World*, 25th ed. SIL International. http://www.ethnologue.com.

Eccles, J. S., & Roeser, R. W. (2011). Schools as developmental contexts during adolescence. *Journal of Research on Adolescence, 21*(1), 225–241.

Eccles, J. S., & Wigfield, A. (2020). From expectancy-value theory to situated expectancy-value theory: A developmental, social cognitive, and sociocultural perspective on motivation. *Contemporary Educational Psychology, 61*, 101859.

Eccles, J., & Midgley, C. (1989). Stage-environment fit: Developmentally appropriate classrooms for young adolescents. in C. Ames & R. Ames (eds.), *Research on motivation in education* (Vol. 3, pp. 139–186). New York: Academic Press.

Echegaray, C. (2017, December 7). From child life patient to child life specialist (Vanderbilt University Medical Center: VUMC Voice). *Employee Spotlight.* https://voice.vumc.org/child-life-patient-child-life-specialist/

Echevarria, J., Frey, N., & Fisher, D. (2015). *What it takes for English learners*. Educational Leadership.

Echols, L., & Graham, S. (2013). Birds of a different feather: How do cross-ethnic friends flock together? *Merrill-Palmer Quarterly, 59*(4), 461–488.

Echols, L., & Ivanich, J. (2021). From "fast friends" to true friends: Can a contact intervention promote friendships in middle school? *Journal of Research on Adolescence*. https://doi.org/10.1111/jora.12622

Eckert-Lind, C., Busch, A. S., Petersen, J. H., Biro, F. M., Butler, G., Bräuner, E. V., & Juul, A. (2020). Worldwide secular trends in age at pubertal onset assessed by breast development among girls: A systematic review and meta-analysis. *JAMA Pediatrics, 174*(4), e195881–e195881. https://doi.org/10.1001/jamapediatrics.2019.5881

Ecton, W. G., & Dougherty, S. M. (2021). Heterogeneity in high school career and technical education outcomes. EdWorkingPaper No. 21-492. *Annenberg Institute for School Reform at Brown University.*

Edde, M., Leroux, G., Altena, E., & Chanraud, S. (2021). Functional brain connectivity changes across the human life span: From fetal development to old age. *Journal of Neuroscience Research, 99*(1), 236–262.

Editors of *The Lancet*. (2010). Retraction — Ileal-lymphoid-nodular hyperplasia, non-specific colitis, and pervasive developmental disorder in children. *The Lancet, 375*(9713), 445. https://doi.org/10.1016/S0140-6736(10)60175-4

Efevbera, Y., & Bhabha, J. (2020). Defining and deconstructing girl child marriage and applications to global public health. *BMC Public Health, 20*(1), 1547. https://doi.org/10.1186/s12889-020-09545-0

Egalite, A. J. (2016). How family background influences student achievement. *Education Next, 16*(2), 70–78.

Egalite, A. J., & Kisida, B. (2018). The effects of teacher match on students' academic perceptions and attitudes. *Educational Evaluation and Policy Analysis, 40*(1), 59–81.

Egan, K. B., Cornwell, C. R., Courtney, J. G., & Ettinger, A. S. (2021). Blood lead levels in US children ages 1–11 years, 1976–2016. *Environmental Health Perspectives, 129*(3), 037003.

Egberts, M. R., Prinzie, P., Deković, M., de Haan, A. D., & van den Akker, A. L. (2015). The prospective relationship between child personality and perceived parenting: Mediation by parental sense of competence. *Personality and Individual Differences, 77*, 193–198.

Eggum-Wilkens, N. D., Lemery-Chalfant, K., Aksan, N., & Goldsmith, H. H. (2015). Self-conscious shyness: Growth during toddlerhood, strong role of genetics, and no prediction from fearful shyness. *Infancy, 20*(2), 160–188. https://doi.org/10.1111/infa.12070

Ehrenthal, D. B., Kuo, H.-H. D., & Kirby, R. S. (2020). Infant mortality in rural and nonrural counties in the United States. *Pediatrics, 146*(5), e20200464. https://doi.org/10.1542/peds.2020-0464

Ehrlich, K. B., & Cassidy, J. (2021). Early attachment and later physical health. In R. A. Thompson, J. A. Simpson, & L. J. Berlin (Eds.), *Attachment: The fundamental questions*. Guilford.

Eid, A., Mhatre, I., & Richardson, J. R. (2019). Gene–environment interactions in Alzheimer's disease: A potential path to precision medicine. *Pharmacology & Therapeutics, 199*, 173–187. https://doi.org/10.1016/j.pharmthera.2019.03.005

Eirich, R., McArthur, B. A., Anhorn, C., McGuinness, C., Christakis, D. A., & Madigan, S. (2022). Association of screen time with internalizing and externalizing behavior problems in children 12 years or younger: A systematic review and meta-analysis. *JAMA Psychiatry, 79*(5), 393–405. https://doi.org/10.1001/jamapsychiatry.2022.0155

Eisenberg, A. R. (1999). Emotion talk among Mexican American and Anglo American mothers and children from two social classes. *Merrill-Palmer Quarterly, 45*, 267–284.

Eisenberg, N. (2020). Findings, issues, and new directions for research on emotion socialization. *Developmental Psychology, 56*(3), 664–670. https://doi.org/10.1037/dev0000906

Eisenberg, N., Cumberland, A., & Spinrad, T. L. (1998). Parental socialization of emotion. *Psychological Inquiry, 9*(4), 241–273.

Eisenberg, N., Eggum-Wilkens, N. D., & Spinrad, T. L. (2015). The development of prosocial behavior. In D. A. Schroeder & W. G. Graziano (Eds.), *The Oxford handbook of prosocial behavior* (pp. 114–136). Oxford University Press.

Eisenberger, N. I., Lieberman, M. D., & Williams, K. D. (2003). Does rejection hurt? An fMRI study of social exclusion. *Science, 302*(5643), 290–292.

Ekas, N. V., Braungart Reiker, J. M., & Messinger, D. S. (2018). The development of infant emotion regulation: Time is of the essence. In P. M. Cole & T. Hollenstein (Eds.), *Emotion regulation: A matter of time* (pp. 49–69). Routledge.

Elder, G. H., & George, L. K. (2016). Age, cohorts, and the life course. In M. J. Shanahan, J. T. Mortimer, & M. Kirkpatrick Johnson (Eds.), *Handbook of the life course* (Vol. 2, pp. 59–85). Springer International Publishing. https://doi.org/10.1007/978-3-319-20880-0_3

Elder, G. H., Jr. (1998). The life course as developmental theory. *Child Development, 69*(1), 1–12.

Elder, G. H., Jr., & Conger, R. D. (2014). *Children of the land*. University of Chicago Press.

Elenbaas, L., Rizzo, M. T., & Killen, M. (2020). A developmental science perspective on social inequality. *Current Directions in Psychological Science, 29*(6), 610–616. https://doi.org/10.1177/0963721420964147

Eligon, J. (2020, June 26). A debate over identity and race asks, are African-Americans "Black" or "black"? *The New York Times.* https://www.nytimes.com/2020/06/26/us/black-african-american-style-debate.html

Eliot, L., Ahmed, A., Khan, H., & Patel, J. (2021). Dump the "dimorphism": Comprehensive synthesis of human brain studies reveals few male-female differences beyond size. *Neuroscience & Biobehavioral Reviews, 125,* 667–697. https://doi.org/10.1016/j.neubiorev.2021.02.026

Elkind, D. (1967). Egocentrism in adolescence. *Child Development, 38*(4), 1025–1034.

Elliott, A. M., & Evans, J. A. (2015). Derogatory nomenclature is still being used: The example of split hand/foot. *American Journal of Medical Genetics. Part A, 167A*(4), 928–929. https://doi.org/10.1002/ajmg.a.36952

Ellis, B. J., & Del Giudice, M. (2019). Developmental adaptation to stress: An evolutionary perspective. *Annual Review of Psychology, 70*(1), 111–139. https://doi.org/10.1146/annurev-psych-122216-011732

Ellis, B. J., Abrams, L. S., Masten, A. S., Sternberg, R. J., Tottenham, N., & Frankenhuis, W. E. (2020). Hidden talents in harsh environments. *Development and Psychopathology, 1,* 19.

Ellis, B. J., Bianchi, J., Griskevicius, V., & Frankenhuis, W. E. (2017). Beyond risk and protective factors: An adaptation-based approach to resilience. *Perspectives on Psychological Science, 12*(4), 561–587. https://doi.org/10.1177/1745691617693054

Ellis, B. J., Boyce, W. T., Belsky, J., Bakermans-Kranenburg, M. J., & Ijzendoorn, M. H. van. (2011). Differential susceptibility to the environment: An evolutionary–neurodevelopmental theory. *Development and Psychopathology, 23*(1), 7–28. https://doi.org/10.1017/S0954579410000611

Ellis, B. J., Del Giudice, M., Dishion, T. J., Figueredo, A. J., Gray, P., Griskevicius, V., Hawley, P. H., Jacobs, W. J., James, J., Volk, A. A., & Wilson, D. S. (2012). The evolutionary basis of risky adolescent behavior: Implications for science, policy, and practice. *Developmental Psychology, 48*(3), 598–623. https://doi.org/10.1037/a0026220

Ellis, B. J., Horn, A. J., Carter, C. S., van IJzendoorn, M. H., & Bakermans-Kranenburg, M. J. (2021). Developmental programming of oxytocin through variation in early-life stress: Four meta-analyses and a theoretical reinterpretation. *Clinical Psychology Review, 86,* 101985. https://doi.org/10.1016/j.cpr.2021.101985

Ellis, B. J., Sheridan, M. A., Belsky, J., & McLaughlin, K. A. (2022). Why and how does early adversity influence development? Toward an integrated model of dimensions of environmental experience. *Development and Psychopathology, 1–25.* https://doi.org/10.1017/S0954579421001838

Ellis, C. T., Skalaban, L. J., Yates, T. S., Bejjanki, V. R., Córdova, N. I., & Turk-Browne, N. B. (2021). Evidence of hippocampal learning in human infants. *Current Biology, 31*(15), 3358–3364.e4. https://doi.org/10.1016/j.cub.2021.04.072

Ellis, Y. G., Cliff, D. P., Janssen, X., Jones, R. A., Reilly, J. J., & Okely, A. D. (2017). Sedentary time, physical activity and compliance with IOM recommendations in young children at childcare. *Preventive Medicine Reports, 7,* 221–226. https://doi.org/10.1016/j.pmedr.2016.12.009

Elmore, R. F. (2009). Schooling adolescents. In R. M. Lerner & L. Steinberg (Eds.), *Handbook of adolescent psychology: Contextual influences on adolescent development* (pp. 193–227). John Wiley & Sons. https://doi.org/10.1002/9780470479193.adlpsy002007

Elsner, C., & Wertz, A. E. (2019). The seeds of social learning: Infants exhibit more social looking for plants than other object types. *Cognition, 183,* 244–255. https://doi.org/10.1016/j.cognition.2018.09.016

Ely, D. M., & Driscoll, A. K. (2020). Infant mortality in the United States, 2018: Data from the period linked birth/infant death file. *National Vital Statistics Reports: From the Centers for Disease Control and Prevention, National Center for Health Statistics, National Vital Statistics System, 69*(7), 1–18.

Embury, C. M., Wiesman, A. I., Proskovec, A. L., Mills, M. S., Heinrichs-Graham, E., Wang, Y.-P., Calhoun, V., & Wilson, T. W. (2019). Neural dynamics of verbal working memory processing in children and adolescents. *Neuroimage, 185,* 191–197.

Endendijk, J. J., Smit, A. K., van Baar, A. L., & Bos, P. A. (2019). Boys' toys, girls' toys: An fMRI study of mothers' neural responses to children violating gender expectations. *Biological Psychology, 148,* 107776. https://doi.org/10.1016/j.biopsycho.2019.107776

England-Mason, G., & Gonzalez, A. (2020). Intervening to shape children's emotion regulation: A review of emotion socialization parenting programs for young children. *Emotion, 20*(1), 98.

English, D., Thompson, R., White, C. R., & Wilson, D. (2015). Why should child welfare pay more attention to emotional maltreatment? *Children and Youth Services Review, 50,* 53–63. https://doi.org/10.1016/j.childyouth.2015.01.010

Enriquez, L. (2011). "Because we feel the pressure and we also feel the support": Examining the educational success of undocumented immigrant Latina/o students. *Harvard Educational Review, 81* (3), 476–500. https://doi.org/10.17763/haer.81.3.w7k703q050143762

Entwisle, D. R., & Astone, N. M. (1994). Some practical guidelines for measuring youth's race/ethnicity and socioeconomic status. *Child Development, 65*(6), 1521–1540. https://doi.org/10.1111/j.1467-8624.1994.tb00833.x

Epstein, M., Madeline, F., Kosterman, R., Bailey, J. A., King, K. M., Vasilenko, S. A., Steeger, C. M., & Hill, K. G. (2018). Adolescent age of sexual initiation and subsequent adult health outcomes. *American Journal of Public Health, 108*(6), 822–828. https://doi.org/10.2105/AJPH.2018.304372

Epstein, R., Blake, J., & González, T. (2017). *Girlhood interrupted: The erasure of black girls' childhood* (SSRN Scholarly Paper ID 3000695). Social Science Research Network. https://doi.org/10.2139/ssrn.3000695

Erberber, E., Stephens, M., Mamedova, S., Ferguson, S., & Kroeger, T. (2015). Socioeconomically disadvantaged students who are academically successful: Examining academic resilience cross-nationally. Policy Brief No. 5. *International Association for the Evaluation of Educational Achievement.*

Erck Lambert, A. B., Parks, S. E., Cottengim, C., Faulkner, M., Hauck, F. R., & Shapiro-Mendoza, C. K. (2019). Sleep-related infant suffocation deaths attributable to soft bedding, overlay, and wedging. *Pediatrics, 143*(5), e20183408. https://doi.org/10.1542/peds.2018-3408

Ereky-Stevens, K., Funder, A., Katschnig, T., Malmberg, L.-E., & Datler, W. (2018). Relationship building between toddlers and new caregivers in out-of-home childcare: Attachment security and caregiver sensitivity. *Early Childhood Research Quarterly, 42,* 270–279. https://doi.org/10.1016/j.ecresq.2017.10.007

Erik Erikson, 91, psychoanalyst who reshaped views of human growth, dies. (1994, May 13). *The New York Times,* B9.

Erikson, E. H. (1959). Identity and the life cycle: Selected papers. *Psychological Issues, 1,* 1–171.

Erikson, E. H. (1968). *Identity: Youth and crisis.* W. W. Norton.

Erikson, E. H. (1969). *Gandhi's truth: On the origins of militant nonviolence.* W. W. Norton.

Erikson, E. H. (1993). *Childhood and society: The landmark work on the social significance of childhood.* W. W. Norton. (Original work published 1950)

Erikson, E. H. (1994a). *Identity and the life cycle.* W. W. Norton.

Erikson, E. H. (1994b). *Identity: Youth and crisis.* W. W. Norton.

Erikson, E. H., & Erikson, J. M. (1998). *The life cycle completed* (Extended version). W. W. Norton.

Ernst, M. M., Kogan, B. A., & Lee, P. A. (2020). Gender identity: A psychosocial primer for providing care to patients with a disorder/difference of sex development and their families [individualized care for patients with intersex (Disorders/differences of sex development): Part 2]. *Journal of Pediatric Urology, 16*(5), 606–611. https://doi.org/10.1016/j.jpurol.2020.06.026

Espelage, D. L., Leemis, R. W., Niolon, P. H., Kearns, M., Basile, K. C., & Davis, J. P. (2020). Teen dating violence perpetration: Protective factor trajectories from middle to high school among adolescents. *Journal of Research on Adolescence, 30*(1), 170–188. https://doi.org/10.1111/jora.12510

Espinoza, P., Penelo, E., Mora, M., Francisco, R., González, M. L., & Raich, R. M. (2019). Bidirectional relations between disordered eating, internalization of beauty ideals, and self-esteem: A longitudinal study with adolescents. *The Journal of Early Adolescence, 39*(9), 1244–1260. https://doi.org/10.1177/0272431618812734

Esposito, G., Setoh, P., Shinohara, K., & Bornstein, M. H. (2017). The development of attachment: Integrating genes, brain, behavior, and environment. *Behavioural Brain Research, 325*(Pt. B), 87–89. https://doi.org/10.1016/j.bbr.2017.03.025

Esrick, E. B., Lehmann, L. E., Biffi, A., Achebe, M., Brendel, C., Ciuculescu, M. F., Daley, H., MacKinnon, B., Morris, E., Federico, A., Abriss, D., Boardman, K., Khelladi, R., Shaw, K., Negre, H., Negre, O., Nikiforow, S., Ritz, J., Pai, S.-Y., . . . Williams, D. A. (2021). Post-transcriptional genetic silencing of BCL11A to treat sickle cell disease. *New England Journal of Medicine, 384*(3), 205–215. https://doi.org/10.1056/NEJMoa2029392

Estrada, E. (2019). *Kids at work.* NYU Press.

Estrada, E., & Hondagneu-Sotelo, P. (2011). Intersectional dignities: Latino immigrant street vendor youth in Los Angeles. *Journal of Contemporary Ethnography, 40*(1), 102–131.

Estrada, E., Ferrer, E., Román, F. J., Karama, S., & Colom, R. (2019). Time-lagged associations between cognitive and cortical development from childhood to early adulthood. *Developmental Psychology, 55*(6), 1338–1352. https://doi.org/10.1037/dev0000716

Estrada, J. N., Huerta, A. H., Hernandez, E., Hernandez, R., & Kim, S. (2018). Socio-ecological risk and protective factors for youth gang involvement. In H. Shapiro (Ed.), *The Wiley handbook on violence in education: Forms, factors, and preventions* (pp. 185–202). John Wiley & Sons.

Ethier, K. A., Kann, L., & McManus, T. (2018). Sexual intercourse among high school students—29 states and United States overall, 2005–2015. *Morbidity and Mortality Weekly Report, 66*(5152), 1393–1397. https://doi.org/10.15585/mmwr.mm665152a1

Evans, W. N., Kearney, M. S., Perry, B., & Sullivan, J. X. (2020). Increasing community college completion rates among low-income students: Evidence from a randomized controlled trial evaluation of a case-management intervention. *Journal of Policy Analysis and Management, 39*(4), 930–965. https://doi.org/10.1002/pam.22256

Evers, K. S., & Wellmann, S. (2016). Arginine vasopressin and copeptin in perinatology. *Frontiers in Pediatrics, 4.* https://doi.org/10.3389/fped.2016.00075

Ewald, P. W., & Swain Ewald, H. A. (2019). Genetics and epigenetics. In M. Brüne & W. Schiefenhövel (Eds.), *The Oxford handbook of evolutionary medicine* (pp. 77–130). Oxford University Press.

Exner-Cortens, D., Wright, A., Claussen, C., & Truscott, E. (2021). A systematic review of adolescent masculinities and associations with internalizing behavior problems and social support. *American Journal of Community Psychology.* https://doi.org/10.1002/ajcp.12492

Ezeugwu, V. E., Mandhane, P. J., Hammam, N., Brook, J. R., Tamana, S. K., Hunter, S., Chikuma, J., Lefebvre, D. L., Azad, M. B., Moraes, T. J., Subbarao, P., Becker, A. B., Turvey, S. E., Rosu, A., Sears, M. R., & Carson, V. (2021). Influence of neighborhood characteristics and weather on movement behaviors at age 3 and 5 years in a longitudinal birth cohort. *Journal of Physical Activity and Health, 18*(5), 571–579. https://doi.org/10.1123/jpah.2020-0827

Fadus, M. C., Ginsburg, K. R., Sobowale, K., Halliday-Boykins, C. A., Bryant, B. E., Gray, K. M., & Squeglia, L. M. (2020). Unconscious bias and the diagnosis of disruptive behavior disorders and ADHD in African American and Hispanic youth. *Academic Psychiatry, 44*(1), 95–102. https://doi.org/10.1007/s40596-019-01127-6

Fadus, M. C., Squeglia, L. M., Valadez, E. A., Tomko, R. L., Bryant, B. E., & Gray, K. M. (2019). Adolescent substance use disorder treatment: An update on evidence-based strategies. *Current Psychiatry Reports, 21*(10), 96. https://doi.org/10.1007/s11920-019-1086-0

Faghiri, A., Stephen, J. M., Wang, Y.-P., Wilson, T. W., & Calhoun, V. D. (2018). Changing brain connectivity dynamics: From early childhood to adulthood. *Human Brain Mapping, 39*(3), 1108–1117.

Faherty, A. N., & Mitra, D. (2020). Emerging adulthoods: A microcultural approach to viewing the parent-child relationship. In B. K. Ashdown & A. N. Faherty (Eds.), *Parents and caregivers across cultures: Positive development from infancy through adulthood* (pp. 205–216). Springer International Publishing. https://doi.org/10.1007/978-3-030-35590-6_14

Fahrenthold, D. A. (2014, May 19). Great Society at 50: LBJ's Job Corps will cost taxpayers $1.7 billion this year. Does it work? *Washington Post.*

Fairchild, G., Hawes, D. J., Frick, P. J., Copeland, W. E., Odgers, C. L., Franke, B., Freitag, C. M., & De Brito, S. A. (2019). Conduct disorder. *Nature Reviews Disease Primers, 5*(1), 1–25. https://doi.org/10.1038/s41572-019-0095-y

Fall, C. H. D., & Kumaran, K. (2019). Metabolic programming in early life in humans. *Philosophical Transactions of the Royal Society B: Biological Sciences,* *374*(1770), 20180123. https://doi.org/10.1098/rstb.2018.0123

Fan, H., Xu, J., Cai, Z., He, J., & Fan, X. (2017). Homework and students' achievement in math and science: A 30-year meta-analysis, 1986–2015. *Educational Research Review, 20,* 35–54. https://doi.org/10.1016/j.edurev.2016.11.003

Fandakova, Y., & Hartley, C. A. (2020). Mechanisms of learning and plasticity in childhood and adolescence. *Developmental Cognitive Neuroscience, 42*(4), 100764. https://doi.org/10.1016/j.dcn.2020.100764

Fandakova, Y., Bunge, S. A., Wendelken, C., Desautels, P., Hunter, L., Lee, J. K., & Ghetti, S. (2018). The importance of knowing when you don't remember: Neural signaling of retrieval failure predicts memory improvement over time. *Cerebral Cortex, 28*(1), 90–102.

Fanger, S. M., Frankel, L. A., & Hazen, N. (2012). Peer exclusion in preschool children's play: Naturalistic observations in a playground setting. *Merrill-Palmer Quarterly (1982–),* 224–254.

Farago, F., Davidson, K. L., & Byrd, C. M. (2019). Ethnic-racial socialization in early childhood: The implications of color-consciousness and colorblindness for prejudice development. In H. E. Fitzgerald, D. J. Johnson, D. B. Qin, F. A. Villarruel, & J. Norder (Eds.), *Handbook of children and prejudice: Integrating research, practice, and policy* (pp. 131–145). Springer International Publishing. https://doi.org/10.1007/978-3-030-12228-7_7

Farhat, T. (2015). Stigma, obesity and adolescent risk behaviors: Current research and future directions. *Current Opinion in Psychology, 5,* 56–66. https://doi.org/10.1016/j.copsyc.2015.03.021

Farmer, V. L., Williams, S. M., Mann, J. I., Schofield, G., McPhee, J. C., & Taylor, R. W. (2017). The effect of increasing risk and challenge in the school playground on physical activity and weight in children: A cluster randomised controlled trial (PLAY). *International Journal of Obesity, 41*(5), 793–800. https://doi.org/10.1038/ijo.2017.41

Farpour-Lambert, N. (2020). Adolescent athletes. In W. Krutsch, H. O. Mayr, V. Musahl, F. Della Villa, P. M. Tscholl, & H. Jones (Eds.), *Injury and Health Risk Management in Sports: A Guide to Decision Making* (pp. 7–15). Springer. https://doi.org/10.1007/978-3-662-60752-7_2

Farr, R. H., Bruun, S. T., Doss, K. M., & Patterson, C. J. (2018). Children's Gender-Typed Behavior from Early to Middle Childhood in Adoptive Families with Lesbian, Gay, and Heterosexual Parents. *Sex Roles, 78*(7), 528–541. https://doi.org/10.1007/s11199-017-0812-5

Farran, D. C. (2016, July 14). Federal Preschool Development Grants: Evaluation needed. *Brookings.* https://www.brookings.edu/research/federal-preschool-development-grants-evaluation-needed/

Fasoli, A. D., & Raeff, C. (2021). How does culture show up in development? Conclusion to the spotlight series on the concept of culture. *Applied Developmental Science, 25*(2), 106–113. https://doi.org/10.1080/10888691.2021.1876301

Fast, A. A., & Olson, K. R. (2018). Gender development in transgender preschool children. *Child Development, 89*(2), 620–637. https://doi.org/10.1111/cdev.12758

Fasteland, M. (2019). Reading the antimodern way: G. Stanley Hall's *Adolescence* and imperialist reading for White American boys. *The Journal of the History of Childhood and Youth, 12* (1), 7–25. https://doi.org/10.1353/hcy.2019.0001

Fatherly. (2015, November 19). *This Is What Kids In 2015 Want To Be When They Grow Up.* Fatherly. https://www.fatherly.com/news/what-kids-want-to-be-when-they-grow-up/

Fatherly. (2017, December 22). *The 2017 Imagination Report: What Kids Want to Be When They Grow Up.* Fatherly. https://www.fatherly.com/love-money/the-2017-imagination-report-what-kids-want-to-be-when-they-grow-up/

Fazel, M., & Betancourt, T. S. (2018). Preventive mental health interventions for refugee children and adolescents in high-income settings. *The Lancet Child & Adolescent Health, 2*(2), 121–132. https://doi.org/10.1016/S2352-4642(17)30147-5

Fedorenko, E., & Thompson-Schill, S. L. (2014). Reworking the language network. *Trends in Cognitive Sciences, 18*(3), 120–126.

Feitoza, A. H. P., Henrique, R. S., Barnett, L. M., Ré, A. H. N., Lopes, V. P., Webster, E. K., Robinson, L. E., Cavalcante, W. A., & Cattuzzo, M. T. (2018). Perceived motor competence in childhood: Comparative study among countries. *Journal of Motor Learning and Development, 6*(2), S337–S350. https://doi.org/10.1123/jmld.2016-0079

Feldman, R. (2020). What is resilience: Aan affiliative neuroscience approach. *World Psychiatry, 19*(2), 132–150. https://doi.org/10.1002/wps.20729

Feldman, R., & Bakermans-Kranenburg, M. J. (2017). Oxytocin: A parenting hormone. *Current Opinion in Psychology, 15*(Supplement C), 13–18. https://doi.org/10.1016/j.copsyc.2017.02.011

Feliciano, C., & Lanuza, Y. R. (2017). An immigrant paradox? Contextual attainment and intergenerational educational mobility. *American Sociological Review, 82*(1), 211–241.

Felitti, V. J., Anda, R. F., Nordenberg, D., Williamson, D. F., Spitz, A. M., Edwards, V., Koss, M. P., & Marks, J. S. (1998). Relationship of childhood abuse and household dysfunction to many of the leading causes of death in adults: The Adverse Childhood Experiences (ACE) Study. *American Journal of Preventive Medicine, 14*(4), 245–258. https://doi.org/10.1016/S0749-3797(98)00017-8

Felmban, W. S., & Klaczynski, P. A. (2019). Adolescents' base rate judgments, metastrategic understanding, and stereotype endorsement. *Journal of Experimental Child Psychology, 178,* 60–85.

Felmlee, D. H., McMillan, C., Inara Rodis, P., & Osgood, D. W. (2018). The evolution of youth friendship networks from 6th to 12th grade: School transitions, popularity and centrality. In D. F. Alwin, D. H. Felmlee, & D. A. Kreager (Eds.), *Social networks and the life course: Integrating the development of human lives and social relational networks* (pp. 161–184). Springer International Publishing. https://doi.org/10.1007/978-3-319-71544-5_8

Feng, Z., Glinskaya, E., Chen, H., Gong, S., Qiu, Y., Xu, J., & Yip, W. (2020). Long-term care system for older adults in China: Policy landscape, challenges, and future prospects. *The Lancet, 396*(10259), 1362–1372. https://doi.org/10.1016/S0140-6736(20)3

Fenson, L., Dale, P. S., Reznick, J. S., Bates, E., Thal, D. J., Pethick, S. J., ... & Stiles, J. (1994). Variability in early communicative development. *Monographs of the society for research in child development,* i–185.

Ferdinand, K. C. (2021). Overcoming barriers to COVID-19 vaccination in African Americans: The need for cultural humility. *American Journal of Public Health, 111*(4), 586–588. https://doi.org/10.2105/AJPH.2020.306135

Ferguson, C. A. (1964). Baby Talk in Six Languages. *American Anthropologist, 66*(6_PART2), 103–114. https://doi.org/10.1525/aa.1964.66.suppl_3.02a00060

Ferguson, C. J., Copenhaver, A., & Markey, P. (2020). Reexamining the findings of the American Psychological Association's 2015 Task Force on Violent Media: A meta-analysis. *Perspectives on Psychological Science, 15*(6), 1423–1443. https://doi.org/10.1177/1745691620927666

Ferguson, C. J., Muñoz, M. E., Garza, A., & Galindo, M. (2014). Concurrent and prospective analyses of peer, television and social media influences on body dissatisfaction, eating disorder symptoms and life satisfaction in adolescent girls. *Journal of Youth and Adolescence, 43*(1), 1–14. https://doi.org/10.1007/s10964-012-9898-9

Ferguson, C. J., & Wang, J. C. (2022). Aggressive video games are not a risk factor for future aggression in youth: A longitudinal study. In *Key Topics in Parenting and Behavior* (pp. 115–127). Cham: Springer Nature Switzerland.

Ferjan Ramírez, N., & Kuhl, P. K. (2016). *Bilingual language learning in children.* University of Washington, Institute for Learning and Brain Sciences.

Ferjan Ramírez, N., Lytle, S. R., & Kuhl, P. K. (2020). Parent coaching increases conversational turns and advances infant language development. *Proceedings of the National Academy of Sciences, 117*(7), 3484–3491.

Fernald, A., & Marchman, V. A. (2012). Individual differences in lexical processing at 18 months predict vocabulary growth in typically-developing and late-talking toddlers. *Child Development, 83*(1), 203–222. https://doi.org/10.1111/j.1467-8624.2011.01692.x

Fernandez, C., McCaffery, H., Miller, A. L., Kaciroti, N., Lumeng, J. C., & Pesch, M. H. (2020). Trajectories of picky eating in low-income US children. *Pediatrics, 145*(6), e20192018. https://doi.org/10.1542/peds.2019-2018

Ferre, C. L., Babik, I., & Michel, G. F. (2020). A perspective on the development of hemispheric specialization, infant handedness, and cerebral palsy. *Cortex, 127*, 208-220.

Ferriss, S. (2015, April 10). How does your state rank on sending students to police? *Time.* https://time.com/3818075/student-police-ranking/

Fiks, A. G., Ross, M. E., Mayne, S. L., Song, L., Liu, W., Steffes, J., McCarn, B., Grundmeier, R. W., Localio, A. R., & Wasserman, R. (2016). Preschool ADHD diagnosis and stimulant use before and after the 2011 AAP Practice Guideline. *Pediatrics, 138*(6), e20162025. https://doi.org/10.1542/peds.2016-2025

Filippa, M., Lordier, L., De Almeida, J. S., Monaci, M. G., Adam-Darque, A., Grandjean, D., Kuhn, P., & Hüppi, P. S. (2020). Early vocal contact and music in the NICU: New insights into preventive interventions. *Pediatric Research, 87*(2), 249–264. https://doi.org/10.1038/s41390-019-0490-9

Finch, H., Hernández Finch, M. E., & Avery, B. (2021). The impact of national and school contextual factors on the academic performance of immigrant students. *Frontiers in Education, 6.* https://www.frontiersin.org/articles/10.3389/feduc.2021.793790

Findlay, B. L., Melucci, A., Dombrovskiy, V., Pierre, J., & Lee, Y.-H. (2019). Children after motor vehicle crashes: Restraint utilization and injury severity. *Journal of Pediatric Surgery, 54*(7), 1411–1415. https://doi.org/10.1016/j.jpedsurg.2018.10.046

Finer, L. B., & Zolna, M. R. (2016). Declines in unintended pregnancy in the United States, 2008–2011. *New England Journal of Medicine, 374*(9), 843–852. https://doi.org/10.1056/NEJMsa1506575

Finkel, E. J. (2019). *The all-or-nothing marriage: How the best marriages work.* Penguin.

Finkelhor, D. (2020). Trends in adverse childhood experiences (ACEs) in the United States. *Child Abuse & Neglect, 108*, 104641. https://doi.org/10.1016/j.chiabu.2020.104641

Finkelstein, D. M., Petersen, D. M., & Schottenfeld, L. S. (2017). Promoting children's physical activity in low-income communities in Colorado: What are the barriers and opportunities? *Preventing Chronic Disease, 14*, 170111. https://doi.org/10.5888/pcd14.170111

Finkelhor, D., Turner, H. A., Shattuck, A., & Hamby, S. L. (2013). Violence, crime, and abuse exposure in a national sample of children and youth: An update. *JAMA pediatrics, 167*(7), 614–621.

Finkelhor, D., Turner, H., Wormuth, B. K., Vanderminden, J., & Hamby, S. (2019). Corporal punishment: Current rates from a national survey. *Journal of Child and Family Studies, 28*(7), 1991–1997. https://doi.org/10.1007/s10826-019-01426-4

Finken, M. J. J., van der Steen, M., Smeets, C. C. J., Walenkamp, M. J. E., de Bruin, C., Hokken-Koelega, A. C. S., & Wit, J. M. (2018). Children born small for gestational age: Differential diagnosis, molecular genetic evaluation, and implications. *Endocrine Reviews, 39*(6), 851–894. https://doi.org/10.1210/er.2018-00083

Finlay, B. B., & Arrieta, M. C. (2017). *Let them eat dirt: How microbes can make your child healthier.* Algonquin Books.

Finsaas, M. C., Kessel, E. M., Dougherty, L. R., Bufferd, S. J., Danzig, A. P., Davila, J., Carlson, G. A., & Klein, D. N. (2020). Early childhood psychopathology prospectively predicts social functioning in early adolescence. *Journal of Clinical Child and Adolescent Psychology, 49*(3), 353–364. https://doi.org/10.1080/15374416.2018.1504298

Fischer, K. W., & Hencke, R. W. (1996). Infants' construction of actions in context: Piaget's contribution to research on early development. *Psychological Science, 7*(4), 204–210.

Fischer, N. M., Duffy, E. Y., & Michos, E. D. (2021). Protecting our youth: Support policy to combat health disparities fueled by targeted food advertising. *Journal of the American Heart Association, 10*(1), e018900. https://doi.org/10.1161/JAHA.120.018900

Fischhoff, B. (2013). The sciences of science communication. *Proceedings of the National Academy of Sciences, 110*(Suppl. 3), 14033–14039. https://doi.org/10.1073/pnas.1213273110

Fisher, A. V., Godwin, K. E., & Seltman, H. (2014). Visual environment, attention allocation, and learning in young children: When too much of a good thing may be bad. *Psychological Science, 25*(7), 1362–1370. https://doi.org/10.1177/0956797614533801

Fisher, C. M., Telljohann, S. K., Price, J. H., Dake, J. A., & Glassman, T. (2015). Perceptions of elementary school children's parents regarding sexuality education. *American Journal of Sexuality Education, 10*(1), 1–20.

Fiske, A., & Holmboe, K. (2019). Neural substrates of early executive function development. *Developmental Review, 52*, 42–62. https://doi.org/10.1016/j.dr.2019.100866

Fivush, R. (2014). Gendered narratives: Elaboration, structure, and emotion in parent-child reminiscing across the preschool years. In C. P. Thompson, D. J. Herrmann, D. Bruce, J. D. Read, D. G. Payne, & M. P. Toglia (Eds.), *Autobiographical memory: Theoretical and applied perspectives* (pp. 79–104). Psychology Press. https://doi.org/10.4324/9781315784250-6

Fivush, R. (2019). Sociocultural developmental approaches to autobiographical memory. *Applied Cognitive Psychology, 33*(4), 489–497. https://doi.org/10.1002/acp.3512

Flaherty, E. G., Stirling, J., & The Committee on Child Abuse and Neglect. (2010). The pediatrician's role in child maltreatment prevention. *Pediatrics, 126*(4), 833–841. https://doi.org/10.1542/peds.2010-2087

Flaherty, M., Hunsicker, D., & Goldin-Meadow, S. (2021). Structural biases that children bring to language learning: A cross-cultural look at gestural input to homesign. *Cognition, 211*, 104608. https://doi.org/10.1016/j.cognition.2021.104608

Flanagan, C., & Gallay, E. (2014). Adolescents' theories of the commons. *Advances in Child Development and Behavior, 46*, 33–55.

Flanagan, I. M. L., Auty, K. M., & Farrington, D. P. (2019). Parental supervision and later offending: A systematic review of longitudinal studies. *Aggression and Violent Behavior, 47*, 215–229. https://doi.org/10.1016/j.avb.2019.06.003

Flavell, J. H. (1979). Metacognition and cognitive monitoring: A new area of cognitive–developmental inquiry. *American Psychologist, 34*(10), 906.

Flavell, J. H. (1996). Piaget's legacy. *Psychological Science, 7*(4), 200–203.

Flaviano, M., & Harville, E. W. (2021). Adverse childhood experiences on reproductive plans and adolescent pregnancy in the Gulf resilience on women's health cohort. *International Journal of Environmental Research and Public Health, 18*(1), 165.

Fleming, A. R. (2009, October 5). Can an intellectually disabled mom raise a gifted daughter? It's working so far for Bonnie and Myra Brown. People.

Flensborg-Madsen, T., & Mortensen, E. L. (2018). Developmental milestones during the first three years as precursors of adult intelligence. *Developmental Psychology, 54*(8), 1434–1444. https://doi.org/10.1037/dev0000545

Flint, T. K. (2020). Responsive play: Creating transformative classroom spaces through play as a reader response. *Journal of Early Childhood Literacy, 20*(2), 385–410. https://doi.org/10.1177/1468798418763991

Floresco, S. B. (2015). The nucleus accumbens: An interface between cognition, emotion, and action. *Annual Review of Psychology, 66*, 25–52.

Floris, D. L., Wolfers, T., Zabihi, M., Holz, N. E., Zwiers, M. P., Charman, T., Tillman, J., Ecker, C., Dell'Acqua, F., Banaschewski, T., Moessnang, C., Baron-Cohen, S., Holt, R., Durston, S., Loth, E., Murphy, D. G. M., Marquand, A., Buitelaar, J. K., Beckmann, C. F., & EU-AIMS Longitudinal European Autism Project Group. (2021). Atypical brain asymmetry in autism — a candidate for clinically meaningful stratification. *Biological Psychiatry: Cognitive Neuroscience and Neuroimaging, 6*(8), 802–812.

Flynn, H. K., Felmlee, D. H., & Conger, R. D. (2017). The social context of adolescent friendships: Parents, peers, and romantic partners. *Youth & Society, 49*(5), 679–705. https://doi.org/10.1177/0044118X14559900

Flynn, H. K., Felmlee, D. H., Shu, X., & Conger, R. D. (2018). Mothers and fathers matter: The influence of parental support, hostility, and problem solving on adolescent friendships. *Journal of Family Issues, 39*(8), 2389–2412. https://doi.org/10.1177/0192513X18755423

Flynn, J. R. (2020). Secular changes in intelligence: The "Flynn effect." In R. J. Sternberg (Ed.), *The Cambridge handbook of intelligence* (pp. 940–963). Cambridge University Press.

Flynn, J. R., & Shayer, M. (2018). IQ decline and Piaget: Does the rot start at the top? *Intelligence, 66*, 112–121. https://doi.org/10.1016/j.intell.2017.11.010

Folayan, M. O., Tantawi, M. E., Ramos-Gomez, F., & Sabbah, W. (2020). Early childhood caries and its associations with sugar consumption, overweight and exclusive breastfeeding in low, middle and high-income countries: An ecological study. *PeerJ, 8*, e9413. https://doi.org/10.7717/peerj.9413

Fomby, P., & Johnson, D. S. (2022). Continuity and change in US children's family composition, 1968–2017. *Demography, 59*(2), 731–760.

Fomby, P., & Osborne, C. (2017). Family instability, multipartner fertility, and behavior in middle childhood. *Journal of Marriage and Family, 79*(1), 75–93.

Fonagy, P., Luyten, P., Allison, E., & Campbell, C. (2016). Reconciling psychoanalytic ideas with attachment theory. In J. Cassidy & P. R. Shaver (Eds.), *Handbook of attachment: Theory, research, and clinical applications* (3rd ed., pp. 780–804). Guilford.

Forbes, M. K., Fitzpatrick, S., Magson, N. R., & Rapee, R. M. (2019). Depression, anxiety, and peer victimization: Bidirectional relationships and associated outcomes transitioning from childhood to adolescence. *Journal of Youth and Adolescence, 48*(4), 692–702. https://doi.org/10.1007/s10964-018-0922-6

Force, L. M., Abdollahpour, I., Advani, S. M., Agius, D., Ahmadian, E., Alahdab, F., Alam, T., Alebel, A., Alipour, V., Allen, C. A., Almasi-Hashiani, A., Alvarez, E. M., Amini, S., Amoako, Y. A., Anber, N. H., Arabloo, J., Artaman, A., Atique, S., Awasthi, A., . . . Bhakta, N. (2019). The global burden of childhood and adolescent cancer in 2017: An analysis of the Global Burden of Disease Study 2017. *The Lancet Oncology, 20*(9), 1211–1225. https://doi.org/10.1016/S1470-2045(19)30339-0

Forger, N. G. (2018). Past, present and future of epigenetics in brain sexual differentiation. *Journal of Neuroendocrinology, 30*(2), e12492. https://doi.org/10.1111/jne.12492

Foronda, C., Baptiste, D. L., & Reinholdt, M. M. (2016). Cultural humility: A concept analysis. *Journal of Transcultural Nursing, 27*(3), 210–217.

Forry, N. (2015, September 21). Consumer education helps parents choose quality child care. *Child Trends.* https://www.childtrends.org/blog/consumer-education-helps-parents-choose-quality-child-care

Forry, N., Iruka, I., Tout, K., Torquati, J., Susman-Stillman, A., Bryant, D., & Daneri, M. P. (2013). *Predictors of quality and child outcomes in family child care settings.* Child Trends.

Forslund, T., Granqvist, P., van IJzendoorn, M. H., Sagi-Schwartz, A., Glaser, D., Steele, M., Hammarlund, M., Schuengel, C., Bakermans-Kranenburg, M. J., Steele, H., Shaver, P. R., Lux, U., Simmonds, J., Jacobvitz, D., Groh, A. M., Bernard, K., Cyr, C., Hazen, N. L., Foster, S., . . . Duschinsky, R. (2021). Attachment goes to court: Child protection and custody issues. *Attachment & Human Development, 1*–52. https://doi.org/10.1080/14616734.2020.1840762

Fortenberry, J. D. (2014). Sexual learning, sexual experience, and healthy adolescent sex. In E. S. Lefkowitz & S. A. Vasilenko (Eds.), *Positive and negative outcomes of sexual behaviors* (pp. 71–86). Jossey-Bass/Wiley.

Fosco, G. M., McCauley, D. M., & Sloan, C. J. (2021). Distal and proximal family contextual effects on adolescents' interparental conflict appraisals: A daily diary study. *Journal of Family Psychology.* https://doi.org/10.1037/fam0000703

Fosco, G. M., Stormshak, E. A., Dishion, T. J., & Winter, C. E. (2012). Family relationships and parental monitoring during middle school as predictors of early adolescent problem behavior. *Journal of Clinical Child & Adolescent Psychology, 41*(2), 202–213.

Fotuhi, O., Ehret, P. J., Kocsik, S., & Cohen, G. L. (2022). Boosting college prospects among low-income students: Using self-affirmation to trigger motivation and a behavioral ladder to channel it. *Journal of Personality and Social Psychology, 122*(2), 187–201. https://doi.org/10.1037/pspa0000283

Fox, M. (2005, September 27). Urie Bronfenbrenner, 88, an authority on child development, dies. *The New York Times.* https://www.nytimes.com/2005/09/27/nyregion/urie-bronfenbrenner-88-an-authority-on-child-development-dies.html

Fox, M., Siddarth, P., Oughli, H. A., Nguyen, S. A., Milillo, M. M., Aguilar, Y., Ercoli, L., & Lavretsky, H. (2021). Women who breastfeed exhibit cognitive benefits after age 50. *Evolution, Medicine, and Public Health, 9*(1), 322–331. https://doi.org/10.1093/emph/eoab027

Fraga, M. F., Ballestar, E., Paz, M. F., Ropero, S., Setien, F., Ballestar, M. L., Heine-Suñer, Cigudosa, J. C., Urioste, M., Benitez, J., Boix-Chornet, M., Sanchez-Aguilera, A., Ling, C., Carlsson, E., Poulsen, P., Vaag, A., Stephan, Z., Spector, T. D., Wu, Y.-Z. . . . Esteller, M. (2005). Epigenetic differences arise during the lifetime of monozygotic twins. *Proceedings of the National Academy of Sciences, 102*(30), 10604–10609.

Fragile Families and Child Wellbeing Study (FFCWS). (2021). *About the Fragile Families and Child Wellbeing Study.* https://fragilefamilies.princeton.edu/about

Fraguas, D., Díaz-Caneja, C. M., Ayora, M., Durán-Cutilla, M., Abregú-Crespo, R., Ezquiaga-Bravo, I., Martín-Babarro, J., & Arango, C. (2021). Assessment of school anti-bullying interventions: A meta-analysis of randomized clinical trials. *JAMA Pediatrics, 175*(1), 44. https://doi.org/10.1001/jamapediatrics.2020.3541

Fraiman, Y. S., Litt, J. S., Davis, J. M., & Pursley, D. M. (2021). Racial and ethnic disparities in adult COVID-19 and the future impact on child health. *Pediatric Research, 89*(5), 1052–1054.

Fraley, R. C. (2019). Attachment in adulthood: Recent developments, emerging debates, and future directions. *Annual Review of Psychology, 70*(1), 401–422. https://doi.org/10.1146/annurev-psych-010418-102813

Fraley, R. C., & Roisman, G. I. (2019). The development of adult attachment styles: Four lessons. *Current Opinion in Psychology, 25*, 26–30.

Franchak, J. M. (2019). Changing opportunities for learning in everyday life: Infant body position over the first year. *Infancy, 24*(2), 187–209.

Franchak, J. M. (2020). The ecology of infants' perceptual-motor exploration. *Current Opinion in Psychology, 32*, 110–114. https://doi.org/10.1016/j.copsyc.2019.06.035

Francis, B., Craig, N., Hodgen, J., Taylor, B., Tereshchenko, A., Connolly, P., & Archer, L. (2020). The impact of tracking by attainment on pupil self-confidence over time: Demonstrating the accumulative impact of self-fulfilling prophecy. *British Journal of Sociology of Education, 41*(5), 626–642. https://doi.org/10.1080/01425692.2020.1763162

Francis, J. K. R., & Gold, M. A. (2017). Long-acting reversible contraception for adolescents: A review. *JAMA Pediatrics, 171*(7), 694–701. https://doi.org/10.1001/jamapediatrics.2017.0598

Francis, L., & Pearson, D. (2019). The recognition of emotional abuse: Adolescents' responses to warning signs in romantic relationships. *Journal of Interpersonal Violence.* https://doi.org/10.1177/0886260519850537

Franck, L. S., & O'Brien, K. (2019). The evolution of family-centered care: From supporting parent-delivered interventions to a model of family integrated care. *Birth Defects Research, 111*(15), 1044–1059. https://doi.org/10.1002/bdr2.1521

Frank, L. (2020). *Out of milk: Infant food insecurity in a rich nation.* UBC Press.

Frank, L. D., Iroz-Elardo, N., MacLeod, K. E., & Hong, A. (2019). Pathways from built environment to health: A conceptual framework linking behavior and exposure-based impacts. *Journal of Transport & Health, 12*, 319–335. https://doi.org/10.1016/j.jth.2018.11.008

Frank, M. C., Braginsky, M., Yurovsky, D., & Marchman, V. A. (2021). *Variability and consistency in early language learning: The Wordbank Project.* MIT Press.

Frankenhuis, W. E. (2019). Modeling the evolution and development of emotions. *Developmental Psychology, 55*(9), 2002.

Frankenhuis, W. E., & Nettle, D. (2020). The strengths of people in poverty. *Current Directions in Psychological Science, 29*(1), 16–21. https://doi.org/10.1177/0963721419881154

Frankenhuis, W. E., & Walasek, N. (2020). Modeling the evolution of sensitive periods. *Developmental Cognitive Neuroscience, 41*, 100715. https://doi.org/10.1016/j.dcn.2019.100715

Frazer, Z., McConnell, K., & Jansson, L. M. (2019). Treatment for substance use disorders in pregnant women: Motivators and barriers. *Drug and Alcohol Dependence, 205*, 107652. https://doi.org/10.1016/j.drugalcdep.2019.107652

Fredstrom, B. K., Rose-Krasnor, L., Campbell, K., Rubin, K. H., Booth-LaForce, C., & Burgess, K. B. (2012). Brief report: How anxiously withdrawn preadolescents think about friendship. *Journal of Adolescence, 35*(2), 451–454.

French, B., Outhwaite, L. A., Langley-Evans, S. C., & Pitchford, N. J. (2020). Nutrition, growth, and other factors associated with early cognitive and motor development in Sub-Saharan Africa: A scoping review. *Journal of Human Nutrition and Dietetics, 33*(5), 644–669. https://doi.org/10.1111/jhn.12795

Freud, S. (1927). Some psychological consequences of the anatomical distinction between the sexes. *The International Journal of Psychoanalysis, 8*, 133–142.

Freud, S. (1964). The interpretation of dreams. In The standard edition of the complete psychological works of Sigmund Freud (J. Strachey, Ed.). Macmillan. (Original work published 1899)

Freud, S. (1968a). Female sexuality (J. Strachey, Trans.). In *The standard edition of the complete psychological works of Sigmund Freud* (Vol. XXI, pp. 223–245). The Hogarth Press. (Original work published 1931)

Freud, S. (1968b). Femininity (J. Strachey, Trans.). In *The standard edition of the complete psychological works of Sigmund Freud* (Vol. XXII, pp. 112–135). The Hogarth Press. (Original work published 1933)

Freud, S. (1977). *A general introduction to psychoanalysis* (J. Strachey, Trans.). W. W. Norton.

Freud, S. (1989). Mourning and melancholia. In *The Freud Reader* (P. Gay, Ed.). New York: W. W. Norton. (Original work published 1917)

Freud, S. (2000). *Three essays on the theory of sexuality* (J. Strachey, Trans.). Basic Books. (Original work published 1905)

Freud, S. (2018). *The Sigmund Freud collection.* Charles River Editors.

Freudenberg, N., Goldrick-Rab, S., & Poppendieck, J. (2019). College students and SNAP: The new face of food insecurity in the United States. *American Journal of Public Health, 109*(12), 1652–1658. https://doi.org/10.2105/AJPH.2019.305332

Freund, J.-D., Linberg, A., & Weinert, S. (2019). Longitudinal interplay of young children's negative affectivity and maternal interaction quality in the context of unequal psychosocial resources. *Infant Behavior and Development, 55*, 123–132. https://doi.org/10.1016/j.infbeh.2019.01.003

Frick, A., Möhring, W., & Newcombe, N. S. (2014). Picturing perspectives: Development of perspective-taking abilities in 4- to 8-year-olds. *Frontiers in Psychology, 5.* https://doi.org/10.3389/fpsyg.2014.00386

Friederici, A. D., Chomsky, N., Berwick, R. C., Moro, A., & Bolhuis, J. J. (2017). Language, mind and brain. *Nature Human Behaviour, 1*(10), 713–722. https://doi.org/10.1038/s41562-017-0184-4

Friedman, L. J. (2000). *Identity's architect: A biography of Erik H. Erikson.* Harvard University Press.

Friso-van den Bos, I., Kroesbergen, E. H., & Van Luit, J. E. H. (2018). Counting and number line trainings in kindergarten: Effects on arithmetic performance and number sense. *Frontiers in Psychology, 9*, 975. https://doi.org/10.3389/fpsyg.2018.00975

Frisvold, D. E. (2015). Nutrition and cognitive achievement: An evaluation of the School Breakfast Program. *Journal of Public Economics, 124*, 91–104.

Frith, U. (2019). Flux of life. *Developmental Cognitive Neuroscience, 38*, 100669. https://doi.org/10.1016/j.dcn.2019.100669

Fritts, R. (2021, June 29). How do babies perceive the world? *MIT Technology Review.* https://www.technologyreview.com/2021/06/29/1025745/how-do-babies-perceive-the-world/

Fritz, J., de Graaff, A. M., Caisley, H., van Harmelen, A.-L., & Wilkinson, P. O. (2018). A systematic review of amenable resilience factors that moderate and/or mediate the relationship between childhood adversity and mental health in young people. *Frontiers in Psychiatry, 9*, 230. https://doi.org/10.3389/fpsyt.2018.00230

Frosh, S. (2013). Psychoanalysis, colonialism, racism. *Journal of Theoretical and Philosophical Psychology, 33*(3), 141–154. https://doi.org/10.1037/a0033398

Frost, D. M., Meyer, I. H., & Hammack, P. L. (2015). Health and well-being in emerging adults' same-sex relationships: Critical questions and directions for research in developmental science. *Emerging Adulthood, 3*(1), 3–13. https://doi.org/10.1177/2167696814535915

Frostenson, S. (2016, February 3). 18 cities in Pennsylvania reported higher levels of lead exposure than Flint. *Vox.* https://www.vox.com/2016/2/3/10904120/lead-exposure-flint-pennsylvania

Fry, R., & Parker, K. (2021, October 5). Rising share of U.S. adults are living without a spouse or partner. *Social & Demographic Trends Project.* Pew Research Center. https://www.pewresearch.org/social-trends/2021/10/05/rising-share-of-u-s-adults-are-living-without-a-spouse-or-partner/

Fryar, C. D., Carroll, M. D., & Afful, J. (2020a). *Prevalence of low weight-for-recumbent length, recumbent length-for-age, and weight-for-age among infants and toddlers from birth to 24 months of age: United States, 1999–2000 through 2017–2018* [Health E Stats]. https://www.cdc.gov/nchs/data/hestat/low-weight-recumbent-17-18/low-weight-recumbent.htm

Fryar, C. D., Carroll, M. D., & Afful, J. (2020b). *Prevalence of high weight-for-recumbent length among infants and toddlers from birth to 24 months of age: United States, 1971–1974 through 2017–2018* [Health E Stats]. https://www.cdc.gov/nchs/data/hestat/high-weight-recumbent-17-18/high-weight-recumbent.htm

Fuhrmann, D., Knoll, L. J., & Blakemore, S.-J. (2015). Adolescence as a sensitive period of brain development. *Trends in Cognitive Sciences, 19*(10), 558–566. https://doi.org/10.1016/j.tics.2015.07.008

Fujiki, M., & Brinton, B. (2017). Pragmatics and social communication in child language disorders. In R. G. Schwartz (Ed.), *Handbook of child language disorders* (2nd ed.). Psychology Press.

Fukao, K., Makino, T., & Settsu, T. (2021). Human capital and economic growth in Japan: 1885–2015. *Journal of Economic Surveys, 35*(3), 710–740. https://doi.org/10.1111/joes.12419

Fuligni, A. J. (1998). Authority, autonomy, and parent–adolescent conflict and cohesion: A study of adolescents from Mexican, Chinese, Filipino, and European backgrounds. *Developmental Psychology, 34*(4), 782.

Fuligni, A. J. (2019). The need to contribute during adolescence. *Perspectives on Psychological Science, 14*(3), 331–343.

Fuligni, A. J. (2020). Is there inequality in what adolescents can give as well as receive?. *Current Directions in Psychological Science, 29*(4), 405–411.

Fuligni, A. J., & Fuligni, A. S. (2009). Immigrant families and the educational development of their children. In *Immigrant Families in Contemporary Society.* Guilford Press.

Fuligni, A. J., Hughes, D. L., & Way, N. (2009). Ethnicity and immigration. In R. M. Lerner & L. Steinberg (Eds.), *Handbook of adolescent psychology: Contextual influences on adolescent development* (Vol. 2, 3rd ed., pp. 527–569). John Wiley & Sons. https://doi.org/10.1002/9780470479193.adlpsy002016

Fuligni, A. J., Smola, X. A., & Al Salek, S. (2021). Feeling needed and useful during the transition to young adulthood. *Journal of Research on Adolescence.*

Fuligni, A. J., & Tsai, K. M. (2015). Developmental flexibility in the age of globalization: Autonomy and identity development among immigrant adolescents. *Annual Review of Psychology, 66*, 411–431.

Fuligni, A. J., Tseng, V., & Lam, M. (1999). Attitudes toward family obligations among American adolescents with Asian, Latin American, and European backgrounds. *Child Development, 70*(4), 1030–1044.

Fuligni, A. J., Witkow, M., & Garcia, C. (2005). Ethnic identity and the academic adjustment of adolescents from Mexican, Chinese, and European backgrounds. *Developmental Psychology, 41*(5), 799.

Fuligni, A. S., Howes, C., Huang, Y., Hong, S. S., & Lara-Cinisomo, S. (2012). Activity settings and daily routines in preschool classrooms: Diverse experiences in early learning settings for low-income children. *Early Childhood Research Quarterly, 27*(2), 198–209. https://doi.org/10.1016/j.ecresq.2011.10.001

Fullana, M. A., Dunsmoor, J. E., Schruers, K. R. J., Savage, H. S., Bach, D. R., & Harrison, B. J. (2020). Human fear conditioning: From neuroscience to the clinic. *Behaviour Research and Therapy, 124*, 103528. https://doi.org/10.1016/j.brat.2019.103528

Fullerton, A. M. (1911). *A handbook of obstetric nursing for nurses, students and mothers.* P. Blakiston's Son. http://archive.org/details/ahandbookobstet01fullgoog

Fullwiley, D. (2021, February 1). DNA and our twenty-first-century ancestors. *Boston Review.* http://bostonreview.net/race/duana-fullwiley-dna-and-our-twenty-first-century-ancestors

Funk, C., Hefferon, M., Kennedy, B., & Johnson, C. (2019). *Trust and mistrust in Americans' views of scientific experts.* Pew Research Center.

Furman, W. (2018). The romantic relationships of youth. In W. M. Bukowski, B. Laursen, & K. H. Rubin (Eds.), *Handbook of peer interactions, relationships, and groups* (2nd ed., pp. 410–428). Guilford.

Furman, W., & Rose, A. J. (2015). Friendships, romantic relationships, and peer relationships. In M. Lamb & R. M. Lerner (Eds.), *Handbook of child psychology and developmental science* (pp. 932–974). Wiley. https://doi.org/10.1002/9781118963418.childpsy322

Furth, C. (1988). Androgynous males and deficient females: Biology and gender boundaries in sixteenth- and seventeenth-century China. *Late Imperial China, 9*(2), 1–31. https://doi.org/10.1353/late.1988.0002

Furukawa, E., Tangney, J., & Higashibara, F. (2012). Cross-cultural continuities and discontinuities in shame, guilt, and pride: A study of children residing in Japan, Korea and the USA. *Self and Identity, 11*(1), 90–113.

Futagi, Y., Toribe, Y., & Suzuki, Y. (2012). The grasp reflex and Moro reflex in infants: Hierarchy of primitive reflex responses. *International Journal of Pediatrics, 2012*, e191562. https://doi.org/10.1155/2012/191562

Gabard-Durnam, L., & McLaughlin, K. A. (2020). Sensitive periods in human development: Charting a course for the future. *Current Opinion in Behavioral Sciences, 36*, 120–128. https://doi.org/10.1016/j.cobeha.2020.09.003

Gabel, A. D., & Scheller, A. (2013). *Sensorimotor development and assessment.* Pearson Clinical Assessment.

Gach, E. J., Ip, K. I., Sameroff, A. J., & Olson, S. L. (2018). Early cumulative risk predicts externalizing behavior at age 10: The mediating role of adverse parenting. *Journal of Family Psychology, 32*(1), 92–102. https://doi.org/10.1037/fam0000360

Gaddis, A., & Brooks-Gunn, J. (1985). The male experience of pubertal change. *Journal of Youth and Adolescence, 14*(1), 61–69.

Gaffney, H., Ttofi, M. M., & Farrington, D. P. (2021). What works in anti-bullying programs? Analysis of effective intervention components. *Journal of School Psychology, 85*, 37–56. https://doi.org/10.1016/j.jsp.2020.12.002

Gagné, T., Sacker, A., & Schoon, I. (2021a). Changes in patterns of social role combinations at ages 25–26 among those growing up in England between 1996 and 2015–16: Evidence from the 1970 British cohort and next steps studies. *Journal of Youth and Adolescence, 50*, 2052–2066. https://doi.org/10.1007/s10964-021-01477-1

Gagné, T., Schoon, I., & Sacker, A. (2021b). Trends in young adults' mental distress and its association with employment: Evidence from the behavioral risk factor surveillance system, 1993–2019. *Preventive Medicine, 150*, 106691. https://doi.org/10.1016/j.ypmed.2021.106691

Gago Galvagno, L. G., De Grandis, M. C., Clerici, G. D., Mustaca, A. E., Miller, S. E., & Elgier, A. M. (2019). Regulation during the second year: Executive function and emotion regulation links to joint attention, temperament, and social vulnerability in a Latin American sample. *Frontiers in Psychology, 10*, 1473. https://doi.org/10.3389/fpsyg.2019.01473

Gaias, L. M., Gal, D. E., Abry, T., Taylor, M., & Granger, K. L. (2018). Diversity exposure in preschool: Longitudinal implications for cross-race friendships and racial bias. *Journal of Applied Developmental Psychology, 59*, 5–15. https://doi.org/10.1016/j.appdev.2018.02.005

Gaigbe-Togbe, V. (2015). *The impact of socio-economic inequalities on early childhood survival: Results from the demographic and health surveys* (Technical Paper No. 2015/1, p. 30). United Nations Population Division.

Galatzer-Levy, I. R., Huang, S. H., & Bonanno, G. A. (2018). Trajectories of resilience and dysfunction following potential trauma: A review and statistical evaluation. *Clinical Psychology Review, 63*, 41–55.

Galla, B. M., Choukas-Bradley, S., Fiore, H. M., & Esposito, M. V. (2021). Values-alignment messaging boosts adolescents' motivation to control social media use. *Child Development, 92*(5), 1717–1734. https://doi.org/10.1111/cdev.13553

Gallagher, D., Andres, A., Fields, D. A., Evans, W. J., Kuczmarski, R., Lowe, W. L., Jr., Lumeng, J. C., Oken, E., Shepherd, J. A., & Sun, S. (2020). Body composition measurements from birth through 5 years: Challenges, gaps, and existing & emerging technologies — A National Institutes of Health Workshop. *Obesity Reviews, 21*(8), e13033.

Galler, J. R., Bringas-Vega, M. L., Tang, Q., Rabinowitz, A. G., Musa, K. I., Chai, W. J., Omar, H., Abdul Rahman, M. R., Abd Hamid, A. I., Abdullah, J. M., & Valdés-Sosa, P. A. (2021). Neurodevelopmental effects of childhood malnutrition: A neuroimaging perspective. *NeuroImage, 231*, 117828. https://doi.org/10.1016/j.neuroimage.2021.117828

Gallois, S., Duda, R., Hewlett, B., & Reyes-García, V. (2015). Children's daily activities and knowledge acquisition: A case study among the Baka from southeastern Cameroon. *Journal of Ethnobiology and Ethnomedicine, 11*(1), 86. https://doi.org/10.1186/s13002-015-0072-9

Gallup, G. G. (1970). Chimpanzees: Self-recognition. *Science, 167*(3914), 86–87. https://doi.org/10.1126/science.167.3914.86

Galton, F. (1883). *Inquiries into human faculty and its development.* Macmillan.

Galupa, R., & Heard, E. (2018). X-chromosome inactivation: A crossroads between chromosome architecture and gene regulation. *Annual Review of Genetics, 52*(1), 535–566. https://doi.org/10.1146/annurev-genet-120116-024611

Galupo, M. P., Cartwright, K. B., & Savage, L. S. (2009). Cross-category friendships and postformal thought among college students. *Journal of Adult Development, 17*(4), 208–214. https://doi.org/10.1007/s10804-009-9089-4

Galván, A. (2013). The teenage brain: Sensitivity to rewards. *Current Directions in Psychological Science, 22*(2), 88–93. https://doi.org/10.1177/0963721413480859

Galván, A. (2017). Adolescence, brain maturation and mental health. *Nature Neuroscience, 20*(4), 503–504.

Galván, A. (2020). The need for sleep in the adolescent brain. *Trends in Cognitive Sciences, 24*(1), 79–89. https://doi.org/10.1016/j.tics.2019.11.002

Galván, A., Hare, T., Voss, H., Glover, G., & Casey, B. J. (2007). Risk-taking and the adolescent brain: Who is at risk? *Developmental Science, 10*(2), F8–F14.

Galvez, M. P., McGovern, K., Teitelbaum, S. L., Windham, G., & Wolff, M. S. (2018). Neighborhood factors and urinary metabolites of nicotine, phthalates, and dichlorobenzene. *Pediatrics, 141*(Supplement 1), S87–S95. https://doi.org/10.1542/peds.2017-1026L

Gándara, P. (2017). The potential and promise of Latino students. *American Educator, 41*(1), 4.

Gándara, P. (2018). The economic value of bilingualism in the United States. *Bilingual Research Journal, 41*(4), 334–343. https://doi.org/10.1080/15235882.2018.1532469

Garbarino, J., & Bruyere, E. (2013). Resilience in the lives of children of war. In C. Fernando & M. Ferrari (Eds.), *Handbook of resilience in children of war* (pp. 253–266). Springer Science & Business Media.

Garceau, C., & Ronis, S. T. (2019). A qualitative investigation of expected versus actual initial sexual experiences before age 16. *Journal of Adolescence, 71*, 38–49.

García Coll, C., Crnic, K., Lamberty, G., Wasik, B. H., Jenkins, R., García, H. V., & McAdoo, H. P. (1996). An integrative model for the study of developmental competencies in minority children. *Child Development, 67*(5), 1891–1914. https://doi.org/10.1111/j.1467-8624.1996.tb01834.x

García Coll, C., Miranda, A. G., Torres, I. B., & Bermudez, J. N. (2018). On becoming cultural beings: A focus on race, gender, and language. *Research in Human Development, 15*(3–4), 332–344. https://doi.org/10.1080/15427609.2018.1491217

García, D. G., & Yosso, T. J. (2020). Recovering our past: A methodological reflection. *History of Education Quarterly, 60*(1), 59–72. https://doi.org/10.1017/heq.2019.50

García, J. S. M., Oinonen, E., Merino, R., & Perosa, G. (2021). Education and inequality in Finland, Spain and Brazil. In P. López-Roldán & S. Fachelli (Eds.), *Towards a comparative analysis of social inequalities between Europe and Latin America* (pp. 105–140). Springer.

Garcia, K. E., Kroenke, C. D., & Bayly, P. V. (2018). Mechanics of cortical folding: Stress, growth and stability. *Philosophical Transactions of the Royal Society B: Biological Sciences, 373*(1759), 20170321. https://doi.org/10.1098/rstb.2017.0321

García-Moya, I., Bunn, F., Jiménez-Iglesias, A., Paniagua, C., & Brooks, F. M. (2019). The conceptualisation of school and teacher connectedness in adolescent research: A scoping review of literature. *Educational Review, 71*(4), 423–444.

Garcia-Sanchez, I. M. (2018). Children as interactional brokers of care. *Annual Review of Anthropology, 47*, 167–184.

Gard, A. M., McLoyd, V. C., Mitchell, C., & Hyde, L. W. (2020). Evaluation of a longitudinal family stress model in a population-based cohort. *Social Development, 29*(4), 1155–1175. https://doi.org/10.1111/sode.12446

Gardner, H. (1999). Are there additional intelligences? The case for naturalist, spiritual, and existential intelligences. In J. Kane (Ed.), *Education, information, and transformation* (pp. 111–131). Prentice Hall.

Gardner, H. (2011). *Frames of mind: The theory of multiple intelligences* (30-year ed.). Basic Books.

Gardstedt, J., Niklasson, A., Aronson, S., Albertsson-Wikland, K., & Holmgren, A. (2019). Menarche and its relation to the pubertal growth spurt. *ESPE Abstracts, 92*, P1–119. http://abstracts.eurospe.org/hrp/0092/hrp0092p1-119

Garenne, M. (2021). Age at menarche in Nigerian demographic surveys. *Journal of Biosocial Science, 53*(5), 745–757. http://dx.doi.org/10.1017/S0021932020000504

Gargano, L., Mason, M. K., & Northridge, M. E. (2019). Advancing oral health equity through school-based oral health programs: An ecological model and review. *Frontiers in Public Health, 7*. https://www.frontiersin.org/article/10.3389/fpubh.2019.00359

Gariepy, G., Danna, S., Gobiņa, I., Rasmussen, M., Gaspar de Matos, M., Tynjälä, J., Janssen, I., Kalman, M., Villeruša, A., Husarova, D., Brooks, F., Elgar, F. J., Klavina-Makrecka, S., Šmigelskas, K., Gaspar, T., & Schnohr, C. (2020). How are adolescents sleeping? Adolescent sleep patterns and sociodemographic differences in 24 European and North American countries. *Journal of Adolescent Health, 66*(6, Supplement), S81–S88. https://doi.org/10.1016/j.jadohealth.2020.03.013

Garmezy, N. E., & Rutter, M. E. (Eds.). (1983). *Stress, coping, and development in children.* Johns Hopkins University Press.

Garon, N. M., Longard, J., Bryson, S. E., & Moore, C. (2012). Making decisions about now and later: Development of future-oriented self-control. *Cognitive Development, 27*(3), 314–322. https://doi.org/10.1016/j.cogdev.2012.05.003

Garratt, R., Bamber, D., Powell, C., Long, J., Brown, J., Turney, N., Chessman, J., Dyson, S., & James-Roberts, I. S. (2019). Parents' experiences of having an excessively crying baby and implications for support services. *Journal of Health Visiting, 7*(3), 132–140. https://doi.org/10.12968/johv.2019.7.3.132

Garrett-Peters, P. T., Castro, V. L., & Halberstadt, A. G. (2017). Parents' beliefs about children's emotions, children's emotion understanding, and classroom adjustment in middle childhood. *Social Development, 26*(3), 575–590.

Gartner, M., Kiang, L., & Supple, A. (2014). Prospective links between ethnic socialization, ethnic and American identity, and well-being among Asian-American adolescents. *Journal of Youth and Adolescence, 43*(10), 1715–1727. https://doi.org/10.1007/s10964-013-0044-0

Gartstein, M. A., & Putnam, S. P. (2018). *Toddlers, parents and culture: Findings from the joint effort toddler temperament consortium.* Routledge.

Gartstein, M. A., & Skinner, M. K. (2018). Prenatal influences on temperament development: The role of environmental epigenetics. *Development and Psychopathology, 30*(4), 1269–1303. https://doi.org/10.1017/S0954579417001730

Gartstein, M. A., Hancock, G. R., & Iverson, S. L. (2018). Positive affectivity and fear trajectories in infancy: Contributions of mother–child interaction factors. *Child Development, 89*(5), 1519–1534. https://doi.org/10.1111/cdev.12843

Gatzke-Kopp, L. M., Warkentien, S., Willoughby, M., Fowler, C., Folch, D. C., & Blair, C. (2021). Proximity to sources of airborne lead is associated with reductions in children's executive function in the first four years of life. *Health & Place, 68*, 102517.

Gaul, D., & Issartel, J. (2016). Fine motor skill proficiency in typically developing children: On or off the maturation track? *Human Movement Science, 46*, 78–85. https://doi.org/10.1016/j.humov.2015.12.011

Gault-Sherman, M. (2012). It's a two-way street: The bidirectional relationship between parenting and delinquency. *Journal of Youth and Adolescence, 41*(2), 121–145.

Gauvain, M. (2020). Vygotsky on learning and development. In A. Slater & P. C. Quinn (Eds.), *Developmental psychology: Revisiting the classic studies* (p. 89). Sage.

Gauvain, M., & Nicolaides, C. (2015). Cognition in childhood across cultures. In L. A. Jensen (Ed.), *The Oxford handbook of human development and culture: An interdisciplinary perspective* (pp. 198–213). Oxford University Press.

Gauvain, M., & Perez, S. (2015). Cognitive development and culture. In L. S. Liben, U. Müller, & R. M. Lerner (Eds.), *Handbook of child psychology and developmental science: Cognitive processes* (pp. 854–896). Wiley.

Gauvain, M., Perez, S. M., & Reisz, Z. (2018). Stability and change in mother–child planning over middle childhood. *Developmental Psychology, 54*(3), 571–585. https://doi.org/10.1037/dev0000456

Gavela-Pérez, T., Garcés, C., Navarro-Sánchez, P., López Villanueva, L., & Soriano-Guillén, L. (2015). Earlier menarcheal age in Spanish girls is related with an increase in body mass index between pre-pubertal school age and adolescence. *Pediatric Obesity, 10*(6), 410–415.

Gavett, B. E., Zhao, R., John, S. E., Bussell, C. A., Roberts, J. R., & Yue, C. (2017). Phishing suspiciousness in older and younger adults: The role of executive functioning. *PLOS ONE, 12*(2), e0171620. https://doi.org/10.1371/journal.pone.0171620

Gavin, K. (2020, September 20). *Loneliness doubled for older adults in first months of COVID-19.* University of Michigan. https://labblog.uofmhealth.org/rounds/loneliness-doubled-for-older-adults-first-months-of-covid-19

Gay, P. (1996). *The naked heart: The bourgeois experience Victoria to Freud* (Vol. 4). W. W. Norton.

Gay, P. (1998). *Freud: A life for our time.* W. W. Norton.

Gaysina, D., Richards, M., Kuh, D., & Hardy, R. (2015). Pubertal maturation and affective symptoms in adolescence and adulthood: Evidence from a prospective birth cohort. *Development and Psychopathology, 27*(4pt1), 1331–1340.

Gazzaniga, M. S. (2005). Forty-five years of split-brain research and still going strong. *Nature Reviews Neuroscience, 6*(8), 653–659.

Geangu, E., Hauf, P., Bhardwaj, R., & Bentz, W. (2011). Infant pupil diameter changes in response to others' positive and negative emotions. *PLOS ONE, 6*(11), e27132.

Gee, D. G. (2016). Sensitive periods of emotion regulation: Influences of parental care on frontoamygdala circuitry and plasticity. *New Directions for Child and Adolescent Development, 153*, 87–110.

Gee, D. G. (2020). Caregiving influences on emotional learning and regulation: Applying a sensitive period model. *Current Opinion in Behavioral Sciences, 36*, 177–184. https://doi.org/10.1016/j.cobeha.2020.11.003

Gee, D. G., Gabard-Durnam, L., Telzer, E. H., Humphreys, K. L., Goff, B., Shapiro, M., Flannery, J., Lumian, D. S., Fareri, D. S., Caldera, C., & Tottenham, N. (2014). Maternal buffering of human amygdala–prefrontal circuitry during childhood but not adolescence. *Psychological Science, 25*(11), 2067–2078. https://doi.org/10.1177/0956797614550878

Geffen, J., & Forster, K. (2018). Treatment of adult ADHD: A clinical perspective. *Therapeutic Advances in Psychopharmacology, 8*(1), 25–32. https://doi.org/10.1177/2045125317734977

Gehlbach, H., Brinkworth, M. E., King, A. M., Hsu, L. M., McIntyre, J., & Rogers, T. (2016). Creating birds of similar feathers: Leveraging similarity to improve teacher–student relationships and academic achievement. *Journal of Educational Psychology, 108*(3), 342.

Gelman, R. (1973). The nature and development of early number concepts. In H. W. Reese (Ed.), *Advances in child development and behavior* (Vol. 7, pp. 115–167). JAI. https://doi.org/10.1016/S0065-2407(08)60441-3

General Social Survey. (2018). [Cross-section [machine-readable data file, 68,846 cases]. Principal Investigator, Michael Davern; Co-Principal Investigators, Rene Bautista, Jeremy Freese, Stephen L. Morgan, and Tom W. Smith; Sponsored by National Science Foundation. – NORC ed. – Chicago: NORC, 2021: NORC at the University of Chicago [producer and distributor]. Data accessed from the GSS Data Explorer website at gssdataexplorer.norc.org.

Generett, G. G., & Olson, A. M. (2020). The stories we tell: How merit narratives undermine success for urban youth. *Urban Education, 55*(3), 394–423.

Gentile, D. A., Reimer, R. A., Nathanson, A. I., Walsh, D. A., & Eisenmann, J. C. (2014). Protective effects of parental monitoring of children's media use: A prospective study. *JAMA Pediatrics, 168*(5), 479–484.

George, C., Kaplan, N., & Main, M. (1985). *Attachment interview for adults* [Unpublished manuscript]. University of California, Berkeley.

George, M. J., Russell, M. A., Piontak, J. R., & Odgers, C. L. (2018). Concurrent and subsequent associations between daily digital technology use and high-risk adolescents' mental health symptoms. *Child Development, 89*(1), 78–88. https://doi.org/10.1111/cdev.12819

Georgieff, M. K., Ramel, S. E., & Cusick, S. E. (2018). Nutritional influences on brain development. *Acta Paediatrica, 107*(8), 1310–1321. https://doi.org/10.1111/apa.14287

Gershenson, S., Hart, C. M. D., Hyman, J., Lindsay, C., & Papageorge, N. W. (2018). *The long-run impacts of same-race teachers* (No. w25254). National Bureau of Economic Research. https://doi.org/10.3386/w25254

Gershoff, E. T., & Font, S. A. (2016). Corporal punishment in U.S. public schools: Prevalence, disparities in use, and status in state and federal policy. *Social Policy Report, 30*, 1.

Gershoff, E. T., & Grogan-Kaylor, A. (2016). Spanking and child outcomes: Old controversies and new meta-analyses. *Journal of Family Psychology, 30*(4), 453.

Gershoff, E., Sattler, K. M. P., & Holden, G. W. (2019). School corporal punishment and its associations with achievement and adjustment. *Journal of Applied Developmental Psychology, 63*, 1–8. https://doi.org/10.1016/j.appdev.2019.05.004

Gervais, M., Jaimovich, N., Siu, H. E., & Yedid-Levi, Y. (2016). What should I be when I grow up? Occupations and unemployment over the life cycle. *Journal of Monetary Economics, 83*, 54–70. https://doi.org/10.1016/j.jmoneco.2016.08.003

Gesell, A. (1928). *Infancy and human growth* (pp. xvii, 418). MacMillan. https://doi.org/10.1037/14664-000

Gettler, L. T., Boyette, A. H., & Rosenbaum, S. (2020). Broadening perspectives on the evolution of human paternal care and fathers' effects on children. *Annual Review of Anthropology, 49*(1), 141–160. https://doi.org/10.1146/annurev-anthro-102218-011216

Gettler, L. T., Kuo, P. X., Sarma, M. S., Trumble, B. C., Burke Lefever, J. E., & Braungart-Rieker, J. M. (2021). Fathers' oxytocin responses to first holding their newborns: Interactions with testosterone reactivity to predict later parenting behavior and father-infant bonds. *Developmental Psychobiology, 63*(5), 1384–1398.

Gewirtz-Meydan, A., & Finkelhor, D. (2020). Sexual abuse and assault in a large national sample of children and adolescents. *Child Maltreatment, 25*(2), 203–214. https://doi.org/10.1177/1077559519873975

Ghandour, R. M., Sherman, L. J., Vladutiu, C. J., Ali, M. M., Lynch, S. E., Bitsko, R. H., & Blumberg, S. J. (2019). Prevalence and treatment of depression, anxiety, and conduct problems in US children. *The Journal of Pediatrics, 206*, 256–267.e3. https://doi.org/10.1016/j.jpeds.2018.09.021

Ghassabian, A., Sundaram, R., Bell, E., Bello, S. C., Kus, C., & Yeung, E. (2016). Gross motor milestones and subsequent development. *Pediatrics, 138*(1), e20154372. https://doi.org/10.1542/peds.2015-4372

Ghavami, N., Katsiaficas, D., & Rogers, L. O. (2016). Toward an intersectional approach in developmental science: The role of race, gender, sexual orientation, and immigrant status. In S. S. Horn, M. D. Ruck, & L. S. Liben (Eds.), *Advances in child development and behavior* (Vol. 50, pp. 31–73). JAI. https://doi.org/10.1016/bs.acdb.2015.12.001

Ghimire, U., Papabathini, S. S., Kawuki, J., Obore, N., & Musa, T. H. (2021). Depression during pregnancy and the risk of low birth weight, preterm birth and intrauterine growth restriction — an updated meta-analysis. *Early Human Development, 152*, 105243. https://doi.org/10.1016/j.earlhumdev.2020.105243

Gibbons, F. X., Fleischli, M. E., Gerrard, M., Simons, R. L., Weng, C. Y., & Gibson, L. P. (2020). The impact of early racial discrimination on illegal behavior, arrest, and incarceration among African Americans. *American Psychologist, 75*(7), 952.

Gibson, E. J. (1988). Exploratory behavior in the development of perceiving, acting, and the acquiring of knowledge. *Annual Review of Psychology, 39*(1), 1–42.

Gibson, E. J., & Walk, R. D. (1960). The "visual cliff." *Scientific American, 202*(4), 64–71.

Gibson, J. J. (1979). *The ecological approach to visual perception: Classic edition.* Psychology Press.

Gibson, J. M., Fisher, M., Clonch, A., MacDonald, J. M., & Cook, P. J. (2020). Children drinking private well water have higher blood lead than those with city water. *Proceedings of the National Academy of Sciences, 117*(29), 16898–16907. https://doi.org/10.1073/pnas.2002729117

Gilchrist, C. P., Thompson, D. K., Kelly, C. E., Beare, R., Adamson, C., Dhollander, T., Lee, K., Treyvaud, K., Matthews, L. G., Tolcos, M., Cheong, J. L. Y., Inder, T. E., Doyle, L. W., Cumberland, A., & Anderson, P. J. (2022). The structural connectome and internalizing and externalizing symptoms at 7 and 13 years in individuals born very preterm and full term. *Biological Psychiatry: Cognitive Neuroscience and Neuroimaging, 7*(4), 424–434. https://doi.org/10.1016/j.bpsc.2021.10.003

Gilkerson, L., Burkhardt, T., Katch, L. E., & Hans, S. L. (2020). Increasing parenting self-efficacy: The Fussy Baby Network® intervention. *Infant Mental Health Journal, 41*(2), 232–245. https://doi.org/10.1002/imhj.21836

Gill, I., & Saavedra, J. (February 1, 2022) We are losing a generation: The devastating impacts of COVID-19. *Voices: World Bank Blogs.* https://blogs.worldbank.org/voices/we-are-losing-generation-devastating-impacts-covid-19

Gill, V. R., Liley, H. G., Erdei, C., Sen, S., Davidge, R., Wright, A. L., & Bora, S. (2021). Improving the uptake of Kangaroo Mother Care in neonatal units: A narrative review and conceptual framework. *Acta Paediatrica, 110*(5), 1407–1416. https://doi.org/10.1111/apa.15705

Gillam-Krakauer, M., & Gowen, C. W., Jr. (2020). Birth asphyxia. *StatPearls.*

Gillen-O'Neel, C., & Fuligni, A. (2013). A longitudinal study of school belonging and academic motivation across high school. *Child Development, 84*(2), 678–692.

Gillen-O'Neel, C., Huynh, V. W., Hazelbaker, T., & Harrison, A. (2021). From kindness and diversity to justice and action: White parents' ethnic–racial socialization goals. *Journal of Family Issues,* 0192513X21996392. https://doi.org/10.1177/0192513X21996392

Gilliam, W. S. (2016). *Early childhood expulsions and suspensions undermine our nation's most promising agent of opportunity and social justice.* Robert

Wood Johnson Foundation. https://scholar.google.com/citations?view_op=view_citation&hl=en&user=wJq1irQAAAAJ&sortby=pubdate&citation_for_view=wJq1irQAAAAJ:Zph67rFs4hoC

Gilliam, W. S., Malik, A. A., Shafiq, M., Klotz, M., Reyes, C., Humphries, J. E., Murray, T., Elharake, J. A., Wilkinson, D., & Omer, S. B. (2021). COVID-19 transmission in US child care programs. *Pediatrics, 147*(1), e2020031971. https://doi.org/10.1542/peds.2020-031971

Gilligan, C. (1977). In a different voice: Women's conceptions of self and of morality. *Harvard Educational Review, 47*(4), 481–517.

Gilligan, C. (1993). *In a different voice: Psychological theory and women's development.* Harvard University Press.

Gilmore, J. H., Langworthy, B., Girault, J. B., Fine, J., Jha, S. C., Kim, S. H., Cornea, E., & Styner, M. (2020). Individual variation of human cortical structure is established in the first year of life. *Biological Psychiatry: Cognitive Neuroscience and Neuroimaging, 5*(10), 971–980. https://doi.org/10.1016/j.bpsc.2020.05.012

Gilmore, J. H., Santelli, R. K., & Gao, W. (2018). Imaging structural and functional brain development in early childhood. *Nature Reviews Neuroscience, 19*(3), 123–137. https://doi.org/10.1038/nrn.2018.1

Gindis, B. (1999). Vygotsky's vision: Reshaping the practice of special education for the 21st century. *Remedial and Special Education, 20*(6), 333–340. https://doi.org/10.1177/074193259902000606

Giofrè, D., Toffalini, E., Altoè, G., & Cornoldi, C. (2017). Intelligence measures as diagnostic tools for children with specific learning disabilities. *Intelligence, 61*, 140–145.

Glick, G. C., & Rose, A. J. (2011). Prospective associations between friendship adjustment and social strategies: Friendship as a context for building social skills. *Developmental Psychology, 47*(4), 1117.

Global School-based Student Health Survey (GSSHS). (2016). *Global School-based Student Health Survey, Bhutan, 2016 fact sheet.* World Health Organization.

Gmeindl, L., Chiu, Y. C., Esterman, M. S., Greenberg, A. S., Courtney, S. M., & Yantis, S. (2016). Tracking the will to attend: Cortical activity indexes self-generated, voluntary shifts of attention. *Attention, Perception, & Psychophysics, 78*(7), 2176–2184.

Gnambs, T., Stasielowicz, L., Wolter, I., & Appel, M. (2020). Do computer games jeopardize educational outcomes? A prospective study on gaming times and academic achievement. *Psychology of Popular Media, 9*(1), 69–82. https://doi.org/10.1037/ppm0000204

Goddings, A.-L., Beltz, A., Peper, J. S., Crone, E. A., & Braams, B. R. (2019). Understanding the role of puberty in structural and functional development of the adolescent brain. *Journal of Research on Adolescence, 29*(1), 32–53. https://doi.org/10.1111/jora.12408

Goddings, A.-L., Viner, R. M., Mundy, L., Romaniuk, H., Molesworth, C., Carlin, J. B., Allen, N. B., & Patton, G. C. (2021). Growth and adrenarche: Findings from the CATS observational study. *Archives of Disease in Childhood.* https://doi.org/10.1136/archdischild-2020-319341

Godleski, S. A., Kamper, K. E., Ostrov, J. M., Hart, E. J., & Blakely-McClure, S. J. (2015). Peer victimization and peer rejection during early childhood. *Journal of Clinical Child and Adolescent Psychology, 44*(3), 380–392. https://doi.org/10.1080/15374416.2014.940622

Godwin, K. E., Almeda, M. V., Seltman, H., Kai, S., Skerbetz, M. D., Baker, R. S., & Fisher, A. V. (2016).

Off-task behavior in elementary school children. *Learning and Instruction, 44*, 128–143.

Godwin, K. E., Seltman, H., Almeda, M., Skerbetz, M. D., Kai, S., Baker, R. S., & Fisher, A. V. (2021). The elusive relationship between time on-task and learning: Not simply an issue of measurement. *Educational Psychology, 41*(4), 502–519. https://doi.org/10.1080/01443410.2021.1894324

Goff, P. A., Jackson, M. C., Di Leone, B. A. L., Culotta, C. M., & DiTomasso, N. A. (2014). The essence of innocence: Consequences of dehumanizing Black children. *Journal of Personality and Social Psychology, 106*(4), 526.

Goldberg, A. E., Kuvalanka, K. A., & Black, K. (2019). Trans students who leave college: An exploratory study of their experiences of gender minority stress. *Journal of College Student Development, 60*(4), 381–400.

Goldberg, A. E., Moyer, A. M., & Kinkler, L. A. (2013). Lesbian, gay, and heterosexual adoptive parents' perceptions of parental bonding during early parenthood. *Couple and Family Psychology: Research and Practice, 2*(2), 146.

Golden, C. R., & McHugh, M. C. (2017). The personal, political, and professional life of Sandra Bem. *Sex Roles, 76*(9), 529–543.

Golden, J. C., & Jacoby, J. W. (2018). Playing princess: Preschool girls' interpretations of gender stereotypes in Disney Princess media. *Sex Roles, 79*(5), 299–313. https://doi.org/10.1007/s11199-017-0773-8

Golden, R. L., Furman, W., & Collibee, C. (2016). The risks and rewards of sexual debut. *Developmental Psychology, 52*(11), 1913.

Goldfarb, E. S., & Lieberman, L. D. (2021). Three decades of research: The case for comprehensive sex education. *Journal of Adolescent Health, 68*(1), 13–27. https://doi.org/10.1016/j.jadohealth.2020.07.036

Goldhaber, D., Kane, T. J., McEachin, A., Morton, E., Patterson, T., & Staiger, D. O. (2022). The consequences of remote and hybrid instruction during the pandemic. Working Paper No. 267-0522. *National Center for Analysis of Longitudinal Data in Education Research (CALDER).*

Goldhaber, D., & Özek, U. (2019). How much should we rely on student test achievement as a measure of success? *Educational Researcher, 48*(7), 479–483.

Goldin, C. (1998). America's graduation from high school: The evolution and spread of secondary schooling in the twentieth century. *The Journal of Economic History, 58*(2), 345–374. https://www.cambridge.org/core/journals/journal-of-economic-history/article/americas-graduation-from-high-school-the-evolution-and-spread-of-secondary-schooling-in-the-twentieth-century/6419955E40943932F792C9F26A3FA5AA

Goldin, C., & Katz, L. F. (1997). *Why the United States led in education: Lessons from secondary school expansion, 1910 to 1940.* National Bureau of Economic Research.

Goldin, C., & Katz, L. F. (2008). Transitions: Career and family life cycles of the educational elite. *American Economic Review, 98*(2), 363–369.

Goldin-Meadow, S. (2015). From action to abstraction: Gesture as a mechanism of change. *Developmental Review, 38*, 167–184.

Goldman, N., Glei, D. A., & Weinstein, M. (2018). Declining mental health among disadvantaged Americans. *Proceedings of the National Academy of Sciences, 115*(28), 7290–7295.

Goldschmidt, L., Langa, M., Alexander, D., & Canham, H. (2021). A review of Kohlberg's theory and its applicability in the South African context through the

lens of early childhood development and violence. *Early Child Development and Care, 191*(7–8), 1066–1078. https://doi.org/10.1080/03004430.2021.1897583

Goldstein, D. (2022, May 22). In the fight over how to teach reading, this guru makes a major retreat. *The New York Times.* https://www.nytimes.com/2022/05/22/us/reading-teaching-curriculum-phonics.html

Goldstein, E. B., & Brockmole, J. (2017). *Sensation and perception.* Cengage Learning.

Goldstein, E. B., & Cacciamani, L. (2021). *Sensation and perception* (11th ed.). Cengage Learning.

Goldstick, J. E., Cunningham, R. M., & Carter, P. M. (2022). Current causes of death in children and adolescents in the United States. *New England Journal of Medicine, 386*(20), 1955–1956. https://doi.org/10.1056/NEJMc2201761

Goldston, D. B., Molock, S. D., Whitbeck, L. B., Murakami, J. L., Zayas, L. H., & Hall, G. C. N. (2008). Cultural considerations in adolescent suicide prevention and psychosocial treatment. *American Psychologist, 63*(1), 14.

Golestanzadeh, M., Riahi, R., & Kelishadi, R. (2020). Association of phthalate exposure with precocious and delayed pubertal timing in girls and boys: A systematic review and meta-analysis. *Environmental Science: Processes & Impacts, 22*(4), 873–894. https://doi.org/10.1039/c9em00512a

Golinkoff, R. M., Hoff, E., Rowe, M. L., Tamis-LeMonda, C. S., & Hirsh-Pasek, K. (2019). Language matters: Denying the existence of the 30-million-word gap has serious consequences. *Child Development, 90*(3), 985–992. https://doi.org/10.1111/cdev.13128

Göllner, R., Damian, R. I., Rose, N., Spengler, M., Trautwein, U., Nagengast, B., & Roberts, B. W. (2017). Is doing your homework associated with becoming more conscientious?. *Journal of Research in Personality, 71*, 1–12.

Golombok, S. (2017). Parenting in new family forms. *Current Opinion in Psychology, 15*, 76–80. https://doi.org/10.1016/j.copsyc.2017.02.004

Golombok, S., Zadeh, S., Freeman, T., Lysons, J., & Foley, S. (2021). Single mothers by choice: Parenting and child adjustment in middle childhood. *Journal of Family Psychology, 35*(2), 192–202. https://doi.org/10.1037/fam0000797

Gómez, R. L., & Edgin, J. O. (2016). The extended trajectory of hippocampal development: Implications for early memory development and disorder. *Developmental Cognitive Neuroscience, 18*, 57–69.

Gómez-López, M., Viejo, C., & Ortega-Ruiz, R. (2019). Psychological well-being during adolescence: Stability and association with romantic relationships. *Frontiers in Psychology, 10*, 1772. https://doi.org/10.3389/fpsyg.2019.01772

Gómez-Roig, M. D., Pascal, R., Cahuana, M. J., García-Algar, O., Sebastiani, G., Andreu-Fernández, V., Martínez, L., Rodríguez, G., Iglesia, I., Ortiz-Arrabal, O., Mesa, M. D., Cabero, M. J., Guerra, L., Llurba, E., Domínguez, C., Zanini, M. J., Foraster, M., Larqué, E., Cabañas, F., . . . Vento, M. (2021). Environmental exposure during pregnancy: Influence on prenatal development and early life: A comprehensive review. *Fetal Diagnosis and Therapy, 48*(4), 245–257. https://doi.org/10.1159/000514884

Gonzalez, C. L. R., & Sacrey, L.-A. R. (2018). The development of the motor system. In R. Gibb & B. Kolb (Eds.), *The neurobiology of brain and behavioral development* (pp. 235–256). Academic Press. https://doi.org/10.1016/B978-0-12-804036-2.00009-1

González, M., Loose, T., Liz, M., Pérez, M., Rodríguez-Vinçon, J. I., Tomás-Llerena, C., & Vásquez-Echeverría, A. (2022). School readiness losses during the COVID-19 outbreak. A comparison of two cohorts of young children. *Child Development*.

Gooch, D., Thompson, P., Nash, H. M., Snowling, M. J., & Hulme, C. (2016). The development of executive function and language skills in the early school years. *Journal of Child Psychology and Psychiatry, 57*(2), 180–187.

Goodman, A. H., Moses, Y. T., & Jones, J. L. (2012). *Race: Are we so different?* John Wiley & Sons.

Goodman, W. B., Dodge, K. A., Bai, Y., Murphy, R. A., & O'Donnell, K. (2021). Effect of a universal postpartum nurse home visiting program on child maltreatment and emergency medical care at 5 years of age: A randomized clinical trial. *JAMA Network Open, 4*(7), e2116024–e2116024. https://doi.org/10.1001/jamanetworkopen.2021.16024

Goodnow, J. J., & Lawrence, J. A. (2015). Children and cultural context. In *Handbook of child psychology and developmental science* (pp. 1–41). American Cancer Society. https://doi.org/10.1002/9781118963418.childpsy419

Gopalan, M., & Brady, S. T. (2020). College students' sense of belonging: A national perspective. *Educational Researcher, 49*(2), 134–137. https://doi.org/10.3102/0013189X19897622

Gopnik, A. (2020). Childhood as a solution to explore–exploit tensions. *Philosophical Transactions of the Royal Society B: Biological Sciences, 375*(1803), 20190502. https://doi.org/10.1098/rstb.2019.0502

Gopnik, A., Frankenhuis, W. E., & Tomasello, M. (2020). Introduction to special issue: 'Life history and learning: How childhood, caregiving and old age shape cognition and culture in humans and other animals.' *Philosophical Transactions of the Royal Society B: Biological Sciences, 375* (1803), 20190489. https://doi.org/10.1098/rstb.2019.0489

Gordon, M. S., & Cui, M. (2018). The intersection of race and community poverty and its effects on adolescents' academic achievement. *Youth & Society, 50*(7), 947–965.

Gordon, R. A., Crosnoe, R., & Wang, X. (2013). Physical attractiveness and the accumulation of social and human capital in adolescence and young adulthood: Assets and distractions. *Monographs of the Society for Research in Child Development, 78*(6), 1.

Gordon, R. A., Kaestner, R., & Korenman, S. (2008). Child care and work absences: Trade-offs by type of care. *Journal of Marriage and Family, 70*(1), 239–254. https://doi.org/10.1111/j.1741-3737.2007.00475.x

Gorham, L. S., & Barch, D. M. (2020). White matter tract integrity, involvement in sports, and depressive symptoms in children. *Child Psychiatry & Human Development, 51*(3), 490–501.

Gottesmann, C. (2009). Discovery of the dreaming sleep stage: A recollection. *Sleep, 32*(1), 15.

Gottlieb, A. (2004). *The afterlife is where we come from.* University of Chicago Press.

Gottlieb, A. (2019). The new childhood studies: Reflections on some recent collaborations between anthropologists and psychologists. *AnthropoChildren*. https://doi.org/10.25518/2034-8517.3162

Gottlieb, G. (2007). Probabilistic epigenesis. *Developmental Science, 10*(1), 1–11. https://doi.org/10.1111/j.1467-7687.2007.00556.x

Gottman, J. (2011). *Raising an emotionally intelligent child.* Simon & Schuster.

Gottman, J. M., & Graziano, W. G. (1983). How children become friends. *Monographs of the Society for Research in Child Development, 48*(3), 1–86.

Gottman, J. M., Katz, L. F., & Hooven, C. (1996). Parental meta-emotion philosophy and the emotional life of families: Theoretical models and preliminary data. *Journal of Family Psychology, 10*(3), 243.

Goyal, M. K., Johnson, T. J., Chamberlain, J. M., Cook, L., Webb, M., Drendel, A. L., Alessandrini, E., Bajaj, L., Lorch, S., Grundmeier, R. W., Alpern, E. R., & Pediatric Emergency Care Applied Research Network (PECARN). (2020). Racial and ethnic differences in emergency department pain management of children with fractures. *Pediatrics, 145*(5), e20193370. https://doi.org/10.1542/peds.2019-3370

Goyer, J. P., Garcia, J., Purdie-Vaughns, V., Binning, K. R., Cook, J. E., Reeves, S. L., Apfel, N., Taborsky-Barba, S., Sherman, D. K., & Cohen, G. L. (2017). Self-affirmation facilitates minority middle schoolers' progress along college trajectories. *Proceedings of the National Academy of Sciences, 114*(29), 7594–7599.

Goyette, T. (2016, May 17). A letter to my husband as I go through postpartum depression. *Discovering Parenthood*. https://www.discoveringparenthood.com/about/

Grabell, A. S., Olson, S. L., Miller, A. L., Kessler, D. A., Felt, B., Kaciroti, N., Wang, L., & Tardif, T. (2015). The impact of culture on physiological processes of emotion regulation: A comparison of US and Chinese preschoolers. *Developmental Science, 18*(3), 420–435.

Grabell, A. S., Santana, A. M., Thomsen, K. N., Gonzalez, K., Zhang, Z., Bivins, Z., & Rahman, T. (2022). Prefrontal modulation of frustration-related physiology in preschool children ranging from low to severe irritability. *Developmental Cognitive Neuroscience, 55*, 101112. https://doi.org/10.1016/j.dcn.2022.101112

Graham, A., Haner, M., Sloan, M. M., Cullen, F. T., Kulig, T. C., & Jonson, C. L. (2020). Race and worrying about police brutality: The hidden injuries of minority status in America. *Victims & Offenders, 15*(5), 549–573. https://doi.org/10.1080/15564886.2020.1767252

Graham, A., Powell, M. A., Anderson, D., Fitzgerald, R., & Taylor, N. J. (2013). *Ethical research involving children.* UNICEF Innocenti Research Centre.

Graham, A. M., Rasmussen, J. M., Entringer, S., Ben Ward, E., Rudolph, M. D., Gilmore, J. H., Styner, M., Wadhwa, P. D., Fair, D. A., & Buss, C. (2019). Maternal cortisol concentrations during pregnancy and sex specific associations with neonatal amygdala connectivity and emerging internalizing behaviors. *Biological Psychiatry, 85*(2), 172–181. https://doi.org/10.1016/j.biopsych.2018.06.023

Graham, J. M. (2018). How do genes affect the risk of having a child with a birth defect? In *Teratology Primer* (3rd ed.). Society for Birth Defects Research & Prevention.

Graham, N., Schultz, L., Mitra, S., & Mont, D. (2017). Disability in middle childhood and adolescence. In *Child and Adolescent Health and Development* (3rd ed.). The International Bank for Reconstruction and Development / The World Bank. PMID: 30212134.

Granat, A., Gadassi, R., Gilboa-Schechtman, E., & Feldman, R. (2017). Maternal depression and anxiety, social synchrony, and infant regulation of negative and positive emotions. *Emotion, 17*(1), 11.

Grandjean, P., & Landrigan, P. J. (2014). Neurobehavioural effects of developmental toxicity. *The Lancet: Neurology, 13*(3), 330–338. https://doi.org/10.1016/S1474-4422(13)70278-3

Granic, I., Lobel, A., & Engels, R. C. (2014). The benefits of playing video games. *American Psychologist, 69*(1), 66.

Granqvist, P., Sroufe, L. A., Dozier, M., Hesse, E., Steele, M., van Ijzendoorn, M. H., Solomon, J., Schuengel, C., Fearon, P., Bakermans-Kranenburg, M., Steele, H., Cassidy, J., Carlson, E., Madigan, S., Jacobvitz, D., Foster, S., Behrens, K., Rifkin-Graboi, A., Gribneau, N., . . . Duschinsky, R. (2017). Disorganized attachment in infancy: A review of the phenomenon and its implications for clinicians and policy-makers. *Attachment & Human Development, 19*(6), 534–558. https://doi.org/10.1080/14616734.2017.1354040

Grant, S., Liao, K., Miller, C., Peterson, S., Elting, L., & Guadagnolo, B. A. (2021). Lower levels of trust in the medical profession among White, younger, and more-educated individuals with cancer. *American Journal of Clinical Oncology, 44*(4), 150–157. https://doi.org/10.1097/COC.0000000000000771

Gray, D. L., Hope, E. C., & Matthews, J. S. (2018). Black and belonging at school: A case for interpersonal, instructional, and institutional opportunity structures. *Educational Psychologist, 53*(2), 97–113. https://doi.org/10.1080/00461520.2017.1421466

Gray, P. (2017). What exactly is play, and why is it such a powerful vehicle for learning? *Topics in Language Disorders, 37*(3), 217–228.

Gray, P. (2018, March 27). Benefits of play revealed in research on video gaming. *Psychology Today.* https://www.psychologytoday.com/us/blog/freedom-learn/201803/benefits-play-revealed-in-research-video-gaming

Gray, P. (2020). Risky play: Why children love and need it. In S. Little, A. Cox, & P. E. Owens (Eds.), *The Routledge handbook of designing public spaces for young people: Processes, practices and policies for youth inclusion* (pp. 39–51). Routledge.

Grayling, A. C. (2010). *Ideas that matter: The concepts that shape the 21st century.* Basic Books.

Gray-Lobe, G., Pathak, P. A., & Walters, C. R. (2021). *The long-term effects of universal preschool in Boston* (No. w28756). National Bureau of Economic Research. https://doi.org/10.3386/w28756

Grayson, G. (2018, January 22). My grandmother was Italian. Why aren't my genes Italian? *NPR.org.* https://www.npr.org/sections/health-shots/2018/01/22/578293890/my-grandmother-was-italian-why-arent-my-genes-italian

Green, R. C., Berg, J. S., Grody, W. W., Kalia, S. S., Korf, B. R., Martin, C. L., McGuire, A. L., Nussbaum, R. L., O'Daniel, J. M., Ormond, K. E., Rehm, H. L., Watson, M. S., Williams, M. S., & Biesecker, L. G. (2013). ACMG recommendations for reporting of incidental findings in clinical exome and genome sequencing. *Genetics in Medicine, 15*(7), 565–574. https://doi.org/10.1038/gim.2013.73

Greenberg, M. T., & Harris, A. R. (2012). Nurturing mindfulness in children and youth: Current state of research. *Child Development Perspectives, 6*(2), 161–166.

Greene, D. J., Koller, J. M., Hampton, J. M., Wesevich, V., Van, A. N., Nguyen, A. L., Hoyt, C. R., McIntyre, L., Earl, E. A., Klein, R. L., Shimony, J. S., Petersen, S. E., Schlaggar, B. L., Fair, D. A., & Dosenbach, N. U. F. (2018). Behavioral interventions for reducing head motion during MRI scans in children. *NeuroImage, 171*, 234–245. https://doi.org/10.1016/j.neuroimage.2018.01.023

Greenfield, P. M. (1997). You can't take it with you: Why ability assessments don't cross cultures. *American Psychologist, 52*(10), 1115–1124. https://doi.org/10.1037/0003-066X.52.10.1115

Greenfield, P. M. (1998). The cultural evolution of IQ. In U. Neisser (Ed.), *The rising curve: Long-term gains in IQ and related measures* (pp. 81–123). American Psychological Association. https://doi.org/10.1037/10270-003

Greenfield, P. M. (2012). Cultural change, human activity, and cognitive development. *Human Development, 55*(4), 229–232.

Greenfield, P. M. (2018). Studying social change, culture, and human development: A theoretical framework and methodological guidelines. *Developmental Review, 50*, 16–30. https://doi.org/10.1016/j.dr.2018.05.003

Greenfield, P. M., Keller, H., Fuligni, A., & Maynard, A. (2003). Cultural pathways through universal development. *Annual Review of Psychology, 54* (1), 461–490. https://doi.org/10.1146/annurev.psych.54.101601.145221

Greenough, W. T., Black, J. E., & Wallace, C. S. (1987). Experience and brain development. *Child Development, 58*(3), 539–559.

Greenspan, L. (2017, April 6). Why are girls starting puberty earlier? *US News & World Report.* https://health.usnews.com/wellness/for-parents/articles/2017-04-06/why-are-girls-starting-puberty-earlier

Gregory, A., & Fergus, E. (2017). Social and emotional learning and equity in school discipline. *The Future of Children, 27*(1), 117–136.

Gregory, A., & Weinstein, R. S. (2008). The discipline gap and African Americans: Defiance or cooperation in the high school classroom. *Journal of School Psychology, 46*(4), 455–475.

Griffith, J. M., Clark, H. M., Haraden, D. A., Young, J. F., & Hankin, B. L. (2021). Affective development from middle childhood to late adolescence: Trajectories of mean-level change in negative and positive affect. *Journal of Youth and Adolescence, 50*(8), 1550–1563. https://doi.org/10.1007/s10964-021-01425-z

Grill, J. (2018). "In England, they don't call you black!" Migrating racialisations and the production of Roma difference across Europe. *Journal of Ethnic and Migration Studies, 44*(7), 1136–1155. https://doi.org/10.1080/1369183X.2017.1329007

Grinshteyn, E., & Hemenway, D. (2019). Violent death rates in the US compared to those of the other high-income countries, 2015. *Preventive Medicine, 123*, 20–26.

Grissom, J. A., & Redding, C. (2016). Discretion and disproportionality: Explaining the underrepresentation of high-achieving students of color in gifted programs. *AERA Online, 2*(1), 1–15.

Groh, A. M., Fearon, R. M. P., van IJzendoorn, M. H., Bakermans-Kranenburg, M. J., & Roisman, G. I. (2017). Attachment in the early life course: Meta-analytic evidence for its role in socioemotional development. *Child Development Perspectives, 11*(1), 70–76. https://doi.org/10.1111/cdep.12213

Grolig, L., Cohrdes, C., Tiffin-Richards, S. P., & Schroeder, S. (2020). Narrative dialogic reading with wordless picture books: A cluster-randomized intervention study. *Early Childhood Research Quarterly, 51*, 191–203.

Grosse Wiesmann, C., Friederici, A. D., Singer, T., & Steinbeis, N. (2020). Two systems for thinking about others' thoughts in the developing brain. *Proceedings of the National Academy of Sciences, 117*(12), 6928–6935. https://doi.org/10.1073/pnas.1916725117

Grossman, A. H., Park, J. Y., Frank, J. A., & Russell, S. T. (2021). Parental responses to transgender and gender nonconforming youth: Associations with parent support, parental abuse, and youths' psychological adjustment. *Journal of Homosexuality, 68*(8), 1260–1277.

Grossmann, I. (2017). Wisdom in context. *Perspectives on Psychological Science, 12*(2), 233–257.

Grossman, J. M., & Charmaraman, L. (2009). Race, context, and privilege: White adolescents' explanations of racial-ethnic centrality. *Journal of Youth and Adolescence, 38*(2), 139–152. https://doi.org/10.1007/s10964-008-9330-7

Grossmann, K., Grossmann, K. E., Spangler, G., Suess, G., & Unzner, L. (1985). Maternal sensitivity and newborns' orientation responses as related to quality of attachment in Northern Germany. *Monographs of the Society for Research in Child Development, 50*(1–2), 233–256. https://doi.org/10.2307/3333836

Grossmann, T. (2020). Early social cognition: Exploring the role of the medial prefrontal cortex. In J. Decety (Ed.), *The social brain: A developmental perspective* (pp. 67–88). MIT Press.

Grossmann, T., & Dela Cruz, K. L. (2021). Insights into the uniquely human origins of understanding other minds. *Behavioral and Brain Sciences.*

Grove, M. A., & Lancy, D. F. (2018). Cultural models of stages in the life course. In S. Crawford, D. M. Hadley, & G. Shepherd (Eds.), *The Oxford handbook of the archaeology of childhood* (pp. 90–103). Oxford University Press.

Grubb, L. K., Powers, M., & Committee on Adolescence. (2020). Emerging issues in male adolescent sexual and reproductive health care. *Pediatrics, 145*(5), e20200627. https://doi.org/10.1542/peds.2020-0627

Grubbs, J. B., & Kraus, S. W. (2021). Pornography use and psychological science: A call for consideration. *Current Directions in Psychological Science, 30*(1), 68–75. https://doi.org/10.1177/0963721420979594

Grubin, D. (2002). *Young Dr. Freud.* https://www.pbs.org/youngdrfreud/pages/family_parenthood.htm

Grugel, J., & Ferreira, F. P. M. (2012). Street working children, children's agency and the challenge of children's rights: evidence from Minas Gerais, Brazil. *Journal of International Development, 24*(7), 828–840.

Grusec, J. E., Danyliuk, T., Kil, H., & O'Neill, D. (2017). Perspectives on parent discipline and child outcomes. *International Journal of Behavioral Development, 41*(4), 465–471.

Gu, X., Tamplain, P. M., Chen, W., Zhang, T., Keller, M. J., & Wang, J. (2021). A mediation analysis of the association between fundamental motor skills and physical activity during middle childhood. *Children, 8*(2), 64. https://doi.org/10.3390/children8020064

Guadalupe, T., Kong, X. Z., Akkermans, S. E. A., Fisher, S. E., & Francks, C. (2021). Relations between hemispheric asymmetries of grey matter and auditory processing of spoken syllables in 281 healthy adults. *Brain Structure and Function.* https://doi.org/10.1007/s00429-021-02220-z

Guan, S.-S. A., Greenfield, P. M., & Orellana, M. F. (2014). Translating into understanding: Language brokering and prosocial development in emerging adults from immigrant families. *Journal of Adolescent Research, 29*(3), 331–355. https://doi.org/10.1177/0743558413520223

Guardabassi, V., & Tomasetto, C. (2020). Weight status or weight stigma? Obesity stereotypes—not excess weight—reduce working memory in school-aged children. *Journal of Experimental Child Psychology, 189*, 104706.

Guilamo-Ramos, V., Benzekri, A., Thimm-Kaiser, M., Dittus, P., Ruiz, Y., Cleland, C. M., & McCoy, W. (2020). A triadic intervention for adolescent sexual health: A randomized clinical trial. *Pediatrics, 145*(5), e20192808. https://doi.org/10.1542/peds.2019-2808

Gülgöz, S., Alonso, D. J., Olson, K. R., & Gelman, S. A. (2021). Transgender and cisgender children's essentialist beliefs about sex and gender identity. *Developmental Science, 24*(6). https://doi.org/10.1111/desc.13115

Gülgöz, S., Glazier, J. J., Enright, E. A., Alonso, D. J., Durwood, L. J., Fast, A. A., Lowe, R., Ji, C., Heer, J., Martin, C. L., & Olson, K. R. (2019). Similarity in transgender and cisgender children's gender development. *Proceedings of the National Academy of Sciences, 116*(49), 24480–24485. https://doi.org/10.1073/pnas.1909367116

Gunderson, E. A., Donnellan, M. B., Robins, R. W., & Trzesniewski, K. H. (2018). The specificity of parenting effects: Differential relations of parent praise and criticism to children's theories of intelligence and learning goals. *Journal of Experimental Child Psychology, 173*, 116–135. https://doi.org/10.1016/j.jecp.2018.03.015

Gunderson, E. A., Sorhagen, N. S., Gripshover, S. J., Dweck, C. S., Goldin-Meadow, S., & Levine, S. C. (2018). Parent praise to toddlers predicts fourth grade academic achievement via children's incremental mindsets. *Developmental Psychology, 54*(3), 397.

Gunderson, L. (2013). Whole-language approaches to reading and writing. In *Instructional models in reading* (pp. 231–258). Routledge.

Güngör, D., Nadaud, P., LaPergola, C. C., Dreibelbis, C., Wong, Y. P., Terry, N., Abrams, S. A., Beker, L., Jacobovits, T., Järvinen, K. M., Nommsen-Rivers, L. A., O'Brien, K. O., Oken, E., Pérez-Escamilla, R., Ziegler, E. E., & Spahn, J. M. (2019). Infant milk-feeding practices and cardiovascular disease outcomes in offspring: A systematic review. *The American Journal of Clinical Nutrition, 109*(Suppl 1), 800S–816S. https://doi.org/10.1093/ajcn/nqy332

Gunn, H. M., Tsai, M.-C., McRae, A., & Steinbeck, K. S. (2018). Menstrual patterns in the first gynecological year: A systematic review. *Journal of Pediatric and Adolescent Gynecology, 31*(6), 557–565.e6. https://doi.org/10.1016/j.jpag.2018.07.009

Gunnar, M. R. (2020). Early adversity, stress, and neurobehavioral development. *Development and Psychopathology, 32*(5), 1555–1562. https://doi.org/10.1017/S0954579420001649

Gunnar, M. R., DePasquale, C. E., Reid, B. M., Donzella, B., & Miller, B. S. (2019). Pubertal stress recalibration reverses the effects of early life stress in postinstitutionalized children. *Proceedings of the National Academy of Sciences, 116*(48), 23984–23988. https://doi.org/10.1073/pnas.1909699116

Guo, X., Yao, D., Cao, Q., Liu, L., Zhao, Q., Li, H., Huang, F., Wang, Y., Qian, Q., Wang, Y., Calhoun, V. D., Johnstone, S. J., Sui, J., & Sun, L. (2020). Shared and distinct resting functional connectivity in children and adults with attention-deficit/hyperactivity disorder. *Translational psychiatry, 10*(1), 1–12.

Gupta, N. D., & Simonsen, M. (2016). Academic performance and type of early childhood care. *Economics of Education Review, 53*, 217–229.

Gupta, P. (2015, October 12). This Navajo woman is planning the first Native American birthing center in the country. *Cosmopolitan.* https://www.cosmopolitan.com/politics/news/a47518/americas-first-native-american-birthing-center/

Güroğlu, B. (2021). Adolescent brain in a social world: Unravelling the positive power of peers from a neurobehavioral perspective. *European Journal of Developmental Psychology, 18*(4), 471–493. https://doi.org/10.1080/17405629.2020.1813101

Guryan, J., Ludwig, J., Bhatt, M. P., Cook, P. J., Davis, J. M., Dodge, K., Farkas, G., Fryer, R. G., Jr., Mayer, S., Pollack, H., & Steinberg, L. (2021). *Not too late: Improving academic outcomes among adolescents.* National Bureau of Economic Research.

Gustafsson, H. C., Young, A. S., Doyle, O., Nagel, B. J., Mackiewicz Seghete, K., Nigg, J. T., Sullivan, E. L., & Graham, A. M. (2021). Trajectories of perinatal depressive symptoms in the context of the COVID-19 pandemic. *Child Development, 92*(5), e749–e763. https://doi.org/10.1111/cdev.13656

Guthold, R., Stevens, G. A., Riley, L. M., & Bull, F. C. (2020). Global trends in insufficient physical activity among adolescents: A pooled analysis of 298 population-based surveys with 1.6 million participants. *The Lancet Child & Adolescent Health, 4*(1), 23–35. https://doi.org/10.1016/S2352-4642(19)30323-2

Guthrie, J. T., Wigfield, A., Humenick, N. M., Perencevich, K. C., Taboada, A., & Barbosa, P. (2006). Influences of stimulating tasks on reading motivation and comprehension. *The Journal of Educational Research, 99*(4), 232–246. https://doi.org/10.3200/JOER.99.4.232-246

Gutiérrez, K. D. (2016). 2011 AERA presidential address: Designing resilient ecologies: Social design experiments and a new social imagination. *Educational Researcher, 45*(3), 187–196.

Guttmacher Institute. (2022). *Minors' Access to STI Services* [State Laws and Policies].

Guyer, A. E., & Jarcho, J. M. (2018). Neuroscience and peer relations. In W. M. Bukowski, B. Laursen, & K. H. Rubin (Eds.), *Handbook of peer interactions, relationships, and groups* (pp. 177–199). Guilford.

Guyer, A. E., Pérez-Edgar, K., & Crone, E. A. (2018). Opportunities for neurodevelopmental plasticity from infancy through early adulthood. *Child Development, 89*(3), 687–697. https://doi.org/10.1111/cdev.13073

Guyer, A. E., Silk, J. S., & Nelson, E. E. (2016). The neurobiology of the emotional adolescent: From the inside out. *Neuroscience & Biobehavioral Reviews, 70*, 74–85.

Guyer, C., & Jenni, O. G. (2017). Sleep in neonates and infants. In J. Stein (ed.), *Reference Module in Neuroscience and Biobehavioral Psychology* (pp. 581–585). Elsevier. https://doi.org/10.1016/b978-0-12-809324-5.01089-0

Ha, T., Kim, H., & McGill, S. (2019). When conflict escalates into intimate partner violence: The delicate nature of observed coercion in adolescent romantic relationships. *Development and Psychopathology, 31*(5), 1729–1739. https://doi.org/10.1017/S0954579419001007

Haandrikman, K. (2019). Partner choice in Sweden: How distance still matters. *Environment and Planning A: Economy and Space, 51*(2), 440–460. https://doi.org/10.1177/0308518X18786726

Haarbauer-Krupa, J., Lee, A. H., Bitsko, R. H., Zhang, X., & Kresnow-Sedacca, M. (2018). Prevalence of parent-reported traumatic brain injury in children and associated health conditions. *JAMA Pediatrics, 172*(11), 1078–1086. https://doi.org/10.1001/jamapediatrics.2018.2740

Habibi, M., Weber, L., Neves, M., Wiegandt, D. L., & Leser, U. (2017). Deep learning with word embeddings improves biomedical named entity recognition. *Bioinformatics, 33*(14), i37–i48.

Hadders-Algra, M. (2018). Early human motor development: From variation to the ability to vary and adapt. *Neuroscience & Biobehavioral Reviews, 90*, 411–427. https://doi.org/10.1016/j.neubiorev.2018.05.009

Haga, M., Tortella, P., Asonitou, K., Charitou, S., Koutsouki, D., Fumagalli, G., & Sigmundsson, H. (2018). Cross-cultural aspects: Exploring motor competence among 7- to 8-year-old children from Greece, Italy, and Norway. *SAGE Open, 8*(2), 2158244018768381. https://doi.org/10.1177/2158244018768381

Hagen, J. W., Lasagna, C. A., & Packett, S. E. (2020). A century of research in child development: The emergence of a new science. In N. Jones, M. Platt, K. D. Mize, & J. Hardin (Eds.), *Conducting research in developmental psychology: A topical guide for research methods utilized across the lifespan* (pp. 1–25). Routledge.

Hagerman, C. J., Ferrer, R. A., Klein, W. M. P., & Persky, S. (2020). Association of parental guilt with harmful versus healthful eating and feeding from a virtual reality buffet. *Health Psychology: Official Journal of the Division of Health Psychology, American Psychological Association, 39*(3), 199–208. https://doi.org/10.1037/hea0000831

Haglund, K. A., & Fehring, R. J. (2010). The association of religiosity, sexual education, and parental factors with risky sexual behaviors among adolescents and young adults. *Journal of Religion and Health, 49*(4), 460–472.

Hahn-Holbrook, J., Haselton, M. G., Dunkel Schetter, C., & Glynn, L. M. (2013). Does breastfeeding offer protection against maternal depressive symptomatology?. *Archives of Women's Mental Health, 16*(5), 411–422.

Haidt, J. (2009). Moral psychology and the misunderstanding of religion. In J. Schloss & M. Murray (Eds.), *The believing primate: Scientific, philosophical, and theological reflections on the origin of religion* (pp. 278–291). Oxford University Press.

Haight, W. (2006). A sociocultural perspective of parent–child play. In D. P. Fromberg & D. Bergen (Eds.), *Play from birth to twelve: Contexts, perspectives, and meanings* (pp. 309–314). Routledge.

Haimovitz, K., & Dweck, C. S. (2016). What predicts children's fixed and growth intelligence mind-sets? Not their parents' views of intelligence but their parents' views of failure. *Psychological Science, 27*(6), 859–869.

Hairston, I. S., Handelzalts, J. E., Lehman-Inbar, T., & Kovo, M. (2019). Mother-infant bonding is not associated with feeding type: A community study sample. *BMC Pregnancy and Childbirth, 19*(1), 125. https://doi.org/10.1186/s12884-019-2264-0

Hajal, N., Neiderhiser, J., Moore, G., Leve, L., Shaw, D., Harold, G., Scaramella, L., Ganiban, J., & Reiss, D. (2015). Angry responses to infant challenges: Parent, marital, and child genetic factors associated with harsh parenting. *Child Development, 86*(1), 80–93. https://doi.org/10.1111/cdev.12345

Hajal, N. J., & Paley, B. (2020). Parental emotion and emotion regulation: A critical target of study for research and intervention to promote child emotion socialization. *Developmental Psychology, 56*(3), 403–417. https://doi.org/10.1037/dev0000864

Halberstadt, A. G., Oertwig, D., & Riquelme, E. H. (2020). Beliefs about children's emotions in Chile. *Frontiers in Psychology, 11*, 34. https://doi.org/10.3389/fpsyg.2020.00034

Hales, B., Scialli, A., & Tassinari, M. (Eds.). (2018). *Teratology primer* (3rd ed.). Society for Birth Defects Research & Prevention.

Halim, M. L. D. (2016). Princesses and superheroes: Social-cognitive influences on early gender rigidity. *Child Development Perspectives, 10*(3), 155–160.

Halim, M. L. D., Martin, C. L., Andrews, N. C., Zosuls, K. M., & Ruble, D. N. (2021). Enjoying each other's company: Gaining other-gender

Halim, M. L. D., Ruble, D. N., Tamis-LeMonda, C. S., Shrout, P. E., & Amodio, D. M. (2017). Gender attitudes in early childhood: Behavioral consequences and cognitive antecedents. *Child Development, 88*(3), 882–899. https://doi.org/10.1111/cdev.12642

Halim, M. L. D., Walsh, A. S., Tamis-LeMonda, C. S., Zosuls, K. M., & Ruble, D. N. (2018). The roles of self-socialization and parent socialization in toddlers' gender-typed appearance. *Archives of Sexual Behavior, 47*(8), 2277–2285.

Halim, M. L., Ruble, D., Tamis-LeMonda, C., & Shrout, P. E. (2013). Rigidity in gender-typed behaviors in early childhood: A longitudinal study of ethnic minority children. *Child Development, 84*(4), 1269–1284.

Hall, Elizabeth. (1970). A Conversation with Jean Piaget and Barbel Inhelder. *Psychology Today, 3*, 25–32, 54–56.

Hall, G. S. (1904). *Adolescence: Its psychology and its relations to physiology, anthropology, sociology, sex, crime, religion and education.* D. Appleton & Company. https://doi.org/10.1037/10616-006

Hall, S. (2021). COVID vaccines and breastfeeding: What the data say. *Nature, 594*(7864), 492–494. https://doi.org/10.1038/d41586-021-01680-x

Halliday, K. E., Witek-McManus, S. S., Opondo, C., Mtali, A., Allen, E., Bauleni, A., Ndau, S., Phondiwa, E., Ali, D., Kachigunda, V., Sande, J. H., Jawati, M., Verney, A., Chimuna, T., Melody, D., Moestue, H., Roschnik, N., Brooker, S. J., & Mathanga, D. P. (2020). Impact of school-based malaria case management on school attendance, health and education outcomes: A cluster randomised trial in southern Malawi. *BMJ Global Health, 5*(1), e001666. https://doi.org/10.1136/bmjgh-2019-001666

Halonen, J. S. (2008). Measure for measure: The challenge of assessing critical thinking. In D. S. Dunn, J. S. Halonen, & R. A. Smith (Eds.), *Teaching critical thinking in psychology: A handbook of best practices* (pp. 59–75). John Wiley & Sons. https://doi.org/10.1002/9781444305173.ch6

Halpern, H. P., & Perry-Jenkins, M. (2016). Parents' gender ideology and gendered behavior as predictors of children's gender-role attitudes: A longitudinal exploration. *Sex Roles, 74*(11), 527–542.

Halpern-Manners, A., Raymo, J. M., Warren, J. R., & Johnson, K. L. (2020). School performance and mortality: The mediating role of educational attainment and work and family trajectories across the life course. *Advances in Life Course Research, 46*, 100362.

Halstead, M. E., Walter, K. D., Moffatt, K., & The Council on Sports Medicine and Fitness. (2018). Sport-related concussion in children and adolescents. *Pediatrics, 142*(6), e20183074. https://doi.org/10.1542/peds.2018-3074

Hamby, S., Taylor, E., Mitchell, K., Jones, L., & Newlin, C. (2020). Poly-victimization, trauma, and resilience: Exploring strengths that promote thriving after adversity. *Journal of Trauma & Dissociation, 21*(3), 376–395. https://doi.org/10.1080/15299732.2020.1719261

Hamel, L. M., Penner, L. A., Albrecht, T. L., Heath, E., Gwede, C. K., & Eggly, S. (2016). Barriers to clinical trial enrollment in racial and ethnic minority patients with cancer. *Cancer Control: Journal of the Moffitt Cancer Center, 23*(4), 327–337.

Hamermesh, D. S., Gordon, R. A., & Crosnoe, R. (2019). *O Youth and Beauty: Children's Looks and Children's Cognitive Development* (Working Paper No. 26412). National Bureau of Economic Research. https://doi.org/10.3386/w26412

Hamilton, L. T. (2016). *Parenting to a Degree: How Family Matters for College Women's Success*. University of Chicago Press.

Hamlat, E. J., McCormick, K. C., Young, J. F., & Hankin, B. L. (2020). Early pubertal timing predicts onset and recurrence of depressive episodes in boys and girls. *Journal of Child Psychology and Psychiatry, and Allied Disciplines, 61*(11), 1266–1274. https://doi.org/10.1111/jcpp.13198

Hammer, P. J. (2019). The Flint Water Crisis, the Karegnondi Water Authority and strategic–structural racism. *Critical Sociology, 45*(1), 103–119. https://doi.org/10.1177/0896920517729193

Hammond, M. D., & Cimpian, A. (2021). "Wonderful but Weak": Children's ambivalent attitudes toward women. *Sex Roles, 84*(1), 76–90. https://doi.org/10.1007/s11199-020-01150-0

Hammond, S. I., Al-Jbouri, E., Edwards, V., & Feltham, L. E. (2017). Infant helping in the first year of life: Parents' recollection of infants' earliest prosocial behaviors. *Infant Behavior and Development, 47*, 54–57. https://doi.org/10.1016/j.infbeh.2017.02.004

Hammond, S. I., & Brownell, C. A. (2018). Happily unhelpful: Infants' everyday helping and its connections to early prosocial development. *Frontiers in Psychology, 9*, 1770. https://doi.org/10.3389/fpsyg.2018.01770

Han, D., & Adolph, K. E. (2020). The impact of errors in infant development: Falling like a baby. *Developmental Science, 24*(5), e13069. https://doi.org/10.1111/desc.13069

Han, Y., Kebschull, J. M., Campbell, R. A. A., Cowan, D., Imhof, F., Zador, A. M., & Mrsic-Flogel, T. D. (2018). The logic of single-cell projections from visual cortex. *Nature, 556*(7699), 51–56. https://doi.org/10.1038/nature26159

Hanifan, L. J. (1916). The rural school community center. *The Annals of the American Academy of Political and Social Science, 67* (1), 130–138. https://doi.org/10.1177/000271621606700118

Hanna-Attisha, M. (2019). *What the eyes don't see: A story of crisis, resistance, and hope in an American city* (Reprint ed.). One World.

Hanna-Attisha, M., Hamp, N., & O'Connell, L. (2022). Promise of early intervention for children exposed to lead. *JAMA Pediatrics, 176*(5), 446–448. https://doi.org/10.1001/jamapediatrics.2022.0017

Hanna-Attisha, M., LaChance, J., Sadler, R. C., & Champney Schnepp, A. (2016). Elevated blood lead levels in children associated with the Flint drinking water crisis: A spatial analysis of risk and public health response. *American Journal of Public Health, 106*(2), 283–290. https://doi.org/10.2105/AJPH.2015.303003

Hanner, E., Braham, E. J., Elliott, L., & Libertus, M. E. (2019). Promoting math talk in adult–child interactions through grocery store signs. *Mind, Brain, and Education, 13*(2), 110–118.

Hanson, D. (2013). Assessing the Harlem children's zone. *Center for Policy Innovation Discussion Paper, 8*.

Hanson, M. H. (2020). Stories: Trauma, theatre, and theory. In K. Knutson, T. Okada, & K. Crowley (Eds.), *Multidisciplinary approaches to art learning and creativity* (pp. 64–85). Routledge.

Hanushek, E. (2020). Quality education and economic development. In B. Panth & R. Maclean (Eds.), *Anticipating and preparing for emerging skills and jobs* (pp. 25–32). Springer.

Hanushek, E. A., Peterson, P. E., Talpey, L. M., & Woessmann, L. (2019). *The unwavering SES achievement gap: Trends in U.S. student performance* (National Bureau of Economic Research No. 25648). National Bureau of Economic Research.

Hanushek, E. A., Schwerdt, G., Woessmann, L., & Zhang, L. (2017). General education, vocational education, and labor-market outcomes over the lifecycle. *Journal of Human Resources, 52*(1), 48–87. https://doi.org/10.3368/jhr.52.1.0415-7074R

Harackiewicz, J. M., & Priniski, S. J. (2018). Improving student outcomes in higher education: The science of targeted intervention. *Annual Review of Psychology, 69*(1), 409–435. https://doi.org/10.1146/annurev-psych-122216-011725

Harden, K. P. (2014). A sex-positive framework for research on adolescent sexuality. *Perspectives on Psychological Science, 9*(5), 455–469.

Harding, J. F., Hughes, D. L., & Way, N. (2017). Racial/ethnic differences in mothers' socialization goals for their adolescents. *Cultural Diversity and Ethnic Minority Psychology, 23*(2), 281–290. https://doi.org/10.1037/cdp0000116

Harel, Y., Zuk, L., Guindy, M., Nakar, O., Lotan, D., & Fattal-Valevski, A. (2017). The effect of subclinical infantile thiamine deficiency on motor function in preschool children. *Maternal & Child Nutrition, 13*(4), e12397.

Hargrove, T. W. (2019). Light privilege? Skin tone stratification in health among African Americans. *Sociology of Race and Ethnicity (Thousand Oaks, Calif.), 5*(3), 370–387. https://doi.org/10.1177/2332649218793670

Harkness, S., & Super, C. M. (2021). Why understanding culture is essential for supporting children and families. *Applied Developmental Science, 25* (1), 14–25. https://doi.org/10.1080/10888691.2020.1789354

Harkness, S., Super, C. M., Mavridis, C. J., Barry, O., & Zeitlin, M. (2013). Culture and early childhood development. In P. R. Britto, P. L. Engle, & C. M. Super (Eds.), *Handbook of early childhood development research and its impact on global policy* (pp. 142–160). Oxford University Press.

Härkönen, J., Bernardi, F., & Boertien, D. (2017). Family dynamics and child outcomes: An overview of research and open questions. *European Journal of Population, 33*(2), 163–184.

Harley, K. G., Berger, K. P., Kogut, K., Parra, K., Lustig, R. H., Greenspan, L. C., Calafat, A. M., Ye, X., & Eskenazi, B. (2019). Association of phthalates, parabens and phenols found in personal care products with pubertal timing in girls and boys. *Human Reproduction, 34*(1), 109–117. https://doi.org/10.1093/humrep/dey337

Harlow, H. F. (1958). The nature of love. *American Psychologist, 13*(12), 673–685. https://doi.org/10.1037/h0047884

Harper, J. (2013, July 6). Ice cream and crime: Where cold cuisine and hot disputes intersect. *Times-Picayune*. https://www.nola.com/news/crime_police/article_ca3c791c-d524-555f-9431-06dc69bcfbe1.html

Harrell-Levy, M. K., & Kerpelman, J. L. (2015). The relationship between perceived transformative class experiences and subsequent prosocial intentions. *Education Research and Perspectives, 42*, 429–458.

Harrington, E. M., Trevino, S. D., Lopez, S., & Giuliani, N. R. (2020). Emotion regulation in early childhood: Implications for socioemotional and academic components of school readiness. *Emotion, 20*(1), 48–53. https://doi.org/10.1037/emo0000667

Harris Poll. (2017). *Accelerating acceptance, 2017.* GLAAD.

Harris, B. (2011). Arnold Gesell's progressive vision: Child hygiene, socialism and eugenics. *History of Psychology, 14*(3), 311–334.

Harris, J. L., & Pomeranz, J. L. (2020). Infant formula and toddler milk marketing: Opportunities to address harmful practices and improve young children's diets. *Nutrition Reviews, 78*(10), 866–883. https://doi.org/10.1093/nutrit/nuz095

Harris, M. A., Donnellan, M. B., Guo, J., McAdams, D. P., Garnier-Villarreal, M., & Trzesniewski, K. H. (2017). Parental co-construction of 5-to 13-year-olds' global self-esteem through reminiscing about past events. *Child Development, 88*(6), 1810–1822.

Harris, M. A., Donnellan, M. B., & Trzesniewski, K. H. (2018). The lifespan self-esteem scale: Initial validation of a new measure of global self-esteem. *Journal of Personality Assessment, 100*(1), 84–95. https://doi.org/10.1080/00223891.2016.1278380

Harstad, E., Shults, J., Barbaresi, W., Bax, A., Cacia, J., Deavenport-Saman, A., Friedman, S., LaRosa, A., Loe, I. M., & Mittal, S. (2021). A2-Adrenergic agonists or stimulants for preschool-age children with attention-deficit/hyperactivity disorder. *JAMA, 325*(20), 2067–2075. https://doi.org/10.1001/jama.2021.6118

Hart, B., & Risley, T. R. (1995). *Meaningful differences in the everyday experience of young American children.* Paul H. Brookes Publishing.

Hart, J. L., & Tannock, M. T. (2019). Rough play: Past, present and potential. In P. K. Smith & J. L. Roopnarine (Eds.), *The Cambridge handbook of play: Developmental and disciplinary perspectives* (pp. 200–221). Cambridge University Press.

Hart, S. L. (2016). Proximal foundations of jealousy: Expectations of exclusivity in the infant's first year of life. *Emotion Review, 8*(4), 358–366. https://doi.org/10.1177/1754073915615431

Hart, S. L. (2020). Jealousy. In D. Güngör (Ed.), *The encyclopedia of child and adolescent development* (pp. 1–13). American Cancer Society. https://doi.org/10.1002/9781119171492.wecad162

Hartanto, A., Toh, W. X., & Yang, H. (2019). Bilingualism narrows socioeconomic disparities in executive functions and self-regulatory behaviors during early childhood: Evidence from the early childhood longitudinal study. *Child Development, 90*(4), 1215–1235.

Harter, S. (1993). Causes and consequences of low self-esteem in children and adolescents. In R. F. Baumeister (Ed.), *Self-esteem: The puzzle of low self-regard* (pp. 87–116). Springer US. https://doi.org/10.1007/978-1-4684-8956-9_5

Harter, S. (2006). Developmental and individual difference perspectives on self-esteem. In D. K. Mroczek & T. D. Little (Eds.), *Handbook of personality development* (pp. 311–334). Lawrence Erlbaum Associates.

Harter, S. (2012). Emerging self-processes during childhood and adolescence. In M. R. Leary & J. P. Tangney (Eds.), *Handbook of self and identity* (2nd ed., pp. 680–715). Guilford.

Harter, S. (2015). *The construction of the self: Developmental and sociocultural foundations.* Guilford.

Hartl, A. C., Laursen, B., & Cillessen, A. H. N. (2015). A survival analysis of adolescent friendships: The downside of dissimilarity. *Psychological Science, 26*(8), 1304–1315. https://doi.org/10.1177/0956797615588751

Hartley, B. L., & Sutton, R. M. (2013). A stereotype threat account of boys' academic underachievement. *Child Development, 84*(5), 1716–1733.

Hartnett, C. S., Fingerman, K. L., & Birditt, K. S. (2018). Without the ties that bind: U.S. young adults who lack active parental relationships. *Advances in Life Course Research, 35*, 103–113. https://doi.org/10.1016/j.alcr.2018.01.004

Hartshorne, J. K., Tenenbaum, J. B., & Pinker, S. (2018). A critical period for second language acquisition: Evidence from 2/3 million English speakers. *Cognition, 177*, 263–277. https://doi.org/10.1016/j.cognition.2018.04.007

Hartup, W. W. (1996). The company they keep: Friendships and their developmental significance. *Child Development, 67*(1), 1–13.

Harvard Kennedy School Institute of Politics. (2021). *Harvard Youth Poll* (41st ed.). Harvard University.

Hasan, Y., Bègue, L., Scharkow, M., & Bushman, B. J. (2013). The more you play, the more aggressive you become: A long-term experimental study of cumulative violent video game effects on hostile expectations and aggressive behavior. *Journal of Experimental Social Psychology, 49*(2), 224–227.

Hashikawa, A. N., Sells, J. M., DeJonge, P. M., Alkon, A., Martin, E. T., & Shope, T. R. (2020). Child care in the time of coronavirus disease-19: A period of challenge and opportunity. *The Journal of Pediatrics, 225*, 239–245. https://doi.org/10.1016/j.jpeds.2020.07.042

Hastings, O. P., & Schneider, D. (2021). Family structure and inequalities in parents' financial investments in children. *Journal of Marriage and Family, 83*(3), 717–736. https://doi.org/10.1111/jomf.12741

Hatano, K., & Sugimura, K. (2017). Is adolescence a period of identity formation for all youth? Insights from a four-wave longitudinal study of identity dynamics in Japan. *Developmental Psychology, 53*(11), 2113.

Haun, D. B. M., & Tomasello, M. (2011). Conformity to peer pressure in preschool children. *Child Development, 82*(6), 1759–1767. https://doi.org/10.1111/j.1467-8624.2011.01666.x

Have, M., Nielsen, J. H., Ernst, M. T., Gejl, A. K., Fredens, K., Grøntved, A., & Kristensen, P. L. (2018). Classroom-based physical activity improves children's math achievement: A randomized controlled trial. *PLOS ONE, 13*(12), e0208787. https://doi.org/10.1371/journal.pone.0208787

Havers, F. P. (2021). Hospitalization of adolescents aged 12–17 years with laboratory-confirmed COVID-19 — COVID-NET, 14 states, March 1, 2020–April 24, 2021. *Morbidity and Mortality Weekly Report, 70*(23), 851–857. https://doi.org/10.15585/mmwr.mm7023e1

Hawi, N. S., & Samaha, M. (2016). To excel or not to excel: Strong evidence on the adverse effect of smartphone addiction on academic performance. *Computers & Education, 98*, 81–89. https://doi.org/10.1016/j.compedu.2016.03.007

Hawks, L., Woolhandler, S., Himmelstein, D. U., Bor, D. H., Gaffney, A., & McCormick, D. (2019). Association between forced sexual initiation and health outcomes among US women. *JAMA Internal Medicine, 179*(11), 1551–1558. https://doi.org/10.1001/jamainternmed.2019.3500

Hawley, P. H. (2015). Social dominance in childhood and its evolutionary underpinnings: Why it matters and what we can do. *Pediatrics, 135*(Supplement 2), S31–S38.

Hawley, P. H. (2016). Eight myths of child social development: An evolutionary approach to power, aggression, and social competence. In D. C. Geary & D. B. Berch (Eds.), *Evolutionary perspectives on child development and education* (pp. 145–166). Springer International Publishing. https://doi.org/10.1007/978-3-319-29986-0_6

Hawley, P. H., & Sinatra, G. M. (2019). Declawing the dinosaurs in the science classroom: Reducing Christian teachers' anxiety and increasing their efficacy for teaching evolution. *Journal of Research in Science Teaching, 56*(4), 375–401. https://doi.org/10.1002/tea.21479

Hay, D. F. (2017). The early development of human aggression. *Child Development Perspectives, 11*(2), 102–106. https://doi.org/10.1111/cdep.12220

Hay, D. F., Paine, A. L., Perra, O., Cook, K. V., Hashmi, S., Robinson, C., Kairis, V., & Slade, R. (2021). Prosocial and aggressive behavior: A longitudinal study. *Monographs of the Society for Research in Child Development, 86*(2), 7–103. https://doi.org/10.1111/mono.12427

Hayne, H., Scarf, D., & Imuta, K. (2015). Childhood memories. *International Encyclopedia of the Social & Behavioral Sciences, 3*, 465–470.

Haynes, L., Ip, A., Cho, I. Y. K., Dimond, D., Rohr, C. S., Bagshawe, M., Dewey, D., Lebel, C., & Bray, S. (2020). Grey and white matter volumes in early childhood: A comparison of voxel-based morphometry pipelines. *Developmental Cognitive Neuroscience, 46*, 100875. https://doi.org/10.1016/j.dcn.2020.100875

Hays-Grudo, J., Morris, A. S., Beasley, L., Ciciolla, L., Shreffler, K., & Croff, J. (2021). Integrating and synthesizing adversity and resilience knowledge and action: The ICARE model. *American Psychologist, 76*(2), 203–215. https://doi.org/10.1037/amp0000766

Hazan, C., & Shaver, P. (1987). Romantic love conceptualized as an attachment process. *Journal of Personality and Social Psychology, 52*(3), 511–524.

He, H., Liu, Q., Li, N., Guo, L., Gao, F., Bai, L., Gao, F., & Lyu, J. (2020). Trends in the incidence and DALYs of schizophrenia at the global, regional and national levels: Results from the Global Burden of Disease Study 2017. *Epidemiology and Psychiatric Sciences, 29*. https://doi.org/10.1017/S2045796019000891

He, X., Wang, H., Chang, F., Dill, S.-E., Liu, H., Tang, B., & Shi, Y. (2021). IQ, grit, and academic achievement: Evidence from rural China. *International Journal of Educational Development, 80*, 102306. https://doi.org/10.1016/j.ijedudev.2020.102306

Headey, D. D., & Alderman, H. H. (2019). The relative caloric prices of healthy and unhealthy foods differ systematically across income levels and continents. *The Journal of Nutrition, 149*(11), 2020–2033. https://doi.org/10.1093/jn/nxz158

Heal, G., & Park, J. (2015). *Goldilocks economies? Temperature stress and the direct impacts of climate change* (No. w21119). National Bureau of Economic Research.

Heavy Head, R. (2007). *Rediscovering Blackfoot science: How First Nations helped develop a keystone of modern psychology*. https://www.sshrc-crsh.gc.ca/society-societe/stories-histoires/story-histoire-eng.aspx?story_id=91

Hebert-Beirne, J. M., O'Conor, R., Ihm, J. D., Parlier, M. K., Lavender, M. D., & Brubaker, L. (2017). A pelvic health curriculum in school settings: The effect on adolescent females' knowledge. *Journal of Pediatric and Adolescent Gynecology, 30*(2), 188–192. https://doi.org/10.1016/j.jpag.2015.09.006

Hecht, C. A., Yeager, D. S., Dweck, C. S., & Murphy, M. C. (2021). Chapter Five — Beliefs, affordances, and adolescent development: Lessons from a decade of growth mindset interventions. In J. J. Lockman (Ed.), *Advances in Child Development and Behavior* (Vol. 61, pp. 169–197). JAI. https://doi.org/10.1016/bs.acdb.2021.04.004

Heckman, J. J., Holland, M. L., Makino, K. K., Pinto, R., & Rosales-Rueda, M. (2017). *An analysis of the memphis nurse-family partnership program* (No. w23610). National Bureau of Economic Research. https://doi.org/10.3386/w23610

Heffer, T., Good, M., Daly, O., MacDonell, E., & Willoughby, T. (2019). The longitudinal association between social-media use and depressive symptoms among adolescents and young adults: An empirical reply to Twenge et al. (2018). *Clinical Psychological Science, 7*(3), 462–470. https://doi.org/10.1177/2167702618812727

Heft-Neal, S., Burney, J., Bendavid, E., Voss, K. K., & Burke, M. (2020). Dust pollution from the Sahara and African infant mortality. *Nature Sustainability, 3*(10), 863–871. https://doi.org/10.1038/s41893-020-0562-1

Heiligman, D. (2009). *Charles and Emma: The Darwins' leap of faith*. Henry Holt.

Helldén, D., Andersson, C., Nilsson, M., Ebi, K. L., Friberg, P., & Alfvén, T. (2021). Climate change and child health: A scoping review and an expanded conceptual framework. *The Lancet Planetary Health, 5*(3), e164–e175. https://doi.org/10.1016/S2542-5196(20)30274-6

Helle, S. (2018). "Only in dress?" Methodological concerns regarding nonbinary gender. In S. L. Budin, M. Cifarelli, A. Garcia-Ventura, & A. Millet Albà (Eds.), *Gender and methodology in the ancient Near East: Approaches from Assyriology and beyond* (pp. 41–53). Edicions Universitat de Barcelona.

Helm, P., & Grønlund, L. (1998). A halt in the secular trend towards earlier menarche in Denmark. *Acta Obstetricia et Gynecologica Scandinavica, 77*(2), 198–200. https://doi.org/10.1080/j.1600-0412.1998.770213.x

Hendry, A., Johnson, M. H., & Holmboe, K. (2019). Early development of visual attention: Change, stability, and longitudinal associations. *Annual Review of Developmental Psychology, 1*, 251–275.

Hennegan, J., Shannon, A. K., Rubli, J., Schwab, K. J., & Melendez-Torres, G. J. (2019). Women's and girls' experiences of menstruation in low- and middle-income countries: A systematic review and qualitative metasynthesis. *PLOS Medicine, 16*(5), e1002803. https://doi.org/10.1371/journal.pmed.1002803

Henrique, A. J., Gabrielloni, M. C., Rodney, P., & Barbieri, M. (2018). Non-pharmacological interventions during childbirth for pain relief, anxiety, and neuroendocrine stress parameters: A randomized controlled trial. *International Journal of Nursing Practice, 24*(3), e12642. https://doi.org/10.1111/ijn.12642

Henry, C. S., & Hubbs-Tait, L. (2013). New directions in authoritative parenting. In R. E. Larzelere, A. S. Morris, & A. W. Harrist (Eds.), *Authoritative parenting: Synthesizing nurturance and discipline for optimal child development* (pp. 237–264). American Psychological Association.

Hepper, P. (2015). Behavior during the prenatal period: Adaptive for development and survival. *Child Development Perspectives, 9*(1), 38–43. https://doi.org/10.1111/cdep.12104

Herbert, A. C., Ramirez, A. M., Lee, G., North, S. J., Askari, M. S., West, R. L., & Sommer, M. (2017). Puberty experiences of low-income girls in the United States: A systematic review of qualitative literature from 2000 to 2014. *Journal of Adolescent Health, 60*(4), 363–379.

Herbert, W. (2010). Heuristics revealed. *APS Observer, 23*(8).

Herkama, S., Saarento, S., & Salmivalli, C. (2017). The KiVa antibullying program: Lessons learned and future directions. In P. Sturmey (Ed.), *The Wiley handbook of violence and aggression* (pp. 1–12). Wiley.

Herman-Giddens, M. E. (2006). Recent data on pubertal milestones in United States children: the secular trend toward earlier development. *International journal of andrology, 29*(1), 241–246.

Hernandez, I. A., Silverman, D. M., & Destin, M. (2021). From deficit to benefit: Highlighting lower-SES students' background-specific strengths reinforces their academic persistence. *Journal of Experimental Social Psychology, 92,* 104080. https://doi.org/10.1016/j .jesp.2020.104080

Hernández, M. M., & Bámaca-Colbert, M. Y. (2016). A behavioral process model of familism. *Journal of Family Theory & Review, 8*(4), 463–483. https://doi .org/10.1111/jftr.12166

Hernández, M. M., Robins, R. W., Widaman, K. F., & Conger, R. D. (2017). Ethnic pride, self-esteem, and school belonging: A reciprocal analysis over time. *Developmental Psychology, 53*(12), 2384–2396. https://doi. org/10.1037/dev0000434

Herriman, M., Schweitzer, M. E., & Volpp, K. G. (2019). The need for an intervention to prevent sports injuries: Beyond "rub some dirt on it." *JAMA Pediatrics, 173*(3), 215–216.

Herting, M. M., Uban, K. A., Gonzalez, M. R., Baker, F. C., Kan, E. C., Thompson, W. K., Granger, D. A., Albaugh, M. D., Anokhin, A. P., Bagot, K. S., Banich, M. T., Barch, D. M., Baskin-Sommers, A., Breslin, F. J., Casey, B. J., Chaarani, B., Chang, L., Clark, D. B., Cloak, C. C., . . . Sowell, E. R. (2021). Correspondence between perceived pubertal development and hormone levels in 9–10 year-olds from the adolescent brain cognitive development study. *Frontiers in Endocrinology, 11,* 549928. https://doi.org/10.3389 /fendo.2020.549928

Hesselmar, B., Sjöberg, F., Saalman, R., Åberg, N., Adlerberth, I., & Wold, A. E. (2013). Pacifier cleaning practices and risk of allergy development. *Pediatrics, 131*(6), e1829–e1837.

Hesson, L. B., & Pritchard, A. L. (2019). Genetics and epigenetics: A historical overview. In L. B. Hesson & A. L. Pritchard (Eds.), *Clinical epigenetics* (pp. 1–46). Springer. https://doi.org/10.1007/978 -981-13-8958-0_1

Hewitt, L., Benjamin-Neelon, S. E., Carson, V., Stanley, R. M., Janssen, I., & Okely, A. D. (2018). Child care centre adherence to infant physical activity and screen time recommendations in Australia, Canada and the United States: An observational study. *Infant Behavior & Development, 50,* 88–97. https://doi .org/10.1016/j.infbeh.2017.11.008

Hicken, M. T., Kravitz-Wirtz, N., Durkee, M., & Jackson, J. S. (2018). Racial inequalities in health: Framing future research. *Social Science & Medicine, 199,* 11–18. https://doi.org/10.1016/j.socscimed.2017.12.027

Hiekel, N., Liefbroer, A. C., & Poortman, A.-R. (2014). Understanding diversity in the meaning of cohabitation across Europe. *European Journal of Population, 30*(4), 391–410. https://doi.org/10.1007 /s10680-014-9321-1

Higgins, L. T., & Xiang, G. (2009). The development and use of intelligence tests in China. *Psychology and Developing Societies, 21*(2), 257–275.

Higgitt, R. (2017). Challenging tropes: Genius, heroic invention, and the longitude problem in the museum. *Isis, 108*(2), 371–380. https://doi.org/10.1086/692691

Hill, A. J., & Zhou, W. (2021). Peer discrimination in the classroom and academic achievement. *Journal of Human Resources,* 0919-10460R3.

Hill, B. (2021). Expanding our understanding and use of the ecological systems theory model for the prevention of maternal obesity: A new socioecological framework. *Obesity Reviews, 22*(3), e13147.

Hill, B., & Rodriguez, A. C. I. (2020). Weight stigma across the preconception, pregnancy, and postpartum periods: A narrative review and conceptual model. *Seminars in Reproductive Medicine, 38*(6), 414–422. https://doi.org/10.1055/s-0041-1723775

Hill, H. A., Yankey, D., Elam-Evans, L. D., Singleton, J. A., & Sterrett, N. (2021). Vaccination coverage by age 24 months among children born in 2017 and 2018—National Immunization Survey–Child, United States, 2018–2020. Morbidity and Mortality Weekly Reports, 70, 1435–1440. http://doi.org/10.15585 /mmwr.mm7041a1external icon.

Hill, J. P., & den Dulk, K. R. (2013). Religion, volunteering, and educational setting: The effect of youth schooling type on civic engagement. *Journal for the Scientific Study of Religion, 52*(1), 179–197. https://doi .org/10.1111/jssr.12011

Hilliard, L. J., & Liben, L. S. (2020). Addressing sexism with children: Young adults' beliefs about bias socialization. *Child Development, 91*(2), 488–507. https://doi.org/10.1111/cdev.13230

Hillis, S., Mercy, J., Amobi, A., & Kress, H. (2016). Global prevalence of past-year violence against children: A systematic review and minimum estimates. *Pediatrics, 137*(3), e20154079. https://doi.org/10.1542 /peds.2015-4079

Hillman, C. H., McAuley, E., Erickson, K. I., Liu-Ambrose, T., & Kramer, A. F. (2018). On mindful and mindless physical activity and executive function: A response to Diamond and Ling (2016). *Developmental Cognitive Neuroscience, 37,* 100529. https://doi.org /10.1016/j.dcn.2018.01.006

Hillman, C. H., Pontifex, M. B., Castelli, D. M., Khan, N. A., Raine, L. B., Scudder, M. R., Drollette, E. S., Moore, R. D., Wu, C.-T., & Kamijo, K. (2014). Effects of the FITKids randomized controlled trial on executive control and brain function. *Pediatrics, 134*(4), e1063–e1071. https://doi.org/10.1542/ peds.2013-3219

Hines, M. (2020). Human gender development. *Neuroscience & Biobehavioral Reviews, 118,* 89–96. https://doi.org/10.1016/j.neubiorev.2020.07.018

Hino, K., Ikeda, E., Sadahiro, S., & Inoue, S. (2021). Associations of neighborhood built, safety, and social environment with walking to and from school among elementary school-aged children in Chiba, Japan. *International Journal of Behavioral Nutrition and Physical Activity, 18*(1), 1–13.

Hinshaw, S. P. (2018). Attention deficit hyperactivity disorder (ADHD): Controversy, developmental mechanisms, and multiple levels of analysis. *Annual Review of Clinical Psychology, 14*(1), 291–316. https://doi.org /10.1146/annurev-clinpsy-050817-084917

Hirsh-Pasek, K. (2021). *Play breeds better thinkers.* Science.

Ho, T. C., Gifuni, A. J., & Gotlib, I. H. (2021). Psychobiological risk factors for suicidal thoughts and behaviors in adolescence: A consideration of the role of puberty. *Molecular Psychiatry.* https://doi.org/10.1038 /s41380-021-01171-5

Hochberg, Z., & Konner, M. (2020). Emerging adulthood, a pre-adult life-history stage. *Frontiers in Endocrinology, 10,* 918. https://doi.org/10.3389 /fendo.2019.00918

Hodder, R. K., O'Brien, K. M., Tzelepis, F., Wyse, R. J., & Wolfenden, L. (2020). Interventions for increasing fruit and vegetable consumption in children aged five years and under. *Cochrane Database of Systematic Reviews,* 5. https://doi.org/10.1002/14651858. CD008552.pub7

Hodel, A. S. (2018). Rapid infant prefrontal cortex development and sensitivity to early environmental experience. *Developmental Review, 48,* 113–144. https:// doi.org/10.1016/j.dr.2018.02.003

Hodges, E. A., Propper, C. B., Estrem, H., & Schultz, M. B. (2020). Feeding during infancy: Interpersonal behavior, physiology, and obesity risk. *Child Development Perspectives, 14*(3), 185–191. https://doi.org/10.1111/cdep.12376

Hodges, T. (2018, October 25). *School engagement is more than just talk.* Gallup.com. https://www.gallup .com/education/244022/school-engagement-talk.aspx

Hoehl, S., Hellmer, K., Johansson, M., & Gredebäck, G. (2017). Itsy bitsy spider: Infants react with increased arousal to spiders and snakes. *Frontiers in Psychology, 8,* 1710. https://doi.org/10.3389/fpsyg.2017.01710

Hoehl, S., Keupp, S., Schleihauf, H., McGuigan, N., Buttelmann, D., & Whiten, A. (2019). 'Overimitation': A review and appraisal of a decade of research. *Developmental Review, 51,* 90–108. https://doi.org /10.1016/j.dr.2018.12.002

Hoelscher, D. M., Brann, L. S., O'Brien, S., Handu, D., & Rozga, M. (2022). Prevention of pediatric overweight and obesity: Position of the Academy of Nutrition and Dietetics based on an umbrella review of systematic reviews. *Journal of the Academy of Nutrition and Dietetics, 122*(2), 410-423.

Hoff, E. (2018). Bilingual development in children of immigrant families. *Child Development Perspectives, 12*(2), 80–86. https://doi.org/10.1111/cdep.12262

Hoff, E., & Core, C. (2015). What clinicians need to know about bilingual development. *Seminars in Speech and Language, 36*(02), 089–099. https://doi.org /10.1055/s-0035-1549104

Hofferth, S. L. (2009). Changes in American children's time—1997 to 2003. *Electronic International Journal of Time Use Research, 6*(1), 26.

Hoffman, M. L. (1977). Personality and social development. *Annual Review of Psychology, 28*(1), 295–321. https://doi.org/10.1146/annurev.ps.28.020177.001455

Höhle, B., Bijeljac-Babic, R., & Nazzi, T. (2020). Variability and stability in early language acquisition: Comparing monolingual and bilingual infants' speech perception and word recognition. *Bilingualism: Language and Cognition, 23*(1), 56–71. https://doi.org /10.1017/S1366728919000348

Høigaard, R., Kovač, V. B., Øverby, N. C., & Haugen, T. (2015). Academic self-efficacy mediates the effects of school psychological climate on academic achievement. *School Psychology Quarterly, 30*(1), 64–74. https://doi.org /10.1037/spq0000056

Holbein, J., Kawashima-Ginsberg, K., & Wang, T. (2021). *Quantifying the effects of protests on voter registration and turnout* (Study II of Protests, Politics, and Power: Exploring the Connections Between Youth Voting and Youth Movements). CIRCLE, Tufts University.

Holbreich, M., Genuneit, J., Weber, J., Braun-Fahrländer, C., Waser, M., & von Mutius, E. (2012). Amish children living in northern Indiana have a very low prevalence of allergic sensitization. *Journal of Allergy and Clinical Immunology, 129*(6), 1671–1673. https:// doi.org/10.1016/j.jaci.2012.03.016

Holden, G. W., Williamson, P. A., & Holland, G. W. (2014). Eavesdropping on the family: A pilot investigation of corporal punishment in the home. *Journal of Family Psychology, 28*(3), 401.

Holland, D., Chang, L., Ernst, T. M., Curran, M., Buchthal, S. D., Alicata, D., Skranes, J., Johansen, H., Hernandez, A., Yamakawa, R., Kuperman, J. M., & Dale, A. M. (2014). Structural growth trajectories and rates of change in the first 3 months of infant brain development. *JAMA Neurology, 71*(10), 1266–1274. https://doi.org/10.1001/jamaneurol.2014.1638

Holland, J., Reynolds, T., & Weller, S. (2007). Transitions, networks and communities: The significance of social capital in the lives of children and young people. *Journal of Youth Studies, 10*(1), 97–116.

Holodynski, M., & Seeger, D. (2019). Expressions as signs and their significance for emotional development. *Developmental Psychology, 55*(9), 1812.

Holt, N. L., Kingsley, B. C., Tink, L. N., & Scherer, J. (2011). Benefits and challenges associated with sport participation by children and parents from low-income families. *Psychology of Sport and Exercise, 12*(5), 490–499. https://doi.org/10.1016/j.psychsport.2011.05.007

Holt-Lunstad, J. (2017). The potential public health relevance of social isolation and loneliness: Prevalence, epidemiology, and risk factors. *Public Policy & Aging Report, 27*(4), 127–130. https://doi.org/10.1093/ppar/prx030

Holzen, K. V., & Nazzi, T. (2020). Emergence of a consonant bias during the first year of life: New evidence from own-name recognition. *Infancy, 25*(3), 319–346. https://doi.org/10.1111/infa.12331

Hong, K., Savelyev, P. A., & Tan, K. T. (2020). Understanding the mechanisms linking college education with longevity. *Journal of Human Capital, 14*(3), 371–400.

Hong, P., Cui, M., Ledermann, T., & Love, H. (2021). Parent-child relationship satisfaction and psychological distress of parents and emerging adult children. *Journal of Child and Family Studies, 30*(4), 921–931. https://doi.org/10.1007/s10826-021-01916-4

Hookway, L., Lewis, J., & Brown, A. (2021). The challenges of medically complex breastfed children and their families: A systematic review. *Maternal & Child Nutrition, 17*(4), e13182. https://doi.org/10.1111/mcn.13182

Hooper, E. G., Wu, Q., Ku, S., Gerhardt, M., & Feng, X. (2018). Maternal emotion socialization and child outcomes among African Americans and European Americans. *Journal of Child and Family Studies, 27*(6), 1870–1880. https://doi.org/10.1007/s10826-018-1020-9

Hopkins, A. A. (1921). Our latest science—eugenics. *Scientific American, 125* (16), 273–279.

Hopkins, M., Weddle, H., Bjorklund Jr, P., Umansky, I. M., & Blanca Dabach, D. (2021). "It's created by a community": Local context mediating districts' approaches to serving immigrant and refugee newcomers. *AERA Open, 7*, 23328584211032234.

Horbar, J. D., Edwards, E. M., Greenberg, L. T., Profit, J., Draper, D., Helkey, D., Lorch, S. A., Lee, H. C., Phibbs, C. S., Rogowski, J., Gould, J. B., & Firebaugh, G. (2019). Racial segregation and inequality in the neonatal intensive care unit for very low-birth-weight and very preterm infants. *JAMA Pediatrics, 173*(5), 455–461. https://doi.org/10.1001/jamapediatrics.2019.0241

Hornbeck, K., Walter, K., & Myrvik, M. (2017). Should potential risk of chronic traumatic encephalopathy be discussed with young athletes? *AMA Journal of Ethics, 19*(7), 686–692. https://doi.org/10.1001/journalofethics.2017.19.7.pfor1-1707.

Hornberger, L. L., Lane, M. A., & The Committee on Adolescence. (2021). Identification and management of eating disorders in children and adolescents. *Pediatrics, 147*(1), e2020040279. https://doi.org/10.1542/peds.2020-040279

Horowitz, S. H., Rawe, J., & Whittaker, M. C. (2017). *The State of Learning Disabilities: Understanding the 1 in 5.* New York: National Center for Learning Disabilities

Horta, B. L. (2019). Breastfeeding: Investing in the future. *Breastfeeding Medicine, 14*(S1), S-11–S-12.

Horton, R., Crawford, G., Freeman, L., Fenwick, A., Wright, C. F., & Lucassen, A. (2019). Direct-to-consumer genetic testing. *BMJ, 367,* l5688. https://doi.org/10.1136/bmj.l5688

Horvath, C. A., & Lee, C. M. (2015). Parenting responses and parenting goals of mothers and fathers of adolescents. *Marriage & Family Review, 51*(4), 337–355. https://doi.org/10.1080/01494929.2014.955938

Horvath, G., Knopik, V. S., & Marceau, K. (2020). Polygenic influences on pubertal timing and tempo and depressive symptoms in boys and girls. *Journal of Research on Adolescence, 30*(1), 78–94. https://doi.org/10.1111/jora.12502

Horváth, K., & Plunkett, K. (2018). Spotlight on daytime napping during early childhood. *Nature and Science of Sleep, 10*, 97–104. https://doi.org/10.2147/NSS.S126252

Hosokawa, M., Imazeki, S., Mizunuma, H., Kubota, T., & Hayashi, K. (2012). Secular trends in age at menarche and time to establish regular menstrual cycling in Japanese women born between 1930 and 1985. BMC Women's Health, 12, 19. http://dx.doi.org/10.1186/1472-6874-12-19

Hostinar, C. E., Sullivan, R. M., & Gunnar, M. R. (2014). Psychobiological mechanisms underlying the social buffering of the hypothalamic–pituitary–adrenocortical axis: A review of animal models and human studies across development. *Psychological Bulletin, 140*(1), 256.

Hou, X. H., Gong, Z. Q., Wang, L. J., Zhou, Y., & Su, Y. (2020). A reciprocal and dynamic development model for the effects of siblings on children's theory of mind. *Frontiers in Psychology, 11*, 2667.

Houdé, O., & Borst, G. (2014). Measuring inhibitory control in children and adults: Brain imaging and mental chronometry. *Frontiers in Psychology, 5*, 616.

Houdé, O., Pineau, A., Leroux, G., Poirel, N., Perchey, G., Lanoë, C., Lubin, A., Turbelin, M., Rossi, S., Simon, G., Delcroix, N., Lamberton, F., Vigneau, M., Wisniewski, G., Vicet, J.-R., & Mazoyer, B. (2011). Functional magnetic resonance imaging study of Piaget's conservation-of-number task in preschool and school-age children: A neo-Piagetian approach. *Journal of Experimental Child Psychology, 110*(3), 332–346.

Hourigan, K. L. (2021). Girls try, boys aim high: Exposing difference in implied ability, activity, and agency of girls versus boys in language on McDonald's happy meal boxes. *Sex Roles, 84*(7), 377–391. https://doi.org/10.1007/s11199-020-01173-7

House, B. R. (2018). How do social norms influence prosocial development? *Current Opinion in Psychology, 20*, 87–91. https://doi.org/10.1016/j.copsyc.2017.08.011

House, B. R., & Tomasello, M. (2018). Modeling social norms increasingly influences costly sharing in middle childhood. *Journal of Experimental Child Psychology, 171*, 84–98.

Howard, A. L., Pals, S., Walker, B., Benevides, R., Massetti, G. M., Oluoch, R. P., Ogbanufe, O., Marcelin, L. H., Cela, T., Mapoma, C. C., Gonese, E., Msungama, W., Magesa, D., Kayange, A., Galloway, K., Apondi, R., Wasula, L., Mugurungi, O., Ncube, G., . . . Patel, P. (2021). Forced sexual initiation and early sexual debut and associated risk factors and health problems among adolescent girls and young women—Violence against children and youth surveys, nine PEPFAR countries, 2007–2018. *Morbidity and Mortality Weekly Report, 70*(47), 1629–1634. https://doi.org/10.15585/mmwr.mm7047a2

Howard, J., Miles, G. E., Rees-Davies, L., & Bertenshaw, E. J. (2017). Play in middle childhood: Everyday play behaviour and associated emotions. *Children & Society, 31*(5), 378–389.

Howard, L. M., & Khalifeh, H. (2020). Perinatal mental health: A review of progress and challenges. *World Psychiatry, 19*(3), 313–327. https://doi.org/10.1002/wps.20769

Howe, N., & Leach, J. (2018). Children's play and peer relations. In W. M. Bukowski, B. Laursen, & K. H. Rubin (Eds.), *Handbook of peer interactions, relationships, and groups* (2nd ed., pp. 222–242). Guilford.

Howe, N., Della Porta, S., Recchia, H., & Ross, H. (2016). "Because if you don't put the top on, it will spill": A longitudinal study of sibling teaching in early childhood. *Developmental Psychology, 52*(11), 1832–1842. https://doi.org/10.1037/dev0000193

Howell, B. R., Styner, M. A., Gao, W., Yap, P.-T., Wang, L., Baluyot, K., Yacoub, E., Chen, G., Potts, T., Salzwedel, A., Li, G., Gilmore, J. H., Piven, J., Smith, J. K., Shen, D., Ugurbil, K., Zhu, H., Lin, W., & Elison, J. T. (2019). The UNC/UMN Baby Connectome Project (BCP): An overview of the study design and protocol development. *NeuroImage, 185*, 891–905. https://doi.org/10.1016/j.neuroimage.2018.03.049

Hoy, M. K., Clemens, J., Martin, C., & Moshfegh, A. (2020). Fruit and vegetable intake among children by level of variety, What we eat in America, NHANES 2013–2016. *Current Developments in Nutrition, 4*(Supplement_2), 206. https://doi.org/10.1093/cdn/nzaa043_057

Hoyert, D. L., & Gregory, E. C. (2020). Cause-of-death data from the fetal death file, 2015–2017. *National Vital Statistics Reports, 69*(4), 1–20.

Hoyniak, C. P., Bates, J. E., Camacho, M. C., McQuillan, M. E., Whalen, D. J., Staples, A. D., Rudasill, K. M., & Deater-Deckard, K. (2022). The physical home environment and sleep: What matters most for sleep in early childhood. *Journal of Family Psychology.* https://doi.org/10.1037/fam0000977

Hoyniak, C. P., Bates, J. E., McQuillan, M. E., Staples, A. D., Petersen, I. T., Rudasill, K. M., & Molfese, V. J. (2020). Sleep across early childhood: implications for internalizing and externalizing problems, socioemotional skills, and cognitive and academic abilities in preschool. *Journal of Child Psychology and Psychiatry, 61*(10), 1080–1091.

Hoyniak, C. P., Bates, J. E., Staples, A. D., Rudasill, K. M., Molfese, D. L., & Molfese, V. J. (2019). Child sleep and socioeconomic context in the development of cognitive abilities in early childhood. *Child Development, 90*(5), 1718–1737. https://doi.org/10.1111/cdev.13042

Hoyos-Quintero, A. M., & García-Perdomo, H. A. (2019). Factors related to physical activity in early childhood: A systematic review. *Journal of Physical Activity and Health, 16*(10), 925–936. https://doi.org/10.1123/jpah.2018-0715

Hraba, J., & Grant, G. (1970). Black is beautiful: A reexamination of racial preference and identification. *Journal of Personality and Social Psychology, 16*(3), 398.

Hrdy, S. B., & Burkart, J. M. (2020). The emergence of emotionally modern humans: Implications for language and learning. *Philosophical Transactions of the Royal Society B: Biological Sciences, 375* (1803), 20190499. https://doi.org/10.1098/rstb.2019.0499

Hruschka, D. J., Medin, D. L., Rogoff, B., & Henrich, J. (2018). Pressing questions in the study of psychological and behavioral diversity. *Proceedings of the National Academy of Sciences, 115*(45), 11366–11368.

Hruska, L. C., Zelic, K. J., Dickson, K. S., & Ciesla, J. A. (2015). Adolescents' co-rumination and stress predict affective changes in a daily-diary paradigm. *International Journal of Psychology, 52*(5), 372–380. https://doi.org/10.1002/ijop.12227

Hsieh, S.-S., Chueh, T.-Y., Morris, T. P., Kao, S.-C., Westfall, D. R., Raine, L. B., Hopman, R. J., Pontifex, M. B., Castelli, D. M., Kramer, A. F., & Hillman, C. H. (2020). Greater childhood cardiorespiratory fitness is associated with better top-down cognitive control: A midfrontal theta oscillation study. *Psychophysiology, 57*(12), e13678. https://doi.org/10.1111/psyp.13678

Huang, C.-Y., & Lamb, M. E. (2014). Are Chinese children more compliant? Examination of the cultural difference in observed maternal control and child compliance. *Journal of Cross-Cultural Psychology, 45*(4), 507–533.

Huber, G. A., & Malhotra, N. (2017). Political homophily in social relationships: Evidence from online dating behavior. *The Journal of Politics, 79*(1), 269–283. https://doi.org/10.1086/687533

Huddleston, J., & Ge, X. (2003). Boys at puberty: Psychosocial implications. In C. Hayward (Ed.), *Gender differences at puberty* (pp. 113–134). Cambridge University Press.

Hudson, J. A., & Mayhew, E. M. Y. (2009). The development of memory in infancy and childhood. *The Development of Memory for Recurring Events,* 69–91.

Hudson, K. N., Ballou, H. M., & Willoughby, M. T. (2020). Short report: Improving motor competence skills in early childhood has corollary benefits for executive function and numeracy skills. *Developmental Science, 24*(4), e13071. https://doi.org/10.1111/desc.13071

Hudson, K. N., Ballou, H. M., & Willoughby, M. T. (2021). Improving motor competence skills in early childhood has corollary benefits for executive function and numeracy skills. *Developmental Science, 24*(4), e13071.

Hudson, M. M., Bhatia, S., Casillas, J., Landier, W., & Section on Hematology/Oncology, C. O. G., American Society of Pediatric Hematology/Oncology. (2021). Long-term follow-up care for childhood, adolescent, and young adult cancer survivors. *Pediatrics, 148*(3), e2021053127. https://doi.org/10.1542/peds.2021-053127

Huelke, D. F. (1998). An overview of anatomical considerations of infants and children in the adult world of automobile safety design. In *Annual Proceedings/Association for the Advancement of Automotive Medicine* (Vol. 42, pp. 93–113). Association for the Advancement of Automotive Medicine.

Hughes, C., & Devine, R. T. (2015). Individual differences in theory of mind from preschool to adolescence: Achievements and directions. *Child Development Perspectives, 9*(3), 149–153. https://doi.org/10.1111/cdep.12124

Hughes, C., Devine, R. T., & Wang, Z. (2018). Does parental mind-mindedness account for cross-cultural differences in preschoolers' theory of mind? *Child Development, 89*(4), 1296–1310.

Hughes, C., Devine, R. T., Ensor, R., Koyasu, M., Mizokawa, A., & Lecce, S. (2014). Lost in translation? Comparing British, Japanese, and Italian children's theory-of-mind performance. *Child Development Research, 2014,* 893492.

Hughes, C., Devine, R. T., Mesman, J., & Blair, C. (2020). Understanding the terrible twos: A longitudinal investigation of the impact of early executive function and parent–child interactions. *Developmental Science, 23*(6), e12979. https://doi.org/10.1111/desc.12979

Hughes, C., McHarg, G., & White, N. (2018). Sibling influences on prosocial behavior. *Current Opinion in Psychology, 20,* 96–101. https://doi.org/10.1016/j.copsyc.2017.08.015

Hughes, D., Del Toro, J., Harding, J. F., Way, N., & Rarick, J. R. D. (2016). Trajectories of discrimination across adolescence: Associations with academic, psychological, and behavioral outcomes. *Child Development, 87*(5), 1337–1351. https://doi.org/10.1111/cdev.12591

Hughes, D. L., Watford, J. A., & Del Toro, J. (2016b). Chapter one—A transactional/ecological perspective on ethnic–racial identity, socialization, and discrimination. In S. S. Horn, M. D. Ruck, & L. S. Liben (Eds.), Advances in child development and behavior (Vol. 51, pp. 1–41). JAI. https://www.sciencedirect.com/science/article/abs/pii/S0065240716300209

Huguley, J. P., Wang, M. T., Vasquez, A. C., & Guo, J. (2019). Parental ethnic–racial socialization practices and the construction of children of color's ethnic–racial identity: A research synthesis and meta-analysis. *Psychological Bulletin, 145*(5), 437.

Huhmann, K. (2020). Menses requires energy: A review of how disordered eating, excessive exercise, and high stress lead to menstrual irregularities. *Clinical Therapeutics, 42*(3), 401–407. https://doi.org/10.1016/j.clinthera.2020.01.016

Huitsing, G., & Monks, C. P. (2018). Who victimizes whom and who defends whom? A multivariate social network analysis of victimization, aggression, and defending in early childhood. *Aggressive Behavior, 44*(4), 394–405.

Huizinga, M., Baeyens, D., & Burack, J. A. (2018). Editorial: Executive Function and Education. *Frontiers in Psychology, 9.* https://doi.org/10.3389/fpsyg.2018.01357

Hulleman, C. S., Barron, K. E., Kosovich, J. J., & Lazowski, R. A. (2016). Student motivation: Current theories, constructs, and interventions within an expectancy-value framework. In A. A. Lipnevich, F. Preckel, & R. D. Roberts (Eds.), *Psychosocial skills and school systems in the 21st century: Theory, research, and practice* (pp. 241–278). Springer International Publishing. https://doi.org/10.1007/978-3-319-28606-8_10

Hulteen, R. M., Barnett, L. M., True, L., Lander, N. J., Cruz, B. del P., & Lonsdale, C. (2020). Validity and reliability evidence for motor competence assessments in children and adolescents: A systematic review. *Journal of Sports Sciences, 38*(15), 1717–1798. https://doi.org/10.1080/02640414.2020.1756674

Human Rights Campaign Foundation. (2018). *Healthcare Equality Index 2018: Rising to the new standard of promoting equitable and inclusive care for lesbian, gay, bisexual, transgender & queer patients and their families.*

Human Rights Watch. (2016). *The education deficit: Failures to protect and fulfill the right to education through global development agendas.* Human Rights Watch.

Human Rights Watch. (2019). *"They are making us into slaves, not educating us": How indefinite conscription restricts young people's rights, access to education in Eritrea.* Human Rights Watch. https://www.hrw.org/report/2019/08/08/they-are-making-us-slaves-not-educating-us/how-indefinite-conscription-restricts

Humphreys, K. L., Miron, D., McLaughlin, K. A., Sheridan, M. A., Nelson, C. A., Fox, N. A., & Zeanah, C. H. (2018). Foster care promotes adaptive functioning in early adolescence among children who experienced severe, early deprivation. *Journal of Child Psychology and Psychiatry, and Allied Disciplines, 59*(7), 811–821. https://doi.org/10.1111/jcpp.12865

Humphreys, K., Guyon-Harris, K., Tibu, F., Nelson, C. A., Fox, N. A., & Zeanah, C. H. (2020). Causal effects of foster care on cognitive ability and adaptive functioning in young adulthood. *Biological Psychiatry, 87*(9), S43–S44. https://doi.org/10.1016/j.biopsych.2020.02.136

Hunley, K. L., Cabana, G. S., & Long, J. C. (2016). The apportionment of human diversity revisited. *American Journal of Physical Anthropology, 160*(4), 561–569. https://doi.org/10.1002/ajpa.22899

Hunt, D. M., & Carvalho, L. S. (2016). The genetics of color vision and congenital color deficiencies. In *Human color vision* (pp. 1–32). Springer. https://doi.org/10.1007/978-3-319-44978-4_1

Huppert, E., Cowell, J. M., Cheng, Y., Contreras-Ibáñez, C., Gomez-Sicard, N., Gonzalez-Gadea, M. L., Huepe, D., Ibanez, A., Lee, K., Mahasneh, R., Malcolm-Smith, S., Salas, N., Selcuk, B., Tungodden, B., Wong, A., Zhou, X., & Decety, J. (2019). The development of children's preferences for equality and equity across 13 individualistic and collectivist cultures. *Developmental Science, 22*(2), e12729.

Hurst, K. (March 11, 2022). Rising share of Americans see women raising children on their own, cohabitation as bad for society. *Pew Research Center.* https://www.pewresearch.org/fact-tank/2022/03/11/rising-share-of-americans-see-women-raising-children-on-their-own-cohabitation-as-bad-for-society/

Hutchins, H. J., Barry, C. M., Wanga, V., Bacon, S., Njai, R., Claussen, A. H., Ghandour, R. M., Lebrun-Harris, L. A., Perkins, K., & Robinson, L. R. (2022). Perceived racial/ethnic discrimination, physical and mental health conditions in childhood, and the relative role of other adverse experiences. *Adversity and Resilience Science,* 1–14.

Hutson, J. A., Taft, J. G., Barocas, S., & Levy, K. (2018). Debiasing desire: Addressing bias & discrimination on intimate platforms. *Proceedings of the ACM on Human-Computer Interaction 2 (CSCW),* 88, 1–18.

Huttenlocher, P. R., & Dabholkar, A. S. (1997). Regional differences in synaptogenesis in human cerebral cortex. *The Journal of Comparative Neurology, 387*(2), 167–178. https://doi.org/10.1002/(SICI)1096-9861(19971020)387:2<167::AID-CNE1>3.0.CO;2-Z

Hutton, J. S., Dudley, J., Horowitz-Kraus, T., DeWitt, T., & Holland, S. K. (2020a). Associations between screen-based media use and brain white matter integrity in preschool-aged children. *JAMA Pediatrics, 174*(1), e193869.

Hutton, J. S., Dudley, J., Horowitz-Kraus, T., DeWitt, T., & Holland, S. K. (2020b). Associations between home literacy environment, brain white matter integrity and cognitive abilities in preschool-age children. *Acta Paediatrica, 109*(7), 1376–1386. https://doi.org/10.1111/apa.15124

Huynh, V. W., & Fuligni, A. J. (2010). Discrimination hurts: The academic, psychological, and physical well-being of adolescents. *Journal of Research on Adolescence, 20*(4), 916–941.

Huynh, V. W., Guan, S.-S. A., Almeida, D. M., McCreath, H., & Fuligni, A. J. (2016). Everyday discrimination and diurnal cortisol during adolescence. *Hormones and Behavior, 80*, 76–81. https://doi.org/10.1016/j.yhbeh.2016.01.009

Hviid, A., Hansen, J. V., Frisch, M., & Melbye, M. (2019). Measles, mumps, rubella vaccination and autism. *Annals of Internal Medicine, 170*(8), 513–520. https://doi.org/10.7326/M18-2101

Hyde, D. C. (2021). The emergence of a brain network for numerical thinking. *Child Development Perspectives.*

Hyde, L. W., Gard, A. M., Tomlinson, R. C., Burt, S. A., Mitchell, C., & Monk, C. S. (2020). An ecological approach to understanding the developing brain: Examples linking poverty, par-enting, neighborhoods, and the brain. *The American Psychologist, 75*(9), 1245–1259. https://doi.org/10.1037/amp0000741

Hygen, B. W., Belsky, J., Stenseng, F., Skalicka, V., Kvande, M. N., Zahl-Thanem, T., & Wichstrøm, L. (2020). Time spent gaming and social competence in children: Reciprocal effects across childhood. *Child Development, 91*(3), 861–875.

Hym, C., Forma, V., Anderson, D. I., Provasi, J., Granjon, L., Huet, V., Carpe, E., Teulier, C., Durand, K., Schaal, B., & Barbu-Roth, M. (2021). Newborn crawling and rooting in response to maternal breast odor. *Developmental Science, 24*(3), e13061. https://doi.org/10.1111/desc.13061

Hyman, S. L., Levy, S. E., Myers, S. M., & Council on Children with Disabilities, Section on Developmental and Behavioral Pediatrics. (2020). Identification, evaluation, and management of children with autism spectrum disorder. *Pediatrics, 145*(1), e20193447. https://doi.org/10.1542/peds.2019-3447

Hymel, S., & Swearer, S. M. (2015). Four decades of research on school bullying: An introduction. *American Psychologist, 70*(4), 293.

Hysing, M., Askeland, K. G., La Greca, A. M., Solberg, M. E., Breivik, K., & Sivertsen, B. (2019). Bullying involvement in adolescence: Implications for sleep, mental health, and academic outcomes. *Journal of Interpersonal Violence.* https://doi.org/10.1177/0886260519853409

Ibbotson, P. (2013). The scope of usage-based theory. *Frontiers in Psychology, 4*, 255.

Ilari, B. (2020). Longitudinal research on music education and child development: Contributions and challenges. *Music & Science, 3*, 2059204320937224. https://doi.org/10.1177/2059204320937224

Incollingo Rodriguez, A. C., Tomiyama, A. J., Guardino, C. M., & Dunkel Schetter, C. (2019). Association of weight discrimination during pregnancy and postpartum with maternal postpartum health. *Health Psychology, 38*(3), 226–237. https://doi.org/10.1037/hea0000711

Inhelder, B., & Piaget, J. (1958). *The growth of logical thinking: From childhood to adolescence* (A. Parsons & S. Milgram, Trans.). Basic Books. https://doi.org/10.1037/10034-000

Inhelder, B., & Piaget, J. (1964). *The early growth of logic in the child.* Routledge.

Inselman, A. L., & Slikker, W. (2018). Is there a safe dose of a medication associated with birth defects? In B. Hales, A. Scialli, & M. Tassinari (Eds.), *Teratology primer* (3rd ed.). Society for Birth Defects Research & Prevention.

International Commission on the Futures of Education (ICFE). (2021). *Reimagining our futures together: A new social contract for education—UNESCO Digital Library.* UNESCO. https://unesdoc.unesco.org/ark:/48223/pf0000379707.locale=en

International Labour Office (ILO). (2020). *Global Employment Trends for Youth: Technology and the future of jobs.* International Labour Organization.

International Labour Office & United Nations Children's Fund (ILO/UNICEF). (2021). *Child Labour: Global estimates 2020, trends and the road forward.*

International Labour Organization (ILO). (2021). *An update on the youth labour market impact of the COVID-19 crisis* [Statistical brief].

Ioverno, S., DeLay, D., Martin, C. L., & Hanish, L. D. (2021). Who engages in gender bullying? The role of homophobic name-calling, gender pressure, and gender conformity. *Educational Researcher, 50*(4), 215–224. https://doi.org/10.3102/0013189X20968067

Ip, K. I., Miller, A. L., Karasawa, M., Hirabayashi, H., Kazama, M., Wang, L., Olson, S. L., Kessler, D., & Tardif, T. (2021). Emotion expression and regulation in three cultures: Chinese, Japanese, and American preschoolers' reactions to disappointment. *Journal of Experimental Child Psychology, 201*, 104972. https://doi.org/10.1016/j.jecp.2020.104972

Ipsos. (2021). *Gender identity and sexual orientation differences by generation.*

Iqbal, M. (2021, March). *Tinder revenue and usage statistics.* Business of Apps. https://www.businessofapps.com/data/tinder-statistics/

Irwin, V., Zhang, J., Wang, X., Hein, S., Wang, K., Roberts, A., York, C., Barmer, A., Bullock Mann, F., Dilig, R., Parker, S., Nachazel, T., Barnett, M., & Purcell, S. (2021). *Report on the condition of education 2021* (NCES 2021-144). National Center for Education Statistics. https://eric.ed.gov/?id=ED612942

Ishihara, T., Sugasawa, S., Matsuda, Y., & Mizuno, M. (2018). Relationship between sports experience and executive function in 6–12-year-old children: Independence from physical fitness and moderation by gender. *Developmental Science, 21*(3), e12555. https://doi.org/10.1111/desc.12555

Isiekwe, G. I., Sofola, O. O., Onigbogi, O. O., Utomi, I. L., & Sanu, O. O. (2016). Dental esthetics and oral health-related quality of life in young adults. *American Journal of Orthodontics and Dentofacial Orthopedics, 150*(4), 627–636.

Ismail, S., Odland, M. L., Malik, A., Weldegiorgis, M., Newbigging, K., Peden, M., Woodward, M., & Davies, J. (2021). The relationship between psychosocial circumstances and injuries in adolescents: An analysis of 87,269 individuals from 26 countries using the Global School-based Student Health Survey. *PLOS Medicine, 18*(9), e1003722. https://doi.org/10.1371/journal.pmed.1003722

Ismail, Z., Elbayoumi, H., Fischer, C. E., Hogan, D. B., Millikin, C. P., Schweizer, T., Mortby, M. E., Smith, E. E., Patten, S. B., & Fiest, K. M. (2017). Prevalence of depression in patients with mild cognitive impairment: A systematic review and meta-analysis.

JAMA Psychiatry, 74(1), 58–67. https://doi.org/10.1001/jamapsychiatry.2016.3162

Israel, A., Brandt, N. D., Grund, S., Köller, O., Lüdtke, O., & Wagner, J. (2021). Personality and psychosocial functioning in early adolescence: Age-differential associations from the self- and parent perspective. *European Journal of Personality.* https://doi.org/10.1177/08902070211005636

Ivars, K., Nelson, N., Theodorsson, A., Theodorsson, E., Ström, J. O., & Mörelius, E. (2015). Development of salivary cortisol circadian rhythm and reference intervals in full-term infants. *PLOS One, 10*(6), e0129502

Ivey-Stephenson, A. Z., Demissie, Z., Crosby, A. E., Stone, D. M., Gaylor, E., Wilkins, N., Lowry, R., & Brown, M. (2020). Suicidal ideation and behaviors among high school students—youth risk behavior survey, United States, 2019. *Morbidity and Mortality Weekly Report Supplements, 69*(1), 47–55. https://doi.org/10.15585/mmwr.su6901a6

Izard, V., Sann, C., Spelke, E. S., & Streri, A. (2009). Newborn infants perceive abstract numbers. *Proceedings of the National Academy of Sciences, 106*(25), 10382–10385. https://doi.org/10.1073/pnas.0812142106

Jaacks, L. M., Vandevijvere, S., Pan, A., McGowan, C. J., Wallace, C., Imamura, F., Mozaffarian, D., Swinburn, B., & Ezzati, M. (2019). The obesity transition: Stages of the global epidemic. *The Lancet. Diabetes & Endocrinology, 7*(3), 231–240. https://doi.org/10.1016/S2213-8587(19)30026-9

Jabès, A., & Nelson, C. A. (2015). 20 years after "The ontogeny of human memory: A cognitive neuroscience perspective, where are we?. *International Journal of Behavioral Development, 39*(4), 293–303.

Jablonski, N. G. (2018). Eye color. In *The international encyclopedia of biological anthropology* (pp. 1–2). Wiley. https://doi.org/10.1002/9781118584538.ieba0541

Jablonski, N. G. (2021). Skin color and race. *American Journal of Physical Anthropology, 175*(2), 437–447. https://doi.org/10.1002/ajpa.24200

Jackman, K., Kreuze, E. J., Caceres, B. A., & Schnall, R. (2020). Bullying and peer victimization of minority youth: Intersections of sexual identity and race/ethnicity. *Journal of School Health, 90*(5), 368–377. https://doi.org/10.1111/josh.12883

Jackson, C. K. (2021). Linking social-emotional learning to long-term success. *Education Next, 21*(1). https://www.proquest.com/docview/2475144933/abstract/2357C9FEBE534776PQ/1

Jackson, C. K., Porter, S. C., Easton, J. Q., Blanchard, A., & Kiguel, S. (2020). School effects on socioemotional development, school-based arrests, and educational attainment. *American Economic Review: Insights, 2*(4), 491–508. https://doi.org/10.1257/aeri.20200029

Jackson, F. M., Rashied-Henry, K., Braveman, P., Dominguez, T. P., Ramos, D., Maseru, N., Darity, W., Waddell, L., Warne, D., Legaz, G., Gupta, R., & James, A. (2020). A prematurity collaborative birth equity consensus statement for mothers and babies. *Maternal and Child Health Journal, 24*(10), 1231–1237. https://doi.org/10.1007/s10995-020-02960-0

Jackson, J. S., Hudson, D., Kershaw, K., Mezuk, B., Rafferty, J., & Tuttle, K. K. (2011). Discrimination, chronic stress, and mortality among black Americans: A life course framework. In R. G. Rogers & E. M. Crimmins (Eds.), *International handbook of adult mortality* (pp. 311–328). Springer Netherlands. https://doi.org/10.1007/978-90-481-9996-9_15

Jackson, L., Pascalis, L. D., Harrold, J., & Fallon, V. (2021). Guilt, shame, and postpartum infant feeding outcomes: A systematic review. *Maternal & Child Nutrition, 17*(3), e13141. https://doi.org/10.1111/mcn.13141

Jackson, M. L., Williams, W. L., Rafacz, S. D., & Friman, P. C. (2020). Encopresis and enuresis. In P. Sturmey (Ed.), *Functional analysis in clinical treatment* (2nd ed., pp. 199–225). Academic Press. https://doi.org/10.1016/B978-0-12-805469-7.00009-7

Jacob, B. A. (2017). *What we know about career and technical education in high school.* Brookings.

Jacobson, L. A., Crocetti, D., Dirlikov, B., Slifer, K., Denckla, M. B., Mostofsky, S. H., & Mahone, E. M. (2018). Anomalous brain development is evident in preschoolers with attention-deficit/hyperactivity disorder. *Journal of the International Neuropsychological Society, 24*(6), 531–539. https://doi.org/10.1017/S1355617718000103

Jahoda, G. (2012). Critical reflections on some recent definitions of "culture." *Culture & Psychology, 18*(3), 289–303. https://doi.org/10.1177/1354067X12446229

James, C., Davis, K., Charmaraman, L., Konrath, S., Slovak, P., Weinstein, E., & Yarosh, L. (2017). Digital life and youth well-being, social connectedness, empathy, and narcissism. *Pediatrics, 140*(Supplement 2), S71–S75. https://doi.org/10.1542/peds.2016-1758F

James-Todd, T. M., Chiu, Y. H., & Zota, A. R. (2016). Racial/ethnic disparities in environmental endocrine disrupting chemicals and women's reproductive health outcomes: Epidemiological examples across the life course. *Current Epidemiology Reports, 3*(2), 161–180.

James-Todd, T., Tehranifar, P., Rich-Edwards, J., Titievsky, L., & Terry, M. B. (2010). The impact of socioeconomic status across early life on age at menarche among a racially diverse population of girls. *Annals of Epidemiology, 20*(11), 836–842. https://doi.org/10.1016/j.annepidem.2010.08.006

Janevic, T., Osypuk, T., Stojanovski, K., Jankovic, J., Gundersen, D., & Rogers, M. (2017). Associations between racial discrimination, smoking during pregnancy and low birthweight among Roma. *European Journal of Public Health, 27*(3), 410–415. https://doi.org/10.1093/eurpub/ckw214

Jang, H., & Reardon, S. F. (2019). States as sites of educational (in)equality: State contexts and the socioeconomic achievement gradient. *AERA Open, 5*(3), 2332858419872459. https://doi.org/10.1177/2332858419872459

Janis, J. A., Ahrens, K. A., & Ziller, E. C. (2019). Female age at first sexual intercourse by rural–urban residence and birth cohort. *Women's Health Issues, 29*(6), 489–498. https://doi.org/10.1016/j.whi.2019.07.004

Janssen, L. H. C., Elzinga, B. M., Verkuil, B., Hillegers, M. H. J., & Keijsers, L. (2021). The link between parental support and adolescent negative mood in daily life: Between-person heterogeneity in within-person processes. *Journal of Youth and Adolescence, 50*(2), 271–285. https://doi.org/10.1007/s10964-020-01323-w

Janssen, X., Martin, A., Hughes, A. R., Hill, C. M., Kotronoulas, G., & Hesketh, K. R. (2020). Associations of screen time, sedentary time and physical activity with sleep in under 5s: A systematic review and meta-analysis. *Sleep Medicine Reviews, 49*, 101226. https://doi.org/10.1016/j.smrv.2019.101226

Jaramillo, J. M., Rendón, M. I., Muñoz, L., Weis, M., & Trommsdorff, G. (2017). Children's self-regulation in cultural contexts: The role of parental socialization theories, goals, and practices. *Frontiers in Psychology, 8*, 923. https://doi.org/10.3389/fpsyg.2017.00923

Jarrett, O. (2016). Doll studies as racial assessments: A historical look at racial attitudes and school desegregation.

In M. M. Patte & J. A. Sutterby (Eds.), *Celebrating 40 years of play research: Connecting our past, present, and future* (pp. 19–38). Hamilton Books. https://www.google.com/books/edition/Celebrating_40_Years_of_Play_Research/3VvnDAAAQBAJ?hl=en&gbpv=1&dq=Jarrett,+2016+doll&pg=PA19&printsec=frontcover

Javdani, S., Sadeh, N., White, H. I., Emerson, E., Houck, C., Brown, L. K., & Donenberg, G. R. (2019). Contextualizing pubertal development: The combination of sexual partners' age and girls' pubertal development confers risk for externalizing but not internalizing symptoms among girls in therapeutic day schools. *Journal of Adolescence, 71*, 84–90. https://doi.org/10.1016/j.adolescence.2019.01.001

Javidi, H., Maheux, A. J., Widman, L., Kamke, K., Choukas-Bradley, S., & Peterson, Z. D. (2020). Understanding adolescents' attitudes toward affirmative consent. *Journal of Sex Research, 57*(9), 1100–1107. https://doi.org/10.1080/00224499.2019.1711009

Jebb, A. T., Tay, L., Diener, E., & Oishi, S. (2018). Happiness, income satiation and turning points around the world. *Nature Human Behaviour, 2*(1), 33–38. https://doi.org/10.1038/s41562-017-0277-0

Jelenkovic, A., Sund, R., Yokoyama, Y., Latvala, A., Sugawara, M., Tanaka, M., Matsumoto, S., Freitas, D. L., Maia, J. A., Knafo-Noam, A., Mankuta, D., Abramson, L., Ji, F., Ning, F., Pang, Z., Rebato, E., Saudino, K. J., Cutler, T. L., Hopper, J. L., . . . Silventoinen, K. (2020). Genetic and environmental influences on human height from infancy through adulthood at different levels of parental education. *Scientific Reports, 10*(1), 7974. https://doi.org/10.1038/s41598-020-64883-8

Jellison, S., Roberts, W., Bowers, A., Combs, T., Beaman, J., Wayant, C., & Vassar, M. (2020). Evaluation of spin in abstracts of papers in psychiatry and psychology journals. *BMJ Evidence-Based Medicine, 25* (5), 178–181. https://doi.org/10.1136/bmjebm-2019-111176

Jenni, O. G. (2020). Typical sleep development. In *The Encyclopedia of Child and Adolescent Development* (pp. 1–16). John Wiley & Sons. https://doi.org/10.1002/9781119171492.wecad035

Jennings, M. K., & Zhang, N. (2005). Generations, political status, and collective memories in the Chinese countryside. *The Journal of Politics, 67*(4), 1164–1189. https://doi.org/10.1111/j.1468-2508.2005.00355.x

Jennings, W., Stoker, G., Willis, H., Valgardsson, V., Gaskell, J., Devine, D., McKay, L., & Mills, M. C. (2021). Lack of trust and social media echo chambers predict COVID-19 vaccine hesitancy. *MedRxiv*, 2021-01. https://doi.org/10.1101/2021.01.26.21250246

Jensen, L. A., & Dost-Gözkan, A. (2015). Adolescent-parent relations in Asian Indian and Salvadoran immigrant families: A cultural-developmental analysis of autonomy, authority, conflict, and cohesion. *Journal of Research on Adolescence, 25*(2), 340–351. https://doi.org/10.1111/jora.12116

Jeon, M., Dimitriou, D., & Halstead, E. J. (2021). A systematic review on cross-cultural comparative studies of sleep in young populations: The roles of cultural factors. *International Journal of Environmental Research and Public Health, 18*(4), 2005.

Jepsen, C., Mueser, P., & Troske, K. (2017). Second chance for high school dropouts? A regression discontinuity analysis of postsecondary educational returns to the GED. *Journal of Labor Economics, 35*(S1), S273–S304.

Jerrim, J. (2014). The unrealistic educational expectations of high school pupils: Is America exceptional?

Unrealistic educational expectations. *The Sociological Quarterly, 55*(1), 196–231. https://doi.org/10.1111/tsq.12049

Jewell, J. A., & Brown, C. S. (2014). Relations among gender typicality, peer relations, and mental health during early adolescence. *Social Development, 23*(1), 137–156.

Jewell, T., Gardner, T., Susi, K., Watchorn, K., Coopey, E., Simic, M., Fonagy, P., & Eisler, I. (2019). Attachment measures in middle childhood and adolescence: A systematic review of measurement properties. *Clinical Psychology Review, 68*, 71–82. https://doi.org/10.1016/j.cpr.2018.12.004

Jhang, Y., & Oller, D. K. (2017). Emergence of functional flexibility in infant vocalizations of the first 3 months. *Frontiers in Psychology, 8*, 300. https://doi.org/10.3389/fpsyg.2017.00300

Jiang, X., Dai, X., Goldblatt, S., Buescher, C., Cusack, T. M., Matson, D. O., & Pickering, L. K. (1998). Pathogen transmission in child care settings studied by using a cauliflower virus DNA as a surrogate marker. *The Journal of Infectious Diseases, 177*(4), 881–888. https://doi.org/10.1086/515253

Jiang, Y., Ekono, M., & Skinner, C. (2015). *Basic facts about low-income children: Children under 18 years, 2013.* National Center for Children in Poverty.

Jimenez, M. E., Wade, R., Lin, Y., Morrow, L. M., & Reichman, N. E. (2016). Adverse experiences in early childhood and kindergarten outcomes. *Pediatrics, 137*(2), e20151839.

Jin, J., & Rounds, J. (2012). Stability and change in work values: A meta-analysis of longitudinal studies. *Journal of Vocational Behavior, 80*(2), 326–339. https://doi.org/10.1016/j.jvb.2011.10.007

Jin, M. K., Jacobvitz, D., Hazen, N., & Jung, S. H. (2011). Maternal sensitivity and infant attachment security in Korea: Cross-cultural validation of the strange situation. *Attachment & Human Development, 14*(1), 33–44. https://doi.org/10.1080/14616734.2012.636656

Joel, S., Eastwick, P. W., Allison, C. J., Arriaga, X. B., Baker, Z. G., Bar-Kalifa, E., Bergeron, S., Birnbaum, G. E., Brock, R. L., Brumbaugh, C. C., Carmichael, C. L., Chen, S., Clarke, J., Cobb, R. J., Coolsen, M. K., Davis, J., de Jong, D. C., Debrot, A., DeHaas, E. C., . . . Wolf, S. (2020). Machine learning uncovers the most robust self-report predictors of relationship quality across 43 longitudinal couples studies. *Proceedings of the National Academy of Sciences, 117*(32), 19061–19071. https://doi.org/10.1073/pnas.1917036117

Joel, S., Eastwick, P. W., & Finkel, E. J. (2017). Is romantic desire predictable? Machine learning applied to initial romantic attraction. *Psychological Science, 28*(10), 1478–1489. https://doi.org/10.1177/0956797617714580

Johander, E., Turunen, T., Garandeau, C. F., & Salmivalli, C. (2021). Different approaches to address bullying in KiVa schools: Adherence to guidelines, strategies implemented, and outcomes obtained. *Prevention Science, 22*(3), 299–310. https://doi.org/10.1007/s11121-020-01178-4

Johns, M. M., Lowry, R., Andrzejewski, J., Barrios, L. C., Demissie, Z., McManus, T., Rasberry, C. N., Robin, L., & Underwood, J. M. (2019). Transgender identity and experiences of violence victimization, substance use, suicide risk, and sexual risk behaviors among high school students — 19 states and large urban school districts, 2017. *Morbidity and Mortality Weekly Report, 68*(3), 67–71. https://doi.org/10.15585/mmwr.mm6803a3

Johns, M. M., Lowry, R., Haderxhanaj, L. T., Rasberry, C. N., Robin, L., Scales, L., Stone, D., & Suarez, N. A. (2020). Trends in violence victimization and suicide risk by sexual identity among high school students — Youth Risk Behavior Survey, United States, 2015–2019. *MMWR Supplements*, 69(1), 19–27. https://doi.org/10.15585/mmwr.su6901a3

Johnson, A., Kirk, R., Rosenblum, K. L., & Muzik, M. (2015). Enhancing breastfeeding rates among African American women: A systematic review of current psychosocial interventions. *Breastfeeding edicine*, 10(1), 45–62. https://doi.org/10.1089/bfm.2014.0023

Johnson, J. D., Green, C. A., Vladutiu, C. J., & Manuck, T. A. (2020). Racial disparities in prematurity persist among women of high socioeconomic status. *American Journal of Obstetrics & Gynecology MFM, 2*(3), 100104.

Johnson, M. H., & de Haan, M. (2015). *Developmental cognitive neuroscience: An introduction*. John Wiley & Sons.

Johnson, R. M., Alvarado, R. E., & Rosinger, K. O. (2021). What's the "problem" of considering criminal history in college admissions? A critical analysis of "ban the box" policies in Louisiana and Maryland. *The Journal of Higher Education, 92*(5), 704–734. https://doi.org /10.1080/00221546.2020.1870849

Johnson, S. B., Riis, J. L., & Noble, K. G. (2016). State of the art review: Poverty and the developing brain. *Pediatrics,* peds.2015-3075. https://doi.org/10.1542 /peds.2015-3075

Johnson, T. J., Winger, D. G., Hickey, R. W., Switzer, G. E., Miller, E., Nguyen, M. B., Saladino, R. A., & Hausmann, L. R. M. (2017). Comparison of physician implicit racial bias toward adults versus children. *Academic Pediatrics, 17*(2), 120–126. https://doi.org /10.1016/j.acap.2016.08.010

Johnston-Goodstar, K., & VeLure Roholt, R. (2017). "Our kids aren't dropping out; they're being pushed out": Native American students and racial microaggressions in schools. *Journal of Ethnic & Cultural Diversity in Social Work, 26*(1–2), 30–47. https://doi.org/10.1080/1 5313204.2016.1263818

Johnston-Robledo, I., & Chrisler, J. C. (2013). The menstrual mark: Menstruation as social stigma. *Sex Roles, 68*(1), 9–18.

Joly, Y., Dalpé, G., Dupras, C., Bévière-Boyer, B., de Paor, A., Dove, E. S., Granados Moreno, P., Ho, C. W. L., Ho, C.-H., Ó Cathaoir, K., Kato, K., Kim, H., Song, L., Minssen, T., Nicolás, P., Otlowski, M., Prince, A. E. R., P. S. Nair, A. P. S., Van Hoyweghen, I., . . . Bombard, Y. (2020). Establishing the international Genetic Discrimination Observatory. *Nature Genetics, 52*(5), 466–468. https://doi.org/10.1038 /s41588-020-0606-5

Jones, C. M., & Rogers, L. O. (2022). "There are stereotypes for everything": Multiracial adolescents navigating racial identity under white supremacy. *Social Sciences, 11*(1), 19.

Jones, C. R. G., Simonoff, E., Baird, G., Pickles, A., Marsden, A. J. S., Tregay, J., Happé, F., & Charman, T. (2018). The association between theory of mind, executive function, and the symptoms of autism spectrum disorder. *Autism Research, 11*(1), 95–109. https://doi.org/10.1002/aur.1873

Jones, D. E., Greenberg, M., & Crowley, M. (2015). Early social-emotional functioning and public health: The relationship between kindergarten social competence and future wellness. *American Journal of Public Health, 105*(11), 2283–2290. https://doi.org/10.2105 /AJPH.2015.302630

Jones, J. M. (2021, February 24). *LGBT identification rises to 5.6% in latest U.S. estimate*. Gallup.com. https:// news.gallup.com/poll/329708/lgbt-identification-rises -latest-estimate.aspx

Jones, J. S., Milton, F., Mostazir, M., & Adlam, A. R. (2020). The academic outcomes of working memory and metacognitive strategy training in children: A double-blind randomized controlled trial. *Developmental Science, 23*(4), e12870. https://doi.org/10.1111/ desc.12870

Jones, J., & Mosher, W. D. (2013). *Fathers' involvement with their children: United States, 2006–2010* (National Health Statistics Reports No. 71). U.S. Department of Health and Human Services.

Jones, M. C., & Furman, W. (2011). Representations of romantic relationships, romantic experience, and sexual behavior in adolescence. *Personal Relationships, 18*(1), 144–164.

Jones, N., Marks, R., Ramirez, R., & Rios-Vargas, M. (2021). 2020 Census illuminates racial and ethnic composition of the country. U.S. Census Bureau. https://www.census.gov/library/stories/2021/08 /improved-race-ethnicity-measures-reveal-united-states -population-much-more-multiracial.html

Jones, N. A., & Sloan, A. (2018). Neurohormones and temperament interact during infant development. *Philosophical Transactions of the Royal Society B: Biological Sciences, 373*(1744), 20170159. https://doi.org /10.1098/rstb.2017.0159

Jones, S. E., & Sliwa, S. (2016). Peer reviewed: School factors associated with the percentage of students who walk or bike to school, school health policies and practices study, 2014. *Preventing Chronic Disease, 13*.

Jones, S. L., Dufoix, R., Laplante, D. P., Elgbeili, G., Patel, R., Chakravarty, M. M., King, S., & Pruessner, J. C. (2019). Larger amygdala volume mediates the association between prenatal maternal stress and higher levels of externalizing behaviors: Sex specific effects in Project Ice Storm. *Frontiers in Human Neuroscience, 13*. https://doi.org/10.3389/fnhum.2019.00144

Jonsson, H., Magnusdottir, E., Eggertsson, H. P., Stefansson, O. A., Arnadottir, G. A., Eiriksson, O., Zink, F., Helgason, E. A., Jonsdottir, I., Gylfason, A., Jonasdottir, A., Jonasdottir, A., Beyter, D., Steingrimsdottir, T., Norddahl, G. L., Magnusson, O. T., Masson, G., Halldorsson, B. V., Thorsteinsdottir, U., . . . Stefansson, K. (2021). Differences between germline genomes of monozygotic twins. *Nature Genetics, 53*(1), 27–34. https://doi.org/10.1038 /s41588-020-00755-1

Jordan, K., & Tseris, E. (2018). Locating, understanding and celebrating disability: Revisiting Erikson's "stages." *Feminism & Psychology, 28*(3), 427–444. https://doi.org/10.1177/0959353517705400

Jordan-Young, R. M., & Karkazis, K. (2019). *Testosterone: An unauthorized biography*. Harvard University Press.

Jovanovic, T., Vance, L. A., Cross, D., Knight, A. K., Kilaru, V., Michopoulos, V., Klengel, T., & Smith, A. K. (2017). Exposure to violence accelerates epigenetic aging in children. *Scientific Reports, 7*(1), 8962. https:// doi.org/10.1038/s41598-017-09235-9

Joyner, K., Manning, W., & Bogle, R. (2017). Gender and the stability of same-sex and different-sex relationships among young adults. *Demography, 54*(6), 2351–2374.

Juang, L. P., & Cookston, J. T. (2009). A longitudinal study of family obligation and depressive symptoms among Chinese American adolescents. *Journal of Family Psychology, 23*(3), 396–404. https://doi.org/10.1037/a0015814

Juang, L. P., Syed, M., Cookston, J. T., Wang, Y., & Kim, S. Y. (2012). Acculturation-based and everyday family conflict in Chinese American families. *New Directions for Child and Adolescent Development, 2012*(135), 13–34. https://doi.org/10.1002/cd.20002

Juvonen, J., & Graham, S. (2014). Bullying in schools: The power of bullies and the plight of victims. *Annual Review of Psychology, 65*(1), 159–185. https://doi.org /10.1146/annurev-psych-010213-115030

Juvonen, J., Lessard, L. M., Rastogi, R., Schacter, H. L., & Smith, D. S. (2019). Promoting social inclusion in educational settings: Challenges and opportunities. *Educational Psychologist, 54*(4), 250–270.

Juvonen, J., & Schacter, H. L. (2018). Bullying in school and online contexts: Social dominance, bystander compliance, and social pain of victims. In A. Rutland, D. Nesdale, & C. S. Brown (Eds.), *The Wiley-Blackwell handbook of group processes in children and adolescents* (pp. 317–332). Wiley-Blackwell.

Juvonen, J., Schacter, H. L., Sainio, M., & Salmivalli, C. (2016). Can a school-wide bullying prevention program improve the plight of victims? Evidence for risk × intervention effects. *Journal of Consulting and Clinical Psychology, 84*(4), 334–344. https://doi.org/10.1037 /ccp0000078

Kabay, S., Wolf, S., & Yoshikawa, H. (2017). "So that his mind will open": Parental perceptions of early childhood education in urbanizing Ghana. *International Journal of Educational Development, 57*, 44–53.

Kaestle, C. E. (2019). Sexual orientation trajectories based on sexual attractions, partners, and identity: A longitudinal investigation from adolescence through young adulthood using a U.S. representative sample. *The Journal of Sex Research, 56*(7), 811–826. https://doi.org /10.1080/00224499.2019.1577351

Kagan, J. (2018). Perspectives on two temperamental biases. *Philosophical Transactions of the Royal Society B: Biological Sciences, 373*(1744), 20170158. https://doi.org /10.1098/rstb.2017.0158

Kågesten, A., Gibbs, S., Blum, R. W., Moreau, C., Chandra-Mouli, V., Herbert, A., & Amin, A. (2016). Understanding factors that shape gender attitudes in early adolescence globally: A mixed-methods systematic review. *PLOS ONE, 11*(6), e0157805. https://doi.org /10.1371/journal.pone.0157805

Kagitcibasi, C. (2005). Autonomy and Relatedness in Cultural Context: Implications for Self and Family. *Journal of Cross-Cultural Psychology, 36*(4), 403–422. https://doi.org/10.1177/0022022105275959

Kagitcibasi, C. (2017). Doing psychology with a cultural lens: A half-century journey. *Perspectives on Psychological Science, 12*(5), 824–832.

Kahn, N. F., & Halpern, C. T. (2018). Associations between patterns of sexual initiation, sexual partnering, and sexual health outcomes from adolescence to early adulthood. *Archives of Sexual Behavior, 47*(6), 1791–1810. https://doi.org/10.1007/s10508-018-1176-9

Kail, R. V., & Ferrer, E. (2007). Processing speed in childhood and adolescence: Longitudinal models for examining developmental change. *Child Development, 78*(6), 1760–1770. https://doi.org /10.1111/j.1467-8624.2007.01088.x

Kajonius, P. J., & Carlander, A. (2017). Who gets ahead in life? Personality traits and childhood background in economic success. *Journal of Economic Psychology, 59*, 164–170.

Kalogrides, D., & Grodsky, E. (2011). Something to fall back on: Community colleges as a safety net. *Social Forces, 89*(3), 853–877. https://doi.org/10.1353/sof.2011.0019

Kan, P. F. (2014). Novel word retention in sequential bilingual children. *Journal of Child Language, 41*(2), 416–438. https://doi.org/10.1017/S0305000912000761

Kanda, H., Ling, J., Tonomura, S., Noguchi, K., Matalon, S., & Gu, J. G. (2019). TREK-1 and TRAAK are principal K+ channels at the nodes of Ranvier for rapid action potential conduction on mammalian myelinated afferent nerves. *Neuron, 104*(5), 960–971. e7. https://doi.org/10.1016/j.neuron.2019.08.042

Kandel, E. R. (2012). *The age of insight: The quest to understand the unconscious in art, mind, and brain, from Vienna 1900 to the present.* Random House.

Kandemir, M., & Sevimli-Celik, S. (2021). No muddy shoes, no dirty clothes! Examining the views of teachers and parents regarding children's outdoor play and learning. *Journal of Adventure Education and Outdoor Learning,* 1–22. https://doi.org/10.1080/14729679.2021.2011339

Kandler, C., Zapko-Willmes, A., Richter, J., & Riemann, R. (2021). Synergistic and dynamic genotype environment interplays in the development of personality differences. In J. F. Rauthmann (Ed.), *The handbook of personality dynamics and processes* (pp. 155–181). Academic Press. https://doi.org/10.1016/B978-0-12-813995-0.00007-8

Kang, E., Klein, E. F., Lillard, A. S., & Lerner, M. D. (2016). Predictors and moderators of spontaneous pretend play in children with and without autism spectrum disorder. *Frontiers in Psychology, 7*, 1577.

Kang, S., & Harvey, E. A. (2020). Racial differences between black parents' and white teachers' perceptions of attention-deficit/hyperactivity disorder behavior. *Journal of Abnormal Child Psychology, 48*(5), 661–672. https://doi.org/10.1007/s10802-019-00600-y

Kanno, Y., & Kangas, S. E. (2014). "I'm not going to be, like, for the AP" English language learners' limited access to advanced college-preparatory courses in high school. *American Educational Research Journal, 51*(5), 848–878. http://journals.sagepub.com/doi/abs/10.3102/0002831214544716

Kansky, J., & Allen, J. P. (2018). Long-term risks and possible benefits associated with late adolescent romantic relationship quality. *Journal of Youth and Adolescence, 47*(7), 1531–1544. https://doi.org/10.1007/s10964-018-0813-x

Kansra, A. R., Lakkunarajah, S., & Jay, M. S. (2020). Childhood and adolescent obesity: A review. *Frontiers in Pediatrics, 8*, 866.

Kantor, L. M., & Lindberg, L. (2020). Pleasure and sex education: The need for broadening both content and measurement. *American Journal of Public Health, 110*(2), 145–148. https://doi.org/10.2105/AJPH.2019.305320

Kapetanovic, S., Rothenberg, W. A., Lansford, J. E., Bornstein, M. H., Chang, L., Deater-Deckard, K., Di Giunta, L., Dodge, K. A., Gurdal, S., Malone, P. S., Oburu, P., Pastorelli, C., Skinner, A. T., Sorbring, E., Steinberg, L., Tapanya, S., Uribe Tirado, L. M., Yotanyamaneewong, S., Peña Alampay, L., . . . Bacchini, D. (2020). Cross-cultural examination of links between parent–adolescent communication and adolescent psychological problems in 12 cultural groups. *Journal of Youth and Adolescence, 49*(6), 1225–1244. https://doi.org/10.1007/s10964-020-01212-2

Kapitány, R., Nelson, N., Burdett, E. R., & Goldstein, T. R. (2020). The child's pantheon: Children's hierarchical belief structure in real and non-real figures. *PLOS ONE, 15*(6), e0234142.

Kaplowitz, P., Bloch, C., & the Section on Endocrinology of the American Academy of Pediatrics. (2016). Evaluation and referral of children with signs of early puberty. *Pediatrics, 137*(1), e20153732. https://doi.org/10.1542/peds.2015-3732

Kapp, S. K. (2020). *Autistic community and the neurodiversity movement: Stories from the frontline* (p. 330). Springer Nature.

Kar, P., Tomfohr-Madsen, L., Giesbrecht, G., Bagshawe, M., & Lebel, C. (2021). Alcohol and substance use in pregnancy during the COVID-19 pandemic. *Drug and Alcohol Dependence,* 108760. https://doi.org/10.1016/j.drugalcdep.2021.108760

Karably, K., & Zabrucky, K. M. (2009). Children's metamemory: A review of the literature and implications for the classroom. *International Electronic Journal of Elementary Education, 2*(1), 32–52.

Karakus, M., Courtney, M., & Aydin, H. (2022). Immigrant students PISA — published 2022. *Educational Assessment, Evaluation and Accountability.* https://doi.org/10.1007/s11092-022-09395-x

Karasik, L. B., Adolph, K. E., Tamis-LeMonda, C. S., & Bornstein, M. H. (2010). WEIRD walking: Cross-cultural research on motor development. *The Behavioral and Brain Sciences, 33*(2–3), 95–96. https://doi.org/10.1017/S0140525X10000117

Karasik, L. B., Tamis-LeMonda, C. S., Ossmy, O., & Adolph, K. E. (2018). The ties that bind: Cradling in Tajikistan. *PLOS One, 13*(10), e0204428. https://doi.org/10.1371/journal.pone.0204428

Kardaras, N. (2016). *Glow kids: How screen addiction is hijacking our kids—and how to break the trance.* St. Martin's Press.

Kariuki, S. N., & Williams, T. N. (2020). Human genetics and malaria resistance. *Human Genetics, 139*(6), 801–811. https://doi.org/10.1007/s00439-020-02142-6

Karl, J. M., Slack, B. M., Wilson, A. M., Wilson, C. A., & Bertoli, M. E. (2019). Increasing task precision demands reveals that the reach and grasp remain subject to different perception-action constraints in 12-month-old human infants. *Infant Behavior and Development, 57*, 101382. https://doi.org/10.1016/j.infbeh.2019.101382

Karn, S., Yu, H., Karna, S., Chen, L., & Qiao, D. (2016). Women's awareness and attitudes towards labor analgesia influencing practice between developed and developing countries. *Advances in Reproductive Sciences, 4*(2), 46–52. https://doi.org/10.4236/arsci.2016.42007

Kärnä, A., Voeten, M., Little, T. D., Alanen, E., Poskiparta, E., & Salmivalli, C. (2013). Effectiveness of the KiVa antibullying program: Grades 1–3 and 7–9. *Journal of Educational Psychology, 105*(2), 535.

Karns, C. M., Isbell, E., Giuliano, R. J., & Neville, H. J. (2015). Auditory attention in childhood and adolescence: An event-related potential study of spatial selective attention to one of two simultaneous stories. *Developmental Cognitive Neuroscience, 13*, 53–67. https://doi.org/10.1016/j.dcn.2015.03.001

Karra, M., Subramanian, S., & Fink, G. (2017). Height in healthy children in low- and middle-income countries: An assessment. *The American Journal of Clinical Nutrition, 105*(1), 121–126. https://doi.org/10.3945/ajcn.116.136705

Kärtner, J., Torréns, M. G., & Schuhmacher, N. (2021). Parental structuring during shared chores and the development of helping across the second year. *Social Development, 30*(2), 374–395. https://doi.org/10.1111/sode.12490

Kassai, R., Futo, J., Demetrovics, Z., & Takacs, Z. K. (2019). A meta-analysis of the experimental evidence on the near- and far-transfer effects among children's executive function skills. *Psychological Bulletin, 145*(2), 165–188. https://doi.org/10.1037/bul0000180

Kato, G. J., Piel, F. B., Reid, C. D., Gaston, M. H., Ohene-Frempong, K., Krishnamurti, L., Smith, W. R., Panepinto, J. A., Weatherall, D. J., Costa, F. F., & Vichinsky, E. P. (2018). Sickle cell disease. *Nature Reviews Disease Primers, 4*(1), 1–22. https://doi.org/10.1038/nrdp.2018.10

Katrinli, S., Stevens, J., Wani, A. H., Lori, A., Kilaru, V., van Rooij, S. J. H., Hinrichs, R., Powers, A., Gillespie, C. F., Michopoulos, V., Gautam, A., Jett, M., Hammamieh, R., Yang, R., Wildman, D., Qu, A., Koenen, K., Aiello, A. E., Jovanovic, T., . . . Smith, A. K. (2020). Evaluating the impact of trauma and PTSD on epigenetic prediction of lifespan and neural integrity. *Neuropsychopharmacology, 45*(10), 1609–1616. https://doi.org/10.1038/s41386-020-0700-5

Katsanis, N. (2016). The continuum of causality in human genetic disorders. *Genome Biology, 17*(1), 233. https://doi.org/10.1186/s13059-016-1107-9

Katz, A. J., Hensel, D. J., Hunt, A. L., Zaban, L. S., Hensley, M. M., & Ott, M. A. (2019). Only yes means yes: Sexual coercion in rural adolescent relationships. *Journal of Adolescent Health, 65*(3), 423–425.

Katz, L. F., & Krueger, A. B. (2016). *The rise and nature of alternative work arrangements in the United States, 1995–2015.* NBER. http://scholar.harvard.edu/files/lkatz/files/katz_krueger_cws_v3. pdf, https://krueger.princeton.edu/sites/default/files/akrueger/files/katz_krueger_cws_-_march_29_20165.pdf

Katz, L. F., Gurtovenko, K., Maliken, A., Stettler, N., Kawamura, J., & Fladeboe, K. (2020). An emotion coaching parenting intervention for families exposed to intimate partner violence. *Developmental Psychology, 56*(3), 638–651. https://doi.org/10.1037/dev0000800

Kaufman, A. S., Raiford, S. E., & Coalson, D. L. (2015). *Intelligent testing with the WISC-V.* Wiley.

Kaufman, S. B. (2019, April 23). Who created Maslow's iconic pyramid? *Scientific American.* https://blogs.scientificamerican.com/beautiful-minds/who-created-maslows-iconic-pyramid/

Kavle, J. A., LaCroix, E., Dau, H., & Engmann, C. (2017). Addressing barriers to exclusive breast-feeding in low- and middle-income countries: A systematic review and programmatic implications. *Public Health Nutrition, 20*(17), 3120–3134. https://doi.org/10.1017/S1368980017002531

Kawakami, F., Tomonaga, M., & Suzuki, J. (2017). The first smile: Spontaneous smiles in newborn Japanese macaques (*Macaca fuscata*). *Primates, 58*(1), 93–101. https://doi.org/10.1007/s10329-016-0558-7

Kazda, L., Bell, K., Thomas, R., McGeechan, K., Sims, R., & Barratt, A. (2021). Overdiagnosis of attention-deficit/hyperactivity disorder in children and adolescents: A systematic scoping review. *JAMA Network Open, 4*(4), e215335–e215335. https://doi.org/10.1001/jamanetworkopen.2021.5335

Kazdin, A. E. (2003). Psychotherapy for children and adolescents. *Annual Review of Psychology, 54*(1), 253–276.

Kazdin, A. E., Glick, A., Pope, J., Kaptchuk, T. J., Lecza, B., Carrubba, E., McWhinney, E., & Hamilton, N. (2018). Parent management training for conduct problems in children: Enhancing treatment to improve therapeutic change. *International Journal of Clinical and Health Psychology, 18*(2), 91–101. https://doi.org/10.1016/j.ijchp.2017.12.002

Keane, L., & Loades, M. (2017). Low self-esteem and internalizing disorders in young people — a systematic review. *Child and Adolescent Mental Health, 22*(1), 4–15.

Kearins, J. M. (1981). Visual spatial memory in Australian aboriginal children of desert regions. *Cognitive Psychology, 13*(3), 434–460. https://doi.org/10.1016/0010-0285(81)90017-7

Kearney, M. S., & Levine, P. B. (2015). Investigating recent trends in the U.S. teen birth rate. *Journal of Health Economics, 41*, 15–29. https://doi.org/10.1016/j.jhealeco.2015.01.003

Kearney, M. S., & Levine, P. B. (2017). Income inequality and the decision to drop out of high school. *Communities & Banking, 28*(1), 11, 13.

Keestra, S. M., Bentley, G. R., la Mora, A. N., Houghton, L. C., Wilson, H., Vázquez-Vázquez, A., Cooper, G. D., Dickinson, F., Griffiths, P., Bogin, B. A., & Varela-Silva, M. I. (2021). The timing of adrenarche in Maya girls, Merida, Mexico. *American Journal of Human Biology, 33*(2), e23465. https://doi.org/10.1002/ajhb.23465

Kehm, R. D., Spector, L. G., Poynter, J. N., Vock, D. M., Altekruse, S. F., & Osypuk, T. L. (2018). Does socioeconomic status account for racial and ethnic disparities in childhood cancer survival? *Cancer, 124*(20), 4090–4097. https://doi.org/10.1002/cncr.31560

Keller, H. (2017). Culture and development: A systematic relationship. *Perspectives on Psychological Science, 12*(5), 833–840. https://doi.org/10.1177/1745691617704097

Keller, H. (2018). Universality claim of attachment theory: Children's socioemotional development across cultures. *Proceedings of the National Academy of Sciences, 115*(45), 11414–11419. https://doi.org/10.1073/pnas.1720325115

Keller, H. (2019). The role of emotions in socialization processes across cultures: Implications for theory and practice. In D. Matsumoto & H. C. Hwang (Eds.), *The handbook of culture and psychology* (pp. 209–231). Oxford University Press.

Keller, H. (2020). Children's socioemotional development across cultures. *Annual Review of Developmental Psychology, 2*(1), 27–46. https://doi.org/10.1146/annurev-devpsych-033020-031552

Keller, H. (2021). Attachment theory: Fact or fancy? In R. A. Thompson, J. A. Simpson, & L. J. Berlin (Eds.), *Attachment: The fundamental questions* (pp. 229–236). Guilford.

Keller, H., & Otto, H. (2009). The cultural socialization of emotion regulation during infancy. *Journal of Cross-Cultural Psychology, 40*(6), 996–1011.

Kelley, A. S., Qin, Y., Marsh, E. E., & Dupree, J. M. (2019). Disparities in accessing infertility care in the United States: Results from the National Health and Nutrition Examination Survey, 2013–16. *Fertility and Sterility, 112*(3), 562–568. https://doi.org/10.1016/j.fertnstert.2019.04.044

Kelly, D. J., Duarte, S., Meary, D., Bindemann, M., & Pascalis, O. (2019). Infants rapidly detect human faces in complex naturalistic visual scenes. *Developmental Science, 22*(6), e12829. https://doi.org/10.1111/desc.12829

Kelly, M. G. (2020). The curious case of the missing tail: Trends among the top 1% of school districts in the United States, 2000–2015. *Educational Researcher, 49*(5), 312–320. https://doi.org/10.3102/0013189X20922999

Kelly, Y., Zilanawala, A., Sacker, A., Hiatt, R., & Viner, R. (2017). Early puberty in 11-year-old girls: Millennium Cohort Study findings. *Archives of Disease in Childhood, 102*(3), 232–237. https://doi.org/10.1136/archdischild-2016-310475

Kempe, A., Saville, A. W., Albertin, C., Zimet, G., Breck, A., Helmkamp, L., Vangala, S., Dickinson, L. M., Rand, C., & Humiston, S. (2020). Parental hesitancy about routine childhood and influenza vaccinations: A national survey. *Pediatrics, 146*(1), e20193852.

Kenney, E. L., & Gortmaker, S. L. (2017). United States adolescents' television, computer, videogame, smartphone, and tablet use: Associations with sugary drinks, sleep, physical activity, and obesity. *The Journal of Pediatrics, 182*, 144–149. https://doi.org/10.1016/j.jpeds.2016.11.015

Kenrick, D. T., Cohen, A. B., Neuberg, S. L., & Cialdini, R. B. (2018). The science of antiscience thinking. *Scientific American, 319*(1), 36–41.

Keresztes, A., Bender, A. R., Bodammer, N. C., Lindenberger, U., Shing, Y. L., & Werkle-Bergner, M. (2017). Hippocampal maturity promotes memory distinctiveness in childhood and adolescence. *Proceedings of the National Academy of Sciences, 114*(34), 9212–9217.

Kerr, M., & Stattin, H. (2000). What parents know, how they know it, and several forms of adolescent adjustment: Further support for a reinterpretation of monitoring. *Developmental Psychology, 36*(3), 366. https://doi.org/10.1037/0012-1649.36.3.366

Kerr, M., Stattin, H., & Pakalniskiene, V. (2008). Parents react to adolescent problem behaviors by worrying more and monitoring less. In M. Kerr, H. Stattin, & R. Engels (Eds.), *What can parents do? New insights into the role of parents in adolescent problem behavior* (pp. 91–112). Wiley.

Kessler, H. S. (2016). Simple interventions to improve healthy eating behaviors in the school cafeteria. *Nutrition Reviews, 74*(3), 198–209.

Kessler, R., Hinkle, B. T., Moyers, A., & Silverberg, B. (2020). Adolescent sexual health: Identity, risk, and screening for sexually transmitted infections. *Primary Care: Clinics in Office Practice, 47*(2), 367–382. https://doi.org/10.1016/j.pop.2020.02.012

Kessler, S. E. (2020). Why care: Complex evolutionary history of human healthcare networks. *Frontiers in Psychology, 11*. https://doi.org/10.3389/fpsyg.2020.00199

Kharbanda, E. O., Vazquez-Benitez, G., Kunin-Batson, A., Nordin, J. D., Olsen, A., & Romitti, P. A. (2020). Birth and early developmental screening outcomes associated with cannabis exposure during pregnancy. *Journal of Perinatology, 40*(3), 473–480. https://doi.org/10.1038/s41372-019-0576-6

Khatiwada, I., & Sum, A. M. (2016). The widening socioeconomic divergence in the U.S. labor market. In I. Kirsch & H. Braun (Eds.), *The dynamics of opportunity in America* (pp. 197–252). Springer.

Khurana, A., Romer, D., Betancourt, L. M., & Hurt, H. (2018). Modeling trajectories of sensation seeking and impulsivity dimensions from early to late adolescence: Universal trends or distinct sub-groups? *Journal of Youth and Adolescence, 47*(9), 1992–2005. https://doi.org/10.1007/s10964-018-0891-9

Kiang, L., & Fuligni, A. J. (2010). Meaning in life as a mediator of ethnic identity and adjustment among adolescents from Latin, Asian, and European American backgrounds. *Journal of Youth and Adolescence, 39*(11), 1253–1264. https://doi.org/10.1007/s10964-009-9475-z

Kiang, L., Mendonça, S., Liang, Y., Payir, A., O'Brien, L. T., Tudge, J. R. H., & Freitas, L. B. L. (2016). If children won lotteries: Materialism, gratitude and imaginary windfall spending. *Young Consumers, 17*(4), 404–418. https://doi.org/10.1108/YC-07-2016-00614

Killedar, A., Lung, T., Petrou, S., Teixeira-Pinto, A., Tan, E. J., & Hayes, A. (2020). Weight status and health-related quality of life during childhood and adolescence: Effects of age and socioeconomic position. *International Journal of Obesity, 44*(3), 637–645. https://doi.org/10.1038/s41366-020-0529-3

Killen, M. (2019). Developing inclusive youth: How to reduce social exclusion and foster equality and equity in childhood. *American Educator, 43*(3), 8.

Killen, M., & Smetana, J. G. (2015). Origins and development of morality. In R. M. Lerner (Ed.), *Handbook of child psychology and developmental science* (pp. 1–49). John Wiley & Sons. https://doi.org/10.1002/9781118963418.childpsy317

Kim, C., & Tamborini, C. R. (2019). Are they still worth it? The long-run earnings benefits of an associate degree, vocational diploma or certificate, and some college. *RSF: The Russell Sage Foundation Journal of the Social Sciences, 5*(3), 64–85. https://doi.org/10.7758/RSF.2019.5.3.04

Kim, C., McGee, S., Khuntia, S., Elnour, A., Johnson-Clarke, F., Mangla, A., Ivengar, P., & Nesbitt, L. (2021). Characteristics of COVID-19 cases and outbreaks at child care facilities—District of Columbia, July–December 2020. *Morbidity and Mortality Weekly Report, 70*(20), 744–748. https://doi.org/10.15585/mmwr.mm7020a3

Kim, D.-J., Davis, E. P., Sandman, C. A., Glynn, L., Sporns, O., O'Donnell, B. F., & Hetrick, W. P. (2019). Childhood poverty and the organization of structural brain connectome. *NeuroImage, 184*, 409–416. https://doi.org/10.1016/j.neuroimage.2018.09.041

Kim, E. (2021, June 21). How Does Treating Gun Violence As A Public Health Crisis Work? One Bronx Program Offers A Potential Flagship Model. Gothamist. https://gothamist.com

Kim, H., Duran, C. A. K., Cameron, C. E., & Grissmer, D. (2018). Developmental relations among motor and cognitive processes and mathematics skills. *Child Development, 89*(2), 476–494. https://doi.org/10.1111/cdev.12752

Kim, J. I., & Kim, G. (2018). Effects on inequality in life expectancy from a social ecology perspective. *BMC Public Health, 18*(1), 243. https://doi.org/10.1186/s12889-018-5134-1

Kim, J., Gilbert, J., Yu, Q., & Gale, C. (2021). Measures matter: A meta-analysis of the effects of educational apps on preschool to grade 3 children's literacy and math skills. *AERA Open, 7*, 23328584211004184. https://doi.org/10.1177/23328584211004183

Kim, M. H., Ahmed, S. F., & Morrison, F. J. (2021). The effects of kindergarten and first grade schooling on executive function and academic skill development: Evidence from a school cutoff design. *Frontiers in Psychology, 11*, 607973. https://doi.org/10.3389/fpsyg.2020.607973

Kim, Y. J., Cha, E. J., Kang, K. D., Kim, B.-N., & Han, D. H. (2016). The effects of sport dance on brain connectivity and body intelligence. *Journal of Cognitive Psychology, 28*(5), 611–617. https://doi.org/10.1080/20445911.2016.1177059

Kimberly, L. L., Folkers, K. M., Friesen, P., Sultan, D., Quinn, G. P., Bateman-House, A., Parent, B., Konnoth, C., Janssen, A., Shah, L. D., Bluebond-Langner, R., & Salas-Humara, C. (2018). Ethical issues in gender-affirming care for youth. *Pediatrics, 142*(6), e20181537. https://doi.org/10.1542/peds.2018-1537

King, C. (2019). *Gods of the upper air: How a circle of renegade anthropologists reinvented race, sex, and gender in the twentieth century.* Knopf Doubleday.

King, L. S., Humphreys, K. L., & Gotlib, I. H. (2019). The neglect–enrichment continuum: Characterizing variation in early caregiving environments. *Developmental Review, 51*, 109–122. https://doi.org/10.1016/j.dr.2019.01.001

King, V., Boyd, L. M., & Pragg, B. (2018). Parent-adolescent closeness, family belonging, and adolescent well-being across family structures. *Journal of Family Issues, 39*(7), 2007–2036. https://doi.org/10.1177/0192513X17739048

King, V., Pragg, B., & Lindstrom, R. (2020). Family relationships during adolescence and stepchilden's educational attainment in young adulthood. *Journal of Marriage and Family, 82*(2), 622–638. https://doi.org/10.1111/jomf.12642

Kingsbury, M. A., & Bilbo, S. D. (2019). The inflammatory event of birth: How oxytocin signaling may guide the development of the brain and gastrointestinal system. *Frontiers in Neuroendocrinology, 55*, 100794. https://doi.org/10.1016/j.yfrne.2019.100794

Kinney, A. B. (1995). *Chinese views of childhood.* University of Hawaii Press.

Kinney, A. B. (2004). *Representations of childhood and youth in early China.* Stanford University Press.

Kinney, H. C., Hefti, M. M., Goldstein, R. D., & Haynes, R. L. (2018). Sudden infant death syndrome. In H. Adle-Biassette, B. N. Harding, & J. Golden (Eds.), *Developmental neuropathology* (pp. 269–280). Wiley. https://doi.org/10.1002/9781119013112.ch25

Kirlic, N., Colaizzi, J. M., Cosgrove, K. T., Cohen, Z. P., Yeh, H. W., Breslin, F., Morris, A. S., Aupperle, R., L., Singh, M. K., & Paulus, M. P. (2021). Extracurricular activities, screen media activity, and sleep may be modifiable factors related to children's cognitive functioning: Evidence from the ABCD Study®. *Child Development, 92*(5), 2035–2052.

Kitayama, S., & Salvador, C. E. (2017). Culture embrained: Going beyond the nature-nurture dichotomy. *Perspectives on Psychological Science, 12*(5), 841–854. https://doi.org/10.1177/1745691617707317

Kitzman, H., Olds, D. L., Knudtson, M. D., Cole, R., Anson, E., Smith, J. A., Fishbein, D., DiClemente, R., Wingood, G., & Caliendo, A. M. (2019). Prenatal and infancy nurse home visiting and 18-year outcomes of a randomized trial. *Pediatrics, 144*(6), e20183876.

Klaczynski, P. A. (2014). Heuristics and biases: Interactions among numeracy, ability, and reflectiveness predict normative responding. *Frontiers in Psychology, 5*, 665.

Klein, W., Graesch, A. P., & Izquierdo, C. (2009). Children and chores: A mixed-methods study of children's household work in Los Angeles families. *Anthropology of Work Review, 30*(3), 98–109.

Klinzing, J. G., Niethard, N., & Born, J. (2019). Mechanisms of systems memory consolidation during sleep. *Nature Neuroscience, 22*(10), 1598–1610.

Kluger, R. (2011). *Simple justice: The history of* Brown v. Board of Education *and Black America's struggle for equality.* Knopf Doubleday.

Knifsend, C. A., Camacho-Thompson, D. E., Juvonen, J., & Graham, S. (2018). Friends in activities, school-related affect, and academic outcomes in diverse middle schools. *Journal of Youth and Adolescence, 47*(6), 1208–1220.

Knight, G. P., Safa, M. D., & White, R. M. B. (2018). Advancing the assessment of cultural orientation: A developmental and contextual framework of multiple psychological dimensions and social identities. *Development and Psychopathology, 30*(5), 1867–1888. https://doi.org/10.1017/S095457941800113X

Knobl, V., Dallacker, M., Hertwig, R., & Mata, J. (2022). Happy and healthy: How family mealtime routines relate to child nutritional health. *Appetite, 171*, 105939. https://doi.org/10.1016/j.appet.2022.105939

Knoll, L. J., Magis-Weinberg, L., Speekenbrink, M., & Blakemore, S.-J. (2015). Social influence on risk perception during adolescence. *Psychological Science, 26*(5), 583–592. https://doi.org/10.1177/0956797615569578

Ko, J. Y., Coy, K. C., Haight, S. C., Haegerich, T. M., Williams, L., Cox, S., Njai, R., & Grant, A. M. (2020). Characteristics of marijuana use during pregnancy—Eight states, pregnancy risk assessment monitoring system, 2017. *Morbidity and Mortality Weekly Report, 69*(32), 1058–1063. https://doi.org/10.15585/mmwr.mm6932a2

Kobak, R., Abbott, C., Zisk, A., & Bounoua, N. (2017). Adapting to the changing needs of adolescents: Parenting practices and challenges to sensitive attunement. *Current Opinion in Psychology, 15*, 137–142. https://doi.org/10.1016/j.copsyc.2017.02.018

Kobin, B. (2019, September 26). Too many "broken hearts"? Elementary school tells fifth graders to stop dating. *The Courier Journal.* https://www.courier-journal.com/story/news/local/indiana/clark/2019/09/26/indiana-elementary-school-jeffersonville-riverside-no-dating-fifth-grade-students/3772740002/

Kochanska, G. (2002). Mutually responsive orientation between mothers and their young children: A context for the early development of conscience. *Current Directions in Psychological Science, 11*(6), 191–195. https://doi.org/10.1111/1467-8721.00198

Kochanska, G., Boldt, L. J., & Goffin, K. C. (2019). Early relational experience: A foundation for the unfolding dynamics of parent–child socialization. *Child Development Perspectives, 13*(1), 41–47. https://doi.org/10.1111/cdep.12308

Kochanska, G., Boldt, L. J., Kim, S., Yoon, J. E., & Philibert, R. A. (2015). Developmental interplay between children's biobehavioral risk and the parenting environment from toddler to early school age: Prediction of socialization outcomes in preadolescence. *Development and Psychopathology, 27*(3), 775.

Koenka, A. C. (2020). Academic motivation theories revisited: An interactive dialog between motivation scholars on recent contributions, underexplored issues, and future directions. *Contemporary Educational Psychology, 61*, 101831.

Koepp, A. E., & Gershoff, E. T. (2022). Amount and type of physical activity as predictors of growth in executive functions, attentional control, and social self-control across 4 years of elementary school. *Developmental Science, 25*(1), e13147.

Kohlberg, L. (1978). Revisions in the theory and practice of moral development. *New Directions for Child and Adolescent Development, 1978*(2), 83–87.

Kohlberg, L. (1981). *The philosophy of moral development: Moral stages and the idea of justice.* Harper & Row.

Kohlberg, L., & Kramer, R. (1969). Continuities and discontinuities in childhood and adult moral development. *Human Development, 12*(2), 93–120.

Kohler, R. (2014). *Jean Piaget.* Bloomsbury.

Kokis, J. V., Macpherson, R., Toplak, M. E., West, R. F., & Stanovich, K. E. (2002). Heuristic and analytic processing: Age trends and associations with cognitive ability and cognitive styles. *Journal of Experimental Child Psychology, 83*, 26–52.

Kolbe, L. J. (2019). School health as a strategy to improve both public health and education. *Annual Review of Public Health, 40*(1), 443–463.

Kolling, T., Graf, F., & Knopf, M. (2016). Cross-cultural perspectives on declarative and nondeclarative memory from infancy to early childhood. *Child Development Perspectives, 10*(1), 28–32. https://doi.org/10.1111/cdep.12158

Kollmayer, M., Schultes, M.-T., Schober, B., Hodosi, T., & Spiel, C. (2018). Parents' judgments about the desirability of toys for their children: Associations with gender role attitudes, gender-typing of toys, and demographics. *Sex Roles, 79*(5), 329–341. https://doi.org/10.1007/s11199-017-0882-4

Kommers, D., Oei, G., Chen, W., Feijs, L., & Oetomo, S. B. (2016). Suboptimal bonding impairs hormonal, epigenetic and neuronal development in preterm infants, but these impairments can be reversed. *Acta Paediatrica, 105*(7), 738–751. https://doi.org/10.1111/apa.13254

Kong, A., Thorleifsson, G., Frigge, M. L., Vilhjalmsson, B. J., Young, A. I., Thorgeirsson, T. E., Benonisdottir, S., Oddsson, A., Halldorsson, B. V., Masson, G., Gudbjartsson, D. F., Helgason, A., Bjornsdottir, G., Thorsteinsdottir, U., & Stefansson, K. (2018). The nature of nurture: Effects of parental genotypes. *Science, 359*(6374), 424–428.

Konrad, C., Hillmann, M., Rispler, J., Niehaus, L., Neuhoff, L., & Barr, R. (2021). Quality of mother-child interaction before, during, and after smartphone use. *Frontiers in Psychology, 12*. https://doi.org/10.3389/fpsyg.2021.616656

Konrad, C., & Seehagen, S. (2020). The effect of napping and nighttime sleep on memory in infants. *Advances in Child Development and Behavior, 60*, 31–56.

Kontou, E., McDonald, N. C., Brookshire, K., Pullen-Seufert, N. C., & LaJeunesse, S. (2020). US active school travel in 2017: Prevalence and correlates. *Preventive Medicine Reports, 17*, 101024.

Koomen, R., Grueneisen, S., & Herrmann, E. (2020). Children delay gratification for cooperative ends. *Psychological Science, 31*(2), 139–148.

Kopala-Sibley, D. C., Cyr, M., Finsaas, M. C., Orawe, J., Huang, A., Tottenham, N., & Klein, D. N. (2020). Early childhood parenting predicts late childhood brain functional connectivity during emotion perception and reward processing. *Child Development, 91*(1), 110–128. https://doi.org/10.1111/cdev.13126

Kopp, C. B. (1989). Regulation of distress and negative emotions: A developmental view. *Developmental Psychology, 25*(3), 343–354. https://doi.org/10.1037/0012-1649.25.3.343

Kosakowski, H. L., Cohen, M. A., Takahashi, A., Keil, B., Kanwisher, N., & Saxe, R. (2022). Selective responses to faces, scenes, and bodies in the ventral visual pathway of infants. *Current Biology, 32*(2), 265–274.e5. https://doi.org/10.1016/j.cub.2021.10.064

Kosakowski, H. L., Cohen, M., Keil, B., Takahashi, A., Nichoson, I., Alves, L., Kanwisher, N., & Saxe, R. (2020). Face selectivity in human infant ventral temporal cortex. *Journal of Vision, 20*(11), 790. https://doi.org/10.1167/jov.20.11.790

Kost, K., Maddow-Zimet, I., & Arpaia, A. (2017). *Pregnancies, births and abortions among adolescents and young women in the United States, 2013: National and state trends by age, race and ethnicity.* Guttmacher Institute.

Köster, M., & Kärtner, J. (2019). Why do infants help? A simple action reveals a complex phenomenon. *Developmental Review, 51*, 175–187. https://doi.org/10.1016/j.dr.2018.11.004

Kotecki, P. (2018). 10 countries at risk of becoming demographic time bombs. *Business Insider.* https://www.businessinsider.com/10-countries-at-risk-of-becoming-demographic-time-bombs-2018-8

Kotowski, J., Fowler, C., & Orr, F. (2021). Bottle-feeding, a neglected area of learning and support for nurses working in child health: An exploratory qualitative study. *Journal of Child Health Care*. https://doi.org/10.1177/13674935211007321

Koyanagi, A., Veronese, N., Vancampfort, D., Stickley, A., Jackson, S. E., Oh, H., Shin, J. I., Haro, J. M., Stubbs, B., & Smith, L. (2020). Association of bullying victimization with overweight and obesity among adolescents from 41 low- and middle-income countries. *Pediatric Obesity, 15*(1), e12571. https://doi.org/10.1111/ijpo.12571

Köymen, B., Lieven, E., Engemann, D. A., Rakoczy, H., Warneken, F., & Tomasello, M. (2014). Children's norm enforcement in their interactions with peers. *Child Development, 85*(3), 1108–1122. https://doi.org/10.1111/cdev.12178

Kozhimannil, K. B., Vogelsang, C. A., Hardeman, R. R., & Prasad, S. (2016). Disrupting the pathways of social determinants of health: Doula support during pregnancy and childbirth. *The Journal of the American Board of Family Medicine, 29*(3), 308–317. https://doi.org/10.3122/jabfm.2016.03.150300

Kozieł, S. M., & Malina, R. M. (2018). Modified maturity offset prediction equations: Validation in independent longitudinal samples of boys and girls. *Sports Medicine, 48*(1), 221–236. https://doi.org/10.1007/s40279-017-0750-y

Kraaijenvanger, E. J., Pollok, T. M., Monninger, M., Kaiser, A., Brandeis, D., Banaschewski, T., & Holz, N. E. (2020). Impact of early life adversities on human brain functioning: A coordinate-based meta-analysis. *Neuroscience & Biobehavioral Reviews, 113*, 62–76. https://doi.org/10.1016/j.neubiorev.2020.03.008

Krashen, S. D. (1999). *Three arguments against whole language and why they are wrong.* Heinemann.

Kreider, R. M., & Lofquist, D. A. (2014). *Adopted children and stepchildren: 2010* (No. P20-572). US Census Bureau. https://www.census.gov/library/publications/2014/demo/p20-572.html

Kreisel, K. M., Spicknall, I. H., Gargano, J. W., Lewis, F. M. T., Lewis, R. M., Markowitz, L. E., Roberts, H., Johnson, A. S., Song, R., St. Cyr, S. B., Weston, E. J., Torrone, E. A., & Weinstock, H. S. (2021). Sexually transmitted infections among US women and men: Prevalence and incidence estimates, 2018. *Sexually Transmitted Diseases, 48*(4), 208–214. https://doi.org/10.1097/OLQ.0000000000001355

Kreski, N., Platt, J., Rutherford, C., Olfson, M., Odgers, C., Schulenberg, J., & Keyes, K. M. (2021). Social media use and depressive symptoms among United States adolescents. *Journal of Adolescent Health, 68*(3), 572–579. https://doi.org/10.1016/j.jadohealth.2020.07.006

Kris, V. (2016). *Work-based learning for youth at risk: Getting employers on board.* OECD.

Kroger, J., & Marcia, J. E. (2011). The identity statuses: Origins, meanings, and interpretations. In S. J. Schwartz, K. Luyckx, & V. L. Vignoles (Eds.), *Handbook of identity theory and research* (pp. 31–53). Springer.

Kroger, J., Martinussen, M., & Marcia, J. E. (2010). Identity status change during adolescence and young adulthood: A meta-analysis. *Journal of Adolescence, 33*(5), 683–698. https://doi.org/10.1016/j.adolescence.2009.11.002

Krol, K. M., Puglia, M. H., Morris, J. P., Connelly, J. J., & Grossmann, T. (2019). Epigenetic modification of the oxytocin receptor gene is associated with emotion processing in the infant brain. *Developmental Cognitive Neuroscience, 37*, 100648. https://doi.org/10.1016/j.dcn.2019.100648

Kroshus, E., Qu, P., Chrisman, S., Herring, S., & Rivara, F. (2021). Socioeconomic status and parent perceptions about the costs and benefits of youth sport. *PLOS ONE, 16*(11), e0258885. https://doi.org/10.1371/journal.pone.0258885

Kross, E., Verduyn, P., Demiralp, E., Park, J., Lee, D. S., Lin, N., Shablack, H., Jonides, J., & Ybarra, O. (2013). Facebook use predicts declines in subjective well-being in young adults. *PLOS ONE, 8*(8), e69841. https://doi.org/10.1371/journal.pone.0069841

Kruszka, P., Addissie, Y. A., Tekendo-Ngongang, C., Jones, K. L., Savage, S. K., Gupta, N., Sirisena, N. D., Dissanayake, V. H. W., Sampath Paththinge, C., Aravena, T., Nampoothiri, S., Yesodharan, D., Girisha, K. M., Patil, S. J., Jamuar, S. S., Goh, J. C-Y., Utari, A., Sihombing, N., Mishra, R., Chitrakar, N. S., . . . Muenke, M. (2020). Turner syndrome in diverse populations. *American Journal of Medical Genetics Part A, 182*(2), 303–313.

Kuhfeld, M., & Lewis, K. (2022). *Student achievement in 2021–22: Cause for hope and continued urgency.* NWEA. https://www.nwea.org/research/publication/student-achievement-in-2021-22-cause-for-hope-and-continued-urgency/

Kuhl, P. K., Ramírez, R. R., Bosseler, A., Lin, J. F. L., & Imada, T. (2014). Infants' brain responses to speech suggest analysis by synthesis. *Proceedings of the National Academy of Sciences, 111*(31), 11238–11245.

Kuhn, D. (2009). Adolescent thinking. In R. M. Lerner & L. Steinberg (Eds.), *Handbook of adolescent psychology: Individual bases of adolescent development* (pp. 152–186). John Wiley & Sons. https://doi.org/10.1002/9780470479193.adlpsy001007

Kühn, S., Gallinat, J., & Mascherek, A. (2022). Effects of computer gaming on cognition, brain structure, and function: A critical reflection on existing literature. *Dialogues in Clinical Neuroscience, 21*(3), 319–330. https://doi.org/10.31887/DCNS.2019.21.3/skuehn

Kühn, S., Gleich, T., Lorenz, R. C., Lindenberger, U., & Gallinat, J. (2014). Playing Super Mario induces structural brain plasticity: Gray matter changes resulting from training with a commercial video game. *Molecular Psychiatry, 19*(2), 265–271.

Kühn, S., Kugler, D. T., Schmalen, K., Weichenberger, M., Witt, C., & Gallinat, J. (2019). Does playing violent video games cause aggression? A longitudinal intervention study. *Molecular Psychiatry, 24*(8), 1220–1234.

Kulawiak, P. R., & Wilbert, J. (2020). Introduction of a new method for representing the sociometric status within the peer group: The example of sociometrically neglected children. *International Journal of Research & Method in Education, 43*(2), 127–145.

Kuo, M., Barnes, M., & Jordan, C. (2019). Do experiences with nature promote learning? Converging evidence of a cause-and-effect relationship. *Frontiers in Psychology, 10.* https://www.frontiersin.org/article/10.3389/fpsyg.2019.00305

Kuper, L. E., Wright, L., & Mustanski, B. (2018). Gender identity development among transgender and gender nonconforming emerging adults: An intersectional approach. *International Journal of Transgenderism, 19*(4), 436–455. https://doi.org/10.1080/15532739.2018.1443869

Kuppens, S., Moore, S. C., Gross, V., Lowthian, E., & Siddaway, A. P. (2020). The enduring effects of parental alcohol, tobacco, and drug use on child well-being: A multilevel meta-analysis. *Development and Psychopathology, 32*(2), 765–778. https://doi.org/10.1017/S0954579419000749

Kurtz-Costes, B., DeFreitas, S. C., Halle, T. G., & Kinlaw, C. R. (2011). Gender and racial favouritism in Black and White preschool girls. *British Journal of Developmental Psychology, 29*(2), 270–287. https://doi.org/10.1111/j.2044-835X.2010.02018.x

Kushner, H. I. (2017). *On the other hand: Left hand, right brain, mental disorder, and history.* JHU Press.

Kuzawa, C. W., & Blair, C. (2019). A hypothesis linking the energy demand of the brain to obesity risk. *Proceedings of the National Academy of Sciences, 116*(27), 13266–13275.

Kuzawa, C. W., Chugani, H. T., Grossman, L. I., Lipovich, L., Muzik, O., Hof, P. R., Wildman, D. E., Sherwood, C. C., Leonard, W. R., & Lange, N. (2014). Metabolic costs and evolutionary implications of human brain development. *Proceedings of the National Academy of Sciences, 111*(36), 13010–13015. https://doi.org/10.1073/pnas.1323099111

Kwan, K. M. W., Shi, S. Y., Nabbijohn, A. N., MacMullin, L. N., VanderLaan, D. P., & Wong, W. I. (2020). Children's appraisals of gender nonconformity: Developmental pattern and intervention. *Child Development, 91*(4), e780–e798.

Kwon, K.-A., Ford, T. G., Salvatore, A. L., Randall, K., Jeon, L., Malek-Lasater, A., Ellis, N., Kile, M. S., Horm, D. M., Kim, S. G., & Han, M. (2020). Neglected elements of a high-quality early childhood workforce: Whole teacher well-being and working conditions. *Early Childhood Education Journal.* https://doi.org/10.1007/s10643-020-01124-7

Kwon, K.-A., Jeon, S., Jeon, L., & Castle, S. (2019). The role of teachers' depressive symptoms in classroom quality and child developmental outcomes in early head start programs. *Learning and Individual Differences, 74*, 101748. https://doi.org/10.1016/j.lindif.2019.06.002

Kwon, S., & O'Neill, M. (2020). Socioeconomic and familial factors associated with gross motor skills among US children aged 3–5 years: The 2012 NHANES National Youth Fitness Survey. *International Journal of Environmental Research and Public Health, 17*(12), 4491. https://doi.org/10.3390/ijerph17124491

Labella, M. H. (2018). The sociocultural context of emotion socialization in African American families. *Clinical Psychology Review, 59*, 1–15. https://doi.org/10.1016/j.cpr.2017.10.006

Labouvie-Vief, G. (1980). Beyond formal operations: Uses and limits of pure logic in life-span development. *Human Development, 23*(3), 141–161. https://doi.org/10.1159/000272546

Labouvie-Vief, G. (2015). Cognitive–Emotional Development from Adolescence to Adulthood. In Integrating Emotions and Cognition Throughout the Lifespan (pp. 89–116). Springer International Publishing. https://doi.org/10.1007/978-3-319-09822-7_6

Lachman, P., Roman, C. G., & Cahill, M. (2013). Assessing youth motivations for joining a peer group as risk factors for delinquent and gang behavior. *Youth Violence and Juvenile Justice, 11*(3), 212–229. https://doi.org/10.1177/1541204012461510

Lachman, R., Lachman, J. L., & Butterfield, E. C. (1979). *Cognitive psychology and information processing: An introduction.* Routledge.

Lacko, A. M., Maselko, J., Popkin, B., & Ng, S. W. (2021). Socio-economic and racial/ethnic disparities in the nutritional quality of packaged food purchases in the USA, 2008–2018. *Public Health Nutrition, 1–13.* https://doi.org/10.1017/S1368980021000367

Lacroix, E., Atkinson, M. J., Garbett, K. M., & Diedrichs, P. C. (2020). One size does not fit all: Trajectories of body image development and their predictors in early adolescence. *Development and Psychopathology*, 1–10. https://doi.org/10.1017/S0954579420000917

Lacroix, E., Atkinson, M. J., Garbett, K. M., & Diedrichs, P. C. (2022). One size does not fit all: Trajectories of body image development and their predictors in early adolescence. *Development and Psychopathology*, 34(1), 285–294. https://doi.org/10.1017/S0954579420000917

Ladd, G. W. (1999). Peer relationships and social competence during early and middle childhood. *Annual Review of Psychology*, 50(1), 333–359.

Lafnitzegger, A., & Gaviria-Agudelo, C. (2022). Vaccine hesitancy in pediatrics. *Advances in Pediatrics*, 69(1), 163–176.

LaForett, D. R., & Mendez, J. L. (2017). Play beliefs and responsive parenting among low-income mothers of preschoolers in the United States. *Early Child Development and Care*, 187(8), 1359–1371.

Lagattuta, K. H., Kramer, H. J., Kennedy, K., Hjortsvang, K., Goldfarb, D., & Tashjian, S. (2015). Beyond Sally's missing marble: Further development in children's understanding of mind and emotion in middle childhood. *Advances in Child Development and Behavior*, 48, 185–217.

Lai, T., & Kao, G. (2018). Hit, robbed, and put down (but not bullied): Underreporting of bullying by minority and male students. *Journal of Youth and Adolescence*, 47(3), 619–635. https://doi.org/10.1007/s10964-017-0748-7

Lalys, L., & Pineau, J.-C. (2014). Age at menarche in a group of French schoolgirls. *Pediatrics International*, 56(4), 601–604. https://doi.org/10.1111/ped.12296

Lam, C. B., McHale, S. M., & Crouter, A. C. (2014). Time with peers from middle childhood to late adolescence: Developmental course and adjustment correlates. *Child Development*, 85(4), 1677–1693. https://doi.org/10.1111/cdev.12235

Lam, J. R., Tyler, J., Scurrah, K. J., Reavley, N. J., & Dite, G. S. (2019). The association between socioeconomic status and psychological distress: A within and between twin study. *Twin Research and Human Genetics*, 22(5), 312–320. https://doi.org/10.1017/thg.2019.91

Lam, K. K. L., & Zhou, M. (2022). Grit and academic achievement: A comparative cross-cultural meta-analysis. *Journal of Educational Psychology*, 114(3), 597.

Lambert, G. H. (2016). Developmental toxicity. *Perspectives in Basic and Applied Toxicology*, 242.

Lamela, D., Figueiredo, B., Bastos, A., & Feinberg, M. (2016). Typologies of post-divorce coparenting and parental well-being, parenting quality and children's psychological adjustment. *Child Psychiatry & Human Development*, 47(5), 716–728.

Lampl, M., & Schoen, M. (2017). How long bones grow children: Mechanistic paths to variation in human height growth. *American Journal of Human Biology*, 29(2), e22983. https://doi.org/10.1002/ajhb.22983

Lancy, D. F. (2018). Work in children's lives. In D. F. Lancy (Ed.), *Anthropological perspectives on children as helpers, workers, artisans, and laborers* (pp. 1–30). Palgrave Macmillan.

Lancy, D. F. (2020). *Child helpers: A multidisciplinary perspective*. Cambridge University Press.

Lancy, D. F. (2021). *Anthropological perspectives on children as helpers, workers, artisans, and laborers*. Palgrave Macmillan.

Landberg, M., Dimitrova, R., & Syed, M. (2018). International perspectives on identity and acculturation in emerging adulthood: Introduction to the special issue. *Emerging Adulthood*, 6(1), 3–6. https://doi.org/10.1177/2167696817748107

Landrigan, P. J., Fuller, R., Fisher, S., Suk, W. A., Sly, P., Chiles, T. C., & Bose-O'Reilly, S. (2019). Pollution and children's health. *Science of The Total Environment*, 650, 2389–2394. https://doi.org/10.1016/j.scitotenv.2018.09.375

Landrum, R. E., Brakke, K., & McCarthy, M. A. (2019). The pedagogical power of storytelling. *Scholarship of Teaching and Learning in Psychology*, 5(3), 247–253. https://doi.org/10.1037/stl0000152

Lange, S. J., Kompaniyets, L., Freedman, D. S., Kraus, E. M., Porter, R., Blanck, H. M., & Goodman, A. B. (2021). Longitudinal trends in body mass index before and during the COVID-19 pandemic among persons aged 2–19 years — United States, 2018–2020. *Morbidity and Mortality Weekly Report*, 70(37), 1278–1283. https://doi.org/10.15585/mmwr.mm7037a3

Lange, S., Probst, C., Rehm, J., & Popova, S. (2018). National, regional, and global prevalence of smoking during pregnancy in the general population: A systematic review and meta-analysis. *The Lancet Global Health*, 6(7), e769–e776.

Laninga-Wijnen, L., Ryan, A. M., Harakeh, Z., Shin, H., & Vollebergh, W. A. (2018). The moderating role of popular peers' achievement goals in 5th-and 6th-graders' achievement-related friendships: A social network analysis. *Journal of Educational Psychology*, 110(2), 289.

Lansford, J. E. (2009). Parental divorce and children's adjustment. *Perspectives on Psychological Science*, 4(2), 140–152.

Lansford, J. E. (2017). An international perspective on parenting and children's adjustment. In N. J. Cabrera & B. Leyendecker (Eds.), *Handbook on positive development of minority children and youth* (pp. 107–122). Springer International Publishing. https://doi.org/10.1007/978-3-319-43645-6_7

Lansford, J. E., & Bornstein, M. H. (2020). Parenting. In W. K. Halford & F. van de Vijver (Eds.), *Cross-cultural family research and practice* (pp. 565–602). Academic Press. https://doi.org/10.1016/B978-0-12-815493-9.00018-1

Lansford, J. E., Godwin, J., Al-Hassan, S. M., Bacchini, D., Bornstein, M. H., Chang, L., Chen, B.-B., Deater-Deckard, K., Di Giunta, L., Dodge, K. A., Malone, P. S., Oburu, P., Pastorelli, C., Skinner, A. T., Sorbring, E., Steinberg, L., Tapanya, S., Alampay, L. P., Uribe Tirado, L. M., & Zelli, A. (2018). Longitudinal associations between parenting and youth adjustment in twelve cultural groups: Cultural normativeness of parenting as a moderator. *Developmental Psychology*, 54(2), 362–377. https://doi.org/10.1037/dev0000416

Lansford, J. E., Godwin, J., McMahon, R. J., Crowley, M., Pettit, G. S., Bates, J. E., Coie, J. D., & Dodge, K. A. (2021). Early physical abuse and adult outcomes. *Pediatrics*, 147(1), e20200873. https://doi.org/10.1542/peds.2020-0873

Lansford, J. E., Godwin, J., Uribe Tirado, L. M., Zelli, A., Al-Hassan, S. M., Bacchini, D., Bombi, A. S., Bornstein, M. H., Chang, L., Deater-Deckard, K., Di Giunta, L., Dodge, K. A., Malone, P. S., Oburu, P., Pastorelli, C., Skinner, A. T., Sorbring, E., Tapanya, S., & Alampay, L. P. (2015). Individual, family, and culture level contributions to child physical abuse and neglect: A longitudinal study in nine countries. *Development and Psychopathology*, 27(4 Pt. 2), 1417–1428. https://doi.org/10.1017/S095457941500084X

Lansford, J. E., Laird, R. D., Pettit, G. S., Bates, J. E., & Dodge, K. A. (2014). Mothers' and fathers' autonomy-relevant parenting: Longitudinal links with adolescents' externalizing and internalizing behavior. *Journal of Youth and Adolescence*, 43(11), 1877–1889. https://doi.org/10.1007/s10964-013-0079-2

Lansford, J. E., Rothenberg, W. A., & Bornstein, M. H. (2021). *Parenting across cultures from childhood to adolescence: Development in nine countries*. Routledge.

Lapan, C., & Boseovski, J. J. (2017). When peer performance matters: Effects of expertise and traits on children's self-evaluations after social comparison. *Child Development*, 88(6), 1860–1872.

Lara, L. A. S., & Abdo, C. H. N. (2016). Age at time of initial sexual intercourse and health of adolescent girls. *Journal of Pediatric and Adolescent Gynecology*, 29(5), 417–423. https://doi.org/10.1016/j.jpag.2015.11.012

Lareau, A. (2011). *Unequal childhoods: Class, race, and family life*. University of California Press.

Lareau, A. (2015). Cultural knowledge and social inequality. *American Sociological Review*, 80(1), 1–27. http://asr.sagepub.com/content/80/1/1.short

Larson, R. W., Moneta, G., Richards, M. H., & Wilson, S. (2002). Continuity, stability, and change in daily emotional experience across adolescence. *Child Development*, 73(4), 1151–1165.

Larson, R. W., Richards, M. H., Moneta, G., Holmbeck, G., & Duckett, E. (1996). Changes in adolescents' daily interactions with their families from ages 10 to 18: Disengagement and transformation. *Developmental Psychology*, 32(4), 744–754. https://doi.org/10.1037/0012-1649.32.4.744

Lassi, M., & Teperino, R. (2020). Introduction to epigenetic inheritance: Definition, mechanisms, implications and relevance. In R. Teperino (Ed.), *Beyond our genes: Pathophysiology of gene and environment interaction and epigenetic inheritance* (pp. 159–173). Springer International Publishing. https://doi.org/10.1007/978-3-030-35213-4_9

Latham, R. M., & Von Stumm, S. (2017). Mothers want extraversion over conscientiousness or intelligence for their children. *Personality and Individual Differences*, 119, 262–265.

Lau, Y.-F. C. (2020). Y chromosome in health and diseases. *Cell & Bioscience*, 10(1), 97. https://doi.org/10.1186/s13578-020-00452-w

Laube, C., van den Bos, W., & Fandakova, Y. (2020). The relationship between pubertal hormones and brain plasticity: Implications for cognitive training in adolescence. *Developmental Cognitive Neuroscience*, 42, 100753. https://doi.org/10.1016/j.dcn.2020.100753

Laue, H. E., Coker, M. O., & Madan, J. C. (2022). The developing microbiome from birth to 3 years: The gut-brain axis and neurodevelopmental outcomes. *Frontiers in Pediatrics*, 10, 815885. https://doi.org/10.3389/fped.2022.815885

Laue, H. E., Karagas, M. R., Coker, M. O., Bellinger, D. C., Baker, E. R., Korrick, S. A., & Madan, J. C. (2021). Sex-specific relationships of the infant microbiome and early-childhood behavioral outcomes. *Pediatric Research*, 1–12. https://doi.org/10.1038/s41390-021-01785-z

Laurito, A., Lacoe, J., Schwartz, A. E., Sharkey, P., & Ellen, I. G. (2019). School climate and the impact of neighborhood crime on test scores. *RSF: The Russell Sage Foundation Journal of the Social Sciences*, 5(2), 141–166.

Lauro, J., Core, C., & Hoff, E. (2020). Explaining individual differences in trajectories of simultaneous bilingual development: Contributions of child and environmental factors. *Child Development*, 91(6), 2063–2082. https://doi.org/10.1111/cdev.13409

Laursen, B., Coy, K. C., & Collins, W. A. (1998). Reconsidering changes in parent-child conflict across adolescence: A meta-analysis. *Child Development, 69*(3), 817–832.

Laursen, B., Little, T. D., & Card, N. A. (2012). *Handbook of developmental research methods.* Guilford.

Lavelli, M., Carra, C., Rossi, G., & Keller, H. (2019). Culture-specific development of early mother–infant emotional co-regulation: Italian, Cameroonian, and West African immigrant dyads. *Developmental Psychology, 55*(9), 1850–1867. https://doi.org/10.1037/dev0000696

Lavigne, M., Birken, C. S., Maguire, J. L., Straus, S., & Laupacis, A. (2017). Priority setting in paediatric preventive care research. *Archives of Disease in Childhood, 102*(8), 748–753. https://doi.org/10.1136/archdischild-2016-312284

Lavoie, J., Nagar, P. M., & Talwar, V. (2017). From Kantian to Machiavellian deceivers: Development of children's reasoning and self-reported use of secrets and lies. *Childhood, 24*(2), 197–211. https://doi.org/10.1177/0907568216671179

Law, E., Fisher, E., Eccleston, C., & Palermo, T. M. (2019). Psychological interventions for parents of children and adolescents with chronic illness. *Cochrane Database of Systematic Reviews, 3*, CD009660. https://doi.org/10.1002/14651858.CD009660.pub4

Lawton, B. L., Foeman, A., & Surdel, N. (2018). Bridging discussions of human history: Ancestry DNA and new roles for Africana studies. *Genealogy, 2*(1), 5. https://doi.org/10.3390/genealogy2010005

Lawton, G., & Ifama, D. (2018). "It made me question my ancestry": Does DNA home testing really understand race? *The Guardian.*

le Roux, K. W., Almirol, E., Rezvan, P. H., Le Roux, I. M., Mbewu, N., Dippenaar, E., & Rotheram-Borus, M. J. (2020). Community health workers impact on maternal and child health outcomes in rural South Africa—A non-randomized two-group comparison study. *BMC Public Health, 20*(1), 1–14.

Leaper, C., & Brown, C. S. (2018). Sexism in childhood and adolescence: Recent trends and advances in research. *Child Development Perspectives, 12*(1), 10–15. https://doi.org/10.1111/cdep.12247

Lebel, C., Treit, S., & Beaulieu, C. (2019). A review of diffusion MRI of typical white matter development from early childhood to young adulthood. *NMR in Biomedicine, 32*(4), e3778. https://doi.org/10.1002/nbm.3778

LeBourgeois, M. K., Hale, L., Chang, A.-M., Akacem, L. D., Montgomery-Downs, H. E., & Buxton, O. M. (2017). Digital media and sleep in childhood and adolescence. *Pediatrics, 140*(Supplement 2), S92–S96. https://doi.org/10.1542/peds.2016-1758J

Lebrun-Harris, L. A., Ghandour, R. M., Kogan, M. D., & Warren, M. D. (2022). Five-year trends in US children's health and well-being, 2016–2020. *JAMA Pediatrics.*

Lebrun-Harris, L. A., Sherman, L. J., Limber, S. P., Miller, B. D., & Edgerton, E. A. (2019). Bullying victimization and perpetration among U.S. children and adolescents: 2016 National Survey of Children's Health. *Journal of Child and Family Studies, 28*(9), 2543–2557. https://doi.org/10.1007/s10826-018-1170-9

Lederer, A. M., & Laing, E. E. (2017). What's in a name? Perceptions of the terms sexually transmitted disease and sexually transmitted infection among late adolescents. *Sexually Transmitted Diseases, 44*(11), 707–711. https://doi.org/10.1097/OLQ.0000000000000682

Lee, C. D., Nelin, L., & Foglia, E. E. (2022). Neonatal resuscitation in 22-week pregnancies. *New England Journal of Medicine, 386*(4), 391–393. https://doi.org/10.1056/NEJMclde2114954

Lee, D. R., McKeith, I., Mosimann, U., Ghosh-Nodyal, A., & Thomas, A. J. (2013). Examining carer stress in dementia: The role of subtype diagnosis and neuropsychiatric symptoms. *International Journal of Geriatric Psychiatry, 28*(2), 135–141.

Lee, E.-Y., Bains, A., Hunter, S., Ament, A., Brazo-Sayavera, J., Carson, V., Hakimi, S., Huang, W. Y., Janssen, I., Lee, M., Lim, H., Silva, D. A. S., & Tremblay, M. S. (2021). Systematic review of the correlates of outdoor play and time among children aged 3–12 years. *International Journal of Behavioral Nutrition and Physical Activity, 18*(1), 41. https://doi.org/10.1186/s12966-021-01097-9

Lee, G. Y., & Kisilevsky, B. S. (2014). Fetuses respond to father's voice but prefer mother's voice after birth. *Developmental Psychobiology, 56*(1), 1–11. https://doi.org/10.1002/dev.21084

Lee, J. M., Wasserman, R., Kaciroti, N., Gebremariam, A., Steffes, J., Dowshen, S., Harris, D., Serwint, J., Abney, D., Smitherman, L., Reiter, E., & Herman-Giddens, M. E. (2016). Timing of puberty in overweight versus obese boys. *Pediatrics, 137*(2), e20150164.

Lee, J., Cheon, Y. M., Wei, X., & Chung, G. H. (2018). The role of ethnic socialization, ethnic identity and self-esteem: Implications for bi-ethnic adolescents' school adjustment. *Journal of Child and Family Studies, 27*(12), 3831–3841. https://doi.org/10.1007/s10826-018-1235-9

Lee, K. (2010). Developmental trajectories of Head Start children's reading and home environment scores: Across ethnicities. *Journal of Social Service Research.*

Lee, K., Quinn, P. C., & Heyman, G. D. (2017). Rethinking the emergence and development of implicit racial bias: A perceptual-social linkage hypothesis. In N. Budwig, E. Turiel, & P. D. Zelazo (Eds.), *New perspectives on human development* (pp. 27–46). Cambridge University Press.

Lee, M. R., & Thai, C. J. (2015). Asian American phenotypicality and experiences of psychological distress: More than meets the eyes. *Asian American Journal of Psychology, 6*(3), 242–251. https://doi.org/10.1037/aap0000015

Lee, P. A., Nordenström, A., Houk, C. P., Ahmed, S. F., Auchus, R., Baratz, A., Dalke, K. B., Liao, L.-M., Lin-Su, K., Looijenga, L. H. J., 3rd, Mazur, T., Meyer-Bahlburg, H. F. L., Mouriquand, P., Quigley, C. A., Sandberg, D. E., Vilain, E., Witchel, S., & the Global DSD Update Consortium. (2016). Global disorders of sex development update since 2006: Perceptions, approach and care. *Hormone Research in Paediatrics, 85*(3), 158–180. https://doi.org/10.1159/000442975

Leerkes, E. M., & Zhou, N. (2018). Maternal sensitivity to distress and attachment outcomes: Interactions with sensitivity to non-distress and infant temperament. *Journal of Family Psychology, 32*(6), 753–761. https://doi.org/10.1037/fam0000420

Lee-St. John, T. J., Walsh, M. E., Raczek, A. E., Vuilleumier, C. E., Foley, C., Heberle, A., Sibley, E., & Dearing, E. (2018). The long-term impact of systemic student support in elementary school: Reducing high school dropout. *AERA Open, 4*(4), 2332858418799085.

Legare, C. H. (2019). The development of cumulative cultural learning. *Annual Review of Developmental Psychology, 1*(1), 119–147. https://doi.org/10.1146/annurev-devpsych-121318-084848

Legare, C. H., Clegg, J. M., & Wen, N. J. (2018). Evolutionary developmental psychology: 2017 redux. *Child Development, 89*, 2282–2287.

Lehnart, J., Neyer, F. J., & Eccles, J. (2010). Long-term effects of social investment: The case of partnering in young adulthood. *Journal of Personality, 78*(2), 639–670. https://doi.org/10.1111/j.1467-6494.2010.00629.x

Lei, L., & South, S. J. (2021). Explaining the decline in young adult sexual activity in the United States. *Journal of Marriage and Family, 83*(1), 280–295.

Leibold, L. J., & Buss, E. (2019). Masked speech recognition in school-age children. *Frontiers in Psychology, 10*, 1981. https://doi.org/10.3389/fpsyg.2019.01981

Lemola, S., Perkinson-Gloor, N., Brand, S., Dewald-Kaufmann, J. F., & Grob, A. (2015). Adolescents' electronic media use at night, sleep disturbance, and depressive symptoms in the smartphone age. *Journal of Youth and Adolescence, 44*(2), 405–418.

Lenhart, A. (2015, August 6). *Teens, technology and friendships.* Pew Research Center: Internet, Science & Tech. http://www.pewinternet.org/2015/08/06/teens-technology-and-friendships/

Lenhart, A., Smith, A., Anderson, M., Duggan, M., & Perrin, A. (2015). Teens, technology and friendships: Video games, social media and mobile phones play an integral role in how teens meet and interact with friends. *Pew Research Center, 1.*

Lennox, S. (2013). Interactive read-alouds — An avenue for enhancing children's language for thinking and understanding: A review of recent research. *Early Childhood Education Journal, 41*(5), 381–389. https://doi.org/10.1007/s10643-013-0578-5

Lenroot, R. K., Gogtay, N., Greenstein, D. K., Wells, E. M., Wallace, G. L., Clasen, L. S., Blumenthal, J. D., Lerch, J., Zijdenbos, A. P., Evans, A. C., Thompson, P. M., & Giedd, J. N. (2007). Sexual dimorphism of brain developmental trajectories during childhood and adolescence. *NeuroImage, 36*(4), 1065–1073. https://doi.org/10.1016/j.neuroimage.2007.03.053

Leonard, H., Khurana, A., & Hammond, M. (2021). Bedtime media use and sleep: Evidence for bidirectional effects and associations with attention control in adolescents. *Sleep Health, 7*(4), 491–499. https://doi.org/10.1016/j.sleh.2021.05.003

Leonard, J. A., Lydon-Staley, D. M., Sharp, S. D. S., Liu, H. Z., Park, A. T., Bassett, D. S., Duckworth, A. L., & Mackey, A. P. (2022). Daily fluctuations in young children's persistence. *Child Development, 93*(2), e222–e236. https://doi.org/10.1111/cdev.13717

Lepper, M. R., & Woolverton, M. (2002). The wisdom of practice: Lessons learned from the study of highly effective tutors. In J. Aronson (Ed.), *Improving academic achievement* (pp. 135–158). Academic Press.

Lerner, R. M. (2021). *Individuals as producers of their own development: The dynamics of person-context coactions.* Routledge.

Lerner, R. M., & Murray, E. D. (2016). Finally! A developmental science that privileges development. *Human Development, 59*(6), 377–385. https://doi.org/10.1159/000455030

Leroy, J. L., Frongillo, E. A., Dewan, P., Black, M. M., & Waterland, R. A. (2020). Can children catch up from the consequences of undernourishment? Evidence from child linear growth, developmental epigenetics, and brain and neurocognitive development. *Advances in Nutrition, 11*(4), 1032–1041. https://doi.org/10.1093/advances/nmaa020

Lessard, L. M., & Juvonen, J. (2020). Weight stigma in the school setting: The role of inclusive weight climate — A commentary. *Journal of School Health*, *90*(7), 507–510. https://doi.org/10.1111/josh.12898

Lessard, L. M., & Juvonen, J. (2022). The academic benefits of maintaining friendships across the transition to high school. *Journal of School Psychology*, *92*, 136–147. https://doi.org/10.1016/j.jsp.2022.03.005

Lessard, L. M., & Puhl, R. M. (2021). Reducing educators' weight bias: The role of school-based anti-bullying policies. *Journal of School Health*, *91*(10), 796–801. https://doi.org/10.1111/josh.13068

Leszczensky, L., & Pink, S. (2019). What drives ethnic homophily? A relational approach on how ethnic identification moderates preferences for same-ethnic friends. *American Sociological Review*, *84*(3), 394–419. https://doi.org/10.1177/0003122419846849

Leszczensky, L., & Stark, T. (2019). Understanding the causes and consequences of segregation in youth's friendship networks: Opportunities and challenges for research. In P. F. Titzmann & P. Jugert (Eds.), *Youth in superdiverse societies* (pp. 233–248). Routledge.

Letourneau, E. J., Brown, D. S., Fang, X., Hassan, A., & Mercy, J. A. (2018). The economic burden of child sexual abuse in the United States. *Child Abuse & Neglect*, *79*, 413–422. https://doi.org/10.1016/j.chiabu.2018.02.020

Levin, D. E., & Carlsson-Paige, N. (2005). *The war play dilemma: What every parent and teacher needs to know*. Teachers College Press.

LeVine, R. A., & LeVine, S. (2016). *Do parents matter? Why Japanese babies sleep soundly, Mexican siblings don't fight, and American families should just relax*. PublicAffairs.

Levy, J., Lankinen, K., Hakonen, M., & Feldman, R. (2021). The integration of social and neural synchrony: A case for ecologically valid research using MEG neuroimaging. *Social Cognitive and Affective Neuroscience*, *16*(1–2), 143–152. https://doi.org/10.1093/scan/nsaa061

Lewis, B. A., Billing, L., Schuver, K., Gjerdingen, D., Avery, M., & Marcus, B. H. (2017). The relationship between employment status and depression symptomatology among women at risk for postpartum depression. *Women's Health*, *13*(1), 3–9.

Lewis, K., Sandilos, L. E., Hammer, C. S., Sawyer, B. E., & Méndez, L. I. (2016). Relations among the home language and literacy environment and children's language abilities: A study of Head Start dual language learners and their mothers. *Early Education and Development*, *27*(4), 478–494.

Lewis, M. (2014). Toward the development of the science of developmental psychopathology. In M. Lewis & K. D. Rudolph (Eds.), *Handbook of developmental psychopathology* (pp. 3–23). Springer Science & Business Media.

Lewis, M. (2017). The emergence of human emotions. In L. F. Barrett, M. Lewis, & J. M. Haviland-Jones (Eds.), *Handbook of emotions* (4th ed., pp. 271–291). Guilford.

Lewis, M., & Brooks-Gunn, J. (1979). Toward a theory of social cognition: The development of self. *New Directions for Child and Adolescent Development*, *1979*(4), 1–20. https://doi.org/10.1002/cd.23219790403

Lewis, M., Takai-Kawakami, K., Kawakami, K., & Sullivan, M. W. (2010). Cultural differences in emotional responses to success and failure. *International Journal of Behavioral Development*, *34*(1), 53–61. https://doi.org/10.1177/0165025409348559

Lewis, T. L., & Maurer, D. (2005). Multiple sensitive periods in human visual development: Evidence from visually deprived children. *Developmental Psychobiology*, *46*(3), 163–183. https://doi.org/10.1002/dev.20055

Lew-Levy, S., Boyette, A. H., Crittenden, A. N., Hewlett, B. S., & Lamb, M. E. (2020). Gender-typed and gender-segregated play among Tanzanian Hadza and Congolese BaYaka hunter-gatherer children and adolescents. *Child Development*, *91*(4), 1284–1301. https://doi.org/10.1111/cdev.13306

Lew-Levy, S., Reckin, R., Lavi, N., Cristóbal-Azkarate, J., & Ellis-Davies, K. (2017). How do hunter-gatherer children learn subsistence skills? *Human Nature*, *28*(4), 367–394. https://doi.org/10.1007/s12110-017-9302-2

Leyva, D., Weiland, C., Shapiro, A., Yeomans-Maldonado, G., & Febles, A. (2022). A strengths-based, culturally responsive family intervention improves Latino kindergarteners' vocabulary and approaches to learning. *Child Development*, *93*(2), 451–467.

Li, C., Mendoza, M., & Milanaik, R. (2017). Touchscreen device usage in infants and toddlers and its correlations with cognitive development. *Pediatrics & Health Research*, *2*(1). https://doi.org/10.21767/2574-2817.100013

Li, G., & Davis, J. T. M. (2019). Sexual experimentation in heterosexual, bisexual, lesbian/gay, and questioning adolescents from ages 11 to 15. *Journal of Research on Adolescence*, *30*(2), 423–439. https://doi.org/10.1111/jora.12535

Li, S., Nguyen, T. L., Wong, E. M., Dugué, P.-A., Dite, G. S., Armstrong, N. J., Craig, J. M., Mather, K. A., Sachdev, P. S., Saffery, R., Sung, J., Tan, Q., Thalamuthu, A., Milne, R. L., Giles, G. G., Southey, M. C., & Hopper, J. L. (2020). Genetic and environmental causes of variation in epigenetic aging across the lifespan. *Clinical Epigenetics*, *12*(1), 158. https://doi.org/10.1186/s13148-020-00950-1

Li, T., Chen, X., Mascaro, J., Haroon, E., & Rilling, J. K. (2017). Intranasal oxytocin, but not vasopressin, augments neural responses to toddlers in human fathers. *Hormones and Behavior*, *93*, 193–202. https://doi.org/10.1016/j.yhbeh.2017.01.006

Li, W., Wang, Z., Wang, G., Ip, P., Sun, X., Jiang, Y., & Jiang, F. (2021). Socioeconomic inequality in child mental health during the COVID-19 pandemic: First evidence from China. *Journal of Affective Disorders*, *287*, 8–14. https://doi.org/10.1016/j.jad.2021.03.009

Li, Y., Li, H., Decety, J., & Lee, K. (2013). Experiencing a natural disaster alters children's altruistic giving. *Psychological Science*, *24*(9), 1686–1695. https://doi.org/10.1177/0956797613479975

Li, Y., Thompson, W. K., Reuter, C., Nillo, R., Jernigan, T., Dale, A., Sugrue, L. P., & ABCD Consortium. (2021). Rates of incidental findings in brain magnetic resonance imaging in children. *JAMA Neurology*. https://doi.org/10.1001/jamaneurol.2021.0306

Lian, Q., Zuo, X., Mao, Y., Zhang, Y., Luo, S., Zhang, S., Lou, C., Tu, X., & Zhou, W. (2018). The impact of the Wenchuan earthquake on early puberty: A natural experiment. *PeerJ*, *6*, e5085.

Liang, M., Simelane, S., Fillo, G. F., Chalasani, S., Weny, K., Canelos, P. S., Jenkins, L., Moller, A.-B., Chandra-Mouli, V., Say, L., Michielsen, K., Engel, D. M. C., & Snow, R. (2019). The state of adolescent sexual and reproductive health. *Journal of Adolescent Health*, *65*(6), S3–S15.

Liberman, Z., Kinzler, K. D., & Woodward, A. L. (2021). Origins of homophily: Infants expect people with shared preferences to affiliate. *Cognition*, *212*, 104695. https://doi.org/10.1016/j.cognition.2021.104695

Lickliter, R., & Witherington, D. C. (2017). Towards a truly developmental epigenetics. *Human Development*, *60*(2–3). https://www.karger.com/Article/Abstract/477996

Lieberman, A. (2019). *What if all children had access to a PreK4 SA?* New America Foundation.

Lieberman, M. D., & Eisenberger, N. I. (2015). The dorsal anterior cingulate cortex is selective for pain: Results from large-scale reverse inference. *Proceedings of the National Academy of Sciences*, *112*(49), 15250–15255.

Liepmann, H. (2018). The impact of a negative labor demand shock on fertility — evidence from the fall of the Berlin Wall. *Labour Economics*, *54*, 210–224.

Lillard, A. S. (2016). *Montessori: The science behind the genius*. Oxford University Press.

Lillard, A. S. (2017). Why do the children (pretend) play? *Trends in Cognitive Sciences*, *21*(11), 826–834. https://doi.org/10.1016/j.tics.2017.08.001

Lillard, A. S., Lerner, M. D., Hopkins, E. J., Dore, R. A., Smith, E. D., & Palmquist, C. M. (2013). The impact of pretend play on children's development: A review of the evidence. *Psychological Bulletin*, *139*(1), 1.

Lim, N. (2016). Cultural differences in emotion: Differences in emotional arousal level between the East and the West. *Integrative Medicine Research*, *5*(2), 105–109. https://doi.org/10.1016/j.imr.2016.03.004

Lima Santos, J. P., Kontos, A. P., Mailliard, S., Eagle, S. R., Holland, C. L., Suss, S. J., Abdul-waalee, H., Stiffler, R. S., Bitzer, H. B., Blaney, N. A., Colorito, A. T., Santucci, C. G., Brown, A., Kim, T., Iyengar, S., Skeba, A., Diler, R. S., Ladouceur, C. D., Phillips, M. L., . . . Versace, A. (2021). White matter abnormalities associated with prolonged recovery in adolescents following concussion. *Frontiers in Neurology*, *12*, 681467. https://doi.org/10.3389/fneur.2021.681467

Limpo, T., & Graham, S. (2020). The role of handwriting instruction in writers' education. *British Journal of Educational Studies*, *68*(3), 311–329. https://doi.org/10.1080/00071005.2019.1692127

Lin, H.-P., Chen, K.-L., Chou, W., Yuan, K.-S., Yen, S.-Y., Chen, Y.-S., & Chow, J. C. (2020). Prolonged touch screen device usage is associated with emotional and behavioral problems, but not language delay, in toddlers. *Infant Behavior and Development*, *58*, 101424. https://doi.org/10.1016/j.infbeh.2020.101424

Lin, Q.-M., Spruyt, K., Leng, Y., Jiang, Y.-R., Wang, G.-H., Dong, S.-M., Mei, H., & Jiang, F. (2019). Cross-cultural disparities of subjective sleep parameters and their age-related trends over the first three years of human life: A systematic review and meta-analysis. *Sleep Medicine Reviews*, *48*, 101203. https://doi.org/10.1016/j.smrv.2019.07.006

Lin, Y., Stavans, M., & Baillargeon, R. (2021). Infants' physical reasoning and the cognitive architecture that supports it. In O. Houdé & G. Borst (Eds.), *Cambridge handbook of cognitive development*. Cambridge University Press.

Linares, R., Bajo, M. T., & Pelegrina, S. (2016). Age-related differences in working memory updating components. *Journal of Experimental Child Psychology*, *147*, 39–52. https://doi.org/10.1016/j.jecp.2016.02.009

Lindberg, L. D., Maddow-Zimet, I., & Marcell, A. V. (2019). Prevalence of sexual initiation before age 13 years among male adolescents and young adults in the United States. *JAMA Pediatrics*, *173*(6), 553–560. https://doi.org/10.1001/jamapediatrics.2019.0458

Lin-Siegler, X., Ahn, J. N., Chen, J., Fang, F.-F. A., & Luna-Lucero, M. (2016). Even Einstein struggled: Effects of learning about great scientists' struggles on high school students' motivation to learn science. *Journal of Educational Psychology, 108*(3), 314–328. https://doi.org/10.1037/edu0000092

Lipina, S. J., Martelli, M. I., Vuelta, B., & Colombo, J. A. (2005). Performance on the A-not-B task of Argentinean infants from unsatisfied and satisfied basic needs homes. *Revista Interamericana de Psicología/Interamerican Journal of Psychology, 39*(1), 49–60.

Lippman, L. H., Ryberg, R., Carney, R., & Moore, K. A. (2015). *Workforce connections: Key "soft skills" that foster youth workforce success: Toward a consensus across fields.* Child Trends.

Listman, J. D., & Dingus-Eason, J. (2018). How to be a deaf scientist: Building navigational capital. *Journal of Diversity in Higher Education, 11* (3), 279–294. https://doi.org/10.1037/dhe0000049

Liston, C., McEwen, B. S., & Casey, B. J. (2009). Psychosocial stress reversibly disrupts prefrontal processing and attentional control. *Proceedings of the National Academy of Sciences, 106*(3), 912–917. https://doi.org/10.1073/pnas.0807041106

Litovsky, R. (2015). Development of the auditory system. In M. J. Aminoff, F. Boller, D. F. Swaab (Eds.), *Handbook of clinical neurology* (Vol. 129, pp. 55–72). Elsevier. https://www.ncbi.nlm.nih.gov/pmc/articles/PMC4612629/

Little, E. E., Legare, C. H., & Carver, L. J. (2019). Culture, carrying, and communication: Beliefs and behavior associated with babywearing. *Infant Behavior and Development, 57*, 101320. https://doi.org/10.1016/j.infbeh.2019.04.002

Liu, B., Du, Y., Wu, Y., Sun, Y., Santillan, M. K., Santillan, D. A., & Bao, W. (2021). Prevalence and distribution of electronic cigarette use before and during pregnancy among women in 38 states of the United States. *Nicotine & Tobacco Research, ntab041*. https://doi.org/10.1093/ntr/ntab041

Liu, C., Moore, G. A., Beekman, C., Pérez-Edgar, K. E., Leve, L. D., Shaw, D. S., Ganiban, J. M., Natsuaki, M. N., Reiss, D., & Neiderhiser, J. M. (2018). Developmental patterns of anger from infancy to middle childhood predict problem behaviors at age 8. *Developmental Psychology, 54*(11), 2090–2100. https://doi.org/10.1037/dev0000589

Liu, D., Chen, D., & Brown, B. B. (2020). Do parenting practices and child disclosure predict parental knowledge? A meta-analysis. *Journal of Youth and Adolescence, 49*(1), 1–16. https://doi.org/10.1007/s10964-019-01154-4

Liu, J., Chen, Y., Stephens, R., Cornea, E., Goldman, B., Gilmore, J. H., & Gao, W. (2021). Hippocampal functional connectivity development during the first two years indexes 4-year working memory performance. *Cortex, 138*, 165–177. https://doi.org/10.1016/j.cortex.2021.02.005

Liu, J. L., Harkness, S., & Super, C. M. (2020). Chinese mothers' cultural models of children's shyness: Ethnotheories and socialization strategies in the context of social change. *New Directions for Child and Adolescent Development, 2020*(170), 69–92. https://doi.org/10.1002/cad.20340

Liu, J., Hayes, M. S., & Gershenson, S. (2022). JUE insight: From referrals to suspensions: New evidence on racial disparities in exclusionary discipline. *Journal of Urban Economics*, 103453. https://doi.org/10.1016/j.jue.2022.103453

Liu, Q., & Wang, Z. (2021). Associations between parental emotional warmth, parental attachment, peer attachment, and adolescents' character strengths. *Children and Youth Services Review, 120*, 105765. https://doi.org/10.1016/j.childyouth.2020.105765

Liu, R. T., Walsh, R. F. L., Sheehan, A. E., Cheek, S. M., & Sanzari, C. M. (2022). Prevalence and correlates of suicide and nonsuicidal self-injury in children: A systematic review and meta-analysis. *JAMA Psychiatry, 79*(7), 718–726. https://doi.org/10.1001/jamapsychiatry.2022.1256

Liu, S., Yu, Q., Li, Z., Cunha, P. M., Zhang, Y., Kong, Z., Lin, W., Chen, S., & Cai, Y. (2020). Effects of acute and chronic exercises on executive function in children and adolescents: A systemic review and meta-analysis. *Frontiers in Psychology*, 11. https://www.frontiersin.org/article/10.3389/fpsyg.2020.554915

Liu, X., Nie, Z., Chen, J., Guo, X., Ou, Y., Chen, G., Mai, J., Gong, W., Wu, Y., Gao, X., Qu, Y., Bell, E. M., Lin, S., & Zhuang, J. (2018). Does maternal environmental tobacco smoke interact with social-demographics and environmental factors on congenital heart defects? *Environmental Pollution, 234*, 214–222. https://doi.org/10.1016/j.envpol.2017.11.023

Livingston, G. (2018, January 18). *U.S. women more likely to have children than a decade ago.* Pew Research Center's Social & Demographic Trends Project. https://www.pewresearch.org/social-trends/2018/01/18/theyre-waiting-longer-but-u-s-women-today-more-likely-to-have-children-than-a-decade-ago/

Livingston, G., & Brown, A. (2017, May 18). *Intermarriage in the U.S. 50 years after loving v. Virginia.* Pew Research Center's Social & Demographic Trends Project. http://www.pewsocialtrends.org/2017/05/18/intermarriage-in-the-u-s-50-years-after-loving-v-virginia/

Lo, C. O., & Porath, M. (2017). Paradigm shifts in gifted education: An examination vis-a-vis its historical situatedness and pedagogical sensibilities. *Gifted Child Quarterly, 61*(4), 343–360.

Lobel, A., Engels, R. C., Stone, L. L., Burk, W. J., & Granic, I. (2017). Video gaming and children's psychosocial wellbeing: A longitudinal study. *Journal of Youth and Adolescence, 46*(4), 884–897.

LoBraico, E. J., Brinberg, M., Ram, N., & Fosco, G. M. (2020). Exploring processes in day-to-day parent–adolescent conflict and angry mood: Evidence for circular causality. *Family Process, 59*(4), 1706–1721. https://doi.org/10.1111/famp.12506

LoBue, V., & Adolph, K. E. (2019). Fear in infancy: Lessons from snakes, spiders, heights, and strangers. *Developmental Psychology, 55*(9), 1889–1907. https://doi.org/10.1037/dev0000675

LoBue, V., Reider, L. B., Kim, E., Burris, J. L., Oleas, D. S., Buss, K. A., Pérez-Edgar, K., & Field, A. P. (2020). The importance of using multiple outcome measures in infant research. *Infancy, 25*(4), 420–437. https://doi.org/10.1111/infa.12339

Locke, J. (1847). *An essay concerning human understanding.* Kay & Troutman. (Original work published 1690)

Locke, J. L., & Bogin, B. (2006). Language and life history: A new perspective on the development and evolution of human language. *Behavioral and Brain Sciences, 29*(3), 259–280.

Loeb, E. L., Kansky, J., Narr, R. K., Fowler, C., & Allen, J. P. (2020). Romantic relationship churn in early adolescence predicts hostility, abuse, and avoidance in relationships into early adulthood. *The Journal of Early Adolescence, 40*(8), 1195–1225. https://doi.org/10.1177/0272431619899477

Loeb, S. (2016). *Missing the target: We need to focus on informal care rather than preschool.* Brookings.

Loebach, J., & Gilliland, J. (2019). Examining the social and built environment factors influencing children's independent use of their neighborhoods and the experience of local settings as child-friendly. *Journal of Planning Education and Research*, 0739456X19828444. https://doi.org/10.1177/0739456X19828444

Logan, K., Cuff, S., Council on Sports Medicine and Fitness, LaBella, C. R., Brooks, M. A., Canty, G., Diamond, A. B., Hennrikus, W., Moffatt, K., Nemeth, B. A., Pengel, K. B., Peterson, A. R., & Stricker, P. R. (2019). Organized sports for children, preadolescents, and adolescents. *Pediatrics, 143*(6), e20190997. https://doi.org/10.1542/peds.2019-0997

Logan, R. W., & McClung, C. A. (2019). Rhythms of life: Circadian disruption and brain disorders across the lifespan. *Nature Reviews Neuroscience, 20*(1), 49–65. https://doi.org/10.1038/s41583-018-0088-y

Logel, C., Hall, W., Page-Gould, E., & Cohen, G. L. (2019). Why is it so hard to change? The role of self-integrity threat and affirmation in weight loss. *European Journal of Social Psychology, 49*(4), 748–759.

Logue, D., Madigan, S. M., Delahunt, E., Heinen, M., Mc Donnell, S. J., & Corish, C. A. (2018). Low energy availability in athletes: A review of prevalence, dietary patterns, physiological health, and sports performance. *Sports Medicine, 48*(1), 73–96.

Lomawaima, K. T., Brayboy, B. M. J., & McCarty, T. L. (2018). Editors' Introduction to the Special Issue: Native American Boarding School Stories. *Journal of American Indian Education, 57*(1), 1–10.

London, R. A. (2019a). *Rethinking Recess: Creating Safe and Inclusive Playtime for All Children in School.* Harvard.

London, R. A. (2019b). The right to play: Eliminating the opportunity gap in elementary school recess. *Phi Delta Kappan, 101*(3), 48–52.

Loomis, A. M. (2018). The role of preschool as a point of intervention and prevention for trauma-exposed children: Recommendations for practice, policy, and research. *Topics in Early Childhood Special Education, 38*(3), 134–145. https://doi.org/10.1177/0271121418789254

López, B. G., Luque, A., & Piña-Watson, B. (2021). Context, intersectionality, and resilience: Moving toward a more holistic study of bilingualism in cognitive science. *Cultural Diversity and Ethnic Minority Psychology*. https://doi.org/10.1037/cdp0000472

Lopez, L. D., Walle, E. A., Pretzer, G. M., & Warlaumont, A. S. (2020). Adult responses to infant prelinguistic vocalizations are associated with infant vocabulary: A home observation study. *PLOS One, 15*(11), e0242232. https://doi.org/10.1371/journal.pone.0242232

López-Vicente, M., Garcia-Aymerich, J., Torrent-Pallicer, J., Forns, J., Ibarluzea, J., Lertxundi, N., González, L., Valera-Gran, D., Torrent, M., Dadvand, P., Vrijheid, M., & Sunyer, J. (2017). Are early physical activity and sedentary behaviors related to working memory at 7 and 14 years of age? *The Journal of Pediatrics, 188*, 35–41.

Lorber, M. F., Del Vecchio, T., & Slep, A. M. S. (2018). The development of individual physically aggressive behaviors from infancy to toddlerhood. *Developmental Psychology, 54*(4), 601–612. https://doi.org/10.1037/dev0000450

LoRe, D., Ladner, P., & Suskind, D. (2018). Talk, read, sing: Early language exposure as an overlooked social determinant of health. *Pediatrics, 142*(3).

Lorek, M., Tobolska-Lorek, D., Kalina-Faska, B., Januszek-Trzciakowska, A., & Gawlik, A. (2019). Clinical and biochemical phenotype of adolescent males with gynecomastia. *Journal of Clinical Research in Pediatric Endocrinology, 11*(4), 388.

Lorenz, K. (1981). *The foundations of ethology.* Springer Science & Business Media.

Lorenzetti, V., Hoch, E., & Hall, W. (2020). Adolescent cannabis use, cognition, brain health and educational outcomes: A review of the evidence. *European Neuropsychopharmacology, 36,* 169–180. https://doi.org/10.1016/j.euroneuro.2020.03.012

Lott, I. T., & Head, E. (2019). Dementia in Down syndrome: Unique insights for Alzheimer disease research. *Nature Reviews Neurology, 15*(3), 135–147. https://doi.org/10.1038/s41582-018-0132-6

Lou, H. C., Rømer Thomsen, K., & Changeux, J.-P. (2020). The molecular organization of self-awareness: Paralimbic dopamine-GABA interaction. *Frontiers in Systems Neuroscience, 14,* 3. https://doi.org/10.3389/fnsys.2020.00003

Louis-Jacques, A. F., & Stuebe, A. M. (2020). enabling breastfeeding to support lifelong health for mother and child. *Obstetrics and Gynecology Clinics, 47*(3), 363–381. https://doi.org/10.1016/j.ogc.2020.04.001

Louv, R. (2008). *Last child in the woods: Saving our children from nature-deficit disorder.* Algonquin Books of Chapel Hill. https://www.google.com/books/edition/Last_Child_in_the_Woods/WnLBBwAAQBAJ?hl=en&gbpv=1&dq=louv+play+&pg=PP1&printsec=frontcover

Loveless, T. (2016, March 24). *2016 Brown Center report on American education: How well are American students learning?* Brookings. https://www.brookings.edu/research/2016-brown-center-report-on-american-education-how-well-are-american-students-learning/

Lowry, R., Johns, M. M., Gordon, A. R., Austin, S. B., Robin, L. E., & Kann, L. K. (2018). Nonconforming gender expression and associated mental distress and substance use among high school students. *JAMA Pediatrics, 172*(11), 1020–1028. https://doi.org/10.1001/jamapediatrics.2018.2140

Loyd, A. B., & Gaither, S. E. (2018). Racial/ethnic socialization for White youth: What we know and future directions. *Journal of Applied Developmental Psychology, 59,* 54–64. https://doi.org/10.1016/j.appdev.2018.05.004

Lozada, M., & Carro, N. (2016). Embodied action improves cognition in children: Evidence from a study based on Piagetian conservation tasks. *Frontiers in Psychology, 7,* 393.

Lubans, D., Richards, J., Hillman, C., Faulkner, G., Beauchamp, M., Nilsson, M., Kelly, P., Smith, J., Raine, L., & Biddle, S. (2016). Physical activity for cognitive and mental health in youth: A systematic review of mechanisms. *Pediatrics, 138*(3).

Luby, J. L., Baram, T. Z., Rogers, C. E., & Barch, D. M. (2020). Neurodevelopmental optimization after early-life adversity: Cross-species studies to elucidate sensitive periods and brain mechanisms to inform early intervention. *Trends in Neurosciences, 43*(10), 744–751. https://doi.org/10.1016/j.tins.2020.08.001

Luciano, E. C., & Orth, U. (2017). Transitions in romantic relationships and development of self-esteem. *Journal of Personality and Social Psychology, 112*(2), 307.

Ludwig, C. A., Callaway, N. F., Fredrick, D. R., Blumenkranz, M. S., & Moshfeghi, D. M. (2016). What colour are newborns' eyes? Prevalence of iris colour in the Newborn Eye Screening Test (NEST) study. *Acta Ophthalmologica, 94*(5), 485–488. https://doi.org/10.1111/aos.13006

Lugo-Candelas, C. I., Harvey, E. A., & Breaux, R. P. (2015). Emotion socialization practices in Latina and European-American mothers of preschoolers with behavior problems. *Journal of Family Studies, 21*(2), 144–162. https://doi-org.mimas.calstatela.edu/10.1080/13229400.2015.1020982

Luhmann, M., Orth, U., Specht, J., Kandler, C., & Lucas, R. E. (2014). Studying changes in life circumstances and personality: It's about time. *European Journal of Personality, 28*(3), 256–266.

Luke, B., Brown, M. B., Wantman, E., Forestieri, N. E., Browne, M. L., Fisher, S. C., Yazdy, M. M., Ethen, M. K., Canfield, M. A., Watkins, S., Nichols, H. B., Farland, L. V., Oehninger, S., Doody, K. J., Eisenberg, M. L., & Baker, V. L. (2021). The risk of birth defects with conception by ART. *Human Reproduction, 36*(1), 116–129. https://doi.org/10.1093/humrep/deaa272

Lum, Z.-A. (2011, March). South Asian students on "Frenchies," ethnic cliques and the new cool. *The Vancouver Observer.*

Luna, B., Garver, K. E., Urban, T. A., Lazar, N. A., & Sweeney, J. A. (2004). Maturation of cognitive processes from late childhood to adulthood. *Child Development, 75*(5), 1357–1372. https://doi.org/10.1111/j.1467-8624.2004.00745.x

Lundberg, K. (2021). *Despite pandemic, civically engaged youth report higher well-being* (CIRCLE / Tisch College Post-Election Youth Poll). Tufts University. https://circle.tufts.edu/latest-research/despite-pandemic-civically-engaged-youth-report-higher-well-being

Lundkvist-Houndoumadi, I., & Thastum, M. (2013). A "Cool Kids" cognitive-behavioral therapy group for youth with anxiety disorders: Part 1, the case of Erik. *Pragmatic Case Studies in Psychotherapy, 9*(2), 122–178.

Lundquist, J. H., & Curington, C. V. (2019). Love me tinder, love me sweet. *Contexts, 18*(4), 22–27. https://doi.org/10.1177/1536504219883848

Lundquist, J. H., & Lin, K. H. (2015). Is love (color) blind? The economy of race among gay and straight daters. *Social Forces, 93*(4), 1423–1449.

Lundy, A., & Trawick-Smith, J. (2021). Effects of active outdoor play on preschool children's on-task classroom behavior. *Early Childhood Education Journal, 49*(3), 463–471. https://doi.org/10.1007/s10643-020-01086-w

Lunkenheimer, E., Lichtwarck-Aschoff, A., Hollenstein, T., Kemp, C. J., & Granic, I. (2016). Breaking the coercive cycle: How parent and child risk factors influence real-time variability in parental responses to child misbehavior. *Parenting, 16*(4), 237–256.

Luthar, S. S., & Ciciolla, L. (2016). What it feels like to be a mother: Variations by children's developmental stages. *Developmental Psychology, 52*(1), 143–154. https://doi.org/10.1037/dev0000062

Luthar, S. S., & Eisenberg, N. (2017). Resilient adaptation among at-risk children: Harnessing science toward maximizing salutary environments. *Child Development, 88*(2), 337–349.

Lynch, A. W. (2018). Identity and literacy practices in a bilingual classroom: An exploration of leveraging community cultural wealth. *Bilingual Research Journal, 41*(2), 117–132. https://doi.org/10.1080/15235882.2018.1452312

Lyons, H. A., Manning, W. D., Longmore, M. A., & Giordano, P. C. (2014). Young adult casual sexual behavior: Life course specific motivations and consequences. *Sociological Perspectives, 57*(1), 79–101. https://doi.org/10.1177/0731121413517557

Lyons, H. A., Manning, W. D., Longmore, M. A., & Giordano, P. C. (2015). Gender and casual sexual activity from adolescence to emerging adulthood: Social and life course correlates. *Journal of Sex Research, 52*(5), 543–557. https://doi.org/10.1080/00224499.2014.906032

Ma, J., Pender, M., & Welch, M. (2016). *Education pays 2016: The benefits of higher education for individuals and society* (Trends in Higher Education Series). College Board. https://eric.ed.gov/?id=ED572548

Ma, J., Pender, M., & Welch, M. (2020). *Education pays 2019: The benefits of higher education for individuals and society* (Trends in Higher Education Series). College Board.

Määttä, S., Laakso, M.-L., Tolvanen, A., Ahonen, T., & Aro, T. (2014). Children with differing developmental trajectories of prelinguistic communication skills: Language and working memory at age 5. *Journal of Speech, Language, and Hearing Research, 57*(3), 1026–1039. https://doi.org/10.1044/2014_JSLHR-L-13-0012

Maccoby, E. E. (1992). The role of parents in the socialization of children: An historical overview. *Developmental Psychology, 28*(6), 1006–1017.

Maccoby, E. E., & Jacklin, C. N. (1987). Gender segregation in childhood. In H. W. Reese (Ed.), *Advances in child development and behavior* (Vol. 20, pp. 239–287). JAI. https://doi.org/10.1016/S0065-2407(08)60404-8

Maccoby, E. E., & Martin, J. A. (1983). Socialization in the context of the family: Parent-child interaction. In P. H. Mussen & E. M. Hetherington (Eds.), *Handbook of child psychology* (pp. 1–101). Wiley.

MacDonald, T. K. (2019). Lactation care for transgender and non-binary patients: Empowering clients and avoiding aversives. *Journal of Human Lactation, 35*(2), 223–226. https://doi.org/10.1177/0890334419830989

Maciejewski, D. F., van Lier, P. A., Branje, S. J., Meeus, W. H., & Koot, H. M. (2015). A 5-year longitudinal study on mood variability across adolescence using daily diaries. *Child Development, 86*(6), 1908–1921.

Mackes, N. K., Golm, D., Sarkar, S., Kumsta, R., Rutter, M., Fairchild, G., Mehta, M. A., Sonuga-Barke, E. J. S., & on behalf of the ERA Young Adult Follow-up Team. (2020). Early childhood deprivation is associated with alterations in adult brain structure despite subsequent envi-ronmental enrichment. *Proceedings of the National Academy of Sciences, 117*(1), 641–649. https://doi.org/10.1073/pnas.1911264116

MacLeod, C. (2009). The invention of heroes. *Nature, 460*(7255), 572–573. https://doi.org/10.1038/460572a

Macmillan, R., & Shanahan, M. J. (2021). Why precarious work is bad for health: Social marginality as key mechanisms in a multi-national context. *Social Forces,* soab006. https://doi.org/10.1093/sf/soab006

MacMullin, L. N., Bokeloh, L. M., Nabbijohn, A. N., Santarossa, A., van der Miesen, A. I., Peragine, D. E., & VanderLaan, D. P. (2021). Examining the relation between gender nonconformity and psychological well-being in children: The roles of peers and parents. *Archives of Sexual Behavior, 50*(3), 823–841.

MacNeilage, P. F. (2008). *The origin of speech* (No. 10). Oxford University Press.

MacPhee, D., & Prendergast, S. (2019). Room for improvement: Girls' and boys' home environments are still gendered. *Sex Roles, 80*(5), 332–346. https://doi.org/10.1007/s11199-018-0936-2

MacPhee, D., Prendergast, S., Albrecht, E., Walker, A. K., & Miller-Heyl, J. (2018). The child-rearing environment and children's mastery motivation as contributors to school readiness. *Journal of Applied Developmental Psychology, 56,* 1–12.

MacSwan, J., Thompson, M. S., Rolstad, K., McAlister, K., & Lobo, G. (2017). Three theories of the effects of language education programs: An empirical evaluation of bilingual and English-only policies. *Annual Review of Applied Linguistics, 37,* 218–240.

MacWhinney, B. (2017). First language acquisition. In M. Aronoff & J. Ress-Miller (Eds.), *The handbook of linguistics* (2nd ed., pp. 397–413). Wiley. https://doi.org /10.1002/9781119072256.ch19

Maddow-Zimet, I., & Kost, K. (2021). *Pregnancies, births and abortions in the United States, 1973–2017: National and state trends by age.* Guttmacher Institute. https://www.guttmacher.org/report/pregnancies-births -abortions-in-united-states-1973-2017

Mader, J. (2020, February 8). How play is making a comeback in kindergarten. *The Hechinger Report.* http:// hechingerreport.org/play-based-kindergarten-makes -a-comeback/

Madigan, S., Browne, D., Racine, N., Mori, C., & Tough, S. (2019). Association between screen time and children's performance on a developmental screening test. *JAMA Pediatrics, 173*(3), 244–250. https://doi.org /10.1001/jamapediatrics.2018.5056

Madigan, S., McArthur, B. A., Anhorn, C., Eirich, R., & Christakis, D. A. (2020). Associations between screen use and child language skills: A systematic review and meta-analysis. *JAMA Pediatrics, 174*(7), 665–675. https://doi.org/10.1001/jamapediatrics.2020.0327

Madigan, S., Racine, N., & Tough, S. (2020). Prevalence of preschoolers meeting vs exceeding screen time guidelines. *JAMA Pediatrics, 174*(1), 93–95. https://doi .org/10.1001/jamapediatrics.2019.4495

Madrigal, A. C. (2017, November 7). Should children form emotional bonds with robots? *The Atlantic.* https:// www.theatlantic.com/magazine/archive/2017/12 /my-sons-first-robot/544137/

Magai, C., & McFadden, S. H. (1995). *The role of emotions in social and personality development: History, theory and research.* Springer Science & Business Media.

Magallón, S., Narbona, J., & Crespo-Eguílaz, N. (2016). Acquisition of motor and cognitive skills through repetition in typically developing children. *PLOS ONE, 11*(7), e0158684. https://doi.org/10.1371 /journal.pone.0158684

Magette, A. L., Durtschi, J. A., & Love, H. A. (2018). Lesbian, gay, and bisexual substance use in emerging adulthood moderated by parent-child relationships in adolescence. *The American Journal of Family Therapy, 46*(3), 272–286.

Magnus, M. C., Guyatt, A. L., Lawn, R. B., Wyss, A. B., Trajanoska, K., Küpers, L. K., Rivadeneira, F., Tobin, M. D., London, S. J., Lawlor, D. A., Millard, L. A. C., & Fraser, A. (2020). Identifying potential causal effects of age at menarche: A Mendelian randomization phenome-wide association study. *BMC Medicine, 18*(1), 71. https://doi.org/10.1186/s12916-020-01515-y

Magnusson, C., & Nermo, M. (2018). From childhood to young adulthood: The importance of self-esteem during childhood for occupational achievements among young men and women. *Journal of Youth Studies, 21*(10), 1392–1410.

Maheux, A. J., Nesi, J., Galla, B. M., Roberts, S. R., & Choukas-Bradley, S. (2021). #Grateful: Longitudinal associations between adolescents' social media use and gratitude during the COVID-19 pandemic. *Journal of Research on Adolescence, 31*(3), 734–747. https://doi.org /10.1111/jora.12650

Mahler, M. S. (1974). Symbiosis and individuation. *The Psychoanalytic Study of the Child, 29*(1), 89–106. https://doi.org/10.1080/00797308.1974.11822615

Mahoney, J. L., Weissberg, R. P., Greenberg, M. T., Dusenbury, L., Jagers, R. J., Niemi, K., Schlinger, M., Schlund, J., Shriver, T. P., VanAusdal, K., & Yoder, N. (2021). Systemic social and emotional learning: Promoting educational success for all preschool to high school students. *American Psychologist, 76*(7), 1128–1142. https://doi.org/10.1037/amp0000701

Mahrer, N. E., O'Hara, K. L., Sandler, I. N., & Wolchik, S. A. (2018). Does shared parenting help or hurt children in high-conflict divorced families? *Journal of Divorce & Remarriage, 59*(4), 324–347. https://doi.org /10.1080/10502556.2018.1454200

Main, M., Kaplan, N., & Cassidy, J. (1985). Security in infancy, childhood, and adulthood: A move to the level of representation. *Monographs of the Society for Research in Child Development, 50*(1–2), 66–104.

Main, M., & Solomon, J. (1986). Discovery of an insecure-disorganized/disoriented attachment pattern. In T. Brazelton (Ed.), *Affective development in infancy* (pp. 95–124). Ablex.

Mak, H. W., Fosco, G. M., & Lanza, S. T. (2021). Dynamic associations of parent–adolescent closeness and friend support with adolescent depressive symptoms across ages 12–19. *Journal of Research on Adolescence, 31*(2), 299–316. https://doi.org/10.1111 /jora.12597

Maldeniya, D., Varghese, A., Stuart, T., & Romero, D. M. (2017). The role of optimal distinctiveness and homophily in online dating. *Proceedings of the International AAAI Conference on Web and Social Media, 11*(1), 616–619.

Male, C., & Q. Wodon. (2017). *Disability gaps in educational attainment and literacy: The price of exclusion.* Disability and Education Notes Series. The World Bank.

Malik, R., Hamm, K., Lee, W. F., Davis, E. E., & Sojourner, A. (2020). *The coronavirus will make child care deserts worse and exacerbate inequality.* Center for American Progress.

Malina, R. M., Kozieł, S. M., Králik, M., Chrzanowska, M., & Suder, A. (2020). Prediction of maturity offset and age at peak height velocity in a longitudinal series of boys and girls. *American Journal of Human Biology,* e23551.

Mallett, C. A. (2016). The school-to-prison pipeline: A critical review of the punitive paradigm shift. *Child and Adolescent Social Work Journal, 33*(1), 15–24.

Malone, J. C. (2014). Did John B. Watson really "found" behaviorism? *The Behavior Analyst, 37*(1), 1–12. https://doi.org/10.1007/s40614-014-0004-3

Malone, J. C. (2017). John B. Watson. In J. Vonk & T. Shackelford (Eds.), *Encyclopedia of animal cognition and behavior* (pp. 978–983). Springer. https://doi.org /10.1007/978-3-319-47829-6

Malti, T., & Dys, S. P. (2018). From being nice to being kind: Development of prosocial behaviors. *Current Opinion in Psychology, 20,* 45-49.

Mamedova, S., & Pawlowski, E. (2019). *Adult literacy in the United States.* Data Point, NCES 2019179. National Center for Education Statistics.

Mamedova, S., & Pawlowski, E. (2020). *Adult numeracy in the United States.* Data Point, NCES 2020-025. National Center for Education Statistics.

Mamedova, S., Stephens, M., Liao, Y., Sennett, J., Sirma, P., & Burg, S. S. (2021). 2012–2016 Program for International Student Assessment Young Adult Follow-up Study (PISA YAFS): How reading and mathematics performance at age 15 relate to literacy and numeracy skills and education, workforce, and life outcomes at age 19 (NCES 2021–029). U.S. Department of Education.

Manczak, E. M., & Gotlib, I. H. (2019). Lipid profiles at birth predict teacher-rated child emotional and social development 5 years later. *Psychological Science, 30*(12), 1780–1789. https://doi.org/10.1177 /0956797619885649

Mandlik, N., & Kamat, D. (2020). Medical anthropology in pediatrics: Improving disparities by partnering with families. *Pediatric Annals, 49*(5), e222–e227. http://dx.doi.org/10.3928/19382359-20200421-02

Manfredi, C., Viellevoye, R., Orlandi, S., Torres-García, A., Pieraccini, G., & Reyes-García, C. A. (2019). Automated analysis of newborn cry: Relationships between melodic shapes and native language. *Biomedical Signal Processing and Control, 53,* 101561. https://doi.org/10.1016/j.bspc.2019.101561

Manfredi-Lozano, M., Roa, J., & Tena-Sempere, M. (2018). Connecting metabolism and gonadal function: novel central neuropeptide pathways involved in the metabolic control of puberty and fertility. *Frontiers in neuroendocrinology, 48,* 37–49.

Mannheim, K. (1970). The problem of generations. *Psychoanalytic Review, 57*(3), 378–404.

Manning, B. L., Roberts, M. Y., Estabrook, R., Petitclerc, A., Burns, J. L., Briggs-Gowan, M., Wakschlag, L. S., & Norton, E. S. (2019). Relations between toddler expressive language and temper tantrums in a community sample. *Journal of Applied Developmental Psychology, 65,* 101070. https://doi.org /10.1016/j.appdev.2019.101070

Manning, K. Y., Long, X., Watts, D., Tomfohr-Madsen, L., Giesbrecht, G. F., & Lebel, C. (2021). Prenatal maternal distress during the COVID-19 pandemic and its effects on the infant brain. *medRxiv.* https://doi.org/10.1101/2021.10.04.21264536

Manning, W. D. (2020). Young adulthood relationships in an era of uncertainty: A case for cohabitation. *Demography, 57*(3), 799–819. https://doi.org/10.1007 /s13524-020-00881-9

Manning, W. D., Smock, P. J., & Fettro, M. N. (2019). Cohabitation and marital expectations among single millennials in the U.S. *Population Research and Policy Review, 38*(3), 327–346. https://doi.org/10.1007 /s11113-018-09509-8

Marans, S., & Hahn, H. (2017). *Enhancing police responses to children exposed to violence: A toolkit for law enforcement.* International Association of Chiefs of Police and Yale Child Study Center, Office of Juvenile Justice and Delinquency Prevention, Office of Justice Programs, U.S. Department of Justice.

Marçal, K. E. (2021). Pathways to adolescent emotional and behavioral problems: An examination of maternal depression and harsh parenting. *Child Abuse & Neglect, 113,* 104917. https://doi.org/10.1016/j .chiabu.2020.104917

Marcelo, A. K., & Yates, T. M. (2019). Young children's ethnic–racial identity moderates the impact of early discrimination experiences on child behavior problems. *Cultural Diversity and Ethnic Minority Psychology, 25*(2), 253.

Marchesini, E., Morfini, M., & Valentino, L. (2021). Recent advances in the treatment of hemophilia: A review. *Biologics: Targets & Therapy, 15,* 221.

Marchi, J., Berg, M., Dencker, A., Olander, E. K., & Begley, C. (2015). Risks associated with obesity in pregnancy, for the mother and baby: A systematic review of reviews. *Obesity Reviews, 16*(8), 621–638. https://doi.org/10.1111/obr.12288

Marcovitch, S., & Zelazo, P. D. (1999). The A-not-B error: Results from a logistic meta-analysis. *Child Development, 70*(6), 1297–1313.

Marcovitch, S., Clearfield, M. W., Swingler, M., Calkins, S. D., & Bell, M. A. (2016). Attentional predictors of 5-month-olds' performance on a looking A-not-B task. *Infant and Child Development, 25*(4), 233–246.

Marcus, J. (2021, October 10). Why college graduation rates are measured over six years instead of four. The Hechinger Report. http://hechingerreport.org/how-the-college-lobby-got-the-government-to-measure-graduation-rates-over-six-years-instead-of-four/

Marengo, D., Longobardi, C., Fabris, M. A., & Settanni, M. (2018). Highly-visual social media and internalizing symptoms in adolescence: The mediating role of body image concerns. *Computers in Human Behavior, 82*, 63–69. https://doi.org/10.1016/j.chb.2018.01.003

Marey-Sarwan, I., Keller, H., & Otto, H. (2016). Stay close to me: Stranger anxiety and maternal beliefs about children's socio-emotional development among Bedouins in the unrecognized villages in the Naqab. *Journal of Cross-Cultural Psychology, 47*(3), 319–332. https://doi.org/10.1177/0022022115619231

Margolis, A. A. (2020). Zone of proximal development, scaffolding and teaching practice. *Cultural-Historical Psychology, 16*(3), 15–26.

Margoni, F., & Surian, L. (2018). Infants' evaluation of prosocial and antisocial agents: A meta-analysis. *Developmental Psychology, 54*(8), 1445.

Marini, S., Davis, K. A., Soare, T. W., Zhu, Y., Suderman, M. J., Simpkin, A. J., Smith, A. D. A. C., Wolf, E. J., Relton, C. L., & Dunn, E. C. (2020). Adversity exposure during sensitive periods predicts accelerated epigenetic aging in children. *Psychoneuroendocrinology, 113*, 104484. https://doi.org/10.1016/j.psyneuen.2019.104484

Marinović, V., & Träuble, B. (2021). Vicarious ostracism and control in young children. *Social Development, 30*(1), 225–238.

Marinović, V., Wahl, S., & Träuble, B. (2017). "Next to you"—Young children sit closer to a person following vicarious ostracism. *Journal of Experimental Child Psychology, 156*, 179–185. https://doi.org/10.1016/j.jecp.2016.11.011

Markey, P. M., Ferguson, C. J., & Hopkins, L. I. (2020). Video game play: Myths and benefits. *American Journal of Play, 13*(1), 87–106.

Marklund, U., Marklund, E., Lacerda, F., & Schwarz, I.-C. (2015). Pause and utterance duration in child-directed speech in relation to child vocabulary size. *Journal of Child Language, 42*(5), 1158–1171. https://doi.org/10.1017/S0305000914000609

Marks, A. K., & García Coll, C. (2018). Education and developmental competencies of ethnic minority children: Recent theoretical and methodological advances. *Developmental Review, 50*, 90–98. https://doi.org/10.1016/j.dr.2018.05.004

Marks, K. J., Whitaker, M., Anglin, O., Milucky, J., Patel, K., Pham, H., Chai, S. J., Kirley, P. D., Armistead, I., McLafferty, S., Meek, J., Yousey-Hindes, K., Anderson, E. J., Openo, K. P., Weigel, A., Henderson, J., Nunez, V. T., Como-Sabetti, K., Lynfield, R., . . . COVID-NET Surveillance Team. (2022). Hospitalizations of children and adolescents with laboratory-confirmed COVID-19 — COVID-NET, 14 States, July 2021–January 2022. *Morbidity and Mortality Weekly Report, 71*(7), 271.

Markus, H. R. (2017). American = independent? *Perspectives on Psychological Science, 12*(5), 855–866. https://doi.org/10.1177/1745691617718799

Marrus, N., Eggebrecht, A. T., Todorov, A., Elison, J. T., Wolff, J. J., Cole, L., Gao, W., Pandey, J., Shen, M. D., Swanson, M. R., Emerson, R. W., Klohr, C. L., Adams, C. M., Estes, A. M., Zwaigenbaum, L., Botteron, K. N., McKinstry, R. C., Constantino, J. N., Evans, A. C., . . . Pruett, J. R., Jr. (2018). Walking, gross motor development, and brain functional connectivity in infants and toddlers. *Cerebral Cortex, 28*(2), 750–763. https://doi.org/10.1093/cercor/bhx313

Marsh, H., Seaton, M., Dicke, T., Parker, P., & Horwood, M. (2019). The centrality of academic self-concept to motivation and learning. In K. Renninger & S. Hidi (Eds.), *The Cambridge handbook of motivation and learning* (pp. 36–62). Cambridge University Press

Marshall, E. A., & Symonds, J. E. (2021). Introduction and overview. In E. A. Marshall & J. E. Symonds (Eds.), *Young adult development at the school-to-work transition: International pathways and processes* (pp. xxi–xxxii). Oxford University Press.

Martin, C. L., Andrews, N. C. Z., England, D. E., Zosuls, K., & Ruble, D. N. (2017). A dual identity approach for conceptualizing and measuring children's gender identity. *Child Development, 88*(1), 167–182. https://doi.org/10.1111/cdev.12568

Martin, C. L., & Halverson, C. F. (1981). A schematic processing model of sex typing and stereotyping in children. *Child Development, 52*(4), 1119–1134. https://doi.org/10.2307/1129498

Martin, C. L., & Ruble, D. N. (2010). Patterns of gender development. *Annual Review of Psychology, 61*, 353–381. https://doi.org/10.1146/annurev.psych.093008.100511

Martin, J., Hamilton, B. E., & Osterman, M. J. K. (2020). *Births in the United States, 2019* (NCHS Data Brief No. 387). https://www.cdc.gov/nchs/products/databriefs/db387.htm

Martin, J. A., Hamilton, B. E., Osterman, M. J. K., & Driscoll, A. K. (2021). Births: Final data for 2019. *National Vital Statistics Reports: From the Centers for Disease Control and Prevention, National Center for Health Statistics, National Vital Statistics System, 70*(2), 1–51.

Martin, M. J., Blozis, S. A., Boeninger, D. K., Masarik, A. S., & Conger, R. D. (2014). The timing of entry into adult roles and changes in trajectories of problem behaviors during the transition to adulthood. *Developmental Psychology, 50*(11), 2473–2484. https://doi.org/10.1037/a0037950

Martínez, E. (2016). *The education deficit: Failures to protect and fulfill the right to education in global development agendas*. Human Rights Watch.

Martinez, G. M., & Abma, J. C. (2020). Sexual activity and contraceptive use among teenagers aged 15–19 in the United States, 2015–2017. *NCHS Data Brief, no 366*. National Center for Health Statistics.

Martinez, M. A., Gutierrez, B. C., Halim, M. L. D., & Leaper, C. (2021). Gender and ethnic variation in emerging adults' recalled dating socialization in relation to current romantic attitudes and relationship experiences. *Sexuality & Culture*. https://doi.org/10.1007/s12119-021-09873-2

Martinez, M. A., Osornio, A., Halim, M. L. D., & Zosuls, K. M. (2019). Gender: Awareness, identity, and stereotyping. In J. B. Benson (Ed.), *Encyclopedia of infant and early child development* (pp. 1–12). Elsevier Science.

Martínez-Patiño, M. J. (2005). Personal account: A woman tried and tested. *The Lancet, 366*, S38. https://doi.org/10.1016/S0140-6736(05)67841-5

Martinez-Torteya, C., D'Amico, J., & Gilchrist, M. (2018). Trauma exposure: Consequences to maternal and offspring stress systems. In M. Muzik & K. L. Rosenblum (Eds.), *Motherhood in the face of trauma: Pathways towards healing and growth* (pp. 85–98). Springer.

Martini, D. N., & Broglio, S. P. (2018). Long-term effects of sport concussion on cognitive and motor performance: A review. *International Journal of Psychophysiology, 132*, 25–30.

Martin-Storey, A., Cheadle, J. E., Skalamera, J., & Crosnoe, R. (2015). Exploring the social integration of sexual minority youth across high school contexts. *Child Development, 86*(3), 965–975. https://doi.org/10.1111/cdev.12352

Martin-Storey, A., & Fish, J. (2019). Victimization disparities between heterosexual and sexual minority youth from ages nine to fifteen. *Child Development, 90*(1), 71–81. https://doi.org/10.1111/cdev.13107

Martos, A. J., Nezhad, S., & Meyer, I. H. (2015). Variations in sexual identity milestones among lesbians, gay men, and bisexuals. *Sexuality Research and Social Policy, 12*(1), 24–33. https://doi.org/http://dx.doi.org/10.1007/s13178-014-0167-4

Marulis, L. M., & Neuman, S. B. (2010). The effects of vocabulary intervention on young children's word learning: A meta-analysis. *Review of Educational Research, 80*(3), 300–335.

Marusak, H. A., Thomason, M. E., Sala-Hamrick, K., Crespo, L., & Rabinak, C. A. (2018). What's parenting got to do with it: Emotional autonomy and brain and behavioral responses to emotional conflict in children and adolescents. *Developmental Science, 21*(4), e12605. https://doi.org/10.1111/desc.12605

Marván, M. L., & Alcalá-Herrera, V. (2019). Menarche: Psychosocial and cultural aspects. In J. M. Ussher, J. C. Chrisler, & J. Perz (Eds.), *Routledge international handbook of women's sexual and reproductive health* (pp. 28–38). Routledge.

Marx, V., & Nagy, E. (2017). Fetal behavioral responses to the touch of the mother's abdomen: A frame-by-frame analysis. *Infant Behavior and Development, 47*, 83–91. https://doi.org/10.1016/j.infbeh.2017.03.005

Marzilli, E., Cerniglia, L., & Cimino, S. (2018). A narrative review of binge eating disorder in adolescence: Prevalence, impact, and psychological treatment strategies. *Adolescent Health, Medicine and Therapeutics, 9*, 17–30. https://doi.org/10.2147/AHMT.S148050

Masek, L. R., McMillan, B. T. M., Paterson, S. J., Tamis-LeMonda, C. S., Golinkoff, R. M., & Hirsh-Pasek, K. (2021a). Where language meets attention: How contingent interactions promote learning. *Developmental Review, 60*, 100961. https://doi.org/10.1016/j.dr.2021.100961

Masek, L. R., Paterson, S. J., Golinkoff, R. M., Bakeman, R., Adamson, L. B., Owen, M. T., Pace, A., & Hirsh-Pasek, K. (2021b). Beyond talk: Contributions of quantity and quality of communication to language success across socioeconomic strata. *Infancy, 26*(1), 123–147.

Maslow, A. H. (1943). A theory of human motivation. *Psychological Review, 50*(4), 370–396. https://doi.org/10.1037/h0054346

Maslow, A. H. (1970). New introduction: Religions, values, and peak-experiences. *Journal of Transpersonal Psychology, 2*(2), 83–90.

Masquelier, B., Hug, L., Sharrow, D., You, D., Mathers, C., Gerland, P., & Alkema, L. (2021). Global, regional, and national mortality trends in youth aged 15–24 years between 1990 and 2019: A systematic analysis. *The Lancet Global Health, 9*(4), e409–e417. https://doi.org/10.1016/S2214-109X(21)00023-1

Massey, W. V., Thalken, J., Szarabajko, A., Neilson, L., & Geldhof, J. (2021). Recess quality and social and behavioral health in elementary school students. *Journal of School Health, 91*(9), 730–740. https://doi.org/10.1111/josh.13065

Massing-Schaffer, M., Nesi, J., Telzer, E. H., Lindquist, K. A., & Prinstein, M. J. (2022). Adolescent peer experiences and prospective suicidal ideation: The protective role of online-only friendships. *Journal of Clinical Child & Adolescent Psychology, 51*(1), 49–60. https://doi.org/10.1080/15374416.2020.1750019

Massonnié, J., Rogers, C. J., Mareschal, D., & Kirkham, N. Z. (2019). Is classroom noise always bad for children? The contribution of age and selective attention to creative performance in noise. *Frontiers in Psychology, 10*, 381.

Masten, A. S., & Cicchetti, D. (2016). Resilience in development: Progress and transformation. In D. Cicchetti (Ed.), *Developmental psychopathology: Risk, resilience, and intervention* (pp. 271–333). Wiley

Masten, A. S., Lucke, C. M., Nelson, K. M., & Stallworthy, I. C. (2021). Resilience in development and psychopathology: Multisystem perspectives. *Annual Review of Clinical Psychology, 17*, 521–549.

Mastro, S., & Zimmer-Gembeck, M. J. (2015). Let's talk openly about sex: Sexual communication, self-esteem and efficacy as correlates of sexual well-being. *European Journal of Developmental Psychology, 12*(5), 579–598. https://doi.org/10.1080/17405629.2015.1054373

Matas, L., Arend, R. A., & Sroufe, L. A. (1978). Continuity of adaptation in the second year: The relationship between quality of attachment and later competence. *Child Development, 49*(3), 547–556. https://doi.org/10.2307/1128221

Mathews, H. M., Hirsch, S. E., Hernández, M., & Kauffman, J. M. (2022). A Sketch of the Problem. In *Navigating Students' Mental Health in the Wake of COVID-19* (pp. 1–19). Routledge.

Mathewson, T. G. (2022, June 6). *"State-sanctioned violence": Inside one of the thousands of schools that still paddles students.* The Hechinger Report. http://hechingerreport.org/state-sanctioned-violence-inside-one-of-the-thousands-of-schools-that-still-paddles-students/

Maunder, R., & Monks, C. P. (2019). Friendships in middle childhood: Links to peer and school identification, and general self-worth. *British Journal of Developmental Psychology, 37*(2), 211–229.

Maurer, D., & Werker, J. F. (2014). Perceptual narrowing during infancy: A comparison of language and faces. *Developmental Psychobiology, 56*(2), 154–178. https://doi.org/10.1002/dev.21177

May, P. A., Chambers, C. D., Kalberg, W. O., Zellner, J., Feldman, H., Buckley, D., Kopald, D., Hasken, J. M., Xu, R., Honerkamp-Smith, G., Taras, H., Manning, M. A., Robinson, L. K., Adam, M. P., Abdul-Rahman, O., Vaux, K., Jewett, T., Elliott, A.

J., Kable, J. A., . . . Hoyme, H. E. (2018). Prevalence of fetal alcohol spectrum disorders in 4 US communities. *JAMA, 319*(5), 474–482. https://doi.org/10.1001/jama.2017.21896

May, P. A., Serna, P., Hurt, L., & DeBruyn, L. M. (2005). Outcome evaluation of a public health approach to suicide prevention in an American Indian Tribal Nation. *American Journal of Public Health, 95*(7), 1238–1244. https://doi.org/10.2105/AJPH.2004.040410

Mayers, A., Hambidge, S., Bryant, O., & Arden-Close, E. (2020). Supporting women who develop poor postnatal mental health: What support do fathers receive to support their partner and their own mental health? *BMC Pregnancy and Childbirth, 20*(1), 359. https://doi.org/10.1186/s12884-020-03043-2

Mayor, J., & Plunkett, K. (2014). Shared understanding and idiosyncratic expression in early vocabularies. *Developmental Science, 17*(3), 412–423. https://doi.org/10.1111/desc.12130

Mazzone, A., Camodeca, M., & Salmivalli, C. (2016). Interactive effects of guilt and moral disengagement on bullying, defending and outsider behavior. *Journal of Moral Education, 45*(4), 419–432.

Mazzone, A., Yanagida, T., Camodeca, M., & Strohmeier, D. (2021). Information processing of social exclusion: Links with bullying, moral disengagement and guilt. *Journal of Applied Developmental Psychology, 75*, 101292.

Mazzoni, S. E., & Carter, E. B. (2017). Group prenatal care. *American Journal of Obstetrics and Gynecology, 216*(6), 552–556. https://doi.org/10.1016/j.ajog.2017.02.006

McAdams, D. P., & Zapata-Gietl, C. (2015). Three strands of identity development across the human life course: Reading Erik Erikson in full. In *The Oxford handbook of identity development* (pp. 81–94). Oxford University Press.

McArthur, B. A., Browne, D., Racine, N., Tough, S., & Madigan, S. (2022). Screen time as a mechanism through which cumulative risk is related to child socioemotional and developmental outcomes in early childhood. *Research on Child and Adolescent Psychopathology*, 1–12.

McArthur, B. A., Eirich, R., McDonald, S., Tough, S., & Madigan, S. (2021). Screen use relates to decreased offline enrichment activities. *Acta Paediatrica, 110*(3), 896–898. https://doi.org/10.1111/apa.15601

McCann, S., Amadó, M. P., & Moore, S. E. (2020). The role of iron in brain development: A systematic review. *Nutrients, 12*(7), 2001. https://doi.org/10.3390/nu12072001

McClelland, M. M., & Cameron, C. E. (2019). Developing together: The role of executive function and motor skills in children's early academic lives. *Early Childhood Research Quarterly, 46*, 142–151. https://doi.org/10.1016/j.ecresq.2018.03.014

McClintock, M. K., & Herdt, G. (1996). Rethinking puberty: The development of sexual attraction. *Current Directions in Psychological Science, 5*(6), 178–183.

McClure, C. C., Cataldi, J. R., & O'Leary, S. T. (2017). Vaccine hesitancy: Where we are and where we are going. *Clinical Therapeutics, 39*(8), 1550–1562.

McConnell, E. A., Birkett, M., & Mustanski, B. (2016). Families matter: Social support and mental health trajectories among lesbian, gay, bisexual, and transgender youth. *Journal of Adolescent Health, 59*(6), 674–680.

McCormack, M., & Savin-Williams, R. (2018). Young men's rationales for non-exclusive gay sexualities.

Culture, Health & Sexuality, 20(8), 929–944. https://doi.org/10.1080/13691058.2017.1398349

McCormick, B. J. J., Caulfield, L. E., Richard, S. A., Pendergast, L., Seidman, J. C., Maphula, A., Koshy, B., Blacy, L., Roshan, R., Nahar, B., Shrestha, R., Rasheed, M., Svensen, E., Rasmussen, Z., Scharf, R. J., Haque, S., Oria, R., Murray-Kolb, L. E., & MAL-ED Network Investigators. (2020). Early life experiences and trajectories of cognitive development. *Pediatrics, 146*(3), e20193660. https://doi.org/10.1542/peds.2019-3660

McCoy, D. C., & Wolf, S. (2018). Changes in classroom quality predict Ghanaian preschoolers' gains in academic and social-emotional skills. *Developmental Psychology, 54*(8), 1582.

McCoy, D. C., Cuartas, J., Behrman, J., Cappa, C., Heymann, J., López Bóo, F., Lu, C., Raikes, A., Richter, L., Stein, A., & Fink, G. (2021). Global estimates of the implications of COVID-19-related preprimary school closures for children's instructional access, development, learning, and economic wellbeing. *Child Development, 92*(5), e883–e899. https://doi.org/10.1111/cdev.13658

McCue, D. (2021, March 8). *After a brief return, young adults quick to move out of parents homes as the pandemic continues.* Housing Perspectives: Joint Center for Housing Studies of Harvard University. https://www.jchs.harvard.edu/blog/after-brief-return-young-adults-quick-move-out-parents-homes-pandemic-continues

McDaniel, B. T., & Coyne, S. M. (2016). Technology interference in the parenting of young children: Implications for mothers' perceptions of coparenting. *The Social Science Journal, 53*(4), 435–443. https://doi.org/10.1016/j.soscij.2016.04.010

McDaniel, B. T., & Radesky, J. S. (2020). Longitudinal associations between early childhood externalizing behavior, parenting stress, and child media use. *Cyberpsychology, Behavior, and Social Networking, 23*(6), 384–391. https://doi.org/10.1089/cyber.2019.0478

McDermott, E. R., Donlan, A. E., & Zaff, J. F. (2019). Why do students drop out? Turning points and long-term experiences. *The Journal of Educational Research, 112*(2), 270–282.

McDermott, E. R., Umaña-Taylor, A. J., & Martinez-Fuentes, S. (2018). Family ethnic socialization predicts better academic outcomes via proactive coping with discrimination and increased self-efficacy. *Journal of Adolescence, 65*, 189–195. https://doi.org/10.1016/j.adolescence.2018.03.011

McDonald, N. M., Perdue, K. L., Eilbott, J., Loyal, J., Shic, F., & Pelphrey, K. A. (2019). Infant brain responses to social sounds: A longitudinal functional near-infrared spectroscopy study. *Developmental Cognitive Neuroscience, 36*, 100638. https://doi.org/10.1016/j.dcn.2019.100638

McDougall, P., & Vaillancourt, T. (2015). Long-term adult outcomes of peer victimization in childhood and adolescence: Pathways to adjustment and maladjustment. *American Psychologist, 70*(4), 300.

McEwen, B. S., & Bulloch, K. (2019). Epigenetic impact of the social and physical environment on brain and body. *Metabolism, 100*, 153941. https://doi.org/10.1016/j.metabol.2019.07.005

McFadden, K. E., Puzio, A., Way, N., & Hughes, D. (2020). Mothers' gender beliefs matter for adolescents' academic achievement and engagement: An examination of ethnically diverse US mothers and adolescents. *Sex Roles, 84*, 166–182.

McFarland, D. A., Moody, J., Diehl, D., Smith, J. A., & Thomas, R. J. (2014). Network ecology and adolescent social structure. *American Sociological Review, 79*(6), 1088–1121. https://doi.org/10.1177/0003122414554001

McFarland, J., Cui, J., Rathbun, A., & Holmes, J. (2018). Trends in high school dropout and completion rates in the United States: 2018. Compendium report. NCES 2019-117. *National Center for Education Statistics.*

McFarland, J., Hussar, B., De Brey, C., Snyder, T., Wang, X., Wilkinson-Flicker, S., & Hinz, S. (2017). *The condition of education 2017* (NCES 2017-144). National Center for Education Statistics.

McFarland, M. J., Hauer, M. E., & Reuben, A. (2022). Half of US population exposed to adverse lead levels in early childhood. *Proceedings of the National Academy of Sciences, 119*(11), e2118631119.

McGillicuddy, D., & Devine, D. (2020). 'You feel ashamed that you are not in the higher group'—Children's psychosocial response to ability grouping in primary school. *British Educational Research Journal, 46*(3), 553–573. https://doi.org/10.1002/berj.3595

McGraw, M. B. (1943). *The neuromuscular maturation of the human infant* (p. 140). Columbia University Press.

McHarg, G., Ribner, A. D., Devine, R. T., & Hughes, C. (2020). Screen time and executive function in toddlerhood: A longitudinal study. *Frontiers in Psychology, 11*, 570392. https://doi.org/10.3389/fpsyg.2020.570392

McInroy, L. B., McCloskey, R. J., Craig, S. L., & Eaton, A. D. (2019). LGBTQ+ youths' community engagement and resource seeking online versus offline. *Journal of Technology in Human Services, 37*(4), 315–333.

McKenzie, K., Murray, G., Murray, A., Delahunty, L., Hutton, L., Murray, K., & O'Hare, A. (2019). Child and Adolescent Intellectual Disability Screening Questionnaire to identify children with intellectual disability. *Developmental Medicine & Child Neurology, 61*(4), 444–450. https://doi.org/10.1111/dmcn.13998

McKinsey Global Institutie. (2021). *The Future of Work After COVID-19.* McKinsey Global Institute.

McKowen, C., & Strambler, M. J. (2009). Developmental antecedents and social and academic consequences of stereotype-consciousness in middle childhood. *Child Development, 80*(6), 1643–1659.

McLaughlin, K. A., Garrad, M. C., & Somerville, L. H. (2015). What develops during emotional development? A component process approach to identifying sources of psychopathology risk in adolescence. *Dialogues in Clinical Neuroscience, 17*(4), 403–410. http://www.ncbi.nlm.nih.gov/pmc/articles/PMC4734878/

McLaughlin, K. A., Weissman, D., & Bitrán, D. (2019). Childhood adversity and neural development: A systematic review. *Annual Review of Developmental Psychology, 1*, 277–312.

McLeod, A., & Winter, J. (2022). *American Indian Traditional Foods in USDA School Meals Programs: A Wisconsin Farm to School Toolkit.* Wisconsin Department of Public Instruction.

McLoyd, V. C., & Hallman, S. K. (2020). Antecedents and correlates of adolescent employment: Race as a moderator of psychological predictors. *Youth & Society, 52*(6), 871–893.

McMahon, R. (2018). The history of transdisciplinary race classification: Methods, politics and institutions, 1840s–1940s. *The British Journal for the History of Science, 51*(1), 41–67. https://doi.org/10.1017/S0007087417001054

McMahon, R. J., & Frick, P. J. (2019). Conduct and oppositional disorders. In M. J. Prinstein, E. A. Youngstrom, E. J. Mash, & R. A. Barkley (Eds.), *Treatment of disorders in childhood and adolescence* (pp. 102–172). Guilford.

McMahon, S. D., Anderman, E. M., Astor, R. A., Espelage, D. L., Martinez, A., Reddy, L. A., & Worrell, F. C. (2022). *Violence against educators and school personnel: Crisis during COVID.* Technical Report. American Psychological Association.

McMakin, D. L., Dahl, R. E., Buysse, D. J., Cousins, J. C., Forbes, E. E., Silk, J. S., Siegle, G. J., & Franzen, P. L. (2016). The impact of experimental sleep restriction on affective functioning in social and nonsocial contexts among adolescents. *Journal of Child Psychology and Psychiatry, 57*(9), 1027–1037.

McManus, C. (2019). Half a century of handedness research: Myths, truths; fictions, facts; backwards, but mostly forwards. *Brain and Neuroscience Advances, 3*, 2398212818820513. https://doi.org/10.1177/2398212818820513

McMullen, M. B. (2018). The many benefits of continuity of care for infants, toddlers, families, and caregiving staff. *Young Children, 73*(3), 38–39. https://www.naeyc.org/resources/pubs/yc/jul2018/benefits-continuity-care

McNeel, B. (2018, July 17). Measuring success at the San Antonio public preschool program. *The Hechinger Report.* http://hechingerreport.org/measuring-success-at-san-antonios-public-preschool-program/

McNeill, J., Howard, S. J., Vella, S. A., Santos, R., & Cliff, D. P. (2018). Physical activity and modified organized sport among preschool children: Associations with cognitive and psychosocial health. *Mental Health and Physical Activity, 15*, 45–52. https://doi.org/10.1016/j.mhpa.2018.07.001

McQuillan, M. E., Kultur, E. C., Bates, J. E., O'Reilly, L. M., Dodge, K. A., Lansford, J. E., & Pettit, G. S. (2018). Dysregulation in children: Origins and implications from age 5 to age 28. *Development and Psychopathology, 30*(2), 695–713. https://doi.org/10.1017/S0954579417001572

McQuillan, M. E., Smith, L. B., Yu, C., & Bates, J. E. (2020). Parents influence the visual learning environment through children's manual actions. *Child Development, 91*(3), e701–e720. https://doi.org/10.1111/cdev.13274

McQuire, C., Daniel, R., Hurt, L., Kemp, A., & Paranjothy, S. (2020). The causal web of foetal alcohol spectrum disorders: A review and causal diagram. *European Child & Adolescent Psychiatry, 29*(5), 575–594. https://doi.org/10.1007/s00787-018-1264-3

Mead, M. (1975). Children's play style: Potentialities and limitations of its use as a cultural indicator. *Anthropological Quarterly, 48*(3), 157–181.

Means, D. R., & Pyne, K. B. (2017). Finding my way: Perceptions of institutional support and belonging in low-income, first-generation, first-year college students. *Journal of College Student Development, 58*(6), 907–924. https://doi.org/10.1353/csd.2017.0071

Means, D. R., Hudson, T. D., & Tish, E. (2019). A snapshot of college access and inequity: Using photography to illuminate the pathways to higher education for underserved youth. *The High School Journal, 102*(2), 139–158. https://doi.org/10.1353/hsj.2019.0003

Medico, D., Pullen Sansfaçon, A., Zufferey, A., Galantino, G., Bosom, M., & Suerich-Gulick, F. (2020). Pathways to gender affirmation in trans youth: A qualitative and participative study with youth and their parents. *Clinical Child Psychology and Psychiatry, 25*(4), 1002–1014. https://doi.org/10.1177/1359104520938427

Meehan, C. L., & Crittenden, A. N. (2016). *Childhood: Origins, evolution, and implications.* University of New Mexico Press.

Meehan, C. L., & Hawks, S. (2013). Cooperative breeding and attachment among the Aka Foragers. In N. Quinn & J. M. Mageo (Eds.), *Attachment reconsidered: Cultural perspectives on a Western theory* (pp. 85–113). Palgrave Macmillan US. https://doi.org/10.1057/9781137386724_4

Meek, J. Y., & Noble, L. (2022). Policy statement: breastfeeding and the use of human milk. *Pediatrics, 150*(1).

Meek, S., Smith, L., Allen, R., Catherine, E., Edyburn, K., Williams, C., Fabes, R., McIntosh, K., Garcia, E., Takanashi, R., Gordon, L., Jimenez-Castellanos, O., Hemmeter, M. L., Giliam, W., & Pontier, R. (2020). *Start with equity: From the early years to the early grades: Data, research and an actionable child equity policy agenda.* Children's Equity Project.

Meeus, W. (2011). The study of adolescent identity formation 2000–2010: A review of longitudinal research. *Journal of Research on Adolescence, 21*(1), 75–94.

Meeus, W. (2016). Adolescent psychosocial development: A review of longitudinal models and research. *Developmental Psychology, 52*(12), 1969–1993. https://doi.org/10.1037/dev0000243

Meeus, W. H. J., Branje, S. J. T., van der Valk, I., & de Wied, M. (2007). Relationships with intimate partner, best friend, and parents in adolescence and early adulthood: A study of the saliency of the intimate partnership. *International Journal of Behavioral Development, 31*(6), 569–580. https://doi.org/10.1177/0165025407080584

Meeus, W., Vollebergh, W., Branje, S., Crocetti, E., Ormel, J., van de Schoot, R., Crone, E. A., & Becht, A. (2021). On imbalance of impulse control and sensation seeking and adolescent risk: An intra-individual developmental test of the dual systems and maturational imbalance models. *Journal of Youth and Adolescence, 50*(5), 827–840. https://doi.org/10.1007/s10964-021-01419-x

Meier, A., & Allen, G. (2009). Romantic relationships from adolescence to young adulthood: Evidence from the National Longitudinal Study of Adolescent Health. *The Sociological Quarterly, 50*(2), 308–335.

Meier, A., Musick, K., Fischer, J., & Flood, S. (2018). Mothers' and fathers' well-being in parenting across the arch of child development. *Journal of Marriage and Family, 80*(4), 992–1004. https://doi.org/10.1111/jomf.12491

Meijer, A., Königs, M., Fels, I. M. J. van der, Visscher, C., Bosker, R. J., Hartman, E., & Oosterlaan, J. (2020). The effects of aerobic versus cognitively demanding exercise interventions on executive functioning in school-aged children: A cluster-randomized controlled trial. *Journal of Sport and Exercise Psychology, 43*(1), 1–13. https://doi.org/10.1123/jsep.2020-0034

Meijer, A., Königs, M., Vermeulen, G. T., Visscher, C., Bosker, R. J., Hartman, E., & Oosterlaan, J. (2020). The effects of physical activity on brain structure and neurophysiological functioning in children: A systematic review and meta-analysis. *Developmental Cognitive Neuroscience, 45*, 100828. https://doi.org/10.1016/j.dcn.2020.100828

Meinhofer, A., & Angleró-Díaz, Y. (2019). Trends in foster care entry among children removed from their homes because of parental drug use, 2000 to 2017. *JAMA Pediatrics, 173*(9), 881–883. https://doi.org/10.1001/jamapediatrics.2019.1738

Meisel, S. N., & Colder, C. R. (2021) An examination of the joint effects of adolescent interpersonal styles and parenting styles on substance use. *Development and Psychopathology,* 1–19. https://doi.org/10.1017/S0954579420001637

Melnitchouk, N., Scully, R. E., & Davids, J. S. (2018). Barriers to breastfeeding for US physicians who are mothers. *JAMA Internal Medicine, 178*(8), 1130–1132. https://doi.org/10.1001/jamainternmed.2018.0320

Meltzer, L. J., Williamson, A. A., & Mindell, J. A. (2021). Pediatric sleep health: It matters, and so does how we define it. *Sleep Medicine Reviews, 57,* 101425. https://doi.org/10.1016/j.smrv.2021.101425

Meltzoff, A. N. (2020). Imitation and modeling. In A. N. Meltzoff & R. A. Williamson (Eds.), *Encyclopedia of infant and early childhood development* (2nd ed., pp. 100–109). Elsevier.

Meltzoff, A. N., & Marshall, P. J. (2018). Human infant imitation as a social survival circuit. *Current Opinion in Behavioral Sciences, 24,* 130–136. https://doi.org/10.1016/j.cobeha.2018.09.006

Meltzoff, A. N., & Moore, M. K. (1977). Imitation of facial and manual gestures by human neonates. *Science, 198*(4312), 75–78.

Mendle, J., Beltz, A. M., Carter, R., & Dorn, L. D. (2019). Understanding puberty and its measurement: Ideas for research in a new generation. *Journal of Research on Adolescence, 29*(1), 82–95. https://doi.org/10.1111/jora.12371

Mendle, J., & Ferrero, J. (2012). Detrimental psychological outcomes associated with pubertal timing in adolescent boys. *Developmental Review, 32*(1), 49–66.

Mendonça, B., Sargent, B., & Fetters, L. (2016). Cross-cultural validity of standardized motor development screening and assessment tools: A systematic review. *Developmental Medicine & Child Neurology, 58*(12), 1213–1222.

Meng, X., Li, S., Duan, W., Sun, Y., & Jia, C. (2017). Secular Trend of Age at Menarche in Chinese Adolescents Born From 1973 to 2004. *Pediatrics, 140*(2). https://doi.org/10.1542/peds.2017-0085

Mennella, J. A., Nolden, A. A., & Bobowski, N. (2018). Measuring sweet and bitter taste in children: Individual variation due to age and taste genetics. In J. C. Lumeng & J. O. Fisher (Eds.), *Pediatric food preferences and eating behaviors* (pp. 1–34). Academic Press. https://doi.org/10.1016/B978-0-12-811716-3.00001-4

Menon, R. (2019). Initiation of human parturition: Signaling from senescent fetal tissues via extracellular vesicle mediated paracrine mechanism. *Obstetrics & Gynecology Science, 62*(4), 199. https://doi.org/10.5468/ogs.2019.62.4.199

Mercer, M. (2013, August 30). *Children as young as 10 can do farm work in some states.* Stateline. http://pew.org/2gMJaEb

Mercurio, M. R., & Carter, B. S. (2020). Resuscitation policies for extremely preterm newborns: Finally moving beyond gestational age. *Journal of Perinatology, 40*(12), 1731–1733. https://doi.org/10.1038/s41372-020-00843-4

Merlo, C. L., Jones, S. E., Michael, S. L., Chen, T. J., Sliwa, S. A., Lee, S. H., Brener, N. D., Lee, S. M., & Park, S. (2020). Dietary and physical activity behaviors among high school students—Youth Risk Behavior Survey, United States, 2019. *MMWR Supplements, 69*(1), 64–76.

Merriam, A. P. (1971). Aspects of sexual behavior among the Bala (Basongye). In D. S. Marshall & R. C. Suggs (Eds.), *Human sexual behavior: Variations in the ethnographic spectrum* (pp. 71–102). Basic Books.

Merrick, M. T., Ford, D. C., Ports, K. A., & Guinn, A. S. (2018). Prevalence of Adverse Childhood Experiences From the 2011-2014 Behavioral Risk Factor Surveillance System in 23 States. *JAMA Pediatrics, 172*(11), 1038–1044. https://doi.org/10.1001/jamapediatrics.2018.2537

Merz, E. C., Wiltshire, C. A., & Noble, K. G. (2019). Socioeconomic inequality and the developing brain: Spotlight on language and executive function. *Child Development Perspectives, 13*(1), 15–20. https://doi.org/10.1111/cdep.12305

Mesman, J. (2021). Video observations of sensitive caregiving "off the beaten track": Introduction to the special issue. *Attachment & Human Development, 23*(2), 115–123. https://doi.org/10.1080/14616734.2020.1828511

Mesman, J., Minter, T., Angnged, A., Cissé, I. A. H., Salali, G. D., & Migliano, A. B. (2018). Universality without uniformity: A culturally inclusive approach to sensitive responsiveness in infant caregiving. *Child Development, 89*(3), 837–850. https://doi.org/10.1111/cdev.12795

Mesman, J., van Ijzendoorn, M. H., & Sagi-Schwartz, A. (2016). Cross-cultural patterns of attachment. In J. Cassidy & P. R. Shaver (Eds.), *Handbook of attachment: Theory, research, and clinical applications* (pp. 852–877). Guilford.

Meter, D. J., & Bauman, S. (2018). Moral disengagement about cyberbullying and parental monitoring: Effects on traditional bullying and victimization via cyberbullying involvement. *The Journal of Early Adolescence, 38*(3), 303–326.

Metzger, A. N., & Hamilton, L. T. (2021). The stigma of ADHD: Teacher ratings of labeled students. *Sociological Perspectives, 64*(2), 258–279.

Mian, N. D., & Gray, S. A. O. (2019). Preschool anxiety: Risk and protective factors. In B. Fisak & P. Barrett (Eds.), *Anxiety in preschool children* (pp. 29–51). Routledge.

Michaelson, L. E., & Munakata, Y. (2020). Same data set, different conclusions: Preschool delay of gratification predicts later behavioral outcomes in a preregistered study. *Psychological Science, 31*(2), 193–201.

Michel, G. F., Babik, I., Nelson, E. L., Campbell, J. M., & Marcinowski, E. C. (2018). Chapter 13: Evolution and development of handedness: An evo–devo approach. In G. S. Forrester, W. D. Hopkins, K. Hudry, & A. Lindell (Eds.), *Progress in brain research* (Vol. 238, pp. 347–374). Elsevier. https://doi.org/10.1016/bs.pbr.2018.06.007

Midgett, A., & Doumas, D. M. (2019). Witnessing bullying at school: The association between being a bystander and anxiety and depressive symptoms. *School Mental Health, 11*(3), 454–463. https://doi.org/10.1007/s12310-019-09312-6

Midgley, N. (2007). Anna Freud: The Hampstead War Nurseries and the role of the direct observation of children for psychoanalysis. *The International Journal of Psychoanalysis, 88*(4), 939–959. https://doi.org/10.1516/V28R-J334-6182-524H

Miech, R. A., Johnston, L. D., O'Malley, P. M., Bachman, J. G., Schulenberg, J. E., & Patrick, M. E. (2021). *Monitoring the future: National Survey Results on Drug Use, 1975–2020. 2020 Volume I: Secondary school students.* University of Michigan Institute for Social Research.

Migration Policy Institute (MPI). (2022). Migration Policy Institute tabulation of data from U.S. Census Bureau, 2019 American Community Survey (ACS) and 1990 Decennial Census; 1990 data were accessed from Steven Ruggles, J. Trent Alexander, Katie Genadek, Ronald Goeken, Matthew B. Schroeder, and Matthew Sobek, Integrated Public Use Microdata Series: Version 5.0 [Machine-readable database]. University of Minnesota, 2010.

Miguel, P. M., Pereira, L. O., Silveira, P. P., & Meaney, M. J. (2019). Early environmental influences on the development of children's brain structure and function. *Developmental Medicine & Child Neurology, 61*(10), 1127–1133. https://doi.org/10.1111/dmcn.14182

Mijs, J. J. B., & Roe, E. L. (2021). Is America coming apart? Socioeconomic segregation in neighborhoods, schools, workplaces, and social networks, 1970–2020. *Sociology Compass, 15*(6), e12884. https://doi.org/10.1111/soc4.12884

Mikulincer, M., & Shaver, P. R. (2019). Attachment orientations and emotion regulation. *Current Opinion in Psychology, 25,* 6–10. https://doi.org/10.1016/j.copsyc.2018.02.006

Mikulincer, M., & Shaver, P. R. (2021). The continuing influence of early attachment orientations viewed from a personality-social perspective on adult attachment. In R. A. Thompson, J. A. Simpson, & L. J. Berlin (Eds.), *Attachment: The fundamental questions* (pp. 211–218). Guilford.

Mikwar, M., MacFarlane, A. J., & Marchetti, F. (2020). Mechanisms of oocyte aneuploidy associated with advanced maternal age. *Mutation Research/Reviews in Mutation Research, 785,* 108320. https://doi.org/10.1016/j.mrrev.2020.108320

Miller, C. E., & Meyers, S. A. (2015). Disparities in school discipline practices for students with emotional and learning disabilities and autism. *Journal of Education and Human Development, 4*(1), 255–267.

Miller, E., Jones, K. A., & McCauley, H. L. (2018). Updates on adolescent dating and sexual violence prevention and intervention. *Current Opinion in Pediatrics, 30*(4), 466.

Miller, J. G. (2018). Physiological mechanisms of prosociality. *Current Opinion in Psychology, 20,* 50–54. https://doi.org/10.1016/j.copsyc.2017.08.018

Miller, J. G., & Hastings, P. D. (2019). Parenting, neurobiology, and prosocial development. In D. J. Laible, G. Carlo, & L. M. Padilla-Walker (Eds.), *The Oxford handbook of parenting and moral development* (pp. 129–144). Oxford University Press.

Miller, J. G., Goyal, N., & Wice, M. (2015). Ethical considerations in research on human development and culture. In *The Oxford handbook of human development and culture* (pp. 14–27). Oxford University Press.

Miller, J. G., Kahle, S., & Hastings, P. D. (2015). Roots and benefits of costly giving: Children who are more altruistic have greater autonomic flexibility and less family wealth. *Psychological Science, 26*(7), 1038–1045.

Miller, P. H. (2011). Piaget's theory: Past, present, and future. In U. Goswami (Ed.), *The Wiley-Blackwell handbook of childhood cognitive development* (pp. 649–672). Wiley-Blackwell.

Miller, S. A. (2017). *Developmental research methods.* Sage.

Miller, S. E., Avila, B. N., & Reavis, R. D. (2020). Thoughtful friends: Executive function relates to social problem solving and friendship quality in middle childhood. *The Journal of Genetic Psychology, 181*(2–3), 78–94.

Miller, T. R., Steinbeigle, R., Lawrence, B. A., Peterson, C., Florence, C., Barr, M., & Barr, R. G. (2018). Lifetime cost of abusive head trauma at ages 0–4, USA. *Prevention Science, 19*(6), 695–704.

Millner, A. J., & Nock, M. K. (2020). Self-injurious thoughts and behaviors. In E. A. Youngstrom, M. J. Prinstein, E. J. Mash, Y R. A. Barkley (Eds.), *Assessment of disorders in childhood and adolescence* (5th ed., pp. 245–267). Guilford.

Mills, K. L., Dumontheil, I., Speekenbrink, M., & Blakemore, S.-J. (2015). Multitasking during social interactions in adolescence and early adulthood. *Royal Society Open Science, 2*(11), 150117. https://doi.org /10.1098/rsos.150117

Mills, K. L., Goddings, A.-L., Herting, M. M., Meuwese, R., Blakemore, S.-J., Crone, E. A., Dahl, R. E., Güroğlu, B., Raznahan, A., Sowell, E. R., & Tamnes, C. K. (2016). Structural brain development between childhood and adulthood: Convergence across four longitudinal samples. *NeuroImage, 141*, 273–281. https://doi.org/10.1016/j.neuroimage.2016.07.044

Mills-Koonce, W. R., Rehder, P. D., & McCurdy, A. L. (2018). The significance of parenting and parent–child relationships for sexual and gender minority adolescents. *Journal of Research on Adolescence, 28*(3), 637–649.

Milner, J. S., & Crouch, J. L. (2013). Assessment of maternal attributions of infant's hostile intent and its use in child maltreatment prevention/intervention efforts. *JAMA Pediatrics, 167*(6), 588–589.

Milojevich, H. M., Machlin, L., & Sheridan, M. A. (2020). Early adversity and children's emotion regulation: Differential roles of parent emotion regulation and adversity exposure. *Development and Psychopathology, 32*(5), 1788–1798. https://doi.org/10.1017 /S0954579420001273

Mindell, J. A., Sadeh, A., Wiegand, B., How, T. H., & Goh, D. Y. (2010). Cross-cultural differences in infant and toddler sleep. *Sleep Medicine, 11*(3), 274–280.

Mingebach, T., Kamp-Becker, I., Christiansen, H., & Weber, L. (2018). Meta-meta-analysis on the effectiveness of parent-based interventions for the treatment of child externalizing behavior problems. *PLOS ONE, 13*(9), e0202855. https://doi.org/10.1371/journal .pone.0202855

Mintz, S. (2004). *Huck's raft: A history of American childhood*. Harvard University Press.

Mintz, S. (2015). *The prime of life*. Harvard University Press.

Miranda, R., Oriol, X., & Amutio, A. (2019). Risk and protective factors at school: Reducing bullies and promoting positive bystanders' behaviors in adolescence. *Scandinavian Journal of Psychology, 60*(2), 106–115. https://doi.org/10.1111/sjop.12513

Mireault, G. C., Crockenberg, S. C., Heilman, K., Sparrow, J. E., Cousineau, K., & Rainville, B. (2018). Social, cognitive, and physiological aspects of humour perception from 4 to 8 months: Two longitudinal studies. *The British Journal of Developmental Psychology, 36*(1), 98–109. https://doi.org/10.1111/bjdp.12216

Miron, O., Yu, K.-H., Wilf-Miron, R., & Kohane, I. S. (2019). Suicide rates among adolescents and young adults in the United States, 2000–2017. *JAMA, 321*(23), 2362–2364. https://doi.org/10.1001 /jama.2019.5054

Mischel, W. (1966). A social learning view of sex differences in behavior. In E. E. Maccoby (Ed.), *The development of sex differences* (pp. 56–81). Stanford University Press.

Mischel, W. (2014). *The marshmallow test: Understanding self-control and how to master it*. Random House.

Mischel, W. (2015). *The marshmallow test: Why self-control is the engine of success*. Little, Brown.

Mischel, W., & Ebbesen, E. B. (1970). Attention in delay of gratification. *Journal of Personality and Social Psychology, 16*(2), 329.

Mischel, W., Shoda, Y., & Rodriguez, M. I. (1989). Delay of gratification in children. *Science, 244*(4907), 933–938.

Mishra, S. (2020). Social networks, social capital, social support and academic success in higher education: A systematic review with a special focus on "underrepresented" students. *Educational Research Review, 29*, 100307. https://doi.org/10.1016/j.edurev.2019.100307

Missikpode, C., Hamann, C. J., & Peek-Asa, C. (2021). Association between driver and child passenger restraint: Analysis of community-based observational survey data from 2005 to 2019. *Journal of Safety Research, 79*, 168–172

Mitchell, C., McLanahan, S., Schneper, L., Garfinkel, I., Brooks-Gunn, J., & Notterman, D. (2017). Father loss and child telomere length. *Pediatrics, 140*(2), e20163245.

Mitter, N., Ali, A., & Scior, K. (2019). Stigma experienced by families of individuals with intellectual disabilities and autism: A systematic review. *Research in Developmental Disabilities, 89*, 10–21.

Miyake, A., Kost-Smith, L. E., Finkelstein, N. D., Pollock, S. J., Cohen, G. L., & Ito, T. A. (2010). Reducing the gender achievement gap in college science: A classroom study of values affirmation. *Science, 330*(6008), 1234–1237.

Miyamoto, Y., Yoo, J., Levine, C. S., Park, J., Boylan, J. M., Sims, T., Markus, H. R., Kitayama, S., Kawakami, N., Karasawa, M., Coe, C. L., Love, G. D., & Ryff, C. D. (2018). Culture and social hierarchy: Self- and other-oriented correlates of socioeconomic status across cultures. *Journal of Personality and Social Psychology, 115*(3), 427–445. https://doi.org/10.1037/pspi0000133

Modecki, K. L., Hagan, M. J., Sandler, I., & Wolchik, S. A. (2015). Latent profiles of nonresidential father engagement six years after divorce predict long-term offspring outcomes. *Journal of Clinical Child & Adolescent Psychology, 44*(1), 123–136.

Modell, J., & Goodman, M. (1990). Historical perspectives. In S. S. Feldman & G. R. Elliott (Eds.), *At the threshold: The developing adolescent* (pp. 93–122). Harvard University Press.

Moffett, L., & Morrison, F. J. (2020). Off-task behavior in kindergarten: Relations to executive function and academic achievement. *Journal of Educational Psychology, 112*(5), 938–955. https://doi.org/10.1037/edu0000397

Moffitt, T. E. (1993). Adolescence-limited and life-course-persistent antisocial behavior: A developmental taxonomy. *Psychological Review, 100*(4), 674. http://psycnet.apa.org/journals/rev/100/4/674/

Moffitt, T. E. (2006). Life-course-persistent versus adolescence-limited antisocial behavior. In D. Cicchetti & D. J. Cohen (Eds.), *Developmental psychopathology: Risk, disorder, and adaptation* (pp. 570–598). John Wiley & Sons.

Moffitt, U., Juang, L. P., & Syed, M. (2020). Intersectionality and youth identity development research in Europe. *Frontiers in Psychology, 11*, 78. https://doi .org/10.3389/fpsyg.2020.00078

Mohamoud, Y. A., Kirby, R. S., & Ehrenthal, D. B. (2021). County poverty, urban–rural classification, and the causes of term infant death: United States, 2012–2015. *Public Health Reports*. https://doi .org/10.1177/0033354921999169

Mohan, H., Verhoog, M. B., Doreswamy, K. K., Eyal, G., Aardse, R., Lodder, B. N., Goriounova, N. A., Asamoah, B., Brakspear, B., Clementine, A. B., Groot, C., van der Sluis, S., Testa-Silva, G., Obermayer, J.,

Boudewijns, Z. S. R. M., Narayanan, R. T., Baayen, J. C., Segev, I., Mansvelder, H. D., . . . Pj, C. (2015). Dendritic and axonal architecture of individual pyramidal neurons across layers of adult human neocortex. *Cerebral Cortex, 25*(12), 4839–4853. https://doi.org /10.1093/cercor/bhv188

Mohanty, A. (2021). *Dynamics of economic well-being: Poverty, 2013–2016* (No. P70BR-172; Current Population Reports). U.S. Census Bureau.

Mojtabai, R., Olfson, M., & Han, B. (2016). National trends in the prevalence and treatment of depression in adolescents and young adults. *Pediatrics, 138*(6), e20161878. https://doi.org/10.1542/peds.2016-1878

Molina, G., Weiser, T. G., Lipsitz, S. R., Esquivel, M. M., Uribe-Leitz, T., Azad, T., Shah, N., Semrau, K., Berry, W. R., Gawande, A. A., & Haynes, A. B. (2015). Relationship between cesarean delivery rate and maternal and neonatal mortality. *JAMA, 314*(21), 2263–2270. https://doi.org/10.1001/jama.2015.15553

Moll, L. C. (2013). *LS Vygotsky and education*. Routledge.

Möllborg, P., Wennergren, G., Almqvist, P., & Alm, B. (2015). Bed sharing is more common in sudden infant death syndrome than in explained sudden unexpected deaths in infancy. *Acta Paediatrica, 104*(8), 777–783.

Mollborn, S., Limburg, A., Pace, J., & Fomby, P. (2022). Family socioeconomic status and children's screen time. *Journal of Marriage and Family, 84*(4), 1129–1151. https://doi.org/10.1111/jomf.12834

Molloy, C., Beatson, R., Harrop, C., Perini, N., & Goldfeld, S. (2021). Systematic review: Effects of sustained nurse home visiting programs for disadvantaged mothers and children. *Journal of Advanced Nursing, 77*(1), 147–161.

Monk, E. P., Esposito, M. H., & Lee, H. (2021). Beholding inequality: Race, gender, and returns to physical attractiveness in the United States. *American Journal of Sociology, 127*(1), 194–241. https://doi.org /10.1086/715141

Monsivais, P., Thompson, C., Astbury, C. C., & Penney, T. L. (2021). Environmental approaches to promote healthy eating: Is ensuring affordability and availability enough? *BMJ, 372*, n549. https://doi.org /10.1136/bmj.n549

Monteiro, R., Rocha, N. B., & Fernandes, S. (2021). Are emotional and behavioral problems of infants and children aged younger than 7 years related to screen time exposure during the coronavirus disease 2019 confinement? An exploratory study in Portugal. *Frontiers in Psychology, 12*, 590279. https://doi.org/10.3389 /fpsyg.2021.590279

Montirosso, R., Provenzi, L., & Mascheroni, E. (2021). The role of protective caregiving in epigenetic regulation in human infants. In L. Provenzi & R. Montirosso (Eds.), *Developmental human behavioral epigenetics* (Vol. 23, pp. 143–156). Academic Press. https://doi.org/10.1016/B978-0-12-819262-7.00008-8

Moodie, J. L., Campisi, S. C., Salena, K., Wheatley, M., Vandermorris, A., & Bhutta, Z. A. (2020). Timing of pubertal milestones in low- and middle-income countries: A systematic review and meta-analysis. *Advances in Nutrition, 11*(4), 951–959. https://doi.org/10.1093 /advances/nmaa007

Moon, C. (2017). Prenatal experience with the maternal voice. In M. Filippa, P. Kuhn, & B. Westrup (Eds.), *Early vocal contact and preterm infant brain development: Bridging the gaps between research and practice* (pp. 25–37). Springer International Publishing. https:// doi.org/10.1007/978-3-319-65077-7_2

Moon, R. Y., & Hauck, F. R. (2016). SIDS risk: It's more than just the sleep environment. *Pediatrics*, peds.2015-3665. https://doi.org/10.1542/peds.2015-3665

Moore, J. (2017). John B. Watson's classical S–R behaviorism. *The Journal of Mind and Behavior, 38*(1), 1–34.

Moore, K. L., Persaud, T. V. N., & Torchia, M. G. (2020). *The developing human — e-book: Clinically oriented embryology*. Elsevier Health Sciences.

Morales, D. X., Prieto, N., Grineski, S. E., & Collins, T. W. (2019). Race/ethnicity, obesity, and the risk of being verbally bullied: A national multilevel study. *Journal of Racial and Ethnic Health Disparities, 6*(2), 245–253. https://doi.org/10.1007/s40615-018-0519-5

Moran, A. J., Khandpur, N., Polacsek, M., & Rimm, E. B. (2019). What factors influence ultra-processed food purchases and consumption in households with children? A comparison between participants and non-participants in the Supplemental Nutrition Assistance Program (SNAP). *Appetite, 134*, 1–8. https://doi.org/10.1016/j.appet.2018.12.009

Morelli, G. A., Chaudhary, N., Gottlieb, A., Keller, H., Murray, M., Quinn, N., & Vicedo, M. (2017). A pluralistic approach to attachment. In H. Keller & K. A. Bard (Eds.), *The cultural nature of attachment: Contextualizing relationships and development* (pp. 140–169). MIT Press.

Morgan, E. H., Schoonees, A., Sriram, U., Faure, M., & Seguin-Fowler, R. A. (2020). Caregiver involvement in interventions for improving children's dietary intake and physical activity behaviors. *Cochrane Database of Systematic Reviews, 1*. https://doi.org/10.1002/14651858.CD012547.pub2

Morgan, P. L. (2021). Unmeasured confounding and racial or ethnic disparities in disability identification. *Educational Evaluation and Policy Analysis, 43*(2), 351–361. https://doi.org/10.3102/0162373721991575

Morgan, P. L., Farkas, G., Cook, M., Strassfeld, N. M., Hillemeier, M. M., Pun, W. H., & Schussler, D. L. (2017). Are black children disproportionately overrepresented in special education? A best-evidence synthesis. *Exceptional Children, 83*(2), 181–198. https://doi.org/10.1177/0014402916664042

Morgan, P. L., Farkas, G., Wang, Y., Hillemeier, M. M., Oh, Y., & Maczuga, S. (2019). Executive function deficits in kindergarten predict repeated academic difficulties across elementary school. *Early Childhood Research Quarterly, 46*, 20–32.

Morgenroth, T., Ryan, M. K., & Peters, K. (2015). The motivational theory of role modeling: How role models influence role aspirants' goals. *Review of General Psychology, 19*(4), 465–483. https://doi.org/10.1037/gpr0000059

Moriguchi, Y., Chevalier, N., & Zelazo, P. D. (2016). Development of executive function during childhood. *Frontiers in Psychology, 7*, 6.

Morning, A., Bruckner, H., & Nelson, A. (2019). Socially desirable reporting and the expression of biological concepts of race. *Du Bois Review: Social Science Research on Race, 16*(2), 439–455. https://doi.org/10.1017/S1742058X19000195

Morris, A. S., Criss, M. M., Silk, J. S., & Houltberg, B. J. (2017). The impact of parenting on emotion regulation during childhood and adolescence. *Child Development Perspectives, 11*(4), 233–238. https://doi.org/10.1111/cdep.12238

Morris, A. S., Cui, L., & Steinberg, L. (2013). Parenting research and themes: What we have learned and where to go next. In R. E. Larzelere, A. S. Morris, & A. W. Harrist (Eds.), *Authoritative parenting: Synthesizing nurturance and discipline for optimal child development* (pp. 35–58). American Psychological Association.

Morris, B. J., & Zentall, S. R. (2014). High fives motivate: The effects of gestural and ambiguous verbal praise on motivation. *Frontiers in Psychology, 5*, 928. https://doi.org/10.3389/fpsyg.2014.00928

Morris, K. S., Seaton, E. K., Iida, M., & Lindstrom Johnson, S. (2020). Racial discrimination stress, school belonging, and school racial composition on academic attitudes and beliefs among Black youth. *Social Sciences, 9*(11), 191. https://doi.org/10.3390/socsci9110191

Morrison, F. J., Kim, M. H., Connor, C. M., & Grammer, J. K. (2019). The causal impact of schooling on children's development: Lessons for developmental science. *Current Directions in Psychological Science, 28*(5), 441–449. https://doi.org/10.1177/0963721419855661

Morrison, M., Tay, L., & Diener, E. (2011). Subjective well-being and national satisfaction: Findings from a worldwide survey. *Psychological Science, 22*(2), 166–171. https://doi.org/10.1177/0956797610396224

Morrison-Beedy, D., & Grove, L. (2018). Adolescent girls' experiences with sexual pressure, coercion, and victimization: # MeToo. *Worldviews on Evidence-Based Nursing, 15*(3), 225–229.

Morrissey, B., Taveras, E., Allender, S., & Strugnell, C. (2020). Sleep and obesity among children: A systematic review of multiple sleep dimensions. *Pediatric Obesity, 15*(4), e12619. https://doi.org/10.1111/ijpo.12619

Morrongiello, B. A. (2018). Preventing unintentional injuries to young children in the home: Understanding and influencing parents' safety practices. *Child Development Perspectives, 12*(4), 217–222.

Morrow, A. S., & Villodas, M. T. (2018). Direct and indirect pathways from adverse childhood experiences to high school dropout among high-risk adolescents. *Journal of Research on Adolescence, 28*(2), 327–341. https://doi.org/10.1111/jora.12332

Mortimer, J. T. (2015). Social change and entry to adulthood. In *Emerging trends in the social and behavioral sciences* (pp. 1–17). American Cancer Society. https://doi.org/10.1002/9781118900772.etrds0305

Mortimer, J. T. (2019). A sociologist's perspective: The historic specificity of development and resilience in the face of increasingly ominous futures. In R. D. Parke & G. H. Elder Jr. (Eds.), *Children in changing worlds: Sociocultural and temporal perspectives* (pp. 287–298). Cambridge University Press. https://doi.org/10.1017/9781108264846.011

Mortimer, J. T. (2020). Youth, jobs, and the future: Problems and prospects. *Contemporary Sociology, 49*(2), 149–151. https://doi.org/10.1177/0094306120902418j

Mortimer, J. T., Vuolo, M., & Staff, J. (2014). Agentic pathways toward fulfillment in work. In A. C. Keller, R. Samuel, M. M. Bergman, & N. K. Semmer (Eds.), *Psychological, educational, and sociological perspectives on success and well-being in career development* (pp. 99–126). Springer Netherlands. https://doi.org/10.1007/978-94-017-8911-0_6

Mortimer, J. T., Zimmer-Gembeck, M. J., Holmes, M., & Shanahan, M. J. (2002). The process of occupational decision making: Patterns during the transition to adulthood. *Journal of Vocational Behavior, 61*(3), 439–465. https://doi.org/10.1006/jvbe.2002.1885

Morton, S., & Brodsky, D. (2016). Fetal physiology and the transition to extrauterine life. *Clinics in Perinatology, 43*(3), 395–407. https://doi.org/10.1016/j.clp.2016.04.001

Moscoviz, L., & Evans, D. K. (2022). *Learning loss and student dropouts during the Covid-19 pandemic: A review of the evidence two years after schools shut down*. Center for Global Development, Working Paper, 609.

Moseson, H., Zazanis, N., Goldberg, E., Fix, L., Durden, M., Stoeffler, A., Hastings, J., Cudlitz, L., Lesser-Lee, B., Letcher, L., Reyes, A., & Obedin-Maliver, J. (2020). The imperative for transgender and gender nonbinary inclusion: Beyond women's health. *Obstetrics & Gynecology, 135*(5), 1059–1068. https://doi.org/10.1097/AOG.0000000000003816

Moss, L. (2019, January 10). UGA middle school garden program expands beyond Athens–Clarke County. *UGA Public Service and Outreach*. https://outreach.uga.edu/uga-middle-school-garden-program-expands-beyond-athens-clarke-county/

Mõttus, R., Briley, D. A., Zheng, A., Mann, F. D., Engelhardt, L. E., Tackett, J. L., Harden, K. P., & Tucker-Drob, E. M. (2019). Kids becoming less alike: A behavioral genetic analysis of developmental increases in personality variance from childhood to adolescence. *Journal of Personality and Social Psychology, 117*(3), 635.

Mousavi Khaneghah, A., Fakhri, Y., Nematollahi, A., & Pirhadi, M. (2020). Potentially toxic elements (PTEs) in cereal-based foods: A systematic review and meta-analysis. *Trends in Food Science & Technology, 96*, 30–44. https://doi.org/10.1016/j.tifs.2019.12.007

Mowen, T. J., & Freng, A. (2019). Is more necessarily better? School security and perceptions of safety among students and parents in the United States. *American Journal of Criminal Justice, 44*(3), 376–394.

Mowen, T. J., & Schroeder, R. D. (2018). Maternal parenting style and delinquency by race and the moderating effect of structural disadvantage. *Youth & Society, 50*(2), 139–159. https://doi.org/10.1177/0044118X15598028

Mpofu, J. J., Cooper, A. C., Ashley, C., Geda, S., Harding, R. L., Johns, M. M., Spinks-Franklin, A., Njai, R., Moyse, D., & Underwood, J. M. (2022). Perceived racism and demographic, mental health, and behavioral characteristics among high school students during the COVID-19 pandemic — Adolescent Behaviors and Experiences Survey, United States, January–June 2021. *MMWR Supplements, 71*(3), 22.

Mucherah, W., Finch, H., White, T., & Thomas, K. (2018). The relationship of school climate, teacher defending and friends on students' perceptions of bullying in high school. *Journal of Adolescence, 62*, 128–139. https://doi.org/10.1016/j.adolescence.2017.11.012

Muelbert, M., Galante, L., Alexander, T., Harding, J. E., Pook, C., & Bloomfield, F. H. (2021). Odor-active volatile compounds in preterm breastmilk. *Pediatric Research, 1*–12. https://doi.org/10.1038/s41390-021-01556-w

Muenks, K., Wigfield, A., & Eccles, J. S. (2018). I can do this! The development and calibration of children's expectations for success and competence beliefs. *Developmental Review, 48*, 24–39. https://doi.org/10.1016/j.dr.2018.04.001

Muhlenkamp, K. (2012, April). Twin studies. *The University of Chicago Magazine*. https://mag.uchicago.edu/science-medicine/twin-studies

Mulder, R. H., Walton, E., Neumann, A., Houtepen, L. C., Felix, J. F., Bakermans-Kranenburg, M. J., Suderman, M., Tiemeier, H., van IJzendoorn, M. H., Relton, C. L., & Cecil, C. A. (2020). Epigenomics of being bullied: Changes in DNA methylation following bullying exposure. *Epigenetics, 15*(6–7), 750–764.

Mulgrew, K. (2020). Puberty and body image. In S. Hupp & J. Jewell (Eds.), *The encyclopedia of child and adolescent development* (pp. 1–9). Wiley. https://doi.org/10.1002/9781119171492.wecad355

Mullally, S. L., & Maguire, E. A. (2014). Learning to remember: The early ontogeny of episodic memory. *Developmental Cognitive Neuroscience, 9,* 12–29. https://doi.org/10.1016/j.dcn.2013.12.006

Mullan, K. (2019). A child's day: Trends in time use in the UK from 1975 to 2015. *The British Journal of Sociology, 70*(3), 997–1024. https://doi.org/10.1111/1468-4446.12369

Mullen, S. (2018). Major depressive disorder in children and adolescents. *Mental Health Clinician, 8*(6), 275–283. https://doi.org/10.9740/mhc.2018.11.275

Mulvey, K. L., Boswell, C., & Niehaus, K. (2018). You don't need to talk to throw a ball! Children's inclusion of language-outgroup members in behavioral and hypothetical scenarios. *Developmental Psychology, 54*(7), 1372.

Mulvihill, A., Matthews, N., Dux, P. E., & Carroll, A. (2021). Preschool children's private speech content and performance on executive functioning and problem-solving tasks. *Cognitive Development, 60,* 101116. https://doi.org/10.1016/j.cogdev.2021.101116

Munakata, Y. (1998). Infant perseveration and implications for object permanence theories: A PDP model of the AB task. *Developmental Science, 1*(2), 161–184.

Munakata, Y., & Michaelson, L. E. (2021). Executive functions in social context: Implications for conceptualizing, measuring, and supporting developmental trajectories. *Annual Review of Developmental Psychology, 3,* 139–163.

Munn-Chernoff, M. A., Johnson, E. C., Chou, Y.-L., Coleman, J. R. I., Thornton, L. M., Walters, R. K., Yilmaz, Z., Baker, J. H., Hübel, C., Gordon, S., Medland, S. E., Watson, H. J., Gaspar, H. A., Bryois, J., Hinney, A., Leppä, V. M., Mattheisen, M., Ripke, S., Yao, S., . . . Agrawal, A. (2021). Shared genetic risk between eating disorder-and substance-use-related phenotypes: Evidence from genome-wide association studies. *Addiction Biology, 26*(1), e12880.

Munro-Kramer, M. L., Fava, N. M., Saftner, M. A., Darling-Fisher, C. S., Tate, N. H., Stoddard, S. A., & Martyn, K. K. (2016). What are we missing? Risk behaviors among Arab-American adolescents and emerging adults. *Journal of the American Association of Nurse Practitioners, 28*(9), 493–502. https://doi.org/10.1002/2327-6924.12352

Munyaradzi, M., Mubaya, R. R., van Reisen, M., & van Stam, G. (2016). Maslow's theory of human motivation and its deep roots in individualism: Interrogating Maslow's applicability in africa. In *Theory, Knowledge, Development and Politics: What Role for the Academy in the Sustainability of Africa?* Langaa RPCIG.

Munzer, T. G., Miller, A. L., Peterson, K. E., Brophy-Herb, H. E., Horodynski, M. A., Contreras, D., Sturza, J., Lumeng, J. C., & Radesky, J. (2018). Media exposure in low-income preschool-aged children is associated with multiple measures of self-regulatory behavior. *Journal of Developmental and Behavioral Pediatrics, 39*(4), 303–309. https://doi.org/10.1097/DBP.0000000000000560

Murano, M. C., Feldt, M. M., & Lantos, J. D. (2020). Parental concerns on short stature: A 15 years follow-up. *The Journal of Pediatrics, 220,* 237–240. https://doi.org/10.1016/j.jpeds.2020.01.010

Murayama, K., Pekrun, R., Suzuki, M., Marsh, H. W., & Lichtenfeld, S. (2016). Don't aim too high for your kids: Parental overaspiration undermines students' learning in mathematics. *Journal of Personality and Social Psychology, 111*(5), 766–779. https://doi.org/10.1037/pspp0000079

Murphy, M. L., Cohen, S., Janicki-Deverts, D., & Doyle, W. J. (2017). Offspring of parents who were separated and not speaking to one another have reduced resistance to the common cold as adults. *Proceedings of the National Academy of Sciences, 114*(25), 6515–6520.

Murray, A., Hall, H., Speyer, L., Carter, L., Mirman, D., Caye, A., & Rohde, L. (2021). Developmental trajectories of ADHD symptoms in a large population-representative longitudinal study. *Psychological Medicine,* 1–7. https://doi.org/10.1017/S0033291721000349

Mustafa, N. S., Bakar, N. H. A., Mohamad, N., Adnan, L. H. M., Fauzi, N. F. A. M., Thoarlim, A., & Ahmad, R. (2020). MDMA and the brain: A short review on the role of neurotransmitters in neurotoxicity. *Basic and Clinical Neuroscience, 11*(4), 381.

Mustanski, B., Kuper, L., & Greene, G. J. (2014). Development of sexual orientation and identity. In D. L. Tolman & L. M. Diamond (Eds.), *APA handbook of sexuality and psychology* (Vol. 1. pp. 597–628). American Psychological Association.

Mutha, P. K., Haaland, K. Y., & Sainburg, R. L. (2012). The effects of brain lateralization on motor control and adaptation. *Journal of Motor Behavior, 44*(6), 455–469. https://doi.org/10.1080/00222895.2012.747482

Myer, G. D., Jayanthi, N., Difiori, J. P., Faigenbaum, A. D., Kiefer, A. W., Logerstedt, D., & Micheli, L. J. (2015). Sport specialization, part I. *Sports Health, 7*(5), 437–442. https://doi.org/10.1177/1941738115598747

Myers, L. J., LeWitt, R. B., Gallo, R. E., & Maselli, N. M. (2017). Baby FaceTime: Can toddlers learn from online video chat?. *Developmental Science, 20*(4), e12430.

Myin-Germeys, I., Kasanova, Z., Vaessen, T., Vachon, H., Kirtley, O., Viechtbauer, W., & Reininghaus, U. (2018). Experience sampling methodology in mental health research: New insights and technical developments. *World Psychiatry, 17*(2), 123–132. https://doi.org/10.1002/wps.20513

Na, M., Jomaa, L., Eagleton, S. G., & Savage, J. S. (2021). Head start parents with or without food insecurity and with lower food resource management skills use less positive feeding practices in preschool-age children. *The Journal of Nutrition, 151*(5), 1294–1301. https://doi.org/10.1093/jn/nxab001

Nabors, L., Stough, C. O., Garr, K., & Merianos, A. (2019). Predictors of victimization among youth who are overweight in a national sample. *Pediatric Obesity, 14*(7), e12516. https://doi.org/10.1111/ijpo.12516

NAEYC Council on the Accreditation of Early Learning Programs (NAEYC). (2019). *NAEYC early learning program accreditation standards and assessment items.* National Association for the Education of Young Children. https://www.naeyc.org/defining-recognizing-high-quality-early-learning-programs

Nagata, J. M., Ganson, K. T., Sajjad, O. M., Benabou, S. E., & Bibbins-Domingo, K. (2021). Prevalence of perceived racism and discrimination among us children aged 10 and 11 years: The Adolescent Brain Cognitive Development (ABCD) study. *JAMA Pediatrics, 175*(8), 861–863. https://doi.org/10.1001/jamapediatrics.2021.1022

Nagy, E. (2011). The newborn infant: A missing stage in developmental psychology. *Infant and Child Development, 20*(1), 3–19.

Nagy, E., Pilling, K., Blake, V., & Orvos, H. (2020). Positive evidence for neonatal imitation: A general response, adaptive engagement. *Developmental Science, 23*(2), e12894. https://doi.org/10.1111/desc.12894

Nakatsuka, N., Moorjani, P., Rai, N., Sarkar, B., Tandon, A., Patterson, N., Bhavani, G. S., Girisha, K. M., Mustak, M. S., Srinivasan, S., Kaushik, A., Vahab, S. A., Jagadeesh, S. M., Satyamoorthy, K., Singh, L., Reich, D., & Thangaraj, K. (2017). The promise of discovering population-specific disease-associated genes in South Asia. *Nature Genetics, 49*(9), 1403–1407. https://doi.org/10.1038/ng.3917

Napolitano, C. M., Sewell, M. N., Yoon, H. J., Soto, C. J., & Roberts, B. W. (2021, June). Social, emotional, and behavioral skills: An integrative model of the skills associated with success during adolescence and across the life span. In *Frontiers in Education* (Vol. 6, p. 679561). Frontiers Media SA.

Nasrullah, M., Muazzam, S., Khosa, F., & Khan, M. M. H. (2017). Child marriage and women's attitude towards wife beating in a nationally representative sample of currently married adolescent and young women in Pakistan. *International Health, 9*(1), 20–28. https://doi.org/10.1093/inthealth/ihw047

Nathan, S., Kemp, L., Bunde-Birouste, A., MacKenzie, J., Evers, C., & Shwe, T. A. (2013). "We wouldn't of made friends if we didn't come to Football United": The impacts of a football program on young people's peer, prosocial and cross-cultural relationships. *BMC Public Health, 13*(1), 1–16.

National Academies of Sciences, Engineering, and Medicine (NASEM). (2016). *Parenting matters: Supporting parents of children ages 0–8.* National Academies Press. https://doi.org/10.17226/21868

National Academies of Sciences, Engineering, and Medicine (NASEM). (2017). *Supporting students' college success: The role of assessment of intrapersonal and interpersonal competencies.* National Academies Press. https://doi.org/10.17226/24697

National Academies of Sciences, Engineering, and Medicine (NASEM). (2018). *Transforming the financing of early care and education.* National Academies Press.

National Academies of Sciences, Engineering, and Medicine (NASEM). (2019). *Monitoring educational equity* (C. Edley, J. Koenig, N. Nielsen, & C. Citro, Eds.). National Academies Press. https://doi.org/10.17226/25389

National Academies of Sciences, Engineering, and Medicine (NASEM). (2020a). *Birth settings in America: Outcomes, quality, access, and choice.*

National Academies of Sciences, Engineering, and Medicine (NASEM). (2020b). *Feeding infants and children from birth to 24 months: Summarizing existing guidance.* National Academies Press. https://doi.org/10.17226/25747

National Association for the Education of Young Children (NAEYC). (2018). *Staff to child ratio and class size.* National Association for the Education of Young Children.

National Association for the Education of Young Children (NAEYC). (2020). *Developmentally appropriate practice: A position statement of the National Association for the Education of Young Children.*

National Association of Charter School Authorizers (NACSA). (2019). *Charter school pipeline analysis.* NACSA.

National Association of School Psychologists. (2017). *Early career spotlight: Rodrigo Enciso, MA, LEP, San Diego Unified School District, San Diego, CA.* National Association of School Psychologists.

National Center for Education Statistics (NCES). (2020, February). *Common Core of Data (CCD), "Public Elementary/Secondary School Universe Survey," 2017–18.*

National Center for Education Statistics (NCES). (2021a). *Condition of education—Status dropout rates and public high school graduation rates.* https://nces.ed.gov/programs/coe/indicator/coj

National Center for Education Statistics (NCES). (2021b). *Young adults neither enrolled in school nor working* (Population Characteristics and Economic Outcomes).

National Center for Education Statistics (NCES). (2022). Enrollment rates of young children. In *Condition of Education.* U.S. Department of Education, Institute of Education Sciences. https://nces.ed.gov/programs/coe/indicator/cfa.

National Center for Health Statistics (NCHS). (2000, May 30). *CDC growth charts: United States.* Centers for Disease Control and Prevention. http://www.cdc.gov/growthcharts/

National Center for Health Statistics (NCHS). (2021, June 18). *Percentage of fair or poor health status for children under age 18 years, United States, 2019.* National Health Interview Survey. https://wwwn.cdc.gov/NHISDataQueryTool/SHS_2019_CHILD3/index.html

National Center for Health Statistics. (2022, May 28). Percentage of ever having asthma for children under age 18 years, United States, 2019–2020; Crude percentage of skin allergies for children under age 18 years, United States, 2018; Crude percentage of food allergies for children under age 18 years, United States, 2018; Crude percentage of respiratory allergies for children under age 18 years, United States, 2018. National Health Interview Survey. Generated interactively. https://wwwn.cdc.gov/NHISDataQueryTool/SHS_child/index.html

National Center for Health Statistics (NCHS), National Vital Statistics System. (2021). *Leading causes of death reports, 1981–2019.* https://www.cdc.gov/injury/wisqars/LeadingCauses.html

National Center on Disability and Journalism (NCDJ). (n.d.). *Disability language style guide.* https://ncdj.org/style-guide/

National Farm to School Network. (2022.). *About.* https://www.farmtoschool.org/about-nfsn

National Health Interview Survey. (2015). *Public-use data file and documentation.* National Center for Health Statistics. http://www.cdc.gov/nchs/nhis/quest_data_related_1997_forward.htm. 2016

National Immunization Survey (NIS). (2021). *Breastfeeding Rates, Breastfeeding Among U.S. Children Born 2011–2018, CDC National Immunization Survey.* Percentage of U.S. children who were breastfed, by birth year and rates of any and exclusive breastfeeding by age among children born in 2018. Centers for Disease Control and Prevention.

National Institute for Early Education Research (NIEER). (2019). *The state of preschool 2019.* Rutgers University.

National Physical Activity Plan Alliance (NPAPA). (2018). *The 2018 United States report card on physical activity for children and youth.*

National Research Council (NRC). (2013). *Reforming juvenile justice: A developmental approach.* National Academies Press.

National Society of Genetic Counselors (NSGC). (2019). *Prenatal testing for adult-onset conditions.* https://www.nsgc.org/Policy-Research-and-Publications/Position-Statements/Position-Statements/Post/prenatal-testing-for-adult-onset-conditions-1

National Student Clearinghouse Research Center (NSCRC). (2022). *Overview: Spring 2022 enrollment estimates.* nsrcresearchcenter.org

National Survey of Children's Health (NSCH). (2011–2012). Data query from the Child and Adolescent Health Measurement Initiative, Data Resource Center for Child and Adolescent Health website. Retrieved [1/20/15] from www.childhealthdata.org

National Survey of Children's Health (NSCH). (2019). [2018–2019 data query, Child and Adolescent Health Measurement Initiative]. Data Resource Center for Child and Adolescent Health supported by the U.S. Department of Health and Human Services, Health Resources and Services Administration (HRSA), Maternal and Child Health Bureau (MCHB). https://mchb.hrsa.gov/data/national-surveys

National Survey of Children's Health (NSCH). (2021). *Child and adolescent health measurement initiative. 2018–2019 National Survey of Children's Health (NSCH) data query.* Data Resource Center for Child and Adolescent Health supported by the U.S. Department of Health and Human Services, Health Resources and Services Administration (HRSA), Maternal and Child Health Bureau (MCHB). www.childhealthdata.org

National Survey of Early Care and Education (NSECE). (2016). *National Survey of Early Care and Education, 2013. Number and characteristics of early care and education (ECE) teachers and caregivers: Initial findings.* National Survey of Early Care and Education. Research and Evaluation, Administration for Children and Families, U.S. Department of Health and Human Services.

Natu, V. S., Gomez, J., Barnett, M., Jeska, B., Kirilina, E., Jaeger, C., Zhen, Z., Cox, S., Weiner, K. S., Weiskopf, N., & Grill-Spector, K. (2019). Apparent thinning of human visual cortex during childhood is associated with myelination. *Proceedings of the National Academy of Sciences, 116*(41), 20750–20759.

Naumova, O. Y., Rychkov, S. Y., Kornilov, S. A., Odintsova, V. V., Anikina, V. O., Solodunova, M. Y., Arintcina, I. A., Zhukova, M. A., Ovchinnikova, I. V., Burenkova, O. V., Zhukova, O. V., Muhamedrahimov, R. J., & Grigorenko, E. L. (2019). Effects of early social deprivation on epigenetic statuses and adaptive behavior of young children: A study based on a cohort of institutionalized infants and toddlers. *PLOS ONE, 14*(3), e0214285. https://doi.org/10.1371/journal.pone.0214285

Navarro, V. M. (2020). Metabolic regulation of kisspeptin—The link between energy balance and reproduction. *Nature Reviews Endocrinology, 16*(8), 407–420. https://doi.org/10.1038/s41574-020-0363-7

Nave, C. S., Edmonds, G. W., Hampson, S. E., Murzyn, T., & Sauerberger, K. S. (2017). From elementary school to midlife: Childhood personality predicts behavior during cognitive testing over four decades later. *Journal of Research in Personality, 67*, 183–189. https://doi.org/10.1016/j.jrp.2016.10.001

Negru-Subtirica, O., Tiganasu, A., Dezutter, J., & Luyckx, K. (2017). A cultural take on the links between religiosity, identity, and meaning in life in religious emerging adults. *British Journal of Developmental Psychology, 35*(1), 106–126.

Nekitsing, C., Blundell-Birtill, P., Cockroft, J. E., & Hetherington, M. M. (2018). Systematic review and meta-analysis of strategies to increase vegetable consumption in preschool children aged 2–5 years. *Appetite, 127*, 138–154. https://doi.org/10.1016/j.appet.2018.04.019

Nelson, C. A., Bhutta, Z. A., Harris, N. B., Danese, A., & Samara, M. (2020). Adversity in childhood is linked to mental and physical health throughout life. *BMJ, 371*, m3048. https://doi.org/10.1136/bmj.m3048

Nelson, C. A., Zeanah, C. H., & Fox, N. A. (2019). How early experience shapes human development: The case of psychosocial deprivation. *Neural Plasticity, 2019*, 1676285. https://doi.org/10.1155/2019/1676285

Nelson, K. (2018). Making memory: Meaning in development of the autobiographical self. In A. Rosa & J. Valsiner (Eds.), *The Cambridge handbook of sociocultural psychology* (pp. 260–273). Cambridge University Press.

Nelson, L. J. (2021). The theory of emerging adulthood 20 years later: A look at where it has taken us, what we know now, and where we need to go. *Emerging Adulthood, 9*(3), 179–188. https://doi.org/10.1177/2167696820950884

Nelson, S. C., Kling, J., Wängqvist, M., Frisén, A., & Syed, M. (2018). Identity and the body: Trajectories of body esteem from adolescence to emerging adulthood. *Developmental Psychology, 54*(6), 1159–1171. https://doi.org/10.1037/dev0000435

Nelson, T. D. (2017). *Ageism: Stereotyping and prejudice against older persons* (2nd ed.). MIT Press.

Neniskyte, U., & Gross, C. T. (2017). Errant gardeners: glial-cell-dependent synaptic pruning and neurodevelopmental disorders. *Nature Reviews Neuroscience, 1.*

Neshteruk, C. D., Mazzucca, S., Østbye, T., & Ward, D. S. (2018). The physical environment in family childcare homes and children's physical activity. *Child: Care, Health and Development, 44*(5), 746-752.

Netsi, E., Santos, I. S., Stein, A., Barros, F. C., Barros, A. J., & Matijasevich, A. (2017). A different rhythm of life: Sleep patterns in the first 4 years of life and associated sociodemographic characteristics in a large Brazilian birth cohort. *Sleep Medicine, 37*, 77–87.

Newcomb, A. F., Bukowski, W. M., & Pattee, L. (1993). Children's peer relations: A meta-analytic review of popular, rejected, neglected, controversial, and average sociometric status. *Psychological Bulletin, 113*(1), 99.

Newheiser, A.-K., Dunham, Y., Merrill, A., Hoosain, L., & Olson, K. R. (2014). Preference for high status predicts implicit outgroup bias among children from low-status groups. *Developmental Psychology, 50*(4), 1081–1090. https://doi.org/10.1037/a0035054

Newland, L. A., Giger, J. T., Lawler, M. J., Roh, S., Brockevelt, B. L., & Schweinle, A. (2019). Multilevel analysis of child and adolescent subjective well-being across 14 countries: Child-and country-level predictors. *Child Development, 90*(2), 395–413.

Newman, R. S., Morini, G., & Chatterjee, M. (2013). Infants' name recognition in on- and off-channel noise. *The Journal of the Acoustical Society of America, 133*(5), EL377–EL383. https://doi.org/10.1121/1.4798269

Newton, A. T., Honaker, S. M., & Reid, G. J. (2020). Risk and protective factors and processes for behavioral sleep problems among preschool and early school-aged children: A systematic review. *Sleep Medicine Reviews, 52*, 101303. https://doi.org/10.1016/j.smrv.2020.101303

Ng'asike, J. T. (2011). Turkana children's sociocultural practices of pastoralist lifestyles and science curriculum and instruction in Kenyan early childhood education. In *Dissertation Abstracts International Section A: Humanities and social sciences* (Vol. 72, Issue 2–A, p. 546). ProQuest Information & Learning.

Ngo, C. T., Alm, K. H., Metoki, A., Hampton, W., Riggins, T., Newcombe, N. S., & Olson, I. R. (2017). White matter structural connectivity and episodic memory in early childhood. *Developmental Cognitive Neuroscience, 28*, 41–53. https://doi.org/10.1016/j.dcn.2017.11.001

Ngo, Q. M., Veliz, P. T., Kusunoki, Y., Stein, S. F., & Boyd, C. J. (2018). Adolescent sexual violence: Prevalence, adolescent risks, and violence characteristics. *Preventive Medicine, 116*, 68–74.

Nguyen, A. J., Bradshaw, C., Townsend, L., & Bass, J. (2020). Prevalence and correlates of bullying victimization in four low-resource countries. *Journal of Interpersonal Violence, 35*(19–20), 3767–3790.

Nguyen, A. M. D., & Benet-Martínez, V. (2013). Biculturalism and adjustment: A meta-analysis. *Journal of Cross-Cultural Psychology, 44*(1), 122–159.

Nguyen, P. T., & Hinshaw, S. P. (2020). Understanding the stigma associated with ADHD: Hope for the future? *The ADHD Report, 28*(5), 1–10, 12. https://doi.org/10.1521/adhd.2020.28.5.1

NICHD Early Child Care Research Network. (2004). Trajectories of physical aggression from toddlerhood to middle childhood: Predictors, correlates, and outcomes. *Monographs of the Society for Research in Child Development, 69*(4), 1–129. https://doi.org/10.1111/j.0037-976x.2004.00312.x

Nicolopoulou, A., Cortina, K. S., Ilgaz, H., Cates, C. B., & de Sá, A. B. (2015). Using a narrative- and play-based activity to promote low-income preschoolers' oral language, emergent literacy, and social competence. *Early Childhood Research Quarterly, 31*, 147–162. https://doi.org/10.1016/j.ecresq.2015.01.006

Nielsen, L. (2017). Re-examining the research on parental conflict, coparenting, and custody arrangements. *Psychology, Public Policy, and Law, 23*(2), 211.

Nielson, M. G., Delay, D., Flannery, K. M., Martin, C. L., & Hanish, L. D. (2020a). Does gender-bending help or hinder friending? The roles of gender and gender similarity in friendship dissolution. *Developmental Psychology, 56*(6), 1157.

Nielson, M. G., Schroeder, K. M., Martin, C. L., & Cook, R. E. (2020b). Investigating the relation between gender typicality and pressure to conform to gender norms. *Sex Roles, 83*, 523–535.

Nigg, J. T., Sibley, M. H., Thapar, A., & Karalunas, S. L. (2020). Development of ADHD: Etiology, heterogeneity, and early life course. *Annual Review of Developmental Psychology, 2*(1), 559.

Nigra, A. E. (2020). Environmental racism and the need for private well protections. *Proceedings of the National Academy of Sciences, 117*(30), 17476–17478. https://doi.org/10.1073/pnas.2011547117

Nijhof, S. L., Vinkers, C. H., van Geelen, S. M., Duijff, S. N., Achterberg, E. J. M., van der Net, J., Veltkamp, R. C., Grootenhuis, M. A., van de Putte, E. M., Hillegers, M. H. J., van der Brug, A. W., Wierenga, C. J., Benders, M. J. N. L., Engels, R. C. M. E., van der Ent, C. K., Vanderschuren, L. J. M. J., & Lesscher, H. M. B. (2018). Healthy play, better coping: The importance of play for the development of children in health and disease. *Neuroscience & Biobehavioral Reviews, 95*, 421–429. https://doi.org/10.1016/j.neubiorev.2018.09.024

Nikkelen, S. W. C., van Oosten, J. M. F., & van den Borne, M. M. J. J. (2020). Sexuality education in the digital era: Intrinsic and extrinsic predictors of online sexual information seeking among youth. *The Journal of Sex Research, 57*(2), 189–199. https://doi.org/10.1080/00224499.2019.1612830

Nikolić, M., Brummelman, E., Colonnesi, C., de Vente, W., & Bögels, S. M. (2018). When gushing leads to blushing: Inflated praise leads socially anxious children to blush. *Behaviour Research and Therapy, 106*, 1–7. https://doi.org/10.1016/j.brat.2018.04.003

Nikolopoulos, H., Mayan, M., MacIsaac, J., Miller, T., & Bell, R. C. (2017). Women's perceptions of discussions about gestational weight gain with health care providers during pregnancy and postpartum: A qualitative study. *BMC Pregnancy and Childbirth, 17*(1), 97. https://doi.org/10.1186/s12884-017-1257-0

Nisbett, R. E., Aronson, J., Blair, C., Dickens, W., Flynn, J., Halpern, D. F., & Turkheimer, E. (2012). Intelligence: New findings and theoretical developments. *American Psychologist, 67*(2), 130–159. https://doi.org/10.1037/a0026699

Nishijima, K., Yoneda, M., Hirai, T., Takakuwa, K., & Enomoto, T. (2019). Biology of the vernix caseosa: A review. *Journal of Obstetrics and Gynaecology Research, 45*(11), 2145–2149. https://doi.org/10.1111/jog.14103

Nist, M. D., Harrison, T. M., & Steward, D. K. (2019). The biological embedding of neonatal stress exposure: A conceptual model describing the mechanisms of stress-induced neurodevelopmental impairment in preterm infants. *Research in Nursing & Health, 42*(1), 61–71. https://doi.org/10.1002/nur.21923

Niu, W. (2020). Intelligence in worldwide perspective: A twenty-first-century update. In R. J. Sternberg (Ed.), *The Cambridge handbook of intelligence* (pp. 893–915). Cambridge University Press.

Nix, R. L., Francis, L. A., Feinberg, M. E., Gill, S., Jones, D. E., Hostetler, M. L., & Stifter, C. A. (2021). Improving toddlers' healthy eating habits and self-regulation: A randomized controlled trial. *Pediatrics, 147*(1), e20193326. https://doi.org/10.1542/peds.2019-3326

Noble, K. G., & Giebler, M. A. (2020). The neuroscience of socioeconomic inequality. *Current Opinion in Behavioral Sciences, 36*, 23–28. https://doi.org/10.1016/j.cobeha.2020.05.007

Noble, K. G., Magnuson, K., Gennetian, L. A., Duncan, G. J., Yoshikawa, H., Fox, N. A., & Halpern-Meekin, S. (2021). Baby's first years: Design of a randomized controlled trial of poverty reduction in the United States. *Pediatrics, 148*(4), e2020049702. https://doi.org/10.1542/peds.2020-049702

Nock, M. K. (2009). Why do people hurt themselves? New insights into the nature and functions of self-injury. *Current Directions in Psychological Science, 18*(2), 78–83.

Nock, M. K., Green, J. G., Hwang, I., McLaughlin, K. A., Sampson, N. A., Zaslavsky, A. M., & Kessler, R. C. (2013). Prevalence, correlates, and treatment of lifetime suicidal behavior among adolescents: Results from the National Comorbidity Survey Replication Adolescent Supplement. *JAMA Psychiatry, 70*(3), 300–310. https://doi.org/10.1001/2013.jamapsychiatry.55

Nogueira Avelar e Silva, R., van de Bongardt, D., van de Looij-Jansen, P., Wijtzes, A., & Raat, H. (2016). Mother– and father–adolescent relationships and early sexual intercourse. *Pediatrics, 138*(6), e20160782. https://doi.org/10.1542/peds.2016-0782

Non, A. L., Román, J. C., Clausing, E. S., Gilman, S. E., Loucks, E. B., Buka, S. L., Appleton, A. A., & Kubzansky, L. D. (2020). Optimism and social support predict healthier adult behaviors despite socially disadvantaged childhoods. *International Journal of Behavioral Medicine, 27*(2), 200–212.

Nong, P., Raj, M., Creary, M., Kardia, S. L. R., & Platt, J. E. (2020). Patient-reported experiences of discrimination in the US health care system. *JAMA Network Open, 3*(12), e2029650. https://doi.org/10.1001/jamanetworkopen.2020.29650

Norbom, L. B., Ferschmann, L., Parker, N., Agartz, I., Andreassen, O. A., Paus, T., Westlye, L. T., & Tamnes, C. K. (2021). New insights into the dynamic development of the cerebral cortex in childhood and adolescence: Integrating macro- and microstructural MRI findings. *Progress in Neurobiology, 204*, 102109. https://doi.org/10.1016/j.pneurobio.2021.102109

Norbury, C. F., & Sonuga-Barke, E. (2017). Editorial: New frontiers in the scientific study of developmental language disorders. *Journal of Child Psychology and Psychiatry, 58*(10), 1065–1067. https://doi.org/10.1111/jcpp.12821

Norbury, C. F., Vamvakas, G., Gooch, D., Baird, G., Charman, T., Simonoff, E., & Pickles, A. (2017). Language growth in children with heterogeneous language disorders: A population study. *Journal of Child Psychology and Psychiatry, 58*(10), 1092–1105. https://doi.org/10.1111/jcpp.12793

NORC. (2021). *Surveys of trust in the U.S. health care system.* American Board of Internal Medicine Foundation.

Norris, A. L., & Orchowski, L. M. (2020). Peer victimization of sexual minority and transgender youth: A cross-sectional study of high school students. *Psychology of Violence, 10*(2), 201–211. https://doi.org/10.1037/vio0000260

Norris, E., van Steen, T., Direito, A., & Stamatakis, E. (2020). Physically active lessons in schools and their impact on physical activity, educational, health and cognition outcomes: A systematic review and meta-analysis. *British Journal of Sports Medicine, 54*(14), 826–838.

Northridge, M. E., Kumar, A., & Kaur, R. (2020). Disparities in access to oral health care. *Annual Review of Public Health, 41*, 513–535. https://doi.org/10.1146/annurev-publhealth-040119-094318

Notini, L., Pang, K. C., Telfer, M., & McDougall, R. (2021). "No one stays just on blockers forever": Clinicians' divergent views and practices regarding puberty suppression for nonbinary young people. *Journal of Adolescent Health, 68*(6), 1189–1196. https://doi.org/10.1016/j.jadohealth.2020.09.028

Ntuli, B., Mokgatle, M., & Madiba, S. (2020). The psychosocial wellbeing of orphans: The case of early school leavers in socially depressed environment in Mpumalanga Province, South Africa. *PLOS ONE, 15*(2), e0229487. https://doi.org/10.1371/journal.pone.0229487

Nucci, L. P., & Turiel, E. (1978). Social interactions and the development of social concepts in preschool children. *Child Development, 49*(2), 400–407.

Núñez, C., García-Alix, A., Arca, G., Agut, T., Carreras, N., Portella, M. J., & Stephan-Otto, C. (2022). *Breastfeeding duration is associated with larger cortical gray matter volumes in children from the ABCD study* (p. 2022.05.23.22274926). medRxiv. https://doi.org/10.1101/2022.05.23.22274926

Nutall, G. C. (1911, April 29). Eugenics and genetics. *Scientific American.* https://doi.org/10.1038/scientificamerican04291911-271supp

Nystrand, C., Feldman, I., Enebrink, P., & Sampaio, F. (2019). Cost-effectiveness analysis of parenting interventions for the prevention of behaviour problems in children. *PLOS ONE, 14*(12), e0225503. https://doi.org/10.1371/journal.pone.0225503

O'Dea, R. E., Lagisz, M., Jennions, M. D., & Nakagawa, S. (2018). Gender differences in individual variation in academic grades fail to fit expected patterns for STEM. *Nature Communications, 9*(1), 3777. https://doi.org/10.1038/s41467-018-06292-0

O'Donnell, K. J., & Meaney, M. J. (2020). Epigenetics, development, and psychopathology. *Annual Review of Clinical Psychology, 16*, 327–350. https://doi.org/10.1146/annurev-clinpsy-050718-095530

O'Hara, L., Ahmed, H., & Elashie, S. (2021). Evaluating the impact of a brief health at Every Size®-informed health promotion activity on body positivity and internalized weight-based oppression. *Body Image, 37*, 225–237. https://doi.org/10.1016/j.bodyim.2021.02.006

O'Hara, M. W., & Engeldinger, J. (2018). Treatment of postpartum depression: Recommendations for the clinician. *Clinical Obstetrics and Gynecology, 61*(3), 604–614. https://doi.org/10.1097/GRF.0000000000000353

O'Keeffe, L. M., Frysz, M., Bell, J. A., Howe, L. D., & Fraser, A. (2020). Puberty timing and adiposity change across childhood and adolescence: Disentangling cause and consequence. *Human Reproduction, 35*(12), 2784–2792. https://doi.org/10.1093/humrep/deaa213

O'Neil, S., Clarke, E., & Peeters Grietens, K. (2017). How to protect your new-born from neonatal death: Infant feeding and medical practices in the Gambia. *Women's Studies International Forum, 60*, 136–143. https://doi.org/10.1016/j.wsif.2016.11.003

O'Sullivan, A., & Monk, C. (2020). Maternal and environmental influences on perinatal and infant development. *Future of Children, 30*(2), 11–34.

Oakley, A. (2018). *Women, peace and welfare: A suppressed history of social reform, 1880–1920.* Policy Press.

Oberle, E., Ji, X. R., Kerai, S., Guhn, M., Schonert-Reichl, K. A., & Gadermann, A. M. (2020). Screen time and extracurricular activities as risk and protective factors for mental health in adolescence: A population-level study. *Preventive Medicine, 141*, 106291. https://doi.org/10.1016/j.ypmed.2020.106291

Obradović, J., & Armstrong-Carter, E. (2020). Addressing educational inequalities and promoting learning through studies of stress physiology in elementary school students. *Development and Psychopathology, 32*(5), 1899–1913.

Ochoa-Bernal, M. A., & Fazleabas, A. T. (2020). Physiologic Events of Embryo Implantation and Decidualization in Human and Non-Human Primates. *International Journal of Molecular Sciences, 21*(6), Article 6. https://doi.org/10.3390/ijms21061973

Odgers, C. L. (2018). Smartphones are bad for some adolescents, not all. *Nature, 554*(7693), 432–434. https://doi.org/10.1038/d41586-018-02109-8

Odgers, C. L., Schueller, S. M., & Ito, M. (2020). Screen time, social media use, and adolescent development. *Annual Review of Developmental Psychology, 2*(1), 485–502. https://doi.org/10.1146/annurev-devpsych-121318-084815

Oh, C., Carducci, B., Vaivada, T., & Bhutta, Z. A. (2022). Interventions to promote physical activity and healthy digital media use in children and adolescents: A systematic review. *Pediatrics, 149*(Supplement 6), e2021053852I. https://doi.org/10.1542/peds.2021-053852I

Oh, W., Bowker, J. C., Santos, A. J., Ribeiro, O., Guedes, M., Freitas, M., Kim, H. K., Song, S., & Rubin, K. H. (2021). Distinct profiles of relationships with mothers, fathers, and best friends and social-behavioral functioning in early adolescence: A cross-cultural study. *Child Development, 92*(6), e1154–e1170. https://doi.org/10.1111/cdev.13610

Oh, W., Volling, B. L., & Gonzalez, R. (2015). Trajectories of children's social interactions with their infant sibling in the first year: A multidimensional approach. *Journal of Family Psychology, 29*(1), 119.

Ohtani, K., & Hisasaka, T. (2018). Beyond intelligence: A meta-analytic review of the relationship among metacognition, intelligence, and academic performance. *Metacognition and Learning, 13*(2), 179–212.

Okonofua, J. A., & Eberhardt, J. L. (2015). Two strikes: Race and the disciplining of young students. *Psychological Science, 26*(5), 617–624. https://doi.org/10.1177/0956797615570365

Okonofua, J. A., Walton, G. M., & Eberhardt, J. L. (2016). A vicious cycle: A social–psychological account of extreme racial disparities in school discipline. *Perspectives on Psychological Science, 11*(3), 381–398. https://doi.org/10.1177/1745691616635592

Okowo-Bele, J.-M. (2015). *Together we can close the immunization gap.* World Health Organization. https://www.who.int/mediacentre/commentaries/vaccine-preventable-diseases/en/

Oladapo, O. T., Diaz, V., Bonet, M., Abalos, E., Thwin, S. S., Souza, H., Perdoná, G., Souza, J. P., & Gülmezoglu, A. M. (2018). Cervical dilatation patterns of 'low-risk' women with spontaneous labour and normal perinatal outcomes: A systematic review. *BJOG: An International Journal of Obstetrics & Gynaecology, 125*(8), 944–954. https://doi.org/10.1111/1471-0528.14930

Olds, D. L., Kitzman, H., Knudtson, M. D., Anson, E., Smith, J. A., & Cole, R. (2014). Effect of home visiting by nurses on maternal and child mortality: Results of a 2-decade follow-up of a randomized clinical trial. *JAMA Pediatrics, 168*(9), 800–806.

Oliver, R., & Nguyen, B. (2018). Teaching young second language learners: Practices in different classroom contexts. In *Teaching young second language learners* (pp. 1–28). Routledge.

Oller, D. K., Caskey, M., Yoo, H., Bene, E. R., Jhang, Y., Lee, C.-C., Bowman, D. D., Long, H. L., Buder, E. H., & Vohr, B. (2019). Preterm and full term infant vocalization and the origin of language. *Scientific Reports, 9*(1), 14734. https://doi.org/10.1038/s41598-019-51352-0

Oller, D. K., Ramsay, G., Bene, E., Long, H. L., & Griebel, U. (2021). Protophones, the precursors to speech, dominate the human infant vocal landscape. *Philosophical Transactions of the Royal Society B, 376*(1836), 20200255.

Olmstead, S. B., McMahan, K. D., & Anders, K. M. (2021). Meanings ascribed to sex and commitment among college-attending and non-college emerging adults: A replication and extension. *Archives of Sexual Behavior, 50*, 2435–2446. https://doi.org/10.1007/s10508-021-02042-4

Olson, S. L., Choe, D. E., & Sameroff, A. J. (2017). Trajectories of child externalizing problems between ages 3 and 10 years: Contributions of children's early effortful control, theory of mind, and parenting experiences. *Development and Psychopathology, 29*(4), 1333–1351. https://doi.org/10.1017/S095457941700030X

Olweus, D. (1978). *Aggression in the schools: Bullies and whipping boys.* Hemisphere.

Olweus, D. (1993). Bully/victim problems among schoolchildren: Long-term consequences and an effective intervention program. In S. Hodgins (Ed.), *Mental disorder and crime* (pp. 317–349). SAGE Publications.

Olweus, D., Limber, S. P., & Breivik, K. (2019). Addressing specific forms of bullying: A large-scale evaluation of the Olweus bullying prevention program. *International Journal of Bullying Prevention, 1*(1), 70–84. https://doi.org/10.1007/s42380-019-00009-7

Olza-Fernández, I., Gabriel, M. A. M., Gil-Sanchez, A., Garcia-Segura, L. M., & Arevalo, M. A. (2014). Neuroendocrinology of childbirth and mother–child attachment: The basis of an etiopathogenic model of perinatal neurobiological disorders. *Frontiers in Neuroendocrinology, 35*(4), 459–472.

Omar, M. T. M. (2020). Religious education in the Arab world: Saudi Arabia, Sudan and Egypt as models. *English Language Teaching, 13*(12), 27–36.

Omura, J. D., Hyde, E. T., Watson, K. B., Sliwa, S. A., Fulton, J. E., & Carlson, S. A. (2019). Prevalence of children walking to school and related barriers—United States, 2017. *Preventive Medicine, 118*, 191–195.

Ong, J. L., Tandi, J., Patanaik, A., Lo, J. C., & Chee, M. W. L. (2019). Large-scale data from wearables reveal regional disparities in sleep patterns that persist across age and sex. *Scientific Reports, 9*(1), 3415. https://doi.org/10.1038/s41598-019-40156-x

Ontai, L. L., Sutter, C., Sitnick, S., Shilts, M. K., & Townsend, M. S. (2019). Parent food-related behaviors and family-based dietary and activity environments: Associations with BMI z-scores in low-income preschoolers. *Childhood Obesity, 16*(S1), S-55–S-63. https://doi.org/10.1089/chi.2019.0105

Orben, A., Tomova, L., & Blakemore, S. J. (2020). The effects of social deprivation on adolescent development and mental health. *The Lancet Child & Adolescent Health, 4*(8), 634–640.

Ordway, M. R., Sadler, L. S., Jeon, S., O'Connell, M., Banasiak, N., Fenick, A. M., Crowley, A. A., Canapari, C., & Redeker, N. S. (2020). Sleep health in young children living with socioeconomic adversity. *Research in Nursing & Health, 43*(4), 329–340.

Orellana, M. F. (2001). The work kids do: Mexican and Central American immigrant children's contributions to households and schools in California. *Harvard Educational Review, 71*(3), 366–390.

Orellana, M. F., & Phoenix, A. (2017). Re-interpreting: Narratives of childhood language brokering over time. *Childhood (Copenhagen, Denmark), 24*(2), 183–196. https://doi.org/10.1177/0907568216671178

Oreskes, N. (2019). *Why trust science?* Princeton University Press.

Organization for Economic Cooperation and Development (OECD). (2015). Program for International Student Assessment (PISA), 2015., Table A5. Average scores of 15-year-old students on the PISA mathematics literacy scale in Massachusetts public schools compared with other participating education systems: 2015. https://nces.ed.gov/surveys/pisa/pisa2015/pisa2015highlights_7_4.asp

Organisation for Economic Co-operation and Development (OECD). (2017). *Starting strong 2017: Key OECD indicators on early childhood education and care.* OECD Publishing.

Organisation for Economic Cooperation and Development (OECD). (2019a). *Luxembourg Country Note: Programme for International Student Assessment (PISA). Results from PISA 2018.* OECD.

Organisation for Economic Co-operation and Development (OECD). (2019b). *Skills matter: Additional results from the Survey of Adult Skills* (OECD Skills Studies). OECD Publishing. https://doi.org/10.1787/1f029d8f-en

Organisation for Economic Co-operation and Development (OECD). (2020). *Is childcare affordable?* (Policy brief on employment, labour and social affairs). OECD.

Organisation for Economic Co-operation and Development (OECD). (2021a). *Age of mothers at childbirth and age-specific fertility* (SF2.3 OECD Family Database).

Organisation for Economic Co-operation and Development (OECD). (2021b). *Beyond Academic Learning: First Results from the Survey of Social and Emotional Skills.* OECD. https://doi.org/10.1787/92a11084-en

Organisation for Economic Co-operation and Development (OECD). (2021c). *Education at a Glance 2021: OECD Indicators*, OECD Publishing, Paris, https://doi.org/10.1787/b35a14e5-en

Organisation for Economic Co-operation and Development (OECD). (2021d). *Young people's concerns during COVID-19: Results from Risks That Matter 2020.* https://read.oecd-ilibrary.org/view/?ref=1099_1099612

-0juxn9tthe&title=Young-people-s-concerns-during-COVID-19-Results-from-Risks-That-Matter-2020

Organisation for Economic Co-operation and Development (OECD). (2022). *Review education policies — Education GPS — OECD: Migrant background.* https://gpseducation.oecd.org/reviewleducationpolicies/#!node=41750&filter=all

Ori, M. R., & Larsen, J. B. (2018). Mercury poisoning in a toddler from home contamination due to skin-lightening cream. *Journal of Pediatrics, 196,* 314–317.

Oron, A. P., Chao, D. L., Ezeanolue, E. E., Ezenwa, L. N., Piel, F. B., Ojogun, O. T., Uyoga, S., Williams, T. N., & Nnodu, O. E. (2020). Caring for Africa's sickle cell children: Will we rise to the challenge? BMC Medicine, *18,* 1–8.

Orth, T., & Rosenfeld, M. (2018). Commitment timing in same-sex and different-sex relationships. *Population Review, 57*(1). https://doi.org/10.1353/prv.2018.0000

Orth, U., Erol, R. Y., & Luciano, E. C. (2018). Development of self-esteem from age 4 to 94 years: A meta-analysis of longitudinal studies. *Psychological Bulletin, 144*(10), 1045–1080. https://doi.org/10.1037/bul0000161

Ortiz, S. O. (2019). On the measurement of cognitive abilities in English learners. *Contemporary School Psychology, 23*(1), 68–86. https://doi.org/10.1007/s40688-018-0208-8

Ortiz, S. O., & Wong, J. Y. T. (2022). Theoretical, empirical and practical issues in testing English learners. In *Fairness in Educational and Psychological Testing: Examining Theoretical, Research, Practice, and Policy Implications of the 2014 Standards.* American Educational Research Association.

Ortiz-Ospina, E. (2020, December 11). Who do we spend time with across our lifetime? Our World in Data. https://ourworldindata.org/time-with-others-lifetime

Ose Askvik, E., van der Weel, F. R. (Ruud), & van der Meer, A. L. H. (2020). The importance of cursive handwriting over typewriting for learning in the classroom: A high-density EEG study of 12-year-old children and young adults. *Frontiers in Psychology, 11,* 1810. https://doi.org/10.3389/fpsyg.2020.01810

Ospina-Betancurt, J., Vilain, E., & Martinez-Patiño, M. J. (2021). The end of compulsory gender verification: Is it progress for inclusion of women in sports? *Archives of Sexual Behavior, 50*(7), 2799–2807. https://doi.org/10.1007/s10508-021-02073-x

Oster, E. (2019). *Cribsheet: A data-driven guide to better, more relaxed parenting, from birth to preschool.* Penguin.

Ostfeld, B. M., Schwartz-Soicher, O., Reichman, N. E., Teitler, J. O., & Hegyi, T. (2017). Prematurity and sudden unexpected infant deaths in the United States. *Pediatrics, 140*(1), e20163334. https://doi.org/10.1542/peds.2016-3334

Ostlund, B. D., Vlisides-Henry, R. D., Crowell, S. E., Raby, K. L., Terrell, S., Brown, M. A., Tinajero, R., Shakiba, N., Monk, C., Shakib, J. H., Buchi, K. F., & Conradt, E. (2019). Intergenerational transmission of emotion dysregulation: Part II. Developmental origins of newborn neurobehavior. *Development and Psychopathology, 31*(3), 833–846. https://doi.org/10.1017/S0954579419000440

Otgaar, H., Howe, M. L., Merckelbach, H., & Muris, P. (2018). Who is the better eyewitness? Sometimes adults but at other times children. *Current Directions in Psychological Science, 27*(5), 378–385.

Ott, M. A., Hunt, A. L., Katz, A. J., & Zaban, L. S. (2020). Tapping into community resiliency in rural adolescent pregnancy prevention: An implementation sciences approach. *Behavioral Medicine, 46*(3–4), 340–352. https://doi.org/10.1080/08964289.2020.1748863

Otto, H., Potinius, I., & Keller, H. (2014). Cultural differences in stranger–child interactions: A comparison between German middle-class and Cameroonian Nso stranger–infant dyads. *Journal of Cross-Cultural Psychology, 45*(2), 322–334. https://doi.org/10.1177/0022022113509133

Otto, H. W. R., Schuitmaker, N., Lamm, B., Abels, M., Serdtse, Y., Yovsi, R., & Tomlinson, M. (2017). Infants' social experiences in three African sociocultural contexts. *Child Development, 88*(4), 1235–1250. https://doi.org/10.1111/cdev.12661

Oudekerk, B., & Morgan, R. E. (2016). *Co-offending among adolescents in violent victimizations, 2004–13.* U.S. Department of Justice, Office of Justice Programs, Bureau of Justice Statistics.

Ou-Yang, M.-C., Sun, Y., Liebowitz, M., Chen, C.-C., Fang, M.-L., Dai, W., Chuang, T.-W., & Chen, J.-L. (2020). Accelerated weight gain, prematurity, and the risk of childhood obesity: A meta-analysis and systematic review. *PLOS ONE, 15*(5), e0232238. https://doi.org/10.1371/journal.pone.0232238

Overton, W. F. (2013). A new paradigm for developmental science: Relationism and relational-developmental systems. *Applied Developmental Science, 17*(2), 94–107. https://doi.org/10.1080/10888691.2013.778717

Overton, W. F. (2015). Processes, relations, and relational-developmental-systems. In *Handbook of child psychology and developmental science.* John Wiley & Sons. https://doi.org/10.1002/9781118963418.childpsy102

Owens, A. (2018). Income segregation between school districts and inequality in students' achievement. *Sociology of Education, 91*(1), 1–27.

Owens, J. (2021). Parental intervention in school, academic pressure, and childhood diagnoses of ADHD. *Social Science & Medicine, 272,* 113746. https://doi.org/10.1016/j.socscimed.2021.113746

Owens-Young, J., & Bell, C. N. (2020). Structural racial inequities in socioeconomic status, urban-rural classification, and infant mortality in US counties. *Ethnicity & Disease, 30*(3), 389–398. https://doi.org/10.18865/ed.30.3.389

Oyserman, D. (2017). Culture three ways: Culture and subcultures within countries. *Annual Review of Psychology, 68,* 435–463.

Oyserman, D., Coon, H. M., & Kemmelmeier, M. (2002). Rethinking individualism and collectivism: Evaluation of theoretical assumptions and meta-analyses. *Psychological Bulletin, 128*(1), 3–72. https://doi.org/10.1037/0033-2909.128.1.3

Oyserman, D., Elmore, K., & Smith, G. (2012). Self, self-concept, and identity. In M. R. Leary & J. P. Tangney (Eds.), *Handbook of self and identity* (2nd ed., pp. 69–104). Guilford.

Özçalışkan, Ş., & Goldin-Meadow, S. (2005). Gesture is at the cutting edge of early language development. *Cognition, 96*(3), B101–B113.

Ozernov-Palchik, O., Sury, D., Turesky, T. K., Yu, X., & Gaab, N. (2021). Longitudinal changes in brain activation underlying reading fluency. *BioRxiv.*

Paavonen, E. J., Saarenpää-Heikkilä, O., Morales-Munoz, I., Virta, M., Häkälä, N., Pölkki, P., Kylliäinen, A., Karlsson, H., Paunio, T., & Karlsson, L. (2020). Normal sleep development in infants: Findings from two large birth cohorts. *Sleep Medicine, 69,* 145–154. https://doi.org/10.1016/j.sleep.2020.01.009

Packer, M. J., & Cole, M. (2020). Culture and human development. In *Oxford research encyclopedia of psychology.* https://doi.org/10.1093/acrefore/9780190236557.013.581

Padilla, J., Jager, J., Updegraff, K. A., McHale, S. M., & Umanña-Taylor, A. J. (2020). Mexican-origin family members' unique and shared family perspectives of familism values and their links with parent-youth relationship quality. *Developmental Psychology, 56*(5), 993–1008. https://doi.org/10.1037/dev0000913

Padilla, N., & Lagercrantz, H. (2020). Making of the mind. *Acta Paediatrica, 109*(5), 883–892. https://doi.org/10.1111/apa.15167

Pahlke, E., Bigler, R. S., & Suizzo, M. A. (2012). Relations between colorblind socialization and children's racial bias: Evidence from European American mothers and their preschool children. *Child Development, 83*(4), 1164–1179.

Palagi, E., Celeghin, A., Tamietto, M., Winkielman, P., & Norscia, I. (2020). The neuroethology of spontaneous mimicry and emotional contagion in human and non-human animals. *Neuroscience & Biobehavioral Reviews, 111,* 149–165. https://doi.org/10.1016/j.neubiorev.2020.01.020

Palmer, S. B., & Abbott, N. (2018). Bystander responses to bias-based bullying in schools: A developmental intergroup approach. *Child Development Perspectives, 12*(1), 39–44.

Panagiotakopoulos, L., Chulani, V., Koyama, A., Childress, K., Forcier, M., Grimsby, G., & Greenberg, K. (2020). The effect of early puberty suppression on treatment options and outcomes in transgender patients. *Nature Reviews Urology, 17*(11), 626–636. https://doi.org/10.1038/s41585-020-0372-2

Panchal, N., Kamal, R., Cox, C., Garfield, R., & Chidambaram, P. (2021). *Mental health and substance use considerations among children during the COVID-19 pandemic.* KFF. https://www.kff.org/coronavirus-covid-19/issue-brief/mental-health-and-substance-use-considerations-among-children-during-the-covid-19-pandemic/

Pang, J., Keh, H. T., Li, X., & Maheswaran, D. (2017). "Every coin has two sides": The effects of dialectical thinking and attitudinal ambivalence on psychological discomfort and consumer choice. *Journal of Consumer Psychology, 27*(2), 218–230.

Paniukov, D., Lebel, R. M., Giesbrecht, G., & Lebel, C. (2020). Cerebral blood flow increases across early childhood. *NeuroImage, 204,* 116224. https://doi.org/10.1016/j.neuroimage.2019.116224

Panofsky, A., & Bliss, C. (2017). Ambiguity and scientific authority: Population classification in genomic science. *American Sociological Review, 82* (1), 59–87. https://doi.org/10.1177/0003122416685812

Pant, R., Kanjlia, S., & Bedny, M. (2020). A sensitive period in the neural phenotype of language in blind individuals. *Developmental Cognitive Neuroscience, 41,* 100744. https://doi.org/10.1016/j.dcn.2019.100744

Pantell, R. H., & Committee on Psychosocial Aspects of Child and Family Health. (2017). The child witness in the courtroom. *Pediatrics, 139*(3).

Paoletti, J. B. (2012). *Pink and blue: Telling the boys from the girls in America.* Indiana University Press.

Papadatou-Pastou, M., Ntolka, E., Schmitz, J., Martin, M., Munafò, M. R., Ocklenburg, S., & Paracchini, S. (2020). Human handedness: A meta-analysis. *Psychological Bulletin, 146*(6), 481–524. https://doi.org/10.1037/bul0000229

Papadimitriou, A. (2016). Timing of puberty and secular trend in human maturation. In P. Kumanov & A. Agarwal (Eds.), *Puberty: Physiology and abnormalities* (pp. 121–136). Springer International Publishing. https://doi.org/10.1007/978-3-319-32122-6_9

Papageorgiou, K. A., Smith, T. J., Wu, R., Johnson, M. H., Kirkham, N. Z., & Ronald, A. (2014). Individual differences in infant fixation duration relate to attention and behavioral control in childhood. *Psychological Science, 25*(7), 1371–1379.

Parade, S. H., Armstrong, L. M., Dickstein, S., & Seifer, R. (2018). Family context moderates the association of maternal postpartum depression and stability of infant temperament. *Child Development, 89*(6), 2118–2135. https://doi.org/10.1111/cdev.12895

Paradies, Y., Bastos, J. L., & Priest, N. (2017). Prejudice, stigma, bias, discrimination, and health. In *The Cambridge handbook of the psychology of prejudice* (pp. 559–581). Cambridge University Press. https://doi.org/10.1017/9781316161579.025

Paradise, R., Mejía-Arauz, R., Silva, K. G., Dexter, A. L., & Rogoff, B. (2014). One, two, three, eyes on me! Adults attempting control versus guiding in support of initiative. *Human Development, 57*(2/3), 131–149.

Parens, E., & Appelbaum, P. S. (2019). On what we have learned and still need to learn about the psychosocial impacts of genetic testing. *Hastings Center Report, 49*(S1), S2–S9. https://doi.org/10.1002/hast.1011

Parent, A. S., Teilmann, G., Juul, A., Skakkebaek, N. E., Toppari, J., & Bourguignon, J. P. (2003). The timing of normal puberty and the age limits of sexual precocity: Variations around the world, secular trends, and changes after migration. *Endocrine Reviews, 24*(5), 668–693.

Parents Together. (2020, April 23). Survey shows parents alarmed as kids' screen time skyrockets during COVID-19 crisis. *ParentsTogether.* https://parents-together.org/survey-shows-parents-alarmed-as-kids-screen-time-skyrockets-during-covid-19-crisis/

Pariser, D., & Forget, B. (2019). The Social Organization of Students in Class Versus in an Online Social Network: Freedom and Constraint in Two Different Settings. In *Mobile Media In and Outside of the Art Classroom: Attending to Identity, Spatiality, and Materiality.* Springer Nature.

Park, H., & Lau, A. S. (2016). Socioeconomic status and parenting priorities: Child independence and obedience around the world: Socioeconomic status and child socialization. *Journal of Marriage and Family, 78*(1), 43–59. https://doi.org/10.1111/jomf.12247

Park, H., Chiang, J. J., Irwin, M. R., Bower, J. E., McCreath, H., & Fuligni, A. J. (2019). Developmental trends in sleep during adolescents' transition to young adulthood. *Sleep Medicine, 60*, 202–210.

Park, I. J. K., Wang, L., Williams, D. R., & Alegría, M. (2018). Coping with racism: Moderators of the discrimination–adjustment link among Mexican-origin adolescents. *Child Development, 89*(3), e293–e310. https://doi.org/10.1111/cdev.12856

Park, M., O'Toole, A., & Katsiaficas, C. (2017). *Dual language learners: A national demographic and policy profile* (Fact sheet). Migration Policy Institute.

Parker, A. E., Halberstadt, A. G., Dunsmore, J. C., Townley, G., Bryant, A., Thompson, J. A., & Beale, K. S. (2012). "Emotions are a window into one's heart": A qualitative analysis of parental beliefs about children's emotions across three ethnic groups. *Monographs of the Society for Research in Child Development, 77*(3), i–144.

Parker, C. M., Hirsch, J. S., Philbin, M. M., & Parker, R. G. (2018). The urgent need for research and interventions to address family-based stigma and discrimination against lesbian, gay, bisexual, transgender, and queer youth. *Journal of Adolescent Health, 63*(4), 383–393. https://doi.org/10.1016/j.jadohealth.2018.05.018

Parker, J. G., & Asher, S. R. (1993). Friendship and friendship quality in middle childhood: Links with peer group acceptance and feelings of loneliness and social dissatisfaction. *Developmental Psychology, 29*(4), 611.

Parker, K., & Horowitz, J. M. (2015). *Parenting in America: Outlook, worries, aspirations are strongly linked to financial situation.* Pew Research Center.

Parker, K., Horowitz, J. M., & Stepler, R. (2017). *On gender differences, no consensus on nature vs. nurture.* Pew Research Center.

Parker, P. D., Jerrim, J., Schoon, I., & Marsh, H. W. (2016). A multination study of socioeconomic inequality in expectations for progression to higher education: The role of between-school tracking and ability stratification. *American Educational Research Journal, 53*(1), 6–32. https://doi.org/10.3102/0002831215621786

Parks, S. E., Erck Lambert, A. B., Hauck, F. R., Cottengim, C. R., Faulkner, M., & Shapiro-Mendoza, C. K. (2021). Explaining sudden unexpected infant deaths, 2011–2017. *Pediatrics, 147*(5).

Parolin, Z., & Curran, M. A. (2021). *Expanded child tax credit leads to further decline in child poverty in August 2021: Monthly child tax credit lifts 3.5 million children out of poverty with second payment* [Poverty and Social Policy Fact Sheet]. Center on Poverty & Social Policy at Columbia University.

Parsons, A. W., Parsons, S. A., Malloy, J. A., Marinak, B. A., Reutzel, D. R., Applegate, M. D., Applegate, A. J., Fawson, P. C., & Gambrell, L. B. (2018). Upper elementary students' motivation to read fiction and nonfiction. *The Elementary School Journal, 118*(3), 505–523. https://doi.org/10.1086/696022

Partanen, E., & Virtala, P. (2017). Prenatal sensory development. In B. Hopkins, E. Geangu, & S. Linkenauger (Eds.), *The Cambridge encyclopedia of child development* (2nd ed., pp. 231–241). Cambridge University Press. https://doi.org/10.1017/9781316216491.041

Parten, M. B. (1932). Social participation among preschool children. *The Journal of Abnormal and Social Psychology, 27*(3), 243.

Paruthi, S., Brooks, L. J., D'Ambrosio, C., Hall, W. A., Kotagal, S., Lloyd, R. M., Malow, B. A., Maski, K., Nichols, C., Quan, S. F., Rosen, C. L., Troester, M. M., & Wise, M. S. (2016a). Consensus statement of the American Academy of Sleep Medicine on the recommended amount of sleep for healthy children: Methodology and discussion. *Journal of Clinical Sleep Medicine, 12*(11), 1549–1561. https://doi.org/10.5664/jcsm.6288

Paruthi, S., Brooks, L. J., D'Ambrosio, C., Hall, W. A., Kotagal, S., Lloyd, R. M., Malow, B. A., Maski, K., Nichols, C., Quan, S. F., Rosen, C. L., Troester, M. M., & Wise, M. S. (2016b). Recommended amount of sleep for pediatric populations: A consensus statement of the American Academy of Sleep Medicine. *Journal of Clinical Sleep Medicine: JCSM : Official Publication of the American Academy of Sleep Medicine, 12*(6), 785–786. https://doi.org/10.5664/jcsm.5866

Pascalis, O., De Haan, M., & Nelson, C. A. (2002). Is face processing species-specific during the first year of life? *Science, 296*(5571), 1321–1323.

Paschall, K., Moore, K. A., Pina, G., & Anderson, S. (2020). *Comparing the national outcome measure of healthy and ready to learn with other well-being and school readiness measures.* Child Trends.

Paschall, K., & Tout, K. (2018, May 1). Most child care settings in the United States are homes, not centers. *Child Trends.* https://www.childtrends.org/blog/most-child-care-providers-in-the-united-states-are-based-in-homes-not-centers

Pasco, M. C., White, R., Iida, M., & Seaton, E. K. (2021). A prospective examination of neighborhood social and cultural cohesion and parenting processes on ethnic-racial identity among US Mexican adolescents. *Developmental Psychology, 57*(5), 783.

Passel, J. S. (2011). Demography of immigrant youth: Past, present, and future. *The Future of Children, 21*(1), 19–41. https://muse.jhu.edu/article/446008/summary

Pastorelli, C., Lansford, J. E., Luengo, B. K., Malone, P. S., Di, L. G., Bacchini, D., Bombi, A. S., Zelli, A., Miranda, M. C., Bornstein, M. H., Tapanya, S., Uribe, L. T., Alampay, L. P., Al-Hassan, S. M., Chang, L., Deater-Deckard, K., Dodge, K. A., Oburu, P., Skinner, A. T., & Sorbring, E. (2016). Positive parenting and children's prosocial behavior in eight countries. *Journal of Child Psychology and Psychiatry, and Allied Disciplines, 57*(7), 824–834. https://doi.org/10.1111/jcpp.12477

Patel, V., Saxena, S., Lund, C., Thornicroft, G., Baingana, F., Bolton, P., Chisholm, D., Collins, P. Y., Cooper, J. L., Eaton, J., Herrman, H., Herzallah, M. M., Huang, Y., Jordans, M. J. D., Kleinman, A., Medina-Mora, M. E., Morgan, E., Niaz, U., Omigbodun, O., . . . Unützer, J. (2018). The Lancet commission on global mental health and sustainable development. *The Lancet, 392*(10157), 1553–1598. https://doi.org/10.1016/S0140-6736(18)31612-X

Patterson, C. J. (2019). Lesbian and gay parenthood. In *Handbook of parenting* (pp. 345–371). Routledge.

Patterson, G. R. (1982). *Coercive family process* (Vol. 3). Castalia Publishing.

Patterson, G. R. (2016). Coercion theory: The study of change. In T. J. Dishion & J. J. Snyder (Eds.), *The Oxford handbook of coercive relationship dynamics* (pp. 7–22). Oxford University Press.

Patterson, G. R., & Dishion, T. J. (1985). Contributions of families and peers to delinquency. *Criminology, 23*(1), 63–79. https://doi.org/10.1111/j.1745-9125.1985.tb00326.x

Patton, G. C., Olsson, C. A., Skirbekk, V., Saffery, R., Wlodek, M. E., Azzopardi, P. S., Stonawski, M., Rasmussen, B., Spry, E., Francis, K., Bhutta, Z. A., Kassebaum, N. J., Mokdad, A. H., Murray, C. J. L., Prentice, A. M., Reavley, N., Sheehan, P., Sweeny, K., Viner, R. M., & Sawyer, S. M. (2018). Adolescence and the next generation. *Nature, 554*(7693), 458–466. https://doi.org/10.1038/nature25759

Pauker, K., Apfelbaum, E. P., & Spitzer, B. (2015). When societal norms and social identity collide: The race talk dilemma for racial minority children. *Social Psychological and Personality Science, 6*(8), 887–895. https://doi.org/10.1177/1948550615598379

Pauker, K., Xu, Y., Williams, A., & Biddle, A. M. (2016). Race essentialism and social contextual differences in children's racial stereotyping. *Child Development, 87*(5), 1409–1422.

Paul, S. E., Hatoum, A. S., Fine, J. D., Johnson, E. C., Hansen, I., Karcher, N. R., Moreau, A. L., Bondy, E., Qu, Y., Carter, E. B., Rogers, C. E., Agrawal, A., Barch, D. M., & Bogdan, R. (2021). Associations between prenatal cannabis exposure and childhood outcomes: Results from the ABCD Study. *JAMA Psychiatry, 78*(1), 64–76. https://doi.org/10.1001/jamapsychiatry.2020.2902

Paulus, M. P., Squeglia, L. M., Bagot, K., Jacobus, J., Kuplicki, R., Breslin, F. J., Bodurka, J., Sheffield Morris, A., Thompson, W. K., Bartsch, H., & Tapert, S. F. (2019). Screen media activity and brain structure in youth: Evidence for diverse structural correlation networks from the ABCD Study. *NeuroImage, 185,* 140–153. https://doi.org/10.1016/j.neuroimage.2018.10.040

Pavlov, I. P. (1928). *Lectures on conditioned reflexes: Twenty-five years of objective study of the higher nervous activity (behaviour) of animals.* (W. H. Gantt, Trans.). Liverwright Publishing Corporation. https://doi.org/10.1037/11081-000

Paynter, M. J. (2019). Medication and facilitation of transgender women's lactation. *Journal of Human Lactation, 35*(2), 239–243. https://doi.org/10.1177/0890334419829729

Peahl, A. F., & Howell, J. D. (2021). The evolution of prenatal care delivery guidelines in the United States. *American Journal of Obstetrics and Gynecology, 224*(4), 339–347. https://doi.org/10.1016/j.ajog.2020.12.016

Pearce, L. D., Hayward, G. M., Chassin, L., & Curran, P. J. (2018). The increasing diversity and complexity of family structures for adolescents. *Journal of Research on Adolescence: The Official Journal of the Society for Research on Adolescence, 28*(3), 591–608. https://doi.org/10.1111/jora.12391

Pearl, M., & Pearl, D. (2015). *To train up a child: Child training for the 21st century.* No Greater Joy Ministries.

Peguero, A. A., Merrin, G. J., Hong, J. S., & Johnson, K. R. (2019). School disorder and dropping out: The intersection of gender, race, and ethnicity. *Youth & Society, 51*(2), 193–218.

Pellegrini, A. D., & Smith, P. K. (1998). The development of play during childhood: Forms and possible functions. *Child Psychology and Psychiatry Review, 3*(2), 51–57.

Pellizzoni, S., Apuzzo, G. M., Vita, C. D., Agostini, T., & Passolunghi, M. C. (2019). Evaluation and training of executive functions in genocide survivors: The case of Yazidi children. *Developmental Science, 22*(5), e12798. https://doi.org/10.1111/desc.12798

Penela, E. C., Walker, O. L., Degnan, K. A., Fox, N. A., & Henderson, H. A. (2015). Early behavioral inhibition and emotion regulation: Pathways toward social competence in middle childhood. *Child Development, 86*(4), 1227–1240.

Peng, P., & Kievit, R. A. (2020). The development of academic achievement and cognitive abilities: A bidirectional perspective. *Child Development Perspectives, 14*(1), 15–20.

Pennestri, M.-H., Burdayron, R., Kenny, S., Béliveau, M.-J., & Dubois-Comtois, K. (2020). Sleeping through the night or through the nights? *Sleep Medicine, 76,* 98–103. https://doi.org/10.1016/j.sleep.2020.10.005

Pennestri, M.-H., Laganière, C., Bouvette-Turcot, A.-A., Pokhvisneva, I., Steiner, M., Meaney, M. J., Gaudreau, H., & on behalf of the Mavan Research Team. (2018). Uninterrupted infant sleep, development, and maternal mood. *Pediatrics, 142*(6), e20174330.

Penniston, T., Reynolds, K., Pierce, S., Furer, P., & Lionberg, C. (2021). Challenges, supports, and postpartum mental health symptoms among non-breastfeeding mothers. *Archives of Women's Mental Health, 24*(2), 303–312. https://doi.org/10.1007/s00737-020-01059-3

Pereira, A., Busch, A. S., Solares, F., Baier, I., Corvalan, C., & Mericq, V. (2021). Total and central adiposity are associated with age at gonadarche and incidence of precocious gonadarche in boys. *The Journal of Clinical Endocrinology & Metabolism, 106*(5), 1352–1361. https://doi.org/10.1210/clinem/dgab064

Perelli-Harris, B., Mynarska, M., Berghammer, C., Berrington, A., Evans, A., Isupova, O., Keizer, R., Klaerner, A., Lappegard, T., & Vignoli, D. (2014). Towards a deeper understanding of cohabitation: Insights from focus group research across Europe and Australia. *Demographic Research, 31*(34), 1043–1078. https://doi.org/10.4054/DemRes.2014.31.34

Pereyra-Elías, R., Quigley, M. A., & Carson, C. (2022). To what extent does confounding explain the association between breastfeeding duration and cognitive development up to age 14? Findings from the UK Millennium Cohort Study. *PLOS One, 17*(5), e0267326.

Perez Rivera, M. B., & Dunsmore, J. C. (2011). Mothers' acculturation and beliefs about emotions, mother–child emotion discourse, and children's emotion understanding in Latino families. *Early Education and Development, 22*(2), 324–354. https://doi.org/10.1080/10409281003702000

Perez, E. (2020, July 2). Black leaders started using the term "people of color" in the 1960s. Now it's a major identity. *Washington Post.* https://www.washingtonpost.com/politics/2020/07/02/people-color-are-protesting-heres-what-you-need-know-about-this-new-identity/

Pérez, I. E., Wu, R., Murray, C. B., & Bravo, D. (2021). An interdisciplinary framework examining culture and adaptation in migrant children and adolescents. *New Directions for Child and Adolescent Development, 2021*(176), 13–39.

Perlman, S. B., Huppert, T. J., & Luna, B. (2016). Functional near-infrared spectroscopy evidence for development of prefrontal engagement in working memory in early through middle childhood. *Cerebral Cortex, 26*(6), 2790–2799. https://doi.org/10.1093/cercor/bhv139

Perone, S., Palanisamy, J., & Carlson, S. M. (2018). Age-related change in brain rhythms from early to middle childhood: Links to executive function. *Developmental Science, 21*(6), e12691.

Perrin, E. M., Rothman, R. L., Sanders, L. M., Skinner, A. C., Eden, S. K., Shintani, A., Throop, E. M., & Yin, H. S. (2014). Racial and ethnic differences associated with feeding- and activity-related behaviors in infants. *Pediatrics,* peds.2013-1326. https://doi.org/10.1542/peds.2013-1326

Perrin, R., Miller-Perrin, C., & Song, J. (2017). Changing attitudes about spanking using alternative biblical interpretations. *International Journal of Behavioral Development, 41*(4), 514–522. https://doi.org/10.1177/0165025416673295

Perry, A. (2019, September 17). Black teachers matter, for students and communities. *The Hechinger Report.* https://hechingerreport.org/black-teachers-matter-for-students-and-communities/

Perry, D. G., & Pauletti, R. E. (2011). Gender and adolescent development. *Journal of Research on Adolescence, 21*(1), 61–74. https://doi.org/10.1111/j.1532-7795.2010.00715.x

Perry, M., Tan, Z., Chen, J., Weidig, T., Xu, W., & Cong, X. S. (2018). Neonatal pain: Perceptions and current practice. *Critical Care Nursing Clinics of North America, 30*(4), 549–561. https://doi.org/10.1016/j.cnc.2018.07.013

Perry, R. E., Blair, C., & Sullivan, R. M. (2017). Neurobiology of infant attachment: Attachment despite adversity and parental programming of emotionality. *Current Opinion in Psychology, 17,* 1–6. https://doi.org/10.1016/j.copsyc.2017.04.022

Perszyk, D. R., Lei, R. F., Bodenhausen, G. V., Richeson, J. A., & Waxman, S. R. (2019). Bias at the intersection of race and gender: Evidence from preschool-aged children. *Developmental Science, 22*(3), e12788. https://doi.org/10.1111/desc.12788

Pertea, M., Shumate, A., Pertea, G., Varabyou, A., Breitwieser, F. P., Chang, Y.-C., Madugundu, A. K., Pandey, A., & Salzberg, S. L. (2018). CHESS: A new human gene catalog curated from thousands of large-scale RNA sequencing experiments reveals extensive transcriptional noise. *Genome Biology, 19*(1), 208. https://doi.org/10.1186/s13059-018-1590-2

Pesando, L. M., Barban, N., Sironi, M., & Furstenberg, F. F. (2021). A sequence-analysis approach to the study of the transition to adulthood in low- and middle-income countries. *Population and Development Review, 47*(3), 719–747.

Pesch, M. H., Levitt, K. J., Danziger, P., & Orringer, K. (2021). Pediatrician's beliefs and practices around rapid infant weight gain: A qualitative study. *Global Pediatric Health, 8.* https://doi.org/10.1177/2333794X21992164

Pesu, L., Viljaranta, J., & Aunola, K. (2016). The role of parents' and teachers' beliefs in children's self-concept development. *Journal of Applied Developmental Psychology, 44,* 63–71. https://doi.org/10.1016/j.appdev.2016.03.001

Petek, G. (2019). *Overview of Special Education in California.* Legislative Analyst's Office.

Peters, S. J. (2021). The challenges of achieving equity within public school gifted and talented programs. *Gifted Child Quarterly,* 00169862211002535.

Peters, S. J., Gentry, M., Whiting, G. W., & McBee, M. T. (2019). Who gets served in gifted education? Demographic representation and a call for action. *Gifted Child Quarterly, 63*(4), 273–287.

Petersen, E. E. (2019). Racial/ethnic disparities in pregnancy-related deaths—United States, 2007–2016. *MMWR. Morbidity and Mortality Weekly Report, 68.* https://doi.org/10.15585/mmwr.mm6835a3

Peterson, C., Slaughter, V., Moore, C., & Wellman, H. M. (2016). Peer social skills and theory of mind in children with autism, deafness, or typical development. *Developmental Psychology, 52*(1), 46.

Peterson, C. C., & Wellman, H. M. (2019). Longitudinal theory of mind (ToM) development from preschool to adolescence with and without ToM delay. *Child Development, 90*(6), 1917–1934. https://doi.org/10.1111/cdev.13064

Petitto, L. A., Katerelos, M., Levy, B. G., Gauna, K., Tétreault, K., & Ferraro, V. (2001). Bilingual signed and spoken language acquisition from birth: Implications for the mechanisms underlying early bilingual language acquisition. *Journal of Child Language, 28*(2), 453–496.

Petitto, L. A., Langdon, C., Stone, A., Andriola, D., Kartheiser, G., & Cochran, C. (2016). Visual sign phonology: Insights into human reading and language from a natural soundless phonology. *Wiley Interdisciplinary Reviews: Cognitive Science, 7*(6), 366–381. https://doi.org/10.1002/wcs.1404

Petitto, L. A., & Marentette, P. F. (1991). Babbling in the manual mode: Evidence for the ontogeny of language. *Science, 251*(5000), 1493–1496. https://doi.org/10.1126/science.2006424

Petrilli, M. J. (2016, July 6). College readiness versus college completion: Variations by race. The Thomas B. Fordham Institute. https://fordhaminstitute.org/national/commentary/college-readiness-versus-college-completion-variations-race

Peven, K., Day, L. T., Ruysen, H., Tahsina, T., KC, A., Shabani, J., Kong, S., Ameen, S., Basnet, O., Haider, R., Rahman, Q. S., Blencowe, H., Lawn, J. E., Rahman, Q. S., Rahman, A. E., Tahsina, T., Zaman, S. B., Ameen, S., Hossain, T., . . . EN-BIRTH Study Group. (2021). Stillbirths including intrapartum timing: EN-BIRTH multi-country validation study. *BMC Pregnancy and Childbirth, 21*(1), 226. https://doi.org /10.1186/s12884-020-03238-7

Pfeifer, J. H., & Allen, N. B. (2021). Puberty initiates cascading relationships between neurodevelopmental, social, and internalizing processes across adolescence. *Biological Psychiatry, 89*(2), 99–108. https://doi.org /10.1016/j.biopsych.2020.09.002

Phadke, V. K., Bednarczyk, R. A., & Omer, S. B. (2020). Vaccine refusal and measles outbreaks in the US. *JAMA, 324*(13), 1344–1345. https://doi.org/10.1001 /jama.2020.14828

Philpott, L. F., Savage, E., Leahy-Warren, P., & FitzGerald, S. (2020). Paternal perinatal depression: A narrative review. *International Journal of Men's Social and Community Health, 3*(1), e1–e15.

Physical Activity Guidelines Advisory Committee. (2018). *2018 physical activity guidelines advisory committee scientific report.* U.S. Department of Health and Human Services. https://health.gov/our-work /physical-activity/current-guidelines/scientific-report

Piaget, J. (1952). *The origins of intelligence in children* (M. Cook, Trans.). W. W. Norton. https://doi.org /10.1037/11494-000

Piaget, J. (1954). *The construction of reality in the child.* Basic Books. https://doi.org/10.1037/11168-000

Piaget, J. (1965). *The moral development.* Free Press.

Piaget, J. (1968). *Six psychological studies* (A. Tenzer, Trans.). Vintage Books.

Piaget, J. (1970). *Science of education and the psychology of the child* (D. Coltman, Trans.). Orion.

Piaget, J. (1971). The theory of stages in cognitive development. In D. R. Green, M. P. Ford, & G. B. Flamer (Eds.), *Measurement and Piaget* (pp. 1–11). McGraw-Hill.

Piaget, J. (2013). *Child's conception of the world: Selected works.* Routledge.

Piaget, J., & Inhelder, B. (1956). *The child's conception of space.* Routledge.

Piaget, J., & Inhelder, B. (1969). *The psychology of the child.* Basic Books.

Piantadosi, S., Byar, D. P., & Green, S. B. (1988). The ecological fallacy. *American Journal of Epidemiology, 127*(5), 893–904.

Piccolo, L. R., Merz, E. C., & Noble, K. G. (2019). School climate is associated with cortical thickness and executive function in children and adolescents. *Developmental Science, 22*(1), e12719. https://doi.org/10.1111 /desc.12719

Piedade, S. R., Hutchinson, M. R., Ferreira, D. M., Cristante, A. F., & Maffulli, N. (2021). The management of concussion in sport is not standardized. A systematic review. *Journal of Safety Research, 76*, 262–268. https://doi.org/10.1016/j.jsr.2020.12.013

Pilkauskas, N. V., & Cross, C. (2018). Beyond the Nuclear Family: Trends in Children Living in Shared Households. *Demography, 55*(6), 2283–2297. https:// doi.org/10.1007/s13524-018-0719-y

Pillai, R. L. I. (2020). We all need a little TLC: An argument for an increased role of child life services in patient care and medical education. *Hospital Pediatrics, 10*(10), 913–917. https://doi.org/10.1542/hpeds.2020-0119

Pinker, S. (1984). *Language learnability and language development.* Harvard University Press.

Pinker, S. (1994). *The language instinct: How the mind creates language.* William Morrow.

Pinquart, M. (2017). Associations of parenting dimensions and styles with externalizing problems of children and adolescents: An updated meta-analysis. *Developmental Psychology, 53*(5), 873.

Pinquart, M., & Ebeling, M. (2020). Students' expected and actual academic achievement: A meta-analysis. *International Journal of Educational Research, 100*, 101524. https://doi.org/10.1016/j.ijer.2019.101524

Pinquart, M., & Kauser, R. (2018). Do the associations of parenting styles with behavior problems and academic achievement vary by culture? Results from a meta-analysis. *Cultural Diversity and Ethnic Minority Psychology, 24*(1), 75.

Pinquart, M., & Pfeiffer, J. P. (2020). Longitudinal associations of the attainment of developmental tasks with psychological symptoms in adolescence: A meta-analysis. *Journal of Research on Adolescence, 30*(S1), 4–14. https://doi.org/10.1111/jora.12462

Pinto, T. M., Samorinha, C., Tendais, I., & Figueiredo, B. (2020). Depression and paternal adjustment and attitudes during the transition to parenthood. *Journal of Reproductive and Infant Psychology, 38*(3), 281–296. https://doi.org/10.1080/02646838.2019.1652256

Piolanti, A., & Foran, H. M. (2021). Efficacy of interventions to prevent physical and sexual dating violence among adolescents: A systematic review and meta-analysis. *JAMA Pediatrics, 176*(2), 142–149.

Piquero, A. R., & Moffitt, T. E. (2010). Life-course persistent offending. In J. R. Adler (Ed.), *Forensic psychology* (pp. 233–254). Willan.

Piras, G. N., Bozzola, M., Bianchin, L., Bernasconi, S., Bona, G., Lorenzoni, G., Buzi, F., Rigon, F., Tonini, G., De Sanctis, V., & Perissinotto, E. (2020). The levelling-off of the secular trend of age at menarche among Italian girls. *Heliyon, 6*(6), e04222. https://doi .org/10.1016/j.heliyon.2020.e04222

Pitts, N. B., Zero, D. T., Marsh, P. D., Ekstrand, K., Weintraub, J. A., Ramos-Gomez, F., Tagami, J., Twetman, S., Tsakos, G., & Ismail, A. (2017). Dental caries. *Nature Reviews Disease Primers, 3*(1), 1–16.

Pitula, C. E., DePasquale, C. E., Mliner, S. B., & Gunnar, M. R. (2019). Peer problems among postinstitutionalized, internationally adopted children: Relations to hypocortisolism, parenting quality, and ADHD symptoms. *Child Development, 90*(3), e339–e355. https://doi.org/10.1111/cdev.12986

Pivnick, L. K., Gordon, R. A., & Crosnoe, R. (2021, July 15). The developmental significance of looks from middle childhood to early adolescence. *Journal of Research on Adolescence.* https://doi.org/10.1111/jora .12644

Planalp, E. M., & Braungart-Rieker, J. M. (2015). Trajectories of regulatory behaviors in early infancy: Determinants of infant self-distraction and self-comforting. *Infancy, 20*(2), 129–159. https://doi.org /10.1111/infa.12068

Planalp, E. M., & Goldsmith, H. H. (2020). Observed profiles of infant temperament: Stability, heritability, and associations with parenting. *Child Development, 91*(3), e563–e580. https://doi.org/10.1111/cdev.13277

Planalp, E. M., van Hulle, C., Lemery-Chalfant, K., & Goldsmith, H. H. (2017). Genetic and environmental contributions to the development of positive affect in infancy. *Emotion, 17*(3), 412–420. https://doi .org/10.1037/emo0000238

Plesons, M., Patkar, A., Babb, J., Balapitiya, A., Carson, F., Caruso, B. A., Franco, M., Hansen, M. M., Haver, J., Jahangir, A., Kabiru, C. W., Kisangala, E., Phillips-Howard, P., Sharma, A., Sommer, M., & Chandra-Mouli, V. (2021). The state of adolescent menstrual health in low- and middle-income countries and suggestions for future action and research. *Reproductive Health, 18*, 31. https://doi.org/10.1186 /s12978-021-01082-2

Plomin, R., & von Stumm, S. (2018). The new genetics of intelligence. *Nature Reviews Genetics, 19*(3), 148.

Poelker, K. E., & Gibbons, J. L. (2019). Sharing and caring: Prosocial behavior in young children around the world. In T. Tulviste, D. L. Best, & J. L. Gibbons (Eds.), *Children's social worlds in cultural context* (pp. 89–102). Springer.

Poirel, N., Borst, G., Simon, G., Rossi, S., Cassotti, M., Pineau, A., & Houdé, O. (2012). Number conservation is related to children's prefrontal inhibitory control: An fMRI study of a Piagetian task. *PLOS ONE, 7*(7), e40802. https://doi.org/10.1371/journal.pone.0040802

Pollak, S. D., Camras, L. A., & Cole, P. M. (2019). Progress in understanding the emergence of human emotion. *Developmental Psychology, 55*(9), 1801. https:// doi.org/10.1037/dev0000789

Pollitt, A. M., Reczek, C., & Umberson, D. (2020). LGBTQ-parent families and health. In *LGBTQ-parent families: Innovations in research and implications for practice.* Springer Nature.

Pomerantz, E. M., Ng, F. F. Y., Cheung, C. S. S., & Qu, Y. (2014). Raising happy children who succeed in school: Lessons from China and the United States. *Child Development Perspectives, 8*(2), 71–76.

Pomerantz, E. M., & Wang, Q. (2009). The role of parental control in children's development in Western and East Asian countries. *Current Directions in Psychological Science, 18*(5), 285–289.

Ponitz, C. E. C., McClelland, M. M., Jewkes, A. M., Connor, C. M., Farris, C. L., & Morrison, F. J. (2008). Touch your toes! Developing a direct measure of behavioral regulation in early childhood. *Early Childhood Research Quarterly, 23*(2), 141–158.

Ponnock, A., Muenks, K., Morell, M., Yang, J. S., Gladstone, J. R., & Wigfield, A. (2020). Grit and conscientiousness: Another jangle fallacy. *Journal of Research in Personality, 89*, 104021.

Pont, S. J., Puhl, R., Cook, S. R., Slusser, W., Section on Obesity, and The Obesity Society. (2017). Stigma experienced by children and adolescents with obesity. *Pediatrics, 140*(6), e20173034. https://doi.org/10.1542 /peds.2017-3034

Ponticorvo, M., Sica, L. S., Rega, A., & Miglino, O. (2020). On the edge between digital and physical: Materials to enhance creativity in children. An application to atypical development. *Frontiers in Psychology, 11*, 755. https://doi.org/10.3389/fpsyg.2020.00755

Popkin, B. M. (2021). Measuring the nutrition transition and its dynamics. *Public Health Nutrition, 24*(2), 318–320. https://doi.org/10.1017 /S136898002000470X

Popova, S., Lange, S., Probst, C., Gmel, G., & Rehm, J. (2017). Estimation of national, regional, and global prevalence of alcohol use during pregnancy and fetal alcohol syndrome: A systematic review and meta-analysis. *The Lancet Global Health, 5*(3), e290–e299. https://doi.org/10.1016/S2214-109X(17)30021-9

Popple, P. R. (2018). *Social work practice and social welfare policy in the United States: A history.* Oxford University Press.

Porche, M. V., Costello, D. M., & Rosen-Reynoso, M. (2016). Adverse family experiences, child mental health, and educational outcomes for a national sample of students. *School Mental Health, 8*(1), 44–60.

Porter, J. R., Sobel, K., Fox, S. E., Bennett, C. L., & Kientz, J. A. (2017). Filtered out: Disability disclosure practices in online dating communities. *Proceedings of the ACM on Human-Computer Interaction 1 (CSCW), 87*, 1–13. https://doi.org/10.1145/3134722

Poskett, J. (2019). *Materials of the mind: Phrenology, race, and the global history of science, 1815–1920.* University of Chicago Press.

Posner, M. I., Rothbart, M. K., & Voelker, P. (2016). Developing brain networks of attention. *Current Opinion in Pediatrics, 28*(6), 720–724. https://doi.org/10.1097/MOP.0000000000000413

Post, E. G., Biese, K. M., Schaefer, D. A., Watson, A. M., McGuine, T. A., Brooks, M. A., & Bell, D. R. (2020). Sport-specific associations of specialization and sex with overuse injury in youth athletes. *Sports Health, 12*(1), 36–42.

Poulin-Dubois, D., Serbin, L. A., Eichstedt, J. A., Sen, M. G., & Beissel, C. F. (2002). Men don't put on make-up: Toddlers' knowledge of the gender stereotyping of household activities. *Social Development, 11*(2), 166–181. https://doi.org/10.1111/1467-9507.00193

Pound, P., Denford, S., Shucksmith, J., Tanton, C., Johnson, A. M., Owen, J., Hutten, R., Mohan, L., Bonell, C., Abraham, C., & Campbell, R. (2017). What is best practice in sex and relationship education? A synthesis of evidence, including stakeholders' views. *BMJ Open, 7*(5), e014791. https://doi.org/10.1136/bmjopen-2016-014791

Povolo, C. A., Reid, J. N., Shariff, S. Z., Welk, B., & Morrow, S. A. (2021). Concussion in adolescence and the risk of multiple sclerosis: A retrospective cohort study. *Multiple Sclerosis Journal, 27*(2), 180–187. https://doi.org/10.1177/1352458520908037

Powell, M. A., Fitzgerald, R. M., Taylor, N., & Graham, A. (2012). *International literature review: Ethical issues in undertaking research with children and young people.* Lismore, NSW: Childwatch International Research Network, Southern Cross University, Centre for Children and Young People, and University of Otago, Centre for Research on Children and Families.

Powell, R. A., Digdon, N., Harris, B., & Smithson, C. (2014). Correcting the record on Watson, Rayner, and Little Albert: Albert Barger as "psychology's lost boy." *American Psychologist, 69*(6), 600.

Powell, R. A., & Schmaltz, R. M. (2020). Did Little Albert actually acquire a conditioned fear of furry animals? What the film evidence tells us. *History of Psychology, 24*(2), 164–181. https://doi.org/10.1037/hop0000176

Pratt, M. E., McClelland, M. M., Swanson, J., & Lipscomb, S. T. (2016). Family risk profiles and school readiness: A person-centered approach. *Early Childhood Research Quarterly, 36*, 462–474.

Pressman, S. (2017). *Rethinking antipoverty policy.* Edward Elgar Publishing. https://www.elgaronline.com/view/9781784717209.00032.xml

Price-Williams, D., Gordon, W., & Ramirez, M. (1969). Skill and conservation: A study of pottery-making children. *Developmental Psychology, 1*(6p1), 769.

Priest, N., Alam, O., Truong, M., Sharples, R., Nelson, J., Dunn, K., Francis, K. L., Paradies, Y., & Kavanagh, A. (2021). Promoting proactive bystander responses to racism and racial discrimination in primary schools: A mixed methods evaluation of the "Speak Out Against Racism" program pilot. *BMC Public Health, 21*(1), 1434. https://doi.org/10.1186/s12889-021-11469-2

Priest, N., Perry, R., Ferdinand, A., Paradies, Y., & Kelaher, M. (2014). Experiences of racism, racial/ethnic attitudes, motivated fairness and mental health outcomes among primary and secondary school students. *Journal of Youth and Adolescence, 43*(10), 1672–1687. https://doi.org/10.1007/s10964-014-0140-9

Priest, N., Slopen, N., Woolford, S., Philip, J. T., Singer, D., Kauffman, A. D., Mosely, K., Davis, M., Ransome, Y., & Williams, D. (2018). Stereotyping across intersections of race and age: Racial stereotyping among White adults working with children. *PLOS ONE, 13*(9), e0201696. https://doi.org/10.1371/journal.pone.0201696

Profit, J., Gould, J. B., Bennett, M., Goldstein, B. A., Draper, D., Phibbs, C. S., & Lee, H. C. (2017). Racial/ethnic disparity in NICU quality of care delivery. *Pediatrics, 140*(3), e20170918. https://doi.org/10.1542/peds.2017-0918

Project Play. (2020, February 25). Survey: African-American youth more often play sports to chase college, pro dreams. *National Youth Sport Parent Survey.* https://www.aspenprojectplay.org/national-youth-sport-survey/african-american-youth-more-often-play-sports-to-chase-college-pro-dreams

Protzko, J. (2017). Raising IQ among school-aged children: Five meta-analyses and a review of randomized controlled trials. *Developmental Review, 46*, 81–101. https://doi.org/10.1016/j.dr.2017.05.001

Protzko, J., & Aronson, J. (2016). Context moderates affirmation effects on the ethnic achievement gap. *Social Psychological and Personality Science, 7*(6), 500–507.

Provenzi, L., Grumi, S., Altieri, L., Bensi, G., Bertazzoli, E., Biasucci, G., Cavallini, A., Decembrino, L., Falcone, R., Freddi, A., Gardella, B., Giacchero, R., Giorda, R., Grossi, E., Guerini, P., Magnani, M. L., Martelli, P., Motta, M., Nacinovich, R., . . . Group, M.-C. S. (2021). Prenatal maternal stress during the COVID-19 pandemic and infant regulatory capacity at 3 months: A longitudinal study. *Development and Psychopathology,* 1–9. https://doi.org/10.1017/S0954579421000766

Prüss-Üstün, A., Wolf, J., Corvalán, C., Bos, R., & Neira, M. (2016). *Preventing disease through healthy environments: A global assessment of the burden of disease from environmental risks.* World Health Organization.

Przybylski, A. K. (2019). Digital screen time and pediatric sleep: Evidence from a preregistered cohort study. *The Journal of Pediatrics, 205*, 218–223.e1. https://doi.org/10.1016/j.jpeds.2018.09.054

Puhl, R. M., Lessard, L. M., Pearl, R. L., Himmelstein, M. S., & Foster, G. D. (2021). International comparisons of weight stigma: Addressing a void in the field. *International Journal of Obesity, 45*, 1976–1985. https://doi.org/10.1038/s41366-021-00860-z

Pujol, J., Fenoll, R., Forns, J., Harrison, B. J., Martínez-Vilavella, G., Macià, D., Alvarez-Pedrerol, M., Blanco-Hinojo, L., González-Ortiz, S., Deus, J., & Sunyer, J. (2016). Video gaming in school children: How much is enough?. *Annals of Neurology, 80*(3), 424–433.

Pulcini, C. D., Zima, B. T., Kelleher, K. J., Houtrow, A. J. (2017). Poverty and trends in 3 common chronic disorders. *Pediatrics, 139*(3), e20162539.

Puleo, A. (2020, July 22). *Roblox played by over half of kids in America.* Game Rant. https://gamerant.com/roblox-player-count-kids-america/

Pullen Sansfaçon, A., Medico, D., Suerich-Gulick, F., & Temple Newhook, J. (2020). "I knew that I wasn't cis, I knew that, but I didn't know exactly": Gender identity development, expression and affirmation in youth who access gender affirming medical care. *International Journal of Transgender Health, 21*(3), 307–320. https://doi.org/10.1080/26895269.2020.1756551

Puri, N., Coomes, E. A., Haghbayan, H., & Gunaratne, K. (2020). Social media and vaccine hesitancy: New updates for the era of COVID-19 and globalized infectious diseases. *Human Vaccines & Immunotherapeutics, 16*(11), 2586–2593. https://doi.org/10.1080/21645515.2020.1780846

Purpura, D. J., Schmitt, S. A., & Ganley, C. M. (2017). Foundations of mathematics and literacy: The role of executive functioning components. *Journal of Experimental Child Psychology, 153*, 15–34. https://doi.org/10.1016/j.jecp.2016.08.010

Puterman, E., Weiss, J., Hives, B. A., Gemmill, A., Karasek, D., Mendes, W. B., & Rehkopf, D. H. (2020). Predicting mortality from 57 economic, behavioral, social, and psychological factors. *Proceedings of the National Academy of Sciences, 117*(28), 16273–16282. https://doi.org/10.1073/pnas.1918455117

Putkinen, V., & Saarikivi, K. (2018). Neural correlates of enhanced executive functions: Is less more? *Annals of the New York Academy of Sciences.* https://doi.org/10.1111/nyas.13645

Putnam, H., & Walsh, K. (2021). *Knowledge of early reading—state teacher preparation and licensure requirements.* National Center for Teacher Quality. https://www.nctq.org/publications/Knowledge-of-Early-Reading----Excerpted-from-State-of-the-States-2021:-Teacher-Preparation-Policy

Putnam, R. D. (2000). Bowling alone: America's declining social capital. In L. Crothers & C. Lockhart (Eds.), *Culture and politics: A reader* (pp. 223–234). Palgrave Macmillan US. https://doi.org/10.1007/978-1-349-62965-7_12

Putnam, S. P., Garstein, M. A., & Rothbart, M. K. (2019). Historical background of the study of temperament and new perspectives on assessment. In R. DelCarmen-Wiggins & A. S. Carter (Eds.), *The Oxford handbook of infant, toddler, and preschool mental health assessment* (pp. 131–156). Oxford University Press.

Putnick, D. L., Bornstein, M. H., Lansford, J. E., Malone, P. S., Pastorelli, C., Skinner, A. T., Sorbring, E., Tapanya, S., Tirado, L. M. U., Zelli, A., Alampay, L. P., Al-Hassan, S. M., Bacchini, D., Bombi, A. S., Chang, L., Deater-Deckard, K., Di Giunta, L., Dodge, K. A., & Oburu, P. (2015). Perceived mother and father acceptance-rejection predict four unique aspects of child adjustment across nine countries. *Journal of Child Psychology and Psychiatry, 56*(8), 923–932.

Putnick, D. L., Hahn, C. S., Hendricks, C., Suwalsky, J. T., & Bornstein, M. H. (2020). Child, mother, father, and teacher beliefs about child academic competence: Predicting math and reading performance in European American adolescents. *Journal of Research on Adolescence, 30*, 298–314.

Puzzanchera, C. (2021). *Juvenile arrests, 2019* (Juvenile Justice Statistics, National Report Series Bulletin). U.S. Department of Justice.

Pynn, S. R., Neely, K. C., Ingstrup, M. S., Spence, J. C., Carson, V., Robinson, Z., & Holt, N. L. (2019). An intergenerational qualitative study of the good parenting ideal and active free play during middle childhood. *Children's Geographies, 17*(3), 266–277. https://doi.org/10.1080/14733285.2018.1492702

Pyra, E., & Schwarz, W. (2019). Puberty: Normal, delayed, and precocious. In S. Llahana, C. Follin, C. Yedinak, & A. Grossman (Eds.), *Advanced practice in endocrinology nursing* (pp. 63–84). Springer International Publishing. https://doi .org/10.1007/978-3-319-99817-6_4

Qi, H., & Roberts, K. P. (2019). Cultural influences on the development of children's memory and cognition. In J. B. Benson (Ed.), *Advances in child development and behavior* (Vol. 56, pp. 183–225). JAI. https://doi .org/10.1016/bs.acdb.2018.11.005

Qian, M. K., Quinn, P. C., Heyman, G. D., Pascalis, O., Fu, G., & Lee, K. (2019). A long-term effect of perceptual individuation training on reducing implicit racial bias in preschool children. *Child Development, 90*(3), e290–e305. https://doi.org/10.1111/ cdev.12971

Qian, M., Heyman, G. D., Quinn, P. C., Messi, F. A., Fu, G., & Lee, K. (2021). Age-related differences in implicit and explicit racial biases in Cameroonians. *Developmental Psychology, 57*(3), 386–396. https://doi.org /10.1037/dev0001149

Qian, M. K., Quinn, P. C., Heyman, G. D., Pascalis, O., Fu, G., & Lee, K. (2017). Perceptual Individuation Training (but not Mere Exposure) Reduces Implicit Racial Bias in Preschool Children. *Developmental Psychology, 53*(5), 845–859. https://doi.org/10.1037/ dev0000290

Qian, Y., Chen, W., & Guo, B. (2020). Zing-Yang Kuo and behavior epigenesis based on animal experiments. *Protein & Cell, 11*(6), 387–390. https://doi.org /10.1007/s13238-018-0516-9

Qiao, D. P., & Xie, Q. W. (2017). Public perceptions of child physical abuse in Beijing. *Child & Family Social Work, 22*(1), 213–225.

Qu, Y., Pomerantz, E. M., Wang, M., Cheung, C., & Cimpian, A. (2016). Conceptions of adolescence: Implications for differences in engagement in school over early adolescence in the United States and China. *Journal of Youth and Adolescence, 45*(7), 1512–1526. https://doi.org/10.1007/s10964-016-0492-4

Qu, Y., Pomerantz, E. M., & Wu, G. (2020a). Countering youth's negative stereotypes of teens fosters constructive behavior. *Child Development, 91*(1), 197–213. https://doi.org/10.1111/cdev.13156

Qu, Y., Rompilla, D. B., Wang, Q., & Ng, F. F.-Y. (2020b). Youth's negative stereotypes of teen emotionality: Reciprocal relations with emotional functioning in Hong Kong and Mainland China. *Journal of Youth and Adolescence, 49*(10), 2003–2019. https://doi.org /10.1007/s10964-020-01303-0

Quereshi, A., & Okonofua, J. (2018). *Locked out of the classroom: How implicit bias contributes to disparities in school discipline.* NAACP Legal Defence Fund, Thurgood Marshall Institute.

Querido, J. G., Warner, T. D., & Eyberg, S. M. (2002). Parenting styles and child behavior in African American families of preschool children. *Journal of Clinical Child and Adolescent Psychology, 31*(2), 272–277.

Quevedo, K., Benning, S. D., Gunnar, M. R., & Dahl, R. E. (2009). The onset of puberty: Effects on the psychophysiology of defensive and appetitive motivation. *Development and Psychopathology, 21*(1), 27–45. https://doi.org/10.1017/S0954579409000030

Quillen, E. E., Norton, H. L., Parra, E. J., Lona-Durazo, F., Ang, K. C., Illiescu, F. M., Pearson, L. N., Shriver, M. D., Lasisi, T., Gokcumen, O., Starr, I., Lin, Y.-L., Martin, A. R., & Jablonski, N. G. (2019). Shades of complexity: New perspectives on the evolution and genetic architecture of human skin. *American Journal of Physical Anthropology, 168*(S67), 4–26. https://doi.org/10.1002/ajpa.23737

Quillian, L., Pager, D., Hexel, O., & Midtbøen, A. H. (2017). Meta-analysis of field experiments shows no change in racial discrimination in hiring over time. *Proceedings of the National Academy of Sciences, 114*(41), 10870–10875. https://doi.org/10.1073/pnas.1706255114

Quinlan, E. B., Barker, E. D., Luo, Q., Banaschewski, T., Bokde, A. L., Bromberg, U., Büchel, C., Desrivières, S., Flor, H., Frouin, V., Garavan, H., Chaarani, B., Gowland, P., Heinz, A., Brühl, R., Martinot, J.-L., Martinot, M.-L. P., Nees, F., Orfanos, D. P., Paus, T., . . . Schumann, G. (2020). Peer victimization and its impact on adolescent brain development and psychopathology. *Molecular Psychiatry, 25*(11), 3066–3076.

Quist, M., Kaciroti, N., Poehlmann-Tynan, J., Weeks, H. M., Asta, K., Singh, P., & Shah, P. E. (2019). Interactive effects of infant gestational age and infant fussiness on the risk of maternal depressive symptoms in a nationally representative sample. *Academic Pediatrics, 19*(8), 917–924. https://doi.org/10.1016/j .acap.2019.02.015

Quitmann, J. H., Bullinger, M., Sommer, R., Rohenkohl, A. C., & Silva, N. M. B. D. (2016). Associations between psychological problems and quality of life in pediatric short stature from patients' and parents' perspectives. *PLOS ONE, 11*(4), e0153953. https://doi.org /10.1371/journal.pone.0153953

Rachwani, J., Herzberg, O., Golenia, L., & Adolph, K. E. (2019). Postural, visual, and manual coordination in the development of prehension. *Child Development, 90*(5), 1559–1568. https://doi.org/10.1111/cdev.13282

Rachwani, J., Tamis-LeMonda, C. S., Lockman, J. J., Karasik, L. B., & Adolph, K. E. (2020). Learning the designed actions of everyday objects. *Journal of Experimental Psychology. General, 149*(1), 67–78. https://doi.org/10.1037/xge0000631

Racine, N., McArthur, B. A., Cooke, J. E., Eirich, R., Zhu, J., & Madigan, S. (2021). Global prevalence of depressive and anxiety symptoms in children and adolescents during COVID-19: A meta-analysis. *JAMA Pediatrics, 175*(11), 1142–1150. https://doi.org /10.1001/jamapediatrics.2021.2482

Racine, N., McArthur, B. A., Cooke, J. E., Eirich, R., Zhu, J., & Madigan, S. (2021). Global prevalence of depressive and anxiety symptoms in children and adolescents during COVID-19: A meta-analysis. *JAMA Pediatrics, 175*(11), 1142–1150.

Radesky, J. (2019). Mobile media and parent–child interaction. In C. Donohue (Ed.), *Exploring key issues in early childhood and technology: Evolving perspectives and innovative approaches* (pp. 85–90). Routledge.

Radesky, J. S. (2021). Young children's online-offline balance. *Acta Paediatrica (Oslo, Norway: 1992), 110*(3), 748–749.

Radwan, C. M. (2019). Toxic metals detected in nearly all baby foods. *Contemporary Pediatrics, 36*(12), 14.

Rae, J. R., Gülgöz, S., Durwood, L., DeMeules, M., Lowe, R., Lindquist, G., & Olson, K. R. (2019). Predicting early-childhood gender transitions. *Psychological Science, 30*(5), 669–681. https://doi.org /10.1177/0956797619830649

Raeff, C. (2016). *Exploring the dynamics of human development: An integrative approach.* Oxford University Press.

Raeff, C., Greenfield, P. M., & Quiroz, B. (2000). Conceptualizing interpersonal relationships in the cultural contexts of individualism and collectivism. *New Directions for Child and Adolescent Development, 2000*(87), 59–74. https://doi.org/10.1002 /cd.23220008706

Raffaelli, M., Kang, H., & Guarini, T. (2012). Exploring the immigrant paradox in adolescent sexuality: An ecological perspective. In C. G. Coll & A. K. Marks (Eds.), *The immigrant paradox in children and adolescents: Is becoming American a developmental risk?* (pp. 109–134). American Psychological Association. https://doi.org/10.1037/13094-005

Rafferty, J., Committee on Psychosocial Aspects of Child and Family Health, Committee on Adolescence, & Section on Lesbian, Gay, Bisexual, and Transgender Health and Wellness. (2018). Ensuring comprehensive care and support for transgender and gender-diverse children and adolescents. *Pediatrics, 142*(4), e20182162. https://doi.org/10.1542 /peds.2018-2162

Raffington, L., Belsky, D. W., Kothari, M., Malanchini, M., Tucker-Drob, E. M., & Harden, K. P. (2021). Socioeconomic disadvantage and the pace of biological aging in children. *Pediatrics, 147*(6). https:// doi.org/10.1542/peds.2020-024406

Ragni, M. V. (2021). Hemophilia as a blueprint for gene therapy. *Science, 374*(6563), 40–41. https://doi.org /10.1126/science.abg0856

Rainbolt, S., Fowler, E. S., & Mansfield, K. C. (2019). High school teachers' perceptions of restorative discipline practices. *NASSP Bulletin, 103*(2), 158–182.

Rakesh, D., Cropley, V., Zalesky, A., Vijayakumar, N., Allen, N. B., & Whittle, S. (2021). Neighborhood disadvantage and longitudinal brain-predicted-age trajectory during adolescence. *Developmental Cognitive Neuroscience, 51*, 101002. https://doi.org/10.1016/j .dcn.2021.101002

Raley, R. K., Weiss, I., Reynolds, R., & Cavanagh, S. E. (2019). Estimating Children's Household Instability Between Birth and Age 18 Using Longitudinal Household Roster Data. *Demography, 56*(5), 1957–1973. https://doi.org/10.1007/s13524-019-00806-1

Raley, R. K., & Sweeney, M. M. (2020). Divorce, repartnering, and stepfamilies: A decade in review. *Journal of Marriage and Family, 82*(1), 81–99.

Ramani, G. B., Daubert, E. N., Lin, G. C., Kamarsu, S., Wodzinski, A., & Jaeggi, S. M. (2020). Racing dragons and remembering aliens: Benefits of playing number and working memory games on kindergartners' numerical knowledge. *Developmental Science, 23*(4), e12908.

Ramey, D. M. (2015). The social structure of criminalized and medicalized school discipline. *Sociology of Education, 88*(3), 181–201.

Ramírez-Esparza, N., García-Sierra, A., & Jiang, S. (2020). The current standing of bilingualism in today's globalized world: A socio-ecological perspective. *Current Opinion in Psychology, 32*, 124–128. https://doi .org/10.1016/j.copsyc.2019.06.038

Ramírez, N. F., & Kuhl, P. K. (2016). *Bilingual language learning in children.* University of Washington, Institute for Learning and Brain Sciences.

Ramos-Gomez, F., Kinsler, J., & Askaryar, H. (2020). Understanding oral health disparities in children as a global public health issue: How dental health professionals can make a difference. *Journal of Public Health Policy, 41*(2), 114–124. https://doi.org/10.1057 /s41271-020-00222-5

Rao, N., & Stewart, S. M. (1999). Cultural influences on sharer and recipient behavior: Sharing in Chinese and Indian preschool children. *Journal of Cross-Cultural Psychology, 30*(2), 219–241.

Rao, W.-W., Zong, Q.-Q., Zhang, J.-W., An, F.-R., Jackson, T., Ungvari, G. S., Xiang, Y., Su, Y.-Y., D'Arcy, C., & Xiang, Y.-T. (2020). Obesity increases the risk of depression in children and adolescents: Results from a systematic review and meta-analysis. *Journal of Affective Disorders, 267*, 78–85. https://doi.org/10.1016/j.jad.2020.01.154

Rapee, R. M., Oar, E. L., Johnco, C. J., Forbes, M. K., Fardouly, J., Magson, N. R., & Richardson, C. E. (2019). Adolescent development and risk for the onset of social-emotional disorders: A review and conceptual model. *Behaviour Research and Therapy, 123*, 103501. https://doi.org/10.1016/j.brat.2019.103501

Raposa, E. B., Rhodes, J., Stams, G. J. J., Card, N., Burton, S., Schwartz, S., Yovienne-Sykes, L. Y., Kanchewa, S., Kupersmidt, J., & Hussain, S. (2019). The effects of youth mentoring programs: A meta-analysis of outcome studies. *Journal of Youth and Adolescence, 48*(3), 423–443.

Rasmussen, B., Maharaj, N., Sheehan, P., & Friedman, H. S. (2019). Evaluating the employment benefits of education and targeted interventions to reduce child marriage. *Journal of Adolescent Health, 65*(1), S16–S24.

Raspa, M., Levis, D. M., Kish-Doto, J., Wallace, I., Rice, C., Barger, B., Green, K. K., & Wolf, R. B. (2015). Examining parents' experiences and information needs regarding early identification of developmental delays: Qualitative research to inform a public health campaign. *Journal of Developmental & Behavioral Pediatrics, 36*(8), 575–585. https://doi.org/10.1097/DBP.0000000000000205

Ratey, J. H., & Hagerman, E. (2013). *Spark: The revolutionary new science of exercise and the brain.* Little, Brown. https://www.amazon.com/Spark-Revolutionary-Science-Exercise-Brain/dp/0316113514

Raval, V. V., & Green, J. H. (2018). Children's developing emotional competence in a global context. In P. A. Kumar, S. T. George, & N. T. Sudhesh (Eds.), *Character strength development: Perspectives from positive psychology* (pp. 160–178). SAGE.

Raval, V., & Walker, B. (2019). Unpacking "culture": Caregiver socialization of emotion and child functioning in diverse families. *Developmental Review, 15.* https://doi.org/10.1016/j.dr.2018.11.001.

Raval, V. V., & Walker, B. L. (2019). Unpacking 'culture': Caregiver socialization of emotion and child functioning in diverse families. *Developmental Review, 51*, 146–174.

Ravindran, N., Berry, D., & McElwain, N. L. (2019). Dynamic bidirectional associations in negative behavior: Mother–toddler interaction during a snack delay. *Developmental Psychology, 55*(6), 1191–1198. https://doi.org/10.1037/dev0000703

Ravindran, N., Hu, Y., McElwain, N. L., & Telzer, E. H. (2020). Dynamics of mother–adolescent and father–adolescent autonomy and control during a conflict discussion task. *Journal of Family Psychology, 34*(3), 312–321. https://doi.org/10.1037/fam0000588

Ré, A. H. N., Okely, A. D., Logan, S. W., da Silva, M. M., Cattuzzo, M. T., & Stodden, D. F. (2020). Relationship between meeting physical activity guidelines and motor competence among low-income school youth. *Journal of Science and Medicine in Sport, 23*(6), 591–595.

Reardon, S. F., & Portilla, X. A. (2016). Recent trends in income, racial, and ethnic school readiness gaps at kindergarten entry. *AERA Open, 2*(3), 2332858416657343.

Reardon, S., Weathers, E. S., Fahle, E. M., Jang, H., & Kalogrides, D. (2019). *Is separate still unequal? New evidence on school segregation and racial academic achievement gaps.* The Educational Opportunity Project at Stanford University. https://edopportunity.org

Rebelo, M. A. B., Vieira, J. M. R., Pereira, J. V., Quadros, L. N., & Vettore, M. V. (2019). Does oral health influence school performance and school attendance? A systematic review and meta-analysis. *International Journal of Paediatric Dentistry, 29*(2), 138–148. https://doi.org/10.1111/ipd.12441

Recksiedler, C., & Settersten, R. A. S., Jr. (2020). How young adults' appraisals of work and family goals changed over the Great Recession: An examination of gender and rural-urban differences. *Journal of Youth Studies, 23*(9), 1217–1233. https://doi.org/10.1080/13676261.2019.1663339

Reddy, A. (2007). The eugenic origins of IQ testing: Implications for post-Atkins litigation. *DePaul Law Review, 57*, 667.

Reddy, V. (2000). Coyness in early infancy. *Developmental Science, 3*(2), 186–192.

Reddy, V. (2019a). Humour as culture in infancy. In E. Loizou & S. L. Recchia (Eds.), *Research on young children's humor: Theoretical and practical implications for early childhood education* (pp. 187–201). Springer International Publishing. https://doi.org/10.1007/978-3-030-15202-4_11

Reddy, V. (2019b). Meeting infant affect. *Developmental Psychology, 55*(9), 2020–2024. https://doi.org/10.1037/dev0000773

Redelmeier, D. A., & Raza, S. (2016). Concussions and repercussions. *PLOS Medicine, 13*(8), e1002104. https://doi.org/10.1371/journal.pmed.1002104

Reed, J., Hirsh-Pasek, K., & Golinkoff, R. M. (2017). Learning on hold: Cell phones sidetrack parent–child interactions. *Developmental Psychology, 53*(8), 1428.

Reese, E., & Neha, T. (2015). Let's kōrero (talk): The practice and functions of reminiscing among mothers and children in Māori families. *Memory, 23*(1), 99–110. https://doi.org/10.1080/09658211.2014.929705

Reetzke, R., Xie, Z., Llanos, F., & Chandrasekaran, B. (2018). Tracing the trajectory of sensory plasticity across different stages of speech learning in adulthood. *Current Biology, 28*(9), 1419–1427.e4. https://doi.org/10.1016/j.cub.2018.03.026

Regalado, A. (2018, February 12). 2017 was the year consumer DNA testing blew up. *Technology Review.* https://www.technologyreview.com/s/610233/2017-was-the-year-consumer-dna-testing-blew-up

Reich, D. (2018, March 23). Opinion | How genetics is changing our understanding of "race." *The New York Times.* https://www.nytimes.com/2018/03/23/opinion/sunday/genetics-race.html

Reid, J. L., Lynn Kagan, S., Brooks-Gunn, J., & Melvin, S. A. (2021). Promoting quality in programs for infants and toddlers: Comparing the family child care and center-based teaching workforce. *Children and Youth Services Review, 122*, 105890. https://doi.org/10.1016/j.childyouth.2020.105890

Reid, V. M., & Dunn, K. (2021). The fetal origins of human psychological development. *Current Directions in Psychological Science*, 0963721420984419. https://doi.org/10.1177/0963721420984419

Reid, V. M., Dunn, K., Young, R. J., Amu, J., Donovan, T., & Reissland, N. (2017). The human fetus preferentially engages with face-like visual stimuli. *Current Biology, 27*(12), 1825–1828.e3. https://doi.org/10.1016/j.cub.2017.05.044

Reigal, R. E., Moral-Campillo, L., Morillo-Baro, J. P., Juarez-Ruiz de Mier, R., Hernández-Mendo, A., &

Morales-Sánchez, V. (2020). Physical exercise, fitness, cognitive functioning, and psychosocial variables in an adolescent sample. *International Journal of Environmental Research and Public Health, 17*(3), 1100.

Reinka, M. A., Quinn, D. M., & Puhl, R. M. (2021). Examining the relationship between weight controllability beliefs and eating behaviors: The role of internalized weight stigma and BMI. *Appetite, 164*, 105257. https://doi.org/10.1016/j.appet.2021.105257

Reissland, N., Einbeck, J., Wood, R., & Lane, A. (2021). Effects of maternal mental health on prenatal movement profiles in twins and singletons. *Acta Paediatrica, 110*(9), 2553–2558. https://doi.org/10.1111/apa.15903

Reissland, N., & Kisilevsky, B. S. (Eds.). (2016). *Fetal development: Research on brain and behavior, environmental influences, and emerging technologies.* Springer International Publishing.

Renaissance Learning. (2022). *What Kids Are Reading: 2022 Edition.* Renaissance Learning. https://www.renaissance.com/wka

Rende, R. (2015). The developmental significance of chores: Then and now. *The Brown University Child and Adolescent Behavior Letter, 31*(1), 1–7.

Rentzou, K., Slutsky, R., Tuul, M., Gol-Guven, M., Kragh-Müller, G., Foerch, D. F., & Paz-Albo, J. (2019). Preschool teachers' conceptualizations and uses of play across eight countries. *Early Childhood Education Journal, 47*(1), 1–14.

Rescorla, L. A. (2019). Assessment of language in young children. In R. DelCarmen-Wiggins & A. S. Carter (Eds.), *The Oxford handbook of infant, toddler, and preschool mental health assessment* (2nd ed., p. 315). Oxford University Press.

Rex, S. M., Kopetsky, A., Bodt, B., & Robson, S. M. (2021). Relationships among the physical and social home food environments, dietary intake, and diet quality in mothers and children. *Journal of the Academy of Nutrition and Dietetics.* https://doi.org/10.1016/j.jand.2021.03.008

Rex-Lear, M., Jensen-Campbell, L. A., & Lee, S. (2019). Young and biased: Children's perceptions of overweight peers. *Journal of Applied Biobehavioral Research, 24*(3), e12161. https://doi.org/10.1111/jabr.12161

Reyna, V. F., & Panagiotopoulos, C. (2020). Morals, money, and risk taking from childhood to adulthood: The neurodevelopmental framework of fuzzy-trace theory. In J. Decety (Ed.), *The social brain: A developmental perspective.* MIT Press.

Reynolds, G. D., & Romano, A. C. (2016). The development of attention systems and working memory in infancy. *Frontiers in Systems Neuroscience, 10*, 15.

Reynolds, J. E., Grohs, M. N., Dewey, D., & Lebel, C. (2019). Global and regional white matter development in early childhood. *NeuroImage, 196*, 49–58. https://doi.org/10.1016/j.neuroimage.2019.04.004

Rhodes, M., & Baron, A. (2019). The development of social categorization. *Annual Review of Developmental Psychology, 1*(1), 359–386. https://doi.org/10.1146/annurev-devpsych-121318-084824

Ribot, K. M., Hoff, E., & Burridge, A. (2018). Language use contributes to expressive language growth: Evidence from bilingual children. *Child Development, 89*(3), 929–940. https://doi.org/10.1111/cdev.12770

Richards, M. J., Bogart, A., & Sheeder, J. (2022). Communication and interpretation of sexual consent and refusal in adolescents and young adults. *Journal of Adolescent Health, 70*(6), 915–921. https://doi.org/10.1016/j.jadohealth.2021.12.013

Richardson, D., & Hiu, C. F. (2018). *Developing a global indicator on bullying of school-aged children* (Innocenti Working Papers). UNICEF. https://www.un-ilibrary.org/content/papers/25206796/160

Richetto, J., & Meyer, U. (2021). Epigenetic modifications in schizophrenia and related disorders: Molecular scars of environmental exposures and source of phenotypic variability. *Biological Psychiatry, 89*(3), 215–226. https://doi.org/10.1016/j.biopsych.2020.03.008

Richmond, E., & Rogol, A. D. (2016). Endocrine responses to exercise in the developing child and adolescent. *Sports Endocrinology, 47*, 58–67.

Richmond, T. K., Thurston, I. B., & Sonneville, K. R. (2021). Weight-focused public health interventions—no benefit, some harm. *JAMA Pediatrics, 175*(3), 238–239. https://doi.org/10.1001/jamapediatrics.2020.4777

Richtel, M. (2021, January 16). Children's screen time has soared in the pandemic, alarming parents and researchers. *The New York Times.* https://www.nytimes.com/2021/01/16/health/covid-kids-tech-use.html

Richter, L. M., Daelmans, B., Lombardi, J., Heymann, J., Boo, F. L., Behrman, J. R., Lu, C., Lucas, J. E., Perez-Escamilla, R., Dua, T., Bhutta, Z. A., Stenberg, K., Gertler, P., & Darmstadt, G. L. (2017). Investing in the foundation of sustainable development: Pathways to scale up for early childhood development. *The Lancet, 389*(10064), 103–118. https://doi.org/10.1016/S0140-6736(16)31698-1

Rico, A., Brener, N. D., Thornton, J., Mpofu, J. J., Harris, W. A., Roberts, A. M., Kilmer, G., Chyen, D., Whittle, L., Leon-Nguyen, M., Lim, C., Saba, A., Bryan, L. N., Smith-Grant, J., & Underwood, J. M. (2022). Overview and methodology of the Adolescent Behaviors and Experiences Survey—United States, January–June 2021. *MMWR Supplements, 71*(3), 1.

Rideout, V. J. (2013). Zero to eight: Children's media use in America 2013. *Common Sense Media.*

Rideout, V., & Robb, M. B. (2019). *The common sense census: Media use by tweens and teens, 2019.* Common Sense Media.

Rideout, V., Peebles, A., Mann, S., & Robb, M. B. (2022). *Common Sense census: Media use by tweens and teens, 2021.* Common Sense.

Rieffe, C., Broekhof, E., Kouwenberg, M., Faber, J., Tsutsui, M. M., & Güroğlu, B. (2016). Disentangling proactive and reactive aggression in children using self-report. *European Journal of Developmental Psychology, 13*(4), 439–451.

Riggins, T., Canada, K. L., & Botdorf, M. (2020). Empirical evidence supporting neural contributions to episodic memory development in early childhood: Implications for childhood amnesia. *Child Development Perspectives, 14*(1), 41–48. https://doi.org/10.1111/cdep.12353

Riggins, T., Geng, F., Botdorf, M., Canada, K., Cox, L., & Hancock, G. R. (2018). Protracted hippocampal development is associated with age-related improvements in memory during early childhood. *NeuroImage, 174*, 127–137. https://doi.org/10.1016/j.neuroimage.2018.03.009

Righi, M. K., Bogen, K. W., Kuo, C., & Orchowski, L. M. (2021). A qualitative analysis of beliefs about sexual consent among high school students. *Journal of Interpersonal Violence, 36*(15–16), NP8290–NP8316.

Rinaldi, P., Caselli, M. C., Di Renzo, A., Gulli, T., & Volterra, V. (2014). Sign vocabulary in deaf toddlers exposed to sign language since birth. *The Journal of Deaf Studies and Deaf Education, 19*(3), 303–318. https://doi.org/10.1093/deafed/enu007

Rippon, G., Eliot, L., Genon, S., & Joel, D. (2021). How hype and hyperbole distort the neuroscience of sex differences. *PLOS Biology, 19*(5), e3001253. https://doi.org/10.1371/journal.pbio.3001253

Ristic, J., & Enns, J. T. (2015). The changing face of attentional development. *Current Directions in Psychological Science, 24*(1), 24–31.

Ritchie, S. J., & Bates, T. C. (2013). Enduring links from childhood mathematics and reading achievement to adult socioeconomic status. *Psychological Science, 24*(7), 1301–1308.

Rivas-Drake, D., & Umaña-Taylor, A. (2019). *Below the surface: Talking with teens about race, ethnicity, and identity.* Princeton University Press.

Rivas-Drake, D., Saleem, M., Schaefer, D. R., Medina, M., & Jagers, R. (2019). Intergroup contact attitudes across peer networks in school: Selection, influence, and implications for cross-group friendships. *Child Development, 90*(6), 1898–1916. https://doi.org/10.1111/cdev.13061

Rivas-Drake, D., Seaton, E. K., Markstrom, C., Quintana, S., Syed, M., Lee, R. M., Schwartz, S. J., Umaña-Taylor, A. J., French, S., Yip, T., & Ethnic and Racial Identity in the 21st Century Study Group. (2014). Ethnic and racial identity in adolescence: Implications for psychosocial, academic, and health outcomes. *Child Development, 85*(1), 40–57. https://doi.org/10.1111/cdev.12200

Rixon, A., Lomax, H., & O'Dell, L. (2019). Childhoods past and present: Anxiety and idyll in reminiscences of childhood outdoor play and contemporary parenting practices. *Children's Geographies, 17*(5), 618–629. https://doi.org/10.1080/14733285.2019.1605047

Roberts, G., Quach, J., Spencer-Smith, M., Anderson, P. J., Gathercole, S., Gold, L., Sia, K.-L., Mensah, F., Rickards, F., Ainley, J., & Wake, M. (2016). Academic outcomes 2 years after working memory training for children with low working memory: A randomized clinical trial. *JAMA Pediatrics, 170*(5), e154568–e154568. https://doi.org/10.1001/jamapediatrics.2015.4568

Roberts, K. J., Binns, H. J., Vincent, C., & Koenig, M. D. (2021). A scoping review: Family and child perspectives of clinic-based obesity treatment. *Journal of Pediatric Nursing, 57*, 56–72.

Robinson, K. H., Smith, E., & Davies, C. (2017). Responsibilities, tensions and ways forward: Parents' perspectives on children's sexuality education. *Sex Education, 17*(3), 333–347.

Roblyer, M. I. Z., Bámaca-Colbert, M. Y., Rojas, S. M., & Cervantes, R. C. (2015). "Our child is not like us": Understanding parent-child conflict among U.S. Latino families. *Family Science Review, 20*(2), 1–22.

Robson, D. A., Allen, M. S., & Howard, S. J. (2020). Self-regulation in childhood as a predictor of future outcomes: A meta-analytic review. *Psychological Bulletin, 146*(4), 324–354. https://doi.org/10.1037/bul0000227

Robson, E., & Evans, R. (2013). Dilemmas of dealing with distress in interviews with children. In M. A. Powell, N. Taylor, R. Fitzgerald, A. Graham, & D. Anderson (Eds.), *Ethical research involving children.* UNICEF Office of Research Innocenti.

Rochadiat, A. M., Tong, S. T., & Novak, J. M. (2018). Online dating and courtship among Muslim American women: Negotiating technology, religious identity, and culture. *New Media & Society, 20*(4), 1618–1639. https://doi.org/10.1177/1461444817702396

Rochat, P. (2018). The ontogeny of human self-consciousness. *Current Directions in Psychological Science, 27*(5), 345–350. https://doi.org/10.1177/0963721418760236

Rochat, P., Dias, M. D., Liping, G., Broesch, T., Passos-Ferreira, C., Winning, A., & Berg, B. (2009). Fairness in distributive justice by 3- and 5-year-olds across seven cultures. *Journal of Cross-Cultural Psychology, 40*(3), 416–442.

Roche, K. M., Caughy, M. O., Schuster, M. A., Bogart, L. M., Dittus, P. J., & Franzini, L. (2014). Cultural orientations, parental beliefs and practices, and Latino adolescents' autonomy and independence. *Journal of Youth and Adolescence, 43*(8), 1389–1403. https://doi.org/10.1007/s10964-013-9977-6

Rodgers, R. F., Damiano, S. R., Wertheim, E. H., & Paxton, S. J. (2017). Media exposure in very young girls: Prospective and cross-sectional relationships with BMIz, self-esteem and body size stereotypes. *Developmental Psychology, 53*(12), 2356–2363. https://doi.org/10.1037/dev0000407

Rodman, A. M., Jenness, J. L., Weissman, D. G., Pine, D. S., & McLaughlin, K. A. (2019). Neurobiological markers of resilience to depression and anxiety following childhood maltreatment: The role of neural circuits supporting the cognitive control of emotion. *Biological Psychiatry, 86*(6), 464–473. https://doi.org/10.1016/j.biopsych.2019.04.033

Rodríguez, S. A., Perez-Brena, N. J., Updegraff, K. A., & Umaña-Taylor, A. J. (2014). Emotional closeness in Mexican-origin adolescents' relationships with mothers, fathers, and same-sex friends. *Journal of Youth and Adolescence, 43*(12), 1953–1968. https://doi.org/10.1007/s10964-013-0004-8

Rodríguez, S., Valle, A., Gironelli, L. M., Guerrero, E., Regueiro, B., & Estévez, I. (2020). Performance and well-being of native and immigrant students: Comparative analysis based on PISA 2018. *Journal of Adolescence, 85*, 96–105.

Rodriguez-Martinez, A., Zhou, B., Sophiea, M. K., Bentham, J., Paciorek, C. J., Iurilli, M. L., Carrillo-Larco, R. M., Bennett, J. E., Di Cesare, M., Taddei, C., Bixby, H., Stevens, G. A., Riley, L. M., Cowan, M. J., Savin, S., Danaei, G., Chirita-Emandi, A., Kengne, A. P., Khang, Y-H., . . . Ezzati, M. (2020). Height and body-mass index trajectories of school-aged children and adolescents from 1985 to 2019 in 200 countries and territories: A pooled analysis of 2181 population-based studies with 65 million participants. *The Lancet, 396*(10261), 1511–1524.

Rodríguez-Vázquez, E., Tena-Sempere, M., & Castellano, J. M. (2020). Mechanisms for the metabolic control of puberty. *Current Opinion in Endocrine and Metabolic Research, 14*, 78–84. https://doi.org/10.1016/j.coemr.2020.06.003

Roebers, C. M. (2017). Executive function and metacognition: Towards a unifying framework of cognitive self-regulation. *Developmental Review, 45*, 31–51.

Roemmich, J. N., & Sinning, W. E. (1997). Weight loss and wrestling training: Effects on growth-related hormones. *Journal of Applied Physiology, 82*(6), 1760–1764. https://doi.org/10.1152/jappl.1997.82.6.1760

Rogers, A. A., Ha, T., Byon, J., & Thomas, C. (2020). Masculine gender-role adherence indicates conflict resolution patterns in heterosexual adolescent couples: A dyadic, observational study. *Journal of Adolescence, 79*, 112–121. https://doi.org/10.1016/j.adolescence.2020.01.004

Rogers, L. O. (2020). "I'm kind of a feminist": Using master narratives to analyze gender identity in middle childhood. *Child Development, 91*(1), 179–196. https://doi.org/10.1111/cdev.13142

Rogers, L. O., & Meltzoff, A. N. (2017). Is gender more important and meaningful than race? An analysis of racial and gender identity among Black, White, and mixed-race children. *Cultural Diversity and Ethnic Minority Psychology, 23*(3), 323.

Rogers, L. O., Rosario, R. J., Padilla, D., & Foo, C. (2021). "[I]t's hard because it's the cops that are killing us for stupid stuff": Racial identity in the sociopolitical context of Black Lives Matter. *Developmental Psychology, 57*(1), 87–101.

Rogers, L. O., & Way, N. (2018). Reimagining social and emotional development: Accommodation and resistance to dominant ideologies in the identities and friendships of boys of color. *Human Development, 61*(6), 311–331. https://doi.org/10.1159/000493378

Rogers, S. J., Estes, A., Lord, C., Munson, J., Rocha, M., Winter, J., Greenson, J., Colombi, C., Dawson, G., Vismara, L. A., Sugar, C. A., Hellemann, G., Whelan, F., & Talbott, M. (2019). A multisite randomized controlled two-phase trial of the Early Start Denver model compared to treatment as usual. *Journal of the American Academy of Child & Adolescent Psychiatry, 58*(9), 853–865. https://doi.org/10.1016/j.jaac.2019.01.004

Rogoff, B. (1990). *Apprenticeship in thinking: Cognitive development in social context.* Oxford University Press.

Rogoff, B. (1998). Cognition as a collaborative process. In W. Damon (Ed.), *Handbook of child psychology: Vol. 2. Cognition, perception, and language* (pp. 679–744). John Wiley & Sons Inc.

Rogoff, B. (2003). *The cultural nature of human development.* Oxford University Press.

Rogoff, B. (2016). Culture and participation: A paradigm shift. *Current Opinion in Psychology, 8*, 182–189. https://doi.org/10.1016/j.copsyc.2015.12.002

Rogoff, B., Callanan, M., Gutiérrez, K. D., & Erickson, F. (2016). The organization of informal learning. *Review of Research in Education, 40*(1), 356–401. https://doi.org/10.3102/0091732X16680994

Rogoff, B., Coppens, A. D., Alcala, L., Aceves-Azuara, I., Ruvalcaba, O., Lopez, A., & Dayton, A. (2017). Noticing learners' strengths through cultural research. *Perspectives on Psychological Science, 12*(5), 876–888. https://doi.org/10.1177/1745691617718355

Rogoff, B., Dahl, A., & Callanan, M. (2018). The importance of understanding children's lived experience. *Developmental Review, 50*, 5–15. https://doi.org/10.1016/j.dr.2018.05.006

Rogoff, B., & Mistry, J. (1985). Memory development in cultural context. In M. Pressley & C. J. Brainerd (Eds.), *Cognitive learning and memory in children* (pp. 117–142). Springer.

Rogoff, B., Sellers, M. J., Pirrotta, S., Fox, N., & White, S. H. (1975). Age of assignment of roles and responsibilities to children. *Human Development, 18*(5), 353–369.

Roisman, G. I., & Groh, A. M. (2021). The legacy of early attachments: Past, present, future. In R. A. Thompson, J. A. Simpson, L. J. Berlin, L. Ahnert, & T. Ai (Eds.), *Attachment: The fundamental questions* (pp. 187–194). Guilford.

Rojas, N. M., Yoshikawa, H., Gennetian, L., Rangel, M. L., Melvin, S., Noble, K., Duncan, G., & Magunson, K. (2020). Exploring the experiences and dynamics of an unconditional cash transfer for low-income mothers: A mixed-methods study. *Journal of Children and Poverty, 26*(1), 64–84. https://doi.org/10.1080/10796126.2019.1704161

Romer, D. (2010). Adolescent risk taking, impulsivity, and brain development: Implications for prevention. *Developmental Psychobiology, 52*(3), 263–276. https://doi.org/10.1002/dev.20442

Romer, D., Reyna, V. F., & Satterthwaite, T. D. (2017). Beyond stereotypes of adolescent risk taking: Placing the adolescent brain in developmental context. *Developmental Cognitive Neuroscience, 27*, 19–34. https://doi.org/10.1016/j.dcn.2017.07.007

Romero, R., Dey, S. K., & Fisher, S. J. (2014). Preterm labor: One syndrome, many causes. *Science (New York, NY), 345*(6198), 760–765. https://doi.org/10.1126/science.1251816

Romito, B., Jewell, J., Jackson, M., AAP Committee on Hospital Care, & Association of Child Life Professionals. (2021). Child life services. *Pediatrics, 147*(1). https://doi.org/10.1542/peds.2020-040261

Romm, K. F., Metzger, A., & Alvis, L. M. (2020). Parental psychological control and adolescent problematic outcomes: A multidimensional approach. *Journal of Child and Family Studies, 29*(1), 195–207. https://doi.org/10.1007/s10826-019-01545-y

Romo, L. F., Mireles-Rios, R., & Lopez-Tello, G. (2014). Latina mothers' and daughters' expectations for autonomy at age 15 (La Quinceanera). *Journal of Adolescent Research, 29*(2), 271–294. https://doi.org/10.1177/0743558413477199

Romo, N. D. (2019). Gone but not forgotten: Violent trauma victimization and the treatment of violence like a disease. *Hospital Pediatrics, 10*(1), 95–97. https://doi.org/10.1542/hpeds.2019-0196

Ronan, L., Alexander-Bloch, A., & Fletcher, P. C. (2020). Childhood obesity, cortical structure, and executive function in healthy children. *Cerebral Cortex, 30*(4), 2519–2528. https://doi.org/10.1093/cercor/bhz257

Ronan, V., Yeasin, R., & Claud, E. C. (2021). Childhood development and the microbiome: The intestinal microbiota in maintenance of health and development of disease during childhood development. *Gastroenterology, 160*(2), 495–506. https://doi.org/10.1053/j.gastro.2020.08.065

Ronkin, E. G., & Tone, E. B. (2020). Working with twin children and their families in mental health care settings. *Professional Psychology: Research and Practice, 51*(3), 237–246. https://doi.org/10.1037/pro0000288

Ronto, R., Wu, J. H., & Singh, G. M. (2018). The global nutrition transition: Trends, disease burdens and policy interventions. *Public Health Nutrition, 21*(12), 2267–2270. https://doi.org/10.1017/S1368980018000423

Roopnarine, J. L., & Davidson, K. L. (2015). Parent–child play across cultures. In J. E. Johnson, S. G. Eberle, T. S. Henricks, & D. Kuschner (Eds.), *The handbook of the study of play* (Vol. 2, pp. 85–100). Rowman & Littlefield.

Roos, L. E., Giuliano, R. J., Beauchamp, K. G., Berkman, E. T., Knight, E. L., & Fisher, P. A. (2020). Acute stress impairs children's sustained attention with increased vulnerability for children of mothers reporting higher parenting stress. *Developmental Psychobiology, 62*(4), 532–543.

Rosado-May, F. J., Urrieta, L., Jr., Dayton, A., & Rogoff, B. (2020). Innovation as a key feature of indigenous ways of learning. In N. S. Nasir, C. D. Lee, R. Pea, & M. McKinney de Royston (Eds.), *Handbook of the cultural foundations of learning* (pp. 79–96). Routledge.

Rosander, K. (2020). Development of gaze control in early infancy. In *Oxford Research Encyclopedia of Psychology*. https://doi.org/10.1093/acrefore/9780190236557.013.825

Rose, A. J., Glick, G. C., Smith, R. L., Schwartz-Mette, R. A., & Borowski, S. K. (2017). Co-rumination exacerbates stress generation among adolescents with depressive symptoms. *Journal of Abnormal Child Psychology, 45*(5), 985–995. https://doi.org/10.1007/s10802-016-0205-1

Rose, A. J., & Smith, R. L. (2018). Gender and peer relationships. In W. M. Bukowski, B. Laursen, & K. H. Rubin (Eds.), *Handbook of peer interactions, relationships, and groups* (pp. 571–589). Guilford.

Rosen, M. L., Hagen, M. P., Lurie, L. A., Miles, Z. E., Sheridan, M. A., Meltzoff, A. N., & McLaughlin, K. A. (2020). Cognitive stimulation as a mechanism linking socioeconomic status with executive function: A longitudinal investigation. *Child Development, 91*(4), e762–e779. https://doi.org/10.1111/cdev.13315

Rosen, R., Visher, M., & Beal, K. (2018). *Career and technical education: Current policy, prominent programs, and evidence.* MDRC.

Rosenbaum, J. E. (2020). Educational and criminal justice outcomes 12 years after school suspension. *Youth & Society, 52*(4), 515–547. https://doi.org/10.1177/0044118X17752208

Rosenberg, K. R. (2021). The evolution of human infancy: Why it helps to be helpless. *Annual Review of Anthropology, 50*(1), 423–440. https://doi.org/10.1146/annurev-anthro-111819-105454

Rosenberg, M. (1963). Parental interest and children's self-conceptions. *Sociometry, 26*(1), 35–49. https://doi.org/10.2307/2785723

Rosenberg, N. A. (2011). A population-genetic perspective on the similarities and differences among worldwide human populations. *Human Biology, 83*(6), 659–684. https://doi.org/10.3378/027.083.0601.

Rosenblum, S. (2018). Inter-relationships between objective handwriting features and executive control among children with developmental dysgraphia. *PLOS ONE, 13*(4), e0196098. https://doi.org/10.1371/journal.pone.0196098

Rosenfeld, M. J. (2017). Marriage, choice, and couplehood in the age of the internet. *Sociological Science, 4*, 490–510.

Rosenfeld, M. J., & Thomas, R. J. (2012). Searching for a mate: The rise of the internet as a social intermediary. *American Sociological Review, 77*(4), 523–547. https://doi.org/10.1177/0003122412448050

Rosenfeld, M. J., Thomas, R. J., & Hausen, S. (2019). Disintermediating your friends: How online dating in the United States displaces other ways of meeting. *Proceedings of the National Academy of Sciences, 116*(36), 17753–17758. https://doi.org/10.1073/pnas.1908630116

Rosenfield, R. L. (2021). Normal and premature adrenarche. *Endocrine Reviews,* bnab009. https://doi.org/10.1210/endrev/bnab009

Rosenke, M., Natu, V. S., Wu, H., Querdasi, F. R., Kular, H., Lopez-Alvarez, N., Grotheer, M., Berman, S., Mezer, A. A., & Grill-Spector, K. (2021). Myelin contributes to microstructural growth in human sensory cortex during early infancy. *BioRxiv,* 2021.03.16.435703. https://doi.org/10.1101/2021.03.16.435703

Rosenthal, N. L., & Kobak, R. (2010). Assessing adolescents' attachment hierarchies: Differences across developmental periods and associations with individual adaptation. *Journal of Research on Adolescence, 20*(3), 678–706. https://doi.org/10.1111/j.1532-7795.2010.00655.x

Rosenzweig, M. R., & Bennett, E. L. (1996). Psychobiology of plasticity: Effects of training and experience on brain and behavior. *Behavioural Brain Research, 78*(1), 57–65. https://doi.org/10.1016/0166-4328(95)00216-2

Roskam, I. (2019). Externalizing behavior from early childhood to adolescence: Prediction from inhibition, language, parenting, and attachment. *Development and Psychopathology, 31*(2), 587–599.

Ross, A., Wood, L., & Searle, M. (2020). The indirect influence of child play on the association between parent perceptions of the neighborhood environment and sense of community. *Health & Place, 65,* 102422. https://doi.org/10.1016/j.healthplace.2020.102422

Ross, J., Yilmaz, M., Dale, R., Cassidy, R., Yildirim, I., & Zeedyk, M. S. (2017). Cultural differences in self-recognition: The early development of autonomous and related selves? *Developmental Science, 20*(3), e12387. https://doi.org/10.1111/desc.12387

Ross, M., & Showalter, T. (2020, December 18). *Millions of young adults are out of school or work. We need an education and employment promise.* Brookings.

Rossi, E., Poulin, F., & Boislard, M. A. (2021). Sexual trajectories during adolescence and adjustment in emerging adulthood. *Emerging Adulthood, 9*(4), 281–291.

Roth, W. D., Yaylacı, Ş., Jaffe, K., & Richardson, L. (2020). Do genetic ancestry tests increase racial essentialism? Findings from a randomized controlled trial. *PLOS ONE, 15*(1), e0227399. https://doi.org/10.1371/journal.pone.0227399

Rothenberg, W. A., Zeitz, S., Lansford, J. E., Bornstein, M. H., Deater-Deckard, K., Dodge, K. A., Malone, P. S., Skinner, A. T., & Steinberg, L. (2021). Four domains of parenting in three ethnic groups in the United States. In J. E. Lansford, W. A. Rothenberg, & M. H. Bornstein (Eds.), *Parenting across cultures from childhood to adolescence: Development in nine countries* (pp. 193–226). Routledge.

Rothman, E. F., Beckmeyer, J. J., Herbenick, D., Fu, T.-C., Dodge, B., & Fortenberry, J. D. (2021). The prevalence of using pornography for information about how to have sex: Findings from a nationally representative survey of U.S. adolescents and young adults. *Archives of Sexual Behavior, 50*(2), 629–646. https://doi.org/10.1007/s10508-020-01877-7

Rothman, E. F., Paruk, J., Espensen, A., Temple, J. R., & Adams, K. (2017). A qualitative study of what US parents say and do when their young children see pornography. *Academic Pediatrics, 17*(8), 844–849.

Rothman, J. (2018, February 3). The philosophy of the midlife crisis. *The New Yorker.* https://www.newyorker.com/books/page-turner/the-philosophy-of-the-midlife-crisis

Rothwell, J. (2020). Assessing the economic gains of eradicating illiteracy nationally and regionally in the United States. *Barbara Bush Foundation for Family Literacy.* https://www.barbarabush.org/reports.

Röttger-Rössler, B. (2020). Research across cultures and disciplines: Methodological challenges in an interdisciplinary and comparative research project on emotion socialization. In M. Schnegg & E. D. Lowe (Eds.), *Comparing cultures: Innovations in comparative ethnography* (pp. 180–200). Cambridge University Press.

Rouse, M. L., Fishbein, L. B., Minshawi, N. F., & Fodstad, J. C. (2017). Historical development of toilet training. In J. L. Matson (Ed.), *Clinical guide to toilet training children* (pp. 1–18). Springer International Publishing. https://doi.org/10.1007/978-3-319-62725-0_1

Rouse, M., & Hamilton, E. (2021). Rethinking sex and the brain: How to create an inclusive discourse in neuroscience. *Mind, Brain, and Education, 15*(2), 163–167. https://doi.org/10.1111/mbe.12285

Rousseau, J.-J. (2010). *Emile, or, On education: Includes Emile and Sophie, or, The solitaries.* UPNE.

Rousseau, P. V., Matton, F., Lecuyer, R., & Lahaye, W. (2017). The Moro reaction: More than a reflex, a ritualized behavior of nonverbal communication. *Infant Behavior and Development, 46,* 169–177. https://doi.org/10.1016/j.infbeh.2017.01.004

Rovee-Collier, C., & Cuevas, K. (2009). Multiple memory systems are unnecessary to account for infant memory development: An ecological model. *Developmental Psychology, 45*(1), 160–174. https://doi.org/10.1037/a0014538

Rovee-Collier, C., & Giles, A. (2010). Why a neuromaturational model of memory fails: Exuberant learning in early infancy. *Behavioural Processes, 83*(2), 197–206. https://doi.org/10.1016/j.beproc.2009.11.013

Rowan-Kenyon, H. T., Savitz-Romer, M., Ott, M. W., Swan, A. K., & Liu, P. P. (2017). Finding conceptual coherence: Trends and alignment in the scholarship on noncognitive skills and their role in college success and career readiness. In M. B. Paulsen (Ed.), *Higher education: Handbook of theory and research* (pp. 141–179). Springer.

Rowe, M. L., Leech, K. A., & Cabrera, N. (2017). Going beyond input quantity: Wh-questions matter for toddlers' language and cognitive development. *Cognitive Science, 41,* 162–179.

Rowe, S. L., Gembeck, M. J. Z., Rudolph, J., & Nesdale, D. (2015). A longitudinal study of rejecting and autonomy-restrictive parenting, rejection sensitivity, and socioemotional symptoms in early adolescents. *Journal of Abnormal Child Psychology, 43*(6), 1107–1118.

Rowland, R., Sass, Z., Ponsonby, A.-L., Pezic, A., Tang, M. L., Vuillermin, P., Gray, L., Burgner, D., & B. I. S. I. Group. (2021). Burden of infection in Australian infants. *Journal of Paediatrics and Child Health, 57*(2), 204–211. https://doi.org/10.1111/jpc.15174

Rowley, K. J., Edmunds, C. C., Dufur, M. J., Jarvis, J. A., & Silveira, F. (2020). Contextualising the achievement gap: Assessing educational achievement, inequality, and disadvantage in high-income countries. *Comparative Education, 56*(4), 459–483.

Rubin, K. H., Barstead, M. G., Smith, K. A., & Bowker, J. C. (2018). Peer relations and the behaviorally inhibited child. In K. Pérez-Edgar & N. A. Fox (Eds.), *Behavioral inhibition: Integrating theory, research, and clinical perspectives* (pp. 157–184). Springer.

Rubin, K. H., Bukowski, W. M., & Bowker, J. C. (2015). Children in peer groups. In M. H. Bornstein, T. Leventhal, & R. M. Lerner (Eds.), *Handbook of child psychology and developmental science: Ecological settings and processes* (pp. 175–222). Wiley. https://doi.org/10.1002/9781118963418.childpsy405

Rubino, F., Puhl, R. M., Cummings, D. E., Eckel, R. H., Ryan, D. H., Mechanick, J. I., Nadglowski, J., Ramos Salas, X., Schauer, P. R., Twenefour, D., Apovian, C. M., Aronne, L. J., Batterham, R. L., Berthoud, H.-R., Boza, C., Busetto, L., Dicker, D., De Groot, M., Eisenberg, D., . . . Dixon, J. B. (2020). Joint international consensus statement for ending stigma of obesity. *Nature Medicine, 26*(4), 485–497. https://doi.org/10.1038/s41591-020-0803-x

Ruble, D. N., & Brooks-Gunn, J. (1982). The experience of menarche. *Child Development, 53*(6), 1557–1566.

Ruble, D. N., Taylor, L. J., Cyphers, L., Greulich, F. K., Lurye, L. E., & Shrout, P. E. (2007). The role of gender constancy in early gender development. *Child Development, 78*(4), 1121–1136. https://doi.org/10.1111/j.1467-8624.2007.01056.x

Rucinski, C. L., Brown, J. L., & Downer, J. T. (2018). Teacher–child relationships, classroom climate, and children's social-emotional and academic development. *Journal of Educational Psychology, 110*(7), 992–1004. https://doi.org/10.1037/edu0000240

Rüdiger, M., & Rozycki, H. J. (2020). It's time to reevaluate the Apgar score. *JAMA Pediatrics, 174*(4), 321–322.

Rudzik, A. E. F., & Ball, H. L. (2021). Biologically normal sleep in the mother-infant dyad. *American Journal of Human Biology, 33*(5), e23589. https://doi.org/10.1002/ajhb.23589

Rueda, M. R., Posner, M. I., & Rothbart, M. K. (2004). Attentional control and self-regulation. *Handbook of Self-Regulation: Research, Theory, and Applications, 2,* 284–299.

Ruffman, T., Lorimer, B., & Scarf, D. (2017). Do infants really experience emotional contagion? *Child Development Perspectives, 11*(4), 270–274. https://doi.org/10.1111/cdep.12244

Rui, N. (2009). Four decades of research on the effects of detracking reform: Where do we stand?—A systematic review of the evidence. *Journal of Evidence-Based Medicine, 2*(3), 164–183. http://onlinelibrary.wiley.com/doi/10.1111/j.1756-5391.2009.01032.x/full

Ruprecht, K., Elicker, J., & Choi, J. Y. (2016). Continuity of care, caregiver–child interactions, and toddler social competence and problem behaviors. *Early Education and Development, 27*(2), 221–239. https://doi.org/10.1080/10409289.2016.1102034

Rutherford, H. J. V., Potenza, M. N., Mayes, L. C., & Scheinost, D. (2020). The application of connectome-based predictive modeling to the maternal brain: Implications for mother–infant bonding. *Cerebral Cortex (New York, NY), 30*(3), 1538–1547. https://doi.org/10.1093/cercor/bhz185

Rutjens, B. T., Sengupta, N., van der Lee, R., van Koningsbruggen, G. M., Martens, J. P., Rabelo, A., & Sutton, R. M. (2021). Science skepticism across 24 countries. *Social Psychological and Personality Science,* 19485506211001330. https://doi.org/10.1177/19485506211001329

Rutland, A., & Killen, M. (2015). A developmental science approach to reducing prejudice and social exclusion: Intergroup processes, social–cognitive development, and moral reasoning. *Social Issues and Policy Review, 9*(1), 121–154.

Rutledge, S. A., Cannata, M., Brown, S. L., & Traeger, D. G. (2020). *Steps to schoolwide success: Systemic practices for connecting social-emotional and academic learning.* Harvard Education Press.

Rutter, C., & Walker, S. (2021). Infant mortality inequities for Māori in New Zealand: A tale of three policies. *International Journal for Equity in Health, 20*(1), 10. https://doi.org/10.1186/s12939-020-01340-y

Ryan, W. S., Legate, N., & Weinstein, N. (2015). Coming out as lesbian, gay, or bisexual: The lasting impact of initial disclosure experiences. *Self and Identity, 14*(5), 549–569.

Ryberg, R., Harris, K. M., & Pearce, L. (2018). *Religiosity of young adults: The National Longitudinal Study of Adolescent to Adult Health* (Add Health Research Brief No. 4). Carolina Population Center, University of Carolina at Chapel Hill.

Rybińska, A., & Morgan, S. P. (2019). Childless expectations and childlessness over the life course. *Social Forces, 97*(4), 1571–1602. https://doi.org/10.1093/sf/soy098

Rysavy, M. A., Li, L., Bell, E. F., Das, A., Hintz, S. R., Stoll, B. J., Vohr, B. R., Carlo, W. A., Shankaran, S., Walsh, M. C., Tyson, J. E., Cotten, C. M., Smith, P. B., Murray, J. C., Colaizy, T. T., Brumbaugh, J. E., & Higgins, R. D. (2015). Between-hospital variation in treatment and outcomes in extremely preterm infants. *New England Journal of Medicine, 372*(19), 1801–1811. https://doi.org/10.1056/NEJMoa1410689

Rytioja, M., Lappalainen, K., & Savolainen, H. (2019). Behavioural and emotional strengths of sociometrically popular, rejected, controversial, neglected, and average children. *European Journal of Special Needs Education, 34*(5), 557–571.

Rzehak, P., Oddy, W. H., Mearin, M. L., Grote, V., Mori, T. A., Szajewska, H., Shamir, R., Koletzko, S., Weber, M., Beilin, L. J., Huang, R.-C., Koletzko, B., & for the WP10 working group of the Early Nutrition Project. (2017). Infant feeding and growth trajectory patterns in childhood and body composition in young adulthood. *The American Journal of Clinical Nutrition, 106*(2), 568–580. https://doi.org/10.3945/ajcn.116.140962

Saarni, C. (1984). An observational study of children's attempts to monitor their expressive behavior. *Child Development, 55*(4), 1504–1513. https://doi.org/10.2307/1130020

Saarni, C. (1999). *The development of emotional competence.* Guilford.

Sadeh, A. (2015). III. Sleep assessment methods. *Monographs of the Society for Research in Child Development, 80*(1), 33–48.

Saey, T. H. (2018, May 22). Consumer DNA testing promises more than it delivers. *Genetics.*

Safa, M. D., & Umaña-Taylor, A. J. (2021). Biculturalism and adjustment among US Latinos: A review of four decades of empirical findings. *Advances in Child Development and Behavior, 61*, 73–127.

Safar, K., & Moulson, M. C. (2020). Three-month-old infants show enhanced behavioral and neural sensitivity to fearful faces. *Developmental Cognitive Neuroscience, 42*, 100759.

Saffran, J. R. (2020). Statistical language learning in infancy. *Child Development Perspectives, 14*(1), 49–54. https://doi.org/10.1111/cdep.12355

Safronova, V. (2021, July 7). A private-school sex educator defends her methods. *The New York Times.* https://www.nytimes.com/2021/07/07/style/sex-educator-methods-defense.html

Saguy, T., Reifen-Tagar, M., & Joel, D. (2021). The gender-binary cycle: The perpetual relations between a biological-essentialist view of gender, gender ideology, and gender-labelling and sorting. *Philosophical Transactions of the Royal Society B: Biological Sciences, 376*(1822), 20200141. https://doi.org/10.1098/rstb.2020.0141

Sahota, A. K., Shapiro, W. L., Newton, K. P., Kim, S. T., Chung, J., & Schwimmer, J. B. (2020). Incidence of nonalcoholic fatty liver disease in children: 2009–2018. *Pediatrics, 146*(6). https://doi.org/10.1542/peds.2020-0771

Sakai, J. (2020). Core concept: How synaptic pruning shapes neural wiring during development and, possibly, in disease. *Proceedings of the National Academy of Sciences of the United States of America, 117*(28), 16096–16099.

Sako, M. (2014). Outsourcing and offshoring of professional services. In B. Hinings, D. Muzio, J. Broschak, & L. Empson (Eds.), *The Oxford handbook of professional service firms* (pp. 327–350). Oxford University Press. http://books.google.com/books?hl=en&lr=&id=JcdQCgAAQBAJ&oi=fnd&pg=PA327&dq=%22professional+services+and+non-professional+business+services.+It%22+%22firms.+We+focus+on+primary+activities+to+test+the+analytical%22+%22on+a+number+of+theories,+and+gauging+whether+different%22+&ots=0OxF26MaZ7&sig=zTUDY_gNhq-l_Evdm9rgre7vdHA

Sala, G., & Gobet, F. (2020). Working memory training in typically developing children: A multilevel meta-analysis. *Psychonomic Bulletin & Review, 27*(3), 423–434. https://doi.org/10.3758/s13423-019-01681-y

Salandy, S., Rai, R., Gutierrez, S., Ishak, B., & Tubbs, R. S. (2019). Neurological examination of the infant. *Clinical Anatomy, 32*(6), 770–777. https://doi.org/10.1002/ca.23352

Salcedo-Arellano, M. J., Dufour, B., McLennan, Y., Martinez-Cerdeno, V., & Hagerman, R. (2020). Fragile X syndrome and associated disorders: Clinical aspects and pathology. *Neurobiology of Disease, 136*, 104740. https://doi.org/10.1016/j.nbd.2020.104740

Salinas, C. (2020). The complexity of the "x" in Latinx: How Latinx/a/o students relate to, identify with, and understand the term Latinx. *Journal of Hispanic Higher Education, 19*(2), 149–168. https://doi.org/10.1177/1538192719900382

Salmela-Aro, K., Tang, X., Symonds, J., & Upadyaya, K. (2021). Student engagement in adolescence: A scoping review of longitudinal studies 2010–2020. *Journal of Research on Adolescence, 31*(2), 256–272.

Salmon, D. A., Dudley, M. Z., Glanz, J. M., & Omer, S. B. (2015). Vaccine hesitancy. *American Journal of Preventive Medicine, 49*(6), S391–S398. https://doi.org/10.1016/j.amepre.2015.06.009

Salmon, K., & Reese, E. (2016). The benefits of reminiscing with young children. *Current Directions in Psychological Science, 25*(4), 233–238.

Salomon, I., & Brown, C. S. (2019). The selfie generation: Examining the relationship between social media use and early adolescent body image. *The Journal of Early Adolescence, 39*(4), 539–560. https://doi.org/10.1177/0272431618770809

Salzmann, J. (1943). *Principles of orthodontics.* Lippincott.

Samek, D. R., Hicks, B. M., Keyes, M. A., Iacono, W. G., & McGue, M. (2017). Antisocial peer affiliation and externalizing disorders: Evidence for gene × environment × development interaction. *Development and Psychopathology, 29*(1), 155–172.

Sameroff, A. J. (2020). It's more complicated. *Annual Review of Developmental Psychology, 2*(1), 1–26. https://doi.org/10.1146/annurev-devpsych-061520-120738

Sameroff, A. J., & Haith, M. M. (1996). Interpreting developmental transitions. In A. Sameroff & M. Haith (Eds.), *The five to seven year shift: The age of reason and responsibility* (pp. 3–30). University of Chicago Press.

Samji, H., Wu, J., Ladak, A., Vossen, C., Stewart, E., Dove, N., Long, D., & Snell, G. (2022). Review: Mental health impacts of the COVID-19 pandemic on children and youth—a systematic review. *Child and Adolescent Mental Health, 27*(2), 173–189. https://doi.org/10.1111/camh.12501

Sampedro-Piquero, P., Alvarez-Suarez, P., & Begega, A. (2018). Coping with stress during aging: The importance of a resilient brain. *Current Neuropharmacology, 16*(3), 284–296. https://doi.org/10.2174/1570159X15666170915141610

Sánchez, B., Garcia-Murillo, Y., Monjaras-Gaytan, L. Y., Thursby, K., Ulerio, G., de los Reyes, W., Salusky, I. R., & Rivera, C. S. (2022). Everyday acts of resistance: Mexican, undocumented immigrant children and adolescents navigating oppression with mentor support. *Journal of Research on Adolescence, 32*(2), 398–416. https://doi.org/10.1111/jora.12755

Sanchez, C. E., Barry, C., Sablok, A., Russell, K., Majors, A., Kollins, S. H., & Fuemmeler, B. F. (2018). Maternal pre-pregnancy obesity and child neurodevelopmental outcomes: A meta-analysis. *Obesity Reviews: An Official Journal of the International Association for the Study of Obesity, 19*(4), 464–484. https://doi.org/10.1111/obr.12643

Sanchez, D., Flannigan, A., Guevara, C., Arango, S., & Hamilton, E. (2017). Links among familial gender ideology, media portrayal of women, dating, and sexual behaviors in African American, and Mexican American adolescent young women: A qualitative study. *Sex Roles, 77*, 453–470. https://doi.org/10.1007/s11199-017-0739-x

Sanchez, O., & Kolodner, M. (2021, October 10). Why racial graduation gaps exist across the nation. *Hechinger Report.* http://hechingerreport.org/why-white-students-are-250-more-likely-to-graduate-than-black-students-at-public-universities/

Sánchez Romero, M. (2018). Care and socialization of children in the European Bronze Age. In S. Crawford, D. Hadley, & G. Shepherd (Eds.), *The Oxford handbook of the archaeology of childhood.* Oxford University Press. https://doi.org/10.1093/oxfordhb/9780199670697.013.18

Sandberg, D. E., & Gardner, M. (2022). Differences/disorders of sex development: Medical conditions at the intersection of sex and gender. *Annual Review of Clinical Psychology, 18*(1), 201–231. https://doi.org/10.1146/annurev-clinpsy-081219-101412

Sanders, J. O., Qiu, X., Lu, X., Duren, D. L., Liu, R. W., Dang, D., Menendez, M. E., Hans, S. D., Weber, D. R., & Cooperman, D. R. (2017). The uniform pattern of growth and skeletal maturation during the human adolescent growth spurt. *Scientific Reports, 7*(1), 16705. https://doi.org/10.1038/s41598-017-16996-w

Sanderson, K. (2021). Why sports concussions are worse for women. *Nature, 596*(7870), 26–28. https://doi.org/10.1038/d41586-021-02089-2

Sandseter, E. B. H., Kleppe, R., & Sando, O. J. (2021). The prevalence of risky play in young children's indoor and outdoor free play. *Early Childhood Education Journal, 49*(2), 303–312.

Sanes, D. H., & Woolley, S. M. (2011). A behavioral framework to guide research on central auditory development and plasticity. *Neuron, 72*(6), 912–929.

Sania, A., Sudfeld, C. R., Danaei, G., Fink, G., McCoy, D. C., Zhu, Z., Fawzi, M. C. S., Akman, M., Arifeen, S. E., Barros, A. J. D., Bellinger, D., Black, M. M., Bogale, A., Braun, J. M., Broek, N. van den, Carrara, V., Duazo, P., Duggan, C., Fernald, L. C. H., . . . Fawzi, W. (2019). Early life risk factors of motor, cognitive and language development: A pooled analysis of studies from low/middle-income countries. *BMJ Open, 9*(10), e026449. https://doi.org/10.1136/bmjopen-2018-026449

Santelli, J. S., Song, X., Garbers, S., Sharma, V., & Viner, R. M. (2017). Global trends in adolescent fertility, 1990–2012, in relation to national wealth, income inequalities, and educational expenditures. *Journal of Adolescent Health, 60*(2), 161–168. https://doi.org/10.1016/j.jadohealth.2016.08.026

Sanz Cortes, M., Chmait, R. H., Lapa, D. A., Belfort, M. A., Carreras, E., Miller, J. L., Brawura Biskupski Samaha, R., Sepulveda Gonzalez, G., Gielchinsky, Y., Yamamoto, M., Persico, N., Santorum, M., Otaño, L., Nicolaou, E., Yinon, Y., Faig-Leite, F., Brandt, R., Whitehead, W., Maiz, N., . . . Nicolaides, K. H. (2021). Experience of 300 cases of prenatal fetoscopic open spina bifida repair: Report of the International Fetoscopic Neural Tube Defect Repair Consortium. *American Journal of Obstetrics and Gynecology, 225*(6), 678.e1–678.e11. https://doi.org/10.1016/j.ajog.2021.05.044

Sarrico, C., McQueen, A., & Samuel, S. (Eds.). (2017). *State of higher education, 2015–2016.* Organisation for Economic Co-operation and Development (OECD) Higher Education Programme (IMHE).

Sassler, S. (2010). Partnering across the life course: Sex, relationships, and mate selection. *Journal of Marriage and the Family, 72*(3), 557–575. https://doi.org/10.1111/j.1741-3737.2010.00718.x

Sassler, S., Michelmore, K., & Qian, Z. (2018). Transitions from sexual relationships into cohabitation and beyond. *Demography, 55*(2), 511–534. https://doi.org/10.1007/s13524-018-0649-8

Sathyanesan, A., Zhou, J., Scafidi, J., Heck, D. H., Sillitoe, R. V., & Gallo, V. (2019). Emerging connections between cerebellar development, behavior, and complex brain disorders. *Nature Reviews Neuroscience, 20*(5), 298–313. https://doi.org/10.1038/s41583-019-0152-2

Sauber-Schatz, E. K., Ederer, D. J., Dellinger, A. M., & Baldwin, G. T. (2016). Vital signs: Motor vehicle injury prevention — United States and 19 comparison countries. *Morbidity and Mortality Weekly Report, 65*(26), 672–677.

Sauber-Schatz, E. K., Thomas, A. M., & Cook, L. J. (2015). Motor vehicle crashes, medical outcomes, and hospital charges among children aged 1–12 years — Crash Outcome Data Evaluation System, 11 states, 2005–2008. *Morbidity and Mortality Weekly Report: Surveillance Summaries, 64*(8), 1–32.

Sauber-Schatz, E. K., West, B. A., Bergen, G., & Centers for Disease Control and Prevention (CDC). (2014). Vital signs: Restraint use and motor vehicle occupant death rates among children aged 0–12 years — United States, 2002-2011. *Morbidity & Mortality Weekly Report, 63*(5), 113–118

Saucedo, M., Bouvier-Colle, M. H., Blondel, B., Bonnet, M. P., Deneux-Tharaux, C., & ENCMM Study Group. (2020). Delivery hospital characteristics and postpartum maternal mortality: A national case–control study in France. *Anesthesia & Analgesia, 130*(1), 52–62.

Saucedo, M., Esteves-Pereira, A. P., Pencolé, L., Rigouzzo, A., Proust, A., Bouvier-Colle, M.-H., & Deneux-Tharaux, C. (2021). Understanding maternal mortality in women with obesity and the role of care they receive: A national case-control study. *International Journal of Obesity, 45*(1), 258–265. https://doi.org/10.1038/s41366-020-00691-4

Sauerteig, L. D. H. (2012). Loss of innocence: Albert Moll, Sigmund Freud and the invention of childhood sexuality around 1900. *Medical History, 56*(2), 156–183. https://doi.org/10.1017/mdh.2011.31

Saulny, S. (2011, January 30). Black? White? Asian? More young Americans choose all of the above. *The New York Times.* https://www.nytimes.com/2011/01/30/us/30mixed.html

Savahl, S., Montserrat, C., Casas, F., Adams, S., Tiliouine, H., Benninger, E., & Jackson, K. (2019). Children's experiences of bullying victimization and the influence on their subjective well-being: A multinational comparison. *Child Development, 90*(2), 414–431.

Savin-Williams, R. C. (2016). Sexual orientation: Categories or continuum? Commentary on Bailey et al. (2016). *Psychological Science in the Public Interest, 17*(2), 37–44. https://doi.org/10.1177/1529100616637618

Savin-Williams, R. C., & Cohen, K. M. (2015). Developmental trajectories and milestones of lesbian, gay, and bisexual young people. *International Review of Psychiatry, 27*(5), 357–366. https://doi.org/10.3109/09540261.2015.1093465

Saxe, G. B. (1988). Candy selling and math learning. *Educational Researcher, 17*(6), 14–21.

Saxe, G. B., & de Kirby, K. (2014). Cultural context of cognitive development. *WIREs Cognitive Science, 5*(4), 447–461. https://doi.org/10.1002/wcs.1300

Saxe-Custack, A., Todem, D., Anthony, J. C., Kerver, J. M., LaChance, J., & Hanna-Attisha, M. (2022). Effect of a pediatric fruit and vegetable prescription program on child dietary patterns, food security, and weight status: A study protocol. *BMC Public Health, 22*(1), 150. https://doi.org/10.1186/s12889-022-12544-y

Sbihi, H., Boutin, R. CT., Cutler, C., Suen, M., Finlay, B. B., & Turvey, S. E. (2019). Thinking bigger: How early-life environmental exposures shape the gut microbiome and influence the development of asthma and allergic disease. *Allergy, 74*(11), 2103–2115. https://doi.org/10.1111/all.13812

Schacter, H. L. (2021). Effects of peer victimization on child and adolescent physical health. *Pediatrics, 147*(1), e2020003434. https://doi.org/10.1542/peds.2020-003434

Schaeffer, K. (2021). *Among many U.S. children, reading for fun has become less common, federal data shows.* Pew Research Center. https://www.pewresearch.org/fact-tank/2021/11/12/among-many-u-s-children-reading-for-fun-has-become-less-common-federal-data-shows/

Schanzenbach, D. W., Nunn, R., Bauer, L., Mumford, M., & Breitwieser, A. (2016). Seven facts on noncognitive skills from education to the labor market. *Washington: The Hamilton Project.*

Scharf, M., & Goldner, L. (2018). "If you really love me, you will do/be. . .": Parental psychological control and its implications for children's adjustment. *Developmental Review, 49*, 16–30. https://doi.org/10.1016/j.dr.2018.07.002

Scheier, L. M., & Griffin, K. W. (2021). Youth marijuana use: A review of causes and consequences. *Current Opinion in Psychology, 38*, 11–18. https://doi.org/10.1016/j.copsyc.2020.06.007

Schenck-Fontaine, A., Lansford, J. E., Skinner, A. T., Deater-Deckard, K., Di Giunta, L., Dodge, K. A., Oburu, P., Pastorelli, C., Sorbring, E., Steinberg, L., Malone, P. S., Tapanya, S., Uribe Tirado, L. M., Alampay, L. P., Al-Hassan, S. M., Bacchini, D., Bornstein, M. H., & Chang, L. (2020). Associations between perceived material deprivation, parents' discipline practices, and children's behavior problems: An international perspective. *Child Development, 91*(1), 307–326. https://doi.org/10.1111/cdev.13151

Schenkelberg, M. A., McIver, K. L., Brown, W. H., & Pate, R. R. (2020). Preschool environmental influences on physical activity in children with disabilities. *Medicine & Science in Sports & Exercise, 52*(12), 2682–2689.

Scherer, A. K. (2015). *Mortuary landscapes of the classic Maya: Rituals of body and soul.* University of Texas Press.

Scherrer, V., & Preckel, F. (2019). Development of motivational variables and self-esteem during the school career: A meta-analysis of longitudinal studies. *Review of Educational Research, 89*(2), 211–258. https://doi.org/10.3102/0034654318819127

Schlegel, A. (1995). A cross-cultural approach to adolescence. *Ethos, 23*(1), 15–32.

Schlegel, A. (2015). The cultural context of adolescent self-regulation. In G. Oettingen & P. M. Gollwitzer (Eds.), *Self-regulation in adolescence* (pp. 288–307). Cambridge University Press.

Schlegel, A., & Barry, H. (1991). *Adolescence: An anthropological inquiry.* Free Press.

Schlesier, J., Roden, I., & Moschner, B. (2019). Emotion regulation in primary school children: A systematic review. *Children and Youth Services Review, 100*, 239–257. https://doi.org/10.1016/j.childyouth.2019.02.044

Schmader, T., & Forbes, C. (2017). Stereotypes and performance. In J. R. Smith & S. A. Haslam (Eds.), *Social psychology: Revisiting the classic studies* (p. 245). Sage.

Schmidt, M., Jäger, K., Egger, F., Roebers, C. M., & Conzelmann, A. (2015). Cognitively engaging chronic physical activity, but not aerobic exercise, affects executive functions in primary school children: A group-randomized controlled trial. *Journal of Sport and Exercise Psychology, 37*(6), 575–591. https://doi.org/10.1123/jsep.2015-0069

Schmidt, M., Mavilidi, M. F., Singh, A., & Englert, C. (2020). Combining physical and cognitive training to improve kindergarten children's executive functions: A cluster randomized controlled trial. *Contemporary Educational Psychology, 63*, 101908.

Schmitt, M. L., Hagstrom, C., Nowara, A., Gruer, C., Adenu-Mensah, N. E., Keeley, K., & Sommer, M. (2021). The intersection of menstruation, school and family: Experiences of girls growing up in urban areas in the U.S.A. *International Journal of Adolescence and Youth, 26*(1), 94–109. https://doi.org/10.1080/02673843.2020.1867207

Schneider, M. (2020, June 25). Census shows white decline, nonwhite majority among youngest. *AP News.* https://apnews.com/article/a3600edf620ccf2759080d00f154c069

Schneider, W., & Ornstein, P. A. (2019). Determinants of memory development in childhood and adolescence. *International Journal of Psychology, 54*(3), 307–315. https://doi.org/10.1002/ijop.12503

Schnitzer, P. G., Dowd, M. D., Kruse, R. L., & Morrongiello, B. A. (2015). Supervision and risk of unintentional injury in young children. *Injury Prevention: Journal of the International Society for Child and Adolescent Injury Prevention, 21*, e63–e70. https://doi.org/10.1136/injuryprev-2013-041128

Schochet, P. Z. (2018). *National job corps study: 20-year follow-up study using tax data.* Princeton, NJ: Mathematica Policy Research.

Schoeppe, S., Duncan, M. J., Badland, H. M., Alley, S., Williams, S., Rebar, A. L., & Vandelanotte, C. (2015). Socio-demographic factors and neighbourhood social cohesion influence adults' willingness to grant children greater independent mobility: A cross-sectional study. *BMC Public Health, 15*(1), 1–8.

Schofield, T. J., Conger, R. D., & Conger, K. J. (2017). Disrupting intergenerational continuity in harsh parenting: Self-control and a supportive partner. *Development and Psychopathology, 29*(4), 1279–1287.

Schonert-Reichl, K. A., Oberle, E., Lawlor, M. S., Abbott, D., Thomson, K., Oberlander, T. F., & Diamond, A. (2015). Enhancing cognitive and social–emotional development through a simple-to-administer mindfulness-based school program for elementary school children: A randomized controlled trial. *Developmental Psychology, 51*(1), 52.

Schoppe-Sullivan, S. J., & Fagan, J. (2020). The evolution of fathering research in the 21st century: Persistent challenges, new directions. *Journal of Marriage and Family, 82*(1), 175–197. https://doi.org/10.1111/jomf.12645

Schrantee, A., Tamminga, H. G., Bouziane, C., Bottelier, M. A., Bron, E. E., Mutsaerts, H. J. M., Zwinderman, A. H., Groote, I. R., Rombouts, S. A. R. B., Lindauer, R. J. L., Klein, S., Niessen, W. J., Opmeer, B. C., Boer, F., Lucassen, P. J. Andersen, S. L., Guerts, H. M., & Reneman, L. (2016). Age-dependent effects of methylphenidate on the human dopaminergic system in young vs adult patients with attention-deficit/hyperactivity disorder: A randomized clinical trial. *JAMA Psychiatry, 73*(9), 955–962.

Schreuders, E., Braams, B. R., Blankenstein, N. E., Peper, J. S., Güroğlu, B., & Crone, E. A. (2018). Contributions of reward sensitivity to ventral striatum activity across adolescence and early adulthood. *Child Development, 89*(3), 797–810. https://doi.org/10.1111/cdev.13056

Schuengel, C., Verhage, M. L., & Duschinsky, R. (2021). Prospecting the attachment research field: A move to the level of engagement. *Attachment & Human Development,* 1–21. https://doi.org/10.1080/14616734.2021.1918449

Schulenberg, J., Patrick, M. E., Maslowsky, J., & Maggs, J. L. (2014). The epidemiology and etiology of adolescent substance use in developmental perspective. In M. Lewis & K. D. Rudolph (Eds.), *Handbook of developmental psychopathology* (pp. 601–620). Springer. https://doi.org/10.1007/978-1-4614-9608-3_30

Schulz, E., Wu, C. M., Ruggeri, A., & Meder, B. (2019). Searching for rewards like a child means less generalization and more directed exploration. *Psychological Science, 30*(11), 1561–1572. https://doi.org/10.1177/0956797619863663

Schulz, J., Bahrami-Rad, D., Beauchamp, J., & Henrich, J. (2018). *The origins of WEIRD psychology* (SSRN Scholarly Paper ID 3201031). Social Science Research Network. https://doi.org/10.2139/ssrn.3201031

Schunk, D. H., & DiBenedetto, M. K. (2016). Self-efficacy theory in education. *Handbook of Motivation at School, 2,* 34–54.

Schuster, R. C., Szpak, M., Klein, E., Sklar, K., & Dickin, K. L. (2019). "I try, I do": Child feeding practices of motivated, low-income parents reflect trade-offs between psychosocial- and nutrition-oriented goals. *Appetite, 136,* 114–123. https://doi.org/10.1016/j.appet.2019.01.005

Schwanitz, K., & Mulder, C. H. (2015). Living arrangements of young adults in Europe. *Comparative Population Studies, 40*(4). http://www.comparativepopulationstudies.de/index.php/CPoS/article/view/158

Schwartz, A. E., Hopkins, B. G., & Stiefel, L. (2021). The effects of special education on the academic performance of students with learning disabilities. *Journal of Policy Analysis and Management, 40*(2), 480–520. https://doi.org/10.1002/pam.22282

Schwartz, C. R., Wang, Y., & Mare, R. D. (2021). Opportunity and change in occupational assortative mating. *Social Science Research, 99,* 102600. https://doi.org/10.1016/j.ssresearch.2021.102600

Schwartz, S. E. O., Kanchewa, S. S., Rhodes, J. E., Cutler, E., & Cunningham, J. L. (2016). "I didn't know you could just ask": Empowering underrepresented college-bound students to recruit academic and career mentors. *Children and Youth Services Review, 64,* 51–59. https://doi.org/10.1016/j.childyouth.2016.03.001

Schwartz, S. J., Zamboanga, B. L., Meca, A., & Ritchie, R. A. (2012). Identity around the world: An overview. *New Directions for Child and Adolescent Development, 2012*(138), 1–18.

Schwartz-Mette, R. A., Shankman, J., Dueweke, A. R., Borowski, S., & Rose, A. J. (2020). Relations of friendship experiences with depressive symptoms and loneliness in childhood and adolescence: A meta-analytic review. *Psychological Bulletin, 146*(8), 664–700. https://doi.org/10.1037/bul0000239

Scott, E. S., Bonnie, R. J., & Steinberg, L. (2016). Young adulthood as a transitional legal category: Science, social change, and justice policy. *Fordham Law Review, 85,* 641. https://heinonline.org/HOL/Page?handle=hein.journals/flr85&id=657&div=&collection=

Scott, K. A., Britton, L., & McLemore, M. R. (2019). The ethics of perinatal care for black women: Dismantling the structural racism in "mother blame" narratives. *The Journal of Perinatal & Neonatal Nursing, 33*(2), 108–115. https://doi.org/10.1097/JPN.0000000000000394

Scott, K. E., Shutts, K., & Devine, P. G. (2020). Parents' expectations for and reactions to children's racial biases. *Child Development, 91*(3), 769–783.

Scott, S. R., & Manczak, E. M. (2021). Peripheral immune correlates of childhood and adolescent peer relationships: A systematic review. *Developmental Psychobiology, 63*(5), 985–996. https://doi.org/10.1002/dev.22119

Scrimgeour, M. B., Davis, E. L., & Buss, K. A. (2016). You get what you get and you don't throw a fit! Emotion socialization and child physiology jointly predict early prosocial development. *Developmental Psychology, 52*(1), 102.

Scudellari, M. (2017). News feature: Cleaning up the hygiene hypothesis. *Proceedings of the National Academy of Sciences, 114*(7), 1433–1436. https://doi.org/10.1073/pnas.1700688114

Sear, R. (2021). The male breadwinner nuclear family is not the "traditional" human family, and promotion of this myth may have adverse health consequences. *Philosophical Transactions of the Royal Society B: Biological Sciences, 376*(1827), 20200020. https://doi.org/10.1098/rstb.2020.0020

Seaton, E. K., & Carter, R. (2019). Perceptions of pubertal timing and discrimination among African American and Caribbean Black girls. *Child Development, 90*(2), 480–488.

Sebastián-Enesco, C., Hernández-Lloreda, M. V., & Colmenares, F. (2013). Two and a half-year-old children are prosocial even when their partners are not. *Journal of Experimental Child Psychology, 116*(2), 186–198. https://doi.org/10.1016/j.jecp.2013.05.007

Section on Endocrinology. (2014). Physical development: What's normal? What's not? (Ages & Stages). *Healthy Children.* https://www.healthychildren.org/English/ages-stages/gradeschool/puberty/Pages/Physical-Development-Whats-Normal-Whats-Not.aspx

Segal, N. L., Craig, J. M., & Umstad, M. P. (2020). Challenge to the assumed rarity of heteropaternal superfecundation: Findings from a case report. *Australian Journal of Forensic Sciences, 52*(5), 547–552. https://doi.org/10.1080/00450618.2019.1616821

Sege, R. D., Siegel, B. S., Council on Child Abuse and Neglect, & Committee on Psychosocial Aspects of Child and Family Health. (2018). Effective discipline to raise healthy children | American Academy of Pediatrics. *Pediatrics, 142*(6). https://doi.org/10.1542/peds.2018-3112

Segura Moreno, C. C., & Diaz Heredia, L. P. (2021). Adaptation to asthma in children: A mat-ter of coping and stress control. *Comprehensive Child and Adolescent Nursing,* 1–12. https://doi.org/10.1080/24694193.2021.1945707

Seijo, D., Fariña, F., Corras, T., Novo, M., & Arce, R. (2016). Estimating the epidemiology and quantifying the damages of parental separation in children and adolescents. *Frontiers in Psychology, 7,* 1611.

Seixas, P. (2018). History in schools. In B. Beverage & N. Wouters (Eds.), *The Palgrave handbook of state-sponsored history after 1945* (pp. 273–288). Palgrave Macmillan UK. https://doi.org/10.1057/978-1-349-95306-6_14

Sejkora, E. K. D., Igler, E. C., & Davies, W. H. (2021). Parent-reported toilet training practices and the role of pediatric primary care providers. *Journal of the American Association of Nurse Practitioners, 33*(8), 620–629. https://doi.org/10.1097/JXX.0000000000000410

Sekhar, D. L., Murray-Kolb, L. E., Kunselman, A. R., Weisman, C. S., & Paul, I. M. (2017). Association between menarche and iron deficiency in non-anemic young women. *PLOS ONE, 12*(5), e0177183.

Selden, N. R. (2019). Right brain? Hemispheric dominance and the United States presidency. *Journal of Neurosurgery, 131*(1), 320–323. https://doi.org/10.3171/2019.3.JNS19510

Selemon, L. D. (2013). A role for synaptic plasticity in the adolescent development of executive function. *Translational Psychiatry, 3*(3), e238–e238.

Selman, R. L. (1980). *The growth of interpersonal understanding: Developmental and clinical analyses.* Academy Press.

Semega, J. U. C., Kollar, M., Shrider, E. A., & Creamer, J. (2020). *Income and poverty in the United States: 2019.* https://www.census.gov/library/publications/2020/demo/p60-270.html

Semenov, A. D., Kennedy, D., & Zelazo, P. D. (2020). Mindfulness and executive function: Implications for learning and early childhood education. In M. S. C. Thomas, D. Mareschal, & I. Dumontheil (Eds.), *Educational neuroscience: Development across the life span* (pp. 298–331). Routledge.

Sender, R., Fuchs, S., & Milo, R. (2016). Revised estimates for the number of human and bacteria cells in the body. *PLOS Biology, 14*(8), e1002533. https://doi.org/10.1371/journal.pbio.1002533

Sesame Workshop. (2016). K is for kind: A national survey on kindness and kids. *Sesame Street.* http://kindness.sesamestreet.org

Setoh, P., Lee, K. J. J., Zhang, L., Qian, M. K., Quinn, P. C., Heyman, G. D., & Lee, K. (2019). Racial categorization predicts implicit racial bias in preschool children. *Child Development, 90*(1), 162–179. https://doi.org/10.1111/cdev.12851

Setoh, P., Wu, D., Baillargeon, R., & Gelman, R. (2013). Young infants have biological expectations about animals. *Proceedings of the National Academy of Sciences, 110*(40), 15937–15942.

Settersten, R. A., Bernardi, L., Härkönen, J., Antonucci, T. C., Dykstra, P. A., Heckhausen, J., Kuh, D., Mayer, K. U., Moen, P., Mortimer, J. T., Mulder, C. H., Smeeding, T. M., van der Lippe, T., Hagestad, G. O., Kohli, M., Levy, R., Schoon, I., & Thomson, E. (2020). Understanding the effects of Covid-19 through a life course lens. *Current Perspectives on Aging and the Life Cycle, 45,* 100360. https://doi.org/10.1016/j.alcr.2020.100360

Settersten, R. A., Ottusch, T. M., & Schneider, B. (2015). Becoming adult: Meanings of markers to adulthood. In R. Scott & S. Koss (Eds.), *Emerging trends in the social and behavioral sciences: An interdisciplinary, searchable, and linkable resource* (pp. 1–16). Wiley.

Sha, Z., Schijven, D., Carrion-Castillo, A., Joliot, M., Mazoyer, B., Fisher, S. E., Crivello, F., & Francks, C. (2021). The genetic architecture of structural left–right asymmetry of the human brain. *Nature Human Behaviour, 5*(9), 1226–1239. https://doi.org/10.1038/s41562-021-01069-w

Shakiba, N., Ellis, B. J., Bush, N. R., & Boyce, W. T. (2020). Biological sensitivity to context: A test of the hypothesized U-shaped relation between early adversity and stress responsivity. *Development and Psychopathology, 32*(2), 641–660.

Shalby, C. (2021, March 31). These community workers are key to the state's vaccine strategy. *Los Angeles Times.* https://www.latimes.com/california/story/2021-03-31/vaccine-outreach-communities-los-angeles

Shanahan, L., Zucker, N., Copeland, W. E., Bondy, C., Egger, H. L., & Costello, E. J. (2015). Childhood somatic complaints predict generalized anxiety and depressive disorders during adulthood in a community sample. *Psychological Medicine, 45*(8), 1721–1730. https://doi.org/10.1017/S0033291714002840

Shanahan, M. J., Mortimer, J. T., & Johnson, M. K. (2016). Introduction: Life course studies—trends, challenges, and future directions. In M. J. Shanahan, J. T. Mortimer, & M. K. Johnson (Eds.), *Handbook of the life course* (pp. 1–23). Springer.

Shannon, C., & Klausner, J. (2018). The growing epidemic of sexually transmitted infections in adolescents: A neglected population. *Current Opinion in Pediatrics, 30*(1), 137–143. https://doi.org/10.1097/MOP.0000000000000578

Shapiro, D., Dundar, A., Huie, F., Wakhungu, P. K., Bhimdiwala, A., Nathan, A., & Hwang, Y. (2018). *Transfer and mobility: A national view of student movement in postsecondary institutions — Fall 2011 cohort* (Signature Report No. 15). National Student Clearinghouse Research Center.

Shapiro-Mendoza, C. K., Camperlengo, L., Ludvigsen, R., Cottengim, C., Anderson, R. N., Andrew, T., Covington, T., Hauck, F. R., Kemp, J., & MacDorman, M. (2014). Classification system for the Sudden Unexpected Infant Death Case Registry and its application. *Pediatrics, 134*(1), e210–e219.

Sharma, S., van Teijlingen, E., Hundley, V., Angell, C., & Simkhada, P. (2016). Dirty and 40 days in the wilderness: Eliciting childbirth and postnatal cultural practices and beliefs in Nepal. *BMC Pregnancy and Childbirth, 16,* 147. https://doi.org/10.1186/s12884-016-0938-4

Sharon, T. (2016). Constructing adulthood markers of adulthood and well-being among emerging adults. *Emerging Adulthood, 4*(3), 161–167. https://doi.org/10.1177/2167696815579826

Sharp, K., Tillery, R., Long, A., Wang, F., Pan, H., & Phipps, S. (2022). Trajectories of resilience and post-traumatic stress in childhood cancer: Consistency of child and parent outcomes. *Health Psychology, 41*(4), 256–267. https://doi.org/10.1037/hea0001132

Shavelson, R. J., Hubner, J. J., & Stanton, G. C. (1976). Self-concept: Validation of construct interpretations. *Review of Educational Research, 46*(3), 407–441.

Shaw, K. A., Maenner, M. J., Bakian, A. V., Bilder, D. A., Durkin, M. S., Furnier, S. M., Hughes, M. M., Patrick, M., Pierce, K., Salinas, A., Shenouda, J.,

Vehorn, A., Warren, Z., Zahorodny, W., Constantino, J. N., DiRienzo, M., Esler, A., Fitzgerald, R. T., Grzybowski, A., . . . Cogswell, M. E. (2021). Early identification of autism spectrum disorder among children aged 4 years—autism and developmental disabilities monitoring network, 11 sites, United States, 2018. *MMWR Surveillance Summaries 2021, 70* (No. SS-10), 1–14.

Shayer, M., & Ginsburg, D. (2009). Thirty years on–a large anti-Flynn effect/(II): 13- and 14-year-olds. Piagetian tests of formal operations norms 1976–2006/7. *British Journal of Educational Psychology, 79*(3), 409–418.

Sheehan, P., Sweeny, K., Rasmussen, B., Wils, A., Friedman, H. S., Mahon, J., Patton, G. C., Sawyer, S. M., Howard, E., Symons, J., Stenberg, K., Chalasani, S., Maharaj, N., Reavley, N., Shi, H., Fridman, M., Welsh, A., Nsofor, E., & Laski, L. (2017). Building the foundations for sustainable development: A case for global investment in the capabilities of adolescents. *The Lancet, 390*(10104), 1792–1806.

Shelleby, E. C., Shaw, D. S., Dishion, T. J., Wilson, M. N., & Gardner, F. (2018). Effects of the family check-up on reducing growth in conduct problems from toddlerhood through school age: An analysis of moderated mediation. *Journal of Consulting and Clinical Psychology, 86*(10), 856.

Shelley, W. W., & Peterson, D. (2019). "Sticks and stones may break my bones, but bullying will get me bangin'": Bullying involvement and adolescent gang joining. *Youth Violence and Juvenile Justice, 17*(4), 385–412.

Shepherd, C. C. J., Li, J., Cooper, M. N., Hopkins, K. D., & Farrant, B. M. (2017). The impact of racial discrimination on the health of Australian Indigenous children aged 5–10 years: Analysis of national longitudinal data. *International Journal for Equity in Health, 16,* 116.

Sherman, L. E., Greenfield, P. M., Hernandez, L. M., & Dapretto, M. (2018). Peer influence via Instagram: Effects on brain and behavior in adolescence and young adulthood. *Child Development, 89*(1), 37–47.

Shermer, M. (1990). Darwin, Freud, and the myth of the hero in science. *Science Communication, 11*(3), 280–301. https://doi.org/10.1177/107554709001100305

Shi, D. S., Whitaker, M., Marks, K. J., Anglin, O., Milucky, J., Patel, K., Pham, H., Chai, S. J., Kawasaki, B., Meek, J., Anderson, E. J., Weigel, A., Henderson, J., Lynfield, R., Ropp, S. L., Muse, A., Bushey, S., Billing, L. M., Sutton, M., . . . Havers, F. P. (2022). Hospitalizations of children aged 5–11 years with laboratory-confirmed COVID-19 — COVID-NET, 14 states, March 2020–February 2022. *Morbidity and Mortality Weekly Report, 71*(16), 574–581. https://doi.org/10.15585/mmwr.mm7116e1

Shih, S.-F., Wagner, A. L., Masters, N. B., Prosser, L. A., Lu, Y., & Zikmund-Fisher, B. J. (2021). Vaccine hesitancy and rejection of a vaccine for the novel coronavirus in the United States. *Frontiers in Immunology, 12,* 558270. https://doi.org/10.3389/fimmu.2021.558270

Shimon-Raz, O., Salomon, R., Bloch, M., Aisenberg Romano, G., Yeshurun, Y., Ulmer Yaniv, A., Zagoory-Sharon, O., & Feldman, R. (2021). Mother brain is wired for social moments. *ELife, 10,* e59436. https://doi.org/10.7554/eLife.59436

Shiner, R. L. (2017). Personality trait structure, processes, and development in childhood and adolescence. *European Journal of Personality, 31,* 567–568.

Shiner, R. L. (2021). Personality development in middle childhood. In O. P. John & R. W. Robins (Eds.), *Handbook of personality: Theory and research* (4th ed., pp. 284–302). Guilford.

Shirtcliff, E. A., Skinner, M. L., Obasi, E. M., & Haggerty, K. P. (2017). Positive parenting predicts cortisol functioning six years later in young adults. *Developmental Science, 20*(6), e12461. https://doi.org/10.1111/desc.12461

Shneidman, L. A., & Goldin-Meadow, S. (2012). Language input and acquisition in a Mayan village: How important is directed speech? *Developmental Science, 15*(5), 659–673. https://doi.org/10.1111/j.1467-7687.2012.01168.x

Shneidman, L., Gaskins, S., & Woodward, A. (2016a). Child-directed teaching and social learning at 18 months of age: Evidence from Yucatec Mayan and US infants. *Developmental Science, 19*(3), 372–381. https://doi.org/10.1111/desc.12318

Shneidman, L., Gweon, H., Schulz, L. E., & Woodward, A. L. (2016b). Learning from others and spontaneous exploration: A cross-cultural investigation. *Child Development, 87*(3), 723–735. https://doi.org/10.1111/cdev.12502

Shoaibi, A., Neelon, B., Østbye, T., & Benjamin-Neelon, S. E. (2019). Longitudinal associations of gross motor development, motor milestone achievement and weight-for-length z score in a racially diverse cohort of US infants. *BMJ Open, 9*(1), e024440. https://doi.org/10.1136/bmjopen-2018-024440

Shoda, Y., Mischel, W., & Peake, P. K. (1990). Predicting adolescent cognitive and self-regulatory competencies from preschool delay of gratification: Identifying diagnostic conditions. *Developmental Psychology, 26*(6), 978.

Shonkoff, J. P., Slopen, N., & Williams, D. R. (2021). Early childhood adversity, toxic stress, and the impacts of racism on the foundations of health. *Annual Review of Public Health, 42*(1), 115–134. https://doi.org/10.1146/annurev-publhealth-090419-101940

Shuffrey, L. C., Firestein, M. R., Kyle, M. H., Fields, A., Alcántara, C., Amso, D., Austin, J., Bain, J. M., Barbosa, J., Bence, M., Bianco, C., Fernández, C. R., Goldman, S., Gyamfi-Bannerman, C., Hott, V., Hu, Y., Hussain, M., Factor-Litvak, P., Lucchini, M., . . . Dumitriu, D. (2022). Association of birth during the COVID-19 pandemic with neurodevelopmental status at 6 months in infants with and without in utero exposure to maternal SARS-CoV-2 infection. *JAMA Pediatrics,* e215563. https://doi.org/10.1001/jamapediatrics.2021.5563

Shulman, E. P., Smith, A. R., Silva, K., Icenogle, G., Duell, N., Chein, J., & Steinberg, L. (2016). The dual systems model: Review, reappraisal, and reaffirmation. *Developmental Cognitive Neuroscience, 17,* 103–117. https://doi.org/10.1016/j.dcn.2015.12.010

Shulman, S., & Connolly, J. (2015). The challenge of romantic relationships in emerging adulthood. In J. J. Arnett (Ed.), *The Oxford handbook of emerging adulthood* (pp. 230–244). Oxford University Press.

Shulman, S., & Scharf, M. (2018). Adolescent psychopathology in times of change: The need for integrating a developmental psychopathology perspective. *Journal of Adolescence, 65,* 95–100.

Shulman, S., Scharf, M., Ziv, I., Norona, J., & Welsh, D. P. (2020). Adolescents' sexual encounters with either romantic or casual partners and the quality of their romantic relationships four years later. *The Journal of Sex Research, 57*(2), 155–165. https://doi.org/10.1080/00224499.2018.1560387

Shulman, S., Seiffge-Krenke, I., Scharf, M., Boiangiu, S. B., & Tregubenko, V. (2016). The diversity of romantic pathways during emerging adulthood and their developmental antecedents. *International Journal of Behavioral Development, 42*(2), 167–174. https://doi.org/10.1177/0165025416673474

Shultz, J., Powers, M., Jewell, J., Taylor, G., & Djuhari, L. (2020). *Prevention of overweight and obesity in children and adolescents: UNICEF advocacy strategy and guidance.* UNICEF.

Shultz, S., Klin, A., & Jones, W. (2018). Neonatal transitions in social behavior and their implications for autism. *Trends in Cognitive Sciences, 22*(5), 452–469. https://doi.org/10.1016/j.tics.2018.02.012

Shumer, D. E., & Araya, A. (2019). Endocrine care of transgender children and adolescents. In L. Poretsky & W. C. Hembree (Eds.), *Transgender medicine: A multidisciplinary approach* (pp. 165–181). Springer International Publishing. https://doi.org/10.1007/978-3-030-05683-4_9

Shutts, K. (2015). Young children's preferences: Gender, race, and social status. *Child Development Perspectives, 9*(4), 262–266. https://doi.org/10.1111/cdep.12154

Shutts, K., Kenward, B., Falk, H., Ivegran, A., & Fawcett, C. (2017). Early preschool environments and gender: Effects of gender pedagogy in Sweden. *Journal of Experimental Child Psychology, 162*, 1–17.

Sibley, M. H., Arnold, L. E., Swanson, J. M., Hechtman, L. T., Kennedy, T. M., Owens, E., Molina, B. S. G., Jensen, P. S., Hinshaw, S. P., Roy, A., Chronis-Tuscano, A., Newcorn, J. H., Rohde, L. A., & MTA Cooperative Group. (2022). Variable patterns of remission from ADHD in the multimodal treatment study of ADHD. *American Journal of Psychiatry, 179*(2), 142–151.

Siegel, R. L., Miller, K. D., Fuchs, H. E., & Jemal, A. (2022). Cancer statistics, 2022. *CA: A Cancer Journal for Clinicians.* https://doi.org/10.3322/caac.21708

Siegel, R. S., & Dickstein, D. P. (2012). Anxiety in adolescents: Update on its diagnosis and treatment for primary care providers. *Adolescent Health, Medicine and Therapeutics, 3*, 1.

Siegler, R. S. (1992). The other Alfred Binet. *Developmental Psychology, 28*(2), 179.

Siegler, R. S. (1999). Strategic development. *Trends in Cognitive Sciences, 3*(11), 430–435. https://doi.org/10.1016/S1364-6613(99)01372-8

Siegler, R. S. (2006). Microgenetic analyses of learning. In D. Kuhn, R. S. Siegler, W. Damon, & R. M. Lerner (Eds.), *Handbook of child psychology: Cognition, perception, and language* (pp. 464–510). John Wiley & Sons.

Siegler, R. S. (2016). Continuity and change in the field of cognitive development and in the perspectives of one cognitive developmentalist. *Child Development Perspectives, 10*(2), 128–133. https://doi.org/10.1111/cdep.12173

Siegler, R. S., & Braithwaite, D. W. (2017). Numerical development. *Annual Review of Psychology, 68*, 187–213.

Siegler, R. S., & Ellis, S. (1996). Piaget on childhood. *Psychological Science, 7*(4), 211–215. https://doi.org/10.1111/j.1467-9280.1996.tb00361.x

Siegler, R. S., Im, S.-H., & Braithwaite, D. (2020). Understanding development requires assessing the relevant environment: Examples from mathematics learning. *New Directions for Child and Adolescent Development, 2020*(173), 83–100. https://doi.org/10.1002/cad.20372

Signore, F., Gulìa, C., Votino, R., De Leo, V., Zaami, S., Putignani, L., Gigli, S., Santini, E., Bertacca, L., Porrello, A., & Piergentili, R. (2020). The role of number of copies, structure, behavior and copy number variations (CNV) of the Y chromosome in male infertility. *Genes, 11*(1), 40. https://doi.org/10.3390/genes11010040

Silbereisen, R. K., & Schmitt-Rodermund, E. (2020). German immigrants in Germany: Adaption of adolescents' timetables for autonomy. In P. Noack, M. Hofer, & J. Youniss (Eds.), *Psychological responses to social change: Human development in changing environments* (pp. 105–128). De Gruyter. https://www.degruyter.com/document/doi/10.1515/9783110877373-009/html

Silver, E., Korja, R., Mainela-Arnold, E., Pulli, E. P., Saukko, E., Nolvi, S., Kataja, E.-L., Karlsson, L., Karlsson, H., & Tuulari, J. J. (2021). A systematic review of MRI studies of language development from birth to 2 years of age. *Developmental Neurobiology, 81*(1), 63–75. https://doi.org/10.1002/dneu.22792

Silvers, J. A., & Guassi Moreira, J. F. (2019). Capacity and tendency: A neuroscientific framework for the study of emotion regulation. *Neuroscience Letters, 693*, 35–39. https://doi.org/10.1016/j.neulet.2017.09.017

Simeonsson, R. J., & Lee, A. (2017). The international classification of functioning, disability and health-children and youth. In S. Castro & O. Palikara (eds.), *An Emerging Approach for Education and Care: Implementing a Worldwide Classification of Functioning and Disability.* Routledge.

Simion, F., & Di Giorgio, E. (2015). Face perception and processing in early infancy: Inborn predispositions and developmental changes. *Frontiers in Psychology, 6*, 969.

Simms, M. D., & Jin, X. M. (2015). Autism, language disorder, and social (pragmatic) communication disorder: DSM-V and differential diagnoses. *Pediatrics in Review, 36*(8), 355–362.

Simon, E. B., Vallat, R., Barnes, C. M., & Walker, M. P. (2020). Sleep loss and the socio-emotional brain. *Trends in Cognitive Sciences, 24*(6), 435–450.

Simon, K. (2013, February 8). A life defined not by disability, but love (Story Corps). *Morning Edition.* National Public Radio.

Simon, L., & Daneback, K. (2013). Adolescents' use of the internet for sex education: A thematic and critical review of the literature. *International Journal of Sexual Health, 25*(4), 305–319. https://doi.org/10.1080/19317611.2013.823899

Simon, T. R., Shattuck, A., Kacha-Ochana, A., David-Ferdon, C. F., Hamby, S., Henly, M., Merrick, M. T., Turner, H. A., & Finkelhor, D. (2018). Injuries from physical abuse: National survey of children's exposure to violence I–III. *American Journal of Preventive Medicine, 54*(1), 129–132. https://doi.org/10.1016/j.amepre.2017.08.031

Simoni, Z. (2021). Social class, teachers, and medicalisation lag: A qualitative investigation of teachers' discussions of ADHD with parents and the effect of neighbourhood-level social class. *Health Sociology Review, 30*(2), 188–203. https://doi.org/10.1080/14461242.2020.1820364

Simons, C., Metzger, S. R., & Sonnenschein, S. (2020). Children's metacognitive knowledge of five key learning processes. *Translational Issues in Psychological Science, 6*(1), 32.

Singer, D. G., Singer, J. L., D'Agostino, H., & DeLong, R. (2009). Children's pastimes and play in sixteen nations: Is free-play declining? *American Journal of Play, 1*(3), 283–312.

Singh, L., Tan, A., & Quinn, P. C. (2021). Infants recognize words spoken through opaque masks but not through clear masks. *Developmental Science, 24*(6), e13117. https://doi.org/10.1111/desc.13117

Singhal, A., Cole, T. J., Fewtrell, M., & Lucas, A. (2004). Breastmilk feeding and lipoprotein profile in adolescents born preterm: Follow-up of a prospective randomised study. *The Lancet, 363*(9421), 1571–1578.

Sinno, S. M., Schuette, C. T., & Hellriegel, C. (2017). The impact of family and community on children's understanding of parental role negotiation. *Journal of Family Issues, 38*(4), 435–456. https://doi.org/10.1177/0192513X15573867

Sinnott, J. (1998). *The development of logic in adulthood: Postformal thought and its applications.* Springer Science & Business Media.

Sinnott, J. D. (2002). Postformal thought and adult development. In J. Demick & C. Andreoletti (Eds.), *Handbook of adult development* (pp. 221–238). Springer.

Sinnott, J. D. (2021). Psychology, politics, and complex thought: A time for postformal thought in politics. In J. D. Sinnott & J. S. Rabin (Eds.), *The psychology of political behavior in a time of change* (pp. 147–176). Springer International Publishing. https://doi.org/10.1007/978-3-030-38270-4_5

Sinnott, J., Hilton, S., Wood, M., & Douglas, D. (2020). Relating flow, mindfulness, cognitive flexibility, and postformal thought: Two studies. *Journal of Adult Development, 27*(1), 1–11. https://doi.org/10.1007/s10804-018-9320-2

Sinnott, J., Hilton, S., Wood, M., Spanos, E., & Topel, R. (2015). Does motivation affect emerging adults' intelligence and complex postformal problem solving? *Journal of Adult Development, 23*(2), 69–78. https://doi.org/10.1007/s10804-015-9222-5

Sironi, M. (2018). Economic conditions of young adults before and after the Great Recession. *Journal of Family and Economic Issues, 39*(1), 103–116. https://doi.org/10.1007/s10834-017-9554-3

Sisk, C. L., & Romeo, R. D. (2020). *Coming of age: The neurobiology and psychobiology of puberty and adolescence.* Oxford University Press.

Sivertsen, B., Harvey, A. G., Reichborn-Kjennerud, T., Torgersen, L., Ystrom, E., & Hysing, M. (2015). Later emotional and behavioral problems associated with sleep problems in toddlers: A longitudinal study. *JAMA Pediatrics, 169*(6), 575–582.

Sivertsen, B., Harvey, A. G., Reichborn-Kjennerud, T., Ystrom, E., & Hysing, M. (2021). Sleep problems and depressive symptoms in toddlers and 8-year-old children: A longitudinal study. *Journal of Sleep Research, 30*(1), e13150. https://doi.org/10.1111/jsr.13150

Skeen, S., Laurenzi, C. A., Gordon, S. L., du Toit, S., Tomlinson, M., Dua, T., Fleischmann, A., Kohl, K., Ross, D., Servili, C., Brand, A. S., Dowdall, N., Lund, C., van der Westhuizen, C., Carvajal-Aguirre, L., Eriksson de Carvalho, C., & Melendez-Torres, G. J. (2019). Adolescent mental health program components and behavior risk reduction: A meta-analysis. *Pediatrics, 144*(2), e20183488. https://doi.org/10.1542/peds.2018-3488

Skelton, A. E., & Franklin, A. (2020). Infants look longer at colours that adults like when colours are highly saturated. *Psychonomic Bulletin & Review, 27*(1), 78–85. https://doi.org/10.3758/s13423-019-01688-5

Skene, K., O'Farrelly, C. M., Byrne, E. M., Kirby, N., Stevens, E. C., & Ramchandani, P. G. (2022). Can guidance during play enhance children's learning and development in educational contexts? A systematic review and meta-analysis. *Child Development.* https://doi.org/10.1111/cdev.13730

Skinner, A. L., & Meltzoff, A. N. (2019). Childhood experiences and intergroup biases among children. *Social Issues and Policy Review, 13*(1), 211–240.

Skinner, B. F. (1938). *The behavior of organisms: An experimental analysis.* Appleton-Century.

Skinner, B. F. (1989). Teaching machines. *Science, 243*(4898), 1535–1535. https://doi.org/10.1126/science .243.4898.1535-b

Skinner, B. F. (2011). *About behaviorism*. Knopf Doubleday.

Skočajić, M. M., Radosavljević, J. G., Okičić, M. G., Janković, I. O., & Žeželj, I. L. (2020). Boys just don't! Gender stereotyping and sanctioning of counter-stereotypical behavior in preschoolers. *Sex Roles, 82*(3), 163–172.

Skopek, J., Triventi, M., & Buchholz, S. (2019). How do educational systems affect social inequality of educational opportunities? The role of tracking in comparative perspective. *Research Handbook on the Sociology of Education*.

Slaughter, V. (2021). Do newborns have the ability to imitate? *Trends in Cognitive Sciences, 25*(5), 377–387. https://doi.org/10.1016/j.tics.2021.02.006

Slaughter, V., Imuta, K., Peterson, C. C., & Henry, J. D. (2015). Meta-analysis of theory of mind and peer popularity in the preschool and early school years. *Child Development, 86*(4), 1159–1174. https://doi .org/10.1111/cdev.12372

Slaughter-Acey, J. C., Sneed, D., Parker, L., Keith, V. M., Lee, N. L., & Misra, D. P. (2019). Skin tone matters: Racial microaggressions and delayed prenatal care. *American Journal of Preventive Medicine, 57*(3), 321–329. https://doi.org/10.1016/j.amepre.2019.04.014

Slemaker, A., Espeleta, H. C., Heidari, Z., Bohora, S. B., & Silovsky, J. F. (2017). Childhood injury prevention: Predictors of home hazards in Latino families enrolled in SafeCare®+. *Journal of Pediatric Psychology, 42*(7), 738–747.

Slobodskaya, H. R., Kozlova, E. A., Han, S. Y., Gartstein, M. A., & Putnam, S. P. (2018). Cross cultural differences in temperament. In M. A. Gartstein & S. P. Putnam (Eds.), *Toddlers, parents, and culture: Findings from the Joint Effort Toddler Temperament Consortium* (pp. 29–37). Routledge. https://doi.org /10.4324/9781315203713-3

Slot, P. L., Mulder, H., Verhagen, J., & Leseman, P. P. (2017). Preschoolers' cognitive and emotional self-regulation in pretend play: Relations with executive functions and quality of play. *Infant and Child Development, 26*(6), e2038.

Smahel, D., Machackova, H., Mascheroni, G., Dedkova, L., Staksrud, E., Ólafsson, K., Livingstone, S., & Hasebrink, U. (2020). EU Kids Online 2020: Survey results from 19 countries. *EU Kids Online*. https://doi.org/10.21953/lse.47fdeqj01ofo

Smale-Jacobse, A. E., Meijer, A., Helms-Lorenz, M., & Maulana, R. (2019). Differentiated instruction in secondary education: A systematic review of research evidence. *Frontiers in Psychology, 10*. https://www.frontiersin .org/articles/10.3389/fpsyg.2019.02366

Smetana, J. G. (2015). Talking the talk and walking the walk: Conversational pathways to moral development. *Human Development, 58*(4–5), 301–307. https://doi.org /10.1159/000439012

Smetana, J. G. (2017). Current research on parenting styles, dimensions, and beliefs. *Current Opinion in Psychology, 15*, 19–25. https://doi.org/10.1016/j .copsyc.2017.02.012

Smetana, J. G., & Rote, W. M. (2019). Adolescent–parent relationships: Progress, processes, and prospects. *Annual Review of Developmental Psychology, 1*, 41–68.

Smith, B., Rogers, S. L., Blissett, J., & Ludlow, A. K. (2020). The relationship between sensory sensitivity, food fussiness and food preferences in children with neurodevelopmental disorders. *Appetite, 150*, 104643. https://doi.org/10.1016/j.appet.2020.104643

Smith, C. E., Blake, P. R., & Harris, P. L. (2013). I should but I won't: Why young children endorse norms of fair sharing but do not follow them. *PLOS ONE, 8*(3), e59510.

Smith, C. E., Noh, J. Y., Rizzo, M. T., & Harris, P. L. (2017). When and why parents prompt their children to apologize: The roles of transgression type and parenting style. *Journal of Family Studies, 23*(1), 38–61. https:// doi.org/10.1080/13229400.2016.1176588

Smith, J. D., Dishion, T. J., Shaw, D. S., Wilson, M. N., Winter, C. C., & Patterson, G. R. (2014). Coercive family process and early-onset conduct problems from age 2 to school entry. *Development and Psychopathology, 26*(4 Pt. 1), 917–932. https://doi.org/10.1017 /S0954579414000169

Smith, J. D., Fu, E., & Kobayashi, M. (2020). Prevention and management of childhood obesity and its psychological and health comorbidities. *Annual Review of Clinical Psychology, 16*, 351–378. https://doi .org/10.1146/annurev-clinpsy-100219-060201

Smith, K. A., Mei, L., Yao, S., Wu, J., Spelke, E., Tenenbaum, J. B., & Ullman, T. D. (2020). The fine structure of surprise in intuitive physics: When, why, and how much? In *Proceedings of the 42nd Annual Meeting of the Cognitive Science Society*.

Smith, K. E., & Pollak, S. E. (2021). Rethinking concepts and categories for understanding the neurodevelopmental effects of childhood adversity. *Perspectives on Psychological Science: A Journal of the Association for Psychological Science, 16*(1), 67–93. https://doi.org /10.1177/1745691620920725

Smith, L. B., Jayaraman, S., Clerkin, E., & Yu, C. (2018). The developing infant creates a curriculum for statistical learning. *Trends in Cognitive Sciences, 22*(4), 325–336. https://doi.org/10.1016/j .tics.2018.02.004

Smith, S. (2018). Befriending the same differently: Ethnic, socioeconomic status, and gender differences in same-ethnic friendship. *Journal of Ethnic and Migration Studies, 44*(11), 1858–1880. https://doi.org/10.1080/1 369183X.2017.1374168

Smith, V. C., Wilson, C. R., & Committee on Substance Use and Prevention. (2016). Families affected by parental substance use. *Pediatrics, 138*(2), e20161575. https://doi.org/10.1542/peds.2016-1575

SmithBattle, L. (2020). Walking on eggshells: An update on the stigmatizing of teen mothers. *MCN: The American Journal of Maternal/Child Nursing, 45*(6), 322–327.

Smith-Bonahue, T., Smith-Adcock, S., & Harman Ehrentraut, J. (2015). "I won't be your friend if you don't!" Preventing and responding to relational aggression in preschool classrooms. *Young Children, 70*(1).

Smock, P. J., & Schwartz, C. R. (2020). The demography of families: A review of patterns and change. *Journal of Marriage and the Family, 82*(1), 9–34. https://doi .org/10.1111/jomf.12612

Snarey, J. R. (2012). Lawrence Kohlberg: His moral biography, moral psychology, and moral pedagogy. In W. E. Pickren, D. A. Dewsbury, & M. Wertheimer (Eds.), *Portraits of pioneers in developmental psychology* (pp. 277–296). Psychology Press.

Snow, C. E., & Matthews, T. J. (2016). Reading and language in the early grades. *The Future of Children, 26*(2), 57–74.

Sobchuk, K., Connolly, S., & Sheehan, D. (2019). Exploring the literature on the benefits of nature and outdoor play and the role of play leaders. *The Journal of the Health and Physical Education Council of the Alberta Teachers Association, 50*(1), 36–45.

Society for Research on Child Development (SRCD) Governing Council. (2021). *Ethical Principles and Standards for Developmental Scientists*. https://www .srcd.org/about-us/ethical-principles-and-standards -developmental-scientists

Söderström, F., Normann, E., Jonsson, M., & Ågren, J. (2021). Outcomes of a uniformly active approach to infants born at 22–24 weeks of gestation. *Archives of Disease in Childhood — Fetal and Neonatal Edition, 106*, 343. https://doi.org/10.1136 /archdischild-2020-320486

Soenens, B., & Vansteenkiste, M. (2020). Taking adolescents' agency in socialization seriously: The role of appraisals and cognitive-behavioral responses in autonomy-relevant parenting. *New Directions for Child and Adolescent Development, 2020*(173), 7–26. https://doi.org /10.1002/cad.20370

Solarin, A. U., Olutekunbi, O. A., Madise-Wobo, A. D., & Senbanjo, I. (2017). Toilet training practices in Nigerian children. *South African Journal of Child Health, 11*(3), 122–128.

Solmi, F., Sharpe, H., Gage, S. H., Maddock, J., Lewis, G., & Patalay, P. (2021). Changes in the prevalence and correlates of weight-control behaviors and weight perception in adolescents in the UK, 1986–2015. *JAMA Pediatrics, 175*(3), 267. https://doi .org/10.1001/jamapediatrics.2020.4746

Somerville, L. H. (2016). Searching for signatures of brain maturity: What are we searching for? *Neuron, 92*(6), 1164–1167. https://doi.org/10.1016/j .neuron.2016.10.059

Somerville, L. H., Haddara, N., Sasse, S. F., Skwara, A. C., Moran, J. M., & Figner, B. (2019). Dissecting "peer presence" and "decisions" to deepen understanding of peer influence on adolescent risky choice. *Child Development, 90*(6), 2086–2103. https://doi.org/10.1111/cdev.13081

Somerville, L. H., Jones, R. M., & Casey, B. J. (2010). A time of change: Behavioral and neural correlates of adolescent sensitivity to appetitive and aversive environmental cues. *Brain and Cognition, 72*(1), 124–133. https://doi.org/10.1016/j.bandc.2009.07.003

Somerville, L. H., Jones, R. M., Ruberry, E. J., Dyke, J. P., Glover, G., & Casey, B. (2013). Medial prefrontal cortex and the emergence of self-conscious emotion in adolescence. *Psychological Science, 24*(8), 1554–1562. https://doi.org/10.1177/0956797613475633

Somerville, L. H., Sasse, S. F., Garrad, M. C., Drysdale, A. T., Abi Akar, N., Insel, C., & Wilson, R. C. (2017). Charting the expansion of strategic exploratory behavior during adolescence. *Journal of Experimental Psychology: General, 146*(2), 155.

Song, S., Su, M., Kang, C., Liu, H., Zhang, Y., McBride-Chang, C., Tardif, T., Li, H., Liang, W., Zhang, Z., & Shu, H. (2015). Tracing children's vocabulary development from preschool through the school-age years: An 8-year longitudinal study. *Developmental Science, 18*(1), 119–131. https://doi.org /10.1111/desc.12190

Song, Y., Broekhuizen, M. L., & Dubas, J. S. (2020). Happy little benefactor: Prosocial behaviors promote happiness in young children from two cultures. *Frontiers in Psychology, 11*, 1398. https://doi.org/10.3389 /fpsyg.2020.01398

Sonlight. (2017, July 17). It's What Camp Is About. Sonlight. https://sonlightcamp.org/2017/07/17/ its-what-camp-is-about/

Sonuga-Barke, E. J. S., Kennedy, M., Kumsta, R., Knights, N., Golm, D., Rutter, M., Maughan, B., Schlotz, W., & Kreppner, J. (2017). Child-to-adult neurodevelopmental and mental health trajectories after early life deprivation: The young adult follow-up of the longitudinal English and Romanian Adoptees study. *The Lancet, 389*(10078), 1539–1548. https://doi.org/10.1016/S0140-6736(17)30045-4

Sorenson Duncan, T., & Paradis, J. (2020). How does maternal education influence the linguistic environment supporting bilingual language development in child second language learners of English? *International Journal of Bilingualism, 24*(1), 46–61. https://doi.org/10.1177/1367006918768366

Sorkhabi, N., & Mandara, J. (2013). Are the effects of Baumrind's parenting styles culturally specific or culturally equivalent? In R. E. Larzelere, A. S. Morris, & A. W. Harrist (Eds.), *Authoritative parenting: Synthesizing nurturance and discipline for optimal child development* (pp. 113–135). American Psychological Association.

Soto, C. J., & Tackett, J. L. (2015). Personality traits in childhood and adolescence: Structure, development, and outcomes. *Current Directions in Psychological Science, 24*(5), 358–362.

Southern Poverty Law Center (SPLC). (2019). *Hate at school.* Southern Poverty Law Center.

Souto, P. H. S., Santos, J. N., Leite, H. R., Hadders-Algra, M., Guedes, S. C., Nobre, J. N. P., Santos, L. R., & Morais, R. L. de S. (2020). Tablet use in young children is associated with advanced fine motor skills. *Journal of Motor Behavior, 52*(2), 196–203.

Sparks, J., Daly, C., Wilkey, B. M., Molden, D. C., Finkel, E. J., & Eastwick, P. W. (2020). Negligible evidence that people desire partners who uniquely fit their ideals. *Journal of Experimental Social Psychology, 90,* 103968. https://doi.org/10.1016/j.jesp.2020.103968

Sparks, S. D. (2018, July 17). Volunteerism declined among young people. *Education Week.* https://www.edweek.org/leadership/volunteerism-declined-among-young-people/2018/07

Spear, L. P. (2009). Heightened stress responsivity and emotional reactivity during pubertal maturation: Implications for psychopathology. *Development and Psychopathology, 21*(1), 87–97. https://doi.org/10.1017/S0954579409000066

Spear, L. P. (2013). Adolescent neurodevelopment. *Journal of Adolescent Health, 52*(2), S7–S13.

Spelke, E. S. (2017). Core knowledge, language, and number. *Language Learning and Development, 13*(2), 147–170. https://doi.org/10.1080/15475441.2016.1263572

Spencer, B., Wambach, K., & Domain, E. W. (2015). African American women's breastfeeding experiences: Cultural, personal, and political voices. *Qualitative Health Research, 25*(7), 974–987. https://doi.org/10.1177/1049732314554097

Spencer, D., Pasterski, V., Neufeld, S. A., Glover, V., O'Connor, T. G., Hindmarsh, P. C., Hughes, I. A., Acerini, C. L., & Hines, M. (2021). Prenatal androgen exposure and children's gender-typed behavior and toy and playmate preferences. *Hormones and Behavior, 127,* 104889.

Spencer, M. B. (2010, April 28). CNN pilot demonstration. *CNN.* http://i2.cdn.turner.com/cnn/2010/images/05/13/expanded_results_methods

Spencer, M. B. (2017). *Privilege and critical race perspectives' intersectional contributions to a systems theory of human development.* Cambridge University Press.

Spencer, S. J., Logel, C., & Davies, P. G. (2016). Stereotype threat. *Annual Review of Psychology, 67*(1), 415–437. https://doi.org/10.1146/annurev-psych-073115-103235

Spielberg, J. M., Olino, T. M., Forbes, E. E., & Dahl, R. E. (2014). Exciting fear in adolescence: Does pubertal development alter threat processing? *Developmental Cognitive Neuroscience, 8,* 86–95.

Spies, E. L., & Klevens, J. (2016). Fatal abusive head trauma among children aged <5 Years — United States, 1999–2014. *Morbidity and Mortality Weekly Report, 65,* 505–509. http://doi.org/10.15585/mmwr.mm6520a1external icon

Spitz, R. A. (1945). Hospitalism. *The Psychoanalytic Study of the Child, 1*(1), 53–74. https://doi.org/10.1080/00797308.1945.11823126

Spruijt-Metz, D. (2011). Etiology, treatment, and prevention of obesity in childhood and adolescence: A decade in review. *Journal of Research on Adolescence, 21*(1), 129–152.

Spyreli, E., McKinley, M. C., & Dean, M. (2021). Parental considerations during complementary feeding in higher income countries: A systematic review of qualitative evidence. *Public Health Nutrition,* 1–31. https://doi.org/10.1017/S1368980021001749

SRCD Governing Council. (2021). *Ethical principles and standards for developmental Scientists.* Society for Research on Child Development. https://www.srcd.org/about-us/ethical-principles-and-standards-developmental-scientist

Sroufe, L. A. (2016). The place of attachment in development. In J. Cassidy & P. R. Shaver (Eds.), *Handbook of attachment: Theory, research, and clinical applications* (Vol. 3, pp. 997–1011). Guilford.

Sroufe, L. A. (2021). Then and now: The legacy and future of attachment research. *Attachment & Human Development, 23*(4), 396–403. https://doi.org/10.1080/14616734.2021.1918450

Ssemata, A. S., Nakitende, J. A., Kizito, S., Whipple, E. C., Bangirana, P., Nakasujja, N., John, C. C., & McHenry, M. S. (2020). Associations of childhood exposure to malaria with cognition and behavior outcomes: A systematic review protocol. *Systematic Reviews, 9,* 174. https://doi.org/10.1186/s13643-020-01434-2

St James-Roberts, I. (2012). *The origins, prevention and treatment of infant crying and sleeping problems: An evidence-based guide for healthcare professionals and the families they support.* Routledge.

St James-Roberts, I., Garratt, R., Powell, C., Bamber, D., Long, J., Brown, J., Morris, S., Dyson, S., Morris, T., Jaicim, N. B., James-Roberts, I. S., Garratt, R., Powell, C., Bamber, D., Long, J., Brown, J., Morris, S., Dyson, S., Morris, T., & Jaicim, N. B. (2019). *A support package for parents of excessively crying infants: Development and feasibility study.* NIHR Journals Library.

St James-Roberts, I., Roberts, M., Hovish, K., & Owen, C. (2015). Video evidence that London infants can resettle themselves back to sleep after waking in the night, as well as sleep for long periods, by 3 months of age. *Journal of Developmental and Behavioral Pediatrics, 36*(5), 324.

Staats, S., van der Valk, I. E., Meeus, W. H. J., & Branje, S. J. T. (2018). Longitudinal transmission of conflict management styles across inter-parental and adolescent relationships. *Journal of Research on Adolescence, 28*(1), 169–185. https://doi.org/10.1111/jora.12324

Staes, N., Smaers, J. B., Kunkle, A. E., Hopkins, W. D., Bradley, B. J., & Sherwood, C. C. (2019). Evolutionary divergence of neuroanatomical organization and related genes in chimpanzees and bonobos. *Cortex: A Journal Devoted to the Study of the Nervous System and Behavior, 118,* 154–164.

Staff, J., Harris, A., Sabates, R., & Briddell, L. (2010). Uncertainty in early occupational aspirations: Role exploration or aimlessness? *Social Forces, 89*(2), 659–683. https://doi.org/10.1353/sof.2010.0088

Staff, J., Mont'Alvao, A., & Mortimer, J. T. (2015). Children at work. In M. H. Bornstein, T. Leventhal, & R. M. Lerner (Eds.), *Handbook of child psychology and developmental science: Ecological settings and processes* (pp. 345–374). John Wiley & Sons. https://doi.org/10.1002/9781118963418.childpsy409

Staff, J., Yetter, A. M., Cundiff, K., Ramirez, N., Vuolo, M., & Mortimer, J. T. (2020). Is adolescent employment still a risk factor for high school dropout? *Journal of Research on Adolescence, 30*(2), 406–422. https://doi.org/10.1111/jora.12533

Stallings, M. C., & Neppl, T. (2021). An examination of genetic and environmental factors related to negative personality traits, educational attainment, and economic success. *Developmental Psychology, 57*(2), 191.

Stanberry, L. R., Thomson, M. C., & James, W. (2018). Prioritizing the needs of children in a changing climate. *PLOS Medicine, 15*(7), e1002627. https://doi.org/10.1371/journal.pmed.1002627

Stanford Graduate School of Business Staff. (2012, May 2). The value of "values affirmation." *Insights by Stanford Business.* https://www.gsb.stanford.edu/insights/value-values-affirmation

Stanford, F. C., & Kyle, T. K. (2018). Respectful language and care in childhood obesity. *JAMA Pediatrics, 172*(11), 1001–1002. https://doi.org/10.1001/jamapediatrics.2018.1912

Stanley, C. T., Petscher, Y., & Catts, H. (2018). A longitudinal investigation of direct and indirect links between reading skills in kindergarten and reading comprehension in tenth grade. *Reading and Writing, 31*(1), 133–153.

Starrs, A. M., Ezeh, A. C., Barker, G., Basu, A., Bertrand, J. T., Blum, R., Coll-Seck, A. M., Grover, A., Laski, L., Roa, M., Sathar, Z. A., Say, L., Serour, G. I., Singh, S., Stenberg, K., Temmerman, M., Biddlecom, A, Popinchalk, A., Summers, C., & Ashford, L. S. (2018). Accelerate progress — sexual and reproductive health and rights for all: Report of the Guttmacher–Lancet Commission. *The Lancet, 391*(10140), 2642–2692.

Staton, S., Rankin, P. S., Harding, M., Smith, S. S., Westwood, E., LeBourgeois, M. K., & Thorpe, K. J. (2020). Many naps, one nap, none: A systematic review and meta-analysis of napping patterns in children 0–12 years. *Sleep Medicine Reviews, 50,* 101247. https://doi.org/10.1016/j.smrv.2019.101247

Stearns, P. N. (2016). *Childhood in world history.* Routledge.

Stearns, P. N. (2017). History of children's rights. In M. D. Ruck, M. Peterson-Badali, & M. Freeman (Eds.), *Handbook of children's rights: Global and multidisciplinary perspectives* (pp. 1–18). Taylor & Francis.

Steele, C. J., & Zatorre, R. J. (2018). Practice makes plasticity. *Nature Neuroscience, 21*(12), 1645–1646.

Steele, C. M., & Aronson, J. (1995). Stereotype threat and the intellectual test performance of African Americans. *Journal of Personality and Social Psychology, 69*(5), 797.

Steene-Johannessen, J., Hansen, B. H., Dalene, K. E., Kolle, E., Northstone, K., Møller, N. C., Grøntved, A., Wedderkopp, N., Kriemler, S., Page, A. S., Puder, J. J., Reilly, J. J., Sardinha, L. B., van Sluijs, E. M. F., Andersen, L. B., van der Ploeg, H., Ahrens, W., Flexeder, C., Standl, M., . . . On behalf of the Determinants of Diet and Physical Activity knowledge hub (DEDIPAC); International Children's Accelerometry Database (ICAD) Collaborators, I. C. and H. C. (2020). Variations in accelerometry measured physical activity and sedentary time across Europe—Harmonized analyses of 47,497 children and adolescents. *International Journal of Behavioral Nutrition and Physical Activity, 17*(1), 38. https://doi.org/10.1186/s12966-020-00930-x

Stefano, L. D., Mills, C., Watkins, A., & Wilkinson, D. (2020). Ectogestation ethics: The implications of artificially extending gestation for viability, newborn resuscitation and abortion. *Bioethics, 34*(4), 371–384. https://doi.org/10.1111/bioe.12682

Stein, R., Kempf, E., Gesing, J., Stanik, J., Kiess, W., & Körner, A. (2019). Pubertal milestones and related hormonal changes among children with obesity. *ESPE Abstracts, 92*, P2–110. https://abstracts.eurospe.org/hrp/0092/hrp0092p2-110

Steinbach, A. (2019). Children's and parents' well-being in joint physical custody: A literature review. *Family Process, 58*(2), 353–369.

Steinberg, L. (2008). A social neuroscience perspective on adolescent risk-taking. *Developmental Review, 28*(1), 78–106. https://doi.org/10.1016/j.dr.2007.08.002

Steinberg, L. (2014). Family structure, parenting practices, and adolescent adjustment: An ecological examination. In E. M. Hetherington (Ed.), *Coping with divorce, single parenting, and remarriage: A risk and resiliency perspective* (pp. 65). Lawrence Erlbaum Associates.

Steinberg, L., & Icenogle, G. (2019). Using developmental science to distinguish adolescents and adults under the law. *Annual Review of Developmental Psychology, 1*, 21–40.

Steinberg, L., Icenogle, G., Shulman, E. P., Breiner, K., Chein, J., Bacchini, D., Chang, L., Chaudhary, N., Giunta, L. D., Dodge, K. A., Fanti, K. A., Lansford, J. E., Malone, P. S., Oburu, P., Pastorelli, C., Skinner, A. T., Sorbring, E., Tapanya, S., Tirado, L. M. U., . . . Takash, H. M. S. (2017). Around the world, adolescence is a time of heightened sensation seeking and immature self-regulation. *Developmental Science, 21*(2), e12532. https://doi.org/10.1111/desc.12532

Steinberg, L., Lamborn, S. D., Darling, N., Mounts, N. S., & Dornbusch, S. M. (1994). Over-time changes in adjustment and competence among adolescents from authoritative, authoritarian, indulgent, and neglectful families. *Child Development, 65*(3), 754–770.

Stenson, A. F., Leventon, J. S., & Bauer, P. J. (2019). Emotion effects on memory from childhood through adulthood: Consistent enhancement and adult gender differences. *Journal of Experimental Child Psychology, 178*, 121–136. https://doi.org/10.1016/j.jecp.2018.09.016

Stephens, R. L., Langworthy, B. W., Short, S. J., Girault, J. B., Styner, M. A., & Gilmore, J. H. (2020). White matter development from birth to 6 years of age: A longitudinal study. *Cerebral Cortex, 30*(12), 6152–6168. https://doi.org/10.1093/cercor/bhaa170

Stern, A. M. (2015). Instituting eugenics in California. In A. M. Stern (Ed.), *Eugenic nation* (pp. 82–110). University of California Press.

Sternberg, R. J. (1985). *Beyond IQ: A triarchic theory of human intelligence*. Cambridge University Press.

Sternberg, R. J. (1997). The concept of intelligence and its role in lifelong learning and success. *American Psychologist, 52*(10), 1030.

Sternberg, R. J. (2015). Still searching for the Zipperumpazoo: A reflection after 40 years. *Child Development Perspectives, 9*(2), 106–110.

Sternberg, R. J. (2017). Some lessons from a symposium on cultural psychological science. *Perspectives on Psychological Science, 12*(5), 911–921. https://doi.org/10.1177/1745691617720477

Sternberg, R. J. (2018a). The triarchic theory of successful intelligence. In D. P. Flanagan & E. M. McDonough (Eds.), *Contemporary intellectual assessment: Theories, tests, and issues* (pp. 174–194). Guilford.

Sternberg, R. J. (2018b). Theories of intelligence. In S. I. Pfeiffer, E. Shaunessy-Dedrick, & M. Foley-Nicpon (Eds.), *APA handbook of giftedness and talent* (pp. 145–161). American Psychological Association. https://doi.org/10.1037/0000038-010

Sternberg, R. J. (2021). *Adaptive intelligence: Surviving and thriving in times of uncertainty*. Cambridge University Press.

Stewart, J. L., Kamke, K., Widman, L., & Hope, E. C. (2021). "They see sex as something that's reproductive and not as something people do for fun": Shortcomings in adolescent girls' sexual socialization from adults. *Journal of Adolescent Research*. https://doi.org/10.1177/07435584211020299

Stewart, J. L., Spivey, L. A., Widman, L., Choukas-Bradley, S., & Prinstein, M. J. (2019). Developmental patterns of sexual identity, romantic attraction, and sexual behavior among adolescents over three years. *Journal of Adolescence, 77*, 90–97. https://doi.org/10.1016/j.adolescence.2019.10.006

Stierman, B., Afful, J., Carroll, M. D., Chen, T. C., Davy, O., Fink, S., Clark, J., Riddles, M. K., & Akinbami, L. J. (2021). National Health and Nutrition Examination Survey 2017–March 2020 prepandemic data files: Development of files and prevalence estimates for selected health outcomes. National Health Statistics Reports.

Stiles, J., & Jernigan, T. L. (2010). The basics of brain development. *Neuropsychology Review, 20*(4), 327–348. https://doi.org/10.1007/s11065-010-9148-4

Stjernholm, Y. V., Charvalho, P. da S., Bergdahl, O., Vladic, T., & Petersson, M. (2021). Continuous support promotes obstetric labor progress and vaginal delivery in primiparous women—A randomized controlled study. *Frontiers in Psychology, 12*. https://www.frontiersin.org/article/10.3389/fpsyg.2021.582823

Stock, S. J., Carruthers, J., Calvert, C., Denny, C., Donaghy, J., Goulding, A., Hopcroft, L. E. M., Hopkins, L., McLaughlin, T., Pan, J., Shi, T., Taylor, B., Agrawal, U., Auyeung, B., Katikireddi, S. V., McCowan, C., Murray, J., Simpson, C. R., Robertson, C., . . . Wood, R. (2022). SARS-CoV-2 infection and COVID-19 vaccination rates in pregnant women in Scotland. *Nature Medicine*, 1–9. https://doi.org/10.1038/s41591-021-01666-2

Stockdale, L. A., Porter, C. L., Coyne, S. M., Essig, L. W., Booth, M., Keenan-Kroff, S., & Schvaneveldt, E. (2020). Infants' response to a mobile phone modified still-face paradigm: Links to maternal behaviors and beliefs regarding technoference. *Infancy, 25*(5), 571–592. https://doi.org/10.1111/infa.12342

Stoll, S., & Lieven, E. (2014). Studying language acquisition cross linguistically. In H. Winskel & P. Pradakannaya (Eds.), *South and southeast Asian psycholinguistics* (pp. 19–35). Cambridge University Press.

Stoltenborgh, M., Bakermans-Kranenburg, M. J., Alink, L. R., & van IJzendoorn, M. H. (2015). The prevalence of child maltreatment across the globe: Review of a series of meta-analyses. *Child Abuse Review, 24*(1), 37–50.

Stone, L. B., & Gibb, B. E. (2015). Brief report: Preliminary evidence that co-rumination fosters adolescents' depression risk by increasing rumination. *Journal of Adolescence, 38*, 1–4. https://doi.org/10.1016/j.adolescence.2014.10.008

Stoskopf, A. (1999). The forgotten history of eugenics. *Rethinking Schools, 13*(3), 12–13.

Stoskopf, A. (2012). Racism in the history of standardized testing: Legacies for today. In W. Au & M. B. Tempel (Eds.), *Pencils down: Rethinking high-stakes testing and accountability in public schools* (pp. 34–39). Rethinking Schools.

Stough, C. (2015, October 9). *Show us your smarts: A very brief history of intelligence testing*. The Conversation. http://theconversation.com/show-us-your-smarts-a-very-brief-history-of-intelligence-testing-45444

Stoute, B. J. (2020). Racism: A challenge for the therapeutic dyad. *American Journal of Psychotherapy, 73*(3), 69–71. https://doi.org/10.1176/appi.psychotherapy.20200043

Stover, C. S., Zhou, Y., Leve, L. D., Neiderhiser, J. M., Shaw, D. S., & Reiss, D. (2015). The relationship between genetic attributions, appraisals of birth mothers' health, and the parenting of adoptive mothers and fathers. *Journal of Applied Developmental Psychology, 41*, 19–27. https://doi.org/10.1016/j.appdev.2015.06.003

Strachan, D. P. (1989). Hay fever, hygiene, and household size. *BMJ: British Medical Journal, 299*(6710), 1259.

Strand, B. H., Knapskog, A.-B., Persson, K., Edwin, T. H., Amland, R., Mjørud, M., Bjertness, E., Engedal, K., & Selbæk, G. (2018). Survival and years of life lost in various aetiologies of dementia, mild cognitive impairment (MCI) and subjective cognitive decline (SCD) in Norway. *PLOS ONE, 13*(9), e0204436. https://doi.org/10.1371/journal.pone.0204436

Strings, S. (2019). *Fearing the black body: The racial origins of fat phobia*. NYU Press.

Strouse, G. A., Troseth, G. L., O'Doherty, K. D., & Saylor, M. M. (2018). Co-viewing supports toddlers' word learning from contingent and noncontingent video. *Journal of Experimental Child Psychology, 166*, 310–326. https://doi.org/10.1016/j.jecp.2017.09.005

Stucke, N. J., Stoet, G., & Doebel, S. (2022). What are the kids doing? Exploring young children's activities at home and relations with externally cued executive function and child temperament. *Developmental Science*, e13226. https://doi.org/10.1111/desc.13226

Studer-Luethi, B., Bauer, C., & Perrig, W. J. (2016). Working memory training in children: Effectiveness depends on temperament. *Memory & Cognition, 44*(2), 171–186. https://doi.org/10.3758/s13421-015-0548-9

Suárez-Orozco, C., López Hernández, G., & Cabral, P. (2021). The rippling effects of unauthorized status: Stress, family separations, and deportation and their implications for belonging and development. In *Trauma and racial minority immigrants: Turmoil, uncertainty, and resistance* (pp. 185–203). American Psychological Association.

Suárez-Orozco, C., Motti-Stefanidi, F., Marks, A., & Katsiaficas, D. (2018). An integrative risk and resilience model for understanding the adaptation of immigrant-origin children and youth. *American Psychologist, 73*(6), 781–796. https://doi.org/10.1037/amp0000265

Suarez-Rivera, C., Smith, L. B., & Yu, C. (2019). Multimodal parent behaviors within joint attention support sustained attention in infants. *Developmental Psychology, 55*(1), 96–109. https://doi.org/10.1037/dev0000628

Subbotsky, E. (2014). The belief in magic in the age of science. *SAGE Open, 4.* https://doi.org/10.1177/2158244014521433

Substance Abuse and Mental Health Services Administration (SAMHSA). (2020). *Key substance use and mental health indicators in the United States: Results from the 2019 National Survey on Drug Use and Health* (HHS Publication No. PEP20-07-01–001; NSDUH Series H-55). Center for Behavioral Health Statistics and Quality, SAMHSA.

Substance Abuse and Mental Health Services Administration (SAMHSA). (2021). *Key substance use and mental health indicators in the United States: Results from the 2020 National Survey on Drug Use and Health.* Center for Behavioral Health Statistics and Quality, SAMHSA. https://www.samhsa.gov/data/

Sudre, G., Mangalmurti, A., & Shaw, P. (2018). Growing out of attention deficit hyperactivity disorder: Insights from the 'remitted' brain. *Neuroscience & Biobehavioral Reviews, 94,* 198–209.

Suggate, S., Schaughency, E., McAnally, H., & Reese, E. (2018). From infancy to adolescence: The longitudinal links between vocabulary, early literacy skills, oral narrative, and reading comprehension. *Cognitive Development, 47,* 82–95. https://doi.org/10.1016/j.cogdev.2018.04.005

Suglia, S. F., Chen, C., Wang, S., Cammack, A. L., April-Sanders, A. K., McGlinchey, E. L., Kubo, A., Bird, H., Canino, G., & Duarte, C. S. (2020). Childhood adversity and pubertal development among Puerto Rican boys and girls. *Psychosomatic Medicine, 82*(5), 487–494. https://doi.org/10.1097/PSY.0000000000000817

Suh, B., & Luthar, S. S. (2020). Parental aggravation may tell more about a child's mental/behavioral health than adverse childhood experiences: Using the 2016 National Survey of Children's Health. *Child Abuse & Neglect, 101,* 104330.

Suizzo, M.-A. (2020). Parent–child relationships. In *The encyclopedia of child and adolescent development* (pp. 1–13). Wiley. https://doi.org/10.1002/9781119171492.wecad408

Suizzo, M.-A., Robinson, C., & Pahlke, E. (2008). African American mothers' socialization beliefs and goals with young children: Themes of history, education, and collective independence. *Journal of Family Issues, 29*(3), 287–316. https://doi.org/10.1177/0192513X07308368

Sukhodolsky, D. G., Smith, S. D., McCauley, S. A., Ibrahim, K., & Piasecka, J. B. (2016). Behavioral interventions for anger, irritability, and aggression in children and adolescents. *Journal of Child and Adolescent Psychopharmacology, 26*(1), 58–64. https://doi.org/10.1089/cap.2015.0120

Suleiman, A. B., & Dahl, R. (2019). Parent–child relationships in the puberty years: Insights from developmental neuroscience. *Family Relations, 68*(3), 279–287. http://dx.doi.org/10.1111/fare.12360

Suleiman, A. B., & Deardorff, J. (2015). Multiple dimensions of peer influence in adolescent romantic and sexual relationships: A descriptive, qualitative perspective. *Archives of Sexual Behavior, 44*(3), 765–775. https://doi.org/10.1007/s10508-014-0394-z

Suleiman, A. B., & Harden, K. P. (2016). The importance of sexual and romantic development in understanding the developmental neuroscience of adolescence. *Developmental Cognitive Neuroscience, 17,* 145–147. https://doi.org/10.1016/j.dcn.2015.12.007

Suleiman, A. B., Galván, A., Harden, K. P., & Dahl, R. E. (2017). Becoming a sexual being: The 'elephant in the room' of adolescent brain development. *Developmental Cognitive Neuroscience, 25,* 209–220.

Sullivan, A., & Brown, M. (2015). Reading for pleasure and progress in vocabulary and mathematics. *British Education Research Journal, 41,* 971–991. https://doi.org/10.1002/berj.3180

Sullivan, J., Moss-Racusin, C., Lopez, M., & Williams, K. (2018). Backlash against gender stereotype-violating preschool children. *PLOS ONE, 13*(4), e0195503. https://doi.org/10.1371/journal.pone.0195503

Sumontha, J., Farr, R. H., & Patterson, C. J. (2017). Children's gender development: Associations with parental sexual orientation, division of labor, and gender ideology. *Psychology of Sexual Orientation and Gender Diversity, 4*(4), 438–450. https://doi.org/10.1037/sgd0000242

Sun, H., Gong, T.-T., Jiang, Y.-T., Zhang, S., Zhao, Y.-H., & Wu, Q.-J. (2019). Global, regional, and national prevalence and disability-adjusted life-years for infertility in 195 countries and territories, 1990–2017: Results from a global burden of disease study, 2017. *Aging (Albany NY), 11*(23), 10952–10991. https://doi.org/10.18632/aging.102497

Sun, H., & Weaver, C. M. (2021). Decreased iron intake parallels rising iron deficiency anemia and related mortality rates in the US population. *The Journal of Nutrition, 151*(7), 1947–1955. https://doi.org/10.1093/jn/nxab064

Sun, H., & Yin, B. (2020). Multimedia input and bilingual children's language learning. *Frontiers in Psychology, 11,* 2023. https://doi.org/10.3389/fpsyg.2020.02023

Sun, J. W., Bai, H. Y., Li, J. H., Lin, P. Z., Zhang, H. H., & Cao, F. L. (2017). Predictors of occupational burnout among nurses: A dominance analysis of job stressors. *Journal of Clinical Nursing, 26*(23–24), 4286–4292.

Sun, Y., Fang, J., Wan, Y., Su, P., & Tao, F. (2020). Association of early-life adversity with measures of accelerated biological aging among children in China. *JAMA Network Open, 3*(9), e2013588–e2013588. https://doi.org/10.1001/jamanetworkopen.2020.13588

Sun, Y., Tao, F., Su, P.-Y., & Collaboration, C. P. R. (2012). National estimates of pubertal milestones among urban and rural Chinese boys. *Annals of Human Biology, 39*(6), 461–467. https://doi.org/10.3109/03014460.2012.712156

Sunderam, S., Kissin, D. M., Zhang, Y., Jewett, A., Boulet, S. L., Warner, L., Kroelinger, C. D., & Barfield, W. D. (2022). Assisted reproductive technology surveillance — United States, 2018. *MMWR Surveillance Summaries, 71*(4), 1–19. https://doi.org/10.15585/mmwr.ss7104a1

Sung, J., Beijers, R., Gartstein, M. A., de Weerth, C., & Putnam, S. P. (2015). Exploring temperamental differences in infants from the United States of America (US) and the Netherlands. *The European Journal of Developmental Psychology, 12*(1), 15–28. https://doi.org/10.1080/17405629.2014.937700

Supanitayanon, S., Trairatvorakul, P., & Chonchaiya, W. (2020). Screen media exposure in the first 2 years of life and preschool cognitive development: A longitudinal study. *Pediatric Research, 88*(6), 894–902. https://doi.org/10.1038/s41390-020-0831-8

Super, C. M., & Harkness, S. (1994). Temperament and the developmental niche. In W. B. Casey & S. C.

McDevitt (Eds.), *Prevention and early intervention: Individual differences as risk factors for the mental health of children: A festschrift for Stella Chess and Alexander Thomas* (pp. 115–125). Brunner/Mazel.

Super, C. M., Harkness, S., Bonichini, S., Welles, B., Zylicz, P. O., Bermudez, M. R., & Palacios, J. (2020). Developmental continuity and change in the cultural construction of the "difficult child": A study in six Western cultures. In S. Harkness & C. M. Super (Eds.), *Cross cultural research on parents: Application to the care and education of children* (pp. 43–68). Wiley. https://doi.org/10.1002/cad.20338

Supplee, L. H., & Duggan, A. (2019). Innovative research methods to advance precision in home visiting for more efficient and effective programs. *Child Development Perspectives, 13*(3), 173–179. https://doi.org/10.1111/cdep.12334

Sutton, A., Lichter, D. T., & Sassler, S. (2019). Rural–urban disparities in pregnancy intentions, births, and abortions among US adolescent and young women, 1995–2017. *American Journal of Public Health, 109*(12), 1762–1769.

Suwanwongse, K., & Shabarek, N. (2020). Epidemiology, clinical features, and outcomes of hospitalized infants with COVID-19 in the Bronx, New York. *Archives De Pediatrie, 27*(7), 400–401. https://doi.org/10.1016/j.arcped.2020.07.009

Swit, C. S., & Slater, N. M. (2021). Relational aggression during early childhood: A systematic review. *Aggression and Violent Behavior, 58,* 101556. https://doi.org/10.1016/j.avb.2021.101556

Switkowski, K. M., Gingras, V., Rifas-Shiman, S. L., & Oken, E. (2020). Patterns of complementary feeding behaviors predict diet quality in early childhood. *Nutrients, 12*(3), 810. https://doi.org/10.3390/nu12030810

Syed, M. (2021). The logic of microaggressions assumes a racist society. *Perspectives on Psychological Science, 16*(5), 926–931.

Syed, M., & Fish, J. (2018). Revisiting Erik Erikson's legacy on culture, race, and ethnicity. *Identity, 18*(4), 274–283. https://doi.org/10.1080/15283488.2018.1523729

Syed, M., Santos, C., Yoo, H. C., & Juang, L. P. (2018). Invisibility of racial/ethnic minorities in developmental science: Implications for research and institutional practices. *American Psychologist, 73*(6), 812–826. https://doi.org/10.1037/amp0000294

Symonds, W. C., Schwartz, R., & Ferguson, R. F. (2011). *Pathways to prosperity: Meeting the challenge of preparing young Americans.* Pathways to Prosperity Project, Harvard Graduate School of Education. http://globalpathwaysinstitute.org/wp-content/uploads/2015/03/Pathways_to_Prosperity_Feb2011-1.pdf

Szepsenwol, O., & Simpson, J. A. (2021). Early attachment from the perspective of life-history theory. In R. A. Thompson, J. A. Simpson, L. J. Berlin, L. Ahnert, & T. Ai (Eds.), *Attachment: The fundamental questions* (pp. 219–228). Guilford.

Szkody, E., Steele, E. H., & McKinney, C. (2020). Effects of parenting styles on psychological problems by self esteem and gender differences. *Journal of Family Issues, 42*(9), 1931–1954 0192513X20958445. https://doi.org/10.1177/0192513X20958445

Szucs, L. E., Lowry, R., Fasula, A. M., Pampati, S., Copen, C. E., Hussaini, K. S., Kachur, R. E., Koumans, E. H., & Steiner, R. J. (2020). Condom and contraceptive use among sexually active high school students — youth risk behavior survey, United States, 2019. *Morbidity and Mortality Weekly Report, 69*(1), 11–18.

Tagi, V. M., & Chiarelli, F. (2020). Obesity and insulin resistance in children. *Current Opinion in Pediatrics, 32*(4), 582–588. https://doi.org/10.1097/MOP.0000000000000913

Takanishi, R., & Le Menestrel, S. (2017). *Promoting the educational success of children and youth learning English: Promising futures.* National Academies Press.

Talma, H., Schönbeck, Y., Dommelen, P. van, Bakker, B., Buuren, S. van, & HiraSing, R. A. (2013). Trends in Menarcheal Age between 1955 and 2009 in the Netherlands. *PLoS One, 8*(4), e60056. http://dx.doi.org/10.1371/journal.pone.0060056

Tamnes, C., & Mills, K. L. (2020). Imaging structural brain development in childhood and adolescence. In D. Poeppel, G. R. Mangun, & M. S. Gazzaniga (Eds.), *The cognitive neurosciences* (Vol. VI, pp. 17–25). MIT Press.

Tan, P. Z., Oppenheimer, C. W., Ladouceur, C. D., Butterfield, R. D., & Silk, J. S. (2020). A review of associations between parental emotion socialization behaviors and the neural substrates of emotional reactivity and regulation in youth. *Developmental Psychology, 56*(3), 516–527. https://doi.org/10.1037/dev0000893

Tandon, P. S., Saelens, B. E., Zhou, C., Kerr, J., & Christakis, D. A. (2013). Indoor versus outdoor time in preschoolers at child care. *American Journal of Preventive Medicine, 44*(1), 85–88.

Tang, H., & Barsh, G. S. (2017). Skin color variation in Africa. *Science, 358* (6365), 867–868. https://doi.org/10.1126/science.aaq1322

Tangherlini, T. R., Shahsavari, S., Shahbazi, B., Ebrahimzadeh, E., & Roychowdhury, V. (2020). An automated pipeline for the discovery of conspiracy and conspiracy theory narrative frameworks: Bridgegate, Pizzagate and storytelling on the web. *PLOS ONE, 15*(6), e0233879. https://doi.org/10.1371/journal.pone.0233879

Tanner-Smith, E. E., Wilson, S. J., & Lipsey, M. W. (2013). The comparative effectiveness of outpatient treatment for adolescent substance abuse: A meta-analysis. *Journal of Substance Abuse Treatment, 44*(2), 145–158. https://doi.org/10.1016/j.jsat.2012.05.006

Tardiff, N., Bascandziev, I., Carey, S., & Zaitchik, D. (2020). Specifying the domain-general resources that contribute to conceptual construction: Evidence from the child's acquisition of vitalist biology. *Cognition, 195*, 104090. https://doi.org/10.1016/j.cognition.2019.104090

Tarokh, L., Saletin, J. M., & Carskadon, M. A. (2016). Sleep in adolescence: Physiology, cognition and mental health. *Neuroscience & Biobehavioral Reviews, 70*, 182–188. https://doi.org/10.1016/j.neubiorev.2016.08.008

Taruscio, D., Baldi, F., Carbone, P., Neville, A. J., Rezza, G., Rizzo, C., & Mantovani, A. (2017). Primary prevention of congenital anomalies: Special focus on environmental chemicals and other toxicants, maternal health and health services and infectious diseases. In M. Posada de la Paz, D. Taruscio, & S. C. Groft (Eds.), *Rare diseases epidemiology: Update and overview* (pp. 301–322). Springer International Publishing. https://doi.org/10.1007/978-3-319-67144-4_18

Tashjian, S. M., Rahal, D., Karan, M., Eisenberger, N., Galván, A., Cole, S. W., & Fuligni, A. J. (2021). Evidence from a randomized controlled trial that altruism moderates the effect of prosocial acts on adolescent well-being. *Journal of Youth and Adolescence, 50*(1), 29–43. https://doi.org/10.1007/s10964-020-01362-3

Tasse, M. J. (2016). Defining intellectual disability: Finally we all agree . . . almost. *Spotlight on Disability Newsletter.* https://www.apa.org/pi/disability/resources/publications/newsletter/2016/09/intellectual-disability

Tate, C. (1996). Freud and his "Negro": Psychoanalysis as ally and enemy of African Americans. *Journal for the Psychoanalysis of Culture & Society, 1*(1), 53–62.

Tatum, B. D. (2017). *Why are all the black kids sitting together in the cafeteria? And other conversations about race.* Basic Books. (Original work published 1997)

Taylor, C. M., & Emmett, P. M. (2019). Picky eating in children: Causes and consequences. *Proceedings of the Nutrition Society, 78*(2), 161–169. https://doi.org/10.1017/S0029665118002586

Taylor, J. L., McPheeters, M. L., Sathe, N. A., Dove, D., Veenstra-VanderWeele, J., & Warren, Z. (2012). A systematic review of vocational interventions for young adults with autism spectrum disorders. *Pediatrics, 130*(3), 531–538. https://doi.org/10.1542/peds.2012-0682

Taylor, J. S., Madhavan, S., Han, R. W., Chandler, J. M., Tenakoon, L., & Chao, S. (2021). Financial burden of pediatric firearm-related injury admissions in the United States. *PLOS ONE, 16*(6), e0252821. https://doi.org/10.1371/journal.pone.0252821

Taylor, K. M., Kioumourtzoglou, M.-A., Clover, J., Coull, B. A., Dennerlein, J. T., Bellinger, D. C., & Weisskopf, M. G. (2018). Concussion history and cognitive function in a large cohort of adolescent athletes. *The American Journal of Sports Medicine, 46*(13), 3262–3270. https://doi.org/10.1177/0363546518798801

Taylor, L., Claire, R., Campbell, K., Coleman-Haynes, T., Leonardi-Bee, J., Chamberlain, C., Berlin, I., Davey, M.-A., Cooper, S., & Coleman, T. (2021). Fetal safety of nicotine replacement therapy in pregnancy: Systematic review and meta-analysis. *Addiction, 116*(2), 239–277. https://doi.org/10.1111/add.15185

Taylor, R. D., Oberle, E., Durlak, J. A., & Weissberg, R. P. (2017). Promoting positive youth development through school-based social and emotional learning interventions: A meta-analysis of follow-up effects. *Child Development, 88*(4), 1156–1171.

Teicher, M. H., & Samson, J. A. (2016). Annual research review: Enduring neurobiological effects of childhood abuse and neglect. *Journal of Child Psychology and Psychiatry, 57*(3), 241–266.

Telzer, E. H., Flannery, J., Humphreys, K. L., Goff, B., Gabard-Durman, L., Gee, D. G., & Tottenham, N. (2015). "The cooties effect": Amygdala reactivity to opposite-versus same-sex faces declines from childhood to adolescence. *Journal of Cognitive Neuroscience, 27*(9), 1685–1696.

Telzer, E. H., & Fuligni, A. J. (2009). Daily family assistance and the psychological well-being of adolescents from Latin American, Asian, and European backgrounds. *Developmental Psychology, 45*(4), 1177.

Telzer, E. H., Fuligni, A. J., Lieberman, M. D., & Galván, A. (2013). The effects of poor quality sleep on brain function and risk taking in adolescence. *Neuroimage, 71*, 275–283.

Templin, M. C. (1957). *Certain language skills in children: Their development and interrelationships.* University of Minnesota Press.

Tereshchenko, A., Bradbury, A., & Archer, L. (2019). Eastern European migrants' experiences of racism in English schools: Positions of marginal whiteness and linguistic otherness. *Whiteness and Education, 4*(1), 53–71. https://doi.org/10.1080/23793406.2019.1584048

Terman, L. M. (1916). The uses of intelligence tests. In L. M. Terman (Ed.), *The measurement of intelligence* (pp. 3–21). Houghton, Mifflin.

Tervalon, M., & Murray-García, J. (1998). Cultural humility versus cultural competence: A critical distinction in defining physician training outcomes in multicultural education. *Journal of Health Care for the Poor and Underserved, 9*(2), 117–125. https://doi.org/10.1353/hpu.2010.0233

Teti, D. M., Cole, P. M., Cabrera, N., Goodman, S. H., & McLoyd, V. C. (2017). Supporting parents: How six decades of parenting research can inform policy and best practice. *Social Policy Report, 30*(5), 1–34.

Tetzner, J., Becker, M., & Brandt, N. D. (2020). Personality-achievement associations in adolescence—examining associations across grade levels and learning environments. *Journal of Personality, 88*(2), 356–372. https://doi.org/10.1111/jopy.12495

Tevington, P. (2018). "You're throwing your life away": Sanctioning of early marital timelines by religion and social class. *Social Inclusion, 6*(2), 140–150.

Thakrar, A. P., Forrest, A. D., Maltenfort, M. G., & Forrest, C. B. (2018). Child mortality in the US and 19 OECD comparator nations: A 50-year time-trend analysis. *Health Affairs, 37*(1), 140–149. https://doi.org/10.1377/hlthaff.2017.0767

The Education Commission & UNICEF. (2022). *Recovering learning: Are children and youth on track in skills development?* The Education Commission and UNICEF.

The Hanen Center (Hanen). (2017). *It takes two to talk: The Hanen program for parents of children with language delays.* The Hanen Center (Ontario).

Thelen, E. (1995). Motor development: A new synthesis. *American Psychologist, 50*(2), 79.

Thelen, E., & Adolph, K. E. (1994). Arnold L. Gesell: The paradox of nature and nurture. In R. D. Parke, P. A. Ornstein, J. J. Rieser, & C. Zahn-Waxler (Eds.), *A century of developmental psychology* (pp. 357–387). American Psychological Association. https://doi.org/10.1037/10155-027

Thibodeau, R. B., Gilpin, A. T., Brown, M. M., & Meyer, B. A. (2016). The effects of fantastical pretend-play on the development of executive functions: An intervention study. *Journal of Experimental Child Psychology, 145*, 120–138.

Thiebaut de Schotten, M., Cohen, L., Amemiya, E., Braga, L. W., & Dehaene, S. (2014). Learning to read improves the structure of the arcuate fasciculus. *Cerebral Cortex, 24*(4), 989–995. https://doi.org/10.1093/cercor/bhs383

Thiem, K. C., Neel, R., Simpson, A. J., & Todd, A. R. (2019). Are black women and girls associated with danger? Implicit racial bias at the intersection of target age and gender. *Personality and Social Psychology Bulletin, 45*(10), 1427–1439.

Thijssen, S., Muetzel, R. L., Bakermans-Kranenburg, M. J., Jaddoe, V. W. V., Tiemeier, H., Verhulst, F. C., White, T., & Ijzendoorn, M. H. V. (2017). Insensitive parenting may accelerate the development of the amygdala–medial prefrontal cortex circuit. *Development and Psychopathology, 29*(2), 505–518. https://doi.org/10.1017/S0954579417000141

Thomaes, S., Brummelman, E., & Sedikides, C. (2017). Why most children think well of themselves. *Child Development, 88*(6), 1873–1884.

Thomala, L. L. (2021). *China: MAUs of online dating and matchmaking apps 2020*. Statistica. https://www.statista.com/statistics/1130445/china-monthly-active-users-of-online-dating-and-matchmaking-apps/

Thomas, A., & Chess, S. (1957). An approach to the study of sources of individual differences in child behavior. *Journal of Clinical & Experimental Psychopathology, 18*, 347–357.

Thomas, A., & Chess, S. (1977). *Temperament and development*. Brunner/Mazel.

Thomas, A., Chess, S., & Birch, H. G. (1970). The origin of personality. *Scientific American, 223*(2), 102–109.

Thomas, E., Buss, C., Rasmussen, J. M., Entringer, S., Ramirez, J. S. B., Marr, M., Rudolph, M. D., Gilmore, J. H., Styner, M., Wadhwa, P. D., Fair, D. A., & Graham, A. M. (2019). Newborn amygdala connectivity and early emerging fear. *Developmental Cognitive Neuroscience, 37*, 100604. https://doi.org/10.1016/j.dcn.2018.12.002

Thomas, F., Renaud, F., Benefice, E., de Meeüs, T., & Guegan, J.-F. (2001). International variability of ages at menarche and menopause: Patterns and main determinants. *Human Biology, 73*(2), 271–290. JSTOR. https://www.jstor.org/stable/41465935

Thomason, M. E., Scheinost, D., Manning, J. H., Grove, L. E., Hect, J., Marshall, N., Hernandez-Andrade, E., Berman, S., Pappas, A., Yeo, L., Hassan, S. S., Constable, R. T., Ment, L. R., & Romero, R. (2017). Weak functional connectivity in the human fetal brain prior to preterm birth. *Scientific Reports, 7*, 39286. https://doi.org/10.1038/srep39286

Thompson, D. K., Matthews, L. G., Alexander, B., Lee, K. J., Kelly, C. E., Adamson, C. L., Hunt, R. W., Cheong, J. L. Y., Spencer-Smith, M., Neil, J. J., Seal, M. L., Inder, T. E., Doyle, L. W., & Anderson, P. J. (2020). Tracking regional brain growth up to age 13 in children born term and very preterm. *Nature Communications, 11*(1), 696. https://doi.org/10.1038/s41467-020-14334-9

Thompson, D. L., & Thompson, S. (2018). Educational equity and quality in K–12 schools: Meeting the needs of all students. *Journal for the Advancement of Educational Research International, 12*(1), 34–46.

Thompson, J. A. (2019). Disentangling the roles of maternal and paternal age on birth prevalence of down syndrome and other chromosomal disorders using a Bayesian modeling approach. *BMC Medical Research Methodology, 19*(1), 1–8.

Thompson, R. A. (2019). Emotion dysregulation: A theme in search of definition. *Development and Psychopathology, 31*(3), 805–815.

Thompson, R., Kaczor, K., Lorenz, D. J., Bennett, B. L., Meyers, G., & Pierce, M. C. (2017). Is the use of physical discipline associated with aggressive behaviors in young children? *Academic Pediatrics, 17*(1), 34–44. https://doi.org/10.1016/j.acap.2016.02.014

Thomsen, L. (2020). The developmental origins of social hierarchy: How infants and young children mentally represent and respond to power and status. *Current Opinion in Psychology, 33*, 201–208. https://doi.org/10.1016/j.copsyc.2019.07.044

Thoreson, R. R. (2017). *"Just let us be": Discrimination against LGBT students in the Philippines*. Human Rights Watch.

Thornhill, J. P., Barkati, S., Walmsley, S., Rockstroh, J., Antinori, A., Harrison, L. B., Palich, R., Nori, A., Reeves, I., Habibi, M. S., Apea, V., Boesecke, C.,

Vandekerchove, L., Yakubovsky, M., Sendagorta, E., Blanco, J. L., Florence, E., Moschese, D., Maltez, J. L., . . . Orkin, C. M. (2022). Monkeypox virus infection in humans across 16 countries — April–June 2022. *New England Journal of Medicine, 387*(8), 679–691.

Thorpe, K., Irvine, S., Pattinson, C., & Staton, S. (2020). Insider perspectives: The "tricky business" of providing for children's sleep and rest needs in the context of early childhood education and care. *Early Years, 40*(2), 221–236.

Tibbetts, Y., Harackiewicz, J. M., Canning, E. A., Boston, J. S., Priniski, S. J., & Hyde, J. S. (2016). Affirming independence: Exploring mechanisms underlying a values affirmation intervention for first-generation students. *Journal of Personality and Social Psychology, 110*(5), 635.

Tijani, A. M., Awowole, I. O., Badejoko, O. O., Badejoko, B. O., Ijarotimi, A. O., & Loto, O. M. (2019). Is menarche really occurring earlier? A study of secondary school girls in Ile-Ife, Nigeria. *Tropical Journal of Obstetrics and Gynaecology, 36*(1), 112–116. https://doi.org/10.4314/tjog.v36i1

Tilburg, W. C. (2017). Policy approaches to improving housing and health. *The Journal of Law, Medicine & Ethics, 45*(1_suppl), 90–93. https://doi.org/10.1177/1073110517703334

Tilley, J. L., Huey Jr, S. J., Farver, J. M., Lai, M. H., & Wang, C. X. (2021). The immigrant paradox in the problem behaviors of youth in the United States: A meta-analysis. *Child Development, 92*(2), 502–516.

Tillman, K. H., Brewster, K. L., & Holway, G. V. (2019). Sexual and romantic relationships in young adulthood. *Annual Review of Sociology, 45*(1), 133–153. https://doi.org/10.1146/annurev-soc-073018-022625

Tilton-Weaver, L. C., Burk, W. J., Kerr, M., & Stattin, H. (2013). Can parental monitoring and peer management reduce the selection or influence of delinquent peers? Testing the question using a dynamic social network approach. *Developmental Psychology, 49*(11), 2057–2070. https://doi.org/10.1037/a0031854

Tilton-Weaver, L., Kerr, M., Pakalniskeine, V., Tokic, A., Salihovic, S., & Stattin, H. (2010). Open up or close down: How do parental reactions affect youth information management? *Journal of Adolescence, 33*(2), 333–346. https://doi.org/10.1016/j.adolescence.2009.07.011

Timmons, K., Cooper, A., Bozek, E., & Braund, H. (2021). The impacts of COVID-19 on early childhood education: Capturing the unique challenges associated with remote teaching and learning in K-2. *Early Childhood Education Journal*. https://doi.org/10.1007/s10643-021-01207-z

TIMSS (Trends in International Mathematics and Science Study), 2019. International Association for the Evaluation of Educational Achievement (IEA), Trends in International Mathematics and Science Study. TIMSS & PIRLS International Study Center, Lynch School of Education, Boston College.

Tinggaard, J., Mieritz, M. G., Sørensen, K., Mouritsen, A., Hagen, C. P., Aksglaede, L., Wohlfahrt-Veje, C., & Juul, A. (2012). The physiology and timing of male puberty. *Current Opinion in Endocrinology, Diabetes and Obesity, 19*(3), 197–203. https://doi.org/10.1097/MED.0b013e3283535614

Tipene-Leach, D., & Abel, S. (2019). Innovation to prevent sudden infant death: The wahakura as an indigenous vision for a safe sleep environment. *Australian Journal of Primary Health, 25*(5), 406–409. https://doi.org/10.1071/PY19033

Titchner, T. J., Aloi, M., & Gupta, P. (2015). Pediatric head injury. *Trauma Reports*. https://www.reliasmedia.com/articles/136065-pediatric-head-injury

Tjaden, J., Rolando, D., Doty, J., & Mortimer, J. T. (2019). The long-term effects of time use during high school on positive development. *Longitudinal and Life Course Studies, 10*(1), 51–85. https://doi.org/10.1332/175795919X15468755933371

TNTP. (2018). The Opportunity Myth: What Students Can Show Us About How School Is Letting Them Down—and How to Fix It. https://tntp.org/assets/documents/TNTP_The-Opportunity-Myth_Web.pdf

Todd, A. R., Thiem, K. C., & Neel, R. (2016). Does seeing faces of young black boys facilitate the identification of threatening stimuli? *Psychological Science, 27*(3), 384–393.

Toe, D., Mood, D., Most, T., Walker, E., & Tucci, S. (2020). The assessment of pragmatic skills in young deaf and hard of hearing children. *Pediatrics, 146*(Supplement 3), S284–S291. https://doi.org/10.1542/peds.2020-0242H

Toffalini, E., Pezzuti, L., & Cornoldi, C. (2017). Einstein and dyslexia: Is giftedness more frequent in children with a specific learning disorder than in typically developing children? *Intelligence, 62*, 175–179. https://doi.org/10.1016/j.intell.2017.04.006

Toh, S. H., Howie, E. K., Coenen, P., & Straker, L. M. (2019). "From the moment I wake up I will use it . . . every day, very hour": A qualitative study on the patterns of adolescents' mobile touch screen device use from adolescent and parent perspectives. *BMC Pediatrics, 19*(1), 1–16.

Tolan, P. H., McDaniel, H. L., Richardson, M., Arkin, N., Augenstern, J., & DuBois, D. L. (2020). Improving understanding of how mentoring works: Measuring multiple intervention processes. *Journal of Community Psychology, 48*(6), 2086–2107.

Tomasello, M. (2006). Acquiring linguistic constructions. In D. Kuhn, R. S. Siegler, W. Damon, & R. M. Lerner (Eds.), *Handbook of child psychology: Cognition, perception, and language* (pp. 255–298). John Wiley & Sons.

Tomasello, M. (2015). The usage-based theory of language acquisition. In E. L. Bavin & L. R. Naigles (Eds.), *The Cambridge Handbook of Child Language* (2nd ed., pp. 89–106). Cambridge University Press. https://doi.org/10.1017/CBO9781316095829.005

Tomasello, M. (2016). Cultural learning redux. *Child Development, 87*(3), 643–653. https://doi.org/10.1111/cdev.12499

Tomasello, M. (2018). The normative turn in early moral development. *Human Development, 61*(4–5), 248–263. https://doi.org/10.1159/000492802

Tomasello, M. (2019). *Becoming human: A theory of ontogeny*. Harvard University Press.

Tomasello, M. (2020). The adaptive origins of uniquely human sociality. *Philosophical Transactions of the Royal Society B: Biological Sciences, 375*(1803), 20190493. https://doi.org/10.1098/rstb.2019.0493

Tomasello, M. (2021). *Becoming human: A theory of ontogeny*. Harvard University Press.

Tomaz, S. A., Jones, R. A., Hinkley, T., Bernstein, S. L., Twine, R., Kahn, K., Norris, S. A., & Draper, C. E. (2019). Gross motor skills of South African preschool-aged children across different income settings. *Journal of Science and Medicine in Sport, 22*(6), 689–694. https://doi.org/10.1016/j.jsams.2018.12.009

Tomova, L., Andrews, J. L., & Blakemore, S.-J. (2021). The importance of belonging and the avoidance of social risk taking in adolescence. *Developmental Review, 61,* 100981. https://doi.org/10.1016/j.dr.2021.100981

Tomporowski, P. D., & Pesce, C. (2019). Exercise, sports, and performance arts benefit cognition via a common process. *Psychological Bulletin, 145*(9), 929–951. https://doi.org/10.1037/bul0000200

Tooley, U. A., Bassett, D. S., & Mackey, A. P. (2021). Environmental influences on the pace of brain development. *Nature Reviews Neuroscience, 22*(6), 372–384. https://doi.org/10.1038/s41583-021-00457-5

Toppe, T. (2020). Social inclusion increases over early childhood and is influenced by others' group membership. *Developmental Psychology, 56*(2), 324. https://doi.org/10.1037/dev0000873

Torppa, M., Niemi, P., Vasalampi, K., Lerkkanen, M.-K., Tolvanen, A., & Poikkeus, A.-M. (2020). Leisure reading (but not any kind) and reading comprehension support each other—A longitudinal study across grades 1 and 9. *Child Development, 91*(3), 876–900. https://doi.org/10.1111/cdev.13241

Tottenham, N. (2020). Early adversity and the neotenous human brain. *Biological Psychiatry, 87*(4), 350–358. https://doi.org/10.1016/j.biopsych.2019.06.018

Tottenham, N., & Gabard-Durnam, L. J. (2017). The developing amygdala: A student of the world and a teacher of the cortex. *Current Opinion in Psychology, 17,* 55–60. https://doi.org/10.1016/j.copsyc.2017.06.012

Towner, S. L., Dolcini, M. M., & Harper, G. W. (2015). Romantic relationship dynamics of urban African American adolescents: Patterns of monogamy, commitment, and trust. *Youth & Society, 47*(3), 343–373. https://doi.org/10.1177/0044118X12462591

Tram, K. H., Saeed, S., Bradley, C., Fox, B., Eshun-Wilson, I., Mody, A., & Geng, E. (2021). Deliberation, dissent, and distrust: Understanding distinct drivers of COVID-19 vaccine hesitancy in the United States. *Clinical Infectious Diseases,* ciab633. https://doi.org/10.1093/cid/ciab633

Tran, S. P., & Raffaelli, M. (2020). Configurations of autonomy and relatedness in a multiethnic U.S. sample of parent-adolescent dyads. *Journal of Research on Adolescence: The Official Journal of the Society for Research on Adolescence, 30*(1), 203–218. https://doi.org/10.1111/jora.12517

Trang, N. H. H. D., Hong, T. K., & Dibley, M. J. (2012). Cohort profile: Ho Chi Minh City youth cohort—changes in diet, physical activity, sedentary behaviour and relationship with overweight/obesity in adolescents. *BMJ Open, 2*(1), e000362.

Trautner, E., McCool-Myers, M., & Joyner, A. B. (2020). Knowledge and practice of induction of lactation in trans women among professionals working in trans health. *International Breastfeeding Journal, 15*(1), 63. https://doi.org/10.1186/s13006-020-00308-6

Trent, M., Dooley, D. G., Douge, J., Section on Adolescent Health, Council on Community Pediatrics, & Committee on Adolescence. (2019). The impact of racism on child and adolescent health. *Pediatrics, 144*(2), e20191765. https://doi.org/10.1542/peds.2019-1765

Trikamjee, T., Comberiati, P., & Peter, J. (2022). Pediatric asthma in developing countries: Challenges and future directions. *Current Opinion in Allergy and Clinical Immunology, 22*(2), 80–85. https://doi.org/10.1097/ACI.0000000000000806

Trinidad, J. E. (2019). Understanding when parental aspirations negatively affect student outcomes: The case of aspiration-expectation inconsistency. *Studies in Educational Evaluation, 60,* 179–188. https://doi.org/10.1016/j.stueduc.2019.01.004

Troller-Renfree, S. V., Brito, N. H., Desai, P. M., Leon-Santos, A. G., Wiltshire, C. A., Motton, S. N., Meyer, J. S., Isler, J., Fifer, W. P., & Noble, K. G. (2020). Infants of mothers with higher physiological stress show alterations in brain function. *Developmental Science, 23*(6), e12976. https://doi.org/10.1111/desc.12976

Troller-Renfree, S. V., Costanzo, M. A., Duncan, G. J., Magnuson, K., Gennetian, L. A., Yoshikawa, H., . . . & Noble, K. G. (2022). The impact of a poverty reduction intervention on infant brain activity. *Proceedings of the National Academy of Sciences, 119*(5).

Troller-Renfree, S. V., Morales, S., Leach, S. C., Bowers, M. E., Debnath, R., Fifer, W. P., . . . & Noble, K. G. (2021). Feasibility of assessing brain activity using mobile, in-home collection of electroencephalography: methods and analysis. *Developmental Psychobiology, 63*(6), e22128.

Tronick, E., Als, H., Adamson, L., Wise, S., & Brazelton, T. B. (1978). The infant's response to entrapment between contradictory messages in face-to-face interaction. *Journal of the American Academy of Child Psychiatry, 17*(1), 1–13.

Tronick, E., & Snidman, N. (2021). Children's reaction to mothers wearing or not wearing a mask during face-to-face interactions. *Social Science Research Network,* 3899140. https://doi.org/10.2139/ssrn.3899140

Trostel, P. A. (2015). *It's not just the money: The benefits of college education to individuals and to society.* Lumina Foundation.

Troude, P., Santin, G., Guibert, J., Bouyer, J., & de La Rochebrochard, E. (2016). Seven out of 10 couples treated by IVF achieve parenthood following either treatment, natural conception or adoption. *Reproductive BioMedicine Online, 33*(5), 560–567. https://doi.org/10.1016/j.rbmo.2016.08.010

Troxel, W., & Wolfson, A. (2016). Sleep science and policy: A focus on school start times. *Sleep Health, 2*(3), 186. https://doi.org/10.1016/j.sleh.2016.07.001

Troyansky, D. G. (2015). *Aging in world history.* Routledge.

Tsai, J. L., Louie, J. Y., Chen, E. E., & Uchida, Y. (2007). Learning what feelings to desire: Socialization of ideal affect through children's storybooks. *Personality and Social Psychology Bulletin, 33*(1), 17–30.

Tsai, J., Becker, D., Sussman, S., Bluthenthal, R., Unger, J. B., & Schwartz, S. J. (2017). Acculturation and risky sexual behavior among adolescents and emerging adults from immigrant families. In S. J. Schwartz & J. Unger (Eds.), *The Oxford handbook of acculturation and health* (p. 301). Oxford University Press.

Tsimicalis, A., Genest, L., Stevens, B., Ungar, W. J., & Barr, R. (2018). The impact of a childhood cancer diagnosis on the children and siblings' school attendance, performance, and activities: A qualitative descriptive study. *Journal of Pediatric Oncology Nursing, 35*(2), 118–131.

Tucker-Drob, E. M. (2017). How do individual experiences aggregate to shape personality development. *European Journal of Personality, 31*(5), 570–571.

Tudor-Locke, C., Craig, C. L., Beets, M. W., Belton, S., Cardon, G. M., Duncan, S., Hatano, Y., Lubans, D. R., Olds, T. S., Raustorp, A., Rowe, D. A., Spence, J. C., Tanaka, S., & Blair, S. N. (2011a). How many steps/day are enough? For children and adolescents. *International Journal of Behavioral Nutrition and Physical Activity, 8*(1), 78. https://doi.org/10.1186/1479-5868-8-78

Tudor-Locke, C., Craig, C. L., Brown, W. J., Clemes, S. A., De Cocker, K., Giles-Corti, B., Hatano, Y., Inoue, S., Matsudo, S. M., Mutrie, N., Oppert, J-M., Rowe, D. A., Schmidt, M. D., Schofield, G. M., Spence, J. C., Teixeira, P. J., Tully, M. A., & Blair, S. N. (2011b). How many steps/day are enough? For adults. *International Journal of Behavioral Nutrition and Physical Activity, 8*(1), 1–17.

Tulchin-Francis, K., Stevens, W., Gu, X., Zhang, T., Roberts, H., Keller, J., Dempsey, D., Borchard, J., Jeans, K., & VanPelt, J. (2021). The impact of the coronavirus disease 2019 pandemic on physical activity in U.S. children. *Journal of Sport and Health Science, 10*(3), 323–332. https://doi.org/10.1016/j.jshs.2021.02.005

Tunmer, W. E., & Herriman, M. L. (1984). The development of metalinguistic awareness: A conceptual overview. *Metalinguistic Awareness in Children,* 12–35.

Turban, J. L., King, D., Carswell, J. M., & Keuroghlian, A. S. (2020). Pubertal suppression for transgender youth and risk of suicidal ideation. *Pediatrics, 145*(2), e20191725. https://doi.org/10.1542/peds.2019-1725

Turiel, E. (1983). *The development of social knowledge: Morality and convention.* Cambridge University Press.

Turiel, E., & Dahl, A. (2019). The development of domains of moral and conventional norms, coordination in decision-making, and the implications of social opposition. In N. Roughley & K. Bayertz (Eds.), *The normative animal? On the anthropological significance of social, moral, and linguistic norms* (pp. 195–213). Oxford University Press.

Turkheimer, E., Pettersson, E., & Horn, E. E. (2014). A phenotypic null hypothesis for the genetics of personality. *Annual Review of Psychology, 65*(1), 515–540. https://doi.org/10.1146/annurev-psych-113011-143752

Turley, P., Meyer, M. N., Wang, N., Cesarini, D., Hammonds, E., Martin, A. R., Neale, B. M., Rehm, H. L., Wilkins-Haug, L., Benjamin, D. J., Hyman, S., Laibson, D., & Visscher, P. M. (2021). Problems with using polygenic scores to select embryos. *New England Journal of Medicine, 385*(1), 78–86. https://doi.org/10.1056/NEJMsr2105065

Turner, P. L., & Mainster, M. A. (2008). Circadian photoreception: Ageing and the eye's important role in systemic health. *British Journal of Ophthalmology 92*(11), 1439–1444.

Turnwald, B. P., Goyer, J. P., Boles, D. Z., Silder, A., Delp, S. L., & Crum, A. J. (2019). Learning one's genetic risk changes physiology independent of actual genetic risk. *Nature Human Behaviour, 3*(1), 48–56. https://doi.org/10.1038/s41562-018-0483-4

Turoman, N., Tivadar, R. I., Retsa, C., Maillard, A. M., Scerif, G., & Matusz, P. J. (2021). The development of attentional control mechanisms in multisensory environments. *Developmental Cognitive Neuroscience, 48,* 100930. https://doi.org/10.1016/j.dcn.2021.100930

Tutty, L. M., Aubry, D., & Velasquez, L. (2020). The "Who Do You Tell?" TM Child sexual abuse education program: Eight years of monitoring. *Journal of Child Sexual Abuse, 29*(1), 2–21. https://doi.org/10.1080/10538712.2019.1663969

Twenge, J. M. (2017, September). Have smartphones destroyed a generation? *The Atlantic.* https://www.theatlantic.com/magazine/archive/2017/09/has-the-smartphone-destroyed-a-generation/534198/

Twenge, J. M. (2019). More time on technology, less happiness? Associations between digital-media use and psychological well-being. *Current Directions in Psychological Science, 28*(4), 372–379. https://doi.org/10.1177/0963721419838244

Twenge, J. M. (2020). Why increases in adolescent depression may be linked to the technological environment. *Current Opinion in Psychology, 32*, 89–94. https://doi.org/10.1016/j.copsyc.2019.06.036

Twenge, J. M., & Campbell, W. K. (2018). Associations between screen time and lower psychological well-being among children and adolescents: Evidence from a population-based study. Preventive Medicine Reports, 12, 271–283. https://doi.org/10.1016/j.pmedr.2018.10.003

Twenge, J. M., Joiner, T. E., Rogers, M. L., & Martin, G. N. (2018a). Increases in depressive symptoms, suicide-related outcomes, and suicide rates among U.S. adolescents after 2010 and links to increased new media screen time. *Clinical Psychological Science, 6*(1), 3–17. https://doi.org/10.1177/2167702617723376

Twenge, J. M., Martin, G. N., & Campbell, W. K. (2018b). Decreases in psychological well-being among American adolescents after 2012 and links to screen time during the rise of smartphone technology. *Emotion, 18*(6), 765–780. https://doi.org/10.1037/emo0000403

Twig, G., Reichman, B., Afek, A., Derazne, E., Hamiel, U., Furer, A., Gershovitz, L., Bader, T., Cukierman-Yaffe, T., Kark, J. D., & Pinhas-Hamiel, O. (2019). Severe obesity and cardio-metabolic comorbidities: A nationwide study of 2.8 million adolescents. *International Journal of Obesity, 43*(7), 1391–1399. https://doi.org/10.1038/s41366-018-0213-z

U.S. Bureau of Labor Statistics. (2021). *College enrollment and work activity of recent high school and college graduates summary* (USDL-21-0721). https://www.bls.gov/news.release/hsgec.nr0.htm

U.S. Bureau of Labor Statistics. (2021). *Employment and unemployment among youth — Summer 2021* (USDL-21-1515).

U.S. Bureau of Labor Statistics. (2021b). *Labor Force Statistics from the Current Population Survey. Household Data Annual Averages. 11b. Employed persons by detailed occupation and age.*

U.S. Bureau of Labor Statistics. (2022). Labor force participation rate — 16–19 yrs [LNS11300012]. FRED, Federal Reserve Bank of St. Louis. https://fred.stlouisfed.org/series/LNS11300012

U.S. Census Bureau. (2020). *America's families and living arrangements: 2020.* https://www.census.gov/data/tables/2020/demo/families/cps-2020.html

U.S. Census Bureau. (2021). *U.S. Census Bureau, Current Population Survey, 2021 Annual Social and Economic Supplement (CPS ASEC (POV34: Single Year of Age — Poverty Status: 2020 Below 100% of Poverty).* U.S. Census Bureau.

U.S. Census Bureau, American Community Survey. (2015). *Detailed languages spoken at home and ability to speak English.* https://www.census.gov/data/tables/2013/demo/2009-2013-lang-tables.html

U.S. Census Bureau, Current Population Survey. (2020). 2020 Annual Social and Economic Supplement, Ages 18–29. Internet Release Date: December 2020.

U.S. Census Bureau, Current Population Survey. (2021, March). Annual Social and Economic Supplements. Accessed October 24, 2021.

U.S. Department of Education. (2016). National Center for Education Statistics, Parent and Family Involvement in Education Survey of the National Household Education Surveys Program (NHES).

U.S. Department of Education. (2019a). *High school transcript study.* U.S. Department of Education, Institute of Education Sciences, National Center for Education Statistics, National Assessment of Educational Progress (NAEP).

U.S. Department of Education. (2019b). Institute of Education Sciences, National Center for Education Statistics, National Assessment of Educational Progress (NAEP), 2019 Reading Assessment. Mathematics Assessment. https://www.nationsreportcard.gov/highlights/mathematics/2019/ https://www.nationsreportcard.gov/reading/nation/achievement/?grade=4

U.S. Department of Education. (2020a). *Results from the 2019 Mathematics and Reading Assessments at Grade 12* [The Nation's Report Card]. U.S. Department of Education.

U.S. Department of Education, National Center for Education Statistics, Integrated Postsecondary Education Data System (IPEDS). (2019–2020, Winter). Graduation rates component. In *Digest of education statistics 2020* (table 326.10).

U.S. Department of Education, Office for Civil Rights. Civil Rights Data Collection, 2017–18, available at http://ocrdata.ed.gov.

U.S. Department of Education, Office of Special Education Programs. (2020b, February). National Center for Education Statistics, Statistics of Public Elementary and Secondary School Systems, 1977–78 and 1980–81; Common Core of Data (CCD), "State non-fiscal survey of public elementary/secondary education," 1990–91 through 2018–19; and National Elementary and Secondary Enrollment Projection Model, 1972 through 2029. In *Annual report to Congress on the implementation of the Individuals with Disabilities Education Act, selected years, 1979 through 2006; and Individuals with Disabilities Education Act (IDEA) database.* https://www2.ed.gov/programs/osepidea/618-data/state-level-data-files/index.html#bcc

U.S. Department of Health and Human Services (USDHHS). (2018). *Physical activity guidelines for Americans* (2nd ed.).

U.S. Department of Health and Human Services (USDHHS), Administration for Health and Families, Administration on Children, Youth and Families, Children's Bureau. (2020). *The AFCARS report: Adoption and foster care analysis and reporting system FY 2019 data (as of June 23, 2020; No. 27).* Children's Bureau.

U.S. Department of Health and Human Services (USDHHS). (2021a). *Child maltreatment 2019.* Administration for Children and Families, Administration on Children, Youth and Families, Children's Bureau. https://www.acf.hhs.gov/cb/research-data-technology/statistics-research/child-maltreatment

U.S. Department of Health and Human Services (USDHHS), Centers for Disease Control and Prevention (CDC), National Center for Health Statistics (NCHS), Division of Vital Statistics. (2021). *Natality public-use data 2016–2019.* CDC WONDER.

U.S. Department of Justice. *Juvenile Arrests, 2019* (Juvenile Justice Statistics: National Report Series Bulletin).

Uccelli, P., Demir-Lira, Ö. E., Rowe, M. L., Levine, S., & Goldin-Meadow, S. (2019). Children's early decontextualized talk predicts academic language proficiency in midadolescence. *Child Development, 90*(5), 1650–1663.

Uecker, J. (2014). Religion and early marriage in the United States: Evidence from the add health study. *Journal for the Scientific Study of Religion, 53*(2), 392–415. https://doi.org/10.1111/jssr.12114

Ullah, F., & Kaelber, D. C. (2021). Using large aggregated de-identified electronic health record data to determine the prevalence of common chronic diseases in pediatric patients who visited primary care clinics. *Academic pediatrics, 21*(6), 1084–1093.

Ullmann, H., Weeks, J. D., & Madans, J. H. (2021). Children living in households that experienced food insecurity: United States, 2019–2020. *NCHS Data Brief, no 432.* National Center for Health Statistics. https://doi.org/10.15620/cdc:113966external icon.

Umaña-Taylor, A. J. (2016). A post-racial society in which ethnic-racial discrimination still exists and has significant consequences for youths' adjustment. *Current Directions in Psychological Science, 25*(2), 111–118. https://doi.org/10.1177/0963721415627858

Umaña-Taylor, A. J., & Hill, N. E. (2020). Ethnic–racial socialization in the family: A decade's advance on precursors and outcomes. *Journal of Marriage and Family, 82*(1), 244–271. https://doi.org/10.1111/jomf.12622

Umaña-Taylor, A. J., Wong, J. J., Gonzales, N. A., & Dumka, L. E. (2012). Ethnic identity and gender as moderators of the association between discrimination and academic adjustment among Mexican-origin adolescents. *Journal of Adolescence, 35*(4), 773–786.

Underwood, J. M., Brener, N., Thornton, J., Harris, W. A., Bryan, L. N., Shanklin, S. L., Deputy, N., Roberts, A. M., Queen, B., Chyen, D., Whittle, L., Lim, C., Yamakawa, Y., Leon-Nguyen, M., Kilmer, G., Smith-Grant, J., Demissie, Z., Jones, S. E., Clayton, H., & Dittus, P. (2020). Overview and methods for the youth risk behavior surveillance system — United States, 2019. *Morbidity and Mortality Weekly Report Supplements, 69*, 1–10. https://doi.org/10.15585/mmwr.su6901a1

UNESCO. (2020). *School enrollment, tertiary (% gross) | Data.* UNESCO Institute of Statistics. https://data.worldbank.org/indicator/SE.TER.ENRR

UNESCO. (2022). *Reimagining our futures together: A new social contract for education.* United Nations.

UNICEF. (2017). *A familiar face: Violence in the lives of children and adolescents.* United Nation's Children's Fund. https://data.unicef.org/resources/a-familiar-face

UNICEF. (2019). *Healthy mothers, healthy babies: Taking stock of maternal health.* UNICEF. https://data.unicef.org/resources/healthy-mothers-healthy-babies/

UNICEF. (2020). *Child protection advocacy briefing: Violence against children* [Advocacy brief].

UNICEF. (2021a). *Data warehouse, global databases, 2021, based on MICS, DHS and other nationally representative household survey data.* https://data.unicef.org/resources/data_explorer/unicef_f/?ag=UNICEF&df=GLOBAL_DATAFLOW&ver=1.0&dq=.MNCH_ANC1+MNCH_ANC4..&startPeriod=2016&endPeriod=2021

UNICEF. (2021b). *The State of the World's Children 2021: On My Mind: Promoting, Protecting and Caring for Children's Mental Health.* UNICEF.

UNICEF. (2021c). *Under-five mortality.* https://data.unicef.org/topic/child-survival/under-five-mortality/

UNICEF. (2022a). *Covid-19 scale of education loss "nearly insurmountable," warns UNICEF: Media Factsheet.* UNICEF.

UNICEF. (2022b, July). *HIV Statistics — Global and Regional Trends.* UNICEF DATA. https://data.unicef.org/topic/hivaids/global-regional-trends/

UNICEF. (2022c). *Primary education.* https://www.unicef.org/education/primary-education

UNICEF & Pure Earth. (2020). *The toxic truth: Children's exposure to lead pollution undermines a generation of future potential* (2nd Ed.). UNICEF

United Nations Convention on the Rights of Persons with Disabilities. (2006, December 13). https://www.ohchr.org/en/hrbodies/crpd/pages/conventionrightspersonswithdisabilities.aspx

United Nations Educational, Scientific and Cultural Organization (UNESCO). (2018). *International technical guidance on sexuality education: An evidence-informed approach.* https://www.unfpa.org/publications/international-technical-guidance-sexuality-education

United Nations Environment Program (UNEP). (2020). *Update on the global status of legal limits on lead in paint.* United Nations, World Bank and the Global Alliance to Eliminate Lead Paint.

United Nations Inter-agency Group for Child Mortality Estimation (UN IGME). (2020). *Levels & trends in child mortality: Report 2020.* United Nations Children's Fund.

United Nations Inter-agency Group for Child Mortality Estimation (UN IGME). (2021). *Levels & trends in child mortality: Report 2021.* UN Inter-agency Group for Child Mortality Estimation (UN IGME).

United Nations, Department of Economic and Social Affairs. (2016). *Youth civic engagement* (UN World Youth Report). United Nations.

Unsworth, S. (2016). Quantity and quality of language input in bilingual language development. In E. Nicoladis & S. Montanari (Eds.), *Bilingualism across the lifespan: Factors moderating language proficiency* (pp. 103–121). American Psychological Association.

Uretsky, M. (2021, August 25). *Photo of you as teen for textbook?* [Personal communication].

Urrila, A. S., Artiges, E., Massicotte, J., Miranda, R., Vulser, H., Bezivin-Frere, P., Lapidaire, W., Lemaitre, H., Penttila, J., Conrod, P. J., Garavan, H., Paillere Martinot, M.-L., & Martinot, J.-L. (2017). Sleep habits, academic performance, and the adolescent brain structure. *Scientific Reports, 7*(1), 41678. https://doi.org/10.1038/srep41678

Ustun, B., Reissland, N., Covey, J., Schaal, B., & Blisset, J. (2022). Flavour sensing in utero and emerging discriminative behaviours in the human fetus. *Psychological Science.*

Vadgama, N., Pittman, A., Simpson, M., Nirmalananthan, N., Murray, R., Yoshikawa, T., De Rijk, P., Rees, E., Kirov, G., Hughes, D., Fitzgerald, T., Kristiansen, M., Pearce, K., Cerveira, E., Zhu, Q., Zhang, C., Lee, C., Hardy, J., & Nasir, J. (2019). De novo single-nucleotide and copy number variation in discordant monozygotic twins reveals disease-related genes. *European Journal of Human Genetics, 27*(7), 1121–1133. https://doi.org/10.1038/s41431-019-0376-7

Vagos, P., da Silva, D. R., & Macedo, S. (2021). The impact of attachment to parents and peers on the psychopathic traits of adolescents: A short longitudinal study. *European Journal of Developmental Psychology*, 1–16. https://doi.org/10.1080/17405629.2021.1890020

Vaish, A., & Hepach, R. (2020). The development of prosocial emotions. *Emotion Review, 12*(4), 259–273.

Vaivada, T., Akseer, N., Akseer, S., Somaskandan, A., Stefopulos, M., & Bhutta, Z. A. (2020). Stunting in childhood: An overview of global burden, trends, determinants, and drivers of decline. *The American Journal of Clinical Nutrition, 112*(Supplement_2), 777S–791S. https://doi.org/10.1093/ajcn/nqaa159

Valentine, C. J. (2020). Nutrition and the developing brain. *Pediatric Research, 87*(2), 190–191. https://doi.org/10.1038/s41390-019-0650-y

Valkenborghs, S. R., Noetel, M., Hillman, C. H., Nilsson, M., Smith, J. J., Ortega, F. B., & Lubans, D. R. (2019). The impact of physical activity on brain structure and function in youth: A systematic review. *Pediatrics, 144*(4), e20184032. https://doi.org/10.1542/peds.2018-4032

Vally, Z., Murray, L., Tomlinson, M., & Cooper, P. J. (2015). The impact of dialogic book-sharing training on infant language and attention: A randomized controlled trial in a deprived South African community. *Journal of Child Psychology and Psychiatry, 56*(8), 865–873.

Van Aggelpoel, T., Vermandel, A., Fraeyman, J., Massart, M., & Hal, G. V. (2019). Information as a crucial factor for toilet training by parents. *Child: Care, Health and Development, 45*(3), 457–462. https://doi.org/10.1111/cch.12653

van Beeck, A. E., Zomer, T. P., van Beeck, E. F., Richardus, J. H., Voeten, H. A., & Erasmus, V. (2016). Children's hand hygiene behaviour and available facilities: An observational study in Dutch day care centres. *The European Journal of Public Health, 26*(2), 297–300.

van Bergen, D. D., Wilson, B. D. M., Russell, S. T., Gordon, A. G., & Rothblum, E. D. (2021). Parental responses to coming out by lesbian, gay, bisexual, queer, pansexual, or two-spirited people across three age cohorts. *Journal of Marriage and Family, 83*(4), 1116–1133. https://doi.org/10.1111/jomf.12731

van Berkel, N., Goncalves, J., Lovén, L., Ferreira, D., Hosio, S., & Kostakos, V. (2019). Effect of experience sampling schedules on response rate and recall accuracy of objective self-reports. *International Journal of Human-Computer Studies, 125*, 118–128. https://doi.org/10.1016/j.ijhcs.2018.12.002

van de Bongardt, D., Yu, R., Deković, M., & Meeus, W. H. J. (2015). Romantic relationships and sexuality in adolescence and young adulthood: The role of parents, peers, and partners. *European Journal of Developmental Psychology, 12*(5), 497–515. https://doi.org/10.1080/17405629.2015.1068689

van den Berg, L., & Verbakel, E. (2021). Trends in singlehood in young adulthood in Europe. *Advances in Life Course Research*, 100449. https://doi.org/10.1016/j.alcr.2021.100449

van den Berg, V., Saliasi, E., de Groot, R. H., Chinapaw, M. J., & Singh, A. S. (2019a). Improving cognitive performance of 9–12 years old children: Just dance? A randomized controlled trial. *Frontiers in Psychology, 10*, 174.

van den Berg, V., Singh, A. S., Komen, A., Hazelebach, C., van Hilvoorde, I., & Chinapaw, M. J. M. (2019b). Integrating juggling with math lessons: A randomized controlled trial assessing effects of physically active learning on maths performance and enjoyment in primary school children. *International Journal of Environmental Research and Public Health, 16*(14), 2452. https://doi.org/10.3390/ijerph16142452

van den Berg, Y. H., Deutz, M. H., Smeekens, S., & Cillessen, A. H. (2017). Developmental pathways to preference and popularity in middle childhood. *Child Development, 88*(5), 1629–1641.

Van den Bergh, B. R., Dahnke, R., & Mennes, M. (2018). Prenatal stress and the developing brain: Risks for neurodevelopmental disorders. *Development and Psychopathology, 30*(3), 743–762. https://doi.org/10.1017/S0954579418000342

Van den Bergh, B. R. H., van den Heuvel, M. I., Lahti, M., Braeken, M., de Rooij, S. R., Entringer, S., Hoyer, D., Roseboom, T., Räikkönen, K., King, S., & Schwab, M. (2020). Prenatal developmental origins of behavior and mental health: The influence of maternal stress in pregnancy. *Neuroscience & Biobehavioral Reviews, 117*, 26–64. https://doi.org/10.1016/j.neubiorev.2017.07.003

van den Noort, M., Struys, E., Bosch, P., Jaswetz, L., Perriard, B., Yeo, S., Barisch, P., Vermeire, K., Lee, S.-H., & Lim, S. (2019). Does the bilingual advantage in cognitive control exist and if so, what are its modulating factors? A systematic review. *Behavioral Sciences, 9*(3), 27. https://doi.org/10.3390/bs9030027

van der Aalsvoort, G., & Broadhead, P. (2016). Working across disciplines to understand playful learning in educational settings. *Childhood Education, 92*(6), 483–493.

van der Doef, S., & Reinders, J. (2018). Stepwise sexual development of adolescents: The Dutch approach to sexuality education. *Nature Reviews Urology, 15*(3), 133–134. https://doi.org/10.1038/nrurol.2018.3

Van der Fels, I. M., Te Wierike, S. C., Hartman, E., Elferink-Gemser, M. T., Smith, J., & Visscher, C. (2015). The relationship between motor skills and cognitive skills in 4–16 year old typically developing children: A systematic review. *Journal of Science and Medicine in Sport, 18*(6), 697–703.

van der Horst, F. C. P., & van der Veer, R. (2010). The ontogeny of an idea: John Bowlby and contemporaries on mother–child separation. *History of Psychology, 13*(1), 25–45. https://doi.org/10.1037/a0017660

Van Der Horst, P. W. (1987). *Chaeremon, Egyptian priest and stoic philosopher: The fragments* (Vol. 101). Brill.

van der Ploeg, R., Steglich, C., & Veenstra, R. (2020). The way bullying works: How new ties facilitate the mutual reinforcement of status and bullying in elementary schools. *Social Networks, 60*, 71–82.

van der Wilt, F., van der Veen, C., van Kruistum, C., & van Oers, B. (2019). Why do children become rejected by their peers? A review of studies into the relationship between oral communicative competence and sociometric status in childhood. *Educational Psychology Review, 31*(3), 699–724.

van Dijk, R., van der Valk, I. E., Deković, M., & Branje, S. (2020). A meta-analysis on interparental conflict, parenting, and child adjustment in divorced families: Examining mediation using meta-analytic structural equation models. *Clinical Psychology Review, 79*, 101861. https://doi.org/10.1016/j.cpr.2020.101861

van Doeselaar, L., Klimstra, T. A., Denissen, J. J., Branje, S., & Meeus, W. (2018). The role of identity commitments in depressive symptoms and stressful life events in adolescence and young adulthood. *Developmental Psychology, 54*(5), 950.

Van Doorn, M. D., Branje, S. J. T., VanderValk, I. E., De Goede, I. H. A., & Meeus, W. H. J. (2011). Longitudinal spillover effects of conflict resolution styles between adolescent-parent relationships and adolescent friendships. *Journal of Family Psychology, 25*(1), 157–161. https://doi.org/10.1037/a0022289

van Gelder, S. (2017, May 24). For new native mothers, a place for culture and comfort. *Yes! Magazine.*

Van Goethem, A., Van Hoof, A., Orobio de Castro, B., Van Aken, M., & Hart, D. (2014). The role of reflection in the effects of community service on adolescent development: A meta-analysis. *Child development, 85*(6), 2114–2130.

Van Hecke, L., Loyen, A., Verloigne, M., van der Ploeg, H. P., Lakerveld, J., Brug, J., De Bourdeaudhuij, I., Ekelund, U., Donnelly, A., Hendriksen, I., & Deforche, B. on Behalf of the DEDIPAC Consortium (2016). Variation in population levels of physical activity in European children and adolescents according to cross-European studies: A systematic literature review within DEDIPAC. *International Journal of Behavioral Nutrition and Physical Activity, 13*(1), 70–91.

van Hoorn, J., Shablack, H., Lindquist, K. A., & Telzer, E. H. (2019). Incorporating the social context into neurocognitive models of adolescent decision-making: A neuroimaging meta-analysis. *Neuroscience & Biobehavioral Reviews, 101*, 129–142. https://doi.org/10.1016/j.neubiorev.2018.12.024

van Hoorn, J., van Dijk, E., Meuwese, R., Rieffe, C., & Crone, E. A. (2016). Peer influence on prosocial behavior in adolescence. *Journal of Research on Adolescence, 26*(1), 90–100. https://doi.org/10.1111/jora.12173

Van Hulle, C. A., Moore, M. N., Lemery-Chalfant, K., Goldsmith, H. H., & Brooker, R. J. (2017). Infant stranger fear trajectories predict anxious behaviors and diurnal cortisol rhythm during childhood. *Development and Psychopathology, 29*(3), 1119–1130. https://doi.org/10.1017/S0954579417000311

van IJzendoorn, M. H., & Bakermans-Kranenburg, M. J. (2021). Integrating temperament and attachment: The differential susceptibility paradigm. In *Attachment theory and research*. Wiley.

van IJzendoorn, M. H., Bakermans-Kranenburg, M. J., Coughlan, B., & Reijman, S. (2020). Annual research review: Umbrella synthesis of meta-analyses on child maltreatment antecedents and interventions: Differential susceptibility perspective on risk and resilience. *Journal of Child Psychology and Psychiatry, 61*(3), 272–290. https://doi.org/10.1111/jcpp.13147

van IJzendoorn, M. H., Bakermans-Kranenburg, M. J., & Juffer, F. (2007). Plasticity of growth in height, weight, and head circumference: Meta-analytic evidence of massive catch-up after international adoption. *Journal of Developmental and Behavioral Pediatrics: JDBP, 28*(4), 334–343. https://doi.org/10.1097/DBP.0b013e31811320aa

van Raalte, A. A., Sasson, I., & Martikainen, P. (2018). The case for monitoring life-span inequality. *Science, 362*(6418), 1002–1004. https://doi.org/10.1126/science.aau5811

van Rosmalen, L., van der Horst, F. C. P., & van der Veer, R. (2016). From secure dependency to attachment: Mary Ainsworth's integration of Blatz's security theory into Bowlby's attachment theory. *History of Psychology, 19*(1), 22–39.

van Rosmalen, L., van der Veer, R., & van der Horst, F. (2015). Ainsworth's strange situation procedure: The origin of an instrument. *Journal of the History of the Behavioral Sciences, 51*(3), 261–284. https://doi.org/10.1002/jhbs.21729

Van Speybroeck, L. (2002). From epigenesis to epigenetics: The case of CH Waddington. *Annals of the New York Academy of Sciences, 981*(1), 61–81.

Vandell, D. L., Simpkins, S. D., & Wegemer, C. M. (2019). Parenting and children's organized activities. In M. H. Bornstein (Ed.), *Handbook of parenting* (pp. 347–379). Routledge.

Vandenbosch, L., Fardouly, J., & Tiggemann, M. (2022). Social media and body image: Recent trends and future directions. *Current Opinion in Psychology, 45*, 101289. https://doi.org/10.1016/j.copsyc.2021.12.002

Vanderminden, J., Hamby, S., David-Ferdon, C., Kacha-Ochana, A., Merrick, M., Simon, T. R., ... &

Turner, H. (2019). Rates of neglect in a national sample: Child and family characteristics and psychological impact. *Child abuse & neglect, 88*, 256–265.

Vanderwall, C., Eickhoff, J., Randall Clark, R., & Carrel, A. L. (2018). BMI z-score in obese children is a poor predictor of adiposity changes over time. *BMC Pediatrics, 18*(1), 187. https://doi.org/10.1186/s12887-018-1160-5

Vanes, L. D., Moutoussis, M., Ziegler, G., Goodyer, I. M., Fonagy, P., Jones, P. B., Bullmore, E. T., & Dolan, R. J. (2020). White matter tract myelin maturation and its association with general psychopathology in adolescence and early adulthood. *Human Brain Mapping, 41*(3), 827–839. https://doi.org/10.1002/hbm.24842

VanTieghem, M., Korom, M., Flannery, J., Choy, T., Caldera, C., Humphreys, K. L., Gabard-Durnam, L., Goff, B., Gee, D. G., Telzer, E. H., Shapiro, M., Louie, J. Y., Fareri, D. S., Bolger, N., & Tottenham, N. (2021). Longitudinal changes in amygdala, hippocampus and cortisol development following early caregiving adversity. *Developmental Cognitive Neuroscience, 48*, 100916. https://doi.org/10.1016/j.dcn.2021.100916

Vargas, C. M., Stines, E. M., & Granado, H. S. (2017). Health-equity issues related to childhood obesity: A scoping review. *Journal of Public Health Dentistry, 77*(S1), S32–S42. https://doi.org/10.1111/jphd.12233

Váša, F., Romero-Garcia, R., Kitzbichler, M. G., Seidlitz, J., Whitaker, K. J., Vaghi, M. M., Kundu, P., Patel, A. X., Fonagy, P., Dolan, R. J., Jones, P. B., Goodyer, I. M., the NSPN Consortium, Vértes, P. E., & Bullmore, E. T. (2020). Conservative and disruptive modes of adolescent change in human brain functional connectivity. *Proceedings of the National Academy of Sciences, 117*(6), 3248–3253. https://doi.org/10.1073/pnas.1906144117

Vasilenko, S. A., & Espinosa-Hernández, G. (2019). Multidimensional profiles of religiosity among adolescents: Associations with sexual behaviors and romantic relationships. *Journal of Research on Adolescence, 29*(2), 414–428. https://doi.org/10.1111/jora.12444

Vasilenko, S. A., Kreager, D. A., & Lefkowitz, E. S. (2015). Gender, contraceptive attitudes, and condom use in adolescent romantic relationships: A dyadic approach. *Journal of Research on Adolescence, 25*(1), 51–62.

Vasilenko, S. A., Kugler, K. C., & Rice, C. E. (2016). Timing of first sexual intercourse and young adult health outcomes. *The Journal of Adolescent Health, 59*(3), 291–297. https://doi.org/10.1016/j.jadohealth.2016.04.019

Vasilenko, S. A., Lefkowitz, E. S., & Welsh, D. P. (2014). Is sexual behavior healthy for adolescents? A conceptual framework for research on adolescent sexual behavior and physical, mental, and social health. *New Directions for Child and Adolescent Development, 2014*(144), 3–19.

Vasileva, M., Graf, R. K., Reinelt, T., Petermann, U., & Petermann, F. (2021). Research review: A meta-analysis of the international prevalence and comorbidity of mental disorders in children between 1 and 7 years. *Journal of Child Psychology and Psychiatry, 62*(4), 372–381.

Vasung, L., Abaci Turk, E., Ferradal, S. L., Sutin, J., Stout, J. N., Ahtam, B., Lin, P.-Y., & Ellen Grant, P. (2019). Exploring early human brain development with structural and physiological neuroimaging. *NeuroImage, 187*, 226–254. https://doi.org/10.1016/j.neuroimage.2018.07.041

Vaziri Flais, S., & American Academy of Pediatrics. (2018). *Caring for your school-age child: Ages 5 to 12* (3rd ed.). Penguin. https://www.penguinrandomhouse.com/books/162244/caring-for-your-school-age-child-3rd-edition-by-american-academy-of-pediatrics-shelly-vaziri-flais-md-faap-editor-in-chief/9780425286043

Vedam, S., Stoll, K., Taiwo, T. K., Rubashkin, N., Cheyney, M., Strauss, N., McLemore, M., Cadena, M., Nethery, E., Rushton, E., Schummers, L., Declercq, E., & the GVtM-US Steering Council. (2019). The Giving Voice to Mothers study: Inequity and mistreatment during pregnancy and childbirth in the United States. *Reproductive Health, 16*(1), 77. https://doi.org/10.1186/s12978-019-0729-2

Veldman, S. L. C., Jones, R. A., Santos, R., Sousa-Sá, E., & Okely, A. D. (2018). Gross motor skills in toddlers: Prevalence and socio-demographic differences. *Journal of Science and Medicine in Sport, 21*(12), 1226–1231. https://doi.org/10.1016/j.jsams.2018.05.001

Velez, G., & Spencer, M. B. (2018). Phenomenology and intersectionality: Using PVEST as a frame for adolescent identity formation amid intersecting ecological systems of inequality. *New Directions for Child and Adolescent Development, 2018*(161), 75–90.

Velez-Agosto, N. M., Soto-Crespo, J. G., Vizcarrondo-Oppenheimer, M., Vega-Molina, S., & Garcia Coll, C. (2017). Bronfenbrenner's bioecological theory revision: Moving culture from the macro into the micro. *Perspectives on Psychological Science, 12*(5), 900–910. https://doi.org/10.1177/1745691617704397

Veliz, P., McCabe, S. E., Eckner, J. T., & Schulenberg, J. E. (2021). Trends in the prevalence of concussion reported by US adolescents, 2016–2020. *JAMA, 325*(17), 1789–1791. https://doi.org/10.1001/jama.2021.1538

Veliz, P., Snyder, M., & Sabo, D. (2019). *The state of high school sports in America: An evaluation of the nation's most popular extracurricular activity*. Women's Sports Foundation.

Venkatesh, S. A. (2006). *Off the books*. Harvard University Press.

Ventura, A. K., Levy, J., & Sheeper, S. (2019). Maternal digital media use during infant feeding and the quality of feeding interactions. *Appetite, 143*, 104415. https://doi.org/10.1016/j.appet.2019.104415

Verbeek, M., van de Bongardt, D., Reitz, E., & Deković, M. (2020). A warm nest or 'the talk'? Exploring and explaining relations between general and sexuality-specific parenting and adolescent sexual emotions. *Journal of Adolescent Health, 66*(2), 210–216. https://doi.org/10.1016/j.jadohealth.2019.08.015

Verbruggen, S. W., Kainz, B., Shelmerdine, S. C., Hajnal, J. V., Rutherford, M. A., Arthurs, O. J., Phillips, A. T. M., & Nowlan, N. C. (2018). Stresses and strains on the human fetal skeleton during development. *Journal of the Royal Society Interface, 15*(138), 20170593. https://doi.org/10.1098/rsif.2017.0593

Verd, S., Ramakers, J., Vinuela, I., Martin-Delgado, M.-I., Prohens, A., & Díez, R. (2021). Does breastfeeding protect children from COVID-19? An observational study from pediatric services in Majorca, Spain. *International Breastfeeding Journal, 16*(1), 83. https://doi.org/10.1186/s13006-021-00430-z

Verkuyten, M. (2016). Further conceptualizing ethnic and racial identity research: The social identity approach and its dynamic model. *Child Development, 87*(6), 1796–1812. https://doi.org/10.1111/cdev.12555

Verkuyten, M., Thijs, J., & Gharaei, N. (2019). Discrimination and academic (dis)engagement of ethnic-racial minority students: A social identity threat perspective. *Social Psychology of Education, 22*(2), 267–290. https://doi.org/10.1007/s11218-018-09476-0

Vermeir, I., & Van de Sompel, D. (2017). How advertising beauty influences children's self-perception and behavior. In Information Resources Management Association (Eds.), *Advertising and branding: Concepts, methodologies, tools, and applications* (pp. 1495–1511). IGI Global. https://doi.org/10.4018/978-1-5225 -1793-1.ch069

Vermillet, A.-Q., Tølbøll, K., Litsis Mizan, S., C. Skewes, J., & Parsons, C. E. (2022). Crying in the first 12 months of life: A systematic review and meta-analysis of cross-country parent-reported data and modeling of the "cry curve." *Child Development, 93*(4), 1201–1222. https://doi.org/10.1111/cdev.13760

Vespa, J. (2017). *The changing economics and demographics of young adulthood: 1975-2016, population characteristics.* U.S. Census Bureau, U.S. Department of Commerce, Economics and Statistics Administration.

Viarouge, A., Houdé, O., & Borst, G. (2019). The progressive 6-year-old conserver: Numerical saliency and sensitivity as core mechanisms of numerical abstraction in a Piaget-like estimation task. *Cognition, 190,* 137–142. https://doi.org/10.1016/j.cognition.2019.05.005

Vicedo, M. (2017). Putting attachment in its place: Disciplinary and cultural contexts. *European Journal of Developmental Psychology, 14*(6), 684–699.

Victora, C. G., Bahl, R., Barros, A. J., França, G. V., Horton, S., Krasevec, J., Murch, S., Sankar, M. J., Walker, N., & Rollins, N. C. (2016). Breastfeeding in the 21st century: Epidemiology, mechanisms, and lifelong effect. *The Lancet, 387*(10017), 475–490.

Vijayakumar, N., de Macks, Z. O., Shirtcliff, E. A., & Pfeifer, J. H. (2018). Puberty and the human brain: Insights into adolescent development. *Neuroscience & Biobehavioral Reviews, 92,* 417–436.

Vijayakumar, N., Youssef, G. J., Allen, N. B., Anderson, V., Efron, D., Hazell, P., Mundy, L., Nicholson, J. M., Patton, G., Seal, M. L., Simmons, J. G., Whittle, S., & Silk, T. (2021a). A longitudinal analysis of puberty-related cortical development. *NeuroImage, 228,* 117684. https://doi.org/10.1016/j.neuroimage.2020.117684

Vijayakumar, N., Youssef, G., Allen, N. B., Anderson, V., Efron, D., Mundy, L., Patton, G., Simmons, J. G., Silk, T., & Whittle, S. (2021b). The effects of puberty and its hormones on subcortical brain development. *Comprehensive Psychoneuroendocrinology, 7,* 100074. https://doi.org/10.1016/j.cpnec.2021.100074

Villalobos Solís, M., Smetana, J. G., & Tasopoulos-Chan, M. (2017). Evaluations of conflicts between Latino values and autonomy desires among Puerto Rican adolescents. *Child Development, 88*(5), 1581–1597.

Villatoro, A. P., DuPont-Reyes, M. J., Phelan, J. C., Painter, K., & Link, B. G. (2018). Parental recognition of preadolescent mental health problems: Does stigma matter? *Social Science & Medicine, 216,* 88–96. https://doi.org/10.1016/j.socscimed.2018.09.040

Visser, B. A., Ashton, M. C., & Vernon, P. A. (2006). g and the measurement of multiple intelligences: A response to Gardner. *Intelligence, 34*(5), 507–510.

Vissing, N. H., Chawes, B. L., Rasmussen, M. A., & Bisgaard, H. (2018). Epidemiology and risk factors of infection in early childhood. *Pediatrics, 141*(6), e20170933. https://doi.org/10.1542/peds.2017-0933

Vittrup, B. (2018). Color blind or color conscious? White American mothers' approaches to racial socialization. *Journal of Family Issues, 39*(3), 668–692. https://doi.org/10.1177/0192513X16676858

Vivekanandarajah, A., Nelson, M. E., Kinney, H. C., Elliott, A. J., Folkerth, R. D., Tran, H., Cotton, J., Jacobs, P., Minter, M., McMillan, K., Duncan, J. R.,

Broadbelt, K. G., Schissler, K., Odendaal, H. J., Angal, J., Brink, L., Burger, E. H., Coldrey, J. A., Dempers, J., . . . Network, P. (2021). Nicotinic receptors in the brainstem ascending arousal system in SIDS with analysis of pre-natal exposures to maternal smoking and alcohol in high-risk populations of the safe passage study. *Frontiers in Neurology, 12,* 636668. https://doi.org/10.3389/fneur.2021.636668

Vöhringer, I. A., Kolling, T., Graf, F., Poloczek, S., Fassbender, I., Freitag, C., Lamm, B., Suhrke, J., Teiser, J., Teubert, M., Keller, H., Lohaus, A., Schwarzer, G., & Knopf, M. (2018). The development of implicit memory from infancy to childhood: On average performance levels and interindividual differences. *Child Development, 89*(2), 370–382. https://doi.org/10.1111/cdev.12749

Volling, B. L. (2012). Family transitions following the birth of a sibling: An empirical review of changes in the firstborn's adjustment. *Psychological Bulletin, 138*(3), 497.

Volling, B. L., Yu, T., Gonzalez, R., Kennedy, D. E., Rosenberg, L., & Oh, W. (2014). Children's responses to mother-infant and father-infant interaction with a baby sibling: Jealousy or joy? *Journal of Family Psychology, 28*(5), 634–644. https://doi.org/10.1037/a0037811

Volpe, J. J. (2019). Dysmaturation of premature brain: Importance, cellular mechanisms, and potential interventions. *Pediatric Neurology, 95,* 42–66. https://doi.org/10.1016/j.pediatrneurol.2019.02.016

von Hofsten, C., & Rosander, K. (2018). The development of sensorimotor intelligence in infants. In J. M. Plumert (Ed.), *Studying the perception-action system as a model system for understanding development* (pp. 73–106). Elsevier Academic Press. https://doi.org/10.1016/bs.acdb.2018.04.003

von Suchodoletz, A., Gestsdottir, S., Wanless, S. B., McClelland, M. M., Birgisdottir, F., Gunzenhauser, C., & Ragnarsdottir, H. (2013). Behavioral self-regulation and relations to emergent academic skills among children in Germany and Iceland. *Early Childhood Research Quarterly, 28*(1), 62–73.

Vreeland, A., Gruhn, M. A., Watson, K. H., Bettis, A. H., Compas, B. E., Forehand, R., & Sullivan, A. D. (2019). Parenting in context: Associations of parental depression and socioeconomic factors with parenting behaviors. *Journal of Child and Family Studies, 28*(4), 1124–1133.

Vrolijk, P., Van Lissa, C. J., Branje, S. J. T., Meeus, W. H. J., & Keizer, R. (2020). Longitudinal linkages between father and mother autonomy support and adolescent problem behaviors: Between-family differences and within-family effects. *Journal of Youth and Adolescence, 49*(11), 2372–2387. https://doi.org/10.1007/s10964-020-01309-8

Vuolo, M., Mortimer, J. T., & Staff, J. (2014). Adolescent precursors of pathways from school to work. *Journal of Research on Adolescence, 24*(1), 145–162.

Vygotsky, L. (1962). *Thought and language.* MIT Press. https://doi.org/10.1037/11193-000

Vygotsky, L. S. (2016). Play and its role in the mental development of the child (N. Veresov & M. Barrs, Trans.). *International Research in Early Childhood Education, 7*(2), 3–25. (Original work published in Russian in 1933)

Vygotsky, L. S., & Cole, M. (1978). *Mind in society: Development of higher psychological processes.* Harvard University Press.

Waasdorp, T. E., Fu, R., Perepezko, A. L., & Bradshaw, C. P. (2021). The role of bullying-related policies: Understanding how school staff respond to bullying situations.

European Journal of Developmental Psychology, 1–16. https://doi.org/10.1080/17405629.2021.1889503

Waddington, C. H. (1952). Selection of the genetic basis for an acquired character. *Nature, 169*(4302), 625–626. https://doi.org/10.1038/169625b0

Wade, M., Sheridan, M. A., Zeanah, C. H., Fox, N. A., Nelson, C. A., & McLaughlin, K. A. (2020). Environmental determinants of physiological reactivity to stress: The interacting effects of early life deprivation, caregiving quality, and stressful life events. *Development and Psychopathology, 32*(5), 1732–1742. https://doi.org/10.1017/S0954579420001327

Wade, M., Zeanah, C. H., Fox, N. A., Tibu, F., Ciolan, L. E., & Nelson, C. A. (2019). Stress sensitization among severely neglected children and protection by social enrichment. *Nature Communications, 10*(1), 1–8.

Wade, R. M., & Harper, G. W. (2020). Racialized sexual discrimination (RSD) in the age of online sexual networking: Are young Black gay/bisexual men (YBGBM) at elevated risk for adverse psychological health? *American Journal of Community Psychology, 65*(3–4), 504–523. https://doi.org/10.1002/ajcp.12401

Wadsworth, D. D., Johnson, J. L., Carroll, A. V., Pangelinan, M. M., Rudisill, M. E., & Sassi, J. (2020). Intervention strategies to elicit MVPA in preschoolers during outdoor play. *International Journal of Environmental Research and Public Health, 17*(2), 650. https://doi.org/10.3390/ijerph17020650

Wagner, D. (2005). *The poorhouse: America's forgotten institution.* Rowman & Littlefield.

Wagner, J., Becker, M., Lüdtke, O., & Trautwein, U. (2015). The first partnership experience and personality development: A propensity score matching study in young adulthood. *Social Psychological and Personality Science, 6*(4), 455–463. https://doi.org/10.1177/1948550614566092

Wahab, A., Wilopo, S. A., Hakimi, M., & Ismail, D. (2020). Declining age at menarche in Indonesia: A systematic review and meta-analysis. *International Journal of Adolescent Medicine and Health, 32*(6). http://dx.doi.org/10.1515/ijamh-2018-0021

Waite-Stupiansky, S. (2017). Jean Piaget's constructivist theory of learning. In L. E. Cohen & S. Waite-Stupiansky (Eds.), *Theories of early childhood education: Developmental, behaviorist, and critical* (pp. 3–17). Taylor & Francis.

Wakefield, A. J., Murch, S. H., Anthony, A., Linnell, J., Casson, D. M., Malik, M., Berelowitz, M., Dhillon, A. P., Thomson, M. A., & Harvey, P. (1998). *Retracted: Ileal-lymphoid-nodular hyperplasia, non-specific colitis, and pervasive developmental disorder in children.* Elsevier.

Wakschlag, L. S., Perlman, S. B., Blair, R. J., Leibenluft, E., Briggs-Gowan, M. J., & Pine, D. S. (2018). The neurodevelopmental basis of early childhood disruptive behavior: Irritable and callous phenotypes as exemplars. *American Journal of Psychiatry, 175*(2), 114–130. https://doi.org/10.1176/appi.ajp.2017.17010045

Walajahi, H., Wilson, D. R., & Hull, S. C. (2019). Constructing identities: The implications of DTC ancestry testing for tribal communities. *Genetics in Medicine, 21*(8), 1744–1750. https://doi.org/10.1038/s41436-018-0429-2

Walhovd, K. B., Fjell, A. M., Giedd, J., Dale, A. M., & Brown, T. T. (2017). Through thick and thin: A need to reconcile contradictory results on trajectories in human cortical development. *Cerebral Cortex, 27*(2), bhv301. https://doi.org/10.1093/cercor/bhv301

Walhovd, K. B., & Lövdén, M. (2020). A lifespan perspective on human neurocognitive plasticity. In D. Poeppel, G. Mangun, & M. S. Gazzaniga (Eds.), *The cognitive neurosciences* (pp. 47–60). MIT Press.

Walker, S. M. (2019). Long-term effects of neonatal pain. *Seminars in Fetal and Neonatal Medicine, 24*(4), 101005. https://doi.org/10.1016/j.siny.2019.04.005

Wallace, D. (2009). *This is water: Some thoughts, delivered on a significant occasion, about living a compassionate life.* Little, Brown.

Wallace, J. B. (2015, March 13). Why children need chores. *Wall Street Journal.* https://www.wsj.com/articles/why-children-need-chores-1426262655

Wallenborn, J. T., Levine, G. A., Carreira dos Santos, A., Grisi, S., Brentani, A., & Fink, G. (2021). Breastfeeding, physical growth, and cognitive development. *Pediatrics, 147*(5). https://doi.org/10.1542/peds.2020-008029

Wallerstein, J. S. (1987). Children after divorce: Wounds that don't heal. *Perspectives in Psychiatric Care, 24*(3–4), 107–113.

Walsh, A., & Leaper, C. (2020). A content analysis of gender representations in preschool children's television. *Mass Communication and Society, 23*(3), 331–355. https://doi.org/10.1080/15205436.2019.1664593

Walters, D. D., Phan, L. T. H., & Mathisen, R. (2019). The cost of not breastfeeding: Global results from a new tool. *Health Policy and Planning, 34*(6), 407–417. https://doi.org/10.1093/heapol/czz050

Walters, F. P., & Gray, S. H. (2018). Addressing sexual and reproductive health in adolescents and young adults with intellectual and developmental disabilities. *Current Opinion in Pediatrics, 30*(4), 451–458. https://doi.org/10.1097/MOP.0000000000000635

Walton, G. M., & Brady, S. T. (2017). The many questions of belonging. In A. J. Elliot, C. S. Dweck, & D. S. Yeager (eds.), *Handbook of competence and motivation: Theory and application* (pp. 272–293). The Guilford Press.

Walton, G. M., & Brady, S. T. (2020). The social-belonging intervention. In G. M. Walton & A. J. Crum (Eds.), *Handbook of wise interventions: How social-psychological insights can help solve problems* (pp. 36–62). Guilford.

Walton, G. M., & Wilson, T. D. (2018). Wise interventions: Psychological remedies for social and personal problems. *Psychological Review, 125*(5), 617.

Wambogo, E. A., Ansai, N., Ahluwalia, N., & Ogden, C. L. (2020, November). Fruit and vegetable consumption among children and adolescents in the United States, 2015–2018. *National Center for Health Statistics Data Brief No. 391.* Centers for Disease Control and Prevention.

Wan, M. W., Fitch-Bunce, C., Heron, K., & Lester, E. (2021). Infant screen media usage and social-emotional functioning. *Infant Behavior and Development, 62,* 101509. https://doi.org/10.1016/j.infbeh.2020.101509

Wanberg, C. R., Ali, A. A., & Csillag, B. (2020). Job seeking: The process and experience of looking for a job. *Annual Review of Organizational Psychology and Organizational Behavior, 7,* 315–337.

Wang, C., Song, S., d'Oleire Uquillas, F., Zilverstand, A., Song, H., Chen, H., & Zou, Z. (2020). Altered brain network organization in romantic love as measured with resting-state fMRI and graph theory. *Brain Imaging and Behavior, 14*(6), 2771–2784. https://doi.org/10.1007/s11682-019-00226-0

Wang, H., Lin, S. L., Leung, G. M., & Schooling, C. M. (2016). Age at onset of puberty and adolescent depression: "Children of 1997" birth cohort. *Pediatrics, 137*(6), e20153231. https://doi.org/10.1542/peds.2015-3231

Wang, M.-T., Degol, J. L., Amemiya, J., Parr, A., & Guo, J. (2020). Classroom climate and children's academic and psychological wellbeing: A systematic review and meta-analysis. *Developmental Review, 57,* 100912. https://doi.org/10.1016/j.dr.2020.100912

Wang, M.-T., Henry, D. A., Smith, L. V., Huguley, J. P., & Guo, J. (2020). Parental ethnic-racial socialization practices and children of color's psychosocial and behavioral adjustment: A systematic review and meta-analysis. *American Psychologist, 75*(1), 1–22. https://doi.org/10.1037/amp0000464

Wang, Q. (2016). Five myths about the role of culture in psychological research. *APS Observer, 30*(1). https://www.psychologicalscience.org/observer/five-myths-about-the-role-of-culture-in-psychological-research

Wang, X., Xie, X., Wang, Y., Wang, P., & Lei, L. (2017). Partner phubbing and depression among married Chinese adults: The roles of relationship satisfaction and relationship length. *Personality and Individual Differences, 110,* 12–17. https://doi.org/10.1016/j.paid.2017.01.014

Wang, Y., & Yip, T. (2020). Sleep facilitates coping: moderated mediation of daily sleep, ethnic/racial discrimination, stress responses, and adolescent well-being. *Child Development, 91*(4), e833–e852.

Wang, Y., Liu, Q., Tang, F., Yan, L., & Qiao, J. (2019). Epigenetic regulation and risk factors during the development of human gametes and early embryos. *Annual Review of Genomics and Human Genetics, 20*(1), 21–40. https://doi.org/10.1146/annurev-genom-083118-015143

Wang, Z., Fong, F. T., & Meltzoff, A. N. (2021). Enhancing same-gender imitation by highlighting gender norms in Chinese pre-school children. *British Journal of Developmental Psychology, 39*(1), 133–152.

Wankoff, L. S. (2011). Warning signs in the development of speech, language, and communication: When to refer to a speech-language pathologist. *Journal of Child and Adolescent Psychiatric Nursing: Official Publication of the Association of Child and Adolescent Psychiatric Nurses, Inc., 24*(3), 175–184. https://doi.org/10.1111/j.1744-6171.2011.00292.x

Wantchekon, K. A., & Umaña-Taylor, A. J. (2021). Relating profiles of ethnic–racial identity process and content to the academic and psychological adjustment of Black and Latinx adolescents. *Journal of Youth and Adolescence, 50*(7), 1333–1352. https://doi.org/10.1007/s10964-021-01451-x

Ward, L. M., & Grower, P. (2020). Media and the development of gender role stereotypes. *Annual Review of Developmental Psychology, 2*(1), 177–199. https://doi.org/10.1146/annurev-devpsych-051120-010630

Warlaumont, A. S., & Finnegan, M. K. (2016). Learning to produce syllabic speech sounds via reward-modulated neural plasticity. *PLOS One, 11*(1), e0145096.

Warnock, D. M., & Hurst, A. L. (2016). "The poor kids' table": Organizing around an invisible and stigmatized identity in flux. *Journal of Diversity in Higher Education, 9*(3), 261.

Warren, A.-S., Goldsmith, K. A., & Rimes, K. A. (2019). Childhood gender-typed behavior and emotional or peer problems: A prospective birth-cohort study. *Journal of Child Psychology and Psychiatry, 60*(8), 888–896. https://doi.org/10.1111/jcpp.13051

Warren, M. (1948). The evolution of a geriatric unit from a public assistance institution, 1935–1947. *Proceedings of the Royal Society of Medicine, 41,* 337–338.

Warren, N. S. (2020). Cultural competency. In B. S. LeRoy, P. McCarthy Veach, & N. P. Callanan (Eds.), *Genetic counseling practice* (pp. 247–270). John Wiley & Sons. https://doi.org/10.1002/9781119529873.ch12

Wartosch, L., Schindler, K., Schuh, M., Gruhn, J. R., Hoffmann, E. R., McCoy, R. C., & Xing, J. (2021). Origins and mechanisms leading to aneuploidy in human eggs. *Prenatal Diagnosis, 41*(5), 620–630. https://doi.org/10.1002/pd.5927

Wass, S. V., Smith, C. G., Clackson, K., Gibb, C., Eitzenberger, J., & Mirza, F. U. (2019). Parents mimic and influence their infant's autonomic state through dynamic affective state matching. *Current Biology, 29*(14), 2415–2422.e4. https://doi.org/10.1016/j.cub.2019.06.016

Wasserberg, M. J. (2014). Stereotype threat effects on African American children in an urban elementary school. *The journal of experimental education, 82*(4), 502–517.

Waters, S. F., West, T. V., Karnilowicz, H. R., & Mendes, W. B. (2017). Affect contagion between mothers and infants: Examining valence and touch. *Journal of Experimental Psychology. General, 146*(7), 1043–1051. https://doi.org/10.1037/xge0000322

Waters, T. E. A., Facompré, C. R., Van de Walle, M., Dujardin, A., De Winter, S., Heylen, J., Santens, T., Verhees, M., Finet, C., & Bosmans, G. (2019). Stability and change in secure base script knowledge during middle childhood and early adolescence: A 3-year longitudinal study. *Developmental Psychology, 55*(11), 2379–2388.

Watson, J. B. (1913). Psychology as the behaviorist views it. *Psychological Review, 20*(2), 158–177. https://doi.org/10.1037/h0074428

Watson, J. B. (1928). *Psychological care of infant and child.* W. W. Norton.

Watson, R. J., Snapp, S., & Wang, S. (2017). What we know and where we go from here: A review of lesbian, gay, and bisexual youth hookup literature. *Sex Roles, 77*(11–12), 801–811. https://doi.org/10.1007/s11199-017-0831-2

Watson, R. J., Wheldon, C. W., & Puhl, R. M. (2020). Evidence of diverse identities in a large national sample of sexual and gender minority adolescents. *Journal of Research on Adolescence, 30*(S2), 431–442. https://doi.org/10.1111/jora.12488

Watt, R. G., Daly, B., Allison, P., Macpherson, L. M. D., Venturelli, R., Listl, S., Weyant, R. J., Mathur, M. R., Guarnizo-Herreño, C. C., Celeste, R. K., Peres, M. A., Kearns, C., & Benzian, H. (2019). Ending the neglect of global oral health: Time for radical action. *The Lancet, 394*(10194), 261–272. https://doi.org/10.1016/S0140-6736(19)31133-X

Watts, N., Amann, M., Ayeb-Karlsson, S., Belesova, K., Bouley, T., Boykoff, M., Byass, P., Cai, W., Campbell-Lendrum, D., Chambers, J., Cox, P. M., Daly, M., Dasandi, N., Davies, M., Depledge, M., Depoux, A., Dominguez-Salas, P., Drummond, P., Ekins, P., . . . Costello, A. (2018). The Lancet Countdown on health and climate change: From 25 years of inaction to a global transformation for public health. *The Lancet, 391*(10120), 581–630. https://doi.org/10.1016/S0140-6736(17)32464-9

Watts, T. W., Duncan, G. J., & Quan, H. (2018). Revisiting the marshmallow test: A conceptual replication investigating links between early delay of gratification and later outcomes. *Psychological Science, 29*(7), 1159–1177. https://doi.org/10.1177/0956797618761661

Waugh, W. E., & Brownell, C. A. (2017). "Help yourself!" What can toddlers' helping failures tell us about the development of prosocial behavior? *Infancy, 22*(5), 665–680. https://doi.org/10.1111/infa.12189

Way, N. (2019). Reimagining boys in the 21st century. *Men and Masculinities, 22*(5), 926–929. https://doi.org/10.1177/1097184X19875170

Way, N., Cressen, J., Bodian, S., Preston, J., Nelson, J., & Hughes, D. (2014). "It might be nice to be a girl . . . Then you wouldn't have to be emotionless": Boys' resistance to norms of masculinity during adolescence. *Psychology of Men & Masculinity, 15*(3), 241–252. https://doi.org/10.1037/a0037262

Weatherhead, D., Arredondo, M. M., Nácar Garcia, L., & Werker, J. F. (2021). The role of audiovisual speech in fast-mapping and novel word retention in monolingual and bilingual 24-month-olds. *Brain Sciences, 11*(1), 114. https://doi.org/10.3390/brainsci11010114

Weaver, C. M., Shaw, D. S., Crossan, J. L., Dishion, T. J., & Wilson, M. N. (2015). Parent–child conflict and early childhood adjustment in two-parent low-income families: Parallel developmental processes. *Child Psychiatry and Human Development, 46*(1), 94–107. https://doi.org/10.1007/s10578-014-0455-5

Weaver, J., & Schofield, T. (2015). Mediation and moderation of divorce effects on children's behavior problems. *Journal of Family Psychology, 29*(1): 39–48. https://doi.org/10.1037/fam0000043

Weaver, J. M., Schofield, T. J., & Papp, L. M. (2018). Breastfeeding duration predicts greater maternal sensitivity over the next decade. *Developmental Psychology, 54*(2), 220.

Weaver, L. T. (2010). In the balance: Weighing babies and the birth of the infant welfare clinic. *Bulletin of the History of Medicine, 84*(1), 30–57. https://doi.org/10.1353/bhm.0.0315

Weber, J., Illi, S., Nowak, D., Schierl, R., Holst, O., von Mutius, E., & Ege, M. J. (2015). Asthma and the hygiene hypothesis. Does cleanliness matter? *American Journal of Respiratory and Critical Care Medicine, 191*(5), 522–529. https://doi.org/10.1164/rccm.201410-1899OC

Webster, E. K., Martin, C. K., & Staiano, A. E. (2019). Fundamental motor skills, screen-time, and physical activity in preschoolers. *Journal of Sport and Health Science, 8*(2), 114–121. https://doi.org/10.1016/j.jshs.2018.11.006

Wechsler, D. (2014). *WISC-V: Technical and interpretive manual.* Pearson.

Weinberger, A. H., Gbedemah, M., Martinez, A. M., Nash, D., Galea, S., & Goodwin, R. D. (2018). Trends in depression prevalence in the USA from 2005 to 2015: Widening disparities in vulnerable groups. *Psychological Medicine, 48*(8), 1308–1315. https://doi.org/10.1017/S0033291717002781

Weininger, E. B., Lareau, A., & Conley, D. (2015). What money doesn't buy: Class resources and children's participation in organized extracurricular activities. *Social Forces, 94*(2), 479–503. https://doi.org/10.1093/sf/sov071

Weintraub, S., Dikmen, S. S., Heaton, R. K., Tulsky, D. S., Zelazo, P. D., Bauer, P. J., Carlozzi, N. E., Slotkin, J., Blitz, D., Wallner-Allen, K., Fox, N. A., Beaumont, J. L., Mungas, D., Nowinski, C. J., Richler, J., Deocampo, J. A., Anderson, J. E., Manly, J. J., Borosh, B., . . . Gershon, R. C. (2013). Cognition assessment using the NIH Toolbox. *Neurology, 80*(11 Suppl. 3), S54–S64. https://doi.org/10.1212/WNL.0b013e3182872ded

Weis, M., Trommsdorff, G., & Muñoz, L. (2016). Children's self-regulation and school achievement in cultural contexts: The role of maternal restrictive control. *Frontiers in Psychology, 7*, 722.

Weisberg, D. S. (2015). Pretend play. *WIREs Cognitive Science, 6*(3), 249–261. https://doi.org/10.1002/wcs.1341

Weisberg, D. S., Hirsh-Pasek, K., Golinkoff, R. M., Kittredge, A. K., & Klahr, D. (2016). Guided play: Principles and practices. *Current Directions in Psychological Science, 25*(3), 177–182.

Weisner, T. S. (2020). Still the most important influence on human development: Culture, context, and methods pluralism. *Human Development, 64*(4–6), 238–244.

Weiss, J. (2020). What is youth political participation? Literature review on youth political participation and political attitudes. *Frontiers in Political Science, 2*, 1. https://doi.org/10.3389/fpos.2020.00001

Weiss, M. J., Ratledge, A., Sommo, C., & Gupta, H. (2019). Supporting community college students from start to degree completion: Long-term evidence from a randomized trial of CUNY's ASAP. *American Economic Journal: Applied Economics, 11*(3), 253–297. https://doi.org/10.1257/app.20170430

Weissbourd, R., Anderson, T. R., Cashin, A., & McIntyre, J. (2017). The talk: How adults can promote young people's healthy relationships and prevent misogyny and sexual harassment. *Harvard Graduate School of Education, 16*(8), 1–46.

Weisz, J. R., Kuppens, S., Eckshtain, D., Ugueto, A. M., Hawley, K. M., & Jensen-Doss, A. (2013). Performance of evidence-based youth psychotherapies compared with usual clinical care: A multilevel meta-analysis. *JAMA Psychiatry, 70*(7), 750–761. https://doi.org/10.1001/jamapsychiatry.2013.1176

Weitbrecht, E. M., & Whitton, S. W. (2020). College students' motivations for "hooking up": Similarities and differences in motives by gender and partner type. *Couple and Family Psychology: Research and Practice, 9*(3), 123–143. https://doi.org/10.1037/cfp0000138

Wellesley College. (2013, November 11). *Wellesley salutes veterans on campus.* Wellesley College. http://www.wellesley.edu/news/2013/11/node/40223

Wellman, H. M. (2018). Theory of mind: The state of the art. *European Journal of Developmental Psychology, 15*(6), 728–755. https://doi.org/10.1080/17405629.2018.1435413

Wellman, H. M., Cross, D., Bartsch, K., & Harris, P. L. (1986). Infant search and object permanence: A meta-analysis of the A-not-B error. *Monographs of the society for Research in Child Development*, 1–67.

Wells, G., Horwitz, J., & Seetharaman, D. (2021, September 14). Facebook knows Instagram is toxic for teen girls, company documents show—WSJ. *Wall Street Journal.* https://www.wsj.com/articles/facebook-knows-instagram-is-toxic-for-teen-girls-company-documents-show-11631620739?mod=hp_lead_pos7&mod=article_inline

Welsh, R. O., & Little, S. (2018). The school discipline dilemma: A comprehensive review of disparities and alternative approaches. *Review of Educational Research, 88*(5), 752–794. https://doi.org/10.3102/0034654318791582

Wende, M. E., Stowe, E. W., Eberth, J. M., McLain, A. C., Liese, A. D., Breneman, C. B., Josey, M. J., Hughey, S. M., & Kaczynski, A. T. (2020). Spatial clustering patterns and regional variations for food and physical activity environments across the United States. *International Journal of Environmental Health Research*, 1–15. https://doi.org/10.1080/09603123.2020.1713304

Wendlandt, N. M., & Rochlen, A. B. (2008). Addressing the college-to-work transition implications for university career counselors. *Journal of Career Development, 35*(2), 151–165. https://doi.org/10.1177/0894845308325646

Wentzel, K. R., Jablansky, S., & Scalise, N. R. (2018). Do friendships afford academic benefits? A meta-analytic study. *Educational Psychology Review, 30*(4), 1241–1267. https://doi.org/10.1007/s10648-018-9447-5

Werblow, J., & Duesbery, L. (2009). The impact of high school size on math achievement and dropout rate. *The High School Journal, 92*(3), 14–23.

Werchan, D. M., Kim, J.-S., & Gómez, R. L. (2021). A daytime nap combined with nighttime sleep promotes learning in toddlers. *Journal of Experimental Child Psychology, 202*, 105006. https://doi.org/10.1016/j.jecp.2020.105006

Werchan, D. M., Lynn, A., Kirkham, N. Z., & Amso, D. (2019). The emergence of object-based visual attention in infancy: A role for family socioeconomic status and competing visual features. *Infancy, 24*(5), 752–767. https://doi.org/10.1111/infa.12309

Werker, J. F. (2018). Speech perception, word learning, and language acquisition in infancy: The voyage continues. *Applied Psycholinguistics, 39*(4), 769–777. https://doi.org/10.1017/S0142716418000243

Werner, E. (2000, May 31). *SRCD oral history interview: Emmy Werner.* Society for Research on Child Development.

Werner, E. (2001, May 10). *Interview with Emmy E. Werner by Orville E. Thompson* [Interview]. University of California, Davis. https://video.ucdavis.edu/media/Emmy+Werner/0_pi0fcs35/25823492

Werner, E. (2003, November). *A lifetime of resilience research: An interview with Emmy Werner, Ph.D.* National Resilience Resource Center at the University of Minnesota.

Werner, E. E. (1989). High-risk children in young adulthood: A longitudinal study from birth to 32 years. *American Journal of Orthopsychiatry, 59*(1), 72–81.

Werner, E. E. (1995). Resilience in development. *Current Directions in Psychological Science, 4*(3), 81–84.

Werner, L. A., & Leibold, L. J. (2017). Auditory development in normal-hearing children. In R. Sewald & A. M. Tharpe (Eds.), *Comprehensive Handbook of Pediatric Audiology* (2nd ed., pp. 67–86). Plural Publishing.

Werth, J. M., Nickerson, A. B., Aloe, A. M., & Swearer, S. M. (2015). Bullying victimization and the social and emotional maladjustment of bystanders: A propensity score analysis. *Journal of School Psychology, 53*(4), 295–308.

Westrupp, E. M., Reilly, S., McKean, C., Law, J., Mensah, F., & Nicholson, J. M. (2020). Vocabulary development and trajectories of behavioral and emotional difficulties via academic ability and peer problems. *Child Development, 91*(2), e365–e382. https://doi.org/10.1111/cdev.13219

Westwell-Roper, C., To, S., Andjelic, G., Lu, C., Lin, B., Soller, L., Chan, E. S., & Stewart, S. E. (2022). Food-allergy-specific anxiety and distress in parents of children with food allergy: A systematic review. *Pediatric Allergy and Immunology, 33*(1), e13695. https://doi.org/10.1111/pai.13695

Weymouth, B. B., Buehler, C., Zhou, N., & Henson, R. A. (2016). A meta-analysis of parent–adolescent conflict: Disagreement, hostility, and youth maladjustment. *Journal of Family Theory & Review, 8*(1), 95–112.

Whalen, D. J., Sylvester, C. M., & Luby, J. L. (2017). Depression and anxiety in preschoolers: A review of the past 7 years. *Child and Adolescent Psychiatric Clinics of North America, 26*(3), 503–522. https://doi .org/10.1016/j.chc.2017.02.006

Wheaton, A. G., & Claussen, A. H. (2021). Short sleep duration among infants, children, and adolescents aged 4 months–17 years — United States, 2016–2018. *Morbidity and Mortality Weekly Report, 70*(38), 1315–1321. https://doi.org/10.15585/mmwr. mm7038a1

Wheaton, A. G., Jones, S. E., Cooper, A. C., & Croft, J. B. (2018). Short sleep duration among middle school and high school students — United States, 2015. *Morbidity and Mortality Weekly Report, 67*(3), 85.

Wheeler, L. A., Zeiders, K. H., Updegraff, K. A., Umaña-Taylor, A. J., Rodríguez de Jesús, S. A., & Perez-Brena, N. J. (2017). Mexican-origin youth's risk behavior from adolescence to young adulthood: The role of familism values. *Developmental Psychology, 53*(1), 126–137. https://doi.org/10.1037/dev0000251

Whincup, P. H., Gilg, J. A., Odoki, K., Taylor, S. J. C., & Cook, D. G. (2001). Age of menarche in contemporary British teenagers: Survey of girls born between 1982 and 1986. *BMJ, 322*(7294), 1095–1096. https://doi.org/10.1136/bmj.322.7294.1095

Whitaker, A., & Losen, D. J. (2019). *The striking outlier: The persistent, painful and problematic practice of corporal punishment in schools.* https://escholarship.org /uc/item/9d19p8wt

Whitaker, T. R., & Snell, C. L. (2016). Parenting while powerless: Consequences of "the talk." *Journal of Human Behavior in the Social Environment, 26*(3–4), 303–309. https://doi.org/10.1080/10911359.2015.1127736

White, E. M., DeBoer, M. D., & Scharf, R. J. (2019). Associations between household chores and childhood self-competency. *Journal of Developmental & Behavioral Pediatrics, 40*(3), 176–182. https://doi.org/10.1097 /DBP.0000000000000637

White, E. S., & Mistry, R. S. (2016). Parent civic beliefs, civic participation, socialization practices, and child civic engagement. *Applied Developmental Science, 20*(1), 44–60. https://doi.org/10.1080/10888691.2015 .1049346

White, J. (2006). *Intelligence, destiny and education: The ideological roots of intelligence testing.* Routledge.

White, R. E., & Carlson, S. M. (2016). What would Batman do? Self-distancing improves executive function in young children. *Developmental Science, 19*(3), 419–426. https://doi.org/10.1111/desc.12314

White, R. E., & Carlson, S. M. (2021). Pretending with realistic and fantastical stories facilitates executive function in 3-year-old children. *Journal of Experimental Child Psychology, 207*, 105090. https://doi .org/10.1016/j.jecp.2021.105090

White, R., Barreto, M., Harrington, J., Kapp, S. K., Hayes, J., & Russell, G. (2020). Is disclosing an autism spectrum disorder in school associated with reduced stigmatization? *Autism, 24*(3), 744–754.

Whitehurst, G. J. "Russ." (2018, March 12). *Betsy DeVos is half-right on test scores, but test scores alone don't make the case for school choice.* Brookings. https://www .brookings.edu/blog/up-front/2018/03/12/betsy-devos -is-half-right-on-test-scores-but-test-scores-alone-dont -make-the-case-for-school-choice/

Whiten, A. (2017). Social learning and culture in child and chimpanzee. *Annual Review of Psychology, 68*(1), 129–154. https://doi.org/10.1146/annurev-psych -010416-044108

Whitney, D. G., & Peterson, M. D. (2019). US national and state-level prevalence of mental health disorders and disparities of mental health care use in children. *JAMA Pediatrics, 173*(4), 389–391. https:// doi.org/10.1001/jamapediatrics.2018.5399

Whitton, S. W., Dyar, C., Newcomb, M. E., & Mustanski, B. (2018). Romantic involvement: A protective factor for psychological health in racially-diverse young sexual minorities. *Journal of Abnormal Psychology, 127*(3), 265–275. https://doi.org/10.1037 /abn0000332

Wick, K., Leeger-Aschmann, C. S., Monn, N. D., Radtke, T., Ott, L. V., Rebholz, C. E., Cruz, S., Gerber, N., Schmutz, E. A., Puder, J. J., Munsch, S., Kakebeeke, T. H., Jenni, O. G., Granacher, U., & Kriemler, S. (2017). Interventions to promote fundamental movement skills in childcare and kindergarten: A systematic review and meta-analysis. *Sports Medicine, 47*(10), 2045–2068. https://doi.org/10.1007/ s40279-017-0723-1

Widman, L., Choukas-Bradley, S., Helms, S. W., Golin, C. E., & Prinstein, M. J. (2014). Sexual communication between early adolescents and their dating partners, parents, and best friends. *The Journal of Sex Research, 51*(7), 731–741. https://doi.org/10.1080 /00224499.2013.843148

Widman, L., Evans, R., Javidi, H., & Choukas-Bradley, S. (2019). Assessment of parent-based interventions for adolescent sexual health: A systematic review and meta-analysis. *JAMA Pediatrics, 173*(9), 866–877. https://doi.org/10.1001/jamapediatrics.2019.2324

Wiersma, R., Haverkamp, B. F., van Beek, J. H., Riemersma, A. M. J., Boezen, H. M., Smidt, N., Corpeleijn, E., & Hartman, E. (2020). Unravelling the association between accelerometer-derived physical activity and adiposity among preschool children: A systematic review and meta-analyses. *Obesity Reviews, 21*(2), e12936. https://doi.org/10.1111/obr.12936

Wigfield, A., & Eccles, J. S. (2020). 35 years of research on students' subjective task values and motivation: A look back and a look forward. In A. J. Elliot (Ed.), *Advances in motivation science* (Vol. 7, pp. 161–198). Elsevier. https://doi.org/10.1016/bs .adms.2019.05.002

Wigfield, A., Eccles, J. S., Fredricks, J. A., Simpkins, S., Roeser, R. W., & Schiefele, U. (2015). Development of achievement motivation and engagement. In R. M. Lerner (Ed.), *Handbook of child psychology and developmental science* (pp. 1–44). John Wiley & Sons. https:// doi.org/10.1002/9781118963418.childpsy316

Wigfield, A., Gladstone, J. R., & Turci, L. (2016). Beyond cognition: Reading motivation and reading comprehension. *Child Development Perspectives, 10*(3), 190–195.

Wijnands, A., Rijt, J. V., & Coppen, P. A. (2021). Learning to think about language step by step: A pedagogical template for the development of cognitive and reflective thinking skills in L1 grammar education. *Language Awareness, 30*(4), 317–335.

Wilbur, T. G., & Roscigno, V. J. (2016). First-generation disadvantage and college enrollment/completion. *Socius, 2*. https://doi.org/10.1177/2378023116664351

Wilkinson, K., Ball, S., Mitchell, S. B., Ukoumunne, O. C., O'Mahen, H. A., Tejerina-Arreal, M., Hayes, R., Berry, V., Petrie, I., & Ford, T. (2021). The

longitudinal relationship between child emotional disorder and parental mental health in the British Child and Adolescent Mental Health surveys 1999 and 2004. *Journal of Affective Disorders, 288*, 58–67. https://doi .org/10.1016/j.jad.2021.03.059

Will, G. J., Crone, E. A., Van Lier, P. A., & Güroğlu, B. (2016). Neural correlates of retaliatory and prosocial reactions to social exclusion: Associations with chronic peer rejection. *Developmental Cognitive Neuroscience, 19*, 288–297.

Willford, J. A., Goldschmidt, L., De Genna, N. M., Day, N. L., & Richardson, G. A. (2021). A longitudinal study of the impact of marijuana on adult memory function: Prenatal, adolescent, and young adult exposures. *Neurotoxicology and Teratology, 84*, 106958.

Williams, C. (2020). New research ignites debate on the '30 Million Word Gap.' *Edutopia.* https://www .edutopia.org/article/new-research-ignites-debate-30 -million-word-gap

Williams, C. D., Byrd, C. M., Quintana, S. M., Anicama, C., Kiang, L., Umaña-Taylor, A. J., Calzada, E. J., Gautier, M. P., Ejesi, K., Tuitt, N. R., Martinez-Fuentes, S., White, L., Marks, A., Rogers, L. O., & Whitesell, N. (2020). A lifespan model of ethnic-racial identity. *Research in Human Development, 17*(2–3), 99–129.

Williams, J. F., Smith, V. C., & the Committee on Substance Abuse. (2015). Fetal alcohol spectrum disorders. *Pediatrics, 136*(5), e1395–e1406. https://doi .org/10.1542/peds.2015-3113

Williams, P. G., Lerner, M. A., Sells, J., Alderman, S. L., Hashikawa, A., Mendelsohn, A., . . . & Weiss-Harrison, A. (2019). School readiness. *Pediatrics, 144*(2)

Williams, R. C., Biscaro, A., & Clinton, J. (2019). Relationships matter: How clinicians can support positive parenting in the early years. *Paediatrics & Child Health, 24*(5), 340–347. https://doi.org/10.1093/pch /pxz063

Williams, S. M., Sirugo, G., & Tishkoff, S. A. (2021). Embracing African genetic diversity. *Med, 2*(1), 19–20. https://doi.org/10.1016/j.medj.2020.12.019

Willoughby, M., Hudson, K., Hong, Y., & Wylie, A. (2021a). Improvements in motor competence skills are associated with improvements in executive function and math problem-solving skills in early childhood. *Developmental Psychology, 57*(9), 1463–1470. https://doi .org/10.1037/dev0001223

Willoughby, T., Heffer, T., Good, M., & Magnacca, C. (2021b). Is adolescence a time of heightened risk taking? An overview of types of risk-taking behaviors across age groups. *Developmental Review, 61*, 100980.

Willumsen, J., & Bull, F. (2020). Development of WHO guidelines on physical activity, sedentary behavior, and sleep for children less than 5 years of age. *Journal of Physical Activity and Health, 17*(1), 96–100. https://doi.org/10.1123/jpah.2019-0457

Wilmouth, J., Menozzi, C., & Bassarsky, L. (2022). *Why population growth matters for sustainable development* (Policy Brief No. 130; Future of the World). United Nations.

Wilson, N., Lee, J. J., & Bei, B. (2019). Postpartum fatigue and depression: A systematic review and meta-analysis. *Journal of Affective Disorders, 246*, 224–233. https://doi.org/10.1016/j.jad.2018.12.032

Wimmer, H., & Perner, J. (1983). Beliefs about beliefs: Representation and constraining function of wrong beliefs in young children's understanding of deception. *Cognition, 13*(1), 103–128. https://doi.org /10.1016/0010-0277(83)90004-5

Winston, C. N. (2016). An existential-humanistic-positive theory of human motivation. *The Humanistic Psychologist, 44*(2), 142–163. https://doi.org/10.1037/hum0000028

Winter, S. (2020). Inclusive and exclusive education for diverse learning needs. In W. Leal Filho, A. M. Azul, L. Brandli, P. G. Özuyar, & T. Wall (Eds.), *Quality Education* (pp. 451–463). Springer International. https://doi.org/10.1007/978-3-319-95870-5_24

Witchel, S. F., & Topaloglu, A. K. (2019). Puberty: Gonadarche and adrenarche. In J. F. Strauss & R. L. Barbieri (Eds.), *Yen & Jaffe's reproductive endocrinology: Physiology, pathophysiology, and clinical management* (8th ed., pp. 394–446.e16). Elsevier. https://doi.org/10.1016/B978-0-323-47912-7.00017-2

Witherington, D. C., & Boom, J. (2019). Conceptualizing the dynamics of development in the 21st century: Process, (inter)action, and complexity. *Human Development, 63*(3–4), 147–152. https://doi.org/10.1159/000504097

Witten, K., Kearns, R., Carroll, P., Asiasiga, L., & Tava'e, N. (2013). New Zealand parents' understandings of the intergenerational decline in children's independent outdoor play and active travel. *Children's Geographies, 11*(2), 215–229.

Wittig, S. M. O., & Rodriguez, C. M. (2019). Emerging behavior problems: Bidirectional relations between maternal and paternal parenting styles with infant temperament. *Developmental Psychology, 55*(6), 1199–1210. https://doi.org/10.1037/dev0000707

Wohlfahrt-Veje, C., Mouritsen, A., Hagen, C. P., Tinggaard, J., Mieritz, M. G., Boas, M., Petersen, J. H., Skakkebæk, N. E., & Main, K. M. (2016). Pubertal onset in boys and girls is influenced by pubertal timing of both parents. *The Journal of Clinical Endocrinology & Metabolism, 101*(7), 2667–2674. https://doi.org/10.1210/jc.2015-1073

Wolf, R. M., & Long, D. (2016). Pubertal development. *Pediatrics in Review, 37*(7), 292–300. https://doi.org/10.1542/pir.2015-0065

Wolfe, V. V., & Kelly, B. M. (2019). Child maltreatment. In M. J. Prinstein, E. A. Youngstrom, E. J. Mash, & R. A. Barkley (Eds.), *Treatment of disorders in childhood and adolescence* (pp. 591–657). Guilford.

Wolke, D., Bilgin, A., & Samara, M. (2017). Systematic review and meta-analysis: Fussing and crying durations and prevalence of colic in infants. *The Journal of Pediatrics, 185*, 55–61.e4. https://doi.org/10.1016/j.jpeds.2017.02.020

Wolke, D., Johnson, S., & Mendonça, M. (2019). The life course consequences of very preterm birth. *Annual Review of Developmental Psychology, 1*(1), 69–92. https://doi.org/10.1146/annurev-devpsych-121318-084804

Wolraich, M. L., Hagan, J. F., Allan, C., Chan, E., Davison, D., Earls, M., & Zurhellen, W. (2019). Clinical practice guideline for the diagnosis, evaluation, and treatment of attention-deficit/hyperactivity disorder in children and adolescents. *Pediatrics, 144*(4).

Wong, A. W., & Landes, S. D. (2021). Expanding understanding of racial-ethnic differences in ADHD prevalence rates among children to include Asians and Alaskan Natives/American Indians. *Journal of Attention Disorders*, 10870547211027932.

Wong, C. L., Ip, W. Y., Kwok, B. M. C., Choi, K. C., Ng, B. K. W., & Chan, C. W. H. (2018). Effects of therapeutic play on children undergoing cast-removal procedures: A randomised controlled trial.

BMJ Open, 8(7), e021071. https://doi.org/10.1136/bmjopen-2017-021071

Wood, D., Bruner, J. S., & Ross, G. (1976). The role of tutoring in problem solving. *Journal of Child Psychology and Psychiatry, 17*(2), 89–100. https://doi.org/10.1111/j.1469-7610.1976.tb00381.x

Wood, M. A., Bukowski, W. M., & Lis, E. (2016). The digital self: How social media serves as a setting that shapes youth's emotional experiences. *Adolescent Research Review, 1*(2), 163–173. https://doi.org/10.1007/s40894-015-0014-8

Woodruff, R. C., Campbell, A. P., Taylor, C. A., Chai, S. J., Kawasaki, B., Meek, J., Anderson, E. J., Weigel, A., Monroe, M. L., Reeg, L., Bye, E., Sosin, D. M., Muse, A., Bennett, N. M., Billing, L. M., Sutton, M., Talbot, H. K., McCaffrey, K., Pham, H., . . . COVID-NET Surveillance Team. (2021). Risk factors for severe COVID-19 in children. *Pediatrics, 149*(1), e2021053418. https://doi.org/10.1542/peds.2021-053418

Woodworth, K. R. (2020). Birth and infant outcomes following laboratory-confirmed SARS-CoV-2 infection in pregnancy — SET-NET, 16 jurisdictions, March 29–October 14, 2020. *MMWR. Morbidity and Mortality Weekly Report, 69*. https://doi.org/10.15585/mmwr.mm6944e2

Woolverton, G. A., & Marks, A. K. (2021). "I just check 'other'": Evidence to support expanding the measurement inclusivity and equity of ethnicity/race and cultural identifications of U.S. adolescents. *Cultural Diversity and Ethnic Minority Psychology.* Advance online publication. https://doi.org/10.1037/cdp0000360

Wootten-Greener, J. (2017, April 3). Child neglect, abuse, drug culture overwhelm Idaho's foster system. *Twin Falls Times-News.* https://magicvalley.com/news/local/child-neglect-abuse-drug-culture-overwhelm-idahos-foster-system/article_2d248905-1558-5f86-8d92-fc064abc0be6.html

Workman, J. (2022). Inequality begets inequality: Income inequality and socioeconomic achievement gradients across the United States. *Social Science Research, 102744.* https://doi.org/10.1016/j.ssresearch.2022.102744

World Bank, UNESCO, UNICEF, Foreign, Commonwealth and Development Office (FCDO), United States Agency for International Development (USAID), & Bill & Melinda Gates Foundation. (2022). *The State of Global Learning Poverty: 2022 Update. Conference Edition.* World Bank, UNESCO, UNICEF, FCDO, USAID, BMGF.

World Health Organization. (2011). *World report on disability 2011.* World Health Organization.

World Health Organization (WHO). (2006). *WHO child growth standards: Length/height-for-age, weight-for-age, weight-for-length, weight-for-height and body mass index-for-age: Methods and development.*

World Health Organization (WHO). (2018a). *Air pollution and child health: Prescribing clean air.* https://www.who.int/publications-detail-redirect/air-pollution-and-child-health

World Health Organization (WHO). (2018b). *The global network for age-friendly cities and communities: Looking back over the last decade, looking forward to the next* (No. WHO/FWC/ALC/18.4).

World Health Organization. (2018c). *WHO recommendations on antenatal care for a positive pregnancy experience: summary: highlights and key messages from the World Health Organization's 2016 global*

recommendations for routine antenatal care (No. WHO/RHR/18.02). World Health Organization.

World Health Organization (WHO). (2019a). *Guidelines on physical activity, sedentary behaviour and sleep for children under 5 years of age.*

World Health Organization (WHO). (2019b). *Trends in maternal mortality 2000 to 2017: Estimates by WHO, UNICEF, UNFPA, World Bank Group and the United Nations Population Division.* https://apps.who.int/iris/handle/10665/327595

World Health Organization (WHO). (2020). *Children: Improving survival and well-being* [Fact sheet]. https://www.who.int/news-room/fact-sheets/detail/children-reducing-mortality

World Health Organization (WHO). (2021). *Suicide worldwide in 2019: Global health estimates.*

World Health Organization (WHO). (2022a). Adolescent and young adult health. Fact Sheet. https://www.who.int/news-room/fact-sheets/detail/adolescents-health-risks-and-solutions

World Health Organization (WHO). (2022b). *WHO recommends groundbreaking malaria vaccine for children at risk* [News release]. World Health Organization. https://www.who.int/news/item/06-10-2021-who-recommends-groundbreaking-malaria-vaccine-for-children-at-risk

World Health Organization (WHO), United Nations Children's Fund (UNICEF), & World Bank (WB). (2021). Levels and trends in child malnutrition: UNICEF / WHO / The World Bank Group joint child malnutrition estimates: Key findings of the 2021 edition. https://apps.who.int/iris/handle/10665/341135

Wörmann, V., Holodynski, M., Kärtner, J., & Keller, H. (2014). The emergence of social smiling: The interplay of maternal and infant imitation during the first three months in cross-cultural comparison. *Journal of Cross-Cultural Psychology, 45*(3), 339–361. https://doi.org/10.1177/0022022113509134

Worthman, C. M., Dockray, S., & Marceau, K. (2019). Puberty and the evolution of developmental science. *Journal of Research on Adolescence, 29*(1), 9–31. https://doi.org/10.1111/jora.12411

Wray-Lake, L., Arruda, E. H., & Schulenberg, J. E. (2020). Civic development across the transition to adulthood in a national U.S. sample: Variations by race/ethnicity, parent education, and gender. *Developmental Psychology, 56*(10), 1948–1967. https://doi.org/10.1037/dev0001101

Wright, P. J., Herbenick, D., & Paul, B. (2020). Adolescent condom use, parent-adolescent sexual health communication, and pornography: Findings from a US probability sample. *Health Communication, 35*(13), 1576–1582.

Wrzus, C., Hänel, M., Wagner, J., & Neyer, F. J. (2013). Social network changes and life events across the life span: A meta-analysis. *Psychological Bulletin, 139*(1), 53–80. https://doi.org/10.1037/a0028601

Wu, L., Feng, X., He, A., Ding, Y., Zhou, X., & Xu, Z. (2017). Prenatal exposure to the Great Chinese Famine and mid-age hypertension. *PLOS One, 12*(5), e0176413. https://doi.org/10.1371/journal.pone.0176413

Wu, Q., & Feng, X. (2020). Infant emotion regulation and cortisol response during the first 2 years of life: Association with maternal parenting profiles. *Developmental Psychobiology, 62*(8), 1076–1091. https://doi.org/10.1002/dev.21965

Wühl, E. (2019). Hypertension in childhood obesity. *Acta Paediatrica, 108*(1), 37–43. https://doi.org/10.1111/apa.14551

Wyshak, G., & Frisch, R. (1982). Evidence for a Secular Trend in Age of Menarche. *The New England Journal of Medicine, 306*, 1033–1035. https://doi.org/10.1056/NEJM198204293061707

Xia, M., Fosco, G. M., Lippold, M. A., & Feinberg, M. E. (2018). A developmental perspective on young adult romantic relationships: Examining family and individual factors in adolescence. *Journal of Youth and Adolescence, 47*(7), 1499–1516. https://doi.org/10.1007/s10964-018-0815-8

Xiao, S. X., Martin, C. L., DeLay, D., & Cook, R. E. (2021). A double-edged sword: Children's intergroup gender attitudes have social consequences for the beholder. *Developmental Psychology, 57*(9), 1510–1524. https://doi.org/10.1037/dev0001065

Xie, M., Fowle, J., Ip, P. S., Haskin, M., & Yip, T. (2021). Profiles of ethnic-racial identity, socialization, and model minority experiences: Associations with well-being among Asian American adolescents. *Journal of Youth and Adolescence, 50*(6), 1173–1188. https://doi.org/10.1007/s10964-021-01436-w

Xu, J. (2019). Learning "merit" in a Chinese preschool: Bringing the anthropological perspective to understanding moral development. *American Anthropologist, 121*(3), 655–666.

Xue, Y., Yang, Y., & Huang, T. (2019). Effects of chronic exercise interventions on executive function among children and adolescents: A systematic review with meta-analysis. *British Journal of Sports Medicine, 53*(22), 1397–1404. https://doi.org/10.1136/bjsports-2018-099825

Yakushko, O. (2019). Eugenics and its evolution in the history of western psychology: A critical archival review. *Psychotherapy and Politics International, 17*(2), e1495. https://doi.org/10.1002/ppi.1495

Yamato, T. P., Maher, C. G., Traeger, A. C., Wiliams, C. M., & Kamper, S. J. (2018). Do schoolbags cause back pain in children and adolescents? A systematic review. *British Journal of Sports Medicine, 52*(19), 1241–1245.

Yan, J., Hou, Y., Shen, Y., & Kim, S. Y. (2021). Family Obligation, Parenting, and Adolescent Outcomes Among Mexican American Families. *The Journal of Early Adolescence,* 02724316211016064. https://doi.org/10.1177/02724316211016064

Yanaoka, K., Michaelson, L. E., Guild, R. M., Dostart, G., Yonehiro, J., Saito, S., & Munakata, Y. (2022). Cultures crossing: The power of habit in delaying gratification. *Psychological Science, 33*(7), 1172–1181.

Yang, F. N., Xie, W., & Wang, Z. (2022). Effects of sleep duration on neurocognitive development in early adolescents in the USA: A propensity score matched, longitudinal, observational study. The Lancet Child & Adolescent Health, 0(0). https://doi.org/10.1016/S2352-4642(22)00188-2

Yang, J. L., Anyon, Y., Pauline, M., Wiley, K. E., Cash, D., Downing, B. J., Greer, E., Kelty, E., Morgan, T. L., & Pisciotta, L. (2018). "We have to educate every single student, not just the ones that look like us": Support service providers' beliefs about the root causes of the school-to-prison pipeline for youth of color. *Equity & Excellence in Education, 51*(3–4), 316–331. https://doi.org/10.1080/10665684.2018.1539358

Yang, N., Waddington, G., Adams, R., & Han, J. (2018). Translation, cultural adaption, and test–retest reliability of Chinese versions of the Edinburgh Handedness Inventory and Waterloo Footedness Questionnaire. *Laterality: Asymmetries of Body, Brain and Cognition, 23*(3), 255–273. https://doi.org/10.1080/1357650X.2017.1357728

Yang, S., Martin, R. M., Oken, E., Hameza, M., Doniger, G., Amit, S., Patel, R., Thompson, J., Rifas-Shiman, S. L., Vilchuck, K., Bogdanovich, N., & Kramer, M. S. (2018). Breastfeeding during infancy and neurocognitive function in adolescence: 16-year follow-up of the PROBIT cluster-randomized trial. *PLOS Medicine, 15*(4), e1002554. https://doi.org/10.1371/journal.pmed.1002554

Yang, Y., & Wang, Q. (2019). Culture in emotional development. In V. LoBue, K. Pérez-Edgar, & K. A. Buss (Eds.), *Handbook of emotional development* (pp. 569–593). Springer International Publishing. https://doi.org/10.1007/978-3-030-17332-6_22

Yang, Z., Wang, X., Wan, X., Wang, M., Qiu, Z., Chen, J., Shi, M., Zhang, S., & Xia, Y. (2022). Pediatric asthma control during the COVID-19 pandemic: A systematic review and meta-analysis. *Pediatric Pulmonology, 57*(1), 20–25. https://doi.org/10.1002/ppul.25736

Yanık, B., & Yasar, M. (2018). An ethnographic approach to peer culture in a Turkish preschool classroom. *International Electronic Journal of Elementary Education, 10*(4), 489–496.

Yaniv, A. U., Salomon, R., Waidergoren, S., Shimon-Raz, O., Djalovski, A., & Feldman, R. (2021). Synchronous caregiving from birth to adulthood tunes humans' social brain. *Proceedings of the National Academy of Sciences, 118*(14). https://doi.org/10.1073/pnas.2012900118

Yap, C. X., Sidorenko, J., Wu, Y., Kemper, K. E., Yang, J., Wray, N. R., Robinson, M. R., & Visscher, P. M. (2018). Dissection of genetic variation and evidence for pleiotropy in male pattern baldness. *Nature Communications, 9*(1), 5407. https://doi.org/10.1038/s41467-018-07862-y

Yaremych, H. E., & Volling, B. L. (2020). Sibling relationships and mothers' and fathers' emotion socialization practices: A within-family perspective. *Early Child Development and Care, 190*(2), 195–209. https://doi.org/10.1080/03004430.2018.1461095

Yasnitsky, A. (2018). *Vygotsky: An intellectual biography.* Routledge.

Yasnitsky, A., & van der Veer, R. (2015). *Revisionist revolution in Vygotsky studies: The state of the art.* Routledge.

Yasui, M., Dishion, T. J., Stormshak, E., & Ball, A. (2015). Socialization of culture and coping with discrimination among American Indian families: Examining cultural correlates of youth outcomes. *Journal of the Society for Social Work and Research, 6*(3), 317–341. https://doi.org/10.1086/682575

Yates, J. (2018). Perspective: The long-term effects of light exposure on establishment of newborn circadian rhythm. *Journal of Clinical Sleep Medicine, 14*(10), 1829–1830.

Yazejian, N., Bryant, D. M., Hans, S., Horm, D., St. Clair, L., File, N., & Burchinal, M. (2017). Child and parenting outcomes after 1 year of Educare. *Child Development, 88*(5), 1671–1688. https://doi.org/10.1111/cdev.12688

Yazejian, N., Bryant, D., Freel, K., & Burchinal, M. (2015). High-quality early education: Age of entry and time in care differences in student outcomes for English-only and dual language learners. *Early Childhood Research Quarterly, 32*(Supplement C), 23–39. https://doi.org/10.1016/j.ecresq.2015.02.002

Ybarra, M. L., Price-Feeney, M., & Mitchell, K. J. (2019). A cross-sectional study examining the (in)congruency of sexual identity, sexual behavior, and romantic attraction among adolescents in the US. *The Journal of Pediatrics, 214*, 201–208.

Ye, J., Betrán, A. P., Vela, M. G., Souza, J. P., & Zhang, J. (2014). Searching for the optimal rate of medically necessary cesarean delivery. *Birth, 41*(3), 237–244. https://doi.org/10.1111/birt.12104

Yeager, D. S., Dahl, R. E., & Dweck, C. S. (2018). Why interventions to influence adolescent behavior often fail but could succeed. *Perspectives on Psychological Science, 13*(1), 101–122.

Yeager, D. S., Purdie-Vaughns, V., Garcia, J., Apfel, N., Brzustoski, P., Master, A., Hessert, W. T., Williams, M. E., & Cohen, G. L. (2014). Breaking the cycle of mistrust: Wise interventions to provide critical feedback across the racial divide. *Journal of Experimental Psychology. General, 143*(2), 804–824. https://doi.org/10.1037/a0033906

Yeager, D. S., & Walton, G. M. (2011). Social-psychological interventions in education: They're not magic. *Review of Educational Research, 81*(2), 267–301.

Yeo, S. C., Jos, A. M., Erwin, C., Lee, S. M., Lee, X. K., Lo, J. C., Chee, M., & Gooley, J. J. (2019). Associations of sleep duration on school nights with self-rated health, overweight, and depression symptoms in adolescents: Problems and possible solutions. *Sleep Medicine, 60*, 96–108.

Yeung, H. H., & Werker, J. F. (2013). Lip movements affect infants' audiovisual speech perception. *Psychological Science, 24*(5), 603–612.

Yip, T. (2014). Ethnic identity in everyday life: The influence of identity development status. *Child Development, 85*(1), 205–219.

Yip, T., Wang, Y., Mootoo, C., & Mirpuri, S. (2019). Moderating the association between discrimination and adjustment: A meta-analysis of ethnic/racial identity. *Developmental Psychology, 55*(6), 1274–1298. https://doi.org/10.1037/dev0000708

Yogeeswaran, K., Verkuyten, M., Osborne, D., & Sibley, C. G. (2018). "I have a dream" of a colorblind nation? Examining the relationship between racial colorblindness, system justification, and support for policies that redress inequalities. *Journal of Social Issues, 74*(2), 282–298. https://doi.org/10.1111/josi.12269

Yoon, E., Adams, K., Clawson, A., Chang, H., Surya, S., & Jérémie-Brink, G. (2017). East Asian adolescents' ethnic identity development and cultural integration: A qualitative investigation. *Journal of Counseling Psychology, 64*(1), 65–79. https://doi.org/10.1037/cou0000181

Yoon, J., & Lee, C. (2019). Neighborhood outdoor play of White and Non-White Hispanic children: Cultural differences and environmental disparities. *Landscape and Urban Planning, 187*, 11–22. https://doi.org/10.1016/j.landurbplan.2019.01.010

York, B. N., Loeb, S., & Doss, C. (2019). One step at a time the effects of an early literacy text-messaging program for parents of preschoolers. *Journal of Human Resources, 54*(3), 537–566.

Yoshida, M., Worlock, K. B., Huang, N., Lindeboom, R. G., Butler, C. R., Kumasaka, N., . . . & Meyer, K. B. (2022). Local and systemic responses to SARS-CoV-2 infection in children and adults. *Nature, 602*(7896), 321–327.

Yoshikawa, H., Weiland, C., & Brooks-Gunn, J. (2016). When does preschool matter? *The Future of Children, 26*(2), 21–35.

Yosso, T. J. (2005). Whose culture has capital? A critical race theory discussion of community cultural wealth. *Race Ethnicity and Education, 8*(1), 69–91. https://doi.org/10.1080/1361332052000341006

Yosso, T. J. (2006). Whose culture has capital? A critical race theory discussion of community cultural wealth. *Race Ethnicity and Education, 8*(1), 69–91. https://doi.org/10.1080/1361332052000341006

Yosso, T. J. (2020). Critical race media literacy for these urgent times. *International Journal of Multicultural Education, 22*(2), 5–13. https://doi.org/10.18251/ijme.v22i2.2685

Yosso, T. J., & Solorzano, D. G. (2005). Conceptualizing a critical race theory in sociology. In M. Romero & E. Margolis (Eds.), *The Blackwell companion to social inequalities* (pp. 117–146). John Wiley & Sons. https://doi.org/10.1002/9780470996973.ch7

Young, N. A. E. (2021). *Childhood disability in the United States: 2019* (ACSBR-006). U.S. Census Bureau. https://www.census.gov/library/publications/2021/acs/acsbr-006.html

YRBS. (2019). *Youth online: High school YRBS — 2019 results.* Centers for Disease Control and Prevention. https://nccd.cdc.gov/youthonline/App/Results.aspx?

Yu, D., Caughy, M. O., Smith, E. P., Oshri, A., & Owen, M. T. (2020). Severe poverty and growth in behavioral self-regulation: The mediating role of parenting. *Journal of Applied Developmental Psychology, 68,* 101135. https://doi.org/10.1016/j.appdev.2020.101135

Yu, E., & Cantor, P. (2016, December 19). Putting PISA results to the test. *The 180 blog.* Turnaround For Children. https://turnaroundusa.org/2015-pisa-analysis/

Yu, Y., & Kushnir, T. (2020). The ontogeny of cumulative culture: Individual toddlers vary in faithful imitation and goal emulation. *Developmental Science, 23*(1), e12862. https://doi.org/10.1111/desc.12862

Yücel, G., Kendirci, M., & Gül, Ü. (2018). Menstrual characteristics and related problems in 9- to 18-year-old Turkish school girls. *Journal of Pediatric and Adolescent Gynecology, 31*(4), 350–355.

Yudell, M., Roberts, D., DeSalle, R., & Rishkoff, S. (2016). Taking race out of human genetics. *Science, 351*(6273), 564–565.

Yun, H.-Y., & Juvonen, J. (2020). Navigating the healthy context paradox: Identifying classroom characteristics that improve the psychological adjustment of bullying victims. *Journal of Youth and Adolescence, 49*(11), 2203–2213. https://doi.org/10.1007/s10964-020-01300-3

Zacharopoulos, G., Sella, F., & Kadosh, R. C. (2021). The impact of a lack of mathematical education on brain development and future attainment. *Proceedings of the National Academy of Sciences, 118*(24). https://doi.org/10.1073/pnas.2013155118

Zaidi, B., & Morgan, S. P. (2017). The second demographic transition theory: A review and appraisal. *Annual Review of Sociology, 43,* 473–492. https://doi.org/10.1146/annurev-soc-060116-053442

Zakin, E. (2011). *Psychoanalytic feminism.* https://stanford.library.sydney.edu.au/entries/feminism-psychoanalysis/

Zamani, Z. (2016). "The woods is a more free space for children to be creative; their imagination kind of sparks out there": Exploring young children's cognitive play opportunities in natural, manufactured and mixed outdoor preschool zones. *Journal of Adventure Education and Outdoor Learning, 16*(2), 172–189. https://doi.org/10.1080/14729679.2015.1122538

Zamir, O., Gewirtz, A. H., Dekel, R., Lavi, T., & Tangir, G. (2020). Mothering under political violence: Post-traumatic symptoms, observed maternal parenting practices and child externalising behaviour. *International Journal of Psychology, 55*(1), 123–132. https://doi.org/10.1002/ijop.12557

Zarrett, N., Liu, Y., Vandell, D. L., & Simpkins, S. D. (2020). The role of organized activities in supporting youth moral and civic character development: A review of the literature. *Adolescent Research Review, 6*(2), 199–227.

Zavala, V. A., Bracci, P. M., Carethers, J. M., Carvajal-Carmona, L., Coggins, N. B., Cruz-Correa, M. R., Davis, M., de Smith, A. J., Dutil, J., Figueiredo, J. C., Fox, R., Graves, K. D., Gomez, S. L., Llera, A., Neuhausen, S. L., Newman, L., Nguyen, T., Palmer, J. R., Palmer, N. R., . . . Fejerman, L. (2021). Cancer health disparities in racial/ethnic minorities in the United States. *British Journal of Cancer, 124*(2), 315–332.

Zeanah, C. H., Gunnar, M. R., McCall, R. B., Kreppner, J. M., & Fox, N. A. (2011). Sensitive periods. *Monographs of the Society for Research in Child Development, 76*(4), 147–162. https://doi.org/10.1111/j.1540-5834.2011.00631.x

Zeiders, K. H., Umaña-Taylor, A. J., Carbajal, S., & Pech, A. (2021). Police discrimination among Black, Latina/x/o, and White adolescents: Examining frequency and relations to academic functioning. *Journal of Adolescence, 90,* 91–99. https://doi.org/10.1016/j.adolescence.2021.06.001

Zeifman, D. M., & St James-Roberts, I. (2017). Parenting the crying infant. *Current Opinion in Psychology, 15,* 149–154.

Zelazo, P. D. (2020). Executive function and psychopathology: A neurodevelopmental perspective. *Annual Review of Clinical Psychology, 16*(1), 431–454. https://doi.org/10.1146/annurev-clinpsy-072319-024242

Zelazo, P. D., & Carlson, S. M. (2020). The neurodevelopment of executive function skills: Implications for academic achievement gaps. *Psychology & Neuroscience, 13*(3), 273.

Zelazo, P. D., & Lee, W. S. C. (2010). Brain development. In *The handbook of life-span development.* Wiley. https://doi.org/10.1002/9780470880166.hlsd001004

Zeng, S., Pereira, B., Larson, A., Corr, C. P., O'Grady, C., & Stone-MacDonald, A. (2021). Preschool suspension and expulsion for young children with disabilities. *Exceptional Children, 87*(2), 199–216. https://doi.org/10.1177/0014402920949832

Zentall, S. R., & Morris, B. J. (2010). "Good job, you're so smart": The effects of inconsistency of praise type on young children's motivation. *Journal of Experimental Child Psychology, 107*(2), 155–163. https://doi.org/10.1016/j.jecp.2010.04.015

Zero to Three. (2016a). *Celebrating all the moms out there. Hey moms — We hear you on Mother's Day and every day.*

Zero to Three. (2016b). *The discipline dilemma: Guiding principles for managing challenging behaviors.*

Zero to Three. (2016c). *Tuning in: Parents of young children tell us what they think, know and need.*

Zhang, Q., Wang, C., Zhao, Q., Yang, L., Buschkuehl, M., & Jaeggi, S. M. (2019). The malleability of executive function in early childhood: Effects of schooling and targeted training. *Developmental Science, 22*(2), e12748. https://doi.org/10.1111/desc.12748

Zhang, X., & Belsky, J. (2020). Three phases of gene × environment interaction research: Theoretical assumptions underlying gene selection. *Development and Psychopathology,* 1–12. https://doi.org/10.1017/S0954579420000966

Zhang, X., Sayler, K., Hartman, S., & Belsky, J. (2021). Infant temperament, early-childhood parenting, and early-adolescent development: Testing alternative models of parenting × temperament interaction. *Development and Psychopathology,* 1–12. https://doi.org/10.1017/S0954579420002096

Zhang, Y., & Ang, S. (2020). Trajectories of union transition in emerging adulthood: Socioeconomic status and race/ethnicity differences in the national longitudinal survey of youth 1997 cohort. *Journal of Marriage and Family, 82*(2), 713–732. https://doi.org/10.1111/jomf.12662

Zhang, Y., Luo, Q., Huang, C.-C., Lo, C.-Y. Z., Langley, C., Desrivières, S., Quinlan, E. B., Banaschewski, T., Millenet, S., Bokde, A. L. W., Flor, H., Garavan, H., Gowland, P., Heinz, A., Ittermann, B., Martinot, J.-L., Artiges, E., Paillère-Martinot, M.-L., Nees, F., . . . for the IMAGEN consortium. (2021). The human brain is best described as being on a female/male continuum: Evidence from a neuroimaging connectivity study. *Cerebral Cortex, 31*(6), 3021–3033. https://doi.org/10.1093/cercor/bhaa408

Zhang, Y., Shi, J., Wei, H., Han, V., Zhu, W.-Z., & Liu, C. (2019). Neonate and infant brain development from birth to 2 years assessed using MRI-based quantitative susceptibility mapping. *NeuroImage, 185,* 349–360. https://doi.org/10.1016/j.neuroimage.2018.10.031

Zheng, L. R., Atherton, O. E., Trzesniewski, K., & Robins, R. W. (2020). Are self-esteem and academic achievement reciprocally related? Findings from a longitudinal study of Mexican-origin youth. *Journal of Personality, 88*(6), 1058–1074. https://doi.org/10.1111/jopy.12550

Zheng, M., Lamb, K. E., Grimes, C., Laws, R., Bolton, K., Ong, K. K., & Campbell, K. (2018). Rapid weight gain during infancy and subsequent adiposity: A systematic review and meta-analysis of evidence. *Obesity Reviews: An Official Journal of the International Association for the Study of Obesity, 19*(3), 321–332. https://doi.org/10.1111/obr.12632

Zheng, M., Rangan, A., Olsen, N. J., & Heitmann, B. L. (2021). Longitudinal association of nighttime sleep duration with emotional and behavioral problems in early childhood: Results from the Danish Healthy Start Study. *Sleep, 44*(1), zsaa138. https://doi.org/10.1093/sleep/zsaa138

Zhou, M., & Bankston III, C. L. (2020). The model minority stereotype and the national identity question: The challenges facing Asian immigrants and their children. *Ethnic and Racial Studies, 43*(1), 233–253.

Zhou, M., & Gonzales, R. G. (2019). Divergent destinies: Children of immigrants growing up in the United States. *Annual Review of Sociology, 45*(1), 383–399.

Zhou, N., Cao, H., & Leerkes, E. M. (2017). Interparental conflict and infants' behavior problems: The mediating role of maternal sensitivity. *Journal of Family Psychology, 31*(4), 464–474. https://doi.org/10.1037/fam0000288

Zhou, X., & Wu, X. (2021). Posttraumatic stress disorder and growth: Examination of joint trajectories in children and adolescents. *Development and Psychopathology,* 1–13.

Zigler, E., & Gilman, E. (1991). The legacy of Jean Piaget. In G. A. Kimble & M. Wertheimer (Eds.), *Portraits of pioneers in psychology* (Vol. 3, Chap. 9). Psychology Press.

Ziv, Y., & Hotam, Y. (2015). Theory and measure in the psychological field: The case of attachment theory and the strange situation procedure. *Theory & Psychology, 25*(3), 274–291. https://doi.org/10.1177/0959354315577970

Zosuls, K. M., Andrews, N. C., Martin, C. L., England, D. E., & Field, R. D. (2016). Developmental changes in the link between gender typicality and peer victimization and exclusion. *Sex Roles, 75*(5), 243–256.

Zreik, G., Oppenheim, D., & Sagi-Schwartz, A. (2017). Infant attachment and maternal sensitivity in the Arab minority in Israel. *Child Development, 88*(4), 1338–1349. https://doi.org/10.1111/cdev.12692

Zubler, J. M., Wiggins, L. D., Macias, M. M., Whitaker, T. M., Shaw, J. S., Squires, J. K., Pajek, J. A., Wolf, R. B., Slaughter, K. S., Broughton, A. S., Gerndt, K. L., Mlodoch, B. J., & Lipkin, P. H. (2022). Evidence-informed milestones for developmental surveillance tools. *Pediatrics, 149*(3), e2021052138. https://doi.org/10.1542/peds.2021-052138

Zucker, J. K., & Patterson, M. M. (2018). Racial socialization practices among White American parents: Relations to racial attitudes, racial identity, and school diversity. *Journal of Family Issues, 39*(16), 3903–3930. https://doi.org/10.1177/0192513X18800766

Zucker, N. L., & Hughes, S. O. (2020). The persistence of picky eating: Opportunities to improve our strategies and messaging. *Pediatrics, 145*(6), e20200893. https://doi.org/10.1542/peds.2020-0893

Zuk, J., & Gaab, N. (2018). Evaluating predisposition and training in shaping the musician's brain: The need for a developmental perspective. *Annals of the New York Academy of Sciences, 1423*(1), 40–50.

Zwaigenbaum, L., Bryson, S. E., Brian, J., Smith, I. M., Sacrey, L., Armstrong, V., Roberts, W., Szatmari, P., Garon, N., Vaillancourt, T., & Roncadin, C. (2021). Assessment of autism symptoms from 6 to 18 months of age using the Autism Observation Scale for Infants in a prospective high-risk cohort. *Child Development, 92*(3), 1187–1198. https://doi.org/10.1111/cdev.13485

Zych, I., Baldry, A. C., Farrington, D. P., & Llorent, V. J. (2019). Are children involved in cyberbullying low on empathy? A systematic review and meta-analysis of research on empathy versus different cyberbullying roles. *Aggression and Violent Behavior, 45,* 83–97.

NAME INDEX

SUBJECT INDEX

Note: Page numbers followed by f indicate figures; those followed by t indicate tables. **Boldface** page numbers indicate key terms.